THE CENTURY WAR BOOK

THE FAMOUS HISTORY OF THE CIVIL WAR BY THE PEOPLE WHO ACTUALLY FOUGHT IT

ARNO PRESS
A New York Times Company
New York • 1978

Library of Congress Cataloging in Publication Data

Main entry under title:

The Century war book.

A condensation of "The Century war series,"
published from Nov. 1884 to Nov. 1887, in the
Century Magazine.
Reprint of the 1894 ed. published by Century
Co., New York under title: Battles and leaders
of the Civil War.
Includes index.
1.   United States—History—Civil War, 1861-
1865—Campaigns and battles.   2.   United States—
History—Civil War 1861-1865—Personal narratives.
I.   The Century.
E470.B34   1978   973.7'3   77-18666
ISBN 0-405-11123-1

Reprint edition 1978 by Arno Press Inc.
Original edition 1894 by the Century Co.

Manufactured in the United States of America

CAMP GOSSIP.

PREFACE TO THE PEOPLE'S PICTORIAL EDITION.

THE present edition of "Battles and Leaders of the Civil War," known familiarly as "The Century War Book," is issued with the idea of bringing its picturesque features before a larger body of readers than has been reached even by the great circulations of the complete book and of THE CENTURY MAGAZINE, upon whose "War Papers" the book is founded. Probably no series of magazine articles ever attracted so wide an interest as the "War Papers" in THE CENTURY. Within six months after the appearance of the first of these articles, the circulation of THE CENTURY was increased one hundred thousand copies. In this unique work many commanders and subordinates have contributed to the history of the heroic deeds of which they were

UNIFORM OF THE 14TH NEW YORK
AT BULL RUN.

a part. General Grant wrote for it four papers on his greatest campaigns, and out of them grew his "Personal Memoirs," which retrieved his fortunes, and added new laurels to his fame. The good temper and the unpartizan character of the articles have been an important means of bringing about a better understanding between the soldiers who were opposed in the War for the Union, and indeed between all the people of the North and the South.

Upon the completion of the "War Papers" in THE CENTURY, the work "Battles and Leaders of the Civil War" was issued under the editorial charge of Robert Underwood Johnson and Clarence Clough Buel, of the staff of THE CENTURY, by whom the war articles had been planned and edited, and to render the book complete many additional articles and illustrations were prepared for it, making the total cost of the four-volume history nearly a quarter of a million dollars.

CHRONOLOGICAL SUMMARY AND RECORD

Of Every Engagement Between the Troops of the Union and of the Confederacy, in the Civil War in the United States, Showing the Total Losses and Casualties in Each Engagement—The Whole Collated and Compiled from the Official Records of the War Department at Washington.

APRIL, 1861

12—Bombardment of Fort Sumter, S. C. No casualties.

15—Evacuation of Fort Sumter, S. C. *Union* 1 killed, 3 wounded. By premature explosion of cannon in firing a salute to the United States flag.

19—Riots in Baltimore, Md. 6th Mass., 26th Pa. *Union* 4 killed, 30 wounded. *Confed.* 9 killed.

MAY, 1861

10—Camp Jackson, Mo. 1st, 3d and 4th Mo. Reserve Corps, 3d Mo. Vols. *Confed.* 639 prisoners.

Riots in St. Louis, Mo. 5th Mo., U. S. Reserves. *Union* 4 killed. *Confed.* 27 killed.

JUNE, 1861

1—Fairfax C. H., Va. Co. B. 2d U. S. Cav. *Union* 1 killed, 4 wounded. *Confed.* 1 killed, 14 wounded.

3—Philippi, W. Va. 1st W. Va., 14th and 16th Ohio, 7th and 9th Ind. *Union* 2 wounded. *Confed.* 16 wounded.

10—Big Bethel, Va. 1st, 2d, 3d, 5th and 7th N. Y., 4th Mass. Detachment of 2d U. S. Artil. *Union* 16 killed, 34 wounded. *Confed.* 1 killed, 7 wounded.

11—Romney, W. Va. 11th Ind. *Union* 1 wounded. *Confed.* 2 killed, 1 wounded.

17—Vienna, Va. 1st Ohio. *Union* 5 killed, 6 wounded. *Confed.* 6 killed.

Booneville, Mo. 2d Mo. (three months') Volunteers, Batteries H and L Mo. Light Artil. *Union* 2 killed, 19 wounded. *Confed.* 14 killed, 20 wounded.

Edwards Ferry, Md. 1st Pa. *Union* 1 killed, 4 wounded. *Confed.* 15 killed.

18—Camp Cole, Mo. Home Guards. *Union* 15 to 25 killed, 25 to 52 wounded. *Confed.* 4 killed, 20 wounded.

26—Patterson Creek or Kelley's Island, Va. 11th Ind. *Union* 1 killed, 1 wounded. *Confed.* 7 killed, 2 wounded.

27—Matthias' Point, Va. Gunboats *Pawnee* and *Freeborn*. *Union* 1 killed, 4 wounded.

JULY, 1861

2—Falling Waters, Md., also called Haynesville or Martinsburg, Md. 1st Wis., 11th Pa. *Union* 8 killed, 15 wounded. *Confed.* 31 killed, 50 wounded.

5—Carthage or Dry Forks, Mo. 3d and 5th Mo., one battery of Mo. Artil. *Union* 13 killed, 31 wounded. *Confed.* 30 killed, 125 wounded, 45 prisoners.

Newport News, Va. 1st Co. 9th N. Y. *Union* 6 wounded. *Confed.* 3 wounded.

6—Middle Creek Fork or Buckhannon, W. Va. One Co. 3d Ohio. *Union* 1 killed, 6 wounded. *Confed.* 7 killed.

7—Great Falls, Md. 8th N. Y. *Union* 2 killed. *Confed.* 12 killed.

8—Laurel Hill or Bealington, W. Va. 14th Ohio, 9th Ind. *Union* 2 killed, 6 wounded.

10—Monroe Station, Mo. 16th Ill., 3d Ia., Hannibal (Mo.) Home Guards. *Union* 3 killed. *Confed.* 4 killed, 20 wounded, 75 prisoners.

11—Rich Mountain, Va. 8th, 10th and 13th Ind., 19th Ohio. *Union* 11 killed, 35 wounded. *Confed.* 60 killed, 140 wounded, 100 prisoners.

12—Barboursville or Red House, Va. 2d Ky. *Union* 1 killed. *Confed.* 10 killed.

Beverly, W. Va. 4th and 9th Ohio. *Confed.* 600 prisoners.

14—Carrick's Ford, W. Va. 14th Ohio, 7th and 9th Ind. *Union* 13 killed, 40 wounded. *Confed.* 20 killed, 10 wounded, 50 prisoners.

16—Millsville or Wentzville, Mo. 8th Mo. *Union* 7 killed, 1 wounded. *Confed.* 7 killed.

17—Fulton, Mo. 3d Mo. Reserves. *Union* 1 killed, 15 wounded.

Scarrytown, W. Va. 2d Ky., 12th and 21st Ohio, 1st Ohio Battery. *Union* 9 killed, 38 wounded.

Martinsburg, Mo. One Co. of 1st Mo. Reserves. *Union* 1 killed, 1 wounded.

Bunker Hill, Va. Detachment of Gen. Patterson's command. *Confed.* 4 killed.

18—Blackburn's Ford, Va. 1st Mass., 2d and 3d Mich., 12th N. Y., Detachment of 2d U. S. Cav., Battery E 3d U. S. Artil. *Union* 19 killed, 38 wounded. *Confed.* 15 killed, 53 wounded.

18 and 19—Harrisonville and Parkersville, Mo. Van Horne's (Mo.) Battalion, Cass Co. Home Guards. *Union* 1 killed. *Confed.* 14 killed.

21—Bull Run or Manassas, Va. 2d Me., 2d N. H., 2d Vt., 1st, 4th and 5th Mass., 1st and 2d R. I., 1st, 2d and 3d Conn., 8th, 11th, 12th, 13th, 16th, 18th, 27th, 29th, 31st, 32d, 35th, 38th, and 39th N. Y., 2d, 8th, 14th, 69th, 71st and 79th N. Y. Militia, 27th Pa., 1st, 2d and 3d Mich., 1st and 2d Minn., 2d Wis., 1st and 2d Ohio, Detachments of 2d, 3d and 8th U. S. Regulars, Battalion of Marines, Batteries D, E, G and M, 2d U. S. Artil., Battery E, 3d Artil., Battery D, 5th Artil., 2d R. I. Battery, Detachments of 1st and 2d Dragoons. *Union* 481 killed, 1,011 wounded, 1,460 missing and captured. *Confed.* 269 killed, 1,483 wounded. *Confed.* Brig.-Gens. Bee and Barton killed.

22—Forsyth, Mo. 1st Ia., 2d Kan., Stanley Dragoons, Totten's Battery. *Union* 3 wounded. *Confed.* 5 killed, 10 wounded.

24—Blue Mills, Mo. 5th Mo. Reserves. *Union* 1 killed, 12 wounded.

26—Lane's Prairie, near Rolla, Mo. Home Guards. *Union* 3 wounded. *Confed.* 1 killed, 3 wounded.

27—Fort Fillmore, N. Mex. 7th U. S. Inft. and U. S. Mounted Rifles, in all 400 men, captured by Confederates.

AUGUST, 1861

2—Dug Springs, Mo. 1st Ia., 3d Mo., five batteries of Mo. Light Artil. *Union* 4 killed, 37 wounded. *Confed.* 40 killed, 41 wounded.

3—Messilla, N. Mex. 7th U. S. Inft. and U. S. Mounted Rifles. *Union* 3 killed, 6 wounded. *Confed.* 12 killed.

5—Athens, Mo. Home Guards, 21st Mo. *Union* 3 killed, 8 wounded. *Confed.* 14 killed, 14 wounded.

Point of Rocks, Md. 28th N. Y. *Confed.* 3 killed, 2 wounded.

7—Hampton, Va. 20th N. Y. *Confed.* 3 killed, 6 wounded.

8—Lovettsville, Va. 19th N. Y. *Confed.* 1 killed, 5 wounded.

10—Wilson's Creek, Mo., also called Springfield and Oak Hill. 6th and 10th Mo. Cav., 2d Kan. Mounted Vols., one Co. of 1st U. S. Cav., 1st Ia., 1st Kan., 1st, 2d, 3d and 5th Mo., Detachments of 1st and 2d U. S. Regulars, Mo. Home Guards, 1st Mo. Light Artil., Battery F 2d U. S. Artil. *Union* 223 killed, 721 wounded, 291 missing. *Confed.* 265 killed, 800 wounded, 30 missing. *Union* Brig.-Gen. Nathaniel Lyon killed.

Potosi, Mo. Mo. Home Guards. *Union* 1 killed. *Confed.* 2 killed, 3 wounded.

17—Brunswick, Mo. 5th Mo. Reserves. *Union* 1 killed, 7 wounded.

19—Charlestown or Bird's Point, Mo. 22d Ill. *Union* 1 killed, 6 wounded. *Confed.* 40 killed.

20—Hawk's Nest, W. Va. 11th Ohio. *Union* 3 wounded. *Confed.* 1 killed, 3 wounded.

26—Cross Lanes or Summerville, W. Va. 7th Ohio. *Union* 5 killed, 40 wounded, 200 captured.

27—Ball's Cross Roads, Va. Two Co.'s 23d N. Y. *Union* 1 killed, 2 wounded.

28 and 29—Fort Hatteras, N. C. 9th, 20th and 99th N. Y. and Naval force. *Union* 1 killed, 2 wounded. *Confed.* 5 killed, 51 wounded, 715 prisoners.

29—Lexington, Mo. Mo. Home Guards. *Confed.* 8 killed.

31—Munson's Hill, Va. Two Cos. 23d N. Y. *Union* 2 killed, 2 wounded.

SEPTEMBER, 1861

1—Bennett's Mills, Mo. Mo. Home Guards. *Union* 1 killed, 8 wounded.

Boone C. H., W. Va. 1st Ky. *Union* 6 wounded. *Confed.* 30 killed.

2—Dallas, Mo. 11th Mo. *Union* 2 killed.

Dry Wood or Ft. Scott, Mo. 5th and 6th Kan., one Co. of 9th Kan. Cav., 1st Kan. Battery. *Union* 4 killed, 9 wounded.

Beher's Mills. 13th Mass. *Confed.* 3 killed, 5 wounded.

10—Carnifex Ferry. 9th, 10th, 12th, 13th, 28th and 47th Ohio. *Union* 16 killed, 102 wounded.

11—Lewinsville, Va. 19th Ind., 3d Vt., 65th N. Y., 79th N. Y. Militia. *Union* 6 killed, 8 wounded.

12—Black River, near Ironton, Mo. Three Cos. 1st Ind. Cav. *Confed.* 5 killed.

12 and 13—Cheat Mountain, W. Va. 13th, 14th, 15th and 17th Ind., 3d,

6th, 24th and 25th Ohio, 2d W. Va. *Union* 9 killed, 12 wounded. *Confed.* 80 wounded.

13—Booneville, Mo. Mo. Home Guards. *Union* 1 killed, 4 wounded. *Confed.* 12 killed, 30 wounded.

14—Confederate Privateer *Judah* destroyed near Pensacola, Fla., by the U. S. Flag-ship *Colorado*. *Union* 3 killed, 15 wounded.

15—Pritchard's Mills, or Darnestown, Va. 28th Pa., 13th Mass. *Union* 1 killed. *Confed.* 8 killed, 75 wounded.

12 to 20—Lexington, Mo. 23d Ill., 8th, 25th and 27th Mo., 13th and 14th Mo. Home Guards, Berry's and Van Horne's Mo. Cav., 1st Ill. Cav. *Union* 42 killed, 108 wounded, 1,624 missing and captured. *Confed.* 25 killed, 75 wounded.

17—Morristown, Mo. 5th, 6th and 9th Kan. Cav., 1st Kan. Battery. *Union* 2 killed, 6 wounded. *Confed.* 7 killed.

Blue Mills, Mo. 3d Ia. *Union* 11 killed, 39 wounded. *Confed.* 10 killed, 60 wounded.

18—Barboursville, W. Va. Ky. Home Guards. *Union* 1 killed, 1 wounded. *Confed.* 7 killed.

21 and 22—Papinsville or Osceola, Mo. 5th, 6th and 9th Kan. Cav. *Union* 17 killed.

22—Eliott's Mills or Camp Crittenden, Mo. 7th Ia. *Union* 1 killed, 5 wounded.

23—Romney or Hanging Rock, W. Va. 4th and 8th Ohio. *Union* 3 killed, 50 wounded. *Confed.* 35 killed.

25—Chapmansville, W. Va. 1st Ky., 34th Ohio. *Union* 4 killed, 9 wounded. *Confed.* 20 killed, 50 wounded.

26—Lucas Bend, Ky. Stewart's Cavalry. *Confed.* 4 killed.

29—Camp Advance, Munson's Hill, Va. 69th Pa., through mistake, fire into the 71st Pa., killing 9 and wounding 25.

OCTOBER, 1861

3—Greenbrier, W. Va. 24th, 25th and 32d Ohio, 7th, 9th, 13th, 14th, 15th and 17th Ind., Battery G, 4th U. S. Artil., Battery A, 1st Mich. Artil. *Union* 8 killed, 32 wounded. *Confed.* 100 killed, 75 wounded.

4—Alamosa, near Ft. Craig, N. Mex. Mink's Cav. and U. S. Regulars. *Confed.* 11 killed, 30 wounded.

Buffalo Hill, Ky. *Union* 20 killed. *Confed.* 50 killed.

8—Hillsborough, Ky. Home Guards. *Union* 3 killed, 2 wounded. *Confed.* 11 killed, 29 wounded.

9—Santa Rosa, Fla. 6th N. Y., Co. A 1st U. S. Artil., Co. H 2d U. S. Artil., Co.'s C and E 3d U. S. Inft. *Union* 14 killed, 29 wounded. *Confed.* 350 wounded.

12—Cameron, Mo. James' Cav. *Union* 1 killed, 4 wounded. *Confed.* 8 killed.

Upton Hill, Ky. 39th Ind. *Confed.* 5 killed, 3 wounded.

Bayles' Cross Roads, La. 79th N. Y. *Union* 4 wounded.

13—Beckwith Farm (12 miles from Bird's Point), Mo. Tuft's Cav. *Union* 2 killed, 5 wounded. *Confed.* 1 killed, 4 wounded.

West Glaze, also called Shanghai, or Henrytown, or Monday's Hollow, Mo. 6th and 10th Mo. Cav. Fremont Battalion Cav. *Confed.* 62 killed.

15—Big River Bridge, near Potosi, Mo. Forty men of 38th Ill. *Union* 1 killed, 6 wounded, 33 captured. *Confed.* 5 killed, 4 wounded.

Lime Creek, Mo. 13th Ill. Inft., 6th Mo. Cav. *Confed.* 63 killed, 40 wounded.

16—Bolivar Heights, Va. Parts of 28th Pa., 3d Wis., 13th Mass. *Union* 4 killed, 7 wounded.

Warsaw, Mo. *Confed.* 3 killed.

17 to 21—Fredericktown and Ironton, Mo. 17th, 20th, 21st, 33d and 38th Ill., 8th Wis., 1st Ind. Cav., Co. A 1st Mo. Light Artil. *Union* 6 killed, 60 wounded. *Confed.* 200 wounded.

19—Big Hurricane Creek, Mo. 18th Mo. *Union* 2 killed, 14 wounded. *Confed.* 14 killed.

21—Ball's Bluff, also called Edwards Ferry, Harrison's Landing, Leesburg, Va. 15th, 20th Mass., 40th N. Y., 71st Pa., Battery B, R. I. Artil. *Union* 223 killed, 226 wounded. *Confed.* 36 killed, 264 wounded, 445 captured and missing. *Union* Acting Brig.-Gen. E. D. Baker killed.

22—Buffalo Mills, Mo. *Confed.* 17 killed.

23—West Liberty, Mo. 2d Ohio, 1st and Loughlin's Ohio Cav., 1st Ohio Artil. *Union* 2 wounded. *Confed.* 10 killed, 5 wounded.

Hodgeville, Ky. Detach. 6th Ind. *Union* 3 wounded. *Confed.* 3 killed, 5 wounded.

25—Zagonyi's Charge, Springfield, Mo. Fremont's Body Guard and White's Prairie Scouts. *Union* 18 killed, 37 wounded. *Confed.* 106 killed.

26—Romney or Mill Creek Mills, W. Va. 4th and 8th Ohio, 7th W. Va., Md. Volunteers, 2d Regt. of Potomac Home Guards, and Ringgold (Pa.) Cav. *Union* 2 killed, 15 wounded. *Confed.* 20 killed, 15 wounded, 50 captured.

Saratoga, Ky. 9th Ill. *Union* 4 wounded. *Confed.* 8 killed, 17 wounded.

27—Plattsburg, Mo. *Confed.* 8 killed.

Spring Hill, Mo. 1st Co. of 7th Mo. Cav. *Union* 5 wounded.

29—Woodbury and Morgantown, Ky. 17th Ky., 3d Ky. Cav. *Union* 1 wounded.

NOVEMBER, 1861

1—Renick, Randolph Co., Mo. *Union* 14 wounded.

6—Little Santa Fé, Mo. 4th Mo., 5th Kan. Cav., Kowald's Mo. Battery. *Union* 2 killed, 6 wounded.

7—Belmont, Mo. 22d, 27th, 30th and 31st Ill., 7th Ia., Battery B 1st Ill. Artil., 2d Co. 15th Ill. Cav. *Union* 90 killed, 173 wounded, 235 missing. *Confed.* 261 killed, 427 wounded, 278 missing.

Galveston Harbor, Tex. U. S. Frigate *Santee* burned the *Royal Yacht.* *Union* 1 killed, 8 wounded. *Confed.* 3 wounded.

Port Royal, S. C. Bombardment by U. S. Navy. *Union* 8 killed, 23 wounded. *Confed.* 11 killed, 39 wounded.

9—Piketown or Fry Mountain, Ky. 2d, 21st, 33d and 59th Ohio, 16th Ky. *Union* 4 killed, 26 wounded. *Confed.* 18 killed, 45 wounded, 200 captured.

10—Guyandott, W. Va. Recruits of 9th W. Va. *Union* 7 killed, 20 wounded. *Confed.* 3 killed, 10 wounded.

Gauley Bridge, W. Va. 11th Ohio, 2d Ky. Cav. *Union* 2 killed, 16 wounded.

11—Little Blue, Mo. 110 men of the 7th Kan. Cav. *Union* 7 killed, 9 wounded.

12—Occoquan Creek, Va. Detach. 1st N. Y. Cav. *Union* 3 killed, 1 wounded.

17—Cypress Bridge, Ky. *Union* 10 killed, 15 wounded.

18—Palmyra, Mo. Detach. 3d Mo. Cav. *Confed.* 3 killed, 5 wounded.

19—Wirt C. H., W. Va. Detach. 1st W. Va. Cav. *Confed.* 1 killed, 5 wounded.

23—Ft. Pickens, Pensacola, Fla. Cos. C and E 3d U. S. Inft., Cos. G and I 6th N. Y., Batteries A, F and L 1st U. S. Artil., and C, H and K 2d U. S. Artil. *Union* 5 killed, 7 wounded. *Confed.* 5 killed, 93 wounded.

24—Lancaster, Mo. 21st Mo. *Union* 1 killed, 2 wounded. *Confed.* 13 killed.

26—Little Blue, Mo. 7th Kan. Cav. *Union* 1 killed, 1 wounded.

Drainesville, Va. 1st Pa. Cav. *Confed.* 2 killed.

29—Black Walnut Creek, near Sedalia, Mo. 1st Mo. Cav. *Union* 15 wounded. *Confed.* 17 killed.

DECEMBER, 1861

3—Salem, Mo. Detach. 10th Mo. Cav. *Union* 6 killed, 10 wounded. *Confed.* 16 killed, 20 wounded.

Vienna, Va. Detach. 3d Pa. Cav. *Union* all captured. *Confed.* 1 killed.

4—Anandale, Va. 30 men of 3d N. J. *Union* 1 killed. *Confed.* 7 killed.

Dunksburg, Mo. Citizens repulse raiders. *Confed.* 7 killed, 10 wounded.

11—Bertrand, Mo. 2d Ill. Cav. *Union* 1 wounded.

13—Camp Allegheny or Buffalo Mountain, W. Va. 9th and 13th Ind., 25th and 32d Ohio, 2d W. Va. *Union* 20 killed, 107 wounded. *Confed.* 20 killed, 96 wounded.

17—Rowlett's Station, also called Mumfordsville or Woodsonville, Ky. 32d Ind. *Union* 10 killed, 22 wounded. *Confed.* 33 killed, 50 wounded.

18—Milford, also called Shawnee Mound, or Blackwater, Mo. 27th Ohio, 8th, 18th, 22d and 24th Ind., 31st Kan., 1st Ia. Cav., Detach. U. S. Cav., 2 Batteries of 1st Mo. Lt. Artil. *Union* 2 killed, 8 wounded. *Confed.* 1,300 captured.

20—Drainesville, Va. 1st, 6th, 9th, 10th and 12th Pa. Reserve Corps, 1st Pa. Artil., 1st Pa. Cav. *Union* 7 killed, 61 wounded. *Confed.* 43 killed, 143 wounded.

21—Hudson, Mo. Detach. 7th Mo. Cav. *Union* 5 wounded. *Confed.* 10 killed.

22—Newmarket Bridge, near Newport News, Va. 20th N. Y. *Union* 6 wounded. *Confed.* 10 killed, 20 wounded.

24—Wadesburg, Mo. Mo. Home Guards. *Union* 2 wounded.

28—Sacramento, Ky. 3d Ky. Cav. *Union* 1 killed, 8 wounded. *Confed.* 30 killed.

Mt. Zion, Mo. Birge's Sharpshooters, 3d Mo. Cav. *Union* 5 killed, 63 wounded. *Confed.* 25 killed, 150 wounded.

JANUARY, 1862

1—Port Royal, S. C. 3d Mich., 47th, 48th and 79th N. Y., 50th Pa. *Union* 1 killed, 10 wounded.

4—Huntersville, Va. Detachments of 25th Ohio, 2d W. Va. and 1st Ind. Cav. *Union* 1 wounded. *Confed.* 1 killed, 7 wounded.

Bath, Va., also including skirmishes at Great Cacapon Bridge, Alpine Station and Hancock. 39th Ill. *Union* 2 killed, 2 wounded. *Confed.* 30 wounded.

Calhoun, Mo. *Union* 10 wounded. *Confed.* 30 wounded.

7—Blue Gap, near Romney, Va. 4th, 5th, 7th and 8th Ohio, 14th Ind., 1st W. Va. Cav. *Confed.* 15 killed.

Jennies' Creek, Ky., also called Paintsville. Four Cos. 1st W. Va. Cav. *Union* 3 killed, 1 wounded. *Confed.* 6 killed, 14 wounded.

8—Charleston, Mo. 10th Ia. *Union* 8 killed, 16 wounded.

Dry Forks, Cheat River, W. Va. One Co. of 2d W. Va. Cav. *Union* 6 wounded. *Confed.* 6 killed.

Silver Creek, Mo., also called Sugar Creek, and Roan's Tan Yard. Detachments of 1st and 2d Mo., 4th Ohio, 1st Iowa Cav. *Union* 5 killed, (6 wounded. *Confed.* 80 wounded.

9—Columbus, Mo. 7th Kan. Cav. *Union* 5 killed.

10—Middle Creek and Prestonburg, Ky. 40th and 42d Ohio, 14th and 22d Ky. *Union* 2 killed, 25 wounded. *Confed.* 40 killed.

19 and **20**—Mill Springs, Ky., also called Logan's Cross Roads, Fishing Creek, Somerset and Beech Grove. 9th Ohio, 2d Minn., 4th Ky., 10th Ind., 1st Ky. Cav. *Union* 38 killed, 194 wounded. *Confed.* 190 killed, 160 wounded. *Confed.* Gen. F. K. Zollikoffer killed.

22—Knob Noster, Mo. 2d Mo. Cav. *Union* 1 killed.

29—Occoquan Bridge, Va. Detachments of 37th N. Y. and 1st N. J. Cav. *Union* 1 killed, 4 wounded. *Confed.* 10 killed.

FEBRUARY, 1862

1—Bowling Green, Ky. One Co. of 2d Ind. Cav. *Confed.* 3 killed, 2 wounded.

6—Fort Henry, Tenn. U. S. Gunboats *Essex, Carondelet, Saint Louis, Cincinnati, Conestoga, Tyler* and *Lexington.* *Union* 40 wounded. *Confed.* 5 killed, 11 wounded.

8—Linn Creek, Va. Detachment of 5th W. Va. *Union* 1 killed, 1 wounded. *Confed.* 8 killed, 7 wounded.

Roanoke Island, N. C. 21st, 23d, 24th, 25th and 27th Mass., 10th Conn., 9th, 51st and 53d N. Y., 9th N. J., 51st Pa., 4th and 5th R. I., U. S. Gunboats *Southfield, Delaware, Stars and Stripes, Louisiana, Hetzel, Commodore Perry, Underwriter, Valley City, Commodore Barney, Hunchback, Ceres, Putnam, Morse, Lockwood, J. N. Seymour, Granite, Brinker, Whitehead, Shawseen, Pickett, Pioneer, Hussar, Vidette, Chasseur.* *Union* 35 killed, 200 wounded. *Confed.* 16 killed, 39 wounded, 2,527 taken prisoners.

10—Elizabeth City, or Cobb's Point, N. C., U. S. Gunboats *Delaware, Underwriter, Louisiana, Seymour, Hetzel, Shawseen, Valley City, Putnam, Commodore Perry, Ceres, Morse, Whitehead* and *Brinker.* *Union* 3 killed.

13—Blooming Gap, Va. 8th Ohio, 7th W. Va., 1st W. Va. Cav. *Union* 2 killed, 5 wounded. *Confed.* 13 killed.

14—Flat Lick Fords, Ky. 49th Ind., 6th Ky. Cav. *Confed.* 4 killed, 4 wounded.

14, 15 and **16**—Fort Donelson, Tenn. 17th and 25th Ky., 11th, 25th, 31st, and 44th Ind., 2d, 7th, 12th and 14th Iowa, 1st Neb., 58th and 76th Ohio, 8th and 13th Mo., 8th Wis., 8th, 9th, 11th, 12th, 17th, 18th, 20th, 28th, 29th, 30th, 31st, 41st, 45th, 46th, 48th, 49th, 57th and 58th Ill., Batteries B and D 1st Ill. Art., D and E 2d Ill. Artil., four Cos. Ill. Cav., Birge's Sharpshooters and six gunboats. *Union* 446 killed, 1,735 wounded, 150 missing. *Confed.* 231 killed, 1,007 wounded, 13,829 prisoners. *Union* Maj.-Gen. John A. Logan wounded.

17—Sugar Creek or Pea Ridge, Mo. 1st and 6th Mo., 3d Ill. Cav. *Union* 5 killed, 9 wounded.

18—Independence, Mo. 2d Ohio Cav. *Union* 1 killed, 3 wounded. *Confed.* 4 killed, 5 wounded.

21—Ft. Craig or Valverde, N. Mex. 1st N. Mex. Cav., 2d Col. Cav., Detachments of 1st, 2d and 5th N. Mex., and of 5th, 7th and 10th U. S. Inft., Hill's and McRae's Batteries. *Union* 62 killed, 140 wounded. *Confed.* 150 wounded.

24—Mason's Neck, Occoquan, Va. 37th N. Y. *Union* 2 killed, 1 wounded.

26—Keytesville, Mo. 6th Mo. Cav. *Union* 2 killed, 1 wounded. *Confed.* 1 killed.

MARCH, 1862

2—Pittsburg Landing, Tenn. 32d Ill. and U. S. Gunboats *Lexington* and *Tyler.* *Union* 5 killed, 5 wounded. *Confed.* 20 killed, 200 wounded.

3—New Madrid, Mo. 5th Iowa, 59th Ind., 39th and 63d Ohio, 2d Mich. Cav., 7th Ill. Cav. *Union* 1 killed, 3 wounded.

5—Occoquan, Va. Detachment of 63d Pa. *Union* 2 killed, 2 wounded.

6, 7 and **8**—Pea Ridge, Ark., including engagements at Bentonville, Leetown and Elkhorn Tavern. 25th, 35th, 36th, 37th, 44th and 59th Ill., 2d, 3d, 12th, 15th, 17th, 24th, and Phelps' Mo., 8th, 18th and 22d Ind., 4th and 9th Iowa, 3d Iowa Cav., 3d and 15th Ill. Cav., 1st, 4th, 5th and 6th Mo. Cav., Batteries B and F 2d Mo. Light Artil., 2d Ohio Battery, 1st Ind. Battery, Battery A 2d Ill. Artil. *Union* 203 killed, 972 wounded, 174 missing. *Confed.* 1,100 killed, 2,500 wounded, 1,600 missing and captured. *Union* Brig-Gen. Asboth and Actg. Brig.-Gen. Carr wounded. *Confed.* Brig.-Gen. B. McCulloch and Actg. Brig.-Gen. James McIntosh killed.

7—Fox Creek, Mo. 4th Mo. Cav. *Union* 5 wounded.

8—Near Nashville, Tenn. 1st Wis., 4th Ohio Cav. *Union* 1 killed, 2 wounded. *Confed.* 4 killed.

9—Mountain Grove, Mo. 10th Mo. Cav. *Union* 10 killed, 2 wounded.

Hampton Roads, Va. 20th Ind., 7th and 11th N. Y., U. S. Gunboats *Monitor, Minnesota, Congress* and *Cumberland.* *Union* 261 killed, 108 wounded. *Confed.* 7 killed, 17 wounded.

10—Burke's Station, Va. One Co. 1st N. Y. Cav. *Union* 1 killed. *Confed.* 3 killed, 5 wounded.

Jacksborough, Big Creek Gap, Tenn. 2d Tenn. *Union* 2 wounded. *Confed.* 2 killed, 4 wounded.

11—Paris, Tenn. Detachments of 5th Iowa and 1st Neb. Cav., Battery K 1st Mo. Art. *Union* 5 killed, 5 wounded. *Confed.* 10 wounded.

12—Lexington, Mo. 1st Iowa Cav. *Union* 1 killed, 1 wounded. *Confed.* 9 killed, 3 wounded.

Near Lebanon, Mo. *Confed.* 13 killed, 5 wounded.

13—New Madrid, Mo. 10th and 16th Ill., 27th, 39th, 43d and 63d Ohio, 3d Mich. Cav., 1st U. S. Inft., Bissell's Mo. Engineers. *Union* 50 wounded. *Confed.* 100 wounded.

14—Newberne, N. C. 51st N. Y., 8th, 10th and 11th Conn., 21st, 23d, 24th, 25th and 27th Mass., 9th N. J., 51st Pa., 4th and 5th R. I. *Union* 91 killed, 466 wounded. *Confed.* 64 killed, 106 wounded, 413 captured.

16—Black Jack Forest, Tenn. Detachments of 4th Ill. and 5th Ohio Cav. *Union* 4 wounded.

18—Salem or Spring River, Ark. Detachments of 6th Mo. and 3d Iowa Cav. *Union* 5 killed, 10 wounded. *Confed.* 100 killed, wounded and missing.

21—Mosquito Inlet, Fla. U. S. Gunboats *Penguin* and *Henry Andrew.* *Union* 8 killed, 8 wounded.

22—Independence or Little Santa Fe, Mo. 2d Kan. *Union* 1 killed, 2 wounded. *Confed.* 7 killed.

23—Carthage, Mo. 6th Kan. Cav. *Union* 1 wounded.

Winchester or Kearnstown, Va. 1st W. Va., 84th and 110th Pa., 5th, 7th, 8th, 29th, 62d and 67th Ohio, 7th, 13th and 14th Ind., 39th Ill., 1st Ohio Cav., 1st Mich. Cav., 1st W. Va. Artil., 1st Ohio Artil., Co. E 4th U. S. Artil. *Union* 103 killed, 440 wounded, 24 missing. *Confed.* 80 killed, 342 wounded, 269 prisoners.

26—Warrensburg or Briar, Mo. Sixty men of 7th Mo. Militia Cav. *Union* 1 killed, 22 wounded. *Confed.* 9 killed, 17 wounded.

Humonsville, Mo. Co. B 8th Mo. Militia Cav. *Union* 5 wounded. *Confed.* 15 wounded.

26, 27 and **28**—Apache Cañon or Glorietta, near Santa Fe, N. Mex. 1st and 2d Colo. Cav. *Union* 32 killed, 75 wounded, 35 missing. *Confed.* 36 killed, 60 wounded, 93 missing.

28—Warrensburg, Mo. 1st Ill. Cav. *Union* 3 killed, 1 wounded. *Confed.* 15 killed.

APRIL, 1862

2—Putnam's Ferry, near Doniphan, Mo. 21st and 38th Ill., 5th Ill. Cav., 16th Ohio Battery and Col. Carlin's Brigade. *Confed.* 3 killed.

4—Great Bethel, Va. Advance of 3d Corps Army of Potomac. *Union* 4 killed, 10 wounded.

Crump's Landing or Adamsville, Tenn. 48th, 70th and 72d Ohio, 5th Ohio Cav. *Union* 2 wounded. *Confed.* 20 wounded.

6 and **7**—Shiloh or Pittsburg Landing, Tenn. Army of Western Tennessee, commanded by Maj.-Gen. U. S. Grant, as follows: 1st Div., Maj.-Gen. J. A. McClernand; 2d Div., Maj.-Gen. C. F. Smith; 3d Div., Brig.-Gen. Lew. Wallace; 4th Div., Brig.-Gen. S. A. Hurlburt; 5th Div., Brig.-Gen. W. T. Sherman; 6th Div., Brig.-Gen. B. M. Prentiss. Army of the Ohio commanded by Maj.-Gen. D. C. Buell, as follows: 2d Div., Brig.-Gen. A. M. D. Cook; 4th Div., Brig.-Gen. W. Nelson; 5th Div., Brig.-Gen. T. L. Crittenden, 21st Brigade of the 6th Div., Gunboats *Tyler* and *Lexington.* *Union* 1,735 killed, 7,882 wounded, 3,956 captured. *Confed.* 1,728 killed, 8,012 wounded, 959 captured. *Union* Brig.-Gen. W. T. Sherman and W. H. L. Wallace wounded and B. M. Prentiss captured. *Confed.* Maj.-Gen. A. S. Johnson, commander-in-chief, and Brig.-Gen. A. H. Gladden killed; Maj.-Gen. W. S. Cheatham and Brig.-Gen. C. Clark, B. R. Johnson, and J. S. Bowen wounded.

8—Island No. 10, Tenn. Maj.-Gen. Pope's command and the Navy, under Flag-officer Foote. *Confed.* 17 killed, 3,000 prisoners.

Near Corinth, Miss. 3d Brigade 5th Div. Army of Western Tennessee and 4th Ill. Cav. *Confed.* 15 killed, 25 wounded, 200 captured.

9—Owen's River, Cal. 2d Cal. Cav. *Union* 1 killed, 2 wounded

10—Ft. Pulaski, Ga. 6th and 7th Conn., 3d R. I., 46th and 48th N. Y., 8th Maine, 15th U. S. Inft., Crew of U. S. S. *Wabash.* *Union* 1 killed. *Confed.* 4 wounded, 360 prisoners.

11—Huntsville, Ala. Army of the Ohio 3d Div. *Confed.* 200 prisoners.

Yorktown, Va. 12th N. Y., 57th and 63d Pa. *Union* 2 killed, 8 wounded.

12—Little Blue River, Mo. *Confed.* 5 killed.

Monterey, Va. 75th Ohio, 1st W. Va. Cav. *Union* 3 wounded.

14—Pollocksville, N. C. *Confed.* 7 wounded.

Diamond Grove, Mo. 6th Kan. Cav. *Union* 1 wounded.

Walkersville, Mo. 2d Mo. Militia Cav. *Union* 2 killed, 3 wounded.
Montavallo, Mo. Two Cos. 1st Iowa Cav. *Union* 2 killed, 6 wounded. *Confed.* 2 killed, 10 wounded.
15—Pechacho Pass, Ariz. 1st Cal. Cav. *Union* 3 killed, 3 wounded.
16—Savannah, Tenn. *Confed.* 5 killed, 65 wounded.
White Marsh or Wilmington Island, Ga. 8th Mich., Battery of R. I. Light Artil. *Union* 10 killed, 35 wounded. *Confed.* 5 killed, 7 wounded.
Lee's Mills, Va. 3d, 4th and 6th Vt., 3d N. Y. Battery and Battery of 5th U. S. Artil. *Union* 35 killed, 129 wounded. *Confed.* 20 killed, 75 wounded, 50 captured.
17—Holly River, W. Va. *Union* 3 wounded. *Confed.* 2 killed.
18—Falmouth, Va. 2d N. Y. Cav. *Union* 5 killed, 16 wounded. *Confed.* 19 captured.
Edisto Island, S. C. 55th Pa., 3d N. H., U. S. S. *Crusader*. *Union* 3 wounded.
18 to **28**.—Forts Jackson and St. Philip, and the capture of New Orleans, La. Commodore Farragut's fleet of war vessels and mortar boats, under Commander D. D. Porter. *Union* 36 killed, 193 wounded. *Confed.* 185 killed, 197 wounded, 400 captured.
19—Talbot's Ferry, Ark. 4th Iowa Cav. *Union* 1 killed. *Confed.* 3 killed.
Camden, N. C., also called South Mills. 9th and 89th N. Y., 21st Mass., 51st Pa., 6th N. H. *Union* 12 killed, 98 wounded. *Confed.* 6 killed, 19 wounded.
23—Grass Lick, W. Va. 3d Md., Potomac Home Brigade. *Union* 3 killed.
25—Fort Macon, N. C. U. S. Gunboats *Daylight, Georgia, Chippewa*, the bark *Gemsbok* and Gen. Parkes's division. *Union* 1 killed, 11 wounded. *Confed.* 7 killed, 18 wounded, 450 captured.
26—Turnback Creek, Mo. 5th Kan. Cav. *Union* 1 killed.
Neosho, Mo. 1st Mo. Cav. *Union* 3 killed, 3 wounded. *Confed.* 30 wounded, 62 prisoners.
In front of Yorktown, Va. Three Cos. 1st Mass. *Union* 3 killed, 16 wounded.
27—Horton's Mills, N. C. 103d N. Y. *Union* 1 killed, 6 wounded. *Confed.* 3 wounded.
28—Paint Rock Railroad Bridge. Twenty-two men of 10th Wis. *Union* 7 wounded.
Cumberland Mountain, Tenn. 16th and 42d Ohio, 22d Ky.
Monterey, Tenn. 2d Iowa Cav. *Union* 1 killed, 3 wounded. *Confed.* 5 killed.
29—Bridgeport, Ala. 3d Div. Army of the Ohio. *Confed.* 72 killed and wounded, 350 captured.

MAY, 1862

1—Clarke's Hollow, W. Va. Co. C 23d Ohio. *Union* 1 killed, 21 wounded.
3—Farmington, Miss. 10th, 16th, 22d, 27th, 42d and 51st Ill., 10th and 16th Mich., Yates's (Ill.) Sharpshooters, 2d Mich. Cav., Battery C 1st Ill. Artil. *Union* 2 killed, 12 wounded. *Confed.* 30 killed.
4—Licking, Mo. 24th Mo., 5th Mo., Militia Cav. *Union* 1 killed, 2 wounded.
Cheese Cake Church, Va. 3d Pa., 1st and 6th U. S. Cav.
5—Lebanon, Tenn. 1st, 4th and 5th Ky. Cav., Detachment of the 7th Pa. *Union* 6 killed, 25 wounded. *Confed.* 66 prisoners.
Lockridge Mills or Dresden, Ky. 5th Iowa Cav. *Union* 4 killed, 16 wounded, 68 missing.
Williamsburg, Va. 3d and 4th Corps, Army of the Potomac. *Union* 456 killed, 1,400 wounded, 372 missing. *Confed.* 1,000 killed, wounded, and captured.
7—West Point or Eltham's Landing, Va. 16th, 31st and 32d N. Y., 95th and 96th Pa., 5th Maine, 1st Mass. Artil., Battery D 2d U. S. Artil. *Union* 49 killed, 104 wounded, 41 missing.
Somerville Heights, Va. 13th Ind. *Union* 2 killed, 7 wounded, 24 missing.
8—McDowell or Bull Pasture, Va. 25th, 32d, 75th and 82d Ohio, 3d W. Va., 1st W. Va. Cav., 1st Conn. Cav., 1st Ind. Battery. *Union* 28 killed, 225 wounded. *Confed.* 100 killed, 200 wounded.
Glendale, near Corinth, Miss. 7th Ill. Cav. *Union* 1 killed, 4 wounded. *Confed.* 30 killed and wounded.
9—Elkton Station, near Athens, Ala. Co. E 37th Ind. *Union* 5 killed, 43 captured. *Confed.* 13 killed.
Slatersville or New Kent C. H., Va. 98th Pa., 2d R. I., 6th U. S. Cav. *Union* 4 killed, 3 wounded. *Confed.* 10 killed, 14 wounded.
10—Fort Pillow, Tenn. U. S. Gunboats *Cincinnati* and *Mound City*. *Union* 3 wounded. *Confed.* 2 killed, 1 wounded.
11—Bloomfield, Mo. 1st Wis. Cav. *Confed.* 1 killed.
13—Monterey, Tenn. Part of Brig.-Gen. M. L. Smith's Brigade. *Union* 2 wounded. *Confed.* 2 killed, 3 wounded.
15—Linden, Va. One Co. of 28th Pa. *Union* 1 killed, 3 wounded, 14 missing.
Fort Darling, James River, Va. U. S. Gunboats *Galena, Port Royal, Naugatuck, Monitor* and *Aroostook*. *Union* 12 killed, 14 wounded. *Confed.* 7 killed, 8 wounded.
Chalk Bluffs, Mo. 1st Wis. Cav. *Union* 1 killed, 3 wounded.
Butler, Bates Co., Mo. 1st Iowa Cav. *Union* 3 killed, 1 wounded.
15, 16 and **18**—Princeton, W. Va. Gen. J. D. Cox's Division. *Union* 30 killed, 70 wounded. *Confed.* 2 killed, 14 wounded.
17—In front of Corinth, Miss. Brig.-Gen. M. L. Smith's Brigade. *Union* 10 killed, 31 wounded. *Confed.* 12 killed.
19—Searcy Landing, Ark. Detachments of 3d and 17th Mo. and 4th Mo. Cav., Battery B 1st Mo. Light Artil. *Union* 18 killed, 27 wounded. *Confed.* 150 killed, wounded and missing.
Clinton, N. C. *Union* 5 wounded. *Confed.* 9 killed.
21—Phillip's Creek, Miss. 2d Div. Army of Tennessee. *Union* 3 wounded.
22—Florida, Mo. Detachment 3d Iowa Cav. *Union* 2 wounded.
Near New Berne, N. C. Co. I 17th Mass. *Union* 3 killed, 8 wounded.
23—Lewisburg, Va. 36th and 44th Ohio, 2d W. Va. Cav. *Union* 14 killed, 60 wounded. *Confed.* 40 killed, 66 wounded, 100 captured.
Front Royal, Va. 1st Md., Detachments of 29th Pa., Capt. Mapes' Pioneers, 5th N. Y. Cav., and 1st Pa. Artil. *Union* 32 killed, 122 wounded, 750 missing.
Buckton Station, Va. 3d Wis., 27th Ind. *Union* 2 killed, 6 wounded. *Confed.* 12 killed.
Ft. Craig, New Mex. 3d U. S. Cav. *Union* 3 wounded.
24—New Bridge, Va. 4th Mich. *Union* 1 killed, 10 wounded. *Confed.* 60 killed and wounded, 27 captured.
Chickahominy, Va. Davidson's Brigade of 4th Corps. *Union* 2 killed, 4 wounded.
25—Winchester, Va. 2d Mass., 29th and 46th Pa., 27th Ind., 3d Wis., 28th N. Y., 5th Conn., Battery M 1st N. Y. Artil., 1st Vt. Cav., 1st Mich. Cav., 5th N. Y. Cav. *Union* 38 killed, 155 wounded, 711 missing.
27—Hanover C. H., Va. 12th, 13th, 14th, 17th, 25th and 44th N. Y., 62d and 83d Pa., 16th Mich., 9th and 22d Mass., 5th Mass. Artil., 2d Maine Artil., Battery F 5th U. S. Artil., 1st U. S. Sharpshooters. *Union* 53 killed, 344 wounded. *Confed.* 200 killed and wounded, 730 prisoners.
Big Indian Creek, near Searcy Landing, Ark. 1st Mo. Cav. *Union* 3 wounded. *Confed*, 5 killed, 25 wounded.
Osceola, Mo. 1st Iowa Cav. *Union* 3 killed, 2 wounded.
28—Wardensville, Va. 3d Md., Potomac Home Brigade, 3d Ind. Cav. *Confed.* 2 killed, 3 wounded.
29—Pocataligo, S. C. 50th Pa., 79th N. Y., 8th Mich., 1st Mass. Cav. *Union* 2 killed, 9 wounded.
30—Booneville, Miss. 2d Iowa Cav., 2d Mich. Cav. *Confed.* 2,000 prisoners.
Front Royal, Va. 1st R. I. Cav. *Union* 5 killed, 8 wounded. *Confed.* 156 captured.
31—Neosho, Mo. 10th Ill. Cav., 14th Mo. Cav. (Militia). *Union* 2 killed, 3 wounded.
Near Washington, N. C. 3d N. Y. Cav. *Union* 1 wounded. *Confed.* 3 killed, 2 wounded.
31 and **June 1**—Seven Pines and Fair Oaks, Va. 2d Corps, 3d Corps and 4th Corps, Army of the Potomac. *Union* 890 killed, 3,627 wounded, 1,222 missing. *Confed.* 2,800 killed, 3,897 wounded, 1,300 missing. *Union* Brig.-Gen'ls O. O. Howard, Naglee, and Wessells wounded. *Confed.* Brig.-Gen. Hatton killed, Gen. J. E. Johnson and Brig.-Gen. Rhodes wounded, Brig.-Gen. Pettigrew captured.

JUNE, 1862

1 and **2**—Strasburg and Staunton Road, Va. 8th W. Va., 60th Ohio, 1st N. J. Cav., 1st Pa. Cav. *Union* 2 wounded.
3—Legare's Point, S. C. 28th Mass., 100th Pa. *Union* 5 wounded.
4—Jasper, Sweden's Cove, Tenn. 79th Pa., 5th Ky. Cav., 7th Pa. Cav., 1st Ohio Battery. *Union* 2 killed, 7 wounded. *Confed.* 20 killed, 20 wounded.
Blackland, Miss. 2d Iowa Cav., 2d Mich. Cav. *Union* 5 killed, 14 wounded.
5—Tranter's Creek, N. C. 24th Mass., Co. I 3d N. Y. Cav., Marine Artil. *Union* 7 killed, 11 wounded.
6—Memphis, Tenn. U. S. Gunboats *Benton, Louisville, Carondelet, Cairo,* and *St. Louis;* and Rams *Monarch* and *Queen of the West*. *Confed.* 80 killed and wounded, 100 captured.
Harrisonburg, Va. 1st N. J. Cav., 1st Pa. Rifles, 6th Ohio, 8th W. Va. *Union* 63 missing. *Confed.* 17 killed, 50 wounded. *Confed.* Gen. Ashby killed.
8—Cross Keys or Union Church, Va. 8th, 39th, 41st, 45th, 54th and 58th N. Y., 2d, 3d, 5th and 8th W. Va., 25th, 32d, 55th, 60th, 73d, 75th and 82d Ohio, 1st and 27th Pa., 1st Ohio Battery. *Union* 125 killed, 500 wounded. *Confed.* 42 killed, 230 wounded. *Confed.* Brig.-Gens. Stewart and Elzey wounded.
9—Port Republic, Va. 5th, 7th, 29th and 66th Ohio, 84th and 110th Pa., 7th Ind., 1st W. Va., Batteries E 4th U. S. and A and L 1st Ohio Artil. *Union* 67 killed, 361 wounded, 574 missing. *Confed.* 88 killed, 535 wounded, 34 missing.
10—James Island, S. C. *Union* 3 killed, 13 wounded. *Confed.* 17 killed, 30 wounded.
11—Monterey, Owen Co., Ky. Capt. Blood's Mounted Provost Guard, 13th Ind. Battery. *Union* 2 killed. *Confed.* 100 captured.
12—Waddell's Farm, near Village Creek, Ark. Detachment of 9th Ill. Cav. *Union* 12 wounded. *Confed.* 28 killed and wounded.
13—Old Church, Va. 5th U. S. Cav. *Confed.* 1 killed.
James Island, S. C. *Union* 3 killed, 19 wounded. *Confed.* 19 killed, 6 wounded.
14—Turnstall Station, Va. *Union* 4 killed, 8 wounded. Bushwackers fire into railway train.
16—Secessionville or Fort Johnson, James Island, S. C. 46th, 47th and 79th N. Y., 3d R. I., 3d N. H., 45th, 97th and 100th Pa., 6th and 7th Conn., 8th Mich., 28th Mass., 1st N. Y. Engineers, 1st Conn. Artil., Battery E 3d U. S. and I 3d R. I. Artil., Co. H 1st Mass. Cav. *Union* 85 killed, 472 wounded, 138 missing. *Confed.* 51 killed, 144 wounded.
17—St. Charles, White River, Ark. 43d and 46th Ind., U. S. Gunboats *Lexington, Mound City, Conestoga* and *St. Louis*. *Union* 105 killed, 30 wounded. *Confed.* 155 killed, wounded and captured.
Warrensburg, Mo. 7th Mo. Cav. (Militia). *Union* 2 killed, 2 wounded.
Smithville, Ark. *Union* 2 killed, 4 wounded. *Confed.* 4 wounded, 15 prisoners.
18—Williamsburg Road, Va. 16th Mass. *Union* 7 killed, 57 wounded. *Confed.* 5 killed, 9 wounded.
21—Battle Creek, Tenn. 2d and 33d Ohio, 10th Wis., 24th Ill., 4th Ohio Cav., 4th Ky. Cav., and Edgarton's Battery. *Union* 4 killed, 3 wounded.
22—Raceland, near Algiers, La. 8th Vt. *Union* 3 killed, 8 wounded.
23—Raytown, Mo. 7th Mo. Cav. *Union* 1 killed, 1 wounded.
25—Oak Grove, Va., also called Kings School House and The Orchards. Hooker's and Kearney's Divisions of the Third Corps, Palmer's Brigade of the Fourth Corps, and part of Richardson's Division of the Second Corps. *Union* 51 killed, 401 wounded, 64 missing. *Confed.* 65 killed, 465 wounded, 11 missing.
Germantown, Tenn. 56th Ohio. *Union* 10 killed.
Little Red River, Ark. 4th Iowa Cav. *Union* 2 wounded.
26 to **29**—Vicksburg, Miss. U. S. Fleet, under command of Commodore Farragut. No casualties recorded.
26 to **July 1**—The Seven Days' Retreat. Army of the Potomac, Maj.-Gen. Geo. B. McClellan commanding, including engagements known as Mechanicsville or Ellison's Mills on the 26th, Gaines' Mills or Cold Harbor and Chickahominy on the 27th, Peach Orchard and Savage Station on the 29th, White Oak Swamp, also called Charles City Cross Roads, Glendale, Nelson's Farm, Frazier's Farm, Turkey Bend and New Market Cross Roads on the 30th and Malvern Hill on July 1st.
Union—First Corps, Brig.-Gen. McCall's Div., 253 killed, 1,240 wounded, 1,581 missing.
Second Corps, Maj.-Gen. E. V. Sumner, 187 killed, 1076 wounded, 848 missing.
Third Corps, Maj.-Gen. Heintzleman, 189 killed, 1,051 wounded, 833 missing.
Fourth Corps, Maj.-Gen. E. D. Keyes, 69 killed, 507 wounded, 201 missing.
Fifth Corps, Maj.-Gen. Fitz-John Porter, 620 killed, 2,460 wounded, 1,198 missing.
Sixth Corps, Maj.-Gen. Franklin, 245 killed, 1,313 wounded, 1,179 missing.
Cavalry, Brig.-Gen. Stoneman, 19 killed, 60 wounded, 97 missing.
Engineers' Corps, 2 wounded, 21 missing.
Total, 1,582 killed, 7,709 wounded, 5,958 missing.
(Maj.-Gen. Sumner and Brig.-Gens. Mead, Brook and Burns, wounded.)
Confed.—Maj.-Gen. Hager's Division, 187 killed, 803 wounded, 360 missing.
Maj.-Gen. Magruder's Division, 258 killed, 1,495 wounded, 30 missing.
Maj.-Gen. Longstreet's Division, 763 killed, 3,929 wounded, 239 missing.
Maj.Gen. Hill's Division, 619 killed, 3,251 wounded.
Maj.-Gen. Jackson's Division, 966 killed, 4,417 wounded, 63 missing.
Maj.-Gen. Holmes' Division, 2 killed, 52 wounded.
Maj.-Gen. Stuart's Cavalry, 15 killed, 30 wounded, 60 missing.
Artillery, Brig.-Gen. Pendleton, 10 killed, 34 wounded.
Total, 2,820 killed, 14,011 wounded, 752 missing.
Brig.-Gens. Griffith, killed, and Anderson, Featherstone and Pender wounded.
27—Williams Bridge, Amite River, La. 21st Ind. *Union* 2 killed, 4 wounded. *Confed.* 4 killed.
Village Creek, Ark. 9th Ill. Cav. *Union* 2 killed, 30 wounded.
Waddell's Farm, Ark. Detachment 3d Iowa Cav. *Union* 4 killed, 4 wounded.
29—Willis Church, Va. Cavalry advance of Casey's Division, Fourth Corps. *Confed.* 2 killed, 15 wounded, 46 captured.
30—Luray, Va. Detachment of Cavalry of Brig.-Gen. Crawford's Command. *Union* 1 killed, 3 wounded.

JULY, 1862

1—Boonville, Miss. 2d Iowa Cav., 2d Mich. Cav. *Union* 45 killed and wounded. *Confed.* 17 killed, 65 wounded.

Morning Sun, Tenn. 57th Ohio. *Union* 4 wounded. *Confed.* 11 killed, 26 wounded.

3—Haxals or Elvington Heights, Va. 14th Ind., 7th W. Va., 4th and 8th Ohio. *Union* 8 killed, 32 wounded. *Confed.* 100 killed and wounded.

6—Grand Prairie, near Aberdeen, Ark. 24th Ind. *Union* 1 killed, 21 wounded. *Confed.* 84 killed and wounded.

7—Bayou Cache, also called Cotton Plant, Round Hill, Hill's Plantation and Bayou de View. 11th Wis., 33d Ill., 8th Ind., 1st Mo. Light Artil., 1st Ind. Cav., 5th and 13th Ill. Cav. *Union* 7 killed, 57 wounded. *Confed.* 110 killed, 200 wounded.

8—Black River, Mo. 5th Kan. Cav. *Union* 1 killed, 3 wounded.

9—Hamilton, N. C. 9th N. Y. and Gunboats *Perry*, *Ceres* and *Shawseen*. *Union* 1 killed, 20 wounded.

Aberdeen, Ark. 24th, 34th, 43d and 46th Ind. Casualties not recorded.

Tompkinsville, Ky. 3d Pa. Cav. *Union* 4 killed, 6 wounded. *Confed.* 10 killed and wounded.

11—Williamsburg, Va. *Confed.* 3 killed.

Pleasant Hill, Mo. 1st Iowa Cav., Mo. Militia. *Union* 10 killed, 19 wounded. *Confed.* 6 killed, 5 wounded.

12—Lebanon, Ky. 28th Ky., Lebanon Home Guards (Morgan's Raid). *Union* 2 killed, 65 prisoners.

Near Culpepper, Va. 1st Md., 1st Vt., 1st W. Va., 5th N. Y. Cav. *Confed.* 1 killed, 5 wounded.

13—Murfreesboro', Tenn. 9th Mich., 3d Minn., 4th Ky. Cav., 7th Pa. Cav., 1st Ky. Battery. *Union* 33 killed, 62 wounded, 800 missing. *Confed.* 50 killed, 100 wounded.

14—Batesville, Ark. 4th Iowa Cav. *Union* 1 killed, 4 wounded.

15—Attempt to destroy 4th Wis., Gunboats *Carondelet*, *Queen of the West*, *Tyler* and *Essex*. *Union* 13 killed, 36 wounded. *Confed.* 5 killed, 9 wounded.

Apache Pass, Ariz. 2d Cal. Cav. *Union* 1 wounded.

Fayetteville, Ark. Detachment of Cavalry, under command of Maj. W. H. Miller. *Confed.* 150 captured.

Near Decatur, Tenn. Detachment of 1st Ohio Cav. *Union* 4 wounded.

17—Cynthiana, Ky. 18th Ky., 7th Ky. Cav., Cynthiana, Newport, Cincinnati and Bracken Co. Home Guards (Morgan's Raid). *Union* 17 killed, 34 wounded. *Confed.* 8 killed, 29 wounded.

18—Memphis, Mo. 2d Mo. Cav., 9th and 11th Mo. State Militia. *Union* 13 killed, 35 wounded. *Confed.* 23 killed.

20 to September **20**—Guerrilla Campaign in Missouri. Gen. Schofield's Command. *Union* 77 killed, 156 wounded, 347 missing. *Confed.* 506 killed, 1,800 wounded, 560 missing.

23—Florida, Mo. Two Cos. 3d Iowa Cav. *Union* 22 wounded. *Confed.* 3 killed.

Columbus, Mo. 7th Mo. Cav. *Union* 2 wounded.

24—Trinity, Ala. Co. E 31st Ohio. *Union* 2 killed, 11 wounded. *Confed.* 12 killed, 30 wounded.

Near Florida, Mo. 3d Iowa Cav. *Union* 1 killed, 2 wounded. *Confed.* 1 killed, 12 wounded.

24 and **25**—Santa Fe, Mo. 3d Iowa Cav. *Union* 2 killed, 13 wounded.

25—Courtland Bridge, Ala. Two Cos. 10th Ky., two Cos. 1st Ohio Cav. *Union* 100 captured.

25 and **26**—Mountain Store and Big Piney, Mo. Three Cos. 3d Mo. Cav., Battery L 2d Mo. Artil. *Confed.* 5 killed.

26—Young's Cross Roads, N. C. 9th N. J., 3d N. Y. Cav. *Union* 7 wounded. *Confed.* 4 killed, 13 wounded.

Greenville, Mo. 3d and 12th Mo. Militia Cav. *Union* 2 killed, 5 wounded.

28—Bayou Barnard, Ind. Ter. 1st, 2d and 3d Kan. Home Guards, 1st Kan. Battery. No casualties recorded.

Moore's Mills, Mo. 9th Mo., 3d Iowa Cav., 2d Mo. Cav., 3d Ind. Battery. *Union* 19 killed, 21 wounded. *Confed.* 30 killed, 100 wounded.

29—Bollinger's Mills, Mo. Two Cos. 13th Mo. *Confed.* 10 killed.

Russelville, Ky. 7th Ind., Russelville Home Guards. *Union* 1 wounded.

Brownsville, Tenn. One Co. 15th Ill. Cav. *Union* 4 killed, 6 wounded. *Confed.* 4 killed, 6 wounded.

30—Paris, Ky. 9th Pa. Cav. *Confed.* 27 killed, 39 wounded.

31—Coggins' Point, opposite Harrison's Landing, Va. U. S. Gunboat Fleet. *Union* 10 killed, 15 wounded. *Confed.* 1 killed, 6 wounded.

AUGUST, 1862

1—Newark, Mo. Seventy-three men of the 11th Mo. State Militia. *Union* 4 killed, 4 wounded, 60 captured. *Confed.* 73 killed and wounded.

2—Ozark or Forsythe, Mo. 14th Mo. State Militia. *Union* 1 wounded. *Confed.* 3 killed, 7 wounded.

Orange C. H., Va. 5th N. Y. Cav., 1st Vt. Cav. *Union* 4 killed, 12 wounded. *Confed.* 11 killed, 52 captured.

Clear Creek or Taberville, Mo. Four Cos. 1st Iowa Cav. *Union* 5 killed, 14 wounded. *Confed.* 11 killed.

Coahomo Co., Miss. 11th Wis. *Union* 5 wounded.

3—Sycamore Church, near Petersburg, Va. 3d Pa. Cav., 5th U. S. Cav. *Union* 2 wounded. *Confed.* 6 wounded.

Chariton Bridge, Mo. 6th Mo. Cav. *Union* 2 wounded. *Confed.* 11 killed, 14 wounded.

Jonesboro', Ark. 1st Wis. Cav. *Union* 4 killed, 2 wounded, 21 missing.

Lauguelle Ferry, Ark. 1st Wis. Cav. *Union* 17 killed, 38 wounded.

4—Sparta, Tenn. Detachments of 4th Ky. and 7th Ind. Cav. *Union* 1 killed.

White Oak Swamp Bridge, Va. 3d Pa. Cav. *Confed.* 10 wounded, 28 captured.

5—Baton Rouge, La. 14th Me., 6th Mich., 7th Vt., 21st Ind., 30th Mass., 9th Conn., 4th Wis., 2d, 4th and 6th Mass. Batteries. *Union* 82 killed, 255 wounded, 34 missing. *Confed.* 84 killed, 316 wounded, 78 missing. *Union* Brig.-Gen. Thomas Williams killed.

Malvern Hill, Va. Portion of Hooker's Div., Third Corps and Richardson's Div., Second Corps and Cavalry, Army of the Potomac. *Union* 3 killed, 11 wounded. *Confed.* 100 captured.

6—Montevallo, Mo. 3d Wis. Cav. *Union* 1 wounded, 3 missing.

Beech Creek, W. Va. 4th W. Va. *Union* 3 killed, 8 wounded. *Confed.* 1 killed, 11 wounded.

Kirksville, Mo. Mo. State Militia. *Union* 28 killed, 60 wounded. *Confed.* 128 killed, 200 wounded.

Matapony or Thornburg, Va. Detachment of King's Division. *Union* 1 killed, 12 wounded, 72 missing.

Tazewell, Tenn. 16th and 42d Ohio, 14th and 22d Ky., 4th Wis. Battery. *Union* 3 killed, 23 wounded, 50 missing. *Confed.* 9 killed, 40 wounded.

7—Trenton, Tenn. 2d Ill. Cav. *Confed.* 30 killed, 20 wounded.

8—Panther Creek, Mo. 1st Mo. Militia Cav. *Union* 1 killed, 4 wounded.

9—Stockton, Mo. Col. McNeil's command of Mo. State Militia. *Confed.* 13 killed, 36 missing.

Cedar Mountain, Va., also called Slaughter Mountain, Southwest Mountain, Cedar Run and Mitchell's Station. Second Corps, Maj.-Gen. Banks; Third Corps, Maj.-Gen. McDowell. Army of Virginia, under command of Maj.-Gen. Pope. *Union* 450 killed, 660 wounded, 290 missing. *Confed.* 229 killed, 1,047 wounded, 31 missing. *Union* Brig.-Gens. Augur, Carroll, and Geary wounded. *Confed.* Brig.-Gen. C. S. Winder killed.

10—Nueces River, Tex. Texas Loyalists. *Union* 40 killed. *Confed.* 8 killed, 14 wounded.

10 to **13**—Grand River, Lee's Ford, Chariton River, Walnut Creek, Compton Ferry, Switzler's Mills and Yellow Creek, Mo. 9th Mo. Militia. *Union* 100 killed and wounded.

11—Independence, Mo. 7th Mo. Militia Cav. *Union* 14 killed, 18 wounded, 312 missing.

Helena, Ark. 2d Wis. Cav. *Union* 1 killed, 2 wounded.

Wyoming C. H., W. Va. Detachment of 37th Ohio. *Union* 2 killed.

Kinderhook, Tenn. Detachments of 3d Ky. and 1st Tenn. Cav. *Union* 3 killed. *Confed.* 7 killed.

12—Galatin, Tenn. 2d Ind., 4th and 5th Ky., 1st Pa. Cav. *Union* 30 killed, 50 wounded, 200 captured. *Confed.* 6 killed, 18 wounded.

13—Galatin, Tenn. 13th and 69th Ohio, 11th Mich., drove the Confederates from the town with slight loss.

Clarendon, Ark. Brig.-Gen. Hovey's Div. of the 13th Corps. *Confed.* 700 captured.

15—Merriweather's Ferry, Tenn. One Co. 2d Ill. Cav. *Union* 3 killed, 6 wounded. *Confed.* 20 killed.

16—Lone Jack, Mo. Mo. Militia Cav. *Union* 60 killed, 100 wounded. *Confed.* 110 killed and wounded.

18—Capture of Rebel steamer *Fairplay*, near Milliken's Bend, La. 58th and 76th Ohio. *Confed.* 40 prisoners.

19—Clarksville, Tenn. 71st Ohio. *Union* 200 captured.

White Oak Ridge, near Hickman, Ky. 2d Ill. Cav. *Union* 2 wounded. *Confed.* 4 killed.

20—Brandy Station, Va. Cavalry of Army of Virginia. *Confed.* 3 killed, 12 wounded.

Edgefield Junction, Tenn. Detachment of 50th Ind. *Confed.* 8 killed, 18 wounded.

Union Mills, Mo. 1st Mo. Cav., 13th Ill. Cav. *Union* 4 killed, 3 wounded. *Confed.* 1 killed.

21—Pinckney Island, S. C. *Union* 3 killed, 3 wounded.

22—Courtland, Tenn. 42d Ill. *Union* 2 wounded. *Confed.* 8 killed.

23—Big Hill, Madison Co., Ky. 3d Tenn., 7th Ky. Cav. *Union* 10 killed, 40 wounded and missing. *Confed.* 25 killed.

23 to **25**—Skirmishes on the Rappahannock at Waterloo Bridge, Lee Springs, Freeman's Ford and Sulphur Springs, Va. Army of Virginia, under Maj.-Gen. Pope. *Confed.* 27 killed, 94 wounded. *Union* Brig.-Gen. Bohlen captured.

23 to Sept. **1**—Pope's Campaign in Virginia. Army of Virginia. *Union* 7,000 killed, wounded and missing. *Confed.* 1,500 killed, 8,000 wounded.

24—Dallas, Mo. 12th Mo. Militia Cav. *Union* 3 killed, 1 wounded.

Coon Creek or Lamar, Mo. *Union* 2 killed, 22 wounded.

25 and **26**—Fort Donelson and Cumberland Iron Works, Tenn. 71st Ohio, 5th Iowa Cav. *Union* 31 killed and wounded. *Confed.* 30 killed and wounded.

Bloomfield, Mo. 13th Ill. Cav. *Confed.* 20 killed and wounded.

26—Rienzi and Kossuth, Miss. 2d Iowa Cav., 7th Kan. Cav. *Union* 5 killed, 12 wounded.

27—Bull Run Bridge, Va. 11th and 12th Ohio, 1st, 2d, 3d and 4th N. J. *Union* Brig.-Gen. G. W. Taylor mortally wounded.

Kettle Run, Va. Maj.-Gen. Hooker's Div. of Third Corps. *Union* 300 killed and wounded. *Confed.* 300 killed and wounded.

28—Readyville or Round Hill, Tenn. 10th Brigade Army of Ohio. *Union* 5 wounded.

28 and **29**—Groveton and Gainesville, Va. First Corps, Maj.-Gen. Sigel, Third Corps, Maj.-Gen. McDowell, Army of Virginia, Hooker's and Kearney's Division of Third Corps, and Reynolds' Division of First Corps, Army of Potomac, Ninth Corps, Maj.-Gen. Reno. *Union* 7,000 killed, wounded and missing. *Confed.* 7,000 killed, wounded and missing.

29—Manchester, Tenn. Two Cos. 18th Ohio, one Co. 9th Mich. *Confed.* 100 killed and wounded.

30—Second Battle of Bull Run or Manassas, Va. Same troops as engaged at Groveton and Gainesville on the 28th and 29th, with the addition of Porter's Fifth Corps. *Union* 800 killed, 4,000 wounded, 3,000 missing. *Confed.* 700 killed, 3,000 wounded.

Bolivar, Tenn. 20th and 78th Ohio, 2d and 11th Ill. Cav., 9th Ind. Art. *Union* 5 killed, 18 wounded, 64 missing. *Confed.* 100 killed and wounded.

McMinnville, Tenn. 26th Ohio, 17th and 58th Ind., 8th Ind. Battery. *Confed.* 1 killed, 20 wounded.

Richmond, Ky. 12th, 16th, 55th, 66th, 69th and 71st Ind., 95th Ohio, 18th Ky., 6th and 7th Ky. Cav., Batteries D and G Mich. Art. *Union* 200 killed, 700 wounded, 4,000 missing. *Confed.* 250 killed, 500 wounded.

31—Medon Station, Tenn. 45th Ill., 7th Mo. *Union* 3 killed, 13 wounded, 43 missing.

Yates' Ford, Ky. 94th Ohio. *Union* 3 killed, 10 wounded.

SEPTEMBER, 1862.

1—Britton's Lane, Tenn. 20th and 30th Ill., 4th Ill. Cav., Foster's (Ohio) Cav., Battery A 2d Ill. Art. *Union* 5 killed, 51 wounded, 52 missing. *Confed.* 179 killed, 100 wounded.

Chantilly, Va. McDowell's Corps, Army of Virginia. Hooker's and Kearney's Divisions of Third Corps, Army of Potomac, Reno's Corps. *Union* 1,300 killed, wounded, and missing. *Confed.* 800 killed, wounded, and missing. *Union* Maj.-Gen. Kearney and Brig.-Gen. Stevens killed.

2—Vienna, Va. 1st Minn. *Union* 1 killed, 6 wounded.

3—Slaughterville, Ky. Foster's (Ohio) Cav. *Confed.* 3 killed, 2 wounded, 25 captured.

6—Washington, N. C. 24th Mass., 1st N. C., 3d N. Y. Cav. *Union* 8 killed, 36 wounded. *Confed.* 30 killed, 100 wounded.

7—Poolesville, Md. 3d Ind. and 8th Ill. Cav. *Union* 2 killed, 6 wounded. *Confed.* 3 killed, 6 wounded.

Clarksville or Rickett's Hill, Tenn. 11th Ill., 13th Wis., 71st Ohio, 5th Iowa Cav., and two batteries. No casualties recorded.

9—Columbia, Tenn. 42d Ill. *Confed.* 18 killed, 45 wounded.

Des Allemands, La. 21st Ind., 4th Wis. *Confed.* 12 killed.

10—Cold Water, Miss. 6th Ill. Cav. *Confed.* 4 killed, 80 wounded.

Fayetteville, W. Va. 34th and 37th Ohio, 4th W. Va. *Union* 13 killed, 80 wounded.

12 to **15**—Harper's Ferry, Va. 39th, 111th, 115th, 125th and 126th N. Y. Militia, 32d, 60th, and 87th Ohio, 9th Vt., 65th Ill., 15th Ind., 1st and 3d Md. Home Brigade, 8th N. Y. Cav., 12th Ill. Cav., 1st Md. Cav., four Batteries of Artil. *Union* 80 killed, 120 wounded, 11,583 missing and captured. *Confed.* 500 killed and wounded.

14—Turner's and Crampton's Gap, South Mountain, Md. First Corps, Maj.-Gen. Hooker; Sixth Corps, Maj.-Gen. Franklin; Ninth Corps, Maj.-Gen. Reno. *Union* 443 killed, 1,806 wounded. *Confed.* 500 killed, 2,343 wounded, 1,500 captured. *Union* Maj.-Gen. Reno killed. *Confed.* Brig.-Gen. Garland killed.

14 to **16**—Mumfordsville, Ky., 18th U. S. Inft., 28th and 33d Ky., 17th, 50th, 60th, 67th, 68th, 74th, 78th, and 89th Ind., Conkle's Battery, 13th Ind. Artil. and Louisville Provost Guard. *Union* 50 killed, 3,566 captured and missing. *Confed.* 714 killed and wounded.

17—Durhamville, Tenn. Detachment of 52d Ind. *Union* 1 killed, 10 wounded. *Confed.* 8 killed.

Antietam or Sharpsburg, Md. First Corps, Maj.-Gen. Hooker; Second Corps, Maj.-Gen. Sumner; Fifth Corps, Maj.-Gen. Fitz-John Porter; Sixth Corps, Maj.-Gen. Franklin; Ninth Corps, Maj.-Gen. Burnside; Twelfth Corps, Maj.-Gen. Williams; Couch's Div., Fourth Corps; Pleasanton's Div. of Cav. *Union* 2,010 killed, 9,416 wounded, 1,043 missing. *Confed.* 3,500 killed, 16,399 wounded, 6,000 missing. *Union* Brig.-Gen. Mansfield killed, Maj.-Gens. Hooker and Richardson, and Brig.-Gens. Rodman, Weber, Sedgwick, Hartsuff, Dana, and Meagher wounded. *Confed.* Brig.-Gens. Branch, Anderson, and Starke killed, Maj.-Gen. Anderson, Brig.-Gens. Toombs, Lawton, Kipley, Rodes, Gregg, Armstead, and Ransom wounded.

19 and **20**—Iuka, Miss. Stanley's and Hamilton's Divisions, Army of the Mississippi, under Maj.-Gen. Rosecrans. *Union* 144 killed, 598 wounded. *Confed.* 263 killed, 692 wounded, 561 captured. *Confed.* Brig.-Gen. Little killed and Whitfield wounded.

20—Blackford's Ford, Sheppardstown, Va. Fifth Corps, Griffith's and Barnes' Brigades. *Union* 92 killed, 131 wounded, 103 missing. *Confed.* 33 killed, 231 wounded.

30—Newtonia, Mo. 1st Brigade Army of Kansas, 4th Brigade Mo. Militia Cav. *Union* 50 killed, 80 wounded, 115 missing. *Confed.* 220 killed, 280 wounded.

OCTOBER, 1862.

1—Floyd's Ford, Ky. 34th Ill., 77th Penna., 4th Ind. Cav. No casualties recorded.

Sheperdstown, Va. 8th Ill., 8th Penna., 3d Ind. Cav., Pennington's Battery. *Union* 12 wounded. *Confed.* 60 killed.

3 and **4**—Corinth, Miss. McKean's, Davies', Hamilton's, and Stanley's Divisons, Army of the Miss. *Union* 315 killed, 1,812 wounded, 232 missing. *Confed.* 1,423 killed, 5,692 wounded, 2,248 missing. *Union* Brig.-Gens. Hacklemans killed and Oglesby wounded.

5—Metamora, on Big Hatchie River, Miss. Hurlbut's and Ord's Divisions. *Union* 500 killed and wounded. *Confed.* 400 killed and wounded.

7—La Vergne, Tenn. Palmer's Brigade. *Union* 5 killed, 9 wounded. *Confed.* 80 killed and wounded, 175 missing.

8—Perryville, Ky. First Corps, Army of the Ohio, Maj.-Gen. McCook, and Third Corps, Brig.-Gen. Gilbert. *Union* 916 killed, 2,943 wounded, 489 missing. *Confed.* 2,500 killed, wounded, and missing. *Union* Brig.-Gens. J. S. Jackson and Terrill killed. *Confed.* Brig.-Gens. Cleburne, Wood, and Brown wounded.

10—Harrodsburg, Ky. Union troops, commanded by Lieut.-Col. Boyle, 9th Ky. Cav. *Confed.* 1,600 captured.

11—La Grange, Ark. Detach. 4th Iowa Cav. *Union* 4 killed, 13 wounded.

17—Lexington, Ky. Detach. 3d and 4th Ohio Cav. *Union* 4 killed, 24 wounded, 350 missing.

18—Haymarket, Va. Detach. 6th Iowa Cav. *Union* 1 killed, 6 wounded, 23 captured.

22—Pocotaligo or Yemassee, S. C. 47th, 55th, and 76th Penna., 48th N. Y., 6th and 7th Conn., 3d and 4th N. H., 3d R. I., 1st N. Y. Engineers, 1st Mass. Cav., Batteries D and M 1st U. S. Artil. and E 3d U. S. Artil. *Union* 43 killed, 258 wounded. *Confed.* 14 killed, 102 wounded.

23—Waverly, Tenn. 83d Ill. *Union* 1 killed, 2 wounded. *Confed.* 40 killed and wounded.

24—Grand Prairie, Mo. Two Battalions Mo. Militia Cav. *Union* 3 wounded. *Confed.* 8 killed, 20 wounded.

28—Clarkson, Mo. Detach. 2d Ill. Artil. *Confed.* 10 killed, 2 wounded.

NOVEMBER, 1862.

1—Philomont, Va. Pleasanton's Cavalry. *Union* 1 killed, 14 wounded. *Confed.* 5 killed, 10 wounded.

2 and **3**—Bloomfield and Union, Loudon Co., Va. Pleasanton's Cavalry. *Union* 2 killed, 10 wounded. *Confed.* 3 killed, 15 wounded.

3—Harrisonville, Mo. 5th and 6th Mo. Cav. *Union* 10 killed, 3 wounded. *Confed.* 6 killed, 20 wounded.

5—Barbee's Cross Roads and Chester Gap, Va. Pleasanton's Cavalry. *Union* 5 killed, 10 wounded. *Confed.* 36 killed.

Nashville, Tenn. 16th and 51st Ill., 69th Ohio, 14th Mich., 78th Pa., 5th Tenn. Cav., 7th Pa. Cav. *Union* 26 wounded. *Confed.* 23 captured.

6—Garrettsburg, Ky. 8th Ky. Cav. *Confed.* 17 killed, 85 wounded.

7—Big Beaver Creek, Mo. 10th Ill., two Cos. Mo. Militia Cav. *Union* 300 captured.

Marianna, Ark. 3d and 4th Iowa, 9th Ill. Cav. *Union* 3 killed, 20 wounded. *Confed.* 50 killed and wounded.

8—Hudsonville, Miss. 7th Kan. Cav., 2d Iowa Cav. *Confed.* 16 killed, 185 captured.

17—Gloucester, Va. 104th Pa. *Union* 1 killed, 3 wounded.

18—Rural Hills, Tenn. 8th Ky. Cav. *Confed.* 16 killed.

24—Beaver Creek, Mo. 21st Iowa, 3d Mo. Cav. *Union* 6 killed, 10 wounded. *Confed.* 5 killed, 20 wounded.

26—Summerville, Miss. 7th Ill. Cav. *Confed.* 28 captured.

28—Cane Hill, Boston Mountain, and Boonsboro', Ark. 1st Division Army of the Frontier. *Union* 4 killed, 36 wounded. *Confed.* 75 killed, 300 wounded.

Hartwood Church, Va. 3d Pa. Cav. *Union* 4 killed, 9 wounded, 200 missing.

DECEMBER, 1862.

1—Charleston and Berryville, Va. 2d Div. 12th Corps. *Confed.* 5 killed, 18 wounded.

5—Coffeeville, Miss. 1st, 2d, and 3d Cav. Brigades, Army of the Tennessee. *Union* 10 killed, 54 wounded. *Confed.* 7 killed, 43 wounded.

Helena, Ark. 30th Iowa, 29th Wis. *Confed.* 8 killed.

7—Prairie Grove or Fayetteville, Ark. 1st, 2d, and 3d Divisions Army of the Frontier. *Union* 167 killed, 798 wounded, 183 missing. *Confed.* 300 killed, 1,200 wounded and missing.

Hartsville, Tenn. 106th and 108th Ohio, 104th Ill., 2d Ind. Cav., 11th Ky. Cav., 13th Ind. Battery. *Union* 55 killed, 1,800 captured. *Confed.* 21 killed, 114 wounded.

9—Dobbin's Ferry, Tenn. 35th Ind., 51st Ohio, 8th and 21st Ky., 7th Ind. Battery. *Union* 5 killed, 48 wounded.

12—Little Bear Creek, Ala. 52d Ill. *Union* 1 killed, 2 wounded. *Confed.* 11 killed, 30 wounded.

12 to **18**.—Foster's expedition to Goldsboro', N. C. 1st, 2d, and 3d Brigades of First Division and Wessell's Brigade of Peck's Division, Dep't of North Carolina. *Union* 90 killed, 478 wounded. *Confed.* 71 killed, 268 wounded, 400 missing.

13—Fredericksburg, Va. Army of the Potomac, Maj.-Gen. Burnside; Second Corps, Maj.-Gen. Couch; Ninth Corps, Maj.-Gen. Wilcox. Right Grand Div., Maj.-Gen. Sumner; First Corps, Maj.-Gen. Reynolds; Sixth Corps, Maj.-Gen. W. F. Smith. Left Grand Div., Maj.-Gen. Franklin; Fifth Corps, Maj.-Gen. Butterfield; Third Corps, Maj.-Gen. Stoneman. Center Grand Div., Maj.-Gen. Hooker. *Union* 1,180 killed, 9,028 wounded, 2,145 missing. *Confed.* 579 killed, 3,870 wounded, 127 missing. *Union* Brig.-Gens. Jackson and Bayard killed and Gibbons and Vinton wounded. *Confed.* Brig.-Gen. T. R. R. Cobb killed and Maxey Gregg wounded.

14—Kingston, N. C. 1st, 2d and 3d Brigades 1st Div. and Wessell's Brigade of Peck's Division, Dep't of North Carolina. *Union* 40 killed, 120 wounded. *Confed.* 50 killed, 75 wounded, 400 missing.

18—Lexington, Tenn. 11th Ill. Cav., 5th Ohio Cav., 2d Tenn. Cav. *Union* 7 killed, 10 wounded, 124 missing. *Confed.* 7 killed, 28 wounded.

20—Holly Springs, Miss. 2d Ill. Cav. *Union* 1,000 captured.

Trenton, Tenn. Detachments 122d Ill., 7th Tenn. Cav., and convalescents. *Union* 1 killed, 250 prisoners. *Confed.* 17 killed, 50 wounded.

21—Davis's Mills, Miss. Six Cos. 25th Ind., two Cos. 5th Ohio Cav. *Union* 3 wounded. *Confed.* 22 killed, 50 wounded, 20 missing.

24—Middleburg, Miss. 115 men of 12th Mich. *Union* 9 wounded. *Confed.* 9 killed, 11 wounded.

Glasgow, Ky. Five Cos. 2d Mich. Cav. *Union* 1 killed, 1 wounded. *Confed.* 3 killed, 3 wounded.

25—Green's Chapel, Ky. Detachment of 4th and 5th Ind. Cav. *Union* 1 killed. *Confed.* 9 killed, 22 wounded.

26—Bacon Creek, Ky. Detachment 2d Mich Cav. *Union* 23 wounded.

27—Elizabethtown, Ky. 91st Ill. 500 men captured by Morgan.

Dumfries, Va. 5th, 7th and 66th Ohio, 12th Ill. Cav., 1st Md. Cav., 6th Maine Battery. *Union* 3 killed, 8 wounded. *Confed.* 25 killed, 40 wounded.

28—Elk Fork, Tenn. 6th and 10th Ky. Cav. *Confed.* 30 killed, 176 wounded, 51 missing.

28 and **29**—Chickasaw Bayou, Vicksburg, Miss. Army of Tennessee. Maj.-Gen. W. T. Sherman—Brig.-Gens. G. W. Morgan's, Frederick Steele's, M. L. Smith's, and A. J. Smith's divisions of the right wing. *Union* 191 killed, 982 wounded, 756 missing. *Confed.* 207 wounded. *Union* Maj.-Gen. M. L. Smith wounded.

30—Wautauga Bridge and Carter's Station, Tenn. 7th Ohio Cav., 9th Pa. Cav. *Union* 1 killed, 2 wounded. *Confed.* 7 killed, 15 wounded, 273 missing.

Jefferson, Tenn. Second Brigade 1st Division Thomas's corps. *Union* 20 killed, 40 wounded. *Confed.* 15 killed, 50 wounded.

Parker's Cross Roads or Red Mound, Tenn. 18th, 106th, 119th and 122d Ill., 27th, 39th and 63d Ohio, 50th Ind., 39th Iowa, 7th Tenn., 7th Wis. Battery. *Union* 23 killed, 139 wounded, 58 missing. *Confed.* 50 killed, 150 wounded, 300 missing.

31 to **Jan. 2**—Murfreesboro' or Stone River, Tenn. Army of the Cumberland, Maj.Gen. Rosecrans. Right Wing, McCook's Corps; Center, Thomas's Corps; Left Wing, Crittenden's Corps. *Union* 1,533 killed, 7,245 wounded, 2,800 missing. *Confed.* 14,560 killed, wounded and missing. *Union* Brig.-Gen. Sill killed and Kirk wounded. *Confed.* Brig.-Gens. Raines and Hanson killed and Chalmers and Davis wounded.

JANUARY, 1863

1—Galveston, Tex. Three Cos. 42d Mass., U. S. Gunboats *Westfield, Harriet Lane, Owasco, Sachem, Clifton,* and *Coryphæus.* *Union* 600 killed, wounded and missing. *Confed.* 50 killed and wounded.

7 and **8**—Springfield, Mo. Mo. Militia, convalescents and citizens. *Union* 14 killed, 144 wounded. *Confed.* 40 killed, 206 wounded and missing. *Union* Brig.-Gen. Brown wounded.

11—Fort Hindman, Ark. Thirteenth Corps, Maj.-Gen. McClernand; Fifteenth Corps, Maj.-Gen. Sherman and gunboats Mississippi squadron. *Union* 129 killed, 831 wounded. *Confed.* 100 killed, 400 wounded, 5,000 prisoners.

Hartsville or Wood's Fork, Mo. 21st Iowa, 99th Ill., 3d Iowa Cav., 3d Mo. Cav., Battery L 2d Mo. Artil. *Union* 7 killed, 64 wounded. *Confed.* Brig.-Gen. McDonald killed.

14—Bayou Teche, La. 8th Vt., 16th and 75th N. Y., 19th Conn., 6th Mich., 21st Ind., 1st La. Cav., 4th and 6th Mass. Battery, 1st Maine Battery, and U. S. Gunboats *Calhoun, Diana, Kinsman* and *Estrella.* *Union* 10 killed. 27 wounded. *Confed.* 15 killed. *Union* Commodore Buchanan killed. *Confed.* Gunboat *Cotton* destroyed.

24—Woodbury, Tenn. Second Division Crittenden's Corps. *Union* 2 killed, 1 wounded. *Confed.* 35 killed, 100 missing.

30—Deserted House or Kelly's Store, near Suffolk, Va. Portion of Maj.-Gen. Peck's forces. *Union* 24 killed, 80 wounded. *Confed.* 50 wounded.

31—Rover, Tenn. 4th Ohio Cav. *Confed.* 12 killed, 12 wounded, 300 captured.

FEBRUARY, 1863

3—Fort Donelson or Cumberland Iron Works, Tenn. 83d Ill., 2d Ill. Artil., one battalion 5th Iowa Cav. *Union* 16 killed, 60 wounded, 50 missing. *Confed.* 140 killed, 400 wounded, 130 missing.

14—Brentsville, Va. 1st Mich. Cav. *Union* 15 wounded.

16—Near Romney, W. Va. Detachments 116th and 122d Ohio. *Union* 72 wounded and captured.

21—Prairie Station, Miss. 2d Iowa Cav. *Union* 1 killed, 3 wounded.

24—Mississippi River below Vicksburg. U. S. Gunboat *Indianola.* *Union* 1 killed, 1 wounded. *Confed.* 35 killed.

MARCH, 1863

1—Bradyville, Tenn. 3d and 4th Ohio Cav., 1st Tenn. Cav. *Union* 1 killed, 6 wounded. *Confed.* 5 killed, 27 wounded, 100 captured.

4—Skeet, N. C. 3d N. Y. Cav. *Union* 3 killed, 15 wounded. *Confed.* 28 wounded.

4 and **5**—Thompson's Station, also called Spring Hill and Unionville, Tenn. 33d and 85th Ind., 22d Wis., 19th Mich., 124th Ohio, 18th Ohio Battery, 2d Mich. Cav., 9th Penna. Cav., 4th Ky. Cav. *Union* 100 killed, 300 wounded, 1,306 captured. *Confed.* 150 killed, 450 wounded.

8—Fairfax C. H., Va. Brig.-Gen. Stoughton and thirty-three men captured by Mosby in his midnight raid.

10—Covington, Tenn. 6th and 7th Ill. Cav. *Confed.* 25 killed.

13 to **April 5**—Fort Pemberton, Miss. Thirteenth Corps, Brig.-Gen. Ross; Seventeenth Corps, Brig.-Gen. Quimby, U. S. Gunboats *Chillicothe* and *DeKalb.* Casualties not recorded.

14—Port Hudson, La. Maj.-Gen. Banks' troops and Admiral Farragut's fleet. *Union* 65 wounded.

16 to **22**—Expedition up Steele's Bayou and at Deer Creek, Miss. 2d Division Fifteenth Corps, Maj.-Gen. Sherman, gunboat fleet, Admiral Porter. Casualties not recorded.

17—Kelly's Ford, Va. 1st and 5th U. S. Regulars, 3d, 4th and 16th Penna., 1st R. I., 6th Ohio, 4th N. Y. Cav., 6th N. Y. Battery. *Union* 9 killed, 35 wounded. *Confed.* 11 killed, 88 wounded.

20—Vaught's Hill, near Milton, Tenn. 105th Ohio, 101st Ind., 80th and 123d Ill., 1st Tenn. Cav., 9th Ind. Battery. *Union* 7 killed, 48 wounded. *Confed.* 63 killed, 300 wounded.

22—Mt. Sterling, Ky. 10th Ky. Cav. *Union* 4 killed, 10 wounded. *Confed.* 8 killed, 13 wounded.

24—Danville, Ky. 18th and 22d Mich., 1st Ky. Cav., 2d Tenn. Cav., 1st Ind. Battery.

Ponchatoula, La. 127th and 165th N. Y., 9th Conn., 14th and 24th Maine, 6th Mich. *Union* 6 wounded. *Confed.* 3 killed, 11 wounded.

25—Brentwood, Tenn. Detachment 22d Wis. and 19th Mich. *Union* 1 killed, 4 wounded, 300 prisoners. *Confed.* 1 killed, 5 wounded.

Franklin and Little Harpeth, Tenn. 4th and 6th Ky. Cav., 9th Penna. Cav., 2d Mich. Cav. *Union* 4 killed, 19 wounded, 40 missing.

28—Pattersonville, La. Gunboat *Diana* with Detachment of 12th Conn. and 160th N. Y. on board. *Union* 4 killed, 14 wounded, 99 missing.

29—Somerville, Tenn. 6th Ill. Cav. *Union* 9 killed, 29 wounded.

30—Dutton's Hill or Somerset, Ky. 1st Ky. Cav., 7th Ohio Cav., 44th and 45th Ohio Mounted Vol. *Union* 10 killed, 25 wounded. *Confed.* 290 killed, wounded and missing.

Point Pleasant, W. Va. One Co. 13th W. Va. *Union* 1 killed, 3 wounded. *Confed.* 20 killed, 25 wounded.

30 to **April 4**—Washington and Rodman's Point, N. C. Maj.-Gen. Foster's command. Casualties not recorded.

APRIL, 1863

2 and 3—Woodbury and Snow Hill, Tenn. 3d and 4th Ohio Cav. *Union* 1 killed, 8 wounded. *Confed.* 50 killed and wounded.

7—Bombardment Fort Sumter, S. C. South Atlantic squadron; *Keokuk, Weehawken, Passaic, Montauk, Patapsco, New Ironsides, Catskill, Nantucket* and *Nahant*. *Union* 2 killed, 20 wounded. *Confed.* 4 killed, 10 wounded.

10—Franklin and Harpeth River, Tenn. 40th Ohio and portion of Granger's Cavalry. *Union* 100 killed and wounded. *Confed.* 19 killed, 35 wounded, 83 missing.

Antioch Station, Tenn. Detachment 10th Mich. *Union* 8 killed, 12 wounded.

12 to 14—Irish Bend and Bisland, La., also called Indian Ridge and Centreville. Nineteenth Corps, Grover's, Emory's, Weitzel's Divisions. *Union* 350 killed, wounded and missing. *Confed.* 400 wounded, 2,000 missing and captured.

12 to May 4—Siege of Suffolk, Va. Troops, Army of Virginia and Department of North Carolina. *Union* 44 killed, 202 wounded. *Confed.* 500 killed and wounded, 400 captured.

15—Dunbar's Plantation, La. 2d Ill. Cav. *Union* 1 killed, 2 wounded.

17 to May 2—Grierson's expedition from La Grange, Tenn., to Baton Rouge, La. 6th and 7th Ill. Cav., 2d Iowa Cav. *Confed.* 100 killed and wounded, 500 prisoners.

18 and 19—Hernando and Coldwater, Miss. Portion of Sixteenth Corps, detachment of Artil., 2d Brigade Cavalry Division. Casualties not recorded.

20—Patterson, Mo. 3d Mo. Militia Cav. *Union* 12 killed, 7 wounded, 41 missing.

24—Tuscumbia, Ala. Sixteenth Corps, 2d Division. Maj.-Gen. Dodge.

White Water, Mo. 1st Wis. Cav. *Union* 2 killed, 6 wounded.

26—Cape Girardeau, Mo. 32d Iowa, 1st Wis. Cav., 2d Mo. Cav., Batteries D and L 1st Mo. Lt. Artil. *Union* 6 killed, 6 wounded. *Confed.* 60 killed, 275 wounded and missing.

27 to May 3—Streight's Raid, Tuscumbia, Ala., to Rome, Ga., including skirmishes at Day's Gap, April 30th; Black Warrior Creek, May 1st and Blount's Farm, May 2d. 3d Ohio, 51st and 73d Ind., 80th Ill., Mounted Inft., two Cos. 1st Ala. Cav. *Union* 12 killed, 69 wounded, 1,466 missing and captured.

27 to May 8—Stoneman's Cavalry Raid in Virginia.

29—Fairmount, W. Va. Detachments 106th N. Y., 6th W. Va. and Va. Militia. *Union* 1 killed, 6 wounded. *Confed.* 100 killed and wounded.

Grand Gulf, Miss. Gunboat fleet. *Union* 26 killed, 54 wounded.

30—Spottsylvania C. H., Va. 6th N. Y. Cav. *Union* 58 killed and wounded.

30 and May 1—Chalk Bluff and St. Francois River, Mo. 2d Mo. Militia, 3d Mo. Cav., 1st Iowa Cav., Battery E 1st Mo. Lt. Artil. *Union* 2 killed, 11 wounded.

MAY, 1863

1—Port Gibson, Miss. (the first engagement in Grant's Campaign against Vicksburg). Thirteenth Corps, Maj.-Gen. McClernand, and 3d Division Seventeenth Corps, Maj.-Gen. McPherson. *Union* 130 killed, 718 wounded. *Confed.* 1,150 killed and wounded, 500 missing. *Confed.* Brig.-Gen. Tracy killed.

1—LaGrange, Ark. 3d Iowa Cav. *Union* 3 killed, 9 wounded, 30 missing.

Monticello, Ky. 2d Tenn. Cav., 1st Ky. Cav., 2d and 7th Ohio Cav., 45th Ohio and 112th Ill. Mounted Inft.

1 to 4—Chancellorsville, Va., including battles of Sixth Corps at Fredericksburg and Salem Heights. Army of the Potomac, Maj.-Gen. Hooker; First Corps, Maj.-Gen. Reynolds; Second Corps, Maj.-Gen. Couch; Third Corps, Maj.-Gen. Sickles; Fifth Corps, Maj.-Gen. Meade; Sixth Corps, Maj.-Gen. Sedgwick; Eleventh Corps, Maj.-Gen. Howard; Twelfth Corps, Maj.-Gen. Slocum. *Union* 1,512 killed, 9,518 wounded, 5,000 missing. *Confed.* 1,581 killed, 8,700 wounded, 2,000 missing. *Union* Maj.-Gen. Berry and Brig.-Gen. Whipple killed, Devens and Kirby wounded. *Confed.* Brig.-Gen. Paxton killed, Lieut.-Gen. T. J. Jackson, Maj.-Gen. A. P. Hill, Brig.-Gens. Hoke, Nichols, Ramseur, McGowan, Heth, and Pender wounded.

3—Warrenton Junction, Va. 1st W. Va. Cav., 5th N. Y. Cav. *Union* 1 killed, 16 wounded. *Confed.* 15 wounded.

4—Siege of Suffolk, Va., raised. (See April 12.)

11—Horse Shoe Bend, Ky. Detachment commanded by Col. R. T. Jacobs. *Union* 10 killed, 20 wounded, 40 missing. *Confed.* 100 killed, wounded, and missing.

12—Raymond, Miss. Seventeenth Corps, Maj.-Gen. McPherson. *Union* 69 killed, 341 wounded. *Confed.* 969 killed and wounded. *Confed.* Gen. Telghman killed.

13—Hall's Ferry. 2d Ill. Cav. *Confed.* 12 killed.

14—Jackson, Miss. Fifteenth Corps, Maj.-Gen. Sherman; Seventeenth Corps, Maj.-Gen. McPherson. *Union* 40 killed, 240 wounded. *Confed.* 450 killed and wounded.

16—Champian Hills, Miss. Hovey's Div. Thirteenth Corps and Seventeenth Corps. *Union* 426 killed, 1,842 wounded, 189 missing. *Confed.* 2,500 killed and wounded, 1,800 missing.

17—Big Black River, Miss. Carr's and Osterhaus's Divisions, Thirteenth Corps, Maj.-Gen. McClernand. *Union* 29 killed, 242 wounded. *Confed.* 600 killed and wounded, 2,500 captured.

18 to July 4—**Siege of Vicksburg. Thirteenth Corps, Fifteenth Corps, and Seventeenth Corps, commanded by Maj.-Gen. U. S. Grant, and gunboat fleet, commanded by Admiral Porter. Assault on Fort Hill on May 19th and general assault on the 20th, in which *Confed.* Brig.-Gen. Green was killed. Three divisions of the Sixteenth Corps and two divisions of the Ninth Corps, and Maj.-Gen. Herron's Division were then added to the besieging forces. *Union* 545 killed, 3,688 wounded, 303 missing. *Confed.* 21,277 killed, wounded, and missing.**

20 to 28—**Clendenin's raid, below Fredericksburg, Va. 8th Ill. Cav. *Confed.* 100 prisoners.**

21—Middleton, Tenn. 4th Mich., 3d Ind., 7th Pa., 3d and 4th Ohio and 4th U. S. Cav., 39th Ind. Mounted Inft. Casualties not recorded.

25—Near Helena, Ark. 3d Iowa and 5th Kan. Cav. *Union* 10 killed, 14 wounded.

27—Lake Providence, La. 47th U. S. Colored. *Union* 1 killed, 1 wounded.

27 to July 9—Siege of Port Hudson, La. *Union* 500 killed, 2,500 wounded. *Confed.* 100 killed, 700 wounded, 6,408 prisoners. *Union* Brig.-Gens. W. T. Sherman and H. E. Paine wounded.

JUNE, 1863

4—Franklin, Tenn. 85th Ind., 7th Ky. Cav., 4th and 6th Ky. Cav., 9th Pa. Cav., 2d Mich. Cav. *Union* 25 killed and wounded. *Confed.* 200 killed and wounded.

5—Franklin's Crossing, Rappahannock River, Va. 26th N. J., 5th Vt., 15th and 50th N. Y. Engineers, supported by 6th Corps. *Union* 6 killed, 35 wounded.

6 to 8—Milliken's Bend, La. 23d Iowa and three regts. colored troops. (No quarter shown.) *Union* 154 killed, 223 wounded, 115 missing. *Confed.* 125 killed, 400 wounded, 200 missing.

9—Monticello and Rocky Gap, Ky. 2d and 7th Ohio Cav., 1st Ky. Cav., 45th Ohio and 2d Tenn. Mounted Inft. *Union* 4 killed, 26 wounded. *Confed.* 20 killed, 80 wounded.

Beverly Ford and Brandy Station, Va. 2d, 3d, and 7th Wis., 2d and 33d Mass., 6th Maine, 86th and 104th N. Y., 1st, 2d, 5th, and 6th U. S. Cav., 2d, 6th, 8th, 9th, and 10th N. Y. Cav., 1st, 6th, and 17th Pa. Cav., 1st Md., 8th Ill., 3d Ind., 1st N. J., 1st Maine Cav. and 3d W. Va. Cav. *Union* 500 killed, wounded, and missing. *Confed.* 700 killed, wounded, and missing.

11—Middleton, Va. 87th Pa., 13th Pa. Cav., Battery L, 5th U. S. Artil. *Confed.* 8 killed, 42 wounded.

13 and 15—Winchester, Va. 2d, 67th, and 87th Pa., 18th Conn., 12th W. Va., 110th, 116th, 122d, and 123d Ohio, 3d, 5th, and 6th Md., 12th and 13th Pa. Cav., 1st N. Y. Cav., 1st and 3d W. Va. Cav., Battery L 5th U. S. Artil., 1st W. Va. Battery, Baltimore Battery, one Co. 14th Mass. Heavy Artil. *Union* 3,000 killed, wounded, and missing. *Confed.* 850 killed, wounded, and missing.

14—Martinsburg, Va. 106th N. Y., 126th Ohio, W. Va. Battery. *Union* 200 missing. *Confed.* 1 killed, 2 wounded.

16—Triplett's Bridge, Ky. 15th Mich., 10th and 14th Ky. Cav., 7th and 9th Mich. Cav., 11th Mich. Battery. *Union* 15 killed, 30 wounded.

17—Aldie, Va. Kilpatrick's Cavalry. *Union* 24 killed, 41 wounded, 89 missing. *Confed.* 100 wounded.

Westport, Mo. Two Cos. 9th Kan. *Union* 14 killed, 6 wounded.

Capture of rebel gunboat *Atlanta* by U. S. ironclad *Weehawken*. *Confed.* 1 killed, 17 wounded, 145 prisoners.

20—Rocky Crossing, Miss. 5th Ohio Cav., 9th Ill. Mounted Inft. *Union* 7 killed, 28 wounded, 30 missing.

20 and 21—La Fourche Crossing, La. Detachments 23d Conn., 176th N. Y., 26th, 42d, and 47th Mass., 21st Ind. *Union* 8 killed, 40 wounded. *Confed.* 53 killed, 150 wounded.

21—Upperville, Va. Pleasanton's Cavalry. *Union* 94 wounded. *Confed.* 20 killed, 100 wounded, 60 missing.

22—Hill's Plantation, Miss. Detachment of 4th Iowa Cav. *Union* 4 killed, 10 wounded, 28 missing.

23—Brashear City, La. Detachments of 114th and 176th N. Y., 23d Conn., 42d Mass., 21st Ind. *Union* 46 killed, 40 wounded, 300 missing. *Confed.* 3 killed, 18 wounded.

23 to 30—Rosecrans' Campaign. Murfreesboro to Tullahoma, Tenn., including Middleton, Hoover's Gap, Beech Grove, Liberty Gap, and Gray's Gap. Army of the Cumberland: Fourteenth, Twentieth, and Twenty-first Corps, Granger's Reserve Corps, and Stanley's Cavalry. *Union* 85 killed, 462 wounded. *Confed.* 1,634 killed, wounded, and captured.

28—Donaldsonville, La. 28th Maine and convalescents, assisted by gunboats. *Confed.* 39 killed, 112 wounded, 150 missing.

29—Westminster, Md. Detachments 1st Del. Cav. *Union* 2 killed, 7 wounded. *Confed.* 3 killed, 15 wounded.

30—Hanover, Pa. Cavalry Corps. *Union* 12 killed, 43 wounded. *Confed.* 75 wounded, 60 missing.

JULY, 1863

1 to 3—Gettysburg, Pa. Army of the Potomac, Maj.-Gen. Geo. G. Meade First Corps, Maj. Gen. Reynolds; Second Corps, Maj. Gen. Hancock Third Corps, Maj.-Gen. Sickles; Sixth Corps, Maj.-Gen. Sedgwick; Eleventh Corps, Maj.-Gen. Howard; Twelfth Corps, Maj.-Gen. Slocum; Cavalry Corps, Maj.-Gen. Pleasanton. *Union* 2,834 killed, 13,709 wounded, 6,643 missing. *Confed.* 3,500 killed, 14,500 wounded, 13,621 missing. *Union* Maj.-Gen. Reynolds, Brig.-Gens. Weed, Zook, and Farnsworth killed; Maj.-Gens. Sickles and Hancock, Brig.-Gens. Paul, Rowley, Gibbons, and Barlow wounded. (Gen. Lucius Fairchild, Commander-in-Chief Grand Army of the Republic, lost his arm on the first day.) *Confed.* Maj.-Gen. Pender, Brig.-Gens. Gurnett, Barksdale, and Semmes killed; Maj.-Gens. Hood, Trimble, and Heth, Brig.-Gens. Kemper, Scales, Anderson, Hampton, Jones, Jenkins, Pettigrew, and Posey wounded.

1 to 26—Morgan's raid into Kentucky, Indiana, and Ohio, finally captured at New Lisbon, Ohio, by Brig.-Gen. Shackleford's Cavalry. *Union* 22 killed, 80 wounded, 790 missing. *Confed.* 86 killed, 385 wounded, 3,000 captured.

4—Helena, Ark. Maj.-Gen. Prentiss's Division of Sixteenth Corps and gunboat *Tyler*. *Union* 57 killed, 117 wounded, 32 missing. *Confed.* 173 killed, 687 wounded, 776 missing.

4 and 5—Bolton and Birdsong Ferry, Miss. Maj.-Gen. Sherman's forces. *Confed.* 2,000 captured.

4 and 5—Monterey Gap and Smithsburg, Md., and Fairfield, Pa. Kilpatrick's Cavalry. *Union* 30 killed and wounded. *Confed.* 30 killed and wounded, 100 prisoners.

5—Lebanon, Ky. 20th Ky. *Union* 9 killed, 15 wounded, 400 missing. *Confed.* 3 killed, 6 wounded.

6—Quaker Bridge, N. C. 17th, 23d, and 27th Mass., 9th N. J., 81st and 158th N. Y., Belger's and Angel's Batteries.

Hagerstown and Williamsport, Md. Kilpatrick's Cavalry.

7 and 9—Iuka, Miss. 10th Mo. and 7th Kan. Cav. *Union* 5 killed, 3 wounded.

7 to 9—Boonsboro, Md. Buford's and Kilpatrick's Cavalry. *Union* 9 killed, 45 wounded.

9 to 16—Jackson, Miss., including engagements at Rienzi, Bolton Depot, Canton, and Clinton. 9th, 13th, 15th, and part of 16th Corps. *Union* 100 killed, 800 wounded, 100 missing. *Confed.* 71 killed, 504 wounded, 764 missing.

10 to Sept. 6—Siege of Fort Wagner, Morris Island, S. C. Troops Department of the South, under command of Maj.-Gen. Gilmore, and U. S. Navy under Admiral Dahlgren. *Union* 1,757 killed, wounded, and missing. *Confed.* 561 killed, wounded, and missing.

12—Ashby Gap, Va. 2d Mass. Cav. *Union* 2 killed, 8 wounded.

13—Yazoo City, Miss. Maj.-Gen. Herron's Division and three gunboats. *Confed.* 250 captured.

Jackson, Tenn. 9th Ill., 3d Mich. Cav., 2d Iowa Cav., and 1st Tenn. Cav. *Union* 2 killed, 20 wounded. *Confed.* 38 killed, 150 wounded.

Donaldsonville, La. Portions of Weitzel's and Grover's Divisions, Nineteenth Corps. *Union* 450 killed, wounded, and missing.

13 to 15—Draft riots in New York City, in which over 1,000 rioters were killed.

14—Falling Waters, Md. 3d Cav. Division Army of the Potomac. *Union* 29 killed, 36 wounded. *Confed.* 125 killed and wounded, 1,500 prisoners. *Confed.* Maj.-Gen. Pettigrew killed.

14—Elk River, Tenn. Advance of the Fourteenth Corps Army of the Cumberland. *Union* 10 killed, 30 wounded. *Confed.* 60 killed, 24 wounded, 100 missing.

Near Bolivar Heights, Va. 1st Conn. Cav. *Confed.* 25 killed.

15—Pulaski, Ala. 3d Ohio and 5th Tenn. Cav. *Confed.* 3 killed, 50 missing.

Halltown, Va. 16th Pa. and 1st Maine Cav. *Union* 25 killed and wounded. *Confed.* 20 killed and wounded.

16—Sheppardstown, Va. 1st, 4th, and 16th Pa., 10th N. Y. and 1st Maine Cav. *Confed.* 25 killed, 75 wounded.

17—Honey Springs, Ind. Ter. 2d, 6th, and 9th Kan. Cav., 2d and 3d Kan. Batteries, 2d and 3d Kan. Indian Home Guards. *Union* 17 killed, 60 wounded. *Confed.* 150 killed, 400 wounded.

Wytheville, W. Va. 34th Ohio, 1st and 2d W. Va. Cav. *Union* 17 killed, 61 wounded. *Confed.* 75 killed, 125 missing.

Canton, Miss. 76th Ohio, 25th and 31st Iowa, 3d, 13th and 17th Mo., 2d Wis. Cav., 5th Ill. Cav., 3d and 4th Iowa Cav., one battery of artillery. Casualties not recorded.

18 to 21—Potter's Cavalry Raid to Tar River and Rocky Mount, N. C. 3d and 12th N. Y. Cav., 1st N. C. Cav. *Union* 60 wounded.

18 to 26—Morgan's Raid into Kentucky, Indiana, and Ohio pursued and captured by Brig.-Gens. Hobson and Shackleford's Cavalry, including skirmishes at Burkesville, Columbia, Green River Bridge, Lebanon, and Bradenburg, Ky., Corydon and Vernon, Ind., capture of the larger part at Buffington Island, Ohio, and final capture at New Lisbon, Ohio, on the 26th. *Union* 33 killed, 97 wounded, 805 missing. *Confed.* 795 killed and wounded, 4,104 captured.

21 to 23—Manassas Gap and Chester Gap, Va. Cavalry advance and Third Corps Army of the Potomac. *Union* 35 killed, 102 wounded. *Confed.* 300 killed and wounded.

26—Pattacassey Creek, N. C. Brig.-Gen. Heckman's troops. *Union* 3 killed, 17 wounded.

30—Irvine, Ky. 14th Ky. Cav. *Union* 4 killed, 5 wounded. *Confed.* 7 killed, 18 wounded.

AUGUST, 1863

1 to **3**—Rappahannock Station, Brandy Station, and Kelly's Ford, Va. Brig.-Gen. Buford's Cav. *Union* 16 killed, 134 wounded.

3—Jackson, La. 73d, 75th, and 78th U. S. Colored Troops. *Union* 2 killed, 2 wounded, 27 missing.

5—Dutch Gap, James River, Va. U. S. Gunboats *Commodore Barney* and *Cohassett. Union* 3 killed, 1 wounded.

7—New Madrid, Mo. One company 24th Mo. *Union* 1 killed, 1 wounded.

9—Sparta, Tenn. Cavalry Army of the Cumberland. *Union* 6 killed, 25 wounded.

13—Grenada, Miss. 9th Ill., 2d Iowa Cav., 3d Mich. Cav., 3d, 4th, 9th, and 11th Ill. Cav. Casualties not recorded.
Pineville, Mo. 6th Mo. Militia Cav. *Confed.* 65 wounded.

14—West Point, White River, Ark. 32d Iowa, with U. S. Gunboats *Lexington, Cricket,* and *Mariner. Union* 2 killed, 7 wounded.

21—Quantrell's plunder and massacre of Lawrence, Kansas, in which 140 citizens were killed and 24 wounded. *Confed.* 40 killed.
Coldwater, Miss. 3d and 4th Iowa Cav., 5th Ill. Cav. *Union* 10 wounded.

24—Coyle Tavern, near Fairfax C. H., Va. 2d Mass. Cav. *Union* 2 killed, 3 wounded. *Confed.* 2 killed, 4 wounded.

25 to **30**—Averill's Raid in W. Va. *Union* 3 killed, 10 wounded, 60 missing.

26—Rocky Gap, near White Sulphur Springs, Va. 3d and 8th W. Va., 2d and 3d W. Va. Cav., 14th Pa. Cav. *Union* 16 killed, 113 wounded. *Confed.* 156 killed and wounded.

25 to **31**—Brownsville, Bayou Metoe and Austin, Ark. Davidson's Cavalry. *Union* 13 killed, 72 wounded.

SEPTEMBER, 1863

1—Barbee's Cross Roads, Va. Detachment 6th Ohio Cav. *Union* 2 killed, 4 wounded.
Devil's Back Bone, Ark. 1st Ark., 6th Mo. Militia, 2d Kan. Cav., 2d Ind. Battery. *Union* 4 killed, 12 wounded. *Confed.* 25 killed, 40 wounded.

5—Limestone Station, Tenn. Five Cos. 100th Ohio. *Union* 12 killed, 20 wounded, 240 missing. *Confed.* 6 killed, 10 wounded.

8—Night attack on Fort Sumter, S. C. Four hundred and thirteen marines and sailors, commanded by Commander Stevens, U. S. N. *Union* 3 killed, 114 missing.

9—Cumberland Gap, Tenn. Shackleford's Cavalry. *Confed.* 2,000 captured.

10—Little Rock, Ark. Maj.-Gen. Steele's troops and Davidson's Cavalry.

11—Ringgold, Ga. Advance of Twenty-first Corps. *Union* 8 killed, 19 wounded. *Confed.* 3 killed, 18 missing.

12—Sterling's Plantation, La. Battery E 1st Mo. Artil. *Union* 3 killed, 3 wounded.

13—Culpeper, Va. 1st, 2d, and 3d Divisions, Cavalry Corps Army of the Potomac. *Union* 3 killed, 40 wounded. *Confed.* 10 killed, 40 wounded, 75 missing.
Lett's Tan Yard, near Chickamauga, Ga. Wilder's Mounted Brigade. *Union* 50 killed and wounded. *Confed.* 10 killed, 40 wounded.

14—Rapidan Station, Va. Cavalry Army of the Potomac. *Union* 8 killed, 40 wounded.
Vidalia, La. 2d Mo. *Union* 2 killed, 4 wounded. *Confed.* 6 killed, 11 wounded.

19—Rapidan Station, Va. Buford's Cavalry. *Union* 4 killed, 19 wounded.

19 and **20**—Chickamauga, Ga. Army of the Cumberland, Maj.-Gen. Rosecrans; Fourteenth Corps, Maj.-Gen. Thomas; Twentieth Corps, Maj.-Gen. McCook; Twenty-first Corps, Maj.-Gen. Crittenden, and Reserve Corps, Maj.-Gen. Granger. *Union* 1,644 killed, 9,262 wounded, 4,945 missing. *Confed.* 2,389 killed, 13,412 wounded, 2,003 missing. *Union* Brig.-Gen. Lytle killed, and Starkweather, Whittaker, and King wounded. *Confed.* Brig.-Gens. Preston, Smith, Deshler, and Helm killed, and Maj.-Gen. Hood, Brig.-Gens. Adams, Gregg, Brown, McNair, Bunn, Preston, Clerburne, Benning, and Clayton wounded.

21—Bristol, Tenn. Shackleford's and Foster's Cavalry. Casualties not recorded.

22—Madison C. H., Tenn. 1st Division Buford's Cav. *Union* 1 killed, 20 wounded.
Blountsville, Tenn. Foster's 2d Brigade Cav. *Union* 5 killed, 22 wounded. *Confed.* 15 killed, 50 wounded, 100 missing.
Rockville, Md. 11th N. Y. Cav. *Confed.* 34 killed and wounded.

26—Calhoun, Tenn. Cavalry Army of the Ohio. *Union* 6 killed, 20 wounded, 40 missing.

27—Moffat's Station, Ark. Detachment 1st Ark. *Union* 2 killed, 2 wounded. *Confed.* 5 killed, 20 wounded.

29—Near Morganzia, La. 19th Iowa, 26th Ind. *Union* 14 killed, 40 wounded, 400 missing.

OCTOBER, 1863

1—Anderson's Gap, Tenn. 21st Ky. *Union* 38 killed and wounded.

2—Anderson's Cross Roads, Tenn. McCook's Cavalry Corps. *Union* 70 killed and wounded. *Confed.* 200 killed and wounded.

3—McMinnville, Tenn. 4th Tenn. *Union* 7 killed, 31 wounded, 350 missing. *Confed.* 23 killed and wounded.

4—Neosho, Mo. Three Cos. 6th Mo. Militia Cav. *Union* 1 killed, 14 wounded, 43 missing.

5—Stockade at Stone River, Tenn. One Co. 19th Mich. *Union* 6 wounded, 44 captured.
Glasgow, Ky. 37th Ky. Mounted Inft. *Union* 3 wounded, 100 missing. *Confed.* 13 wounded.

6—Quantrell's attack on the escort of Maj.-Gen. Blunt, at Baxter Springs, Ark., robbing and murdering the prisoners. *Union* 54 killed, 18 wounded, 5 missing.

7—Near Farmington, Tenn. 1st, 3d, and 4th Ohio Cav., 2d Ky. Cav., Long's 2d Cav. Division, and Wilder's Brigade Mounted Inft. *Union* 15 killed, 60 wounded. *Confed.* 10 killed, 60 wounded, 240 missing.

10—Rapidan, Va. Buford's Cavalry. *Union* 20 wounded.
James City, also called Robertson's Run, Va. Pleasanton's Cavalry. *Union* 10 killed, 40 wounded.
Blue Springs, Tenn. Ninth Corps Army of the Ohio and Shackleford's Cav. *Union* 100 killed, wounded, and missing. *Confed.* 66 killed and wounded, 150 missing.

11—Henderson's Mill, Tenn. 5th Ind. Cav. *Union* 11 wounded. *Confed.* 30 killed and wounded.
Colliersville, Tenn. 66th Ind., 13th U. S. Reg. *Union* 15 killed, 50 wounded.

12—Jefferson, Va. 2d Cavalry Division Army of the Potomac. *Union* 12 killed, 80 wounded, 400 missing.

12 and **13**—Ingham's Mills and Wyatts, Miss. 2d Iowa Cav. *Union* 45 killed and wounded. *Confed.* 50 killed and wounded.
Culpeper and White Sulphur Springs, Va. Cavalry Corps Army of the Potomac. *Union* 8 killed, 46 wounded.
Merrill's Crossing to Lamine Crossing, Mo. Mo. Enrolled Militia, 1st Mo. Militia Battery, 1st, 4th, and 7th Mo. Militia Cav. *Union* 16 killed. *Confed.* 53 killed, 70 wounded.
Blountville, Tenn. 3d Brigade of Shackleford's Cavalry. *Union* 6 wounded. *Confed.* 8 killed, 26 wounded.
Bulltown, Va. Detachments of 6th and 11th W. Va. *Confed.* 9 killed, 60 wounded.

14—Auburn, Va. Portion of 1st Division Second Corps. *Union* 11 killed, 42 wounded. *Confed.* 8 killed, 24 wounded.
Bristoe Station, Va. Second Corps, portion of 5th Corps, 2d Cavalry Division Army of the Potomac. *Union* 51 killed, 329 wounded. *Confed.* 750 killed and wounded, 450 missing. *Union* Brig.-Gen. Malone killed. *Confed.* Brig.-Gens. Cooke, Posey, and Kirkland wounded.

15—McLean's Ford or Liberty Mills, Va. New Jersey Brigade of Third Corps. *Union* 2 killed, 25 wounded. *Confed.* 60 killed and wounded.

15 to **18**—Canton, Brownsville, and Clinton, Miss. Portion of Fifteenth and Seventeenth Corps. *Confed.* 200 killed and wounded.

16—Cross Timbers, Mo. 18th Iowa. *Confed.* 2 killed, 8 wounded.

17—Tampa Bay, Fla. Destruction of two blockade runners by U. S. Gunboats *Tahoma* and *Adele. Union* 3 killed, 10 wounded.

18—Charlestown, W. Va. 9th Md. *Union* 12 killed, 13 wounded, 379 missing.
Berrysville, Va. 34th Mass., 17th Ind. Battery. *Union* 2 killed, 4 wounded. *Confed.* 5 killed, 20 wounded.

19—Buckland Mills, Va. 3d Division of Kilpatrick's Cav. *Union* 20 killed, 60 wounded, 100 missing. *Confed.* 10 killed, 40 wounded.

20 and **22**—Philadelphia, Tenn. 45th Ohio Mounted Inft., 1st, 11th, and 12th Ky. Cav., 24th Ind. Battery. *Union* 20 killed, 80 wounded, 354 missing. *Confed.* 15 killed, 82 wounded, 111 missing.

21—Cherokee Station, Ala. 1st Division Fifteenth Corps. *Union* 7 killed, 37 wounded. *Confed.* 40 killed and wounded.

22—Beverly Ford, Va. 2d Penna. and 1st Me. Cav. *Union* 6 killed.

25—Pine Bluff, Ark. 5th Kan. and 1st Ind. Cav. *Union* 11 killed, 27 wounded. *Confed.* 53 killed, 164 wounded.

26—Cane Creek, Ala. 1st Division Fifteenth Corps. *Union* 2 killed, 6 wounded. *Confed.* 10 killed, 30 wounded.
Vincent's Cross Roads, or Bay Springs, Miss. 1st Alabama (Union) Cav. *Union* 14 killed, 25 wounded.

27—Brown's Ferry, Tenn. Detachment of 2d Brigade, 2d Division of Fourth Corps. *Union* 5 killed, 21 wounded.
Wauhatchie, Tenn. Eleventh Corps and 2d Division of Twelfth Corps. *Union* 77 killed, 339 wounded. *Confed.* 300 killed, 1,200 wounded.

28—Leiper's Ferry, Tenn. 11th and 37th Ky., 112th Ill. *Union* 2 killed, 5 wounded.

29—Cherokee Station, Ala. First Division of Fifteenth Corps. Casualties not recorded.

NOVEMBER, 1863

3—Centerville and Piney Factory, Tenn. Detachments from various regiments, under Lieut.-Col. Scully. *Confed.* 15 killed.
Grand Coteau, La. 3d and 4th Divisions of Thirteenth Corps. *Union* 26 killed, 124 wounded, 576 missing. *Confed.* 60 killed, 320 wounded, 65 missing.

3 and **4**—Colliersville, and Moscow, Tenn. Cavalry Brigade of Sixteenth Corps. *Union* 6 killed, 57 wounded. *Confed.* 100 wounded.

6—Rogersville, Tenn. 7th Ohio Cav., 2d Tenn. Mounted Inft., 2d Ill. Battery. *Union* 5 killed, 12 wounded, 650 missing. *Confed.* 10 killed, 20 wounded.
Droop Mountain, Va. 10th W. Va., 28th Ohio, 14th Penna. Cav., 2d and 5th W. Va. Cav., Battery B, W. Va. Artil. *Union* 31 killed, 94 wounded. *Confed.* 50 killed, 250 wounded, 100 missing.

7—Rappahannock Station, Va. 5th Wis., 5th and 6th Maine, 49th and 119th Penna., 121st N. Y., supported by balance of Sixth and portion of Fifth Corps. *Union* 370 killed and wounded. *Confed.* 11 killed, 98 wounded, 1,629 missing.
Kelly's Ford, Va. 1st U. S. Sharpshooters, 40th N. Y., 1st and 20th Ind., 3d and 5th Mich., 110th Penna., supported by remainder of Third Corps. Union 70 killed and wounded. *Confed.* 5 killed, 59 wounded, 295 missing.

8—Clarksville, Ark. 3d Wis. Cav. *Union* 2 killed.
Muddy Run, near Culpeper, Va. 1st Division Cavalry Division Army of the Potomac. *Union* 4 killed, 25 wounded.

11—Natchez, Miss. 58th U. S. Colored. *Union* 4 killed, 6 wounded. *Confed.* 4 killed, 8 wounded.

13—Trinity River, Cal. Two Cos. 1st Battalion Cal. Inft. *Union* 2 wounded.

14—Huff's Ferry, Tenn. 111th Ohio, 107th Ill., 11th and 13th Ky., 23d Mich., 24th Mich. Battery. *Union* 100 killed and wounded.
Rockford, Tenn. 1st Ky. Cav., 45th Ohio Mounted Inft. *Union* 25 wounded.
Marysville, Tenn. 11th Ky. Cav. *Union* 100 killed and wounded.

15—Loudon Creek, Tenn. 111th Ohio. *Union* 4 killed, 12 wounded. *Confed.* 6 killed, 10 wounded.

16—Campbell's Station, Tenn. Ninth Corps, 2d Division of Twenty-third Corps, Sanders' Cav. *Union* 60 killed, 340 wounded. *Confed.* 570 killed and wounded.

17—Mount Jackson, Va. 1st N. Y. Cav. *Union* 2 killed, 3 wounded. *Confed.* 27 missing.

17 to **Dec. 4**—Siege of Knoxville, Tenn. Army of the Ohio, commanded by Maj.-Gen. Burnside, complete casualties not recorded. At Fort Sanders, Nov. 29th, the losses were, *Union* 20 killed, 80 wounded. *Confed.* 80 killed, 400 wounded, 300 captured.

19—Union City, Tenn. 2d Ill. Cav. *Union* 1 killed. *Confed.* 11 killed, 53 captured.

23 to **25**—Chattanooga, Lookout Mountain, Orchard Knob and Missionary Ridge, Tenn. Fourth and Fourteenth Corps, Army of the Cumberland, Maj.-Gen. Geo. H. Thomas; Eleventh, Geary's Division of the Twelfth, and the Fifteenth Corps Army of the Tennessee, Maj.-Gen. W. T. Sherman. *Union* 757 killed, 4,529 wounded, 330 missing. *Confed.* 361 killed, 2,181 wounded, 6,142 missing.

24—Sparta, Tenn. 1st Tenn. and 9th Penna. Cav. *Confed.* 1 killed, 2 wounded.

26 to **28**—Operations at Mine Run, Va., including Raccoon Ford, New Hope, Robertson's Tavern, Bartlett's Mills and Locust Grove. First Corps, Second Corps, Third Corps, Fifth Corps, Sixth Corps, and 1st and 2d Cavalry Divisions Army of the Potomac. *Union* 100 killed, 400 wounded. *Confed.* 100 killed, 400 wounded.

27—Cleveland, Tenn. 2d Brigade of 2d Cavalry Division. *Confed.* 200 captured.
Ringgold and Taylor's Ridge, Ga. Portions of Twelfth, Fourteenth, and Fifteenth Corps. *Union* 68 killed, 351 wounded. *Confed.* 50 killed, 200 wounded, 230 missing.

27 to **29**—Fort Esperanza, Tex. Portions of 1st and 2d Divisions Thirteenth Corps. *Union* 1 killed, 2 wounded. *Confed.* 1 killed.

DECEMBER, 1863

1 to **4**—Ripley and Moscow Station, Miss., and Salisbury, Tenn. 2d Brigade Cavalry Division of Sixteenth Corps. *Union* 175 killed and wounded. *Confed.* 15 killed, 40 wounded. *Union* Col. Hatch, commanding, wounded.

2—Walker's Ford, W. Va. 65th, 116th, and 118th Ind., 21st Ohio Battery, 5th Ind. Cav., 14th Ill. Cav. *Union* 9 killed, 39 wounded. *Confed.* 25 killed, 50 wounded.

7—Creelsboro, Ky., and Celina, Tenn. 13th Ky. Cav. *Confed.* 15 killed.

8 to **21**—Averill's Raid in Southwestern Va. *Union* 6 killed, 5 wounded. *Confed.* 200 prisoners.

10 to **14**—Bean's Station and Morristown, Tenn. Shackleford's Cavalry. *Union* 700 killed and wounded. *Confed.* 932 killed and wounded, 150 prisoners.

17 to **26**—Rodney and Port Gibson, Miss. Miss. Marine Brigade. *Union* 2 killed.

19—Barren Fork, Ind. Ter. 1st and 3d Kan., Indian Home Guards. *Confed.* 50 killed.

24 and **25**—Bolivar and Summerville, Tenn. 7th Ill. Cav. *Union* 3 killed, 8 wounded.

28—Charlestown, Tenn. Detachments of 2d Mo. and 4th Ohio Cav. guarding wagon train. *Union* 2 killed, 15 wounded. *Confed.* 8 killed, 39 wounded, 121 captured.

29—Talbot's Station and Mossy Creek, Tenn. 1st Brigade, 2d Division Twenty-third Corps, 1st Tenn. Cav., 1st Wis. Cav., 2d and 4th Ind. Cav., 24th Ind. Battery.

30—St. Augustine, Fla. 10th Conn., 24th Mass. *Union* 4 killed. Greenville, N. C. Detachments of 12th N. Y., 1st N. C. and 23d N. Y. Battery. *Union* 1 killed, 6 wounded. *Confed.* 6 killed.

Waldron, Ark. 2d Kan. Cav. *Union* 2 killed, 6 wounded.

JANUARY, 1864

1 to **10**—Rectortown and London Heights, Va. 1st Md. Cav., Potomac Home Brigade. *Union* 29 killed and wounded, 41 missing. *Confed.* 4 killed, 10 wounded.

3—Jonesville, Va. Detachment 16th Ill. Cav., 22d Ohio Battery. *Union* 12 killed, 48 wounded, 300 missing. *Confed.* 4 killed, 12 wounded.

7—Martin's Creek, Ark. 11th Mo. Cav. *Union* 1 killed, 1 wounded.

12—Mayfield, Ky. 58th Ill. *Union* 1 killed, 1 wounded. *Confed.* 2 killed.

13—Mossy Creek, Tenn. McCook's Cav. *Confed.* 14 killed.

14—Bealton, Va. One Co. 9th Mass. *Union* 2 wounded. *Confed.* 3 killed, 12 wounded.

16 and **17**—Dandridge, Tenn. Fourth Corps and Cav. Division of Army of the Ohio. *Union* 150 wounded.

20—Tracy City, Tenn. Detachment 20th Conn. *Union* 2 killed.

23—Rolling Prairie, Ark. 11th Mo. Cav. *Union* 11 killed.

24—Baker Springs, Ark. 2d and 6th Kan. Cav. *Union* 1 killed, 2 wounded, *Confed.* 6 killed, 2 wounded.

Tazewell, Tenn. 34th Ky., 116th and 18th Ind., 11th Tenn. Cav., 11th Mich. Battery. *Confed.* 31 killed.

27—Fair Gardens or Kelly's Ford, Tenn. Sturgis's Cavalry. *Union* 100 killed and wounded. *Confed.* 65 killed, 100 captured.

28—Tunnel Hill, Ga. Part of Fourteenth Corps. *Union* 2 wounded. *Confed.* 32 wounded.

29—Medley, W. Va. 1st and 14th W. Va., 23d Ill., 2d Md., Potomac Home Brigade, 4th W. Va. Cav., Ringgold (Pa.) Cav. *Union* 10 killed, 70 wounded. *Confed.* 100 wounded.

FEBRUARY, 1864

1—Smithfield, Va. Detachments 99th N. Y., 21st Conn., 20th N. Y. Cav., 3d Pa. Artil., and marines from U. S. Gunboats *Minnesota* and *Smith Briggs*. *Union* 90 missing.

1 to **3**—Bachelor Creek, Newport Barracks, and New Berne, N. C. 132d N. Y., 9th Vt., 17th Mass., 2d N. C., 12th N. Y. Cav., 3d N. Y. Artil. *Union* 16 killed, 50 wounded, 280 missing. *Confed.* 5 killed, 30 wounded.

1 to **March 8**—Expedition up the Yazoo River, Miss. 11th Ill., 47th U. S. Colored, 3d U. S. Colored Cav., and a portion of Porter's Fleet of Gunboats. *Union* 35 killed, 121 wounded. *Confed.* 35 killed, 90 wounded.

3 to **March 5**—Expedition from Vicksburg to Meridian, Miss., including Champion Hills, Raymond, Clinton, Jackson, Decatur, Chunky Station, occupation of Meridian, Lauderdale Springs, and Marion, Miss. Two Divisions of the Sixteenth and three of the Seventeenth Corps, with the 5th Ill., 4th Iowa, 10th Mo. and Foster's (Ohio) Cav. *Union* 56 killed, 138 wounded, 105 missing. *Confed.* 503 killed and wounded, 212 captured.

5—Qualltown, N. C. Detachment of 14th Ill. Cav. *Union* 3 killed, 6 wounded. *Confed.* 50 captured, including Maj.-Gen. Vance.

Cape Girardeau, Mo. 2d Mo. Militia Cav. *Confed.* 7 killed.

6—Bolivar, Tenn. Detachment of 7th Ind. Cav. *Union* 1 killed, 3 wounded. *Confed.* 30 wounded.

Morton's Ford, Va. Portion of Second Corps. *Union* 10 killed, 201 wounded. *Confed.* 100 missing.

7—Barnett's Ford, Va. Brig.-Gen. Merritt's Cav. *Union* 20 killed and wounded.

Vidalia, La. 30th Mo., 64th U. S. Colored, 6th U. S. Artil., Colored. *Confed.* 6 killed, 10 wounded.

9—Morgan's Mills, Ark. Detachments of 4th Ark., 11th Mo. Cav., 1st Neb. Cav. *Union* 1 killed, 4 wounded. *Confed.* 65 killed and wounded.

9 to **14**—Barber's Place, St. Mary's River, Lake City and Gainesville, Fla. 40th Mass. Mounted Inft. and Independent (Mass.) Cav. *Union* 4 killed, 16 wounded. *Confed.* 4 killed, 48 wounded.

10 to **25**—Smith's Raid from Germantown, Tenn., into Mississippi. Smith's and Grierson's Cav. Divisions. *Union* 43 killed, 267 wounded. *Confed.* 50 wounded, 300 captured.

12—Rock House, W. Va. 14th Ky. *Confed.* 12 killed, 4 wounded.

14—Ross Landing, Ark. 51st U. S. Colored. *Union* 13 killed, 7 wounded. Brentsville, Va. 13th Pa. Cav. *Union* 4 killed, 1 wounded.

14 and **15**—Waterproof, La. 49th U. S. Colored and U. S. Gunboat *Forest Rose*. *Union* 8 killed, 14 wounded. *Confed.* 15 killed.

19—Grosse Tete Bayou, La. 4th Wis. Cav. *Union* 2 wounded. *Confed.* 4 killed, 6 wounded.

Near Batesville, Ark. 4th Ark., 11th Mo. Cav. *Union* 3 killed, 4 wounded. *Confed.* 6 killed, 10 wounded.

20—Holston River, Tenn. 4th Tenn. *Union* 2 killed, 3 wounded. *Confed.* 5 killed, 10 wounded.

Olustee or Silver Lake, Fla. 47th, 48th and 115th N. Y., 7th Conn., 7th N. H., 40th Mass., 8th and 54th U. S. Colored, 1st N. C. Colored, 1st Mass. Cav., 1st and 3d U. S. Artil., 3d R. I. Artil. *Union* 193 killed, 1,175 wounded, 460 missing. *Confed.* 100 killed, 400 wounded.

22—Mulberry Gap, Tenn. 9th Tenn. Cav. *Union* 13 killed and wounded, 256 captured.

Drainesville, Va. Detachment of 2d Mass. Cav. *Union* 10 killed, 7 wounded, 57 captured. *Confed.* 2 killed, 4 wounded.

Johnson's Mills, Tenn. Detachment of 24 men 5th Tenn. Cav., captured and massacred by Ferguson's guerrillas.

23 and **March 18**—Calf Killer Creek, Tenn. 5th Tenn. Cav. *Union* 8 killed, 3 wounded. *Confed.* 33 killed.

25 to **27**—Buzzard Roost, Tunnel Hill and Rocky Face, Ga. Fourth and Fourteenth Corps and Cavalry Corps Army of the Cumberland. *Union* 17 killed, 272 wounded. *Confed.* 20 killed, 120 wounded.

27 and **28**—Near Canton, Miss. Foraging Detachments of 3d and 32d Iowa. *Union* 2 killed, 5 wounded. *Confed.* 3 killed, 15 wounded.

28 to **March 4**—Kilpatrick's Raid, Stevensburg to Richmond, Va. Kilpatrick's Cavalry. *Union* 330 killed, wounded and captured. *Confed.* 308 killed, wounded and captured.

MARCH, 1864

1—Stanardsville and Burton's Ford, Rapidan, Va. Custer's Cav. *Union* 10 wounded. *Confed.* 30 captured.

2—Harrisonburg, La. Porter's Miss. Squadron. *Union* 2 killed, 14 wounded.

5—Panther Springs, Tenn. One Co. 3d Tenn. *Union* 2 killed, 8 wounded. 22 captured. *Confed.* 30 wounded.

7—Decatur, Ala. Army of the Tennessee, commanded by Brig.-Gen. Dodge.

9—Suffolk, Va. 2d U. S. Colored Cav. *Union* 8 killed, 1 wounded. *Confed.* 25 wounded.

14—Fort De Russy, La. Detachments of Sixteenth and Seventeenth Corps and Porter's Miss. Squadron. *Union* 7 killed, 41 wounded. *Confed.* 5 killed, 4 wounded, 260 prisoners.

15—Clarendon, Ark. 8th Mo. Cav. *Union* 1 killed, 3 wounded.

17—Manchester, Tenn. 5th Tenn. Cav. *Confed.* 21 killed.

21—Henderson Hills, La. Detachments of Sixteenth Corps and Cavalry Division Nineteenth Corps. *Union* 1 wounded. *Confed.* 8 killed, 250 captured.

24—Union City, Ky. 7th Tenn. Cav. 450 men captured by Forrest.

25—Fort Anderson, Paducah, Ky. 122d Ill., 16th Ky. Cav., 8th U. S. Colored Artil. *Union* 14 killed, 46 wounded. *Confed.* 10 killed, 40 wounded. *Confed.* Brig.-Gen. Thompson killed.

26 to **30**—Longview and Mt. Elba, Ark. 28th Wis., 5th Kan. Cav., 7th Mo. Cav. *Union* 4 killed, 18 wounded. *Confed.* 12 killed, 35 wounded, 300 captured.

28—Charleston, Ill. Attack on 5th Ill. by mob of Copperheads while returning to the front on veteran furlough. *Union* 2 killed, 8 wounded. *Confed.* 3 killed, 4 wounded, 12 prisoners.

29—Bolivar, Tenn. 6th Tenn. Cav. *Union* 8 killed, 35 wounded.

31—Near Snydersville, Miss. 3d U. S. Colored Cav. *Union* 16 killed, 3 wounded. *Confed.* 3 killed, 7 wounded.

APRIL, 1864

1—Augusta, Ark. 3d Minn., 8th Mo. Cav. *Union* 8 killed, 16 wounded. *Confed.* 15 killed, 45 wounded.

2—Spoonville, Ark. 29th Iowa, 9th Wis., 50th Ind., with 1st Mo. Cav. *Union* 10 killed, 35 wounded. *Confed.* 100 killed and wounded.

Crump's Hill or Piney Woods, La. 14th N. Y. Cav., 2d La., 2d Ill., and 16th Mo. Cav., 5th U. S. Colored Artil. *Union* 20 wounded. *Confed.* 10 killed, 25 wounded.

3—Okalona, Ark. 27th Wis., 40th Iowa, 77th Ohio, 43d Ill., 1st Mo. Cav., 13th Ill. Cav. *Union* 16 killed, 74 wounded. *Confed.* 75 killed and wounded.

4—Campti, La. 35th Iowa, 5th Minn., 2d and 18th N. Y. Cav., 3d R. I. Cav. *Union* 10 killed, 18 wounded. *Confed.* 3 killed, 12 wounded.

4 to **6**—Elkins' Ford, Ark. 43d Ind., 29th and 36th Iowa, 1st Iowa Cav., Battery E 2d Mo. Light Artil. *Union* 5 killed, 33 wounded. *Confed.* 18 killed, 30 wounded.

5—Roseville, Ark. Seventy-five men of 2d and 6th Kan. Cav., in engagement with guerrillas. *Union* 19 killed, 11 wounded. *Confed.* 15 killed, 25 wounded, 11 captured.

Stone's Farm. Twenty-six men of 6th Kan. Cav., in engagement with guerrillas. 11, including Asst. Surg. Fairchild, captured and massacred.

6—Quicksand Creek, Ky. Co. I 14th Ky. *Confed.* 10 killed, 7 wounded.

7—Wilson's Farm, La. Advance Cavalry of Nineteenth Corps. *Union* 14 killed, 39 wounded. *Confed.* 15 killed, 40 wounded, 100 captured.

Near Port Hudson, La. Detachment 118th Ill., 3d Ill. Cav., 21st N. Y. Battery. *Union* 1 killed, 4 wounded.

8 and **9**—Sabine Cross Roads and Pleasant Hills, La. Portions of Thirteenth, Sixteenth and Nineteenth Corps and Cavalry Division Army of Dept. of the Gulf. *Union* 300 killed, 1,600 wounded, 2,100 missing. *Confed.* 600 killed, 2,400 wounded, 500 missing. *Union* Maj.-Gen. Franklin and Brig.-Gen. Ransom wounded. *Confed.* Maj.-Gen. Moulton and Brig.-Gen. Parsons killed.

10 to **13**—Prairie D'Ann, Ark. 3d Division Seventh Corps. *Union* 100 killed and wounded. *Confed.* 50 killed and wounded.

12—Pleasant Hill Landing, La. Seventeenth Corps and U. S. Gunboats *Osage* and *Lexington*. *Union* 7 wounded. *Confed.* 200 killed and wounded.

13—Moscow, Ark. 18th Iowa, 6th Kan. Cav., 2d Ind. Battery. *Union* 5 killed, 17 wounded. *Confed.* 30 killed and wounded.

13 and **14**—Paintsville and Half-Mount, Ky. Ky. Volunteers. *Union* 4 wounded. *Confed.* 25 killed, 25 wounded.

14—Smithfield or Cherry Grove, Va. 9th N. J., 23d and 25th Mass., 118th N. Y. *Union* 5 wounded. *Confed.* 6 wounded.

15—Bristoe Station, Va. 13th Pa. Cav. *Union* 1 killed, 2 wounded.

15 and **16**—Liberty P. O., and occupation of Camden, Ark. 29th Iowa, 50th Ind., 9th Wis. *Union* 255 killed and wounded.

17—Decatur, Ala. 25th Wis. *Union* 2 wounded.

17 to **20**—Plymouth, N. C. 85th N. Y., 103d Pa., 16th Conn. and the Navy. *Union* 20 killed, 80 wounded, 1,500 missing. *Confed.* 500 killed, wounded and missing. Lieut.-Com. Flusser, U. S. N., killed.

18—Poison Springs, eight miles from Camden, Ark. Forage train guarded by 18th Iowa, 79th U. S. Colored, 6th Kan. Cav. *Union* 113 killed, 88 wounded, 68 missing.

Boyken's Mills, S. C. 54th Mass., U. S. Colored. *Union* 2 killed, 18 wounded.

21—Cotton Plate, Cache River, Ark. 8th Mo. Cav. *Union* 5 killed, 2 wounded.

Red Bone, Miss., 2d Wis. Cav. *Union* 1 killed, 6 wounded.

22—Near Tunica Bend, Red River, La. Three Cos. 3d R. I. Cav. *Union* 2 killed, 17 wounded.

23—Nickajack Trace, Ga. Detachment of 92d Ill. *Union* 5 killed, 9 wounded, 22 taken prisoners, of whom 12 were shot down and 6 died from wounds.

23 and **24**—Moneti's Bluff, Cane River and Cloutersville, La. Portion of Thirteenth, Seventh and Nineteenth Corps. *Union* 350 killed and wounded. *Confed.* 400 killed and wounded.

25—Mark's Mills, Ark. 36th Iowa, 77th Ohio, 43d Ill., 1st Ind. Cav., 7th Mo. Cav., Battery E 2d Mo. Light Artil. *Union* 100 killed, 250 wounded, 100 missing. *Confed.* 110 killed, 228 wounded, 40 missing.

25 and **26**—Wautauga Bridge, Tenn. 10th Mich. Cav. *Union* 3 killed, 9 wounded.

26—Moro Creek, Ark. 33d and 40th Iowa, 5th Kan., 2d and 4th Mo., 1st Iowa Cav. *Union* 5 killed, 14 wounded.

29—Princeton, Ark. 40th Iowa, 43d Ill., 6th Kan. Cav., 3d Ill. Battery. Casualties not recorded.

30—Jenkins' Ferry, Saline River, Ark. 3d Division of Seventh Corps *Union* 200 killed, 955 wounded. *Confed.* 300 killed, 800 wounded.

MAY, 1864

1—Jacksonville, Fla. 7th U. S. Colored. *Union* 1 killed.

1 to **8**—Hudnot's Plantation and near Alexandria, La. Cavalry of Thirteenth and Nineteenth Corps. *Union* 33 killed, 87 wounded. *Confed.* 25 killed, 100 wounded.

2—Gov. Moor's Plantation, La. Foraging of Detachment of 83d Ohio and 3d R. I. Cav. *Union* 2 killed, 10 wounded.

3—Red Clay, Ga. 1st Division of McCook's Cav. *Union* 10 killed and wounded.

Richland, Ark. 2d Ark. Cav. *Union* 20 killed.

4—Doubtful Cañon, Ariz. Detachment of 5th Cav. and 1st Cal. Cav. *Union* 1 killed, 6 wounded. *Confed.* 10 killed, 20 wounded.

4 to **12**—Kautz's Cavalry Raid from Suffolk, Wall's Bridge, Stoney Creek Station, Jarrett's Station, White's Bridge to City Point, Va. 5th and 11th Pa. Cav., 3d N. Y. Cav., 1st D. C. Cav., 8th N. Y. Battery. *Union* 10 killed, wounded and missing. *Confed.* 20 wounded, 50 prisoners.

4 to **13**—Yazoo City expedition, including Benton and Vaughn, Miss. 11th, 72d and 76th Ill., 5th Ill. Cav., 3d U. S. Colored Cav., 7th Ohio Battery. *Union* 5 killed, 20 wounded.

5—Ram *Albermarle*, Roanoke River, N. C. U. S. Gunboats, *Ceres*, *Commodore Hull*, *Mattabesett*, *Sassacus*, *Seymour*, *Wyalusing*, *Miama* and *Whitehead*. *Union* 5 killed, 26 wounded. *Confed.* 57 captured.

Dunn's Bayou, Red River, La. 56th Ohio, on board U. S. Gunboat

Signal, steamer *Covington* and transport *Warner*. *Union* 35 killed, 65 wounded, 150 missing.

5 to 7—Wilderness, Va. Army of the Potomac, Maj.-Gen. George G. Meade; Second Corps, Maj.-Gen. Hancock; Fifth Corps, Maj.-Gen. Warren; Sixth Corps, Maj.-Gen. Sedgwick; Ninth Corps, Maj.-Gen. Burnside and Sheridan's Cavalry. *Union* 5,597 killed, 21,463 wounded, 10,677 missing. *Confed.* 2,000 killed, 6,000 wounded, 3,400 missing. *Union* Brig.-Gens. Wadsworth, Hays and Webb killed. *Confed.* Gens. Jones and Pickett killed, and Longstreet, Pegram, Stafford, Hunter and Jennings wounded.

5 to 9—Rocky Face Ridge, Ga., including Tunnel Hill, Mill Creek Gap and Buzzard's Roost. Army of the Cumberland, Maj.-Gen. Thomas; Army of the Tennessee, Maj.-Gen. McPherson. Army of the Mississippi, Maj.-Gen. Sherman. *Union* 200 killed, 637 wounded. *Confed.* 600 killed and wounded.

6—James River, near City Point, Va. U. S. Gunboat *Commodore Jones*. *Union* 23 killed, 48 wounded.

6 and 7—Richmond and Petersburg Railroad, near Chester Station, Va. Portion of Tenth and Eighteenth Corps. *Union* 48 killed, 256 wounded. *Confed.* 50 killed, 200 wounded.

7—Bayou La Mourie, La. Portion of Sixteenth Corps. *Union* 10 killed, 31 wounded.

8—Todd's Tavern, Va. 2d Division Cavalry Corps Army of the Potomac. *Union* 40 killed, 150 wounded. *Confed.* 30 killed, 150 wounded.

8 to 18—Spottsylvania, Fredericksburg Road, Laurel Hill and Ny River, Va. Army of the Potomac, Maj.-Gen. Meade; Second Corps, Maj.-Gen. Hancock; Fifth Corps, Maj.-Gen. Warren; Sixth Corps, Maj.-Gen. Wright; Ninth Corps, Maj.-Gen. Burnside and Sheridan's Cavalry. *Union* 4,177 killed, 19,687 wounded, 2,577 missing. *Confed.* 1,000 killed, 5,000 wounded, 3,000 missing. *Union* Maj.-Gen. Sedgwick and Brig.-Gens. Rice, Owens and Stevenson killed; Brig.-Gens. Robertson, Bartlett, Morris and Baxter wounded. *Confed.* Gens. Daniels and Perrin killed, Hayes and Walker wounded and Maj.-Gen. Ed. Johnson and Brig.-Gen. Stewart captured.

9—Varnell's Station, Ga. 1st Div. McCook's Cav. *Union* 4 killed, 25 wounded.

9 and 10—Swift Creek or Arrowfield Church, Va. Tenth and Eighteenth Corps. *Union* 90 killed, 400 wounded. *Confed.* 500 missing.

Cloyd's Mountain and New River Bridge, Va. 12th, 23d, 34th and 36th Ohio, 9th 11th, 14th and 15th W. Va., 3d and 4th Pa. Reserves. *Union* 126 killed, 585 wounded. *Confed.* 600 killed and wounded, 300 missing.

9 to 13—Sheridan's Cavalry Raid in Virginia, engagements Beaver Dam Station, South Anna Bridge, Ashland and Yellow Tavern. *Union* 50 killed, 174 wounded, 200 missing. *Confed.* killed and wounded not recorded, 100 prisoners. *Confed.* Maj.-Gen. J. E. B. Stuart killed and J. B. Gordon wounded.

12 to 16—Fort Darling, Drury's Bluff, Va. Tenth and Eighteenth Corps. *Union* 422 killed, 2,380 wounded, 210 missing. *Confed.* 400 killed, 2,000 wounded, 100 missing.

12 to 17—Kautz's Raid on Petersburg and Lynchburg Railroad, Va. *Union* 6 killed, 28 wounded.

13 to 16—Resaca, Ga. Fourth, Fourteenth, Twentieth and Cavalry Corps, Army of the Cumberland, Maj.-Gen. Thomas; Fifteenth and Sixteenth Corps, Army of the Tennessee, Maj.-Gen. McPherson, and Twenty-third Corps, Army of the Ohio, Maj.-Gen. Schofield. *Union* 600 killed, 2,147 wounded. *Confed.* 300 killed, 1,500 wounded, 1,000 missing. *Confed.* Brig.-Gen. Wadkins killed.

15—Mount Pleasant Landing, La. 67th U. S. Colored. *Union* 3 killed, 5 wounded.

New Market, Va. Maj.-Gen. Sigel's command. *Union* 120 killed, 560 wounded, 240 missing. *Confed.* 85 killed, 320 wounded.

Tanner's Bridge, Ga. 2d Division Cavalry, Army of the Cumberland. *Union* 2 killed, 16 wounded.

16 to 30—Bermuda Hundred, Va. Tenth and Eighteenth Corps, Army of the James. *Union* 200 killed, 1,000 wounded. *Confed.* 3,000 killed, wounded and missing.

17 and 18—Adairsville and Calhoun, Ga. Fourth Corps, Maj.-Gen. Howard. Casualties not recorded.

18—Rome and Kingston, Ga. 2d Division of Fourteenth Corps and Cavalry Army of the Cumberland. *Union* 16 killed, 59 wounded.

Bayou De Glaize or Calhoun Station, La. Portions of Sixteenth, Seventeenth and Cavalry of Nineteenth Corps. *Union* 60 killed, 300 wounded. *Confed.* 500 killed and wounded.

19 to 22—Cassville, Ga. Twentieth Corps, Maj.-Gen. Hooker. *Union* 10 killed, 46 wounded.

21—Mt. Pleasant, Miss. 4th Mo. Cav. *Union* 2 killed, 1 wounded.

23 to 27—North Anna River, Jericho Ford or Taylor's Bridge and Talopotomy Creek, Va. Second, Fifth and Ninth Corps, Army of the Potomac, Maj.-Gen. Meade. *Union* 223 killed, 1,460 wounded, 290 missing. *Confed.* 2,000 killed and wounded.

24—Holly Springs, Miss. 4th Mo. Cav. *Union* 1 killed, 2 wounded.

Wilson's Wharf, Va. 10th U. S. Colored, 1st D. C. Cavalry, Battery B U. S. Colored Artil. *Union* 2 killed, 24 wounded. *Confed.* 20 killed, 100 wounded.

Nashville, Tenn. 15th U. S. Colored. *Union* 4 killed, 8 wounded.

25 to June 4—Dallas, Ga., also called New Hope Church and Allatoona Hills.

Fourth, Fourteenth, Twentieth and Cavalry Corps, Army of the Cumberland, Maj.-Gen. Thomas; Twenty-third Corps, Maj.-Gen. Schofield; Fifteenth, Sixteenth and Seventeenth Corps Army of the Tennessee, Maj.-Gen. McPherson—Army of the Mississippi, Maj.-Gen. Sherman. *Union* 2,400 killed, wounded and missing. *Confed.* 3,000 killed, wounded and missing. *Confed.* Maj.-Gen. Walker killed.

25—Cassville Station, Ga. 1st and 11th Ky. Cav. *Union* 8 killed, 16 wounded. *Confed.* 2 killed, 6 wounded.

26—Torpedo explosion on Bachelor's Creek, N. C. 132d and 158th N. Y., 58th Pa. *Union* 35 killed, 19 wounded.

26 to 29—Decatur and Moulton, Ala. 1st, 3d and 4th Ohio Cav., 2d Cavalry Division. *Union* 48 killed and wounded. *Confed.* 60 killed and wounded.

27 and 28—Hanoverton, Hawe's Shop and Salem Church, Va. 1st and Second Divisions Cavalry Corps, Maj.-Gen. Sheridan. *Union* 25 killed, 119 wounded, 200 missing. *Confed.* 475 killed, wounded and missing.

30—Hanover and Ashland, Va. Wilson's Cavalry. *Union* 26 killed, 130 wounded.

Old Church, Va. Torbett's Cavalry. *Union* 16 killed, 74 wounded.

JUNE, 1864

1 to 12—Cold Harbor, Va., including Gaines's Mills, Salem Church and Hawe's Shop. Second, Fifth, Sixth, Ninth and Eighteenth Corps and Sheridan's Cavalry. *Union* 1,905 killed, 10,570 wounded, 2,456 missing. *Confed.* 1,200 killed and wounded, 500 missing. *Union* Brig.-Gens. Brookes and Byrnes killed and Tyler, Stannard and Johnson wounded. *Confed.* Brig.-Gens. Doles and Keitt killed and Kirkland, Finnegan, Law and Lane wounded.

2—Bermuda Hundred, Va. Tenth Corps. *Union* 25 killed, 100 wounded. *Confed.* 100 killed and wounded.

3 to 6—Panther Gap and Buffalo Gap, W. Va. Hayes's Brigade of 2d Division Army of West Virginia. *Union* 25 killed and wounded. *Confed.* 25 killed and wounded.

5—Piedmont, W. Va. Portion of Army of West Virginia, commanded by Maj.-Gen. Hunter. *Union* 130 killed, 650 wounded. *Confed.* 460 killed, 1,450 wounded, 1,060 missing. *Confed.* Gen. W. E. Jones killed.

6—Lake Chicot, Ark. Sixteenth Corps. *Union* 40 killed, 70 wounded. *Confed.* 100 killed and wounded.

9—Point of Rocks, Md. 2d U. S. Colored Cav. *Union* 2 killed.

Mt. Sterling, Ky. Burbridge's Cavalry. *Union* 35 killed, 150 wounded. *Confed.* 50 killed, 200 wounded, 250 captured.

9 to 30—Kenesaw Mountain, Marietta or Big Shanty, Ga., including general assault on the 27th, Pine Mt., Golgotha, Culp's House and Powder Springs. Fourth, Fourteenth and Twentieth Corps, Army of the Cumberland, Maj.-Gen. Thomas; Fifteenth, Sixteenth and Seventeenth Corps, Army of the Tennessee, Maj.-Gen. McPherson; Twenty-third Corps, Maj.-Gen. Schofield; Army of the Mississippi, Maj.-Gen. W. T. Sherman. *Union* 1,370 killed, 6,500 wounded, 800 missing. *Confed.* 1,100 killed and wounded, 3,500 missing. *Union* Brig.-Gens. Harker and McCook killed. *Confed.* Lieut.-Gen. Leonidas Polk killed.

10—Petersburg, Va. Portion of Tenth Corps and Kautz's Cav. *Union* 20 killed, 67 wounded.

Brice's Cross Roads, near Guntown, Miss. 81st, 95th, 108th, 113th, 114th and 120th Ill., 72d and 95th Ohio, 9th Minn., 93d Ind., 55th and 59th U. S. Colored, Brig.-Gen. Grierson's Cavalry, the 4th Mo., 2d N. J., 19th Pa., 7th and 9th Ill., 7th Ind., 3d and 4th Iowa, and 10th Kan. Cav., 1st Ill. and 6th Ind. Batteries, Battery F 2d U. S. Colored Artil. *Union* 223 killed, 394 wounded, 1,623 missing. *Confed.* 131 killed, 475 wounded.

Cynthiana and Kellar's Bridge, Ky. 168th and 171st Ohio. *Union* 21 killed, 71 wounded, 980 captured by Morgan's Raiders.

10 and 11—Lexington, W. Va. 2d Division Army of West Virginia. *Union* 6 killed, 18 wounded.

11—Cynthiana, Ky. Burbridge's Cav. Attack on Morgan's Raiders. *Union* 150 killed and wounded. *Confed.* 300 killed and wounded, 400 captured.

11 and 12—Trevilian Station, Va. Sheridan's Cavalry. *Union* 85 killed, 490 wounded, 160 missing. *Confed.* 370 missing.

13—White Oak Swamp Bridge, Va. Wilson's and Crawford's Cav. *Union* 50 killed, 250 wounded.

14—Lexington, Mo. Detachment 1st Mo. Cav. *Union* 8 killed, 1 wounded.

15—Samaria Church, Malvern Hill, Va. Wilson's Cav. *Union* 25 killed, 3 wounded. *Confed.* 100 killed and wounded.

15 to 19—Petersburg, Va. (Commencement of the siege that continued to its fall, April 2, 1865). Tenth and Eighteenth Corps, Army of the James, Maj.-Gen. B. F. Butler; Second, Fifth, Sixth and Ninth Corps, Army of the Potomac, Maj.-Gen. Geo. G. Meade. *Union* 1,298 killed, 7,474 wounded, 1,814 missing.

16—Otter Creek, near Liberty, Va. Hunter's Command in advance of the Army of West Virginia. *Union* 3 killed, 15 wounded.

17 and 18—Lynchburg, Va. Sullivan's and Crook's Divisions and Averill's and Duffie's Cav., Army of the West Virginia. *Union* 100 killed, 500 wounded, 100 missing. *Confed.* 200 killed amd wounded.

19—Capture of the *Alabama*, off Cherbourg, France, by U. S. Steamer *Kearsarge*. *Union* 3 wounded. *Confed.* 9 killed, 21 wounded, 70 captured.

20 to 30—In front of Petersburg, Va. Fifth, Ninth, Tenth and Eighteenth Corps. *Union* 112 killed, 506 wounded, 800 missing. *Union* Gens. Chamberlain and Eagan wounded.

21—Salem, Va. Averill's Cav. *Union* 6 killed, 10 wounded. *Confed.* 10 killed and wounded.

Naval engagement on the James River, near Dutch Gap. Casualties not recorded.

Buford's Gap, Va. 23d Ohio. *Union* 15 killed.

22—White River, Ark. Three Cos. 12th Iowa, and U. S. Gunboat *Lexington*. *Union* 2 killed, 4 wounded. *Confed.* 2 killed, 3 wounded.

22 and 23—Weldon Railroad, Williams' Farm or Jerusalem Plank Road, Va. Second, Sixth and 1st Division of Fifth Corps, Army of the Potomac. *Union* 604 killed, 2,494 wounded, 2,217 missing. *Confed.* 300 wounded, 200 missing.

22 to 30—Wilson's Raid on the Weldon Railroad, Va. Kautz's and Wilson's Cav. *Union* 92 killed, 317 wounded, 734 missing. *Confed.* 365 killed and wounded.

23 and 24—Jones's Bridge and Samaria Church, Va. Torbett's and Gregg's Cavalry Divisions. *Union* 54 killed, 235 wounded, 300 missing. *Confed.* 250 killed and wounded.

25 to 29—Clarendon, St. Charles River, Ark. 126th Ill. and 11th Mo., 9th Iowa and 3d Mich. Cav., Battery D 2d Mo. Artil. *Union* 200 wounded. *Confed.* 200 wounded, 200 missing.

JULY, 1864

1 to 31—In front of Petersburg, including Deep Bottom, New Market, and Malvern Hill, on the 27th, and mine explosion on the 30th. Second, Fifth, Ninth, Tenth and Eighteenth Corps. *Union* 898 killed, 4,060 wounded, 3,110 missing. *Confed.* loss at Deep Bottom, 400 killed, 600 wounded, 200 missing.

2—Pine Bluff, Ark. 64th U. S. Col. *Union* 6 killed.

Fort Johnson, James Island, S. C. Troops of Department of the South. *Union* 19 killed, 97 wounded, 135 missing.

2 to 5—Nickajack Creek or Smyrna, Ga. Troops under command of Maj.-Gen. Sherman. *Union* 60 killed, 310 wounded. *Confed.* 100 killed and wounded.

3—Leetown, Va. 10th W. Va., 1st N. Y. Cav. *Union* 3 killed, 12 wounded.

Hammack's Mills, W. Va. 153d Ohio Natl. Guard. *Union* 3 killed, 7 wounded.

3 to 9—Expedition from Vicksburg to Jackson, Miss. 1st Division Seventeenth Corps. *Union* 150 wounded. *Confed.* 200 wounded.

4—Vicksburg, Miss. 48th U. S. Colored. *Union* 1 killed, 7 wounded.

4 to 5—Coleman's Plantation, near Port Gibson, Miss. 52d U. S. Colored. *Union* 6 killed, 18 wounded.

4 to 7—Bolivar and Maryland Heights. Maj.-Gen. Sigel's Reserve Division. *Union* 20 killed, 80 wounded.

5—Hagerstown, Md. 1st Md. Cavalry, Potomac Home Brigade. *Union* 2 killed, 6 wounded.

5 to 7—John's Island, S. C. Maj.-Gen. Foster's troops. *Union* 16 killed, 82 wounded. *Confed.* 20 killed, 80 wounded.

5 to 18—Smith's Expedition, La Grange, Tenn., to Tupelo, Miss. 1st and 3d Divisions Sixteenth Corps, one Brigade U. S. Colored Troops and Grierson's Cavalry. *Union* 85 killed, 567 wounded. *Confed.* 110 killed, 600 wounded.

6—Little Blue, Mo. 2d Col. Cav. *Union* 8 killed, 1 wounded.

6 to 10—Chattahoochee River, Ga. Army of the Ohio, Maj.-Gen. Schofield; Army of the Tennessee, Maj.-Gen. McPherson; Army of the Cumberland, Maj.-Gen. Thomas; Army of the Mississippi, Maj.-Gen. W. T. Sherman. *Union* 80 killed, 450 wounded, 200 missing.

7—Solomon's Gap and Middleton, Md. 8th Ill. Cav., Potomac Home Brigade and Alexander's Baltimore Battery. *Union* 5 killed, 20 wounded.

9—Monocacy, Md. 1st and 2d Brigades of 3d Division Sixth Corps, and Detachment of Eighth Corps. *Union* 90 killed, 579 wounded, 1,290 missing. *Confed.* 400 wounded.

11 to 22—Rosseau's Raid in Alabama and Georgia, including Ten Islands and Stone's Ferry, Ala., and Auburn and Chewa Station, Ga. 8th Ind., 5th Iowa, 8th Ohio, 2d Ky. and 4th Tenn. Cav., Battery E 1st Mich. Artil. *Union* 3 killed, 30 wounded. *Confed.* 95 killed and wounded.

12—Fort Stevens, Washington, D. C. Twenty-second Corps, 1st and 2d Divisions Sixth Corps, Marines, Home Guards, citizens and convalescents. *Union* 54 killed, 319 wounded. *Confed.* 500 killed and wounded.

Lee's Mills, near Ream's Station, Va. 2d Division Gregg's Cav. *Union* 3 killed, 13 wounded. *Confed.* 25 killed and wounded.

14—Farr's Mills, Ark. One Co. 4th Ark. Cav. *Union* 1 killed, 7 wounded. *Confed.* 4 killed, 6 wounded.

14 and 15—Ozark, Mo. 14th Kan. Cav. *Union* 2 killed, 1 wounded.

16 and 17—Grand Gulf, Port Gibson, Miss. 72d and 76th Ill., 53d U. S. Colored, 2d Wis. Cav. Casualties not recorded.

17 and **18**—Snicker's Gap and Island Ford, Va. Army of West Virginia, Maj.-Gen. Crook and portion of Sixth Corps. *Union* 30 killed, 181 wounded, 100 missing.

18—Ashby's Gap, Va. Duffie's Cav. *Union* 200 killed and wounded.

19 and **20**—Darksville, Stevenson's Depot and Winchester, Va. Averill's Cav. *Union* 38 killed, 175 wounded. *Confed.* 300 wounded, 300 captured.

20—Peach Tree Creek, Ga. Fourth, Fourteenth and Twentieth Corps, Maj.-Gen. Geo. H. Thomas. *Union* 300 killed, 1,410 wounded. *Confed.* 1,113 killed, 2,500 wounded, 1,183 missing. *Confed.* Brig.-Gens. Featherstone, Long, Pett's and Stevens killed.

22—Atlanta, Ga. (Hood's first sortie.) Fifteenth, Sixteenth and Seventeenth Corps, Maj.-Gen. McPherson. *Union* 500 killed, 2,141 wounded, 1,000 missing. *Confed.* 2,482 killed, 4,000 wounded, 2,017 missing. *Union* Maj.-Gen. McPherson and Brig.-Gen. Greathouse killed.

22—Decatur, Ga. 2d Brigade of the 4th Division of Sixteenth Corps. *Confed.* Maj.-Gen. Walker killed.

23 and **24**—Kernstown and Winchester, Va. Portion of Army of West Virginia. *Union* 1,200 killed and wounded. *Confed.* 600 killed and wounded.

26—Wallace's Ferry, Ark. 15th Ill. Cav., 60th and 56th U. S. Colored Troops, Co. E 2d U. S. Colored Artil. *Union* 16 killed, 32 wounded. *Confed.* 150 wounded.

26 to **31**—Stoneman's Raid to Macon, Ga. Stoneman's and Garrard's Cav. *Union* 100 killed and wounded, 900 missing.

26 to **31**—McCook's Raid to Lovejoy Station, Ga. 1st Wis., 5th and 8th Iowa, 2d and 8th Ind., 1st and 4th Tenn., and 4th Ky. Cavalry. *Union* 100 killed and wounded, 500 missing.

27—Mazzard Prairie, Fort Smith, Ark. Two hundred men of 6th Kan. Cav. *Union* 12 killed, 17 wounded, 152 captured. *Confed.* 12 killed, 20 wounded.

28—Atlanta, Ga. (Second sortie at Ezra Chapel.) Fifteenth, Sixteenth and Seventeenth Corps, Maj.-Gen. Howard. *Union* 100 killed, 600 wounded. *Confed.* 642 killed, 3,000 wounded, 1,000 missing.

28 to **Sept. 22**—Siege of Atlanta, Ga. Army of the Military Division of the Mississippi, Maj.-Gen. W. T. Sherman. Casualties not recorded.

29—Clear Springs, Md. 12th and 14th Penna. Cav. *Confed.* 17 killed and wounded.

30—Lee's Mills, Va. Davis's Cav. *Union* 2 killed, 11 wounded.
Lebanon, Ky. One Co. 12th Ohio Cav. *Confed.* 6 killed.

AUGUST, 1864

1 to **31**—In front of Petersburg, Va. Second, Fifth, Ninth and Eighteenth Corps. *Union* 87 killed, 484 wounded.

2—Green Springs, W. Va. 153d Ohio. *Union* 1 killed, 5 wounded, 90 missing. *Confed.* 5 killed, 22 wounded.

5—Donaldsonville, La. 11th N. Y. Cav. *Union* 60 missing.

5 to **23**—Forts Gaines and Morgan, Mobile Harbor, Ala. Thirteenth Corps and Admiral Farragut's fleet of war vessels. *Union* 75 killed, 100 drowned by sinking of the *Tecumseh*, 170 wounded. *Confed.* 2,344 captured.

6—Plaquemine, La. 4th Wis. Cav., 14th R. I. Heavy Artil. *Union* 2 killed.

7—Moorefield, Va. 14th Penna., 8th Ohio, 1st and 3d W. Va., and 1st N. Y. Cav. *Union* 9 killed, 22 wounded. *Confed.* 100 killed and wounded, 400 missing.

7 to **14**—Tallahatchie River, Abbeville, Oxford and Hurricane Creek, Miss. Hatch's Cav. and Mower's Command of Sixteenth Corps. Casualties not recorded.

9—Explosion of ammunition at City Point, Va. *Union* 70 killed, 130 wounded.

10 and **11**—Berryville Pike, Sulphur Springs Bridge and White Post, Va. Torbett's Cav. *Union* 34 killed, 90 wounded, 200 missing.

13—Near Snicker's Gap, Va. 144th and 149th Ohio. *Union* 4 killed, 10 wounded, 200 missing. *Confed.* 2 killed, 3 wounded.

14—Gravel Hill, Va. Gregg's Cav. *Union* 3 killed, 18 wounded.

14 to **16**—Dalton, Ga. 2d Mo. and 14th U. S. Colored.

14 to **18**—Strawberry Plains, Va. Second and Tenth Corps and Gregg's Cav. *Union* 400 killed, 1,755 wounded, 1,400 missing. *Confed.* 1,000 wounded.

15—Fisher's Hill, near Strasburg, Va. Sixth and Eighth Corps and 1st Cav. Division Army of the Potomac. *Union* 30 wounded.

16—Crooked Run, Front Royal, Va. Merritt's Cav. *Union* 13 killed, 58 wounded. *Confed.* 30 killed, 150 wounded, 300 captured.

17—Gainesville, Fla. 75th Ohio Mounted Inft. *Union* 16 killed, 30 wounded, 102 missing.
Winchester, Va. New Jersey Brigade of Sixth Corps and Wilson's Cav. *Union* 50 wounded, 250 missing.

18, 19 and **21**—Six-Mile House, Weldon Railroad, Va. Fifth and Ninth Corps and Kautz's and Gregg's Cav. *Union* 212 killed, 1,155 wounded, 3,176 missing. *Confed.* 2,000 wounded, 2,000 missing. *Confed.* Brig.-Gens. Saunders and Lamar killed and Claigman, Barton, Finnegan and Anderson wounded.

18 to **22**—Kilpatrick's Raid on the Atlanta Railroad. *Union* 400 wounded.

19—Snicker's Gap, Pike, Va. Detachment of 5th Mich. Cav. *Union* 30 killed, 3 wounded (all prisoners taken, and the wounded, were put to death by Mosby).
Martinsburg, Va. Averill's Cav. *Union* 25 killed and wounded.

19—Pine Bluff, Tenn. River, Tenn. Detachment of Co. B 83d Ill. Mounted Inft. *Union* 8 killed, and mutilated by guerrillas.

21—Summit Point, Berryville and Flowing Springs, Va. Sixth Corps and Merritt's and Wilson's Cav. *Union* 600 killed and wounded. *Confed.* 400 killed and wounded.
Memphis, Tenn. Detachments of 8th Iowa, 108th and 113th Ill., 39th, 40th and 41st Wis., 61st U. S. Colored, 3d and 4th Iowa Cav., Battery G 1st Mo. Lt. Artil. *Union* 30 killed, 100 wounded. *Confed.* 100 killed and wounded.

21 and **22**—College or Oxford Hill, Miss. 4th Iowa, 11th and 21st Mo., 3d Iowa Cav., 12th Mo. Cav. *Confed.* 15 killed.

23—Abbeville, Miss. 10th Mo., 14th Iowa, 5th and 7th Minn., 8th Wis. *Union* 20 wounded. *Confed.* 15 killed.

24—Fort Smith, Ark. 11th U. S. Colored. *Union* 1 killed, 13 wounded.
Jones's Hay Station and Ashley Station, Ark. 9th Iowa and 8th and 11th Mo. Cav. *Union* 5 killed, 41 wounded. *Confed.* 60 wounded.

24 and **25**—Bermuda Hundred, Va. Tenth Corps. *Union* 31 wounded. *Confed.* 61 missing.

24 to **27**—Halltown, Va. Portion of Eighth Corps. *Union* 39 killed, 178 wounded. *Confed.* 130 killed and wounded.

25—Smithfield and Sheperdstown or Kearneysville, Va. Merritt's and Wilson's Cav. *Union* 20 killed, 61 wounded, 100 missing. *Confed.* 300 killed and wounded.
Ream's Station, Va. Second Corps and Gregg's Cav. *Union* 127 killed, 546 wounded, 1,769 missing. *Confed.* 1,500 killed and wounded.

27 and **28**—Holly Springs, Miss. 14th Iowa, 11th U. S. Colored Artil., 10th Mo. Cav. *Union* 1 killed, 2 wounded.

29—Smithfield, Va. 3d Div. Sixth Corps and Torbett's Cav. *Union* 10 killed, 90 wounded. *Confed.* 200 killed and wounded.

31—Block House, No. 5, Nashville and Chattanooga Railroad, Tenn. 115th Ohio. *Union* 3 killed, *Confed.* 25 wounded.

31 and **Sept. 1**—Jonesboro', Ga. Fifteenth, Sixteenth, Seventeenth and Davis's Cavalry Divisions of Fourteenth Corps. *Union* 1,149 killed and wounded. *Confed.* 2,000 killed, wounded and missing. *Confed.* Brig.-Gens. Anderson, Cummings and Patten killed.

SEPTEMBER, 1864

1 to **8**—Rosseau's pursuit of Wheeler in Tenn. Rosseau's Cav., 1st and 4th Tenn., 2d Mich., 1st Wis., 8th Iowa, 2d and 8th Ind., and 6th Ky. *Union* 10 killed, 30 wounded. *Confed.* 300 killed, wounded and captured.

1 to **Oct. 30**—In front of Petersburg. Army of the Potomac. *Union* 170 killed, 822 wounded, 812 missing. *Confed.* 1,000 missing.

2—Fall of Atlanta, Ga. Twentieth Corps. *Confed.* 200 captured.

2 to **6**—Lovejoy Station, Ga. Fourth and Twenty-third Corps. Casualties not recorded.

3 and **4**—Berryville, Va. Eighth and Nineteenth Corps and Torbett's Cav. *Union* 30 killed, 182 wounded, 100 missing. *Confed.* 25 killed, 100 wounded, 70 missing.

4—Greenville, Tenn. 9th and 13th Tenn., and 10th Mich. Cav. *Union* 6 wounded. *Confed.* 10 killed, 60 wounded, 75 missing. *Confed.* Gen. John Morgan killed.

6—Searcy, Ark. Detachment 9th Iowa Cav. *Union* 2 killed, 6 wounded.

10—Capture of Fort Hell, Va. 99th Pa., 20th Ind., 2d U. S. Sharpshooters. *Union* 20 wounded. *Confed.* 90 prisoners.

13—Lock's Ford, Va. Torbett's Cav. *Union* 2 killed, 18 wounded. *Confed.* 181 captured.

16—Sycamore Church, Va. 1st D. C. and 13th Pa. Cav. *Union* 400 killed, wounded and captured. *Confed.* 50 killed and wounded.

16 and **18**—Fort Gibson, Ind. Ter. 79th U. S. Colored and 2d Kan. Cav. *Union* 38 killed, 48 missing.

17—Belcher's Mills, Va. Kautz's and Gregg's Cav. *Union* 25 wounded.

19 to **22**—Winchester and Fisher's Hill, Va. Sixth, Eighth and 1st and 2d Divisions of the Nineteenth Corps. Averill's and Torbett's Cav., Maj.-Gen. Phil. Sheridan. *Union* 693 killed, 4,033 wounded, 623 missing. *Confed.* 3,250 killed and wounded, 3,600 captured. *Union* Brig.-Gens. Russell and Mulligan killed, and McIntosh, Upton and Chapman wounded. *Confed.* Maj.-Gen. Rhodes and Brig.-Gens. Gordon and Goodwin killed, and Fitz-Hugh Lee, Terry, Johnson and Wharton wounded.

23—Athens, Ala. 106th, 110th and 114th U. S. Colored, 3d Tenn. Cav., reinforced by 18th Mich. and 102d Ohio. *Union* 950 missing. *Confed.* 5 killed, 25 wounded.
Rockport, Mo. 3d Mo. Militia Cav. *Union* 10 killed.

24—Fayette, Mo. 9th Mo. Militia Cav. *Union* 3 killed, 5 wounded. *Confed.* 6 killed, 30 wounded.

26 and **27**—Pilot Knob or Ironton, Mo. 47th and 50th Mo., 14th Iowa, 2d and 3d Mo. Cav., Battery H 2d Mo. Lt. Artil. *Union* 28 killed, 56 wounded, 100 missing. *Confed.* 1,500 killed and wounded.

27—Centralia, Mo. Three Co.'s 39th Mo., massacred by Price. *Union* 122 killed, 2 wounded.
Marianna, Fla. 7th Vt., 82d U. S. Colored and 2d Maine Cav. *Union* 32 wounded. *Confed.* 81 missing.

28 and **30**—New Market Heights or Laurel Hill, Va. Tenth and Eighteenth Corps and Kautz's Cav. *Union* 400 killed, 2,029 wounded. *Confed.* 2,000 killed and wounded.

29—Centreville, Tenn. 2d Tenn. Mounted Inft. *Union* 10 killed, 25 wounded.

29 and **30**—Leesburg and Harrison, Mo. 14th Iowa, 2d Mo. Militia Cav., Battery H 2d Mo. Lt. Artil.

30 and **Oct. 1**—Poplar Springs Church, Va. 1st Div. Fifth Corps and 2d Div. Ninth Corps. *Union* 141 killed, 788 wounded, 1,756 missing. *Confed.* 800 wounded, 100 missing.
Arthur's Swamp, Va. Gregg's Cav. *Union* 60 wounded, 100 missing.

OCTOBER, 1864

2—Waynesboro, Va. Portion of Custer's and Merritt's Cav. *Union* 50 killed and wounded.
Saltville, Va. 11th and 13th Ky. Cav., 12th Ohio, 11th Mich., 5th and 6th U. S. Colored Cav., 26th, 30th, 35th, 37th, 39th, 40th and 45th Ky. Mounted Inft. *Union* 54 killed, 190 wounded, 104 missing. *Confed.* 18 killed, 71 wounded, 21 missing.

5—Jackson, La. 23d Wis., 1st Tex., and 1st La. Cav., 2d and 4th Mass. Battery. *Union* 4 killed, 10 wounded.
Allatoona, Ga. 7th, 12th, 50th, 57th and 93d Ill., 39th Iowa, 4th Minn., 18th Wis. and 12th Wis. Battery. *Union* 142 killed, 352 wounded, 212 missing. *Confed.* 231 killed, 500 wounded, 411 missing.

7—New Market, Va. 3d Div. Custer's Cav. *Union* 56 missing.

7 to **11**—Jefferson City, California and Boonsville, Mo. (Price's Invasion.) 1st, 4th, 5th, 6th and 7th Mo. Militia Cav., 15th Mo. Cav., 17th Ill. Cav., Battery H 2d Mo. Lt. Artil.

7 and **13**—Darbytown Road, Va. Tenth Corps and Kautz's Cav. *Union* 105 killed, 502 wounded, 206 missing. *Confed.* 1,100 killed and wounded, 350 missing. *Confed.* Gen. Gregg killed.

9—Tom's Brook, Fisher's Hill or Strasburg, Va. Merritt's, Custer's and Torbett's Cav. *Union* 9 killed, 67 wounded. *Confed.* 100 killed and wounded, 180 missing.

10—East Point, Miss. 61st U. S. Colored. *Union* 16 killed, 20 wounded.

11—Fort Donelson, Tenn. Detachment 4th U. S. Colored Heavy Artil. *Union* 4 killed, 9 wounded. *Confed.* 3 killed, 23 wounded.

12—Reconnaissance to Strasburg, Va. Maj.-Gen. Emory's and Crook's troops. *Union* 30 killed, 144 wounded, 40 missing.

13—Dalton, Ga. Troops under Col. Johnson, 44th U. S. Colored. *Union* 400 missing.
Buzzard Roost, Ga. One Co. 115th Ill. *Union* 5 killed, 36 wounded, 60 missing.

15—Glasgow, Mo. 43d Mo., and detachments of 17th Ill., 9th Mo. Militia, 13th Mo. Cav., 62d U. S. Colored. *Union* 400 wounded and missing. *Confed.* 50 killed and wounded.

19—Lexington, Mo. 5th, 11th, 15th and 16th Kan. Cav., 3d Wis. Cav. Casualties not recorded.
Cedar Creek, Va. (Sheridan's Ride.) Sixth Corps, Eighth Corps, and 1st and 2d Divisions Nineteenth Corps, Merritt's, Custer's and Torbett's Cav. *Union* 588 killed, 3,516 wounded, 1,801 missing. *Confed.* 3,000 killed and wounded, 1,200 missing. *Union* Brig.-Gens. Bidwell and Thorburn killed, Maj.-Gens. Wright, Ricketts and Grover and Brig.-Gens. Ketchem, McKenzie, Penrose, Hamlin, Devins, Duval and Lowell wounded. *Confed.* Maj.-Gen. Ramseur killed and Battle and Conner wounded.

21 and **22**—Little Blue and Independence, Mo. Kansas Militia, 2d and 5th Mo. Militia, 2d Col. Cav., 5th, 7th, 11th, 15th and 16th Kan. Cav., 1st, 2d, 4th, 6th, 7th, 8th and 9th Mo. Militia Cav. Casualties not recorded.

23—Hurricane Creek, Miss. 1st Iowa and 9th Kan. Cav. *Union* 1 killed, 2 wounded.

26 to **29**—Decatur, Ala. 18th Mich., 102d Ohio, 68th Ind., and 14th U. S. Colored. *Union* 10 killed, 45 wounded, 100 missing. *Confed.* 100 killed, 300 wounded.

27—Hatcher's Run, Va. Gregg's Cav., 2d and 3d Divisions Second Corps, Fifth and Ninth Corps. *Union* 156 killed, 1,047 wounded, 699 missing. *Confed.* 200 killed, 600 wounded, 200 missing

27 and **28**—Fair Oaks, Va. Tenth and Eighteenth Corps and Kautz's Cav. *Union* 120 killed, 783 wounded, 400 missing. *Confed.* 60 killed, 311 wounded, 80 missing.

28—Destruction of the rebel ram *Albemarle*, by Lieut. Cushing and thirteen marines. *Union* 3 wounded, 11 captured.
Morristown, Tenn. Gen. Gillem's Cav. *Union* 8 killed, 42 wounded. *Confed.* 240 missing.

28 and **30**—Newtonia, Mo. Col. Blunt's Cav. in pursuit of Price. *Confed.* 250 wounded.

29—Beverly W. Va. 8th Ohio Cav. *Union* 8 killed, 25 wounded, 13 missing. *Confed.* 17 killed, 27 wounded, 92 missing.

30—Near Brownsville, Ark. 7th Iowa and 11th Mo. Cav. *Union* 2 killed.

NOVEMBER, 1864

1 to 4—Union Station, Tenn. 10th Mo. Cav. *Union* 2 killed, 2 wounded, 26 missing.

5—Fort Sedgwick or Fort Hell, Va. Second Corps. *Union* 5 killed, 10 wounded. *Confed.* 15 killed, 35 wounded.

9—Atlanta, Ga. 2d Division, Twentieth Corps. *Confed.* 20 killed and wounded.

12—Newtown and Cedar Springs, Va. Merritt's, Custer's and Powell's Cav. *Union* 84 killed, 100 missing. *Confed.* 150 missing.

13—Bull's Gap, Tenn. 8th, 9th and 13th Tenn. Cav. *Union* 5 killed, 36 wounded, 200 missing.

16—Lovejoy Station and Bear Creek Station, Ga. Kilpatrick's Cav. *Confed.* 50 captured.

17—Bermuda Hundred, Va. 209th Pa. *Union* 10 wounded, 120 missing. *Confed.* 10 wounded.

18—Myerstown, Va. Detachment 91st Ohio. *Union* 60 killed and wounded.

20—Macon, Ga. 10th Ohio Cav., 9th Pa. Cav., 92d Ill. Mounted Inft., 10th Wis. Battery.

21—Griswoldville, Ga. Walcott's Brigade, 1st Division, Fifteenth Corps and 1st Brigade 3d Division Cav. *Union* 10 killed, 52 wounded. *Confed.* 50 killed, 200 wounded, 400 missing.

Rood's Hill, Va. Torbett's Cav. *Union* 18 killed, 52 wounded.

Lawrenceburg, Campbellville and Lynnville, Tenn. Hatch's Cav. *Union* 75 killed and wounded. *Confed.* 50 killed and wounded.

26—Saundersville, Ga. 3d Brigade 1st Division Twentieth Corps. *Union* 100 missing.

26 to 29—Sylvan Grove, Waynesboro', Browne's Cross Roads. Kilpatrick's Cav. *Union* 46 wounded. *Confed.* 600 killed and wounded.

29 and 30—Spring Hill and Franklin, Tenn. Fourth and Twenty-third Corps and Cavalry. *Union* 189 killed, 1,033 wounded, 1,104 missing. *Confed.* 1,750 killed, 3,800 wounded, 702 missing. *Union* Maj.-Gens. Stanley and Bradley wounded. *Confed.* Maj.-Gen. Cleborne, Brig.-Gens. Adams, Williams, Strahl, Geist and Granberry killed; Maj.-Gen. Brown and Brig.-Gens. Carter, Manigault. Quarles, Cockerell and Scott wounded.

30—Honey Hill or Grahamsville, S. C. 25th Ohio, 56th and 155th N. Y., 26th, 32d, 35th and 102d U. S. Colored, 54th and 55th Mass. Colored. *Union* 66 killed, 645 wounded.

DECEMBER, 1864

1—Stony Creek Station, Weldon Railroad, Va. Gregg's Cav. *Union* 40 wounded. *Confed.* 175 captured.

Twelve miles from Yazoo City, Miss. Detachment of 2d Wis. Cav. *Union* 5 killed, 9 wounded, 25 missing.

1 to 14—In front of Nashville, Tenn. Fourth, Twenty-third and 1st and 2d Division of Sixteenth Corps and Wilson's Cav. *Union* 16 killed, 100 wounded.

1 to 31—In front of Petersburg. Army of the Potomac. *Union* 40 killed, 329 wounded.

2 and 3—Block-house No. 2, Mill Creek, Chattanooga, Tenn. Detachment 115th Ohio, 44th and two Cos. 14th U. S. Colored. *Union* 12 killed, 46 wounded, 57 missing.

3—Thomas's Station, Ga. 92d Ill. Mounted Inft. *Union* 2 killed, 1 wounded.

4—Block-house No. 7, Tenn. Gen. Milroy's troops. *Union* 100 wounded. *Confed.* 100 killed and wounded.

5 to 8—Murfreesboro', Tenn. Gen. Rosseau's troops. *Union* 30 killed, 175 wounded. *Confed.* 197 missing.

6—White Post, Va. Fifty men of 21st N. Y. Cav. *Union* 30 wounded.

6 to 9—Deveaux's Neck, S. C. 56th and 155th N. Y., 25th and 107th Ohio, 26th, 33d, 34th and 102d U. S. Colored, 54th and 55th Mass. Colored, 3d R. I. Artil. and U. S. Gunboats. *Union* 39 killed, 390 wounded, 200 missing. *Confed.* 400 killed and wounded.

7 to 9—Eden Station, Ogeechee River, Ga. Fifteenth and Seventeenth Corps right wing of Sherman's Army.

7 to 11—Weldon Railroad Expedition. Fifth Corps, 3d Division of Second Corps, and 2d Division Cavalry Corps, Army of the Potomac. *Union* 100 wounded.

8 and 9—Hatcher's Run, Va. 1st Division, Second Corps, 3d and 13th Pa. Cav., 6th Ohio Cav. *Union* 125 killed and wounded.

8 to 28—Raid to Gordonsville, Va. Merritt's and Custer's Cav. *Union* 43 wounded.

10 to 21—Siege of Savannah, Ga. Fourteenth, Fifteenth, Seventeenth and Twentieth Corps of Sherman's Army. *Union* 200 wounded. *Confed.* 800 missing.

12 to 21—Stoneman's Raid from Bean's Station, Tenn., to Saltville, Va., including Abingdon, Glade Springs and Marion. *Union* 20 killed, 123 wounded. *Confed.* 126 wounded, 500 missing.

13—Fort McAllister, Ga. 2d Division of Fifteenth Corps. *Union* 24 killed, 110 wounded. *Confed.* 250 missing.

14—Memphis, Tenn. 4th Iowa Cav. *Union* 3 killed, 6 wounded.

15 and 16—Nashville, Tenn. Fourth Corps, 1st and 3d Divisions Thirteenth Corps, Twenty-third Corps, Wilson's Cav., and Detachments colored troops, convalescents. *Union* 400 killed, 1,740 wounded. *Confed.* 4,462 missing.

17—Franklin, Tenn. Wilson's Cav. *Confed.* 1,800 wounded and sick captured.

17 to 19—Mitchell's Creek, Fla., and Pine Barren Creek, Ala. 82d and 97th U. S. Colored. *Union* 9 killed, 53 wounded, 11 missing.

20—Lacey's Springs. Custer's Cav. *Union* 2 killed, 22 wounded, 40 missing.

25—Fort Fisher, N. C. Tenth Corps and North Atlantic Squadron. *Union* 8 killed, 38 wounded. *Confed.* 3 killed, 55 wounded, 280 missing.

28—Egypt Station, Miss. 4th and 11th Ill. Cav., 7th Ind., 4th and 10th Mo., 2d Wis., 2d N. J., 1st Miss. and 3d U. S. Colored Cav. *Union* 23 killed, 88 wounded. *Confed.* 500 captured. *Confed.* Brig.-Gen. Gholson killed.

JANUARY, 1865

2—Franklin, Miss. 4th and 11th Ill. Cav., 3d U. S. Colored Cav. *Union* 4 killed, 9 wounded. *Confed.* 20 killed, 30 wounded.

2 and 3—Nauvoo and Thornhill, Ala. 15th Pa. Cav., Detachments of 10th, 12th and 13th Ind. Cav. and 2d Tenn. Cav. *Union* 1 killed, 2 wounded. *Confed.* 3 killed, 2 wounded, 95 captured, and Hood's supply and pontoon train destroyed.

11—Beverly, W. Va. 34th Ohio and 8th Ohio Cav. *Union* 5 killed, 20 wounded, 583 missing.

12 to 15—Fort Fisher, N. C. Portions of Twenty-fourth and Twenty-fifth Corps and Porter's Gunboats. *Union* 184 killed, 749 wounded. *Confed.* 400 killed and wounded, 2,083 captured.

14 to 16—Pocataligo, S. C. Seventeenth Corps. *Union* 25 wounded.

16—Explosion of the magazine at Fort Fisher, N. C. *Union* 25 killed, 66 wounded.

25 to Feb. 9—Combahee River and River's Bridge, Salkahatchie, S. C. Fifteenth and Seventeenth Corps. *Union* 138 killed and wounded.

FEBRUARY, 1865

5 to 7—Dabney's Mills, Hatcher's Run, Va. Fifth Corps and 1st Division Sixth Corps and Gregg's Cav. *Union* 232 killed, 1,062 wounded, 186 missing. *Confed.* 1,200 killed and wounded, Brig.-Gens. Morrow, Smyth, Davis, Gregg, Ayres, Sickels and Gwynn wounded. *Confed.* Gen. Pegram killed and Sorrell wounded.

8 to 14—Williston, Blackville and Aiken, S. C. Kilpatrick's Cav. *Confed.* 240 killed and wounded, 100 missing.

10—James Island, S. C. Maj.-Gen. Gilmore's command. *Union* 20 killed, 76 wounded. *Confed.* 20 killed and 70 wounded.

11—Sugar Loaf Battery, Federal Point, N. C. Portions of Twenty-fourth and Twenty-fifth Corps. *Union* 14 killed, 114 wounded.

15 to 17—Congaree Creek and Columbia, S. C. Fifteenth Corps. *Union* 20 killed and wounded.

18—Ashby Gap, Va. Detachment 14th Pa. Cav. *Union* 6 killed, 19 wounded, 64 missing.

18 to 22—Fort Anderson, Town Creek and Wilmington, N. C. Twenty-third and Twenty-fourth Corps and Porter's Gunboats. *Union* 40 killed, 204 wounded. *Confed.* 70 killed, 400 wounded, 375 missing.

22—Douglas Landing, Pine Bluff, Ark. 13th Ill. Cav. *Union* 40 wounded. *Confed.* 26 wounded.

27 to March 25—Sheridan's Raid in Virginia. 1st and 3d Divisions Cavalry Corps. *Union* 35 killed and wounded. *Confed.* 1,667 prisoners.

MARCH, 1865

6—Olive Branch, La. 4th Wis. Cav. *Union* 3 killed, 2 wounded. Natural Bridge, Fla. 2d and 99th U. S. Colored. *Union* 22 killed, 46 wounded.

8 to 10—Wilcox's Bridge, N. C. Palmer's, Carter's and Ruger's Divisions. *Union* 80 killed, 421 wounded, 600 missing. *Confed.* 1,500 killed, wounded and missing.

16—Averysboro', N. C. Twentieth Corps and Kilpatrick's Cav. *Union* 77 killed, 477 wounded. *Confed.* 108 killed, 540 wounded, 217 missing.

19 to 21—Bentonville, N. C. Fourteenth, Fifteenth, Seventeenth and Twentieth Corps and Kilpatrick's Cav. *Union* 191 killed, 1,168 wounded, 287 missing. *Confed.* 267 killed, 1,200 wounded, 1,625 missing.

20 to April 6—Stoneman's Raid into Southwestern Va. and North Carolina. Palmer's, Brown's and Miller's Cavalry Brigades.

22 to April 24—Wilson's Raid, Chickasaw, Ala., to Macon, Ga. *Union* 63 killed, 345 wounded, 63 missing. *Confed.* 22 killed, 38 wounded, 6,766 prisoners.

25—Fort Steadman, in front of Petersburg, Va. 1st and 3d Divisions Ninth Corps. *Union* 68 killed, 337 wounded, 506 missing. *Confed.* 800 killed and wounded, 1,881 missing, assault of the Second and Sixth Corps. *Union* 103 killed, 864 wounded, 209 missing. *Confed.* 834 captured.

26 to April 9—Siege of Mobile, Ala., including Spanish Fort and Port Blakely. Thirteenth and Sixteenth Corps and U. S. Navy. *Union* 213 killed, 1,211 wounded. *Confed.* 500 killed and wounded, 2,952 missing and captured.

29—Quaker Road, Va. Warren's Fifth Corps and Griffin's 1st Division, Army of the Potomac. *Union* 55 killed, 306 wounded. *Confed.* 135 killed, 400 wounded, 100 missing.

31—Boydton and White Oak Roads, Va. Second and Fifth Corps. *Union* 177 killed, 1,134 wounded, 556 missing. *Confed.* 1,000 wounded, 235 missing.

Dinwiddie C. H., Va. 1st, 2d and 3d Cavalry Divisions Army of the Potomac. *Union* 67 killed, 354 wounded. *Confed.* 400 killed and wounded.

APRIL, 1865

1—Five Forks, Va. 1st, 2d and 3d Cavalry Divisions and Fifth Corps. *Union* 124 killed, 706 wounded. *Confed.* 3,000 killed and wounded, 5,500 captured.

2—Fall of Petersburg, Va. Second, Sixth, Ninth and Twenty-fourth Corps. *Union* 296 killed, 2,565 wounded, 500 missing. *Confed.* 3,000 prisoners.

3—Namozin Church and Willicomack, Va. Custer's Cavalry. *Union* 10 killed, 85 wounded.

3—Fall of Richmond, Va. *Confed.* 6,000 prisoners, of whom 5,000 were sick and wounded.

5—Amelia Springs, Va. Crook's Cav. *Union* 20 killed, 96 wounded.

6—Sailor's Creek, Va. Second and Sixth Corps and Sheridan's Cav. *Union* 166 killed, 1,014 wounded. *Confed.* 1,000 killed, 1,800 wounded, 6,000 prisoners.

High Bridge, Appomattox River, Va. Portion of Twenty-fourth Corps. *Union* 10 killed, 31 wounded, 1,000 missing and captured.

7—Farmville, Va. Second Corps. *Union* 655 killed and wounded.

8 and 9—Appomattox C. H., Va. Twenty-fourth Corps, one Division of the Twenty-fifth Corps and Sheridan's Cav. *Union* 200 killed and wounded. *Confed.* 500 killed.

9—Lee surrendered to the Armies of the Potomac and James; Lieut.-Gen. U. S. Grant. *Confed.* 26,000 prisoners.

17—Surrender of Mosby to Maj.-Gen. Hancock. *Confed.* 700 prisoners.

26—Johnson surrendered to the Armies of the Tennessee, Georgia and Ohio; Maj.-Gen. W. T. Sherman. *Confed.* 29,924 prisoners.

MAY, 1865

10—Capture of Jefferson Davis at Irwinsville, Ga. 1st Wis. and 4th Mich. Cav. *Union* 2 killed, 4 wounded, caused by the pursuing parties firing into each other.

Tallahassee, Fla. Surrender of Sam Jones's command to Detachment of Wilson's Cav.; Maj.-Gen. McCook. *Confed.* 8,000 prisoners.

11—Chalk Bluff, Ark. Surrender of Jeff. Thompson's command to forces under Gen. Dodge. *Confed.* 7,454 prisoners.

13—Palmetto Ranche, Tex. 34th Ind., 62d U. S. Colored and 2d Tex. Cav. *Union* 118 killed and wounded.

26—Surrender of Kirby Smith to Maj.-Gen. Canby's command. *Confed.* 20,000 prisoners.

For Mrs Lucy G. Speed, from whose pious hand I accepted the present of an Oxford Bible twenty years ago. Washington, D.C. October 3, 1861. A Lincoln

ABRAHAM LINCOLN.
From a photograph sent to Mrs. Lucy G. Speed, Oct. 3, 1861.

WASHINGTON ON THE EVE OF THE WAR.

BY CHARLES P. STONE, BRIGADIER-GENERAL, U. S. V.
Inspector-General of the District of Columbia at the outbreak of the War.

ALL who knew Washington in the days of December, 1860, know what thoughts reigned in the minds of thinking men. Whatever their daily occupations, they went about them with their thoughts always bent on the possible disasters of the near future. The country was in a curious and alarming condition: South Carolina had already passed an ordinance of secession, and other States were preparing to follow her lead. The only regular troops near the capital of the country were 300 or 400 marines at the marine barracks, and 3 officers and 53 men of ordnance at the Washington arsenal. The old militia system had been abandoned (without being legally abolished), and Congress had passed no law establishing a new one. The only armed volunteer organizations in the District of Columbia were: The Potomac Light Infantry, 1 company, at Georgetown; the National Rifles, 1 company, in Washington; the Washington Light Infantry, of about 160 men, and another small organization called the National Guard Battalion. It had been evident for months that, on assembling in December, Congress would have far different work to consider than the organization of the District of Columbia militia. Nor in the delicate position of affairs would it be the policy of President Buchanan, at the outset of the session, to propose the military organization of the Federal District. It was also evident that, should he be so disposed, the senators

A Lincoln

From a photograph taken about 1860 by Hesler, of Chicago; from the original negative owned by George B. Ayres, Philadelphia.

and representatives of the Southern States would oppose and denounce the project. What force, then, would the Government have at its disposal in the Federal District for the simple maintenance of order in case of need? Evidently but a handful; and as to calling thither promptly any regular troops, that was out of the question, since they had already been distributed by the Southern sympathizers to the distant frontiers of the Indian country,—Texas, Utah, New Mexico, Oregon, and Washington Territory. Months would have been necessary to concentrate at Washington, in that season, a force of three thousand regular troops. Even had President Buchanan been desirous of bringing troops to the capital, the feverish condition of the public mind would, as the executive believed, have been badly affected by any movement of the kind, and the approaching crisis might have been precipitated. I saw at once that the only force which could be readily made of service was a volunteer force raised from among the well-disposed men of the District, and that this must be organized, if at all, under the old law of 1799. By consultation with gentlemen well ac-

ABRAHAM LINCOLN.
From a photograph taken March 6, 1865.

quainted with the various classes of Washington society, I endeavored to learn what proportion of the able-bodied population could be counted on to sustain the Government should it need support from the armed and organized citizens.

On the 31st of December, 1860, Lieutenant-General Scott, General-in-Chief of the army (who had his head-quarters in New York), was in Washington. The President, at last thoroughly alarmed at the results of continued concessions to secession, had summoned him for consultation. On the evening of that day I went to pay my respects to my old commander, and was received by him at Wormley's hotel. He chatted pleasantly with me for a few minutes, recalling past service in the Mexican war, etc.; and when the occasion presented itself, I remarked that I was glad to see him in good spirits, for that proved to me that he took a more cheerful view of the state of public affairs than he had on his arrival — more cheerful than we of Washington had dared to take during the past few days.

"Yes, my young friend," said the general, "I feel more cheerful about the affairs of the country than I did this morning; for I believe that a safer policy than has hitherto been followed will now be adopted. The policy of entire conciliation, which has so far been pursued, would soon have led to ruin. We are now in such a state that a policy of pure force would precipitate a crisis for which we are not prepared. A mixed policy of force and conciliation is now necessary, and I believe it will be adopted and carried out." He then looked at his watch, rose, and said: "I must be with the President in a quarter of an hour," and ordered his carriage. He walked up and down the dining-room, but suddenly stopped and faced me, saying: "How is the feeling in the District of Columbia? What proportion of the population would sustain the Government by force, if necessary?"

"It is my belief, General," I replied, "that two-thirds of the fighting stock of this population would sustain the Government in defending itself, if called upon. But

3

WILLIAM H. SEWARD.

Secretary of State throughout Mr. Lincoln's Administration.
From a daguerreotype taken about 1851.

EDWIN M. STANTON.

Secretary of War. Appointed Jan. 15, 1862.

The Washington Light Infantry organization and the National Guard were old volunteers composed of Washington people, and were almost to a man faithful to the Government. Of their officers, Major-General Weightman, though aged, and Major-General Force, aged and infirm, were active, and true as steel; Brigadier-Generals Bacon and Carrington were young, active, and true. Brigadier-General Robert Ould, who took no part in the preparations of the winter, joined the Confederates as soon as Virginia passed her ordinance of secession, and his known sentiments precluded consultation with him.

Having thus studied the ground, and taken the first necessary steps toward security, I commenced the work of providing a force of volunteers. I addressed individual letters to some forty well-known and esteemed gentlemen of the District, informing each one that it would be agreeable to the Government should he in his neighborhood raise and organize a company of volunteers for the preservation of order in the District. To some of these letters I received no replies to some I received replies courteously declining the service; to some I received letters sarcastically declining; but to many I received replies enthusiastically accepting the service. In about six weeks thirty-three companies of infantry and riflemen and two troops of cavalry were on the lists of the District volunteer force; and all had been uniformed, equipped, and put under frequent drill.

The Northern Liberties fire-companies brought their quota; the Lafayette Hose Company was prompt to enroll; the masons, the carpenters, the stone-cutters, the painters, and the German turners responded: each corporation formed its companies and drilled industriously. Petty rivalries disappeared, and each company strove to excel the others in drill and discipline. While the newly organized companies thus strove to perfect themselves, the older organizations resumed their drills and filled their ranks with good recruits. . . .

While the volunteer force for the support of the Government was organizing, another force with exactly the opposite purpose was in course of formation. I learned that the great hall over Beach's livery-stable was nightly filled with men who were actively drilled. Doctor B——, of well-known secession tendencies, was the moving spirit of these men, and he was assisted by other citizens of high standing, among whom was a connection of Governor Letcher of Virginia. The numbers of these occu-

pants of Beach's hall increased rapidly, and I found it well to have a skilful New York detective officer, who had been placed at my disposition, enrolled among them. These men called themselves "National Volunteers," and in their meetings openly discussed the seizure of the national capital at the proper moment. They drilled industriously, and had regular business meetings, full reports of which were regularly laid before me every following morning by "the New York member." In the meeting at which the uniform to be adopted was discussed, the vote was for gray Kentucky jeans, with the Maryland button. A cautious member suggested that they must remember that, in order to procure arms, it would be "necessary to get the requisition signed by 'Old Stone,' and if he saw that they had adopted the Maryland button, and not that of the United States, he might suspect them and refuse the issue of arms!" Doctor B—— supported the idea of the Maryland button, and said that, if Stone refused the arms, the Governor of Virginia would see them furnished, etc.

they are uncertain as to what can be done or what the Government desires to have done, and they have no rallying-point."

The general walked the room again in silence. The carriage came to the door, and I accompanied him toward it. As he was leaving, he turned suddenly, looked me in the face, placed his hand on my shoulder, and said:

"These people have no rallying-point. Make yourself that rallying-point!"

The next day I was commissioned by the President colonel in the staff and Inspector-General of the District of Columbia. I was mustered into the service of the United States from the 2d day of January, 1861, on the special requisition of the General-in-Chief, and thus was the first of two and a half millions called into the military service of the Government to defend it against secession. . . .

An office was assigned me in the War Department, convenient to the army-registers and near the Secretary of War, who kindly gave orders that I should at all times be admitted to his cabinet without waiting, and room was made for me in the office of Major-General Weightman, the senior major-general of the District, where each day I passed several hours in order to confer with him, and to be able promptly to obtain his authority for any necessary order.

SALMON P. CHASE.
Secretary of the Treasury from the beginning of Mr. Lincoln's
Administration until July 1, 1864.

HANNIBAL HAMLIN.
Vice-President of the United States from
March 4, 1861, to March 4, 1865. (From a photograph.)

GIDEON WELLES.
Secretary of the Navy throughout Mr. Lincoln's Administration.

SIMON CAMERON.
Secretary of War from March 4, 1861, until Jan. 15, 1862.
From a photograph.

These gentlemen probably little thought that a full report of their remarks would be read the next morning by "Old Stone" to the General-in-Chief. . . .

I must now go back a little in time, to mention one fact which will show in how weak and dangerous a condition our Government was in the latter part of January and the early part of February, 1861. The invitations which I had issued for the raising of companies of volunteers had, as already stated, been enthusiastically responded to, and companies were rapidly organized. The preparatory drills were carried on every night, and I soon found that the men were sufficiently advanced to receive their arms. I began to approve the requisitions for arms; but, to my great astonishment, the captains who first received the orders came back to me, stating that the Ordnance Department had refused to issue any arms! On referring to the Ordnance Office, I was informed by the Chief of Ordnance that he had received, the day before, an order not to issue any arms to the District of Columbia troops, and that this order had come from the President!

I went immediately to the Secretary of War (Mr. Holt) and informed him of the state of affairs, telling him at the same time that I did not feel disposed to be employed in child's play, organizing troops which could not be armed, and that unless the order in question should be immediately revoked there was no use for me in my place, and that I must at once resign. Mr. Holt told me that I was perfectly right; that unless the order should be revoked there was no use in my holding my place, and he added, with a smile, "And I will also say, Colonel, there will be no use in my holding my place any longer. Go to the President, Colonel, and talk to him as you have talked to me."

I went to the White House, and was received by Mr. Buchanan. I found him sitting at his writing-table, in his dressing-gown, wearied and worried.

I opened at once the subject of arms, and stated the necessity of immediate issue, as the refusal of arms would not only stop the instruction of the volunteers, which they needed sadly, but would make them lose all confidence in the Government and break up the organizations. I closed by saying that, while I begged his pardon for saying it, in case he declined to revoke his order I must ask him to accept my resignation at once.

Mr. Buchanan was evidently in distress of mind, and said :

"Colonel, I gave that order acting on the advice of the District Attorney, Mr. Robert Ould."

"Then, Mr. President," I replied, "the District Attorney has advised your Excellency very badly."

"But, Colonel, the District Attorney is an old resident of Washington, and he knows all the little jealousies which exist here. He tells me that you have organized a company from the Northern Liberty Fire Company."

"Not only one, but two excellent companies in the Northern Liberty, your Excellency."

"And then, the District Attorney tells me you have organized another company from among the members of the Lafayette Hose Company."

"Yes, your Excellency, another excellent company."

"And the District Attorney tells me, Colonel, that there is a strong feeling of enmity between those fire-companies, and, if arms are put in their hands, there will be danger of bloodshed in the city."

"Will your Excellency excuse me if I say that the District Attorney talks nonsense, or worse, to you? If the Northern Liberties and the Lafayette Hose men wish to fight, can they not procure hundreds of arms in the shops along the avenue? Be assured, Mr. President, that the people of this District are thinking now of other things than old ward feuds. They are thinking whether or not the Government of the United States is to allow itself to crumble out of existence by its own weakness. And I believe that the District Attorney knows that as well as I do. If the companies of volunteers are not armed, they will disband, and the Government will have nothing to protect it in case of even a little disturbance. Is it not better for the public peace, your Excellency, even if the bloody feud exists (which I believe is forgotten in a greater question),— is it not better to have these men organized and under the discipline of the Government?"

The President hesitated a moment, and then said :

" I don't know that you are not right, Colonel; but you must take the responsibility on you that no bloodshed results from arming these men."

I willingly accepted this responsibility. The prohibitory order was revoked. My companies received their arms, and made good use of them, learning the manual of arms in a surprisingly short time. Later, they made good use of them in sustaining the Government which had furnished them against the faction which soon became its public enemy, including Mr. Robert Ould, who, following his convictions (no doubt as honestly as I was following mine), gave his earnest services to his State against the Federal Government.

I think that the country has never properly appreciated the services of those District of Columbia volunteers. It certainly has not appreciated the difficulties surmounted in their organization. Those volunteers were citizens of the Federal District, and therefore had not at the time, nor have they ever had since, the powerful stimulant of State feeling, nor the powerful support of a State government, a State's pride, a State press to set forth and make much of their services.

WINFIELD SCOTT, BREVET LIEUTENANT-GENERAL, U. S. A.
General Scott was General-in-Chief of the army until November 1, 1861, when he was placed upon the retired list on his own application, and was succeeded by Major-General George B. McClellan. He died at West Point in May, 1866, in his eightieth year.

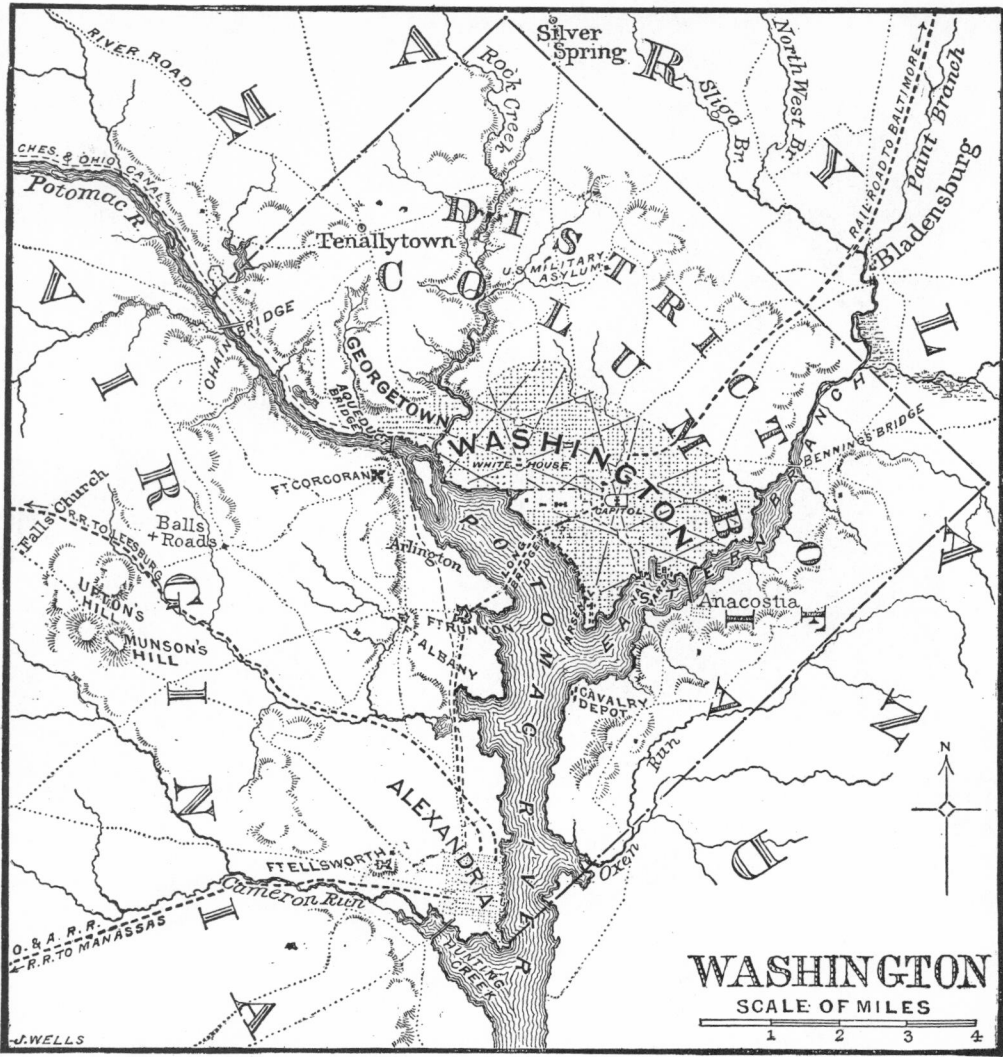

WASHINGTON
SCALE OF MILES
1 2 3 4

They did their duty quietly, and they did it well and faithfully. Although not mustered into the service and placed on pay until after the fatal day when the flag was fired upon at Sumter, yet they rendered great service before that time in giving confidence to the Union men, to members of the national legislature, and also to the President in the knowledge that there was at least a small force at its disposition ready to respond at any moment to his call. It should also be remembered of them, that the first troops mustered into the service were sixteen companies of these volunteers; and that, during the dark days when Washington was cut off from communication with the North, when railway bridges were burned and tracks torn up, when the Potomac was blockaded, these troops were the only reliance of the Government for guarding the public departments, for preserving order and for holding the bridges and

other outposts; that these were the troops which recovered possession of the railway from Washington to Annapolis Junction and made practicable the reopening of communications. They also formed the advance guard of the force which first crossed the Potomac into Virginia and captured the city of Alexandria.

Moreover, these were the troops which insured the regular inauguration on the steps of the Capitol of the constitutionally elected President. I firmly believe that without them Mr. Lincoln would never have been inaugurated. I believe that tumults would have been created, during which he would have been killed, and that we should have found ourselves engaged in a struggle, without preparation, and without a recognized head at the capital. In this I may be mistaken, of course, as any other man may be mistaken; but it was then my opinion, when I had many sources of informa-

tion at my command, and it remains my opinion now, when, after the lapse of many years and a somewhat large experience, I look back in cool blood upon those days of political madness.

One day, after the official declaration of the election of Mr. Lincoln, my duties called me to the House of Representatives; and while standing in the lobby waiting for the member with whom I had business, I conversed with a distinguished officer from New York. We were leaning against the sill of a window which overlooked the steps of the Capitol, where the President-elect usually stands to take the oath of office. The gentleman grew excited as we discussed the election of Mr. Lincoln, and pointing to the portico he exclaimed:

"He will never be inaugurated on those steps!"

"Mr. Lincoln," I replied, "has been constitutionally elected President of the United States. You may be sure that, if he lives until the fourth day of March, he will be inaugurated on those steps."

As I spoke, I noticed for the first time how per-

fectly the wings of the Capitol flanked the steps in question; and on the morning of the 4th of March I saw to it that each window of the two wings was occupied by two riflemen.

I received daily numerous communications from various parts of the country, informing me of plots to prevent the arrival of the President-elect at the capital. These warnings came from St. Louis, from Chicago, from Cincinnati, from Pittsburg, from New York, from Philadelphia, and especially from Baltimore. Every morning I reported to General Scott on the occurrences of the night and the information received by the morning's mail; and every evening I rendered an account of the day's work and received instructions for the night. General Scott also received numerous warnings of danger to the President-elect, which he would give me to study and compare. Many of the communications were anonymous and vague. But, on the other hand, many were from calm and wise men, one of whom became, shortly afterward, a cabinet minister; one was a railway

CAPTAIN GRANT.

From a daguerreotype (one-fourth of the above size) given by him
to Mrs. Grant, and worn by her on a wristlet.

LIEUT. U. S. GRANT AND GEN. ALEX. HAYS.

BRIGADIER-GENERAL U. S. GRANT.

From a photograph taken in 1861.

president, another a distinguished ex-governor of a State, etc. In every case where the indications were distinct, they were followed up to learn if real danger existed. So many clear indications pointed to Baltimore, that three good detectives of the New York police force were constantly employed there. These men reported frequently to me, and their statements were constantly compared with the information received from independent sources.

Doubtless, Mr. Lincoln, at his home in Springfield, Ill., received many and contradictory reports from the capital, for he took his own way of obtaining information. One night, between eleven o'clock and midnight, while I was busy in my study over the papers of the day and evening, a card was brought to me bearing the name "Mr. Leonard Swett," and upon it was written in the well-known hand of General Scott, "Colonel Stone, Inspector-General, may converse freely with Mr. Swett." Soon a tall gentleman of marked features entered my room. At first I thought it was Mr. Lincoln himself, so much, at first glance, did Mr. Swett's face resemble the portraits I had seen of Mr. Lincoln, and so nearly did his height correspond with that attributed to the President-elect. But I quickly found that the gentleman's card bore his true name, and that Mr. Swett had come directly from Mr. Lincoln, having his full confidence, to see for him the state of affairs in Washington, and

report to him in person. Mr. Swett remained several days in the capital, had frequent and long conversations with General Scott and myself (and I suppose also with many others), and with me visited the armories of some of the volunteer companies. As he drove with me to the railway station on his departure, Mr. Swett said:

"Mr. Lincoln, and in fact almost everybody, is ignorant of the vast amount of careful work which has been done here this winter, by General Scott and yourself, to insure the existence of the Government and to render certain and safe the inauguration of Mr. Lincoln. He will be very grateful to both." I replied, with more sincerity than tact:

"Mr. Lincoln has no cause to be grateful to me. I was opposed to his election, and believed in advance that it would bring on what is evidently coming, a fearful war. The work which I have done has not been done for him, and he

THE WASHINGTON ARSENAL.

need feel under no obligations to me. I have done my best toward saving the Government of the country and to insure the regular inauguration of the constitutionally elected President on the 4th of next month."

As President Lincoln approached the capital, it became certain that desperate attempts would be made to prevent his arriving there. To be thoroughly informed as to what might be expected in Baltimore, I directed a detective to be constantly near the chief of police and to keep up relations with him; while two others were instructed to watch without the knowledge and independent of the chief of police. The officer who was near the chief of police reported regularly, until near the last, that there was no danger in Baltimore; but the others discovered a band of desperate men plotting for the destruction of Mr. Lincoln during his passage through the city and by affiliat-

ing with them, these detectives obtained the details of the plot.

Mr. Lincoln passed through Baltimore in advance of the time announced for the journey (in accordance with advice given by me to Mr. Seward, and which was carried by Mr. Frederick W. Seward to Mr. Lincoln), and arrived safe at Washington on the morning of the day he was to have passed through Baltimore. But the plotting to prevent his inauguration continued; and there was only too good reason to fear that an attempt would be made against his life during the passage of the inaugural procession from Willard's Hotel, where Mr. Lincoln lodged, to the Capitol.

On the afternoon of the 3d of March, General Scott held a conference at his headquarters, there being present his staff, General Sumner, and myself, and then was arranged the programme of the procession. President Buchanan was to drive to Willard's Hotel, and call upon the President-elect. The two were to ride in the same carriage, between double files of a squadron of the District of Columbia cavalry. The company of sappers and miners were to march in front of the presidential carriage, and the infantry and riflemen of the District of Columbia were to follow it. Riflemen in squads were to be placed on the roofs of certain commanding houses which I had selected, along Pennsylvania Avenue, with orders to watch the windows on the opposite side and to fire upon them in case any at-

INAUGURATION OF ABRAHAM LINCOLN, MARCH 4, 1861.
Process reproduction of an imperfect photograph.

SOUTH OR GARDEN SIDE OF THE WHITE HOUSE.—TREASURY BUILDING IN
THE DISTANCE.

THE WHITE HOUSE AT NIGHT.

tempt should be made to fire from those windows on the presidential carriage. The small force of regular cavalry which had arrived was to guard the side-street crossings of Pennsylvania Avenue, and to move from one to another during the passage of the procession. A battalion of District of Columbia troops were to be placed near the steps of the Capitol, and riflemen in the windows of the wings of the Capitol. On the arrival of the presidential party at the Capitol, the troops were to be stationed so as to return in the same order after the ceremony.

To illustrate the state of uncertainty in which we were at that time concerning men, I may here state that the lieutenant-colonel, military secretary of the General-in-Chief, who that afternoon recorded the conclusions of the General in conference, and who afterward wrote out for me the instructions regarding the disposition of troops, resigned his commission that very night, and departed for the South, where he joined the Confederate army.

During the night of the 3d of March, notice was brought me that an attempt would be made to blow up the platform on which the President would stand to take the oath of office. I immediately placed men under the steps, and at daybreak a trusted battalion of District troops (if I remember rightly, it was the National Guard, under Colonel Tait) formed in a semicircle at the foot of the great stairway, and prevented all entrance from without. When the crowd began to assemble in front of the portico, a large number of policemen in plain clothes were scattered through the mass to observe closely, to place themselves near any person who might act suspiciously, and to strike down any hand which might raise a weapon.

At the appointed hour, Mr. Buchanan was escorted to Willard's hotel, which he entered. There I found a number of mounted "marshals of the day," and posted them around the carriage, within the cavalry guard. The two Presidents were saluted by the troops as they came out of the hotel

and took their places in the carriage. The procession started. During the march to the Capitol I rode near the carriage, and by an apparently clumsy use of my spurs managed to keep the horses of the cavalry in an uneasy state, so that it would have been very difficult for even a good marksman to get an aim at one of the inmates of the carriage between the prancing horses.

After the inaugural ceremony, the President and the ex-President were escorted in the same order to the White House. Arrived there, Mr. Buchanan walked to the door with Mr. Lincoln, and there bade him welcome to the House and good-morning. The infantry escort formed in line from the gate of the White House to the house of Mr. Ould, whither Mr. Buchanan drove, and the cavalry escorted his carriage. The infantry line presented arms to the ex-President as he passed, and the cavalry escort saluted as he left the carriage and entered the house. Mr. Buchanan turned on the steps, and gracefully acknowledged the salute. The District of Columbia volunteers had

given to President Lincoln his first military salute and to Mr. Buchanan his last.

NOTE.—In December, 1860, the military forces of the United States consisted of 1108 officers and 15,259 men of the regular army; total, 16,367.

ROTUNDA OF THE CAPITOL IN 1861.

MAJOR ROBERT ANDERSON.
Commanding Officer of the Garrison at Fort Sumter. (From a photograph.)

FORT SUMTER.

FROM MOULTRIE TO SUMTER.

BY ABNER DOUBLEDAY, BREVET MAJOR-GENERAL, U. S. A., RETIRED.
Captain U. S. A., and Executive Officer under Major Anderson at Fort Sumter.

AS senior captain of the 1st Regiment of United States Artillery, I had been stationed at Fort Moultrie, Charleston Harbor, two or three years previous to the outbreak of 1861. There were two other forts in the harbor. Of these, Fort Sumter was unoccupied, being in an unfinished state, while Castle Pinckney was in charge of a single ordnance sergeant. The garrison of Fort Moultrie consisted of 2 companies that had been reduced to 65 men, who with the band raised the number in the post to 73. Fort Moultrie had no strength; it was merely a sea battery. No one ever imagined it would be attacked by our own people; and if assailed by foreigners, it was supposed that an army of citizen-soldiery would be there to defend it. It was very low, the walls having about the height of an ordinary room. It was little more, in fact, than the old fort of Revolutionary time of which the father of Major Robert Anderson had been a defender. The sand had drifted from the sea against the wall, so that cows would actually scale the ramparts. In 1860 we applied to have the fort put in order, but the quartermaster-general, afterward the famous Joseph E. Johnston, said the matter did not pertain to his department. We were then apprehend-

MAJOR ANDERSON AND EIGHT OF HIS OFFICERS.
Process reproduction of an imperfect photograph. The picture, though dim, has the value of a fac-simile.

ing trouble, for the signs of the times indicated that the South was drifting toward secession, though the Northern people could not be made to believe this, and regarded our representation to this effect as nonsense. I remember that at that time our engineer officer, Captain J. G. Foster, was alone, of the officers, in thinking there would be no trouble. We were commanded by a Northern man of advanced age, Colonel John L. Gardner, who had been wounded in the war of 1812 and had served with credit in Florida and Mexico. November 15th, 1860, Mr. Floyd, the Secretary of War, relieved him and put in command Major Robert Anderson of Kentucky, who was a regular officer. Floyd thought the new commander could be relied upon to carry out the Southern programme, but we never believed that Anderson took command with a knowledge of that programme or a desire that it should succeed. He simply obeyed orders; he had to obey or leave the army. Anderson was a Union man and, in the incipiency, was perfectly willing to chastise South Carolina in case she should attempt any revolutionary measures. His feeling as to coercion changed when he found that all the Southern States had joined South Carolina, for he looked upon the conquest of the South as hopeless.

Soon after his arrival, which took place on the 21st of November, Anderson wanted the sand removed from the walls of Moultrie, and urged that it be done. Suddenly the Secretary of War seemed to adopt this view. He pretended there was danger of war with England, with reference to Mexico, which was absurd; and under this pretext was seized with a sudden zeal to put the harbor of Charleston in condition,—to be turned over to the Confederate forces. He appropriated $150,000 for Moultrie, and $80,000 to finish Sumter. There was not much to be made out of Fort Moultrie, with all our efforts, because it was hardly defensible; but Major Anderson strove to strengthen it.

He put up heavy gates to prevent Charleston secessionists from entering, and made a little man-hole through which visitors had to crawl in and out.

We could get no additional ammunition, but Colonel Gardner had managed to procure a six months' supply of food from the North before the trouble came. The Secretary of War would not let us have a man in the way of reinforcement, the plea being that reinforcements would irritate the people. The secessionists could hardly be restrained from attacking us, but the leaders kept them back, knowing that our workmen were laboring in their interests, at the expense of the United States. When Captain Truman Seymour was sent with a party to the United States arsenal in Charleston to get some friction primers and a little ammunition, a crowd interfered and drove his men back. It became evident, as I told Anderson, that we could not defend the fort, because the houses around us on Sullivan's Island looked down into Moultrie, and could be occupied by our enemies. At last it was rumored that two thousand riflemen had been detailed to shoot us down from the tops of those houses. I proposed to anticipate the enemy and burn the dwellings, but Anderson would not take so decided a step at a time when the North did not believe there was going to be war. It was plain that the only thing to be done was to slip over the water to Fort Sumter, but Anderson said he had been assigned to Fort Moultrie, and that he must stay there. We were then in a very peculiar position. It was commonly believed that we would not be supported even by the North, as the Democrats had been bitterly opposed to the election of Lincoln; that at the first sign of war twenty thousand men in sympathy with the South would rise in New York. Moreover, the one to whom we soldiers always looked up as to a father—the Secretary of War—seemed to be devising arrangements to have us made away

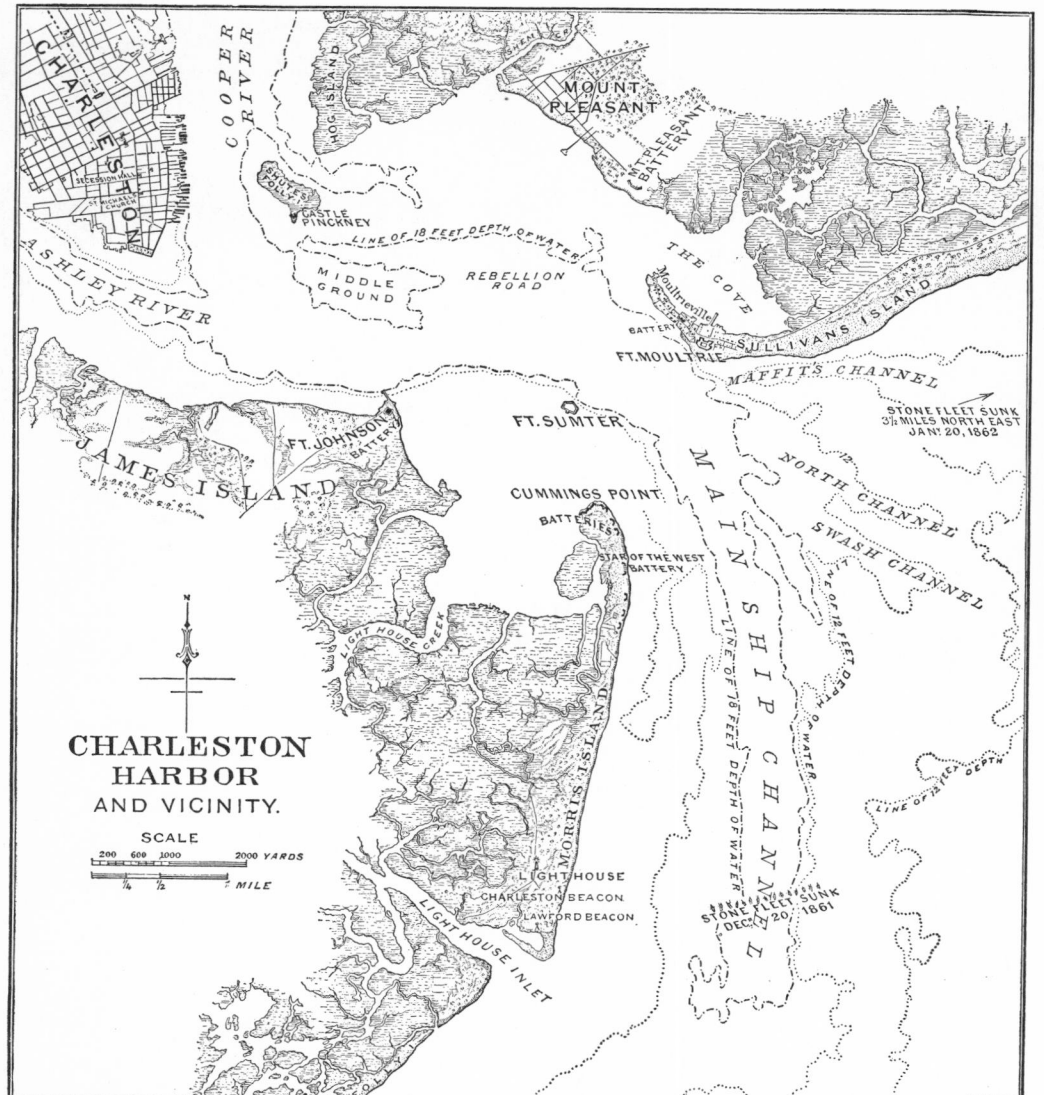

CHARLESTON
HARBOR
AND VICINITY.

SCALE

THE HOT-SHOT FURNACE, FORT MOULTRIE.
From a photograph.

FORT SUMTER AFTER THE BOMBARDMENT.
From a sketch made in April, 1861.

with. We believed that in the event of an outbreak from Charleston few of us would survive; but it did not greatly concern us, since that risk was merely a part of our business, and we intended to make the best fight we could. The officers, upon talking the matter over, thought they might control any demonstration at Charleston by throwing shells into the city from Castle Pinckney. But, with only sixty-four soldiers and a brass band, we could not detach any force in that direction.

Finally, Captain Foster, who had misapprehended the whole situation, and who had orders to put both Moultrie and Sumter in perfect order, brought several hundred workmen from Baltimore. Unfortunately, these were nearly all in sympathy with the Charlestonians, many even wearing secession badges.

Bands of secessionists were now patrolling near us by day and night. We were so worn out with guard-duty—watching them—that on one occasion my wife and Captain Seymour's relieved us on guard, all that was needed being some one to give the alarm in case there was an attempt to break in. Foster thought that out of his several hundred workmen he could get a few Union men to drill at the guns as a garrison in Castle Pinckney, but they rebelled the moment they found they were expected to act as artillerists, and said that they were not there as warriors. It was said that when the enemy took possession of the castle, some of these workmen were hauled from under beds and from other hiding-places.

The day before Christmas I asked Major Anderson for wire to make an entanglement in front of my part of the fort, so that any one who should charge would tumble over the wires and could be shot at our leisure. I had already caused a slop-ing picket-fence to be projected over the parapet on my side of the works so that scaling-ladders could not be raised against us. The discussion in Charleston over our proceedings was of an amusing character. This wooden *fraise* puzzled the Charleston militia and editors; one of the latter said: "Make ready your sharpened stakes, but you will not intimidate freemen."

When I asked Anderson for the wire, he said I should have a mile of it, with a peculiar smile that puzzled me for the moment. He then sent for Hall, the post quartermaster, bound him to secrecy, and told him to take three schooners and some barges which had been chartered for the purpose of taking the women and children and six months' supply of provisions to Fort Johnson, opposite Charleston. He was instructed when the secession patrols should ask what this meant, to tell them we were sending off the families of the officers and men to the North because they were in the way. The excuse was plausible, and no one interfered. We were so closely watched that we could make no movement without demands being made as to the reason of it. On the day we left—the day after Christmas—Anderson gave up his own mess, and came to live with me as my guest. In the evening of that day I went to notify the major that tea was ready. Upon going to the parapet for that purpose, I found all the officers there, and noticed something strange in their manner. The problem was solved when Anderson walked up to me and said: "Captain, in twenty minutes you will leave this fort with your company for Fort Sumter." The order was startling and unexpected, and I thought of the immediate hostilities of which the movement would be the occasion. I rushed over to my company quarters and informed my men, so that they

RUINS OF THE CASEMATES NEAR THE SALLY-PORT, AND
OF THE FLAG-STAFF.
From photographs.

THE SALLY-PORT OF FORT SUMTER.
From a photograph taken from the wharf.

THE SEA BATTERY OF FORT MOULTRIE.
From a photograph taken before the war.

might put on their knapsacks and have everything in readiness. This took about ten minutes. Then I went to my house, told my wife that there might be fighting, and that she must get out of the fort as soon as she could and take refuge behind the sand-hills. I put her trunks out of the sally-port, and she followed them. Then I started with my company to join Captain Seymour and his men. We had to go a quarter of a mile through the little town of Moultrieville to reach the point of embarkation. It was about sunset, the hour of the siesta, and fortunately the Charleston militia were taking their afternoon nap. We saw nobody, and soon reached a low line of sea-wall under which were hidden the boats in charge of the three engineers, for Lieutenants Snyder and Meade had been sent by Floyd to help Captain Foster do the work on the forts. The boats had been used in going back and forward in the work of construction, manned by ordinary workmen, who now vacated them for our use. Lieutenant Snyder said to me in a low tone: "Captain, those boats are for your men." So saying, he started with his own party up the coast. When my thirty men were embarked I went straight for Fort Sumter. It was getting dusk. I made slow work in crossing over, for my men were not expert oarsmen. Soon I saw the lights of the secession guard-boat coming down on us. I told the men to take off their coats and cover up their muskets, and I threw my own coat open to conceal my buttons. I wished to give the impression that it was an officer in charge of laborers. The guard-ship stopped its paddles and inspected us in the gathering darkness, but concluded we were all right and passed on. My party was the first to reach Fort Sumter.

We went up the steps of the wharf in the face of an excited band of secession workmen, some of whom were armed with pistols. One or two Union men among them cheered, but some of the others said angrily: "What are these soldiers doing here? what is the meaning of this?" Ordering my men to charge bayonets, we drove the workmen into the center of the fort. I took possession of the guard-room commanding the main entrance and placed

sentinels. Twenty minutes after, Seymour arrived with the rest of the men. Meantime Anderson had crossed in one of the engineer boats. As soon as the troops were all in we fired a cannon, to give notice of our arrival to the quartermaster, who had anchored at Fort Johnson with the schooners carrying the women and children. He immediately sailed up to the wharf and landed his passengers and stores. Then the workmen of secession sympathies were sent aboard the schooners to be taken ashore.

Lieutenant Jefferson C. Davis of my company had been left with a rear-guard at Moultrie. These, with Captain Foster and Assistant-Surgeon Crawford, stood at loaded columbiads during our passage, with orders to fire upon the guard-boats and sink them if they tried to run us down. On withdrawing, the rear-guard spiked the guns of the fort, burned the gun-carriages on the front looking toward Sumter, and cut down the flag-staff. Mrs. Doubleday first took refuge at the house of the post sutler, and afterward with the family of Chaplain Harris, with whom she sought shelter behind the sand-hills. When all was quiet they paced the beach, anxiously watching Fort Sumter. Finding that the South Carolinians were ignorant of what had happened, we sent the boats back to procure additional supplies.

The next morning Charleston was furious. Messengers were sent out to ring every door-bell and convey the news to every family. The governor sent two or three of his aides to demand that we return to Moultrie. Anderson replied in my hearing that he was a Southern man, but that he had been assigned to the defense of Charleston Harbor, and intended to defend it.

Chaplain Harris was a spirited old man. He had lived at Charleston most of his life, and knew the South Carolinians well. He visited Fort Sumter on our first day there and made a prayer at the raising of the flag, after which he returned to his home at Moultrieville. One day he went to the commander of Fort Moultrie and said to him: "Will any impediment be put in the way of my going over to Fort Sumter?" The reply was: "Oh, no, parson; I reckon we'll give you a pass." The chaplain

answered: "I did n't ask you for a pass, sir. I am a United States officer, and will go to any United States fort without your permission. I asked you a different question: whether you would prevent my going by force." He was not allowed to cross, after that.

We had no light and were obliged to procure some if possible, for the winter nights were long. There was much money due the workmen who had been discharged, and the secessionists sent them over to demand their pay. Mrs. Doubleday came in the same boat with them, and managed to ship us a box of candles at the same time; she also brought a bandbox full of matches. At the same time Mrs. Seymour reached us stealthily in a boat rowed by two little boys. Mrs. Foster was already there. Anderson thought there was going to be trouble, so he requested the ladies to return to Moultrieville that night. The next day they went to a Charleston hotel, where they were obliged to keep very quiet and have their meals served privately in their rooms. After a day or two they left for the North, on account of the feeling in the city.

From December 26th until April 12th, we busied ourselves in preparing for the expected attack, and our enemies did the same on all sides of us. Anderson apparently did not want reinforcements, and he shrank from civil war. He endured all kinds of hostile proceedings on the part of the secessionists, in the hope that Congress would make some compromise that would save slavery and the Union together.

Soon after daylight on the 9th of January, with my glass I saw a large steamer pass the bar and enter the Morris Island Channel. It was the *Star of the West*, with reinforcements and supplies for us. When she came near the upper part of the island the secessionists fired a shot at her. I hastened to Major Anderson's room, and was ordered by him to have the long roll beaten and to post the men at the barbette guns. By the time we reached the parapet the transport coming to our relief had approached so near that Moultrie opened fire. Major Anderson would not allow us to return the fire, so the transport turned about and steamed seaward. Anderson asked for

an explanation of the firing from Governor Pickens, and announced that he would allow no vessel to pass within range of the guns of Sumter if the answer was unsatisfactory. Governor Pickens replied that he would renew the firing under like circumstances. I think Major Anderson had received an intimation that the *Star of the West* was coming, but did not believe it. He thought General Scott would send a man-of-war instead of a merchant vessel. Great secrecy was observed in loading her, but the purpose of the expedition got into the newspapers, and, of course, was telegraphed to Charleston. Bishop Stevens of the Methodist Church stated in a speech made by him on Memorial Day in the Academy of Music, New York, that he aimed the first gun against the *Star of the West*. I aimed the first gun on our side in reply to the attack on Fort Sumter.

Sure that we would all be tasked to the utmost in the coming conflict, and be kept on the alert by day and night, I desired to get all the sleep I could beforehand, and lay down on a cot bedstead in the magazine nearest to Morris Island,— one of the few places that would be shell-proof when the fire opened. About 4 A. M. on the 12th, Major Anderson came to me as his executive officer, and informed me that the enemy would fire upon us as soon as it was light enough to see the fort. He said he would not return it until it was broad daylight, the idea being that he did not desire to waste his ammunition.

We have not been in the habit of regarding the signal shell fired from Fort Johnson as the first gun of the conflict, although it was undoubtedly aimed at Fort Sumter. Edmund Ruffin of Virginia is usually credited with opening the attack by firing the first gun from the iron-clad battery on Morris Island. The ball from that gun struck the wall of the magazine where I was lying, penetrated the masonry, and burst very near my head. As the smoke from this explosion came in through the ventilators of the magazine, and as the floor was strewn with powder where the flannel cartridges had been filled, I thought for a moment the place was on fire.

When it was fully light we took breakfast lei-

that I will mention. As the fire against us came from all directions, a shot from Sullivan's Island struck near the lock of the magazine, and bent the copper door, so that all access to the few cartridges we had there was cut off. Just previous to this the officers had been engaged, amid a shower of shells, in vigorous efforts to cut away wood-work which was dangerously near the magazine.

After the surrender we were allowed to salute our flag with a hundred guns before marching out, but it was very dangerous and difficult to do so; for, owing to the recent conflagration, there were fire and sparks all around the cannon, and it was not easy to find a safe place of deposit for the cartridges. It happened that some flakes of fire had entered the muzzle of one of the guns after it was sponged. Of course, when the gunner attempted to ram the cartridge down it exploded prematurely, killing Private Daniel Hough instantly, and setting fire to a pile of cartridges underneath, which also exploded, seriously wounding five men. Fifty guns were fired in the salute.

With banners flying, and with drums beating "Yankee Doodle," we marched on board the transport that was to take us to the steamship *Baltic*, which drew too much water to pass the bar and was anchored outside. We were soon on our way to New York.

With the first shot against Sumter the whole North became united. Mobs went about New York and made every doubtful newspaper and private house display the Stars and Stripes. When we reached that city we had a royal reception. The streets were alive with banners.

SOME EFFECTS OF THE BOMBARDMENT.
From a photograph.

battles and skirmishes in many parts of the field of war. Anderson, Foster, Seymour, Crawford, Davis, and myself became major-generals of volunteers. Norman J. Hall, who rendered brilliant service at Gettysburg, became a colonel, and would doubtless have risen higher had he not been compelled by ill health to retire. Talbot became an assistant adjutant-general with the rank of captain, but died before the war had fairly begun. He was not with us during the bombardment, as he had been sent as a special messenger to Washington with despatches. Lieutenant Snyder of the engineers, a most promising young officer, also died at the very commencement of hostilities.

Only one of our number left us and joined the Confederacy,—Lieutenant R. K. Meade of the engineers, a Virginian. His death occurred soon after.

NOTE.— Under an order from Secretary Stanton, the same flag that was lowered April 14th, 1861, was raised again over Sumter, by Major (then General) Anderson, on April 14th, 1865.

A CASEMATE GUN DURING THE CONFLAGRATION.

surely before going to the guns, our food consisting of pork and water.

The first night after the bombardment we expected that the naval vessels outside would take advantage of the darkness to send a fleet of boats with reinforcements of men and supplies of provisions, and as it was altogether probable that the enemy would also improvise a fleet of small boats to meet those of the navy, it became an interesting question, in case parties came to us in this way, to decide whether we were admitting friends or enemies. However, the night passed quietly away without any demonstration.

Captain Chester, in his paper which follows, has omitted a fact

INTERIOR OF SUMTER AFTER THE BOMBARDMENT.
Showing the gate and the gorge wall; also one of the 8-inch columbiads set as mortars, bearing on Morris Island. (From a photograph.)

Our men and officers were seized and forced to ride on the shoulders of crowds wild with enthusiasm. When we purchased anything merchants generally refused all compensation. Fort Hamilton, where we were stationed, was besieged with visitors, many of whom were among the most highly distinguished in all walks of life. The Chamber of Commerce of New York voted a bronze medal to each officer and soldier of the garrison.

We were soon called upon to take an active part in the war, and the two Sumter companies were sent under my command to reinforce General Patterson's column, which was to serve in the Shenandoah Valley. Our march through Pennsylvania was a continuous ovation. Flowers, fruits, and delicacies of all kinds were showered upon us, and the hearts of the people seemed overflowing with gratitude for the very little we had been able to accomplish.

Major Anderson was made a brigadier-general in the regular army, and assigned to command in his native State, Kentucky; but his system had been undermined by his great responsibilities; he was threatened with softening of the brain and was obliged to retire from active service. The other officers were engaged in

INTERIOR OF FORT SUMTER.
The 10-inch columbiad bearing on Charleston. (From a photograph.)

INTERIOR OF SUMTER AFTER THE SURRENDER.
Showing the 8-inch columbiads planted as mortars, and the Confederate flag flying from the derrick by which the guns were raised to the upper tier. (From a photograph.)

FORT JOHNSON. IRON-CLAD BATTERY, CUMMING'S POINT. FORT SUMTER. FORT MOULTRIE.

BURSTING OF THE SIGNAL-SHELL FROM FORT JOHNSON OVER FORT SUMTER.

THE SOUTHWEST OR GORGE FRONT OF FORT SUMTER.
Showing the gate wharf, and esplanade, Machicoulis galleries on the parapet, and the effect of the fire from
Cumming's Point and Fort Johnson.   (From a photograph.)

SUMTER. GUARD-BOAT. CHARLESTON. CASTLE PINCKNEY. MOULTRIE.

MAJOR ANDERSON'S MEN CROSSING IN BOATS TO FORT SUMTER.
From a war-time sketch.

INSIDE THE FORT.

BY JAMES CHESTER, CAPTAIN THIRD ARTILLERY,
U. S. A.
A member of the garrison at Fort Sumter.

THE opening of the bombardment was a some-what dramatic event. A relieving fleet was approaching, all unknown to the Sumter garrison, and General Beauregard, perhaps with the hope of tying Major Anderson's hands in the expected fight with that fleet, had opened negotiations with him on the 11th of April looking toward the evac-uation of the fort. But Major Anderson declined to evacuate his post till compelled by hunger. The last ounce of breadstuffs had been consumed, and matters were manifestly approaching a crisis. It was evident from the activity of the enemy that something important was in the wind. That night we retired as usual. Toward half-past three on the morning of the 12th we were startled by a gun fired in the immediate vicinity of the fort, and many rose to see what was the matter. It was soon learned that a steamer from the enemy de-sired to communicate with Major Anderson, and a small boat under a flag of truce was received and delivered the message. Although no formal an-nouncement of the fact was made, it became gen-erally known among the men that in one hour General Beauregard would open his batteries on Sumter.

The men waited about for some time in expecta-tion of orders, but received none, except an in-formal order to go to bed, and the information that reveille would be sounded at the usual hour. This was daylight, fully two hours off, so some of the men did retire. The majority perhaps remained up, anxious to see the opening, for which purpose they had all gone on the ramparts. Except that the flag was hoisted, and a glimmer of light was visible at the guard-house, the fort looked so dark and silent as to seem deserted. The morning was dark and raw. Some of the watchers surmised that Beauregard was "bluffing," and that there would be no bombardment. But promptly at 4:30 A. M. a flash as of distant lightning in the direction of Mount Pleasant, followed by the dull roar of a mortar, told us that the bombardment had begun. The eyes of the watchers easily detected and fol-lowed the burning fuse which marked the course of the shell as it mounted among the stars, and then descended with ever-increasing velocity, until it landed inside the fort and burst. It was a capi-

tal shot. Then the batteries opened on all sides, and shot and shell went screaming over Sumter as if an army of devils were swooping around it. As a rule the guns were aimed too high, but all the mortar practice was good. In a few minutes the novelty disappeared in a realizing sense of danger, and the watchers retired to the bomb-proofs, where they discussed probabilities until reveille.

Habits of discipline are strong among old sol-diers. If it had not been for orders to the con-trary, the men would have formed for roll-call on the open parade, as it was their custom to do, al-though mortar-shells were bursting there at the lively rate of about one a minute. But they were formed under the bomb-proofs, and the roll was called as if nothing unusual was going on. They were then directed to get breakfast, and be ready to fall in when "assembly" was beaten. The breakfast part of the order was considered a grim joke, as the fare was reduced to the solitary item of fat pork, very rusty indeed. But most of the men worried down a little of it, and were "ready" when the drum called them to their work.

By this time it was daylight, and the effects of the bombardment became visible. No serious damage was being done to the fort. The enemy had concentrated their fire on the barbette bat-teries, but, like most inexperienced gunners, they were firing too high. After daylight their shooting improved, until at 7:30 A. M., when "assembly" was beaten in Sumter, it had become fairly good. At "assembly" the men were again paraded and the orders of the day announced. The garrison was divided into two reliefs, and the tour of duty at the guns was to be four hours. Captain Doubleday being the senior captain, his battery took the first tour.

There were three points to be fired upon,—the Morris Island batteries, the James Island batteries, and the Sullivan's Island batteries. With these last was included the famous iron-clad floating bat-tery, which had taken up a position off the western end of Sullivan's Island to command the left flank of Sumter. Captain Doubleday divided his men into three parties: the first, under his own imme-diate command, was marched to the casemate guns bearing on Morris Island; the second, under Lieu-tenant Jefferson C. Davis, manned the casemate guns bearing on the James Island batteries; and the third—without a commissioned officer until Dr. Crawford joined it—was marched by a sergeant to the guns bearing on Sullivan's Island. The guns

in the lower tier, which were the only ones used during the bombardment,—except surreptitiously without orders,—were 32 and 42-pounders, and some curiosity was felt as to the effect of such shot on the iron-clad battery. The gunners made ex-cellent practice, but the shot were seen to bounce off its sides like peas. After battering it for about an hour and a half, no visible effect had been pro-duced, although it had perceptibly slackened its fire, perhaps to save ammunition. But it was evident that throwing 32-pounder shot at it, at a mile range, was a waste of iron, and the attention of the gunners was transferred to Fort Moultrie.

Moultrie was, perhaps, a less satisfactory target than the iron-clad. It was literally buried under sand-bags, the very throats of the embrasures being closed with cotton-bales. The use of cotton-bales was very effective as against shot, but would have been less so against shell. The fact that the em-brasures were thus closed was not known in Sum-ter till after the bombardment. It explained what was otherwise inexplicable. Shot would be seen to strike an embrasure, and the gunner would feel that he had settled one gun for certain, but even while he was receiving the congratulations of his comrades the supposed disabled gun would reply. That the cotton-bales could not be seen from Sum-ter is not surprising. The sand-bag casemates which covered the guns were at least eighteen feet thick, and the cotton-bale shutter was no doubt ar-ranged to slide up and down like a portcullis inside the pile of sand-bags. The gunners of Sumter, not knowing of the existence of these shutters, di-rected their shot either on the embrasures for the purpose of disabling the enemy's guns, or so as to graze the sand-bag parapet for the purpose of reach-ing the interior of the work. The practice was very good, but the effect, for reasons already stated, was inconsiderable. . . .

The smoke which enveloped the Confederate batteries during the first day, while not so thick as to entirely to obscure them, was sufficiently so to make visual aiming extremely unreliable; and dur-ing the second day, when Sumter was on fire, no-thing could be seen beyond the muzzles of our own guns. But the aiming arrangements, due to the foresight and ingenuity of Captain Doubleday, enabled us to fire with as much accuracy when we could not see the object as when we could. . . .

The first night of the bombardment was one of great anxiety. The fleet might send reinforce-ments; the enemy might attempt an assault. Both would come in boats; both would answer in English. It would be horrible to fire upon friends; it would be fatal not to fire upon enemies. The night was dark and chilly. Shells were dropping into the fort at regular intervals, and the men were tired, hungry, and out of temper. Any party that approached that night would have been rated as enemies upon general principles. Fortunately nobody appeared; reveille sounded, and the men oiled their appetites with the fat pork at the usual hour by way of breakfast.

The second day's bombardment began at the same hour as did the first; that is, on the Sumter side. The enemy's mortars had kept up a very slow fire all night, which gradually warmed up after daylight as their batteries seemed to awaken, until its vigor was about equal to their fire of the day before. The fleet was still off the bar— perhaps waiting to see the end. Fire broke out once or twice in the officers' quarters, and was ex-tinguished. It broke out again in several places at once, and we realized the truth and let the quarters burn. They were firing red-hot shot. This was about 9 o'clock. As soon as Sumter was noticed to be on fire the secessionists increased the fire of their batteries to a maximum. In the

CONFEDERATE MORTAR-BATTERY ON MORRIS ISLAND.
Commanded by Lieutenant C. R. Holmes.
From a photograph.

perfect storm of shot and shell that beat upon us from all sides, the flag-staff was shot down, but the old flag was rescued and nailed to a new staff. This, with much difficulty, was carried to the ramparts and lashed to some chassis piled up there for a traverse.

We were not sorry to see the quarters burn. They were a nuisance. Built for fire-proof buildings, they were not fire-proof. Neither would they burn up in a cheerful way. The principal cisterns were large iron tanks immediately under the roof. These had been riddled, and the quarters below had been deluged with water. Everything was wet and burned badly, yielding an amount of pungent piney smoke which almost suffocated the garrison.

The scene inside the fort as the fire gained headway and threatened the magazine was an exciting one. It had already reached some of our stores of loaded shells and shell-grenades. These must be saved at all hazard. Soldiers brought their blankets and covered the precious projectiles, and thus the most of them were saved. But the magazine itself was in danger. Already it was full of smoke, and the flames were rapidly closing in upon it. It was evident that it must be closed, and it would be many hours before it could be opened again. During these hours the fire must be maintained with such powder as we could secure outside the magazine. A number of barrels were rolled out for this purpose, and the magazine door — already almost too hot to handle — was closed.

It was the intention to store the powder taken from the magazine in several safe corners, covering it with damp soldiers' blankets. But safe corners were hard to find, and most of the blankets were already in use covering loaded shells. The fire was raging more fiercely than ever, and safety demanded that the uncovered powder be thrown overboard. This was instantly done, and if the tide had been high we should have been well rid of it. But the tide was low, and the pile of powder-barrels rested on the riprapping in front of the embrasure. This was observed by the enemy, and some shell guns were turned upon the pile, producing an explosion which blew the gun at that embrasure clear out of battery, but it did no further damage.

The fire had now enveloped the magazine, and the danger of an explosion was imminent. Powder had been carried out all the previous day, and it was more than likely that enough had sifted through the cartridge-bags to carry the fire into the powder-chamber. Major Anderson, his head erect as if on parade, called the men around him; directed that a shot be fired every five minutes; and mentioned that there was some danger of the magazine exploding. Some of the men, as soon as they learned what the real danger was, rushed to the door of the magazine and hurriedly dug a trench in front of it, which they kept filled with water until the danger was considered over. . . . It was during this excitement that ex-Senator Wigfall of Texas visited the fort. . . . Wigfall's conference was not of long duration. . . . About 7 o'clock in the evening another white flag brought the announcement that the terms agreed upon between General Beauregard and Major Anderson had been confirmed, and that we would leave Fort Sumter the following day; which we did, after saluting our flag with fifty guns.

GENERAL G. T. BEAUREGARD.
In command of the Confederate force which bombarded Fort Sumter.

THE CONFEDERATE SIDE AT SUMTER.

BY STEPHEN D. LEE, LIEUTENANT-GENERAL, C. S. A.
Captain, C. S. A., and Aide-de-camp to General Beauregard during the bombardment.

AFTER the evacuation of Fort Moultrie, although Major Anderson was not permitted by the South Carolina authorities to receive any large supply of provisions, yet he received a daily mail, and fresh beef and vegetables from the city of Charleston, and was unmolested at Fort Sumter. He continued industriously to strengthen the fort. The military authorities of South Carolina, and afterward of the Confederate States, took possession of Fort Moultrie, Castle Pinckney, the arsenal, and other United States property in the vicinity. They also remounted the guns at Fort Moultrie, and constructed batteries on Sullivan's, Morris, and James islands, and at other places, looking to the reduction of Fort Sumter if it should become necessary; meantime leaving no stone unturned to secure from the authorities at Washington a quiet evacuation of the fort. Several arrangements to accomplish this purpose were almost reached, but failed. Two attempts were made to reinforce and supply the garrison: one by the steamer *Star of the West*, which tried to reach the fort, January 9th, 1861, and was driven back by a battery on Morris Island, manned by South Carolina troops; the

FRANCIS W. PICKENS,
Governor of South Carolina, 1861.
From a photograph.

other just before the bombardment of Sumter, April 12th. The feeling of the Confederate authorities was that a peaceful issue would finally be arrived at; but they had a fixed determination to use force, if necessary, to occupy the fort. They did not desire or intend to take the initiative, if it could be avoided. So soon, however, as it was clearly understood that the authorities at Washington had abandoned peaceful views, and would assert the power of the United States to supply Fort Sumter, General Beauregard, the commander of the Confederate forces at Charleston, in obedience to the command of his Government at Montgomery, proceeded to reduce the fort. His arrangements were about complete, and on April 11th he demanded of Major Anderson the evacuation of Fort Sumter. He offered to transport Major Anderson and his command to any port in the United States; and to allow him to move out of the fort with company arms and property, and all private property, and to salute his flag in lowering it. This demand was delivered to Major Anderson at 3:45 P. M., by two aides of General Beauregard, James Chesnut, Jr., and myself. At 4:30 P. M. he handed us his reply, refusing to accede to the demand; but added, "Gentlemen, if you do not batter the fort to pieces about us, we shall be starved out in a few days."

The reply of Major Anderson was put in General Beauregard's hands at 5:15 P. M., and he was also told of this informal remark. Anderson's reply and remark were communicated to the Confederate authorities at Montgomery. The Secretary of War, L. P. Walker, replied to Beauregard as follows:

"Do not desire needlessly to bombard Fort Sumter. If Major Anderson will state the time at which, as indicated by him, he will evacuate, and agree that in the meantime he will not use his guns against us, unless ours should be employed against Fort Sumter, you are authorized thus to avoid the effusion of blood. If this, or its equivalent, be refused, reduce the fort as your judgment decides to be most practicable."

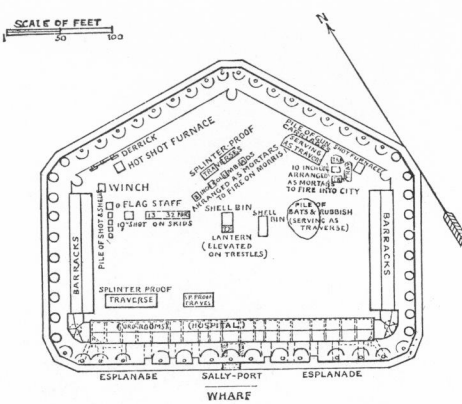

GROUND-PLAN OF FORT SUMTER.
Based on an official drawing.

The same aides bore a second communication to Major Anderson, based on the above instructions, which was placed in his hands at 12:45 A. M., April 12th. His reply indicated that he would evacuate the fort on the 15th, provided he did not in the meantime receive contradictory instructions from his Government, or additional supplies, but he declined to agree not to open his guns upon the Confederate troops, in the event of any hostile demonstration on their part against his flag. Major Anderson made every possible effort to retain the aides till daylight, making one excuse and then another for not replying. Finally, at 3:15 A. M., he delivered his reply. In accordance with their instructions, the aides read it and, finding it unsatisfactory, gave Major Anderson this notification:

"FORT SUMTER, S. C., April 12th, 1861, 3:20 A. M.—SIR: By authority of Brigadier-General Beauregard, commanding the Provisional Forces of the Confederate States, we have the honor to notify you that he will open the fire of his batteries on Fort Sumter in one hour from this time. We have the honor to be very respectfully, Your obedient servants, JAMES CHESNUT, JR., *Aide-de-camp.* STEPHEN D. LEE, *Captain C. S. Army, Aide-de-camp.*"

The above note was written in one of the casemates of the fort, and in the presence of Major Anderson and several of his officers. On receiving it he was much affected. He seemed to realize the full import of the consequences, and the great responsibility of his position. Escorting us to the boat at the wharf, he cordially pressed our hands in farewell, remarking, "If we never meet in this world again, God grant that we may meet in the next."

The boat containing the two aides and also Roger A. Pryor, of Virginia, and A. R. Chisolm, of South Carolina, who were also members of General Beauregard's staff, went immediately to Fort Johnson on James Island, and the order to fire the signal gun was given to Captain George S. James, commanding the battery at that point. It was then 4 A. M. Captain James at once aroused his command, and arranged to carry out the order. He was a great admirer of Roger A. Pryor, and said to him, "You are the only man to whom I would give up the honor of firing the first gun of the war;" and he offered to allow him to fire the first gun of the war. Pryor, on receiving the offer, was very much agitated. With a husky voice he said, "I could not

fire the first gun of the war." His manner was almost similar to that of Major Anderson as we left him a few moments before on the wharf at Fort Sumter. Captain James would allow no one else but himself to fire the gun.

The boat with the aides of General Beauregard left Fort Johnson before arrangements were complete for the firing of the gun, and laid on its oars, about one-third the distance between the fort and Sumter, there to witness the firing of "the first gun of the war" between the States. It was fired from a ten-inch mortar at 4:30 A. M., April 12th, 1861. Captain James was a skilful officer, and the firing of the shell was a success. It burst immediately over the fort, apparently about one hundred feet above. The firing of the mortar woke the echoes from every nook and corner of the harbor, and in this the dead hour of night, before dawn, that shot was a sound of alarm that brought every soldier in the harbor to his feet, and every man, woman, and child in the city of Charleston from their beds. A thrill went through the whole city. It was felt that the Rubicon was passed. No one thought of going home; unused as their ears were to the appalling sounds, or the vivid flashes from the batteries, they stood for hours fascinated with horror. After the second shell the different batteries opened their fire on Fort Sumter, and by 4:45 A. M. the firing was general and regular. It was a hazy, foggy morning. About daylight, the boat with the aides reached Charleston, and they reported to General Beauregard.

Fort Sumter did not respond with her guns till 7:30 A. M. The firing from this fort, during the entire bombardment, was slow and deliberate, and marked with little accuracy. The firing continued without intermission during the 12th, and more slowly during the night of the 12th and 13th. No material change was noticed till 8 A. M. on the 13th, when the barracks in Fort Sumter were set on fire by hot shot from the guns of Fort Moultrie. As soon as this was discovered, the Confederate batteries redoubled their efforts, to prevent the fire being extinguished. Fort Sumter fired at little longer intervals, to enable the garrison to

fight the flames. This brave action, under such a trying ordeal, aroused great sympathy and admiration on the part of the Confederates for Major Anderson and his gallant garrison; this feeling was shown by cheers whenever a gun was fired from Sumter. It was shown also by loud reflections on the "men-of-war" outside the harbor.

About 12:30 the flag-staff of Fort Sumter was shot down, but it was soon replaced. As soon as General Beauregard heard that the flag was no longer flying, he sent three of his aides, William Porcher Miles, Roger A. Pryor, and myself, to offer, and also to see if Major Anderson would receive or needed, assistance in subduing the flames inside the fort. Before we reached it, we saw the United States flag again floating over it, and began to return to the city. Before going far, however, we saw the Stars and Stripes replaced by a white flag. We turned about at once and rowed rapidly to the fort. We were directed, from an embrasure, not to go to the wharf, as it was mined, and the fire was near it. We were assisted through an embrasure and conducted to Major Anderson. Our mission being made known to him, he replied, "Present my compliments to General Beauregard, and say to him I thank him for his kindness, but need no assistance." He further remarked that he hoped the worst was over, that the fire had settled over the magazine, and, as it had not exploded, he thought the real danger was about over. Continuing, he said, "Gentlemen, do I understand you come direct from General Beauregard?" The reply was in the affirmative. He then said, "Why! Colonel Wigfall has just been here as an aide too, and by authority of General Beauregard, and proposed the same terms of evacuation offered on the 11th instant." We informed the major that we were not authorized to offer terms; that we were direct from General Beauregard, and that Colonel Wigfall, although an aide-de-camp to the general, had been detached, and had not seen the general for several days. Major Anderson at once stated, "There is a misunderstanding on my part, and I will at once run up my flag and open fire again." After consul-

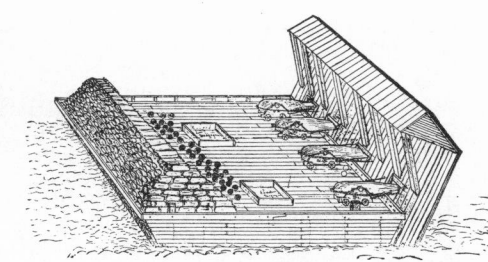

THE IRON-CLAD FLOATING BATTERY.
This battery commanded the left flank of Fort Sumter.
From a plan by Colonel Joseph A. Yates.

tation, we requested him not to do so until the matter was explained to General Beauregard, and requested Major Anderson to reduce to writing his understanding with Colonel Wigfall, which he did. However, before we left the fort, a boat arrived from Charleston, bearing Major D. R. Jones, assistant adjutant-general on General Beauregard's staff, who offered substantially the same terms to Major Anderson as those offered on the 11th, and also by Colonel Wigfall, and which were now accepted.

Thus fell Fort Sumter, April 13th, 1861. At this time fire was still raging in the barracks, and settling steadily over the magazine. All egress was cut off except through the lower embrasures. Many shells from the Confederate batteries, which had fallen in the fort and had not exploded, as well as the hand-grenades used for defense, were exploding as they were reached by the fire. The wind was driving the heat and smoke down into the fort and into the casemates, almost causing suffocation. Major Anderson, his officers and men were blackened by smoke and cinders, and showed signs of fatigue and exhaustion from the trying ordeal through which they had passed.

It was soon discovered, by conversation, that it was a bloodless battle; not a man had been killed or seriously wounded on either side during the entire bombardment of nearly forty hours. Congratulations were exchanged on so happy a result. Major Anderson stated that he had instructed his officers only to fire on the batteries and forts, and not to fire on private property.

The terms of evacuation offered by General Beauregard were generous, and were appreciated by Major Anderson. The garrison was to embark on the 14th, after running up and saluting the United States flag, and to be carried to the United States fleet. A soldier killed during the salute was buried inside the fort, the new Confederate garrison uncovering during the impressive ceremonies. Major Anderson and his command left the harbor, bearing with them the respect and admiration of the Confederate soldiers. It was conceded that he had done his duty as a soldier holding a most delicate trust.

This first bombardment of Sumter was but its "baptism of fire." During subsequent attacks by land and water, it was battered by the heaviest Union artillery. Its walls were completely crushed, but the tons of iron projectiles imbedded in its ruins added strength to the inaccessible mass that surrounded it and made it impregnable. It was never taken, but the operations of General Sherman, after his march to the sea, compelled its evacuation, and the Stars and Stripes were again raised over it, April 14th, 1865.

FORT SUMTER AT THE CLOSE OF THE WAR.
From a sketch made at the time.

JEFFERSON DAVIS.
President of the Confederate States of America. (From a photograph.)

THE CONFEDERATE GOVERNMENT.

IN an article on "The Confederate Government at Montgomery," Mr. R. Barnwell Rhett, editor of the Charleston "Mercury," 1860–62, a son of the chairman of the South Carolina delegation to the Confederate convention, says:

. . . On the 20th of December, 1860, South Carolina passed unanimously the first ordinance of secession. . . . On her invitation, six other Southern States sent delegates to a convention in Montgomery, Alabama, for the purpose of organizing a Confederacy. On the 4th of February, 1861, this convention assembled. The material which constituted it was of a mixed character. There were members who were constitutionally timid and unfit by character and temperament to participate in such work as was on hand. Others had little knowledge of public affairs on a large scale, and had studied neither the resources of the South nor the conduct of the movement. A number of them, however, were men of ripe experience and statesmanlike grasp of the situation — men of large knowledge, with calm, strong, clear views of the policies to be pursued. Alexander H. Stephens characterized this convention as "the ablest body with which he ever served, and singularly free from revolutionary spirit."

ROBERT TOOMBS.
First Secretary of State of the Confederacy; Member of the Confederate Senate; Brigadier-General, C. S. A.
From a photograph.

HOWELL COBB.
President of the First Confederate Congress; Major-General, C. S. A.
From a photograph.

In the organization of the convention, Howell Cobb was chosen to preside and J. J. Hooper, of Montgomery, to act as secretary. It was decided to organize a provisional government under a provisional constitution, which was adopted on the 8th of February. On the 9th a provisional President and Vice-President were elected, who were installed in office on the 18th to carry the government into effect. In regard to this election, it was agreed that when four delegations out of the six should settle upon men, the election should take place. Jefferson Davis was put forward by the Mississippi delegation and Howell Cobb by that of Georgia. The Florida delegation proposed to vote for whomsoever South Carolina should support. The South Carolina delegation offered no candidate and held no meeting to confer upon the matter. The chairman, Mr. R. Barnwell Rhett, did not call them together. . . . On taking the vote in the convention (February 9th) Georgia gave hers to Mr. Cobb, and the other States theirs to Mr. Davis. Georgia then changed her vote, which elected Mr. Davis unanimously. Mr. Alexander H. Stephens was chosen Vice-President. Mr. Rhett was made chairman of the committee to notify the President-elect, and to present him to the convention for inauguration. This office he performed in complimentary style, reflecting the estimate of Mr. Barnwell rather than his own fears. Within six weeks the Provisional Congress found out that they had made a mistake, and that there was danger of a division into an administration and an anti-administration party, which might paralyze the Government. To avoid this, and to confer all power on the President, they resorted to secret sessions.

Mr. Davis offered the office of Secretary of State to Mr. Barnwell, but he declined it, and recommended Mr. C. G. Memminger, also of South Carolina, for the Treasury portfolio, which was promptly accorded to him. Both of these gentlemen had been coöperationists, and up to the last had opposed secession. Mr. Barnwell would not have been sent to the State convention from Beaufort but for the efforts of Edmund Rhett, an influential State senator. Of Mr. Memminger it was said that when a bill was on its passage through the Legislature of South Carolina in 1859, appropriating a sum of money for the purchase of arms, he had slipped in an amendment which had operated to prevent Governor Gist from drawing the money and procuring the arms. In Charleston he was known as an active friend of the free-school system and orphan house, a moral and charitable Episcopalian, and a lawyer, industrious, shrewd, and thrifty. As chairman of the Committee on Ways and Means in the House of Representatives, he was familiar with the cut-and-dried plan of raising the small revenue necessary to carry on the government of South Carolina. Such was his record and experience when appointed to the cabinet of Mr. Davis. Mr. Memminger received no recommendation for this office from the South Carolina

delegation; nor did the delegation from any State, so far as known, attempt to influence the President in the choice of his cabinet.

Mr. Robert Toombs, of Georgia, was appointed Secretary of State. This was in deference to the importance of his State and the public appreciation of his great mental powers and thorough earnestness, not for the active part he had taken in the State convention in behalf of secession. In public too fond of sensational oratory, in counsel he was a man of large and wise views.

Mr. Leroy Pope Walker, of Alabama, was appointed Secretary of War on the recommendation of Mr. William L. Yancey. Ambitious, without any special fitness for this post, and overloaded, he accepted the office with the understanding that Mr. Davis would direct and control its business, which he did. After differing with the President as to the number of arms to be imported, and the number of men to be placed in camp in the winter of 1861–62 (being in favor of very many more than the President), he wisely resigned.

Mr. Stephen R. Mallory, of Florida, was appointed Secretary of the Navy. He was a gentleman of unpretending manners and ordinary good sense, who had served in the Senate with Mr. Davis, and had been chairman of the Committee on Naval Affairs. With some acquaintance with officers of the United States Navy, and some knowledge of nautical matters, he had small comprehension of the responsibilities of the office. His efforts were feeble and dilatory, and he utterly failed to provide for keeping open the seaports of the Confederacy. But he was one of the few who remained in the cabinet to the end.

Mr. Judah P. Benjamin, of Louisiana, was appointed Attorney-General, and held that office until the resignation of Mr. Walker, when he was transferred to the post of Secretary of War. Upon the fall of New Orleans, public indignation compelled a change, and he was made Secretary of State. A man of great fertility of mind and resource and of facile character, he was the factotum of the President, performed his bidding in various ways, and gave him the benefit of his brains in furtherance of the views of Mr. Davis. . . .

Although a provisional government was more free to meet emergencies and correct mistakes, it was determined to proceed to the formation of a permanent government. . . . The committee, of which Mr. Rhett was chairman, agreed at its first meeting that the Constitution of the United States should be adopted with only such alterations as experience has proved desirable, and to avoid latitudinarian constructions. Most of the important amendments were adopted on motion of the chairman. . . . The permanent constitution was adopted on the 11th of March, 1861, and went into operation, with the permanent government, at Richmond, on the 18th of February, 1862, when the Provisional Congress expired. . . .

ALEXANDER H. STEPHENS.
Vice-President of the Confederacy.
From a photograph.

JOHN H. REAGAN.
Confederate Postmaster-General.

CHRISTOPHER G. MEMMINGER.
First Secretary of the Treasury of the
Confederacy.

WILLIAM L. YANCEY.
Member of the Confederate Senate; Confederate Commissioner to
Europe in 1861.   (From a photograph.)

JUDAH P. BENJAMIN.
Confederate Attorney-General until Sept. 17, 1861; Second
Secretary of War; Third Secretary of State.   (From a photograph.)

ROBERT BARNWELL RHETT.
Chairman of Committee on Foreign Affairs, Confederate
Provisional Congress.   (From a photograph.)

LEROY POPE WALKER.
First Confederate Secretary of War.
From a photograph.

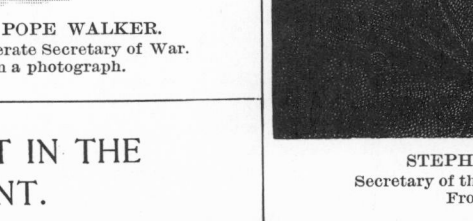

STEPHEN R. MALLORY.
Secretary of the Navy to the Confederacy.
From a photograph.

PORTRAITS OF MEN PROMINENT IN THE CONFEDERATE GOVERNMENT.

SECESSION HALL, CHARLESTON.
Scene of the passage of the Ordinance of Secession.
From a photograph.

If any one attempts to haul down the American flag, shoot him on the spot. —

John A. Dix

Secretary of the Treasury.

FACSIMILE OF THE CONCLUSION OF GENERAL DIX'S "AMERICAN FLAG" DESPATCH.

January 18th, 1861, three days after he had entered on his duties as Secretary of the Treasury to President Buchanan, General Dix sent W. Hemphill Jones, chief clerk of one of the Treasury bureaus, to the South, for the purpose of saving the revenue-cutters at New Orleans, Mobile, and Galveston. January 29th, Mr. Jones telegraphed from New Orleans that the captain of the revenue-cutter *McClelland* refused to obey the Secretary's orders. It was seven in the evening when the despatch was received. Immediately Secretary Dix wrote the following reply:

"Treasury Department, January 29, 1861. Tell Lieutenant Caldwell to arrest Captain Breshwood, assume command of the cutter, and obey the order I gave through you. If Captain Breshwood, after arrest, undertakes to interfere with the command of the cutter, tell Lieutenant Caldwell to consider him as a mutineer, and treat him accordingly. If any one attempts to haul down the American flag, shoot him on the spot.

"JOHN A. DIX,
"Secretary of the Treasury."

MAJOR-GENERAL JOHN A. DIX.
From a photograph.

WAR PREPARATIONS IN THE NORTH.

BY JACOB D. COX, MAJOR-GENERAL, U. S. V., EX-GOVERNOR OF OHIO, EX-SECRETARY OF THE INTERIOR.

A member of the Ohio Senate on the outbreak of the War; made a brigadier-general in the Ohio quota, April 23d, 1861.

THE wonderful outburst of national feeling in the North in the spring of 1861 has always been a thrilling and almost supernatural thing to those who participated in it. The classic myth that the resistless terror which sometimes unaccountably seized upon an army was the work of the god Pan might seem to have its counterpart in the work of a national divinity rousing a whole people, not to terror, but to a sublime enthusiasm of self-devotion. To picture it as a whole is impossible. A new generation can only approximate a knowledge of the feelings of that time by studying in detail some separate scenes of the drama that had a continent for its stage. The writer can only tell what happened under his eye. The like was happening everywhere from Maine to Kansas. What is told is simply a type of the rest.

On Friday, the twelfth day of April, 1861, the Senate of Ohio was in session, trying to go on in the ordinary routine of business, but with a sense of anxiety and strain which was caused by the troubled condition of national affairs. The passage of "ordinances of secession" by one after another of the Southern States, and even the assembling of a provisional Confederate government at Montgomery,

had not wholly destroyed the hope that some peaceful way out of our troubles would be found; yet the gathering of an army on the sands opposite Fort Sumter was really war, and if a hostile gun were fired, we knew it would mean the end of all effort at arrangement. Hoping almost against hope that blood would not be shed, and that the pageant of military array and of a secession government would pass by, we tried to give our thoughts to business; but there was no heart in it, and the "morning hour" lagged, for we could not work in earnest, and we were unwilling to adjourn.

Suddenly a Senator came in from the lobby in an excited way, and, catching the chairman's eye, exclaimed, "Mr. President, the telegraph announces that the secessionists are bombarding Fort Sumter!" There was a solemn and painful hush, but it was broken in a moment by a woman's shrill voice from the spectators' seats, crying, "Glory to God!" It startled every one, almost as if the enemy were in the midst. But it was the voice of a radical friend of the slave, Abby Kelly Foster, who, after a lifetime of public agitation, believed that only through blood could his freedom be won, and who had shouted the fierce cry of joy that the

question had been submitted to the decision of the sword. With most of us, the gloomy thought that civil war had begun in our own land overshadowed everything else; this seemed too great a price to pay for any good,—a scourge to be borne only in preference to yielding what was to us the very groundwork of our republicanism, the right to enforce a fair interpretation of the Constitution through the election of President and Congress.

The next day we learned that Major Anderson had surrendered, and the telegraphic news from all the Northern States showed plain evidence of a popular outburst of loyalty to the Union, following a brief moment of dismay. That was the period when the flag — *The Flag* — flew out to the wind from every housetop in our great cities, and, when, in New York, wildly excited crowds marched the streets demanding that the suspected or the lukewarm should show the symbol of nationality as a committal to the country's cause. He that is not for us is against us, was the deep, instinctive feeling. . . .

A few days after the surrender of Sumter, Stephen A. Douglas passed through Columbus on his way to Washington, and, in response to the calls of a spontaneous gathering of people, spoke to them from the window of his bedroom in the hotel. There had been no thought for any of the common surroundings of a public meeting. There were no torches, no music. A dark mass of men filled full

the dimly lit street, and called for Douglas with an earnestness of tone wholly different from the enthusiasm of common political gatherings. He came half-dressed to his window, and, without any light near him, spoke solemnly to the people upon the terrible crisis which had come upon the nation. Men of all parties were there: his own followers to get some light as to their duty; the Breckinridge Democrats ready, most of them, repentantly to follow a Northern leader now that their Southern associates were in armed opposition to the Government; the Republicans eager to know whether so potent an influence was to be unreservedly on the side of the nation. I remember well the serious solicitude with which I listened to his opening sentences as I leaned against the railing of the State House park, trying in vain to see more than a dim outline of the man as he stood at the unlighted window. His deep, sonorous tones rolled down through the darkness from above us, an earnest, measured voice, the more solemn, the more impressive, because we could not see the speaker, and it came to us literally as "a voice in the night,"—the night of our country's unspeakable trial. There was no uncertainty in his tone; the Union must be preserved and the insurrection must be crushed; he pledged his hearty support to Mr. Lincoln's administration in doing this; other questions must stand aside till the national authority should be everywhere recognized. I do not

VIEW OF WASHINGTON FROM THE SIGNAL CAMP, GEORGETOWN HEIGHTS.
From a sketch made at the time.

think we greatly cheered him,—it was, rather, a deep Amen that went up from the crowd. We went home breathing more freely in the assurance we now felt that, for a time at least, no organized opposition to the Federal Government and its policy of coercion could be formidable in the North.

Yet the situation hung upon us like a nightmare. Garfield and I were lodging together at the time, our wives being kept at home by family cares, and when we reached our sitting-room, after an evening session of the Senate, we often found ourselves involuntarily groaning, "Civil war in *our* land!" The shame, the folly, the outrage, seemed too great to believe, and we half hoped to awake from it as from a dream. Among the painful remembrances of those days is the ever-present weight at the heart which never left me till I found relief in the active duties of camp life at the close of the month. I went about my duties (and I am sure most of those with whom I associated did the same) with the half-choking sense of a grief I dared not think of; like one who is dragging himself to the ordinary labors of life from some terrible and recent bereavement.

We talked of our personal duty, and though both Garfield and myself had young families, we were agreed that our activity in the organization and support of the Republican party made the duty of supporting the Government by military service come peculiarly home to us. He was, for the moment, somewhat trammeled by his half-clerical position, but he very soon cut the knot. My own path seemed unmistakably plain. He, more care-

ful for his friend than for himself, urged upon me his doubts whether my physical strength was equal to the strain that would be put upon it. "I," said he, "am big and strong, and if my relations to the church and the college can be loosened, I shall have no excuse for not enlisting; but you are slender and will break down." It is true I then looked slender for a man six feet high; yet I had confidence in the elasticity of my constitution, and the result justified me, while it also showed how liable one is to mistake in such things. Garfield found that he had a tendency to weakness of the alimentary system, which broke him down on every cam-

paign in which he served, and led to his retiring from the army at the close of 1863. My own health, on the other hand, was strengthened by outdoor life and exposure, and I served to the end with growing physical vigor.

When Mr. Lincoln issued his first call for troops, the existing laws made it necessary that these should be fully organized and officered by the several States. Then, the treasury was in no condition to bear the burden of war expenditures, and, till Congress could assemble, the President was forced to rely on the States for means to equip and transport their own men. This threw upon the

RICHMOND, VIRGINIA, IN 1861.
From a sketch.

19

governors and legislatures of the loyal States responsibilities of a kind wholly unprecedented. A long period of profound peace had made every military organization seem almost farcical. A few independent companies formed the merest shadow of an army, and the State militia proper was only a nominal thing. It happened, however, that I held a commission as brigadier in this State militia, and my intimacy with Governor Dennison led him to call upon me for such assistance as I could render in the first enrollment and organization of the Ohio quota. Arranging to be called to the Senate chamber when my vote might be needed, I gave my time chiefly to such military matters as the governor appointed. Although, as I have said, my military commission had been a nominal thing, and in fact I had never worn a uniform, I had not wholly neglected theoretic preparation for such work. For some years, the possibility of a war of secession had been one of the things which were forced upon the thoughts of reflecting people, and I had given some careful study to such books of tactics and of strategy as were within easy reach. I had especially been led to read military history with critical care, and had carried away many valuable ideas from that most useful means of military education. I had, therefore, some notion of the work before us, and could approach its problems with less loss of time, at least, than if I had been wholly ignorant.

My commission as brigadier-general in the Ohio quota in national service was dated the 23d of April. . . .

THE NEW YORK SEVENTH AT CAMP
CAMERON, WASHINGTON.

THE NEW YORK SEVENTH MARCHING DOWN BROADWAY, APRIL 19, 1861.

A MILITIA UNIFORM OF '61.
After the New York Seventh's Memorial Statue
in the Central Park.

GOING TO THE FRONT.

RECOLLECTIONS OF A PRIVATE, BY WARREN LEE GOSS.

. . . It was the news that the 6th Massachusetts regiment had been mobbed by roughs on their passage through Baltimore which gave me the war fever. And yet when I read Governor John A. Andrew's instructions to have the hero martyrs "preserved in ice and tenderly sent forward," somehow, though I felt the pathos of it, I could not reconcile myself to the ice. Ice in connection with patriotism did not give me agreeable impressions of war, and when I came to think of it, the stoning of the heroic "Sixth" did n't suit me; it detracted from my desire to die a soldier's death.

I lay awake all night thinking the matter over, with the "ice" and "brick-bats" before my mind. However, the fever culminated that night, and I resolved to enlist.

"Cold chills" ran up and down my back as I got out of bed after the sleepless night, and shaved preparatory to other desperate deeds of valor. I was twenty years of age, and when anything unusual was to be done, like fighting or courting, I shaved.

With a nervous tremor convulsing my system, and my heart thumping like muffled drum-beats, I stood before the door of the recruiting-office, and, before turning the knob to enter, read and re-read the advertisement for recruits posted thereon, until I knew all its peculiarities. The promised chances for "travel and promotion" seemed good, and I thought I might have made a mistake in considering war so serious after all. "Chances for travel!" I must confess now, after four years of soldiering,

that the "chances for travel" were no myth; but "promotion" was a little uncertain and slow.

I was in no hurry to open the door. Though determined to enlist, I was half inclined to put it off awhile; I had a fluctuation of desires; I was faint-hearted and brave; I wanted to enlist, and yet — Here I turned the knob, and was relieved. I had been more prompt, with all my hesitation, than the officer in his duty; he was n't in. Finally he came, and said: "What do you want, my boy?" "I want to enlist," I responded, blushing deeply with up-welling patriotism and bashfulness. Then the surgeon came to strip and examine me. In justice to myself, it must be stated that I signed the rolls without a tremor. It is common to the most of humanity, I believe, that, when confronted with actual danger, men have less fear than in its contemplation. I will, however, make one exception in favor of the first shell I heard uttering its blood-curdling hisses, as though a steam locomotive were traveling the air. With this exception I have found the actual dangers of war always less terrible face to face than on the night before the battle.

My first uniform was a bad fit: my trousers were too long by three or four inches; the flannel shirt was coarse and unpleasant, too large at the neck and too short elsewhere. The forage cap was an ungainly bag with pasteboard top and leather visor; the blouse was the only part which seemed decent; while the overcoat made me feel like a little nubbin of corn in a large preponderance of husk. Nothing except "Virginia mud" ever took down my ideas of military pomp quite so low.

After enlisting I did not seem of so much consequence as I had expected. There was not so much excitement on account of my military ap-

pearance as I deemed justly my due. I was taught my facings, and at the time I thought the drill-master needlessly fussy about shouldering, ordering, and presenting arms. At this time men were often drilled in company and regimental evolutions long before they learned the manual of arms, because of the difficulty of obtaining muskets. These we obtained at an early day, but we would willingly have resigned them after carrying them for a few hours. The musket, after an hour's drill, seemed heavier and less ornamental than it had looked to be. The first day I went out to drill, getting tired of doing the same things over and over, I said to the drill-sergeant: "Let's stop this fooling and go over to the grocery." His only reply was addressed to a corporal: "Corporal, take this man out and drill him like h—l"; and the corporal did! I found that suggestions were not so well appreciated in the army as in private life, and that no wisdom was equal to a drill-master's "Right face," "Left wheel," and "Right, oblique, march." It takes a raw recruit some time to learn that he is not to think or suggest, but obey. Some never do learn. I acquired it at last, in humility and mud, but it was tough. Yet I doubt if my patriotism, during my first three weeks' drill, was quite knee-high. Drilling looks easy to a spectator, but it is n't. Old soldiers who read this will remember their green recruithood and smile assent. After a time I had cut down my uniform so that I could see out of it, and had conquered the drill sufficiently to see through it. Then the word came: On to Washington!

Our company was quartered at a large hotel near the railway station in the town in which it had been recruited. Bunks had been fitted up within

A MOTHER'S PARTING GIFT.

PENNSYLVANIA AVENUE, WASHINGTON.
From a sketch made in 1861.

DRILLING A RAW RECRUIT.

a part of the hotel but little used. We took our meals at the public table, and found fault with the style. Six months later we would have considered ourselves aristocratic to have slept in the hotel stables with the meal-bin for a dining-table. One morning there was great excitement at the report that we were going to be sent to the front. Most of us obtained a limited pass and went to see our friends for the last time, returning the same night. Many of our schoolmates came in tears to say good-by. We took leave of them all with heavy hearts, for, lightly as I may here seem to treat the subject, it was no light thing for a boy of twenty to start out for three years into the unknown dangers of a civil war. Our mothers—God bless them!—had brought us something good to eat— pies, cakes, doughnuts, and jellies. It was one way in which a mother's heart found utterance. The young ladies (sisters, of course) brought an invention, usually made of leather or cloth, containing needles, pins, thread, buttons, and scissors, so that nearly every recruit had an embryo tailor's shop, with the goose outside. One old lady, in the innocence of her heart, brought her son an umbrella. We did not see anything particularly laughable about it at the time, but our old drill-sergeant did. Finally we were ready to move; our tears were wiped away, our buttons were polished, and our muskets were as bright as emery paper could make them.

"Wad" Rider, a member of our company, had come from a neighboring State to enlist with us. He was about eighteen years of age, red-headed, freckled-faced, good-natured, and rough, with a wonderful aptitude for crying or laughing from sympathy. Another comrade, whom I will call

Jack, was honored with a call from his mother, a little woman, hardly reaching up to his shoulder, with a sweet, motherly, care-worn face. At the last moment, though she had tried hard to preserve her composure, as is the habit of New England people, she threw her arms around her boy's neck, and with an outburst of sobbing and crying, said: "My dear boy, my dear boy, what will your poor old mother do without you? You are going to fight for your country. Don't forget your mother, Jack; God bless you, God bless you!" We felt as if the mother's tears and blessing were a benediction over us all. There was a touch of nature in her homely sorrow and solicitude over her big boy, which drew tears of sympathy from my eyes as I thought of my own sorrowing mother at home. The sympathetic Wad Rider burst into tears and sobs. His eyes refused, as he expressed it, to "dry up," until, as we were moving off, Jack's mother, rushing toward him with a bundle tied like a wheat-sheaf, called out in a most pathetic voice, "Jack! Jack! you've forgotten to take your pennyroyal." We all laughed, and so did Jack, and I think the laugh helped him more than the cry did. Everybody had said his last word, and the cars were off. Handkerchiefs were waved at us from all the houses we passed; we cheered till we were hoarse, and then settled back and swung our handkerchiefs.

Just here let me name over the contents of my knapsack, as a fair sample of what all the volunteers started with. There were in it a pair of trousers, two pairs of drawers, a pair of thick boots, four pairs of stockings, four flannel shirts, a blouse, a looking-glass, a can of peaches, a bottle of cough-mixture, a button-stick, chalk, razor and strop, the "tailor's shop" spoken of above, a Bible, a small volume of Shakspere, and writing utensils. To its

top was strapped a double woolen blanket and a rubber one. Many other things were left behind because of lack of room in or about the knapsack.

On our arrival in Boston we were marched through the streets—the first march of any consequence we had taken with our knapsacks and equipments. Our dress consisted of a belt about the body, which held a cartridge-box and bayonet, a cross-belt, also a haversack and tin drinking-cup, a canteen, and, last but not least, the knapsack strapped to the back. The straps ran over, around, and about one, in confusion most perplexing to our unsophisticated shoulders, the knapsack constantly giving the wearer the feeling that he was being pulled over backward. My canteen banged against my bayonet, both tin cup and bayonet badly interfered with the butt of my musket, while my cartridge-box and haversack were constantly flopping up and down—the whole jangling like loose harness and chains on a runaway horse. As we marched into Boston Common, I involuntarily cast my eye about for a bench. But for a former experience in offering advice, I should have proposed to the captain to "chip in" and hire a team to carry our equipments. Such was my first experience in war harness. Afterward, with hardened muscles, rendered athletic by long marches and invigorated by hardships, I could look back upon those days and smile, while carrying a knapsack as lightly as my heart. That morning my heart was as heavy as my knapsack. At last the welcome orders came: "Prepare to open ranks! Rear, open order, march! Right dress! Front! Order arms! Fix bayonets! Stack arms! Unsling knapsacks! In place, rest!"

The tendency of raw soldiers at first is to overload themselves. On the first long march the reaction sets in, and the recruit goes to the opposite extreme, not carrying enough, and thereby becom-

ing dependent upon his comrades. Old soldiers preserve a happy medium. I have seen a new regiment start out with a lot of indescribable material, including sheet-iron stoves, and come back after a long march covered with more mud than baggage, stripped of everything except blankets, haversacks, canteens, muskets, and cartridge-boxes.

During that afternoon in Boston, after marching and countermarching, or, as one of our farmer-boy recruits expressed it, after "hawing and geeing" about the streets, we were sent to Fort Independence for the night for safe-keeping. A company of regulars held the fort, and the guards walked their posts with an uprightness that was astonishing. Our first impression of them was that there was a needless amount of "wheel about and turn about, and walk just so," and of saluting and presenting arms. We were all marched to our quarters within the fort, where we unslung our knapsacks. After the first day's struggle with a knapsack, the general verdict was, "got too much of it." At supper-time we were marched to the dining-barracks, where our bill of fare was beef-steak, coffee, wheat bread, and potatoes, but not a sign of milk or butter. It struck me as queer when I heard that the army was never provided with butter and milk.

The next day we started for Washington, by rail. We marched through New York's crowded streets without awakening the enthusiasm we thought our due; for we had read of the exciting scenes attending the departure of the New York 7th for Washington, on the day the 6th Massachusetts was mobbed in Baltimore. . . . We arrived in Baltimore late at night, and we marched through its deserted streets unmolested. . . .

VIRGINIA SCENES IN '61.

BY CONSTANCE CARY HARRISON.
Author of "Sweet Bells Out of Tune," "The Anglomaniacs," "Flower de Hundred," etc., etc.

THE only association I have with my old home in Virginia that is not one of unmixed happiness relates to the time immediately succeeding the execution of John Brown at Harper's Ferry. Our homestead was in Fairfax County, at some distance from the theater of that tragic episode; and, belonging as we did to a family among the first in the State to manumit slaves,—our grandfather having set free those that came to him by inheritance, and the people who served us being hired from their owners and remaining in our employ through years of kindliest relations,—there seemed to be no especial reason for us to share in the apprehension of an uprising of the blacks. But there was the fear—unspoken, or pooh-poohed at by the men who were mouth-pieces for our community—dark, boding, oppressive, and altogether hateful. I can remember taking it to bed with me at night, and awaking suddenly oftentimes to confront it through a vigil of nervous terror, of which it never occurred to me to speak to any one. The notes of whip-poor-wills in the sweet-gum swamp near the stable, the mutterings of a distant thunder-storm, even the rustle of the night wind in the oaks that shaded my window, filled me with nameless dread. In the daytime it seemed impossible to associate suspicion with those familiar tawny or sable faces that surrounded us. We had seen them for so many years smiling or saddening with the family joys or sorrows; they were so guileless, so patient, so satisfied. What subtle influence was at work that should transform them into tigers thirsting for our blood? The idea was preposterous. But when evening came again, and with it the hour when the colored people (who in summer and autumn weather kept astir half the night) assembled themselves together for dance or prayer-meeting, the ghost that refused to be laid was again at one's elbow. Rusty bolts were drawn and rusty fire-arms loaded. A watch was set where never before had eye or ear been lent to such a service. In short, peace had flown from the borders of Virginia.

Although the newspapers were full of secession talk and the matter was eagerly discussed at our tables, I cannot remember that, as late as Christmas-time of the year 1860, coming events had cast any definite shadow on our homes. The people in our neighborhood, of one opinion with their dear and honored friend, Col. Robert

UNIFORM OF THE SIXTH MASSACHUSETTS.
The regiment that was mobbed while passing through Baltimore.

FEDERAL HILL, BALTIMORE.
From a sketch made on the day of the occupation by General Butler.

On the 27th of April, 1861, General B. F. Butler was assigned to the command of the Department of Annapolis, which did not include Baltimore. On the 5th of May, with two regiments and a battery of artillery, he moved from Washington to the Relay House, on the Baltimore and Ohio Railway, 7 miles from Baltimore, at the junction of the Washington branch. He fortified this position, and on the 13th entered Baltimore and occupied and fortified Federal Hill, overlooking the harbor and commanding the city. On the 15th he was followed in command of the Department by General George Cadwalader, who was succeeded on the 11th of June by General N. P. Banks, who administered the Department until succeeded by General John A. Dix, July 23, 1861. On the 22d of May General Butler assumed command at Fort Monroe, Va.

E. Lee, of Arlington, were slow to accept the startling suggestion of disruption of the Union. At any rate, we enjoyed the usual holiday gathering of kinsfolk in the usual fashion. The old Vaucluse house, known for many years past as a center of cheerful hospitality in the county, threw wide open its doors to receive all the members who could be gathered there of a large family circle. The woods about were despoiled of holly and spruce, pine and cedar, to deck the walls and wreathe the picture-frames. On Christmas Eve we had a grand rally of youths and boys belonging to the "clan," as they loved to call it, to roll in a yule log, which was deposited upon a glowing bed of coals in the big "red-parlor" fire-place, and sit about it afterward, welcoming the Christmas in with goblets of egg-nog and apple-toddy.

"Where shall we be a year hence?" some one asked at a pause in the merry chat; and, in the brief silence that followed, arose a sudden spectral thought of war. All felt its presence; no one cared to speak first of its grim possibilities.

On Christmas Eve the following year the old house lay in ruins, a sacrifice by Union troops to military necessity; the forest giants that kept watch around her walls had been cut down and made to serve as breastworks for a fort erected on the Vaucluse property as part of the defenses of Washington. Of the young men and boys who took

part in that holiday festivity, all were in the active service of the South,—one of them, alas! soon to fall under a rain of shot and shell beside his gun at Fredericksburg; the youngest of the number had left his mother's knee to fight at Manassas, and found himself, before the year was out, a midshipman aboard the Confederate steamer *Nashville*, on her cruise in distant seas!

My first vivid impression of war-days was during a ramble in the neighboring woods one Sunday afternoon in spring, when the young people in a happy band set out in search of wild flowers. Pink honeysuckles, blue lupine, beds of fairy flax, anemones, and ferns in abundance sprang under the canopy of young leaves on the forest boughs, and the air was full of the song of birds and the music of running waters. We knew every mossy path far and near in those woods; every tree had been watched and cherished by those who went before us, and dearer than any other spot on earth was our tranquil, sweet Vaucluse. Suddenly the shrill whistle of a locomotive struck the ear, an unwonted sound on Sunday. "Do you know what that means?" said one of the older cousins who accompanied the party. "It is the special train carrying Alexandria volunteers to Manassas,

and to-morrow I shall follow with my company." Silence fell upon our little band. A cloud seemed to come between us and the sun. It was the beginning of the end too soon to come.

The story of one broken circle is the story of another at the outset of such a war. Before the week was over, the scattering of our household, which no one then believed to be more than temporary, had begun. Living as we did upon ground likely to be in the track of armies gathering to confront each other, it was deemed advisable to send the children and young girls into a place more remote from chances of danger. Some weeks later, the heads of the household, two widowed sisters, whose sons were at Manassas, drove away from their home in their carriage at early morning, having spent the previous night in company with a half-grown lad digging in the cellar hasty graves for the interment of two boxes of old English silver-ware, heir-looms in the family, for which there was no time to provide otherwise. Although the enemy were long encamped immediately above it after the house was burnt the following year, this silver was found there when the war had ended; it was lying loose in the earth, the boxes having rotted away.

The point at which our family reunited within the Confederate lines was Bristoe, the station next beyond Manassas, a cheerless railway inn; a part of the premises was used as a country grocery store; and there quarters were secured for us with a view to being near the army. By this time all our kith and kin of fighting age had joined the volunteers. One cannot picture accommodations more forlorn than these eagerly taken for us and for other families attracted to Bristoe by the same powerful magnet. The summer sun poured its burning rays upon whitewashed walls unshaded by a tree. Our bedrooms were almost uninhabitable by day or night, our fare the plainest. From the windows we beheld only a flat, uncultivated country, crossed by red-clay roads, then ankle-deep in dust. We learned to look for all excitement to the glittering lines of railway track, along which continually thundered trains bound to and from the front. It was impossible to allow such a train to pass without running out upon the platform to salute it, for in this way we greeted many

PORTRAITS OF CONFEDERATE PRIVATES.
From ambrotypes found after the war in the dead-letter office, Richmond. Accompanying letters suggest that the warlike attitude was a favorite pose for pictures intended for sisters and sweethearts.

an old friend or relative buttoned up in the smart gray uniform, speeding with high hope to the scene of coming conflict. Such shouts as went up from sturdy throats while we stood waving hands, handkerchiefs, or the rough woolen garments we were at work upon! Then fairly awoke the spirit that made of Southern women the inspiration of Southern men throughout the war. Most of the young fellows we knew and were cheering onward wore the uniform of privates, and for the right to wear it had left homes of ease and luxury. To such we gave our best homage; and from that time forth the youth who was lukewarm in the cause or unambitious of military glory fared uncomfortably in the presence of the average Confederate maiden.

Thanks to our own carriage, we were able during those rallying days of June to drive frequently to visit "the boys" in camp, timing the expeditions to include battalion drill and dress parade, and taking tea afterward in the different tents. Then were the gala days of war, and our proud hosts hastened to produce home dainties despatched from the faraway plantations — tears and blessings interspersed amid the packing; though I have seen a pretty girl persist in declining other fare, to make her meal upon raw biscuit and huckleberry-pie compounded by the bright-eyed amateur cook of a well-beloved mess. Feminine heroism could no farther go.

And so the days wore on until the 17th of July, when a rumor from the front sent an electric shock through our circle. The enemy were moving forward! On the morning of the 18th those who had been able to sleep at all awoke early to listen for the first guns of the engagement of Blackburn's Ford. Deserted as the women at Bristoe were by every male creature old enough to gather news, there was, for us, no way of knowing the progress of events during the long, long day of waiting, of watching, of weeping, of praying, of rushing out upon the railway track to walk as far as we dared in the direction whence came that intolerable booming of artillery. The cloud of dun smoke arising over Manassas became heavier in volume as the day progressed. Still, not a word of tidings, till toward afternoon there came limping up a single, very dirty, soldier with his arm in a sling. What a heaven-send he was, if only as an escape-valve for our pent-up sympathies! We seized him, we washed him, we cried over him, we glorified him until the man was fairly bewildered. Our best endeavors could only develop a pin-scratch of a wound on his right hand; but when our hero had laid in a substantial meal of bread and meat, we plied him with trembling questions, each asking news of some staff or regiment or company. It has since occurred to me that he was a humorist in disguise. His invariable reply, as he looked from one to the other of his satellites, was: "The —— Virginia, marm? Why, of coase. They war n't no two ways o' thinkin' 'bout that ar reg'ment. They just *kivered* tharselves with glory!"

A little later two wagon-loads of slightly wounded claimed our care, and with them came authentic news of the day. Most of us received notes on paper torn from a soldier's pocket-book and grimed with gunpowder, containing assurance of the safety of our own. At nightfall a train carrying more

wounded to the hospitals at Culpeper made a halt at Bristoe; and, preceded by men holding lanterns, we went in among the stretchers with milk, food, and water to the sufferers. One of the first discoveries I made, bending over in that fitful light, was a young officer whom I knew to be a special object of solicitude with one of my comrades in the search; but he was badly hurt, and neither he nor she knew the other was near until the train had moved on. The next day, and the next, were full of burning excitement over the impending general engagement, which people then said would decide the fate of the young Confederacy. Fresh troops came by with every train, and we lived only to turn from one scene to another of welcome and farewell. On Saturday evening arrived a message from General Beauregard, saying that early on Sunday an engine and car would be put at our disposal, to take us to some point more remote from danger. We looked at one another, and, tacitly agreeing the gallant general had sent not an order but a suggestion, declined his kind proposal.

Another unspeakably long day, full of the straining anguish of suspense. Dawning bright and fair, it closed under a sky darkened by cannon-smoke. The roar of guns seemed never to cease. First, a long sullen boom; then a sharper rattling fire, painfully distinct; then stragglers from the field, with varying rumors: at last, the news of victory; and, as before, the wounded, to force our numbed faculties into service. One of the group, the mother of an only son barely fifteen years of age, heard that her boy, after being in action all the early part of the day, had through sheer fatigue fallen asleep upon the ground, where he was found resting peacefully amidst the roar of the guns.

A few days later we rode over the field. The trampled grass had begun to spring again, and wild flowers were blooming around carelessly made graves. From one of these imperfect mounds of clay I saw a hand extended; and when, years afterward, I visited the tomb of Rousseau beneath the Panthéon in Paris, where a sculptured hand bearing a torch protrudes from the sarcophagus, I thought of that mournful spectacle upon the field of Manassas. Fences were everywhere thrown down; the undergrowth of the woods was riddled with shot; here and there we came upon spiked guns, disabled gun-carriages, cannon-balls, blood stained blankets and dead horses. We were glad enough to turn away and gallop homeward.

With August heats and lack of water, Bristoe was forsaken for quarters near Culpeper, where my mother went into the soldiers' barracks, sharing soldiers' accommodations, to nurse the wounded. In September quite a party of us, upon invitation, visited the different headquarters. We stopped over-night at Manassas, five ladies, sleeping upon a couch made of rolls of cartridge-flannel, in a tent guarded by a faithful sentry. I remember the comical effect of the five bird-cages (of a kind without which no self-respecting young woman of that day would present herself in public) suspended upon a line running across the upper part of our tent,

ON THE WAY TO MANASSAS. A VIRGINIA SCENE IN '61.

after we had reluctantly removed them in order to adjust ourselves for repose. Our progress during that memorable visit was royal; an ambulance with a picked troop of cavalrymen had been placed at our service, and the convoy was "personally conducted" by a pleasing variety of distinguished officers. It was at this time, after a supper at the headquarters of the "Maryland line" at Fairfax, that the afterward universal war-song, "My Maryland!" was put afloat upon the tide of army favor. We were sitting outside a tent in the warm starlight of an early autumn night, when music was proposed. At once we struck up Randall's verses to the tune of the old college song, "Lauriger Horatius," — a young lady of the party, Jennie Cary, of Baltimore, having recently set them to this music before leaving home to share the fortunes of the Confederacy. All joined in the ringing chorus; and, when we finished, a burst of applause came from some soldiers listening in the darkness behind a belt of trees. Next day the melody was hummed far and near through the camps, and in due time it had gained the place of favorite song in the army. Other songs sung that evening, which afterward had a great vogue, were one beginning "By blue Patapsco's billowy dash," and "The years glide slowly by, Lorena."

Another incident of note, during the autumn of '61, was that to my cousins, Hetty and Jennie Cary, and to me was intrusted the making of the first three battle-flags of the Confederacy. They were jaunty squares of scarlet crossed with dark blue edged with white, the cross bearing stars to indicate the number of the seceded States. We set our best stitches upon them, edged them with golden fringes, and, when they were finished, despatched one to Johnston, another to Beauregard, and the third to Earl Van Dorn, then commanding infantry at Manassas. The banners were received with all possible enthusiasm; were toasted, fêted, and cheered abundantly. After two years, when Van Dorn had been killed in Tennessee, mine came back to me, tattered and storm-stained from long and honorable service in the field. . . .

NOTE. — The Confederates called the first battle of the war "Manassas," after Manassas Plains. The Federals gave it the name "Bull Run," after a stream of water.

LISTENING FOR THE FIRST GUN AT MANASSAS.

BRIGADIER-GENERAL IRVIN McDOWELL.
In command of the Union forces at Bull Run. (From a photograph.)

THE BATTLE OF BULL RUN.

THE STORY OF THE BATTLE FROM THE UNION SIDE.

BY JAMES B. FRY, BREVET MAJOR-GENERAL, U. S. A.
At Bull Run, Captain and Assistant Adjutant-General on McDowell's staff.

. . . After the firing of the first gun upon Sumter, the two sides were equally active in marshaling their forces on a line along the border States from the Atlantic coast of Virginia in the east to Kansas in the west. Many of the earlier collisions along this line were due rather to special causes or local feeling than to general military considerations. The prompt advance of the Union forces under McClellan to West Virginia was to protect that new-born free State. Patterson's movement to Hagerstown and thence to Harper's Ferry was to prevent Maryland from joining or aiding the rebellion, to re-open the Baltimore and Ohio railroad, and prevent invasion from the Shenandoah Valley. The Southerners, having left the Union and set up the Confederacy upon the principle of State rights, in violation of that principle invaded the State of Kentucky in opposition to her apparent purpose of armed neutrality. That made Kentucky a field of early hostilities, and helped to anchor her

to the Union. Missouri was rescued from secession through the energy of General F. P. Blair and her other Union men, and by the indomitable will of Captain Lyon of the regular army, whose great work was accomplished under many disadvantages. In illustration of the difficulty with which the new condition of affairs penetrated the case-hardened bureauism of long peace, it may be mentioned that the venerable adjutant-general of the army, when a crisis was at hand in Missouri, came from a consultation with the President and Secretary Cameron, and with a sorry expression of countenance and an ominous shake of the head exclaimed, "It's bad, very bad; we're giving that young man Lyon a great deal too much power in Missouri."

Early in the contest another young Union officer came to the front. Major Irvin McDowell was appointed brigadier-general May 14th. He was forty-three years of age, of unexceptionable habits and great physical powers. His education, begun in

CAPTAIN JAMES B. RICKETTS, AFTERWARD MAJOR-GENERAL.

CAPTAIN CHARLES GRIFFIN, AFTERWARD MAJOR-GENERAL.

"The batteries of Ricketts and Griffin, by their fine discipline, wonderful daring, and matchless skill, were the prime features in the fight. The battle was not lost till they were lost."—GENERAL JAMES B. FRY.

France, was continued at the United States Military Academy, from which he was graduated in 1838. Always a close student, he was well informed outside as well as inside his profession. Distinguished in the Mexican war, intensely Union in his sentiments, full of energy and patriotism, outspoken in his opinions, highly esteemed by General Scott, on whose staff he had served, he at once secured the confidence of the President and the Secretary of War, under whose observation he was serving in Washington. Without political antecedents or acquaintances, he was chosen for advancement on account of his record, his ability, and his vigor.

Northern forces had hastened to Washington upon the call of President Lincoln, but prior to May 24th they had been held rigidly on the north side of the Potomac. On the night of May 23d–24th, the Confederate pickets being then in sight of the Capitol, three columns were thrown across the river by General J. K. F. Mansfield, then commanding the Department of Washington, and a line from Alexandria below to chain-bridge above Washington was intrenched under guidance of able engineers. On the 27th Brigadier-General Irvin McDowell was placed in command south of the Potomac.

By the 1st of June the Southern Government had been transferred from Montgomery to Richmond, and the capitals of the Union and of the Confederacy stood defiantly confronting each other. General Scott was in chief command of the Union forces, with McDowell south of the Potomac, confronted by his old classmate, Beauregard, hot from the capture of Fort Sumter.

General Patterson, of Pennsylvania, a veteran of the war of 1812 and the war with Mexico, was in command near Harper's Ferry, opposed by General Joseph E. Johnston. The Confederate President, Davis, then in Richmond, with General

R. E. Lee as military adviser, exercised in person general military control of the Southern forces. The enemy to be engaged by McDowell occupied what was called the "Alexandria line," with headquarters at Manassas, the junction of the Orange and Alexandria with the Manassas Gap railroad. The stream known as Bull Run, some three miles in front of Manassas, was the line of defense. On Beauregard's right, 30 miles away, at the mouth of Aquia Creek, there was a Confederate brigade of 3000 men and 6 guns under General Holmes. The approach to Richmond from the Lower Chesapeake, threatened by General B. F. Butler, was guarded by Confederates under Generals Huger and Magruder. On Beauregard's left, sixty miles distant, in the lower Shenandoah Valley and separated from him by the Blue Ridge Mountains, was the Confederate army of the Shenandoah under command of General Johnston. Beauregard's authority did not extend over the forces of Johnston, Huger, Magruder, or Holmes, but Holmes was with him before the battle of Bull Run, and so was Johnston, who, as will appear more fully hereafter, joined at a decisive moment.

Early in June Patterson was pushing his column against Harper's Ferry, and on the 3d of that month McDowell was called upon by General Scott to submit "an estimate of the number and composition of a column to be pushed toward Manassas Junction and perhaps the Gap, say in 4 or 5 days, to favor Patterson's attack upon Harper's Ferry." McDowell had then been in command at Arlington less than a week, his raw regiments south of the Potomac were not yet brigaded, and this was the first intimation he had of offensive operations. He reported June 4th that 12,000 infantry, 2 batteries, 6 or 8 companies of cavalry, and a reserve of 5000 ready to move from Alexandria would be required. Johnston, however, gave up Harper's Ferry to Patterson, and the diversion by McDowell

THE HENRY HOUSE, FROM STONEWALL JACKSON'S POSITION.

TWO VIEWS OF THE MAIN BATTLE-GROUND.

THE ROBINSON HOUSE, FROM STONEWALL JACKSON'S POSITION.

was not ordered. But the public demand for an advance became imperative — stimulated perhaps by the successful dash of fifty men of the 2d United States Cavalry, under Lieutenant C. H. Tompkins, through the enemy's outposts at Fairfax Court House on the night of June 1st, and by the unfortunate result of the movement of a regiment under General Schenck toward Vienna, June 9th, as well as by a disaster to some of General Butler's troops on the 10th at Big Bethel, near Fort Monroe. On the 24th of June, in compliance with verbal instructions from General Scott, McDowell submitted a "plan of operations and the composition of the force required to carry it into effect." He estimated the Confederate force at Manassas Junction and its dependencies at 25,000 men, assumed that his movements could not be kept secret and that the enemy would call up additional forces from all quarters, and added: "If General J. E. Johnston's force is kept engaged by Major-General Patterson, and Major-General Butler occupies the force now in his vicinity, I think they will not be able to bring up more than ten thousand men, so we may calculate upon having to do with about 35,000 men." And as it turned out, that was about the number he "had to do with." For the advance, McDowell asked "a force of 30,000 of all arms, with a reserve of 10,000." He knew that Beauregard had batteries in position at several places in front of Bull Run and defensive works behind the Run and at Manassas Junction. The stream being fordable at many places, McDowell proposed in his plan of operations to turn the enemy's position and force him out of it by seizing or threatening his communications. Nevertheless, he said in his report:

"Believing the chances are greatly in favor of the enemy's accepting battle between this and the Junction,

and that the consequences of that battle will be of the greatest importance to the country, as establishing the prestige in this contest, on the one side or the other,— the more so as the two sections will be fairly represented by regiments from almost every State,— I think it of great consequence that, as for the most part our regiments are exceedingly raw and the best of them, with few exceptions, not over steady in line, they be organized into as many small fixed brigades as the number of regular colonels will admit, . . . so that the men may have as fair a chance as the nature of things and the comparative inexperience of most will allow."

This remarkably sound report was approved, and McDowell was directed to carry his plan into effect July 8th. But the government machinery worked slowly and there was jealousy in the way, so that the troops to bring his army up to the strength agreed upon did not reach him until the 16th.

Beauregard's Army of the Potomac at Manassas consisted of the brigades of Holmes, Bonham, Ewell, D. R. Jones, Longstreet, Cocke, and Early, and of 3 regiments of infantry, 1 regiment and 3 battalions of cavalry, and 6 batteries of artillery, containing in all 27 guns, making an aggregate available force on the field of Bull Run of about 23,000 men. Johnston's army from the Shenandoah consisted of the brigades of Jackson, Bee, Bartow, and Kirby Smith, 2 regiments of infantry not brigaded, 1 regiment of cavalry (12 companies), and 5 batteries (20 guns), making an aggregate at Bull Run of 8340.

McDowell's army consisted of 5 divisions: Tyler's First Division, containing 4 brigades (Keyes's, Schenck's, W. T. Sherman's, and Richardson's); Hunter's Second Division, containing 2 brigades (Andrew Porter's and Burnside's); Heintzelman's Third Division, containing 3 brigades (Franklin's, Willcox's, and Howard's); Runyon's Fourth Divi-

sion (9 regiments not brigades); and Miles's Fifth Division, containing 2 brigades (Blenker's and Davies's)—10 batteries of artillery, besides 2 guns attached to infantry regiments, 49 guns in all, and 7 companies of regular cavalry. Of the foregoing forces, 9 of the batteries and 8 companies of infantry were regulars, and 1 small battalion was marines. The aggregate force was about 35,000 men. Runyon's Fourth Division was 6 or 7 miles in the rear guarding the road to Alexandria, and, though counted in the aggregate, was not embraced in McDowell's order for battle.

There was an ill-suppressed feeling of sympathy with the Confederacy in the Southern element of Washington society; but the halls of Congress resounded with the eloquence of Union speakers. Martial music filled the air, and war was the topic wherever men met. By day and night the tramp of soldiers was heard, and staff-officers and orderlies galloped through the streets between the headquarters of Generals Scott and McDowell. Northern enthusiasm was unbounded. "On to Richmond!" was the war-cry. Public sentiment was irresistible, and in response to it the army advanced. It was a glorious spectacle. The various regiments were brilliantly uniformed according to the esthetic taste of peace, and the silken banners they flung to the breeze were unsoiled and untorn. The bitter realities of war were nearer than we knew.

McDowell marched on the afternoon of July 16th, the men carrying three days' rations in their haversacks; provision wagons were to follow from Alexandria the next day. On the morning of the 18th his forces were concentrated at Centreville, a point about 20 miles west of the Potomac and 6 or 7 miles east of Manassas Junction. Beauregard's outposts fell back without resistance. Bull Run,

flowing south-easterly, is about half-way between Centreville and Manassas Junction, and owing to its abrupt banks, the timber with which it was fringed, and some artificial defenses at the fords, was a formidable obstacle. The stream was fordable, but all the crossings for eight miles, from Union Mills on the south to the Stone Bridge on the north, were defended by Beauregard's forces. The Warrenton Turnpike, passing through Centreville, leads nearly due west, crossing Bull Run at the Stone Bridge. The direct road from Centreville to Manassas crosses Bull Run at Mitchell's Ford, half a mile or so above another crossing known as Blackburn's Ford. Union Mills was covered by Ewell's brigade, supported after the 18th by Holmes's brigade; McLean's Ford, next to the north, was covered by D. R. Jones's brigade; Blackburn's Ford was defended by Longstreet's brigade, supported by Early's brigade; Mitchell's Ford was held by Bonham's brigade, with an outpost of two guns and an infantry support east of Bull Run; the stream between Mitchell's Ford and the Stone Bridge was covered by Cocke's brigade; the Stone Bridge on the Confederate left was held by Evans with 1 regiment and Wheat's special battalion of infantry, 1 battery of 4 guns, and two companies of cavalry.

McDowell was compelled to wait at Centreville until his provision wagons arrived and he could issue rations. His orders having carried his leading division under Tyler no farther than Centreville, he wrote that officer at 8:15 A. M. on the 18th, "Observe well the roads to Bull Run and to Warrenton. Do not bring on an engagement, but keep up the impression that we are moving on Manassas." McDowell then went to the extreme left of his line to examine the country with reference to a

SUDLEY SPRINGS FORD, LOOKING NORTH.
From a sketch made in 1884.

RUINS OF THE STONE BRIDGE.
Looking along the Warrenton Turnpike toward the battle-field.

sudden movement of the army to turn the enemy's right flank. The reconnoissance showed him that the country was unfavorable to the movement, and he abandoned it. While he was gone to the left, Tyler, presumably to "keep up the impression that we were moving on Manassas," went forward from Centreville with a squadron of cavalry and two companies of infantry for the purpose of making a reconnoissance of Mitchell's and Blackburn's fords along the direct road to Manassas. The force of the enemy at these fords has just been given. Reaching the crest of the ridge overlooking the valley of Bull Run, and a mile or so from the stream, the enemy was seen on the opposite bank, and Tyler brought up Benjamin's artillery, 2 20-pounder rifled guns, Ayres's field battery of 6 guns, and Richardson's brigade of infantry. The 20-pounders opened from the ridge, and a few shots were exchanged with the enemy's batteries. Desiring more information than the long-range cannonade afforded, Tyler ordered Richardson's brigade and a section of Ayres's battery, supported by a squadron of cavalry, to move from the ridge across the open bottom of Bull Run and take position near the stream and have skirmishers "scour the thick woods" which skirted it. Two regiments of infantry, 2 pieces of artillery, and a squadron of cavalry moved down the slope into the woods and opened fire, driving Bonham's outpost to the cover of intrenchments across the stream. The brigades of Bonham and Longstreet, the latter being reinforced for the occasion by Early's brigade, responded at short range to the fire of the Federal reconnoitering force and drove it back in disorder. Tyler reported that having satisfied

himself "that the enemy was in force," and ascertained "the position of his batteries," he withdrew. This unauthorized reconnoissance, called by the Federals the affair at Blackburn's Ford, was regarded at the time by the Confederates as a serious attack, and was dignified by the name of the "battle of Bull Run," the engagement of the 21st being called by them the battle of Manassas. The Confederates, feeling that they had repulsed a heavy and real attack, were encouraged by the result. The Federal troops, on the other hand, were greatly depressed. The regiment which suffered most was completely demoralized, and McDowell thought that the depression of the repulse was felt throughout his army, and produced its effect upon the Pennsylvania regiment and the New York battery, which insisted (their terms having expired) upon their discharge, and on the 21st, as he expressed it, "marched to the rear to the sound of the enemy's cannon." Even Tyler himself felt the depressing effect of his repulse, if we may judge by his cautious and feeble action on the 21st when dash was required.

The operations of the 18th confirmed McDowell in his opinion that with his raw troops the Confederate position should be turned instead of attacked in front. Careful examination had satisfied him that the country did not favor a movement to turn the enemy's right. On the night of the 18th the haversacks of his men were empty, and had to be replenished from the provision wagons, which were late in getting up. Nor had he yet determined upon his point or plan of attack. While resting and provisioning his men, he devoted the 19th and 20th to a careful examination by his en-

gineers of the enemy's position and the intervening country. His men, not soldiers, but civilians in uniform, unused to marching, hot, weary, and footsore, dropped down as they had halted and bivouacked on the roads about Centreville. Notwithstanding Beauregard's elation over the affair at Blackburn's Ford on the 18th, he permitted the 19th and 20th to pass without a movement to follow up the advantage he had gained. During these two days, McDowell carefully examined the Confederate position, and made his plan to manœuvre the enemy out of it. Beauregard ordered no aggressive movement until the 21st, and then, as appears from his own statement, through miscarriage of orders and lack of apprehension on the part of subordinates, the effort was a complete *fiasco*, with the comical result of frightening his own troops, who, late in the afternoon, mistook the return of one of their brigades for an attack by McDowell's left, and the serious result of interfering with the pursuit after he had gained the battle of the 21st.

But Beauregard, though not aggressive on the 19th and 20th, was not idle within his own lines. The Confederate President had authorized Johnston, Beauregard's senior, to use his discretion in moving to the support of Manassas, and Beauregard, urging Johnston to do so, sent railway transportation for the Shenandoah forces. But, as he states, "he at the same time submitted the alternative proposition to Johnston that, having passed the Blue Ridge, he should assemble his forces, press forward by way of Aldie, northwest of Manassas, and fall upon McDowell's right rear," while he, Beauregard, "prepared for the operation at the first sound of the conflict, should strenuously

assume the offensive in front." "The situation and circumstances specially favored the signal success of such an operation," says Beauregard. An attack by two armies moving from opposite points upon an enemy, with the time of attack for one depending upon the sound of the other's cannon, is hazardous even with well-disciplined and well-seasoned troops, and is next to fatal with raw levies. Johnston chose the wiser course of moving by rail to Manassas, thus preserving the benefit of "interior lines," which, Beauregard says, was the "sole military advantage at the moment that the Confederates possessed."

The campaign which General Scott required McDowell to make was undertaken with the understanding that Johnston should be prevented from joining Beauregard. With no lack of confidence in himself, McDowell was dominated by the feeling of subordination and deference to General Scott which at that time pervaded the whole army, and General Scott, who controlled both McDowell and Patterson, assured McDowell that Johnston should not join Beauregard without having "Patterson on his heels." Yet Johnston's army, nearly nine thousand strong, joined Beauregard, Bee's brigade and Johnston in person arriving on the morning of the 20th, the remainder about noon on the 21st. Although the enforced delay at Centreville enabled McDowell to provision his troops and gain information upon which to base an excellent plan of attack, it proved fatal by affording time for a junction of the opposing forces. On the 21st of July General Scott addressed a despatch to McDowell, saying: "It is known that a strong reinforcement left Winchester on the afternoon of the 18th, which

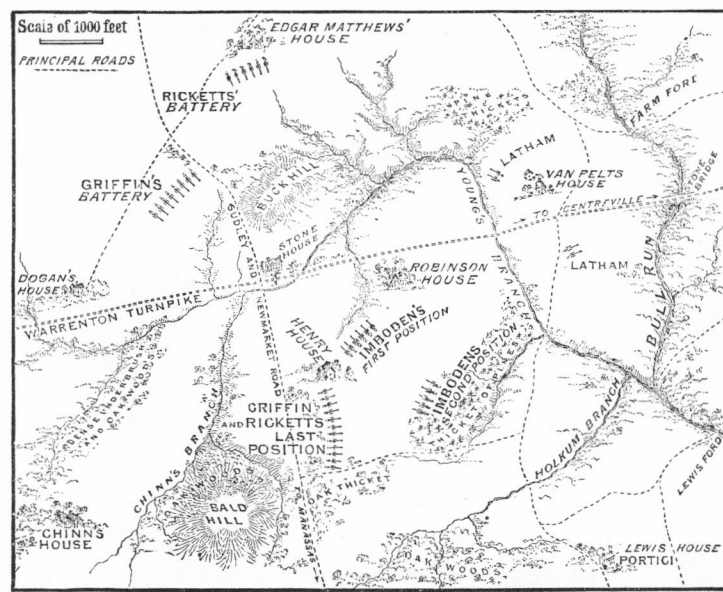

PLAN OF THE BULL RUN BATTLE-FIELD.

A CHARGE TO RECAPTURE RICKETTS'S AND GRIFFIN'S BATTERIES.

you will also have to beat. Four new regiments will leave to-day to be at Fairfax Station to-night. Others shall follow to-morrow—twice the number if necessary." When this despatch was penned, McDowell was fighting the "strong reinforcement" which left Winchester on the 18th. General Scott's report that Beauregard had been reinforced, the information that four regiments had been sent to McDowell, and the promise that twice the number would be sent if necessary, all came too late—and Patterson came not at all.

During the 19th and 20th the bivouacs of McDowell's army at Centreville, almost within cannon-range of the enemy, were thronged by visitors, official and unofficial, who came in carriages from Washington, bringing their own supplies. They were under no military restraint, and passed to and fro among the troops as they pleased, giving the scene the appearance of a monster military picnic. Among others, the venerable Secretary of War, Cameron, called upon McDowell. Whether due to a naturally serious expression, to a sense of responsibility, to a premonition of the fate of his brother who fell upon the field on the 21st, or to other cause, his countenance showed apprehension of evil; but men generally were confident and jovial.

McDowell's plan of battle, promulgated on the 20th, was to turn the enemy's left, force him from his defensive position, and, "if possible, destroy the railroad leading from Manassas to the Valley of Virginia, where the enemy has a large force." He did not know when he issued this order that Johnston had joined Beauregard, though he suspected it. Miles's Fifth Division, with Richardson's brigade of Tyler's division and a strong force of artillery, was to remain in reserve at Centreville, prepare defensive works there, and threaten Blackburn's Ford. Tyler's First Division, which was on the turnpike in advance, was to move at 2:30 A. M., threaten the Stone Bridge, and open fire upon it at

daybreak. This demonstration was to be vigorous, its first purpose being to divert attention from the movements of the turning column. As soon as Tyler's troops cleared the way, Hunter's Second Division, followed by Heintzelman's Third Division, was to move to a point on the Warrenton Turnpike about one or two miles east of Stone Bridge, and there take a country road to the right, cross the Run at Sudley Springs, come down upon the flank and rear of the enemy at the Stone Bridge, and force him to open the way for Tyler's division to cross there and attack, fresh and in full force.

Tyler's start was so late and his advance was so slow as to hold Hunter and Heintzelman 2 or 3 hours on the mile or two of the turnpike between their camps and the point at which they were to turn off for the flank march. This delay, and the fact that the flank march proved difficult and some 12 miles instead of about 6 as was expected, were of serious moment. The flanking column did not cross at Sudley Springs until 9:30 instead of 7, the long march, with its many interruptions, tired out the men, and the delay gave the enemy time to discover the turning movement. Tyler's operations against the Stone Bridge were feeble and ineffective. By 8 o'clock Evans was satisfied that he was in no danger in front, and perceived the movement to turn his position. He was on the left of the Confederate line, guarding the point where the Warrenton Turnpike, the great highway to the field, crossed Bull Run, the Confederate line of defense. He had no instructions to guide him in the emergency that had arisen. But he did not hesitate. Reporting his information and purpose to the adjoining commander, Cocke, and leaving 4 companies of infantry to deceive and hold Tyler at the bridge, Evans before 9 o'clock turned his back upon the point he was set to guard, marched a mile away, and, seizing the high ground to the north of Young's Branch of Bull Run, formed line

of battle at right angles to his former line, his left resting near the Sudley Springs road, by which Burnside with the head of the turning column was approaching, thus covering the Warrenton Turnpike and opposing a determined front to the Federal advance upon the Confederate left and rear. In his rear to the south lay the valley of Young's Branch, and rising from that was the higher ridge or plateau on which the Robinson House and the Henry House were situated, and on which the main action took place in the afternoon. Burnside, finding Evans across his path, promptly formed line of battle and attacked about 9:45 A. M. Hunter, the division commander, who was at the head of Burnside's brigade directing the formation of the first skirmish line, was severely wounded and taken to the rear at the opening of the action. Evans not only repulsed but pursued the troops that made the attack upon him. Andrew Porter's brigade of Hunter's division followed Burnside closely and came to his support. In the mean time Bee had formed a Confederate line of battle with his and Bartow's brigades of Johnston's army on the Henry house plateau, a stronger position than the one held by Evans, and desired Evans to fall back to that line; but Evans, probably feeling bound to cover the Warrenton Turnpike and hold it against Tyler as well as against the flanking column, insisted that Bee should move across the valley to his support, which was done.

After Bee joined Evans, the preliminary battle continued to rage upon the ground chosen by the latter. The opposing forces were Burnside's and Porter's brigades, with one regiment of Heintzelman's division on the Federal side, and Evans's, Bee's, and Bartow's brigades on the Confederate side. The Confederates were dislodged and driven back to the Henry house plateau, where Bee had previously formed line and where what Beauregard called "the mingled remnants of Bee's, Bartow's, and Evans's commands" were re-formed

under cover of Stonewall Jackson's brigade of Johnston's army.

The time of this repulse, as proved by so accurate an authority as Stonewall Jackson, was before 11:30 A. M., and this is substantially confirmed by Beauregard's official report made at the time. Sherman and Keyes had nothing to do with it. They did not begin to cross Bull Run until noon. Thus, after nearly two hours' stubborn fighting with the forces of Johnston, which General Scott had promised should be kept away, McDowell won the first advantage; but Johnston had cost him dearly.

During all this time Johnston and Beauregard had been waiting near Mitchell's Ford for the development of the attack they had ordered by their right upon McDowell at Centreville. The gravity of the situation upon their left had not yet dawned upon them. What might the result have been if the Union column had not been detained by Tyler's delay in moving out in the early morning, or if Johnston's army, to which Bee, Bartow, and Jackson belonged, had not arrived?

But the heavy firing on the left soon diverted Johnston and Beauregard from all thought of an offensive movement with their right, and decided them, as Beauregard has said, "to hurry up all available reinforcements, including the reserves that were to have moved upon Centreville, to our left, and fight the battle out in that quarter." Thereupon Beauregard ordered "Ewell, Jones, and Longstreet to make a strong demonstration all along their front on the other side of Bull Run, and ordered the reserves, Holmes's brigade with six guns, and Early's brigade, to move swiftly to the left," and he and Johnston set out at full speed for the point of conflict, which they reached while Bee was attempting to rally his men about Jackson's brigade on the Henry house plateau. McDowell had waited in the morning at the point on the Warrenton Turnpike where his flanking column

THE ROBINSON HOUSE.
This is the house shown in the illustrations on pages 25 and 32.
From a war-time photograph.

THE SUDLEY SPRINGS ROAD.
Looking toward Sudley Springs from the slope of the Henry House hill.

turned to the right, until the troops, except Howard's brigade, which he halted at that point, had passed. He gazed silently and with evident pride upon the gay regiments as they filed briskly but quietly past in the freshness of the early morning, and then, remarking to his staff, "Gentlemen, that is a big force," he mounted and moved forward to the field by way of Sudley Springs. He reached the scene of actual conflict somewhat earlier than Johnston and Beauregard did, and, seeing the enemy driven across the valley of Young's Branch and behind the Warrenton Turnpike, at once sent a swift aide-de-camp to Tyler with orders to "press the attack" at the Stone Bridge. Tyler acknowledged that he received this order by 11 o'clock. It was Tyler's division upon which McDowell relied for the decisive fighting of the day. He knew that the march of the turning column would be fatiguing, and when by a sturdy fight it had cleared the Warrenton Turnpike for the advance of Tyler's division, it had, in fact, done more than its fair proportion of the work. But Tyler did not attempt to force the passage of the Stone Bridge, which, after about 8 o'clock, was defended by only four companies of infantry, though he admitted that by the plan of battle, when Hunter and Heintzelman had attacked the enemy in the vicinity of the Stone Bridge, "he was to force the passage of Bull Run at that point and attack the enemy in flank." Soon after McDowell's arrival at the front, Burnside rode up to him and said that his brigade had borne the brunt of the battle, that it was out of ammunition, and that he wanted permission to withdraw, refit and fill cartridge-boxes. McDowell in the excitement of the occasion gave reluctant consent, and the brigade, which certainly had done nobly, marched to the rear, stacked arms, and took no further part in the fight. Having sent the order to Tyler to press his attack, and orders to

the rear of the turning column to hurry forward, McDowell, like Beauregard, rushed in person into the conflict, and by the force of circumstances became for the time the commander of the turning column and the force actually engaged, rather than the commander of his whole army. With the exception of sending his adjutant-general to find and hurry Tyler forward, his subsequent orders were mainly or wholly to the troops under his own observation. Unlike Beauregard, he had no Johnston in rear with full authority and knowledge of the situation to throw forward reserves and reinforcements. It was not until 12 o'clock that Sherman received orders from Tyler to cross the stream, which he did at a ford above the Stone Bridge, going to the assistance of Hunter. Sherman reported to McDowell on the field and joined in the pursuit of Bee's forces across the valley of Young's Branch. Keyes's brigade, accompanied by Tyler in person, followed across the stream where Sherman forded, but without uniting with the other forces on the field, made a feeble advance upon the slope of the plateau toward the Robinson house, and then about 2 o'clock filed off by flank to its left and, sheltered by the east front of the bluff that forms the plateau, marched down Young's Branch out of sight of the enemy and took no further part in the engagement. McDowell did not know where it was, nor did he then know that Schenck's brigade of Tyler's division did not cross the Run at all.

The line taken up by Stonewall Jackson upon which Bee, Bartow, and Evans rallied on the southern part of the plateau was a very strong one. The ground was high and afforded the cover of a curvilinear wood with the concave side toward the Federal line of attack. According to Beauregard's official report made at the time, he had upon this part of the field, at the beginning, 6500 infantry, 13 pieces of artillery, and 2 companies of cavalry,

and this line was continuously reinforced from Beauregard's own reserves and by the arrival of the troops from the Shenandoah Valley.

To carry this formidable position, McDowell had at hand the brigades of Franklin, Willcox, Sherman, and Porter, Palmer's battalion of regular cavalry, and Ricketts's and Griffin's regular batteries. Porter's brigade had been reduced and shaken by the morning fight. Howard's brigade was in reserve, and only came into action late in the afternoon. The men, unused to field service, and not yet over the hot and dusty march from the Potomac, had been under arms since midnight. The plateau, however, was promptly assaulted, the northern part of it was carried, the batteries of Ricketts and Griffin were planted near the Henry house, and McDowell clambered to the upper story of that structure to get a glance at the whole field. Upon the Henry house plateau, of which the Confederates held the southern and the Federals the northern part, the tide of battle ebbed and flowed as McDowell pushed in Franklin's, Willcox's, Sherman's, Porter's, and at last Howard's brigades, and as Beauregard put into action reserves which Johnston sent from the right and reinforcements which he hurried forward from the Shenandoah Valley as they arrived by cars. On the plateau, Beauregard says, the disadvantage of his "smooth-bore guns" was reduced by the shortness of range." The short range was due to the Federal advance, and the several struggles for the plateau were at close quarters and gallant on both sides. The batteries of Ricketts and Griffin, by their fine discipline, wonderful daring, and matchless skill, were the prime features in the fight. The battle was not lost till they were lost. When in their advanced and perilous position, and just after their infantry supports had been driven over the slopes, a fatal mistake occurred. A regiment of infantry came out of the woods on

Griffin's right, and as he was in the act of opening upon it with canister, he was deterred by the assurance of Major Barry, the chief of artillery, that it "was a regiment sent by Colonel Heintzelman to support the battery." A moment more and the doubtful regiment proved its identity by a deadly volley, and, as Griffin states in his official report, "every cannoneer was cut down and a large number of horses killed, leaving the battery (which was without support excepting in name) perfectly helpless." The effect upon Ricketts was equally fatal. He, desperately wounded, and Ramsay, his lieutenant, killed, lay in the wreck of the battery. Beauregard speaks of his last advance on the plateau as "leaving in our final possession the Robinson and Henry houses, with most of Ricketts's and Griffin's batteries, the men of which were mostly shot down where they bravely stood by their guns." Having become separated from McDowell, I fell in with Barnard, his chief engineer, and while together we observed the New York Fire Zouaves, who had been supporting Griffin's battery, fleeing to the rear in their gaudy uniforms, in utter confusion. Thereupon I rode back to where I knew Burnside's brigade was at rest, and stated to Burnside the condition of affairs, with the suggestion that he form and move his brigade to the front. Returning, I again met Barnard, and as the battle seemed to him and me to be going against us, and not knowing where McDowell was, with the concurrence of Barnard, as stated in his official report, I immediately sent a note to Miles, telling him to move two brigades of his reserve up to the Stone Bridge and telegraph to Washington to send forward all the troops that could be spared.

After the arrival of Howard's brigade, McDowell for the last time pressed up the slope to the plateau, forced back the Confederate line, and regained possession of the Henry and Robinson houses and of the lost batteries. But there were no longer cannoneers to man or horses to move these guns that had done so much. By the arrival upon this part of the field of his own reserves and Kirby Smith's brigade of Johnston's army about half-past three, Beauregard extended his left to outflank McDowell's shattered, shortened, and disconnected line, and the Federals left the field about half-past four. Until then they had fought wonderfully well for raw troops. There were no fresh forces on the field to support or encourage them, and the men seemed to be seized simultaneously by the conviction that it was no use

UNIFORM OF THE 2D OHIO AT BULL RUN.
From a photograph.

to do anything more and they might as well start home. Cohesion was lost, the organizations with some exceptions being disintegrated, and the men quietly walked off. There was no special excitement except that arising from the frantic efforts of officers to stop men who paid little or no attention to anything that was said. On the high ground by the Matthews house, about where Evans had taken position in the morning to check Burnside, McDowell and his staff, aided by other officers, made a desperate but futile effort to arrest the masses and form them into line. There, I went to Arnold's battery as it came by, and advised that he unlimber and make a stand as a rallying-point, which he did, saying he was in fair condition and ready to fight as long as there was any fighting to be done. But all efforts failed. The stragglers moved past the guns, in spite of all that could be done, and, as stated in his report, Arnold at my direction joined Sykes's battalion of infantry of Porter's brigade and Palmer's battalion of cavalry, all of the regular army, to cover the rear, as the men trooped back in great disorder across Bull Run. There were some hours of daylight for the Confederates to gather the fruits of victory, but a few rounds of shell and canister checked all the pursuit that was attempted, and the occasion called for no sacrifices or valorous deeds by the stanch regulars of the rear-guard. There was no panic, in the ordinary meaning of the word, until the retiring soldiers, guns, wagons, congressmen, and carriages were fired upon, on the road east of Bull Run. Then the panic began, and the bridge over Cub Run being rendered impassable for vehicles by a wagon that was upset upon it, utter confusion set in: pleasure-carriages, gun-carriages, and ammunition wagons which could not be put across the Run were abandoned, and blocked the way, and stragglers broke and threw aside their muskets and cut horses from their harness and rode off upon them. In leaving the field the men took the same routes, in a general way, by which they had reached it. Hence when the men of Hunter's and Heintzelman's divisions got back to Centreville, they had walked about 25 miles. That night they walked back to the Potomac, an additional distance of 20 miles; so that these un-

disciplined and unseasoned men within 36 hours walked fully 45 miles, besides fighting from about 10 A. M. until 4 P. M. on a hot and dusty day in July. McDowell in person reached Centreville before sunset, and found there Miles's division with Richardson's brigade and 3 regiments of Runyon's division, and Hunt's, Tidball's, Ayres's, and Greene's batteries and one or two fragments of batteries, making about 20 guns. It was a formidable force, but there was a lack of food, and the mass of the army was completely demoralized. Beauregard had about an equal force which had not been in the fight, consisting of Ewell's, Jones's, and Longstreet's brigades and some troops of other brigades. McDowell consulted the division and brigade commanders who were at hand upon the question of making a stand or retreating. The verdict was in favor of the latter, but a decision of officers one way or the other was of no moment; the men had already decided for themselves and were streaming away to the rear, in spite of all that could be done. They had no interest or treasure in Centreville, and their hearts were not there. Their tents, provisions, baggage, and letters from home were upon the banks of the Potomac, and no power could have stopped them short of the camps they had left less than a week before. As before stated, most of them were sovereigns in uniform, not soldiers. McDowell accepted the situation, detailed Richardson's and Blenker's brigades to cover the retreat, and the army, a disorganized mass, with some creditable exceptions, drifted as the men pleased away from the scene of action. There was no pursuit, and the march from Centreville was as barren of opportunities for the rear-guard as the withdrawal from the field of battle had been. When McDowell reached Fairfax Court House in the night, he was in communication with Washington and exchanged telegrams with General Scott, in one of which the old hero said, "We are not discouraged"; but that despatch did not lighten the gloom in which it was received. McDowell was so tired that while sitting on the ground writing a despatch he fell asleep, pencil in hand, in the middle of a sentence. His adjutant-general aroused him; the despatch was finished, and the weary ride to the Potomac resumed. When the unfortunate commander dismounted at Arlington next forenoon in a soaking rain, after 32 hours in the saddle, his disastrous campaign of 6 days was closed.

The first martial effervescence of the country was over. The three-months men went home, and the three-months chapter of the war ended — with the South triumphant and confident; the North disappointed but determined.

THE NEW HENRY HOUSE
Showing the Union monument of the first battle.
From a photograph taken in 1884.

THE LONG BRIDGE, WASHINGTON.
The Troops retreating from Bull Run came into the capital over this bridge.

IN WASHINGTON AFTER THE BATTLE.
BY WALT WHITMAN.

THE scene in Washington after the battle has been graphically described by Walt Whitman, from whose "Specimen Days and Collect" (Philadelphia: Rees, Welch & Co.) we make these extracts:

"The defeated troops commenced pouring into Washington over the Long Bridge at daylight on Monday, 22d — day drizzling all through with rain. The Saturday and Sunday of the battle (20th, 21st) had been parched and hot to an extreme — the dust, the grime and smoke, in layers, sweated in, follow'd by other layers again sweated in, absorb'd by those excited souls — their clothes all saturated with the clay-powder filling the air — stirr'd up everywhere on the dry roads and trodden fields by the regiments, swarming wagons, artillery, etc.—all the men with this coating of murk and sweat and rain, now recoiling back, pouring over the Long Bridge — a horrible march of twenty miles, returning to Washington baffled, humiliated, panic-struck. Where are the vaunts and the proud boasts with which you went forth? Where are your banners, and your bands of music, and your ropes to bring back your prisoners? Well, there is n't a band playing — and there is n't a flag but clings ashamed and lank to its staff.

"The sun rises, but shines not. The men appear, at first sparsely and shame-faced enough, then thicker, in the streets of Washington — appear in Pennsylvania Avenue, and on the steps and basement entrances. They come along in disorderly mobs, some in squads, stragglers, companies. Occasionally, a rare regiment, in perfect order, with its officers (some gaps, dead, the true braves), marching in silence, with lowering faces, stern, weary to sinking, all black and dirty, but every man with his musket, and stepping alive; but these are the exceptions. Sidewalks of Pennsylvania Avenue, Fourteenth street, etc., crowded, jamm'd with citizens, darkies, clerks, everybody, lookers-on; women in the windows, curious expressions from faces, as those swarms of dirt-cover'd return'd soldiers there (will they never end?) move by; but nothing said, no comments (half our lookers-on 'secesh' of the most venomous kind — they say nothing; but the devil snickers in their faces). During the forenoon, Washington gets all over motley with these defeated soldiers — queer-looking objects, strange eyes and faces, drench'd (the steady rain drizzles

on all day) and fearfully worn, hungry, haggard, blister'd in the feet. Good people (but not over-many of them either) hurry up something for their grub. They put wash-kettles on the fire, for soup, for coffee. They set tables on the sidewalks — wagon-loads of bread are purchas'd, swiftly cut in stout chunks. Here are two aged ladies, beautiful, the first in the city for culture and charm; they stand with store of eating and drink at an improvis'd table of rough plank, and give food, and have the store replenish'd from their house every half-hour all that day; and there in the rain they stand, active, silent, white-hair'd, and give food, though the tears stream down their cheeks, almost without intermission, the whole time. Amid the deep excitement, crowds and motion, and desperate eagerness, it seems strange to see many, very many, of the soldiers sleeping — in the midst of all, sleeping sound. They drop down anywhere, on the steps of houses, up close by the basements or fences, on the sidewalk, aside on some vacant lot, and deeply sleep. A poor seventeen- or eighteen-year old boy lies there, on the stoop of a grand house; he sleeps so calmly, so profoundly. Some clutch their muskets firmly even in sleep. Some in squads; comrades, brothers, close together — and on them, as they lay, sulkily drips the rain. . . .

"But the hour, the day, the night pass'd, and whatever returns, an hour, a day, a night like that can never again return. The President, recovering himself, begins that very night — sternly, rapidly sets about the task of reorganizing his forces, and placing himself in positions for future and surer work. If there were nothing else of Abraham Lincoln for history to stamp him with, it is enough to send him with his wreath to the memory of all future time, that he endured that hour, that day, bitterer than gall — indeed, a crucifixion day — that it did not conquer him — that he unflinchingly stemm'd it, and resolv'd to lift himself and the Union out of it."

NOTE.— The revised losses at the battle of Bull Run are as follows: Federal, 16 officers and 444 enlisted men killed; 78 officers and 1046 enlisted men wounded; 50 officers and 1262 enlisted men missing; 25 pieces of artillery and a large quantity of small arms. Confederate, 25 officers and 362 enlisted men killed; 63 officers and 1519 enlisted men wounded; 1 officer and 12 enlisted men missing.

From a photograph taken after the war.

R E Lee J. E. Johnston

BATTERY, FORWARD!

THE CONFEDERATE SIDE AT BULL RUN.

IN THE THICK OF THE FIGHT.

BY JOHN D. IMBODEN, BRIGADIER-GENERAL, C. S. A.

Commanding a battery of artillery at Bull Run.

. . . It was at this time that McDowell committed, as I think, the fatal blunder of the day, by ordering both Ricketts's and Griffin's batteries to cease firing and move across the turnpike to the top of the Henry Hill, and take position on the west side of the house. The short time required to effect the change enabled Beauregard to arrange his new line of battle on the highest crest of the hill, southeast of the Henry and Robinson houses, in the edge of the pines. If one of the Federal batteries had been left north of Young's Branch, it could have so swept the hill-top where we re-formed, that it would have greatly delayed, if not wholly have prevented, us from occupying the position. And if we had been forced back to the next hill, on which stands the Lewis house, Sherman, who had crossed Bull Run not far above the Stone Bridge at a farm ford, would have had a fair swing at our right flank, to say nothing of the effect of the artillery playing upon us from beyond Bull Run.

When my retiring battery met Jackson, and he assumed command of us, I reported that I had remaining only three rounds of ammunition for a single gun, and suggested that the caissons be sent to the rear for a supply. He said, "No, not now—wait till other guns get here, and then you can withdraw your battery, as it has been so torn to pieces, and let your men rest."

During the lull in front, my men lay about, exhausted from want of water and food, and black with powder, smoke, and dust. Lieutenant Harman and I had amused ourselves training one of the guns on a heavy column of the enemy, who were advancing toward us, in the direction of the Chinn house, but were still 1200 to 1500 yards away. While we were thus engaged, General Jackson rode up and said that three or four batteries were approaching rapidly, and that we might soon retire. I asked permission to fire the three rounds of shrapnel left to us, and he said, "Go ahead." I picked up a charge (the fuse was cut and ready) and rammed it home myself, remarking to Harman, "Tom, put in the primer and pull her off." I forgot to step back far enough from the muzzle,

and, as I wanted to see the shell strike, I squatted to be under the smoke, and gave the word "Fire." Heavens! what a report. Finding myself full twenty feet away, I thought the gun had burst. But it was only the pent-up gas, that, escaping sideways as the shot cleared the muzzle, had struck my side and head with great violence. I recovered in time to see the shell explode in the enemy's ranks. The blood gushed out of my left ear, and from that day to this it has been totally deaf. The men fired the other two rounds, and limbered up and moved away, just as the Rockbridge Artillery, under Lieutenant Brockenbrough, came into position, followed a moment later by the Leesburg Artillery, under Lieutenant Henry Heaton. Pendleton, supposed by me still to be captain of the first, as Rogers was of the second, were not with their batteries when they unlimbered. But Heaton and Brockenbrough were equal to the occasion. Heaton had been under my command with his battery at the Point of Rocks, below Harper's Ferry, the previous May, and was a brave and skilful young officer. Several other batteries soon came into line, so that by the time Griffin and Ricketts were in position near the Henry house, we had, as I now remember, 26 fresh guns ready for them.

The contest that ensued was terrific. Jackson ordered me to go from battery to battery and see that the guns were properly aimed and the fuses cut the right length. This was the work of but a few minutes. On returning to the left of the line of guns, I stopped to ask General Jackson's permission to rejoin my battery. The fight was just then hot enough to make him feel well. His eyes fairly blazed. He had a way of throwing up his left hand with the open palm toward the person he was addressing, and as he told me to go, he made this gesture. The air was full of flying missiles, and as he spoke he jerked down his hand, and I saw that blood was streaming from it. I exclaimed, "General, you are wounded." He replied, as he drew a handkerchief from his breast-pocket, and began to bind it up, "Only a scratch—a mere scratch," and galloped away along his line.

To save my horse, I had hitched him in a little

THE McLEAN HOUSE.
General Beauregard's headquarters near Manassas. (From a photograph.)

CONFEDERATE FORTIFICATIONS ABOUT MANASSAS JUNCTION.
This view is from a photograph taken in March, 1862. It represents the works substantially as
they were at the time of the battle.

gully some fifty yards or more in the rear. And to reach him, I had to pass the six hundred infantry of Hampton's Legion, who were lying down in supporting distance of our artillery, then all in full play. While I was untying my horse, a shell exploded in the midst of Hampton's infantry, killing several and stampeding 15 or 20 nearest the spot. I tried to rally them; but one huge fellow, musket in hand, and with bayonet fixed, had started on a run. I threw myself in his front with drawn sword, and threatened to cut him down, whereupon he made a lunge at me. I threw up my left arm to ward off the blow, and the bayonet-point ran under the wristband of my red flannel shirt, and raked the skin of my arm from wrist to shoulder. The blow knocked me sprawling on the ground, and the fellow got away. I tore off the dangling shirt-sleeve, and was bare-armed as to my left, the remainder of the fight.

I overtook my battery on the hill near the Lewis house, which was used as a hospital. In a field in front I saw General Johnston and his staff grouped on their horses, and under fire from numerous shells that reached that hill. I rode up to him, reported our ammunition all gone, and requested to know

where I could find the ordnance wagons and get a fresh supply. Observing the sorry plight of the battery and the condition of the surviving men and horses, he directed me to remove them farther to the rear to a place of perfect safety, and return myself to the field, where I might be of some service.

I took the battery back perhaps a mile, where we found a welcome little stream of water. Being greatly exhausted, I rested for perhaps an hour, and returned to the front with Sergeant Joseph Shumate.

When we regained the crest of the Henry plateau, the enemy had been swept from it, and the retreat had begun all along the line. We gazed upon the scene for a time, and, hearing firing between the Lewis house and the Stone Bridge, we rode back to see what it meant. Captain Lindsay Walker had arrived from Fredericksburg with his six-Parrott-gun battery, and from a high hill was shelling the fugitives beyond Bull Run as they were fleeing in wild disorder to the shelter of the nearest woods. Colonel J. E. B. Stuart, at the head of a body of yelling cavalry with drawn sabers, was sweeping round the base of the hill we were on, to cross the Run and fall upon the enemy. . . .

THE END OF THE BATTLE.

BY G. T. BEAUREGARD, GENERAL, C. S. A.

A brigadier-general in command of the Confederate Army of the Potomac at Bull Run.
General Jos. E. Johnston was in supreme command.

. . . It was now between half-past two and three o'clock; a scorching sun increased the oppression of the troops, exhausted from incessant fighting, many of them having been engaged since the morning. Fearing lest the Federal offensive should secure too firm a grip, and knowing the fatal result that might spring from any grave infraction of my line, I determined to make another effort for the recovery of the plateau, and ordered a charge of the entire line of battle, including the reserves, which at this crisis I myself led into action. The

movement was made with such keeping and dash that the whole plateau was swept clear of the enemy, who were driven down the slope and across the turnpike on our right and the valley of Young's Branch on our left, leaving in our final possession the Robinson and Henry houses, with most of Ricketts's and Griffin's batteries, the men of which were mostly shot down where they bravely stood by their guns. Fisher's 6th North Carolina, directed to the Lewis house by Colonel Jordan from Manassas, where it had just arrived, and thence to the

field by General Johnston, came up in happy time to join in this charge on the left. Withers's 18th Virginia, which I had ordered up from Cocke's brigade, was also on hand in time to follow and give additional effect to the charge, capturing, by aid of the Hampton Legion, several guns, which were immediately turned and served upon the broken ranks of the enemy by some of our officers. This handsome work, which broke the Federal fortunes of the day, was done, however, at severe cost. The soldierly Bee, and the gallant, impetuous Bartow, whose day of strong deeds was about to close with such credit, fell a few rods back of the Henry house, near the very spot whence in the morning they had first looked forth upon Evans's struggle with the enemy. Colonel Fisher also fell at the very head of his troops. Seeing Captain Ricketts, who was badly wounded in the leg, and having known him in the old army, I paused from my anxious duties to ask him whether I could do anything for him. He answered that he wanted to be sent back to Washington. As some of our prisoners were there held under threats of not being treated as prisoners of war, I replied that that must depend upon how our prisoners were treated, and ordered him to be carried to the rear. I mention this, because the report of the Federal Committee on the Conduct of the War exhibits Captain Ricketts as testifying that I only approached him to say that he would be treated as our prisoners might be treated. I sent my own surgeons to care for him, and allowed his wife to cross the lines and accompany him to Richmond; and my adjutant-general, Colonel Jordan, escorting her to the car that carried them to that city, personally attended to the comfortable placing of the wounded enemy for the journey.

That part of the enemy who occupied the woods

beyond our left and across the Sudley road had not been reached by the headlong charge which had swept their comrades from the plateau; but the now arriving reinforcements (Kershaw's 2d and Cash's 8th South Carolina) were led into that quarter. Kemper's battery also came up, preceded by its commander, who, while alone, fell into the hands of a number of the enemy, who took him prisoner, until a few moments later, when he handed them over to some of our own troops accompanying his battery. A small plateau, within the southwest angle of the Sudley and turnpike cross-roads, was still held by a strong Federal brigade — Howard's troops, together with Sykes's battalion of regulars; and while Kershaw and Cash, after passing through the skirts of the oak wood along the Sudley road, engaged this force, Kemper's battery was sent forward by Kershaw along the same road, into position near where a hostile battery had been captured, and whence it played upon the enemy in the open field.

Quickly following these regiments came Preston's 28th Virginia, which, passing through the woods, encountered and drove back some Michigan troops, capturing Brigadier-General Willcox. It was now about 3 o'clock, when another important reinforcement came to our aid — Elzey's brigade, 1700 strong, of the Army of the Shenandoah, which, coming from Piedmont by railroad, had arrived at Manassas station, 6 miles in rear of the battle-field, at noon, and had been without delay directed thence toward the field by Colonel Jordan, aided by Major T. G. Rhett, who that morning had passed from General Bonham's to General Johnston's staff. Upon nearing the vicinity of the Lewis house, the brigade was directed by a staff-officer sent by General Johnston toward the left of the field. As it reached the oak wood, just across the Sudley road, led by General Kirby Smith, the latter fell severely wounded; but the command devolved upon Colonel Elzey, an excellent officer, who was now guided by Captain D. B. Harris of the Engineers, a highly accomplished officer of my staff, still farther to the left and through the woods, so as to form an extension of the line of the preceding reinforcements. Beckham's battery, of the same command, was hurried forward by the Sudley road and around the woods into position near the Chinn house; from a well-selected point of action, in full view of the enemy that filled the open fields west of the Sudley road, it played with deadly and decisive effect upon their ranks, already under the fire of Elzey's brigade. Keyes's Federal brigade, which had made its way across the turnpike in rear of the Stone Bridge, was lurking along under cover of the ridges and a wood in order to turn my line on the right, but was easily repulsed by Latham's battery, already placed in position over that approach by Captain Harris, aided by Alburtis's battery, oppor-

RALLYING THE TROOPS OF BEE, BARTOW, AND EVANS, BEHIND THE ROBINSON HOUSE.

the arrival upon their flank of the Shenandoah forces marching from railroad trains halted *en route* with that aim — errors that have been repeated by a number of writers, and by an ambitious but superficial French author.

There were certain sentiments of a personal character clustering about this first battle, and personal anxiety as to its issue, that gladly accepted this theory. To this may be added the general readiness to accept a sentimental or ultra-dramatic explanation — a sorcery wrought by the delay or arrival of some force, or the death or coming of somebody, or any other single magical event — whereby history is easily caught, rather than to seek an understanding of that which is but the gradual result of the operation of many forces, both of opposing design and actual collision, modified more or less by the falls of chance. The personal sentiment, though natural enough at the time, has no place in any military estimate, or place of any kind at this day. The battle of Manassas was,

tunely sent to Latham's left by General Jackson, and supported by fragments of troops collected by staff-officers. Meanwhile the enemy had formed a line of battle of formidable proportions on the opposite height, and stretching in crescent outline, with flanks advanced, from the Pittsylvania (Carter) mansion on their left across the Sudley road in rear of Dogan's, and reaching toward the Chinn house. They offered a fine spectacle as they threw forward a cloud of skirmishers down the opposite slope, preparatory to a new assault against the line on the plateau. But their right was now severely pressed by the troops that had successively arrived; the forces in the southwest angle of the Sudley and Warrenton cross-roads were driven from their position, and as Early's brigade, which, by direction of General Johnston, had swept around by the rear of the woods through which Elzey had passed, appeared on the field, his line of march bore upon the flank of the enemy, now retiring in that quarter.

This movement by my extreme left was masked by the trend of the woods from many of our forces on the plateau; and bidding those of my staff and escort around me raise a loud cheer, I despatched the information to the several commands, with orders to go forward in a common charge. Before the full advance of the Confederate ranks the enemy's whole line, whose right was already yielding, irretrievably broke, fleeing across Bull Run by every available direction. Major Sykes's regulars, aided by Sherman's brigade, made a steady and

handsome withdrawal, protecting the rear of the routed forces, and enabling many to escape by the Stone Bridge. Having ordered in pursuit all the troops on the field, I went to the Lewis house, and, the battle being ended, turned over the command to General Johnston. Mounting a fresh horse,— the fourth on that day,—I started to press the pursuit which was being made by our infantry and cavalry, some of the latter having been sent by General Johnston from Lewis's Ford to intercept the enemy on the turnpike. I was soon overtaken, however, by a courier bearing a message from Major T. G. Rhett, General Johnston's chief-of-staff on duty at Manassas railroad station, informing me of a report that a large Federal force, having pierced our lower line on Bull Run, was moving upon Camp Pickens, my depot of supplies near Manassas. I returned, and communicated this important news to General Johnston. Upon consultation it was deemed best that I should take Ewell's and Holmes's brigades, which were hastening up to the battle-field, but too late for the action, and fall on this force of the enemy, while reinforcements should be sent me from the pursuing forces, who were to be recalled for that purpose. To head off the danger and gain time, I hastily mounted a force of infantry behind the cavalrymen then present, but, on approaching the line of march near McLean's Ford, which the Federals must have taken, I learned that the news was a false alarm, caught from the return of Gen-

eral Jones's forces to this side of the Run, the similarity of the uniforms and the direction of their march having convinced some nervous person that they were a force of the enemy. It was now almost dark, and too late to resume the broken pursuit; on my return I met the coming forces, and, as they were very tired, I ordered them to halt and bivouac for the night where they were.

After giving such attention as I could to the troops, I started for Manassas, where I arrived about 10 o'clock, and found Mr. Davis at my headquarters with General Johnston. Arriving from Richmond late in the afternoon, Mr. Davis had immediately galloped to the field, accompanied by Colonel Jordan. They had met between Manassas and the battle-field the usual number of stragglers to the rear, whose appearance belied the determined array then sweeping the enemy before it, but Mr. Davis had the happiness to arrive in time to witness the last of the Federals disappearing beyond Bull Run. The next morning I received from his hand at our breakfast-table my commission, dated July 21st, as General in the Army of the Confederate States, and after his return to Richmond the kind congratulations of the Secretary of War and of General Lee, then acting as military adviser to the President.

It was a point made at the time at the North that, just as the Confederate troops were about to break and flee, the Federal troops anticipated them by doing so, being struck into this precipitation by

like any other battle, a progression and development from the deliberate counter-employment of the military resources in hand, affected by accidents, as always, but of a kind very different from those referred to. My line of battle, which twice had not only withstood the enemy's attack, but had taken the offensive and driven him back in disorder, was becoming momentarily stronger from the arrival, at last, of the reinforcements provided for; and if the enemy had remained on the field till the arrival of Ewell and Holmes, they would have been so strongly outflanked that many who escaped would have been destroyed or captured. . . .

As to immediate results and trophies, we captured a great many stands of arms, batteries, equipments, standards, and flags, one of which was sent to me, through General Longstreet, as a personal compliment by the Texan "crack shot," Colonel B. F. Terry, who lowered it from its mast at Fairfax Court House, by cutting the halyards by means of his unerring rifle, as our troops next morning reoccupied that place. We captured also many prisoners, including a number of surgeons, whom (the first time in war) we treated not as prisoners, but as guests. Calling attention to their brave devotion to their wounded, I recommended to the War Department that they be sent home without exchange, together with some other prisoners, who had shown personal kindness to Colonel Jones, of the 4th Alabama, who had been mortally wounded early in the day.

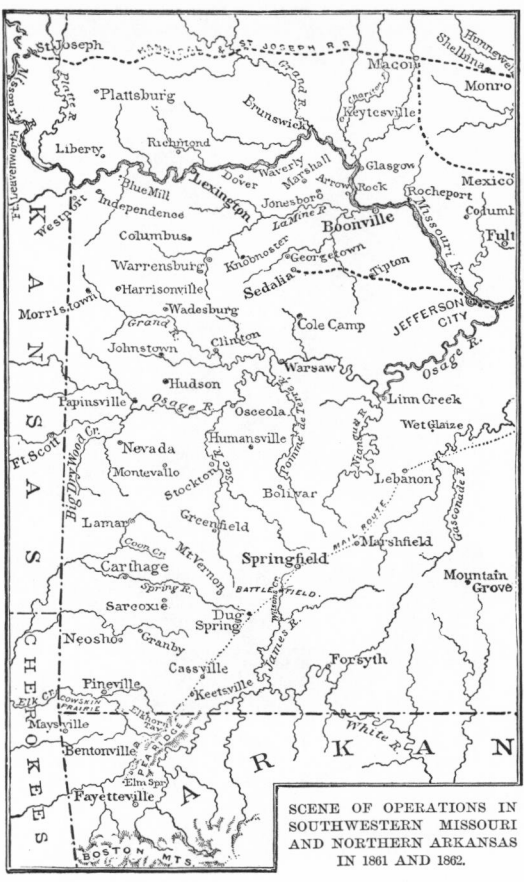

SCENE OF OPERATIONS IN
SOUTHWESTERN MISSOURI
AND NORTHERN ARKANSAS
IN 1861 AND 1862.

NARRATIVE OF EVENTS IN 1861.

VIRGINIA.—Major-General George B. McClellan, during the early summer, had defeated the Confederates in West Virginia and thus gained control of the State. Owing to the prestige of his successes here he was appointed to the command of the Army of the Potomac, which was organized immediately after McDowell's defeat at Bull Run.

On the 31st of October General Scott resigned the command of the armies, and McClellan was appointed to succeed him. McClellan performed the duties of General-in-Chief until March, 1862, and in that capacity directed the operations of all the armies east and west.

During the fall General W. S. Rosecrans opposed Robert E. Lee in West Virginia. The affair of Ball's Bluff on the Upper Potomac took place between a detachment of the Army of the Potomac under General C. P. Stone and a Confederate force belonging to Gen. Jos. E. Johnston's army. In the meantime operations were progressing elsewhere.

MISSOURI.—On May 10 Captain Nathaniel Lyon dispersed a Confederate camp near St. Louis and saved the Missouri Arsenal. The Missouri Confederates, under Sterling Price and Governor Claiborne F. Jackson, were forced across the border into Arkansas. On the 5th of July Colonel Franz Sigel, who had followed on the heels of the retreating Confederates with a small force, was defeated at Carthage in southwestern Missouri by Gov. Jackson. On the 25th of July General John C. Frémont reached St. Louis as the commander of the Western Military Department, which embraced Missouri. The main Union army in the field in the State at that time was at Lexington. It was commanded by Lyon, who had been promoted to brigadier-general. The Confederates confronting Lyon numbered about 10,000.

OFF TO THE WAR.

WILSON'S CREEK, AND THE DEATH OF LYON.

BY WILLIAM M. WHERRY, SIXTH U. S. INFANTRY, BREVET BRIGADIER-GENERAL, U. S. V.
At Wilson's Creek aide-de-camp to General Lyon.

ABOUT the middle of July, 1861, the Army of the Union in southwest Missouri, under General Nathaniel Lyon, was encamped in and near the town of Springfield, and numbered approximately 6200 men, of whom about 500 were ill-armed and undisciplined "Home Guards." The organized troops were in all 5868, in four brigades. By the 9th of August these were reduced to an aggregate of about 5300 men, with the 500 Home Guards additional. . . .

On the 8th of August a march in force was planned for the following night, to make an attack on the enemy's front at Wilson's Creek at daylight. From this intention General Lyon was dissuaded, after having called together the principal officers to receive their instructions. Many of the troops were exhausted, and all were tired; moreover, some supplies having arrived from Rolla, it was deemed wise to clothe and shoe the men as far as practicable, and to give them another day for recuperation.

On the 9th it was intended to march that evening with the whole force united, as agreed upon the 8th, and attack the enemy's left at daylight, and Lyon's staff were busied in visiting the troops and seeing that all things were in order. During the morning Colonel Sigel visited Lyon's headquarters, and had a prolonged conference, the result of which was that Colonel Sigel was ordered to detach his brigade, the 3d and 5th Missouri, one six-gun battery, one company of the 1st U. S. Cavalry, under Captain Eugene A. Carr, and one company of the 2d Dragoons, under Lieutenant Charles E. Farrand, for an attack upon the enemy from the south, while Lyon with the remainder of his available force should attack on the north.

The troops were put in march in the evening; those about Springfield immediately under General Lyon moving out to the west on the Little York road until joined by Sturgis's command from their camps, when they turned to the south across the prairie. The head of the main column reached the point where the enemy's pickets were expected to be found, about 1 A. M., and went into bivouac. Sigel's force, consisting of 1200 men and six pieces of artillery, moved four miles down the Fayetteville road, and then, making a long détour to the left by a by-road, arrived within a mile of the enemy's camp and rear at daylight.

In the vicinity of the Fayetteville road crossing, the creek acquires considerable depth, and in most places has rough, steep, and rather high banks, rendering fording difficult. On the left side the hills assume the proportion of bluffs; on the right or western bank, the ground is a succession of broken ridges, at that time covered for the most part with trees and a stunted growth of scrub oaks with dense foliage, which in places became an almost impenetrable tangle. Rough ravines and deep gullies cut up the surface.

The Confederates were under command of General Ben. McCulloch. On the west side of the stream, "Old Pap" Price, with his sturdy Missourians, men who in many later battles bore themselves with a valor and determination that won the plaudits of their comrades and the admiration of their foes, was holding the point south of Wilson's Creek, selected by Lyon for attack. Price's command consisted of five bodies of Missourians under Slack, Clark, Parsons, McBride, and Rains, the last-named being encamped farther up the stream. On the bluffs on the east side of the creek were Hébert's 3d Louisiana and McIntosh's Arkansas regiment, and, farther south, Pearce's brigade and two batteries, while other troops, under Greer, Churchill, and Major, were in the valley along the Fayetteville road, holding the extreme of the Confederate position.

Lyon put his troops in motion at early dawn on

BRIGADIER-GENERAL NATHANIEL LYON.
The Hero of the West in 1861. Killed at Wilson's Creek.

the 10th, and about 4 o'clock struck Rains's most advanced picket, which escaped and gave warning of the attack, of which General Price was informed just as he was about to breakfast. Captain Plummer's battalion of regular infantry was the advance, followed by Osterhaus's two companies of the 2d Missouri Volunteers, and Totten's battery. A body of 200 mounted Home Guards was on Plummer's left. Having reached the enemy's pickets, the infantry was deployed as skirmishers, Plummer to the left and Osterhaus to the right, and Lieutenant-Colonel Andrews, with the 1st Missouri Infantry, was brought up in support of the battery. Advancing a mile and a half and crossing a brook tributary to the creek, the Union skirmishers met and pushed the Confederate skirmishers up the slope. This disclosed a considerable force of the enemy, along a ridge perpendicular to the line of march and to the valley of the creek, which was attacked by the 1st Missouri and the 1st Kansas, assisted by Totten's battery, who drove back the Confederates on the right to the foot of the slope beyond.

Plummer on the left early became separated from

THE BATTLE-FIELD OF WILSON'S CREEK AS SEEN FROM BEHIND PEARCE'S CAMP ON THE EAST SIDE OF THE CREEK. (From photographs.)

BRIGADIER-GENERAL JAMES McINTOSH, C. S. A.
Commanding the 2d Arkansas Mounted Rifles at Wilson's Creek. Killed at Pea Ridge. (From a photograph.)

the main body by a deep ravine terminating in a swampy piece of ground, beyond which lay a corn-field which he entered, encountering a large force, the main part of which was the Louisiana regiment. These troops fought with determined valor and checked Plummer's progress. DuBois's battery was moved up to a hill on the left, supported by Osterhaus's battalion, the 1st Iowa, and the 2d Kansas, and opened a deadly fire with shells upon the corn-field, with such marked effect as to throw the Confederates into disorder and enable Plummer to draw off his command in good order across the ravine.

A momentary lull occurred at this time, except on our extreme right, where Price's Missourians opposed the 1st Missouri and attempted to turn that flank, but the 2d Kansas by its timely arrival and gallant attack bore back Price's overwhelming numbers and saved the flank. Meanwhile Totten's battery, which had been brought into action by

section and by piece as the conformation of the ground would admit, performed extraordinary service. Steele's regular infantry was added to its support. Price's troops had fought with great bravery and determination, advancing and retiring two or three times before they were compelled to give way on the lower slope of the ridge they had occupied. Many times the firing was one continuous roar.

The lull enabled the enemy to readjust his lines and bring up fresh troops, having accomplished which, Price made a determined advance along nearly the whole of Lyon's front. He charged fiercely in lines of three or four ranks, to within thirty or forty yards, pouring in a galling fire and directing his most determined efforts against Totten's battery, for which Woodruff's, which was pitted against it, was no match at all.

Every available man of Lyon's was now brought into action and the battle raged with redoubled energy on both sides. For more than an hour the balance was about even, one side gaining ground only to give way in its turn to the advance of the other, till at last the Confederates seemed to yield, and a suspension of the fury took place. . . .

About this time great anxiety began to be felt for the fate of Sigel's command. Shortly after Lyon's attack the sound of battle had been heard in the rear of the enemy's line. It continued but a short time, and was renewed shortly afterward for a very brief period only, when it ceased altogether. . . . By 10 o'clock Sigel was out of the fight, and the enemy could turn his whole force upon Lyon.

Meantime a body of troops was observed moving down the hill on the east bank of Wilson's Creek toward Lyon's left, and an attack by other troops from that direction was anticipated. Schofield deployed eight companies of the 1st Iowa and led them in person to repel this. They did so most gallantly after a sanguinary contest, effectually assisted by the fire from DuBois's battery, which alone drove back the column on the opposite side of the stream before it began a crossing.

Lyon, accompanied by an aide and his six or eight orderlies, followed closely the right of the Iowa regiment. After proceeding a short distance, his attention was called by the aide to a line of men drawn up on the prolongation of the left of our main line and nearly perpendicular to the 1st Iowa as it

moved to the eastward. A party of horsemen came out in front of this line of the enemy and proceeded to reconnoiter. General Price and Major Emmett Mac Donald (who had sworn that he would not cut his hair till the Confederacy was acknowledged) were easily recognized. General Lyon started as if to confront them, ordering his party to "draw pistols and follow" him, when the aide protested against his exposing himself to the fire of the line, which was partly concealed by the mass of dense underbrush, and asked if he should not bring up some other troops. To this Lyon assented, and directed the aide to order up the 2d Kansas. The general advanced a short distance, joining two companies of the 1st Iowa, left to protect an exposed position.

Colonel Mitchell of the 2d Kansas, near DuBois's battery, sent his lieutenant-colonel, Blair, to Lyon to ask to be put in action, and the two messengers passed each other without meeting. Lyon repeated his order for the regiment to come forward. The regiment moved promptly by the flank, and as it approached Lyon he directed the two companies of Iowa troops to go forward with it, himself leading the column, swinging his hat. A murderous fire was opened from the thick brush, the 2d Kansas deployed rapidly to the front and with the two companies of the 1st Iowa swept over the hill, dislodging the enemy and driving them back into the next ravine; but while he was at the head of the column, and pretty nearly in the first fire, a ball penetrated Lyon's left breast, inflicting a mortal wound. He slowly dismounted, and as he fell into the arms of his faithful orderly, Lehmann, he exclaimed, "Lehmann, I am killed," and almost immediately expired. . . .

The engagement on different parts of the line lasted about half an hour after Lyon's death, when the Confederates gave way, and silence reigned for nearly the same length of time. Many of the senior officers having been disabled, Sturgis assumed command, and the principal officers were summoned for consultation. This council and the suspended hostilities were soon abruptly terminated by the appearance of the Confederates along our entire front, where the troops had been readjusted in more compact form and were now more determined and cooler than ever. A battery planted in the front began to use shrapnel and canister. . . .

THE SIEGE OF LEXINGTON.

BY COLONEL JAMES A. MULLIGAN, U. S. V.
Commander of the garrison at Lexington, Mo.

NOTE.— General Price hastened from Wilson's Creek battle-field, northward toward Lexington, and by the middle of September had completely invested the place with 18,000 men. The garrison was composed of Illinois and Missouri troops and numbered about 3500. The commandant, Colonel Mulligan, had received orders to hold Lexington at all hazards, and on the 11th of September began intrenching College Hill, a broad eminence overlooking Lexington and the Missouri River. His narrative describes the chief events of the siege.

. . . We waited until the morning of the 12th, vigilantly and without sleep, when a messenger rushed in, saying, "Colonel, the enemy are pushing across the bridge in overwhelming force." With a glass we could see them as they came, General Price riding up and down the lines, urging his men on. Two companies of the Missouri 13th were ordered out, and, with Company K of the Irish Brigade, quickly checked the enemy, drove him back, and burned the bridge.

The enemy now made a détour, and approached the town once more, by the Independence road. Six companies of the Missouri 13th and the Illinois cavalry were ordered out, and met them in the Lexington Cemetery, just outside the town, where the fight raged furiously over the dead. We succeeded in keeping the enemy in check, and in the meantime the work with the shovel went bravely on until we had thrown up breastworks three or four feet high.

BRIGADIER-GENERAL WM. Y. SLACK, C. S. A.
In command of a division at Wilson's Creek. Mortally wounded at Pea Ridge. (From a photograph.)

THE HOSPITAL.

THE COLLEGE, FRONTING SOUTH.

THE BATTLE OF LEXINGTON, MO., AS SEEN FROM GENERAL PARSONS' POSITION.
After a contemporary drawing.

BRIG.-GEN. FELIX K. ZOLLICOFFER, C. S. A.
In command of the First Brigade of the Confederate
Army at Mill Springs. Killed in the battle.
From a photograph.

BRIGADIER-GENERAL SPEED S. FRY, U. S. V.
Colonel of the 4th Kentucky regiment, whose men
shot Gen. Zollicoffer. (From a photograph.)

At 9 o'clock on the morning of the 18th the enemy were seen approaching. The Confederate force had been increased to 18,000 men with 16 pieces of cannon. They came as one dark moving mass, their guns beaming in the sun, their banners waving, and their drums beating — everywhere, as far as we could see, were men, men, men, approaching grandly. Our earthworks covered an area of about eighteen acres, surrounded by a ditch, and protected in front by what were called "confusion pits" and by mines. Our men stood firm behind the breastworks, none trembled or paled, and a solemn silence prevailed.

The enemy opened a terrible fire with their cannon on all sides, which we answered with determination and spirit. Our spies had brought intelligence, and had all agreed that it was the intention of the enemy to make a grand rush, overwhelm us, and bury us in the trenches of Lexington.

. . . On the morning of the 19th the firing was resumed and continued all day. Our officers had told the men that if they could hold out until the 19th we should certainly be reinforced, and all through that day the men watched anxiously for the appearance of the friendly flag under which aid was to reach them, and listened eagerly for the sound of friendly cannon. But they looked and listened in vain, and all day long they fought without water, their parched lips cracking, their tongues swollen.

The morning of the 20th broke, but no reinforcements had come, and still the men fought on. The enemy appeared that day with an artifice which was destined to overreach us and secure to them the possession of our intrenchments. They had constructed a movable breastwork of hemp bales, rolled them before their lines up the hill, and advanced under this cover. All our efforts could not retard the advance of these bales. Round-shot and bullets were poured against them, but they would only rock a little and then settle back. Heated shot were fired with the hope of setting them on fire, but they had been soaked and would not burn. Thus for hours the fight continued. Our cartridges were now nearly used up, many of our brave fellows had fallen and it was evident that the fight must soon cease, when at 3 o'clock an orderly came, saying that the enemy had sent a flag of truce. With the flag came a note from General Price, asking "why the firing had ceased." I returned it, with the reply written on the back, "General, I hardly know, unless you have surrendered." He at once took pains to assure me that this was not the case. I then discovered that the major of another regiment, in spite of orders, had raised a white flag.

Our ammunition was about gone. We were out of rations, and had been without water for days, and many of the men felt like giving up the post, which it seemed impossible to hold longer. They were ordered back to the breastworks, and told to use up all their powder, then defend themselves as best they could, but to hold their place. Then a council of war was held in the college, and the question of surrender was put to the officers, and a ballot was taken, only two out of six votes being cast in favor of fighting on. Then the flag of truce was sent out with our surrender.

NARRATIVE OF EVENTS IN 1861-2 — CONTINUED.

TENNESSEE and KENTUCKY. — On September 3 Major-General Leonidas Polk, Confederate commander in West Tennessee, sent a force into Kentucky to occupy Columbus on the Mississippi River. Two days later Brigadier-General Ulysses S. Grant moved a Union force from Cairo, Illinois, and occupied Paducah, Kentucky. At the same time General Felix K. Zollicoffer marched a brigade of Confederates from East Tennessee through Cumberland Gap to Cumberland Ford, and General Simeon B. Buckner moved from Camp Boone, near Clarksville, and occupied Bowling Green, Kentucky. On the Union side, General Robert Anderson, the hero of Sumter, was in command of the Department of Kentucky, with headquarters at Louisville, with W. T. Sherman second in command, while General George H. Thomas, in command of the Union forces at Camp Dick Robinson, bent all his energies in the direction of a successful movement into East Tennessee. On the 15th of November General Don Carlos Buell became commander of the Department of the Ohio, which included Kentucky. He planned the movement of a heavy column up the Cumberland and Tennessee rivers by water to unite with another column moving east of Bowling Green, by land on Nashville, aiming at the same time by strong demonstrations at Columbus and Bowling Green to keep the Confederates who were stationed there fully occupied.

Thus in the beginning of 1862 the Confederate line extended from Columbus on the Mississippi through Forts Henry and Donelson to Bowling Green, Mill Springs, and Cumberland Gap.

General Albert Sidney Johnston commanded the Confederate army of the West, with a base at Nashville. He purposed to defend the northern border of Tennessee.

The first important event on the main line was the capture of Forts Henry and Donelson in February, 1862. During the interval Thomas, who had been directed to enter East Tennessee, left Lebanon January 1, and marched toward Cumberland Gap. The middle of January found him with a part of his force, numbering about 2500, in Zollicoffer's front near Mill Springs on the Cumberland.

MILL SPRINGS, AND THE DEATH OF GENERAL ZOLLICOFFER.

BY R. M. KELLY, COLONEL, U. S. V.

Of Colonel Fry's regiment (the 4th Kentucky), afterward colonel of the regiment.

General George B. Crittenden had shortly before the appearance of Thomas assumed command of the Confederates on the Cumberland. He recognized that the position intrenched by Zollicoffer on the north of the river was untenable, and that the withdrawal of his forces would be attended with great risk.

. . . The only chance for a satisfactory issue was to attack Thomas before he could concentrate. Thomas's force comprised the 9th Ohio and 2d Minnesota of Colonel Robert L. McCook's brigade, the 10th Indiana and 4th Kentucky of Colonel Mahlon D. Manson's brigade, Kenny's and Wetmore's Ohio batteries, a battalion of Michigan engineers and Colonel Frank Wolford's 1st Kentucky cavalry. Crittenden ordered a movement to begin at midnight on the 18th of January, 1862, in the following order: General Zollicoffer's brigade, consisting of two cavalry companies, a Mississippi regiment, three Tennessee regiments, and a battery in front; next, the brigade of General Carroll, composed of three Tennessee regiments and a section of artillery. An Alabama regiment and two cavalry regiments, intended as a reserve, closed the column. After a march of nine miles over muddy roads and through the rain, his cavalry about daylight encountered Wolford's pickets, who after firing fell back on the reserve, consisting of two companies of the 10th Indiana, and with them made a determined stand, in which they were promptly supported by Wolford with the rest of his battalion, and soon after by the rest of the 10th Indiana, ordered up by Manson, who had been advised by courier from Wolford of the attack. Colonel Manson proceeded in person to order forward the 4th Kentucky and the battery of his brigade and to report to General

THE "DE KALB," FORMERLY THE "ST. LOUIS."
Type of the "Carondelet," "Cincinnati," "Louisville," "Mound City," "Cairo," and "Pittsburg."
From a photograph.

MAP OF THE REGION OF FOOTE'S OPERATIONS.

CAPTAIN JAMES B. EADS.

Thomas. On his way he notified Colonel Van Cleve, of the 2d Minnesota. As Manson dashed through the camp of the 4th Kentucky shouting for Colonel Speed S. Fry, and giving warning of the attack, the men, wearied with the muddy march of the day before, were just beginning to crawl out of their tents to roll-call. Forming rapidly, Fry led them at double-quick in the direction of the firing. Having no one to place him, on coming in sight of the enemy, he took position along a fence in the edge of the woods, with his right resting near the Mill Springs road. In front of him was an open field, across which the enemy were advancing from the shelter of woodland on the opposite side. A ravine ran through the open field parallel to Fry's front, heading near the road on his right, with steep sides in his front, but sloping gradually beyond his left. Before Fry's arrival Zollicoffer had deployed his brigade, and had forced Wolford and the 10th Indiana to fall back, almost capturing the horses of Wolford's men, who were fighting on foot. A portion of Wolford's command, under his immediate charge, and Vanardsall's company of the 10th Indiana, rallied on the 4th Kentucky when it appeared, the remainder of the 10th falling back to its encampment, where it re-formed its lines. Fry was at once subjected to a severe attack. The enemy in his front crawled up under shelter of the ravine to within a short distance of his lines before delivering their fire, and, Fry, mounting the fence, in stentorian tones denounced them as dastards, and defied them to stand up on their feet and come forward like men.

A little lull in the firing occurring at this juncture, Fry rode a short distance to the right to get a better view of the movement of the enemy in that direction. The morning was a lowering one, and the woods were full of smoke. As Fry turned to regain his position he encountered a mounted officer whose uniform was covered with a water-proof coat. After approaching till their knees touched, the stranger said to Fry: "We must not fire on our own men"; and nodding his head to his left, he said, "Those are our men." Fry said, "Of course not. I would not do so intentionally"; and he began to move toward his regiment, when turning he saw another mounted man riding from the trees who fired and wounded Fry's horse. Fry at once fired on the man who had accosted him, and several of his men, observing the incident, fired at the same time. The shots were fatal, and the horseman fell dead, pierced by a pistol-shot in his breast and by two musket-balls. It was soon ascertained that it was Zollicoffer himself who had fallen. In the meantime, the enemy were pressing Fry in front and overlapping his right. On his right front only the fence separated the combatants. The left of his regiment not being assailed, he moved two companies from that flank to his right. As he was making this change General Thomas appeared on the field, and at once placed the 10th Indiana in position to cover Fry's exposed flank.

The fall of Zollicoffer and the sharp firing that followed caused two of his regiments to retreat in confusion. Crittenden then brought up Carroll's brigade to the support of the other two, and ordered a general advance. . . .

———

NOTE.— Thomas defeated Crittenden at Mill Springs, and about the same time (January 10) Colonel James A. Garfield defeated the Confederates on the Big Sandy River, under Humphrey Marshall. With the retreat of Marshall the last Confederate force was, for the time being, driven from Kentucky.

RECOLLECTIONS OF FOOTE AND THE GUN-BOATS.

BY CAPTAIN JAMES B. EADS.

NOTE.— Of the services of Captain Eads to the Western flotilla, the Rev. C. B. Boynton says, in his "History of the Navy": "During the month of July, 1861, the Quartermaster-General advertised for proposals to construct a number of iron-clad gun-boats for service on the Mississippi River. The bids were opened on the 5th of August, and Mr. Eads was found to be the best bidder for the whole number, both in regard to the time of completion and price. . . . On the 7th of August, 1861, Mr. Eads signed a contract with Quartermaster-General Meigs to construct these seven vessels ready for their crews and armaments in sixty-five days."

SOON after the surrender of Fort Sumter, while in St. Louis, I received a letter from Attorney-General Bates, dated Washington, April 17th, in which he said: "Be not surprised if you are called here suddenly by telegram. If called, come instantly. In a certain contingency it will be necessary to have the aid of the most thorough knowledge of our Western rivers and the use of steam on them, and in that event I have advised that you should be consulted." The call by telegram followed close upon the letter. I hurried to Washington, where I was introduced to the Secretary of the Navy, the Hon. Gideon Welles, and to Captain G. V. Fox, afterward Assistant Secretary. In the August following I was to construct 7 gun-boats, which, according to the contract, were to draw 6 feet of water, carry 13 heavy guns each, be plated with 2½-inch iron, and have a speed of 9 miles an hour. The De Kalb (at first called the St. Louis) was the type of the other six, named the Carondelet, Cincinnati, Louisville, Mound City, Cairo, and Pittsburg. They were 175 feet long, 51½ feet beam; the flat sides sloped at an angle of about thirty-five degrees, and the front and rear casemates corresponded with the sides, the stern-wheel being entirely covered by the rear casemate. Each was pierced for three bow guns, eight broadside guns (four on a side), and two stern guns. Before these seven gun-boats were completed, I engaged to convert the snag-boat Benton into an armored vessel of still larger dimensions.

After completing the seven and despatching them down the Mississippi to Cairo, I was requested by Foote (who then went by the title of "flag-officer," the title of admiral not being recognized at that time in our navy), as a special favor to him, to accompany the Benton, the eighth one of the fleet, in her passage down to Cairo. It was in December, and the water was falling rapidly.

The Benton had been converted from the U. S. snag-boat Benton into the most powerful iron-clad of the fleet. She was built with two hulls about twenty feet apart, very strongly braced together. She had been purchased by General Frémont while he was in command of the Western Department, and had been sent to my ship-yard for alteration into a gun-boat. I had the space between the two hulls planked, so that a continuous bottom extended from the outer side of one hull to the outer side of the other. The upper side was decked over in the same manner; and by extending the outer sides of the two hulls forward until they joined each other at a new stem, which received them; the twin boats became one wide, strong, and substantial hull. The new bottom did not extend to the stern of the hull, but was brought up to the deck fifty feet forward of the stern, so as to leave a space for a central wheel with which the boat was to be propelled. This wheel was turned by the original engines of the snag-boat, each of the engines having formerly turned an independent wheel on the outside of the twin boat. In this

REAR-ADMIRAL ANDREW HULL FOOTE.
From a photograph.

THE GUN-BOATS "TYLER" AND "LEXINGTON" ENGAGING THE BATTERIES OF
COLUMBUS, KY., DURING THE BATTLE OF BELMONT.
After a sketch by Rear-Admiral Walke.

manner the *Benton* became a war vessel of about seventy-five feet beam, a greater breadth, perhaps, than that of any war vessel then afloat. She was about two hundred feet long. A slanting casemate, covered with iron plates, was placed on her sides and across her bow and stern; and the wheel was protected in a similar manner. The casemate on the sides and bow was covered with iron 3½ inches thick; the wheel-house and stern with lighter plates, like the first seven boats built by me. She carried 16 guns,—7 32-pounders, 2 9-inch guns, and 7 army 42-pounders.

The wish of Admiral Foote to have me see this boat safely to Cairo was prompted by his knowledge that I had had experience in the management of steamboats upon the river, and his fear that she would be detained by grounding. Ice had just begun to float in the Mississippi when the *Benton* put out from my ship-yard at Carondelet for the South. Some 30 or 40 miles below St. Louis she grounded. Under the direction of Captain Winslow, who commanded the vessel, Lieutenant Bishop, executive officer of the ship, an intelligent and energetic young man, set the crew at work. An anchor was put out for the purpose of hauling her off. My advice was not asked with reference to this first proceeding, and although I had been

requested by Admiral Foote to accompany the vessel, he had not instructed the captain so far as I knew, to be guided by my advice in case of difficulty. After they had been working all night to get the boat afloat, she was harder on than ever; moreover, the water had fallen about six inches. I then volunteered the opinion to Captain Winslow that if he would run hawsers ashore in a certain direction, directly opposite to that in which he had been trying to move the boat, she could be got off. He replied, very promptly, "Mr. Eads, if you will undertake to get her off, I shall be very willing to place the entire crew under your direction." I at once accepted the offer; and Lieutenant Bishop was called up and instructed to obey my directions. Several very large hawsers had been put on board of the boat for the fleet at Cairo. One of the largest was got out and secured to a large tree on the shore, and as heavy a strain was put upon it as the cable would be likely to bear. As the water was still falling, I ordered out a second one, and a third, and a fourth, until five or six eleven-inch hawsers were heavily strained in the effort to drag the broad-bottomed vessel off the bar. There were three steam capstans on the bow of the vessel, and these were used in tightening the strain by luffs upon the hawsers. One of the hawsers was led

through a snatch-block fastened by a large chain to a ring-bolt in the side of the vessel. I was on the upper deck of the vessel near Captain Winslow when the chain which held this lock broke. It was made of iron one and one-eighth inches in diameter, and the link separated into three pieces. The largest, being one-half of the link, was found on the shore at a distance of at least five hundred feet. Half of the remainder struck the iron plating on the bow of the boat, making an indentation half the thickness of one's finger in depth. The third piece struck Captain Winslow on the fleshy part of the arm, cutting through his coat and the muscles of his arm. The wound was a very painful one, but he bore it as might be expected. The iron had probably cut an inch and a half into the arm between the shoulder and the elbow. In the course of the day the *Benton* was floated, and proceeded on her voyage down the river without further delay. Captain Winslow soon after departed for his home on leave of absence. On his recovery he was placed in command of the *Kearsarge*, and to that accident he owed, perhaps, the fame of being the captor of the *Alabama*.

When the *Benton* arrived at Cairo she was visited by all the officers of the army and navy stationed there, and was taken, on that or the following day, on a trial trip a few miles down the river. The *Essex*, in command of Captain William D. Porter, was lying four or five miles below the mouth of the Ohio on the Kentucky shore. As the *Benton* passed up, on her return from this little expedition, Captain Porter offered his congratulations to Foote on the apparent excellence of the boat. "Yes," replied Foote, "but she is almost too slow."

"Plenty fast enough to fight with," was Porter's rejoinder.

Very soon after this (early in the spring of 1862) I was called to Washington, with the request to prepare plans for still lighter iron-clad vessels, the draught of those which I had then completed being only about six feet. The later plans were for vessels that should be capable of going up the Tennessee and the Cumberland. As rapidly as possible I prepared and presented for the inspection of Secretary Welles and his able assistant, Captain Fox, plans of vessels drawing five feet. They were not

acceptable to Captain Fox, who said: "We want vessels much lighter than that."

"But you want them to carry a certain thickness of iron?" I replied.

"Yes, we want them to be proof against heavy shot,—to be plated and heavily plated,—but they must be of much lighter draught."

After the interview I returned with the plans to my hotel, and commenced a revision of them; and in the course of a few days I presented the plans for the *Osage* and the *Neosho*. . . . Each vessel had a rotating turret, carrying two eleven-inch guns, the turret being six inches thick, but extending only a few feet above the deck of the vessel. I was very anxious to construct these turrets after a plan which I had devised, quite different from the Ericsson or Coles systems, and in which the guns should be operated by steam. But, within a month after the engagement at Fort Donelson, the memorable contest between the *Merrimac* and the *Monitor* occurred, whereupon the Navy Department insisted on Ericsson turrets being placed upon these two vessels.

At the same time the department was anxious to have four larger vessels for operations on the lower Mississippi River, which should have two turrets each, and it consented that I should place one of my turrets on each of two of these vessels (the *Chickasaw* and the *Milwaukee*) at my own risk, to be replaced with Ericsson's in case of failure. These were the first turrets in which the guns were manipulated by steam, and they were fired every forty-five seconds. . . . While perfecting those plans, I prepared the designs for the larger vessels (the *Chickasaw*, *Milwaukee*, *Winnebago*, and *Kickapoo*), and when these were approved by Captain Fox and the officers of the navy to whom they were submitted at Washington, Mr. Welles expressed the wish that I should confer with Admiral Foote about them before proceeding to build them, inasmuch as the experience which he had had at Forts Henry and Donelson and elsewhere would be of great value, and might enable him to suggest improvements in them. I therefore hastened from Washington to Island Number Ten, a hundred miles below Cairo, on the Mississippi River, where Foote's flotilla was then engaged. . . .

BETWEEN DECKS—SERVING THE GUNS.
After a drawing by Rear-Admiral Walke.

THE ATTACK UPON FORT HENRY.
After a drawing by Rear-Admiral Walke.

THE GUN-BOATS AT BELMONT AND FORT HENRY.

BY HENRY WALKE, REAR-ADMIRAL, U. S. N.
In command of the Union gun-boats at Belmont, and commander of the "Carondelet" at Fort Henry.

. . . Flag-Officer Foote arrived at Cairo September 12th, and relieved Commander John Rodgers of the command of the station. The first operations of the Western flotilla consisted chiefly of reconnoissances on the Mississippi, Ohio, Cumberland, and Tennessee rivers. At this time it was under the control of the War Department, and acting in coöperation with the army under General Grant, whose headquarters were at Cairo.

On the evening of the 6th of November, 1861, I received instructions from General Grant to proceed down the Mississippi with the wooden gun-boats *Tyler* and *Lexington* on a reconnoissance, and as convoy to some half-dozen transport steamers; but I did not know the character of the service expected of me until I anchored for the night, seven or eight miles below Cairo. Early the next morning, while the troops were being landed near Belmont, Missouri, opposite Columbus, Kentucky, I attacked the Confederate batteries, at the request of General Grant, as a diversion, which was done with some effect. But the superiority of the enemy's batteries on the bluffs at Columbus, both in the number and the quality of his guns, was so great that it would have been too hazardous to have remained long under his fire with such frail vessels as the *Tyler* and *Lexington*, which were only expected to protect the land forces in case of a repulse. Having accomplished the object of the attack, the gun-boats withdrew, but returned twice during the day and renewed the contest. During the last of these engagements a cannon-ball passed obliquely through the side, deck, and scantling of the *Tyler*, killing one man and wounding others. This convinced me of the necessity of withdrawing my vessels, which had been moving in a circle to confuse the enemy's gunners. We fired a few more broadsides, therefore, and, perceiving that the firing had ceased at Belmont, an ominous circumstance, I returned to the landing, to protect the

army and transports. In fact, the destruction of the gun-boats would have involved the loss of our army and our depot at Cairo, the most important one in the West.

Soon after we returned to the landing-place our troops began to appear, and the officers of the gun-boats were warned by General McClernand of the approach of the enemy. The Confederates came *en masse* through a cornfield, and opened with musketry and light artillery upon the transports, which were filled, or being filled, with our retreating soldiers. A well-directed fire from the gun-boats made the enemy fly in the greatest confusion.

Flag-Officer Foote was at St. Louis when the battle of Belmont was fought, and made a report to the Secretary of the Navy of the part which the gun-boats took in the action, forwarding my official report to the Navy Department. The officers of the vessels were highly complimented by General Grant for the important aid they rendered in this battle; and in his second official report of the action he made references to my report. It was impossible for me to inform the flag-officer of the general's intentions, which were kept perfectly secret.

During the winter of 1861–62, an expedition was planned by Flag-Officer Foote and Generals Grant and McClernand against Fort Henry, situated on the eastern bank of the Tennessee River, a short distance south of the line between Kentucky and Tennessee. In January the ironclads were brought down to Cairo, great efforts were made to prepare them for immediate service, but only four of the ironclads could be made ready as soon as required.

On the morning of the 2d of February the flag-officer left Cairo with the four armoured vessels above named, and the wooden gun-boats *Tyler*, *Lexington*, and *Conestoga*, and in the evening reached the Tennessee River. On the 4th the fleet anchored six miles below Fort Henry. The next day, while

reconnoitering, the *Essex* received a shot which passed through the pantry and the officers' quarters, and visited the steerage. On the 5th the flag-officer inspected the officers and crew at quarters, addressed them, and offered a prayer. . . .

The 6th dawned mild and cheering, with a light breeze, sufficient to clear away the smoke. At 10:20 the flag-officer made the signal to prepare for battle, and at 10:50 came the order to get under way and steam up to Panther Island, about two miles below Fort Henry. At 11:35, having passed the foot of the island, we formed in line and approached the fort four abreast,—the *Essex* on the right, then the *Cincinnati*, *Carondelet*, and *St. Louis*. For want of room the last two were interlocked, and remained so during the fight.

As we slowly passed up this narrow stream, not a sound could be heard nor a moving object seen in the dense woods which overhung the dark and swollen river. The gun-crews of the *Carondelet* stood silent at their posts, impressed with the serious and important character of the service before them. About noon the fort and the Confederate flag came suddenly into view, the barracks, the new earth-works, and the great guns well manned. The captains of our guns were men-of-war's men, good shots, and had their men well drilled.

The flag-steamer, the *Cincinnati*, fired the first shot as the signal for the others to begin. At once the fort was ablaze with the flame of her eleven heavy guns. The wild whistle of their rifle-shells was heard on every side of us. On the *Carondelet* not a word was spoken more than at ordinary drill, except when Matthew Arthur, captain of the starboard bow-gun, asked permission to fire at one or two of the enemy's retreating vessels, as he could not at that time bring his gun to bear on the fort. He fired one shot, which passed through the upper cabin of a hospital-boat, whose flag was not seen, but injured no one. The *Carondelet* was struck in about thirty places by the enemy's heavy shot and shell. Eight struck within two feet of the bow-ports, leading to the boilers, around which barricades had been built—a precaution which I always took be-

fore going into action, and which on several occasions prevented an explosion. The *Carondelet* fired 107 shell and solid shot; none of her officers or crew was killed or wounded. . . .

After nearly an hour's hard fighting, the captain of the *Essex*, going below, and complimenting the First Division for their splendid execution, asked them if they did not want to rest and give three cheers, which were given with a will. But the feelings of joy on board the *Essex* were suddenly changed by a calamity which is thus described in a letter to me from James Laning, second master of the *Essex*:

A shot from the enemy pierced the casemate just above the port-hole on the port side, then through the middle boiler, killing in its flight Acting Master's Mate S. B. Brittan, Jr., and opening a chasm for the escape of the scalding steam and water. . . .

The *Essex* before the accident had fired seventy shots from her two 9-inch guns. A powder boy, Job Phillips, fourteen years of age, coolly marked down upon the casemate every shot his gun had fired, and his account was confirmed by the gunner in the magazine. Her loss in killed, wounded, and missing was thirty-two.

The *St. Louis* was struck seven times. She fired one hundred and seven shots during the action. No one on board the vessel was killed or wounded.

Flag-Officer Foote during the action was in the pilot-house of the *Cincinnati*, which received thirty-two shots. Her chimneys, after-cabin, and boats, were completely riddled. Two of her guns were disabled. The only fatal shot she received passed through the larboard front, killing one man and wounding several others. I happened to be looking at the flag-steamer when one of the enemy's heavy shot struck her. It had the effect, apparently, of a thunderbolt, ripping her side-timbers and scattering the splinters over the vessel. She did not slacken her speed, but moved on as though nothing unexpected had happened. . . . The Confederate soldiers fought as valiantly and as skilfully as the Union sailors. Only after a most determined resistance, and after all his heavy guns had been silenced, did Gen. Tilghman lower his flag. . . .

MAJOR-GENERAL LEW WALLACE, U. S. V.
In command of the Third Division of the Union army at Fort Donelson.
From a war-time photograph.

THE CAPTURE OF FORT DONELSON.

BY LEW WALLACE, MAJOR-GENERAL, U. S. V.
In command of the Third Division, under General U. S. Grant.

. . . On the morning of the 13th of February General Grant, with about twenty thousand men, was before Fort Donelson. We have had a view of the army in the works ready for battle; a like view of that outside and about to go into position of attack and assault is not so easily to be given. At dawn the latter host rose up from the bare ground, and, snatching bread and coffee as best they could, fell into lines that stretched away over hills, down hollows, and through thickets, making it impossible for even colonels to see their regiments from flank to flank.

Pausing to give a thought to the situation, it is proper to remind the reader that he is about to witness an event of more than mere historical interest. He is about to see the men of the North and Northwest and of the South and Southwest enter for the first time into a strife of arms; on one side, the best blood of Tennessee, Kentucky, Alabama, Mississippi, and Texas, aided materially by fighting representatives from Virginia; on the other, the best blood of Illinois, Ohio, Indiana, Iowa, Missouri, and Nebraska.

We have now before us a spectacle seldom witnessed in the annals of scientific war — an army behind field-works erected in a chosen position waiting quietly while another army very little superior in numbers proceeds at leisure to place it in a state of siege. Such was the operation General Grant had before him at daybreak of the 13th of February. Let us see how it was accomplished and how it was resisted.

In a clearing about two miles from Dover there was a log-house, at the time occupied by a Mrs. Crisp. As the road to Dover ran close by, it was made the headquarters of the commanding general. All through the night of the 12th the coming and going was incessant. Smith was ordered to find a position in front of the enemy's right wing which would place him face to face with Buckner. McClernand's order was to establish himself on the enemy's left, where he would be opposed to Pillow.

A little before dawn Birge's sharp-shooters were astir. Theirs was a peculiar service. Each was a preferred marksman, and carried a long-range Henry rifle, with sights delicately arranged as for target practice. In action each was perfectly independent. They never manœuverd as a corps. When the time came they were asked, "Canteens full?" "Biscuits for all day?" Then their only order, "All right; hunt your holes, boys." Thereupon they dispersed, and, like Indians, sought cover to please themselves behind rocks and stumps, or in hollows. Sometimes they dug holes; sometimes they climbed into trees. Once in a good location, they remained there the day.

MAJOR-GENERAL JOHN A. McCLERNAND, U. S. V.
In command of the First Division of the Union army at Fort Donelson.

At night they would crawl out and report in camp. This morning, as I have said, the sharp-shooters dispersed early to find places within easy range of the breastworks.

The movement by Smith and McClernand was begun about the same time. A thick wood fairly screened the former. The latter had to cross an open valley under fire of two batteries, one on Buckner's left, the other on a high point jutting from the line of outworks held by Colonel Heiman of Pillow's command. Graves commanded the first, Maney the second; both were of Tennessee. As always in situations where the advancing party is ignorant of the ground and of the designs of the enemy, resort was had to skirmishers, who are to the main body what antennæ are to insects. Theirs it is to unmask the foe. Unlike sharp-shooters, they act in bodies. Behind the skirmishers, the batteries started out to find positions, and through the brush and woods, down the hollows, up the hills the guns and caissons were hauled. Nowadays it must be a very steep bluff in face of which the good artillerist will stop or turn back. At Donelson, however, the proceeding was generally slow and toilsome. The officer had to find a vantage ground first; then with axes a road to it was hewn out; after which, in many instances, the men, with the prolonges over their shoulders, helped the horses along. In the gray of the dawn, the sharp-shooters were deep in their deadly game; as the sun came up, one battery after another opened fire, and was instantly and gallantly answered; and all the time behind the hidden sharp-shooters, and behind the skirmishers, who occasionally stopped to take a hand in the fray, the regiments marched, route-step, colors flying, after their colonels.

About 11 o'clock Commander Walke, of the *Carondelet*, engaged the water-batteries. The air was then full of the stunning music of battle, though as yet not a volley of musketry had been heard. Smith, nearest the enemy at starting, was first in place; and there, leaving the fight to his sharp-shooters and skirmishers and to his batteries, he reported to the chief in the log-house, and, like an old soldier, calmly waited orders. McClernand, following a good road, pushed on rapidly to the high grounds on the right. The appearance of his column in the valley covered by the two Confederate batteries provoked a furious shelling from them. On the double-quick his men

MAJOR-GENERAL C. F. SMITH, U. S. V.
In command of the Second Division of the Union army at Fort Donelson.

passed through it; and when, in the wood beyond, they resumed the route-step and saw that nobody was hurt, they fell to laughing at themselves. The real baptism of fire was yet in store for them.

When McClernand arrived at his appointed place, and extended his brigades, it was discovered that the Confederate outworks offered a front too great for him to envelop. To attempt to rest his right opposite their extreme left would necessitate a dangerous attenuation of his line and leave him without reserves. Over on their left, moreover, ran the road passing from Dover on the south to Charlotte and Nashville, which it was of the highest importance to close hermetically so that there would be no communication left General Floyd except by the river. If the road to Charlotte were left to the enemy, they might march out at their pleasure.

The insufficiency of his force was thus made apparent to General Grant, and whether a discovery of the moment or not, he set about its correction. He knew a reinforcement was coming up the river under convoy of Foote; besides which a brigade, composed of the 8th Missouri and the 11th Indiana infantry and Battery A, Illinois, had been left behind at Forts Henry and Heiman under myself. A courier was despatched to me with an order to bring my command to Donelson. I ferried my troops across the Tennessee in the night, and reported with them at headquarters before noon the next day. The brigade was transferred to General Smith; at the same time an order was put into my hand assigning me to command the Third Division, which was conducted to a position between Smith and McClernand, enabling the latter to extend his line well to the left and cover the road to Charlotte.

Thus on the 14th of February the Confederates were completely invested, except that the river above Dover remained to them. The supineness of General Floyd all this while is to this day incomprehensible. A vigorous attack on the morning of the 13th might have thrown Grant back upon Fort Henry. Such an achievement would have more than offset Foote's conquest. The *morale* to be gained would have alone justified the attempt. But with McClernand's strong division on the right, my own in the center, and C. F. Smith's on the left, the opportunity was gone. On the side of General Grant, the possession of the river was all that was wanting; with that Grant could force the fighting, or wait the certain approach of the grimmest enemy of the besieged — starvation.

It is now — morning of the 14th — easy to see and understand with something more than approximate exactness the oppositions of the two forces. Smith is on the left of the Union army opposite Buckner. My division, in the center, confronts Colonels Heiman. Drake, and Davidson, each with a brigade. McClernand, now well over on the right, keeps the road to Charlotte and Nashville against the major part of Pillow's left wing. The infantry on both sides are in cover

REAR-ADMIRAL HENRY WALKE, U. S. N.,
Commander of the "Carondelet," at Fort Donelson.

behind the crests of the hills or in thick woods, listening to the ragged fusillade which the sharp-shooters and skirmishers maintain against each other almost without intermission. There is little pause in the exchange of shells and round shot. The careful chiefs have required their men to lie down. In brief, it looks as if each party were inviting the other to begin.

These circumstances, the sharp-shooting and cannonading, ugly as they may seem to one who thinks of them under comfortable surroundings, did in fact serve a good purpose the day in question in helping the men to forget their sufferings of the night before. It must be remembered that the weather had changed during the preceding afternoon: from

THE POSITION OF THE GUN-BOATS AND THE WEST BANK.
Fort Donelson is in the farther distance on the extreme left. The upper picture, showing Isaac Williams's house, is a continuation of the right of the lower view. (From a photograph taken in 1884.)

suggestions of spring it turned to intensified winter. From lending a gentle hand in bringing Foote and his ironclads up the river, the wind whisked suddenly around to the north and struck both armies with a storm of mixed rain, snow, and sleet. All night the tempest blew mercilessly upon the unsheltered, fireless soldier, making sleep impossible. Inside the works, nobody had overcoats; while thousands of those outside had marched from Fort Henry as to a summer fête, leaving coats, blankets, and knapsacks behind them in the camp. More than one stout fellow has since admitted, with a laugh, that nothing was so helpful to him that horrible night as the thought that the wind, which seemed about to turn his blood into icicles, was serving the enemy the same way; they, too, had to stand out and take the blast. Let us now go back to the preceding day, and bring up an incident of McClernand's swing into position.

About the center of the Confederate outworks there was a V-shaped hill, marked sharply by a ravine on its right and another on its left. This Colonel Heiman occupied with his brigade of five regiments — all of Tennessee but one. The front presented was about 2500 feet. In the angle of the V, on the summit of the hill, Captain Maney's battery, also of Tennessee, had been planted. Without protection of any kind, it nevertheless completely swept a large field to the left across which an assaulting force would have to come in order to get at Heiman or at Drake, next on the south.

Maney, on the point of the hill, had been active throughout the preceding afternoon, and had succeeded in drawing the fire of some of McClernand's

THE CRISP FARM—GENERAL GRANT'S HEADQUARTERS.

FRONT VIEW OF MRS. CRISP'S HOUSE.

guns. The duel lasted until night. Next morning it was renewed with increased sharpness, Maney being assisted on his right by Graves's battery of Buckner's division, and by some pieces of Drake's on his left.

McClernand's advance was necessarily slow and trying. This was not merely a logical result of unacquaintance with the country and the dispositions of the enemy; he was also under an order from General Grant to avoid everything calculated to bring on a general engagement. In Maney's well-served guns he undoubtedly found serious annoyance, if not a positive obstruction. Concentrating guns of his own upon the industrious Confederate, he at length fancied him silenced and the enemy's infantry on the right thrown into confusion — circumstances from which he hastily deduced a favorable chance to deliver an assault. For that purpose he reinforced his Third Brigade, which was nearest the offending battery, and gave the necessary orders.

Up to this time, it will be observed, there had not been any fighting involving infantry in line. This was now to be changed. Old soldiers, rich with experience, would have regarded the work proposed with gravity; they would have shrewdly cast up an account of the chances of success, not to speak of the chances of coming out alive; they would have measured the distance to be passed, every foot of it under the guns of three batteries, Maney's in the center, Graves's on their left, and Drake's on their right — a direct line of fire doubly crossed. Nor would they have omitted the reception awaiting them from the rifle-pits. They were to descend a hill entangled for two hundred yards with underbrush, climb an opposite ascent partly shorn of timber; make way through an abatis of tree-tops; then, supposing all that successfully accomplished, they would be at last in face of an enemy whom it was possible to reinforce with all the reserves of the garrison — with the whole garrison, if need be. A veteran would have surveyed the three regiments selected for the honorable duty with many misgivings. Not so the men themselves. They were not old soldiers. Recruited but recently from farms and shops, they accepted the assignment heartily and with youthful confidence in their prowess. It may be doubted if a man in the ranks gave a thought to the questions, whether the attack was to be supported while making, or followed up if successful, or whether it was part of a gen-

eral advance. Probably the most they knew was that the immediate objective before them was the capture of the battery on the hill.

The line when formed stood thus from the right: the 49th Illinois, then the 17th, and then the 48th, Colonel Haynie. At the last moment, a question of seniority arose between Colonels Morrison and Haynie. The latter was of opinion that he was the ranking officer. Morrison replied that he would conduct the brigade to the point from which the attack was to be made, after which Haynie might take the command, if he so desired.

Down the hill the three regiments went, crashing and tearing through the undergrowth. Heiman, on the lookout, saw them advancing. Before they cleared the woods, Maney opened with shells. At the foot of the descent, in the valley, Graves joined his fire to Maney's. There Morrison reported to Haynie, who neither accepted nor refused the command. Pointing to the hill, he merely said, "Let us take it together." Morrison turned away, and rejoined his own regiment. Here was confusion in the beginning, or worse, an assault begun without a head. Nevertheless, the whole line went forward. On a part of the hillside the trees were yet standing. The open space fell to Morrison and his 49th, and paying the penalty of the exposure, he outstripped his associates. The men fell rapidly; yet the living rushed on and up, firing as they went. The battery was the common target. Maney's gunners, in relief against the sky, were shot down in quick succession. His first lieutenant (Burns) was one of the first to suffer. His second lieutenant (Massie) was mortally wounded. Maney himself was hit; still he stayed, and his guns continued their punishment; and still the farmer lads and shop boys of Illinois clung to their purpose. With marvelous audacity they pushed through the abatis and reached a point within forty yards of the rifle-pits. It actually looked as if the prize were theirs. The yell of victory was rising in their throats. Suddenly the long line of yellow breastworks before them, covering Heiman's five regiments, crackled and turned into flame. The forlorn hope stopped —staggered—braced up again — shot blindly through the smoke at the smoke of the new enemy, secure in his shelter. Thus for fifteen minutes the Illinoisans stood fighting. The time is given on the testimony of the opposing leader himself. Morrison was knocked out of his saddle by a musket-ball, and disabled; then the men went down the hill. At its foot they rallied round their flags and renewed the assault. Pushed down again, again they rallied, and a third time climbed to the enemy. This time the battery set fire to the dry leaves on the ground, and the heat and smoke became stifling. It was not possible for brave men to endure more. Slowly, sullenly, frequently pausing to return a shot, they went back for the last time; and in going their ears and souls were riven with the shrieks of their wounded comrades, whom the flames crept down upon and smothered and charred where they lay.

Considered as a mere exhibition of courage, this assault, long maintained against odds,—twice repulsed, twice renewed,—has been seldom excelled. One hundred and forty-nine men of the 17th and 49th were killed and wounded. Haynie reported 1 killed and 8 wounded.

There are few things connected with the operations against Fort Donelson so relieved of uncertainty as this: that when General Grant at Fort Henry became fixed in the resolution to undertake the movement, his primary object was the capture of the force to which the post was intrusted. To effect their complete environment, he relied upon Flag-Officer Foote and his gun-boats, whose astonishing success at Fort Henry justified the extreme of confidence.

Foote arrived on the 14th, and made haste to enter upon his work. The *Carondelet* (Commander Walke) had been in position since the 12th. Behind a low out-put of the shore, for two days, she maintained a fire from her rifled guns, happily of greater range than the best of those of the enemy.

EXPLOSION OF A GUN ON BOARD THE "CARONDELET" DURING THE ATTACK ON FORT DONELSON.
See page 46. (After a sketch by Rear-Admiral Walke.)

At 9 o'clock on the 14th, Captain Culbertson, looking from the parapet of the upper battery beheld the river below the first bend full of transports, landing troops under cover of a fresh arrival of gun-boats. The disembarkation concluded, Foote was free. He waited until noon. The captains in the batteries mistook his deliberation for timidity. The impinging of their shot on his iron armor was heard distinctly in the fort a mile and a half away. The captains began to doubt if he would come at all. But at 3 o'clock the boats took position under fire; the *Louisville* on the right, the *St. Louis* next, then the *Pittsburgh*, then the *Carondelet*, all iron-clad.

Five hundred yards from the batteries, and yet Foote was not content! In the Crimean war the allied French and English fleets, of much mightier ships, undertook to engage the Russian shore batteries, but little stronger than those at Donelson. The French on that occasion stood off 1800 yards. Lord Lyons fought his *Agamemnon* at a distance of 800 yards. Foote forged ahead within 400 yards of his enemy, and was still going on. His boat had been hit between wind and water; so with the *Pittsburgh* and *Carondelet*. About the guns the floors were slippery with blood, and both surgeons and carpenters were never so busy. Still the four

boats kept on, and there was great cheering; for not only did the fire from the shore slacken; the lookouts reported the enemy running. It seemed that fortune would smile once more upon the fleet, and cover the honors of Fort Henry afresh at Fort Donelson. Unhappily, when about 350 yards off the hill a solid shot plunged through the pilot-house of the flag-ship, and carried away the wheel. Near the same time the tiller-ropes of the *Louisville* were disabled. Both vessels became unmanageable and began floating down the current. The eddies turned them round like logs. The *Pittsburgh* and *Carondelet* closed in and covered them with their hulls.

Seeing this turn in the fight, the captains of the batteries rallied their men, who cheered in their turn, and renewed the contest with increased will and energy. A ball got lodged in their best rifle. A corporal and some of his men took a log fitting the bore, leaped out on the parapet, and rammed the missile home. "Now, boys," said a gunner in Bidwell's battery, "see me take a chimney!" The flag of the boat and the chimney fell with the shot.

When the vessels were out of range, the victors looked about them. The fine form of their embrasures was gone; heaps of earth had been cast over their platforms. In a space of twenty-four

feet they had picked up as many shot and shells. The air had been full of flying missiles. For an hour and a half the brave fellows had been rained upon; yet their losses had been trifling in numbers. Each gunner had selected a ship and followed her faithfully throughout the action, now and then uniting fire on the *Carondelet*. The Confederates had behaved with astonishing valor. Their victory sent a thrill of joy through the army. The assault on the outworks, the day before, had been a failure. With the repulse of the gun-boats the Confederates scored success number two, and the communication by the river remained open to Nashville. The winds that blew sleet and snow over Donelson that night were not so unendurable as they might have been.

The night of the 14th of February fell cold and dark, and under the pitiless sky the armies remained in position so near to each other that neither dared light fires. Overpowered with watching, fatigue, and the lassitude of spirits which always follows a strain upon the faculties of men like that which is the concomitant of battle, thousands on both sides lay down in the ditches and behind logs and whatever else would in the least shelter them from the cutting wind, and tried to sleep. Very few closed their eyes. Even the horses, after their manner, betrayed the suffering they were enduring.

That morning General Floyd had called a council of his chiefs of brigades and divisions. He expressed the opinion that the post was untenable, except with fifty thousand troops. He called attention to the heavy reinforcements of the Federals, and suggested an immediate attack upon their right wing to reopen land communication with Nashville, by way of Charlotte. The proposal was agreed to unanimously. General Buckner proceeded to make dispositions to cover the retreat, in the event the sortie should be successful. Shortly after noon, when the movement should have begun, the order was countermanded at the instance of Pillow. Then came the battle with the gun-boats.

In the night the council was recalled, with general and regimental officers in attendance. The situation was again debated, and the same conclusion reached. According to the plan resolved upon, Pillow was to move at dawn with his whole division, and attack the right of the besiegers. Gen-

McALLISTER'S BATTERY IN ACTION.

Captain Edward McAllister's Illinois battery did good service on the 13th. In his report he says: "I selected a point, and about noon opened on the four-gun battery through an opening in which I could see the foe. Our fire was promptly returned with such precision that they cut our right wheel on howitzer number three in two. I had no spare wheel, and had to take one off the limber to continue the fight. I then moved all my howitzers over to the west slope of the ridge and loaded under cover of it, and ran the pieces up by hand until I could get the exact elevation. The recoil would throw the guns back out of sight, and thus we continued the fight until the enemy's battery was silenced."

eral Buckner was to be relieved by troops in the forts, and with his command to support Pillow by assailing the right of the enemy's center. If he succeeded, he was to take post outside the intrenchments on the Wynn's Ferry road to cover the retreat. He was then to act as rear-guard. Thus early, leaders in Donelson were aware of the mistake into which they were plunged. Their resolution was wise and heroic. Let us see how they executed it.

Preparations for the attack occupied the night. The troops for the most part were taken out of the rifle-pits and massed over on the left to the number of ten thousand or more. The ground was covered with ice and snow; yet the greatest silence was observed. It seems incomprehensible that columns mixed of all arms, infantry, cavalry, and artillery, could have engaged in simultaneous movement, and not have been heard by some listener outside. One would think the jolting and rumble of heavy gun-carriages would have told the story. But the character of the night must be remembered. The pickets of the Federals were struggling for life against the blast, and probably did not keep good watch.

Oglesby's brigade held McClernand's extreme right. Here and there the musicians were beginning to make the woods ring with reveille, and the numbed soldiers of the line were rising from their icy beds and shaking the snow from their frozen garments. As yet, however, not a company had "fallen in." Suddenly the pickets fired, and with the alarm on their lips rushed back upon their comrades. The woods on the instant became alive.

The regiments formed, officers mounted and took their places; words of command rose loud and eager. By the time Pillow's advance opened fire on Oglesby's right, the point first struck, the latter was fairly formed to receive it. A rapid exchange of volleys ensued. The distance intervening between the works on one side and the bivouac on the other was so short that the action began before Pillow could effect a deployment. His brigades came up in a kind of echelon, left in front, and passed "by regiments left into line," one by one, however; the regiments quickly took their places, and advanced without halting. Oglesby's Illinoisans were now fully awake. They held their ground, returning in full measure the fire that they received. The Confederate Forrest rode around as if to get in their rear,* and it was then give and take, infantry against infantry. The semi-echelon movement of the Confederates enabled them, after an interval, to strike W. H. L. Wallace's brigade, on Oglesby's left. Soon Wal-

* Colonel John McArthur, originally of General C. F. Smith's division, but then operating with McClernand, was there, and though at first discomfited, his men beat the cavalry off, and afterward shared the full shock of the tempest with Oglesby's troops.—L. W.

MAP OF FORT DONELSON, AS INVESTED BY GENERAL GRANT.
Based on the official map by General J. B. McPherson.

lace was engaged along his whole front, now prolonged by the addition to his command of Morrison's regiments. The first charge against him was repulsed; whereupon he advanced to the top of the rising ground behind which he had sheltered his troops in the night. A fresh assault followed, but, aided by a battery across the valley to his left, he repulsed the enemy a second time. His men were steadfast, and clung to the brow of the hill as if it were theirs by holy right. An hour passed, and yet another hour, without cessation of the fire. Meantime the woods rang with a monstrous clangor of musketry, as if a million men were beating empty barrels with iron hammers.

Buckner flung a portion of his division on McClernand's left, and supported the attack with his artillery. The enfilading fell chiefly on W. H. L. Wallace. McClernand, watchful and full of resources, sent batteries to meet Buckner's batteries. To that duty Taylor rushed with his Company B; and McAllister pushed his three 24-pounders into position and exhausted his ammunition in the duel. The roar never slackened. Men fell by the score, reddening the snow with their blood. The smoke, in pallid white clouds, clung to the under-brush and tree-tops as if to screen the combatants from each other. Close to the ground the flame of musketry and cannon tinted everything a lurid red. Limbs dropped from the trees on the heads below, and the thickets were shorn as by an army of cradlers. The division was under peremptory orders to hold its position to the last extremity, and Colonel Wallace was equal to the emergency.

It was now 10 o'clock, and over on the right Oglesby was beginning to fare badly. The pressure on his front grew stronger. The "rebel yell," afterward a familiar battle-cry on many fields, told of ground being gained against him. To add to his doubts, officers were riding to him with a sickening story that their commands were getting out of ammunition, and asking where they could go for a supply. All he could say was to take what was in the boxes of the dead and wounded. At last he realized that the end was come. His right companies began to give way, and as they retreated, holding up their empty cartridge-boxes, the enemy were emboldened, and swept more fiercely around his flank, until finally they appeared in his rear.

GLIMPSE OF THE CUMBERLAND
RIVER WHERE THE GUN-BOATS
FIRST APPEARED.

Looking north from the highest
earth-works of Fort Donelson. (From
a photograph taken in 1884.)

DOVER TAVERN—GENERAL BUCKNER'S HEADQUARTERS
AND THE SCENE OF THE SURRENDER.

From a photograph taken in 1884.

CAPTAIN JOHN A. RAWLINS, U. S. V.

Assistant-Adjutant-General on General Grant's staff.
From a photograph taken in 1861.

He then gave the order to retire the division.

W. H. L. Wallace from his position looked off to his right and saw but one regiment of Oglesby's in place, maintaining the fight, and that was John A. Logan's 31st Illinois. Through the smoke he could see Logan riding in a gallop behind his line; through the roar in his front and the rising yell in his rear, he could hear Logan's voice in fierce entreaty to his "boys." Near the 31st stood W. H. L. Wallace's regiment, the 11th Illinois, under Lieutenant-Colonel Ransom. The gaps in the ranks of the two were closed up always toward the colors. The ground at their feet was strewn with their dead and wounded; at length the common misfortune overtook Logan. To keep men without cartridges under fire sweeping them front and flank would be cruel, if not impossible; and seeing it, he too gave the order to retire, and followed his decimated companies to the rear. The 11th then became the right of the brigade, and had to go in turn. Nevertheless, Ransom changed front to rear coolly, as if on parade, and joined in the general retirement. Forrest charged them and threw them into a brief confusion. The greater portion clung to their colors, and made good their retreat. By 11 o'clock Pillow held the road to Charlotte and the whole of the position occupied at dawn by the First Division, and with it the dead and all the wounded who could not get away.

Pillow's part of the programme, arranged in the council of the night before, was accomplished. The country was once more open to Floyd. Why did he not avail himself of the dearly bought opportunity, and march his army out?

Without pausing to consider whether the Confederate general could now have escaped with his troops, it must be evident that he should have made the effort. Pillow had discharged his duty well. With the disappearance of W. H. L. Wallace's brigade, it only remained for the victor to deploy his regiments into column and march into the country. The road was his. Buckner was in position to protect Colonel Head's withdrawal from the trenches opposite General Smith on the right; that done, he was also in position to cover the retreat. Buckner had also faithfully performed his task.

On the Union side the situation at this critical time was favorable to the proposed retirement. My division in the center was weakened by the despatch of one of my brigades to the assistance of General McClernand; in addition to which my orders were to hold my position. As a point of still greater importance, General Grant had gone on board the *St. Louis* at the request of Flag-Officer Foote, and he was there in consultation with that officer, presumably uninformed of the disaster which had befallen his right. It would take a certain time for him to return to the field and dispose his forces for pursuit. It may be said with strong assurance, consequently, that Floyd could have put his men fairly *en route* for Charlotte before the Federal commander could have interposed an obstruction to the movement. The real difficulty was in the hero of the morning, who now made haste to blight his laurels. General Pillow's vanity whistled itself into ludicrous exaltation. Imagining General Grant's whole army defeated and fleeing in rout for Fort Henry and the transports on the river, he deported himself accordingly. He began by ignoring Floyd. He rode to Buckner and accused him of shameful conduct. He sent an aide to the nearest telegraph station with a despatch to Albert Sidney Johnston, then in command of the Department, asseverating, "on the honor of a soldier," that the day was theirs. Nor did he stop at that. The victory, to be available, required that the enemy should be followed with energy. Such was a habit of Napoleon. Without deigning even to consult his chief, he ordered Buckner to move out and attack the Federals. There was a gorge, up which a road ran toward our central position, or rather what had been our central position. Pointing to the gorge and the road, he told Buckner that was his way and bade him attack in force. There was nothing to do but obey; and when Buckner had begun the movement, the wise programme decided upon the evening before was wiped from the slate.

When Buckner reluctantly took the gorge road marked out for him by Pillow, the whole Confederate army, save the detachments on the works, was virtually in pursuit of McClernand, retiring by the Wynn's Ferry road—falling back, in fact, upon my position. My division was now to feel the weight of Pillow's hand; if they should fail, the fortunes of the day would depend upon the veteran Smith.

When General McClernand perceived the peril threatening him in the morning, he sent an officer to me with a request for assistance. This request I referred to General Grant, who was at the time in consultation with Foote. Upon the turning of Oglesby's flank, McClernand repeated his request, with such a representation of the situation that, assuming the responsibility, I ordered Colonel Cruft to report with his brigade to McClernand. Cruft set out promptly. Unfortunately a guide misdirected him, so that he became involved in the retreat, and was prevented from accomplishing his object.

I was in the rear of my single remaining brigade, in conversation with Captain Rawlins, of Grant's staff, when a great shouting was heard behind me on the Wynn's Ferry road, whereupon I sent an orderly to ascertain the cause. The man reported the roads and woods full of soldiers apparently in rout. An officer then rode by at full speed, shouting "All 's lost! Save yourselves!" A hurried consultation was had with Rawlins, at the end of which the brigade was put in motion toward the enemy's works, on the very road by which Buckner was pursuing under Pillow's mischievous order. It happened also that Colonel W. H. L. Wallace had dropped into the same road with such of his command as stayed by their colors. He came up riding and at a walk, his leg over the horn of his saddle. He was perfectly cool, and looked like a farmer from a hard day's plowing. "Good morning," I said. "Good morning," was the reply. "Are they "pursuing you?" "Yes." "How far are they behind?" That instant the head of my command appeared on the road. The colonel calculated, then answered: "You will have about time to form line of battle right here." "Thank you. Good day." "Good day."

At that point the road began to dip into the gorge; on the right and left there were woods, and in front a dense thicket. An order was despatched to bring Battery A forward at full speed. Colonel John A. Thayer, commanding the brigade, formed it on the double-quick into line; the 1st Nebraska and the 58th Illinois on the right, and the 58th Ohio, with a detached company, on the left. The battery came up on the run and swung across the road, which had been left open for it. Hardly had it unlimbered before the enemy appeared, and firing began. For ten minutes or thereabouts the scenes of the morning were re-enacted. The Confederates struggled hard to perfect their deployments. The woods rang

THE BIVOUAC IN THE SNOW ON THE LINE OF BATTLE—QUESTIONING A PRISONER.

with musketry and artillery. The brush on the slope of the hill was mowed away with bullets. A great cloud arose and shut out the woods and the narrow valley below. Colonel Thayer and his regiments behaved with great gallantry, and the assailants fell back in confusion and returned to the intrenchments. W. H. L. Wallace and Oglesby reformed their commands behind Thayer, supplied them with ammunition, and stood at rest waiting for orders. There was then a lull in the battle. Even the cannonading ceased, and everybody was asking, What next?

Just then General Grant rode up to where General McClernand and I were in conversation. He was almost unattended. In his hand there were some papers, which looked like telegrams. Wholly unexcited, he saluted and received the salutations of his subordinates. Proceeding at once to business, he directed them to retire their commands to the heights out of cannon-range, and throw up works. Reinforcements were *en route*, he said, and it was advisable to await their coming. He was then informed of the mishap to the First Division, and that the road to Charlotte was open to the enemy.

In every great man's career there is a crisis exactly similar to that which now overtook General Grant, and it cannot be better described than as a crucial test of his nature. A mediocre person would have accepted the news as an argument for persistence in his resolution to enter upon a siege. Had General Grant done so, it is very probable his history would have been then and there concluded. His admirers and detractors are alike invited to study him at this precise juncture. It cannot be doubted that he saw with painful distinctness the effect of the disaster to his right wing. His face flushed slightly. With a sudden grip he crushed the papers in his hand. But in an instant these signs of disappointment or hesitation — as the reader pleases — cleared away. In his ordinary quiet voice he said, addressing himself to both officers, "Gentlemen, the position on the right must be retaken." With that he turned and galloped off.

Seeing in the road a provisional brigade, under Colonel Morgan L. Smith, consisting of the 11th Indiana and the 8th Missouri Infantry, going, by order of General C. F. Smith, to the aid of the First Division, I suggested that if General McClernand would order Colonel Smith to report to me, I would attempt to recover the lost ground; and, the order having been given, I reconnoitered the hill, determined upon a place of assault, and arranged my order of attack. I chose Colonel Smith's regiments to lead, and for that purpose conducted them to the crest of a hill opposite a steep bluff covered by the enemy. The two regiments had been formerly of my brigade. I knew they had been admirably drilled in the Zouave tactics, and my confidence in Smith and in George F. McGinnis, colonel of the 11th, was implicit. I was sure they would take their men to the top of the bluff. Colonel Cruft was put in line to support them on the right. Colonel Ross, with his regiments, the 17th and 49th, and the 46th, 57th, and 58th Illinois, were put as support on the left. Thayer's brigade was held in reserve. These dispositions filled the time till about 2 o'clock in the afternoon, when heavy cannonading, mixed with a long roll of musketry, broke out over on the left, whither it will be necessary to transfer the reader.

The veteran in command on the Union left had contented himself with allowing Buckner no rest, keeping up a continual sharp-shooting. Early in the morning of the 14th he made a demonstration of assault with three of his regiments, and though he purposely withdrew them, he kept the menace standing, to the great discomfort of his *vis-à-vis*. With the patience of an old soldier, he waited the pleasure of the general commanding, knowing that when the time came he would be called upon. During the battle of the gun-boats he rode through his command and grimly joked with them. He who never permitted the slightest familiarity from a subordinate could yet indulge in fatherly pleasantries with the ranks when he thought circumstances justified them. He never for a moment doubted the courage of volunteers; they were not regulars — that was all. If properly led, he believed they would storm the gates of his Satanic Majesty. Their hour of trial was now come.

From his brief and characteristic conference with McClernand and myself, General Grant rode to General C. F. Smith. What took place between them is not known, further than that he ordered an assault upon the outworks as a diversion in aid of the assault about to be delivered on the right. General Smith personally directed his chiefs of brigade to get their regiments ready. Colonel John Cook by his order increased the number of his skirmishers already engaged with the enemy.

Taking Lauman's brigade, General Smith began the advance. They were under fire instantly. The guns in the fort joined in with the infantry who were at the time in the rifle-pits, the great body of the Confederate right wing being with General Buckner. The defense was greatly favored by the ground, which subjected the assailants to a double fire from the beginning of the abatis. The men have said that "it looked too thick for a rabbit to get through." General Smith, on his horse, took position in the front and center of the line. Occasionally he turned in the saddle to see how the alignment was kept. For the most part, however, he held his face steadily toward the enemy. He was, of course, a conspicuous object for the sharpshooters in the rifle-pits. The air around him twittered with Minié bullets. Erect as if on review, he rode on, timing the gait of his horse with the movement of his colors. A soldier said: "I was nearly scared to death, but I saw the old man's white mustache over his shoulder, and went on."

On to the abatis the regiments moved without hesitation, leaving a trail of dead and wounded behind. There the fire seemed to get trebly hot, and there some of the men halted, whereupon, seeing the hesitation, General Smith put his cap on the point of his sword, held it aloft, and called out, "No flinching now, my lads! Here—this is the way! Come on!" He picked a path through the jagged limbs of the trees, holding his cap all the time in sight; and the effect was magical. The men swarmed in after him, and got through in the best order they could—not all of them, alas! On the other side of the obstruction they took the sem-

MAJOR-GENERAL GIDEON J. PILLOW, C. S. A.
Commander of the Confederate army at Donelson at the opening of the siege.

BRIGADIER-GENERAL JOHN B. FLOYD, C. S. A.
Commander of a division at Donelson and successor to Pillow.

The three Confederate chiefs of brigade intrusted by General Johnston with the defense of Nashville at Donelson, were John B. Floyd, Gideon J. Pillow and Simon B. Buckner. Generals Floyd and Pillow escaped from the fort before surrender, leaving General Buckner in command.

LIEUT.-GENERAL SIMON B. BUCKNER, C. S. A.
In command of the Confederate army at Donelson at the time
of the surrender.

blance of re-formation and charged in after their chief, who found himself then between the two fires. Up the ascent he rode; up they followed. At the last moment the keepers of the rifle-pits clambered out and fled. The four regiments engaged in the feat—the 25th Indiana, and the 2d, 7th, and 14th Iowa—planted their colors on the breastwork. Later in the day, Buckner came back with his division; but all his efforts to dislodge Smith were vain.

We left my division about to attempt the recapture of the hill, which had been the scene of the combat between Pillow and McClernand. If only on account of the results which followed that assault, in connection with the heroic performance of General C. F. Smith, it is necessary to return to it.

Riding to my old regiments,—the 8th Missouri and the 11th Indiana,—I asked them if they were ready. They demanded the word of me. Waiting a moment for Morgan L. Smith to light a cigar, I called out, "Forward it is, then!" They were directly in front of the ascent to be climbed. Without stopping for his supports, Colonel Smith led them down into a broad hollow, and catching sight of the advance, Cruft and Ross also moved forward. As the two regiments began the climb, the 8th Missouri slightly in the lead, a line of fire ran along the brow of the height. The flank companies cheered while deploying as skirmishers. Their Zouave prac-

tice proved of excellent service to them. Now on the ground, creeping when the fire was hottest, running when it slackened, they gained ground with astonishing rapidity, and at the same time maintained a fire that was like a sparkling of the earth. For the most part the bullets aimed at them passed over their heads and took effect in the ranks behind them. Colonel Smith's cigar was shot off close to his lips. He took another and called for a match. A soldier ran up and gave him one. "Thank you. Take your place now. We are almost up," he said, and, smoking, spurred his horse forward. A few yards from the crest of the height the regiments began loading and firing as they advanced. The defenders gave way. On the top there was a brief struggle, which was ended by Cruft and Ross with their supports.

The whole line then moved forward simultaneously, and never stopped until the Confederates were within the works. There had been no occasion to call on the reserves. The road to Charlotte was again effectually shut, and the battle-field of the morning, with the dead and wounded lying where they had fallen, was in possession of the Third Division, which stood halted within easy musket-range of the rifle-pits. It was then about half-past 3 o'clock in the afternoon. I was reconnoitering the works of the enemy preliminary to charging them, when Colonel Webster, of General Grant's staff, came to me and repeated the order to

fall back out of cannon-range and throw up breastworks. "The general does not know that we have the hill," I said. Webster replied: "I give you the order as he gave it to me." "Very well," said I, "give him my compliments, and say that I have received the order." Webster smiled and rode away. The ground was not vacated, though the assault was deferred. In assuming the responsibility, I had no doubt of my ability to satisfy General Grant of the correctness of my course; and it was subsequently approved.

When night fell, the command bivouacked without fire or supper. Fatigue parties were told off to look after the wounded; and in the relief given there was no distinction made between friend and foe. The labor extended through the whole night, and the surgeons never rested. By sunset the conditions of the morning were all restored. The Union commander was free to order a general assault next day or resort to a formal siege.

A great discouragement fell upon the brave men inside the works that night. Besides suffering from wounds and bruises and the dreadful weather, they were aware that though they had done their best they were held in a close grip by a superior enemy. A council of general and field officers was held at headquarters, which resulted in a unanimous resolution that if the position in front of General Pillow had not been reoccupied by the Federals in strength, the army should effect its re-

treat. A reconnoissance was ordered to make the test. Colonel Forrest conducted it. He reported that the ground was not only reoccupied, but that the enemy were extended yet farther around the Confederate left. The council then held a final session.

General Simon B. Buckner, as the junior officer present, gave his opinion first; he thought he could not successfully resist the assault which would be made by daylight by a vastly superior force. But he further remarked, that as he understood the principal object of the defense of Donelson was to cover the movement of General Albert Sidney Johnston's army from Bowling Green to Nashville, if that movement was not completed he was of opinion that the defense should be continued at the risk of the destruction of the entire force. General Floyd replied that General Johnston's army had already reached Nashville, whereupon General Buckner said that "it would be wrong to subject the army to a virtual massacre, when no good could result from the sacrifice, and that the general officers owed it to their men, when further resistance was unavailing, to obtain the best terms of capitulation possible for them."

Both Generals Floyd and Pillow acquiesced in the opinion. Ordinarily the council would have ended at this point, and the commanding general would have addressed himself to the duty of obtaining terms. He would have called for pen, ink, and paper, and prepared a note for despatch to the commanding general of the opposite force. But there were circumstances outside the mere military situation which at this juncture pressed themselves into consideration. As this was the first surrender of armed men banded together for war upon the general government, what would the Federal authorities do with the prisoners? This question was of application to all the gentlemen in the council. It was lost to view, however, when General Floyd announced his purpose to leave with two steamers which were to be down at daylight, and to take with him as many of his division as the steamers could carry away.

General Pillow then remarked that there were no two persons in the Confederacy whom the Yankees would rather capture than himself and General Floyd (who had been Buchanan's Secretary of War, and was under indictment at Washington). As to the propriety of his accompanying General Floyd, the latter said, coolly, that the question was one for every man to decide for himself. Buckner was of the same view, and added that as for himself he regarded it as his duty to stay with his men and share their fate, whatever it might be. Pillow persisted in leaving. Floyd then directed General Buckner to consider himself in command. Immediately after the council was concluded, General Floyd prepared for his departure. His first move was to have his brigade drawn up. The peculiarity of the step was that, with the exception of one, the 20th Mississippi regiment, his regiments were all Virginians. A short time before daylight the two steamboats arrived. Without loss of time the general hastened to the river, embarked with his Virginians, and at an early hour cast loose from the shore, and in good time, and safely, he reached Nashville. He never satisfactorily explained upon what principle he appropriated all the transportation on hand to the use of his particular command.

Colonel Forrest was present at the council, and when the final resolution was taken, he promptly announced that he neither could nor would surrender his command. The bold trooper had no qualms upon the subject. He assembled his men, all as hardy as himself, and after reporting once more at headquarters, he moved out and plunged into a slough formed by backwater from the river. An icy crust covered its surface, the wind blew

fiercely, and the darkness was unrelieved by a star. There was fearful floundering as the command followed him. At length he struck dry land, and was safe. He was next heard of at Nashville.

General Buckner, who throughout the affair bore himself with dignity, ordered the troops back to their positions and opened communications with General Grant, whose laconic demand of "unconditional surrender," in his reply to General Buckner's overtures, became at once a watchword of the war.

The Third Division was astir very early on the 16th of February. The regiments began to form and close up the intervals between them, the intention being to charge the breastworks south of

Hd Qrs, Army in the Field
Camp near Donelson, Feb.y 16th 1862

Gen. S. B. Buckner,
Confed. Army,

Sir;

Yours of this date proposing
Armistice, and appointment of Commissioners,
to settle terms of Capitulation is just received.
No terms except an unconditional and immediate
surrender can be accepted.

I propose to move immediately upon
your works.

I am Sir, very respectfully
your obt. Sert.
U. S. Grant
Brig. Gen.

FACSIMILE OF THE ORIGINAL "UNCONDITIONAL SURRENDER" DISPATCH.

Dover about breakfast-time. In the midst of the preparation a bugle was heard and a white flag was seen coming from the town toward the pickets. I sent my adjutant-general to meet the flag half-way and inquire its purpose. Answer was returned that General Buckner had capitulated during the night, and was now sending information of the fact to the commander of the troops in this quarter, that there might be no further bloodshed. The division was ordered to advance and take possession of the works and of all public property and prisoners. Leaving that agreeable duty to the brigade commanders, I joined the officer bearing the flag, and with my staff rode across the trench and into the town, till we came to the door of the old tavern al-

ready described, where I dismounted. The tavern was the headquarters of General Buckner, to whom I sent my name; and, being an acquaintance, I was at once admitted.

I found General Buckner with his staff at breakfast. He met me with politeness and dignity. Turning to the officers at the table, he remarked: "General Wallace, it is not necessary to introduce you to these gentlemen; you are acquainted with them all." They arose, came forward one by one, and gave their hands in salutation. I was then invited to breakfast, which consisted of corn bread and coffee, the best the gallant host had in his kitchen. We sat at the table about an hour and a half, when General Grant arrived and took temporary possession of the tavern as his headquarters. Later in the morning the army marched in and completed the possession.

ON BOARD THE GUN-BOAT "CARONDELET."

The following is an extract from Rear-Admiral Walke's account of the naval attack on Fort Donelson:
. . . "As we drew nearer, the enemy's fire greatly increased in force and effect. . . . Soon a 128-pounder struck our anchor, smashing it into flying bolts, and bounded over the vessel, taking away a part of our smoke-stack. . . Another shot took away the remaining boat-davits and the boat with them; and still they came, harder and faster, taking flag-staffs and smoke-stacks, and tearing off the side armor as lightning tears the bark from a tree. Our men fought desperately, but, under the excitement of the occasion, loaded too hastily, and the port rifled gun exploded.

"One of the crew, in his account of the explosion soon after it occurred, said: 'I was serving the gun with shell. When it exploded it knocked us all down, killing none, but wounding over a dozen men and spreading dismay and confusion among us. For about two minutes I was stunned, and at least five minutes elapsed before I could tell what was the matter. When I found out that I was more scared than hurt, although suffering from the gunpowder which I had inhaled, I looked forward and saw our gun lying on the deck, split in three pieces. Then the cry ran through the boat that we were on fire, and my duty as pump-man called me to the pumps. While I was there, two shots entered our bow-ports and killed four men and wounded several others. They were borne past me, three with their heads off. The sight almost sickened me, and I turned my head away. Our master's mate came soon after and ordered us to our quarters at the gun. I told him the gun had burst, and that we had caught fire on the upper deck from the enemy's shell. He then said: 'Never mind the fire; go to your quarters.' Then I took a station at the starboard tackle of another rifled bow-gun and remained there until the close of the fight.' The carpenter and his men extinguished the flames."

MAJOR-GENERAL STERLING PRICE, C. S. A.
Commanding the Missouri State Guard at Pea Ridge. (From a photograph.)

THE PEA RIDGE CAMPAIGN.

BY FRANZ SIGEL, MAJOR-GENERAL, U. S. V.
General commanding the First and Second Divisions at Pea Ridge.

THE battle of Pea Ridge (or Elkhorn Tavern, as the Confederates named it) was fought on the 7th and 8th of March, 1862, one month before the battle of Shiloh. It was the first clear and decisive victory gained by the North in a pitched battle west of the Mississippi River, and until Price's invasion of 1864, the last effort of the South to carry the war into the State of Missouri, except by abortive raids. . . .

The battle of Pea Ridge was the first respite gained by the almost incessant activity and the unflinching courage of our little army, — the Army of the Southwest. It was not a "great" battle, like that of Gettysburg or Chattanooga; it was not of such preponder- ating national importance; it did not "break the backbone of the Rebellion," but it virtu- ally cleared the Southwest of the enemy, gave peace to the people of Missouri, at least for the next two years, and made it possible for our veterans to reinforce the armies under Buell, Rosecrans, Grant, and Sherman. It was a battle of all kinds of surprises and ac- cidents, of good fighting and good manœuv- ering. Van Dorn was evidently "surprised" when he found that his plan to take St. Louis, and to carry the war into Illinois in April, 1862, was anticipated by our unex- pected appearance; he was badly "surprised" when on the 6th of March, instead of "gob- bling up" my two divisions at McKissick's farm, as he confidently expected, he only met a rear-guard of 600 men, which he could not gobble up during nearly 6 hours of its march of 6 miles; he was also surprised to find, on his détour around our left flank and rear, that the road was at different places so blocked up, that instead of arriving in our rear, on the road to Springfield, with the divisions of Price at daylight of the 7th, he did not reach that point before 10 o'clock in the morning, by which de- lay Price's and McCulloch's forces became separated and could not assist each other at the decisive moment, while we gained time to make our preparations for the recep- tion of both. Finally, on the 8th, Van Dorn was greatly "surprised to find himself suddenly confronted by a new, unexpected force," attacked in flank and rear, and com- pelled to retreat. On the other hand, Curtis was "sur- prised" by the sudden turn things had taken, and much disappointed because the enemy did not make the attack against our front, a position not only very strong by na- ture, presenting a chain of high hills, but also strength- ened by intrenchments and abatis, the access to it being also protected and impeded by a deep creek running along our line of defense. He would have been much more "sur- prised" had it not been for the discovery, by our scouting parties, of the enemy's flanking movement.

In a strategical and tactical point of view, the battle of Pea Ridge forms a counterpart to the battle of Wilson's Creek. In the latter battle *we* were the outflanking party, approaching the camp of McCulloch and Price by a night march, completely surprising and attacking their forces in the morning, but making our attack in front and rear, without being able to communicate with and assist each other. My own brigade of 1118 men, which had gained the enemy's rear, was beaten first, and then the forces of General Lyon, 4282 men, after a heroic resistance were compelled to leave the field. The enemy held the "in- terior lines," and could throw readily his forces from one point to the other. At Pea Ridge the same advantage was with *our* army, although the enemy had better facil- ities of communication between his left and right wing, by the road leading from Bentonville to Elkhorn Tavern, than we had had at Wilson's Creek. There we had had to meet substantially the same troops we encountered at Pea Ridge, with the exception of the Indian Brigade under Pike.

From the result of the battles of Wilson's Creek and Pea Ridge, it will be seen that the manœuver of outflanking and "marching into the enemy's rear" is not always suc- cessful. It was not so at Wilson's Creek, when we had approached, unobserved, within cannon-shot of the en- emy's lines; however, we were only 5400 against about 11,000, while at Pea Ridge the enemy had 16,202 men in action against our 10,500. In a manœuver of that kind, the venture of a smaller army to surprise and "bag" an enemy whose forces are concentrated, and who holds the "interior lines" or "inside track," will always be great, unless the enemy's troops are inferior in quality, or other- wise at a disadvantage.

The movement of Van Dorn during the night of the 6th was bold, well conceived, and would probably have been more successful if it had not been pushed too far out. If Van Dorn had formed his line with the left of Price's forces resting on the heights, west of Elkhorn Tavern, and McCulloch's immediately on its right, he would have gained three or four hours' time, and could have swept down upon us before 8 o'clock in the morning, when no preparations had been made to receive him; his two wings (Price's and McCulloch's) would not have been sep- arated from each other by an interval of several miles, and his communications between Bentonville and his position would have been protected. Instead of following this

MAJOR-GENERAL EARL VAN DORN, C. S. A.
In chief command of the Confederate forces at
Pea Ridge. (From a photograph.)

course of action demanded by the unforeseen im- pediment on the road, he passed several miles farther to the northeast, and after gaining the Springfield road, he shifted the whole of Price's forces around to the southeast (toward the Hunts- ville road), consuming again much valuable time. In fact, instead of commencing his attack by the left at daylight on the 7th, as he expected to do, he did not commence it earnestly before 2 P. M., and instead of gaining the desirable position on the heights and fields which my divisions occupied the next day, he made his attack in Cross Timber Hollow, where our inferior forces had the advan- tage of defense and of concealing their weakness in the woods, ravines, and gullies of that wilder- ness. Price's troops fought very bravely, but so did ours. . . . Price's 6500 men with 38 guns could not overwhelm about 4500 with 23 guns (including the reinforcements from the First and Second Divisions). . . .

The death of McCulloch was not only fatal to his troops, but also a most serious blow to Van Dorn. Until 2 o'clock on the 7th, the latter had confidently expected to hear of successful action against our left wing; but he received no answer to the de- spatch he had sent, and began to push forward his own wing. He succeeded, and when night fell made his headquarters at Elkhorn Tavern, where Carr and Major Weston of our army had been in the morning. But here he stopped. He says that by some misunderstanding the troops in the ad- vance were called back (as they were at Shiloh); the true reason for their withdrawal, however, seems to have been their satisfaction with what they had done, and the assurance of completing the work in the morning.

MAJOR-GENERAL SAMUEL R. CURTIS, U. S. V.
Commanding the Union Army at Pea Ridge.

MAJOR-GENERAL FRANZ SIGEL, U. S. V.
Commanding First and Second Divisions at Pea Ridge.

SHARP FIGHTING AT PEA RIDGE,
—FROM THE CONFEDERATE SIDE.

Mr. Hunt P. Wilson, who was a member of Guibor's Confederate battery, has given the "St. Louis Republican" a spirited description of the contest on the Confederate right in the first day's fight. He thus describes the Confederate advance:

. . . "The column entered by what is called Cross Timber Hollow. Some of the ridges are 150 feet high. In the valley of this defile is located what is known as the tan-yard, three-quarters of a mile from Elkhorn Tavern. From the tan-yard there is a gradual ascent. . . .

"The fire in front began to lull, and Slack's brigade

HILL'S ARKANSAS AND TEXAS TROOPS.   GENERAL STERLING PRICE.   GUIBOR'S BATTERY.   ELKHORN TAVERN.
FROST'S BRIGADE.   BURBRIDGE'S, WHITFIELD'S, AND SLACK'S REGIMENTS.   CHURCHILL'S ARKANSAS AND TEXAS TROOPS.   BLEDSOE'S AND GORHAM'S BATTERIES.

LAST HOUR OF THE BATTLE OF PEA RIDGE, MARCH 8, 1862.
Advance of the Union forces to retake the position at Elkhorn Tavern. From a painting by Hunt P. Wilson, in possession of the Southern Historical Society, St. Louis.

with Rives's and Burbridge's regiments came up on a left-wheel, with Rains on their left, across to the hollow, and the whole line charged up with a wild cheer. Captain Guibor, who well understood how to fight artillery in the brush, took all the canister he could lay his hands on, and with two guns went up in the charge with the infantry. General Rains's brigade on the left, led by Colonel Walter Scott O'Kane, and Major Rainwater made a brilliant dash at the redoubt and battery which had been throwing on them for an hour or more from its position in an old field. Eight guns were captured along the line. The Federal troops, being dislodged from the woods, began forming in the fields and planted some new batteries back of the knobs in the rear. And now the fight grew furious. Gorham's battery could not hold its position, and fell back to its old place. Guibor planted his two guns directly in front of the tavern and opened at close quarters with grape and canister on the Federal line, in which great confusion was evident, as officers could be seen trying to rally and re-form their men.

"The entire Confederate line was charging up to the Elkhorn Tavern; Colonel Carr, the Federal cavalry commander, had withdrawn his command from the bench of the mountain on the Confederate right. The Illinois Battery, at first planted in the horse-lot west of the tavern, had limbered to the rear and taken a new position in the fields. The Federal Mountain Howitzer Battery had also moved away. The 8th Iowa Battery, which had poured such a hot fire down the road upon Guibor and Gorham, had by this time lost the use of two of its guns, dismounted by the fire of Guibor's battery, but

continued to fight its two remaining guns until the Confederate regiment of Colonel Clint Burbridge was upon them; when, their horses being killed, that regiment took them in, and at nightfall brought them down the road. To the left on the Van Winkle road the [Confederate] batteries of McDonald, Bledsoe, and Wade had been engaged in a severe artillery duel in which the Federal batteries held their own until the Confederate infantry got within range, when they were forced back, leaving two guns captured by Rains's men led by the gallant O'Kane. The cavalry on the extreme left, under General John B. Clark and Colonel Robert McCulloch, had turned the Federal right wing, and the latter's entire line was falling back to meet reinforcements hurrying to their assistance from Sugar Creek on their left rear. The Federals placed 18 or 20 guns to command the tavern. Guibor moved up with the Confederate line, or a little in advance, and formed in battery in the narrow road in front of the tavern, losing several horses in the movement. And now commenced a hot fight. The rapid fire of the twenty pieces of Federal artillery . . . commenced waving and blazing in his front, while the two guns were replying with grape and canister. Now came the crisis. A regiment of United States infantry moved out of the timber on the left front of the guns about one hundred yards distant, with a small field intervening, the fences around it leveled to the ground. On Guibor's right was the tavern, on his left a blacksmith's shop, and in the lot some corn-cribs. Behind these buildings 'Rock' Champion had placed his company of cavalry to protect their horses from thickly flying bullets. Rock's

quick eye saw the bright bayonets as they were pushing through the brush, and, riding up, he yelled in his rough-and-ready style, 'Guibor, they're flankin' you!' 'I know it, but I can't spare a gun to turn on them,' was the reply. There was no supporting infantry on his left. Said Rock, 'I'll charge them!' This meant to attack a full regiment of infantry advancing in line, 700 or 800 strong, with 22 men. . . . Galloping back a few paces to his little band, his clear, ringing voice could be heard by friend and enemy. 'Battalion, forward, trot, march, gallop, march, charge!' and with a wild yell in they went, their gallant chief in the lead, closely followed by 'Sabre Jack' Murphy, an old regular dragoon; Fitzsimmons, Coggins, O'Flaherty, Pomeroy, and the others. The last named were old British dragoons; three of them had ridden with the heavy squadrons at Balaklava, and all well knew what was in front of them. . . . Within thirty seconds they were right in the midst of the surprised Federal infantry, shouting, slashing, shooting. Corporal Casey charged on foot. Guibor's two guns were at the same time turned left oblique and deluged the Federal left with canister. The result was precisely what Champion had foreseen, and proved his reckless courage was directed by good judgment. The attack was a clear surprise, the result a stampede; the infantry fired an aimless, scattering volley—then, expecting a legion of horsemen to fall on them, fled in confusion. Champion did not follow. Knowing when to stop as well as to commence, he secured their flag and quickly returned to the battery which he had saved, with a loss of only three of his gallant rough-riders."

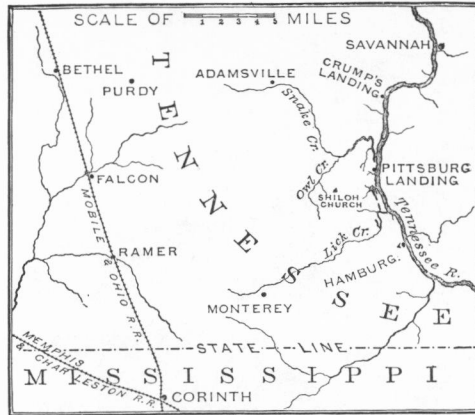

OUTLINE MAP OF THE SHILOH CAMPAIGN.

BRIGADIER-GENERAL W. H. L. WALLACE, U. S. V.
Killed at Shiloh.

DONELSON TO SHILOH.

The Union victory at Pea Ridge set free the Northern troops in Missouri to unite with the armies east of the Mississippi. On the Confederate side Van Dorn and Price marched their troops eastward to unite them with the armies under Albert Sidney Johnston and Beauregard, which had fallen back from the Tennessee line after the capture of Fort Donelson by Grant, and were concentrating at Corinth, Miss., to protect the Memphis and Charleston railway. The victorious army at Donelson, and the Army of the Ohio under Buell, were directed by General Halleck to move up the Tennessee River — that is, south — and cut the Memphis and Charleston road east of Corinth. Grant's army reached Pittsburg Landing early in April. While lying in camp awaiting the arrival of Buell it was attacked early on the morning of the 6th. Buell arrived that afternoon and evening, and on the 7th the united Union forces drove the Confederates back to Corinth. None of the troops from Pea Ridge reached the field in time to participate, and the contest lay between the forces which had confronted each other on the Tennessee line all winter. Johnston was killed at Shiloh, and a few weeks later Beauregard evacuated Corinth, thus yielding up to the North all that had been fought for at Shiloh.

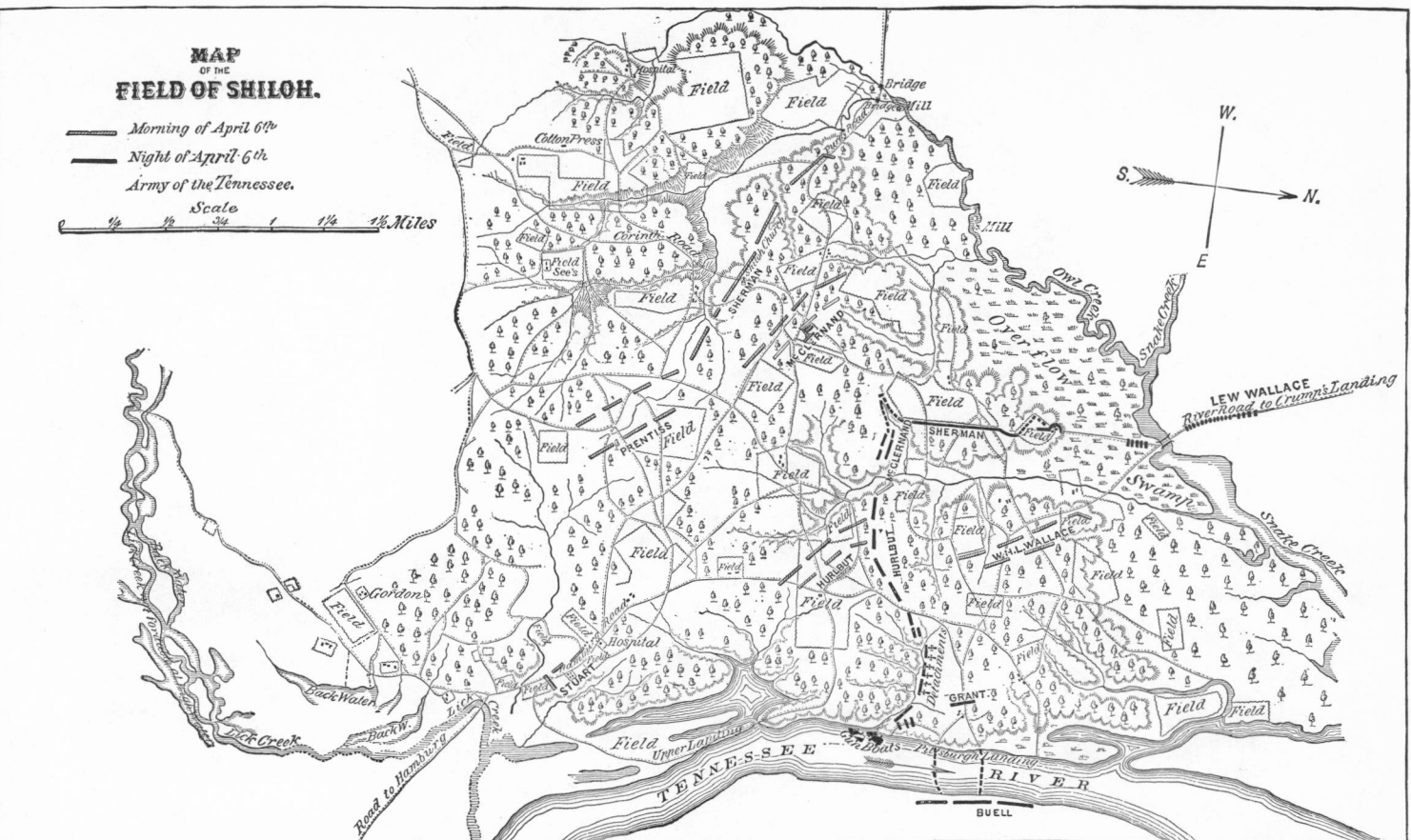

MAP OF THE FIELD OF SHILOH AS REVISED BY GENERAL GRANT.
From General Grant's "Memoirs," by permission of Charles L. Webster & Co.

THE BATTLE OF SHILOH.

THE UNION SIDE.

[BY ULYSSES S. GRANT, GENERAL, U. S. A.
Brigadier-General commanding the Union Army of the Tennessee at Shiloh.

THE battle of Shiloh, or Pittsburg Landing, fought on Sunday and Monday, the 6th and 7th of April, 1862, has been perhaps less understood, or, to state the case more accurately, more persistently misunderstood, than any other engagement between National and Confederate troops during the entire rebellion. Correct reports of the battle have been published, notably by Sherman, Badeau, and, in a speech before a meeting of veterans, by General Prentiss; but all of these appeared long subsequent to the close of the rebellion, and after public opinion had been most erroneously formed.

Events had occurred before the battle, and others subsequent to it, which determined me to make no report to my then chief, General Halleck, further than was contained in a letter, written immediately after the battle, informing him that an engagement had been fought, and announcing the result. The occurrences alluded to are these: After the capture of Fort Donelson, with over fifteen thousand effec-

tive men and all their munitions of war, I believed much more could be accomplished without further sacrifice of life.

Clarksville, a town between Donelson and Nashville, in the State of Tennessee, and on the east bank of the Cumberland, was garrisoned by the enemy. Nashville was also garrisoned, and was probably the best-provisioned depot at the time in the Confederacy. Albert Sidney Johnston occupied Bowling Green, Ky., with a large force. I believed, and my information justified the belief, that these places would fall into our hands without a battle, if threatened promptly. I determined not to miss this chance. But being only a district commander, and under the immediate orders of the department commander, General Halleck, whose headquarters were at St. Louis, it was my duty to communicate to him all I proposed to do, and to get his approval, if possible. I did so communicate, and, receiving no reply, acted upon my own judgment. The result proved that my information

was correct, and sustained my judgment. What, then, was my surprise, after so much had been accomplished by the troops under my immediate command between the time of leaving Cairo, early in February, and the 4th of March, to receive from my chief a despatch of the latter date, saying: "You will place Major-General C. F. Smith in command of expedition, and remain yourself at Fort Henry. Why do you not obey my orders to report strength and positions of your command?" I was left virtually in arrest on board a steamer, without even a guard, for about a week, when I was released and ordered to resume my command.

Again: Shortly after the battle of Shiloh had been fought, General Halleck moved his headquarters to Pittsburg Landing, and assumed command of the troops in the field. Although next to him in rank, and nominally in command of my old district and army, I was ignored as much as if I had been at the most distant point of territory within my jurisdiction; and although I was in command of all the troops engaged at Shiloh, I was not permitted to see one of the reports of General Buell or his subordinates in that battle, until they were published by the War Department, long after the event. In consequence, I never myself made a full report of this engagement.

ULYSSES S. GRANT.
In command of the Union forces at the battle of Shiloh. (From a photograph taken, probably, in 1863.)

ALBERT SIDNEY JOHNSTON.
In command of the Confederate forces at the battle of Shiloh. (From a photograph taken in Salt Lake City in 1860, at the age of fifty-seven.)

When I was restored to my command, on the 13th of March, I found it on the Tennessee River, part at Savannah and part at Pittsburg Landing, nine miles above, and on the opposite or western bank. I generally spent the day at Pittsburg, and returned by boat to Savannah in the evening. I was intending to remove my headquarters to Pittsburg, where I had sent all the troops immediately upon my reassuming command, but Buell, with the Army of the Ohio, had been ordered to reinforce me from Columbia, Tenn. He was expected daily, and would come in at Savannah. I remained, therefore, a few days longer than I otherwise should have done, for the purpose of meeting him on his arrival.

General Lew Wallace, with a division, had been placed by General Smith at Crump's Landing, about five miles farther down the river than Pittsburg, and also on the west bank. His position I regarded as so well chosen that he was not moved from it until the Confederate attack in force at Shiloh.

The skirmishing in our front had been so continuous from about the 3d of April up to the determined attack, that I remained on the field each night until an hour when I felt there would be no further danger before morning. In fact, on Friday, the 4th, I was very much injured by my horse falling with me and on me while I was trying to get to the front, where firing had been heard. The night was one of impenetrable darkness, with rain pouring down in torrents; nothing was visible to the eye except as revealed by the frequent flashes of lightning. Under these circumstances I had to trust to the horse, without guidance, to keep the road. I had not gone far, however, when I met General W. H. L. Wallace and General (then Colonel) McPherson coming from the direction of the front. They said all was quiet so far as the enemy was concerned. On the way back to the boat my horse's feet slipped from under him, and he fell with my leg under his body. The extreme softness of the ground, from the excessive rains of the few preceding days, no doubt saved me from a severe injury and protracted lameness. As it was, my ankle was very much injured; so much so, that my boot had to be cut off. During the battle, and for two or three days after, I was unable to walk except with crutches.

On the 5th General Nelson, with a division of Buell's army, arrived at Savannah, and I ordered him to move up the east bank of the river, to be in a position where he could be ferried over to Crump's Landing or Pittsburg Landing, as occasion required. I had learned that General Buell himself would be at Savannah the next day, and desired to meet me on his arrival. Affairs at Pittsburg Landing had been such for several days that I did not want to be away during the day. I determined, therefore, to take a very early breakfast and ride out to meet Buell, and thus save time. He had arrived on the evening of the 5th, but had not advised me of the fact, and I was not aware of it until some time after. While I was at breakfast, however, heavy firing was heard in the direction of Pittsburg Landing, and I hastened there, sending a hurried note to Buell, informing him of the reason why I could not meet him at Savannah. On the way up the river I directed the despatch-boat to run in close to Crump's Land-ing, so that I could communicate with General Lew Wallace. I found him waiting on a boat, apparently expecting to see me, and I directed him to get his troops in line ready to execute any orders he might receive. He replied that his troops were already under arms and prepared to move.

Up to that time I had felt by no means certain that Crump's Landing might not be the point of attack. On reaching the front, however, about 8 A. M., I found that the attack on Shiloh was unmistakable, and that nothing more than a small guard, to protect our transports and stores, was needed at Crump's. Captain A. S. Baxter, a quartermaster on my staff, was accordingly directed to go back and order General Wallace to march immediately to Pittsburg, by the road nearest the river. Captain Baxter made a memorandum of his order. About 1 P. M., not hearing from Wallace, and being much in need of reinforcements, I sent two more of my staff, Colonel James B. McPherson and Captain W. R. Rowley, to bring him up with his division. They reported finding him marching toward Purdy, Bethel, or some point west from the river,

MAJOR-GEN. THOMAS L. CRITTENDEN, U. S. V.

MAJOR-GENERAL THOMAS J. WOOD, U. S. V.

PITTSBURG LANDING.

MAJOR-GEN. ALEXANDER McD. McCOOK, U. S. V.

MAJOR-GENERAL B. M. PRENTISS, U. S. V.

and farther from Pittsburg by several miles than when he started. The road from his first position was direct, and near the river. Between the two points a bridge had been built across Snake Creek by our troops, at which Wallace's command had assisted, expressly to enable the troops at the two places to support each other in case of need. Wallace did not arrive in time to take part in the first day's fight. General Wallace has since claimed that the order delivered to him by Captain Baxter was simply to join the right of the army, and that the road over which he marched would have taken him to the road from Pittsburg to Purdy, where it crosses Owl Creek, on the right of Sherman; but this is not where I had ordered him nor where I wanted him to go. I never could see, and do not now see, why any order was necessary further than to direct him to come to Pittsburg Landing, without specify-

ing by what route. His was one of three veteran divisions that had been in battle, and its absence was severely felt. Later in the war, General Wallace would never have made the mistake that he

* Since the publication in "The Century" of my article on "The Battle of Shiloh" I have received from Mrs. W. H. L. Wallace, widow of the gallant general who was killed in the first day's fight of that battle, a letter from General Lew Wallace to him, dated the morning of the 5th. At the date of this letter it was well known that the Confederates had troops out along the Mobile and Ohio railroad west of Crump's Landing and Pittsburg Landing, and were also collecting near Shiloh. This letter shows that at that time General Lew Wallace was making preparations for the emergency that might happen for the passing of reinforcements between Shiloh and his position, extending from Crump's Landing westward; and he sends the letter over the road running from Adamsville to the Pittsburg Landing and Purdy road. These two roads intersect nearly a mile west of the crossing of the latter over Owl Creek, where our right rested. In this letter General Lew Wallace advises General W. H. L. Wallace that he will send "to-morrow" (and his letter also says "April 5th," which is the same day the letter was dated and which, therefore, must have been written on the 4th) some cavalry to report to him at his headquarters, and suggesting the propriety of General W. H. L. Wallace's sending a company back with them for the purpose of having the cavalry at the two landings familiarize themselves with the road, so that they could "act promptly in case of emergency as guides to and from the different camps."

This modifies very materially what I have said, and what has been said by others, of the conduct of General Lew Wallace at the battle of Shiloh. It shows that he naturally, with no more experience than he had at the time in the profession of arms, would take the particular road that he did start upon in the absence of orders to move by a different road.

committed on the 6th of April, 1862.* I presume his idea was that by taking the route he did, he would be able to come around on the flank or rear of the enemy, and thus perform an act of heroism

The mistake he made, and which probably caused his apparent dilatoriness, was that of advancing some distance after he found that the firing, which would be at first directly to his front and then off to the left, had fallen back until it had got very much in rear of the position of his advance. This falling back had taken place before I sent General Wallace to move up to Pittsburg Landing, and, naturally, my order was to follow the road nearest the river. But my order was verbal, and to a staff-officer who was to deliver it to General Wallace, so that I am not competent to say just what order the general actually received.

General Wallace's division was stationed, the First Brigade at Crump's Landing, the Second out two miles, and the Third two and a half miles out. Hearing the sounds of battle, General Wallace early ordered his First and Third brigades to concentrate on the Second. If the position of our front had not changed, the road which Wallace took would have been somewhat shorter to our right than the River road. U. S. GRANT.
MOUNT McGREGOR, N. Y., June 21, 1885.

In a letter to General Grant, written Sept. 16, 1884, General Wallace said, in part: "The fact is, I was the victim of a mistake. Captain Baxter's omission from the order you gave him for transmission to me — the omission of the road you wanted me to take in coming up, viz., *the lower or River Road to Pittsburg Landing* — was the cause of my movement at noon. It is also the key of explanation of all that followed. That I took the directest and shortest road to effect a junction with the right of the army, and marched promptly upon receipt of the order, are the best evidence I could have furnished of an actual desire to do my duty, and share the fortunes of the day with you, whether they were good or bad."

that would redound to the credit of his command, as well as to the benefit of his country.

Shiloh was a log meeting-house, some two or three miles from Pittsburg Landing, and on the ridge which divides the waters of Snake and Lick creeks, the former entering into the Tennessee just north of Pittsburg Landing, and the latter south. Shiloh was the key to our position, and was held by Sherman. His division was at that time wholly raw, no part of it ever having been in an engagement, but I thought this deficiency was more than made up by the superiority of the commander. McClernand was on Sherman's left, with troops that had been engaged at Fort Donelson, and were therefore veterans so far as Western troops had become such at that stage of the war. Next to McClernand came Prentiss, with a raw division, and on the extreme left, Stuart, with one brigade of Sherman's division. Hurlbut was in rear of Prentiss, massed, and in reserve at the time of the onset. The division of General C. F. Smith was

FIRST POSITION OF WATERHOUSE'S BATTERY.
From a sketch made shortly after the battle.

CONFEDERATE CHARGE UPON PRENTISS'S CAMP ON SUNDAY MORNING.

on the right, also in reserve. General Smith was sick in bed at Savannah, some nine miles below, but in hearing of our guns. His services on those two eventful days would no doubt have been of inestimable value had his health permitted his presence. The command of his division devolved upon Brigadier-General W. H. L. Wallace, a most estimable and able officer,—a veteran, too, for he had served a year in the Mexican war, and had been with his command at Henry and Donelson. Wallace was mortally wounded in the first day's engagement, and with the change of commanders thus necessarily effected in the heat of battle, the efficiency of his division was much weakened.

The position of our troops made a continuous line from Lick Creek, on the left, to Owl Creek, a branch of Snake Creek, on the right, facing nearly south, and possibly a little west. The water in all these streams was very high at the time, and contributed to protect our flanks. The enemy was compelled, therefore, to attack directly in front. This he did with great vigor, inflicting heavy losses on the National side, but suffering much heavier on his own.

The Confederate assaults were made with such disregard of losses on their own side, that our line of tents soon fell into their hands. The ground on which the battle was fought was undulating, heavily timbered, with scattered clearings, the woods giving some protection to the troops on both sides. There was also considerable underbrush. A number of attempts were made by the enemy to turn our right flank, where Sherman was posted, but every effort was repulsed with heavy loss. But the front attack was kept up so vigorously that, to prevent the success of these attempts to get on our

flanks, the National troops were compelled several times to take positions to the rear, nearer Pittsburg Landing. When the firing ceased at night, the National line was all of a mile in rear of the position it had occupied in the morning.

In one of the backward moves, on the 6th, the division commanded by General Prentiss did not fall back with the others. This left his flanks exposed, and enabled the enemy to capture him, with about 2200 of his officers and men. General Badeau gives 4 o'clock of the 6th as about the time this capture took place. He may be right as to the time, but my recollection is that the hour was later. General Prentiss himself gave the hour as half-past five. I was with him, as I was with each of the division commanders that day, several times, and my recollection is that the last time I was with him was about half-past four, when his division was standing up firmly, and the general was as cool as if expecting victory. But no matter whether it was four or later, the story that he and his command were surprised and captured in their camps is without any foundation whatever. If it had been true, as currently reported at the time, and yet believed by thousands of people, that Prentiss and his division had been captured in their beds, there would not have been an all-day struggle with the loss of thousands killed and wounded on the Confederate side.

With the single exception of a few minutes after the capture of Prentiss, a continuous and unbroken line was maintained all day from Snake Creek or its tributaries on the right to Lick Creek or the Tennessee on the left, above Pittsburg. There was no hour during the day when there was not heavy firing and generally hard fighting at some point on

the line, but seldom at all points at the same time. It was a case of Southern dash against Northern pluck and endurance.

Three of the five divisions engaged on Sunday were entirely raw, and many of the men had only received their arms on the way from their States to the field. Many of them had arrived but a day or two before, and were hardly able to load their muskets according to the manual. Their officers were equally ignorant of their duties. Under these circumstances, it is not astonishing that many of the regiments broke at the first fire. In two cases, as I now remember, colonels led their regiments from the field on first hearing the whistle of the enemy's bullets. In these cases the colonels were constitutional cowards, unfit for any military position. But not so the officers and men led out of danger by them. Better troops never went upon a battle-field than many of these officers and men afterward proved themselves to be who fled panic-stricken at the first whistle of bullets and shell at Shiloh.

During the whole of Sunday I was continuously engaged in passing from one part of the field to another, giving directions to division commanders. In thus moving along the line, however, I never deemed it important to stay long with Sherman. Although his troops were then under fire for the first time, their commander, by his constant presence with them, inspired a confidence in officers and men that enabled them to render services on that bloody battle-field worthy of the best of veterans. McClernand was next to Sherman, and the hardest fighting was in front of these two divisions. McClernand told me on that day, the 6th, that he profited much by having so able a commander sup-

porting him. A casualty to Sherman that would have taken him from the field that day would have been a sad one for the troops engaged at Shiloh. And how near we came to this! On the 6th Sherman was shot twice, once in the hand, once in the shoulder, the ball cutting his coat and making a slight wound, and a third ball passed through his hat. In addition to this he had several horses shot during the day.

The nature of this battle was such that cavalry could not be used in front; I therefore formed ours into line, in rear, to stop stragglers, of whom there were many. When there would be enough of them to make a show, and after they had recovered from their fright, they would be sent to reinforce some part of the line which needed support, without regard to their companies, regiments, or brigades.

On one occasion during the day, I rode back as far as the river and met General Buell, who had just arrived; I do not remember the hour, but at that time there probably were as many as four or five thousand stragglers lying under cover of the river-bluff, panic-stricken, most of whom would have been shot where they lay, without resistance, before they would have taken muskets and marched to the front to protect themselves. This meeting between General Buell and myself was on the despatch-boat used to run between the landing and Savannah. It was brief, and related specially to his getting his troops over the river. As we left the boat together, Buell's attention was attracted by the men lying under cover of the bank. I saw him berating them and trying to shame them into joining their regiments. He even threatened them with shells from the gun-boats near by. But it was all to no effect. Most of these men afterward proved them-

MAJOR-GENERAL HENRY W. HALLECK, U. S. A.
In command of the Department of the Mississippi at the time of the Battle of Shiloh.

FORD WHERE THE NEW HAMBURG ROAD CROSSES LICK CREEK.

selves as gallant as any of those who saved the battle from which they had deserted. I have no doubt that this sight impressed General Buell with the idea that a line of retreat would be a good thing just then. If he had come in by the front instead of through the stragglers in the rear, he would have thought and felt differently. Could he have come through the Confederate rear, he would have witnessed there a scene similar to that of our own. The distant rear of an army engaged in battle is not the best place from which to judge correctly what is going on in front. Later in the war, while occupying the country between the Tennessee and the Mississippi, I learned that the panic in the Confederate lines had not differed much from that within our own. Some of the country people estimated the stragglers from Johnston's army as high as twenty thousand. Of course this was an exaggeration.

The situation at the close of Sunday was as follows: Along the top of the bluff just south of the log-house which stood at Pittsburg Landing, Colonel J. D. Webster, of my staff, had arranged twenty or more pieces of artillery facing south, or up the river. This line of artillery was on the crest of a hill overlooking a deep ravine opening into the Tennessee. Hurlburt, with his division intact, was on the right of this artillery, extending west and possibly a little north. McClernand came next in the general line, looking more to the west. His division was complete in its organization and ready for any duty. Sherman came next, his right extending to Snake Creek. His command, like the other two, was complete in its organization and ready, like its chief, for any service it might be called upon to render. All three divisions were, as a matter of course, more or less shattered and depleted in numbers from the terrible battle of the day. The division of W. H. L. Wallace, as much from the disorder arising from changes of division and brigade commanders, under heavy fire, as from any other cause, had lost its organization, and did not occupy a place in the line as a division; Prentiss's command was gone as a division, many of its members having been killed, wounded, or captured. But it had rendered valiant service before its final dispersal, and had contributed a good share to the defense of Shiloh.

There was, I have said, a deep ravine in front of our left. The Tennessee River was very high, and there was water to a considerable depth in the ravine. Here the enemy made a last desperate effort to turn our flank, but was repelled. The gun-boats *Tyler* and *Lexington*, Gwin and Shirk commanding, with the artillery under Webster, aided the army and effectually checked their further progress. Before any of Buell's troops had reached the west bank of the Tennessee, firing had almost entirely ceased; anything like an attempt on the part of the enemy to advance had absolutely ceased. There was some artillery firing from an unseen enemy, some of his shells passing beyond us; but I do not remember that there was the whistle of a single musket-ball heard. As his troops arrived in the dusk, General Buell marched several of his regiments part way down the face of the hill, where they fired briskly for some minutes, but I do not think a single man engaged in this firing received an injury; the attack had spent its force.

General Lew Wallace, with 5000 effective men, arrived after firing had ceased for the day, and was placed on the right. Thus night came, Wallace came, and the advance of Nelson's division came, but none — unless night — in time to be of material service to the gallant men who saved Shiloh on that first day, against large odds. Buell's loss on the 6th of April was two men killed and one wounded, all members of the 36th Indiana Infantry. The Army of the Tennessee lost on that day at least 7000 men. The presence of two or three regiments of his army on the west bank before firing ceased had not the slightest effect in preventing the capture of Pittsburg Landing.

So confident was I before firing had ceased on the 6th that the next day would bring victory to our arms if we could only take the initiative, that I visited each division commander in person before any reinforcements had reached the field. I directed them to throw out heavy lines of skirmishers in the morning as soon as they could see, and push them forward until they found the enemy, following with their entire divisions in supporting distance, and to engage the enemy as soon as found. To Sherman I told the story of the assault at Fort Donelson, and said that the same tactics would win at Shiloh. Victory was assured when Wallace arrived even if there had been no other support. The enemy received no reinforcements. He had suffered heavy losses in killed, wounded, and straggling, and his commander, General Albert Sidney Johnston, was dead. I was glad, however, to see the reinforcements of Buell and credit them with doing all there was for them to do. During the night of the 6th, the remainder of Nelson's division, Buell's army, crossed the river, and were ready to advance in the morning, forming the left wing. Two other divisions, Crittenden's and McCook's, came up the river from Savannah in the transports, and were on the west bank early on the 7th. Buell commanded them in person. My command was thus nearly doubled in numbers and efficiency.

During the night rain fell in torrents, and our troops were exposed to the storm without shelter. I made my headquarters under a tree a few hundred yards back from the river-bank. My ankle was so much swollen from the fall of my horse the Friday night preceding, and the bruise was so painful, that I could get no rest. The drenching rain would have precluded the possibility of sleep, without this additional cause. Some time after midnight, growing restive under the storm and the continuous pain, I moved back to the log-house on the bank. This had been taken as a hospital, and

THE "HORNETS' NEST"—PRENTISS' TROOPS AND HICKENLOOPER'S BATTERY REPULSING HARDEE'S TROOPS—GIBSON'S BRIGADE CHARGING HURLBUT'S TROOPS.
These cuts form one picture relating to the battle of the first day. From the Cyclorama of Shiloh at Chicago. By permission.

all night wounded men were being brought in, their wounds dressed, a leg or an arm amputated, as the case might require, and everything being done to save life or alleviate suffering. The sight was more unendurable than encountering the enemy's fire, and I returned to my tree in the rain.

The advance on the morning of the 7th developed the enemy in the camps occupied by our troops before the battle began, more than a mile back from the most advanced position of the Confederates on the day before. It is known now that they had not yet learned of the arrival of Buell's command. Possibly they fell back so far to get

the shelter of our tents during the rain, and also to get away from the shells that were dropped upon them by the gun-boats every fifteen minutes during the night.

The position of the Union troops on the morning of the 7th was as follows: General Lew Wallace on the right, Sherman on his left; then McClernand, and then Hurlbut. Nelson, of Buell's army, was on our extreme left, next to the river; Crittenden was next in line after Nelson, and on his right; McCook followed, and formed the extreme right of Buell's command. My old command thus formed the right wing, while the troops directly under Buell constituted the left wing of the army. These relative positions were retained during the entire day, or until the enemy was driven from the field.

In a very short time the battle became general all along the line. This day everything was favorable to the Federal side. We had now become the attacking party. The enemy was driven back all day, as we had been the day before, until finally he beat a precipitate retreat. The last point held by him was near the road leading from the landing to Corinth, on the left of Sherman and right of McClernand. About 3 o'clock, being near that point, and seeing that the enemy was giving way everywhere else, I gathered up a couple of regiments, or parts of regiments, from troops near by, formed them in line of battle and marched them forward, going in front myself to prevent premature or long-range firing. At this point there was a clearing between us and the

enemy favorable for charging, although exposed. I knew the enemy were ready to break, and only wanted a little encouragement from us to go quickly and join their friends who had started earlier. After marching to within musket-range, I stopped and let the troops pass. The command, "Charge," was given, and was executed with loud cheers and with a run, when the last of the enemy broke.

During this second day of the battle I had been moving from right to left and back, to see for myself the progress made. In the early part of the afternoon, while riding with Colonel James B. McPherson, and Major J. P. Hawkins, then my chief commissary, we got beyond the left of our troops. We were moving along the northern edge of a clearing, very leisurely, toward the river above the landing. There did not appear to be an enemy to our right, until suddenly a battery with musketry opened upon us from the edge of the woods on the other side of the clearing. The shells and balls whistled about our ears very fast for about a minute. I do not think it took us longer than that to get out of range and out of sight. In the sudden start we made, Major Hawkins lost his hat. He did not stop to pick it up. When we arrived at a perfectly safe position we halted to take an account of damages. McPherson's horse was panting as if ready to drop. On examination it was found that a ball had struck him forward of the flank just back of the saddle, and had gone entirely through. In a few minutes the poor beast dropped dead; he had given no sign of injury until we came to a stop. A ball had struck the metal scabbard of my sword, just below the hilt, and broken it nearly off; before the battle was over, it had broken off entirely. There were three of us: one had lost a horse, killed, one a hat, and one a

sword-scabbard. All were thankful that it was no worse.

After the rain of the night before and the frequent and heavy rains for some days previous, the roads were almost impassable. The enemy, carrying his artillery and supply trains over them in his retreat, made them still worse for troops following. I wanted to pursue, but had not the heart to order the men who had fought desperately for two days, lying in the mud and rain whenever not fighting, and I did not feel disposed positively to order Buell, or any part of his command, to pursue. Although the senior in rank at the time, I had been so only a few weeks. Buell was, and had been for some time past, a department commander, while I commanded only a district. I did not meet Buell in person until too late to get troops ready and pursue with effect; but had I seen him at the moment of the last charge, I should have at least requested him to follow.

The enemy had hardly started in retreat from his last position, when, looking back toward the river, I saw a division of troops coming up in beautiful order, as if going on parade or review. The commander was at the head of the column, and the staff seemed to be disposed about as they would have been had they been going on parade. When the head of the column came near where I was standing, it was halted, and the commanding officer, General A. McD. McCook, rode up to where I was and appealed to me not to send his division any farther, saying that they were worn out with marching and fighting. This division had marched on the 6th from a point ten or twelve miles east of Savannah, over bad roads. The men had also lost rest during the night while crossing the Tennessee, and had been engaged in the battle of the 7th. It was not, however, the rank and file or the junior

NEW SHILOH CHURCH.
On the site of the log chapel which was destroyed after the battle.

CONFEDERATES.

IN THE "HORNETS' NEST"—W. H. L. WALLACE'S LINE.

GEN. W. H. L. WALLACE.

IN THE "HORNETS' NEST"—W. H. L. WALLACE'S LINE.

These cuts form one picture relating to the first day's battle. From the Cyclorama of Shiloh at Chicago. By permission.

officers who asked to be excused, but the division commander.* I rode forward several miles the day after the battle, and found that the enemy had dropped much, if not all, of their provisions, some ammunition, and the extra wheels of their caissons, lightening their loads to enable them to get off their guns. About five miles out we found their field-hospital abandoned. An immediate pursuit must have resulted in the capture of a considerable number of prisoners and probably some guns.

Shiloh was the severest battle fought at the West

*In an article on the battle of Shiloh, which I wrote for "The Century" magazine, I stated that General A. McD. McCook, who commanded a division of Buell's army, expressed some unwillingness to pursue the enemy on Monday, April 7th, because of the condition of his troops. General Badeau, in his history, also makes the same statement, on my authority. Out of justice to General McCook and his command, I must say that they left a point twenty-two miles east of Savannah on the morning of the 6th. From the heavy rains of a few days previous, and the passage of trains and artillery, the roads were necessarily deep in mud, which made marching slow. The division had not only marched through this mud the day before, but it had been in the rain all night without rest. It was engaged in the battle of the second day, and did as good service as its position allowed. In fact, an opportunity occurred for it to perform a conspicuous act of gallantry which elicited the highest commendation from division commanders in the Army of the Tennessee. General Sherman, both in his memoirs and report, makes mention of this fact. General McCook himself belongs to a family which furnished many volunteers to the army. I refer to these circumstances with minuteness because I did General McCook injustice in my article in "The Century," though not to the extent one would suppose from the public press. I am not willing to do any one an injustice, and if convinced that I have done one, I am always willing to make the fullest admission.

U. S. GRANT.

MOUNT McGREGOR, N. Y., June 21, 1885.

during the war, and but few in the East equaled it for hard, determined fighting. I saw an open field, in our possession on the second day, over which the Confederates had made repeated charges the day before, so covered with dead that it would have been possible to walk across the clearing, in any direction, stepping on dead bodies, without a foot touching the ground. On our side National and Confederate were mingled together in about equal proportions; but on the remainder of the field nearly all were Confederates. On one part, which had evidently not been plowed for several years, probably because the land was poor, bushes had grown up, some to the height of eight or ten feet. There was not one of these left standing unpierced by bullets. The smaller ones were all cut down.

Contrary to all my experience up to that time, and to the experience of the army I was then commanding, we were on the defensive. We were without intrenchments or defensive advantages of any sort, and more than half the army engaged the first day was without experience or even drill as soldiers. The officers with them, except the division commanders, and possibly two or three of the brigade commanders, were equally inexperienced in war. The result was a Union victory that gave the men who achieved it great confidence in themselves ever after.

The enemy fought bravely, but they had started out to defeat and destroy an army and capture a position. They failed in both, with very heavy loss in killed and wounded, and must have gone back discouraged and convinced that the "Yankee" was not an enemy to be despised.

After the battle I gave verbal instructions to division commanders to let the regiments send out parties to bury their own dead, and to detail par-

ties, under commissioned officers from each division, to bury the Confederate dead in their respective fronts, and to report the numbers so buried. The latter part of these instructions was not carried out by all; but they were by those sent from Sherman's division, and by some of the parties sent out by McClernand. The heaviest loss sustained by the enemy was in front of these two divisions.

The criticism has often been made that the Union troops should have been intrenched at Shiloh; but up to that time the pick and spade had been but little resorted to at the West. I had, however, taken this subject under consideration soon after reassuming command in the field. McPherson, my only military engineer, had been directed to lay out a line to intrench. He did so, but reported that it would have to be made in rear of the line of encampment as it then ran. The new line, while it would be nearer the river, was yet too far away from the Tennessee, or even from the creeks, to be easily supplied with water from them; and in case of attack, these creeks would be in the hands of the enemy. Besides this, the troops with me, officers and men, needed discipline and drill more than they did experience with the pick, shovel, and axe. Reinforcements were arriving almost daily, composed of troops that had been hastily thrown together into companies and regiments—fragments of incomplete organizations, the men and officers strangers to each other. Under all these circumstances I concluded that

drill and discipline were worth more to our men than fortifications.

General Buell was a brave, intelligent officer, with as much professional pride and ambition of a commendable sort as I ever knew. I had been two years at West Point with him, and had served with him afterward, in garrison and in the Mexican war, several years more. He was not given in early life or in mature years to forming intimate acquaintances. He was studious by habit, and commanded the confidence and respect of all who knew him. He was a strict disciplinarian, and perhaps did not distinguish sufficiently between

SHILOH SPRING, IN THE RAVINE SOUTH OF THE CHAPEL.
From a photograph taken in 1884.

SLAVES LABORING AT NIGHT ON THE CONFEDERATE EARTHWORKS AT CORINTH.

BIVOUAC OF THE FEDERAL TROOPS, SUNDAY NIGHT.

the volunteer who "enlisted for the war" and the soldier who serves in time of peace. One system embraced men who risked life for a principle, and often men of social standing, competence, or wealth, and independence of character. The other includes, as a rule, only men who could not do as well in any other occupation. General Buell became an object of harsh criticism later, some going so far as to challenge his loyalty. No one who knew him ever believed him capable of a dishonorable act, and nothing could be more dishonorable than to accept high rank and command in war and then betray the trust. When I came into command of the army, in 1864, I requested the Secretary of War to restore General Buell to duty.

After the war, during the summer of 1865, I traveled considerably through the North, and was everywhere met by large numbers of people. Every one had his opinion about the manner in which the war had been conducted; who among the generals had failed, how, and why. Correspondents of the press were ever on hand to hear every word dropped, and were not always disposed to report correctly what did not confirm their preconceived notions, either about the conduct of the war or the individuals concerned in it. The opportunity frequently occurred for me to defend General Buell against what I believed to be most unjust charges. On one occasion a correspondent put in my mouth the very charge I had so often refuted — of disloyalty. This brought from General Buell a very severe retort, which I saw in the New York "World" some time before I received the letter itself. I could very well understand his grievance at seeing untrue and disgraceful charges apparently sustained by an officer who, at the time, was at the head of the army. I replied to him, but not through the press. I kept no copy of my letter, nor did I ever see it in print; neither did I receive an answer to it.

General Albert Sidney Johnston, who commanded the Confederate forces at the beginning of the battle, was disabled by a wound in the afternoon of the first day. His wound, as I understood afterward, was not necessarily fatal, or even dangerous. But he was a man who would not abandon what he deemed an important trust in the face of danger, and consequently continued in the saddle, commanding, until so exhausted by the loss of blood that he had to be taken from his horse, and soon after died. The news was not long in reaching our side, and, I suppose, was quite an encouragement to the National soldiers. I had known Johnston slightly in the Mexican war, and later as an officer in the regular army. He was a man of high character and ability. His contemporaries at West Point, and officers generally who came to know him personally later, and who remained on our side, expected him to prove the most formidable man to meet that the Confederacy would produce. Nothing occurred in his brief command of an army to prove or disprove the high estimate that had been placed upon his military ability.*

General Beauregard was next in rank to Johnston, and succeeded to the command, which he retained to the close of the battle and during the subsequent retreat on Corinth, as well as in the siege of that place. His tactics have been severely criticized by Confederate writers, but I do not be-

* In his "Personal Memoirs" General Grant says: "I once wrote that 'nothing occurred in his brief command of an army to prove or disprove the high estimate that had been placed upon his military ability'; but after studying the orders and despatches of Johnston I am compelled to materially modify my views of that officer's qualifications as a soldier. My judgment now is that he was vacillating and undecided in his actions."

lieve his fallen chief could have done any better under the circumstances. Some of these critics claim that Shiloh was won when Johnston fell, and that if he had not fallen the army under me would have been annihilated or captured. *Ifs* defeated the Confederates at Shiloh. There is little doubt that we would have been disgracefully beaten *if* all the shells and bullets fired by us had passed harmlessly over the enemy, and *if* all of theirs had taken effect. Commanding generals are liable to be killed during engagements; and the fact that when he was shot Johnston was leading a brigade to induce it to make a charge which had been repeatedly ordered, is evidence that there was neither the universal demoralization on our side nor the unbounded confidence on theirs which has been claimed. There was, in fact, no hour during the day when I doubted the eventual defeat of the enemy, although I was disappointed that reinforcements so near at hand did not arrive at an earlier hour.

The Confederates fought with courage at Shiloh, but the particular skill claimed I could not, and still cannot, see; though there is nothing to criticize except the claims put forward for it since. But the Confederate claimants for superiority in strategy, superiority in generalship, and superiority in dash and prowess are not so unjust to the Union troops engaged at Shiloh as are many Northern writers. The troops on both sides were American, and united they need not fear any foreign foe. It is possible that the Southern man started in with a little more dash than his Northern brother; but he was correspondingly less enduring.

The endeavor of the enemy on the first day was simply to hurl their men against ours — first at one point, then at another, sometimes at several points at once. This they did with daring and energy,

until at night the rebel troops were worn out. Our effort during the same time was to be prepared to resist assaults wherever made. The object of the Confederates on the second day was to get away with as much of their army and material as possible. Ours then was to drive them from our front, and to capture or destroy as great a part as possible of their men and material. We were successful in driving them back, but not so successful in captures as if further pursuit could have been made. As it was, we captured or recaptured on the second day about as much artillery as we lost on the first; and, leaving out the one great capture of Prentiss, we took more prisoners on Monday than the enemy gained from us on Sunday. On the 6th Sherman lost 7 pieces of artillery, McClernand 6, Prentiss 8, and Hurlbut 2 batteries. On the 7th Sherman captured 7 guns, McClernand 3, and the Army of the Ohio 20.

At Shiloh the effective strength of the Union force on the morning of the 6th was 33,000. Lew Wallace brought five thousand more after nightfall. Beauregard reported the enemy's strength at 40,955. According to the custom of enumeration in the South, this number probably excluded every man enlisted as musician, or detailed as guard or nurse, and all commissioned officers,— everybody who did not carry a musket or serve a cannon. With us everybody in the field receiving pay from the Government is counted. Excluding the troops who fled, panic-stricken, before they had fired a shot, there was not a time during the 6th when we had more than 25,000 men in line. On the 7th Buell brought twenty thousand more. Of his remaining two divisions, Thomas's did not reach the field during the engagement; Wood's arrived before firing had ceased, but not in time to be of much service.

CHECKING THE CONFEDERATE ADVANCE ON THE EVENING OF THE FIRST DAY.

VICINITY OF
THE "HORNETS' NEST."
From photographs taken in 1885.

Our loss in the two days' fight was 1754 killed, 8408 wounded, and 2885 missing. Of these 2103 were in the Army of the Ohio. Beauregard reported a total loss of 10,699, of whom 1728 were killed, 8012 wounded, and 959 missing. This estimate must be incorrect. We buried, by actual count, more of the enemy's dead in front of the divisions of McClernand and Sherman alone than here reported, and four thousand was the estimate of the burial parties for the whole field. Beauregard reports the Confederate force on the 6th at over 40,000, and their total loss during the two days at 10,699; and at the same time declares that he could put only 20,000 men in battle on the morning of the 7th.

The navy gave a hearty support to the army at Shiloh, as indeed it always did, both before and subsequently, when I was in command. The nature of the ground was such, however, that on this occasion it could do nothing in aid of the troops until sundown on the first day. The country was broken and heavily timbered, cutting off all view of the battle from the river, so that friends would be as much in danger from fire from the gun-boats as the foe. But about sundown, when the National troops were back in their last position, the right of the enemy was near the river and exposed to the fire of the two gun-boats, which was delivered with vigor and effect. After nightfall, when firing had entirely ceased on land, the commander of the fleet informed himself, proximately, of the position of our troops, and suggested the idea of dropping a shell within the lines of the enemy every fifteen minutes during the night. This was done with effect, as is proved by the Confederate reports.

Up to the battle of Shiloh, I, as well as thousands of other citizens, believed that the rebellion against the Government would collapse suddenly and soon if a decisive victory could be gained over any of its armies. Henry and Donelson were such victories. An army of more than 21,000 men was captured or destroyed. Bowling Green, Columbus, and Hick-man, Ky., fell in consequence, and Clarksville, and Nashville, Tenn., the last two with an immense amount of stores, also fell into our hands. The Tennessee and Cumberland rivers, from their mouths to the head of navigation, were secured. But when Confederate armies were collected which not only attempted to hold a line farther south, from Memphis to Chattanooga, Knoxville and on to the Atlantic, but assumed the offensive, and made such a gallant effort to regain what had been lost, then, indeed, I gave up all idea of saving the Union except by complete conquest. Up to that time it had been the policy of our army, certainly of that portion commanded by me, to protect the property of the citizens whose territory was invaded, without regard to their sentiments, whether Union or Secession. After this, however, I regarded it as humane to both sides to protect the persons of those found at their homes, but to consume everything that could be used to support or supply armies. Protection was still continued over such supplies as were within lines held by us, and which we expected to continue to hold. But such supplies within the reach of Confederate armies I regarded as contraband as much as arms or ordnance stores. Their destruction was accomplished without bloodshed, and tended to the same result as the destruction of armies. I continued this policy to the close of the war. Promiscuous pillaging, however, was discouraged and punished.

Instructions were always given to take provisions and forage under the direction of commissioned officers, who should give receipts to owners, if at home, and turn the property over to officers of the quartermaster or commissary departments, tò be issued as if furnished from our Northern depots. But much was destroyed without receipts to owners when it could not be brought within our lines, and would otherwise have gone to the support of secession and rebellion. This policy, I believe, exercised a material influence in hastening the end.

FIGHTING AT SHILOH.

FROM "SHILOH REVIEWED," BY DON CARLOS BUELL, MAJOR-GENERAL, U. S. V.

In command of the Army of the Ohio, at Shiloh.

. . . Prentiss's vigilance gave the first warning of the actual danger, and in fact commenced the contest. On Saturday, disquieted by the frequent appearance of the enemy's cavalry, he increased his pickets, though he had no evidence of the presence of a large force. Early Sunday morning one of these picket-guards, startled no doubt by the hum of forty thousand men half a mile distant, waking up for battle, went forward to ascertain the cause, and soon came upon the enemy's pickets, which it promptly attacked. It was then a quarter past 5 o'clock, and all things being ready, the Confederate general, accepting the signal of the pickets, at once gave the order to advance. Previously, however, General Prentiss, still apprehensive, had sent forward Colonel Moore of the 21st Missouri, with five companies to strengthen the picket-guard. On the way out Colonel Moore met the guard returning to camp with a number of its men killed and wounded. Sending the latter on to camp and calling for the remaining companies of his regiment, he proceeded to the front in time to take a good position on the border of a cleared field, and opened fire upon the enemy's skirmishers, checking them for a while; but the main body forced him back upon the division with a considerable list of wounded, himself among the number. All this occurred in front of Sherman's camp, not in front of Prentiss's. This spirited beginning, unexpected on both sides, gave the first alarm to the divisions of Sherman and Prentiss. The latter promptly formed his division at the first news from the front, and moved a quarter of a mile in advance of his camp, where he was attacked before Sherman was under arms. He held his position until the enemy on his right passed him in attacking Sherman, whose left regiment immediately broke into rout. He then retired in some disorder, renewing the resistance in his camp, but forced back in still greater disorder, until at 9 o'clock he came upon the line which Hurlbut and W. H. L. Wallace were forming half a mile in rear.

Upon the first alarm in his camp, which was simultaneous with the attack upon Sherman, McClernand rapidly got under arms, and endeavored to support Sherman's left with his Third Brigade, only two hundred yards in rear, while he placed his First and Second Brigades in inverted order still farther to the rear and left, to oppose the enemy's columns pouring in upon his left flank through the opening on Sherman's left; but his Third Brigade was forced back with the fugitives from Sherman's broken line by the advancing enemy, and endeavored with only partial success to form on the right of McClernand's line, which at first was formed with the left a little south, and the center north of the Corinth road. Before the formation was completed the line was compelled to retire by the pressure on its front and left flank, with the loss of 6 pieces of artillery, but it re-formed 300 yards in rear.

Hildebrand's brigade had now disappeared in complete disorder from the front, leaving three pieces of artillery in the hands of the enemy. Buckland formed promptly at the first alarm, and in

The stump in the field on the right is said to mark the spot where General Albert Sidney Johnston was killed. The point of woods beyond the field is supposed to be the place which the Confederates called the "Hornets' Nest." The "peach orchard" was a little to the left of the field in the middle ground, and behind the house (in the lower picture) which is across the road from the field in which General Johnston was killed.

MAJOR-GENERAL DON CARLOS BUELL, U. S. V.

WOOD AND UNDERBRUSH CALLED THE "HORNETS' NEST."
From a photograph taken in 1885.

order to keep the enemy back endeavored by Sherman's direction to throw a regiment beyond Oak Creek, which covered his front at a distance of two hundred yards, but on reaching the brow of the low hill bordering the stream the enemy was encountered on the hither side. Nevertheless the brigade resisted effectively for about two hours the efforts of the assailants to cross the boggy stream in force. The enemy suffered great loss in these efforts, but succeeded at last. Before being quite forced back, Buckland received orders from Sherman to form line on the Purdy road four hundred yards in rear, to connect with McClernand's right. Orders were also given to McDowell, who had not yet been engaged, to close to the left on the same line. These orders were in effect defeated in both cases, and five pieces of artillery lost by faults in the execution and the rapid advance of the enemy. Sherman's division as an organized body disappeared from the field from this time until the close of the day. McDowell's brigade preserved a sort of identity for a while. Sherman reports that at "about 10:30 A. M. the enemy had made a furious attack on General

McClernand's whole front. Finding him pressed, I moved McDowell's brigade against the left flank of the enemy, forced him back some distance, and then directed the men to avail themselves of every cover — trees, fallen timber, and a wooded valley to our right." It sounds like the signal to disperse, and a little after 1 o'clock the brigade and regiments are seen no more. Some fragments of the division and the commander himself attached themselves to McClernand's command, which now, owing to its composite and irregular organization, could hardly be denominated a division.

The contest which raged in McClernand's camp was of a fluctuating character. The ground was lost and won more than once, but each ebb and flow of the struggle left the Union side in a worse condition. In his fifth position McClernand was driven to the camp of his First Brigade, half of his command facing to the south and half to the west, to meet the converging attack of the enemy. His nominal connection with the left wing of the army across the head of Tillman's Hollow had been severed, by the dispersion or defeat of the detached commands

that formed it. Another reverse to his thinned ranks would drive him over the bluff into Owl Creek bottom, and perhaps cut him off from the river. He determined, therefore, between 2 and 3 o'clock to retire across Tillman's Hollow in the direction of the landing. That movement was effected with a good deal of irregularity, but with the repulse of a small body of pursuing cavalry, and a new line was formed on the opposite ridge along the River road, north of Hurlbut's headquarters. Leaving the right wing, as it may be called, in this position prior to the attack of 4 o'clock, which drove it still farther back, we will return to the current of events in the left wing.

With Stuart on the extreme left, as with the other commanders, the presence of the enemy was the first warning of danger. He was soon compelled to fall back from his camp to a new position, and presently again to a third, which located him on the prolongation and extreme left of the line formed by Hurlbut and W. H. L. Wallace, but without having any connection with it. As soon as the first advance of the enemy was known, these two commanders were called upon by those in front for support. In the absence of a common superior it was sent forward by regiments or brigades in such a manner as seemed proper to the officer appealed to, and after that was left to its own devices. It seldom formed the connection desired, or came under the direction of a common superior. Indeed, the want of cohesion and concert in the Union ranks is conspicuously indicated in the official reports. A regiment is rarely overcome in front, but falls back because the regiment on its right or left has done so, and exposed its flank. It continues its backward movement at least until it is well under shelter, thus exposing the flank of its neighbor, who then must also needs fall back. Once in operation, the process repeats itself indefinitely. In a broken and covered country which affords occasional rallying-points and obstructs the pursuit, it proceeds step by step. On an open field, in the presence of light artillery and cavalry, it would run rapidly into general rout.

This outflanking, so common in the Union reports at Shiloh, is not a mere excuse of the inferior commanders. It is the practical consequence of the absence of a common head, and the judicious use of reserves to counteract partial reverses and preserve the front of battle. The want of a general direction is seen also in the distribution of Hurlbut's and Wallace's divisions. Hurlbut sent a brigade under Colonel Veatch to support Sherman's left; Wallace sent one under General McArthur to the opposite extreme to support Stuart; and the two remaining brigades of each were between the extremes — Wallace on Veatch's left, but not in connection with it, and Hurlbut on McArthur's right, also without connection. Stuart himself with his brigade was two miles to the left of Sherman's division to which he belonged. When the three Confederate lines were brought together successively at the front, there was, of course, a great apparent mingling of organizations; but it was not in their case attended with the confusion that might be supposed, because each division area was thereby supplied with a triple complement of brigade and division officers, and the whole front was under the close supervision of four remarkably efficient corps commanders. The evils of disjointed command are plainly to be seen in the arrangement of the Federal line, but the position of the left wing after the forced correction of the first faulty disposition of Hurlbut's brigades was exceedingly strong, and in the center was held without a break against oft-repeated assaults from 9 o'clock until 5 o'clock. From 12 until 2 it was identical with the second position taken by Nelson and Crittenden on Monday, and it was equally formidable against attack from both directions. Its peculiar feature consisted in a wood in the center, with a thick undergrowth, flanked on either side by open fields, and with open but sheltering woods in front and rear. The Confederates gave the name of "Hornets' Nest" to the thicket part of it on Sunday, and it was in the open ground on the east flank that General Johnston was killed. . . .

A UNION BATTERY TAKEN BY SURPRISE.

SCENE OF GENERAL ALBERT SIDNEY JOHNSTON'S DEATH.
From a photograph taken in the summer of 1884.

THE CONFEDERATE SIDE AT SHILOH

BY WILLIAM PRESTON JOHNSTON, COLONEL, C. S. A.,
SON OF ALBERT SIDNEY JOHNSTON,
The commander of the Confederate forces, killed at Shiloh.

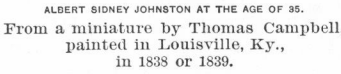

ALBERT SIDNEY JOHNSTON AT THE AGE OF 35.
From a miniature by Thomas Campbell,
painted in Louisville, Ky.,
in 1838 or 1839.

. . . The sun set on Saturday evening in a cloudless sky, and night fell calm, clear, and beautiful. Long before the dawn of Sunday the forest was alive with silent preparations for the ensuing contest, and day broke upon a scene so fair that it left its memory on thousands of hearts. The sky was clear overhead, the air fresh, and when the sun rose in full splendor, the advancing host passed the word from lip to lip that it was the "sun of Austerlitz."

General Johnston, usually so self-contained, felt the inspiration of the scene, and welcomed with exultant joy the long-desired day. His presence inspired all who came near him. His sentences, sharp, terse, and clear, had the ring of victory in them. Turning to his staff, as he mounted, he exclaimed: "To-night we will water our horses in the Tennessee River." It was thus that he formulated his plan of battle; it must not stop short of entire victory. To Randall L. Gibson, who was commanding a Louisiana brigade, he said: "I hope you may get through safely to-day, but *we must win a victory*." To Colonel John S. Marmaduke, who had served under him in Utah, he said, placing his hand on his shoulder: "My son, we must this day conquer or perish." To the ambitious Hindman, who had been in the vanguard from the beginning, he said: "You have *earned* your spurs as a major-general. Let this day's work win them." With such words, as he rode from point to point, he raised a spirit in that host which swept away the serried lines of the conquerors of Donelson. Friend and foe alike testify to the enthusiastic courage and ardor of the Southern soldiers that day.

General Johnston's strategy was completed. He was face to face with his foe, and that foe all unaware of his coming. His front line, composed of the Third Corps and Gladden's brigade, was under Hardee, and extended from Owl Creek to Lick Creek, more than three miles. Hindman's division of two brigades occupied the center, Cleburne's brigade had the left, and Gladden's the right wing—an effective total in the front line of 9024. The second line was commanded by Bragg. He had two divisions: Withers's, of two brigades, on the right, and Ruggles's, of three brigades, on the left. The brigades were, in order from right to left, as follows: Chalmers, Jackson, Gibson, Anderson, Pond. This second line was 10,731 strong. The third line, or reserve, was composed of the First Corps, under Polk, and three brigades under Breckinridge. Polk's command was massed in columns of brigades on the Bark road near Mickey's, and Breckinridge's on the road from Monterey toward the same point. Polk was to advance on the left of the Bark road, at an interval of about eight hundred paces from Bragg's line; and Breckinridge, to the right of that road, was to give support wherever it should become necessary. Polk's corps, 9136 strong in infantry and artillery, was composed of two divisions: Cheatham's on the left, made up of Bushrod R. Johnson's and Stephens's brigades, and Clark's on his right, formed of A. P. Stewart's and Russell's brigades. It followed Bragg's line at a distance of about eight hundred yards. Breckinridge's reserve was composed of Trabue's, Bowen's, and Statham's brigades, with a total, infantry and artillery, of 6439. The cavalry, about 4300 strong, guarded the flanks or was detached on outpost duty; but, both from the newness and imperfection of their organization, equipment, and drill, and from the rough and wooded character of the ground, they could do little service that day. The effectives of all arms that marched out to battle were about 39,630, or, exclusive of cavalry, 35,330.

The Federal army numbered present 49,232, and present for duty 41,543. But at Crump's Landing, five or six miles distant, was General Lew Wallace's division with 8820 present, and 7771 men

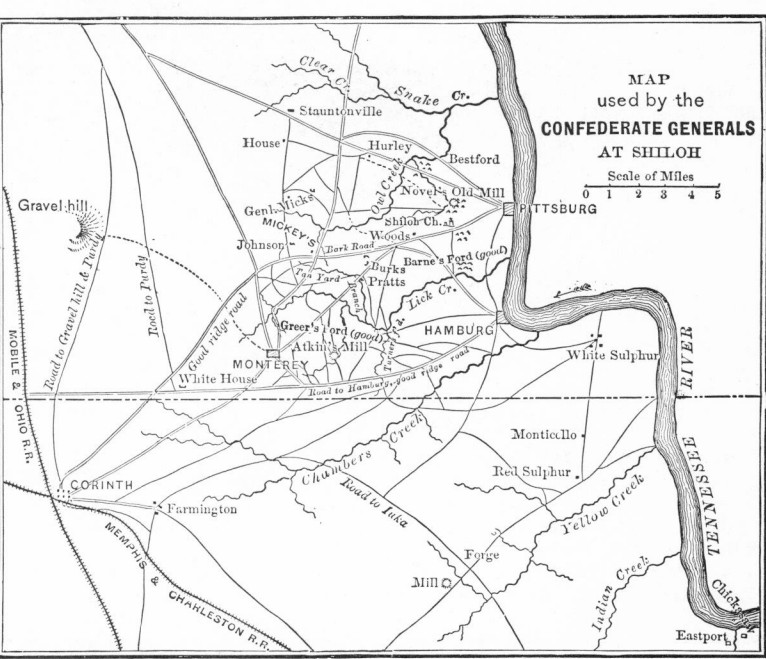

MAP used by the CONFEDERATE GENERALS AT SHILOH
Scale of Miles
0 1 2 3 4 5

From the "Life of General A. S. Johnston," by W. P. Johnston. (D. Appleton & Co.)

present for duty. General Nelson's division of Buell's army had arrived at Savannah on Saturday morning, and was now about five miles distant; Crittenden's division also had arrived on the morning of the 6th. So that Grant, with these three divisions, may be considered as having about 22,000 men in immediate reserve, without counting the remainder of Buell's army, which was near by.*

As General Johnston and his staff were taking their coffee, the first gun of the battle sounded.

* General Grant takes no account of these in his narratives of the battle, and talks as though he were outnumbered instead of outgeneraled. It was his business to get these troops there in time, especially if he was not surprised.—W. P. J.

CONFEDERATE TYPE OF 1862.

WOUNDED AND STRAGGLERS ON THE WAY TO THE LANDING, AND
AMMUNITION-WAGONS GOING TO THE FRONT.

LIEUTENANT-GENERAL W. J. HARDEE, C. S. A.
From a photograph.

"Note the hour, if you please, gentlemen," said General Johnston. It was fourteen minutes past 5. They immediately mounted and galloped to the front.

Some skirmishing on Friday between the Confederate cavalry and the Federal outposts, in which a few men were killed, wounded, and captured on both sides, had aroused the vigilance of the Northern commanders to some extent. Sherman reported on the 5th to Grant that two regiments of infantry and one of cavalry were in his front, and added: "I have no doubt that nothing will occur to-day more than some picket firing. . . . I do not apprehend anything like an attack on our position." In his "Memoirs" he says: "I did not believe they designed anything but a strong demonstration." He said to Major Ricker that an advance of Beauregard's army "could not be possible. Beauregard was not such a fool as to leave his base of operations and attack us in ours— *mere reconnaissance in force.*" This shows a curious coincidence with the actual state of General Beauregard's mind on that day. And Grant telegraphed Halleck on Saturday night: "The main force of the enemy is at Corinth. . . . One division of Buell's column arrived yesterday. . . . I have scarcely the faintest idea of an attack (general one) being made upon us."

Nevertheless, some apprehension was felt among the officers and men of the Federal army, and General Prentiss had thrown forward Colonel Moore, with the 21st Missouri regiment, on the Corinth road. Moore, feeling his way cautiously, encountered Hardee's skirmish-line under Major Hardcastle, and, thinking it an outpost, assailed it vigorously. Thus really the Federals began the fight. The struggle was brief, but spirited. The 8th and 9th Arkansas came up. Moore fell wounded. The Missourians gave way, and Shaver's brigade pursued them. Hindman's whole division moved on, following the ridge and drifting to the right, and drove in the grand guards and outposts until they struck Prentiss's camps. Into these they burst, overthrowing all before them.

To appreciate the suddenness and violence of the blow, one must read the testimony of eye-witnesses. General Bragg says, in a sketch of Shiloh made for the writer: "Contrary to the views of such as urged an abandonment of the attack, the enemy was found utterly unprepared, many being surprised and captured in their tents, and others, though on the outside, in costumes better fitted to the bedchamber than to the battle-field." General Preston says: "General Johnston then went to the camp assailed, which was carried between 7 and 8 o'clock. The enemy were evidently surprised. The breakfasts were on the mess tables, the baggage unpacked, the knapsacks, stores, colors, and ammunition abandoned."

The essential feature of General Johnston's strategy had been to get at his enemy as quickly as possible, and in as good order. In this he had succeeded. His plan of battle was as simple as his strategy. It had been made known in his order of battle, and was thoroughly understood by every brigade commander. The orders of the 3d of April were, that "every effort should be made to turn the *left flank of the enemy,* so as to cut off his line of retreat to the Tennessee River and *throw him back on Owl Creek, where he will be obliged to surrender.*" It is seen that, from the first, these orders were carried out in letter and spirit; and, so long as General Johnston lived, the success of this movement was complete. *The battle was fought precisely as it was planned.* The first, and

almost only, censure of this plan was made by Colonel Jordan, confidential adviser and historian of General Beauregard, who now claims to have made this plan. The instructions delivered to General Johnston's subordinates on the previous day were found sufficient for their conduct on the battle-field. But, to accomplish this, his own personal presence and inspiration and direction were often necessary with these enthusiastic but raw troops. He had personal conference on the field with most of his generals, and led several brigades into battle. The criticism upon this conduct, that he exposed himself unnecessarily, is absurd to those who know how important rapid decision and instantaneous action are in the crisis of conflict. His lines of battle were pushed rapidly to the front, and as gaps widened in the first lines, they were filled by brigades of the second and third. One of Breckinridge's brigades (Trabue's) was sent to the left to support Cleburne and fought under Polk the rest of the day; and the other two were led to the extreme right, only Chalmers being beyond them. Gladden, who was on Hindman's right, and had a longer distance to traverse to strike some of Prentiss's brigades further to the left, found them better prepared, but, after a sanguinary resistance, drove them from their camps. In this bitter struggle Gladden fell mortally wounded. Chalmers's brigade, of Bragg's line, came in on Gladden's right, and his Mississippians drove the enemy, under Stuart, with the bayonet

half a mile. He was about to charge again, when General Johnston came up, and moved him to the right, and brought John K. Jackson's brigade into the interval. Prentiss's left and Stuart's brigade retreated sullenly, not routed, but badly hammered.

With Hindman as a pivot, the turning movement began from the moment of the overthrow of Prentiss's camps. While the front attacks were made all along the line with a desperate courage which would have swept any ordinary resistance from the field, and with a loss which told fearfully on the assailants, they were seconded by assaults in flank which invariably resulted in crushing the Federal line with destructive force and strewing the field with the wounded and the dead. The Federal reports complain that they were flanked and outnumbered, which is true; for, though fewer, the Confederates were probably stronger at every given point throughout the day except at the center called the "Hornets' Nest," where the Federals eventually massed nearly two divisions. The iron flail of war beat upon the Federal front and right flank with the regular and ponderous pulsations of some great engine, and these assaults resulted in a crumbling process which was continually but slowly going on, as regiment and brigade and division yielded to the continuous and successive blows. There has been criticism that there were no grand assaults by divisions and corps. In a broken, densely wooded and unknown country, and with the mode of attack in parallel lines, this was impossible, but the attack was unremitting and the fact is that there were but few lulls in the contest. The fighting was a grapple and a death-struggle all day long, and, as one brigade after another wilted before the deadly fire of the stubborn Federals, still another was pushed into the combat and kept up the fierce assault. A breathing-spell, and the shattered command would gather itself up and resume its work of destruction. These were the general aspects of the battle.

When the battle began Hindman, following the

60

THE SIEGE-BATTERY, ABOVE THE LANDING.

A part of the "last line" in the first day's battle. (From a photograph taken a few days after the battle.)

ABOVE THE LANDING—THE STORE, AND A PART OF THE NATIONAL CEMETERY.

From a photograph taken in 1884.

ridge, had easy ground to traverse; but Cleburne's large brigade on his left, with its supports, moving over a more difficult country, was slower in getting upon Sherman's front. That general and his command were aroused by the long roll, the advancing musketry, and the rush of troops to his left, and he got his division in line of battle and was ready for the assault of Cleburne, which was made about 8 o'clock. General Johnston, who had followed close after Hindman, urging on his attack, saw Cleburne's brigade begin its advance, and then returned to where Hindman was gathering his force for another assault. Hardee said of Cleburne that he "moved quickly through the fields, and, though far outflanked by the enemy on our left, rushed forward under a terrific fire from the serried ranks drawn up in front of the camp. A morass covered his front, and, being difficult to pass, caused a break in this brigade. Deadly volleys were poured upon the men from behind bales of hay and other defenses, as they advanced; and after a series of desperate charges they were compelled to fall back. Supported by the arrival of the second line, Cleburne, with the remainder of his troops, . . . entered the enemy's encampment, which had been forced on the center and right by . . . Gladden's, Wood's, and Hindman's brigades."

While Sherman was repelling Cleburne's attack, McClernand sent up three Illinois regiments to reinforce his left. But General Polk led forward Bushrod R. Johnson's brigade, and General Charles Clark led Russell's brigade, against Sherman's left, while General Johnston himself put A. P. Stewart's brigade in position on their right. Supported by part of Cleburne's line, they attacked Sherman and McClernand fiercely. Polk said: "The resistance at this point was as stubborn as at any other point on the field." Clark and Bushrod R. Johnson fell badly wounded. Hildebrand's Federal brigade was swept from the field, losing in the onslaught 300 killed and wounded, and 94 missing.

Wood's brigade, of Hindman's division, joined in this charge on the right. As they hesitated at the crest of a hill, General Johnston came to the front and urged them to the attack. They rushed forward with the inspiring "rebel yell," and with Stewart's brigade enveloped the Illinois troops. In ten minutes the latter melted away under the fire, and were forced from the field. In this engagement John A. McDowell's and Veatch's Federal brigades, as well as Hildebrand's, were demolished and heard of no more. Buckland retreated and took position with McClernand. In these attacks Anderson's and Pond's Confederate brigades joined with great vigor and severe loss, but with unequal fortune. The former had one success after another; the latter suffered a series of disasters; and yet an equal courage animated them. Gladden's brigade made a final desperate and successful charge on Prentiss's line. The whole Federal front, which had been broken here and there, and was getting ragged, gave way under this hammering process on front and flank, and fell back across a ravine to another strong position behind the Hamburg and Purdy road in rear of Shiloh. Sherman's route of retreat was marked by the thick-strewn corpses of his soldiers. At last, pressed back toward both Owl Creek and the river, Sherman and McClernand found safety by the interposition on their left flank of W. H. L. Wallace's fresh division. Hurlbut and Wallace had advanced about 8 o'clock, so that Prentiss's command found a refuge in the intervals of the new and formidable Federal line, with Stuart on the left and Sherman's shattered division on the right.

General Johnston had pushed Chalmers to the right and front, sweeping down the left bank of Lick Creek, driving in pickets, until he encountered Stuart's Federal brigade on the Pittsburg and Hamburg road. Stuart was strongly posted on a steep hill near the river, covered with thick undergrowth, and with an open field in front.

McArthur was to his right and rear in the woods. Jackson attacked McArthur, who fell back; and Chalmers went at Stuart's brigade. This command reserved its fire until Chalmers's men were within forty yards, and then delivered a heavy and destructive volley; but, after a hard fight, the Federals were driven back. Chalmers's right rested on the Tennessee River bottom-lands, and he fought down the bank toward Pittsburg Landing. The enemy's left was completely turned and the Federal army was now crowded on a shorter line, a mile or more to the rear of its first position, with many of their brigades *hors de combat*. The new line of battle was established before 10 o'clock. All the Confederate troops were then in the front line, except two of Breckinridge's brigades, Bowen's and Statham's, which were moving to the Confederate right, and soon occupied the interval to the left of Chalmers and Jackson. Hardee, with Cleburne and Pond, was pressing Sherman slowly but steadily back. Bragg and Polk met about half-past 10 o'clock, and by agreement Polk led his troops against McClernand, while Bragg directed the operations against the Federal center. A gigantic contest now began which lasted more than five hours. In the impetuous rush forward of regiments to fill the gaps in the front line, even the brigade organization was broken; but though there was dislocation of commands, there was little loss of effective force. The Confederate assaults were made by rapid and often unconnected charges along the line. They were repeatedly checked, and often repulsed. Sometimes counter-charges drove them back for short distances; but, whether in assault or recoil, both sides saw their bravest soldiers fall in frightful numbers. The Confederates came on in motley garb, varying from the favorite gray and domestic "butternut" to the blue of certain Louisiana regiments, which paid dearly the penalty of doubtful colors. Over them waved flags and pennons as various as their uniforms. At each charge

there went up a wild yell, heard above the roar of artillery; only the Kentuckians, advancing with measured step, sang in chorus their war-song: "Cheer, boys, cheer; we'll march away to battle."

On the Federal left center W. H. L. Wallace's and Hurlbut's divisions were massed, with Prentiss's fragments, in a position so impregnable, and thronged with such fierce defenders, that it won from the Confederates the memorable title of the "Hornets' Nest." Here, behind a dense thicket on the crest of a hill, was posted a strong force of as hardy troops as ever fought, almost perfectly protected by the conformation of the ground, and by logs and other rude and hastily prepared defenses. To assail it an open field had to be passed, enfiladed by the fire of its batteries. No figure of speech would be too strong to express the deadly peril of assault upon this natural fortress. For five hours brigade after brigade was led against it. Hindman's brigades, which earlier had swept everything before them, were reduced to fragments, and paralyzed for the remainder of the day. A. P. Stewart's regiments made fruitless assaults. Then Bragg ordered up Gibson's brigade. Gibson himself, a knightly soldier, was aided by colonels three of whom afterward became generals. The brigade made a gallant charge; but, like the others, recoiled from the fire it encountered. Under a cross-fire of artillery and musketry it at last fell back with very heavy loss. Gibson asked that artillery should be sent him; but it was not at hand, and Bragg sent orders to charge again. The colonels thought it hopeless; but Gibson led them again to the attack, and again they suffered a bloody repulse.

The brigade was four times repulsed, but maintained its ground steadily, until W. H. L. Wallace's position was turned, when, renewing its forward movement in conjunction with Cheatham's command, it helped to drive back its stout opponents. Cheatham, charging with Stephens's brigade on Gibson's right, across an open field, had been caught

UNION CAMP, BOWLING GREEN, KY.

From a lithograph. On the hill are seen the Confederate fortifications that were erected by General Buckner.

PITTSBURG LANDING.

Viewed from the ferry landing on the opposite shore. (From a photograph taken in 1885.)

under a murderous cross-fire, but fell back in good order, and, later in the day, came in on Breckinridge's left in the last assault when Prentiss was captured. This bloody fray lasted till nearly 4 o'clock, without making any visible impression on the Federal center. But when its flanks were turned, these assaulting columns, crowding in on its front, aided in its capture.

General Johnston was with the right of Statham's brigade, confronting the left of Hurlbut's division, which was behind the crest of a hill, with a depression filled with chaparral in its front. Bowen's brigade was further to the right in line with Statham's, touching it near this point. The Confederates held the parallel ridge in easy musket-range; and "as heavy fire as I ever saw during the war," says Governor Harris, was kept up on both sides for an hour or more. It was necessary to cross the valley raked by this deadly ambuscade and assail the opposite ridge in order to drive the enemy from his stronghold. When General Johnston came up and saw the situation, he said to his staff: "They are offering stubborn resistance here. I shall have to put the bayonet to them." It was the crisis of the conflict. The Federal key was in his front. If his assault were successful, their left would be completely turned, and the victory won. He determined to charge. He sent Governor Harris, of his staff, to lead a Tennessee regiment; and, after a brief conference with Breckinridge, whom he loved and admired, that officer, followed by his staff, appealed to the soldiers. As he encouraged them with his fine voice and manly bearing, General Johnston rode out in front and slowly down the line. His hat was off. His sword rested in its scabbard. In his right hand he held a little tin cup, the memorial of an incident that had occurred earlier in the day. Passing through a captured camp, he had taken this toy, saying, "Let this be my share of the spoils to-day." It was this plaything which, holding it between two fingers, he employed more effectively in his natural and simple gesticulation than most men could have used a sword. His presence was full of inspiration. He sat his thoroughbred bay, "Fire-eater," with easy command. His voice was persuasive, encouraging, and compelling. His words were few; he said: "Men! they are stubborn; we must use the bayonet." When he reached the center of the line, he turned. "I will lead you!" he cried, and moved toward the enemy. The line was already thrilling and trembling with that irresistible ardor which in battle decides the day. With a mighty shout Bowen's and Statham's brigades moved forward at a charge. A sheet of flame and a mighty roar burst from the Federal stronghold. The Confederate line withered; but there was not an instant's pause. The crest was gained. The enemy were in flight.

THE DEATH OF GENERAL JOHNSTON.

General Johnston had passed through the ordeal seemingly unhurt. His horse was shot in four places; his clothes were pierced by missiles; his boot-sole was cut and torn by a Minié; but if he himself had received any severe wound, he did not know it. At this moment Governor Harris rode up from the right. After a few words, General Johnston sent him with an order to Colonel Statham, which having delivered, he speedily returned. In the mean time, knots and groups of Federal soldiers kept up a desultory fire as they retreated upon their supports, and their last line, now yielding, delivered volley after volley as they sullenly retired. By the chance of war, a Minié ball from one of these did its fatal work. As he sat there, after his wound, Captain Wickham says that Colonel O'Hara, of his staff, rode up, and General Johnston said to him, "We must go to the left, where the firing is heaviest," and then gave him an order, which O'Hara rode off to obey. Governor Harris returned, and, finding him very pale, asked him, "General, are you wounded?" He answered, in a very deliberate and emphatic tone: "Yes, and, I fear, seriously." These were his last words. Harris and Wickham led his horse back under cover of the hill, and lifted him from it. They searched at random for the wound, which had cut an artery in his leg, the blood flowing into his boot. When his brother-in-law, Preston, lifted his head, and addressed him with passionate grief, he smiled faintly, but uttered no word. His life rapidly ebbed away, and in a few moments he was dead.

His wound was not necessarily fatal. General Johnston's own knowledge of military surgery was adequate for its control by an extemporized tourniquet had he been aware or regardful of its nature. Dr. D. W. Yandell, his surgeon, had attended his person during most of the morning; but, finding a large number of wounded men, including many Federals, at one point, General Johnston had ordered Yandell to stop there, establish a hospital, and give them his services. He said to Yandell: "These men were our enemies a moment ago; they are our prisoners now. Take care of them." Yandell remonstrated against leaving him, but he was peremptory. Had Yandell remained with him, he would have had little difficulty with the wound.

Governor Harris, and others of General Johnston's staff, promptly informed General Beauregard of his death, and General Beauregard assumed command, remaining at Shiloh Church, awaiting the issue of events.

Up to the moment of the death of the commander-in-chief, in spite of the dislocation of the commands, there was the most perfect regularity in the development of the plan of battle. In all the seeming confusion there was the predominance of intelligent design; a master mind, keeping in clear view its purpose, sought the weak point in the defense, and, by massing his troops upon the enemy's left, kept turning that flank. With the disadvantage of inferior numbers, General Johnston brought to bear a superior force on each particular point, and, by a series of rapid and powerful blows, broke the Federal army to pieces.

Now was the time for the Confederates to push their advantage, and, closing in on the rear of Prentiss and Wallace, to finish the battle. But, on the contrary, there came a lull in the conflict on the right, lasting more than an hour from half-past 2, the time at which General Johnston fell. It is true that the Federals fell back and left the field, making some desultory resistance, and the Confederates went forward deliberately, occupying their positions, and thus helping to envelop the Federal center; but Breckinridge's two brigades did not make another charge that day, and there was no further general direction or concerted movement. The determinate purpose to capture Grant that day was lost sight of. The strong arm was withdrawn, and the bow remained unbent. Elsewhere there were bloody, desultory combats, but they tended to nothing.

About half-past 3 the contest, which had throbbed with fitful violence for five hours, was renewed with the utmost fury. While an ineffectual struggle was going on at the center, a number of batteries opened upon Prentiss's right flank, the center of what remained of the Federals. The opening of so heavy a fire, and the simultaneous though unconcerted advance of the whole Confederate line, resulted at first in the confusion of the enemy, and then in the death of W. H. L. Wallace and the surrender of Prentiss.

LIEUTENANT-GENERAL
JOHN C. BRECKINRIDGE, C. S. A.
From a photograph.

PREACHING AT THE UNION CAMP DICK ROBINSON, KY.
Sketched from a lithograph.

BIRTHPLACE OF ALBERT SIDNEY JOHNSTON,
WASHINGTON, KY.
From a photograph.

These generals have received scant justice for their stubborn defense. They agreed to hold their position at all odds, and did so until Wallace received his fatal wound and Prentiss was surrounded and captured with nearly three thousand men. This delay was the salvation of Grant's army.

General Breckinridge's command closed in on the Federal left and rear; General Polk crushed their right center by the violence of his assault; and in person, with Marshall J. Smith's Crescent regiment, received the surrender of many troops. General Prentiss gave up his sword to Colonel Russell. Bragg's troops, wrestling at the front, poured in over the "Hornets' Nest," and shared in the triumph. Polk ordered his cavalry to charge the fleeing enemy, and Colonel Miller rode down and captured a 6-gun battery. His men "watered their horses in the Tennessee River." All now felt that the victory was won. Bragg, Polk, Hardee, Breckinridge, all the corps commanders, were at the front, and in communication. Their generals were around them. The hand that had launched the thunder-bolt of war was cold, but its influence still nerved this host and its commanders. A line of battle was formed, and all was ready for the last fell swoop, to compel an "unconditional surrender" by General Grant.

The only position on the high grounds left to the Federals was held by Colonel Webster, of Grant's staff, who had collected some twenty guns or more and manned them with volunteers. Soon after 4 o'clock Chalmers and Jackson, proceeding down the river-bank while Prentiss's surrender was going on, came upon this position. The approaches were bad from that direction; nevertheless, they attacked resolutely, and, though repeatedly repulsed, kept up their assaults till nightfall. At one time

they drove some gunners from their guns, and their attack has been generally mistaken by Federal writers for the final assault of the Confederate army—*which was never made.* The Federal generals and writers attribute their salvation to the repulse of Chalmers, and the honor is claimed respectively for Webster's artillery and for Ammen's brigade of Buell's army, which came up at the last moment. But neither they nor all that was left of the Federal army could have withstood five minutes the united advance of the Confederate line, which was at hand and ready to deal the death-stroke. Their salvation came from a different quarter. Bragg, in his monograph written for the use of the writer in preparing the "Life of A. S. Johnston," gives the following account of the close of the battle:

"Concurring testimony, especially that of the prisoners on both sides,—our captured being present and witnesses to the demoralization of the enemy, and their eagerness to escape or avoid further slaughter by surrender,—left no doubt but that a persistent, energetic assault would soon have been crowned by a general yielding of his whole force. About one hour of daylight was left to us. The enemy's gun-boats, his last hope, took position opposite us in the river, and commenced a furious cannonade at our supposed position. From the elevation necessary to reach the high bluff on which we were operating, this proved all 'sound and fury signifying nothing,' and did not in the slightest degree mar our prospects or our progress. Not so, however, in our rear, where these heavy shells fell among the reserves and stragglers; and to the utter dismay of the commanders on the field, the troops were seen to abandon their inspiring work, and to retire sullenly from the contest when danger was almost past, and victory, so dearly purchased, was almost certain."

Polk, Hardee, Breckinridge, Withers, Gibson, Gilmer, and all who were there confirm this statement. General Buell says of Grant's army that there were "not more than five thousand men in ranks and available on the battle-field at nightfall. . . . The

rest were either killed, wounded, captured, or scattered in inextricable and hopeless confusion for miles along the banks of the river." General Nelson describes them as "cowering under the river-bank, . . . frantic with fright and utterly demoralized."

At this crisis came from General Beauregard an order for the withdrawal of the troops, of which his chief of staff says: "General Beauregard, in the mean time, observing the exhausted, widely scattered condition of his army, directed it to be brought out of battle, collected and restored to order as far as practicable, and to occupy for the night the captured encampments of the enemy. This, however, had been done in chief part by the officers in immediate command of the troops before the order was generally distributed." For this last allegation, or that the army was exhausted, there is not the slightest warrant. When Beauregard's staff-officer gave Bragg this order he said: "Have you promulgated this order to the command?" The officer replied: "I have." General Bragg then said: "If you had not I would not obey it. *The battle is lost.*"

The concurrent testimony of the generals and soldiers *at the front* is at one on all essential points. General Beauregard at Shiloh, two miles in the rear, with the *débris* of the army surging back upon him, the shells bursting around him, sick with his two months' previous malady, pictured in his imagination a wreck at the front, totally different from the actual condition there. Had this officer been with Bragg, and not greatly prostrated and suffering from severe sickness, I firmly believe his order would have been to advance, not to retire. And this in spite of his theory of his plan of battle, which he sums up as follows, and which is so different from General Johnston's: "By a rapid and vigorous attack on General Grant, it was expected he would be beaten back into his transports and the river, or captured in time to enable us to profit by the victory, and remove to the rear all the stores

and munitions that would fall into our hands in such an event before the arrival of General Buell's army on the scene. It was never contemplated, however, to retain the position thus gained and abandon *Corinth, the strategic point of the campaign.*" Why, then, did General Beauregard stop short in his career? Sunday evening it was not a question of retaining, but of gaining, Pittsburg Landing. Complete victory was in his grasp, and he threw it away. General Gibson says: "General Johnston's death was a tremendous catastrophe. There are no words adequate to express my own conception of the immensity of the loss to our country. Sometimes the hopes of millions of people depend upon one head and one arm. The West perished with Albert Sidney Johnston, and the Southern country followed.

Monday was General Beauregard's battle, and it was well fought. But in recalling his troops from the heights which commanded the enemy's landing, he gave away a position which during the night was occupied by Buell's twenty thousand fresh troops, who thus regained the high grounds that had been won at such a cost. Lew Wallace, too, had come up 6500 strong. Moreover, the orders had been conveyed by Beauregard's staff to brigades and even regiments to withdraw, and the troops wandered back over the field, without coherence, direction, or purpose, and encamped where chance provided for them. All array was lost, and, in the morning, they met the attack of nearly thirty thousand fresh and organized troops, with no hope of success except from their native valor and the resolute purpose roused by the triumph of Sunday. Their fortitude, their courage, and the free offering of their lives were equal to the day before. But it was a retreat, not an assault. They retired slowly and sullenly, shattered, but not overthrown, to Corinth, *the strategic point of General Beauregard's campaign.*

THE SECOND DAY'S FIGHTING AT SHILOH.

BY G. T. BEAUREGARD, GENERAL, C. S. A.
After the death of General Albert Sidney Johnston, General Beauregard took command.

. . . Of the second day's battle my sketch shall be very brief. It began with daylight, and this time Buell's army was the attacking force.

Our widely scattered forces, which it had been impossible to organize in the night after the late hour at which they were drawn out of action, were gathered in hand for the exigency as quickly as possible. Generals Bragg, Hardee, and Breckinridge hurried to their assigned positions—Hardee, now to the extreme right, where were Chalmers's and Jackson's brigades of Bragg's corps; General Bragg to the left, where were assembled brigades and fragments of his own troops, as also of Clark's division, Polk's corps, with Trabue's brigade of Kentuckians; Breckinridge was on the left of Hardee. This left a vacant space to be occupied by General Polk, who during the night had gone with Cheatham's division back nearly to Hardee's position on the night of the 5th of April. But just at the critical time, to my great pleasure, General Polk came upon the field with that essential division.

By 7 P. M. the night before, all of Nelson's division had been thrown across the Tennessee, and during the night had been put in position between General Grant's disarrayed forces and our own; Crittenden's division, carried from Savannah by water and disembarked at midnight, was forced through the mob of demoralized soldiers that thronged the riverside and established half a mile in advance, to the left of Nelson. Lew Wallace's division of General Grant's army also had found its way after dark on the 6th across Snake Creek from Crump's Landing to the point near the bridge where General Sherman had rallied the remains of two of his brigades. Rousseau reached the field by water, at daylight, while two other brigades of the same division (McCook's) were close at hand. Thus, at the instant when the battle was opened we had to face at least 23,000 fresh troops, including 3 battalions of regulars, with at least 48 pieces of artillery. On the Confederate side there was not a man who had not taken part in the battle of the day before. The casualties of that day had not been under 6500 officers and men, independent of stragglers; consequently not more than 20,000 infantry could be mustered that morning. The Army of the Ohio in General Buell's hands had been made exceptionally well-trained soldiers for that early period of the war.

The extreme Federal right was occupied by General Lew Wallace's division, while the space intervening between it and Rousseau's brigade was filled with from 5000 to 7000 men gathered during the night and in the early morning from General Grant's broken organizations.

After exchanging some shots with Forrest's cavalry, Nelson's division was confronted with a composite force embracing Chalmers's brigade, Moore's Texas Regiment, with other parts of Withers's division; also the Crescent Regiment of New Orleans and the 26th Alabama, supported by well-posted batteries, and so stoutly was Nelson received that his division had to recede somewhat. Advancing again, however, about 8 o'clock, now reinforced by Hazen's brigade, it was our turn to retire with the loss of a battery. But rallying and taking the offensive, somewhat reinforced, the Confederates were able to recover their lost ground and guns, inflicting a sharp loss on Hazen's brigade, that narrowly escaped capture. Ammen's brigade was also seriously pressed and must have been turned but for the opportune arrival and effective use of Terrill's regular battery of McCook's division.

In the mean time Crittenden's division became involved in the battle, but was successfully kept at bay for several hours by the forces under Hardee and Breckinridge, until it was reinforced by two brigades of McCook's division, which had been added to the attacking force on the field after the battle had been joined, the force of fresh troops being thus increased by at least five thousand men. Our troops were being forced to recede, but slowly; it was not, however, until we were satisfied that we had now to deal with at least three of Buell's divisions as well as with General Lew Wallace's, that I determined to yield the field in the face of so manifestly profitless a combat.

By 1 o'clock General Bragg's forces on our left, necessarily weakened by the withdrawal of a part of his troops to reinforce our right and center, had become so seriously pressed that he called for aid. Some remnants of Louisiana, Alabama, and Tennessee regiments were gathered up and sent forward to support him as best they might, and I went with him personally. General Bragg, now taking the offensive, pressed his adversary back. This was about 2 P. M. My headquarters were still at Shiloh Church.

The odds of fresh troops alone were now too great to justify the prolongation of the conflict. So, directing Adjutant-General Jordan to select at once a proper position in our near rear, and there establish a covering force including artillery, I despatched my staff with directions to the several

THE LAST STAND MADE BY THE CONFEDERATE LINE.
General Beauregard at Shiloh Chapel sending his aides to the corps commanders with orders to begin the retreat. This was at two o'clock on Monday. The tents are part of Sherman's camp, which was reoccupied by him Monday evening.

corps commanders to prepare to retreat from the field, first making a show, however, at different points of resuming the offensive. These orders were executed, I may say, with no small skill, and the Confederate army began to retire at 2.30 P. M. without apparently the least perception on the part of the enemy that such a movement was going on. There was no flurry, no haste shown by officers or men; the spirit of all was admirable. Stragglers dropped into line; the caissons of the batteries were loaded up with rifles; and when the last of our troops had passed to the rear of the covering force, from the elevated ground it occupied, and which commanded a wide view, not a Federal regiment or even a detachment of cavalry was anywhere to be seen as early as 4 P. M.

General Breckinridge, with the rear-guard, bivouacked that night not more than two miles from Shiloh. He withdrew three miles farther on the 8th, and there remained for several days without being menaced.

Our loss in the two days was heavy, reaching 10,699.*

The field was left in the hands of our adversary, as also some captured guns, which were not taken away for want of horses, but in exchange we carried off at least 30 pieces of his artillery, with 26 stands of colors, and nearly 3000 prisoners of war; also a material acquisition of small arms and accouterments which our men had obtained on Sunday instead of their inferior weapons.

* See General Grant's remarks on page 57.

THE UNION FLEET IN THE PORT ROYAL EXPEDITION.

NOTE.—In the summer of 1861 and the winter of 1861-62 several engagements took place on the coast of the Carolinas, including operations at Hatteras Island, Roanoke Island, New Berne, Port Royal, and elsewhere. The above illustration shows the Union fleet under Flag-Officer Du Pont engaging the Confederate forts off Port Royal. The forts were captured; the harbor came into the possession of the Federals, and afforded an admirable base for subsequent operations on the Atlantic seaboard.

LINE-OF-BATTLE SHIP OF THE SEVENTEENTH CENTURY.

THE UNION AND CONFEDERATE NAVIES.

BY JAMES RUSSELL SOLEY, PROFESSOR, U. S. N.

IN order to understand the condition of the United States navy in 1861, it is necessary to glance at the state of affairs during the twenty years before the war. Until the year 1840, naval science during a long period had made but little progress. The various improvements in construction, in equipment, and in ordnance that had been introduced before this date had come about very slowly and gradually, and though numerous small mechanical devices had been adopted from time to time, and old ones had been rendered more efficient, no marked changes had taken place in the art of naval war. Ships were essentially what they had been for two hundred years, and they were rigged, propelled, armed, and fought upon essentially the same principles. But toward the year 1840, the introduction of steam as a motive power marked the beginning of a new era,—an era of developments so rapid and of changes so radical that only the most progressive and elastic minds could follow them. The sailing-vessel was about to be laid aside, except for purposes of training. In the next few years it was replaced, first by the paddle-wheel steamer, then by the screw, then by the twin-screw. The rig of the ship was next altered, and her spars and sail-spread reduced until they were merely auxiliary. Gradually it was realized that the danger from falling spars in an engagement was a disadvantage often out of all proportion to the benefits of auxiliary sail-power, and vessels were built with no spars above the deck but a signal-pole forward and aft. Steam brought with it also a new weapon. The ram, which had

been the principal engine of naval warfare in the Greek and Roman galleys, had disappeared in the Middle Ages when galleys were superseded by sailing-ships. The latter, being dependent upon the wind for their motive power and direction, could not attack an enemy end-on, and hence the ram became useless. Soon after the introduction of steam a few men of inquiring and fertile minds, among them Commodore Matthew Perry and Mr. Charles Ellet, a distinguished civil engineer, perceived that the steam-engine placed a ship-of-war in the same situation as the galleys of the classical period, and that the ram might be employed on the modern vessel to much greater advantage than in ancient times. Presently, the whole system of naval tactics underwent a change, due to the same cause. The close-hauled line ahead, the order of battle for two hundred years and more, gave place to the direct attack in line abreast. To utilize the guns in this new order of battle, they must no longer be mounted in broadside, but upon elevated citadels, giving them a wider sweep around the horizon. Meantime the guns had undergone a change, and were becoming vastly more powerful. First they were adapted to fire shells, which had hitherto been confined to mortars; next the calibers were increased, then rifling was adopted, giving greater range, accuracy, and penetration, and

ROMAN WAR-GALLEY.
From Ancient Terra-cotta Model.

finally breech-loaders came into use. Following closely upon the improvements in guns, came the idea of protecting the sides of vessels with a light armor, at first of bar iron or of two-inch plates, developed by experiment after experiment into masses of solid steel, twenty-two inches in thickness. Last of all came the torpedo, of which a slight and tentative use had been made as early as 1776, but which only made its way into successful and general employment in the war of 1861.

There were signs of the dawn of this revolution before 1840, and its culmination was only reached during the war. But the twenty years between 1840 and 1860 were those in which the movement was really accomplished. During this period the naval administration had endeavored to follow the changes that were taking place, but it had not fully caught up with them. It had begun by building heavy side-wheelers, first the *Mississippi* and *Missouri* and next the *Powhatan* and *Susquehanna*. Efficient as these latter vessels were considered in 1847, when they were begun, and even in 1850, when they were launched, their model was promptly dropped when the submarine screw was introduced in place of the vulnerable paddle-wheel. The six screw-frigates were accordingly built in 1855, and they were regarded with admiration by naval men abroad as well as at home. The *Niagara*, the largest of these, was a ship of 4500 tons. The other five, the *Roanoke*, *Colorado*, *Merrimac*, *Minnesota*, and *Wabash*, had a tonnage somewhat over 3000. All of them were heavily armed, and they formed, or were supposed to form, the chief element of naval strength of the United States. This reliance of the Government upon its large frigates would seem to have been well grounded, and if a war had arisen with a maritime enemy supplied with vessels of the same general type,

they would have given a good account of themselves. In the civil war, however, the enemy had no ordinary vessels of war to be met and conquered in ocean duels, and the waters upon his coast at points vulnerable to naval attack were too shallow to admit the frigates. Hence none of them performed any service at all proportionate to their size and cost of maintenance, except in two or three isolated cases of bombardment, as at Hatteras Inlet, Port Royal, and Fort Fisher.

Of a much more useful type for general service were the twelve screw sloops-of-war built in 1858. There were five of these of the first class, among them the *Hartford*, *Brooklyn*, and *Richmond*, which gave and took so many heavy blows while fighting in Farragut's West Gulf Squadron. Hardly less important were the sloops of the second class, of which the *Iroquois* and *Dacotah* were the largest and most typical examples. To the same group belonged the *Pawnee*, a vessel of peculiar construction, whose constant service was hardly surpassed in efficiency and importance by any other ship of her size on the Atlantic coast. Besides the sloops, there were a few other steamers of miscellaneous dimensions and character, some of which had been purchased and altered for naval use; and these comprised all that the Government had secured toward the creation of a modern steam fleet.

The normal strength of the United States navy, if it is to be a navy at all, cannot be figured at much less than from 80 to 100 vessels, and this was the number in 1861. But of the actual total of 90, as shown by the navy list, 50 were sailing ships,—line-of-battle ships, frigates, sloops, and brigs,—which, splendid vessels as they had been in their day, were now as obsolete as the galleys of Themistocles. It was in placing a false reliance upon these vessels that the Government was at fault: it should have recognized in the course of twenty years that their day was gone forever, that they were of no more use than if they did not exist, that they would only be the slaughter-houses of their gallant crews in an encounter with a modern

THE BURNING OF THE FRIGATE "MERRIMAC" AND OF THE GOSPORT NAVY YARD.

antagonist; and it should by that time have replaced every one of them by war-ships of the period. . . .

The South entered upon the war without any naval preparation, and with very limited resources by which its deficiencies could be promptly supplied. Indeed, it would hardly be possible to imagine a great maritime country more destitute of means for carrying on a naval war than the Confederate States in 1861.

No naval vessels, properly speaking, came into their possession, except the *Fulton*, an old side-wheeler built in 1837, and at this time laid up at Pensacola, and the sunken and half-destroyed hulks at Norfolk, of which only one, the *Merrimac*,

could be made available for service. The seizures of other United States vessels included six revenue-cutters, the *Duane* at Norfolk, and *William Aiken* at Charleston, the *Lewis Cass* at Mobile, the *Robert McClelland* and the *Washington* at New Orleans, and the *Henry Dodge* at Galveston; three coast-survey vessels, the schooners *Petrel* and *Twilight*, and the steam-tender *Firefly*; and six or eight light-house tenders. As all of these were small, and most of them were sailing vessels, they were of little value.

Several coasting or river steamers belonging to private owners, which were lying in Southern waters when the war broke out, were taken or purchased by the Confederate Government. . . .

THE FIGHT BETWEEN THE "MONITOR" AND "MERRIMAC."

BUILDING THE "MERRIMAC," AND THE CONFEDERATE SIDE IN THE BATTLE.

BY JOHN TAYLOR WOOD, COLONEL, C. S. A.
Lieutenant on the "Merrimac."

THE engagement in Hampton Roads on the 8th of March, 1862, between the Confederate iron-clad *Virginia*, or the *Merrimac* (as she is known at the North), and the United States wooden fleet, and that on the 9th between the *Virginia* and the *Monitor*, was, in its results, in some respects the most momentous naval conflict ever witnessed. No battle was ever more widely discussed or produced a greater sensation. It revolutionized the navies of the world. Line-of-battle ships, those huge, overgrown craft, carrying from eighty to one hundred and twenty guns and from five hundred

to twelve hundred men, which, from the destruction of the Spanish Armada to our time, had done most of the fighting, deciding the fate of empires, were at once universally condemned as out of date. Rams and iron-clads were in future to decide all naval warfare. In this battle old things passed away, and the experience of a thousand years of battle and breeze was forgotten. The naval supremacy of England vanished in the smoke of this fight, it is true, only to reappear some years later more commanding than ever. The effect of the news was best described by the London "Times,"

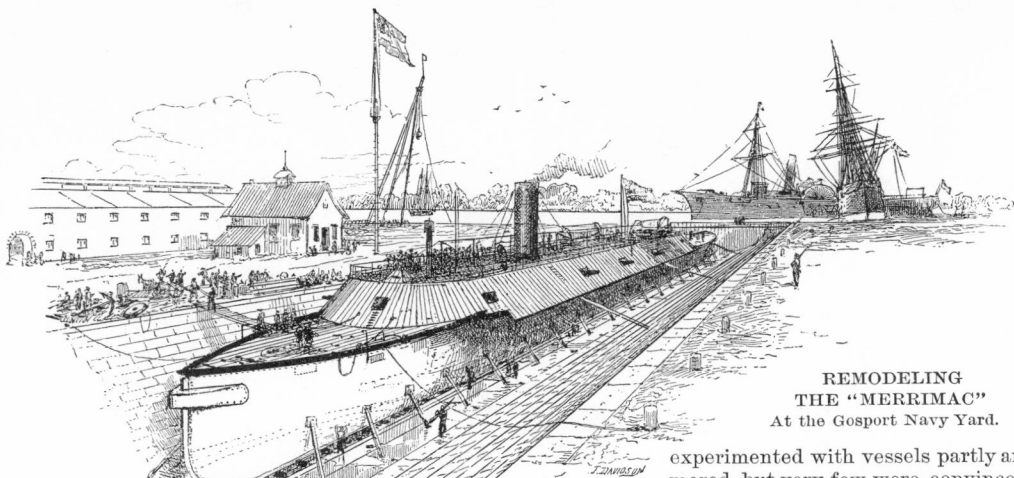

REMODELING
THE "MERRIMAC"
At the Gosport Navy Yard.

which said: "Whereas we had available for immediate purposes one hundred and forty-nine first-class war-ships, we have now two, these two being the *Warrior* and her sister *Ironside*. There is not now a ship in the English navy apart from these two that it would not be madness to trust to an engagement with that little *Monitor*." The Admiralty at once proceeded to reconstruct the navy, cutting down a number of their largest ships and converting them into turret or broadside iron-clads.

The same results were produced in France, which had but one sea-going iron-clad, *La Gloire*, and this one, like the *Warrior*, was only protected amidships. The Emperor Napoleon promptly appointed a commission to devise plans for rebuilding his navy. And so with all the maritime powers. In this race the United States took the lead, and at the close of the war led all the others in the numbers and efficiency of its iron-clad fleet.

It is true that all the great powers had already

experimented with vessels partly armored, but very few were convinced of their utility, and none had been tried by the test of battle, if we except a few floating batteries, thinly clad, used in the Crimean War.

In the spring of 1861 Norfolk and its large naval establishment had been hurriedly abandoned by the Federals, why no one could tell. It is about twelve miles from Fort Monroe, which was then held by a large force of regulars. A few companies of these, with a single frigate, could have occupied and commanded the town and navy yard and kept the channel open. However, a year later, it was as quickly evacuated by the Confederates, and almost with as little reason. But of this I will speak later.

The yard was abandoned to a few volunteers, after it was partly destroyed, and a large number of ships were burnt. Among the spoils were upward of twelve hundred heavy guns, which were scattered among Confederate fortifications from the Potomac to the Mississippi. Among the ships burnt and sunk was the frigate *Merrimac* of 3500 tons and 40 guns,

THE UNITED STATES FRIGATE "MERRIMAC"
Before and after conversion into an iron-clad.

CROSS-SECTION OF
"MERRIMAC."
From a drawing by John L. Porter,
Constructor.

a — 4 inches of iron.
b — 22 inches of wood.

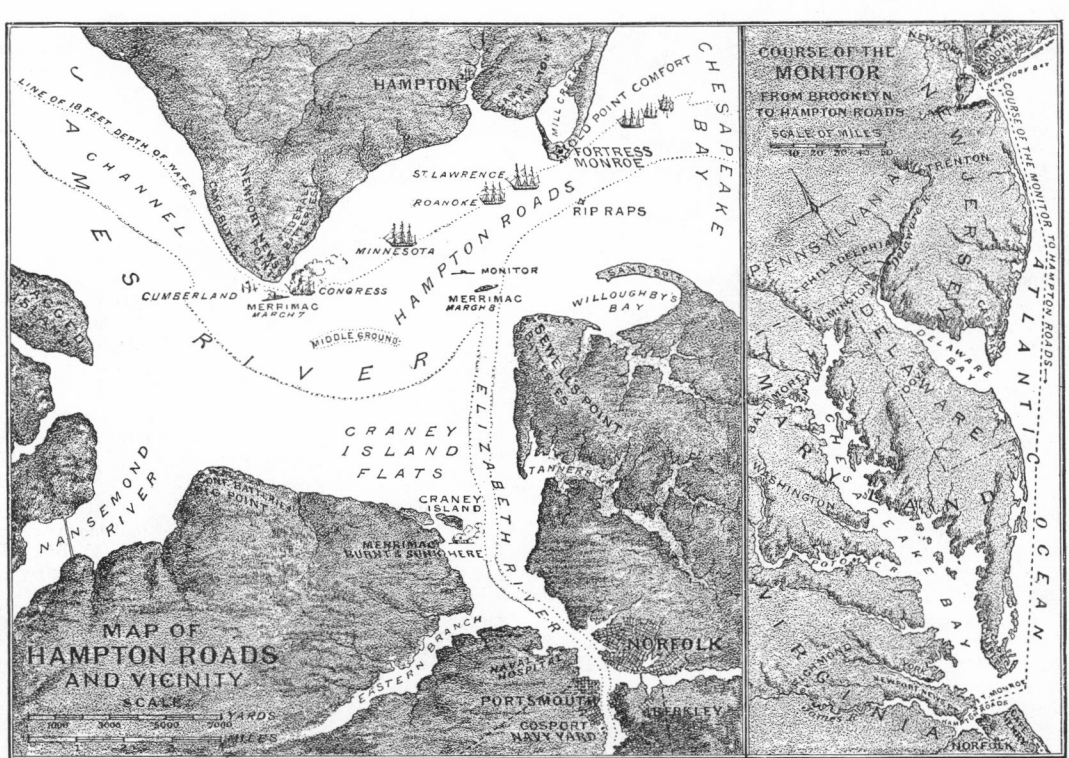

afterward rechristened the *Virginia*, and so I will call her. During the summer of 1861 Lieutenant John M. Brooke, an accomplished officer of the old navy, who with many others had resigned, proposed to Secretary Mallory to raise and rebuild this ship as an iron-clad. His plans were approved, and orders were given to carry them out. She was raised and cut down to the old berth-deck. Both ends for seventy feet were covered over, an when the ship was in fighting trim were just awash. On the midship section, 170 feet in length, was built at an angle of 45 degrees a roof of pitch-pine and oak 24 inches thick, extending from the water-line to a height over the gun-deck of 7 feet. Both ends of the shield were rounded so that the pivot-guns could be used as bow and stern chasers or quartering. Over the gun-deck was a light grating, making a promenade about twenty feet wide. The wood backing was covered with iron plates, rolled at the Tredegar works, two inches thick and eight wide. The first tier was put on horizontally, the second up and down,—in all to the thickness of four inches, bolted through the wood-work and clinched. The prow was of cast-iron, projecting four feet, and badly secured, as events proved. The rudder and propeller were entirely unprotected. The pilot-house was forward of the smokestack, and covered with the same thickness of iron as the sides. The motive power was the same that had always been in the ship. Both of the engines and boilers had been condemned on her return from her last cruise, and were radically defective. Of course, the fire and sinking had not improved them. We could not depend upon them for six hours at a time. A more ill-contrived or unreliable pair of engines could only have been found in some vessels of the United States navy.

Lieutenant Catesby ap R. Jones was ordered to superintend the armament, and no more thoroughly competent officer could have been selected. To his experience and skill as her ordnance and executive officer was due the character of her battery, which proved so efficient. It consisted of 2 7-inch rifles, heavily reinforced around the breech with 3-inch steel bands, shrunk on. These were the first heavy guns so made, and were the bow and stern pivots. There were also 2 6-inch rifles of the same make, and 6 9-inch smooth-bore broad-side,—10 guns in all.

During the summer and fall of 1861 I had been stationed at the batteries on the Potomac at Evansport and Aquia Creek, blockading the river as far as possible. In January, 1862, I was ordered to the *Virginia* as one of the lieutenants, reporting to Commodore French Forrest, who then commanded the navy yard at Norfolk. Commodore Franklin Buchanan was appointed to the command,—an energetic and high-toned officer, who combined with daring courage great professional ability, standing deservedly at the

head of his profession. In 1845 he had been selected by Mr. Bancroft, Secretary of the Navy, to locate and organize the Naval Academy, and he launched that institution upon its successful career. Under him were as capable a set of officers as ever were brought together in one ship. But of man-of-war's men or sailors we had scarcely any. The South was almost without a maritime population. In the old service the majority of officers were from the South, and all the seamen from the North.

Every one had flocked to the army, and to it we had to look for a crew. Some few seamen were found in Norfolk, who had escaped from the gun-boat flotilla in the waters of North Carolina, on their occupation by Admiral Goldsborough and General Burnside. In hopes of securing some

men from the army, I was sent to the headquarters of General Magruder at Yorktown, who was known to have under his command two battalions from New Orleans, among whom might be found a number of seamen. The general, though pressed for want of men, holding a long line with scarcely a brigade, gave me every facility to secure volunteers. With one of his staff I visited every camp, and the commanding officers were ordered to parade their men, and I explained to them what I wanted. About 200 volunteered, and of this number I selected 80 who had had some experience as seamen or gunners. Other commands at Richmond and Petersburg were visited, and so our crew of three hundred was made up. They proved themselves to be as gallant and trusty a body of men as any one would wish to command, not only

in battle, but in reverse and retreat.

Notwithstanding every exertion to hasten the fitting out of the ship, the work during the winter progressed but slowly, owing to delay in sending the iron sheathing from Richmond. At this time the only establishment in the South capable of rolling iron plates was the Tredegar foundry. Its resources were limited, and the demand for all kinds of war material most pressing. And when we reflect upon the scarcity and inexperience of the workmen, and the great changes necessary in transforming an ordinary iron workshop into an arsenal in which all the machinery and tools had to be improvised, it is astonishing that so much was accomplished. The unfinished state of the vessel interfered so with the drills and exercises that we had but little opportunity of getting things into shape. It should be remembered that the ship was an experiment in naval architecture, differing in every respect from any then afloat. The officers and the crew were strangers to the ship and to each other. Up to the hour of sailing she was crowded with workmen. Not a gun had been fired, hardly a revolution of the engines had been made, when we cast off from the dock and started on what many thought was an ordinary trial trip, but which proved to be a trial such as no vessel that ever floated had undergone up to that time. From the start we saw that she was slow, not over five knots; she steered so badly that, with her great length, it took from thirty to forty minutes to turn. She drew twenty-two feet, which confined us to a comparatively narrow channel in the Roads; and, as I have before said, the engines were our weak point. She was as unmanageable as a water-logged vessel.

It was at noon on the 8th of March that we steamed down the Elizabeth River. Passing by our batteries, lined with troops, who cheered us as we passed, and through the obstructions at Craney Island, we took the south channel and headed for Newport News. At anchor at this time off Fort Monroe were the frigates *Minnesota*, *Roanoke*, and *St. Lawrence*, and several gun-boats. The first two were sister ships of the *Virginia* before the war; the last was a sailing frigate of fifty guns. Off Newport News, seven miles above, which was strongly fortified and held by a large Federal garrison, were anchored the frigate *Congress*, 50 guns, and the sloop *Cumberland*, 30. The day was calm, and the last two ships were swinging lazily by their anchors. [The tide was at its height about 1:40 P.M.] Boats were hanging to the lower booms, washed clothes in the rigging. Nothing indicated that we were expected; but when we came within three-quarters of a mile, the boats were dropped astern, booms got alongside, and the *Cumberland* opened with her heavy pivots, followed by the *Congress*, the gun-boats, and the shore batteries.

We reserved our fire until within easy range,

BIRD'S-EYE VIEW OF THE ENGAGEMENT BETWEEN THE "MONITOR" AND THE "MERRIMAC."

MAPS OF THE "MONITOR" AND "MERRIMAC" FIGHT, AND THE COURSE OF THE "MONITOR" FROM BROOKLYN TO HAMPTON ROADS.

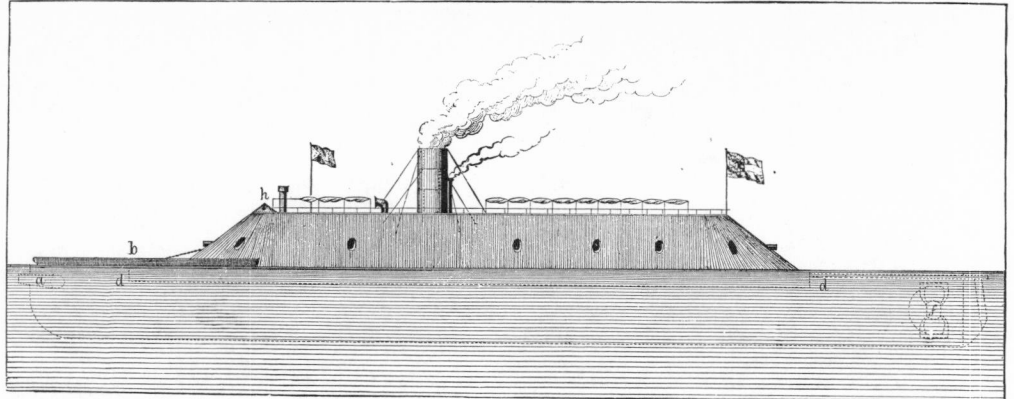

a PROW, OF STEEL.
b WOODEN BULWARK.
h PILOT-HOUSE.

THE "MERRIMAC."
From a sketch made the day before the fight.

Lt. B. L. Blackford, del. March 7, 1862.
d d IRON UNDER WATER.
f PROPELLER.

tunity of using the after-pivot, of which I had charge. As we swung, the *Congress* came in range, nearly stern-on, and we got in three raking shells. She had slipped her anchor, loosed her foretop-sail, run up the jib, and tried to escape, but grounded. Turning, we headed for her and took a position within two hundred yards, where every shot told. In the mean time the *Cumberland* continued the fight, though our ram had opened her side wide enough to drive in a horse and cart. Soon she listed to port and filled rapidly. The crew were driven by the advancing water to the spar-deck, and there worked her pivot-guns until she went down with a roar, the colors still flying. No ship was ever fought more gallantly. The *Congress* continued the unequal contest for more than an hour after the sinking of the *Cumberland*. Her losses were terrible, and finally she ran up the white flag.

As soon as we had hove in sight, coming down the harbor, the *Roanoke*, *St. Lawrence*, and *Minnesota*, assisted by tugs, had got under way, and started up from Old Point Comfort to join their consorts. They were under fire from the batteries at Sewell's Point, but the distance was too great to effect much. The first two, however, ran aground not far above Fort Monroe, and took but little part in the fight. The *Minnesota*, taking the middle or swash channel, steamed up half-way between Old Point Comfort and Newport News, when she grounded, but in a position to be actively engaged.

Previous to this we had been joined by the James River squadron, which had been at anchor a few miles above, and came into action most gallantly, passing the shore batteries at Newport News under a heavy fire, and with some loss. It consisted of the *Yorktown* (or *Patrick Henry*), 12 guns, Captain John R. Tucker; *Jamestown*, 2 guns, Lieut.-Commander J. N. Barney; and *Teaser*, 1 gun, Lieut.-Commander W. A. Webb.

As soon as the *Congress* surrendered, Commander Buchanan ordered the gun-boats *Beaufort*, Lieut.-Commander W. H. Parker, and *Raleigh*, Lieut.-Commander J. W. Alexander, to steam alongside, take off her crew, and set fire to the ship. Lieutenant Pendergrast, who had succeeded Lieutenant Smith, who had been killed, surrendered to Lieutenant Parker, of the *Beaufort*. Delivering his sword and colors, he was directed by Lieutenant

Parker to return to his ship and have the wounded transferred as rapidly as possible. All this time the shore batteries and small-arm men were keeping up an incessant fire on our vessels. Two of the officers of the *Raleigh*, Lieutenant Tayloe and Midshipman Hutter, were killed while assisting the Union wounded out of the *Congress*. A number of the enemy's men were killed by the same fire. Finally it became so hot that the gun-boats were obliged to haul off with only thirty prisoners, leaving Lieutenant Pendergrast and most of his crew on board, and they all afterward escaped to the shore by swimming or in small boats. While this was going on, the white flag was flying at her mainmasthead. Not being able to take possession of his prize, the commodore ordered hot shot to be used, and in a short time she was in flames fore and aft. While directing this, both himself and his flag-lieutenant, Minor, were severely wounded. The command then devolved upon Lieutenant Catesby Jones.

It was now 5 o'clock, nearly two hours of daylight, and the *Minnesota* only remained. She was aground and at our mercy. But the pilots would not attempt the middle channel with the ebb tide and approaching night. So we returned by the south channel to Sewell's Point and anchored, the *Minnesota* escaping, as we thought, only until morning.

Our loss in killed and wounded was twenty-one. The armor was hardly damaged, though at one time our ship was the focus on which were directed at least one hundred heavy guns, afloat and ashore. But nothing outside escaped. Two guns were disabled by having their muzzles shot off. The ram was left in the side of the *Cumberland*. One anchor, the smoke-stack, and the steam-pipes were shot away. Railings, stanchions, boat-davits, everything was swept clean. The flag-staff was repeatedly knocked over, and finally a boarding-pike was used. Commodore Buchanan and the other wounded were sent to the Naval Hospital, and after making preparations for the next day's fight, we slept at our guns, dreaming of other victories in the morning.

But at daybreak we discovered, lying between us and the *Minnesota*, a strange-looking craft, which we knew at once to be Ericsson's *Monitor*, which had long been expected in Hampton Roads, and of

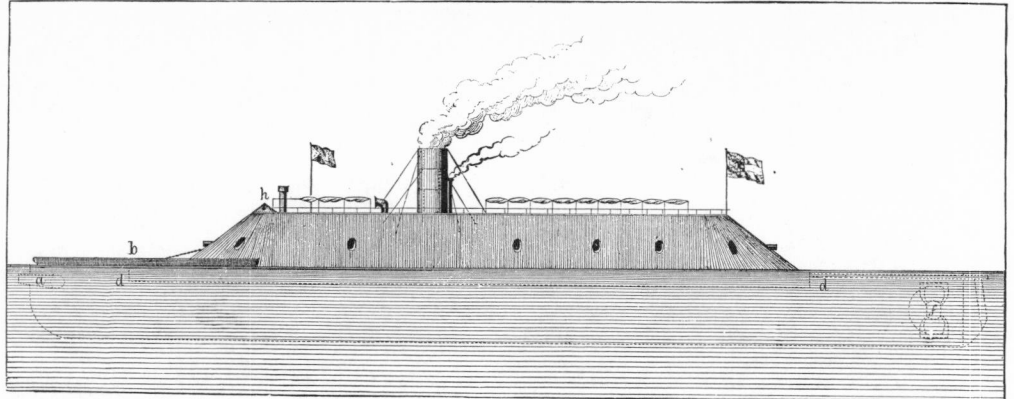

COMMANDERS OF THE "VIRGINIA" (OR "MERRIMAC").
Franklin Buchanan, Admiral, C. S. N.   Josiah Tattnall, Commodore, C. S. N.

when the forward pivot was pointed and fired by Lieutenant Charles Simms, killing and wounding most of the crew of the after pivot-gun of the *Cumberland*. Passing close to the *Congress*, which received our starboard broadside, and returned it with spirit, we steered direct for the *Cumberland*,

striking her almost at right angles, under the fore-rigging on the starboard side. The blow was hardly perceptible on board the *Virginia*. Backing clear of her, we went ahead again, heading up the river, helm hard-a-starboard, and turned slowly. As we did so, for the first time I had an oppor-

COLONEL JOHN TAYLOR WOOD, C. S. A.
Lieutenant on the "Merrimac." (From an oil portrait.)

THE "MERRIMAC" RAMMING THE "CUMBERLAND."

LIEUTENANT GEORGE U. MORRIS, U. S. N.*
Acting-Commander of the "Cumberland."

which, from different sources, we had a good idea. She could not possibly have made her appearance at a more inopportune time for us, changing our plans, which were to destroy the *Minnesota*, and then the remainder of the fleet below Fort Monroe. She appeared but a pygmy compared with the lofty frigate which she guarded. But in her size was one great element of her success. I will not attempt a description of the *Monitor*; her build and peculiarities are well known.

After an early breakfast, we got under way and steamed out toward the enemy, opening fire from our bow pivot, and closing in to deliver our starboard broadside at short range, which was returned promptly from her 11-inch guns. Both vessels then turned and passed again still closer. The *Monitor* was firing every seven or eight minutes, and nearly every shot struck. Our ship was working worse and worse, and after the loss of the smoke-stack, Mr. Ramsey, chief engineer, reported that the draught was so poor that it was with great difficulty he could keep up steam. Once or twice the ship was on the bottom. Drawing 22 feet of water, we were confined to a narrow channel, while the *Monitor*, with only 12 feet immersion, could take any position, and always have us in range of her guns. Orders were given to concentrate our fire on the pilot-house, and with good result, as we afterward learned. More than two hours had passed, and we had made no impression on the enemy so far as we could discover, while our wounds were slight. Several times the *Monitor* ceased firing, and we were in hopes she was disabled, but the revolution again of her turret and the heavy blows of her 11-inch shot on our sides soon undeceived us.

Coming down from the spar-deck, and observing a division standing "at ease," Lieutenant Jones inquired:

"Why are you not firing, Mr. Eggleston?"

"Why, our powder is very precious," replied the lieutenant; "and after two hours' incessant firing I find that I can do her about as much damage by snapping my thumb at her every two minutes and a half."

Lieutenant Jones now determined to run her down or board her. For nearly an hour we manœuvered for a position. Now "Go ahead!" now "Stop!" now "Astern!" The ship was as unwieldy as Noah's ark. At last an opportunity offered. "Go ahead, full speed!" But before the ship gathered headway, the *Monitor* turned, and our disabled ram only gave a glancing blow, effecting nothing. Again she came up on our quarter, her bow against our side, and at this distance fired twice. Both shots struck about half-way up the shield, abreast of the after pivot, and the impact forced the side in bodily two or three inches. All the crews of the after guns were knocked over by the concussion, and bled from the nose or ears. Another shot at the same place would have penetrated. While alongside, boarders were called

THE "MERRIMAC" PASSING THE CONFEDERATE BATTERY ON CRANEY ISLAND, ON HER WAY TO ATTACK THE FEDERAL FLEET.

away; but she dropped astern before they could get on board. And so, for six or more hours, the struggle was kept up. At length, the *Monitor* withdrew over the middle ground where we could not follow, but always maintaining a position to protect the *Minnesota*. To have run our ship ashore on a falling tide would have been ruin. We awaited her return for an hour; and at 2 o'clock P. M. steamed to Sewell's Point, and thence to the dockyard at Norfolk, our crew thoroughly worn out from the two days' fight.

Although there is no doubt that the *Monitor* first retired—for Captain Van Brunt, commanding the *Minnesota*, so states in his official report—the battle was a drawn one so far as the two vessels engaged were concerned. But in its general results the advantage was with the *Monitor*. Our casualties in the second day's fight were only a few wounded.

This action demonstrated for the first time the

* In the absence of Captain Radford, the command of the *Cumberland* devolved upon the executive officer, Lieutenant Morris, from whose official report we quote the following: "At thirty minutes past three the water had gained upon us, notwithstanding the pumps were kept actively employed to a degree that, the forward-magazine being drowned, we had to take powder from the after-magazine for the ten-inch gun. At thirty-five minutes past three the water had risen to the main hatchway, and the ship canted to port, and we delivered a parting fire—each man trying to save himself by jumping overboard. Timely notice was given, and all the wounded who could walk were ordered out of the cockpit; but those of the wounded who had been carried into the sick-bay and on the berth-deck were so mangled that it was impossible to save them. . . . I should judge we have lost upward of one hundred men. I can only say, in conclusion, that all did their duty, and we sank with the American flag flying at the peak." When summoned to surrender, Morris replied, "Never! I'll sink alongside!"

LIEUTENANT JOSEPH B. SMITH, U. S. N.*
Acting Commander of the "Congress."
From a photograph.

THE "MERRIMAC" DRIVING THE "CONGRESS" FROM HER ANCHORAGE.

CAPTAIN G. J. VAN BRUNT, U. S. N.
Commander of the "Minnesota." (From a photograph.)

THE UNION SIDE.

IN THE "MONITOR" TURRET.

BY S. DANA GREENE, COMMANDER, U. S. N.
Executive Officer of the "Monitor."

power and efficiency of the ram as a means of offense. The side of the *Cumberland* was crushed like an egg-shell. The *Congress* and *Minnesota*, even with our disabled bow, would have shared the same fate but that we could not reach them on account of our great draught.

It also showed the power of resistance of two ironclads, widely differing in construction, model, and armament, under a fire which in a short time would have sunk any other vessel then afloat.

The *Monitor* was well handled, and saved the *Minnesota* and the remainder of the fleet at Fort Monroe. But her gunnery was poor. Not a single shot struck us at the water-line, where the ship was utterly unprotected and where one would have been fatal. Or had the fire been concentrated on any one spot, the shield would have been pierced; or had larger charges been used, the result would have been the same. Most of her shot struck us obliquely, breaking the iron of both courses, but not injuring the wood backing. When struck at right angles, the backing would be broken but not penetrated. We had no solid projectiles, except a few of large windage, to be used as hot shot, and, of course, made no impression on the turret. But in all this it should be borne in mind that both vessels were on their trial trip, both were experimental, and both were receiving their baptism of fire.

On our arrival at Norfolk, Commodore Buchanan

*According to the pilot of the *Cumberland*, Lieutenant Smith was killed by a shot. His death was fixed at 4:20 P. M. by Lieutenant Pendergrast, next in command, who did not hear of it until ten minutes later. When his father, Commodore Joseph Smith, who was on duty at Washington, saw by the first despatch from Fort Monroe that the *Congress* had shown the white flag, he said, quietly, "Joe 's dead!" After speaking of the death of Lieutenant Smith, Lieutenant Pendergrast says, in his official report: "Seeing that our men were being killed without the prospect of any relief from the *Minnesota*, . . . not being able to get a single gun to bear upon the enemy, and the ship being on fire in several places, upon consultation with Commander William Smith we deemed it proper to haul down our colors." Lieutenant Smith's sword was sent to his father by the enemy under a flag of truce.

sent for me. I found him at the Naval Hospital, badly wounded and suffering greatly. He dictated a short despatch to Mr. Mallory, Secretary of the Navy, stating the return of the ship and the result of the two days' fight, and directed me to proceed to Richmond with it and the flag of the *Congress*, and make a verbal report of the action, condition of the *Virginia*, etc.

I took the first train for Petersburg and the capital. The news had preceded me, and at every station I was warmly received, and to listening crowds was forced to repeat the story of the fight. Arriving at Richmond, I drove to Mr. Mallory's office and with him went to President Davis's, where we met Mr. Benjamin, who, a few days afterward, became Secretary of State, Mr. Seddon, afterward Secretary of War, General Cooper, Adjutant-General, and a number of others. I told at length what had occurred on the previous two days, and what changes and repairs were necessary to the *Virginia*. As to the future, I said that in the *Monitor* we had met our equal, and that the result of another engagement would be very doubtful. Mr. Davis made many inquiries as regarded the ship's draught, speed, and capabilities, and urged the completion of the repairs at as early a day as possible. The conversation lasted until near midnight. During the evening the flag of the *Congress*, which was a very large one, was brought in, and to our surprise, in unfolding it, we found it in some places saturated with blood. On this discovery it was quickly rolled up and sent to the Navy Department, where it remained during the war; it doubtless burned with that building when Richmond was evacuated.

The news of our victory was received everywhere in the South with the most enthusiastic rejoicing.

Coming, as it did, after a number of disasters in the South and West, it was particularly grateful. Then again, under the circumstances, so little was expected from the navy that this success was entirely unlooked for. So, from one extreme to the other, the most extravagant anticipations were formed of what the ship could do. For instance: the blockade could be raised, Washington leveled to the ground, New York laid under contribution, and so on. At the North, equally groundless alarm was felt. As an example of this, Secretary Welles relates what took place at a Cabinet meeting called by Mr. Lincoln on the receipt of the news. "'The *Merrimac*,' said Stanton, 'will change the whole character of the war; she will destroy, *seriatim*, every naval vessel; she will lay all the cities on the seaboard under contribution. I shall immediately recall Burnside; Port Royal must be abandoned. I will notify the governors and municipal authorities in the North to take instant measures to protect their harbors.' He had no doubt, he said, that the monster was at this moment on her way to Washington; and, looking out of the window, which commanded a view of the Potomac for many miles, 'Not unlikely, we shall have a shell or cannon-ball from one of her guns in the White House before we leave this room.' Mr. Seward, usually buoyant and self-reliant, overwhelmed with the intelligence, listened in responsive sympathy to Stanton, and was greatly depressed, as, indeed, were all the members." . . .

A few days later we went down again to within gun-shot of the Rip-Raps, and exchanged a few rounds with the fort, hoping that the *Monitor* would come out from her lair into open water. Had she done so, a determined effort would have been made to carry her by boarding. . . .

THE keel of the most famous vessel of modern times, Captain Ericsson's first ironclad, was laid in the ship-yard of Thomas F. Rowland, at Greenpoint, Brooklyn, in October, 1861, and on the 30th of January, 1862, the novel craft was launched. On the 25th of February she was commissioned and turned over to the Government, and nine days later left New York for Hampton Roads, where, on the 9th of March, occurred the memorable contest with the *Merrimac*. On her next venture on the open sea she foundered off Cape Hatteras in a gale of wind (December 29th). During her career of less than a year she had no fewer than five different commanders; but it was the fortune of the writer to serve as her only executive officer, standing upon her deck when she was launched, and leaving it but a few minutes before she sank. So hurried was the preparation of the *Monitor* that the mechanics worked upon her day and night up to the hour of her departure, and little opportunity was offered to drill the crew at the guns, to work the turret, and to become familiar with the other unusual features of the vessel. The crew was, in fact, composed of volunteers. Lieutenant Worden, having been authorized by the Navy Department to select his men from any ship-of-war in New York harbor, addressed the crews of the *North Carolina* and *Sabine*, stating fully to them the probable dangers of the passage to Hampton Roads, and the certainty of having important service to perform after arriving. The sailors responded enthusiastically, many more volunteering than were required. Of the crew Captain Worden said, in his official report of the battle, "A better one no naval commander ever had the honor to command."

70

THE EXPLOSION ON THE BURNING "CONGRESS."

We left New York in tow of the tug-boat *Seth Low* at 11 A. M. of Thursday, the 6th of March. On the following day a moderate breeze was encountered, and it was at once evident that the *Monitor* was unfit as a sea-going craft. Nothing but the subsidence of the wind prevented her from being shipwrecked before she reached Hampton Roads. The berth-deck hatch leaked in spite of all we could do, and the water came down under the turret like a waterfall. It would strike the pilot-house and go over the turret in beautiful curves, and it came through the narrow eye-holes in the pilot-house with such force as to knock the helmsman completely round from the wheel. The waves also broke over the blower-pipes, and the water came down through them in such quantities that the belts of the blower-engines slipped, and the engines consequently stopped for lack of artificial draught, without which, in such a confined place, the fires could not get air for combustion. Newton and Stimers, followed by the engineer's force, gallantly rushed into the engine-room and fire-room to remedy the evil, but they were unable to check the inflowing water, and were nearly suffocated with escaping gas. They were dragged out more dead than alive, and carried to the top of the turret, where the fresh air gradually revived them. The water continued to pour through the hawse-hole, and over and down the smoke-stacks and blower-pipes, in such quantities that there was imminent danger that the ship would founder. The steam-pumps could not be operated because the fires had been nearly extinguished, and the engine-room was uninhabitable on account of the suffocating gas with which it was filled. The hand-pumps were then rigged and worked, but they had not enough force to throw the water out through the top of the turret,—the only opening,—and it was useless to bail, as we had to pass the buckets up through the turret, which made it a very long operation. Fortunately, toward evening the wind

and the sea subsided, and, being again in smooth water, the engine was put in operation. But at midnight, in passing over a shoal, rough water was again encountered, and our troubles were renewed, complicated this time with the jamming of wheel-ropes, so that the safety of the ship depended entirely on the strength of the hawser which connected her with the tug-boat. The hawser, being new, held fast; but during the greater part of the night we were constantly engaged in fighting the leaks, until we reached smooth water again, just before daylight.

It was at the close of this dispiriting trial trip, in which all hands had been exhausted in their efforts to keep the novel craft afloat, that the *Monitor* passed Cape Henry at 4 P. M. on Saturday, March 8th. At this point was heard the distant booming of heavy guns, which our captain rightly judged to be an engagement with the *Merrimac*, twenty miles away. He at once ordered the vessel stripped of her sea-rig, the turret keyed up, and every preparation made for battle. As we approached Hampton Roads we could see the fine old *Congress* burning brightly, and soon a pilot came on board and told of the arrival of the *Merrimac*, the disaster to the *Cumberland* and the *Congress*, and the dismay of the Union forces. The *Monitor* was pushed with all haste, and reached the *Roanoke* (Captain Marston), anchored in the Roads, at 9 P. M. Worden immediately reported his arrival to Captain Marston, who suggested that he should go to the assistance of the *Minnesota*, then aground off Newport News. As no pilot was available, Captain Worden accepted the volunteer services of Acting Master Samuel Howard, who earnestly sought the duty. An atmosphere of gloom pervaded the fleet, and the pygmy aspect of the new-comer did not inspire confidence among those who had witnessed the destruction of the day before. Skilfully piloted by Howard, we proceeded on our way, our path illumined by the blaze

of the *Congress*. Reaching the *Minnesota*, hard and fast aground, near midnight, we anchored, and Worden reported to Captain Van Brunt. Between 1 and 2 A. M. the *Congress* blew up—not instantaneously, but successively. Her powder-tanks seemed to explode, each shower of sparks rivaling

the other in its height, until they appeared to reach the zenith,—a grand but mournful sight. Near us, too, at the bottom of the river, lay the *Cumberland*, with her silent crew of brave men, who died while fighting their guns to the water's edge, and whose colors were still flying at the peak.

ESCAPE OF PART OF THE CREW OF THE "CONGRESS."

JOHN L. WORDEN, REAR-ADMIRAL, U. S. N.
Commander of the "Monitor" in the engagement with the "Merrimac."
From a photograph taken in 1875.

PART OF THE CREW OF THE "MONITOR."
From a photograph taken soon after the fight.

NOTE.—The pride of Worden in his crew was warmly reciprocated by his men, and found expression in the following letter, written to him while he was lying in Washington disabled by his wound. We take it from Professor Soley's volume, "The Blockade and the Cruisers" (Charles Scribner's Sons).

HAMPTON ROADS, April 24th, 1862. U. S. MONITOR. TO OUR DEAR AND HONORED CAPTAIN. DEAR SIR: These few lines is from your own crew of the *Monitor*, with their kindest Love to you their Honored Captain, hoping to God that they will have the pleasure of welcoming you back to us again soon, for we are all ready able and willing to meet Death or anything else, only give us back our Captain again. Dear Captain, we have got your Pilot-house fixed and all ready for you when you get well again; and we all sincerely hope that soon we will have the pleasure of welcoming you back to it. . . . We are waiting very patiently to engage our Antagonist if we could only get a chance to do so. The last time she came out we all thought we would have the Pleasure of sinking her. But we all got disappointed, for we did not fire one shot, and the Norfolk papers says we are cowards in the *Monitor*—and all we want is a chance to show them where it lies with you for our Captain We can teach them who is cowards. But there is a great deal that we would like to write to you but we think you will soon be with us again yourself. But we all join in with our kindest love to you, hoping that God will restore you to us again and hoping that your sufferings is at an end now, and we are all so glad to hear that your eyesight will be spaired to you again. We would wish to write more to you if we have your kind Permission to do so but at present we all conclude by tendering to you your kindest Love and affection, to our Dear and Honored Captain. We remain untill Death your Affectionate Crew.

THE MONITOR BOYS.

To Captain Worden.

The dreary night dragged slowly on; the officers and crew were up and alert, to be ready for any emergency. At daylight on Sunday the *Merrimac* and her consorts were discovered at anchor near Sewell's Point. At about half-past 7 o'clock the enemy's vessels got under way and steered in the direction of the *Minnesota*. At the same time the *Monitor* got under way, and her officers and crew took their stations for battle. Captain Van Brunt, of the *Minnesota*, officially reports, "I made signal to the *Monitor* to attack the enemy," but the signal was not seen by us; other work was in hand, and Commander Worden required no signal.

The pilot-house of the *Monitor* was situated well forward, near the bow; it was a wrought-iron structure, built of logs of iron nine inches thick, bolted through the corners, and covered with an iron plate two inches thick, which was not fastened down, but was kept in place merely by its weight. The sight-holes or slits were made by inserting quarter-inch plates at the corners between the upper set of logs and the next below. The structure projected four feet above the deck, and was barely large enough inside to hold three men standing. It presented a flat surface on all sides and on top. The steering-wheel was secured to one of the logs on the front side. The position and shape of this structure should be carefully born in mind.

Worden took his station in the pilot-house, and by his side were Howard, the pilot, and Peter Williams, quartermaster, who steered the vessel throughout the engagement. My place was in the turret, to work and fight the guns; with me were Stodder and Stimers and sixteen brawny men, eight to each gun. John Stocking, boatswain's mate, and Thomas Lochrane, seaman, were gun-captains. Newton and his assistants were in the engine- and fire-rooms, to manipulate the boilers and engines, and most admirably did they perform this important service from the beginning to the close of the action. Webber had charge of the powder division on the berth-deck, and Joseph Crown, gunner's mate, rendered valuable service in connection with this duty.

The physical condition of the officers and men of the two ships at this time was in striking contrast.

The *Merrimac* had passed the night quietly near Sewell's Point, her people enjoying rest and sleep, elated by thoughts of the victory they had achieved that day, and cheered by the prospects of another easy victory on the morrow. The *Monitor* had barely escaped shipwreck twice within the last thirty-six hours, and since Friday morning, forty-eight hours before, few if any of those on board had closed their eyes in sleep or had anything to eat but hard bread, as cooking was impossible. She was surrounded by wrecks and disaster, and her efficiency in action had yet to be proved.

Worden lost no time in bringing it to a test. Getting his ship under way, he steered direct for the enemy's vessels, in order to meet and engage them as far as possible from the *Minnesota*. As he approached, the wooden vessels quickly turned and left. Our captain, to the "astonishment" of Captain Van Brunt (as he states in his official report), made straight for the *Merrimac*, which had already commenced firing; and when he came within short range, he changed his course so as to come alongside of her, stopped the engine, and gave the order, "Commence firing!" I triced up the port, ran out the gun, and, taking deliberate aim, pulled the lockstring. The *Merrimac* was quick to reply, returning a rattling broadside (for she had ten guns to our two), and the battle fairly began. The turrets and other parts of the ship were heavily struck, but the shots did not penetrate; the tower was intact, and it continued to revolve. A look of confidence passed over the men's faces, and we believed the *Merrimac* would not repeat the work she had accomplished the day before.

The fight continued with the exchange of broadsides as fast as the guns could be served and at very short range, the distance between the vessels frequently being not more than a few yards. Worden skilfully manœuvred his quick-turning vessel, trying to find some vulnerable point in his adversary. Once he made a dash at her stern, hoping to disable her screw, which he thinks he missed by not more than two feet. Our shots ripped the iron of the *Merrimac*, while the reverberation of her shots against the tower caused anything but a pleasant sensation. While Stodder, who was stationed at the machine which controlled the revolving motion of the turret, was incautiously leaning against the side of the tower, a large shot struck in the vicinity and disabled him. He left the turret and went below, and Stimers, who had assisted him, continued to do the work.

The drawbacks to the position of the pilot-house were soon realized. We could not fire ahead nor within several points of the bow, since the blast from our own guns would have injured the people in the pilot-house, only a few yards off. Keeler and Toffey passed the captain's orders and messages to me, and my inquiries and answers to him, the speaking-tube from the pilot-house to the turret having been broken early in the action. They performed their work with zeal and alacrity, but, both being landsmen, our technical communications sometimes miscarried. The situation

THE "MONITOR." THE ENCOUNTER AT SHORT RANGE. THE "MERRIMAC."

was novel: a vessel of war was engaged in desperate combat with a powerful foe; the captain, commanding and guiding, was inclosed in one place, and the executive officer, working and fighting the guns, was shut up in another, and communication between them was difficult and uncertain. It was this experience which caused Isaac Newton, immediately after the engagement, to suggest the clever plan of putting the pilot-house on top of the turret, and making it cylindrical instead of square; and his suggestions were subsequently adopted in this type of vessel.

As the engagement continued, the working of the turret was not altogether satisfactory. It was difficult to start it revolving, or, when once started, to stop it, on account of the imperfections of the novel machinery, which was now undergoing its first trial. Stimers was an active, muscular man, and did his utmost to control the motion of the turret; but, in spite of his efforts, it was difficult, if not impossible, to secure accurate firing. The conditions were very different from those of an ordinary broadside gun, under which we had been trained on wooden ships. My only view of the world outside of the tower was over the muzzles of the guns, which cleared the ports by only a few inches. When the guns were run in, the port-holes were covered by heavy iron pendulums,

pierced with small holes to allow the iron rammer and sponge handles to protrude while they were in use. To hoist these pendulums required the entire gun's crew and vastly increased the work inside the turret.

The effect upon one shut up in a revolving drum is perplexing, and it is not a simple matter to keep the bearings. White marks had been placed upon the stationary deck immediately below the turret to indicate the direction of the starboard and port sides, and the bow and stern; but these marks were obliterated early in the action. I would continually ask the captain, "How does the *Merrimac* bear?" He replied, "On the starboard-beam," or "On the port-quarter," as the case might be. Then the difficulty was to determine the direction of the starboard-beam, or port-quarter, or any other bearing. It finally resulted, that when a gun was ready for firing, the turret would be started on its revolving journey in search of the target, and when found it was taken "on the fly," because the turret could not be accurately controlled. Once the *Merrimac* tried to ram us; but Worden avoided the direct impact by the skilful use of the helm, and she struck a glancing blow, which did no damage. At the instant of collision I planted a solid 180-pound shot fair and square upon the forward part of her casemate. Had the gun been loaded with

thirty pounds of powder, which was the charge subsequently used with similar guns, it is probable that this shot would have penetrated her armor; but the charge being limited to fifteen pounds, in accordance with peremptory orders to that effect from the Navy Department, the shot rebounded without doing any more damage than possibly to start some of the beams of her armor-backing.

It is stated by Colonel Wood, of the *Merrimac*, that when that vessel rammed the *Cumberland* her ram, or beak, was broken off and left in that vessel. In a letter to me, about two years since, he described this ram as "of cast-iron, wedge-shaped, about 1500 pounds in weight, 2 feet under water, and projecting 2½ feet from the stem." A ram of this description, had it been intact, would have struck the *Monitor* at that part of the upper hull where the armor and backing were thickest. It is very doubtful if, under any headway that the *Merrimac* could have acquired at such short range, this ram could have done any injury to this part of the vessel. That it could by no possibility have reached the thin lower hull is evident from a glance at the drawing of the *Monitor*, the overhang or upper hull being constructed for the express purpose of protecting the vital part of the vessel.

The battle continued at close quarters without apparent damage to either side. After a time, the

supply of shot in the turret being exhausted, Worden hauled off for about fifteen minutes to replenish. The serving of the cartridges, weighing but fifteen pounds, was a matter of no difficulty; but the hoisting of the heavy shot was a slow and tedious operation, it being necessary that the turret should remain stationary, in order that the two scuttles, one in the deck and the other in the floor of the turret, should be in line. Worden took advantage of the lull, and passed through the port-hole upon the deck outside to get a better view of the situation. He soon renewed the attack, and the contest continued as before.

Two important points were constantly kept in mind: first, to prevent the enemy's projectiles from entering the turret through the port-holes,—for the explosion of a shell inside, by disabling the men at the guns, would have ended the fight, as there was no relief gun's crew on board; second, not to fire into our own pilot-house. A careless or impatient hand, during the confusion arising from the whirligig motion of the tower, might let slip one of our big shot against the pilot-house. For this and other reasons I fired every gun while I remained in the turret.

COMMANDER SAMUEL DANA GREENE, U. S. N.
Executive officer of the "Monitor." (From a war-time photograph.)

ARRIVAL OF THE "MONITOR" AT HAMPTON ROADS.

ON THE GUN-DECK OF THE "MERRIMAC."

Soon after noon a shell from the enemy's gun, the muzzle not ten yards distant, struck the forward side of the pilot-house directly in the sight-hole, or slit, and exploded, cracking the second iron log and partly lifting the top, leaving an opening. Worden was standing immediately behind this spot, and received in his face the force of the blow, which partly stunned him, and, filling his eyes with powder, utterly blinded him. The injury was known only to those in the pilot-house and its immediate vicinity. The flood of light rushing through the top of the pilot-house, now partly open, caused Worden, blind as he was, to believe that the pilot-house was seriously injured, if not destroyed; he therefore gave orders to put the helm to starboard and "sheer off." Thus the *Monitor* retired temporarily from the action, in order to ascertain the extent of the injuries she had received. At the same time Worden sent for me, and leaving Stimers the only officer in the turret, I went forward at once, and found him standing at the foot of the ladder leading to the pilot-house.

He was a ghastly sight, with his eyes closed and the blood apparently rushing from every pore in the upper part of his face. He told me that he was seriously wounded, and directed me to take command. I assisted in leading him to a sofa in his cabin, where he was tenderly cared for by Doctor Logue, and then I assumed command. Blind and suffering as he was, Worden's fortitude never forsook him; he frequently asked from his bed of pain of the progress of affairs, and when told that the *Minnesota* was saved, he said, "Then I can die happy."

When I reached my station in the pilot-house, I found that the iron log was fractured and the top partly open; but the steering gear was still intact, and the pilot-house was not totally destroyed, as had been feared. In the confusion of the moment resulting from so serious an injury to the commanding officer, the *Monitor* had been moving without direction. Exactly how much time elapsed from the moment that Worden was wounded until I had reached the pilot-house and completed the examination of the injury at that point, and determined what course to pursue in the damaged condition of the vessel, it is impossible to state; but it could hardly have exceeded twenty minutes at the utmost. During this time the *Merrimac*, which was leaking badly, had started in the direction of the Elizabeth River; and, on taking my station in the pilot-house and turning the vessel's head in the direction of the *Merrimac*, I saw that she was already in retreat. A few shots were fired at the retiring vessel, and she continued on to Norfolk. I returned with the *Monitor* to the side of the *Minnesota*, where preparations were being made to abandon the ship, which was still aground. Shortly afterward Worden was transferred to a tug, and that night he was carried to Washington.

The fight was over. We of the *Monitor* thought, and still think, that we had gained a great victory. This the Confederates have denied. But it has never been denied that the object of the *Merrimac* on the 9th of March was to complete the destruction of the Union fleet in Hampton Roads, and that she was completely foiled and driven off by the *Monitor*; nor has it been denied that at the close of the engagement the *Merrimac* retreated to Norfolk, leaving the *Monitor* in possession of the field.

In this engagement Captain Worden displayed the highest qualities as an officer and man. He was in his prime (forty-four years old), and carried with him the ripe experience of twenty-eight years in the naval service. He joined the ship a sick man, having but recently left a prison in the South. He was nominated for the command by the late Admiral Joseph Smith, and the result proved the wisdom of the choice. Having accepted his orders against the protests of his physicians and the entreaties of his family, nothing would deter him from the enterprise. He arrived on the battle-ground amidst the disaster and gloom, almost despair, of the Union people, who had little faith that he could beat back the powerful *Merrimac*, after her experience with the *Cumberland* and *Congress*. Without encouragement, single-handed, and without specific orders from any source, he rose above the atmosphere of doubt and depression which surrounded him, and with unflinching nerve and undaunted courage he hurled his little, untried vessel against his huge, well-proved antagonist, and won the battle. He was victor in the first ironclad battle of the world's history.

The subsequent career of the *Monitor* needs but a few words.

On the day after the fight I received the following letter from Mr. Fox, Assistant Secretary of the Navy:

"U. S. Steamer *Roanoke*, Old Point, March 10th, 1862.

My dear Mr. Greene: Under the extraordinary circumstances of the contest of yesterday, and the responsibilities devolving upon me, and your extreme youth, I have suggested to Captain Marston to send on board the *Monitor*, as temporary commanding, Lieutenant Selfridge, until the arrival of Commodore Goldsborough, which will be in a few days. I appreciate your position, and you must appreciate mine, and serve with the same zeal and fidelity. With the kindest wishes for you all, most truly, G. V. Fox."

For the next two months we lay at Hampton Roads. Twice the *Merrimac* came out of the Elizabeth River, but did not attack. We, on our side, had received positive orders not to attack in the comparatively shoal waters above Hampton Roads, where the Union fleet could not manœuver. The *Merrimac* protected the James River, and the *Monitor* protected the Chesapeake. Neither side had an ironclad in reserve, and neither wished to bring on an engagement which might disable its only armored vessel in those waters.

With the evacuation of Norfolk and the destruction of the *Merrimac*, the *Monitor* moved up the James River with the squadron under the command of Commander John Rodgers, in connection with McClellan's advance upon Richmond by the Peninsula. We were engaged for four hours at Fort Darling, but were unable to silence the guns or destroy the earthworks. Probably no ship was ever devised which was so uncomfortable for her crew, and certainly no sailor ever led a more disagreeable life than we did on the James River, suffocated with heat and bad air if we remained below, and a target for sharp-shooters if we came on deck.

With the withdrawal of McClellan's army, we returned to Hampton Roads, and in the autumn were ordered to Washington, where the vessel was repaired. We returned to Hampton Roads in November, and sailed thence (December 29th) in tow of the steamer *Rhode Island*, bound for Beaufort, N. C. Between 11 P. M. and midnight on the following night the *Monitor* went down in a gale, a few miles south of Cape Hatteras. Four officers and twelve men were drowned, forty-nine people being saved by the boats of the steamer. It was impossible to keep the vessel free of water, and we presumed that the upper and lower hulls thumped themselves apart. No ship in the world's history has a more imperishable place in naval annals than the *Monitor*. Not only by her providential arrival at the right moment did she secure the safety of Hampton Roads and all that depended on it, but the idea which she embodied revolutionized the system of naval warfare which had existed from the earliest recorded history.

LIEUTENANT CATESBY AP R. JONES OF THE "MERRIMAC."

IN THE TURRET OF THE "MONITOR."

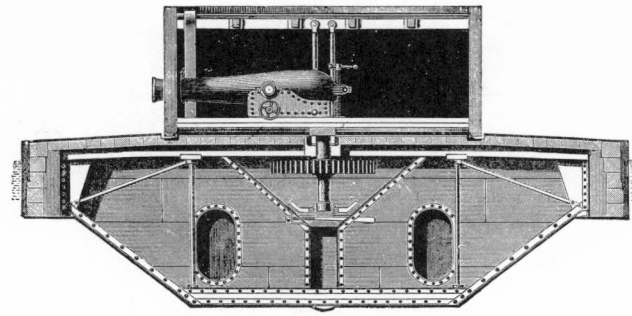

TRANSVERSE SECTION OF THE "MONITOR" THROUGH THE CENTER OF THE TURRET.

THE BUILDING OF THE "MONITOR."

BY CAPTAIN JOHN ERICSSON, INVENTOR OF THE "MONITOR."

THE introduction of General Paixhans's brilliant invention, the shell-gun, in 1824, followed, in 1858, by the successful application of armor-plating to the steam-frigate *La Gloire*, under Napoleon III., compelled an immediate change in naval construction which startled the maritime countries of Europe, especially England, whose boasted security behind her "wooden walls" was shown to be a complete delusion. The English naval architects, however, did not overlook the fact that their French rivals, while producing a gun which rendered wooden navies almost useless, had also by their armor-plating provided an efficient protection against the destructive Paixhans shells.

Accordingly, the Admiralty without loss of time laid the keel of the *Warrior*, an armored iron steam-frigate 380 feet long, 58 feet beam, 26 feet draught, and 9200 tons displacement. The work being pushed with extraordinary vigor, this iron-clad ship was speedily launched and equipped, the admiration of the naval world.

Shortly after the adoption of armor-plating as an essential feature in the construction of vessels of war, the Southern States seceded from the Union, some of the most efficient of the United States naval officers resigning their commissions. Their loss was severely felt by the Navy Department at Washington; nor was it long before the presence of great professional skill among the officers of the naval administration of the Confederate States became manifest. Indeed, the utility of the armor-plating adopted by France and England proved to be bet-

ter understood at Richmond than at Washington. While the Secretary of the Navy, Mr. Welles, and his advisers were discussing the question of armor, news reached Washington that the partly burnt and scuttled steam-frigate *Merrimac*, at the Norfolk Navy Yard, had been raised and cut down to her berth-deck, and that a very substantial structure of timber, resembling a citadel with inclined sides, was being erected on that deck.

The Navy Department at Washington early in August advertised for plans and offers for iron-clad steam-batteries to be built within a stipulated time. My attention having been thus called to a subject which I had thoroughly considered during a series of years, I was fully prepared to present plans of an impregnable steam-battery of light draught, suitable to navigate the shallow rivers and harbors of the Confederate States. Availing myself of the services of a friend who chanced to be in Washington at the time, proposals were at once submitted to a board of naval officers appointed by the President; and the plans presented by my friend being rejected by the board, I immediately set out for Washington and laid the matter personally before its members, all of whom proved to be well-informed and experienced naval experts. Contrary to anticipation, the board permitted me to present a theoretical demonstration concerning the stability of the new structure, doubt of which was the principal consideration which had caused the rejection of the plan presented. In less than an hour I succeeded in demonstrating to the entire satisfaction of the board appointed by President Lincoln that the design was thoroughly practical, and based on sound theory. The Secretary of the Navy accordingly accepted my proposal to build an iron-

clad steam-battery, and instructed me verbally to commence the construction forthwith. Returning immediately to New York, I divided the work among three leading mechanical establishments, furnishing each with detailed drawings of every part of the structure; the understanding being that the most skilful men and the best tools should be employed; also that work should be continued during night-time when practicable. The construction of nearly every part of the battery accordingly commenced simultaneously, all hands working with the utmost diligence, apparently confident that their exertions would result in something of great benefit to the national cause. Fortunately no trouble or delay was met at any point; all progressed satisfactorily; every part sent on board from the workshops fitted exactly the place for which it was intended. As a consequence of these favorable circumstances, the battery, with steam-machinery complete, was launched in one hundred days from the laying of the keel-plate. It should be mentioned that at the moment of starting on the inclined ways toward its destined element, the novel fighting-machine was named *Monitor*.

Before entering on a description of this *fighting-machine* I propose to answer the question frequently asked: What circumstances dictated its size and peculiar construction?

1. The work on the *Merrimac* had progressed so far that no structure of large dimensions could possibly be completed in time to meet her.

2. The well-matured plan of erecting a citadel of considerable dimensions on the ample deck of the razeed *Merrimac* admitted of a battery of heavy ordnance so formidable that no vessel of the ordinary type, of small dimensions, could withstand its fire.

3. The battery designed by the naval authorities of the Confederate States, in addition to the advantage of ample room and numerous guns, presented a formidable front to an opponent's fire by being inclined to such a degree that shot would be readily deflected. Again, the inclined sides, composed of heavy timbers well braced, were covered with two thicknesses of bar iron, ingeniously combined, well calculated to resist the spherical shot peculiar to the Dahlgren and Rodman system of naval ordnance adopted by the United States navy.

4. The shallow waters on the coast of the Southern States called for very light draught; hence the

upper circumference of the propeller of the battery would be exposed to the enemy's fire unless thoroughly protected against shot of heavy caliber. A difficulty was thus presented which apparently could not be met by any device which would not seriously impair the efficiency of the propeller.

5. The limited width of the navigable parts of the Southern rivers and inlets presented an obstacle rendering manœuvering impossible; hence it would not be practicable at all times to turn the battery so as to present a broadside to the points to be attacked.

6. The accurate knowledge possessed by the adversary of the distance between the forts on the river-banks within range of his guns, would enable him to point the latter with such accuracy that unless every part of the sides of the battery could be made absolutely shot-proof, destruction would be certain. It may be observed that the accurate knowledge of range was an advantage in favor of the Southern forts which placed the attacking steam-batteries at great disadvantage.

7. The difficulty of manipulating the anchor within range of powerful fixed batteries presented difficulties which called for better protection to the crew of the batteries than any previously known.

Several minor points familiar to the naval artillerist and naval architect presented considerations which could not be neglected by the constructor of the new battery; but these must be omitted in our brief statement, while the foregoing, being of vital importance, have demanded special notice.

The plans on pages 76 and 77 represent a longitu-

CAPTAIN JOHN ERICSSON.

FLOATING CIRCULAR CITADEL.
Submitted to the French Directory in 1798.

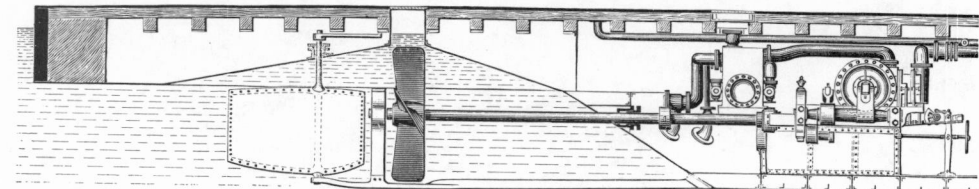

1. AFT SECTION. LONGITUDINAL PLAN THROUGH THE CENTER LINE OF THE ORIGINAL "MONITOR."

dinal section through the center line of the battery, which, for want of space on the page, has been divided into three sections, viz., the aft, central, and forward sections, which for ready reference will be called *aft, central,* and *forward*.

Referring particularly to the upper and lower sections, it will be seen that the hull consists of an upper and lower body joined together in the horizontal plane not far below the water-line. The length of the upper part of the hull is 172 feet, beam 41 feet; the length of the lower hull being 122 feet, beam 34 feet. The depth from the under side of deck to the keel-plate is 11 feet 2 inches, draught of water at load-line 10 feet.

Let us now examine separately the three sectional representations.

Forward Section. The anchor-well, a cylindrical perforation of the overhanging deck, near the bow, first claims our attention. The object of this well being to protect the anchor when raised, it is lined with plate iron backed by heavy timbers, besides being protected by the armor-plating bolted to the outside of the overhang. It should be noticed that this method proved so efficient that in no instance did the anchor-gear receive any injury during the several engagements with the Confederate batteries, although nearly all of the monitors of the *Passaic* class were subjected to rapid fire at short range in upward of twenty actions. It will be remembered that the unprotected anchor of the *Merrimac* was shot away during the short battle with the *Congress* and the *Cumberland*. Having described the method of protecting the anchors, the mechanism adopted for manipulating the same

remains to be explained. Referring to the illustration, it will be seen that a windlass is secured under the deck-beams near the anchor-well. The men working the handles of this mechanism were stationed in the hold of the vessel, and hence were most effectually protected against the enemy's shot, besides being completely out of sight. The Confederate artillerists were at first much surprised at witnessing the novel spectacle of vessels approaching their batteries, then stopping and remaining stationary for an indefinite time while firing, and then again departing, apparently without any intervention of anchor-gear. Our examination of this gear and the anchor-well affords a favorable opportunity of explaining the cause of Lieutenant Greene's alarm, mentioned in a statement recently published by a military journal, concerning a mysterious sound emanating from the said well during the passage of the *Monitor* from New York to Fort Monroe. Lieutenant Greene says that the sound from the anchor-well "resembled the death-groans of twenty men, and was the most dismal, awful sound [he] ever heard." Let us endeavor to trace to some physical cause this portentous sound. The reader will find, on close examination, that the chain-cable which suspends the anchor passes through an aperture ("hawse-pipe") on the after side of the well, and that this pipe is very near the water-line; hence the slightest vertical depression of the bow will occasion a flow of water into the vessel. Obviously, any downward motion of the overhang will cause the air confined in the upper part of the well, when covered, to be blown through the hawse-pipe along with the admitted water, thereby producing a very discordant sound, repeated at every rise and fall of the bow during pitching. Lieutenant Greene also states that, apart from the reported sound, the vessel was flooded by the water which entered

through the hawse-pipe; a statement suggesting that this flooding was the result of faulty construction, whereas it resulted from gross oversight on the part of the executive officer,—namely, in going to sea without stopping the opening round the chain-cable at the point where it passes through the side of the anchor-well.

The pilot-house is the next important object represented in the forward section of the illustration now under consideration. This structure is situated 10 feet from the anchor-well, its internal dimensions being 3 feet 6 inches long, 2 feet 8 inches wide, 3 feet 10 inches high above the plating of the deck; the sides consisting of solid blocks of wrought iron, 12 inches deep and 9 inches thick, firmly held down at the corner by 3-inch bolts passing through the iron-plated deck and deck-beams. The wheel, which by means of ordinary tiller-ropes operates the rudder, is placed within the pilot-house, its axle being supported by a bracket secured to the iron blocks as shown by the illustration. An ordinary ladder resting on the bottom of the vessel leads to the grated floor of the pilot-house. In order to afford the commanding officer and the pilot a clear view of objects before and on the sides of the vessel, the first and second iron blocks from the top are kept apart by packing pieces at the corners; long and narrow sight-holes being thereby formed extending round the pilot-house, and giving a clear view which sweeps round the entire horizon, all but that part which is hidden by the turret, hardly twelve degrees on each side of the line of keel. Regarding the adequacy of the elongated sight-hole formed between the iron blocks in the manner described, it should be

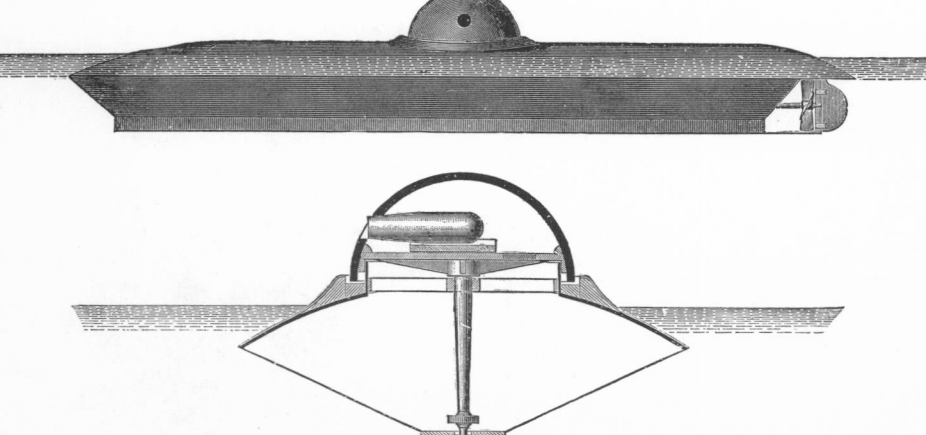

SIDE ELEVATION AND TRANSVERSE SECTION (THROUGH THE CENTER LINE OF ITS REVOLVING SEMI-SPHERICAL TURRET) OF AN IRON-CLAD STEAM-BATTERY.
Plans of which were submitted by Captain Ericsson to Napoleon III. in September, 1854.

SIDE ELEVATION OF A FLOATING REVOLVING CIRCULAR TOWER.
Published by Abraham Bloodgood in 1807.

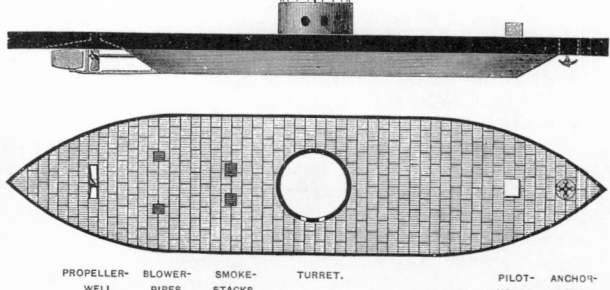

PROPELLER-WELL   BLOWER-PIPES   SMOKE-STACKS   TURRET   PILOT-HOUSE   ANCHOR-WELL

SIDE ELEVATION AND DECK-PLAN OF THE "MONITOR."

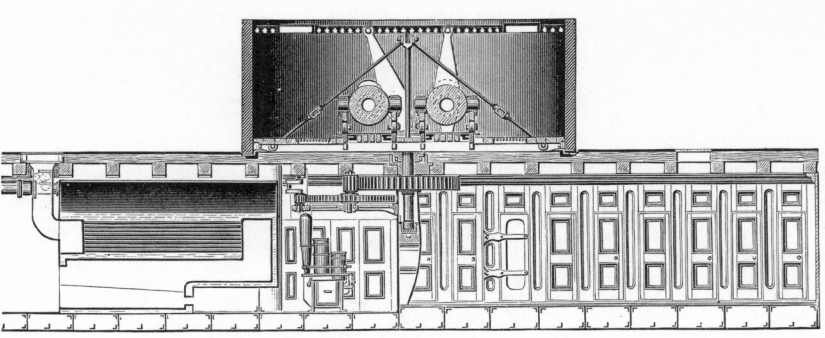

2. CENTRAL SECTION.

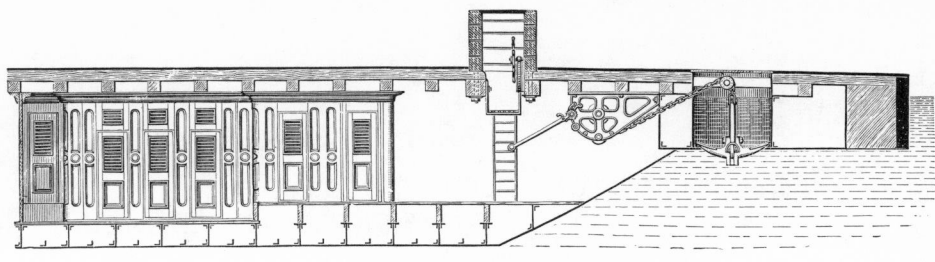

3. FORWARD SECTION.

borne in mind that an opening of five-eighths of an inch affords a vertical view 80 feet high at a distance of only 200 yards. More is not needed, a fact established during trials instituted by experts before the constructor delivered the vessel to the Government. Unfortunately the sight-holes were subsequently altered, the iron blocks being raised and the opening between them increased to such an extent that at sea, to quote Lieutenant Greene's report, the water entered "with such force as to knock the helmsman completely round from the wheel." It may be shown that but for the injudicious increase of the sight-holes, the commander of the *Monitor* would not have been temporarily blinded during the conflict at Hampton Roads, although he placed his vessel in such an extraordinary position that, according to Lieutenant Greene's report, "a shell from the enemy's gun, the muzzle not ten yards distant [from the side of the *Monitor*], struck the forward side of the pilot-house." The size of the sight-hole after the injudicious increase, may be inferred from the reported fact that the blast caused by the explosion of the Confederate shell on striking the outside of the pilot-house had the power of "partly lifting the top." This "top," it should be observed, consisted of an iron plate two inches thick, let down into an appropriate groove, but not bolted down—a circumstance which called forth Lieutenant Greene's disapprobation. The object of the constructor in leaving the top plate of the pilot-house loose, so as to be readily pushed up from below, was that of affording egress to the crew in case of accident. Had the monitor *Tecumseh*, commanded by Captain T. A. M. Craven, when struck by a torpedo during the conflict in Mobile Bay, August 5th, 1864, been provided with a similar loose plate over the main hatch, the fearful calamity of drowning officers and crew would have been prevented. In referring to this untoward event, it should be observed that means had been provided in all the sea-going monitors to afford egress in case of injury to the hull: an opening in the turret-floor, when placed above a corresponding opening in the deck, formed a free passage to the turret, the top of which was provided with sliding hatches. Apparently the officer in charge of the turret-gear of Captain Craven's vessel was not at his post, as he ought to have been during action, or else he had not been taught the imperative duty of placing the turret in such a position that these openings would admit of a free passage from below. Lieutenant Greene's report with reference to the position of the pilot-house calls for particular no-

tice, his assertion being that he "could not fire ahead within several points of the bow." The distance between the center of the turret and the pilot-house being fifty-five feet, while the extreme breadth of the latter is only five feet, it will be found that by turning the turret through an angle of only *six degrees* from the center line of the vessel, the shot will clear the pilot-house, a structure too substantial to suffer from the mere aërial current produced by the flight of the shot. Considering that the *Monitor*, as reported by Lieutenant Greene, was a "quick-turning vessel," the disadvantage of not being able to fire over the bow within *six degrees* of the line of keel is insignificant. Captain Coles claimed for his famous iron-clad turret-ship the advantage of an all-round fire, although the axis of his turret-guns had many times greater deviation from the line of keel than that of the *Monitor*.

The statement published by Lieutenant Greene, that the chief engineer of the vessel immediately after the engagement in Hampton Roads "suggested the clever plan of putting the pilot-house on top of the turret," is incorrect and calls for notice. The obvious device of placing the pilot-house in the center and above the turret was carefully considered before the *Monitor* turret was constructed, but could not be carried out for these reasons:

1. The turret of the battery was too light to support a structure large enough to accommodate the commanding officer, the pilot, and the steering-gear, under the severe condition of absolute impregnability against solid shot from guns of 10-inch caliber employed by the Confederates.

2. A central stationary pilot-house connected with the turret involved so much complication and additional work (see description of turret and pilot-houses further on), that had its adoption not been abandoned the *Monitor* would not have been ready to proceed to Hampton Roads until the beginning of April, 1862. The damage to the national cause which might have resulted from that delay is beyond computation.

The next important part of the battery delineated on the forward section of the illustration, namely, the quarters of the officers and crew, will now be considered; but before entering on a description it should be mentioned that in a small turret-vessel built for fighting, only one-half of the crew need be accommodated at a time, as the other half should be in and on the turret, the latter being always covered with a water-proof awning. Referring again to the forward and to part of the central section, it will be seen that the quarters extend from the transverse bulkhead under the turret to within five feet of the pilot-house, a distance of fifty feet; the forward portion, twenty-four feet in length, being occupied by the officers' quarters and extending across the battery from side to side. The height of the aft part of these quarters is 8 feet 6 inches under the deck-beams; while the height of the whole of the quarters of the crew is 8 feet 6 inches. . . .

Apart from the ample size of the quarters on board the vessel, shown by the illustration, it should be mentioned that the system adopted for ventilating those quarters furnishes an abundant supply of

fresh air by the following means. Two centrifugal blowers, driven by separate steam-engines, furnished seven thousand cubic feet of atmospheric air per minute by the process of suction through standing pipes on deck. . . .

Turret Department. The most important object delineated on the *central* section of the illustration, namely, the rotating turret, will now be considered; but before describing this essential part of the monitor system, it will be well to observe that the general belief is quite erroneous that a revolving platform, open or covered, is a novel design. So far from that being the case, this obvious device dates back to the first introduction of artillery. . . .

The origin of rotating circular gun-platforms being disposed of, the consideration of the central section of the illustration will now be resumed. It will be seen that the turret which protects the guns and gunners of the *Monitor* consists simply of a short cylinder resting on the deck, covered with a grated iron roof provided with sliding hatches. This cylinder is composed of eight thicknesses of wrought-iron plates, each one inch thick, firmly riveted together, the inside course, which extends below the rest, being accurately faced underneath. A flat, broad ring of bronze is let into the deck, its upper face being very smooth in order to form a water-tight joint with the base of the turret without the employment of any elastic packing, a peculiar feature of the turrets of the monitors, as will be seen further on. Unfortunately, before the *Monitor* left New York for Hampton Roads, it was suggested at the Navy Yard to insert a plaited hemp rope between the base of the turret and the bronze ring, for the purpose of making the joint perfectly water-tight. As might have been supposed, the rough and uneven hemp rope did not form a perfect joint; hence during the passage a great leak was observed at intervals as the sea washed over the decks. "The water came down under the turret like a waterfall," says Lieutenant Greene in his report. It will be proper to observe in this place that the "foundering" of the *Monitor* on its way to Charleston was not caused by the "separation of the upper and lower part of the hull," as was imagined by persons who possessed no knowledge of the method adopted by the builders in joining the upper and lower hulls. Again, those who asserted that the plates had been torn asunder at the junction of the hulls did not consider that severe strain cannot take place in a structure nearly submerged. The easy motion at sea, peculiar to the monitors, was pointed out by several of their commanders. Lieutenant Greene in his report to the Secretary of the Navy, dated on board the *Monitor*, March 27th, 1862, says with reference to sea-going qualities:

"During her passage from New York her roll was very easy and slow and not at all deep. She pitched very little and with no strain whatever." . . .

TRANSVERSE SECTION OF THE HULL OF THE ORIGINAL MONITOR.

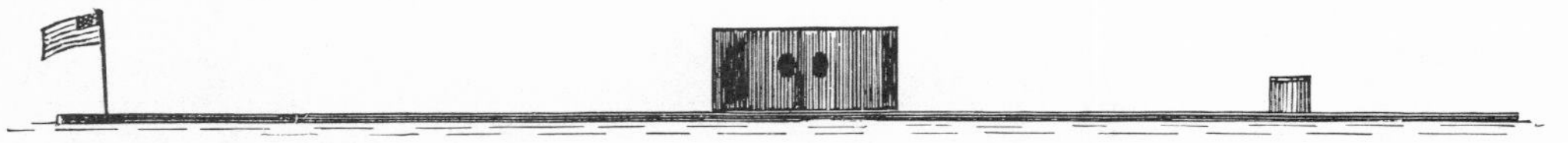

THE "MONITOR" IN BATTLE TRIM.

The true cause of the foundering of the *Monitor* was minutely explained to the writer some time after the occurrence by the engineer, a very intelligent person, who operated the centrifugal pumping-machine of the vessel at the time. According to his statement, oakum was packed under the base of the turret before going to sea, in order to make sure of a water-tight joint; but this expedient failed altogether, the sea gradually washing out the oakum in those places where it had been loosely packed, thereby permitting so large a quantity of water to enter under the turret, fully sixty-three feet in circumference, that the centrifugal pumping-machine had not sufficient power to expel it. The hull consequently filled gradually and settled, until at the expiration of about four hours the *Monitor* went to the bottom. It will be asked, in view of the preceding explanation of the construction of the monitor turrets, namely, that the smooth base of the turret forms a water-tight joint with the ring on the deck, why was oakum packed under the turret before going to Charleston? The commander of the vessel, Captain Bankhead, in his report of the foundering, adverts to the admission of water under the turret, but does not duly consider the serious character of the leak, sixty-three feet in length. Captain Bankhead evidently had not carefully investigated the matter when he attributed the accident to an imaginary separation of the upper and lower hull. It should be observed, in justice to this officer, that having commanded the *Monitor* only during a brief period he possessed but an imperfect knowledge of his vessel, and probably knew nothing regarding the consequence of employing packing,— namely, that it might cause "water to come down under the turret like a waterfall," as previously reported by the second officer in command. It is proper to mention as a mitigating circumstance in favor of the second officer, Lieutenant Greene, that previous to the battle in Hampton Roads he had "never performed any but midshipman duty." The important question, therefore, must remain unanswered, whether in the hands of an older and more experienced executive officer the *Monitor*, like the other vessels of her type, might not have reached Charleston in safety. . . .

NOTE.—During the summer of 1862 the *Monitor* served in the James River squadron, and took part in the attack on Fort Darling. On December 29th, at daybreak, she left Fort Monroe for Charleston to fight the powerful Confederate rams which had virtually raised the blockade of that port by destroying several Union ships of the blockading squadron. Her convoy on the trip was the sidewheel steamer *Rhode Island*, and to hasten the speed of the *Monitor* the *Rhode Island* took her in tow with two long 12-inch hawsers. At dark on the 29th the vessels were off Hatteras, where they encountered a heavily rolling sea. Water in volumes swept the *Monitor's* decks and at 8 o'clock signals of distress were burned for the *Rhode Island* to render assistance. The tow-lines were ordered to be cut, and the lives of two of the crew were lost in carrying out the order. At 10 o'clock the *Monitor's* anchor was lowered and all her steam-power was directed to the pumps. The subsequent fate of the ship and crew is described in the article following.

THE LOSS OF THE "MONITOR."

BY FRANCIS B. BUTTS, A SURVIVOR OF THE CREW.

. . . The clouds now began to separate, a moon of about half-size beamed out upon the sea, and the *Rhode Island*, now a mile away, became visible. Signals were being exchanged, and I felt that the *Monitor* would be saved, or at least that the captain would not leave his ship until there was no hope of saving her. I was sent below to see how the water stood in the ward-room. I went forward to the cabin and found the water just above the soles of my shoes, which indicated that there must be more than a foot in the vessel. I reported this to the captain, and all hands were set to bailing,— bailing out the ocean as it seemed,— but the object was to employ the men, as there now seemed to be danger of excitement among them. I kept employed most of the time, taking the buckets from them through the hatchway on top of the turret. They seldom would have more than a pint of water in them, however, the remainder having been spilled in passing from one man to another.

The weather was clear, but the sea did not cease rolling in the least, and the *Rhode Island*, with the two lines wound up in her wheel, was tossing at the mercy of the sea, and came drifting against our sides. A boat that had been lowered was caught between the vessels and crushed and lost. Some of our seamen bravely leaped down on deck to guard our sides, and lines were thrown to them from the deck of the *Rhode Island*, which now lay her whole length against us, floating off astern, but not a man would be the first to leave his ship, although the captain gave orders to do so. I was again sent to examine the water in the ward-room, which I found to be more than two feet above the deck; and I think I was the last person who saw Engineer G. H. Lewis as he lay seasick in his bunk, apparently watching the water as it grew deeper and deeper, and aware what his fate must be. He called me as I passed his door, and asked if the pumps were working. I replied that they were. "Is there any hope?" he asked; and feeling a little moved at the scene, and knowing certainly what must be his end, and the darkness that stared at us all, I replied, "As long as there is life there is hope." "Hope and hang on when you are wrecked" is an old saying among sailors. I left the ward-room, and learned that the water had gained so as to choke up the main pump. As I was crossing the berth-deck I saw our ensign, Mr. Frederickson, hand a watch to Master's Mate Williams, saying, "Here, this is yours; I may be lost"— which, in fact, was his fate. The watch and chain were both of unusual value. Williams received them into his hand, then with a hesitating glance at the time-piece said, "This thing may be the means of sinking me," and threw it upon the deck. There were three or four cabin-boys pale and prostrate with seasickness, and the cabin-cook, an old African negro, under great excitement, was scolding them most profanely.

As I ascended the turret-ladder the sea broke over the ship, and came pouring down the hatchway with so much force that it took me off my feet; and at the same time the steam broke from the boiler-room, as the water had reached the fires, and for an instant I seemed to realize that we had gone down. Our fires were out, and I heard the water blowing out of the boilers. I reported my observations to the captain, and at the same time saw a boat alongside. The captain again gave orders for the men to leave the ship, and fifteen, all of whom were seamen and men whom I had placed my confidence upon, were the ones who crowded the first boat to leave the ship. I was disgusted at witnessing the scramble, and, not feeling in the least alarmed about myself, resolved that I, an "old haymaker," as landsmen are called, would stick to the ship as long as my officers. I saw three of these men swept from the deck and carried leeward on the swift current.

Bailing was now resumed. I occupied the turret all alone, and passed buckets from the lower hatchway to the man on the top of the turret. I took off my coat— one that I had received from home only a few days before (I could not feel that our noble little ship was yet lost)— and, rolling it up with my boots, drew the tompion from one of the guns, placed them inside, and replaced the tompion. A black cat was sitting on the breech of one of the guns, howling one of those hoarse and solemn tunes which no one can appreciate who is not filled with the superstitions which I had been taught by the sailors, who are always afraid to kill a cat. I would almost as soon have touched a ghost, but I caught her, and, placing her in another gun, replaced the wad and tompion; but I could still hear that distressing howl. As I raised my last bucket to the upper hatchway no one was there to take it. I scrambled up the ladder and found that we below had been deserted. I shouted to those on the berth-deck, "Come up; the officers have left the ship, and a boat is alongside."

As I reached the top of the turret I saw a boat made fast on the weather quarter filled with men. Three others were standing on deck trying to get on board. One man was floating leeward, shouting in vain for help; another, who hurriedly passed me and jumped down from the turret, was swept off by a breaking wave and never rose. I was excited, feeling that it was the only chance to be saved. I made a loose line fast to one of the stanchions, and let myself down from the turret, the ladder having been washed away. The moment I struck the deck the sea broke over it and swept me as I had seen it sweep my shipmates. I grasped one of the smoke-stack braces and, hand-over-hand, ascended, to keep my head above water. It required all my strength to keep the sea from tearing me away. As it swept from the vessel I found myself dangling in the air nearly at the top of the smoke-stack. I let myself fall, and succeeded in reaching a life-line that encircled the deck by means of short stanchions, and to which the boat was attached. The sea again broke over us, lifting me feet upward as I still clung to the life-line. I thought I had nearly measured the depth of the ocean, when I felt the turn, and as my head rose above the water I was somewhat dazed from being so nearly drowned, and spouted up, it seemed, more than a gallon of water that had found its way into my lungs. I was then about twenty feet from the other men, whom I found to be the captain and one seaman; the other had been washed overboard and was now struggling in the water. The men in the boat were pushing back on their oars to keep the boat from being washed on to the *Monitor's* deck, so that the boat had to be hauled in by the painter about ten or twelve feet. The first lieutenant, S. D. Greene, and other officers in the boat were shouting, "Is the captain on board?" and, with severe struggles to have our voices heard above the roar of the wind and sea, we were shouting, "No," and trying to haul in the boat, which we at last succeeded in doing. The captain, ever caring for his men, requested us to get in, but we both, in the same voice, told him to get in first. The moment he was over the bows of the boat Lieutenant Greene cried, "Cut the painter! cut the painter!" I thought, "Now or lost," and in less time than I can explain it, exerting my strength beyond imagination, I hauled in the boat, sprang, caught on the gunwale, was pulled into the boat with a boat-hook in the hands of one of the men, and took my seat with one of the oarsmen. The other man, named Thomas Joice, managed to get into the boat in some way, and he was the last man saved. . . .

After a fearful and dangerous passage over the frantic seas, we reached the *Rhode Island*, which still had the tow-line caught in her wheel and had drifted perhaps two miles to leeward. We came alongside under the lee bows, where the first boat, that had left the *Monitor* nearly an hour before, had just discharged its men; but we found that getting on board the *Rhode Island* was a harder task than getting from the *Monitor*. . . .

It was half-past 12, the night of the 31st of December, 1862, when I stood on the forecastle of the *Rhode Island*, watching the red and white lights that hung from the pennant-staff above the turret, and which now and then were seen as we would perhaps both rise on the sea together, until at last, just as the moon had passed below the horizon, they were lost, and the *Monitor*, whose history is familiar to us all, was seen no more. . . .

VIEW SHOWING THE EFFECT OF SHOT ON THE "MONITOR" TURRET.
From a photograph taken soon after the engagement.

SINKING OF THE "MONITOR."

"AN AFFAIR OF OUTPOSTS."

McCLELLAN ORGANIZING THE GRAND ARMY.

BY PHILIPPE, COMTE DE PARIS.
Aide-de-Camp to General McClellan.

NO one has denied that McClellan was a marvelous organizer. Every veteran of the Army of the Potomac will be able to recall that extraordinary time when the people of the North devoted all their native energy and spirit of initiative to the raising of enormous levies of future combatants and their military equipment,—and when infantry battalions, squadrons of cavalry, and batteries of artillery sprung, as it were, from the earth in a night, and poured in from all sides upon the barren wastes of vacant building-lots that then went to the making up of fully three-quarters of the Federal capital.

It was in the midst of this herculean task of organization that two French aides-de-camp were assigned to duty as military attachés on McClellan's staff. His brilliant operations in Western Virginia against Lee,—who had not yet revealed the full extent of his military genius, and whom McClellan was destined to find again in his front but a year later,—the successes of Laurel Hill and Rich Mountain, gave evidence of what might be expected of the inexperienced troops placed in McClellan's hands. He had already shown rare strategic ability, and the President had confided to him the task of creating the Army of the Potomac from the disorganized bands who had fallen back on Washington under the brave and unfortunate McDowell. Surrounded for the most part by young officers, he was himself the most youthful of us all, not only by reason of his physical vigor, the vivacity of his impressions, the noble candor of his character, and his glowing patriotism, but also, I may add, by his inexperience of men. His military bearing breathed a spirit of frankness, benevolence, and firmness. His look was piercing, his voice gentle, his temper equable, his word of command clear and definite. His encouragement was most affectionate, his reprimand couched in terms of perfect politeness. Discreet, as a military or political chief should be, he was slow in bestowing his confidence; but, once given, it was never withdrawn. Himself perfectly loyal to his friends, he knew how to inspire others with an absolute devotion.

Unfortunately for himself, McClellan succeeded too quickly and too soon to the command of the principal army of the republic. His lieutenants were as new to the work as he—they had not been tested. Public opinion in the army itself—a judge all the more relentless for the very reason that discipline gives it no opportunity to express itself—had as yet been able neither to pronounce on them, nor to ratify the preferences of the general-in-chief. Paradoxical as it may seem, would it not really have been better could McClellan have received a check at first, as Grant did at Belmont, rather than to have begun with the brilliant campaign in West Virginia which won for him the *sobriquet* of "The Young Napoleon"? Just at the time when I joined his staff the exacting confidence of the people and the Government was laying on him an almost superhuman task. In forging the puissant weapon which, later, snatched from his grasp, was destined, in the hands of the Great Hammerer, to bray the army of Lee, he acquired an imperishable title to the gratitude of his compatriots. He wrought, will it be said, for the glory of his successors? No! He labored for his country, even as a private soldier who dies for her, with no thought of fame. In order to give to his weapon every perfection, he soon learned to resist the impatient solicitations of both the people and the Government.

At the end of September, 1861, while yet under the orders of General Scott, McClellan represented the ardent and impatient spirit of men chafing at the slowness of a chief whose faculties had been chilled by the infirmities of age.

Nevertheless, McClellan's first care was to place the capital beyond all peradventure of being carried by sudden attack: on the one hand, for the sake of reassuring the inhabitants and the political organism within its limits; and, on the other, that the army might be at liberty to act independently when it should be called to the field, leaving a sufficient garrison only to secure the defense of the city. He knew that an army tied up about a place it has to protect is virtually paralyzed. The events of 1870 have only too fully confirmed this view.

CAPTAIN LE CLERC.   DUC DE CHARTRES.   COMTE DE PARIS.   PRINCE DE JOINVILLE.   CAPTAIN MOHAIN.

THE ORLÉANS PRINCES AND SUITE AT DINNER.
From a photograph.

An engineer of distinction, McClellan himself devised in all its details the system of defensive works from Alexandria to Georgetown. He gave his daily personal supervision to the execution of this work, alternating outdoor activity with office business. Tireless in the saddle, he was equally indefatigable with the pen. Possessed of a methodical and exact mind, he comprehended the organization of his army in every minute detail. The creation of all the material of war necessary to its existence and action was extraordinary proof of the wonderful readiness of the Americans in an emergency. . . .

But the season advanced. The army was being formed. At the end of September the enemy had fallen back on Fairfax Court House, leaving to us at Munson's Hill a few Quaker guns of logs and pasteboard. The time for action seemed to have come. The rigors of winter in Virginia hardly make themselves felt before the beginning of December. By the 17th of October the enemy had again retreated. The Army of the Potomac replied with a commensurate advance. But this was a *faux pas*. The blunder was consummated at Ball's Bluff. . . .

McClellan, once invested with supreme command, proved himself more of a temporizer than his predecessor [General Scott], and, as will soon be seen, his premature promotion to this post was the cause of all his subsequent mortification and misfortune. . . .

Without giving him the full rank enjoyed by Scott, the President had given him full command of the armies of the republic. It should be said that he had the right to this position as the oldest major-general of the regular army. In assuming his new function he did not give up his own personal and particular direction of the Army of the Potomac. Here he was right; for he could neither have found any one to whom he might safely confide his own proper work of organization, nor could he have left the command of the first army of the republic without condemning himself to perpetual prison in the bureau at Washington. . . .

PROVOST GUARD, WASHINGTON.
From a sketch made in 1862.

THE NORTH FRONT OF THE WAR DEPARTMENT, WASHINGTON.
From a war-time photograph.

McClellan's care . . . was to perfect and strengthen his army; but, above all, not to compromise the safety of his forces by any attempt at operations on the other side of the Potomac. Grand reviews established, to the satisfaction of the inexperienced, the fact of progress in the equipment, instruction, and drill of the troops. At Bailey's Cross-roads might have been seen a rendezvous of 50,000 men, with all the paraphernalia of a campaign, a large number of cavalry, and a formidable array of artillery. No such spectacle had ever been seen in the United States; the novelty of the display caused the liveliest interest among the inhabitants of Washington. But to a European, not the least curious part of the pageant was the President, with his entire Cabinet, in citizens' dress, boldly caracoling at the head of a brilliant military *cortége*, and riding down the long lines of troops to the rattle of drums, the flourish of trumpets, and the loud huzzas of the whole army. While his aides-de-camp were engaged in the field, McClellan worked ceaselessly with the Secretaries of War and of the Navy, Simon Cameron and Gideon Welles, preparing great expeditions, half military and half naval, that should plant the national flag on the principal points of the enemy's coast, and secure convenient bases for future operations. The success won at Port Royal encouraged the Federal Government in these projects. McClellan himself had brought back from the Crimea a personal experience which enabled him, better than any one else, to preside over the details of preparation.

One day, I think it was the 20th of December, General McClellan, ordinarily so assiduous, did not appear at headquarters. The next day it was learned that he was ill. Three days later his life was in danger. Exhausted with work, his robust physique was seized with a typhoid of the most serious type. . . . His absence paralyzed work at headquarters. He had not regularly delegated his powers. His father-in-law and chief of staff, General Marcy, did not dare to act definitely in his

name. McClellan had made the mistake of not creating a general field-staff service, with a duly appointed chief of staff. This might have aided him in securing a consistent *ensemble* of military operations. . . . On his return to the duties of his office [January 13], he realized that during his absence important changes had been arranged. On the 15th of January, Mr. Cameron was superseded by Mr. Stanton, a celebrated lawyer, who was spoken of as one of the coming men of the Democratic party. McClellan, who knew and appreciated him, had, before his illness, contributed materially to Stanton's nomination by recommending him earnestly to the President. But he was not slow to regret this. Mr. Stanton, endowed with a remarkable faculty for work, rendered incontestable service in the organization of the armies; but, fearing the growing importance of those who commanded them, and wishing to impose his authority, he was instrumental, more than any one else, in developing in Mr. Lincoln's mind the idea of directing military operations in person, from the depths of the White House itself. The personal intervention of the President, provoked by the inconsiderate impatience of the public and the precipitate solicitations of McClellan's political adversaries, first declared itself in a singular order, kept a secret as regards the public at the time, but given to the press on March 11th. This order ["President's General War Order No. 1"], dated the 27th of January, directed all the armies of the republic to take the field on the same day, that is, on the 22d of February, in honor of Washington's birthday! In the West, where the rivers were open, everything was in readiness. Moreover, the order of the President was not necessary to warrant Grant, already under orders from McClellan, in beginning the campaign, and Grant anticipated that order. His début was as a lightning-stroke. His victory at Fort Donelson, followed by the capitulation of 15,000 Confederates, was the return for Bull Run. The impression created throughout the whole army was profound. The Federal volunteers took heart again. The

confidence of the Army of the Potomac was redoubled. The general was now restored to health. The weather had moderated. The time had at last come for this army to act. . . .

At the very moment when all seemed ready for the realization of his grand design, two unforeseen circumstances arose to thwart the calculations of McClellan. The first was the sudden evacuation of Manassas by the Confederates. I do not believe that this could be attributed to indiscretions following the councils of war at Washington. I prefer, rather, to ascribe it to the military sagacity of the great soldier who then commanded the Army of Northern Virginia. His positions at Manassas were protected only by the snow and ice which paralyzed the Federals. With the opening of the season he would be obliged to withdraw behind the Rappahannock. This movement brought the Southern army nearer to Richmond, at the same time placing it on the Urbana route, thus making a landing there impossible for us, and permitting Lee to anticipate McClellan on the Virginia peninsula. McClellan would not give up his plan of approaching Richmond from the southeast. Fort Monroe, occupied by the Federals, was chosen as the new point of debarkation, and the pursuit of the enemy on the road from Manassas to Fredericksburg had no other object than to deceive him as to the intentions of the Federals. The army, after having feigned pursuit, was ordered to concentrate near Alexandria, the rendezvous of the grand flotilla which McClellan awaited with so much impatience.

But on the 12th of March another unexpected event again caused consternation among the officers of the staff. The indefatigable newsdealers, who followed the army almost to the very line of battle, had brought papers from Washington, in which we read a decree ["President's War Order No. 3"], dated March 11th, in effect relieving McClellan from the direction in chief of the armies of the United States, the pretext being that McClellan had not taken the field on the 22d of February. It was recalled to mind that on that very day,

McClellan, on going upon the floor of the House of Representatives, had been greeted by a triple salvo of applause, a demonstration flattering enough, but damaging to a general, whose functions forbid even the suspicion of political partisanship. The measure in question was inept, since it virtually restricted McClellan within the Department of the Potomac, excluding West Virginia, then assigned to Frémont. The measure was especially disastrous in suppressing all general direction of military operations, and disintegrating the *ensemble*. It had been decided that Scott was too superannuated to attend to this general direction; it was not for the purpose of abolishing it entirely that command had been confided to younger and more energetic hands. Unfortunately, at this moment Mr. Lincoln had the weakness to think that he himself could effectively exercise the supreme control, assigned him in form, it is true, by a figment of the national Constitution. As for McClellan, the President's decision was mortifying in its method, Lincoln having delayed its promulgation till after the departure of his general, and having left it to be communicated to the latter by the daily papers. Yet McClellan would have consoled himself, had not this measure been followed by others still more harassing, and of a nature to completely cripple intelligent action. But he was relieved of an immense responsibility; he was left at the head of an army eager to follow his lead, eager for battle, and confident of victory under his orders. He alone seemed to preserve his *sang-froid* in the midst of officers of all grades who flocked to his headquarters at Fairfax Court House as the news spread rapidly from camp-fire to camp-fire. Among these officers were stanch supporters, secret foes, those jealous of his fame, would-be worshipers of the rising sun, and, last but not least, indiscreet and compromising friends. In this evil hour McClellan felt how sternly patriotic duty demanded of him that he should hide the mortification he felt at this wound to his feelings as an officer and a man. He sought for consolation only in the sympathy and confidence of his soldiers.

CAMPAIGNING TO NO PURPOSE.

RECOLLECTIONS OF A PRIVATE.—II. BY WARREN LEE GOSS.

WHILE we were in camp at Washington in February, 1862, we were drilled to an extent which to the raw "thinking soldier" seemed unnecessary. Our colonel was a strict disciplinarian. His efforts to drill out of us the methods of action and thought common to citizens, and to substitute in place thereof blind, unquestioning obedience to military rules, were not always appreciated at their true value. In my company there was an old drill-sergeant (let us call him Sergeant Hackett) who was in sympathetic accord with the colonel. He had occasion to reprove me often, and, finally, to inflict a blast of profanity at which my self-respect rebelled. Knowing that swearing was a breach of discipline, I waited confidently upon the colonel, with the manner of one gentleman calling upon another. After the usual salute, I opened complaint by saying: "Colonel, Mr. Hackett has —" The colonel interrupted me angrily, and, with fire in his eye, exclaimed: "*Mister?* There are no misters in the army." "I thought, sir —" I began apologetically. "Think? think?" he cried. "What right have *you* to think? *I* do the thinking for this regiment! Go to your quarters!"

I did not tarry. There seemed to be no common ground on which he and I could argue questions of personal etiquette. But I should do injustice to his character as a commander if I failed to illustrate another manner of reproof which he sometimes applied.

One day, noticing a corporal in soiled gloves, he said: "Corporal, you set a bad example to the men with your soiled gloves. Why do you?"

"I've had no pay, sir, since entering the service, and can't afford to hire washing."

The colonel drew from his pocket a pair of gloves

TROOPER OF THE VIRGINIA CAVALRY, 1861.

CONFEDERATE PRISONERS.

spotlessly white, and, handing them to the corporal, said: "Put on those; I washed them myself!"

This was an unforgotten lesson to the whole regiment that it was a soldier's duty to attend himself to his personal neatness.

In a camp of soldiers, rumor, with her thousand tongues, is always speaking. The rank and file and under-officers of the line are not taken into the confidence of their superiors. Hence the private soldier is usually in ignorance as to his destination. What he lacks in information is usually made up in surmise and conjecture; every hint is caught at and worked out in possible and impossible combinations. He plans and fights imaginary battles. He manoeuvers for position, with pencil and chalk, on fanciful fields, at the same time knowing no more of the part he is actually performing in some great or little plan than the knapsack he bears. He makes some shrewd guesses (the Yankee's birthright), but he knows absolutely nothing. It is this which makes the good-will and confidence of the rank and file in the commander so important a factor in the *morale* of an army.

How we received the report, or whence it came, I know not, but it was rumored one morning that we were about to move. The order in reality came at last, to the distress and dismay of the sutlers, and the little German woman who kept the grocery round the corner. We left her disconsolate over the cakes, pies, and goodies which had been liberally purchased, but which were yet unpaid for, when we fell into two ranks, were counted off, and marched to conquer the prejudices of other sutlers.

We took the cars on February 25th, and were hurried through a number of little sleepy-looking villages of Maryland. The next morning found us at Sandy Hook, about half a mile from Harper's Ferry; thence, after about three hours' delay, we marched to a place opposite the promontory on and around which is situated the picturesque village of Harper's Ferry, at the confluence of the Potomac and Shenandoah rivers.

It was cold at our camping-place, between the

canal and the river. There were no rations awaiting our arrival, and we were suffering from the hunger so common to soldiers. Who ever saw one off duty who was not in pursuit of something to eat? We could n't get anything for love or money. We had at last reached a place where the people showed some of the distress incident to war, and a strong disinclination to feed or believe in us. We were grieved, but it could n't be helped.

The bridge from the Maryland to the Virginia or Harper's Ferry shore had been destroyed by fire, leaving only the granite abutments (which were afterward built upon again), and we were soon set at work conveying some flat-bottomed scows from Sandy Hook to Harper's Ferry. As early as 9 o'clock about one hundred men came down opposite the ferry, just above the old bridge, and broke into little groups, in military precision. Four or five with spades and other implements improvised a wooden abutment on the shore; another party rowed against the stream, moored a scow, and let it drift down until it was opposite the wooden abutment; then a party of ten advanced, each two men carrying a claw-balk, or timbers fitted with a claw, one of which held the gunwale of the boat, the other the shore abutment. Twenty men now came down on the left with planks, one inch thick, six inches wide, and fifteen feet long, narrowed at each end; these they laid across the five joists or balks, and returned on the right. Another party meanwhile moored another boat, which dropped down-stream opposite the one already bridged; five joists, each twenty feet long, were laid upon the gunwale by five men; these were fastened by those in the boat, by means of ropes, to cleats or hooks provided for the purpose on the side of the scows, which were shoved off from the shore until the shore end of the balk rested upon the shore boat. These were covered with planks in the same manner as before; side-rails of joists were lashed down with ropes to secure the whole. So one after another of the boats was dropped into position until a bridge several hundred feet long reached from the Maryland to the Virginia shore, for the passage of artillery and every description of muni-

tions for an army. Owing to the force of the current, a large rope-cable was stretched from shore to shore fifty feet above the bridge, and the upper end of each boat was stayed to the cable by a smaller rope. The rushing bent the bridge into a half-moon curve. The clock-like precision with which these men worked showed them to be the drilled engineers and pontoniers of the regular army. After the bridge was built, a slight, short man, with sandy hair, in military dress, came out upon it and congratulated the engineers on their success. This unassuming man was George B. McClellan, commander of the Army of the Potomac.

It was on this boat-bridge that the army of General Banks crossed to the Virginia shore in 1862. Officers were not allowed to trot their horses; troops in crossing were given the order, "Route step," as the oscillation of the cadence step or trotting horse is dangerous to the stability of a bridge of any kind.

I crossed the bridge soon after it was laid, visited Jefferson Rock, the ruins of the burned armory, and the town in general. The occasional crack of a musket among the hills on the other side of the Shenandoah told that the enemy's scouts were still there. Colonel Geary's men were engaged in driving them from the hills, preparatory to the advance of General Banks. During the day fifteen or twenty were captured and marched through the town, presenting a generally shabby and unmilitary appearance. They did not impress me as they did afterward, when charging on our lines with their unmusical yell and dauntless front.

The ruins of the burned armory of the United States were noticeable from the Maryland shore; also the masses of men moving in ceaseless tramp over the long and almost crescent-like bridge. The murmur of many voices, the mellow, abrupt call of the negro drivers to their mules, the glistening arms of the infantry reflected in the sunlight, the dull rumble of artillery wheels and baggage-wagons, live in memory to-day as one of the pictures of "war's wrinkled front," framed in the routine of more ordinary scenes.

The next day we were sent by rail back to Washington, and into camp upon our old grounds. A few mornings afterward an inspection was ordered. It came with the usual hurry and parade. Knapsacks and equipments were in shining order; every musket, bayonet, and button, boot, and belt, as bright as rubbing and fear of censure or police duty could make them. Inspection over, the last jingle of ramrod in resounding musket was heard, and we were dismissed, with an intimation that on the morrow we were to go on a march. . . .

A CONFEDERATE OF 1862.

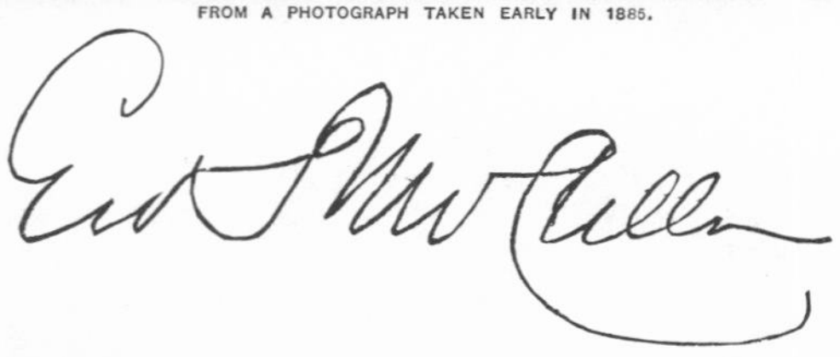

FORT MONROE—PARADE OF THE 3D PENNSYLVANIA ARTILLERY.
From a photograph.

THE PENINSULAR CAMPAIGN.

BY GEORGE B. McCLELLAN, MAJOR-GENERAL, U. S. A.
General-in-Chief of the United States army during the first part of the Peninsular Campaign.

. . . On the 1st of November, upon the retirement of General Winfield Scott, I succeeded to the command of all the armies, except the Department of Virginia, which comprised the country within sixty miles of Fort Monroe. Upon assuming the general command, I found that the West was far behind the East in its state of preparation, and much of my time and large quantities of material were consumed in pushing the organization of the Western armies. Meanwhile the various coast expeditions were employed in seizing important points of the enemy's sea-board, to facilitate the prevention of blockade-running, and to cut or threaten the lines of communication near the coast, with reference to subsequent operations.

The plan of campaign which I adopted for the spring of 1862 was to push forward the armies of Generals Halleck and Buell to occupy Memphis, Nashville, and Knoxville, and the line of the Memphis and Danville Railroad, so as to deprive the enemy of that important line, and force him to adopt the circuitous routes by Augusta, Branchville, and Charleston. It was also intended to seize Washington, North Carolina, at the earliest practicable moment, and to open the Mississippi by effecting a junction between Generals Halleck and Butler. This movement of the Western armies was to be followed by that of the Army of the Potomac from Urbana, on the lower Rappahannock to West Point and Richmond, intending, if we failed to gain Richmond by a rapid march, to cross the James and attack the city in rear, with the James as a line of supply. . . .

The Government soon manifested great impatience in regard to the opening of the Baltimore and Ohio Railroad and the destruction of the Confederate batteries on the Potomac. The first object could be permanently attained only by occupying the Shenandoah Valley with a force strong enough to resist any attack by the Confederate army then at Manassas; the second only by a general advance of the Army of the Potomac, driving the enemy back of the Rapidan. My own view was that the movement of the Army of the Potomac from Urbana would accomplish both of these objects, by forcing the enemy to abandon all his positions and fall back on Richmond. I was therefore unwilling to interfere with this plan by a premature advance, the effect of which must be either to commit us to the overland route, or to minimize the advantages of the Urbana movement. I wished to hold the enemy at Manassas to the last moment —if possible until the advance from Urbana had actually commenced, for neither the reopening of the railroad nor the destruction of the batteries was worth the danger involved. . . .

When Manassas had been abandoned by the enemy and he had withdrawn behind the Rapidan, the Urbana movement lost much of its promise, as the enemy was now in position to reach Richmond before we could do so. The alternative remained of making Fort Monroe and its vicinity the base of operations.

The plan first adopted was to commence the movement with the First Corps as a unit, to land north of Gloucester and move thence on West Point; or, should circumstances render it advisable, to land a little below Yorktown to turn the defenses between that place and Fort Monroe. The Navy Department were confident that we could rely upon their vessels to neutralize the *Merrimac* and aid materially in reducing the batteries on the York River, either by joining in the attack or by running by them and gaining their rear. As transports arrived very slowly, especially those for horses, and the great impatience of the Government grew apace, it became necessary to embark divisions as fast as vessels arrived, and I decided to land them at Fort Monroe, holding the First Corps to the last, still intending to move it in mass to turn Gloucester. On the 17th of March the leading division embarked at Alexandria. The campaign was undertaken with the intention of taking some 145,000 troops, to be increased by a division of 10,000 drawn from the troops in the vicinity of Fort Monroe, giving a total of 155,000. Strenuous efforts were made to induce the President to take away Blenker's German division of 10,000 men, Of his own volition he at first declined, but the day before I left Washington he yielded to the non-military pressure and reluctantly gave the order, thus reducing the expected force to 145,000.

. . . On the 12th of March, I learned that there had appeared in the daily papers the order relieving me from the general command of all the armies and confining my authority to the Department of the Potomac. I had received no previous intimation of the intention of the Government in this respect. Thus, when I embarked for Fort Monroe on the 1st of April, my command extended from Philadelphia to Richmond, from the Alleghanies, including the Shenandoah, to the Atlantic; for an order had been issued a few days previous placing Fort Monroe and the Department of Virginia under my command, and authorizing me to withdraw from the troops therein ten thousand, to form a division to be added to the First Corps.

The fortifications of Washington were at this time completed and armed. I had already given instructions for the refortification of Manassas, the reopening of the Manassas Gap Railroad, the protection of its bridges by block-houses, the intrenchment of a position for a brigade at or near the railroad crossing of the Shenandoah, and an intrenched post at Chester Gap. I left about 42,000 troops for the immediate defense of Washington, and more than 35,000 for the Shenandoah Valley—an abundance to insure the safety of Washington and to check any attempt to recover the lower Shenandoah and threaten Maryland. Beyond this force, the reserves of the Northern States were all available.

On my arrival at Fort Monroe on the 2d of April, I found five divisions of infantry, Sykes's brigade of regulars, two regiments of cavalry, and a portion of the reserve artillery disembarked. Another cavalry regiment and the part of a fourth had arrived, but were still on shipboard; comparatively few wagons had come. On the same day came a telegram stating that the Department of Virginia was withdrawn from my control, and forbidding me to form the division of ten thousand men without General Wool's sanction. I was thus deprived of the command of the base of operations, and the ultimate strength of the army was reduced to 135,000—another serious departure from the plan of campaign. Of the troops disembarked, only four divisions, the regulars, the majority of the reserve artillery, and a part of the cavalry, could be moved, in consequence of the lack of transportation. Casey's division was unable to leave Newport News until the 16th, from the impossibility of supplying it with wagons.

The best information obtainable represented the Confederate troops around Yorktown as numbering at least fifteen thousand, with about an equal force at Norfolk; and it was clear that the army lately at Manassas, now mostly near Gordonsville, was in position to be thrown promptly to the Peninsula. It was represented that Yorktown was surrounded by strong earthworks, and that the Warwick River, instead of stretching across the Peninsula to Yorktown,—as proved to be the case,—came down to Lee's Mills from the North, running parallel with and not crossing the road from Newport News to Williamsburg. It was also known that there were intrenched positions of more or less strength at Young's Mills, on the Newport News road, and at Big Bethel, Howard's Bridge, and Ship's Point, on or near the Hampton and Yorktown road, and at Williamsburg.

On my arrival at Fort Monroe, I learned, in an interview with Flag-Officer Goldsborough, that he could not protect the James as a line of supply, and that he could furnish no vessels to take an active part in the reduction of the batteries at York and Gloucester or to run by and gain their rear. He could only aid in the final attack after our land batteries had essentially silenced their fire.

I thus found myself with 53,000 men in condition to move, faced by the conditions of the problem just stated. Information was received that Yorktown was already being reinforced from Norfolk, and it was apprehended that the main Confederate army would promptly follow the same course. I therefore determined to move at once with the force in hand, and endeavor to seize a point—near the Halfway House—between Yorktown and Williamsburg, where the Peninsula is reduced to a narrow neck, and thus cut off the retreat of the Yorktown garrison and prevent the arrival of reinforcements.

MAJOR-GENERAL GEORGE B. McCLELLAN, U. S. A.
From a war-time photograph.

The advance commenced on the morning of the 4th of April, and was arranged to turn successively the intrenchments on the two roads; the result being that, on the afternoon of the 5th, the Third Corps was engaged with the enemy's outposts in front of Yorktown and under the artillery fire of the place. The Fourth Corps came upon Lee's Mills and found it covered by the unfordable line of the Warwick, and reported the position so strong as to render it impossible to execute its orders to assault. Thus, all things were brought to a stand-still, and the intended movement on the Halfway House could not be carried out. Just at this moment came a telegram, dated the 4th, informing me that the First Corps was withdrawn from my command. Thus, when too deeply committed to recede, I found that another reduction of about 43,000, including several cavalry regiments withheld from me, diminished my paper force to 92,000, instead of the 155,000 on which the plans of the campaign had been founded, and with which it was intended to operate. The number of men left behind, sick and from other causes incident to such a movement, reduced the total for duty to some 85,000, from which must be deducted all camp, depot, and train guards, escorts, and non-combatants, such as cooks, servants, orderlies, and extra-duty men in the various staff-departments, which reduced the numbers actually available for battle to some 67,000 or 68,000.

The order withdrawing the First Corps also broke up the Department of the Potomac, forming out of it the Department of the Shenandoah, under General Banks, and the Department of the Rappahannock, under General McDowell, the latter including Washington. I thus lost all control of the depots at Washington, as I had already been deprived of the control of the base at Fort Monroe and of the ground subsequently occupied by the depot at White House. The only territory remaining under my command was the paltry triangle between the departments of the Rappahannock and Virginia; even that was yet to be won from the enemy. I was thus relieved from the duty of providing for

MAP OF THE PENINSULAR CAMPAIGN.

MAJOR-GEN. SAMUEL P. HEINTZELMAN, U. S. V.

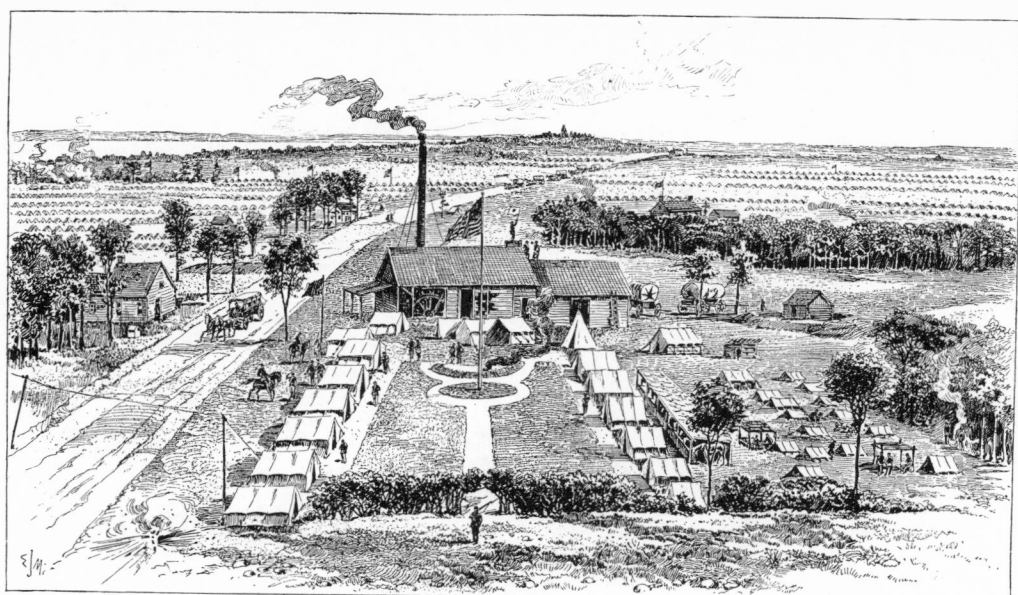

HEADQUARTERS OF GENERAL HEINTZELMAN, COMMANDING THE THIRD ARMY CORPS AT HOWE'S SAW-MILL, BEFORE YORKTOWN.
From a sketch made at the time.

MAJOR-GENERAL JOHN E. WOOL, U. S. A.

the safety of Washington, and deprived of all control over the troops in that vicinity. Instead of one directing head controlling operations which should have been inseparable, the region from the Alleghanies to the sea was parceled out among four independent commanders.

On the 3d of April, at the very moment of all others when it was most necessary to push recruiting most vigorously, to make good the inevitable losses in battle and by disease, an order was issued from the War Department discontinuing all recruiting for the volunteers and breaking up all their recruiting stations. Instead of a regular and permanent system of recruiting, whether by voluntary enlistment or by draft, a spasmodic system of large drafts was thereafter resorted to, and, to a great extent, the system of forming new regiments. The results were wasteful and pernicious. There were enough, or nearly enough, organizations in the field, and these should have been constantly maintained at the full strength by a regular and constant influx of recruits, who, by association with their veteran comrades, would soon have become efficient. The new regiments required much time to become useful, and endured very heavy and unnecessary losses from disease and in battle owing to the inexperience of the officers and men. A course more in accordance with the best-established military principles and the uniform experience of war would have saved the country millions of treasure and thousands of valuable lives.

Then, on the 5th of April, I found myself with 53,000 men in hand, giving less than 42,000 for battle, after deducting extra-duty men and other non-combatants. In our front was an intrenched line, apparently too strong for assault, and which I had now no means of turning, either by land or water. I now learned that 85,000 would be the maximum force at my disposal, giving only some 67,000 for battle. Of the three divisions yet to join, Casey's reached the front only on the 17th, Richardson's on the 16th, and Hooker's commenced arriving at Ship Point on the 10th. Whatever may have been said afterward, no one at the time — so far as my knowledge extended — thought an assault practicable without certain preliminary siege opera-

tions. At all events, my personal experience in this kind of work was greater than that of any officer under my command; and after personal reconnoissances more appropriate to a lieutenant of engineers than to the commanding general, I could neither discover nor hear of any point where an assault promised any chance of success. We were thus obliged to resort to siege operations in order to silence the enemy's artillery fire, and open the way to an assault. All the batteries would have been ready to open fire on the 5th, or, at latest, on the morning of the 6th of May, and it was determined to assault at various points the moment the heavy batteries had performed their allotted task; the navy was prepared to participate in the attack as soon as the main batteries were silenced; the *Galena*, under that most gallant and able officer, John Rodgers, was to take part in the attack, and would undoubtedly have run the batteries at the earliest possible moment; but during the night

of the 3d and 4th of May the enemy evacuated his positions, regarding them as untenable under the impending storm of heavy projectiles.

Meanwhile, on the 22d of April, Franklin's division of McDowell's corps had joined me by water, in consequence of my urgent calls for reinforcements.

The moment the evacuation of Yorktown was known, the order was given for the advance of all the disposable cavalry and horse batteries, supported by infantry divisions, and every possible effort was made to expedite the movement of a column by water upon West Point, to force the evacuation of the lines at Williamsburg, and, if possible, cut off a portion of the enemy's force and trains.

The heavy storms which had prevailed recommenced on the afternoon of the 4th, and not only impeded the advance of troops by land, but delayed the movement by water so much that it was

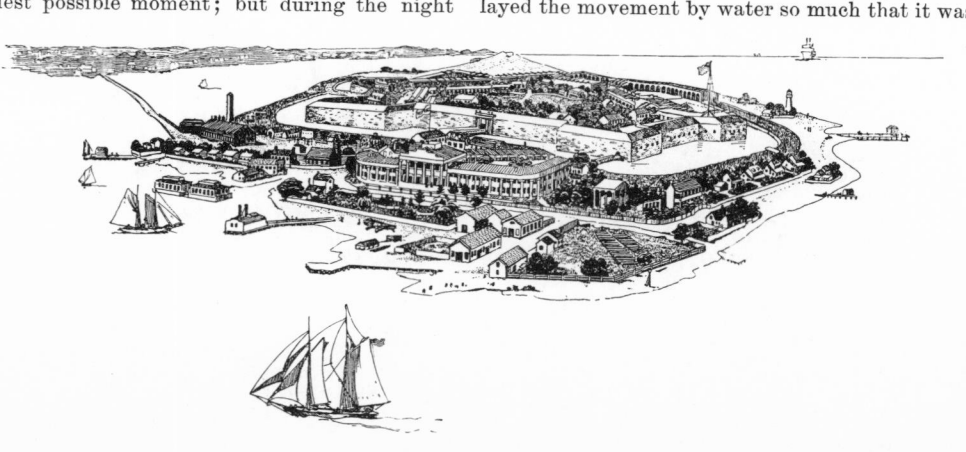

FORT MONROE AND THE OLD HYGEIA HOTEL.

not until the morning of the 7th that the leading division — Franklin's — disembarked near West Point and took up a suitable position to hold its own and cover the landing of reinforcements. This division was attacked not long after it landed, but easily repulsed the enemy.

Meanwhile the enemy's rear-guard held the Williamsburg lines against our advance, except where Hancock broke through, until the night of the 5th, when they retired.

The army was now divided; a part at the mouth of the Pamunkey, a part at Williamsburg, and a part at Yorktown prepared to ascend the York River. The problem was to reunite them without giving the enemy the opportunity of striking any fraction with his whole force. This was accomplished on the 10th, when all the divisions were in communication, and the movement of concentration continued as rapidly as circumstances permitted, so that on the 15th the headquarters and the divisions of Franklin, Porter, Sykes, and Smith reached Cumberland Landing; Couch and Casey being near New Kent Court House, Hooker and Kearny near Roper's Church, and Richardson and Sedgwick near Eltham. On the 15th and 16th, in the face of dreadful weather and terrible roads, the divisions of Franklin, Porter, and Smith were advanced to White House, and a depot established. On the 18th the Fifth and Sixth Corps were formed, so that the organization of the Army of the Potomac was now as follows: Second Corps, Sumner — Divisions, Sedgwick and Richardson; Third Corps, Heintzelman — Divisions, Kearny and Hooker; Fourth Corps, Keyes — Divisions, Couch and Casey; Fifth Corps, F. J. Porter — Divisions, Morell and Sykes and the Reserve Artillery; Sixth Corps, Franklin — Divisions, Smith and Slocum.

The cavalry organization remained unchanged, and we were sadly deficient in that important arm, as many of the regiments belonging to the Army of the Potomac were among those which had been retained near Washington.

The question now arose as to the line of operations to be followed: that of the James on the one hand, and, on the other, the line from White House as a base, crossing the upper Chickahominy.

The army was admirably placed for adopting either, and my decision was to take that of the James, operating on either bank as might prove advisable, but always preferring the southern. I had urgently asked for reinforcements to come by water, as they would thus be equally available for either line of operations. The destruction of the *Merrimac* on the 11th of May had opened the James River to us, and it was only after that date that it became available. My plan, however, was changed by orders from Washington. A telegram of the 18th from the Secretary of War informed me that McDowell would advance from Fredericksburg, and directed me to extend the right of the Army of the Potomac to the north of Richmond, in order to establish communication with him. The same order required me to supply his troops from our depots at White House. Herein lay the failure of the campaign, as it necessitated the division of the army by the Chickahominy, and caused great delay in constructing practicable bridges across that stream; while if I had been able to cross to the James, reinforcements would have reached me by water rapidly and safely, the army would have been united and in no danger of having its flank turned, or its line of supply interrupted, and the attack could have been much more rapidly pushed.

I now proceeded to do all in my power to insure success on the new line of operations thus imposed upon me. On the 20th of May our light troops reached the Chickahominy at Bottom's Bridge, which they found destroyed. I at once ordered Casey's division to ford the stream and occupy the heights beyond, thus securing a lodgment on the right bank. Heintzelman was moved up in support of Keyes. By the 24th, Mechanicsville was carried, so that the enemy was now all together on the other side of the river. Sumner was near the railroad, on the left bank of the stream; Porter and Franklin were on the same bank near Mechanicsville.

It is now time to give a brief description of the Chickahominy. This river rises some fifteen miles northwestward of Richmond, and unites with the James about forty miles below that city. Our operations were on the part between Meadow and Bottom's bridges, covering the approaches to Richmond from the east. Here the river at its

SECTION OF THE ENCAMPMENT OF THE ARMY OF THE POTOMAC NEAR WHITE HOUSE, VA.
Process reproduction of a photograph.

"We were now [middle of May] encamped on the old Custis place, at present owned by General Fitzhugh Lee [Gen. W. H. F. Lee] of the Rebel cavalry service. On every side of us were immense fields of wheat, which, but for the presence of armies, promised an abundant harvest. . . . It was marvelous that such quiet could exist where a hundred thousand men were crowded together, yet almost absolute stillness reigned throughout the vast camp during the whole of this pleasant Sabbath." — From George T. Stevens's "Three Years in the Sixth Corps." The picture represents the space occupied by about one brigade.

ordinary stage is some forty feet wide, fringed with a dense growth of heavy forest-trees, and bordered by low marshy lands, varying from half a mile to a mile in width. Within the limits above mentioned the firm ground, above high-water mark, seldom approaches the river on either bank, and in no place did the high ground come near the stream on both banks. It was subject to frequent, sudden and great variations in the volume of water, and a single violent storm of brief duration sufficed to cause an overflow of the bottom-lands for many days, rendering the river absolutely impassable without long and strong bridges. When we reached the river it was found that all the bridges, except that at Mechanicsville, had been destroyed. The right bank, opposite New, Mechanicsville, and Meadow bridges, was bordered by high bluffs, affording the enemy commanding positions for his batteries, enfilading the approaches, and preventing the rebuilding of important bridges. We were thus obliged to select other less exposed points for our crossings. Should McDowell effect the promised junction, we could turn the head-waters of the Chickahominy, and attack Richmond from the

north and northwest, still preserving our line of supply from White House. But with the force actually available such an attempt would expose the army to the loss of its communications and to destruction in detail; for we had an able and savage antagonist, prompt to take advantage of any error on our part. The country furnished no supplies, so that we could not afford a separation from our depots. All the information obtained showed that Richmond was intrenched, that the enemy occupied in force all the approaches from the east, that he intended to dispute every step of our advance, and that his army was numerically superior. Early on the 24th of May I received a telegram from the President, informing me that McDowell would certainly march on the 26th, suggesting that I should detach a force to the right to cut off the retreat of the Confederate force in front of Fredericksburg, and desiring me to march cautiously and safely. On the same day another despatch came, informing me that, in consequence of Stonewall Jackson's advance down the Shenandoah, the movement of McDowell was suspended. Next day the President again telegraphed that the

movement against General Banks seemed so general and connected as to show that the enemy could not intend a very desperate defense of Richmond; that he thought the time was near when I "must either attack Richmond or give up the job, and come back to the defense of Washington." I replied that all my information agreed that the mass of the enemy was still in the immediate vicinity of Richmond, ready to defend it, and that the object of Jackson's movement was probably to prevent reinforcements being sent to me. ·. . The campaign had taken its present position in consequence of the assurance that I should be joined by McDowell's corps. As it was now clear that I could not count with certainty upon that force, I had to do the best I could with the means at hand.

The first necessity was to establish secure communications between the two parts of the army, necessarily separated by the Chickahominy. Richmond could be attacked only by troops on the right bank. As the expectation of the advance of McDowell was still held out, and that only by the land route, I could not yet transfer the base to the James, but was obliged to retain it on the Pamunkey, and therefore to keep on the left bank a force sufficient to protect our communications and cover the junction of McDowell. It was still permissible to believe that sufficient attention would be paid to the simplest principle of war to push McDowell rapidly on Jackson's heels, when he made his inevitable return march to join the main Confederate army and attack our right flank. The failure of McDowell to reach me at or before the critical moment was due to the orders he received from Washington. The bridges over the Chickahominy first built were swept away by the floods, and it became necessary to construct others more solid and with long log approaches, a slow and difficult task, generally carried on by men working in the water and under fire.

The work was pushed as rapidly as possible, and on the 30th of May the corps of Heintzelman and Keyes were on the right bank of the Chickahominy, the most advanced positions being somewhat strengthened by intrenchments; Sumner's corps was on the left bank, some six miles above Bottom's Bridge; Porter's and Franklin's corps were on the left bank opposite the enemy's left. During the day and night of the 30th torrents of

SUMNER'S MARCH TO REINFORCE COUCH AT FAIR OAKS.

Lieutenant Edmund Kirby, Battery I, First U. S. Artillery, says in his official report: "The roads were almost impassable for artillery, and I experienced great difficulty in getting my guns along. I was obliged at times to unlimber and use the prolonge, the cannoneers being up to their waists in water. About 4 30 P. M. I was within three-quarters of a mile of Fair Oaks Station, with three pieces [twelve-pounder Napoleons] and one caisson, the remainder of the battery being in the rear, and coming up as fast as circumstances would permit."

SUMNER'S CORPS CROSSING THE OVERFLOWED "GRAPEVINE" BRIDGE
TO REINFORCE COUCH AT FAIR OAKS.
From a sketch made at the time.

rain fell, inundating the whole country and threatening the destruction of our bridges.

Well aware of our difficulties, our active enemy, on the 31st of May, made a violent attack upon Casey's division, followed by an equally formidable one on Couch, thus commencing the battle of Fair Oaks or Seven Pines. Heintzelman came up in support, and during the afternoon Sumner crossed the river with great difficulty, and rendered such efficient service that the enemy was checked. In the morning his renewed attacks were easily repulsed, and the ground occupied at the beginning of the battle was more than recovered; he had failed in the purpose of the attack. The ground was now so thoroughly soaked by the rain, and the bridges so much injured, that it was impracticable to pursue the enemy or to move either Porter or Franklin to the support of the other corps on the south bank. Our efforts were at once concentrated upon the restoration of the old and the building of new bridges.

On the 1st of June the Department of Virginia, including Fort Monroe, was placed under my command. On the 2d the Secretary telegraphed that as soon as Jackson was disposed of in the Shenandoah, another large body of troops would be at my service; on the 5th, that he intended sending a part of General McDowell's force as soon as it could return from Front Royal (in the Shenandoah Valley, near Manassas Gap, and about one hundred and fifteen miles northwest of Richmond), probably as many as I wanted; on the 11th, that McCall's force had embarked to join me on the day preceding, and that it was intended to send the residue of General McDowell's force to join me as speedily as possible, and that it was clear that a strong force was operating with Jackson for the purpose of preventing the forces there from joining me.

On the 26th the Secretary telegraphed that the forces of McDowell, Banks, and Frémont would be consolidated as the Army of Virginia, and would operate promptly in my aid by land.

Fortunately for the Army of the Potomac, however, I entertained serious doubts of the aid promised by the land route, so that, on the 18th, I ordered a number of transports, with supplies of all kinds, to be sent up the James, under convoy of the gunboats, so that I might be free to cut loose from the Pamunkey and move over to the James, should circumstances enable me or render it desirable to do so.

The battle of Fair Oaks was followed by storms of great severity, continuing until the 20th of June, and adding vastly to the difficulties of our position, greatly retarding the construction of the bridges and of the defensive works regarded as necessary to cover us in the event of a repulse, and making the ground too difficult for the free movements of troops.

On the 19th Franklin's corps was transferred to the south side of the Chickahominy, Porter's corps, reinforced by McCall's division (which, with a few additional regiments, had arrived on the 12th and 13th), being left alone on the north side.

This dangerous distribution was necessary in order to concentrate sufficient force on the south side to attack Richmond with any hope of success; and, as I was still told that McDowell would arrive by the overland route, I could not yet change the base to the James.

It was not until the 25th that the condition of the ground and the completion of the bridges and intrenchments left me free to attack. On that day the first step was taken, in throwing forward the left of our picket-line, in face of a strong opposition, to gain ground enough to enable Sumner and Heintzelman to support the attack to be made next day by Franklin on the rear of Old Tavern. The successful issue of this attack would, it was supposed, drive the enemy from his positions on the heights overlooking Mechanicsville, and probably enable us to force him back into his main line of works. We would then be in position to reconnoiter the lines carefully, determine the points of attack, and take up a new base and line of supply if expedient.

During the night of the 24th information arrived confirming the anticipation that Jackson was

MAJOR-GENERAL EDWIN V. SUMNER, U. S. V.

MAJOR-GENERAL DARIUS N. COUCH, U. S. V.

HEADQUARTERS OF BRIGADIER-GENERAL JOHN SEDGWICK, ON THE LEESBURG TURNPIKE, NEAR WASHINGTON.
From a sketch made in January, 1862.

WHITE HOUSE, THE HOME OF GENERAL W. H. LEE, McCLELLAN'S BASE OF SUPPLIES ON THE PAMUNKEY.
From sketches made at the time.

RUINS OF THE WHITE HOUSE, WHICH WAS BURNED JUNE 28, DURING THE "CHANGE OF BASE."

moving to attack our right and rear, but I persisted in the operation intended for the 25th, partly to develop the strength of the enemy opposite our left and center, and with the design of attacking Old Tavern on the 26th, if Jackson's advance was so much delayed that Porter's corps would not be endangered.

Late in the afternoon of the 25th, Jackson's advance was confirmed, and it was rendered probable that he would attack next day. All hope of the advance of McDowell's corps in season to be of any service had disappeared; the dangerous position of the army had been faithfully held to the last moment. After deducting the garrisons in rear, the railroad guards, non-combatants, and extra-duty men, there were not more than 75,000 men for battle. The enemy, with a force larger than this, the strong defenses of Richmond close at hand in his rear, was free to strike on either flank. I decided then to carry into effect the long-considered plan of abandoning the Pamunkey and taking up the line of the James.

The necessary orders were given for the defense of the depots at the White House to the last moment and its final destruction and abandonment; it was also ordered that all possible stores should be pushed to the front while communications were open.

The ground to the James had already been reconnoitered with reference to this movement. During the night of the 26th Porter's siege-guns and wagon-trains were brought over to the south side of the Chickahominy. During the afternoon of that day his corps had been attacked in its position on Beaver Dam Creek, near Mechanicsville, and the enemy repulsed with heavy losses on their part. It was now clear that Jackson's corps had taken little or no part in this attack, and that his blow would fall farther to the rear. I therefore ordered the Fifth Corps to fall back and take posi-

tion nearer the bridges, where the flanks would be more secure. This was skilfully effected early on the 27th, and it was decided that this corps should hold its position until night. All the corps commanders on the south side were on the 26th directed to be prepared to send as many troops as they could spare in support of Porter on the next day. All of them thought the enemy so strong in their respective fronts as to require all their force to hold their positions.

Shortly after noon on the 27th the attack commenced upon Porter's corps, in its new position near Gaines's Mill, and the contest continued all day with great vigor. . . .

[For accounts of the battle of Gaines's Mill, as well as of others in the "Seven Days'" series, see articles by Generals Fitz-John Porter, James Longstreet, and D. H. Hill.]

I now bent all my energies to the transfer of the army to the James, fully realizing the very delicate nature of a flank march, with heavy trains, by a single road, in face of an active enemy, but confident that I had the army well in hand and that it would not fail me in the emergency. I thought that the enemy would not anticipate that movement, but would assume that all my efforts would be directed to cover and regain the old depots; and the event proved the correctness of this supposition. It seemed certain that I could gain one or two days for the movement of the trains, while he remained uncertain as to my intentions; and that was all I required with such troops as those of the Army of the Potomac.

During the night of the 27th I assembled the corps commanders at headquarters, informed them of my intentions, and gave them their orders. Keyes's corps was ordered to move at once, with its trains, across White Oak Swamp, and occupy positions on the farther side, to cover the passage of the remainder of the army. By noon of the 28th

this first step was accomplished. During the 28th Sumner, Heintzelman, and Franklin held essentially their old positions; the trains converged steadily to the White Oak Swamp and crossed as rapidly as possible, and during this day and the succeeding night Porter followed the movement of Keyes's corps and took position to support it.

Early on the 28th, when Franklin's corps was drawing in its right to take a more concentrated position, the enemy opened a sharp artillery fire and made at one point a spirited attack with two Georgia regiments, which were repulsed by the two regiments on picket.

Sumner's and Heintzelman's corps and Smith's division of Franklin's were now ordered to abandon their intrenchments, so as to occupy, on the morning of the 29th, a new position in rear, shorter than the old and covering the crossing of the swamp. This new line could easily be held during the day, and these troops were ordered to remain there until dark, to cover the withdrawal of the rest of the trains, and then cross the swamp and occupy the positions about to be abandoned by Keyes's and Porter's corps. Meanwhile Slocum's division had been ordered to Savage's Station in reserve, and, during the morning, was ordered across the swamp to relieve Keyes's corps. This was a critical day; for the crossing of the swamp by the trains must be accomplished before its close, and their protection against attack from Richmond must be assured, as well as communication with the gun-boats.

A sharp cavalry skirmish on the Quaker road indicated that the enemy was alive to our movement, and might at any moment strike in force to intercept the march to the James. The difficulty was not at all with the movement of the troops, but with the immense trains that were to be moved

virtually by a single road, and required the whole army for their protection. With the exception of the cavalry affair on the Quaker road, we were not troubled during this day south of the swamp, but there was severe fighting north of it. Sumner's corps evacuated their works at daylight and fell back to Allen's farm, nearly two miles west of Savage's Station, Heintzelman being on their left. Here Sumner was furiously attacked three times, but each time drove the enemy back with much loss.

Soon afterward Franklin, having only one division with him, ascertained that the enemy had repaired some of the Chickahominy bridges and

UNION MORTAR-BATTERY BEFORE YORKTOWN.

was advancing on Savage's Station, whereupon he posted his division at that point and informed Sumner, who moved his corps to the same place, arriving a little after noon.

About 4 P. M. Sumner and Franklin—three divisions in all—were sharply attacked, mainly by the Williamsburg road; the fighting continued until between 8 and 9 P. M., the enemy being at all times thoroughly repulsed, and finally driven from the field.

Meanwhile, through a misunderstanding of his orders, and being convinced that the troops of Sumner and Franklin at Savage's Station were ample for the purpose in view, Heintzelman withdrew his troops during the afternoon, crossed the swamp at Brackett's Ford, and reached the Charles City road with the rear of his column at 10 P. M.

Slocum reached the position of Keyes's corps early in the afternoon, and, as soon as the latter was thus relieved, it was ordered forward to the James, near Malvern Hill, which it reached, with all its artillery and trains, early on the 30th. Porter was ordered to follow this movement and prolong the line of Keyes's corps to our right. The trains were pushed on in rear of these corps and massed under cover of the gun-boats as fast as they reached the James, at Haxall's plantation. As soon as the fighting ceased with the final repulse of the enemy, Sumner and Franklin were ordered to cross the swamp; this was effected during the night, the rear-guard crossing and destroying the bridge at 5 A. M. on the 30th. All the troops and trains were now between the swamp and the James, and the first critical episode of the movement was successfully accomplished.

The various corps were next pushed forward to establish connection with Keyes and Porter, and hold the different roads by which the enemy could advance from Richmond and strike our line of march. I determined to hold the positions now taken until the trains had all reached a place of safety, and then concentrate the army near the James, where it could enjoy a brief rest after the fatiguing battles and marches through which it was passing, and then renew the advance on Richmond.

General Franklin, with Smith's division of his own corps, Richardson's of the Second, and Naglee's brigade, was charged with the defense of the White Oak Swamp crossing. Slocum held the ground thence to the Charles City road; Kearny from that road to the Long Bridge road; McCall on his left; Hooker thence to the Quaker road; Sedgwick at Nelson's farm, in rear of McCall and Kearny. The Fifth Corps was at Malvern Hill, the Fourth at Turkey Bridge. The trains moved on during this day, and at 4 P. M. the last reached Malvern Hill and kept on to Haxall's, so that the most difficult part of the task was accomplished, and it only

CAMP OF THE UNION ARMY NEAR WHITE HOUSE ON THE PAMUNKEY RIVER, McCLELLAN'S BASE OF OPERATIONS AGAINST RICHMOND.

remained for the troops to hold their ground until nightfall, and then continue the march to the positions selected near Malvern Hill.

The fighting on this day (June 30th) was very severe, and extended along the whole line. It first broke out between 12 and 1, on General Franklin's command, in the shape of a fierce artillery fire, which was kept up through the day and inflicted serious losses. The enemy's infantry made several attempts to cross near the old bridge and below, but was in every case thrown back. Franklin held his position until after dark, and during the night fell back to Malvern. At half-past 2 Slocum's left was attacked in vain on the Charles City road. At about 3 McCall was attacked, and, after 5 o'clock, under the pressure of heavy masses, he was forced back; but Hooker came up from the left, and Sedgwick from the rear, and the two together not only stopped the enemy, but drove him off the field.

At about 4 P. M. heavy attacks commenced on Kearny's left, and three ineffectual assaults were made. The firing continued until after dark. About

midnight Sumner's and Heintzelman's corps and McCall's division withdrew from the positions they had so gallantly held, and commenced their march to Malvern, which they reached unmolested soon after daybreak. Just after the rear of the trains reached Malvern, about 4 P. M., the enemy attacked Porter's corps, but were promptly shaken off.

Thus, on the morning of July 1st, the army was concentrated at Malvern, with the trains at Haxall's in rear. The supplies which had been sent from White House on the 18th were at hand in the James.

After consultation with Commodore Rodgers, I decided that Harrison's Landing was a better position for the resting-place of the army, because the channel passed so close to City Point as to enable the enemy to prevent the passage of transports if we remained at Malvern. It was, however, necessary to accept battle where we were, in order to give ample time for the trains to reach Harrison's, as well as give the enemy a blow that would check his farther pursuit. . . .

Although the result of this bloody battle was a complete victory on our part, it was necessary, for the reasons already given, to continue the movement to Harrison's, whither the trains had been pushed during the night of the 30th of June and the day of the 1st of July. Immediately after the final repulse the orders were given for the withdrawal of the army. The movement was covered by Keyes's corps. So complete was the enemy's discomfiture, and so excellent the conduct of the rear-guard, that the last of the trains reached Harrison's after dark on the 3d, without loss and unmolested by the enemy.

This movement was now successfully accomplished, and the Army of the Potomac was at last in a position on its true line of operations, with its trains intact, no guns lost save those taken in battle, when the artillerists had proved their heroism and devotion by standing to their guns until the enemy's infantry were in the midst of them.

During the "Seven Days" the Army of the Potomac consisted of 143 regiments of infantry, 55 batteries, and less than 8 regiments of cavalry, all told. The opposing Confederate army consisted of 187 regiments of infantry, 79 batteries, and 14 regiments of cavalry. The losses of the two armies from June 25th to July 2d were:

Killed. Wounded. Missing. Total.
Confederate Army.......2,823.....13,703.....3,323....19,749
Army of the Potomac...1,734..... 8,062....6,053....15,849

The Confederate losses in killed and wounded alone were greater than the total losses of the Army of the Potomac in killed, wounded, and missing.

No praise can be too great for the officers and men who passed through these seven days of battle, enduring fatigue without a murmur, successfully meeting and repelling every attack made upon them, always in the right place at the right time, and emerging from the fiery ordeal a compact army of veterans, equal to any task that brave and disciplined men can be called upon to undertake. They needed now only a few days of well-earned repose, a renewal of ammunition and supplies, and reinforcements to fill the gaps made in their ranks by so many desperate encounters, to be prepared to advance again, with entire confidence, to meet their worthy antagonists in other battles. It was, however, decided by the authorities at Washington, against my earnest remonstrances, to abandon the position on the James, and the campaign. The Army of the Potomac was accordingly withdrawn, and it was not until two years later that it again found itself under its last commander at substantially the same point on the bank of the James. It was as evident in 1862 as in 1865 that there was the true defense of Washington, and that it was on the banks of the James that the fate of the Union was to be decided.

VIEW FROM UNION MORTAR-BATTERY No. 4, LOOKING TOWARD YORKTOWN.

"GET THAT TEAM OUT OF THE MUD!"

SKIRMISH AT LEE'S MILLS BEFORE YORKTOWN, APRIL 16, 1862.
From a sketch made at the time.

THE SIEGE OF YORKTOWN.

RECOLLECTIONS OF A PRIVATE—III. BY WARREN LEE GOSS.

. . . One morning we broke camp and went marching up the Peninsula. The roads were very poor and muddy with recent rains, and were crowded with the indescribable material of the vast army which was slowly creeping through the mud over the flat, wooded country. It was a bright day in April—a perfect Virginia day; the grass was green beneath our feet, the buds of the trees were just unrolling into leaves under the warming sun of spring, and in the woods the birds were singing. The march was at first orderly, but under the unaccustomed burden of heavy equipments and knapsacks, and the warmth of the weather, the men straggled along the roads, mingling with the baggage-wagons, ambulances, and pontoon trains, in seeming confusion. . . .

The baggage-trains were a notable spectacle. To each baggage-wagon were attached four or six mules, driven usually by a colored man, with only one rein, or line, and that line attached to the bit of the near leading mule, while the driver rode in a saddle upon the near wheel mule. Each train was accompanied by a guard, and while the guard urged the drivers the drivers urged the mules. The drivers were usually expert, and understood well the wayward, sportive natures of the creatures over whose destinies they presided. On our way to Yorktown our pontoon and baggage trains were sometimes blocked for miles, and the heaviest trains were often unloaded by the guard to facilitate their removal from the mud. It did seem at times as if there were needless delays with the trains, partly due, no doubt, to fear of danger ahead. While I was guarding our pontoon train, after leaving Big Bethel, the teams stopped all along the line. Hurrying to the front, I found one of the leading teams badly mired, but not enough to justify the stopping of the whole train. The lazy colored driver was comfortably asleep in the saddle. "Get that team out of the mud!" I yelled, bringing him to his senses. He flourished his long whip, shouted his mule lingo at the team, and the mules pulled frantically, but not together. "Can't you make your mules pull together?" I inquired. "Dem mules pull right smart!" said the driver. Cocking and capping my unloaded musket, I brought it to the shoulder and again commanded the driver, "Get that team out of the mud!" The negro rolled his eyes wildly and woke up all over. He first patted his saddle mule, spoke to each one, and then, flourishing his long whip with a crack like a pistol, shouted, "Go 'long dar! What I feed yo' fo'?" and the mule team left the slough in a very expeditious manner.

When procuring luxuries of eggs or milk, we paid the people at first in silver, and they gave us local scrip in change; but we found on attempting to pay it out again that they were rather reluctant to receive it, even at that early stage in Confederate finance, and much preferred Yankee silver or notes.

On the afternoon of April 5th, 1862, the advance of our column was brought to a standstill, with the right in front of Yorktown, and the left by the enemy's works at Lee's mills [map p. 83]. We pitched our camp on Wormley Creek, near the Moore house, on the York River, in sight of the enemy's water-battery and their defensive works at Gloucester Point. One of the impediments to an immediate attack on Yorktown was the difficulty of using light artillery in the muddy fields in our front, and at that time the topography of the country ahead was but little understood, and had to be learned by reconnoissance in force. We had settled down to the siege of Yorktown; began bridging the streams between us and the enemy, constructing and improving the roads for the rapid transit of supplies, and for the advance. The first parallel was opened about a mile from the enemy's fortifications, extending along the entire front of their works, which reached from the York River on the left to Warwick Creek on the right, along a line about four miles in length. Fourteen batteries and three redoubts were planted, heavily armed with ordnance.

We were near Battery No. 1, not far from the York River. On it were mounted several 200-pounder guns, which commanded the enemy's water-batteries. One day I was in a redoubt on the left, and saw General McClellan with the Prince de Joinville, examining the enemy's works through their field-glasses. They very soon drew the fire of the observant enemy, who opened with one of their heavy guns on the group, sending the first shot howling and hissing over and very close to their heads; another, quickly following it, struck in the parapet of the redoubt. The French prince, seemingly quite startled, jumped and glanced nervously around, while McClellan quietly knocked the ashes from his cigar.

Several of our war-vessels made their appearance in the York River, and occasionally threw a shot at the enemy's works; but most of them were kept busy at Hampton Roads, watching for the ironclad *Merrimac*, which was still afloat. The firing from the enemy's lines was of little consequence, not amounting to over ten or twelve shots each day, a number of these being directed at the huge balloon which went up daily on a tour of inspection, from near General Fitz-John Porter's headquarters. One day the balloon broke from its mooring of ropes and sailed majestically over the enemy's works; but fortunately for its occupants it soon met a counter-current of air which returned it safe to our lines. The month of April was a dreary one, much of the time rainy and uncomfortable. It was a common expectation among us that we were about to end the rebellion. One of my comrades wrote home to his father that we should probably finish up the war in season for him to be at home to teach the village school the following winter; in fact, I believe he partly en-

WHARF, YORK RIVER. MCCLELLAN'S HEADQUARTERS. NELSON HOUSE.
VIEW OF MAIN STREET, YORKTOWN—THE UNION TROOPS MARCHING IN.
From a sketch made May 4, 1862.

MAJOR-GENERAL OLIVER O. HOWARD, U. S. A.
Facsimile reproduction of a photograph taken before the
Battle of Seven Pines, on the second day of which
General Howard lost his right arm.

MAJOR-GENERAL GUSTAVUS W. SMITH, C. S. A.

MAJOR-GENERAL BENJAMIN HUGER, C. S. A.

MAJOR-GENERAL DAVID B. BIRNEY, U. S. V.

MANASSAS TO SEVEN PINES.

BY JOSEPH E. JOHNSTON, GENERAL, C. S. A.
Confederate commander at Manassas; also commander on the Peninsula until the close of the
first day's battle at Seven Pines.

. . . On the 23d of May, Keyes's Federal corps crossed to the south side of the Chickahominy, and a detachment attacked Hatton's Confederate brigade, which was in observation near Savage's Station. The detachment was driven back, and Hatton's object having been accomplished (to learn whether the enemy had crossed the stream), he was recalled. I was advised to hold that position with the army, but preferred to let the enemy advance, which would increase the interval between his left and the right, which was beyond the Chickahominy. McDowell's corps of 40,000 men was then at Fredericksburg, observed by a division under Brigadier-General J. R. Anderson; and a large Confederate brigade, under Brigadier-General Branch, was at Gordonsville.

On the 24th our cavalry was driven across the Chickahominy, principally at Mechanicsville. This extension of the right wing of the enemy to the west made me apprehend that the two detachments (Anderson and Branch) above mentioned might be cut off. They were therefore ordered to fall back to the Chickahominy. Near Hanover Court House the brigade was attacked by Porter's corps and driven off, escaping with a loss of 66 killed, and 177 wounded, as General Branch reported. A division was formed of Anderson's and Branch's troops, to the command of which Major-General A. P. Hill was assigned.

That evening General Anderson sent word that his scouts left near Fredericksburg reported that McDowell's troops were marching southward. As the object of this march was evidently the junction of this corps with the main army, I determined to attack McClellan before McDowell could join him; and the major-generals were desired to hold their troops ready to move. But at night, when those officers were with me to receive instructions for the expected battle, General J. E. B. Stuart, who

also had a detachment of cavalry observing McDowell's corps, reported that it had returned to Fredericksburg. As my object was to bring on the inevitable battle before McClellan should receive an addition of 40,000 men to his forces, this intelligence made me return to my first design— that of attacking McClellan's left wing on the Williamsburg road as soon as, by advancing, it had sufficiently increased its distance from his right, north of the Chickahominy.

The morning of the 30th, armed reconnoissances were made under General D. H. Hill's direction— on the Charles City road by Brigadier-General Rodes, and on the Williamsburg road by Brigadier-General Garland. The latter found Federal outposts five miles from Richmond— or two miles west of Seven Pines— in such strength as indicated that a corps was near. On receiving this information from General Hill, I informed him that he would lead an attack on the enemy next morning. Orders were given for the concentration of twenty-two of our twenty-eight brigades against McClellan's left wing, about two-fifths of his army. Our six other brigades were guarding the river from New Bridge to Meadow Bridge, on our extreme left. Longstreet and Huger were directed to conduct their divisions to D. H. Hill's position on the Williamsburg road, and G. W. Smith to march with his to the junction of the Nine-mile road with the New Bridge road, where Magruder was with four brigades.

Longstreet, as ranking officer of the troops on the Williamsburg road, was instructed verbally to form D. H. Hill's division as first line, and his own as second, across the road at right angles, and to advance in that order to attack the enemy; while Huger's division should march by the right flank along the Charles City road, to fall upon the enemy's flank when our troops were engaged with

him in front. Federal earthworks and abatis that might be found were to be turned. G. W. Smith was to protect the troops under Longstreet from attack by those of the Federal right wing across the Chickahominy; and, if such transfer should not be threatened, he was to fall upon the enemy on the Williamsburg road. Those troops were formed in four lines, each being a division. Casey's was a mile west of Seven Pines, with a line of skirmishers a half mile in advance; Couch's was at Seven Pines and Fair Oaks— the two forming Keyes's corps. Kearny's division was near Savage's Station, and Hooker's two miles west of Bottom's Bridge— the two forming Heintzelman's corps.

Longstreet's command of the right was to end when the troops approached Seven Pines and I should be present to direct the movements, after which each major-general would command his own division. The rain began to fall violently in the afternoon of the 30th, and continued all night. In the morning the little streams near our camps were so much swollen as to make it probable that the Chickahominy was overflowing its banks and cutting the communication between the wings of

gaged to teach it. Another wrote to his mother: "We have got them hemmed in on every side, and the only reason they don't run is because they can't." We had at last corduroyed every road and bridged every creek; our guns and mortars were in position; Battery No. 1 had actually opened on the enemy's works, Saturday, May 3d, 1862, and it was expected that our whole line would open on them in the morning. About 2 o'clock of Saturday night, or rather of Sunday morning, while on guard duty, I observed a bright illumination, as if a fire had broken out within the enemy's lines. Several guns were fired from their works during the early morning hours, but soon after daylight of May 4th it was reported that they had abandoned their works in our front, and we very quickly found the report to be true. As soon as I was relieved from guard duty, I went over on "French leave" to view our enemy's fortifications. They were prodigiously strong. A few tumble-down tents and houses and seventy pieces of heavy ordnance had been abandoned as the price of the enemy's safe retreat.

As soon as it was known that the Confederates had abandoned the works at Yorktown, the commanding general sent the cavalry and horse artillery under Stoneman in pursuit to harass the retreating column. . . .

the Federal Army. Being confident that Longstreet and D. H. Hill, with their forces united, would be successful in the earlier part of the action against adversaries formed in several lines, with wide intervals between them, I left the immediate control on the Williamsburg road to them, under general instructions, and placed myself on the left, where I could soonest learn of the approach of Federal reinforcements from their right. For this scouts were sent forward to discover all movements that might be made by the enemy.

The condition of the ground and little streams delayed the troops in marching; yet those of Smith, Longstreet, and Hill were in position quite early enough. But the soldiers from Norfolk, who had seen garrison service only, were unnecessarily stopped in their march by a swollen rivulet. This unexpected delay led to interchange of messages for several hours between General Longstreet and myself, I urging Longstreet to begin the fight, he replying. But, near 2 o'clock, that officer was requested to go forward to the attack; the hands of my watch marked 3 o'clock at the report of the first field-piece. The Federal advance line — a long line of skirmishers, supported by several regiments — was encountered at 3 o'clock. The greatly superior numbers of the Confederates soon drove them back to the main position of Casey's division. It occupied a line of rifle-pits, strengthened by a redoubt and abatis. Here the resistance was very obstinate; for the Federals, commanded by an officer of skill and tried courage, fought as soldiers generally do under good leaders; and time and vigorous efforts of superior numbers were required to drive them from their ground. But the resolution of Garland's and G. B. Anderson's brigades, that pressed forward on our left through an open field, under a destructive fire; the admirable service of Carter's and Bondurant's batteries, and a skilfully combined attack upon the Federal left, under General Hill's direction, by Rodes's brigade in front and that of Rains in flank, were at last successful, and the enemy abandoned their intrenchments. Just then reinforcements from Couch's division came up, and an effort was made to recover the position. But it was to no purpose; for two regiments of R. H. Anderson's brigade reinforced Hill's troops, and the Federals were driven back to Seven Pines.

BURNING HORSES, AND BURYING THE DEAD, AT THE TWIN HOUSES NEAR CASEY'S REDOUBT, AFTER THE SECOND DAY'S FIGHT.

Keyes's corps (Casey's and Couch's divisions) was united at Seven Pines and reinforced by Kearny's division, coming from Savage's Station. But the three divisions were so vigorously attacked by Hill that they were broken and driven from their intrenchments, the greater part along the Williamsburg road to the intrenched line west of Savage's Station. Two brigades of their left, however, fled to White Oak Swamp.

General Hill pursued the enemy a mile; then, night being near, he re-formed his troops, facing toward the Federals. Longstreet's and Huger's divisions, coming up, were formed between Hill's line and Fair Oaks.

For some cause the disposition on the Charles City road was modified. Two of General Huger's brigades were ordered to advance along that road, with three of Longstreet's under Brigadier-General Wilcox. After following that road some miles, General Wilcox received orders to conduct his troops to the Williamsburg road. On entering it, he was ordered to the front, and two of his regiments joined Hill's troops near and approaching Seven Pines.

When the action just described began, the mus-

ketry was not heard at my position on the Nine-mile road, from the unfavorable condition of the air; and I supposed for some time that we were hearing only an artillery duel. But a staff-officer was sent to ascertain the facts. He returned at 4 o'clock with intelligence that our infantry as well as artillery had been engaged an hour, and all were pressing on vigorously. As no approach of troops from beyond the Chickahominy had been discovered, I hoped that the enemy's bridges were impassable, and therefore desired General Smith to move toward Seven Pines, to be ready to coöperate with our right. He moved promptly along the Nine-mile road, and his leading regiment soon became engaged with the Federal skirmishers and their reserves, and in a few minutes drove them off.

On my way to Longstreet's left, to combine the action of the two bodies of troops, I passed the head of General Smith's column near Fair Oaks, and saw the camps of about a brigade in the angle between the Nine-mile road and the York River Railroad, and the rear of a column of infantry moving in quick time from that point toward the Chickahominy by the road to the Grapevine ford. A few minutes after this, a battery near the point

where this infantry had disappeared commenced firing upon the head of the Confederate column. A regiment sent against it was received with a volley of musketry, as well as canister, and recoiled. The leading brigade, commanded by Colonel Law, then advanced, and so much strength was developed by the enemy that General Smith brought his other brigades into action on the left of Law's. An obstinate contest began, and was maintained on equal terms, although we engaged superior numbers on ground of their own choosing.

I had passed the railroad a few hundred yards with Hood's brigade when the firing commenced, and stopped to see it terminated. But being confident that the enemy opposing us were those whose camp I had just seen, and therefore only a brigade, I did not doubt that General Smith was more than strong enough to cope with them. Therefore, General Hood was directed to go on in such a direction as to connect his right with Longstreet's left and take his antagonists in flank. The direction of that firing was then nearly southwest from Fair Oaks. It was then about 5 o'clock.

In that position my intercourse with Longstreet was maintained through staff-officers, who were assisted by General Stuart of the cavalry, which was then unemployed; their reports were all of steady progress.

At Fair Oaks, however, no advantage was gained on either side, and the contest was continued with unflagging courage. It was near half-past 6 o'clock before I admitted to myself that Smith was engaged, not with a brigade, as I had obstinately thought, but with more than a division; but I thought that it would be injudicious to engage Magruder's division, our only reserve, so late in the day.

The firing was then violent at Seven Pines, and within a half hour the three Federal divisions were broken and driven from their position in confusion. It was then evident, however, from the obstinacy of our adversaries at Fair Oaks, that the battle would not be decided that day. I said so to the staff-officers near me, and told them that each regiment must sleep where it might be standing when the firing ceased for the night, to be ready to renew it at dawn next morning.

About half-past 7 o'clock I received a musket-shot in the shoulder, and was unhorsed soon after by a heavy fragment of shell which struck my

AFTER THE BATTLE OF SEVEN PINES.

Pettit's battery in Fort Richardson, in front of Fair Oaks Station, between the
Nine-mile road and the railroad.

AFTER THE BATTLE OF SEVEN PINES—PUTTING THE WOUNDED ON CARS.

TWO DAYS OF BATTLE AT SEVEN PINES (FAIR OAKS).

BY GUSTAVUS W. SMITH, MAJOR-GENERAL, C. S. A.

Commander of the left wing at the battle of Seven Pines, and during a portion of the
second day acting commander of the Army.

breast. I was borne from the field — first to a house on the roadside, thence to Richmond. The firing ceased before I had been carried a mile from it. The conflict at Fair Oaks was terminated by darkness only. . . .

The operations of the Confederate troops in this battle were very much retarded by the broad ponds of rain-water,— in many places more than knee-deep,— by the deep mud, and by the dense woods and thickets that covered the ground.

Brigadier-General Hatton was among the killed, and Brigadier-Generals Pettigrew and Hampton were severely wounded. The latter kept his saddle, and served to the end of the action. Among the killed on the Williamsburg road were Colonels Moore, of Alabama, Jones, and Lomax.

The troops on the ground at nightfall were: on the Confederate side, 22 brigades, more than half of which had not been in action; and on the Federal side 6 divisions in 3 corps, two-thirds of which had fought, and half of which had been totally defeated.

Two Federal divisions were at Fair Oaks, and three and a half at Savage's, three miles off, and half an one two miles nearer Bottom's Bridge. The Southern troops were united, and in a position to overwhelm either fraction of the Northern army, while holding the other in check.

Officers of the Federal army have claimed a victory at Seven Pines. The Confederates had such evidences of victory as cannon, captured intrenchments, and not only sleeping on the field, but passing the following day there, so little disturbed by the Federal troops as to gather, in woods, thickets, mud, and water, 6700 muskets and rifles. Besides, the Federal army had been advancing steadily until the day of this battle; after it they made not another step forward, but employed themselves industriously in intrenching. . . .

WHERE the Williamsburg "old stage" road is intersected by the Nine-mile road, at a point seven miles east of Richmond was fought the first great contest between the Confederate Army of Northern Virginia and the Federal Army of the Potomac. The junction of these two roads is called Seven Pines. About one mile from Seven Pines, where the Nine-mile road crosses the Richmond and the York River Railroad, there is a station called Fair Oaks. Before the action ended there was a good deal of fighting near the latter place. The Federals called the action of May 31st and June 1st the battle of Fair Oaks. . . .

When the signal for attack was given, only two regiments of Rodes's brigade had reached Hill's position on the Williamsburg road, about one thousand yards in front of the Federal picket-line. But the other regiments of this brigade came up soon after. At 1 o'clock the signal-guns were fired, and Hill's division at once moved forward. . . .

Whilst Hill's troops were coming into position, their movements had been reported to General Silas Casey, who commanded the Federal first line of defense. He at once ordered one regiment to go forward about eight hundred yards on the Williamsburg road, and support the picket-line; the working parties were called in, batteries harnessed up, and the troops formed, ready to take their assigned places. In a short time the Confederate signal-guns were heard, and the division was ordered into position to resist attack. The camps of these troops were immediately in rear of the earthworks. Palmer's brigade on the left, Wessells's in the center, and Naglee's brigade were detached,

supporting the picket-line, as already stated. About one-half of this division was placed in the rifle-pits on the right and left of the redoubt; the others were put in front, with orders to contest the advance of the Confederates against the first abatis, and Spratt's battery was placed four hundred yards in advance of the earthworks, on the north side of the road, closely supported by three regiments of Naglee's brigade and one of Palmer's.

In moving to attack, Rodes's brigade was on the south side of the road, supported by Rains; Garland's brigade, on the north side of the road, was supported by G. B. Anderson. All were in the dense and marshy woods, wading through water occasionally from two to three feet deep, the whole way obstructed by undergrowth, which often prevented commanders from seeing more than one company of their men at a time. General Hill had taken the precaution to order every man to wear in action a white strip of cloth around his hat as a battle-badge. Garland moved a few minutes before Rodes was ready. His skirmishers soon struck the Federal picket-line, and the shock of Garland's brigade fell upon the small regiment of raw troops that had been ordered into the woods to support the Federal pickets. That regiment fell back to the abatis just in time to prevent being enveloped and destroyed. And it was soon driven through the abatis in great disorder. . . .

In the mean time the contest around the battery at the abatis was close and desperate. Rodes's brigade was hotly engaged on the south side of the road and General Hill had ordered Carter's battery

to the front. The Federals stubbornly held their ground, and Hill now detached General Rains to make a wide flank movement through the woods to the right in order to turn the left of Casey's earthworks. From the edge of the wood, south of the Williamsburg road, Rains's brigade commenced firing on the flank and rear of the troops posted in Casey's rifle-pits. General Hill says:

"I now noticed commotion in the camps and redoubt, and indications of evacuating the position. Rodes took skilful advantage of this commotion, and moved up his brigade in beautiful order and took possession of the redoubt and rifle-pits."

Pending this contest for Casey's earthworks, General Keyes had sent two regiments from the second line direct to Casey's assistance, and a short time before those works were carried he sent General Couch, with two regiments, to attack the Confederate left, and thus relieve the pressure on Casey's front. Before Couch could get into position Casey's line was carried, and General Keyes made immediate preparations for the defense of the line at Seven Pines, held by Couch's division. Peck's brigade was on the left, Devens's in the center, and the regiments of Abercrombie's brigade, that had not been detached, were on the right. Casey's troops, in falling back from their earthworks, endeavored to make a stand at the abatis in front of Couch's line, and General Keyes sent forward one regiment of Devens's brigade to assist in checking the advance of the Confederates. Casey's men were driven through the abatis, and the regiment of Devens's brigade was hurled back in disorder, and could not be rallied until they had retreated beyond the earthworks from which they had advanced. A large proportion of the men of Palmer's and Wessells's brigades having been thrown into great disorder whilst retiring through the second abatis, and finding the earthworks of

MAJOR-GENERAL ERASMUS D. KEYES, U. S. V.

WOUNDED FROM THE BATTLE OF SEVEN PINES, IN THE STREETS OF RICHMOND.

MAJOR-GENERAL JOHN B. MAGRUDER, C. S. A.

the second line already crowded, continued to retreat; but some of them, with nearly the whole of Naglee's brigade, remained upon the field. The Confederates in the immediate front of Seven Pines were now pressing into the second abatis, and there seemed to be strong probability that they would soon break through it and carry the earthworks of Keyes's second line. Thus, after more than two hours' close and bloody fighting, Hill's division un-aided had captured the Federal first line of defense, and was closely pressing upon their second line. Hill then sent to Longstreet for another brigade. In a few minutes "the magnificent brigade of R. H. Anderson" came to Hill's support. . . .

It has already been shown that on May 31st the Confederates struck Keyes's corps, isolated at Seven Pines, with four brigades, and increased the attacking force to five brigades after Keyes had been reinforced by Heintzelman. June 1st, the Confederate attack was made against the left wing of French's brigade, which, with one regiment of Howard's brigade on its left, formed the front line of Richardson's division. On the left of that division was Birney's brigade of Kearny's division. . . .

In this attack the regiment of Howard's brigade on the extreme left of Richardson's front line was broken, fell back behind the second line, and was not again in action. The regiment next to it on the right was forced back a short distance. The left of Richardson's front line was so rudely shaken that all available means were used to strengthen it; a battery and Meagher's brigade were put in to cover the gap, and Burns's brigade, previously detached to cover the communications with the bridges, was recalled and hurriedly sent by General Sumner to Richardson's assistance. . . .

It was about 8 A. M. when General Howard, with two regiments of his brigade, relieved the left wing of French's brigade and took up the fighting. Just at that time the three regiments of Birney's brigade south of the railroad, whose strong advanced guards had been slowly driven back, were rapidly thrown forward. The regiment next the railroad struck the flank of the Confederates just at the time Howard was advancing against their front; and

under these two attacks the Confederates gave way in great disorder. The center regiment, of Birney's three, met with but little resistance until it struck a Confederate force in strong position on a wood road parallel to and three hundred to four hundred yards south of the railroad, in front of the left wing of French's brigade. The two regiments of Howard's brigade, in their forward movement, soon struck the same Confederates in the densely tangled wood. These three Federal regiments, after repeated efforts to dislodge the Confederates,—Pickett's brigade,—were repulsed with severe losses, and resumed position in the lines from which they had advanced.

General Howard was wounded just as his two regiments were coming to close quarters with Pickett's brigade. . . .

General Smith here refers to events in front of Longstreet's command on the Williamsburg road June 1st. His narrative proceeds with an account of his (Smith's) efforts, as temporary commander of the army, to have Longstreet renew the attacks that day. He received from Longstreet two notes dated 10 A. M. and 10:30 A. M., respectively, stating that apparently he (Longstreet) was confronted by the entire Union army, and asking reinforcements. A third message, dated 1:30 P. M., read: "The next attack will be from Sumner's division. I think that if we can whip it we shall be comparatively safe. . . . I sincerely hope that we may succeed against them in their next effort. Oh, that I had ten thousand men more!" General Smith concludes:

To complete this sketch of the battle of Seven Pines, it is essential to mention that when I received General Longstreet's note, dated 1.30 P. M., June 1st, which ended with the exclamation, "Oh, that I had ten thousand men more!" General Lee had just taken command of the army. He seemed very much impressed by the state of affairs on the Williamsburg road, as depicted in General Longstreet's note. I assured him, however, that Longstreet was mistaken in supposing that the whole Federal army was opposed to him; that I had

several hours before nearly stripped the Chickahominy, between New Bridge and Mechanicsville, in order to send him reinforcements; and that the danger to Richmond, if any, was not then on the Williamsburg road, if it ever had been.

General Lee gave me no orders that day. The fact that Longstreet's and D. H. Hill's divisions were sent back to their former camps induces me to believe that this was in compliance with orders given by General Lee to General Longstreet—perhaps for the reason that on May 31st we had not fully succeeded in crushing one Federal corps isolated at Seven Pines, and on June 1st had lost all the ground beyond Seven Pines that we had gained the day previous.

I was completely prostrated on the 2d of June by an attack of paralysis, no symptom of which was manifested within eighteen hours after Lee relieved me of the command of the army. But for that misfortune, I would certainly have required all subordinates to report to me events that took place on the field in their respective commands whilst I was in control of the army.

The detailed reports of regimental and brigade commanders on both sides in this battle show many instances of close, persistent, and bloody fighting, such as have been seldom equaled by any troops on any field. Cases of temporary confusion and disorder occurred, but fair examination shows there was good reason for this. In reference to the general management, however, it may well be said that General McClellan committed a grave error in allowing Keyes's corps to remain isolated for several days within easy striking distance of General Johnston's army. The intention of the latter to throw Longstreet's division against Keyes's exposed and weak right flank was the best plan that could have been adopted. The first great blunder consisted in Longstreet's taking his division from the Nine-mile road to the Williamsburg road, and

the next in placing six brigades on the Charles City road, where there was no enemy. . . .

It is not proposed to speculate here upon what might have happened on the second day, if General Longstreet had made any attempt to carry out the orders he received to renew the attack. But it may be well to emphasize the fact that if Longstreet's division had promptly moved on the Nine-mile road at daybreak, May 31st, and been put in close action on that side, whilst D. H. Hill's division attacked in front,—as Johnston certainly intended,—there would have been no occasion to make excuses for the failure of complete Confederate success in wiping out Keyes's corps, early in the morning of May 31st, before it could have been reinforced by either Heintzelman or Sumner.

NOTE.—On the 15th of May, the Union gun-boats opened fire on the forts at Drewry's Bluff, twelve miles below Richmond, and soon after Johnston's army retired, opening the way for McClellan's advance to within seven miles of Richmond, whose citizens believed at this time that the Confederate authorities would be compelled to evacuate the city. The archives were shipped to Columbia, S. C., the public treasure was kept on cars ready for transportation to a place of safety. Confidence was restored before the battle of Seven Pines. On May 25th and 26th, Lieutenant F. C. Davis, of the 3d Pennsylvania Cavalry, with eleven men rode from Bottom's Bridge, by way of White Oak Bridge and Charles City Court House, to the James River and communicated with the gun-boat fleet. After the battle of Seven Pines, General Lee determined to defend Richmond on the line then held by his army. This fact, in connection with the success of General Jackson in freeing the Shenandoah Valley of Union forces, restored the confidence of the people at Richmond. A large draft of soldiers from the ranks furnished a laboring force to build intrenchments, and slaves in the counties around Richmond were impressed for the work.

On the 18th of June, Brigadier-General Cuvier Grover's brigade, of Hooker's division, made a reconnoissance between the Williamsburg road and the railroad, and found the Confederates in force behind earthworks. The divisions of Hooker and Kearny advanced on the 25th to a point called Oak Grove, about four miles from Richmond, in front of Seven Pines. This was the nearest approach to Richmond during the investment by McClellan.

STUART'S RIDE AROUND McCLELLAN.

BY W. T. ROBINS, COLONEL, C. S. A.

THE battle of "Seven Pines," or "Fair Oaks," had been fought with no result. The temporary success of the Confederates early in the engagement had been more than counterbalanced by the reverses they sustained on the second day, and the two armies lay passively watching each other in front of Richmond. At this time the cavalry of Lee's army was commanded by General J. E. B. Stuart, and this restless officer conceived the idea of flanking the right wing of the Federal army near Ashland, and moving around to the rear, to cross the Chickahominy River at a place called Sycamore Ford, in New Kent County, march over to the James River, and return to the Confederate lines near Deep Bottom, in Henrico County. In carrying out this plan, Stuart would completely encircle the army of General McClellan. At the time of this movement the writer was adjutant of the 9th Virginia cavalry. When the orders were issued from headquarters directing the several commands destined to form the expedition to prepare three days' rations, and the ordnance officers to issue sixty rounds of ammunition to each man, I remember the surmises and conjectures as to our destination. The officers and men were in high spirits in anticipation of a fight, and when the bugles rang out "Boots and Saddles," every man was ready. The men left behind in camp were bewailing their luck, and those forming the detail for the expedition were elated at the prospect of some excitement. "Good-by, boys; we are going to help old Jack drive the Yanks into the Potomac!" I heard one of them shout to those left behind.

On the afternoon of June 12th we went out to the Brooke turnpike, preparatory to the march. The cavalry column was the 9th Virginia, commanded by Colonel W. H. F. Lee, the 1st Virginia, led by Colonel Fitz Lee, and the Jeff Davis Legion, under Colonel Martin. A section of the Stuart Horse Artillery, commanded by Captain Pelham, accompanied the expedition. The whole numbered twelve hundred men. The first night was passed in bivouac in the vicinity of Ashland, and orders were issued enforcing strict silence and forbidding the use of fires, as the success of the expedition would depend upon secrecy and celerity. On the following morning, at the break of dawn, the troopers were mounted and the march was begun without a bugle blast, and the column headed direct for Hanover Court House, distant about

CAVALRY ORDERLY.
From a photograph.

DUEL BETWEEN A UNION CAVALRYMAN AND A CONFEDERATE TROOPER.

two hours' ride. Here we had the first sight of the enemy. A scouting party of the 5th U. S. Cavalry was in the village, but speedily decamped when our troops were ascertained to be Confederates. One prisoner was taken after a hot chase across country. We now moved rapidly to Hawes's Shop, where a Federal picket was surprised and captured without firing a shot. Hardly had the prisoners been disarmed and turned over to the provost guard when the Confederate advance was driven in upon the main body by a squadron of Federal cavalry, sent out from Old Church to ascertain by reconnoissance whether the report of a Confederate advance was true or false. General Stuart at once ordered Colonel W. H. F. Lee, commanding the regiment leading the column, to throw forward a squadron to meet the enemy. Colonel Lee directed Captain Swann, chief of the leading squadron of his regiment, to charge with the saber. Swann moved off at a trot, and, turning a corner of the road, saw the enemy's squadron about two hundred yards in front of him. The order to charge was given, and the men dashed forward in fine style. The onset was so sudden that the Federal cavalry broke and scattered in confusion. The latter had a start of barely two hundred yards, but the Confederate yell that broke upon the air lent them wings, and only a few fell into our hands. The rest made their escape after a chase of a mile and a half. Now the road became very narrow, and the brush on either side was a place so favorable for an ambuscade that Captain Swann

deemed it prudent to draw rein and sound the bugle to recall his men. Stuart, who had been marching steadily onward with the main body of the Confederate column, soon arrived at the front, and the advance-guard, which I had all along commanded, was directed to move forward again. I at once dismounted the men, and pushed forward up a hill in my front. Just beyond the hill, I ran into a force of Federal cavalry drawn up in column of fours, ready to charge. Just as my advance-guard was about to run into him, I heard their commanding officer give the order to charge. I fell back and immediately notified General Stuart of the presence of the enemy. Captain Latané, commanding a squadron of the 9th Virginia, was directed to move forward and clear the road. He moved up the hill at a trot, and when in sight of the enemy in the road gave the command to charge, and with a yell the men rushed forward. At the top of the hill, simultaneously with Latané's order to charge, a company of Federal cavalry, deployed as skirmishers in the woods on the right of the road, were stampeded, and rushed back into the woods to make good their retreat to their friends. The head of Latané's squadron, then just fairly up the hill, was in the line of their retreat and was separated from the rest of the squadron, cut off by the rush of the Federals, and borne along with them up the road toward the enemy. I was riding at the side of Latané, and just at the time when the Federal company rushed back into the road Captain Latané fell from his horse, shot dead.

The rush of the Federals separated myself and six of the leading files of the squadron from our friends, and we were borne along by the flying Federals. Although the Federal cavalry both in front and rear were in full retreat, our situation was perilous in the extreme. Soon we were pushed by foes in our rear into the ranks of those in our front, and a series of hand-to-hand combats ensued. To shoot or to cut us down was the aim of every Federal as he neared us, but we did what we could to defend ourselves. Every one of my comrades was shot or cut down, and I alone escaped unhurt. After having been borne along by the retreating enemy for perhaps a quarter of a mile, I leaped my horse over the fence into the field and so got away.

Now came the rush of the Confederate column, sweeping the road clear, and capturing many prisoners. At this point my regiment was relieved by the 1st Virginia, and Colonel Lee continued the pursuit. The Federals did not attempt to make a stand until they reached Old Church. Here their officers called a halt, and made an attempt to rally to defend their camp. Fitz Lee soon swept them out, and burned their camp. They made no other attempt to stand, and we heard no more of them as an organized body, but many prisoners were taken as we passed along. We had surprised them, taken them in detail, and far outnumbered them at all points. The Federal forces, as we afterward learned, were commanded by General Philip St. George Cooke, father-in-law to General Stuart, to whom the latter sent a polite message. The casualties in this skirmish were slight — one man killed on each side, and about fifteen or twenty wounded on the Confederate side, mostly saber cuts. . . .

We were soon far in rear of McClellan's army, which lay directly between us and Richmond. It was thought probable that the Federal cavalry was concentrating in *our* rear to cut off our retreat. We kept straight on, by Smith's store, through New Kent County to Tunstall's station, on the York River Railroad. . . .

The full moon lighted us on our way as we passed along the River road, and frequently the windings of the road brought us near to and in sight of the James River, where lay the enemy's fleet. In the gray twilight of the dawn of Sunday, we passed the "Double Gates," "Strawberry Plains," and "Tighlman's gate" in succession. At "Tighlman's" we could see the masts of the fleet, not far off. Happily for us, the banks were high, and I imagine they had no lookout in the rigging, and we passed by unobserved. The sight of the enemy's fleet had aroused us somewhat, when "Who goes there?" rang out on the stillness of the early morning. The challenger proved to be a vidette of the 10th Virginia Cavalry, commanded by Colonel J. Lucius Davis, who was picketing that road. Soon I was shaking hands with Colonel Davis and receiving his congratulations. . . .

We lost one man killed and a few wounded, and no prisoners. The most important result was the confidence the men had gained in themselves and in their leaders. The country rang out with praises of the men who had raided entirely around General McClellan's powerful army, bringing prisoners and plunder from under his very nose. The Southern papers were filled with accounts of the expedition, none accurate, and most of them marvelous.

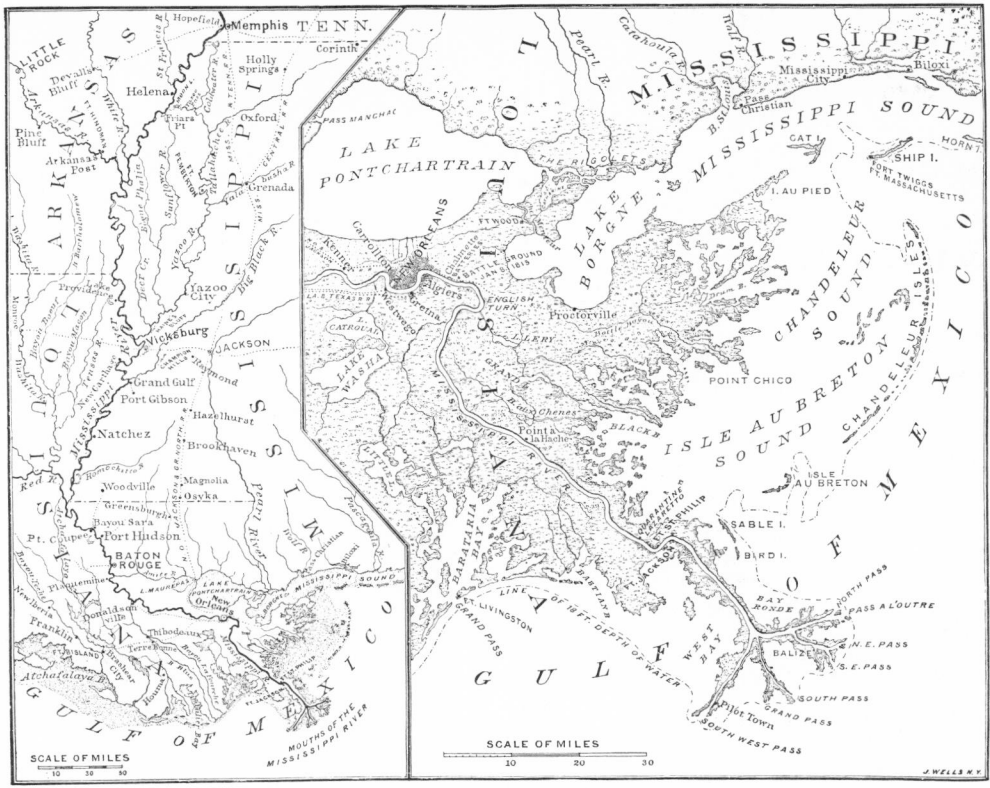

MAPS OF THE LOWER MISSISSIPPI.

THE OPENING OF THE LOWER MISSISSIPPI AND THE CAPTURE OF NEW ORLEANS.

THE UNION SIDE.

BY DAVID D. PORTER, ADMIRAL, U. S. N.
Commander of the Fleet of Mortar-Batteries under Flag-Officer Farragut.

THE most important event of the War of the Rebellion, with the exception of the fall of Richmond, was the capture of New Orleans and the forts Jackson and St. Philip, guarding the approach to that city. To appreciate the nature of this victory, it is necessary to have been an actor in it, and to be able to comprehend not only the immediate results to the Union cause, but the whole bearing of the fall of New Orleans on the Civil War, which at that time had attained its most formidable proportions.

Previous to fitting out the expedition against New Orleans, there were eleven Southern States in open rebellion against the Government of the United States, or, as it was termed by the Southern people, in a state of secession. Their harbors were all more or less closed against our ships-of-war, either by the heavy forts built originally by the General Government for their protection, or by torpedoes and sunken vessels. Through four of these seceding States ran the great river Mississippi, and both of its banks, from Memphis to its mouth, were lined with powerful batteries. On the west side of the river were three important

States, Louisiana, Arkansas, and Texas, with their great tributaries to the Mississippi,—the White, the Arkansas, and the Red,—which were in a great measure secure from the attacks of the Union forces. These States could not only raise half a million soldiers, but could furnish the Confederacy with provisions of all kinds, and cotton enough to supply the Rebel Government with the sinews of war. New Orleans was the largest Southern city, and contained all the resources of modern warfare, having great workshops where machinery of the most powerful kind could be built, and having artisans capable of building ships in wood or iron, casting heavy guns, or making small arms. The people of the city were in no way behind the most zealous secessionists in energy of purpose and in hostility to the Government of the United States.

The Mississippi is thus seen to have been the backbone of the Rebellion, which it should have been the first duty of the Federal Government to break. At the very outset of the war it should have been attacked at both ends at the same time, before the Confederates had time to fortify its banks or to turn the guns in the Government forts against the

D. G. Farragut
Admiral, U. S. N.

95

"CLIFTON" AND "WESTFIELD," ALTERED NEW YORK CITY FERRY-BOATS.　　　"OWASCO."　　　"HARRIET LANE."

MORTAR-STEAMERS ATTACKING THE WATER-BATTERY OF FORT JACKSON.

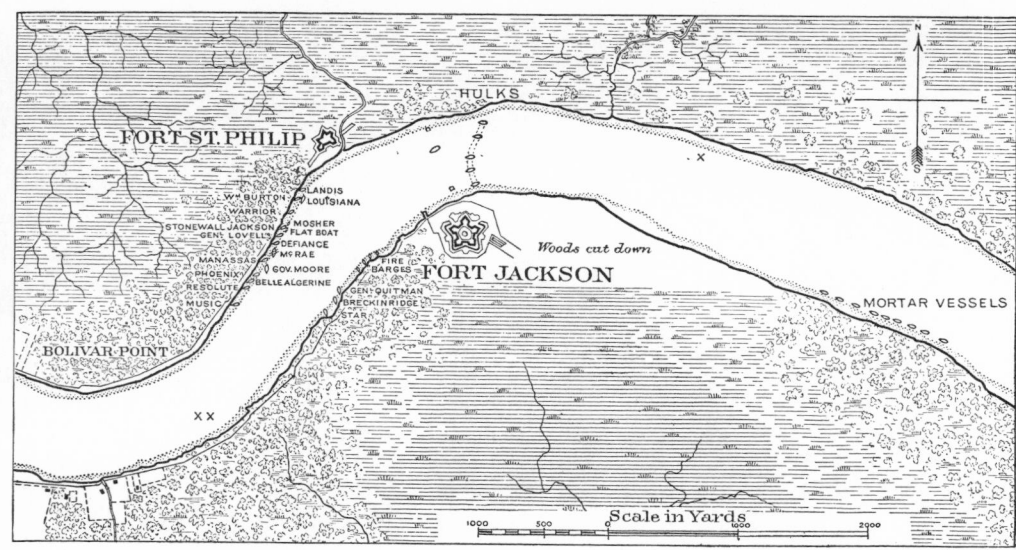

MAP SHOWING THE DEFENSES OF THE MISSISSIPPI AND THE POSITIONS OF THE MORTAR-FLEET AT THE OPENING OF THE BOMBARDMENT.

Union forces. A dozen improvised gun-boats would have held the entire length of the river if they had been sent there in time. The efficient fleet with which Du Pont, in November, 1861, attacked and captured the works at Port Royal could at that time have steamed up to New Orleans and captured the city without difficulty. Any three vessels could have passed Forts Jackson and St. Philip a month after the commencement of the war, and could have gone on to Cairo, if necessary, without any trouble. But the Federal Government neglected to approach the mouth of the Mississippi until a year after hostilities had commenced, except to blockade. The Confederates made good use of this interval, putting forth all their resources and fortifying not only the approaches to New Orleans, but both banks of the river as far north as Memphis.

. . . . . .

Farragut experienced great difficulty in getting the larger vessels over the bar. The *Hartford* and *Brooklyn* were the only two that could pass without lightening. The *Richmond* stuck fast in the mud every time she attempted to cross. The *Mississippi* drew two feet too much water, and the *Pensacola*, after trying several times to get over, ran on a wreck a hundred yards away from the channel. There she lay, with her propeller half out of water, thumping on the wreck as she was driven in by the wind and sea. Pilots had been procured at Pilot Town, near by; but they were either treacherous or nervous, and all their attempts to get the heavy ships over the bar were failures. Farragut felt extremely uncomfortable at the prospect before him, but I convinced him that I could get the vessels over if he would place them under my control, and he consented to do so. I first tried with the *Richmond* (Commander Alden), and, although she had grounded seven times when in charge of a pilot, I succeeded at the first attempt, crossed the bar, and anchored off Pilot Town. The next trial was with the frigate *Mississippi*. The vessel was lightened as much as possible by taking out her spars, sails, guns, provisions,

and coal. All the steamers of the mortar-fleet were then sent to her assistance, and after eight days' hard work they succeeded in pulling the *Mississippi* through. To get the *Pensacola* over looked even more difficult. I asked Captain Bailey to lend me the *Colorado* for a short time, and with this vessel I went as close as possible to the *Pensacola*, ran out a stream-cable to her stern, and, by backing hard on the *Colorado*, soon released her from her disagreeable position. The next day at 12 o'clock I passed her over the bar and anchored her off Pilot Town.

The U. S. Coast Survey steamer *Sachem*, commanded by a very competent officer, Mr. F. H. Gerdes, had been added to the expedition for the purpose of sounding the bar and river channel, and also to establish points and distances which should serve as guides to the commander of the mortar-flotilla. Mr. Gerdes and his assistants selected the positions of the bomb-vessels, furnished all the commanders of vessels with reliable charts, triangulated the river for eight miles below the forts, and planted small poles with white flags on the banks opposite the positions of the different vessels, each flag marked with the name of a vessel and the distance from the mouth of its mortar to the center of the fort. The boats of the surveyors were frequently attacked by sharp-shooters, who fired from concealed positions among the bushes of the river bank. During the bombardment the Coast Survey officers were employed day and night in watching that the vessels did not move an inch from their places, and

SECTION OF FORT ST. PHILIP DURING THE ENGAGEMENT.

The details of the fort drawn from a photograph.

the good effect of all this care was shown in the final result of the mortar practice.

Having finished the preliminary work, on the 16th of April Farragut moved up his fleet to within three miles of the forts, and informed me that I might commence the bombardment as soon as I was ready. The ships all anchored as they came up, but not in very good order, which led to some complications.

The place which I had selected for the first and third divisions of the mortar-vessels was under the lee of a thick wood on the right bank of the river, which presented in the direction of the fort an almost impenetrable mass. The forts could be plainly seen from the mast-heads of the mortar-schooners, which had been so covered with brush that the Confederate gunners could not distinguish them from the trees. The leading vessel of the first division, of seven vessels, under Lieutenant-Commanding Watson Smith, was placed at a point distant 2850 yards from Fort Jackson and 3680 yards from Fort St. Philip. The third division, commanded by Lieutenant Breese, came next in order, and the second division, under Lieutenant Queen, I placed on the east side of the river, the head of the line being 3680 yards from Fort Jackson.

The vessels now being in position, the signal was given to open fire; and on the morning of the 18th of April the bombardment fairly commenced, each mortar vessel having orders to fire once in ten minutes. The moment that the mortars belched forth their shells, both Jackson and St. Philip replied with

great fury; but it was some time before they could obtain our range, as we were well concealed behind our natural rampart. The enemy's fire was rapid, and, finding that it was becoming rather hot, I sent Lieutenant Guest up to the head of the line to open fire on the forts with his 11-inch pivot. This position he maintained for one hour and fifty minutes, and only abandoned it to fill up with ammunition. In the meantime the mortars on the left bank (Queen's division) were doing splendid work, though suffering considerably from the enemy's fire.

I went on board the vessels of this division to see how they were getting on, and found them so cut up that I considered it necessary to remove them, with Farragut's permission, to the opposite shore, under cover of the trees, near the other vessels, which had suffered but little. They held their position, however, until sundown, when the enemy ceased firing.

At 5 o'clock in the evening Fort Jackson was seen to be on fire, and, as the flames spread rapidly, the Confederates soon left their guns. There were many conjectures among the officers of the fleet as to what was burning. Some thought that it was a fire-raft, and I was inclined to that opinion myself until I had pulled up the river in a boat and, by the aid of a night-glass, convinced myself that the fort itself was in flames. This fact I at once reported to Farragut.

At nightfall the crews of the mortar-vessels were completely exhausted; but when it became known that every shell was falling inside of the fort, they redoubled their exertions and increased the rapidity of their fire to a shell every five minutes, or in all two hundred and forty shells an hour. During the night, in order to allow the men to rest, we slackened our fire, and only sent a shell once every half hour. Thus ended the first day's bombardment, which was more effective than that of any other day during the siege.

Next morning the bombardment was renewed and continued night and day until the end, with a result that is thus described in a letter from Colonel

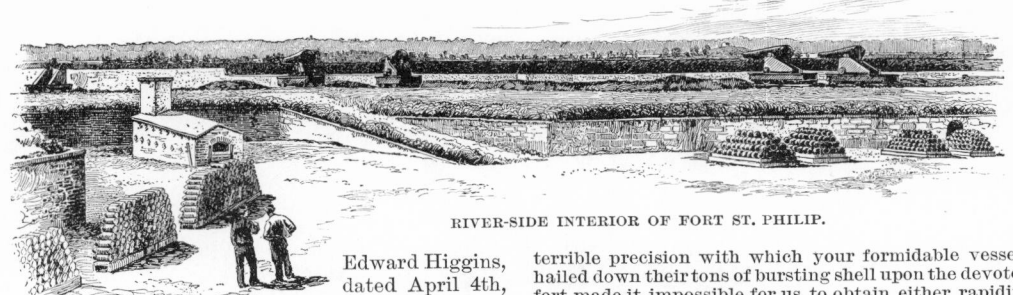

RIVER-SIDE INTERIOR OF FORT ST. PHILIP.

Edward Higgins, dated April 4th, 1872, which I received in answer to my inquiry on the subject:

"Your mortar-vessels were placed in position on the afternoon of the 17th of April, 1862, and opened fire at once upon Fort Jackson, where my headquarters were established. The practice was excellent from the commencement of the fire to the end, and continued without intermission until the morning of the 24th of April, when the fleet passed at about 4 o'clock. Nearly every shell of the many thousand fired at the fort lodged inside of the works. On the first night of the attack the citadel and all buildings in rear of the fort were fired by bursting shell, and also the sand-bag walls that had been thrown around the magazine doors. The fire, as you are aware, raged with great fury, and no effort of ours could subdue it. At this time, and nearly all this night, Fort Jackson was helpless; its magazines were inaccessible, and we could have offered no resistance to a passing fleet. The next morning a terrible scene of destruction presented itself. The wood-work of the citadel being all destroyed, and the crumbling walls being knocked about the fort by the bursting shells, made matters still worse for the garrison. The work of destruction from now until the morning of the 24th, when the fleet passed, was incessant.

"I was obliged to confine the men most rigidly to the casemates, or we should have lost the best part of the garrison. A shell, striking the parapet over one of the magazines, the wall of which was seven feet thick, penetrated five feet and failed to burst. If that shell had exploded, your work would have ended. Another burst near the magazine door, opening the earth and burying the sentinel and another man five feet in the same grave. The parapets and interior of the fort were completely honeycombed, and the large number of sand-bags with which we were supplied alone saved us from being blown to pieces a hundred times, our magazine doors being much exposed.

"On the morning of the 24th, when the fleet passed, the terrible precision with which your formidable vessels hailed down their tons of bursting shell upon the devoted fort made it impossible for us to obtain either rapidity or accuracy of fire, and thus rendered the passage comparatively easy. There was no very considerable damage done to our batteries, but few of the guns being dismounted by your fire; everything else in and around the fort was destroyed."

I was not ignorant of the state of affairs in the fort; for, on the third day of the bombardment, a deserter presented himself and gave us an account of the havoc created by our shells, although I had doubts of the entire truth of his statements. He represented that hundreds of shells had fallen into the fort, breaking in the bomb-proofs, setting fire to the citadel, and flooding the interior by cutting the levees. He also stated that the soldiers were in a desperate and demoralized condition. This was all very encouraging to us, and so stimulated the crews of the mortar-boats that they worked with unflagging zeal and energy. I took the deserter to Farragut, who, although impressed by his statement, was not quite prepared to take advantage of the opportunity; for at this time the line of hulks across the river was considered an insurmountable obstruction, and it was determined to examine and, if possible, remove it before the advance of the fleet.

On the night of the 20th an expedition was fitted out for the purpose of breaking the chain which was supposed to extend from one shore to the other. Two steamers, the *Pinola*, Lieutenant Crosby, and *Itasca*, Lieutenant Caldwell, were detailed for the purpose and placed under the direction of Captain Bell, chief-of-staff. Although the attempt was made under cover of darkness, the sharp eyes of the Confederate gunners soon discovered their ene-

DAVID D. PORTER, ADMIRAL, U. S. N.
In command of the mortar-fleet at Forts Jackson and St. Philip.

mies, and the whole fire of Fort Jackson was concentrated upon them. I had been informed of the intended movement by Farragut, so was ready to redouble the fire of the mortars at the proper time with good effect. In Farragut's words: "Commander Porter, however, kept up such a tremendous fire on them from the mortars that the enemy's shot did the gun-boats no injury, and the cable was separated and their connection broken sufficiently to pass through on the left bank of the river."

The work of the mortar-fleet was now almost over. We had kept up a heavy fire night and day for nearly 5 days — about 2800 shells every 24 hours; in all about 16,800 shells. The men were nearly worn out for want of sleep and rest. The ammunition was giving out, one of the schooners was sunk, and although the rest had received little actual damage from the enemy's shot, they were badly shaken up by the concussion of the mortars.

On the 23d instant I represented the state of affairs to the flag-officer, and he concluded to move on past the works, which I felt sure he could do with but little loss to his squadron. He recognized the importance of making an immediate attack, and called a council of the commanders of vessels, which resulted in a determination to pass the forts that night. The movement was postponed, however, until the next morning, for the reason that the carpenters of one of the larger ships were at work down the river, and the commander did not wish to proceed without them. The ironclad *Louisiana* had now made her appearance, and her commander was being strongly urged by General Duncan to drop down below the forts [see the map, p. 96] and open fire upon the fleet with his heavy rifle-guns. On the 22d General Duncan wrote to Commander Mitchell from Fort Jackson:

FARRAGUT'S FLAG-SHIP THE "HARTFORD."

THE "CAYUGA" BREAKING THROUGH THE CONFEDERATE FLEET.

THE CONFEDERATE "RIVER DEFENSE" RAM "STONEWALL JACKSON."

"It is of vital importance that the present fire of the enemy should be withdrawn from us, which you alone can do. This can be done in the manner suggested this morning under the cover of our guns, while your work on the boat can be carried on in safety and security. Our position is a critical one, dependent entirely on the powers of endurance of our casemates, many of which have been completely shattered, and are crumbling away by repeated shocks; and, therefore, I respectfully but earnestly again urge my suggestion of this morning on your notice. Our magazines are also in danger."

Fortunately for us, Commander Mitchell was not equal to the occasion, and the *Louisiana* remained tied up to the bank, where she could not obstruct the river, or throw the Union fleet into confusion while passing the forts.

While Farragut was making his preparations, the enemy left no means untried to drive the mortar-boats from their position. A couple of heavy guns in Fort St. Philip kept up a continual fire on the head of the mortar column, and the Confederates used their mortars at intervals, but only succeeded in sinking one mortar-schooner and damaging a few others. A body of riflemen was once sent out against us from the forts, but it was met by a heavy fire and soon repulsed.

Two o'clock on the morning of the 24th instant was fixed upon as the time for the fleet to start, and Farragut had previously given the necessary orders to the commanders of vessels, instructing them to prepare their ships for action by sending down their light spars, painting their hulls mud-color, etc.; also to hang their chain-cables over the sides abreast the engines, as a protection against the enemy's shot. He issued the following "General Order":

"UNITED STATES FLAG-SHIP *Hartford*, MISSISSIPPI RIVER, "April 20th, 1862.

"The flag-officer, having heard all the opinions expressed by the different commanders, is of the opinion that whatever is to be done will have to be done quickly, or we shall be again reduced to a blockading squadron, without the means of carrying on the bombardment, as we have nearly expended all the shells and fuses, and material for making cartridges. He has always entertained the same opinions which are expressed by Commander Porter; that is, there are three modes of attack, and the question is, which is the one to be adopted? His own opinion is that a combination of two should be made, viz.: the forts should be run, and when a force is once above the forts, to protect the troops, they should be landed at quarantine from the gulf side by bringing them through the bayou, and then our forces should

move up the river, mutually aiding each other as it can be done to advantage.

"When, in the opinion of the flag-officer, the propitious time has arrived, the signal will be made to weigh and advance to the conflict. If, in his opinion, at the time of arriving at the respective positions of the different divisions of the fleet, we have the advantage, he will make the signal for close action, No. 8, and abide the result, conquer or to be conquered, drop anchor or keep under way, as in his opinion is best.

"Unless the signal above mentioned is made, it will be understood that the first order of sailing will be formed after leaving Fort St. Philip, and we will proceed up the river in accordance with the original opinion expressed. The programme of the order of sailing accompanies this general order, and the commanders will hold themselves in readiness for the service as indicated. Very respectfully, your obedient servant, D. G. FARRAGUT, Flag-Officer West Gulf Blockading Squadron."

Farragut's first plan was to lead the fleet with his flag-ship, the *Hartford*, to be closely followed by the *Brooklyn*, *Richmond*, *Pensacola*, and *Mississippi*, thinking it well to have his heavy vessels in the van, where they could immediately crush any naval force that might appear against them. This plan was a better one than that afterward adopted; but he was induced to change the order of his column by the senior commanders of the fleet, who represented to him that it was unwise for the commander-in-chief to take the brunt of the battle. They finally obtained his reluctant consent to an arrangement by which Captain Bailey was to lead in the gun-boat *Cayuga*, commanded by Lieutenant N. B. Harrison,—a good selection, as it afterward proved, for these officers were gallant and competent men, well qualified for the position. Captain Bailey

MORTAR-SCHOONERS ENGAGED AGAINST FORT JACKSON.
Distance of leading schooner from the fort, 2850 yards. Duration of fire, six days.
Total number of shells fired, 16,800.

had volunteered for the service, and left nothing undone to overcome Farragut's reluctance to give up what was then considered the post of danger, though it turned out to be less hazardous than the places in the rear.

The mortar-flotilla steamers under my command were directed to move up before the fleet weighed anchor, and to be ready to engage the water-batteries of Fort Jackson as the fleet passed. These batteries mounted some of the heaviest guns in the defenses, and were depended upon to do efficient work.

The commanders of vessels were informed of the change of plan, and instructed to follow in line according to the subjoined order of attack:

At 2 o'clock on the morning of April 24th all of the Union vessels began to heave up their anchors. It was a still, clear night, and the click of the capstans, with the grating of the chain-cables as they passed through the hawse-holes, made a great noise, which we feared would serve as a warning to our enemies. This conjecture proved to be correct, for the Confederates were on the alert in both forts and steamers to meet the invaders. One fact only was in our favor, and that was the division of their forces under three different heads, which prevented unanimity of action. In every other respect the odds were against us.

Before Farragut ascended the river, the French admiral and Captain Preedy, of the English frigate *Mersey*, had both been up as far as the forts and had communicated with the military commanders. On their return, they gave discouraging accounts of the defenses, and pronounced it impossible for our fleet to pass them. This, of course, did not tend to cheer our sailors. There were some in the fleet who were doubtful of success, and there was not that confidence on our side that should have existed on such an occasion; but when it was seen that the river obstructions and rafts had been washed away by the currents, and that there appeared to be an open way up the river, every one became more hopeful.

The entire fleet did not get fully under way until half-past 2 A. M. The current was strong, and although the ships proceeded as rapidly as their steam-power would permit, our leading vessel, the *Cayuga*, did not get under fire until a quarter of 3 o'clock, when both Jackson and St. Philip opened on her at the same moment. Five steamers of the mortar-flotilla took their position below the water-battery of Fort Jackson, at a distance of less than two hundred yards, and, pouring in grape, canister, and shrapnel, kept down the fire of that battery. The mortars opened at the same moment with great fury, and the action commenced in earnest.

ORDER OF ATTACK.

First Division,
CAPTAIN THEODORUS BAILEY.

Cayuga.
Pensacola.
Mississippi.
Oneida.
Varuna.
Katahdin.
Kineo.
Wissahickon.

Center Division,
FLAG-OFFICER FARRAGUT.

Hartford.
Brooklyn.
Richmond.

Third Division,
CAPTAIN H. H. BELL.

Sciota.
Iroquois.
Kennebec.
Pinola.
Itasca.
Winona.

Captain Bailey, in the *Cayuga,* followed by the other vessels of his division in compact order, passed the line of obstructions without difficulty. He had no sooner attained this point, however, than he was obliged to face the guns of Fort St. Philip, which did him some damage before he was able to fire a shot in return. He kept steadily on, however, and as soon as his guns could be brought to bear, poured in grape and canister with good effect and passed safe above. He was here met by the enemy's gun-boats, and, although he was beset by several large steamers at the same time, he succeeded in driving them off. The *Oneida* and *Varuna* came to the support of their leader, and by the rapid fire of their heavy guns soon dispersed the enemy's flotilla. This was more congenial work for our men and officers than that through which they had just passed, and it was soon evident that the coolness and discipline of our navy gave it a great advantage over the fleet of the enemy.

Bailey dashed on up the river, followed by his division, firing into everything they met; and soon after the head of the flag-officer's division had passed the forts, most of the river craft were disabled, and the battle was virtually won. This was evident even to Lieutenant-Colonel Higgins, who, when he saw our large ships pass by, ex-

MORTAR-FLEET IN THE DISTANCE.

WRECKS OF CONFEDERATE RIVER FLEET.   MORTAR-STEAMERS ATTACKING WATER-BATTERY, FORT JACKSON.   "RICHMOND."   FORT JACKSON.

FORT ST. PHILIP AND CONFEDERATE IRON-CLAD "LOUISIANA."   FARRAGUT'S DIVISION OF THE FLEET, LED BY THE "HARTFORD."   "MANASSAS," CONFEDERATE.   "IROQUOIS."   "MCRAE," CONFEDERATE.

CONFEDERATE RAMS AND SINKING VESSELS.   REAR VESSEL OF BAILEY'S DIVISION.

BIRD'S-EYE VIEW OF THE PASSAGE OF THE FORTS BELOW NEW ORLEANS, APRIL 24, 1862. THE SECOND DIVISION IN ACTION, 4:15 A. M.

claimed, "Better go to cover, boys; our cake is all dough!"

In the meantime the *Varuna,* being a swift vessel, passed ahead of the other ships in the division, and pushed on up the river after the fleeing enemy, until she found herself right in the midst of them. The Confederates, supposing in the dark that the *Varuna* was one of their own vessels, did not attack her until Commander Boggs made himself known by delivering his fire right and left. One shot exploded the boiler of a large steamer crowded with troops, and she drifted ashore; three other vessels were driven ashore in flames. At daylight the *Varuna* was attacked by the *Governor Moore,* a powerful steamer, fitted as a ram, and commanded by Lieutenant Beverley Kennon, late of the U. S. Navy. This vessel raked the *Varuna* with her bow-gun along the port gangway, killing 5 or 6 men; and while the Union vessel was gallantly returning this fire, her side was pierced twice by the iron prow of the ram. The Confederate ram *Stonewall Jackson* also attacked the *Varuna,* ramming her twice about amidships; the *Varuna* at the same moment punished her severely with grape and canister from her 8-inch guns, and finally drove her out of action in a disabled condition and in flames. But the career of the *Varuna* was ended; she began to fill rapidly, and her gallant commander was obliged to run her into shoal water, where she soon went to the bottom. Captain Lee, of the *Oneida,* seeing that his companion needed assistance, went to his relief, and rescued the officers and men of the *Varuna.* The two Confederate rams were set on fire by their crews and abandoned. Great gallantry was displayed on both sides during the conflict of these smaller steamers, which really bore the brunt of the battle, and the Union commanders showed great skill in managing their vessels.

Bailey's division may be said to have swept everything before it. The *Pensacola,* with her heavy batteries, drove the men from the guns at Fort St. Philip, and made it easier for the ships astern to get by. Fort St. Philip had not been at all damaged by the mortars, as it was virtually beyond their reach, and it was from the guns of that work that our ships received the greatest injury.

As most of the vessels of Bailey's division swept past the turn above the forts, Farragut came upon the scene with the *Hartford* and *Brooklyn.* The other ship of Farragut's division, the *Richmond,* Commander James Alden, got out of the line and passed up on the west side of the river, near where I was engaged with the mortar-steamers in silencing the water-batteries of Fort Jackson. At this moment the Confederates in Fort Jackson had nearly all been driven from their guns by bombs from the mortar-boats and the grape and canister from the steamers. I hailed Alden, and told him to pass close to the fort and in the eddy, and he would receive little damage. He followed this advice, and passed by very comfortably.

By this time the river had been illuminated by two fire-rafts, and everything could be seen as by the light of day. I could see every ship and gun-boat as she passed up as plainly as possible, and noted all their positions.

It would be a difficult undertaking at any time to keep a long line of vessels in compact order when ascending a crooked channel against a three-and-a-half-knot current, and our commanders found it to be especially so under the present trying circumstances. The *Iroquois,* Commander De Camp, as gallant an officer as ever lived, got out of line and passed up ahead of her consorts; but De Camp made good use of his opportunity by engaging and driving off a ram and the gun-boat *McRae,* which attacked him as soon as he had passed Fort Jackson. The *McRae* was disabled and her commander (Huger) mortally wounded. The *Iroquois* was much cut up by Fort St. Philip and the gun-boats, but did not receive a single shot from Fort Jackson, although passing within fifty yards of it.

While the events above mentioned were taking place, Farragut had engaged Fort St. Philip at close quarters with his heavy ships, and had driven the men from their guns. He was passing on up the river, when his flag-ship was threatened by a new and formidable adversary. A fire-raft in full blaze was seen coming down the river, guided toward the *Hartford* by a tug-boat, the *Mosher.* It seemed impossible to avoid this danger, and as the helm was put to port in the attempt to do so, the flag-ship ran upon a shoal. While in this position the fire-raft was pushed against her, and in a minute she was enveloped in flames half-way up to her

FLAG-SHIP "HARTFORD" ATTACKED BY A FIRE-RAFT, PUSHED BY THE CONFEDERATE
TUG-BOAT "MOSHER."

THE CONFEDERATE CRUISER "SUMTER," CAPTAIN SEMMES, LEAVING
NEW ORLEANS, JUNE 18, 1861.
From a sketch made at the time.

tops, and was in a condition of great peril. The fire department was at once called away, and while the *Hartford's* batteries kept up the fight with Fort St. Philip, the flames were extinguished and the vessel backed off the shoal into deep water,—a result due to the coolness of her commander and the good discipline of the officers and men. While the *Hartford* was in this perilous position, and her entire destruction was threatened, Farragut showed all the qualities of a great commander. He walked up and down the poop as coolly as though on dress-parade, while Commander Wainwright directed the firemen in putting out the flames. At times the fire would rush through the ports and almost drive the men from the guns.

"Don't flinch from that fire, boys," sang out Farragut; "there's a hotter fire than that for those who don't do their duty! Give that rascally little tug a shot, and don't let her go off with a whole coat!" The *Mosher* was sunk.

While passing the forts the *Hartford* was struck thirty-two times in hull and rigging, and had 3 men killed and 10 wounded.

The *Brooklyn*, Captain Thomas T. Craven, followed as close after the flag-ship as the blinding smoke from guns and fire-rafts would admit, and the garrison of the fort was again driven to cover by the fire of her heavy battery. She passed on with severe punishment, and was immediately attacked by the most powerful vessel in the Confederate fleet, excepting the *Louisiana*—the ram *Manassas*, commanded by Lieutenant Warley, a gallant young officer of the old service. The blow that the *Manassas* struck the *Brooklyn* did but little apparent injury, and the ram slid off in the dark to seek other prey. (It must be remembered that these scenes were being enacted on a dark night, and in an atmosphere filled with dense smoke, through which our commanders had to grope their way, guided only by the flashes of the guns in the forts and the fitful light of burning vessels and rafts.) The *Brooklyn* was next attacked by a large steamer, which received her broadside at the dis-

tance of twenty yards, and drifted out of action in flames. Notwithstanding the heavy fire which the *Brooklyn* had gone through, she was only struck seventeen times in the hull. She lost 9 men killed and 26 wounded.

When our large ships had passed the forts, the affair was virtually over. Had they all been near the head of the column, the enemy would have been crushed at once, and the flag-ship would have passed up almost unhurt. As it was, the *Hartford* was more exposed and imperiled than any of her consorts, and that at a time when, if anything had happened to the commander-in-chief, the fleet would have been thrown into confusion.

The forts had been so thoroughly silenced by the ships' guns and mortars that when Captain Bell came along in the little *Sciota*, at the head of the third division, he passed by nearly unharmed. All the other vessels succeeded in getting by, except the *Itasca*, Lieutenant Caldwell, the *Winona*, Lieutenant Nichols, and the *Kennebec*, Lieutenant Russell. The first two vessels, having kept in line, were caught at daylight below the forts without support, and, as the current was swift and they were slow steamers, they became mere targets for the Confederates, who now turned all that was left of their fighting power upon them. Seeing their helpless condition, I signaled them to retire, which they did after being seriously cut up. The *Itasca* had a shot through her boiler, and was so completely riddled that her commander was obliged to run her ashore just below the mortar-fleet in order to prevent her sinking. She had received fourteen shot and shell through her hull, but her list of killed and wounded was small. Had not the people

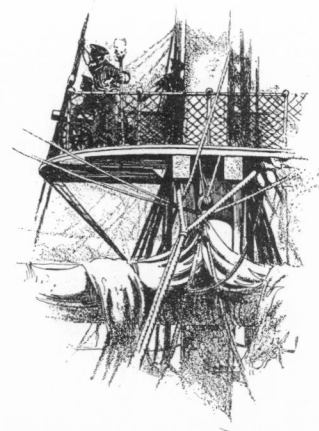

THE MAINTOP OF THE "HARTFORD,"
WITH HOWITZER.

100

in the forts been completely demoralized, they would have sunk these two vessels in ten minutes.

While these events were taking place, the mortar-steamers had driven the men from the water-batteries and had kept up a steady fire on the walls of Fort Jackson. Although at first sight my position in front of these batteries, which mounted six of the heaviest guns in the Confederate works (1 10-inch and 2 8-inch Columbiads, 1 10-inch sea-coast mortar, and 2 rifled 32-pounders), seemed a very perilous one, it was not at all so. I ran the steamers close alongside of the levee just below the water-batteries, and thus protected their hulls below the firing-decks. I got in my first broadside just as the middle of Bailey's column was opened upon by Fort Jackson. The enemy responded quickly, but our fire was so rapid and accurate that in ten minutes the water-battery was deserted. I had 25 8-inch and 32-pounders on one side and 2 11-inch pivot-guns. During the remainder of the action I devoted most of my attention to the battlements of the main fort, firing an occasional shot at the water-battery. The *Harriet Lane* had two men killed, but the only damage done to the vessels was to their masts and rigging, their hulls having been well protected by the levees.

While engaged on this duty I had an excellent opportunity of witnessing the movements of Farragut's fleet, and, by the aid of powerful night-glasses, I could almost distinguish persons on the vessels. The whole scene looked like a beautiful panorama. From almost perfect silence—the steamers moving slowly through the water like phantom ships—one incessant roar of heavy cannon commenced, the Confeder-

ate forts and gun-boats opening together on the head of our line as it came within range. The Union vessels returned the fire as they came up, and soon the guns of our fleet joined in the thunder, which seemed to shake the very earth. A lurid glare was thrown over the scene by the burning rafts, and, as the bomb-shells crossed each other and exploded in the air, it seemed as if a battle were taking place in the heavens as well as on the earth. It all ended as suddenly as it had commenced. In one hour and ten minutes after the vessels of the fleet had weighed anchor, the affair was virtually over, and Farragut was pushing on toward New Orleans, where he was soon to crush the last hope of Rebellion in that quarter by opening the way for the advance of the Union army.

From what I had seen of the conflict I did not greatly fear for the safety of our ships. Now and then a wreck came floating by, all charred and disabled, but I noted that these were side-wheel vessels, and none of ours.

I must refer here to a gallant affair which took place between the *Mississippi* and the ram *Manassas*. The latter vessel proved the most troublesome of the Confederate fleet. She had rammed the *Brooklyn* and the *Mississippi* at different times during the action.

At early daylight, as the vessels approached the quarantine above the forts, the *Manassas* was seen coming up the river as rapidly as her steam would allow.

As she approached the fleet, Flag-Officer Farragut directed Commander Smith in the *Mississippi* to turn and run her down. The order was instantly obeyed by the *Mississippi* turning and going at the ram at full speed; but when it was expected to see the *Manassas* annihilated, the vessels being within fifty yards of each other, the ram put her helm hard-a-port, dodged the *Mississippi*, and ran ashore, where her crew deserted her. Commander Smith set fire to her, and then so riddled her with shot that she was dislodged from the

THE CONFEDERATE IRONCLAD "LOUISIANA."
On the way to Fort St. Philip.

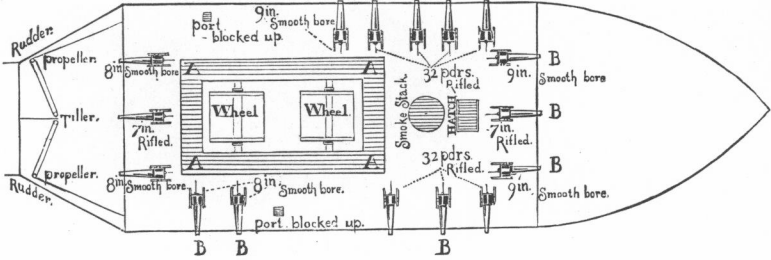

THE PLAN OF THE "LOUISIANA." *
After a sketch made by commander J. K. Mitchell, about the time of the engagement.
A A, Bulkhead around wheels.   B B, Guns used in action.

EXPLOSION OF THE CONFEDERATE IRONCLAD, "LOUISIANA."

CHARLES F. McINTOSH, C. S. N.
Commander of the "Louisiana."

bank and drifted below the forts, where she blew up and sank.

Previous to this a kind of guerrilla warfare had been carried on, and most of the enemy's river-boats had been run ashore or otherwise destroyed, while the *Varuna* lay sunk at the bank with two of her adversaries wrecked beside her, a monument to the gallantry of Commander Boggs.

When the fleet had passed the forts, and there was no longer any necessity for me to hold my position, I dropped down the river with the steamers to where the mortar-boats were anchored, and gave the signal to cease firing. I knew that our squadron had failed to destroy all of the enemy's fleet. The ironclad *Louisiana* lay at the bank apparently uninjured, the *McRae* was at anchor close to Fort Jackson, and three other vessels whose

*Mr. William C. Whittle, who was third lieutenant on the *Louisiana* during the contest against Farragut's fleet in the Mississippi, has sent to the Editors the following statement concerning her armament:

"The hull of the *Louisiana* was almost entirely submerged. Upon this were built her heavy upper works, intended to contain her battery, machinery, etc. This extended to within about twenty-five feet of her stem and stern, leaving a little deck forward and aft, nearly even with the water, and surrounded by a slight bulwark. The structure on the hull had its ends and sides inclined inward and upward from the hull, at an angle of about forty-five degrees, and covered with T railroad iron, the lower layer being firmly bolted to the woodwork, and the upper layer driven into it from the end so as to form a nearly solid plate and a somewhat smooth surface. This plating resisted the projectiles of Farragut's fleet (none of which perforated our side), although one of his largest ships lay across and touching our stem, and in that position fired her heavy guns. Above this structure was an open deck which was surrounded by a sheet-iron bulwark about four feet high, which was intended as a protection against sharp-shooters and small arms, but was entirely inefficient, as the death of our gallant commander, McIntosh, and those who fell around him, goes to prove. The plan for propelling the *Louisiana* was novel and abortive. She had two propellers aft, which we never had an opportunity of test-

character I could not make out were moving back and forth from one shore to the other. This looked serious, for such a force, if properly handled, was superior to mine; and I had to provide immediately against contingencies. There were now seven efficient gun-boats under my command, and I at once prepared them to meet the enemy. My plan was to get as many of my vessels as possible alongside of the *Louisiana*, each one to make fast to her, let go two anchors, and then "fight it out on that line."

Meantime Farragut was speeding on his way up the river with all his fleet except the *Mississippi* and one or two small gun-boats, which were left to guard the lazaretto. On his way up the flag-officer encountered more Confederate batteries at Chalmette, the place made famous by the battle of January 8th, 1815. . . .

Farragut made short work of them, however, and our fleet, meeting with no further resistance, passed on and anchored before New Orleans. . . .

ing. The novel conception, which proved entirely inefficient, was that right in the center section of the vessel there was a large well in which worked the two wheels, one immediately forward of the other. I suppose they were so placed to be protected from the enemy's fire. The machinery of these two wheels was in order when my father, Commodore W. C. Whittle, the naval commanding officer at New Orleans, against his better judgment, was compelled to send the vessel down to the forts. The vessel left New Orleans on the 20th of April, I think. The work on the propellers was incomplete, the machinists and mechanics being still on board, and most of the guns were not mounted. The center wheels were started, but were entirely inefficient, and, as we were drifting helplessly down the stream, tow-boats had to be called to take us down to the point about half a mile above Fort St. Philip, on the left side of the river, where we tied up to the bank with our bow down-stream. Thus, as Farragut's fleet came up and passed, we could only use our bow-guns and the starboard broadside. Moreover, the port-holes for our guns were entirely faulty, not allowing room to train the guns either laterally or in elevation. I had practical experience of this fact, for I had immediate charge of the bow division when a vessel of Admiral Farragut's fleet got across our stem, and I could only fire through and through her at point-blank instead of depressing my guns and sinking her."

THE "BROOKLYN" AT THE PASSAGE OF THE FORTS.

BY COMMANDER JOHN RUSSELL BARTLETT,
U. S. N.
An officer of the "Brooklyn" in the action described.

. . . The present article is intended merely as a personal narrative of the passage of the forts as seen from the deck of the *Brooklyn*. This vessel was a flush-deck sloop-of-war, carrying 22 9-inch guns, 1 80-pounder Dahlgren rifle, and 1 30-pounder Parrott rifle. A small poop-deck extended about fifteen feet from the taffrail, and under this were the steering-wheel and binnacles. I was a midshipman on board doing lieutenant's duty, having charge of a regular watch and in command of a division of guns. My division consisted of 4 guns (2 guns' crews) at the after end of the ship. The guns were numbered in pairs 10 and 11. The No. 11 gun on the starboard side was shifted over to the port side under the poop-deck, and both the No. 11 guns were manned by the marines. It was expected that our principal work would be with our port battery directed against Fort Jackson on the right bank. My two crews manned the No. 10 gun on each side, and also prepared to man the 30-pounder on the poop if occasion should require. On each side of the poop there was a ladder to the main deck. While steaming up to the hulks and until it was necessary for me to be at my guns, I stood on the port ladder with my head above the rail, where I could watch our approach to the forts, and I mounted this ladder several times to see what was going on as we advanced.

On the poop were Captain Craven, Midshipman John Anderson, who had volunteered a few days before from the *Montgomery*, which did not take part in the action, Captain's Clerk J. G. Swift, afterward a graduate of West Point and a lieutenant in the army, and two quartermasters. There was a small piece of ratline stuff carried around the poop, about waist-high. Captain Craven stood at the forward edge of the poop with his hands on this line, and did not move during the whole passage. I had the good fortune during the war to serve with many brave commanders, but I have never met in the service, or out of it, a man of such consummate coolness, such perfect apparent indifference to danger as Admiral Craven. As I write, I hear the sad news of his death.

At 2 o'clock on the morning of the 24th two red lights were hoisted at the peak of the flag-ship as a signal to get under way. All hands had been on deck since midnight to see that everything about the deck and guns was ready for action, and when the decks were wet down and sanded, it really began to look as if we were going to have some pretty hot business on our hands. The anchor was hove up with as little noise as possible, and at half-past 2 we steamed off, following the *Hartford* toward the entrance to the opening which had been made in the obstructions. The Confederates opened fire about 3 o'clock, when the advance division came in sight and range of the forts, and as we passed ahead of the mortar-vessels we also came in range; but the forts were so far ahead that we could not bring our broadside guns to bear. For twenty minutes we stood silent beside the guns, with the shot and shell from Forts St. Philip and Jackson passing over us and bursting everywhere in the air. As we came to the obstruction the water-battery on the Fort Jackson side opened a most destructive fire, and here the *Brooklyn* received her first shot. We gave the water-battery a broadside of grape. With our own smoke and the smoke from the vessels immediately ahead, it was impossible to direct the ship, so that we missed the opening between hulks and brought up on the chain. We dropped back and tried again; this time the chain broke, but we swung alongside of one of the hulks, and the stream-anchor, hanging on the starboard quarter, caught, tore along the hulk, and then parted its lashings. The cable secured us just where the Confederates had the range of their guns, but somebody ran up with an ax and cut the hawser, and we began to steam up the river. A few moments later there was a sudden jar, and the engines stopped. The propeller had no doubt struck some hard object, but no one knew the cause of the stoppage; and as Craven called out, "Stand by the starboard anchor," and a fatal pause under the enemy's fire seemed imminent, a thrill of alarm ran through the ship. The alarm was groundless, however, as no injury was done, and presently the engines started again, and the ship moved on.

THE "BROOKLYN" ATTACKED BY THE CONFEDERATE RAM "MANASSAS."

The *Manassas* was described by her commander, Lieutenant Warley, as "a tug-boat that had been converted into a ram, covered with half-inch iron, and had a 32-pounder carronade; her crew consisted of thirty-five persons, officers and men. She was perforated in the fight by shot and shell as if she had been made of paper."

Admiral Melancton Smith thus describes his encounter with the ram: "Having discovered the *Manassas* stealing up along the St. Philip side of the river behind me, I signaled Farragut for permission to attack, which was given. The *Mississippi* turned in mid-stream and tried to run down the ram, barely missing her, but driving her ashore, when her crew escaped, fired at by the *Kineo*, which had not yet anchored. The ram's engines were found to be still in motion, but the approach of a burning wreck compelled me to abandon the idea of attaching a hawser. Her machinery was destroyed by my boats, and after receiving a broadside or two from the *Mississippi*, she floated down the river in flames and blew up."

There were many fire-rafts, and these and the flashing of the guns and bursting shells made it almost as light as day, but the smoke from the passing fleet was so thick that at times one could see nothing ten feet from the ship. While entangled with the rafts, the *Brooklyn* was hulled a number of times; one shot from Fort Jackson struck the rail just at the break of the poop and went nearly across, plowing out the deck in its course. Another struck Barney Sands, the signal quartermaster, and cut his body almost in two. The first lieutenant, Lowry, coming along at the time, inquired who it was, and understanding the response to be "Bartlett," instead of "Barney," he passed the word that he had sent down "all that was left of poor Bartlett." As he came on deck and was about in all parts of the ship during the fight, he gave the men news of the progress of the fight and of the casualties, and for once I was completely out of existence.

The ship was now clear of the hulks and steamed up the river, throwing shells and shrapnel into Fort Jackson as fast as the guns could be loaded and fired. When just abreast of the fort a shot struck the side of the port of No. 9 gun on the port side, and at the same time a shell burst directly over the gun. The first captain's head was cut off and nine of the gun's crew were wounded. I was standing amidships between the two No. 10 guns, and was struck on the back by the splinters and thrown to the deck. I was on my feet in a moment and turned to my port gun. There were only two men standing at it, the first loader and the first sponger, who were leaning against the side of the ship: the others were all flat on deck, one of them directly in the rear of the gun. The gun had just been loaded, and I pulled this man to one side, clear of the recoil, and fired the gun. It was a time when every one felt that he must do something. After the discharge of the gun the men on the deck got

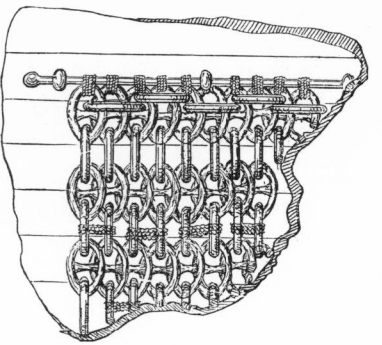

SECTION OF CHAIN ARMOR PLACED ON THE SIDE OF THE "BROOKLYN" TO PROTECT HER BOILERS.
From a sketch lent by Commander Bartlett.

up and came to their places. None of them were seriously hurt. The captain of the gun found a piece of shell inside his cap, which did not even scratch his head; another piece went through my coat-sleeve.

Just after passing Fort Jackson we saw a bright glare on the starboard quarter, and a moment after Captain Craven said, in his deep bass voice, "One bell!" (to slow down), and then, "Two bells!" (to stop her). I went up the poop ladder, and there in plain sight on the left bank, just below Fort St. Philip, was the *Hartford*, with a fire-raft alongside and with flames running up the rigging on the tarred rope to the mast-head.* The tug *Mosher* was near by, but I did not see the ram *Manassas*. It was evidently Craven's intention when he saw Farragut's trouble to go to his rescue. As the engine stopped, the *Brooklyn* dropped down, her head swinging to starboard, until she was on a line between Fort Jackson and the *Hartford*. The fort immediately opened fire on the *Brooklyn* with renewed energy, and she would have been blown out of the water had not the enemy aimed too high and sent the shot through the rigging, boats, and hammock-nettings, many of them just clearing the rail. The port battery was manned, and shell and shrapnel were fired as fast as the guns could be loaded. The *Brooklyn* remained under the fire of Fort Jackson until Craven saw Farragut free from the fire-raft, and then she steamed ahead. This was one of the coolest and bravest

*Commander Albert Kautz, who was at this time lieutenant on the *Hartford*, in a letter to the Editors thus describes this memorable scene:

"No sooner had Farragut given the order 'Hard-a-port,' than the current gave the ship a broad sheer, and her bows went hard up on a mud bank. As the fire-raft came against the port side of the ship, it became enveloped in flames. We were so near to the shore that from the bowsprit we could reach the tops of the bushes, and such a short distance above Fort St. Philip that we could distinctly hear the gunners in the casemates give their orders; and as they saw Farragut's flag at the mizzen, by the bright light, they fired with frightful rapidity. Fortunately they did not make sufficient allowance for our close proximity, and the iron hail passed over our bulwarks, doing but little damage. On the deck of the ship it was bright as noonday, but out over the majestic river, where the smoke of many guns was intensified by that of the pine-knots of the fire-rafts, it was dark as the blackest midnight. For a moment it looked as though the flag-ship was indeed doomed, but the firemen were called away, and with the energy of

REAR-ADMIRAL THOMAS T. CRAVEN, U. S. N.
In command of the "Brooklyn."

acts that I saw during the war, but it was not mentioned in any official report or newspaper account at the time. In fact, the *Brooklyn's* passage of the forts was hardly noticed by the newspaper correspondents, as Craven had old-fashioned ideas and would allow no reporters on board. I am glad, even at this late date, that I can put on record this act of heroism.

As the *Hartford* lay aground with the fire-raft alongside, her crew were at their work, and I saw the flag-officer distinctly on the port side of the poop looking toward us. From this point the *Brooklyn* steamed ahead, toward Fort St. Philip, and passed close to the fort, firing grape from the starboard battery. When she first came abreast of the fort there was a long blaze of musketry from the parapet, but it soon stopped when she got to work. We were at this time less than one hundred feet from the bank, and the *Hartford* had passed ahead. The barbette guns of the fort not being depressed sufficiently, we received no damage while passing, but we were so close that the powder scorched the faces and clothes of the men. A bullet entered the port of No. 1 gun and struck Lieutenant James O'Kane, who had charge

despair rushed aft to the quarter-deck. The flames, like so many forked tongues of hissing serpents, were piercing the air in a frightful manner that struck terror to all hearts. As I crossed from the starboard to the port side of the deck, I passed close to Farragut, who, as he looked forward and took in the situation, clasped his hands high in air, and exclaimed, 'My God, is it to end in this way!'

"Fortunately it was not to end as it at that instant seemed, for just then Master's Mate Allen, with the hose in his hand, jumped into the mizzen rigging, and the sheet of flame succumbed to a sheet of water. It was but the dry paint on the ship's side that made the threatening flame, which went down before the fierce attack of the fireman as rapidly as it had sprung up. As the flames died away the engines were backed 'hard,' and, as if providentially, the ram *Manassas* [mistake] struck the ship a blow under the counter, which shoved her stern in against the bank, causing her bow to slip off. The ship was again free; and a loud, spontaneous cheer rent the air, as the crew rushed to their guns with renewed energy."

of the first division, in the leg. He fell to the deck, but would not allow himself to be carried below until he had himself fired two of the broadside guns into Fort St. Philip. But the most uncomfortable position on board the ship, during this part of the engagement, was that of the quartermaster, Thomas Hollins, who stood in the starboard main chains, heaving the lead and calling out the soundings. The outside of the ship near him was completely peppered with bullets, and the flames from the enemy's guns seemed almost to reach him; still he stood coolly at his post, and when abreast of the fort he was heard calling out, "Only thirteen feet, sir."

As we passed clear of Fort St. Philip, Captain Craven gave orders to load the starboard battery with solid shot. He had seen the ironclad *Louisiana* moored just above the fort. She gave us one or two shots, but when we came directly abeam of her, she closed her port shutters and received our broadside. We could hear our shot strike against her iron sides. We gave but one broadside and then sheered out into the river. A 9-inch shell, fired by the *Louisiana*, struck the *Brooklyn* about a foot above the water-line, on the starboard side of the cutwater, near the wood ends, forced its way for three feet through the dead-wood and timbers, and remained there. At New Orleans this shot was cut out, and it was found that in their hurry the gunners had neglected to remove the lead patch from the fuse, so that the shell did not explode. Had it done so it would have blown the whole bow off, and the *Brooklyn* would have gone to the bottom.

As we swung out into the current and steamed up the river, we began to see the vessels ahead fighting with the Confederate gun-boats, and a few moments later the cry came aft, "A steamer coming down on our port bow." We could see two smoke-stacks and the black smoke from them. I took a look from the poop ladder, and saw a good-sized river steamer coming down on us, crowded with men on her forward deck, as if ready to board. The order had already been given, "Stand by to repel boarders," and to load with shrapnel; the

COMMANDER PORTER RECEIVING CONFEDERATE OFFICERS ON THE "HARRIET LANE."

fuses were cut to burn one second. As she approached, Craven gave the vessel a sheer to starboard, and we began with No. 1 gun, the guns aft following in quick succession, the shells bursting almost immediately as they left the guns. There was a rush of steam, shrieks from the people on board the steamer, and, when it came time for my No. 10 gun to fire, the steamer was lost in the smoke. This was the only one of the river flotilla which we encountered or fired into. Just after our engagement with this steamer, a column of black smoke, which came from the dreaded *Manassas*, was seen on the starboard side, and the cry was passed along by men who were looking out of the ports, "The ram, the ram!" Craven called out, "Give her four bells! Put your helm hard-a-starboard!" Then I saw the smoke-stacks of the *Manassas* and the flash from her gun, and the next moment I was nearly thrown on the deck by the concussion, caused by her striking us just amidships. The ram was going full speed but against the current, and, with our helm to starboard, the blow was not at right angles to our keel, though nearly so. I ran to the No. 10 port, the gun being in, and looked out, and saw her almost directly alongside. A man came out of her little hatch aft, and ran forward along the port side of the deck, as far as the smoke-stacks, placed his hand against one, and looked to see what damage the ram had done. I saw him turn, fall

over, and tumble into the water, but did not know at the moment what caused his sudden disappearance, until I asked the quartermaster, who was leadsman in the chains, if he had seen him fall.

"Why, yes, sir," said he, "I saw him fall overboard,—in fact, I helped him; for I hit him alongside of the head with my hand-lead."

No guns were fired at the ram from the starboard battery; all the crews a moment before had been at the port guns. As the *Manassas* drifted by I ran up on the poop, calling the gun's crew with me, to see if I could hit her with the 30-pounder Parrott, but we were unable to depress it sufficiently, at its high elevation, to bring it to bear before she was lost to sight in the smoke. The shot which she had fired came through the chain and planking, above the berth-deck, through a pile of rigging placed against the ship's side, and just entered the sand-bags placed to protect the steam-drum.

A few moments after this incident a vessel passed on our starboard side, not ten feet from us, and I could see through the port the men loading a pivot-gun. She was directly abreast of No. 10 gun and I took the lock-string to fire, when a cry came from on board the vessel, "Don't fire, it is the *Iroquois*!" At the same moment, Lieutenant Lowry also shouted from near the mainmast, "Don't fire!" Seeing the black smoke pouring

from her stack, and noticing that it was abaft the mainmast, I called to Captain Craven, "It can't be the *Iroquois*! It is not one of our vessels, for her smoke-stack is abaft her mainmast!" Captain Craven, however, repeated the order, "Don't fire!" and I obeyed. I was sure it was one of the Confederate gun-boats, but it was my duty to obey orders, and thus the Confederate gun-boat *McRae* escaped being sunk by the *Brooklyn*; for the gun had been depressed, and a 9-inch shell would have gone through her deck and out below the water-line.

Just after leaving Fort St. Philip a shot came in on the starboard quarter and went across the deck, taking off a marine's head and wounding three other men. Lieutenant Lowry came along about this time, and I heard him report to Captain Craven that Lieutenant O'Kane had been wounded. Craven directed him to put me in charge of the First Division, to which Lowry answered:

"I sent poor Bartlett down below half an hour ago cut in two."

"Oh, no, you did not," said Craven; "he is on deck close to you."

Lowry turned and was as much surprised as if he had seen a ghost, and told me to run forward and take charge of the First Division. There had been terrible havoc here. The powder-man of the pivot-gun had been struck by a shell, which exploded and blew him literally to atoms, and parts of his body were scattered all over the forecastle. . . . It was now almost daylight, and we could see the crews of the deserted boats running for cover to the woods a little way back. Shortly after, the *Brooklyn* came up with the other vessels and anchored near a point where there had been an encampment of troops. They only remained long enough to land and bury the dead. The commanding officers assembled on board the *Hartford* to offer their congratulations to the flag-officer. . . .

FIRING AT THE "VARUNA" THROUGH THE BOW OF THE "GOVERNOR MOORE."

THE CONFEDERATE SIDE.

BY BEVERLEY KENNON, CAPTAIN, LA. S. N.
Commander of the "Governor Moore" in this engagement.

. . . The *Governor Moore*, which was anchored near Fort St. Philip opposite Fort Jackson, could not have been surprised at any time. I slept for the most part only during the day, and but rarely at night. At 8 P. M. four sentinels were always posted on the spar-deck and wheel-houses, and a quartermaster in the pilot-house; an anchor and engine-room watch was set; the chain was unshackled and the fires were banked; both guns were carefully pointed at the opening in the obstructions through which the enemy had to pass to reach us. The vessel being secured as firmly as if at a dock, effective firing of her guns was assured. Every opening in the vessel's side through which a light might be seen was kept closed. At dark the vessel's holds and decks and magazines were brightly lighted to save delay in the event of a sudden call to quarters. Two guns' crews were ready for service, and the officer of the deck and myself were always at hand.

The evening previous to the battle I reported to General Duncan, the commander of the two forts, my observations on the enemy's movements as seen by myself from the mast-head. Yet to my knowledge no picket boat was sent down by us, or any means adopted to watch the enemy and guard against surprise. The result was they were abreast the forts before some of our vessels fired a shot. In a few moments this space was filled with smoke from the guns and exploded shells, intensifying the darkness of the night. A slackening of

the fire on both sides was necessary, since neither could distinguish friend from foe. In some places no object was distinguishable until directly upon it, when it was as soon lost to view, yet the United States squadron steamed ahead, blindfolded, as it were, through the darkness and confusion, soon to find themselves in places of absolute safety and with comparatively few casualties.

At about 3:30 A. M. (April 24th, 1862) an unusual noise down the river attracted my attention. As we expected to be attacked at any moment I descended the ladder to near the water, where I distinctly heard the paddles of a steamer (the *Mississippi*). I saw nothing on reaching the deck, but instantly fired the after gun, the one forward being fired by the sentry there; at the same moment the water-batteries of Fort Jackson and Fort St. Philip let drive, followed in an instant by a general discharge from all the available guns in the forts, and both batteries of the advancing fleet, mounting 192 guns, and Commander Porter's squadron of 7 vessels, mounting 53 guns, which attacked Fort Jackson's flank below the obstructions. There was also a splendid practice from 19 Federal mortars, which fired their 13-inch shells at intervals (between the vessels) of 10 seconds.

The bursting of every description of shells quickly following their discharge, increased a hundred-fold the terrific noise and fearfully grand and magnificent pyrotechnic display which centered in a space of about 1200 yards in width. The ball had not more than fairly opened before the enemy's ships were between the forts, and the Uncle Sam of my earlier days had the key to the valley of the Mississippi again in his breeches-pocket, for which he

THE "STONEWALL JACKSON" RAMMING THE "VARUNA."

had to thank his gallant navy and the stupidity, tardiness, ignorance, and neglect of the authorities in Richmond.

The first gun fired brought my crew to their stations. We had steam within 3 minutes, it having been ordered by that hour; the cable was slipped, when we delayed a moment for Lieutenant Warley to spring the *Manassas*, then inside of us, across the channel. A little tug-boat, the *Belle Algerine*, now fouled us—to her mortal injury. By the time we started, the space between the forts was filling up with the enemy's vessels, which fired upon us as they approached, giving us grape, canister, and shell. My vessel being a large one, we had too little steam and elbow-room in the now limited and crowded space to gather sufficient headway to strike a mortal blow on ramming. So rather than simply "squeeze" my adversary, I made haste slowly by moving close under the east bank to reach the bend above, where I would be able to turn down-stream ready for work. I took this course also, to avoid being fired and run into by the Confederate rams moored above me; but the ground for this fear was soon removed, as, on getting near them, I saw that one had started for New Orleans, while the telegraph steamer *Star*, ram *Quitman*, and one other had been set afire at their berths on the right bank, and deserted before any of the enemy had reached them, and were burning brightly. They being in a clear space were in full view, and I was close to them. Another reason for leaving our berth directly under Fort St. Philip, where the *Louisiana*, *McRae*, and *Manassas* also lay, was to get clear of the cross-fire of the forts, and that of each ship of the enemy as they passed up close to us, for we sustained considerable damage and losses as we moved out into the stream.

When we were turning at the head of the reach we found ourselves close to the United States steamer *Oneida*, 10 guns, with the United States steamer *Cayuga*, 4 guns, on our port beam. On being hailed with "What ship is that?" I replied, "United States steamer *Mississippi*," to deceive,

she being a side-wheel vessel also, but, seeing our distinguishing light, the *Oneida* raked with her starboard broadside at a few feet distance; the *Cayuga* delivered her fire thirty yards distant; the *Pensacola*, 25 guns, a little farther from us, at one fire with shrapnel from the howitzers in her tops cleared out 12 men at our bow-gun. Beyond her the firing of single guns in quick succession, as some vessel unseen to any one was moving rapidly up-stream, attracted my attention. At the same instant the United States steamer *Pinola*, 5 guns, close to on our port quarter, delivered her fire, kill-

REAR-ADMIRAL CHARLES S. BOGGS, U. S. N
In command of the "Varuna."

THE "PENSACOLA" DISABLING THE "GOVERNOR MOORE."

Captain H. W. Morris of the *Pensacola* says, in his report: "The ram [*Governor Moore*], after having struck the *Varuna* gun-boat, and forced her to run on shore to prevent sinking, advanced to attack this ship, coming down on us right ahead. She was perceived by Lieutenant F. A. Roe just in time to avoid her by sheering the ship, and she passed close on our starboard side, receiving, as she went by, a broadside from us." Until I read this, I thought the vessel that did us most damage was the *Oneida*, the other vessels being astern of her. Captain Lee of the *Oneida* in his report speaks of firing into the *Governor Moore*.—B. K.

CAPTAIN BEVERLEY KENNON, LA. S. N.

Commander of the "Governor Moore." (From a tintype.)

THE "GOVERNOR MOORE" IN FLAMES.

The Union ships in their order, beginning with the left, are the "Oneida," the "Pinola," the sunken "Varuna," the "Iroquois," and, in the foreground, the "Pensacola."

ing five men in our bunkers. This combined attack killed and wounded a large number of men, and cut the vessel up terribly. Suddenly two, then one Confederate ram darted through the thick smoke from the right to the left bank of the river, passing close to all of us. They missed the channel for New Orleans, grounded on and around the point next above and close to Fort St. Philip; one was fired and deserted, and blew up soon after as we passed her; the others were disabled and were soon abandoned by their crews. One (the *Resolute*) was after taken possession of later by men from the Confederate steamer *McRae*. I do not know what became of the other, the smoke was so dense. All this passed in a few moments. Suddenly I saw between my vessel and the burning *Quitman*, close to us on the west bank, a large, two-masted steamer rushing up-stream like a racer, belching "black smoke," firing on each burning vessel as she passed, and flying her distinguishing white light at the mast-head and red light at the peak. I thought of General Lovell, not far ahead of her on board the passenger steamer *Doubloon*, and quickly made a movement to follow this stranger in the hope of being able to delay or destroy her. Besides, the four or even more large ships so close to us, but obscured from view, needed but a little more room, and one good chance and a fair view of us, quickly to annihilate my old "tinder-box" of a ship. I therefore slipped out in the smoke and darkness around us after the advancing stranger, which proved to be the *Varuna*, Captain Charles S. Boggs, mounting 8 8-inch guns

and 2 30-pounder rifles, with a complement of about 200 persons. My whereabouts remained unknown to my former adversaries until all of them came to the *Varuna's* assistance at 6:20 A. M., nine miles above, where she sank, and where parts of her wreck are yet to be seen (1885).

When I started after the *Varuna*, I shot away our blue distinguishing light at the mast-head with a musket, as to have hauled it down would have attracted notice. We could see her, as she was in a clear space, and her lights showed her position. But she soon lost sight of us, for, besides being somewhat in the smoke, there were back of us at this location moderately high trees thickly placed, the spaces filled with a luxuriant undergrowth, making a high dark wall or background on both sides of the river. Until we got clear of this, there was nothing to attract attention toward us, the *Varuna* being half a mile ahead, as shown by her lights. Her engines were working finely and driv-

ing her rapidly on her "spurt." * We too, by using oil on our coal, had all the steam we needed. My old ship, shaking all over and fairly dancing through the water, was rapidly lessening the distance between us.

As soon as we reached an open space we hoisted a white light at our mast-head and a red light at the peak. This ruse worked successfully, as the

* Lieutenant C. H. Swasey, of the *Varuna*, remarks in his report upon the slowness of the *Varuna* at this point: "Owing to the small amount of steam we then had (17 pounds), he [Kennon] soon began to come up with us."

sequel proves. Since our existence depended upon closing with her before she made us out, I urged the men to resist the temptation to fire, and to be quiet and patient, otherwise we would soon be put under water from the effects of her broadsides. We were now one and a half miles from the forts, and one mile from where we gave chase. On our port bow and the *Varuna's* port beam, close under the land, I saw the runaway ram *Stonewall Jackson* making slow progress for want of steam, but working hard to get out of danger. She did not notice us. The *Varuna* could not have seen her or would have fired at her. We soon left the *Stonewall Jackson* astern. Four miles more and we were nearly abreast of Szymanski's regiment at Chalmette camp. Still the *Varuna* had not recognized us. I wanted assistance from that regiment, for I could now see that I had a far superior vessel to mine on my hands. I hoped also for assistance from the ram *Stonewall Jackson*, now a mile or two on our quarter, and from the Confederate States gun-boat *Jackson*, over one mile above us, serving as guard-boat at the quarantine station. To secure all this assistance I had but to show our colors and make ourselves known. The day was just dawning, and there was no smoke about us; so as a bid for help from the sources named, we hauled down the enemy's distinguishing lights and opened fire for the first time upon the *Varuna*, distant about one hundred yards, and with a surprise to her people plainly to be seen. This shot missed her! She replied quickly with one or more guns, when a running fight commenced, she raking us with such guns as she could bring to bear, but not daring the risk of a sheer to deliver her broadside, as we were too close upon her. Her former great superiority was now reduced

THE "GOVERNOR MOORE," AT THE END OF THE FIGHT.

MAJOR-GENERAL MANSFIELD LOVELL, C. S. A.
Commander of Confederate Department No. 1,
with headquarters at New Orleans.

THE UNITED STATES STEAMER "MISSISSIPPI" ATTEMPTING TO RUN DOWN THE
CONFEDERATE RAM "MANASSAS."

MELANCTON SMITH,
REAR-ADMIRAL, U. S. N.
In command of the "Mississippi."
Drawn from a photograph.

to a lower figure than that of our two guns, for we, having assumed the offensive, had the advantage, and maintained it until she sank.

Our hoped-for and expected aid never came from any source. So far from it, the gun-boat *Jackson*, lying at quarantine, slipped her cable when the fight commenced, firing two shots at both of us, believing us both enemies (one striking our foremast), and started with all haste for the head-waters of the Mississippi, delaying at New Orleans long enough for her people with their baggage to be landed, when Lieutenant F. B. Renshaw, her commander, burnt her at the levee! The infantry at Chalmette camp could not help us, and the "ram" *Stonewall Jackson*, as it then seemed to us, would not!

Then I saw that we had to fight the *Varuna* alone. On finding our bow-gun useless because it was mounted too far abaft the knight-heads to admit of sufficient depression to hull the enemy, then close under our bows, and noting that every shell from the enemy struck us fair, raking the decks, killing former wounded and well men, and wounding others, I realized that something had to be done and that quickly. I then depressed the bow-gun to a point *inside our bow* and fired it, hoping to throw its shell into the engine-room or boiler of the chase. It went through our deck all right, but struck the hawse-pipe, was deflected, and passed through the *Varuna's* smoke-stack. It was soon fired again through this hole in our bows, the shell

striking the *Varuna's* pivot-gun, where it broke or burst, and killed and wounded several men. Until we had finished reloading, the *Varuna* was undecided what to do, when suddenly and to my surprise she ported her helm.

Not wishing to avoid her fire any longer, being quite near to her, we put our helm to port and received the fire from her pivot-gun and rifles in our port bow, but as her shot struck us, under the cover of the smoke our helm was put hard to starboard,—she not righting hers quickly enough,—and before she could recover herself, we rammed her near the starboard gangway, receiving her starboard broadside and delivering our one shot as we struck her. Her engines stopped suddenly. We backed clear, gathered headway again, and rammed her a second time as near the same place as possible. Before separating, the two vessels dropped alongside each other for a couple of minutes and exchanged musket and pistol shots to some injury to their respective crews, but neither vessel fired a large gun. I expected to be boarded at this time and had had the after gun loaded with a light charge and three stand of canister, and pointed fore and aft ready for either gangway. It was an opportunity for the *Varuna's* two hundred men to make a second Paul Jones of their commander, but it was not embraced. As for ourselves, we had neither the men to board nor to repel boarders. The vessels soon parted, hostilities between them ceased, and the *Varuna* was beached to prevent her sinking in deep water. Then, and not until then, did the *Varuna's* people know that any other Confederate vessel than mine was within several miles of her. Suddenly the ram *Stonewall Jackson*, having to pass the *Varuna* to reach New Orleans, rammed deep into the latter's port gangway. When close upon her, the *Varuna* delivered such of her port broadside guns as could be brought to bear. The *Stonewall Jackson* backed

clear, steamed about four miles up the river, and was beached on the opposite bank, fired, and deserted. Her wreck is there now. Having but one gun, and that mounted aft, she did not fire it. Soon after the *Stonewall Jackson* struck the *Varuna* the latter finished sinking, leaving her topgallant forecastle out of the water, and upon it her crew took refuge.

The United States ships *Oneida*, *Iroquois*, *Pensacola*, *Pinola*, and *Cayuga* were now rapidly approaching and near at hand. I started down-stream to meet and try to ram one of them. On passing abreast the *Varuna* some thoughtless man, knowing her forecastle rifle was loaded, fired it and killed and wounded five of our men, one officer included. Had I returned the fire with our after gun, which was loaded with canister, at the crowd of people closely packed upon and near that little shelf, the damage to life and limb would have been fearful. But not a shot did we fire at her after she was disabled.

We had proceeded down-stream but a short distance when Mr. Duke, the first lieutenant, then at conn, where, though wounded, he had remained throughout the fight doing his duty like a brave man, exclaimed, "Why do this? We have no men left; I'll be —— if I stand here to be murdered," so he slapped the helm hard-a-starboard. As we came round, the enemy's ships, being near, fired a shower of heavy projectiles which struck the vessel in every part. One gun was dismounted. The boats had already been destroyed. The wheel-ropes, the head of the rudder, the slide of the engine, and a large piece of the walking-beam were shot away; the latter fell on the cylinder-head and cracked it, and filled the engine-room with steam, driving every man out of it. The head of the jib was now hoisted, and with a strong current on the port bow, assisted by the headway left on the vessel, we succeeded in reaching the river-bank just above the *Varuna's* wreck, where the anchor was let go to prevent drifting into deep water to sink, the last heavy firing having struck the vessel on and under her water-line. At this place she was

destroyed by fire, her colors burning at her peak. The vessel was not disabled until this last attack upon her, although much cut up. By it no one on the *Governor Moore* outside the cotton bulkhead protection to the engine, except those in the magazine- and shell-room, escaped being struck by shot, bullets, or splinters. Additional men were killed, several more of the wounded were killed, and others wounded. It should be remembered that my vessel had been under a terrific fire for 3 hours, in a narrow river with unruffled surface, and at close quarters, from vessels [the *Oneida*, *Cayuga*, *Pensacola*, and *Varuna*] mounting in the aggregate over 30 of the heaviest guns afloat. Out of 93 all told we lost 57 killed and 17 wounded, of whom 4 died in the hospital.

NEW ORLEANS BEFORE THE CAPTURE.

BY GEORGE W. CABLE.

The famous novelist, author of "Old Creole Days," etc., was a lad in New Orleans at the time of the capture, and later served in Company I, 4th Mississippi Cavalry (Confederate).

. . . There had come a great silence upon trade. Long ago the custom-warehouses had begun to show first a growing roominess, then emptiness, and then had remained shut, and the iron bolts and cross-bars of their doors were gray with cobwebs. One of them, in which I had earned my first wages as a self-supporting lad, had been turned into a sword-bayonet factory, and I had been turned out. For some time later the Levee had kept busy; but its stir and noise had gradually declined, faltered, turned into the commerce of war and the clatter of calkers and ship-carpenters, and faded out. Both receipts and orders from the interior country had shrunk and shrunk, and the

CONFEDERATE SHARP-SHOOTERS AND SWAMP HUNTERS ATTACKING MORTAR-BOATS.

THE UNION FLEET ARRIVING AT NEW ORLEANS.

brave, steady fellows, who at entry and shipping and cash and account desks could no longer keep a show of occupation, had laid down the pen, taken up the sword and musket, and followed after the earlier and more eager volunteers. There had been one new, tremendous sport for moneyed men for a while, with spoils to make it interesting. The sea-going tow-boats of New Orleans were long, slender side-wheelers, all naked power and speed, without either freight or passenger room, each with a single tall, slim chimney and hurrying walking-beam, their low, taper hulls trailing behind scarcely above the water, and perpetually drenched with the yeast of the wheels. Some merchants of the more audacious sort, restless under the strange new quiet of Tchoupitoulas street, had got letters of mark and reprisal, and let slip these sharp-nosed deerhounds upon the tardy, unsuspecting ships that came sailing up

to the Passes unaware of the declaration of war. But that game too was up.

The blockade had closed in like a prison-gate: the lighter tow-boats, draped with tarpaulins, were huddled together under Slaughterhouse Point, with their cold boilers and motionless machinery yielding to rust; the more powerful ones had been moored at the long wharf vacated by Morgan's Texas steamships; there had been a great hammering, and making of chips, and clatter of railroad iron, turning these tow-boats into iron-clad cotton gun-boats, and these had crawled away, some up and some down the river, to be seen in that harbor no more. At length only the foundries, the dry-docks across the river, and the ship-yard in suburb Jefferson, where the great ram *Mississippi* was being too slowly built, were active, and the queen of Southern commerce, the city that had once believed it was to

be the greatest in the world, was absolutely out of employment.

There was, true, some movement of the sugar and rice crops into the hands of merchants who had advanced the money to grow them; and the cotton-presses and cotton-yards were full of cotton, but there it all stuck; and when one counts in a feeble exchange of city for country supplies, there was nothing more. Except — yes — that the merchants had turned upon each other, and were now engaged in a mere passing back and forth among themselves in speculation the daily diminishing supply of goods and food. Some were too noble to take part in this, and dealt only with consumers. I remember one odd little old man, an extensive wholesale grocer, who used to get tipsy all by himself every day, and go home so, but who would not speculate on the food of a distressed city. He had not got down to that.

Gold and silver had long ago disappeared. Confederate money was the currency; and not merely was the price of food and raiment rising, but the value of the money was going down. The State, too, had a paper issue, and the city had another. Yet with all these there was first a famine of small change, and then a deluge of "shinplasters." Pah! What a mess it was! The boss butchers and the keepers of drinking-houses actually took the lead in issuing "money." The current joke was that you could pass the label of an olive-oil bottle, because it was greasy, smelt bad, and bore an autograph — Plagniol Frères, if I remember rightly. I did my first work as a cashier in those days, and I can remember the smell of my cash-drawer yet. Instead of five-cent pieces we had car-tickets. How the grimy little things used to stick together! They would pass and pass until they were so soft and illegible with grocers' and butchers' handling that you could tell only by some faint show of their original color what company had issued them. Rogues did a lively business in "split tickets," literally splitting them and making one ticket serve for two.

Decay had come in. In that warm, moist climate it is always hungry, and wherever it is allowed to feed, eats with a greed that is strange

to see. With the wharves, always expensive and difficult to maintain, it made havoc. The occasional idle, weather-stained ship moored beside them, and resting on the water almost as light and void as an empty peascod, could hardly find a place to fasten to. The streets fell into sad neglect, but the litter of commerce was not in them, and some of their round-stone pavements after a shower would have the melancholy cleanness of weather-bleached bones. How quiet and lonely the harbor grew! The big dry-docks against the farther shore were all empty. Now and then a tug fussed about, with the yellow river all to itself; and one or two steamboats came and went each day, but they moved drowsily, and, across on the other side of the river, a whole fleet of their dingy white sisters lay tied up to the bank, *sine die*. My favorite of all the sea-steamers, the little *Habana*, that had been wont to arrive twice a month from Cuba, disgorge her Spanish-American cargo, and bustle away again, and that I had watched the shipwrights, at their very elbows, razee and fit with three big, raking masts in place of her two small ones, had long ago slipped down the river and through the blockaders, and was now no longer the *Habana*, but the far-famed and dreaded *Sumter*.

The movements of military and naval defense lent some stir. The old revenue-cutter *Washington*, a graceful craft, all wings, no steam, came and went from the foot of Canal street. She was lying there when Farragut's topmasts hove in sight across the low land at English Turn. Near by, on her starboard side, lay a gun-boat, moored near the spot where the "lower coast" packet landed daily, to which spot the crowd used to rush sometimes to see the commanding officer, Major-General Mansfield Lovell, ride aboard, bound down the river to the forts. Lovell was a lithe, brown-haired man of forty-odd, a very attractive figure, giving the eye, at first glance, a promise of much activity. He was a showy horseman, visibly fond of his horse. He rode with so long a stirrup-leather that he simply stood astride the saddle, as straight as a spear; and the idlers of the landing

REAR-ADMIRAL THEODORUS BAILEY, U. S. N.
Captain in command of the first division of the Union fleet.

CAPTAIN THEODORUS BAILEY AND LIEUTENANT GEORGE H. PERKINS ON THEIR
WAY TO DEMAND THE SURRENDER OF NEW ORLEANS.

LIEUTENANT THOMAS B. HUGER,
C. S. N.
In command of the "McRae."

loved to see him keep the saddle and pass from the wharf to the steamboat's deck on her long, narrow stage-plank without dismounting.

Such petty breaks in the dreariness got to be scarce and precious toward the last. Not that the town seemed so desolate then as it does now, as one tells of it; but the times were grim.

Opposite the rear of the store where I was now employed—for it fronted in Common street and stretched through to Canal—the huge, unfinished custom-house reared its lofty granite walls, and I used to go up to its top now and then to cast my eye over the broad city and harbor below. When I did so, I looked down upon a town that had never been really glad again after the awful day of Shiloh. She had sent so many gallant fellows to help Beauregard, and some of them so young,—her last gleaning,—that when, on the day of their departure, they marched with solid column and firm-set, unsmiling mouths down the long gray lane made by the open ranks of those old Confederate Guards, and their escort broke into cheers and tears, and waved their gray shakos on the tops of their bayonets, and seized the dear lads' hands as they passed in mute self-devotion and steady tread, while the trumpets sang "Listen to the Mocking-bird," that was the last time; the town never cheered with elation afterward; and when the people next uncovered, it was in silence, to let the body of Albert Sidney Johnston, their great chevalier, pass slowly up St.

Charles street behind the muffled drums, while on their quivering hearts was written as with a knife the death-roll of that lost battle. One of those—a former school-mate of mine—who had brought that precious body walked beside the bier, with the stains of camp and battle on him from head to foot. The war was coming very near.

Many of the town's old forms and habits of peace held fast. The city, I have said, was under martial law; yet the city management still went through its old routines. The volunteer fire department was as voluntary and as redundantly riotous as ever. The police courts, too, were as cheerful as of old. The public schools had merely substituted "Dixie," the "Marseillaise," and the "Bonnie Blue Flag," for "Hail Columbia" and the "Star-Spangled Banner," and were running straight along. There was one thing besides, of which many of us knew nothing at the time,—a system of espionage, secret, diligent, and fierce, that marked down every man suspected of sympathy with the enemy in a book whose name was too vile to find place on any page. This was not the military secret service,—that is to be expected wherever there is war,—nor

any authorized police, but the scheme of some of the worst of the villains who had ruled New Orleans with the rod of terror for many years—the "Thugs."

But the public mind was at a transparent heat. Everybody wanted to know of everybody else, "Why don't you go to the front?" Even the gentle maidens demanded tartly, one of another, why their brothers or lovers had not gone long ago, though, in truth, the laggards were few indeed. The very children were fierce. For now even we, the uninformed, the lads and women, knew the enemy was closing down upon us. Of course we confronted the fact very valorously, we boys and mothers and sisters—and the newspapers. Had we not inspected the fortifications ourselves? Was not every man in town ready to rush into them at the twelve taps of the fire-alarm bells? Were we not ready to man them if the men gave out? Nothing

afloat could pass the forts. Nothing that walked could get through our swamps. The *Mississippi*—and, in fact, she was a majestically terrible structure, only let us *complete* her—would sweep the river clean.

But there was little laughter. Food was dear; the destitute poor were multiplying terribly; the market men and women, mainly Germans, Gascon-French, and Sicilians, had lately refused to take the shinplaster currency, and the city authority had forced them to accept it. There was little to laugh at. The Mississippi was gnawing its levees and threatening to plunge in upon us. The city was believed to be full of spies.

I shall not try to describe the day the alarm-bells told us the city was in danger and called every man to his mustering-point. The children poured out from the school-gates and ran crying to their homes, meeting their sobbing mothers at their thresholds. The men fell into ranks. I was left entirely alone in charge of the store in which I was employed. Late in the afternoon, receiving orders to close it, I did so, and went home. But I did not stay. I went to the river-side. There until far into the night I saw hundreds of drays carrying cotton out of the presses and yards to the wharves, where it was fired. The glare of those sinuous miles of flame set men and women weeping and wailing thirty miles away on the farther shore of Lake Pontchartrain. But the next day was the day of terrors. During the night fear, wrath, and sense of betrayal had run through the people as the fire had run through the cotton. You have seen, perhaps, a family fleeing with lamentations and wringing of hands out of a burning house: multiply it by thousands upon thousands; that was

MAJOR-GENERAL BENJAMIN F. BUTLER, U. S. V.
Commander of the Military forces of the New Orleans Expedition.

PIERRE SOULÉ.
From a daguerreotype taken about 1851.

New Orleans, though the houses were not burning. The firemen were out; but they cast fire on the waters, putting the torch to the empty ships and cutting them loose to float down the river.

Whoever could go was going. The great mass, that had no place to go to or means to go with, was beside itself. "Betrayed! betrayed!" it cried, and ran in throngs from street to street, seeking some vent, some victim for its wrath. I saw a crowd catch a poor fellow at the corner of Maga- zine and Common streets, whose crime was that he looked like a stranger and might be a spy. He was the palest living man I ever saw. They swung him to a neighboring lamp-post, but the Foreign Legion was patroling the town in strong squads, and one of its lieutenants, all green and gold, leaped with drawn sword, cut the rope, and saved the man. This was but one occurrence: there were many like it. I stood in the rear door of our store, Canal street, soon after reopening it. The junior of the firm was within. I called him to look toward the river. The masts of the cutter *Washington* were slowly tipping, declining, sinking—down she went. The gun-boat moored next to her began to smoke all over and then to blaze. My employers fell into ranks and left the city—left their goods and their affairs in the hands of one mere lad (no stranger would have thought I had reached fourteen) and one big German porter. I closed the doors, sent the porter to his place in the Foreign Legion, and ran to the levee to see the sights.

What a gathering! The riff-raff of the wharves, the town, the gutters. Such women—such wrecks of women! And all the juvenile rag-tag. The lower steamboat landing, well covered with sugar, rice, and molasses, was being rifled. The men smashed; the women scooped up the smashings. The river was overflowing the top of the levee. A rain-storm began to threaten. "Are the Yan- kee ships in sight?" I asked of an idler. He pointed out the tops of their naked masts as they showed up across the huge bend of the river. They were engaging the batteries at Camp Chal- mette—the old field of Jackson's renown. Pres- ently that was over. Ah, me! I see them now as they come slowly round Slaughterhouse Point into full view, silent, grim, and terrible; black with men, heavy with deadly portent; the long-ban- ished Stars and Stripes flying against the frowning sky. Oh, for the *Mississippi*! the *Mississippi*! Just then she came down upon them. But how? Drifting helplessly, a mass of flames.

The crowds on the levee howled and screamed with rage. The swarming decks answered never a word; but one old tar on the *Hartford*, standing with lanyard in hand beside a great pivot-gun, so plain to view that you could see him smile, silently patted its big black breech and blandly grinned.

And now the rain came down in sheets. About 1 or 2 o'clock in the afternoon (as I remember), I being again in the store with but one door ajar, came a roar of shoutings and imprecations and crowding feet down Common street. "Hurrah for

SCENE AT THE CITY HALL—HAULING DOWN THE STATE FLAG.*

FORT JACKSON IN 1885.

Jeff Davis! Hurrah for Jeff Davis! Shoot them! Kill them! Hang them!" I locked the door on the outside, and ran to the front of the mob, bawling with the rest, "Hurrah for Jeff Davis!" About every third man there had a weapon out. Two officers of the United States navy were walking abreast, unguarded and alone, looking not to right or left, never frowning, never flinching, while the mob screamed in their ears, shook cocked pistols in their faces, cursed and crowded, and gnashed upon them. So through the gates of death those two men walked to the City Hall to demand the town's surrender. It was one of the bravest deeds I ever saw done.

Later events, except one, I leave to other pens. An officer from the fleet stood on the City Hall roof about to lower the flag of Louisiana. In the street beneath gleamed the bayonets of a body of marines. A howitzer pointed up and another down the street. All around swarmed the mob. Just then Mayor Monroe—lest the officer above should be fired upon, and the howitzers open upon the crowd—came out alone and stood just before one of the howitzers, tall, slender, with folded arms, eying the gunner. Down sank the flag. Captain Bell, tall and stiff, marched off with the flag rolled under his arm, and the howitzers clanking behind. Then cheer after cheer rang out for Monroe. And now, I dare say, every one is well pleased that, after all, New Orleans never lowered her colors with her own hands.

* General Beauregard, in a letter to Admiral Preble, in 1872, says this flag had thirteen stripes, four blue, six white, and three red, commencing at the top, with the colors as written. The Union was red, with its sides equal to the width of seven stripes. In its center was a single pale-yellow five-pointed star.—A. K.

INCIDENTS OF THE OCCUPATION OF NEW ORLEANS.

BY ALBERT KAUTZ, CAPTAIN, U. S. N.

AT 1 o'clock P. M. of the 25th of April, 1862, Farragut's squadron having completed its memorable passage of Forts Jackson and St. Philip, and having silenced the Chalmette batteries, anchored in front of the city of New Orleans in a drenching rain.

Captain Theodorus Bailey, being second in command, claimed the privilege of carrying ashore the demand for the surrender of the city. This was accorded him by the flag-officer, and the captain, accompanied by Lieutenant George H. Perkins (now captain), at once proceeded to the City Hall. Mayor Monroe took the ground that as General Lovell had not yet left the city, the demand should be made on him. At the captain's request the mayor sent for the general, who in a few moments appeared with his staff. General Lovell said he would not surrender the city, adding that he had already withdrawn his soldiers, and that at the close of the interview he had intended to join his command. Captain Bailey had to return and report to Farragut that there was no one on shore willing to surrender the city. Two or three gentlemen had accompanied Captain Bailey and Lieutenant Perkins to the City Hall, and after the interview Colonel W. S. Lovell and one other of the general's staff escorted them to the landing.

The mob, overawed by the frowning batteries of the ships, really seemed dazed and did not offer to assault the Union officers. On the following morning, however, the people in the streets began to wonder whether anything more was going to be done, and became more violent and boisterous.

Farragut determined to make a formal demand for the surrender on Mayor Monroe, and at 10 o'clock on the morning of the 26th he sent me ashore, with instructions to deliver the official demand to the mayor. My little force on leaving the Hartford consisted of Midshipman John H. Read and a marine guard of twenty men under command of Second Lieutenant George Heisler. We landed on the levee in front of a howling mob, which thronged the river-front as far as the eye could reach. It was expected that I would take the marines with me to the City Hall, as a body-guard, and Farragut informed me that if a shot was fired at us by the mob, he would open fire from all the ships and level the town. The marines were drawn up in line, and I attempted to reason with the mob, but soon found this impossible. I then thought to clear the way by bringing the marines to an aim, but women and children were shoved to the front, while the angry mob behind them shouted: "Shoot, you —— Yankees, shoot!" The provocation was certainly very great, and nothing but the utter absence of respectability in the faces of the people caused me to refrain from giving the order to fire.

Fortunately at this critical moment I discovered an officer of the City Guards, whom I hailed and told that I wished to communicate with the mayor. He begged me to leave the marines on the levee, for he felt sure that to march them through the streets at this time would provoke a conflict. As my object was to communicate with the mayor without unnecessary shedding of blood, I sent the marine guard back to the ship, retaining only one non-commissioned officer, with a musket.

I tied my handkerchief on the bayonet, and with Midshipman Read and this man took up the march for the City Hall. We were cursed and jostled by the mob which filled the streets, but no actual violence was offered us. We found the mayor in the City Hall with his council. The Hon. Pierre Soulé was also there, having doubtless been called in as an adviser. The mayor declined to surrender the city formally, but said as we had the force we could take possession.

While we were in the City Hall a mob came up from the lower part of the city with an American ensign, and when they saw us they tore the flag to shreds, and threw them in the open window at us. I did not comprehend the meaning of this singular and wild demonstration at the time, but afterward learned that on the morning of this same day Farragut had instructed Captain H. W. Morris of the Pensacola, then at anchor abreast of the United States Mint, to hoist a flag on that building, it being United States property. Captain Morris accordingly sent Lieutenant Stillwell with some officers and men from the ship, and the flag was hoisted. It was up only a short time when Mumford hauled it down. It was seized by the mob, which paraded it through the streets with fife and drum until they reached the City Hall, where it was destroyed, as above described. I afterward happened to be present when Farragut reported the hauling down of this flag to General Butler, and I heard the latter say, "I will make an example of that fellow by hanging him." Farragut smiled and remarked, "You know, General, you will have to catch him before you can hang him." General Butler said, "I know that, but I will catch him, and then hang him." History attests how well he kept his word, and there is no doubt but that this hanging proved a wholesome lesson.

The mob soon appeared to be growing more violent, and above the general din was heard an occasional invitation to "the —— Yankees" to "come out and be run up to lamp-posts." At this time Mr. Soulé suggested to me that it would save much trouble to all concerned if I would take my party in a carriage from the rear exit of the hall, the mayor's secretary, Mr. Marion Baker, going with us, while he addressed the mob. He did not hope to have the mob obey him, he only expected to hold it long enough to give us time to get to the landing; and he accomplished his undertaking admirably. Few people ever knew what an important service Mr. Soulé thus rendered to New Orleans.

Farragut fully approved my action. I was not expected to bring a satisfactory answer from the mayor, for he was really helpless and had no control over the city. All he could say was, "Come and take the city; we are powerless." . . .

ENTRANCE TO FORT ST. PHILIP,—1884.

THE BATTLE OF GAINES'S MILL.
From a photograph of the painting by the Prince de Joinville, 1862, made from personal observation.
Persons represented : 1. Gen. F. J. Porter ; 2. Gen. G. W. Morell ; 3. Gen. George G. Meade (on horseback in the distance), and the following aides-de-camp : 4. Comte de Paris ; 5. Colonel Radowitz ; 6. Major Hammerstein ; 7. Duc de Chartres ; 8. Captain Mason.

MAJOR-GENERAL FITZ-JOHN PORTER, U. S. V.

HANOVER COURT HOUSE AND GAINES'S MILL.

(*Continuing " The Peninsular Campaign," from page 94.*)

BY FITZ-JOHN PORTER, MAJOR-GENERAL, U. S. V.
Union Commander at Hanover Court House and Gaines's Mill.

UNDER the direction of General McClellan certain measures for the protection of the right flank of the army in its advance upon Richmond were put in my hands, beginning simultaneously with the march of the army from the Pamunkey. Among these were the clearing of the enemy from the upper Peninsula as far as Hanover Court House or beyond, and, in case General McDowell's large forces, then at Fredericksburg, were not to join us, the destruction of railroad and other bridges over the South and Pamunkey rivers, in order to prevent the enemy in large force from getting into our rear from that direction, and in order, further, to cut the Virginia Central Railroad, the one great line of the enemy's communications between Richmond and Northern Virginia.

A portion of this duty had been accomplished along the Pamunkey as far as was deemed prudent by Colonel G. K. Warren's forces, posted at Old Church, when on the 26th of May, preparatory to an immediate advance upon Richmond, General McClellan directed me to complete the duty above specified, so that the enemy in Northern Virginia, then occupying the attention of McDowell, Banks, and Frémont, could not be suddenly thrown upon our flank and rear nor otherwise strengthen the enemy in Richmond. I was allowed to adopt my own plans, and to select such additional forces as I deemed necessary.

At 4 A. M. on the 27th General G. W. Morell, commanding the division consisting of J. H. Martindale's, Daniel Butterfield's, and James McQuade's brigades, marched from New Bridge preceded by an advance-guard of two regiments of cavalry and

a battery of artillery under command of General W. H. Emory. At the same hour Colonel Warren with his brigade moved from Old Church. . . . In a pelting storm of rain, through deep mud and water for about 14 miles, the command struggled and pushed its way to Peake's Station on the Virginia Central Railroad, 2 miles from Hanover Court House, where we came in presence of the enemy.

At once a force of infantry (Colonel C. A. Johnson's 25th New York Volunteers and Berdan's Sharp-shooters), protected by artillery, was sent forward to hold the enemy in check, pending the arrival of Morell, who was slowly pushing along the swampy roads. Cavalry and artillery were sent to the left along the Ashland road, to guard our flank and destroy the railroad and telegraph at the crossing. On Martindale's arrival he was sent in support of this force, and with it soon became engaged with very persistent opponents. Butterfield was sent to the front, where, deploying in line, he moved rapidly upon the enemy, put them to flight, and captured many prisoners and one cannon and caisson.

CONFEDERATE RETREAT THROUGH MECHANICSVILLE BEFORE THE ADVANCE OF McCLELLAN'S ARTILLERY, MAY 24TH.

As the enemy gave way, the troops were pushed on toward Hanover Court House in pursuit of the fleeing foe and to strike their camp, which I had been informed was near by, but which was found abandoned. Suddenly the signal officers notified me of a large force attacking our flank and rear, and especially the troops under Martindale. At once the infantry were faced about, and at double-quick step hastened to the aid of their imperiled comrades. McQuade's brigade, on arriving opposite the contending forces, moved in line to the attack. Butterfield, now in rear as faced about, pushed his brigade through the woods and fell with vigor upon the enemy's flank. The united attack quickly routed the enemy, inflicting heavy losses in killed and wounded and prisoners. . . .

After the battle of Fair Oaks, during the greater part of the month of June, 1862, the Army of the Potomac, under General McClellan, and the Army of Northern Virginia, under General Lee, confronted each other, east of Richmond. The two armies were of nearly equal strength. McClellan's forces, divided by the Chickahominy, were extended south of that stream, from New Bridge to White Oak Swamp, leaving north of the river only the Fifth Army Corps. The Confederate troops faced the Federal army throughout its length, from White Oak Swamp to New Bridge, and thence up the right bank of the Chickahominy, covering the important crossings at Mechanicsville and Meadow Bridge, north of the city. . . .

In the middle of June General McClellan intrusted to me the management of affairs on the north bank of the Chickahominy, and confided to me his plans as well as his hopes and apprehensions. His plans embraced defensive arrangements against an attack from Richmond upon our weak right flank. We did not fear the results of such an attack if made by the forces from Richmond alone; but if, in addition, we were to be attacked by Jackson's forces, suspicions of whose approach [from the Shenandoah Valley] were

PHILIP ST. GEORGE COOKE,
BREVET MAJOR-GENERAL, U. S. A.
From a photograph.

UNION ARTILLERY AT MECHANICSVILLE SHELLING THE CONFEDERATE WORKS
SOUTH OF THE CHICKAHOMINY.

PROFESSOR T. S. C. LOWE OBSERVING THE BATTLE
OF SEVEN PINES FROM HIS BALLOON "IN-
TREPID" ON THE NORTH SIDE OF
THE CHICKAHOMINY.

already aroused, we felt that we should be in peril. But as Jackson had thus far prevented McDowell from joining us, we trusted that McDowell, Banks, and Frémont, who had been directed to watch Jackson, would be able to prevent him from joining Lee, or, at least, would give timely warning of his escape from their front and follow close upon his heels.

With McClellan's approval, my command was distributed as follows:

General Geo. G. Meade's brigade of General Geo. A. McCall's division of Pennsylvania Reserves was posted at Gaines's house, protecting a siege-battery controlling New Bridge; Generals John F. Reynolds's and Truman Seymour's brigades held the rifle-pits skirting the east bank of Beaver Dam Creek and the field-works covering the only crossings near Mechanicsville and Ellerson's Mill. . . . Cooke's cavalry, near Cold Harbor, guarded the right rear and scouted toward Hanover Court House, while Morell's and Sykes's divisions were conveniently camped so as to cover the bridge-crossings and to move quickly to any threatened point.

Such was the situation on the 24th of June, when, at midnight, General McClellan telegraphed me that a pretended deserter, whom I had that day

sent him, had informed him that Jackson was in the immediate vicinity, ready to unite with Lee in an attack upon my command. . . . Reynolds, who had special charge of the defenses of Beaver Dam Creek and of the forces at and above Mechanicsville, was at once informed of the situation. He prepared to give our anticipated visitors a warm welcome. . . .

Early on the 26th I was informed of a large increase of forces opposite Reynolds, and before noon the Confederates gave evidence of their intention to cross the river at Meadow Bridge and Mechanicsville, while from our cavalry scouts along the Virginia Central Railroad came reports of the approach from the north of large masses of troops.

Thus the attitude of the two armies toward each other was changed. Yesterday, McClellan was rejoicing over the success of his advance toward Richmond, and he was confident of reinforcement by McDowell. To-day, all the united available forces in Virginia were to be thrown against his right flank, which was not in a convenient position to be supported. The prizes now to be contended for were: on the part of McClellan, the safety of his right wing, protection behind his intrenchments with the possibility of being able to remain there, and the gain of sufficient time to enable him to effect a change of base to the James; on the part of Lee, the destruction of McClellan's right wing, and, by drawing him from his intrenchments and attacking him in front, the raising of the siege of Richmond.

The morning of Thursday, June 26th, dawned clear and bright, giving promise that the day would be a brilliant one. The formation of the ground south of the Chickahominy opposite Mechanics-

ville, and west to Meadow Bridge, largely concealed from view the forces gathered to execute an evidently well-planned and well-prepared attack upon my command. . . . In the northern and western horizon vast clouds of dust arose, indicating the movements of Jackson's advancing forces. They were far distant, and we had reason to believe that the obstacles to their rapid advance, placed in their way by detachments sent for that purpose, would prevent them from making an attack that day. As before stated, we did not fear Lee alone; we did fear his attack, combined with one by Jackson on our flank. . . .

About 2 o'clock P. M., on the 26th, the boom of a single cannon in the direction of Mechanicsville resounded through our camps. This was the signal which had been agreed upon, to announce the fact that the enemy were crossing the Chickahominy. The curtain rose; the stage was prepared for the first scene of the tragedy. At once tents were struck, wagons packed and sent to the rear to cross to the right bank of the Chickahominy. The several divisions were promptly formed, and took the positions to which they had previously been assigned. General McCall assumed command at Beaver Dam Creek; Meade joined him, taking position behind Seymour; Martindale and General Charles Griffin, of Morell's division, went, respectively, to the right and rear of Reynolds; Butterfield was directed to support General Cooke's, and subsequently Martindale's right, while Sykes was held ready to move wherever needed. Reynolds and Seymour prepared for action and concealed their men.

About 3 o'clock the enemy, under Longstreet, D. H. and A. P. Hill, in large bodies commenced rapidly to cross the Chickahominy almost simul-

taneously at Mechanicsville, Meadow Bridge, and above, and pushed down the left bank, along the roads leading to Beaver Dam Creek. In accordance with directions previously given, the outposts watching the access to the crossings fell back after slight resistance to their already designated position on the east bank of Beaver Dam Creek, destroying the bridges as they retired.

After passing Mechanicsville the attacking forces were divided, a portion taking the road to the right to Ellerson's Mill, while the larger body directed their march to the left into the valley of Beaver Dam Creek, upon the road covered by Reynolds. Apparently unaware, or regardless, of the great danger in their front, this force moved on with animation and confidence, as if going to parade, or engaging in a sham battle. Suddenly, when half-way down the bank of the valley, our men opened upon it rapid volleys of artillery and infantry, which strewed the road and hillside with hundreds of dead and wounded, and drove the main body of the survivors back in rapid flight to and beyond Mechanicsville. So rapid was the fire upon the enemy's huddled masses clambering back up the hill, that some of Reynolds's ammunition was exhausted, and two regiments were relieved by the 4th Michigan and 14th New York of Griffin's brigade. On the extreme right a small force of the enemy secured a foothold on the east bank, but it did no harm, and retired under cover of darkness.

The forces which were directed against Seymour at Ellerson's Mill made little progress. Seymour's direct and Reynolds's flank fire soon arrested them and drove them to shelter, suffering even more disastrously than those who had attacked Reynolds. Late in the afternoon, greatly strengthened, they renewed the attack with spirit and energy, some

THE UNION DEFENSES AT ELLERSON'S MILL.
From a sketch made at the time.

**CAPTURE OF ABANDONED UNION GUNS
AT GAINES'S MILLS.**
From a sketch made at the time.

reaching the borders of the stream, but only to be repulsed with terrible slaughter, which warned them not to attempt a renewal of the fight. Little depressions in the ground shielded many from our fire, until, when night came on, they all fell back beyond the range of our guns. . . .

General McClellan had joined me on the battle-field at an early hour in the afternoon. While we discussed plans for the immediate future, numerous and unvarying accounts from our outposts and scouts toward the Pamunkey warned us of the danger impending on the arrival of Jackson, and necessitated a decision as to which side of the Chickahominy should be held in force. He left me late at night, about 1 A. M. (June 27th), with the expectation of receiving information on his arrival at his own headquarters from the tenor of which he would be enabled to decide whether I should hold my present position or withdraw to a well-selected and more advantageous one east of Gaines's Mill, where I could protect the bridges across the Chickahominy, over which I must retire if compelled to leave the left bank. He left General Barnard, of the Engineers, with me, to point out the new line of battle in case he should decide to withdraw me from Beaver Dam Creek. The orders to withdraw reached me about 3 o'clock A. M., and were executed as rapidly as possible.

The position selected for the new stand was east of Powhite Creek, about six miles from Beaver Dam Creek. The line of battle was semicircular, the extremities being in the valley of the Chicka-hominy, while the intermediate portion occupied the high grounds along the bank of a creek and curved around past McGehee's to Elder Swamp. Part of the front was covered by the ravine of the creek. The east bank was lined with trees and

underbrush, which afforded concealment and protection to our troops and artillery. . . . Before sunrise of the 27th the troops were withdrawn from Beaver Dam Creek and sent to their new position east of Powhite Creek, destroying the bridges across it after them. . . .

Our new line of battle was well selected and strong, though long and requiring either more troops to man it than I had, or too great a thinning of my line by the use of the reserves. The east bank of the creek, from the valley of the Chickahominy to its swampy sources, was elevated, sloping, and timbered. The bed of the stream was nearly dry, and its west bank gave excellent protection to the first line of infantry posted under it to receive the enemy descending the cleared field sloping to it. The swampy grounds along the sources of the creek were open to our view in front for hundreds of yards, and were swept by the fire of infantry and artillery. The roads from Gaines's Mill and Old Cold Harbor, along which the enemy were compelled to advance, were swept by artillery posted on commanding ground.

Along the ground thus formed and close to its border were posted the divisions of Morell and Sykes,—the latter on the right. . . . McCall's division formed a second line, near the artillery in reserve, in rear of Morell, and immediately behind the woods on the left. Reynolds, the first to leave Beaver Dam Creek, had gone to Barker's Mill to cover the approaches from Cold Harbor and Despatch Station to Grapevine Bridge; but, hearing the battle raging on our left, and having no enemy in his front, while Emory, of Cooke's cavalry, with artillery, was near at hand to do the duty assigned to him, he hastened to join McCall, arriving opportunely in rear of Griffin's left. . . .

Believing my forces too small to defend successfully this long line, I asked General Barnard, when he left me, to represent to General McClellan the necessity of reinforcements to thicken and to fill vacant spaces in my front line. . . . While withdrawing from Beaver Dam, I had seen, to my delight, General H. W. Slocum's division of Franklin's corps crossing the river to my assistance. McClellan had promised to send it, and I needed it; it was one of the best divisions of the army. . . . But to our disappointment, through some misunderstanding, the division was almost immediately recalled to Franklin. In response, however, to a later call, it returned at a time when it was greatly needed, and rendered invaluable services. . . .

The Confederates, under Longstreet and A. P. Hill, following us from Mechanicsville, moved cautiously by the roads leading by Dr. Gaines's house to New Cold Harbor, and by 2 P. M. had formed lines of battle behind the crest of the hills east of Powhite Creek. These lines were parallel to ours, and extended from the valley of the Chickahominy through New Cold Harbor around Morell's front, so as nearly to reach Warren's brigade—the left of Sykes's division. At Gaines's Mill, Colonel Thomas Cass's gallant 9th Massachusetts Volunteers of Griffin's brigade obstinately resisted A. P. Hill's crossing, and were so successful in delaying his advance, after crossing, as to compel him to employ large bodies to force the regiment back to the main line. This brought on a contest which extended to Morell's center and over Martin's front—on his right—and lasted from 12:30 to near 2 o'clock—Cass and his immediate supports falling back south of the swamps. This persistent and prolonged resistance gave to this battle one of its well-known names.

Another column of the enemy, D. H. Hill's, from Beaver Dam Creek, and Jackson's column, from

Northern Virginia, with which it had united, came opposite my right front from the direction of Old Cold Harbor and deployed, connecting with A. P. Hill's on the left and extending to our right beyond McGehee's. The advance column of these troops came a little earlier than those under Longstreet and A. P. Hill, but were more cautious and for some hours not so aggressive. Believing that they were passing on down the river to intercept our communications, and thinking that I might strike them to good advantage while in motion, I asked permission to follow, intending to attack with Sykes's division and Emory of Cooke's cavalry, leaving Morell and McCall to hold the other lines in check. Information, however, soon poured in, convincing me that this force was larger than any I could use against them, and that still larger forces were forming to attack our left and center. This compelled me to keep my troops united and under cover, and also again to ask aid from the south bank of the Chickahominy. My first message to General McClellan was not delivered, as already stated; my second one was responded to by the speedy arrival of Slocum.

Soon after 2 P. M., A. P. Hill's force, between us and New Cold Harbor, again began to show an aggressive disposition, independent of its own troops on its flanks, by advancing from under cover of the woods, in lines well formed and extending, as the contest progressed, from in front of Martin's battery to Morell's left. Dashing across the intervening plains, floundering in the swamps, and struggling against the tangled brushwood, brigade after brigade seemed almost to melt away before the concentrated fire of our artillery and infantry; yet others pressed on, followed by supports as dashing and as brave as their predecessors, despite their heavy losses and the disheartening effect of having to clamber over many of their

RUINS OF GAINES'S MILL, LOOKING EAST.
From a photograph made in the spring of 1885.

At the time of the battle, this building was of five stories, and was, it is said, one of the finest grist-mills in Virginia. The wooden structure, dovetailed into the ruins, now covers but one pair of burrs. The mill was not injured in the fight, but was burned by Sheridan's cavalry in May, 1864, the fire extending to a dwelling-house which stood just beyond the mill. The main conflict was a mile farther to the south-east, but the ridge shown in the picture was the scene of a most gallant resistance to the Confederate advance by the 9th Massachusetts regiment, acting as a rear-guard to Porter's corps. The road to New Cold Harbor and the battle-ground runs to the right.

UNION FIELD-HOSPITAL AT SAVAGE'S STATION, AFTER THE BATTLE OF GAINES'S MILL.
From a photograph taken before the army withdrew, early on the morning of June 30th.

disabled and dead, and to meet their surviving comrades rushing back in great disorder from the deadly contest. For nearly two hours the battle raged, extending more or less along the whole line to our extreme right. The fierce firing of artillery and infantry, the crash of the shot, the bursting of shells, and the whizzing of bullets, heard above the roar of artillery and the volleys of musketry, all combined was something fearful.

Regiments quickly replenished their exhausted ammunition by borrowing from their more bountifully supplied and generous companions. Some withdrew, temporarily, for ammunition, and fresh regiments took their places ready to repulse, sometimes to pursue, their desperate enemy, for the purpose of retaking ground from which we had been pressed and which it was necessary to occupy in order to hold our position.

The enemy were repulsed in every direction. An ominous silence reigned. It caused the inference that their troops were being gathered and massed for a desperate and overwhelming attack. To meet it, our front line was concentrated, reinforced, and arranged to breast the avalanche, should it come. I again asked for additional reinforcements. French's and Meagher's brigades, of Sumner's corps, were sent forward by the com-

manding general, but did not arrive till near dark. . . . All available means were used by which I could be kept informed so that I could provide, in the best possible manner, for the many rapid changes and wants suddenly springing up. The Prince de Joinville and his two nephews—the Comte de Paris and Duc de Chartres—and Colonels Gantt, Radowitz, and Hammerstein, from the commanding general's staff, joined me as volunteer aides. . . .

During the greater part of the afternoon, D. H. Hill's troops, in detachments, were more or less aggressive on the right. The silence which followed the repulse, already referred to, lasted but a short time. The renewed attacks raged with great fierceness and fury, with slight intermission, along the most of our front, till after 5 o'clock. Large and numerous bodies of infantry from the direction of Old Cold Harbor, under cover of artillery, directed their attacks upon Sykes's division and Martin's battery; others, from the west side of Powhite Creek, were hurled in rapid succession against Martindale and Butterfield. These furious attacks were successfully repelled, but were immediately renewed by fresh troops. . . . At 4 o'clock, when Slocum arrived, all our reserves were exhausted. His brigades were necessarily separated

and sent where most needed. Newton's brigade, being in advance, was led to the right of Griffin, there to drive back the enemy and retake ground only held by the enemy for an instant. Taylor's brigade filled vacant spaces in Morell's division, and Bartlett's was sent to Sykes, just in time to render invaluable service, both in resisting and attacking. . . .

About 6:30, preceded by a silence of half an hour, the attack was renewed all along the line with the same apparent determination to sweep us by the force of numbers from the field, if not from existence. The result was evidently a matter of life or death to our opponent's cause. This attack, like its predecessors, was successfully repulsed throughout its length. . . .

As if for a final effort, as the shades of evening were coming upon us, and the woods were filled with smoke, limiting the view therein to a few yards, the enemy again massed his fresher and reformed regiments, and threw them in rapid succession against our thinned and wearied battalions, now almost without ammunition, and with guns so foul that they could not be loaded rapidly. . . . The attacks, though coming like a series of apparently irresistible avalanches, had thus far made no inroads upon our firm and disciplined ranks. Even in this last attack we successfully resisted, driving

back our assailants with immense loss, or holding them beyond our lines, except in one instance, near the center of Morell's line, where by force of numbers and under cover of the smoke of battle our line was penetrated and broken; this at a point where I least expected it. This was naturally the weakest point of our line, owing to the closer proximity of the woods held by the enemy. Under his cover they could form, and with less exposure in time and ground than elsewhere, and launch their battalions in quick succession upon our men. I believed I had guarded against the danger by strongly and often reinforcing the troops holding this part of the line. Here the greater part of McCall's and Slocum's forces were used. Just preceding this break, to my great surprise, I saw cavalry, Rush's Lancers, which I recognized as ours, rushing in numbers through our lines on the left, and carrying off with sudden fright the limbers of our artillery, then prepared to pour their irresistible fire into a pursuing foe. With no infantry to support, and with apparent disaster before them, such of the remainder of these guns as could be moved were carried from the field; some deliberately, others in haste, but not in confusion.

In no other place was our line penetrated or shaken. The right, seeing our disaster, fell back

UNION TROOPS BUILDING THE CORDUROY APPROACHES TO GRAPEVINE BRIDGE.
It was mainly by this bridge that the Union troops were withdrawn the night after the battle of Gaines's Mill.

THE BATTLE OF SAVAGE'S STATION.
From a sketch made at the time.

McClellan's Change of Base and Malvern Hill.

BY DANIEL H. HILL, LIEUTENANT-GENERAL, C. S. A.
Commander of a Division at Malvern Hill.

united and in order, but were compelled to leave behind two guns, the horses of which had been killed. The troops on the left and center retired, some hastily, but not in confusion, often turning back to repulse and pursue the advancing enemy. All soon rallied in rear of the Adams house behind Sykes and the brigades of French and Meagher sent to our aid, and who now, with hearty cheers, greeted our battalions as they retired and re-formed. We lost in all twenty-two cannon; some of these broke down while we were withdrawing, and some ran off the bridges at night while we were crossing to the south bank of the Chickahominy. . . .

This loss of guns, General Porter states, was due to an ill-timed charge by Cooke's cavalry.

At night I was called to General McClellan's headquarters, where the chiefs of corps, or their representatives, were gathered. The commanding general, after hearing full reports, was of the opinion that the final result would be disastrous if we undertook longer to hold the north bank of the river with my command in the condition in which it was left by a hard fight and the loss of rest for two nights. In this opinion all concurred; and I was then instructed to withdraw to the south bank and destroy the bridges after me. The plans to move to the James River were then explained, together with the necessity for the movement, and the orders were given for their execution.

My command was safely withdrawn to the south bank of the river, and the bridges were destroyed soon after sunrise on the 28th. . . .

FIVE of the six Confederate divisions north of the Chickahominy at the close of the battle of Gaines's Mill remained in bivouac all the next day (June 28th), it being deemed too hazardous to force the passage of the river. Ewell was sent with his division to Despatch Station on the York River Railroad. He found the station and the railroad-bridge burnt. J. E. B. Stuart, who followed the retreating Federal cavalry to White House on the Pamunkey, found ruins of stations and stores all along the line. These things proved that General McClellan did not intend to retreat by the short line of the York River Railroad; but it was possible he might take the Williamsburg road. General Lee, therefore, kept his troops on the north side of the river, that he might be ready to move on the Federal flank, should that route be attempted. New Bridge was repaired on Saturday (the 28th), and our troops were then ready to move in either direction. The burnings and explosions in the Federal camp Saturday afternoon and night showed that General McClellan had determined to abandon his strong fortifications around Richmond. Ewell, who was watching him at Bottom's Bridge, and the cavalry, holding the crossings lower down, both reported that there was no attempt at the Williamsburg route. Longstreet and A. P. Hill were sent across the river at New Bridge early on Sunday morning to move down the Darbytown road to the Long Bridge road to intercept the retreat to the James River. . . .

In pursuance of General Lee's plan, Huger was directed (on the 29th) to take the Charles City road to strike the retreating column below White Oak Swamp. Holmes was to take possession of Malvern Hill, and Magruder to follow the line of retreat, as soon as the works were abandoned. The abandonment became known about sunrise on Sunday morning, but Grapevine Bridge was not completed till sunset. Jackson then crossed his corps at that point, my division leading. We bivouacked that night near Savage's Station, where McLaws's division had had a severe fight a few hours before. Just at dawn on Monday, the 30th, we were in motion, when I discovered what appeared to be a line of battle drawn up at the station, but which proved to be a line of sick and of hospital attendants, 2500 in number. About half a mile from the station we saw what seemed to be an entire regiment of Federals cold in death, and learned that a Vermont regiment [the 5th] had been in the desperate charge upon the division of McLaws, and had suffered great loss [killed, 31; wounded, 143]. . . .

We reached White Oak Swamp about noon,

and there found another hospital camp, with about five hundred sick in it. Truly, the Chickahominy swamps were fatal to the Federal forces. A high bluff was on our side of the little stream called White Oak, and a large uncultivated field on the other side. In this field could be seen a battery of artillery, supported by a brigade of infantry — artillerists and infantry lying down and apparently asleep. Under cover of Thomas T. Munford's 2d Virginia cavalry, thirty-one field-pieces were placed upon the bluff, and were ordered to open fire as soon

RUNNING AMMUNITION TRAINS INTO THE CHICKAHOMINY.

THE ARTILLERY ENGAGEMENT AT WHITE
OAK BRIDGE.
From a sketch made at the time.
The view is from Franklin's position south of
the bridge, Jackson's and D. H. Hill's troops
being seen in the distance.

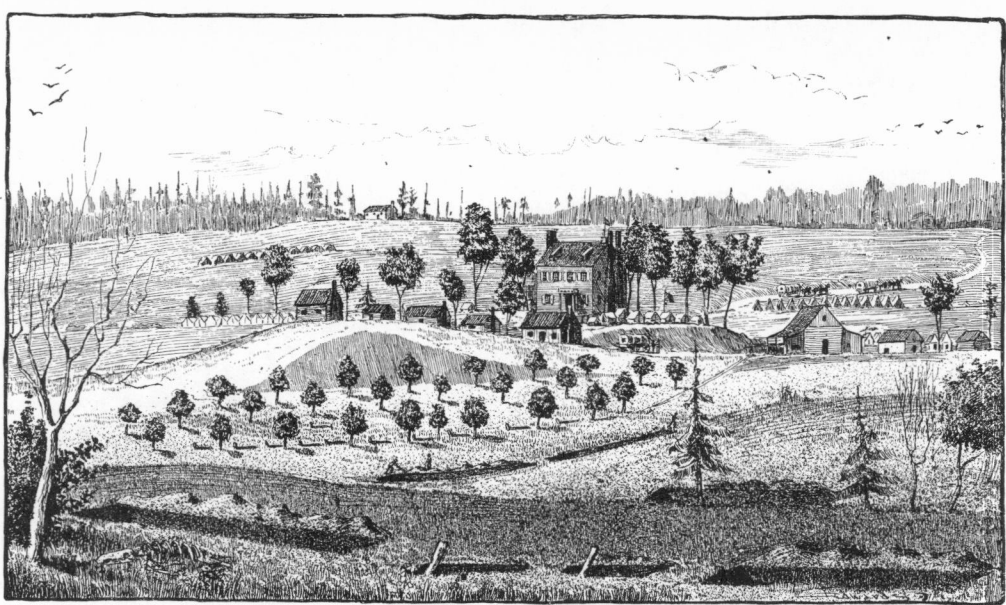

VIEW OF SAVAGE'S STATION FROM THE NORTH SIDE OF THE RAILROAD.
From a sketch made before the battle.

The railroad passes close to the south side of Savage's house. In the foreground are shown burial trenches, and in the peach orchard the graves of officers. The negro cabins on the left were used by the Sanitary Commission; the barn, on the right, was a hospital, but most of the wounded were sheltered in the tents.

as the cavalry mask was removed. The battery fired its loaded guns in reply, and then galloped off, followed by its infantry supports and the long lines of infantry farther back in the field. Munford crossed his regiment over the ford, and Jackson and myself went with him to see what had become of the enemy. We soon found out. The battery had taken up a position behind a point of woods, where it was perfectly sheltered from our guns, but could play upon the broken bridge and ford, and upon every part of the uncultivated field. It opened with grape and canister upon us, and we retired rapidly. Fast riding in the wrong direction is not military, but it is sometimes healthy.

LIEUTENANT-GENERAL DANIEL H. HILL, C. S. A.

We had taken one prisoner, a drunken Irishman, but he declined the honor of going back with us, and made fight with his naked fists. A soldier asked me naïvely whether he should shoot the Irishman or let him go. I am glad that I told him to let the man go, to be a comfort to his family. That Irishman must have had a charmed life. He was under the shelter of his gum-cloth coat hung on a stick, near the ford, when a citizen fired at him four times, from a distance of about fifty paces; and the only recognition that I could see the man make was to raise his hand as if to brush off a fly. One of the shells set the farm-house on fire. We learned from the owner that Franklin's corps was in front of us.

Our cavalry returned by the lower ford, and pronounced it perfectly practicable for infantry. But Jackson did not advance. Why was this? It was the critical day for both commanders, but especially for McClellan. With consummate skill he had crossed his vast train of five thousand wagons and his immense parks of artillery safely over White Oak Swamp, but he was more exposed now than at any time in his flank march. Three columns of attack were converging upon him, and a strong corps was pressing upon his rear. Escape seemed impossible for him, but he *did* escape, at the same time inflicting heavy damage upon his pursuers. General Lee, through no fault in his plans, was to see his splendid prize slip through his hands. Longstreet and A. P. Hill struck the enemy at Frayser's farm (or Glendale) at 3 P. M. on the 30th, and, both being always ready for a fight, immediately attacked. Magruder, who followed them down the Darbytown road, was ordered to the assistance of General Holmes on the New Market road, who was not then engaged, and their two divisions took no part in the action. Huger,

on the Charles City road, came upon Franklin's left flank, but made no attack. I sent my engineer officer, Captain W. F. Lee, to him through the swamp, to ask him whether he could not engage Franklin. He replied that the road was obstructed by fallen timber. So there were five divisions within sound of the firing, and within supporting distance, but not one of them moved. Longstreet and A. P. Hill made a desperate fight, contending against Sumner's corps, and the divisions of McCall, Kearny, and Hooker; but they failed to gain possession of the Quaker road, upon which McClellan was retreating. That night Franklin glided silently by them. He had to pass within easy range of the artillery of Longstreet and Hill, but they did not know he was there. It had been a gallant fight on their part. General Lee reported: "Many prisoners, including a general of division, McCall, were captured, and several batteries, with some thousands of small-arms, were taken." But as an obstruction to the Federal retreat, the fight amounted to nothing.

Major Dabney, in his life of Jackson, thus comments on the inaction of that officer: "On this occasion it would appear, if the vast interests dependent upon General Jackson's coöperation with the proposed attack upon the center were considered, that he came short of the efficiency in action for which he was everywhere else noted." After showing how the crossing of White Oak might have been effected, Dabney adds: "The list of casualties would have been larger than that presented on the 30th, of one cannoneer wounded; but how much shorter would have been the bloody list filled up the next day at Malvern Hill? This temporary eclipse of Jackson's genius was proba-

bly to be explained by physical causes. The labor of the previous days, the sleeplessness, the wear of gigantic cares, with the drenching of the comfortless night, had sunk the elasticity of his will and the quickness of his invention for the nonce below their wonted tension. And which of the sons of man is so great as never to experience this?" I think that an important factor in this inaction was Jackson's pity for his own corps, worn out by long and exhausting marches, and reduced in numbers by its numerous sanguinary battles. He thought that the garrison of Richmond ought now to bear the brunt of the fighting. None of us knew that the veterans of Longstreet and A. P. Hill were unsupported; nor did we even know that the firing that we heard was theirs. Had all our troops been at Frayser's farm, there would have been no Malvern Hill.

Jackson's genius never shone when he was under the command of another. It seemed then to be shrouded or paralyzed. Compare his inertness on this occasion with the wonderful vigor shown a few weeks later at Slaughter's [Cedar] Mountain in the stealthy march to Pope's rear, and later still in the capture of Harper's Ferry. MacGregor on his native heath was not more different from MacGregor in prison than was Jackson his own master from Jackson in a subordinate position. He wrote once to Richmond requesting that he might have "fewer orders and more men." That was the keynote to his whole character. The hooded falcon cannot strike the quarry.

The gentleman who tried his "splendid rifle" on the drunken Irishman was the Rev. L. W. Allen. Mr. Allen had been raised in that neighborhood, and knew Malvern Hill well. He spoke of its commanding height, the difficulties of approach to it, its amphitheatrical form and ample area, which would enable McClellan to arrange his 350 field-guns tier above tier and sweep the plain in every direction. I became satisfied that an attack upon the concentrated Federal army so splendidly posted, and with such vast superiority in artillery, could only be fatal to us. The anxious thought then was, Have Holmes and Magruder been able to keep McClellan from Malvern Hill? General Holmes arrived at Malvern at 10 : 30 A. M. on the 30th, with 5170 infantry, 4 batteries of artillery, and 130 improvised or irregular cavalry. He did not attempt to occupy the hill, although only 1500 Federals had yet reached it. Our cavalry had passed over it on the afternoon of the 29th, and had had a sharp skirmish with the Federal cavalry on the Quaker road.

As General Holmes marched down the river, his troops became visible to the gun-boats, which opened fire upon

THE REAR-GUARD AT WHITE OAK SWAMP—SHOWING GENERAL W. F. SMITH'S DIVISION, FRANKLIN'S CORPS.
Drawn by Julian Scott after his painting owned by the Union League Club, New York.

He lost 2 killed, 49 wounded, 2 pieces of artillery, and 6 caissons. The guns and caissons, General Porter states, were afterward abandoned by the Federals. General Holmes occupied the extreme Confederate right the next day, July 1st, but he took no part in the attack upon Malvern Hill, believing, as he says in his official report, "that it was out of the question to attack the strong position of Malvern Hill from that side with my inadequate force."

Mahone's brigade had some skirmishing with Slocum's Federal division on the 30th, but nothing else was done on that day by Huger's division. Thus it happened that Longstreet and A. P. Hill, with the fragments of their divisions which had been engaged at Gaines's Mill, were struggling alone, while Jackson's whole corps and the divisions of Huger, Magruder, Holmes, McLaws, and my own were near by.

Jackson moved over the swamp early on the first of July, Whiting's division leading. Our

them, throwing those awe-inspiring shells familiarly called by our men "lamp-posts," on account of their size and appearance. Their explosion was very much like that of a small volcano, and had a very demoralizing effect upon new troops, one of whom expressed the general sentiment by saying: "The Yankees throwed them lamp-posts about too careless like." The roaring, howling gun-boat shells were usually harmless to flesh, blood, and bones, but they had a wonderful effect upon the nervous system. General Junius Daniel, a most gallant and accomplished officer, who had a brigade under General Holmes, gave me an incident connected with the affair on the 30th, known as the "Battle of Malvern Cliff." General Holmes, who was very deaf, had gone into a little house concealed from the boats by some intervening woods, and was engaged in some business when the bellowing of the "lamp-posts" began. The irregular cavalry stampeded and made a brilliant charge to the rear. The artillerists of two guns of Graham's Petersburg battery were also panic-struck, and cutting their horses loose mounted them, and, with dangling traces, tried to catch up with the fleet-footed cavaliers. The infantry

troops were inexperienced in the wicked ways of war, having never been under fire before. The fright of the fleeing cavalry would have pervaded their ranks also with the same mischievous result but for the strenuous efforts of their officers, part of whom were veterans. Some of the raw levies crouched behind little saplings to get protection from the shrieking, blustering shells. At this juncture General Holmes, who, from his deafness, was totally unaware of the rumpus, came out of the hut, put his hand behind his right ear, and said : "I thought I heard firing." Some of the pale-faced infantry thought that they also had heard firing.

Part of Wise's brigade joined Holmes on the 30th, with two batteries of artillery and two regiments of cavalry. His entire force then consisted of 5820 infantry, 6 batteries of artillery, and 2 regiments of cavalry. He remained inactive until 4 P. M., when he was told that the Federal army was passing over Malvern Hill in a demoralized condition. He then opened upon the supposed fugitives with six rifled guns, and was speedily undeceived in regard to the disorganization in the Army of the Potomac by a reply from thirty guns,

which in a brief time silenced his own. The audacity of the Federals and the large number of their guns (which had gone in advance of the main body of Porter's corps) made General Holmes believe that he was about to be attacked, and he called for assistance, and, by Longstreet's order, Magruder was sent to him. After a weary march, Magruder was recalled to aid Longstreet ; but the day was spent in fruitless marching and countermarching, so that his fine body of troops took no part in what might have been a decisive battle at Frayser's farm. General Holmes was a veteran soldier of well-known personal courage, but he was deceived as to the strength and intentions of the enemy. General Porter says that the force opposed to General Holmes consisted of Warren's brigade and the Eleventh U. S. Infantry ; in all, 1500 infantry and 30 pieces of artillery. Here was afforded an example of the proneness to overestimate the number of troops opposed to us. The Federals reported Holmes to have 25,000 men, and he thought himself confronted by a large part of McClellan's army. That night he fell back to a stronger position, thinking apparently that there would be an "on to Richmond" movement by the River road.

march was much delayed by the crossing of troops and trains. At Willis's Church I met General Lee. He bore grandly his terrible disappointment of the day before, and made no allusion to it. I gave him Mr. Allen's description of Malvern Hill, and presumed to say, "If General McClellan is there in force, we had better let him alone." Longstreet laughed and said, "Don't get scared, now that we have got him whipped." It was this belief in the demoralization of the Federal army that made our leader risk the attack. It was near noon when Jackson reached the immediate neighborhood of Malvern Hill. Some time was spent in reconnoitering, and in making tentative efforts with our few batteries to ascertain the strength and position of the enemy. I saw Jackson helping with his own hands to push Reilly's North Carolina battery farther forward. It was soon disabled, the woods around us being filled with shrieking and exploding shells. I noticed an artilleryman seated comfortably behind a very large tree, and apparently feeling very secure. A moment later a shell passed through the huge tree and took off the man's head. This gives an idea of the great power of the Federal rifled artillery. Whiting's

MAJOR-GENERAL WILLIAM B. FRANKLIN, U. S. V.

From a photograph taken in August, 1862, when General Franklin was temporarily at home on sick leave.

WOODBURY'S BRIDGE ACROSS THE CHICKAHOMINY.

GENERAL GEORGE A. McCALL, U. S. V.

At the battle of Frayser's Farm, General McCall was captured by the Confederates after a most exciting experience in repelling several charges upon batteries. In his report he says: "I rode forward to ascertain whether some men of the Fourth which I had left a little in advance were still on the ground,—they had, as I afterward learned, joined Kearny,—and I had not proceeded more than 100 yards, before I rode right into the Forty-Seventh Virginia Regiment, which, being drawn up under some trees, was not seen by me in the obscurity of the evening, until I had ridden in among them, and thus became a prisoner."

division was ordered to the left of the Quaker road, and mine to the right; Ewell's was in reserve. Jackson's own division had been halted at Willis's Church. The divisions of Magruder, Huger, and McLaws were still farther over to my right. Those of Longstreet and A. P. Hill were in reserve on the right and were not engaged. At length we were ordered to advance. The brigade of General George B. Anderson first encountered the enemy, and its commander was wounded and borne from the field. His troops, however, crossed the creek and took position in the woods, commanded by Colonel C. C. Tew, a skilful and gallant man. Rodes being sick, his brigade was commanded by that peerless soldier, Colonel J. B. Gordon. Ripley, Garland, and Colquitt also got over without serious loss. My five brigade commanders and myself now made an examination of the enemy's position. He was found to be strongly posted on a commanding hill, all the approaches to which could be swept by his artillery and were guarded by swarms of infantry, securely sheltered by fences, ditches, and ravines. Armistead was immediately on my right. We remained a long while awaiting orders, when I received the following:

"July 1st, 1862.

"GENERAL D. H. HILL: Batteries have been established to act upon the enemy's line. If it is broken, as is probable, Armistead, who can witness the effect of the fire, has been ordered to charge with a yell. Do the same.

"R. H. CHILTON, A. A. G."

crushed in a minute. Not knowing what to do under the circumstances, I wrote to General Jackson that the condition upon which the order was predicted was not fulfilled, and that I wanted instructions. He replied to advance when I heard the shouting. We did advance at the signal, and after an unassisted struggle for an hour and a half, and after meeting with some success, we were compelled to fall back under cover of the woods. Magruder advanced at the same signal, having portions of the divisions of Huger and McLaws, comprising the brigades of Mahone, Wright, Barksdale, Ransom, Cobb, Semmes, Kershaw, Armistead, and G. T. Anderson; but he met with some delay, and did not get in motion till he received a second order from General Lee, and we were then beaten. . . .

Truly, the courage of the soldiers was sublime! Battery after battery was in their hands for a few moments, only to be wrested away by fresh troops of the enemy. If one division could effect this much, what might have been done had the other nine coöperated with it! General Lee says:

"D. H. Hill pressed forward across the open field and engaged the enemy gallantly, breaking and driving back his first line; but a simultaneous advance of the other troops not taking place, he found himself unable to maintain the ground he had gained against the overwhelming numbers and the numerous batteries of the enemy. Jackson sent to his support his own division, and that part of Ewell's which was in reserve; but ow-

A similar order was sent to each division commander. However, only one battery of our artillery came up at a time, and each successive one, as it took position, had fifty pieces turned upon it, and was

ing to the increasing darkness, and the intricacy of the forest and swamp, they did not arrive in time to render the desired assistance. Hill was therefore compelled to abandon part of the ground that he had gained, after suffering severe loss and inflicting heavy damage upon the enemy."

I never saw anything more grandly heroic than the advance after sunset of the nine brigades under Magruder's orders. Unfortunately, they did not move together, and were beaten in detail. As each brigade emerged from the woods, from fifty to one hundred guns opened upon it, tearing great gaps in its ranks; but the heroes reeled on and were shot down by the reserves at the guns, which a few squads reached. Most of them had an open field half a mile wide to cross, under the fire of field-artillery in front, and the fire of the heavy ordnance of the gunboats in their rear. It was not war — it was murder. . . .

The battle of Malvern Hill was a disaster to the Confederates, and the fourteen brigades that had been so badly repulsed were much demoralized. But there were six divisions intact, and they could have made a formidable fight on the 2d. . . .

Throughout this campaign we attacked just when and where the enemy wished us to attack. This was owing to our ignorance of the country and lack of reconnoissance of the successive battle-fields. Porter's weak point at Gaines's Mill was his right flank. A thorough examination of the

ground would have disclosed that; and had Jackson's command gone in on the left of the road running by the McGehee house, Porter's whole position would have been turned and the line of retreat cut off. . . . The battle, with all its melancholy results, proved, however, that the Confederate infantry and Federal artillery, side by side on the same field, need fear no foe on earth.

Both commanders had shown great ability. McClellan, if not always great in the advance, was masterly in retreat, and was unquestionably the greatest of Americans as an organizer of an army. Lee's plans were perfect; and had not his dispositions for a decisive battle at Frayser's farm miscarried, through no fault of his own, he would have won a most complete victory. It was not the least part of his greatness that he did not complain of his disappointment, and that he at no time sought a scapegoat upon which to lay a failure. As reunited Americans, we have reason to be proud of both commanders.

THE PARSONAGE, NEAR MALVERN HILL.

This house was in the rear of the Confederate line, which was formed in the woods shown in the background. It was used as a Confederate hospital after the fight. The road is the Church road (known also as the Quaker road), and the view is from near C. W. Smith's, which was for a short time the headquarters of General Lee. Here the trees were riddled with bullets and torn with shell, and in 1885, when this view was photographed, the corn was growing out of many a soldier's grave.

THE BATTLE OF MALVERN HILL.

THE UNION SIDE.

BY FITZ-JOHN PORTER, MAJOR-GENERAL, U. S. V.

Commander of the Center and Left Wing at Malvern Hill.

BEFORE the battle of Gaines's Mill (already described by me in these pages), a change of base from the York to the James River had been anticipated and prepared for by General McClellan. After the battle this change became a necessity, in presence of a strong and aggressive foe, who had already turned our right, cut our connection with the York River, and was also in large force behind the intrenchments between us and Richmond. The transfer was begun the moment our position became perilous. It now involved a series of battles by day and marches by night which brought into relief the able talents, active foresight, and tenacity of purpose of our commander, the unity of action on the part of his subordinates, and the great bravery, firmness, and confidence in their superiors on the part of the rank and file.

These conflicts from the beginning of the Seven Days' fighting were the engagement at Oak Grove, the battles of Beaver Dam Creek and Gaines's Mill, the engagements at Golding's and Garnett's farms, and at Allen's farm or Peach Orchard; the

battle of Savage's Station; the battle of Glendale (or Charles City cross-roads); the action of Turkey Creek, and the battle of Malvern Hill. Each was a success to our army, the engagement of Malvern Hill being the most decisive. The result of the movement was that on the 2d of July our army was safely established at Harrison's Landing, on the James, in accordance with General McClellan's design. The present narrative will be confined to events coming under my own observation, and connected with my command, the Fifth Army Corps.

Saturday, June 28th, 1862, the day after the battle of Gaines's Mill, my corps spent in bivouac at the Trent farm on the south bank of the Chickahominy. Artillery and infantry detachments guarded the crossings at the sites of the destroyed bridges. Our antagonists of the 27th were still north of the river, but did not molest us. We rested and recuperated as best we could, amid the noise of battle close by, at Garnett's and Golding's farms, in which part of Franklin's corps was

MALVERN HILL, FROM THE DIRECTION OF TURKEY ISLAND BRIDGE.
From a sketch made soon after the war.

VIEW FROM MALVERN HILL, LOOKING TOWARD THE JAMES.
From a photograph taken in 1885.

This view is taken from near the position of Tyler's siege-guns. The engagement of Malvern Cliff, or Turkey Island bridge, on the 30th of June, between Generals Warren and Holmes, took place on the road at the foot of the hill which passes near the house in the middle-ground. The bridge is to the left on this road. The winding stream is Turkey Creek.

engaged, refilling the empty cartridge-boxes and haversacks, so as to be in readiness for immediate duty. . . .

Between 2 and 9 P. M. on the 28th, my corps was in motion and marched by the way of Savage Station to the south side of White Oak Swamp; and at the junction of the roads from Richmond (Glendale) to be prepared to repel attacks from the direction of that city. General Morell, leading the advance, aided General Woodbury, of the engineer corps, to build the causeways and bridges necessary for the easy passage of the trains and troops over the swamps and streams. Sykes and McCall followed at 5 and 9 o'clock, respectively, McCall being accompanied by Hunt's Artillery Reserve.

We expected to reach our destination, which was only ten miles distant, early on the 29th; but, in consequence of the dark night and of the narrow and muddy roads, cut up and blocked by numerous trains and herds of cattle, the head of the column did not arrive till 10 A. M., the rear not until midnight. McCall arrived latest, and all were greatly fatigued.

The enemy not having appeared at Glendale on the afternoon of the 29th, and other troops arriving to take the place of mine, General McClellan ordered me to move that night by the direct road to the elevated and cleared lands (Malvern Hill)

on the north bank of Turkey Creek, there to select and hold a position behind which the army and all its trains could be withdrawn with safety. General Keyes was to move by a different road and form to my right and rear.

Again the dangers and difficulties of night marches attended us, followed by the consequent delay, which, though fortunately it was counterbalanced by the slowness of our opponents in moving to the same point, endangered the safety of our whole army. Although we started before dark, and were led by an intelligent cavalry officer who had passed over the route and professed to know it, my command did not reach Turkey Creek, which was only five miles distant, until 9 A. M. on the 30th. In fact, we were misled up the Long Bridge road toward Richmond until we came in contact with the enemy's pickets. Then we returned and started anew.

Our new field of battle embraced Malvern Hill, just north of Turkey Creek and Crew's Hill, about one mile farther north. The forces which on this occasion came under my control, and were engaged in or held ready to enter the contest, were my own corps, consisting of Morell's, Sykes's, and McCall's divisions, Colonel H. J. Hunt's Artillery Reserve of one hundred pieces, including Colonel R. O. Tyler's Connecticut siege artillery, Couch's division of Keyes's corps, the brigades of John C.

**BREVET BRIGADIER-GENERAL
JAMES McQUADE, U. S. V.**
At Malvern Hill colonel of the 14th New York.
Died in 1885.

THE MAIN BATTLE-FIELD—VIEW OF THE UNION POSITION FROM THE WOODED KNOLL SHOWN ON THE FOLLOWING PAGE.

Caldwell and Thomas F. Meagher of Sumner's corps, and the brigade of D. E. Sickles of Heintzelman's corps. Though Couch was placed under my command, he was left uncontrolled by me, as will be seen hereafter. The other brigades were sent to me by their respective division commanders, in anticipation of my needs or at my request.

This new position, with its elements of great strength, was better adapted for a defensive battle than any with which we had been favored. It was elevated, and was more or less protected on each flank by small streams or by swamps, while the woods in front through which the enemy had to pass to attack us were in places marshy, and the timber so thick that artillery could not be brought up, and even troops were moved in it with difficulty. Slightly in rear of our line of battle on Crew's Hill the reserve artillery and infantry were held for immediate service. The hill concealed them from the view of the enemy and sheltered them to some extent from his fire. These hills, both to the east and west, were connected with the adjacent valleys by gradually sloping plains, except at the Crew house, where for a little distance the slope was quite abrupt, and was easily protected by a small force. With the exception of the River road, all the roads from Richmond, along which the enemy would be obliged to approach, meet in front of Crew's Hill. This hill was flanked with ravines, enfiladed by our fire. The ground in front was sloping, and over it our artillery and infantry, themselves protected by the crest and ridges, had clear sweep for their fire. In all directions, for several hundred yards, the

land over which an attacking force must advance was almost entirely cleared of forest and was generally cultivated.

I reached Malvern Hill some two hours before my command on Monday, June 30th; each division, as it came upon the field, was assigned to a position covering the approaches from Richmond along the River road and the debouches from the New Market, Charles City, and Williamsburg roads. Warren, with his brigade of about six hundred men, took position on the lowlands to the left, to guard against the approach of the enemy along the River road, or over the low, extensive, and cultivated plateau beyond and extending north along Crew's Hill. Warren's men were greatly in need of rest. The brigade had suffered greatly at Gaines's Mill, and was not expected to perform much more than picket duty, and it was large enough for the purpose designed, as it was not probable that any large force would be so reckless as to advance on that road. Warren was supported by the 11th U. S. Infantry, under Major Floyd Jones, and late in the afternoon was strengthened by Martin's battery of 12-pounders and a detachment of the 3d Pennsylvania cavalry under Lieutenant Frank W. Hess.

On the west side of Malvern Hill, overlooking Warren were some thirty-six guns, some of long range, having full sweep up the valley and over the cleared lands north of the River road. . . .

Major Charles S. Lovell, commanding Colonel William Chapman's brigade of Sykes's division, supported some of these batteries, and, with the brigade

of Buchanan on his right, in a clump of pines, extended the line northward, near the Crew (sometimes called the Mellert) house.

Morell, prolonging Sykes's line on Crew's Hill, with headquarters at Crew's house, occupied the right of the line extending to the Quaker road. To his left front, facing west, was the 14th New York Volunteers, under Colonel McQuade, with a section of Captain W. B. Weeden's Battery C, 1st

BERDAN'S SHARP-SHOOTERS (OF MORELL'S DIVISION)
SKIRMISHING IN THE MEADOW WHEAT-FIELD.

Rhode Island Artillery, both watching the Richmond road and the valley, and protecting our left. On their right, under cover of a narrow strip of woods, skirting the Quaker road, were the brigades of Martindale and Butterfield, while in front of these, facing north, was Griffin's brigade. All were supporting batteries of Morell's division, commanded by Captain Weeden and others, under the general supervision of Griffin, a brave and skilled artillery officer.

About 3 o'clock on Monday the enemy were seen approaching along the River road, and Warren and Hunt made all necessary dispositions to receive them. About 4 o'clock the enemy advanced and opened fire from their artillery upon Warren and Sykes and on the extreme left of Morell, causing a few casualties in Morell's division. In return for this intrusion the concentrated rapid fire of the artillery was opened upon them, soon smashing one battery to pieces, silencing another, and driving back their infantry and cavalry in rapid retreat, much to the satisfaction of thousands of men watching the result. The enemy left behind in possession of Warren a few prisoners, two guns and six caissons, the horses of which had been killed. The battery which had disturbed Morell was also silenced by this fire of our artillery. On this occasion the gun-boats in the James made apparent their welcome presence and gave good support by bringing their heavy guns to bear upon the enemy. Though their fire caused a few casualties among our men, and inflicted but little, if any, injury upon the enemy, their large shells, bursting amid the enemy's troops far beyond the attacking force, carried great moral influence with them, and naturally tended, in addition to the effect of our artillery, to prevent any renewed attempt to cross the open valley on our left. This attacking force formed a small part of Wise's brigade of Holmes's division. They were all raw troops, which accounts for their apparently demoralized retreat. This affair is known as the action of Turkey Bridge or Malvern Cliff.

Our forces lay on their arms during the night, in substantially the positions I have described, patiently awaiting the attack expected on the following day.

THE MAIN BATTLE-FIELD—VIEW OF THE CONFEDERATE POSITION FROM THE UNION LINE NEAR THE WEST HOUSE.

MAJOR-GENERAL GEORGE W. MORELL, U. S. V.

McCall's division of Pennsylvania Reserves, now under General Truman Seymour, arrived during the night and was posted just in front of the Malvern house, and was held in reserve, to be called upon for service only in case of absolute necessity.

Early on Tuesday our lines were re-formed and slightly advanced to take full advantage of the formation of the ground, the artillery of the front line being re-posted in commanding positions, and placed under General Griffin's command, but under Captain Weeden's care, just behind the crest of the hill. The infantry was arranged between the artillery to protect and be protected by its neighbors, and prepared to be thrown forward, if at any time advisable, so as not to interfere with the artillery fire.

The corps of Heintzelman and Sumner had arrived during the night and taken position in the order named to the right and rear of Couch's division, protecting that flank effectively toward Western Run. They did not expect to be seriously engaged, but were ready to resist attack and to give assistance to the center and left, if circumstances should require it. At an early hour in the day Sumner kindly sent me Caldwell's brigade, as he thought I might need help. This brigade I placed near Butterfield, who was directed to send it forward wherever it should be needed or called for. He sent it to Couch at an opportune moment early in the day.

General McClellan, accompanied by his staff, visited our lines at an early hour, and approved my measures and those of General Couch, or changed them where it was deemed advisable. Though he left me in charge of that part of the field occupied by Couch, I at no time undertook to control that general, or even indicated a desire to do so, but with full confidence in his ability, which was justified by the result of his action, left him free to act in accordance with his own judgment. I co-operated with him fully, however, having Morell's batteries, under Weeden, posted so as to protect his front, and sending him help when I saw he needed it. The division of Couch, though it suffered severely in the battle of Fair Oaks, had seen less service and met with fewer losses in these "Seven Days' battles" than any one of my three, and was prepared with full ranks to receive an attack, seeming impatient and eager for the fight. Its conduct soon confirmed this impression. Batteries of Hunt's Artillery Reserve were sent to him when needed—and also Caldwell's brigade, voluntarily sent to me early in the day by Sumner, and Sickles's brigade, borrowed of Heintzelman for the purpose.

About 10 A. M. the enemy's skirmishers and artillery began feeling for us along our line; they kept up a desultory fire until about 12 o'clock, with no severe injury to our infantry, who were well masked, and who revealed but little of our strength or position by retaliatory firing or exposure.

Up to this time, and until nearly 1 o'clock, our infantry were resting upon their arms and waiting the moment, certain to come, when the column of the enemy rashly advancing would render it necessary to expose themselves. Our desire was to hold the enemy where our artillery would be most destructive, and to reserve our infantry ammunition for close quarters to repel the more determined assaults of our obstinate and untiring foe. Attacks by brigade were made upon Morell, both on his left front and on his right, and also upon Couch; but our artillery, admirably handled, without exception, was generally sufficient to repel all such efforts and to drive back the assailants in confusion, and with great loss.

While the enemy's artillery was firing upon us

REPULSE OF THE CONFEDERATES ON THE SLOPE OF CREW'S HILL.

General Sumner withdrew part of his corps to the slope of Malvern Hill, to the right of the Malvern house, which descended into the valley of Western Run. Then, deeming it advisable to withdraw all our troops to that line, he ordered me to fall back to the Malvern house; but I protested that such a movement would be disastrous, and declined to obey the order until I could confer with General McClellan, who had approved of the disposition of our troops. Fortunately Sumner did not insist upon my complying with the order, and, as we were soon vigorously attacked, he advanced his troops to a point where he was but little disturbed by the enemy, but from which he could quickly render aid in response to calls for help or where need for help was apparent.

The spasmodic, though sometimes formidable attacks of our antagonists, at different points along our whole front, up to about 4 o'clock, were presumably demonstrations or feelers, to ascertain our strength, preparatory to their engaging in more serious work. An ominous silence, similar to that which had preceded the attack in force along our whole line at Gaines's Mill, now intervened, until, at about 5 : 30 o'clock; the enemy opened upon both Morell and Couch with artillery from nearly the whole of his front, and soon afterward pressed forward his columns of infantry, first on one and then on the other, or on both. As if moved by a reckless disregard of life, equal to that displayed at Gaines's Mill, with a determination to capture our army, or destroy it by driving us into the river, regiment after regiment, and brigade after brigade, rushed at our batteries; but the artillery of both Morell and Couch mowed them down with shrapnel, grape, and canister; while our infantry, withholding their fire until the enemy were within short range, scattered the remnants of their columns, sometimes following them up and capturing prisoners and colors.

As column after column advanced, only to meet the same disastrous repulse, the sight became one of the most interesting imaginable. The havoc made by the rapidly bursting shells from guns arranged so as to sweep any position far and near, and in any direction, was fearful to behold. Pressed to the extreme as they were, the courage of our men was fully tried. The safety of our army—the life of the Union—was felt to be at stake. In one case the brigades of Howe, Abercrombie, and Palmer, of Couch's division, under impulse, gallantly pushed after the retreating foe, captured colors, and advantageously advanced the right of the line, but at considerable loss and great risk. The brigades of Morell, cool, well-disciplined, and easily controlled, let the enemy return after each repulse, but permitted few to escape their fire. Colonel McQuade, on Morell's left, with the 14th New York, against orders and at the risk of defeat and disaster, yielding to impulse, gallantly dashed forward and repulsed an attacking party. Assisted by Buchanan of Sykes's division, Colonel Rice, with the 44th New York Volunteers, likewise drove a portion of the enemy from the field, taking a flag bearing the inscription "Seven Pines." Colonel Hunt, directing the artillery, was twice dismounted by having his horse shot under him, but though constantly exposed continued his labors until after dark. General Couch, who also dismounted in like manner, took advantage of every opportunity to make his opponents feel his blows.

It is not to be supposed that our men, though concealed by the irregularities of the ground, were not sufferers from the enemy's fire. The fact is that before they exposed themselves by pursuing

SUPPLYING THE HUNGRY ARMY AT HARRISON'S LANDING.
From a war-time sketch.

DUMMIES AND QUAKER GUNS.
These were left in the works at Harrison's Landing on the evacuation by the army of the Potomac.

the enemy, the ground was literally covered with the killed and wounded from dropping bullets and bursting shells and their contents; but they bravely bore the severe trial of having to remain inactive under a damaging fire.

As Morell's front ranks became thinned out and the ammunition was exhausted, other regiments eagerly advanced; all were stimulated by the hope of a brilliant and permanent success, and nerved by the approving shouts of their comrades and the cry of "Revenge, boys!" "Remember McLane!" "Remember Black!" "Remember Gove!" or "Remember Cass!" Black and McLane and Gove had been killed at Gaines's Mill; Woodbury and Cass were then lying before them. Colonel McQuade

BERKELEY, HARRISON'S LANDING.
This house was the birthplace of General (afterward President) William Henry Harrison.

was the only regimental commander of Griffin's brigade who escaped death during the Seven Days, and he was constantly exposed.

During that ominous silence of which I have spoken, I determined that our opponents should reap no advantage, even if our lines yielded to attack, and therefore posted batteries, as at Gaines's Mill, to secure against the disaster of a break in our lines, should such a misfortune be ours. For this purpose I sent Weed, Carlisle, and Smead, with their batteries, to the gorge of the roads on Crew's Hill, from which the enemy must emerge in pursuit if he should break our lines; instructing them to join in the fight if necessary, but not to permit the advance of the foe, even if it must be arrested at the risk of firing upon friends. To these Colonel Hunt added three batteries of horse artillery. Though they were all thus posted, and their guns loaded with double canister, "they were," as Captain Smead reported, "very happy to find their services not needed on that occasion."

It was at this time, in answer to my call for aid, that Sumner sent me Meagher, and Heintzelman sent Sickles, both of whom reached me in the height of battle, when, if ever, fresh troops would renew our confidence and insure our success. While riding rapidly forward to meet Meagher, who was approaching at a "double-quick" step, my horse fell, throwing me over his head, much to my discomfort both of body and mind. On rising and remounting I was greeted with hearty cheers, which alleviated my chagrin. This incident gave rise to the report, spread through the country, that I was wounded. Fearing that I might fall into the hands of the enemy, and if so that my diary and despatch-book of the campaign, then on my person, would meet with the same fate and reveal information to the injury of our

cause, I tore it up, scattering the pieces to the winds, as I rode rapidly forward, leading Meagher into action. I have always regretted my act as destroying interesting and valuable memoranda of our campaign.

Advancing with Meagher's brigade, accompanied by my staff, I soon found that our forces had successfully driven back their assailants. Determined, if possible, satisfactorily to finish the contest, regardless of the risk of being fired upon by our artillery in case of defeat, I pushed on beyond our lines into the woods held by the enemy. About fifty yards in front of us, a large force of the enemy suddenly rose and opened with fearful volleys upon our advancing line. I turned to the brigade, which thus far had kept pace with my horse, and found it standing "like a stone-wall," and returning a fire more destructive than it received and from which the enemy fled. The brigade was planted. My presence was no longer needed, and I sought General Sickles, whom I found giving aid to Couch. I had the satisfaction of learning that night that a Confederate detachment, undertaking to turn Meagher's left, was met by a portion of the 69th New York Regiment, which, advancing, repelled the attack and captured many prisoners.

After seeing that General Sickles was in a proper position, I returned to my own corps, where I was joined by Colonel Hunt with some 32-pounder howitzers. Taking those howitzers, we rode forward beyond our lines, and, in parting salutation to our opponents, Colonel Hunt sent a few shells, as a warning of what would be ready to welcome them on the morrow if they undertook to disturb us. . . .

Almost at the crisis of the battle — just before the advance of Meagher and Sickles — the gun-boats on the James River opened their fire with

the good intent of aiding us, but either mistook our batteries at the Malvern house for those of the enemy, or were unable to throw their projectiles beyond us. If the former was the case, their range was well estimated, for all their shot landed in or close by Tyler's battery, killing and wounding a few of his men. Fortunately members of our excellent signal-service corps were present as usual on such occasions, and the message signaled to the boats, "For God's sake, stop firing," promptly relieved us from further damage and the demoralization of a "fire in the rear." Reference is occasionally seen in Confederate accounts of this battle to the fearful sounds of the projectiles from those gun-boats. But that afternoon not one of their projectiles passed beyond my headquarters; and I have always believed and said, as has General Hunt, that the enemy mistook the explosions of shells from Tyler's siege-guns and Kusserow's 32-pounder howitzers, which Hunt had carried forward, for shells from the gun-boats. . . .

Thus ended the memorable "Seven Days' battles," which, for severity and for stubborn resistance and endurance of hardships by the contestants, were not surpassed during the war. Each antagonist accomplished the result for which he aimed: one insuring the temporary relief of Richmond; the other gaining security on the north bank of the James, where the Union army, if our civil and military authorities were disposed, could be promptly reinforced, and from whence only, as subsequent events proved, it could renew the contest successfully. Preparations were commenced and dispositions were at once made under every prospect, if not direct promise, of large reinforcements for a renewal of the struggle on the south side of the James, and in the same manner as subsequently brought a successful termination of the war. . . .

RUSH'S LANCERS—THE SIXTH PENNSYLVANIA CAVALRY.
From a sketch made in 1862.

"THE SEVEN DAYS," INCLUDING FRAYSER'S FARM.

THE CONFEDERATE SIDE.

BY JAMES LONGSTREET, LIEUTENANT-GENERAL, C. S. A.
Commander of a division of Lee's army during "The Seven Days' Battles."

FRAYSER'S FARM-HOUSE, FROM THE QUAKER
OR CHURCH ROAD, LOOKING SOUTH.
From a photograph taken in 1885.

This house was used as General Sumner's headquarters and as a hospital during the battle. The fighting took place from half to three-quarters of a mile to the right, or westward. The National Cemetery is shown in the middle distance.

WHEN General Joseph E. Johnston was wounded at the battle of Seven Pines, and General Lee assumed his new duties as commander of the Army of Northern Virginia, General Stonewall Jackson was in the Shenandoah Valley, and the rest of the Confederate troops were east and north of Richmond in front of General George B. McClellan's army, then encamped about the Chickahominy River, 100,000 strong, and preparing for a regular siege of the Confederate capital. The situation required prompt and successful action by General Lee. Very early in June he called about him, on the noted Nine-mile road near Richmond, all his commanders, and asked each in turn his opinion of the military situation. I had my own views, but did not express them, believing that if they were important it was equally important that they should be unfolded privately to the commanding general. The next day I called on General Lee, and suggested my plan for driving the Federal forces away from the Chickahominy. McClellan had a small force at Mechanicsville, and farther back, at Beaver Dam Creek, a considerable portion of his army in a stronghold that was simply unassailable from the front. The banks of Beaver Dam Creek were so steep as to be impassable except on bridges. I proposed an echelon movement, and suggested that Jackson be called down from the Valley, and passed to the rear of the Federal right, in order to turn the position behind Beaver Dam, while the rest of the Confederate forces who were to engage in the attack could cross the Chickahominy at points suitable for the

succession in the move, and be ready to attack the Federals as soon as they were thrown from their position. After hearing me, General Lee sent General J. E. B. Stuart on his famous ride around McClellan. The dashing horseman, with a strong reconnoitering force of cavalry, made a forced reconnoissance, passing above and around the Federal forces, recrossing the Chickahominy below them, and returning safe to Confederate headquarters. He made a favorable report of the situation and the practicability of the proposed plan. On the 23d of June General Jackson was summoned to General Lee's headquarters, and was there met by General A. P. Hill, General D. H. Hill, and my-

NELSON'S HOUSE.   WILLIS CHURCH.   PENNSYLVANIA RESERVES.

GENERAL HEINTZELMAN'S HEADQUARTERS AT NELSON'S HOUSE, JUNE 30.
From a sketch made at the time.

self. A conference resulted in the selection of the 26th as the day on which we should move against the Federal position at Beaver Dam. General Jackson was ordered down from the Valley. General A. P. Hill was to pass the Chickahominy with part of his division, and hold the rest in readiness to cross at Meadow Bridge, following Jackson's swoop along the dividing ridge between the Pamunkey and the Chickahominy. D. H. Hill and I were ordered to be in position on the Mechanicsville pike early on the 26th, ready to cross the river at Mechanicsville Bridge as soon as it was cleared by the advance of Jackson and A. P. Hill.

Thus matters stood when the morning of the 26th arrived. The weather was clear, and the roads were in fine condition. Everything seemed favorable to the move. But the morning passed and we received no tidings from Jackson. As noon approached, General Hill, who was to move behind Jackson, grew impatient at the delay and begged permission to hurry him up by a fusillade. General Lee consented, and General Hill opened his batteries on Mechanicsville, driving the Federals off. When D. H. Hill and I crossed at the Mechanicsville Bridge we found A. P. Hill severely engaged, trying to drive the Federals from their strong position behind Beaver Dam Creek. Without Jackson to turn the Federal right, the battle could not be ours. Although the contest lasted until some time after night, the Confederates made no progress. The next day the fight was renewed, and the position was hotly contested by the Federals until 7 o'clock in the morning, when the advance of Jackson speedily caused the Federals to abandon their position, thus ending the battle.

It is easy to see that the battle of the previous day would have been a quick and bloodless Confederate victory if Jackson could have reached his position at the time appointed. In my judgment the evacuation of Beaver Dam Creek was very unwise on the part of the Federal commanders. We had attacked at Beaver Dam, and had failed to make an impression at that point, losing several thousand men and officers. This demonstrated that the position was safe. If the Federal commanders knew of Jackson's approach on the 26th, they had ample time to reinforce Porter's right before Friday morning (27th) with men and field defenses, to such extent as to make the remainder of the line to the right secure against assault. So that the Federals in withdrawing not only abandoned a strong position, but gave up the *morale* of their success, and transferred it to our somewhat disheartened forces; for, next to Malvern Hill, the sacrifice at Beaver Dam was unequaled in demoralization during the entire summer.

From Beaver Dam we followed the Federals closely, encountering them again under Porter beyond Powhite Creek, where the battle of Gaines's Mill occurred. General A. P. Hill, being in advance, deployed his men and opened the attack without consulting me. A very severe battle followed. I came up with my reserve forces and was preparing to support Hill, who was suffering very severely, when I received an order from General Lee to make a demonstration against the Federal left, as the battle was not progressing to suit him. I threw in three brigades opposite the Federal left and engaged them in a severe skirmish with infantry and artillery. The battle then raged with great fierceness. General Jackson was again missing, and General Lee grew fearful of the result. Soon I received another message from General Lee, saying that unless I could do something the day seemed to be lost. I then determined to make the heaviest attack I could. The position in front of me was very strong. An open field led down to a difficult

THE UNION RETREAT FROM THE CHICKAHOMINY.
From a sketch made on the field at the time.

The scene is near McClellan's headquarters at Dr. Trent's farm, before day-light on Sunday, June 29th; the Sixth Corps (Franklin's) is falling back; the fires are from the burning of commissary stores and forage; the artillery in position covers the approaches from the Chickahominy, the artillerymen resting underneath the guns. The regiment in the middle-ground is the 16th New York, who wore straw hats, and were, partly in consequence, such conspicuous targets for the enemy that in the Seven Days' fighting they lost 228 men.

ravine a short distance beyond the Powhite Creek. From there the ground made a steep ascent, and was covered with trees and slashed timber and hastily made rifle-trenches. General Whiting came to me with two brigades of Jackson's men and asked me to put him in. I told him I was just organizing an attack and would give him position. My column of attack then was R. H. Anderson's and Pickett's brigades, with Law's and Hood's of Whiting's division. We attacked and defeated the Federals on their left, capturing many thousand stand of arms, fifty-two pieces of artillery, a large quantity of supplies, and many prisoners — among them General Reynolds, who afterward fell at Gettysburg. The Federals made some effort to reinforce and recover their lost ground, but failed, and during the afternoon and night withdrew their entire forces from that side of the Chickahominy, going in the direction of James River. On the 29th General Lee ascertained that McClellan was marching toward the James. He determined to make a vigorous move and strike the enemy a severe blow. He decided to intercept them in

the neighborhood of Charles City cross-roads, and with that end in view planned a pursuit as follows : I was to march to a point below Frayser's farm with General A. P. Hill. General Holmes was to take up position below me on the New Market or River road, to be in readiness to coöperate with me and to attack such Federals as would come within his reach. Jackson was to pursue closely the Federal rear, crossing at the Grapevine Bridge, and coming in on the north of the cross-roads. Huger was to attend to the Federal right flank, and take position on the Charles City road west of the cross-roads. Thus we were to envelop the Federal rear and make the destruction of that part of McClellan's army sure. To reach my position south of the cross-roads, I had about sixteen miles to march. I marched 14 miles on the 29th, crossing over into the Darbytown road and moving down to its intersection, with the New Market road, where I camped for the night, about 3 miles southwest of Frayser's farm. On the morning of the 30th I moved two miles nearer up and made preparation to intercept the Federals as they retreated toward

James River. General McCall, with a division of ten thousand Federals, was at the cross-roads and about Frayser's farm. My division, being in advance, was deployed in front of the enemy. I placed such of my batteries as I could find position for, and kept Hill's troops in my rear. As I had twice as far to march as the other commanders, I considered it certain that Jackson and Huger would be in position when I was ready. After getting my troops in position I called upon General A. P. Hill to throw one of his brigades to cover my right and to hold the rest of his troops in readiness to give pursuit when the enemy had been dislodged. My line extended from near the Quaker road across the New Market road to the Federal right. The ground upon which I approached was much lower than that occupied by General McCall, and was greatly cut up by ravines and covered with heavy timber and tangled undergrowth. On account of these obstructions we were not disturbed while getting into position, except by the firing of a few shots that did no damage. Holmes got into position below me on the New Market road, and was afterward joined by Magruder, who had previously made an unsuccessful attack on the Federal rearguard at Savage's Station.

By 11 o'clock our troops were in position, and we waited for the signal from Jackson and Huger. Everything was quiet on my part of the line, except occasional firing between my pickets and McCall's. I was in momentary expectation of the signal. About half-past 2 o'clock artillery firing was heard on my left, evidently at the point near White Oak Swamp where Huger was to attack. I very naturally supposed this firing to be the expected signal, and ordered some of my batteries to reply, as a signal that I was ready to coöperate. While the order to open was going around to the batteries, President Davis and General Lee, with their staff and followers, were with me in a little open field near the rear of my right. We were in pleasant conversation, anticipating fruitful results from the fight, when our batteries opened. Instantly the Federal batteries responded most spitefully. It was impossible for the enemy to see us as we sat on our horses in the little field, surrounded by tall, heavy timber and thick undergrowth; yet a battery by chance had our range and exact distance, and poured upon us a terrific

CHARGE OF CONFEDERATES UPON RANDOL'S BATTERY AT FRAYSER'S FARM.

The contest for this battery was one of the most severe encounters of the day. The Confederates (the 55th and 60th Virginia regiments) advanced out of formation, in wedge shape, and with trailing arms, and began a hand-to-hand conflict over the guns, which were finally yielded to them.

fire. The second or third shell burst in the midst of us, killing two or three horses and wounding one or two men. Our little party speedily retired to safer quarters. The Federals doubtless had no idea that the Confederate President, commanding general, and division commanders were receiving point-blank shot from their batteries. Colonel Micah Jenkins was in front of us, and I sent him an order to silence the Federal battery, supposing that he could do so with his long-range rifles. He became engaged, and finally determined to charge the battery. That brought on a general fight between my division and the troops in front of us. Kemper on my right advanced his brigade over difficult ground and captured a battery. Jenkins moved his brigade forward and made a bold fight. He was followed by the other four brigades successively.

The enemy's line was broken, and he was partly dislodged from his position. The batteries were taken, but our line was very much broken up by the rough ground we had to move over, and we were not in sufficiently solid form to maintain a proper battle. The battle was continued, however, until we encountered succor from the corps of Generals Sumner and Heintzelman, when we were obliged to halt and hold the position the enemy had left. This line was held throughout the day, though at times, when vigorous combinations were made against me, McCall regained points along his line. Our counter-movements, however, finally pushed him back again, and more formidable efforts from our adversary were required. Other advances were made, and reinforcements came to the support of the Federals, who contested the line with varying fortune, sometimes recovering batteries we had taken, and again losing them. Finally McCall's division was driven off,

and fresh troops seemed to come in to their relief. Ten thousand men of A. P. Hill's division had been held in reserve, in the hope that Jackson and Huger would come up on our left, enabling us to dislodge the Federals, after which Hill's troops could be put in fresh to give pursuit, and follow them down to Harrison's Landing. Jackson found Grapevine Bridge destroyed and could not reach his position; while for some unaccountable reason Huger failed to take part, though near enough to do so. As neither Jackson nor Huger came up, and as night drew on, I put Hill in to relieve my troops. When he came into the fight the Federal line had been broken at every point except one. He formed his line and followed up in the position occupied by my troops. By night we succeeded in getting the entire field, though all of it was not actually occupied until we advanced in pursuit next day. As the enemy moved off they continued the fire of their artillery upon us from various points, and it was after 9 o'clock when the shells ceased to fall. Just before dark General McCall, while looking up a fragment of his division, found us where he supposed his troops were, and was taken prisoner. At the time he was brought in General Lee happened to be with us. As I had known General McCall pleasantly in our service together in the 4th Infantry, I moved to offer my hand as he dismounted. At the first motion, however, I saw he did not regard the occasion as one for renewing the old friendship, and I merely offered him some of my staff as an escort to Richmond. But for the succoring forces, which should have been engaged by Jackson, Huger, Holmes, and Magruder, McCall would have been entirely dislodged by the first attack. All of our other forces were within a radius of 3 miles, and in easy hearing of the battle, yet of the 50,000 none came in to coöperate.

A SAMPLE OF THE CHICKAHOMINY SWAMP.
From a photograph of 1862.

(Jackson should have done more for me than he did. When he wanted me at the Second Manassas, I marched two columns by night to clear the way at Thoroughfare Gap, and joined him in due season.) Hooker claimed at Glendale to have rolled me up and hurriedly thrown me over on Kearny,—tennis-like, I suppose; but McCall showed in his supplementary report that Hooker could as well claim, with a little tension of the hyperbole, that he had thrown me over the moon. On leaving Frayser's farm the Federals withdrew to Malvern Hill, and Lee concentrated his forces and followed them.

On the morning of July 1st, the day after the battle at Frayser's farm, we encountered the enemy at Malvern Hill, and General Lee asked me to make a reconnoissance and see if I could find a good position for the artillery. I found position offering good play for batteries across the Federal left over to the right, and suggested that sixty pieces should

be put in while Jackson engaged the Federal front. I suggested that a heavy play of this cross-fire on the Federals would so discomfit them as to warrant an assault by infantry. General Lee issued his orders accordingly, and designated the advance of Armistead's brigade as the signal for the grand assault. Later it was found that the ground over which our batteries were to pass into position on our right was so rough and obstructed that of the artillery ordered for use there only one or two batteries could go in at a time. As our guns in front did not engage, the result was the enemy concentrated the fire of fifty or sixty guns upon our isolated batteries, and tore them into fragments in a few minutes after they opened, piling horses upon each other and guns upon horses. Before night, the fire from our batteries failing of execution, General Lee seemed to abandon the idea of an attack. He proposed to me to move around to the left with my own and A. P. Hill's division, turning

James Longstreet [signature]

OPENING OF THE BATTLE OF FRAYSER'S FARM.
Slocum's artillery engaged with that of Huger, at Brackett's, on the Charles City Road. (From a sketch made at the time.)

Federal position we put out our skirmish-lines, and I ordered an advance, intending to make another attack, but revoked it on Jackson urging me to wait until the arrival of General Lee. Very soon General Lee came, and, after carefully considering the position of the enemy and of their gunboats on the James, decided that it would be better to forego any further operations. Our skirmish-lines were withdrawn, and we ordered our troops back to their old lines around Richmond . . . .

The Seven Days' Fighting, although a decided Confederate victory, was a succession of mishaps. If Jackson had arrived on the 26th,—the day of his own selection,—the Federals would have been driven back from Mechanicsville without a battle. His delay there, caused by obstructions placed in his road by the enemy, was the first mishap. He was too late in entering the fight at Gaines's Mill, and the destruction of Grapevine Bridge kept him from reaching Frayser's farm until the day after that battle. If he had been there, we might have destroyed or captured McClellan's army. Huger was in position for the battle of Frayser's farm, and after his batteries had misled me into opening the fight he subsided. . . .

General McClellan was a very accomplished soldier and a very able engineer, but hardly equal to the position of field-marshal as a military chieftain. He organized the Army of the Potomac cleverly, but did not handle it skilfully when in actual battle. Still I doubt if his retreat could have been better handled, though the rear of his army should have been more positively either in his own hands or in the hands of Sumner. Heintzelman crossed the White Oak Swamp prematurely and left the rear of McClellan's army exposed, which would have been fatal had Jackson come up and taken part in Magruder's affair of the 29th near Savage's Station.

I cannot close this sketch without referring to the Confederate commander when he came upon the scene for the first time. General Lee was an unusually handsome man, even in his advanced life. He seemed fresh from West Point, so trim was his figure and so elastic his step. Out of battle he was as gentle as a woman, but when the clash of arms came he loved fight, and urged his battle with wonderful determination. As a usual thing he was remarkably well-balanced—always so, except on one or two occasions of severe trial when he failed to maintain his exact equipoise. Lee's orders were always well considered and well chosen. He depended almost too much on his officers for their execution. Jackson was a very skilful man against such men as Shields, Banks, and Frémont, but when pitted against the best of the Federal commanders he did not appear so well. Without doubt the greatest man of rebellion times, the one matchless among forty millions for the peculiar difficulties of the period, was Abraham Lincoln.

"GIN'L LONGSTREET'S BODY-SARVANT, SAH, ENDU'IN' DE WAH!"

the Federal right. I issued my orders accordingly for the two divisions to go around and turn the Federal right, when in some way unknown to me the battle was drawn on. We were repulsed at all points with fearful slaughter, losing six thousand men and accomplishing nothing.

The Federals withdrew after the battle, and the next day I moved on around by the route which it was proposed we should take the day before. I followed the enemy to Harrison's Landing, and Jackson went down by another route in advance of Lee. As soon as we reached the front of the

LEE'S CAMPAIGN AGAINST POPE AND THE SECOND BULL RUN.

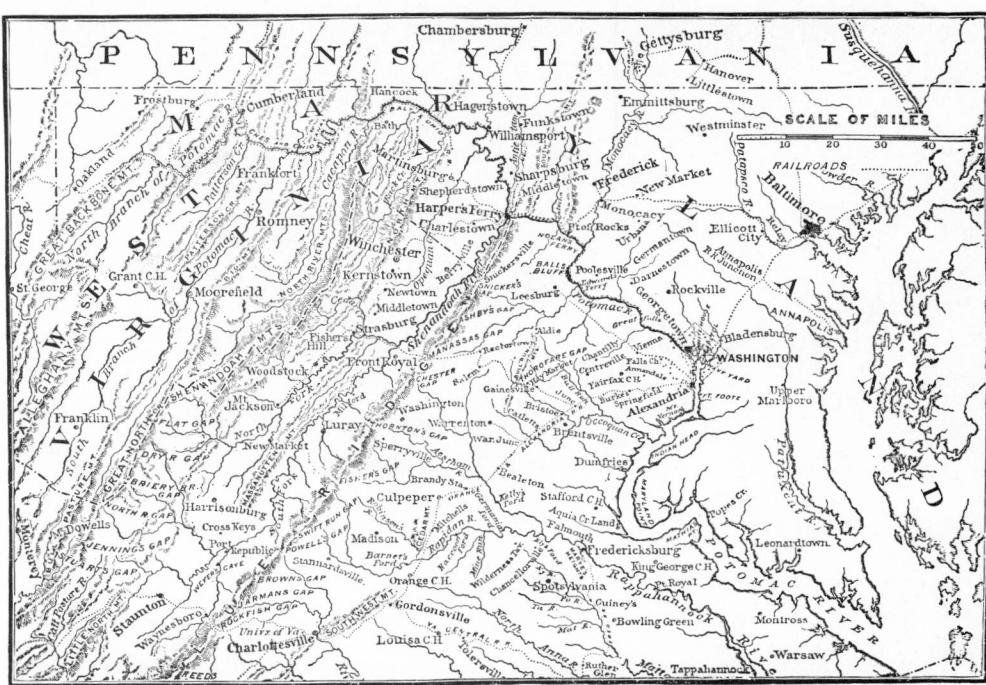

OUTLINE MAP OF THE CAMPAIGN.

NARRATIVE OF EVENTS.

On the 27th of June, 1862, General John Pope, after the capture of New Madrid and Island Number Ten, was transferred from the command of the Army of the Mississippi, to the newly constituted Army of Virginia. That army was composed of the detached corps of Frémont, Banks, and McDowell, stationed in Northern Virginia. Two days later, Frémont was superseded by Sigel. Banks and Sigel moved from the Shenandoah Valley to the Rappahannock line, where McDowell was already encamped. During July, while Pope was engaged in concentrating his forces along the Rappahannock, McClellan's army lay on the James River, and Lee's occupied the defensive lines of Richmond. Meanwhile, on July 11, Gen. H. W. Halleck was transferred from the command of the Western Department, and appointed General-in-chief of the United States forces. Thereafter, until he was superseded by Grant, in March, 1864, he directed the movement of all the armies in the field. At the close of July Halleck planned the withdrawal of McClellan's army from the Peninsula, and its union with that of Pope on the Rappahannock line. In order to facilitate the removal of these forces from Lee's front, Pope was instructed to manœuvre with his army beyond the Rappahannock toward Gordonsville. Lee despatched Stonewall Jackson with three divisions to meet Pope. On August 9 Jackson fought Bank's isolated corps at Cedar Mountain, in the angle between the Rapidan and Rappahannock rivers, and then, although victorious in the battle, retired south of the Rapidan, Pope following him with his entire army until he reached the north bank of that stream. On the 13th Lee marched from Richmond with Longstreet's command and Stuart's cavalry to reinforce Jackson. Finding his troops outnumbered, Pope retreated behind the Rappahannock (Aug. 20). From this point, the narratives of the movements of Lee and Pope preliminary to the second battle of Bull Run will be found in General Longstreet's article, "Our March Against Pope." Between the 20th and 27th of August the several corps of McClellan's army were transferred from the James River to Alexandria and Acquia Creek — the last named a landing on the Potomac convenient to the left flank of Pope's army. About the same time Burnside's Corps (the Ninth), from North Carolina, joined Pope, and to that corps was added later, the Kanawha Division, a reinforcement from Western Virginia, under Gen. J. D. Cox.

OUR MARCH AGAINST POPE.

BY JAMES LONGSTREET, LIEUTENANT-GENERAL, C. S. A.

Commander of the right wing of Lee's army at the Second Battle of Bull Run.

. . . By the Seven Days' fighting around Richmond General Lee frustrated McClellan's plans for a siege. At the end of that campaign Lee retired to Richmond, and McClellan withdrew his forces to Westover Landing, where intrenchments and gun-boats made him secure from attack. As his new position, thus guarded and protected by the navy, was not assailable, General Lee, resuming the defensive at Richmond, resolved to strike out by his left in the direction of Washington, with the idea that the Army of the Potomac might be forced to abandon the James River, in defense of its own capital, threatened by this move.

Contemporaneously with our operations on the Chickahominy, the Washington authorities had been organizing the Army of Virginia of three efficient corps d'armée; and, continuing the search for a young Napoleon, had assigned General Pope, fresh from the West, with his new laurels, to command this select organization. This army, under its dashing leader, was at the same time moving toward Richmond by the Orange and Alexandria Railway, so that our move by the left had also in view the Army of Virginia, as the first obstacle in the way of relief to Richmond — an obstacle to be removed, if possible, before it could be greatly reinforced from other commands. . . .

With the double purpose of drawing McClellan away from Westover, and of checking the advance of the new enemy then approaching from Washington by the Orange and Alexandria Railroad,

General Lee sent Stonewall Jackson to Gordonsville, while I remained near Richmond to engage McClellan in case he should attempt an advance upon the Confederate capital. Jackson had his own division and that of General R. S. Ewell, and later A. P. Hill was sent to reinforce him. McDowell was already in coöperation with Pope, part of his command, however, being still at Fredericksburg. On the 9th of August Jackson encountered the enemy near Slaughter or Cedar Mountain. There the battle of Cedar Run was fought and the Federals were repulsed. . . .

At that time General Lee was feeling very certain that Richmond was in no immediate danger from an advance by McClellan's forces. He therefore began at once preparations for a vigorous campaign against Pope. Divisions under Generals R. H. Anderson, Lafayette McLaws, J. G. Walker, and D. H. Hill were left to watch McClellan, with instructions to follow the main body of the army as soon as the Federals were drawn away from Westover.

On the 13th of August my command was ordered to Gordonsville, and General Lee accompanied me there. Jackson's troops were stationed on the left of the Orange and Alexandria Railroad, and I went into camp on the right of Gordonsville.

Northward was the Rapidan River, several miles distant. Farther on, at Culpeper Court House, was the army of Pope, and farther still was the Rappahannock River. . . .

Realizing the situation, General Lee determined on speedy work, and gave orders that his army should cross the Rapidan on the 18th and make battle. He was exceedingly anxious to move at once, before Pope could get reinforcements. For some reason not fully explained, our movements were delayed and we did not cross the Rapidan until the 20th. In the mean time a despatch to General Stuart was captured by Pope, which gave information of our presence and contemplated ad-

LONGSTREET'S MARCH THROUGH THOROUGHFARE GAP.

THE BATTLE OF CEDAR MOUNTAIN—VIEW FROM THE UNION LINES.
The picture shows the artillery duel and deployment of troops before the main attack toward the right, in the middle distance. (From a sketch made at the time.)

VIEW FROM THE HENRY HILL DURING THE ATTACK UPON JACKSON, ABOUT FOUR O'CLOCK, AUGUST 30TH.
From a sketch made at the time.

vance. This, with information Pope already had, caused him to withdraw to a very strong position behind the Rappahannock River, and there, instead of at Culpeper Court House, where the attack was first meant to be made, General Lee found him. I approached the Rappahannock at Kelly's Ford, and Jackson approached higher up at Beverly Ford, near the Orange and Alexandria Railroad bridge.

We reached the river on the morning of the 21st, without serious opposition, and found Pope in an almost unassailable position, with heavy reinforcements summoned to his aid. General Lee's intention was to force a passage and make the attack before Pope could concentrate. We hoped to be able to interpose, and to strike Pope before McClellan's reinforcements could reach him. We knew at that time that McClellan was withdrawing from Westover. . . .

Pending our movements southwest of the Rappahannock, General Stuart had been making an effort to go around Pope's army, but, fearing to remain on the Washington side of the river in the face of such floods as had come, recrossed with some important despatches he had captured by a charge upon Pope's headquarters train. This correspondence confirmed the information we already had, that the Federal army on the James under McClellan and the Federal troops in the Kanawha Valley under Cox had been ordered to reinforce Pope. Upon receipt of that information, General Lee was more anxious than ever to cross at once. Pope, however, was on the alert, and Lee found he could not attack him to advantage in his stronghold behind the Rappahannock. Lee therefore decided to change his whole plan, and was gratified, on looking at the map, to find a very comfortable way of turning Pope out of his position. It was by moving Jackson off to our left, and far to the rear of the Federal army, while I remained in front with thirty thousand men to engage him in case he should offer to fight.

On the 25th Jackson crossed the Rappahannock at Hinson's Mill, four miles above Waterloo Bridge, and that night encamped at Salem. The next day

he passed through Thoroughfare Gap and moved on by Gainesville, and when sunset came he was many miles in the rear of Pope's army, and between it and Washington. This daring move must have staggered the Federal commander. . . . On the afternoon of the 26th, Pope's army broke away from its strong position to meet Jackson's daring and unexpected move. General Lee decided that I should follow at once, and asked whether I would prefer to force a passage of the river, now rapidly falling, or take the route by which Jackson had gone. From the crossing along the route to Warrenton were numerous strongly defensive positions where a small force could have detained me an uncertain length of time. I therefore decided to take Jackson's route, and on the 26th I started. On the 28th, just before night, I arrived at Thoroughfare Gap. As we approached, a report was made to me that the pass was unoccupied, and we

VIEW OF JACKSON'S POSITION AS SEEN FROM GROVETON CORNERS.
The farthest ridge is the line of the unfinished railway. Jackson's center occupied the ground in the right of the picture. There, on elevated open ground, the front of a deep cut, stands the Union monument. (From a photograph taken in 1884.)

went into bivouac on the west side of the mountain, sending a brigade under Anderson down to occupy the pass. As the Confederates neared the gap from one side, Ricketts's division of Federals approached from the other and took possession of the east side. . . . This sudden interposition of a force at a mountain pass indicated a purpose on the part of the adversary to hold me in check, while overwhelming forces were being brought against Jackson. This placed us in a desperate strait; for we were within relieving distance, and must adopt prompt and vigorous measures that would burst through all opposition. Three miles north was Hopewell Gap, and it was necessary to get possession of this in advance of the Federals, in order to have that vantage-ground for a flank movement, at the same time that we forced our way by footpaths over the mountain heights at Thoroughfare Gap. During the night I sent Wilcox with

three brigades through that pass, while Hood was climbing over the mountain at Thoroughfare by a trail. We had no trouble in getting over, and our apprehensions were relieved at the early dawn of the 29th by finding that Ricketts had given up the east side of the gap and was many hours in advance of us, moving in the direction of Manassas Junction. His force, instead of marching around Jackson, could have been thrown against his right and rear. If Ricketts had made this move, and the forces in front had coöperated with him, such an attack, well handled, might have given us serious trouble before I reached the field.

As we found the pass open at early dawn, and a clean road in front, we marched leisurely to unite our forces on Manassas plains. Before reaching Gainesville we heard the artillery combat in front, and our men involuntarily quickened their steps. Our communications with Jackson were quite regular, and as he had not expressed a wish that we should hurry, our troops were allowed to take their natural swing under the inspiration of impending battle. As we approached the field the fire seemed to become more spirited, and gave additional impulse to our movements. . . .

Passing through Gainesville we filed off to the left down the turnpike, and soon came in sight of the troops held at bay by Jackson. Our line of march brought us in on the left and rear of the Federals. . . .

The two great armies were now face to face upon the memorable field of 1861; both in good defensible positions, and both anxious to find a point for an entering wedge into the stronghold of the adversary. It appeared easy for us, except for the unknown quantity at Manassas Junction, to overleap the Federal left and strike a decisive blow. This force at the Junction was a thorn in our side which could not be ignored. General Lee was quite disappointed by my report against immediate attack along the turnpike, and insisted that by throwing some of the brigades beyond the Federal left their position would be broken up, and a favorable field gained. While talking the matter over, General Stuart reported the advance

COLLISION ON THURSDAY, AUGUST 28TH, BETWEEN REYNOLDS'S DIVISION AND JACKSON'S RIGHT WING.

THE BATTLE OF GROVETON, AUGUST 29TH, AS SEEN FROM CENTREVILLE.

of heavy forces from the direction of Manassas Junction against my right. It proved to be McDowell and Porter. I called over three brigades, under Wilcox, and prepared to receive the attack. Battle was not offered, and I reported to General Lee some time afterward that I did not think the force on my right was strong enough to attack us. General Lee urged me to go in, and of course I was anxious to meet his wishes. At the same time I wanted, more than anything else, to know that my troops had a chance to accomplish what they might undertake. The ground before me was greatly to the advantage of the Federals, but if the attack had come from them it would have been a favorable opportunity for me. After a short while, McDowell moved toward the Federal right, leaving Porter in front of my right with nine thousand men. My estimate of his force, at the time, was ten thousand. General Lee, finding that attack was not likely, again became anxious to bring on the battle by attacking down the Groveton pike. I suggested that, the day being far spent, it might be as well to advance just before night upon a forced reconnoissance, get our troops into the most favorable positions, and have all things ready for battle at daylight the next morning. To this he reluctantly gave consent, and our plans were laid accordingly. Wilcox returned to position on the left of the turnpike. Orders were given for an advance, to be pursued under cover of night until the main position could be carefully examined. It so happened that an order to advance was issued on the other side at the same time, so that the encounter was something of a surprise on both sides. A very spirited engagement was the result, we being successful, so far at least as to carry our point, capturing a piece of artillery and making our reconnoissance before midnight. As none of the reports received of the Federal positions favored attack, I so explained to General Lee, and

our forces were ordered back to their original positions. The gun which we had captured was ordered to be cut down, spiked, and left on the ground.

When Saturday, the 30th, broke, we were a little apprehensive that Pope was going to get away from us, and Pope was afraid that we were going to get away from him. He telegraphed to Washington that I was in full retreat and he was preparing to follow, while we, thinking he was trying to escape, were making arrangements for moving by our left across Bull Run, so as to get over on the Little River pike and move down parallel to his lines and try to interpose between him and Washington. We had about completed our arrangements, and took it for granted that Pope would move out that night by the Warrenton and Centreville pike, and that we could move parallel with him along the Little River pike. General Lee was still anxious to give Pope battle on Manassas plains, but had given up the idea of attacking him in his strong position.

Shortly before nine on the 30th, Pope's artillery began to play a little, and not long afterward some of his infantry force was seen in motion. We did not understand that as an offer of battle, but merely as a display to cover his movements to the rear. Later a considerable force moved out and began to attack us on our left, extending and engaging the whole of Jackson's line. Evi-

dently Pope supposed that I was gone, as he was ignoring me entirely. His whole army seemed to surge up against Jackson as if to crush him with an overwhelming mass. At the critical moment I happened to be riding to the front of my line to find a place where I might get in for my share of the battle. I reached a point a few rods in front of my line on the left of the pike where I could plainly see the Federals as they rushed in heavy masses against the obstinate ranks of the Confederate left. It was a grand display of well-organized attack, thoroughly concentrated and operating cleverly. So terrible was the onslaught that Jackson sent to me and begged for reinforcements. About the same time I received an order from General Lee to the same effect. To retire from my advanced position in front of the Federals and get to Jackson would have taken an hour and a half. I had discovered a prominent position that commanded a view of the great struggle, and realizing the opportunity, I quickly ordered out three batteries, making twelve guns. Lieut. Wm. H. Chapman's Dixie Battery [Virginia] of four guns was the first to report, and was placed in position to rake the Federal ranks that seemed determined to break

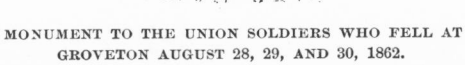

MONUMENT TO THE UNION SOLDIERS WHO FELL AT GROVETON AUGUST 28, 29, AND 30, 1862.

through Jackson's lines. In a moment a heavy fire of shot and shell was being poured into the thick columns of the enemy, and in ten minutes their stubborn masses began to waver and give back. For a moment there was chaos; then order returned and they re-formed, apparently to renew the attack. Meanwhile my other eight pieces reported to me, and from the crest of the little hill the fire of twelve guns cut them down. As the cannon thundered the ranks broke, only to be formed again with dogged determination. A third time the batteries tore the Federals to pieces, and as they fell back under this terrible fire, I sprung everything to the charge. My troops leaped forward with exultant yells, and all along the line we pushed forward. Farther and still farther back we pressed them, until at 10 o'clock at night we had the field; Pope was across Bull Run, and the victorious Confederates lay down on the battle-ground to sleep, while all around were strewn thousands — friend and foe, sleeping the last sleep together.

The next morning the Federals were in a strong position at Centreville. I sent a brigade across Bull Run under General Pryor, and occupied a point over there near Centreville. As our troops proceeded to bury their dead, it began to rain, as it had done on the day after the first battle of Manassas. As soon as General Lee could make his preparations, he ordered Jackson to cross Bull Run near Sudley's and turn the position of the Federals occupying Centreville; and the next day, September 1st, I followed him. But the enemy discovered our turning movement, abandoned Centreville, and put out toward Washington. On the evening of September 1st Jackson encountered a part of the Federal force at Ox Hill [or Chantilly], and, attacking it, had quite a sharp engagement. I came up just before night and found his men retiring in a good deal of confusion. I asked Jackson

DEATH OF GENERAL PHILIP KEARNY, SEPTEMBER 1, 1862.

him. His body was sent over the lines under a flag of truce. The forces we had been fighting at Ox Hill proved to be the rear-guard covering the retreat of the Federals into Washington. They escaped and we abandoned further pursuit. . . .

The entire Bull Run campaign up to Ox Hill was clever and brilliant. It was conceived entirely by General Lee, who held no such consultation over it as he had done in beginning the Seven Days' campaign. The movement around Pope was not as strong as it should have been. A skilful man could have concentrated against me or Jackson, and given us severe battles in detail. I suppose Pope tried to get too many men against Jackson before attacking. If he had been satisfied with a reasonable force he might have overwhelmed him. General Pope, sanguine by nature, was not careful enough to keep himself informed about the movements of his enemy. . . . I was graduated with Pope at West Point. He was a handsome, dashing fellow, and a splendid cavalryman, sitting his horse beautifully. I think he stood at the head for riding. He did not apply himself to his books very closely. He studied about as much as I did, but knew his lessons better. We were graduated in 1842, but Pope saw little of active service till the opening of the Civil War. When he assumed command of the Army of Virginia he was in the prime of life, less than forty years old, and had lost little if any of the dash and grace of his youth. D. H. Hill, Lafayette McLaws, Mansfield Lovell, Gustavus W. Smith, R. H. Anderson, A. P. Stewart, and Earl Van Dorn were among the Confederate commanders who were graduated in the same class with me. Of the Federal commanders, there were of that class — besides Pope — Generals John Newton, W. S. Rosecrans, George Sykes, Abner Doubleday, and others less prominent. Stonewall Jackson came on four years after my class. General Lee had preceded us about fourteen years. General Ewell, who was hurt in this battle, was in the same class with Tecumseh Sherman and George H. Thomas. A truer soldier and nobler spirit than Ewell never drew sword. "Jeb" Stuart was a very daring fellow, and the best cavalryman America ever produced. At the Second Manassas, soon after we heard of the advance of McDowell and Porter, Stuart came up and made a report to General Lee. When he had done so General Lee said he had no orders at that moment, but he requested Stuart to wait awhile. Thereupon Stuart turned round in his tracks, lay down on the ground, put a stone under his head and instantly fell asleep. General Lee rode away, and in an hour returned. Stuart was still sleeping. Lee asked for him, and Stuart sprang to his feet and said, "Here I am, General."

General Lee replied, "I want you to send a message to your troops over on the left to send a few more cavalry over to the right."

"I would better go myself," said Stuart, and with that he swung himself into the saddle and rode off at a rapid gallop, singing as loud as he could, "Jine the cavalry." . . .

A STRAGGLER ON THE LINE OF MARCH.

A CONFEDERATE PRIVATE IN THE SECOND BULL RUN CAMPAIGN.

BY ALLEN C. REDWOOD, 55TH VIRGINIA REGIMENT, C. S. A.

. . . Friday morning early, we started in what we supposed to be the right direction, guided by the firing, which more and more betokened that the fight was on. Once we stopped for a few moments at a field-hospital to make inquiries, and were informed that our brigade was farther along to the right. General Ewell, who had lost his leg the evening before, was carried by on a stretcher while we were there. Very soon we heard sharp musketry over a low ridge which we had been skirting, and almost immediately we became involved with stragglers from that direction — Georgians, I think they were. It looked as if a whole line was giving way, and we hurried on to gain our own colors before it should grow too hot. The proverbial effect of bad company was soon apparent. We were halted by a Louisiana major, who was trying to rally these fragments upon his own command. My companion took the short cut out of the scrape by showing his "sick-permit," and was allowed to pass; mine, alas! had been left in my cartridge-box with my other belongings in that unlucky ambulance. The major was courteous but firm; he listened to my story with more attention than I could have expected, but attached my person all the same. "Better stay with us, my boy, and if you do your duty I'll make it right with your company officers when the fight's over. They won't find fault with you when they know you've

what the situation was, and added that his men seemed to be pretty well dispersed. He said, "Yes, but I hope it will prove a victory."

I moved my troops out and occupied the lines where he had been, relieving the few men who were on picket. Just as we reached there General Kearny, a Federal officer, came along looking for his line, that had disappeared. It was raining in the woods, and was so late in the day that a Federal was not easily distinguished from a Confederate. Kearny did not seem to know that he was in the Confederate line, and our troops did not notice that he was a Federal. He began to inquire about some command, and in a moment or so the men saw that he was a Federal officer. At the same moment he realized where he was. He was called upon to surrender, but instead of doing so he wheeled his horse, lay flat on the animal's neck, clapped spurs into his sides and dashed off. Instantly a half-dozen shots rang out, and before he had gone thirty steps he fell. He had been in the army all his life, and we knew him and respected

A LOUISIANA "PELICAN."

been in with the 'Pelicans,'" he added, as he assigned me to company "F."

The command was as unlike my own as it was possible to conceive. Such a congress of nations only the cosmopolitan Crescent City could have sent forth, and the tongues of Babel seemed resurrected in its speech; English, German, French, and Spanish, all were represented, to say nothing of Doric brogue and local "gumbo." There was, moreover, a vehemence of utterance and gesture curiously at variance with the reticence of our Virginians. In point of fact, we burned little powder that day, and my promised distinction as a "Pelican" pro tem. was cheaply earned. The battalion did a good deal of counter-marching, and some skirmishing, but most of the time we were acting as support to a section of Cutshaw's battery. The tedium of this last service my companions relieved by games of "seven up," with a greasy, well-thumbed deck, and in smoking cigarettes, rolled with great dexterity, between the deals. Once, when a detail was ordered to go some distance under fire to fill the canteens of the company, a hand was dealt to determine who should go, and the decision was accepted by the loser without demur. Our numerous shifts of position

SUPPER AFTER A HARD MARCH.

completely confused what vague ideas I had of the situation, but we must have been near our extreme left at Sudley Church, and never very far from my own brigade, which was warmly engaged that day and the day following. Toward evening we were again within sight of Sudley Church. I could see the light of fires among the trees, as if cooking for the wounded was going on, and the idea occurred to me that there I could easily learn the exact position of my proper command. Once clear of my major and his polyglot "Pelicans," the rest would be plain sailing.

My flank movement was easily effected, and I suddenly found myself the *most* private soldier on that field; there seemed to be nobody else anywhere near. I passed a farm-house, which seemed to have been used as a hospital, and where I picked up a Zouave fez. Some cavalrymen were there, one of whom advised me "not to go down there," but as he gave no special reason and did not urge his views, I paid no heed to him, but went on my way down a long barren slope, ending in a small water-course at the bottom, beyond which the ground rose abruptly and was covered by small growth. The deepening twilight and strange solitude about me, with a remembrance of what had happened a year ago on this same ground, made me feel uncomfortably lonely. By this time I was close to the stream, and while noting the lay of the land on the opposite bank with regard to choice of a crossing-place, I became aware of a man observing me from the end of the cut above. I could not distinguish the color of his uniform, but the crown of his hat tapered suspiciously, I thought, and instinctively I dropped the butt of my rifle to the ground and reached behind me for a cartridge.

"Come here!" he called;—his accent was worse than his hat. "Who are you?" I responded as I executed the movement of "tear cartridge." He laughed and then invited me to "come and see." Meanwhile I was trying to draw my rammer, but this operation was arrested by the dry click of several gunlocks, and I found myself covered by half a dozen rifles, and my friend of the steeple-crown, with less urbanity in his intonation, called out to me to "drop that." In our brief intercourse he had acquired a curious influence over me. I did so.

My captors were of Kearny's division, on picket. They told me they thought I was deserting until they saw me try to load. I could not account for their being where they were, and when they informed me that they had Jackson surrounded and that he must surrender next day, though I openly scouted the notion, I must own the weight of evidence seemed to be with them. The discussion of this and kindred topics was continued until a late hour that night with the sergeant of the guard at Kearny's headquarters, where I supped in unwonted luxury on hard-tack and "genuine" coffee, the sergeant explaining that the fare was no better because of our destruction of their supplies at the Junction. Kearny's orderly gave me a blanket, and so I passed the night. We were astir early in the morning (August 30th), and I saw Kearny as he passed with his staff to the front,—a spare, erect, military figure, looking every inch the fighter he was. He fell three days later, killed by some of my own brigade.

Near the Stone Bridge I found about 500 other prisoners, mostly stragglers picked up along the line of our march. Here my polite provost-sergeant turned me over to other guardians, and after draw-

ing rations, hard-tack, coffee, and sugar, we took the road to Centreville. That thoroughfare was thronged with troops, trains, and batteries, and we had to stand a good deal of chaff on the way, at our forlorn appearance. We were a motley crowd enough, certainly, and it *did* look as if our friends in blue were having their return innings. More than once that day as I thought of the thin line I had left, I wondered how the boys were doing, for disturbing rumors came to us as we lay in a field near Centreville, exchanging rude badinage across the cordon of sentries surrounding us. Other prisoners came in from time to time who brought the same unvarying story, "Jackson hard-pressed —no news of Longstreet yet." So the day wore on. Toward evening there was a noticeable stir in the camps around us, a continual riding to and fro of couriers and orderlies, and now we thought we could hear more distinctly the deep-toned, jarring growl which had interjected itself at intervals all the afternoon through the trivial buzz about us. Watchful of indications, we noted, too, that the drift of wagons and ambulances was *from* the battle-field, and soon orders came for us to take the road in the same direction. The cannonading down the pike was sensibly nearer now, and at times we could catch even the roll of musketry, and once we thought we could distinguish, far off and faint, the prolonged, murmurous sound familiar to our ears as the charging shout of the gray people—but this may have been fancy. All the same, we gave tongue to the cry, and shouts of "Longstreet! Longstreet's at 'em, boys! Hurrah for Longstreet!" went up from our ranks, while the guards trudged beside us in sulky silence. . . .

CONFEDERATE CAMP-SERVANT ON THE MARCH.

CHARGE OF UNION CAVALRY UPON THE CONFEDERATE ADVANCE NEAR BRANDY STATION, AUGUST 20, 1862.

THE SECOND BATTLE OF BULL RUN.

BY JOHN POPE, MAJOR-GENERAL, U. S. A.
Union Commander at the Second Battle of Bull Run.

. . . Under the changed condition of things brought about by General McClellan's retreat to James River, and the purpose to withdraw his army [from the Peninsula] and unite it with that under my command, the campaign of the Army of Virginia was limited to the following objects:

1. To cover the approaches to Washington from any enemy advancing from the direction of Richmond, and to oppose and delay its advance to the last extremity, so as to give all the time possible for the withdrawal of the Army of the Potomac from the James River.

2. If no heavy forces of the enemy moved north, to operate on their lines of communication with Gordonsville and Charlottesville, so as to force Lee to make heavy detachments from his force at Richmond and facilitate to that extent the withdrawal of the Army of the Potomac.

Halleck was of the opinion that the junction of the two armies could be made on the line of the Rappahannock, and my orders to hold fast to my communications with Fredericksburg, through which place McClellan's army was to make its junction with the Army of Virginia, were repeated positively.

The decision of the enemy to move north with the bulk of his army was promptly made and vigorously carried out, so that it became apparent, even before General McClellan began to embark his army, that the line of the Rappahannock was too far to the front. That fact, however, was not realized by Halleck until too late for any change which could be effectively executed. . . .

Under the orders heretofore referred to, the concentration of the corps of the Army of Virginia was completed, Sigel's corps being at Sperryville, Banks's at Little Washington, and Ricketts's division of McDowell's corps at Waterloo Bridge. I assumed the command in person July 29th, 1862. . . .

It is only necessary to say that the course of these operations made it plain enough that the Rappahannock was too far to the front, and that the movements of Lee were too rapid and those of McClellan too slow to make it possible, with the small force I had, to hold that line, or to keep open communication with Fredericksburg without being turned on my right flank by Lee's whole army and cut off altogether from Washington.

On the 21st of August, being then at Rappahannock Station, my little army confronted by nearly the whole force under General Lee, which had compelled the retreat of McClellan to Harrison's Landing, I was positively assured that two days more would see me largely enough reinforced by the Army of the Potomac to be not only secure, but to assume the offensive against Lee, and I was instructed to hold on "and fight like the devil."

I accordingly held on till the 26th of August, when, finding myself to be outflanked on my right by the main body of Lee's army, while Jackson's corps having passed Salem and Rectortown the day before were in rapid march in the direction of Gainesville and Manassas Junction, and seeing that none of the reinforcements promised me were likely to arrive, I determined to abandon the line of the Rappahannock and communications with Fredericksburg, and concentrate my whole force in the direction of Warrenton and Gainesville, to cover the Warrenton pike, and still to confront the enemy rapidly marching to my right.

Stonewall Jackson's movement on Manassas Junction was plainly seen and promptly reported, and I notified General Halleck of it. He informed me on the 23d of August that heavy reinforcements would begin to arrive at Warrenton Junction on the next day (24th), and as my orders still held me to the Rappahannock I naturally supposed that these troops would be hurried forward to me with all speed. Franklin's corps especially, I asked, should be sent rapidly to Gainesville. I also telegraphed Colonel Herman Haupt, chief of railway transportation, to direct one of the strongest divisions coming forward, and to be at Warrenton Junction on the 24th, to be put in the works at Manassas Junction. A cavalry force had been sent forward to observe the Thoroughfare Gap early on the morning of the 26th, but nothing was heard from it.

On the night of August 26th Jackson's advance, having passed Thoroughfare Gap, struck the Orange and Alexandria Railroad at Manassas Junction, and made it plain to me that all of the reinforcements and movements of the troops promised me had altogether failed. Had Franklin been even at Centreville, or had Cox's and Sturgis's divisions been as far west as Bull Run on that day, the movement of Jackson on Manassas Junction would not have been practicable.

As Jackson's movement on Manassas Junction marks the beginning of the second battle of Bull Run, it is essential to a clear understanding of subsequent operations to give the positions of the army under my command on the night of August 26th, as also the movements and operations of the enemy as far as we knew them. . . .

The troops were disposed as follows: McDowell's corps and Sigel's corps were at Warrenton under general command of General McDowell, with Banks's corps at Fayetteville as a reserve. Reno's corps was directed upon the Warrenton turnpike to take post three miles east of Warrenton. Porter's corps was near Bealeton Station moving slowly toward Warrenton Junction; Heintzelman at Warrenton Junction, with very small means to move in any direction.

Up to this time I had been placed by the positive orders of General Halleck much in the position of a man tied by one leg and fighting with a person much his physical superior and free to move in any direction. . . .

The movements of the enemy toward my right forced me either to abandon the line of the Rappahannock and the communications with Fredericksburg, or to risk the loss of my army and the almost certain loss of Washington. Of course between these two alternatives I could not hesitate in a choice. I considered it my duty, at whatever sacrifice to my army and myself, to retard, as far as I could, the

BREVET MAJOR-GEN. CUVIER GROVER, U. S. V.
From a photograph.

On Friday afternoon Grover's brigade, of Hooker's division, charged Jackson's center before Kearny's successful and bloody charge on Jackson's left. Grover led 5 regiments, altogether about 1500 men, and in 20 minutes lost 486, or nearly one-third, of his command.

movement of the enemy toward Washington, until I was certain that the Army of the Potomac had reached Alexandria.

The movement of Jackson presented the only opportunity which had offered to gain any success over the superior forces of the enemy. I determined, therefore, on the morning of the 27th of August to abandon the line of the Rappahannock and throw my whole force in the direction of Gainesville and Manassas Junction, to crush any force of the enemy that had passed through Thoroughfare Gap, and to interpose between Lee's army and Bull Run. Having the interior line of operations, and the enemy at Manassas being inferior in force, it appeared to me, and still so appears, that with even ordinary promptness and energy we might feel sure of success.

RETREAT OF THE UNION TROOPS ACROSS THE RAPPAHANNOCK AT RAPPAHANNOCK STATION.

BREVET MAJOR-GEN. JOHN W. GEARY, U. S. V.

MAJOR-GENERAL ROBERT C. SCHENCK, U. S. V.

MAJOR-GENERAL JOHN POPE, U. S. A.
From a photograph taken early in the war.

In the mean time heavy forces of the enemy still confronted us at Waterloo Bridge, while his main body continued its march toward our right, following the course of Hedgman's River (the Upper Rappahannock). I accordingly sent orders, early on the 27th of August, to General McDowell to move rapidly on Gainesville by the Warrenton pike with his own corps, reinforced by Reynolds's division and Sigel's corps. I directed Reno, followed by Kearny's division of Heintzelman's corps, to move on Greenwich, so as to reach there that night, to report thence at once to General McDowell, and to support him in operations against the enemy which were expected near Gainesville. With Hooker's division of Heintzelman's corps I moved along the railroad toward Manassas Junction, to reopen our communications and to be in position to coöperate with the forces along the Warrenton pike.

On the afternoon of that day a severe engagement took place between Hooker's division and Ewell's division of Jackson's corps, near Bristoe Station, on the railroad. Ewell was driven back along the railroad, but at dark still confronted Hooker along the banks of Broad Run. The loss in this action was about three hundred killed and wounded on each side. Ewell left his dead, many of his wounded, and some of his baggage on the field.

I had not seen Hooker for many years, and I remembered him as a very handsome young man, with florid complexion and fair hair, and with a figure agile and graceful. As I saw him that afternoon on his white horse riding in rear of his line of battle, and close up to it, with the excitement of battle in his eyes, and that gallant and chivalric appearance which he always presented under fire, I was struck with admiration. As a corps commander, with his whole force operating under his own eye, it is much to be doubted whether Hooker had a superior in the army.

The railroad had been torn up and the bridges burned in several places just west of Bristoe Station. I therefore directed General Banks, who had reached Warrenton Junction, to cover the railroad trains at that place until General Porter marched, and then to run back the trains toward Manassas as far as he could and rebuild the railroad bridges. Captain Merrill of the Engineers was also directed to repair the railroad track and bridges toward Bristoe. This work was done by that accomplished officer as far east as Kettle Run on the 27th, and the trains were run back to that point next morning.

At dark on the 27th Hooker informed me that his ammunition was nearly exhausted, only five rounds to the man being on hand. Before this time it had become apparent that Jackson, with his whole force, was south of the Warrenton pike and in the immediate neighborhood of Manassas Junction.

McDowell reached his position at Gainesville during the night of the 27th, and Kearny and Reno theirs at Greenwich. It was clear on that night that we had completely interposed between Jackson and the enemy's main body, which was still west of the Bull Run range, and in the vicinity of White Plains.

In consequence of Hooker's report, and the weakness of the small division which he commanded, and to strengthen my right wing moving in the direction of Manassas, I sent orders to Porter at dark, which reached him at 9 P. M., to move forward from Warrenton Junction at 1 A. M. night, and to report to me at Bristoe Station by daylight next morning (August 28th).

There were but two courses left to Jackson by this sudden movement of the army. He could not retrace his steps through Gainesville, as that place was occupied by McDowell with a force equal if not superior to his own. To retreat through Centreville would carry him still farther away from

the main body of Lee's army. It was possible, however, to mass his whole force at Manassas Junction and assail our right (Hooker's division), which had fought a severe battle that afternoon, and was almost out of ammunition. Jackson, with A. P. Hill's division, retired through Centreville. Thinking it altogether within the probabilities that he might adopt the other alternative, I sent the orders above mentioned to General Porter. . . .

At 9 o'clock on the night of the 27th, satisfied of Jackson's position, I sent orders to General McDowell at Gainesville to push forward at the earliest dawn of day upon Manassas Junction, resting his right on the Manassas Gap Railroad and extending his left to the east. I directed General Reno at the same time to march from Greenwich, also direct on Manassas Junction, and Kearny to move from the same place upon Bristoe Station. This move of Kearny was to strengthen my right at Bristoe and unite the two divisions of Heintzelman's corps.

Jackson began to evacuate Manassas Junction during the night (the 27th) and marched toward Centreville and other points of the Warrenton pike west of that place, and by 11 o'clock next morning was at and beyond Centreville and north of the Warrenton pike. I arrived at Manassas Junction shortly after the last of Jackson's force had moved off, and immediately pushed forward Hooker, Kearny, and Reno upon Centreville, and sent orders to Porter to come forward to Manassas Junction. I

also wrote McDowell the situation and directed him to call back to Gainesville any part of his force which had moved in the direction of Manassas Junction, and march upon Centreville along the Warrenton pike with the whole force under his command to intercept the retreat of Jackson toward Thoroughfare Gap. With King's division in advance, McDowell, marching toward Centreville, encountered late in the afternoon the advance of Jackson's corps retreating toward Thoroughfare Gap. Late in the afternoon, also, Kearny drove the rear-guard of Jackson out of Centreville and occupied that place with his advance beyond it toward Gainesville. A very severe engagement occurred between King's division and Jackson's forces near the village of Groveton on the Warrenton pike, which was terminated by the darkness, both parties maintaining their ground. . . .

The engagement of King's division was reported to me about 10 o'clock at night near Centreville. I felt sure then, and so stated, that there was no escape for Jackson. On the west of him were McDowell's corps, Sigel's corps, and Reynolds's division, all under command of McDowell. On

THE "DEEP CUT."
From a sketch made in 1884.

STARKE'S BRIGADE FIGHTING WITH STONES NEAR THE "DEEP CUT."

If this picture were extended a little to the left it would include the Union monument seen in the picture below.

the east of him, and with the advance of Kearny nearly in contact with him on the Warrenton pike, were the corps of Reno and Heintzelman. Porter was supposed to be at Manassas Junction, where he ought to have been on that afternoon.

I sent orders to McDowell (supposing him to be with his command), and also direct to General King, several times during that night and once by his own staff-officer, to hold his ground at all hazards, to prevent the retreat of Jackson toward Lee, and that at daylight our whole force from Centreville and Manassas would assail him from the east, and he would be crushed between us. I sent orders also to General Kearny at Centreville to move forward cautiously that night along the Warrenton pike; to drive in the pickets of the enemy, and to keep as closely as possible in contact with him during the night, resting his left on the Warrenton pike and throwing his right to the north, if practicable, as far as the Little River pike, and at daylight next morning to assault vigorously with his right advance, and that Hooker and Reno would certainly be with him shortly after daylight. I sent orders to General Porter, who I supposed was at Manassas Junction, to move upon Centreville at dawn, stating to him the position of our forces, and that a severe battle would be fought that morning (the 29th).

With Jackson at and near Groveton, with McDowell on the west, and the rest of the army on the east of him, while Lee, with the mass of his army, was still west of Thoroughfare Gap, the sit-

uation for us was certainly as favorable as the most sanguine person could desire, and the prospect of crushing Jackson, sandwiched between such forces, were certainly excellent. There is no doubt, had General McDowell been with his command when King's division of his corps became engaged with the enemy, he would have brought forward to its support both Sigel and Reynolds, and the result would have been to hold the ground west of Jackson at least until morning brought against him also the forces moving from the direction of Centreville.

To my great disappointment and surprise, however, I learned toward daylight the next morning (the 29th) that King's division had fallen back toward Manassas Junction, and that neither Sigel nor Reynolds had been engaged or had gone to the support of King. The route toward Thoroughfare Gap had thus been left open by the wholly unexpected retreat of King's division, due to the fact that he was not supported by Sigel and Rey-

THE UNION MONUMENT NEAR THE "DEEP CUT."
From a sketch made in 1884.

nolds, and an immediate change was necessary in the disposition of the troops under my command. Sigel and Reynolds were near Groveton, almost in contact with Jackson; Ricketts had fallen back toward Bristoe from Thoroughfare Gap, after offering (as might have been expected) ineffectual resistance to the passage of the Bull Run range by very superior forces; King had fallen back to Manassas Junction; Porter was at Manassas Junction or near there; Reno and Hooker near Centreville; Kearny at Centreville and beyond toward Groveton; Jackson near Groveton with his whole corps; Lee with the main army of the enemy, except three brigades of Longstreet which had passed Hopewell Gap, north of Thoroughfare Gap.

The field of battle was practically limited to the space between the old railroad grade from Sudley to Gainesville if prolonged across the Warrenton pike and the Sudley Springs road east of it. The railroad grade indicates almost exactly the line occupied by Jackson's force, our own line confronting it from left to right.

The ridge which bounded the valley of Dawkins's Branch on the west, and on which were the Hampton Cole and Monroe houses, offered from the Monroe house a full view of the field of battle from right to left, and the Monroe house being on the crest of the ridge overlooked and completely commanded the approach to Jackson's right by the Warrenton turnpike. To the result of the battle this ridge was of the last importance, and, if seized and held by noon, would absolutely have prevented any reinforcement of Jackson's right from the direction of Gainesville. The northern slope of this ridge was held by our troops near the Douglass house, near which, also, the right of Jackson's line rested. The advance of Porter's corps at Dawkins's Branch was less than a mile and a half from the Monroe house, and the road in his front was one of several which converged on that point.

The whole field was free from obstacles to movement of troops and nearly so to manœuvers, with only a few eminences, and these of a nature to have been seized and easily held by our troops even against very superior numbers. The ground was gently undulating and the water-courses insignificant, while the intersecting system of roads and lanes afforded easy communication with all parts of the field. It would be difficult to find anywhere in Virginia a more perfect field of battle than that on which the second battle of Bull Run was fought.

About daylight, therefore, on the 29th of August, almost immediately after I received information of the withdrawal of King's division toward Manassas

Junction, I sent orders to General Sigel, in the vicinity of Groveton, to attack the enemy vigorously at daylight and bring him to a stand if possible. He was to be supported by Reynolds's division. I instructed Heintzelman to push forward from Centreville toward Gainesville on the Warrenton pike at the earliest dawn with the divisions of Kearny and Hooker, and gave orders also to Reno with his corps to follow closely in their rear. They were directed to use all speed, and as soon as they came up with the enemy to establish communication with Sigel, and to attack vigorously and promptly. I also sent orders to General Porter at Manassas Junction to move forward rapidly with his own corps and King's division of McDowell's corps, which was there also, upon Gainesville by the direct route from Manassas Junction to that place. I urged him to make all possible speed, with the purpose that he should come up with the enemy or connect himself with the left of our line near where the Warrenton pike is crossed by the road from Manassas Junction to Gainesville.

Shortly after sending this order I received a note from General McDowell, whom I had not been able to find during the night of the 28th, dated Manassas Junction, requesting that King's division be not taken from his command. I immediately sent a joint order, addressed to Generals McDowell and Porter, repeating the instructions to move forward with their commands toward Gainesville, and informing them of the position and movements of Sigel and Heintzelman.

Sigel attacked the enemy at daylight on the morning of the 29th about a mile east of Groveton, where he was joined by the divisions of Hooker and Kearny. Jackson fell back, but was so closely pressed by these forces that he was obliged to make a stand. He accordingly took up his position along and behind the old railroad embankment extending along his entire front, with his left near Sudley Springs and his right just south of the Warrenton pike. His batteries, some of them of heavy caliber, were posted behind the ridges in the open ground, while the mass of his troops were sheltered by woods and the railroad embankment.

THE RETREAT OVER THE STONE BRIDGE, SATURDAY EVENING, AUGUST 30TH.

I arrived on the field from Centreville about noon, and found the opposing forces confronting each other, both considerably cut up by the severe action in which they had been engaged since daylight. Heintzelman's corps (the divisions of Hooker and Kearny) occupied the right of our line toward Sudley Springs. Sigel was on his left, with his line extending a short distance south of the Warrenton pike, the division of Schenck occupying the high ground to the left (south) of the pike. The extreme left was held by Reynolds. Reno's corps had reached the field and the most of it had been pushed forward into action, leaving four regiments in reserve behind the center of the line of battle. Immediately after I reached the ground, General Sigel reported to me that his line was weak, that the divisions of Schurz and Steinwehr were much cut up and ought to be drawn back from the front. I informed him that this was impossible, as there were no troops to replace them, and that he must hold his ground; that I would not immediately push his troops again into action, as the corps of McDowell and Porter were moving forward on the road from Manassas Junction to Gainesville, and must very soon be in position to fall upon the enemy's right flank and possibly on his rear. I rode along the front of our line and gave the same information to Heintzelman and Reno. . . .

The troops were permitted to rest for a time, and to resupply themselves with ammunition. From 1:30 to 4 o'clock P. M. very severe conflicts occurred repeatedly all along the line, and there was a continuous roar of artillery and small-arms, with scarcely an intermission. About two o'clock in the afternoon three discharges of artillery were heard on the extreme left of our line or right of the enemy's, and I for the moment, and naturally, believed that Porter and McDowell had reached their positions and were engaged with the enemy. I heard only three shots, and as nothing followed I was at a loss to know what had become of these corps, or what was delaying them, as before this hour they should have been, even with ordinary marching, well up on our left. Shortly afterward I received information that McDowell's corps was advancing to join the left of our line by the Sudley Springs road, and would probably be up within two hours [that is, about 4 P. M.] At 4:30 o'clock I sent a peremptory order to General Porter, who was at or near Dawkins's Branch, about four or five miles distant from my headquarters, to push forward at once into action on the enemy's right, and if possible on his rear, stating to him

generally the condition of things on the field in front of me. At 5:30 o'clock, when General Porter should have been going into action in compliance with this order, I directed Heintzelman and Reno to attack the enemy's left. The attack was made promptly and with vigor and persistence, and the left of the enemy was doubled back toward his center. After a severe and bloody action of an hour Kearny forced the position on the left of the enemy and occupied the field of battle there.

By this time General McDowell had arrived on the field, and I pushed his corps, supported by Reynolds, forward at once into action along the Warrenton pike toward the enemy's right, then said to be falling back. This attack along the pike was made by King's division near sunset; but, as Porter made no movement whatever toward the field, Longstreet, who was pushing to the front, was able to extend his lines beyond King's left with impunity, and King's attack did not accomplish what was expected, in view of the anticipated attack which Porter was ordered to make, and should have been making at the same time.

From 5 o'clock in the day until some time after dark the fighting all along our lines was severe and bloody, and our losses were very heavy. . . .

When the battle ceased on the 29th of August, we were in possession of the field on our right, and occupied on our left the position held early in the day, and had every right to claim a decided success. What that success might have been, if a corps of twelve thousand men who had not been in battle that day had been thrown against Longstreet's right while engaged in the severe fight that afternoon, I need not indicate. To say that General Porter's non-action during that whole day was wholly unexpected and disappointing, and that it provoked severe comment on all hands, is to state the facts mildly.*

* Porter was courtmartialed and cashiered. In 1878 a board of officers retried the case, and an entirely new light was thrown upon the circumstances. It was shown that Porter's action "saved the Union army from disaster on the 29th of August." Eventually, by act of Congress, Porter once more received a commission in the army of the United States, and on August 7, 1886, was placed on the retired list.

COLLECTING THE WOUNDED.

In his "Recollections of a Private" Warren Lee Goss says: "At the end of the first day's battle, August 29, so soon as the fighting ceased, many sought without orders to rescue comrades lying wounded between the opposing lines. There seemed to be an understanding between the men of both armies that such parties were not to be disturbed in their mission of mercy. After the failure of the attempt of Grover and Kearny to carry the railroad embankment, the Confederates followed their troops back and formed a line in the edge of the woods. When the fire had died away along the darkling woods, little groups of men from the Union lines went stealthily about, bringing in the wounded from the exposed positions. Blankets attached to poles or muskets often served as stretchers to bear the wounded to the ambulances and surgeons. There was a great lack here of organized effort to care for our wounded. Vehicles of various kinds were pressed into service. The removal went on during the entire night, and tired soldiers were roused from their slumbers by the plaintive cries of comrades passing in the comfortless vehicles. In one instance a Confederate and a Union soldier were found cheering each other on the field. They were put into the same Virginia farm-cart and sent to the rear."

Every indication during the night of the 29th and up to 10 o'clock on the morning of the 30th pointed to the retreat of the enemy from our front. Paroled prisoners of our own army, taken on the evening of the 29th, who came into our lines on the morning of the 30th, reported the enemy retreating during the whole night in the direction of and along the Warrenton pike (a fact since confirmed by Longstreet's report). Generals McDowell and Heintzelman, who reconnoitered the position held by the enemy's left on the evening of the 29th, also confirmed this statement. They reported to me the evacuation of these positions by the enemy, and that there was every indication of their retreat in the direction of Gainesville. On the morning of the 30th, as may be easily believed, our troops, who had been marching and fighting

almost continuously for many days, were greatly exhausted. They had had little to eat for two days, and artillery and cavalry horses had been in harness and under the saddle for ten days, and had been almost out of forage for the last two days. It may be readily imagined how little these troops, after such severe labors and hardships, were in condition for further active marching and fighting. . . .

Between 12 and 2 o'clock during the day I advanced Porter's corps, supported by King's division of McDowell's corps, and supported also on their left by Sigel's corps and Reynolds's division, to attack the enemy along the Warrenton pike. At the same time the corps of Heintzelman and Reno on our right were directed to push forward to the left and front toward the pike and attack the

IN CULPEPER DURING THE OCCUPATION BY POPE.

enemy's left flank. For a time Ricketts's division of McDowell's corps was placed in support of this movement. I was obliged to assume the aggressive or to fall back, as from want of provisions I was not able to await an attack from the enemy or the result of any other movement he might make.

Every moment of delay increased the odds against us, and I therefore pushed forward the attack as rapidly as possible. Soon after Porter advanced to attack along the Warrenton pike and the assault was made by Heintzelman and Reno on the right, it became apparent that the enemy was massing his forces as fast as they arrived on the right of Jackson, and was moving forward to force our left. General McDowell was therefore directed to recall Ricketts's division from our right, and put it so as to strengthen our left thus threatened.

Porter's corps was repulsed after some severe fighting, and began to retire, and the enemy advancing to the assault, our whole line was soon furiously engaged. The main attack of the enemy was made against our left, but was met with stubborn resistance by the divisions of Schenck and Reynolds, and the brigade of Milroy, who was soon reinforced on the left by Ricketts's division. The action was severe for several hours, the enemy bringing up heavy reserves and pouring mass after mass of his troops on our left. He was able also to present at least an equal force all along our line of battle. Porter's corps was halted and re-formed, and as soon as it was in condition it was pushed forward to the support of our left, where it rendered distinguished service, especially the brigade of regulars under Colonel (then Lieutenant-Colonel) Buchanan.

McLean's brigade of Schenck's division, which was posted in observation on our left flank, and in support of Reynolds, became exposed to the attack of the enemy on our left when Reynolds's division was drawn back to form line to support Porter's corps, then retiring from their attack, and it was fiercely assailed by Hood and Evans, in greatly superior force. This brigade was com-

manded in person by General Schenck, the division commander, and fought with supreme gallantry and tenacity. The enemy's attack was repulsed several times with severe loss, but he returned again and again to the assault. . . .

Reno's corps was withdrawn from our right center late in the afternoon and thrown into action on our left, where the assaults of the enemy were persistent and unintermitting. Notwithstanding the disadvantages under which we labored, our troops held their ground with the utmost firmness and obstinacy. The loss on both sides was heavy. By dark our left had been forced back half or three-fourths of a mile, but still remained firm and unbroken and still held the Warrenton pike on our rear, while our right was also driven back equally far, but in good order and without confusion. At dark the enemy took possession of the Sudley Springs road, and was in position to threaten our line of communication *via* stone bridge. After 6 o'clock in the evening I learned, accidentally, that Franklin's corps had arrived at a point about 4 miles east of Centreville, or 12 miles in our rear, and that it was only about 8000 strong.

The result of the battle of the 30th convinced me that we were no longer able to hold our position so far to the front, and so far away from the absolute necessaries of life, suffering, as were men and horses, from fatigue and hunger, and weakened by the heavy losses in battle. About 8 o'clock in the evening, therefore, I sent written orders to the corps commanders to withdraw leisurely to Centreville. . . .

Franklin's corps arrived at Centreville late on the afternoon of the 30th; Sumner's the next day. What was then thought by the Government of our operations up to this time is shown in the subjoined despatch:

WASHINGTON, August 31st, 1862. 11 A. M.

MY DEAR GENERAL: You have done nobly. Don't yield another inch if you can avoid it. All reserves are being sent forward. . . . I am doing all I can for you and your noble army. God bless you and it. . . .

H. W. HALLECK, General-in-Chief.

ROUTE STEP.

JACKSON'S RAID AROUND POPE.

BY W. B. TALIAFERRO, MAJOR-GENERAL, C. S. A.
Commander of Stonewall Jackson's own Division.

ON the morning of the 25th of August, 1862, Stonewall Jackson, with Ewell's and A. P. Hill's divisions, and his own old division under my command, marched northward from Jeffersonton, Virginia, to cut Pope's communications and destroy his supplies. Quartermasters and commissaries, with their forage and subsistence stores, were left behind, their white tilted wagons parked conspicuously. The *impedimenta* which usually embarrass and delay a marching column had been reduced to a few ambulances and a limited ordnance train; three days' meager rations had been cooked and stowed away in haversacks and pockets; and tin cans and an occasional frying-pan constituted the entire camp-equipage. The men had rested and dried off, and as they marched out they exulted with the inspiration of the balmy summer atmosphere, and the refreshing breezes which swept down from the Blue Mountains.

No man save one in that corps, whatever may have been his rank, knew our destination. The men said of Jackson that his piety expressed itself in obeying the injunction, "Let not thy left hand know what thy right hand doeth." No intelligence of intended Confederate movements ever reached the enemy by any slip of his. The orders to his division chiefs were like this: "March to a cross-road; a staff-officer there will inform you which fork to take; and so to the next fork, where you will find a courier with a sealed direction pointing out the road."

This extreme reticence was very uncomfortable and annoying to his subordinate commanders, and was sometimes carried too far; 'but it was the real secret of the reputation for ubiquity which he acquired, and which was so well expressed by General McClellan in one of his despatches: "I am afraid of Jackson; he will turn up where least expected."

Naturally our destination was supposed to be Waterloo Bridge, there to force the passage of the river; but the road leading to Waterloo was passed, and the northward march continued. The Rappahannock (locally the Hedgeman) is here confined in narrow limits by bold hills and rocky cliffs, and some miles above the bridge there is a road through these crossing the river at Hinson's Mills. The picturesque surroundings of the ford at this place and the cool bath into which the men plunged were not the less enjoyed because of the unexpected absence of opposition by the enemy; and after the inevitable delay which accompanies any crossing of a water-course by an army, Jackson's corps stood on the same side of the river with the entire Federal army.

After crossing, Colonel Thomas T. Munford's 2d Virginia Cavalry picketed the roads leading in the direction of the enemy, whose whole force, now confronting Longstreet alone, was massed within lines drawn from Warrenton and Waterloo on the north to the Orange and Alexandria Railroad (now called the Midland) on the south. But Jackson's course was not directed toward the enemy. We were marching toward the lower Valley of Virginia, with our destination shrouded in mystery.

From the crossing at Hinson's Mills, Jackson's course still took the same direction — through the little village of Orlean, along the base of a small mountain which crops up in Fauquier County, and on to the little town of Salem, where his "foot cavalry," after a march of over twenty-six miles on a midsummer's day, rested for the night. At dawn on the 26th the route was resumed — this day at right angles with the direction of that of the preceding, and now, with faces set to the sunrise, the troops advanced toward the Bull Run Mountains, which loomed up across the pathway. . . .

At Gainesville, on the Warrenton and Alexandria turnpike, we were overtaken by Stuart, who, with Fitz Lee's and Robertson's brigades, had crossed the Rappahannock that morning and pursued nearly the same route with Jackson; and our subsequent movements were greatly aided and influenced by the admirable manner in which the cavalry was employed and managed by Stuart and his accomplished officers. . . .

Wearied as they were, with a march of over thirty miles, Jackson determined, nevertheless, to tax still further the powers of endurance of his men. At Manassas Junction was established a vast depot of quartermaster's, commissary, and ordnance stores; and it was also a "city of refuge" for many runaway negroes of all ages and of both sexes. The extent of the defenses, and of the force detailed for its protection, could not be known; but as it was far in the rear of the Federal army, not very distant from Alexandria, and directly on the line of communication and reinforcement, it was not probable that any large force had been detached for its protection. General Stonewall Jackson's habit in the valley had been to make enforced requisitions upon the Federal commissaries for his subsistence supplies; and the tempting opportunity of continuing this policy and rationing his hungry command, as well as inflicting almost irreparable loss upon the enemy, was not to be neglected. General Trimble volunteered to execute the enterprise with five hundred men, and

his offer was readily accepted; but "to increase the prospect of success," Stuart, with a portion of his cavalry, was ordered to coöperate with him. The enemy were not taken by surprise, and opened with their artillery upon the first intimation of attack, but their force was too small; their cannon were taken at the point of the bayonet, and without the loss of a man killed, and with but fifteen

MAJOR-GENERAL J. E. B. STUART, C. S. A.

RAID UPON A UNION BAGGAGE-TRAIN BY STUART'S CAVALRY.

wounded, the immense stores, eight guns, and three hundred prisoners fell into our hands.* Early next morning A. P. Hill's division and mine were moved to the Junction, Ewell's remaining at Bristoe.

Our troops at Manassas had barely been placed in position before a gallant effort was made by General Taylor, with a New Jersey brigade, to drive off the supposed raiding party and recapture the stores; but, rushing upon overwhelming numbers, he lost his own life, two hundred prisoners, and the train that had transported them from Alexandria. The railroad bridge over Bull Run was destroyed, severing communication with Alexandria, the roads were picketed, and Fitz Lee's cavalry pushed forward as far as Fairfax Court

* NOTE.—What a prize it was! Here were long warehouses full of stores; cars loaded with boxes of new clothing *en route* to General Pope, but destined to adorn the "backs of his enemies"; camps, sutlers' shops—"no eating up" of good things. In view of the abundance, it was not an easy matter to determine what we should eat and drink and wherewithal we should be clothed; one was limited in his choice to only so much as he could personally transport, and the one thing needful in each individual case was not always readily found. However, as the day wore on, an equitable distribution of our wealth was effected by barter, upon a crude and irregular tariff in which the rule of supply and demand was somewhat complicated by fluctuating estimates of the imminence of marching orders. A mounted man would offer large odds in shirts or blankets for a pair of spurs or a bridle; and while in anxious quest of a pair of shoes I fell heir to a case of cavalry half-boots, which I would gladly have exchanged for the object of my search. For a change of underclothing and a pot of French mustard I owe grateful thanks to the major of the 12th Pennsylvania Cavalry, with regrets that I could not use his library. Whisky was, of course, at a high premium, but a keg of "lager"—a drink less popular then than now—went begging in our company.—*From a Confederate private's account of the capture of Manassas.*

House on the turnpike and Burke's Station on the railroad. The long march of over fifty-six miles in two days entitled Jackson's men to a holiday, and the day of rest at Manassas Junction was fully enjoyed. There was no lack or stint of good cheer, in the way of edibles, from canned meats to caramels.

Stonewall Jackson had now severed the communications of the enemy, broken down the bridges behind them, and destroyed their enormous reserve supplies. . . . His march had been made with such celerity, his flanks guarded with such consummate skill, that he was in no hurry to execute those tactical movements which he recognized as essential to his safety and to the delivery of his heaviest blows. On one flank, Fitz Lee was as near to Alexandria as to Manassas Junction; and, on the other, Munford and Rosser were in advance of Bristoe. Jackson was resting—as a man full of life and vigor, ready to start into action at the first touch—but he rested in the consciousness of security. The Federal commander, around whose flank and rear fourteen brigades of infantry, two of cavalry, and eighteen light batteries had passed, was also resting—but in profound ignorance. On the 26th he ordered Heintzelman "to send a regiment" from Warrenton to Manassas, "to repair the wires and protect the railroad." Aroused, however, on the evening of the 27th, to some appreciation of the condition of affairs, he sent one division (Hooker's) of Heintzelman's corps to Bristoe, which attacked the brigades of Lawton, Early, and Forno (Hays's) of Ewell's division, who successively retired, as they had been directed to do, with little loss, upon the main body at Manassas Junction.

At his leisure, Jackson now proceeded to execute his projected movements. A. P. Hill was

JACKSON'S TROOPS PILLAGING THE UNION DEPOT OF SUPPLIES AT MANASSAS JUNCTION.

The results of Jackson's raid on Manassas Junction included the capture of eight pieces of artillery, more than 300 prisoners, 175 horses, 200 new tents, 50,000 pounds of bacon, 1000 barrels of corned beef, 2000 barrels of salt pork, and 2000 barrels of flour.

ordered to Centreville, Ewell to cross Bull Run at Blackburn's Ford and follow the stream to the stone bridge, and my division by the Sudley road, to the left of the other routes, to the vicinity of Sudley Mills, north of the Warrenton pike, where the whole command was to be concentrated. The immense accumulation of stores and the captured trains were set on fire about midnight and destroyed, and at night the troops took up their march, Jackson accompanying his old division then under my command. The night was starlit but moonless, and a slight mist or haze which settled about the earth made it difficult to distinguish objects at any distance. Still, little encumbered by baggage, and with roads free from the blockade of trains, the march was made without serious impediment or difficulty. The enemy was again deceived. A. P. Hill's march to Centreville was mistaken for that of the whole command; Jackson was supposed to be between Bull Run and Washington; and now, instead of a regiment, the whole Federal army was ordered to concentrate on Manassas for the pursuit. . . .

The two divisions, after marching some distance to the north of the turnpike, finding no enemy, were halted and rested, and the prospect of an engagement on that afternoon [the 28th] seemed to disappear with the lengthening shadows. The enemy did not come—he could not be found—

the Warrenton pike, along which it was supposed he would march, was in view—but it was as free from Federal soldiery as it had been two days before, when Jackson's men had streamed along its highway. . . . Late in the afternoon, the Federal columns were discovered passing, and the Confederate line, formed parallel to the turnpike, moved rapidly forward to the attack. There was no disposition on the part of the Federals to avoid the onset, but, on the contrary, they met us half-way.

It was a sanguinary field; none was better contested during the war. The Federal artillery was admirably served, and at one time the annihilation of our batteries seemed inevitable, so destructive was the fire; but the Confederate guns, although forced to retire and seek new positions, responded with a determination and pluck unshaken by the fiery tempest they had encountered. . . .

During our engagement at Groveton the white puffs in the air, seen away off to the Confederate right, and the sounds of sharp but distant explosions coming to our ears, foretold the passage of Thoroughfare Gap; and the next day, before noon, Longstreet's advance, under Hood, mingled their hurrahs with those of our men. The march and the manœuvers of Jackson had been a success; the army was reunited, and ready, under its great head, to strike with both of its strong arms the blows he should direct.

IN THE WAKE OF BATTLE.

RALLYING BEHIND THE TURNPIKE FENCE AT ANTIETAM.

LEE'S INVASION OF MARYLAND AND THE BATTLE OF ANTIETAM.

NARRATIVE OF EVENTS.

Immediately after the collision of the armies of Lee and Pope at Chantilly, Va., Sept. 1, 1862, Lee set his columns in motion to invade the North. At that time the forces under Pope, and those previously commanded by McClellan, were encamped around Alexandria, Va. McClellan had been assigned to the command of the defenses of Washington. On September 3 he moved three corps to the Maryland side of the Potomac to guard Washington from an attack on the Northwest. Lee's advance reached Frederick, Md., September 5, and on the 8th a proclamation to the people of Maryland was issued by the Confederate leader. By the 7th the remainder of the Union army assigned to active service against Lee had crossed into Maryland, and on the 9th began the march to meet the enemy. That day Lee issued the famous "Special Orders No. 191," dividing his forces with a view to invading Pennsylvania. Jackson was to recross into Virginia and capture the fortified posts of Harper's Ferry and Martinsburg, while Longstreet, passing over South Mountain, was to take a position in Western Maryland and guard that region against attack on the north and east. These movements were to be followed by a reunion of Lee's forces in Maryland and the prosecution of the march northward.

The "Lost Order" of General Lee (No. 191, as above; see General Longstreet's account of "Beginning the Campaign") reached General McClellan's hands late on the 13th of September. The Army of the Potomac was at that time approaching South Mountain from the direction of Washington. The Twelfth Corps halted at Frederick on the afternoon of the 13th, while the Ninth Corps passed on to Middletown. During the night, Pleasonton's cavalry reconnoitered the passes of South Mountain. On the 14th the Ninth Corps, supported by the First, drove D. H. Hill's Confederate division from Turner's and Fox's Gaps, and at the same time the Sixth Corps, constituting the left wing of McClellan's army, carried Crampton's Gap. Both passes had been occupied by Longstreet's troops, who in the main held their positions against vigorous assault until night covered their retreat. Union loss, 2,000 men.

The next day the First, Second, Fifth, Ninth, and Twelfth Corps crossed over South Mountain at Turner's and Fox's Gaps and marched in pursuit of Longstreet and D. H. Hill, who retired to the west bank of Antietam Creek, there to await the return of Stonewall Jackson's forces from the Virginia side of the Potomac. The Sixth Corps, passing through Crampton's Gap, halted at the western base of the mountain, in order to guard the main flank of the Union army from an attack on the south by the Confederates around Harper's Ferry. On the 17th it marched to the Antietam battle-field.

BEGINNING THE CAMPAIGN — FROM THE CONFEDERATE SIDE.

BY JAMES LONGSTREET, LIEUTENANT-GENERAL, C. S. A.
Commanding a wing of Lee's army in Maryland.

WHEN the Second Bull Run campaign closed we had the most brilliant prospects the Confederates ever had. We then possessed an army which, had it been kept together, the Federals would never have dared attack. With such a splendid victory behind us, and such bright prospects ahead, the question arose as to whether or not we should go into Maryland. General Lee, on account of our short supplies, hesitated a little, but I reminded him of my experience in Mexico, where sometimes we were obliged to live two or three days on green corn. I told him we could not starve at that season of the year so long as the fields were loaded with "roasting ears." Finally he determined to go on, and accordingly crossed the river and went to Frederick City. On the 6th of September some of our cavalry, moving toward Harper's Ferry, became engaged with some of the Federal artillery near there. General Lee proposed that I should organize a force, and surround the garrison and capture it. I objected, and urged that our troops were worn with marching and were on short rations, and that it would be a bad idea to divide our forces while we were in the enemy's country, where he could get information, in six or eight hours, of any movement we might make. The Federal army, though beaten at the Second Manassas, was not disorganized, and it would certainly come out to look for us, and we should guard against being caught in such a condition. Our army consisted of a superior quality of soldiers, but it was in no condition to divide in the enemy's country. I urged that we should keep it well in hand, recruit our strength, and get up supplies, and then we could do anything we pleased. General Lee made no reply to this, and I supposed the Harper's Ferry scheme was abandoned. A day or two after we had reached Frederick City, I went up to General Lee's tent and found the front walls closed. I inquired for the general, and he, recognizing my voice, asked me to come in. I went in, and found Jackson there. The two were discussing the move against Harper's Ferry, both heartily approving it. They had gone so far that it seemed useless for me to offer any further opposition, and I only suggested that Lee should use his entire army in the move instead of sending off a large portion of it to Hagerstown as he intended to do. General Lee so far changed the wording of his order as to require me to halt at Boonsboro' with General D. H. Hill; Jackson being ordered to Harper's Ferry via Bolivar Heights, on the south side; McLaws by the Maryland Heights on the north, and Walker, via Loudoun Heights, from the southeast. This was afterward changed, and I was sent on to Hagerstown, leaving D. H. Hill alone at South Mountain.

The movement against Harper's Ferry began on the 10th. Jackson made a wide, sweeping march around the Ferry, passing the Potomac at Williamsport, and moving from there on toward Martinsburg, and turning thence upon Harper's Ferry to make his attack by Bolivar Heights. McLaws made a hurried march to reach Maryland Heights before Jackson could get in position, and succeeded in doing so. With Maryland Heights in our possession the Federals could not hold their position there. McLaws put 200 or 300 men to each piece of his artillery and carried it up the heights, and was in position when Jackson came on the heights opposite. Simultaneously Walker appeared upon Loudoun Heights, south of the Potomac and east of the Shenandoah, thus completing the combination against the Federal garrison. The surrender of the Ferry, and the twelve thousand Federal troops there, was a matter of only a short time.

If the Confederates had been able to stop with that, they might have been well contented with their month's campaign. They had had a series of successes and no defeats; but the division of the army to make this attack on Harper's Ferry was a fatal error, as the subsequent events showed.

While a part of the army had gone toward Harper's Ferry I had moved up to Hagerstown. In the mean time Pope had been relieved and McClellan was in command of the army, and with ninety thousand refreshed troops was marching forth to avenge the Second Manassas. The situation was a very serious one for us. McClellan was close upon us. As we moved out of Frederick he came on and occupied that place, and there he came across a lost copy of the order assigning position to the several commands in the Harper's Ferry move.

This "Lost Order" has been the subject of much severe comment by Virginians who have written of the war. It was addressed to D. H. Hill, and they charged that its loss was due to him, and that the failure of the campaign was the result of the lost order. As General Hill has proved that he never received the order at his headquarters it must have been lost by some one else. . . .

McClellan, after finding the order, moved with more confidence on toward South Mountain, where D. H. Hill was stationed as a Confederate rear-guard with five thousand men under his command. As I have stated, my command was at Hagerstown, thirteen miles farther on. General Lee was with me, and on the night of the 13th we received information that McClellan was at the foot of South Mountain with his great army. General Lee ordered me to march back to the mountain early the next morning.

We marched as hurriedly as we could over a hot and dusty road, and reached the mountain about 3 o'clock in the afternoon, with the troops much scattered and worn. In riding up the mountain to join General Hill I discovered that everything was in such disjointed condition that it would be impossible for my troops and Hill's to hold the mountain against such forces as McClellan had there, and wrote a note to General Lee, in which I stated that fact, and cautioned him to make his arrangements to retire that night. We got as many troops up as we could, and by putting in detachments here and there managed to hold McClellan in check until night, when Lee ordered the withdrawal to Sharpsburg. . . .

JACKSON'S CAPTURE OF HARPER'S FERRY.

BY JOHN G. WALKER, MAJOR-GENERAL, C. S. A.
Commanding a Confederate Division at Harper's Ferry.

. . . Late in the afternoon, September 10th, a courier from General Lee delivered me a copy of his famous "Special Orders No. 191," directing me to coöperate with Jackson and McLaws in the capture of Harper's Ferry. . . . Informed of the presence of a superior Federal force at Cheek's Ford, where I was ordered to pass the Potomac, and learning that the crossing at the Point of Rocks was practicable, I moved my division to that place, and succeeding in landing everything safe on the Virginia shore by daylight of the 11th.

About the same time a heavy rain set in, and as the men were much exhausted by their night march, I put them into bivouac. I would here remark that the Army of Northern Virginia had long since discarded their tents, capacious trunks, carpet-bags, bowie-knives, mill-saw swords, and six-shooters, and had reduced their "kits" to the simplest elements and smallest dimensions.

Resuming our march on the morning of the 12th, we reached Hillsboro', and halted for the night. During the night I was sent for from the village inn by a woman who claimed my attendance on the ground that she was just from Washington, and had

FROM WALKER'S POSITION ON LOUDOUN HEIGHTS.   LOUDOUN HEIGHTS.
View of the Union camp and position on Maryland Heights; Harper's Ferry below.

very important information to give me. Answering the call, I found seated in the hotel parlor a young woman of perhaps twenty-five, of rather prepossessing appearance, who claimed to have left Washington the morning before, with important information from "our friends" in the Federal capital which she could communicate only to General Lee himself, and wished to know from me where he could be found. I saw at once that I had to do with a Federal spy; but as I did not wish to be encumbered with a woman prisoner, I professed ignorance of General Lee's whereabouts, and advised her to remain quietly at the hotel, as I should, no doubt, have some information for her the next morning. Before resuming our march the next day I sent her under guard to Leesburg, directing the provost-marshal at that place to hold her for three or four days and then release her.

Resuming the march at daylight on the 13th, we reached the foot of Loudoun Heights about 10 o'clock. Here I was joined by a detachment of signal men and Captain White's company of Maryland cavalry. I detached two regiments — the 27th North Carolina and 30th Virginia — under Colonel J. R. Cooke, directing him to ascend Loudoun Mountain and take possession of the heights, but, in case he found no enemy, not to reveal his presence to the garrison of Harper's Ferry. I sent with him the men of the Signal Corps, with orders to open communication if possible with Jackson, whose force ought to be in the neighborhood, coming from the west. I then disposed of the remainder of the division around the point of the mountain, where it abuts on the Potomac.

About 2 P. M. Colonel Cook reported that he had taken unopposed possession of Loudoun Heights, but that he had seen nothing of Jackson, yet from the movements of the Federals he thought he was close at hand. By 8 o'clock the next morning five long-range Parrott rifles were on the top of the mountain in a masked position, but ready to open fire. About half-past 10 o'clock my signal party succeeded in informing Jackson of my position and my readiness to attack. . . . As soon as he was informed that McLaws was in possession of Maryland Heights, Jackson signaled me substantially the following despatch: "Harper's Ferry is now completely invested. I shall summon its commander to surrender. Should he refuse I shall give him twenty-four hours to remove the noncombatants, and then carry the place by assault. *Do not fire unless forced to.*"

Jackson at this time had, of course, no reason to suspect that McClellan was advancing in force, and doubtless supposed, as we all did, that we should have abundant leisure to rejoin General Lee at Hagerstown. But about noon I signaled to Jackson that an action seemed to be in progress at Crampton's Gap, that the enemy had made his appearance in Pleasant Valley in rear of McLaws, and that I had no doubt McClellan was advancing in force.

To this message Jackson replied that it was, he thought, no more than a cavalry affair between Stuart and Pleasonton. It was now about half-past 12 and every minute the sound of artillery in the direction of South Mountain was growing louder, which left no doubt on my mind of the advance of the whole Federal army. If this were

the case, it was certain that General Lee would be in fearful peril should the capture of Harper's Ferry be much longer delayed. I thereupon asked permission to open fire, but receiving no reply, I determined to be "forced." For this purpose I placed the two North Carolina regiments under Colonel (afterward Major-General, and now U. S. Senator) M. W. Ransom, which had relieved those under Cooke, in line of battle in full view of the Federal batteries on Bolivar Heights. As I expected, they at once opened a heavy, but harmless, fire upon my regiments, which afforded me the wished-for pretext. Withdrawing the infantry to the safe side of the mountain, I directed my batteries to reply.

About an hour after my batteries opened fire those of A. P. Hill and Lawton followed suit, and about 3 o'clock those of McLaws. But the range from Maryland Heights being too great, the fire of McLaws's guns was ineffective, the shells bursting in mid-air without reaching the enemy. From my position on Loudoun Heights my guns had a plunging fire on the Federal batteries a thousand feet below me and did great execution. By 5 o'clock our combined fire had silenced all the opposing batteries except one or two guns east of Bolivar Heights, which kept up a plucky but feeble response until night put a stop to the combat.

During the night of the 14th–15th, Major (afterward Brigadier-General) R. Lindsay Walker, chief of artillery of A. P. Hill's division, succeeded in crossing the Shenandoah with several batteries, and placing them in such a position on the slope of Loudoun Mountain, far below me, as to command the enemy's works. McLaws got his batteries into position nearer the enemy, and at daylight of the 15th the batteries of our five divisions were pouring their fire on the doomed garrison. The fire of my batteries, however, was at random, as the enemy's position was entirely concealed by a dense fog clinging to the sides of the mountain far below. But my artillerists trained their guns by the previous day's experience, and delivered their fire through the fog.

The Federal batteries replied promptly, and for more than an hour maintained a spirited fire; but after that time it grew more and more feeble until about 8 o'clock, when it ceased altogether, and the garrison surrendered. Owing to the fog I was ignorant of what had taken place, but, surmising it, I soon ordered my batteries to cease firing. Those of Lawton, however, continued some minutes later. This happened unfortunately, as Colonel Dixon S. Miles, the Federal commander, was at this time mortally wounded by a fragment of shell while waving a white flag in token of surrender.

It was pleasing to us, perched upon the top of the mountain, to know that more than twelve thousand "boys in blue" below us were stacking arms. Such a situation has its pathetic side too, for after the first feeling of exultation has passed there comes one of sympathy for the humiliation of the brave men, who are no longer enemies but unfortunate fellow-soldiers.

Some hours later, accompanied by two of my staff, I rode into Harper's Ferry, and we were interested in seeing our tattered Confederates fraternizing in the most cordial manner with their well-dressed prisoners. . . .

MAJOR-GENERAL JOHN G. WALKER, C. S. A.

STONEWALL JACKSON IN MARYLAND.

BY HENRY KYD DOUGLAS, COLONEL, C. S. A.
Aide-de-Camp on the Staff of General Jackson.

ON the 3d of September, 1862, the Federal army under General Pope having been confounded, General Lee turned his columns toward the Potomac, with Stonewall Jackson in front. On the 5th of September Jackson crossed the Potomac at White's Ford, a few miles beyond Leesburg. The passage of the river by the troops marching in fours, well closed up, the laughing, shouting, and singing as a brass band in front played "Maryland, my Maryland," was a memorable experience. The Marylanders in the corps imparted much of their enthusiasm to the other troops, but we were not long in finding out that if General Lee had hopes that the decimated regiments of his army would be filled by the sons of Maryland he was doomed to a speedy and unqualified disappointment. However, before we had been in Maryland many hours, one enthusiastic citizen presented Jackson with a gigantic gray mare. She was a little heavy and awkward for a war-horse, but as the general's "Little Sorrel" had a few days before been temporarily stolen, the present was a timely one, and he was not disposed to "look a gift horse in the mouth." Yet the present proved almost a Trojan horse to him, for the next morning when he mounted his new steed, and touched her with his spur, the loyal and undisciplined beast reared straight into the air, and, standing erect for a moment, threw herself backward, horse and rider rolling upon the ground. The general was stunned and severely bruised, and lay upon the ground for some time before he could be removed. He was then placed in an ambulance, where he rode during the day's march, having turned his command over to his brother-in-law, General D. H. Hill, the officer next in rank.

Early that day the army went into camp near Frederick, and Generals Lee, Longstreet, Jackson, and for a time "Jeb" Stuart, had their headquarters near one another in Best's grove. Hither in crowds came the good people of Frederick, especially the ladies, as to a fair. General Jackson, still suffering from his hurt, kept to his tent, busying himself with maps and official papers, and declined to see visitors. Once, however, when he had been called to General Lee's tent, two young girls waylaid him, paralyzed him with smiles and embraces and questions, and then jumped into their carriage and drove off rapidly, leaving him there, cap in hand, bowing, blushing, and speechless. But once safe in his tent he was seen no more that day. The next evening, Sunday, he went into Frederick for the first time to attend church, and there being no service in the Presbyterian Church he went to the German Reformed. As usual he fell asleep, but this time more soundly than was his wont. His head sunk upon his breast, his cap dropped from his hands to the floor, the prayers of the congregation did not disturb him, and only the choir and the deep-toned organ awakened him. Afterward I learned that the minister was credited with much loyalty and courage because he had prayed for the President of the United States in the very presence of Stonewall Jackson. Well, the general did n't hear the

JACKSON'S MEN WADING THE POTOMAC AT WHITE'S FORD.

prayer, and if he had he would doubtless have felt like replying as General Ewell did, when asked at Carlisle, Pennsylvania, if he would permit the usual prayer for President Lincoln—"Certainly; I'm sure he needs it."

General Lee believed that Harper's Ferry would be evacuated as soon as he interposed between it and Washington. But he did not know that Halleck, and not McClellan, held command of it. When he found that it was not evacuated he knew some one had blundered, and took steps to capture the garrison and stores. On Tuesday, the 9th, he issued an order, directing General Jackson to move the next morning, cross the Potomac near Sharpsburg, and envelop Harper's Ferry on the Virginia side. In the same order he directed General McLaws to march on Harper's Ferry by way of Middletown and seize Maryland Heights, and General Walker to cross the Potomac below Harper's Ferry and take Loudoun Heights, all to be in position on the 12th, except Jackson, who was first to capture, if possible, the troops at Martinsburg.

Early on the 10th Jackson was off. In Frederick he asked for a map of Chambersburg and its vicinity, and made many irrelevant inquiries about roads and localities in the direction of Pennsylvania. To his staff, who knew what little value these inquiries had, his questions only illustrated his well-known motto, "Mystery, mystery is the secret of success." I was then assistant inspector-general on his staff, and also aide-de-camp. It was my turn this day to be intrusted with the knowledge of his purpose. Having finished this public inquiry, he took me aside, and after asking me about the different fords of the Potomac between Williamsport and Harper's Ferry, told me

that he was ordered to capture the garrison at Harper's Ferry, and would cross either at Williamsport or Shepherdstown, as the enemy might or might not withdraw from Martinsburg. I did not then know of General Lee's order.

The troops being on the march, the general and staff rode rapidly out of town and took the head of the column. Just a few words here in regard to Mr. Whittier's touching poem, "Barbara Frietchie." An old woman, by that now immortal name, did live in Frederick in those days, but she never saw General Jackson, and General Jackson never saw "Barbara Frietchie." I was with him every minute of the time he was in that city,— he was there only twice,— and nothing like the scene so graphically described by the poet ever happened. Mr. Whittier must have been misinformed as to the incident.*

On the march that day, the captain of the cavalry advance, just ahead, had instructions to let no civilian go to the front, and we entered each village we passed before the inhabitants knew of our coming. In Middletown two very pretty girls,

* With reference to this statement Mr. Whittier said on the 10th of June, 1886: "The poem 'Barbara Frietchie' was written in good faith. The story was no invention of mine. It came to me from sources which I regarded as entirely reliable; it had been published in newspapers, and had gained public credence in Washington and Maryland before my poem was written. I had no reason to doubt its accuracy then, and I am still constrained to believe that it had foundation in fact. If I thought otherwise, I should not hesitate to express it. I have no pride of authorship to interfere with my allegiance to truth." Mr. Whittier, writing March 7th, 1888, states that he "also received letters from several other responsible persons wholly or partially confirming the story, among whom was the late Dorothea L. Dix."

with ribbons of red, white, and blue floating from their hair, and small Union flags in their hands, rushed out of a house as we passed, came to the curbstone, and with much laughter waved their flags defiantly in the face of the general. He bowed and raised his hat, and, turning with his quiet smile to his staff, said: "We evidently have no friends in this town." And this is about the way he would have treated Barbara Frietchie!

Having crossed South Mountain, at Turner's Gap, the command encamped for the night within a mile of Boonsboro'. Here General Jackson must determine whether he would go on to Williamsport or turn toward Shepherdstown. . . . The next morning, having learned that the Federal troops still occupied Martinsburg, General Jackson took the direct road to Williamsport. He there forded the Potomac, the troops now singing, and the bands playing, "Carry me back to ole Virginny!" . . . The next morning the Confederates entered Martinsburg. . . .

General Jackson lost little time in contemplating his victory [the capture of Harper's Ferry, described on page 140]. When night came, he started for Shepherdstown with J. R. Jones and Lawton, leaving directions to McLaws and Walker to follow the next morning. He left A. P. Hill behind to finish up with Harper's Ferry. His first order had been to take position at Shepherdstown to cover Lee's crossing into Virginia, but, whether at his own suggestion or not, the order was changed, and after daylight on the 16th he crossed the Potomac there and joined Longstreet at Sharpsburg. General McClellan had, by that time, nearly all his army in position on the east bank of the Antietam, and General Lee was occupying the irregular range of high ground to the west of it,

MAJOR-GENERAL JESSE L. RENO, U. S. V.
Killed at Fox's Gap.

"STONEWALL" JACKSON AS FIRST LIEUT. OF ARTILLERY, U. S. A.
From an ambrotype taken August 20, 1847.

with the Potomac in his rear. Except some sparring between Hooker and Hood on our left, the 16th was allowed to pass without battle, fortunately for us. In the new dispositions of that evening, Jackson was placed on the left of Lee's army.

The first onset, early on the morning of the 17th, told what the day would be. The impatient Hooker, with the divisions of Meade, Doubleday, and Ricketts, struck the first blow, and Jackson's old division caught it and struck back again. Between such foes the battle soon waxed hot. Step by step and marking each step with dead, the thin Confederate line was pushed back to the wood around the Dunker Church. Here Lawton, Starke (commanding in place of Jones, already wounded), and D. H. Hill with part of his division, engaged Meade. And now in turn the Federals halted and fell back, and left their dead by Dunker Church. Next Mansfield entered the fight, and beat with resistless might on Jackson's people. The battle here grew angry and bloody. Starke was killed, Lawton wounded, and nearly all their general and field officers had fallen; the sullen Confederate line again fell back, killing Mansfield and wounding Hooker, Crawford, and Hartsuff.

And now D. H. Hill led in the rest of his division; Hood also took part to the right and left, front and rear, of Dunker Church. The Federal line was again driven back, while artillery added its din to the incessant rattle of musketry. Then Sumner, with the fresh division of Sedgwick, re-formed the Federal line and renewed the offensive. Hood was driven back, and Hill partly; the Dunker Church wood was passed, the field south of it entered, and the Confederate left turned. Just then McLaws, hurrying from Harper's Ferry, came upon the field, and hurled his men against the victorious Sedgwick. He drove Sedgwick back into the Dunker wood, and beyond it, into the open ground. Farther to our right, the pendulum of battle had been swinging to and fro, with D. H. Hill and R. H. Anderson hammering away at French and Richardson, until the sunken road became historic as "Bloody Lane." Richardson was mortally wounded, and Hancock assumed command of his division.

For a while there was a lull in the storm. It was early in the day, but hours are fearfully long in battle. About noon Franklin, with Slocum and W. F. Smith, marched upon the field to join the unequal contest. Smith tried his luck and was repulsed. Sumner then ordered a halt. Jackson's fight was over, and a strange silence reigned around Dunker Church.

General Lee had not visited the left that day. As usual he trusted to Jackson to fight his own battle, and work out salvation in his own way. How well he did it, against the ablest and fiercest of McClellan's lieutenants, history has told.

During all this time Longstreet, stripped of his troops,—sent to the help of Jackson,—held the right almost alone, with his eye on the center. He was now called into active work on his own front, for there were no unfought troops in Lee's army at Sharpsburg; every soldier on that field tasted battle.

General Burnside, with his corps of fourteen thousand men, had been lying all day beyond the bridge which now bears his name. Ordered to cross at 8 o'clock he managed to get over at 1, and by 3 was ready to advance. He moved against the hill which D. R. Jones held with his little division of 2500 men. Longstreet was watching this advance. Jackson was at General Lee's headquarters on a knoll in rear of Sharpsburg. A. P. Hill

A GLIMPSE OF STONEWALL JACKSON.

was coming, but had not arrived, and it was apparent that Burnside must be stayed, if at all, with artillery. One of the sections, transferred to the right from Jackson at the request of General Lee, was of the Rockbridge Artillery, and as it galloped by, the youngest son of the general-in-chief, Robert E. Lee, Jr., a private at the guns, black with the grime and powder of a long day's fight, stopped a moment to salute his father and then rushed after his gun. Where else in this war was the son of a commanding general a private in the ranks?

Going to put this section in place, I saw Burnside's heavy line move up the hill, and the earth seemed to tremble beneath their tread. It was a splendid and fearful sight, but for them to beat back Jones's feeble line was scarcely war. The artillery tore, but did not stay them. They pressed forward until Sharpsburg was uncovered, and Lee's line of retreat was at their mercy. But then, just then, A. P. Hill, picturesque in his red battle-shirt, with 3 of his brigades, 2500 men, who had marched that day 17 miles from Harper's Ferry and had waded the Potomac, appeared upon the scene. Tired and footsore, the men forgot their woes in that supreme moment, and with no breathing time braced themselves to meet the coming shock. They met it and stayed it. The blue line staggered and hesitated, and, hesitating, was lost. At the critical moment A. P. Hill was always at his strongest. Quickly advancing his battle-flags, his line moved forward, Jones's troops rallied on him, and in the din of musketry and artillery on either flank the Federals broke over the field. Hill did not wait for his other brigades, but held the vantage gained until Burnside was driven back to the Antietam and under the shelter of heavy guns. The day was done. Again A. P. Hill, as at Manassas, Harper's Ferry, and elsewhere, had struck with the right hand of Mars. No wonder that both Lee and Jackson, when, in the delirium of their last moments on earth, they stood again to battle, saw the form of A. P. Hill leading his columns on; but it is a wonder and a shame that the grave of this valiant Virginian in Hollywood cemetery has not a stone to mark it and keep it from oblivion.

The battle at Sharpsburg was the result of unforeseen circumstances and not of deliberate purpose. It was one of the bloodiest of the war, and a defeat for both armies. The prestige of the day was with Lee, but when on the night of the 18th he recrossed into Virginia, although, as the Comte de Paris says, he "left not a single trophy of his nocturnal retreat in the hands of the enemy," he left the prestige of the result with McClellan. . . .

AN ORDERLY AT HEADQUARTERS.

GENERAL VIEW OF THE BATTLE OF ANTIETAM.

This sketch was made on the hill behind McClellan's head-quarters, which is seen in the hollow on the left. Sumner's corps is seen in line of battle in the middle ground, and Franklin's is advancing in column to his support. The smoke in the left background is from a bursting Confederate caisson. The column of smoke is from the burning house and barn of S. Mumma, who gave the ground on which the Dunker Church stands, and after whom, in the Confederate reports, the church is frequently called "St. Mumma's." On the right is the East Wood, the scene of the conflict between Mansfield and Jackson.

GENERAL McCLELLAN RIDING THE LINE OF BATTLE AT ANTIETAM.
General McClellan rode his black horse, "Daniel Webster," which, on account of the difficulty of keeping pace with him, was better known to the staff as "that devil Dan."

FROM THE PENINSULA TO ANTIETAM — THE UNION SIDE.

POSTHUMOUS NOTES
BY GENERAL GEORGE B. McCLELLAN.
Commander of the Army of the Potomac at Antietam.

IT is not proposed to give in this article a detailed account of the battles of South Mountain and Antietam, but simply a sketch of the general operations of the Maryland campaign of 1862 intended for general readers, especially for those whose memory does not extend back to those exciting days, and whose knowledge is derived from the meager accounts in so-called histories, too often intended to mislead and pander to party prejudices rather than to seek and record the truth.

A great battle can never be regarded as a "solitaire," a jewel to be admired or condemned for itself alone, and without reference to surrounding objects and circumstances. A battle is always one link in a long chain of events; the culmination of one series of manœuvers, and the starting-point of another series — therefore it can never be fully understood without reference to preceding and subsequent events.

Restricted as this narrative is intended to be, it is nevertheless necessary to preface it by a brief story of the antecedent circumstances.

In an article already published, I have narrated the events of the Peninsular campaign up to the time when, at the close of the Seven Days' battles, the Army of the Potomac was firmly established on its proper line of operations, the James River.

So long as life lasts the survivors of those glorious days will remember with quickened pulse the attitude of that army when it reached the goal for which it had striven with such transcendent heroism. Exhausted, depleted in numbers, bleeding at every pore, but still proud and defiant, and strong in the consciousness of a great feat of arms heroically accomplished, it stood ready to renew the struggle with undiminished ardor whenever its commander should give the word. It was one of those magnificent episodes which dignify a nation's history, and are fit subjects for the grandest efforts of the poet and the painter.

At the close of such a series of battles and marches the returns of the killed, wounded, and missing by no means fully measure the temporary decrease of strength; there were also many thousands unfitted for duty for some days by illness, demoralization, and fatigue. The first thing to be done was to issue supplies from the vessels already sent to the James, and to allow the men some little time to rest and recover their strength after the great fatigue and nervous tension they had undergone.

In order to permit a small number to watch over the safety of the whole army, and at the same time to prepare the way for ulterior operations, so that when the army advanced again upon Richmond by either bank of the James its base of supplies might be secure with a small guard, the position was rapidly intrenched, the work being completed about the 10th of July.

Prior to the 10th of July two brigades of Shields's division, numbering about 5300 men, had joined the army, bringing its numbers for duty up to 89,549, officers and men, about the same strength as that with which it entered upon the siege of Yorktown, the reinforcements received in the shape of the divisions of Franklin and McCall, the brigades of Shields, and a few regiments from Fort Monroe having slightly more than made good the losses in battle and by disease. But among these 89,000 for duty on the 10th of July were included all the extra duty men employed as teamsters, and in the various administrative services, and, with the further deductions necessary for camp guards, guards of communications, depots and trains, flank detachments, etc., reduced the numbers actually available for offensive battle to not more than [60,000].

A few days sufficed to give the men the necessary rest, and to renew the supplies exhausted on the march across the Peninsula; the army was once more in condition to undertake any operation justified by its numbers, and was in an excellent position to advance by either bank of the James. [End of finished draft.]

. . . .

It was at last upon its true line of operations, which I had been unable to adopt at an earlier day in consequence of the Secretary of War's peremptory order of the 18th of May, requiring the right wing to be extended to the north of Richmond in order to establish communication with General McDowell. General McDowell was then under orders to advance from Fredericksburg, but never came, because, in spite of his earnest protest, these orders were countermanded from Washington, and he was sent upon a fruitless expedition toward the Shenandoah instead of being permitted to join me, as he could have done, at the time of the affair of Hanover Court House.

I urged in vain that the Army of the Potomac should remain on the line of the James, and that it should resume the offensive as soon as reinforced to the full extent of the means in possession of the Government. Had the Army of the Potomac been permitted to remain on the line of the James, I would have crossed to the south bank of that river, and while engaging Lee's attention in front of Malvern, would have made a rapid movement in force on Petersburg, having gained which, I would have operated against Richmond and its communications from the west, having already gained those from the south.

Subsequent events proved that Lee did not move northward from Richmond with his army until assured that the Army of the Potomac was actually on its way to Fort Monroe; and they also proved that so long as the Army of the Potomac was on the James, Washington and Maryland would have been entirely safe under the protection of the fortifications and a comparatively small part of the troops then in that vicinity; so that Burnside's troops and a large part of the Union Army of Virginia might, with entire propriety, have been sent by water to join the army under my command, which — with detachments from the West — could easily have been brought up to more than 100,000 men disposable on the actual field of battle.

In spite of my most pressing and oft-repeated entreaties, the order was insisted upon for the abandonment of the Peninsula line and the return of the Army of the Potomac to Washington in order to support General Pope, who was in no danger so long as the Army of the Potomac remained on the James. With a heavy heart I relinquished the position gained at the cost of so much time and blood.

As an evidence of my good faith in opposing this movement it should be mentioned that General Halleck had assured me, verbally and in writ-

GENERAL McCLELLAN AND PRESIDENT LINCOLN AT ANTIETAM.

NOTE.—The Proclamation of Emancipation was published September 22d, three days after the withdrawal of Lee to Virginia, and was communicated to the army officially on September 24th.

On October 1st President Lincoln visited the army to see for himself if it was in no condition to pursue Lee into Virginia. General McClellan says in his general report: "His Excellency the President honored the Army of the Potomac with a visit, and remained several days, during which he went through the different encampments, reviewed the troops, and went over the battle-fields of South Mountain and Antietam. I had the opportunity during this visit to describe to him the operations of the army since the time it left Washington, and gave him my reasons for not following the enemy after he crossed the Potomac." In "McClellan's Own Story" he says that the President "more than once assured me that he was fully satisfied with my whole course from the beginning; that the only fault he could possibly find was that I was too prone to be sure that everything was ready before acting, but that my actions were all right when I started. I

said to him that I thought a few experiments with those who acted before they were ready would probably convince him that in the end I consumed less time than they did."

After the President's return to Washington, October 5th, Halleck telegraphed to McClellan under date of October 6th: "The President directs that you cross the Potomac and give battle to the enemy or drive him south," etc.

On October 7th McClellan, in "General Orders No. 163," referred to the Proclamation of Emancipation. He warned the army of the danger to military discipline of heated political discussions, and reminded them that the "remedy for political errors, if any are committed, is to be found only in the action of the people at the polls." On October 5th General McClellan had said, in a letter to his wife [see "McClellan's Own Story," page 655], "Mr. Aspinwall [W. H., of New York] is decidedly of the opinion that it is my duty to submit to the President's proclamation and quietly continue doing my duty as a soldier. I presume he is right, and am at least sure that he is honest in his opinion. I shall surely give his views full consideration."

ing, that I was to command all the troops in front of Washington, including those of Generals Burnside and Pope — a promise that was not carried into effect.

As the different divisions of the Army of the Potomac reached Aquia Creek and the vicinity of Washington they were removed from my command, even to my personal escort and camp guard,

CONFEDERATE DEAD AT THE CROSS-ROADS BY WISE'S HOUSE AT FOX'S GAP.
From a sketch made the day after the battle.

so that on the 30th of August, in reply to a telegram from him, I telegraphed General Halleck from Alexandria, "I have no sharp-shooters except the guard around my camp. I have sent off every man but those, and will now send them with the train as you direct. I will also send my only remaining squadron of cavalry with General Sumner. I can do no more. You now have every man of the Army of the Potomac who is within my reach." I had already sent off even my headquarters wagons — so far as landed — with ammunition to the front. . . .

On the 1st of September I met General Halleck at his office in Washington, who by verbal order directed me to take charge of Washington and its defenses, but expressly prohibited me from exercising any control over the active troops under General Pope.

At this interview I informed General Halleck that from information received through one of my aides I was satisfied that affairs were not progressing favorably at the front, and urged him to go out in person to ascertain the exact state of the case. He declined doing this, but finally sent Colonel Kelton, his adjutant-general.

Next morning while at breakfast at an early hour I received a call from the President, accompanied by General Halleck.

The President informed me that Colonel Kelton had returned and represented the condition of affairs as much worse than I had stated to Halleck on the previous day; that there were thirty thousand stragglers on the roads; that the army was entirely defeated and falling back to Washington in confusion. He then said that he regarded Washington as lost, and asked me if I would, under the circumstances, consent to accept command of all the forces. Without one moment's hesitation and without making any conditions whatever, I at once said that I would accept the command and would stake my life that I would save the city. They then left, the President verbally placing me in entire command of the city and of the troops falling back upon it from the front.

I at once sent for my staff-officers and despatched them on various duties; some to the front with orders for the disposition of such corps as they met, others to see to the prompt forwarding of

ammunition and supplies to meet the retreating troops. In a very short time I had made all the requisite preparations and was about to start to the front in person to assume command as far out as possible, when a message came to me from General Halleck informing me that it was the President's order that I should not assume command until the troops had reached the immediate vicinity of the fortifications. I therefore waited until the afternoon, when I rode out to Upton's Hill, the most advanced of the detached works covering the capital.

Soon after arriving there the head of Hatch's command of infantry arrived, immediately followed by Generals Pope and McDowell escorted by a regiment, or part of a regiment, of cavalry. I obtained what information I could from General Pope and despatched the few remaining aides with me to meet the troops on the roads leading in on the left, with final orders to them, when quite a heavy distant artillery firing broke out in the direction of the Chantilly and Vienna road. Asking General Pope what that was, he replied it was probably an attack on Sumner, who commanded the rear-guard in that direction; in reply to another question he said that he thought it probably a serious affair. He and McDowell then asked if I had any objection to their proceeding to Washington. I said that they might do so, but that I was going to the firing. They then proceeded on with their escort while, with a single aide (Colonel Colburn) and three orderlies, I struck across country to intercept the column on our right by the shortest line. It was a little after dark when I reached the column.

I leave to others who were present the description of what then occurred: the frantic cheers of welcome that extended for miles along the column; the breaking of ranks and the wild appeals of the men that I should then and there take them back on the line of retreat and let them snatch victory out of defeat. Let it suffice to say that before the day broke the troops were all in position to repulse attack, and that Washington was safe.

On the 3d it was clear that the enemy intended an invasion of Maryland and Pennsylvania by crossing the Upper Potomac; I therefore moved the Second, Ninth, and Twelfth Corps to the Maryland side of the Potomac in position to meet any attack upon the city on that side.

As soon as this was done I reported the fact to

General Halleck, who asked what general I had placed in command of those three corps; I replied that I had made no such detail, as I should take command in person if the enemy appeared in that direction. He then said that my command included only the defenses of Washington and did not extend to any active column that might be moved out beyond the line of works; that no decision had yet been made as to the commander of the active army. He repeated the same thing on more than one occasion before the final advance to South Mountain and Antietam took place.

I should here state that the only published order ever issued in regard to the extent of my command after my interview with the President on the morning of the 2d was the following:

"WAR DEPARTMENT,
"ADJUTANT-GENERAL'S OFFICE,
"WASHINGTON, September 2, 1862.
"Major-General McClellan will have command of the fortifications of Washington and of all the troops for the defense of the capital.
"By order of MAJOR-GENERAL HALLECK.
"E. D. TOWNSEND,
"Assis't Adjutant-General."

A-

So long as life lasts the survivors of those glorious days will remember with quickened pulse the attitude of that army of the Potomac when it reached the post for which it had striven with such transcendent heroism. Exhausted, depleted in numbers, bleeding at every pore, but still proud and defiant, & strong in the consciousness of a great feat of arms heroically accomplished, it stood ready to renew the struggle with undiminished ardor whenever its commander should give the word. It was one of those magnificent episodes which that dignify a nation's history, and an fit subject for the grandest effort of the poet & the painter.

FACSIMILE OF A PART OF GENERAL McCLELLAN'S LAST MANUSCRIPT. [SEE PAGE 143.]

After General McClellan had written the article on the Peninsular campaign [see p. 82], he was requested to write an account of the battle of Antietam, which he promised to do at his leisure. He had kept the promise in mind, and as occasion served had sketched introductory portions of the proposed article. In the morning after his sudden death, these manuscript pages were found on his table, with some others freshly written, possibly on the previous day or evening. There was also an unsealed note to one of the editors (in reply to one he had received), in which he said that he would at once proceed with the article and finish it.

It was his custom in writing for the press to make a rapid but complete sketch, often abbreviating words and leaving blanks for matter to be copied from documents, and then to rewrite the entire article for publication. It would seem that in this case he had first in mind the consideration stated in the second paragraph of the article, and he had given his attention to the history of the army, from the close of the Seven Days' battles to the advance from Washington toward South Mountain and Antietam. There was no manuscript relating to later events. He had commenced what appears to be his final copy of this first portion of the article, but had completed only about three pages of foolscap, which extend in the print below to a place indicated.

It is an interesting fact that in this final copy the paragraph commencing with the words "So long as life lasts" was apparently the last written, being on a separate page and indicated by a letter A for insertion where it stands. This tribute of admiration for the army which loved him as he loved them was among the last thoughts, if it was not the very last, which his pen committed to paper.

Although this introduction to the account of Antietam is but his first sketch, and not in the final shape he would have given it for publication, it is so comprehensive and complete, and contains so much that is of historical importance, that his literary executor has considered it his duty to allow its publication in "The Century" in the form in which General McClellan left it, and thus as far as possible fulfil a promise made in the last hours of his life.

WILLIAM C. PRIME,
Literary Executor of General McClellan.

had survived I would, no doubt, have been tried for assuming authority without orders, and, in the state of feeling which so unjustly condemned the innocent and most meritorious General F. J. Porter, I would probably have been condemned to death. I was fully aware of the risk I ran, but the path of duty was clear and I tried to follow it. It was absolutely necessary that Lee's army should be met, and in the state of affairs I have briefly described there could be no hesitation on my part as to doing it promptly. Very few in the Army of the Potomac doubted the favorable result of the next collision with the Confederate army, but in other quarters not a little doubt prevailed, and the desire for very rapid movements, so loudly expressed after the result was gained, did not make itself heard during the movements preceding the battles; quite the contrary was the case, as I was more than once cautioned that I was moving too rashly and exposing the capital to an attack from the Virginia side.

As is well known, the result of General Pope's operations had not been favorable, and when I finally resumed command of the troops in and around Washington they were weary, disheartened, their organization impaired, their clothing, ammunition, and supplies in a pitiable condition.

The Army of the Potomac was thoroughly exhausted and depleted by its desperate fighting and severe marches in the unhealthy regions of the Chickahominy, and afterward, during the Second Bull Run campaign; its trains, administration services, and supplies were disorganized or lacking in consequence of the rapidity and manner of its removal from the Peninsula, as well as from the nature of its operations during the Second Bull Run campaign. In the departure from the Peninsula, trains, supplies, cavalry, and artillery in many instances had necessarily been left at Fort Monroe and Yorktown for lack of vessels, as the important point was to remove the infantry divisions rapidly to the support of General Pope. The divisions of the Army of Virginia were also exhausted and weakened, and their trains were disorganized and their supplies deficient by reason of the movements in which they had been engaged.

A few days after this and before I went to the front, Secretary Seward came to my quarters one evening and asked my opinion of the condition of affairs at Harper's Ferry, remarking that he was not at ease on the subject. Harper's Ferry was not at that time in any sense under my control, but I told Mr. Seward that I regarded the arrangements there as exceedingly dangerous; that in my opinion the proper course was to abandon the position and unite the garrison (about ten thousand men) to the main army of operations, for the reason that its presence at Harper's Ferry would not hinder the enemy from crossing the Potomac; that if we were unsuccessful in the approaching battle, Harper's Ferry would be of no use to us and its garrison necessarily would be lost; that if we were successful we would immediately recover the post without any difficulty, while the addition of ten thousand men to the active army would be an important factor in securing success. I added that if it were determined to hold the position the existing arrangements were all wrong, as it would be easy for the enemy to surround and capture the garrison, and that the garrison ought, at least, to be withdrawn to the Maryland Heights, where they could resist attack until relieved.

The Secretary was much impressed by what I said, and asked me to accompany him to General Halleck and repeat my statement to him. I acquiesced, and we went together to General Halleck's quarters, where we found that he had retired for the night. But he received us in his bedroom, when, after a preliminary explanation by the Secretary as to the interview being at his request, I said to Halleck precisely what I had stated to Mr. Seward.

Halleck received my statement with ill-concealed contempt—said that everything was all right as it was; that my views were entirely erroneous, etc., and soon bowed us out, leaving matters at Harper's Ferry precisely as they were.

On the 7th of September, in addition to the three corps already mentioned (the Second, Ninth, and Twelfth), the First and Sixth Corps, Sykes's division of the Fifth Corps, and Couch's division of the Fourth Corps, were also on the Maryland side of the river; the First and Ninth Corps at Leesboro'; the Second and Twelfth in front of Rockville;. the Sixth Corps at Rockville; Couch's division at Offutt's Cross-roads; Sykes's division at Tenally-town.

As the time had now arrived for the army to advance, and I had received no orders to take command of it, but had been expressly told that the assignment of a commander had not been decided, I determined to solve the question for myself, and when I moved out from Washington with my staff and personal escort I left my card with *P. P. C.* written upon it, at the White House, War Office, and Secretary Seward's house, and went on my way.

I was afterward accused of assuming command without authority, for nefarious purposes, and in fact I fought the battles of South Mountain and Antietam with a halter around my neck, for if the Army of the Potomac had been defeated and I

FOX'S GAP. THE APPROACH TO WISE'S FIELD—WISE'S FIELD AS SEEN FROM THE PASTURE NORTH OF THE ROAD.

The Old Sharpsburg or Braddock road lies between the stone wall and the rail fence. The left distance shows the Middle-town valley and the Catoctin range, from which the Ninth Corps, temporarily commanded by General Jesse L. Reno, approached to the attack on South Mountain, September 14. The stump in the middle of the field beyond the wall is near where Reno fell. Part of the struggle was for the wooded crest on the left of the field. General Reno reached the scene about sunset and desiring to know why his troops (Sturgis's division) did not go forward to the summit, went to the skirmish line to examine for himself. He was shot down by the enemy posted among the rocks and trees. The firing on that part of the battle-field continued until late in the evening. The house is Wise's, at the crossing of the ridge and Old Sharpsburg roads. The Confederates here were posted behind a stone wall. The well at Wise's house was filled with the Confederate dead.

Had General Lee remained in front of Washington it would have been the part of wisdom to hold our own army quiet until its pressing wants were fully supplied, its organization was restored, and its ranks were filled with recruits — in brief, until it was prepared for a campaign. But as the enemy maintained the offensive and crossed the Upper Potomac to threaten or invade Pennsylvania, it became necessary to meet him at any cost notwithstanding the condition of the troops, to put a stop to the invasion, save Baltimore and Washington, and throw him back across the Potomac. Nothing but sheer necessity justified the advance of the Army of the Potomac to South Mountain and Antietam in its then condition, and it is to the eternal honor of the brave men who composed it that under such adverse circumstances they gained those victories. The work of supply and reorganization was continued as best we might while on the march, and even after the close of the battles [September 14th–17th] so much remained to be done to place the army in condition for a campaign, that the delay which ensued was absolutely unavoidable, and the army could not have entered upon a new campaign one day earlier than it did. It must then be borne constantly in mind that the purpose of advancing from Washington was simply to meet the necessities of the moment by frustrating Lee's invasion of the Northern States, and, when that was accomplished, to push with the utmost rapidity the work of reorganization and supply so that a new campaign might be promptly inaugurated with the army in condition to prosecute it to a successful termination without intermission.

The advance from Washington was covered by the cavalry, under General Pleasonton, which was pushed as far to the front as possible, and was soon in constant contact with the enemy's cavalry, with whom several well-conducted and successful affairs occurred.

Partly in order to move men freely and rapidly,

partly in consequence of the lack of accurate information as to the exact position and intention of Lee's army, the troops advanced by three main

VIEW FROM TURNER'S GAP, LOOKING SOUTHEAST.
From a photograph taken in 1886.

roads: that part near the Potomac by Offutt's Cross-roads and the mouth of the Seneca; that by Rockville to Frederick, and that by Brookville and Urbana to New Market. We were then in condition to act according to the development of the enemy's plans, and to concentrate rapidly in any position. If Lee threatened our left flank by moving down the river road, or by crossing the Potomac at any of the fords from Coon's Ferry upward, there were enough troops on the river road to hold him in check until the rest of the army could move over to support them; if Lee took up a position behind the Seneca near Frederick the whole army could be rapidly concentrated in that direction to attack him in force; if he moved upon Baltimore the entire army could rapidly be thrown in his rear and his retreat would be cut off; if he moved by Gettysburg or Chambersburg upon York or Carlisle we were equally in position to throw ourselves in his rear.

The first requisite was to gain accurate information as to Lee's movements, and the second, to push the work of supply and reorganization as rapidly as possible.

General Lee and I knew each other well. In the days before the war we served together in Mexico, and we had commanded against each other in the Peninsula. I had the highest respect for his ability as a commander, and knew that he was a general not to be trifled with or carelessly afforded an opportunity of striking a fatal blow. Each of us naturally regarded his own army as the better, but each entertained the highest respect for the endurance, courage, and fighting qualities of the opposing army; and this feeling extended to the officers and men. It was perfectly natural under these circumstances that both of us should exercise a certain amount of caution — I in my endeavors to ascertain Lee's strength, positions, and intentions before I struck the fatal blow; he to abstain from any extended movements of invasion, and to hold his army well in hand until he could be satisfied as to the condition of the Army of the Potomac after its Second Bull Run campaign, and as to the intentions of its commander. . . .

THE PRY HOUSE, McCLELLAN'S HEADQUARTERS AT ANTIETAM.

UNION SIGNAL STATION ON ELK MOUNTAIN,
FIVE OR SIX MILES SOUTH-EAST OF
SHARPSBURG.

LEE'S HEADQUARTERS IN SHARPSBURG.

This house, which was the residence of Jacob H. Grove, is noted in Sharpsburg as the place where Lee held a conference with Longstreet and D. H. Hill. But Lee's headquarters tents were pitched in a small grove on the right of the Shepherdstown road, just outside the town.

McCLELLAN'S POPULARITY WITH HIS ARMY.

"Though a quarter of a century has passed since 'those darkest days of the war,'" writes Mr. George Kimbal of Boston in a letter to the editors, "I still retain a vivid remembrance of the sudden and complete change which came upon the face of affairs when General McClellan was restored to command. At the time, I was serving in Company A, 12th Massachusetts Volunteers, attached to Rickett's division.

"The announcement of McClellan's restoration came to us in the early evening of the 2d of September, 1862, just after reaching Hall's Hill, weary from long marching and well-nigh disheartened by recent reverses. The men were scattered about in groups, discussing the events of their ill-starred campaign, and indulging in comments that were decidedly uncomplimentary to those who had been responsible for its mismanagement. We did not know, of course, the exact significance of all that had happened, as we afterward learned it, but being mainly thinking men, we were able to form pretty shrewd guesses as to where the real difficulty lay. Suddenly, while these mournful consultations were in full blast, a mounted officer, dashing past our bivouac, reined up enough to shout, ' "Little Mac" is back here on the road, boys!' The scene that followed can be more easily imagined than described. From extreme sadness we passed in a twinkling to a delirium of delight. A Deliverer had come. A real 'rainbow of promise' had appeared suddenly in the dark political sky. The feeling in our division upon the return of General McClellan had its counterpart in all the others, for the Army of the Potomac loved him as it never loved any other leader. In a few days we started upon that long march into Maryland, and whenever General McClellan appeared among his troops, from the crossing of the Potomac at Washington to the grapple with Lee at Antietam, it was the signal for the most spontaneous and enthusiastic cheering I ever listened to or participated in. Men threw their caps high into the air, and danced and frolicked like school-boys, so glad were they to get their old commander back again. It is true that McClellan had always been fortunate in being able to excite enthusiasm among his troops, but demonstrations at this time took on an added and noticeable emphasis from the fact that he had been recalled to command after what the army believed to be an unwise and unjust suspension. The climax seemed to be reached, however, at Middletown, where we first caught sight of the enemy. Here, upon our arrival, we found General McClellan sitting upon his horse in the road. The enemy occupied a gap in the South Mountain, a mile or two beyond. Reno and Hatch were fighting, and the smoke of their guns could be seen half-way up the mountain. As each organization passed the general, the men became apparently forgetful of everything but their love for him. They cheered and cheered again, until they became so hoarse they could cheer no longer. It seemed as if an intermission had been declared in order that a reception might be tendered to the general-in-chief. A great crowd continually surrounded him, and the most extravagant demonstrations were indulged in. Hundreds even hugged the horse's legs and caressed his head and mane. While the troops were thus surging by, the general continually pointed with his finger to the gap in the mountain through which our path lay. It was like a great scene in a play, with the roar of the guns for an accompaniment. Another enthusiastic demonstration that I remember occurred in the afternoon of the 17th at Antietam, when the general rode along our line of battle.

ROSTRUM IN NATIONAL CEMETERY AT ANTIETAM.

On Memorial Day, 1885, General McClellan addressed from this rostrum a large assembly of "Grand Army" men.

ANTIETAM—THE CONFEDERATE SIDE.

THE DEFENSE OF SHARPSBURG.

BY JAMES LONGSTREET, LIEUTENANT-GENERAL, C. S. A.

Commander of Lee's right and center at Antietam.*

. . . On the afternoon of the 15th of September my command and Hill's crossed the Antietam Creek, and took position in front of Sharpsburg, my command filing into position on the right of the Sharpsburg and Boonsboro' turnpike, and D. H. Hill's division on the left. Soon after getting into position we found our left, at Dunker Church, the weak point, and Hood, with two brigades, was changed from my right to guard this point, leaving General D. H. Hill between the parts of my command.

That night, after we heard of the fall of Harper's Ferry, General Lee ordered Stonewall Jackson to march to Sharpsburg as rapidly as he could come. Then it was that we should have retired from Sharpsburg and gone to the Virginia side of the Potomac.

The moral effect of our move into Maryland had been lost by our discomfiture at South Mountain, and it was then evident we could not hope to concentrate in time to do more than make a respectable retreat, whereas by retiring before the battle we could have claimed a very successful campaign.

On the forenoon of the 15th, the blue uniforms of the Federals appeared among the trees that crowned the heights on the eastern bank of the Antietam. The number increased, and larger and

*The battle which the Federals called "Antietam," after a creek, was called "Sharpsburg" by the Confederates, after a village. [See map on page 149.]

larger grew the field of blue until it seemed to stretch as far as the eye could see, and from the tops of the mountains down to the edges of the stream gathered the great army of McClellan. It was an awe-inspiring spectacle as this grand force settled down in sight of the Confederates, then shattered by battles and scattered by long and tiresome marches. On the 16th Jackson came and took position with part of his command on my left. Before night the Federals attacked my left and gave us a severe fight, principally against Hood's division, but we drove them back, holding well our ground. After nightfall Hood was relieved from the position on the left, ordered to replenish his ammunition, and be ready to resume his first position on my right in the morning. General Jackson's forces, who relieved Hood, were extended to our left, reaching well back toward the Potomac, where most of our cavalry was. Toombs had joined us with two of his regiments, and was placed as guard on the bridge on my right. Hooker, who had thrown his corps against my left in the afternoon was reinforced by the corps of Sumner and Mansfield. Sykes's division was also drawn into position for the impending battle. Burnside was over against my right, threatening the passage of the Antietam at that point. On the morning of the 17th the Federals were in good position along the Antietam, stretching up and down and across it to our left for three miles. They had a good position for their guns, which were of the most approved make and metal. Our position overcrowned theirs a little, but our guns were inferior and our ammunition was very imperfect.

Back of McClellan's line was a high ridge, upon

SUMNER'S ADVANCE.

French's division closing in upon Roulette's barns and house—Richardson's division continuing the line far to the left.

CHARGE OF IRWIN'S BRIGADE (SMITH'S DIVISION) AT THE DUNKER CHURCH.

General Wm. F. Smith, commanding the Second Division of Franklin's corps, went to the assistance of French. On getting into position, for the most part to the right of French, General Smith in his report, says: "Finding that the enemy were advancing, I ordered forward the Third Brigade (Colonel Irwin's), who, passing through the regular battery then commanded by Lieutenant Thomas (Fourth Artillery), charged upon the enemy and drove them gallantly until abreast the little church at the point of woods, the possession of which had been so fiercely contested. At this point a severe flank fire from the woods was received." The brigade rallied behind the crest of a slope. [See note to map, p. 149.]

which was his signal station overlooking every point of our field. D. R. Jones's brigades of my command deployed on the right of the Sharpsburg pike, while Hood's brigades awaited orders. D. H. Hill was on the left extending toward the Hagerstown-Sharpsburg pike, and Jackson extended out from Hill's left toward the Potomac. The battle opened heavily with the attacks of the corps of Hooker, Mansfield, and Sumner against our left center, which consisted of Jackson's right and D. H. Hill's left. So severe and persistent were these attacks that I was obliged to send Hood to support our center. The Federals forced us back a little, however, and held this part of our position to the end of the day's work. With new troops and renewed efforts McClellan continued his attacks upon this point from time to time, while he brought his forces to bear against other points. The line swayed forward and back like a rope exposed to rushing currents. A force too heavy to be withstood would strike and drive in a weak point till we could collect a few fragments, and in turn force back the advance till our lost ground was recovered. A heroic effort was made by D. H. Hill, who collected some fragments and led a charge to drive back and recover our lost ground at the center. He soon found that his little band was too much exposed on its left flank, and was obliged to abandon the attempt. Thus the battle ebbed and flowed with terrific slaughter on both sides.

The Federals fought with wonderful bravery and the Confederates clung to their ground with heroic courage as hour after hour they were mown down like grass. The fresh troops of McClellan literally tore into shreds the already ragged army of Lee, but the Confederates never gave back.

I remember at one time they were surging up against us with fearful numbers. I was occupying the left over by Hood, whose ammunition gave out. He retired to get a fresh supply. Soon after the Federals moved up against us in great masses.

We were under the crest of a hill occupying a position that ought to have been held by from four to six brigades. The only troops there were Cooke's regiment of North Carolina infantry, and they were without a cartridge. As I rode along the line with my staff I saw two pieces of the Washington Artillery (Miller's battery), but there were not enough men to man them. The gunners had been either killed or wounded. This was a fearful situation for the Confederate center. I put my staff-officers to the guns while I held their horses. It was easy to see that if the Federals broke through our line there, the Confederate army would be cut in two and probably destroyed, for we were already badly whipped, and were only holding our ground by sheer force of desperation. Cooke sent me word that his ammunition was out. I replied that he must hold his position as long as he had a man left. He responded that he would show his colors as long as there was a man alive to hold them up. We loaded up our little guns with canister and sent a rattle of hail into the Federals as they came up over the crest of the hill.

That little battery shot harder and faster, with a sort of human energy, as though it realized that it was to hold the thousands of Federals at bay or the battle was lost. So warm was the reception we gave them that they dodged back behind the crest of the hill. We sought to make them believe we had many batteries before them. As the Federals would come up they would see the colors of the North Carolina regiment waving placidly and then would receive a shower of canister. We made it lively while it lasted. In the mean time General Chilton, General Lee's chief of staff, made his way to me and asked, "Where are the troops you are holding your line with?" I pointed to my two pieces and to Cooke's regiment, and replied, "There they are; but that regiment hasn't a cartridge."

Chilton's eyes popped as though they would come out of his head; he struck spurs to his horse and away he went to General Lee. I suppose he made some remarkable report, although I did not see General Lee again until night. After a little a shot came across the Federal front, plowing the ground in a parallel line. Another and another, each nearer and nearer their line. This enfilade fire, so distressing to soldiers, was from a battery on D. H. Hill's line, and it soon beat back the attacking column.

Meanwhile R. H. Anderson and Hood came to our support and gave us more confidence. It was a little while only until another assault was made against D. H. Hill, and extending far over toward our left, where McLaws and Walker were supporting Jackson. In this desperate effort the lines seemed to swing back and forth for many minutes, but at last they settled down to their respective positions, the Confederates holding with a desperation which seemed to say, "We are here to die."

Meanwhile General Lee was over toward our right, where Burnside was trying to cross to the attack. Toombs, who had been assigned as guard at that point, did handsome service. His troops were footsore and worn from marching, and he had only four hundred men to meet the Ninth Corps. The little band fought bravely, but the Federals were pressing them slowly back. The delay that Toombs caused saved that part of the battle, however, for at the last moment A. P. Hill came in to reinforce him, and D. H. Hill discovered a good place for a battery and opened with it. Thus the Confederates were enabled to drive the Federals back, and when night settled down the army of Lee was still in possession of the field. But it was dearly bought, for thousands of brave soldiers were dead on the field and many gallant commands were torn as a forest in a cyclone. It was heart-rending to see how Lee's army had been slashed by the day's fighting.

Nearly one-fourth of the troops who went into the battle were killed or wounded. We were so badly crushed that at the close of the day ten thousand fresh troops could have come in and taken Lee's army and everything it had. But McClellan did not know it, and [apparently] feared, when Burnside was pressed back, that Sharpsburg was a Confederate victory, and that he would have to retire. As it was, when night settled down both armies were content to stay where they were.

AFTER THE BATTLE—POSITION OF THE CONFEDERATE BATTERIES IN FRONT OF DUNKER CHURCH.

NOTE TO MAP.

On the afternoon of September 16th, Hooker's corps crossed at the two fords and the bridge north of McClellan's headquarters.

A.—From near sunset till dark Hooker engaged Hood's division (of Longstreet's corps) about the "East Wood," marked A on the map. Hood was relieved by two brigades of Jackson's corps, which was in and behind the Dunker Church wood (or West Wood), C.

B.—At dawn on the 17th, Hooker and Jackson began a terrible contest which raged in and about the famous corn-field, B, and in the woods, A and C. Jackson's reserves regained the corn-field. Hartsuff's brigade, of Hooker's corps, and Mansfield's corps charged through the corn-field into the Dunker Church wood, General Mansfield being mortally wounded in front of the East Wood.

Jackson, with the aid of Hood, and a part of D. H. Hill's division, again cleared the Dunker Church wood. J. G. Walker's division, taken from the extreme right of the Confederate line, charged in support of Jackson and Hood.

C.—Sumner's corps formed line of battle in the center, Sedgwick's division facing the East Wood, through which it charged over the corn-field again, and through Dunker Church wood to the edge of the fields beyond. McLaws's division (of Longstreet's corps), just arrived from Harper's Ferry, assisted in driving out Sedgwick, who was forced to retreat northward by the Hagerstown pike.

D.—About the time that Sedgwick charged, French and Richardson, of Sumner's corps, dislodged D. H. Hill's line from Roulette's house.

E.—Hill re-formed in the sunken road, since known as the "Bloody Lane," where his position was carried by French and Richardson, the latter being mortally wounded in the corn-field, E.

F.—Irwin and Brooks, of Franklin's corps, moved to the support of French and Richardson. At the point F, Irwin's brigade was repelled.

G.—D. H. Hill, reinforced by R. H. Anderson's division of Longstreet's corps, fought for the ground about Piper's house.

H.—Stuart attempted a flank movement north of the Dunker Church wood, but was driven back by the thirty guns under Doubleday.

J.—Pleasonton, with a part of his cavalry and several batteries, crossed the Boonsboro' bridge as a flank support to Richardson, and to Burnside on the south. Several battalions of regulars from Porter's corps came to his assistance, and made their way well up to the hill which is now the National Cemetery.

K.—Toombs (of Longstreet) had defended the lower bridge until Burnside moved Rodman and Scammon to the fords below.

L.—Then Toombs hurried south to protect the Confederate flank. Sturgis and Crook charged across the Burnside bridge and gained the heights. Toombs was driven away from the fords.

M.—After 3 o'clock, Burnside's lines, being reformed, completed the defeat of D. R. Jones's division (of Longstreet), and on the right gained the outskirts of Sharpsburg. Toombs, and the arriving brigades of A. P. Hill, of Jackson's corps, saved the village and regained a part of the lost ground.

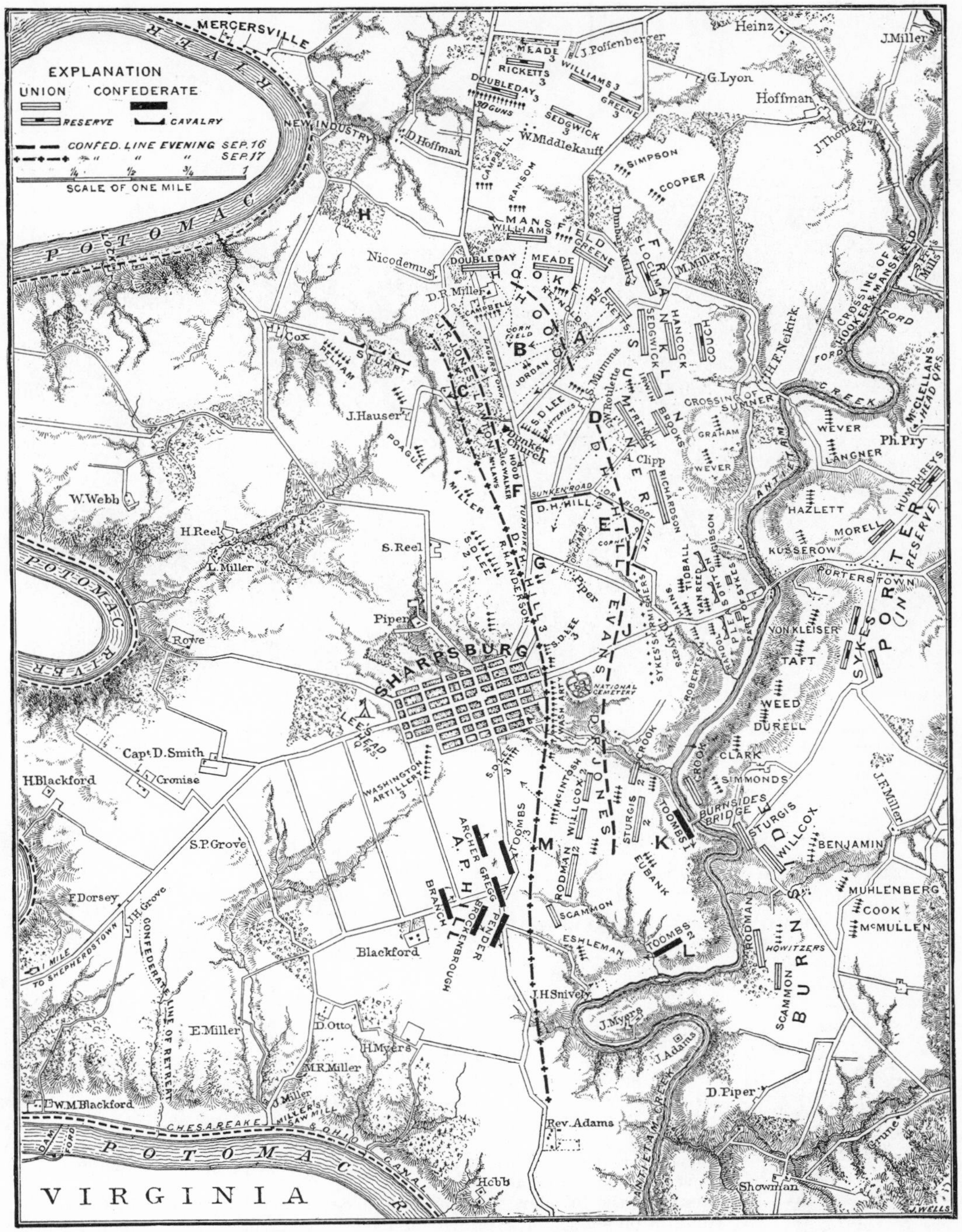

During the progress of the battle of Sharpsburg, General Lee and I were riding along my line and D. H. Hill's, when we received a report of movements of the enemy and started up the ridge to make a reconnoissance. General Lee and I dismounted, but Hill declined to do so. I said to Hill, "If you insist on riding up there and drawing the fire, give us a little interval so that we may not be in the line of the fire when they open upon you." General Lee and I stood on the top of the crest with our glasses, looking at the movements of the Federals on the rear left. After a moment I turned my glass to the right—the Federal left. As I did so, I noticed a puff of white smoke from the mouth of a cannon. "There is a shot for you," I said to General Hill. The gunner was a mile away, and the cannon-shot came whisking through the air for three or four seconds and took off the front legs of the horse that Hill sat on and let the animal down upon his stumps. The horse's head was so low and his croup so high that Hill was in a most ludicrous position. With one foot in the stirrup he made several efforts to get the other leg over the croup, but failed. Finally we prevailed upon him to try the other end of the horse, and he got down. He had a third horse shot under him before the close of the battle. That shot at Hill was the second best shot I ever saw. The best was at Yorktown. There a Federal officer came out in front of our line, and sitting down to his little platting-table began to make a map. One of our officers carefully sighted a gun, touched it off, and dropped a shell into the hands of the man at the little table.

When the battle was over and night was gathering, I started to Lee's headquarters to make my report. In going through the town, I passed a house that had been set afire and was still burning. The family was in great distress, and I stopped to do what I could for them. By that I was detained until after the other officers had reached headquarters and made their reports. My delay caused some apprehension on the part of General Lee that I had been hurt; in fact, such a report had been sent him. When I rode up and dismounted he seemed much relieved, and, coming to me very

hurriedly for one of his dignified manner, threw his arms upon my shoulders and said:

"Here is my old war-horse at last."

When all the reports were in, General Lee decided that he would not be prepared the next day for offensive battle, and would prepare only for defense, as we had been doing.

The next day [the 18th] the Federals failed to advance, and both armies remained in position. During the day some of the Federals came over under a flag of truce to look after their dead and wounded. The following night we withdrew, passing the Potomac with our entire army. . . .

General Lee was not satisfied with the result of the Maryland campaign, and seemed inclined to attribute the failure to the Lost Despatch; though I believe he was more inclined to attribute the loss of the despatch to the fault of a courier or to other negligence than that of the officer to whom it was directed.

Our men came in so rapidly after the battle that renewed hope of gathering his army in great strength soon caused Lee to look for other and new prospects, and to lose sight of the lost campaign.

But at Sharpsburg was sprung the keystone of the arch upon which the Confederate cause rested. Jackson was quite satisfied with the campaign, as the Virginia papers made him the hero of Harper's Ferry, although the greater danger was with McLaws, whose service was the severer and more important. Lee lost nearly 20,000 by straggling in this campaign—almost twice as many as were captured at Harper's Ferry. . . .

THE FIELD OF ANTIETAM.

BURNSIDE'S BRIDGE AT ANTIETAM—I.

This picture, after a photograph taken in 1885, is a view of the Confederate position from the slope of the hill occupied by the Union batteries before a crossing was effected. At the time of the battle the buildings had not been erected, and the Confederate hill-side was covered with trees. A Confederate battery on the left enfiladed the crossing. Union sharp-shooters took advantage of the stone wall on the right of the approach to the bridge. The continuation of the road to Sharpsburg is seen on the right across the bridge. [See notes under cuts on page 151, and map and note on page 149.]

BURNSIDE'S BRIDGE—II.

This picture, after a photograph taken in 1885, is a view of the Union position from the hill where Confederate artillery was planted to enfilade the bridge. From a point below, the 2d Maryland and the 6th New Hampshire charged up the road, but they were swept by such a murderous fire that only a few reached the bridge and sought shelter behind the stone wall above. Subsequently, the bridge was carried by the 51st Pennsylvania, Colonel Robert B. Potter, and the 51st New York, Colonel John F. Hartrauft, charging from the pines on the hill-side.

THE UNION SIDE.

IN THE RANKS WITH HAWKINS'S ZOUAVES AT SOUTH MOUNTAIN AND ANTIETAM.

BY DAVID L. THOMPSON, CO. G, 9TH NEW YORK VOLUNTEERS.

UNIFORM OF HAWKINS'S ZOUAVES.

ON the 5th of September, 1862, Hawkins's Zouaves, as a part of Burnside's corps from Fredericksburg, landed at Washington to assist in the defense of the capital, then threatened by Lee's first invasion of Maryland, and, as events proved, to join in the pursuit of the invaders. Here, in pursuance of a measure for shortening the baggage-train which had lately been decided on, we were deprived of our Sibley tents — those cumbersome, conical caravansaries, in which eighteen men lie upon the ground with their feet toward the center. . . .

We marched at last, and on the 12th of September entered Frederick, wondering all the way what the enemy meant. We of the ranks little suspected what sheaves he was gathering in at Harper's Ferry, behind the curtain of his main body. We guessed, however, as usual, and toward evening began to get our answer. He was right ahead, his rear-guard skirmishing with our advance. We came up at the close of the fight at Frederick, and, forming line of battle, went at double-quick through corn-fields, potato patches, gardens, and backyards — the German washerwomen of the 103d New York regiment going in with us on the run. It was only a measure of precaution, however, the cavalry having done what little there was to do in the way of driving out of the city a Confederate rear-guard not much inclined to stay. . . .

The 14th of September we crossed the Catoctin range of mountains, reaching the summit about noon, and descended its western slope into the beautiful valley of Middletown. Half-way up the valley's western side we halted for a rest, and turned to look back on the moving host. It was a scene to linger in the memory. The valley in which Middletown lies is four or five miles wide, as I remember it, and runs almost due north and south between the parallel ranges of Catoctin and South Mountains. From where we stood the landscape lay below us, the eye commanding the oppo-

site slope of the valley almost at point-blank. An hour before, from the same spot, it had been merely a scene of quiet pastoral beauty. All at once, along its eastern edge the heads of the columns began to appear, and grew and grew, pouring over the ridge and descending by every road, filling them completely and scarring the surface of the gentle landscape with the angry welts of war. By the farthest northern road — the farthest we could see — moved the baggage wagons, the line stretching from the bottom of the valley back to the top of the ridge, and beyond, only the canvas covers of the wagons revealing their character. We knew that each dot was a heavily loaded army wagon, drawn by six mules and occupying forty feet of road at least. Now they looked like white beads on a string. So far away were they that no motion was perceptible. The constant swelling of the end of the line down in the valley, where the teams turned into the fields to park, gave evidence that in this way it was being slowly reeled along the way. The troops were marching by two roads farther south. The Confederates fighting on the western summit must have seen them plainly. Half a mile beyond us the column broke abruptly, filing off into line of battle, right and left, across the fields. From that point backward and downward, across the valley and up the farther slope, it stretched with scarcely a gap, every curve and zigzag of the way defined more sharply by its som-

ber presence. Here, too, on all the distant portions of the line, motion was imperceptible, but could be inferred from the casual glint of sunlight on a musket-barrel miles away. It was 3 o'clock when we resumed our march, turning our backs upon the beautiful, impressive picture — each column a monstrous, crawling, blue-black snake, miles long, quilled with the silver slant of muskets at a "shoulder," its sluggish tail writhing slowly up over the distant eastern ridge, its bruised head weltering in the roar and smoke upon the crest above, where was being fought the battle of South Mountain.

We were now getting nearer to the danger line, the rattle of musketry going on incessantly in the edges of the woods, and behind the low stone fences that seamed the mountain-side. Then we came upon the fringes of the contest — slightly wounded men scattered along the winding road on their way to the hospital, and now and then a squad of prisoners, wounded and unwounded together, going under guard to the rear.

The brigade was ordered to the left of the road to support a regular battery posted at the top of a steep slope, with a corn-field on the left, and twenty yards or so in front, a thin wood. We formed behind the battery and a little down the slope — the 89th on the left, the 9th next, then the 103d. We had been in position but a few minutes when a stir in front advised us of something unusual

THE CHARGE ACROSS THE BURNSIDE BRIDGE.

In his report General Sturgis describes as follows the charge across the bridge: "Orders arrived from General Burnside to carry the bridge at all hazards. I then selected the Fifty-first New York and the Fifty-first Pennsylvania from the Second Brigade, and directed them to charge with the bayonet. They started on their mission of death full of enthusiasm, and, taking a route less exposed than the regiments [Second Maryland and Sixth New Hampshire] which had made the effort before them, rushed at a double-quick over the slope leading to the bridge and over the bridge itself, with an impetuosity which the enemy could not resist; and the Stars and Stripes were planted on the opposite bank at 1 o'clock P. M., amid the most enthusiastic cheering from every part of the field from where they could be seen."

afoot, and the next moment the Confederates burst out of the woods, and made a dash at the battery. We had just obeyed a hastily given order to lie down, when the bullets whistled over our heads, and fell far down the slope behind us. Then the guns opened at short range, full-shotted with grape and canister. The force of the charge was easily broken, for though it was vigorously made it was not sustained — perhaps was not intended to be, as the whole day's battle had been merely an effort of the enemy to check our advance till he could concentrate for a general engagement. As the Confederates came out of the woods their line touched ours on the extreme left only, and there at an acute angle, their men nearly treading on those of the 89th, who were on their faces in the corn-field, before they discovered them. At that instant the situation just there was ideally, cruelly advantageous to us. The Confederates stood before us not twenty feet away, the full intention of destruction on their faces — but helpless, with empty muskets. The 89th simply rose up and shot them down.

It was in this charge that I first heard the "rebel yell"; not the deep-breasted Northern cheer, given in unison and after a struggle, to signify an advantage gained, but a high shrill yelp, uttered without concert, and kept up continually when the fighting was approaching a climax, as an incentive to further effort. This charge ended the contest for the day on that part of the line. Pickets were set well forward in the woods, and we remained some time

in position, waiting. How a trivial thing will often thrust itself upon the attention in a supreme moment was well exemplified here. All about us grew pennyroyal, bruised by the tramping of a hundred feet, and the smell of it has always been associated in my memory with that battle.

Before the sunlight faded, I walked over the narrow field. All around lay the Confederate dead — undersized men mostly, from the coast district of North Carolina, with sallow, hatchet faces, and clad in "butternut" — a color running all the way from a deep coffee-brown up to the whitish-brown of ordinary dust. As I looked down on the poor, pinched faces, worn with marching and scant fare, all enmity died out. There was no "secession" in those rigid forms, nor in those fixed eyes staring blankly at the sky. Clearly it was not "their war." Some of our men primed their muskets afresh with the finer powder from the cartridge-boxes of the dead. With this exception, each remained untouched as he had fallen. Darkness came on rapidly, and it grew very chilly. As little could be done at that hour in the way of burial, we unrolled the blankets of the dead, spread them over the bodies, and then sat down in line, munching a little on our cooked rations in lieu of supper, and listening to the firing, which was kept up on the right, persistently. By 9 o'clock this ceased entirely. Drawing our blankets over us, we went to sleep, lying upon our arms in line as we had stood, living Yankee and dead Confederate side by side, and indistinguishable. This was Sunday.

BURNSIDE'S ATTACK UPON SHARPSBURG.

In this attack Willcox's division (the right of the line) charged into the village. Colonel Fairchild, commanding a brigade in Rodman's division, on the left of the line (which included Hawkins's Zouaves, seen at the stone wall in the picture), describes as follows in his report the advance upon Sharpsburg after the hill above the bridge had been gained: "We continued to advance to the opposite hill under a tremendous fire from the enemy's batteries, up steep embankments. Arriving near a stone fence, the enemy — a brigade composed of South Carolina and Georgia regiments — opened on us with musketry. After returning their fire I immediately ordered a charge, which the whole brigade gallantly responded to, moving with alacrity and steadiness. Arriving at the fence, behind which the enemy were awaiting us, receiving their fire, losing large numbers of our men, we charged over the fence, dislodging them and driving them from their positions down the hill toward the village, a stand of regimental colors belonging to a South Carolina regiment being taken by Private Thomas Hare, Company D, 89th New York Volunteers, who was afterward killed. We continued to pursue the enemy down the hill. Discovering that they were massing fresh troops on our left, I went back and requested General Rodman to bring up rapidly the Second Brigade to our support, which he did, they engaging the enemy, he soon afterward falling badly wounded. . . . The large force advancing on our left flank compelled us to retire from the position, which we could have held had we been properly supported."

The next morning, receiving no orders to march, we set to work collecting the arms and equipments scattered about the field, and burying the dead. The weather being fine, bowers were built in the woods — generally in fence corners — for such of the wounded as could not be moved with safety; others, after stimulants had been given, were helped down the mountain to the rude hospitals. Before we left the spot, some of the country people living thereabout, who had been scared away by the firing, ventured back, making big eyes at all they saw, and asking most ridiculous questions. One was, whether we were from Mexico! Those belated echoes, it seemed, were still sounding in the woods of Maryland.

At Antietam our corps — the Ninth, under Burnside — was on the extreme left, opposite the stone bridge. Our brigade stole into position about half-past 10 o'clock on the night of the 16th. No lights were permitted, and all conversation was carried on in whispers. As the regiment was moving past the 103d New York to get to its place, there occurred, on a small scale and without serious results, one of those unaccountable panics often noticed in crowds, by which each man, however brave individually, merges his individuality for the moment, and surrenders to an utterly causeless fear. When

everything was at its darkest and stealthiest one of the 103d stumbled over the regimental dog, and in trying to avoid treading on it, staggered against a stack of muskets and knocked them over. The giving way of the two or three men upon whom they fell was communicated to others in a sort of wave movement of constantly increasing magnitude, reinforced by the ever-present apprehension of attack, till two regiments were in confusion. In a few seconds order was restored, and we went on to our place in the line — a field of thin corn sloping toward the creek, where we sat down on the plowed ground and watched for a while the dull glare on the sky of the Confederate camp-fires behind the hills. We were hungry, of course, but, as no fires were allowed, we could only mix our ground coffee and sugar in our hands and eat them dry. I think we were the more easily inclined to this crude disposal of our rations from a feeling that for many of us the need of drawing them would cease forever with the following day.

All through the evening the shifting and placing had gone on, the moving masses being dimly described in the strange half lights of earth and sky. There was something weirdly impressive yet unreal in the gradual drawing together of those whispering armies under cover of the night — something of

NORTH OF THE DUNKER CHURCH—A UNION CHARGE THROUGH THE CORN-FIELD.

UNION BURIAL PARTY AT ANTIETAM.
From a photograph.

awe and dread, as always in the secret preparation for momentous deeds. By 11 o'clock the whole line, four miles or more in length, was sleeping, each corps apprised of its appointed task, each battery in place.

It is astonishing how soon, and by what slight causes, regularity of formation and movement are lost in actual battle. Disintegration begins with the first shot. To the book-soldier all order seems destroyed, months of drill apparently going for nothing in a few minutes. Next after the most powerful factor in this derangement—the enemy—come natural obstacles and the inequalities of the ground. One of the commonest is a patch of trees. An advancing line lags there inevitably,

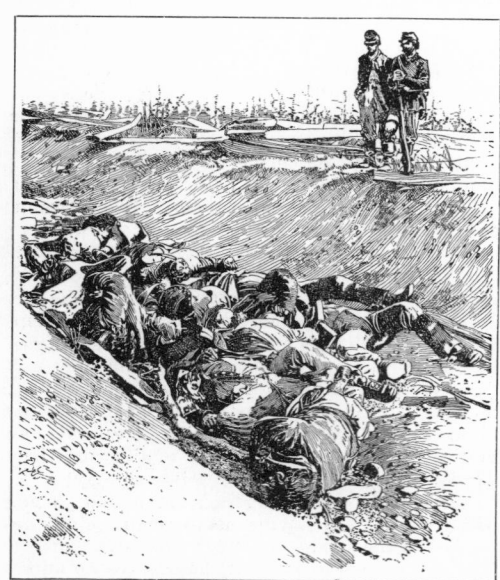

CONFEDERATE DEAD (OF D. H. HILL'S DIVISION)
IN THE SUNKEN ROAD.

the rest of the line swinging around insensibly, with the view of keeping the alignment, and so losing direction. The struggle for the possession of such a point is sure to be persistent. Wounded men crawl to a wood for shelter, broken troops re-form behind it, a battery planted in its edge will stick there after other parts of the line have given way. Often a slight rise of ground in an open field, not noticeable a thousand yards away, becomes, in the keep of a stubborn regiment, a powerful head-land against which the waves of battle roll and break, requiring new dispositions and much time to clear it. A stronger fortress than a casual railroad embankment often proves, it would be difficult to find; and as for a sunken road, what possibilities of victory or disaster lie in that obstruction let Waterloo and Fredericksburg bear witness.

At Antietam it was a low, rocky ledge, prefaced by a corn-field. There were woods, too, and knolls, and there were other corn-fields; but the student of that battle knows one corn-field only—*the* corn-field, now historic, lying a quarter of a mile north of Dunker Church, and east of and bordering the Hagerstown road. About it and across it, to and fro, the waves of battle swung almost from the first, till by 10 o'clock in the morning, when the struggle was over, hundreds of men lay dead among its peaceful blades.

While these things were happening on the right, the left was not without its excitement. A Confederate battery discovered our position in our corn-field, as soon as it was light enough to see, and began to shell us. As the range became better we were moved back and ordered to boil coffee in the protection of a hollow. The general plan of battle appears to have been to break through the Confederate left, following up the advantage with a constantly increasing force, sweep him away from the fords, and so crowd his whole army down into the narrow peninsula formed by the Potomac and Antietam Creek. Even the non-military eye, however, can see that the tendency of such a plan

would be to bring the two armies upon concentric arcs, the inner and shorter of which must be held by the enemy, affording him the opportunity for reinforcement by interior lines—an immense advantage only to be counteracted by the utmost activity on our part, who must attack vigorously where attacking at all, and where not, imminently threaten. Certainly there was no imminence in the threat of our center or left—none whatever of the left, only a vague consciousness of whose existence even seems to have been in the enemy's mind, for he flouted us all the morning with hardly more than a meager skirmish line, while his coming troops, as fast as they arrived upon the ground, were sent off to the Dunker Church.

So the morning wore away, and the fighting on the right ceased entirely. That was fresh anxiety—the scales were turning perhaps, but which way? About noon the battle began afresh. This must have been Franklin's men of the Sixth Corps, for the firing was nearer, and they came up behind the center. Suddenly a stir beginning far up on the right, and running like a wave along the line, brought the regiment to its feet. A silence fell on every one at once, for each felt that the momentous "now" had come. Just as we started I saw, with a little shock, a line-officer take out his watch to note the hour, as though the affair beyond the creek were a business appointment which he was going to keep.

When we reached the brow of the hill the fringe of trees along the creek screened the fighting entirely, and we were deployed as skirmishers under their cover. We sat there two hours. All that time the rest of the corps had been moving over the stone bridge and going into position on the other side of the creek. Then we were ordered over at a ford which had been found below the bridge, where the water was waist-deep. One man was shot in mid-stream. At the foot of the slope on the opposite side the line was formed and we moved up through the thin woods. Reaching the level we lay down behind a battery which seemed to have been disabled. There, if anywhere, I should have

remembered that I was soaking wet from my waist down. So great was the excitement, however, that I have never been able to recall it. Here some of the men, going to the rear for water, discovered in the ashes of some hay-ricks which had been fired by our shells the charred remains of several Confederates. After long waiting it became noised along the line that we were to take a battery that was at work several hundred yards ahead on the top of a hill. This narrowed the field, and brought us to consider the work before us more attentively.

Right across our front, two hundred feet or so away, ran a country road bordered on each side by a snake fence. Beyond this road stretched a plowed field several hundred feet in length, sloping up to the battery, which was hidden in a corn-field. A stone fence, breast-high, inclosed the field on the left, and behind it lay a regiment of Confederates, who would be directly on our flank if we should attempt the slope. The prospect was far from encouraging, but the order came to get ready for the attempt.

Our knapsacks were left on the ground behind us. At the word a rush was made for the fences. The line was so disordered by the time the second fence was passed that we hurried forward to a shallow undulation a few feet ahead, and lay down among the furrows to re-form, doing so by crawling up into line. A hundred feet or so ahead was a similar undulation to which we ran for a second shelter. The battery, which at first had not seemed to notice us, now, apprised of its danger, opened fire upon us. We were getting ready now for the charge proper, but were still lying on our faces. Lieutenant-Colonel Kimball was ramping up and down the line. The discreet regiment behind the fence was silent. Now and then a bullet from them cut the air over our heads, but generally they were reserving their fire for that better shot which they knew they would get in a few minutes. The battery, however, whose shots at first went over our heads, had depressed its guns so as to shave the surface of the ground. Its fire was beginning to tell. I remember looking behind and seeing an

SCENE AT THE RUINS OF MUMMA'S HOUSE AND BARNS.

SHARPSBURG BRIDGE OVER THE ANTIETAM.

officer riding diagonally across the field — a most inviting target — instinctively bending his head down over his horse's neck, as though he were riding through driving rain. While my eye was on him I saw, between me and him, a rolled overcoat with its straps on bound into the air and fall among the furrows. One of the enemy's grape-shot had plowed a groove in the skull of a young fellow and had cut his overcoat from his shoulders. He never stirred from his position, but lay there face downward — a dreadful spectacle. A moment after, I heard a man cursing a comrade for lying on him heavily. He was cursing a dying man. As the range grew better, the firing became more rapid, the situation desperate and exasperating to the last degree. Human nature was on the rack, and there burst forth from it the most vehement, terrible swearing I have ever heard. Certainly the joy of conflict was not ours that day. The suspense was only for a moment, however, for the order to charge came just after. Whether the regiment was thrown into disorder or not, I never knew. I only remember that as we rose and started all the fire that had been held back so long was loosed. In a second the air was full of the hiss of bullets and the hurtle of grape-shot. The mental strain was so great that I saw at that moment the singular effect mentioned, I think, in the life of Goethe on a similar occasion — the whole landscape for an instant turned slightly red. I see again, as I saw it then in a flash, a man just in front of me drop his musket and throw up his hands, stung into vigorous swearing by a bullet behind the ear. Many men fell going up the hill, but it seemed to be all over in a moment, and I found myself passing a hollow where a dozen wounded men lay — among them our sergeant-major, who was calling me to come down. He had caught sight of the blanket rolled across my back,

and called me to unroll it and help to carry from the field one of our wounded lieutenants.

When I returned from obeying this summons the regiment (?) was not to be seen. It had gone in on the run, — what there was left of it, — and had disappeared in the corn-field about the battery. There was nothing to do but lie there and await developments. Nearly all the men in the hollow were wounded, one man — a recruit named Devlin, I think — frightfully so, his arm being cut short off. He lived a few minutes only. All were calling for water, of course, but none was to be had. We lay there till dusk — perhaps an hour, when the fighting ceased. During that hour, while the bullets snipped the leaves from a young locust-tree growing at the edge of the hollow and powdered us with the fragments, we had time to speculate on many things — among others, on the impatience with which men clamor, in dull times, to be led into a fight. We heard all through the war that the army "was eager to be led against the enemy." It must have been so, for truthful correspondents said so, and editors confirmed it. But when you came to hunt for this particular itch, it was always the next regiment that had it. The truth is, when bullets are whacking against tree-trunks, and solid shot are cracking skulls like egg-shells, the consuming passion in the breast of the average man is to get out of the way. Between the physical fear of going forward and the moral fear of turning back, there is a predicament of exceptional awkwardness from which a hidden hole in the ground would be a wonderfully welcome outlet.

Night fell, preventing further struggle. Of 600 men of the regiment who crossed the creek, at 3 o'clock that afternoon, 45 were killed and 176 wounded. The Confederates had possession of that part of the field over which we had moved, and just

after dusk they sent out detachments to collect arms and bring in prisoners. When they came to our hollow all the unwounded and slightly wounded there were marched to the rear — prisoners of the 15th Georgia. . . .

The next morning we were marched — about six hundred of us, fragments of a dozen different commands — to the Potomac, passing through Sharpsburg. We crossed the Potomac by the Shepherdstown ford, and bivouacked in the yard of a house near the river, remaining there all day. The next morning (the 19th) shells began to come from over the river, and we were started on the road to Richmond with a mixed guard of cavalry and infantry. When we reached Winchester we were quartered for a night in the court-house yard, where we were beset by a motley crew who were eager to exchange the produce of the region for greenbacks. . . .

From Winchester we were marched to Staunton, where we were put on board cattle-cars and forwarded at night, by way of Gordonsville, to Richmond, where we entered Libby Prison. We were not treated with special severity, for Libby was not at that time the hissing it afterward became. . . .

HOOKER'S BATTLE AT THE CORN-FIELD.

Of the early morning fight for the control of the corn-field, General Hooker says in his report:

"We had not proceeded far before I discovered that a heavy force of the enemy had taken possession of a corn-field (I have since learned about a thirty-acre field) in

my immediate front, and, from the sun's rays falling on their bayonets projecting above the corn, could see that the field was filled with the enemy, with arms in their hands, standing apparently at 'support arms.' Instructions were immediately given for the assemblage of all of my spare batteries near at hand, of which I think there were five or six, to spring into battery on the right of this field, and to open with canister at once. In the time I am writing every stalk of corn in the northern and greater part of the field was cut as closely as could have been done with a knife, and the slain lay in rows precisely as they had stood in their ranks a few moments before.

"It was never my fortune to witness a more bloody, dismal battle-field. Those that escaped fled in the opposite direction from our advance, and sought refuge behind the trees, fences, and stone ledges nearly on a line with the Dunker Church, etc., as there was no resisting this torrent of death-dealing missives. . . . The whole morning had been one of unusual animation to me, and fraught with the grandest events. The conduct of my troops was sublime, and the occasion almost lifted me to the skies, and its memories will ever remain near me. My command followed the fugitives closely until we had passed the corn-field a quarter of a mile or more, when I was removed from my saddle in the act of falling out of it from loss of blood, having previously been struck without my knowledge."

UNION HOSPITAL IN A BARN NEAR ANTIETAM CREEK.
After a sketch made at the time.

SOUTH-EASTERN STRETCH OF THE SUNKEN ROAD, OR "BLOODY LANE."
From a photograph taken in 1885.

A SOUTHERN WOMAN'S RECOLLECTIONS OF ANTIETAM.

BY MARY BEDINGER MITCHELL.

. . . On the 17th of September cloudy skies looked down upon the two armies facing each other on the fields of Maryland. It seems to me now that the roar of that day began with the light, and all through its long and dragging hours its thunder formed a background to our pain and terror. If we had been in doubt as to our friends' whereabouts on Sunday, there was no room for doubt now. There was no sitting at the windows now and counting discharges of guns, or watching the curling smoke. We went about our work with pale faces and trembling hands, yet trying to appear composed for the sake of our patients, who were much excited. We could hear the incessant explosions of artillery, the shrieking whistles of the shells, and the sharper, deadlier, more thrilling roll of musketry; while every now and then the echo of some charging cheer would come, borne by the wind, and as the human voice pierced that demoniacal clangor we would catch our breath and listen, and try not to sob, and turn back to the forlorn hospitals, to the suffering at our feet and before our eyes, while imagination fainted at thought of those other scenes hidden from us beyond the Potomac.

On our side of the river there were noise, confusion, dust; throngs of stragglers; horsemen galloping about; wagons blocking each other, and teamsters wrangling; and a continued din of shouting, swearing, and rumbling, in the midst of which men were dying, fresh wounded arriving, surgeons amputating limbs and dressing wounds, women going in and out with bandages, lint, medicines, food. An ever-present sense of anguish, dread, pity, and I fear, hatred — these are my recollections of Antietam.

When night came we could still hear the sullen guns and hoarse, indefinite murmurs that succeeded the day's turmoil. That night was dark and lowering and the air heavy and dull. Across the river innumerable camp-fires were blazing, and we could but too well imagine the scenes that they were lighting. We sat in silence, looking into each other's tired faces. There were no impatient words, few tears; only silence, and a drawing close together, as if for comfort. We were almost hopeless, yet clung with desperation to the thought that we were hoping. But in our hearts we could not believe that anything human could have escaped from that appalling fire. On Thursday the two armies lay idly facing each other, but we could not be idle. The wounded continued to arrive until the town was quite unable to hold all the disabled and suffering. They filled every building and overflowed into the country round, into farm-houses, barns, corn-cribs, cabins — wherever four walls and a roof were found together. Those able to travel were sent on to Winchester and other towns back from the river, but their departure seemed to make no appreciable difference. There were six churches, and they were all full; the Odd Fellows' Hall, the Freemasons', the little Town Council room, the barn-like place known as the Drill Room, all the private houses after their capacity, the shops and empty buildings, the school-houses — every inch of space, and yet the cry was for room.

The unfinished Town Hall had stood in naked ugliness for many a long day. Somebody threw a few rough boards across the beams, placed piles of straw over them, laid down single planks to walk upon, and lo, it was a hospital at once. The stone warehouses down in the ravine and by the river had been passed by, because low and damp and undesirable as sanitariums, but now their doors and windows were thrown wide, and, with barely time allowed to sweep them, they were all occupied, even the "old blue factory," an antiquated, crazy, dismal building of blue stucco that peeled off in great blotches, which had been shut up for years, and was in the last stages of dilapidation.

On Thursday night we heard more than usual sounds of disturbance and movement, and in the morning we found the Confederate army in full retreat. General Lee crossed the Potomac under cover of the darkness, and when the day broke the greater part of his force — or the more orderly portion of it — had gone on toward Kearneysville and Leetown. General McClellan followed to the river, and without crossing got a battery in position on Douglas's Hill, and began to shell the retreating army, and, in consequence, the town. What before was confusion grew worse; the retreat became a stampede. The battery may not have done a very great deal of execution, but it made a fearful noise. It is curious how much louder guns sound when they are pointed at you than when turned the other way! And the shell, with its long-drawn screeching, though no doubt less terrifying than the singing Minié ball, has a way of making one's hair stand on end. Then, too, every one who has had any experience in such things, knows how infectious fear is, how it grows when yielded to, and how, when you once begin to run, it soon seems impossible to run fast enough; whereas, if you can manage to stand your ground, the alarm lessens and sometimes disappears.

Some one suggested that yellow was the hospital color, and immediately everybody who could lay hands upon a yellow rag hoisted it over the house. The whole town was a hospital; there was scarcely a building that could not with truth seek protection under that plea, and the fantastic little strips were soon flaunting their ineffectual remonstrance from every roof-tree and chimney. When this specific failed the excitement became wild and ungovernable. It would have been ludicrous had it not produced so much suffering. The danger was less than it seemed, for McClellan, after all, was not bombarding the town, but the army, and most of the shells flew over us and exploded in the fields; but aim cannot always be sure, and enough shells fell short to convince the terrified citizens that their homes were about to be battered down over their ears. The better people kept some outward coolness, with perhaps a feeling of "*noblesse oblige*"; but the poorer classes acted as if the town were already in a blaze, and rushed from their houses with their families and household goods to make their way into the country. The road was thronged, the streets blocked; men were vociferating, women crying, children screaming; wagons, ambulances, guns, caissons, horsemen, footmen, all mingled — nay, even wedged and jammed together — in one struggling, shouting mass. The negroes were the worst, and with faces of a ghastly ash-color, and staring eyes, they swarmed into the fields, carrying their babies, their clothes, their pots and kettles, fleeing from the wrath behind them. The comparison to a hornets' nest attacked by boys is not a good one, for there was no "fight" shown; but a disturbed ant-hill is altogether inadequate. They fled widely and camped out of range, nor would they venture back for days.

Had this been all, we could afford to laugh now, but there was another side to the picture that lent it an intensely painful aspect. It was the hurrying crowds of wounded. Ah me! those maimed and bleeding fugitives! When the firing commenced the hospitals began to empty. All who were able to pull one foot after another, or could bribe or beg comrades to carry them, left in haste. In vain we implored them to stay; in vain we showed them the folly, the suicide, of the attempt; in vain we argued, cajoled, threatened, ridiculed; pointed out that we were remaining and that there was less danger here than on the road. There is no sense or reason in a panic. The cannon were bellowing upon Douglas's Hill, the shells whistling and shrieking, the air full of shouts and cries; we had to scream to make ourselves heard. The men replied that the "Yankees" were crossing; that the town was to be burned; that *we* could not be made prisoners, but they could; that, anyhow, they were going as far as they could walk, or be carried. . . .

ANTIETAM SCENES.

BY CHARLES CARLETON COFFIN.

(Army Correspondent.)

THE cannon were thundering when at early morn, September 17th, 1862, I mounted my horse at Hagerstown, where I had arrived the preceding day, as an army correspondent, upon its evacuation by the Confederates. The people of the town, aroused by the cannonade, were at the windows of the houses or in the streets, standing in groups, listening to the reverberations rolling along the valley. The wind was south-west, the clouds hanging low and sweeping the tree-tops on South Mountain.

The cannonade, reverberating from cloud to mountain and from mountain to cloud, became a continuous roar, like the unbroken rolling of a thunder-storm. The breeze, being in our direction, made the battle seem much nearer than it was. I was fully seven miles from Hooker's battle-field.

I turned down the Hagerstown and Sharpsburg turnpike at a brisk gallop, although I knew that Lee's army was in possession of the thoroughfare by the toll-gate which then stood about two miles north of Sharpsburg. A citizen who had left his home, to be beyond harm during the battle, had given me the information. The thought uppermost in my mind was to gain the left flank of the Confederate army, mingle with the citizens, and so witness the battle from the Confederate side. It would be a grand accomplishment if successful. It would give me a splendid opportunity to see the make-up of the Confederate army. It would be like going behind the scenes of a theater. I was in citizens' dress, splashed with mud, and wore a dilapidated hat.

While wondering what would be the outcome of the venture, I came upon a group of farmers, who were listening with dazed countenances to the uproar momentarily increasing in volume. It was no longer alone the boom of the batteries, but a rattle of musketry — at first like pattering drops upon a roof; then a roll, crash, roar, and rush, like a mighty ocean billow upon the shore chafing the pebbles, wave on wave, — with deep and heavy explosions of the batteries, like the crashing of thunderbolts. I think the currents of air must have had something to do with the effect of sound. The farmers were walking about nervously undecided, evidently, whether to flee or to remain.

"I would n't go down the pike if I were you," said one, addressing me. "You will ride right into the Rebs."

"That is just where I would like to go."

"You can't pass yourself off for a Reb; they 'll see, the instant they set eyes on you, that you are a Yank. They 'll gobble you up and take you to

BETWEEN THE LINES DURING A TRUCE.

Richmond," said the second. No doubt I acted wisely in leaving the turnpike and riding to gain the right flank of the Union line. . . . Ammunition trains were winding up the hill from the road leading to Keedysville.

Striking across the fields, I soon came upon the grounds on Hoffman's farm selected for the field-hospitals. Even at that hour of the morning it was an appalling sight. The wounded were lying in rows awaiting their turn at the surgeon's tables. The hospital stewards had a corps of men distributing straw over the field for their comfort.

Turning from the scenes of the hospital, I ascended the hill and came upon the men who had been the first to sweep across the Hagerstown pike, past the toll-gate, and into the Dunker Church woods, only to be hurled back by Jackson, who had established his line in a strong position behind outcropping limestone ledges.

"There are not many of us left," was the mournful remark of an officer.

I learned the story of the morning's engagement, and then rode to the line of batteries on the ridge by the house of J. Poffenberger; if my memory serves me there were thirty guns in position there, pointing south-west. There was a lull in the

strife. All was quiet in the woods along the turnpike, and in the corn-field beyond D. R. Miller's house, — so quiet that I thought I would ride on to the front line, not knowing that the brigade lying upon the ground near the cannon was the advanced line of the army. I rode through Poffenberger's door-yard, and noticed that a Confederate cannon-shot had ripped through the building; another had upset a hive of bees, and the angry insects had taken their revenge on the soldiers. I walked my horse down the pike past the toll-gate.

"Hold on!" It was the peremptory hail of a Union soldier crouching under the fence by the roadside. "Where are you going?"

"I thought I would go out to the front!"

"The front! you have passed it. This is the picket line. If you know what is good for yourself, you 'll skedaddle mighty quick. The Rebs are in the corn right out there."

I acted upon the timely advice and retreated to a more respectful distance; and none too soon, for a moment later the uproar began again — solid shot tearing through the woods and crashing among the trees, and shells exploding in unexpected places. I recall a round shot that came ricochetting over the ground, cutting little furrows, tossing the earth into the air, as the plow of the locomotive

turns its white furrow after a snow-storm. Its speed gradually diminished, and a soldier was about to catch it, as if he were at a game of baseball, but a united yell of "Look out!" "Don't!" "Take care!" "Hold on!" caused him to desist. Had he attempted it, he would have been knocked over instantly.

Turning from the conflict on the right, I rode down the line, toward the center, forded the Antietam and ascended the hill east of it to the large square mansion of Mr. Pry, where General McClellan had established his headquarters. The general was sitting in an arm-chair in front of the house. His staff were about him; their horses, saddled and bridled, were hitched to the trees and fences. Stakes had been driven in the earth in front of the house, to which were strapped the headquarters telescopes, through which a view of the operations and movements of the two armies could be obtained. . . .

The Fifth Corps, under Fitz-John Porter, was behind the ridge extending south toward the bridge, where the artillery of the Ninth Corps was thundering. Porter, I remember, was with McClellan, watching the movements of the troops across the Antietam — French's and Richardson's divisions, which were forming in the fields east of Roulette's and Mumma's houses. What a splendid sight it was! How beautifully the lines deployed! The clouds which had hung low all the morning had lifted, and the sun was shining through the rifts, its bright beams falling on the flags and glinting from gun-barrel and bayonet. Upon the crest of the hill south of the Dunker Church, I could see Confederates on horseback, galloping, evidently with orders; for, a few moments later, there was another gleam in the sunshine from the bayonets of their troops, who were apparently getting into position to resist the threatened movement of French and Richardson.

Memory recalls the advance of the line of men in blue across the meadow east of Roulette's. They reach the spacious barn, which divides the line of men as a rock parts the current of a river, flowing around it, but uniting beyond. The orchard around the house screens the movement in part. I see the blue uniforms beneath the apple-trees. The line halts for alignment. The skirmishers are in advance. There are isolated puffs of smoke, and then the Confederate skirmishers scamper up the hill and disappear. Up the slope moves the line to the top of a knoll. Ah! what a crash! A white cloud, gleams of lightning, a yell, a hurrah, and then up in the corn-field a great commotion, men firing into each other's faces, the Confederate line breaking, the ground strewn with prostrate forms. The Confederate line in "Bloody Lane" has been annihilated, the center pierced. . . .

Gen. W. S. Rosecrans [signature]

During the summer of 1862, while the Confederate armies under Generals J. E. Johnston and R. E. Lee, and the Union armies under Generals McClellan and Pope, contended in the East, the military situation in the West was comparatively uneventful. The first important collision after Shiloh involving the antagonists of that decisive field, took place at Iuka, Miss., September 19, two days after Antietam.

The battle of Shiloh (April 5 and 6) resulted in the retreat of the Confederates, led by Beauregard, to Corinth. General Halleck, assuming personal command of the Union forces opposed to Beauregard, immediately besieged Corinth, where all of the Confederate troops in the southwest were assembled. Halleck's army comprised the armies under Grant, Buell, and Pope. Beauregard evacuated Corinth, May 30, and fell back southward, halting at Tupelo. Halleck occupied Corinth, repaired the Memphis and Charleston R.R. and sent Buell along that line eastward to threaten Chattanooga. On June 27, General Braxton Bragg succeeded Beauregard in command of the Confederate forces in Mississippi. About that time Halleck and Pope were transferred from the Corinth army to another field, and Grant succeeded to the chief command in Mississippi. Late in July Bragg set out to invade the North, and proceeded with 35,000 men from Tupelo to Chattanooga, Tennessee. [See Colonel Urquhart's article, "Bragg's Advance and Retreat," page 159.] The Confederates remaining in Mississippi after Bragg's departure were left under the command of Generals Van Dorn and Price, who had crossed to the east of the Mississippi after the battle of Pea Ridge, Arkansas (March 8).

Buell was placed on the defensive by Bragg's northward movement, and gradually fell back from the Alabama and Tennessee borders toward his base at Nashville, and received reinforcements from the Union armies around Corinth. Under instructions from Bragg to prevent Grant from reinforcing Buell, Price attempted to march into western Tennessee, and in September reached Iuka, in Northern Mississippi. With a small column of Grant's army, Rosecrans defeated Price at Iuka, September 19, and drove him southward again. Price then joined his forces to Van Dorn's, and their united armies attacked Rosecrans at Corinth, October 3 and 4, and were repulsed.

Meanwhile Bragg, preceded by Forrest's and Morgan's mounted raiders crossed through eastern Tennessee into Kentucky. He reached Glasgow September 12, and issued a proclamation to Kentuckians. On the 16th, he captured the Union post at Munfordville, with 4000 prisoners. A subordinate column, under General E. Kirby Smith, marched from Knoxville, Tennessee, in August, defeated the Union force under General William Nelson at Richmond, Kentucky, on the 30th, and turned the strong Union position at Cumberland Gap, which was evacuated September 17. At the same time a column of Confederate infantry, and the cavalry brigades of Colonels Morgan and Duke, marched to the west bank of the Ohio River and threatened Cincinnati. Buell concentrated his army at Louisville, and marching from there to cope with Bragg, encountered him at Perryville, October 8.

Perryville was indecisive, but Bragg retreated to Knoxville, and the Union army, led by Rosecrans, who succeeded Buell October 29, advanced to Nashville. In December, Bragg occupied Murfreesboro' threatening Nashville, and Rosecrans marched from Nashville on the 26th to attack him. The decisive battle of Murfreesboro' (Union, "Stone's River") followed. [See Colonel G. C. Kniffin's article, p. 161, and General Crittenden's, p. 163.]

THE BATTLE OF IUKA.

BY C. S. HAMILTON, MAJOR-GENERAL, U. S. V.
Commander of a division at Iuka.

IUKA is a little village on the Memphis and Charleston railway, in northern Mississippi, about thirty miles east of Corinth. In September, 1862, the Confederate authorities, to prevent reinforcements being sent by the Federal commander in Mississippi to Buell in Kentucky, sent General Sterling Price with his army corps to Iuka. A regiment of Union troops stationed at Iuka evacuated the place, leaving a considerable quantity of army stores, as also quite an amount of cotton. The latter was destroyed, the former made use of, and Price settled down, apparently at his leisure, under the nose of Grant's force, whose headquarters were at Corinth. As soon as definite information was had of this position of Price, Grant took immediate steps to beat him up. A combined attack was planned, by which Rosecrans with his two divisions (Hamilton's and Stanley's) was to move on Iuka from the south, while Ord, with a similar column, was to approach Iuka from the west. This he did, taking position within about six miles of the village, where he was to await Rosecrans's attack. . . .

[General Hamilton personally led the troops which opened the fight and was an eye-witness of all that he here describes.]

On the halting of my troops, the battalion of skirmishers was pushed rapidly forward in the direction of Iuka. An advance of four hundred yards brought them in the immediate presence of the enemy. I was immediately in rear of the skirmishers, and, taking in the situation at a glance, dashed back to the head of the column. If this should become enveloped by the enemy, a rout was inevitable, and our force would be doubled back on itself. I threw the leading regiment, the 5th Iowa, across the road, moving it a short distance to the right, and ordered up the nearest battery, which was placed in position on the road, and to the left of the first regiment in position. Colonel Sanborn was active in bringing up other regiments, and getting them into line. Just as the first regiment was placed, the enemy opened one of his batteries with canister. The charge passed over our heads, doing no damage beyond bringing down a shower of twigs and leaves. The Confederates were in line ready for action. Why they did not move forward and attack us at once is not understood. Their delay, which enabled us to form the nearest three regiments in line of battle before the attack began, was our salvation. An earlier attack would have enveloped the head of the column, and brought a disastrous rout.

Meantime not a moment was lost. A second regiment, and a third, with all the rapidity that men could exercise, were added to our little line; and while the Confederates were moving to the front, we had managed to get a battle-line of three regiments into position. It was then the storm of battle opened. The opposing infantry lines were within close musketry shot. Our battery was handled with energy, and dealt death to the enemy. The Confederate batteries had ceased firing, their line of fire having been covered by the

FILLMORE STREET, CORINTH.

GROUP OF UNION SOLDIERS AT CORINTH.

advance of their infantry. Our own infantry held their ground nobly against the overwhelming force moving against them, and we were enabled to add another regiment to the line of battle. At the first musketry fire of the enemy, most of the horses of our battery were killed, and the pieces could not be removed from the field. The fight became an infantry duel. I never saw a hotter or more destructive engagement. General Price says in his official report, "The fight began, and was waged with a severity I have never seen surpassed." . . .

September 21st our troops were back in their old encampments at Jacinto. Just two weeks later, the same divisions and brigades were measured against each other on the field of Corinth.

THE BATTLE OF CORINTH.

BY WILLIAM S. ROSECRANS, MAJOR-GENERAL, U. S. V., BREVET MAJOR-GENERAL, U. S. A.
Commander of the Union army at the battle of Corinth.

NOTE.—The battle of Corinth, Miss., was fought on the 3d and 4th of October 1862, between the combined forces of Generals Earl Van Dorn and Sterling Price of the Confederacy, and the Union divisions of Generals David S. Stanley, Charles S. Hamilton, Thomas A. Davies, and Thomas J. McKean, under General W. S. Rosecrans, commander of the Third Division of the District of West Tennessee.
The conflict on the 3d resulted in the Union forces retiring and the Confederates advancing. General Rosecrans describes the struggle of the second day over the intrenchments around the town, as follows:

. . . As the troops had been on the move since the night of October 2d, and had fought all day of the 3d (which was so excessively hot that we were obliged to send water around in wagons), it became my duty to visit their lines and see that the weary troops were surely in position. I returned to my tent at three o'clock in the morning of October 5th, after having seen everything accomplished and the new line in order. It was about a mile in extent and close to the edge of the north side of the town. About 4 o'clock I lay down. At half-past 4 the enemy opened with a six-gun battery. Our batteries, replying, soon silenced it, but I had no time for breakfast. The troops got very little. They had not been allowed to build fires during the night, and were too tired to intrench.

The morning opened clear, and soon grew to be hot. It must have been ninety-four degrees in the shade. The enemy began to extend his infantry line across the north of the town. I visited the lines and gave orders to our skirmishers to fall back the moment it was seen that the enemy was developing a line of battle. About 8 o'clock his left, having crossed the Mobile and Ohio Railroad, got into position behind a spur of table-land, to reach which they had moved by the flank for about half a mile. When they began to advance in line of battle they were not over three hundred yards distant.

I told McKean on the left to be very watchful of his front lest the enemy should turn his left, and directed General Stanley to hold the reserve of his command ready either to help north of the town or to aid McKean if required. I visited Battery Robinett and directed the chief of artillery, Colonel Lothrop, to see to the reserve artillery, some batteries of which were parked in the public square of the town; then the line of Davies's division, which was in nearly open ground, with a few logs, here and there, for breastworks, and then on his extreme right Sweeny's brigade, which had no cover save a slight ridge, on the southwest slope of which, near the crest, the men were lying down. Riding along this line, I observed the Confederate forces emerging from the woods west of the railroad and crossing the open ground toward the Purdy road. Our troops lying on the ground could see the flags of the enemy and the glint of the sunlight on their bayonets. It was about 9 o'clock in the morning. The air was still and fiercely hot. . . .

The Confederates, from behind a spur of the Purdy ridge, advanced splendidly to the attack. The unfavorable line occupied by Davies's division made the resistance on that front inadequate. The troops gave way; the enemy pursued; but the cross-fire from the Union batteries on our right soon thinned their ranks. Their front line was broken, and the heads of their columns melted away. Some of the enemy's scattered line got into the edge of the town; a few into the reserve artillery, which led to the impression that they had captured forty pieces of artillery. But they were soon driven out by Stanley's reserve, and fled, taking nothing away.

At this time, while going to order Hamilton's division into action on the enemy's left, I saw the L-shaped porch of a large cottage packed full of Confederates. I ordered Lieutenant Lorenzo D. Immell, with two field-pieces, to give them grape and canister. After one round, only the dead and dying were left on the porch. Reaching Hamilton's division I ordered him to send Sullivan's brigade forward. It moved in line of battle in open

QUARTERS AT CORINTH OCCUPIED BY THE 52D ILLINOIS VOLUNTEERS DURING THE WINTER OF 1862-3.

THE DEFENSE OF BATTERY ROBINETT.
From a war-time sketch.

43D OHIO. 63D OHIO. 39TH OHIO.

GRAVE OF COLONEL WILLIAM P. ROGERS.
Looking toward Corinth from the embankment of Fort Robinett. (From a photograph taken in 1884).

ground a little to the left of Battery Powell. Before its splendid advance the scattered enemy, who were endeavoring to form a line of battle, about 1 P. M. gave way and went back into the woods, from which they never again advanced.

Meanwhile there had been terrific fighting at Battery Robinett. The roar of artillery and musketry for two or three hours was incessant. Clouds of smoke filled the air and obscured the sun. I witnessed the first charge of the enemy on this part of the line before I went over to Hamilton. The first repulse I did not see because the contestants were clouded in smoke. It was an assault in column. There were three or four assaulting columns of regiments, probably a hundred yards apart. The enemy's left-hand column had tried to make its way down into the low ground to the right of Robinett, but did not make much progress. The other two assaulting columns fared better, because they were on the ridge, where the fallen timber was scarcer. I ordered the 27th Ohio and 11th Missouri to kneel in rear of the right of Robinett, so as to get out of range of the enemy's fire, and the moment he had exhausted himself to charge with the bayonet. The third assault was made just as I was seeing Sullivan into the fight. I saw the enemy come upon the ridge while Battery Robinett was belching its fire at them. After the charge had failed I saw the 27th Ohio and the 11th Missouri chasing them with bayonets.

The head of the enemy's main column reached within a few feet of Battery Robinett, and Colonel Rogers, who was leading it, colors in hand, dis-

mounted, planted a flag-staff on the bank of the ditch, and fell there, shot by one of our drummer-boys, who, with a pistol, was helping to defend Robinett. I was told that Colonel Rogers was the fifth standard-bearer who had fallen in that last desperate charge. It was about as good fighting on the part of the Confederates as I ever saw. The columns were plowed through and through by

THE GROUND IN FRONT OF BATTERY ROBINETT.
From a photograph taken after the battle.

our shot, but they steadily closed up and moved forward until they were forced back.

Just after this last assault I heard for the first time the word "ranch." Passing over the field on our left, among the dead and dying, I saw leaning against the root of a tree a wounded lieutenant of an Arkansas regiment who had been shot through the foot. As I offered him some water, he said, "Thank you, General; one of your men just gave me some." I said, "Whose troops are you?" He replied, "Cabell's." I said, "It was pretty hot fighting here." He answered, "Yes, General, you licked us good, *but we gave you the best we had in the ranch*."

Before the enemy's first assault on Robinett, I inspected the woods toward our left where I knew Lovell's division to be. I said to Colonel Joseph A. Mower, afterward commander of the Sev-

enteenth Army Corps, and familiarly known as "Fighting Joe Mower," "Colonel, take the men now on the skirmish line, and find out what Lovell is doing." He replied, "Very well, General." As he was turning away I added, "Feel them, but don't get into their fingers." He answered significantly: "*I'll feel them!*" Before I left my position Mower had entered the woods, and soon I heard a tremendous crash of musketry in that direction. His skirmishers fell back into the fallen timber, and the adjutant reported to me: "General, I think the enemy have captured Colonel Mower; I think he is killed." Five hours later when we captured the enemy's field-hospitals, we found that Colonel Mower had been shot in the back of the neck and taken prisoner. Expressing my joy at his safety, he showed that he knew he had been unjustly reported to me the day before as intoxicated, by saying: "Yes, General, but if they had reported me for being 'shot in the neck' to-day instead of yesterday, it would have been correct."

About 2 o'clock we found that the enemy did not intend to make another attack. Faint from exhaustion I sought the shade of a tree, from which point I saw three bursts of smoke and said to my staff, "They have blown up some ammunition-wagons, and are going to retreat. We must push them." I was all the more certain of this, because, having failed, a good commander like Van Dorn would use the utmost despatch in putting the forests between him and his pursuing foe. . . .

I rode along the lines of the commands, told them that, having been moving and fighting for three days and two nights, I knew they required rest, but that they could not rest longer than was absolutely necessary. I directed them to proceed to their new camps, provide five days' rations, take some needed rest, and be ready early next morning for the pursuit.

General McPherson, sent from Jackson with five good regiments to help us, arrived and bivouacked in the public square a little before sunset. Our pursuit of the enemy was immediate and vigorous.

GENERAL BRAXTON BRAGG, C. S. A.

BRAGG'S ADVANCE AND RETREAT.

INCLUDING PERRYVILLE AND MURFREESBORO' — THE CONFEDERATE SIDE.

BY DAVID URQUHART, COLONEL C. S. A.
A member of Gen. Bragg's staff.

GENERAL BRAGG'S Kentucky campaign has drawn on him more criticism than any other part of his career as a military commander. During that memorable march I rode at his side from day to day, and it was his habit to confide to me his hopes and fears.

About the end of June, 1862, General Bragg was visited by many prominent citizens of Kentucky, who had abandoned their homes, and who assured him that Kentuckians were thoroughly loyal to the South, and that as soon as they were given an opportunity it would be proved. Fired with this idea, he planned his offensive campaign. On the 21st of July, 1862, the movement of the Army of Mississippi from Tupelo was ordered. The infantry moved by rail, the artillery and cavalry across the country. Headquarters were established at Chattanooga on the 29th. On the 30th Major-General Kirby Smith visited General Bragg at that point,

and it was arranged that Smith should move at once against the Federal forces under General George W. Morgan in Cumberland Gap. In this interview General Bragg was very certain that he would begin his forward move in ten or fifteen days at latest, and if Kirby Smith was successful in his operation against Morgan he would be on his offensive against Buell. Kirby Smith took the field on the 13th of August, 1862. On the 28th, after some inevitable delays, Bragg crossed the Tennessee, his right wing, under Polk, 13,537 strong; the left wing, under Hardee, 13,763 strong,—total effective, 27,320 rank and file.

General Bragg by this time was deeply impressed with the magnitude of his undertaking. He had lost faith somewhat in the stories that had been told him of Kentucky's desire to join the South, but he proposed to give the people a chance of so doing by the presence of Southern troops. At the same time he was resolved to do nothing to imperil the safety of his army, whose loss, he felt, would be a crushing blow to the Confederacy. He reached Carthage on the 9th of September. On the 12th he was at Glasgow, Kentucky, where he issued a proclamation to Kentuckians. About that time also the corps of Polk and Hardee were or-

UNION FORT AT MUNFORDVILLE, CAPTURED BY BRAGG, SEPTEMBER 17, 1862.

dered to unite. Buell was now moving on Bowling Green from the South. On the 16th our army surrounded and invested Munfordville, and General Wilder, with its garrison of four thousand men, was forced to capitulate. General Kirby Smith, having found Morgan's position impregnable, detached a part of his forces to invest it, and, advancing on Lexington, defeated the Federal forces encountered at Richmond, Ky. He was relying on an early junction with General Bragg.

On the 17th of September Generals Polk and Hardee were called to a council at Munfordville. With the map and the cavalry despatches outspread before him, General Bragg placed General Buell and his army in our rear, with Munfordville on the direct line of his march to Louisville, the assumed objective point of his movement, General Bragg then explaining his plan, which was discussed and approved by his lieutenants. Our advance was then resumed, leaving General Buell to pursue his march unmolested. This action was subsequently severely criticized by military men, and at the time it was greatly deplored by many officers of his command. At 1 o'clock on the morning of the 18th of September, indeed, Bragg was on the point of rescinding the order to continue the march, and of directing instead an immediate offensive movement against Buell. The importance of recovering Nashville induced the proposed change of operation. But, upon further consideration, he reverted to his previous plans, saying to me with emphasis, "This campaign must be won by marching, not by fighting." He used similar language at subsequent stages of the campaign before the battle of Perryville. At the moment he evinced no regret at having allowed Buell to pass on our left flank.

The success of the column under Kirby Smith in its combat at Richmond, Ky., elated him. He was worried by the delays that retarded his junction with that officer, and was greatly relieved when all the Confederate forces in Kentucky were united at Lexington. . . .

It was now the eve of the battle of Perryville,

and Kirby Smith, at Salvisa, twenty miles to the northeast, was calling for reinforcements, as he was confident that the feint was against Perryville, and that the main attack would surely fall on him. Thus urged, General Bragg, against his own judgment, yielded, and detached two of his best divisions (Withers's and Cheatham's) to Smith's aid. The former division could not be recalled in time, and the latter arrived the morning of the battle. Having placed General Polk in command of the troops, Bragg had gone to Frankfort, the capital of the State of Kentucky, to witness the inauguration of the secessionist governor, Hawes. The inaugural was being read when the booming of cannon, shortly followed by despatches from our cavalry outposts, announced the near presence of the enemy. As the hall was chiefly filled by the military, who hurried away to their respective commands, the governor was obliged to cut short his inaugural address.

The field of Perryville was an open and beautiful rolling country, and the battle presented a grand panorama. There was desperate fighting on both sides. I saw a Federal battery, with the Union flag planted near its guns, repulse six successive Confederate charges before retiring, saving all but one gun, and eliciting praise for their bravery from their desperate foes.

About dark, Polk, convinced that some Confederate troops were firing into each other, cantered up to the colonel of the regiment that was firing, and asked him angrily what he meant by shooting his own friends. The colonel, in a tone of surprise, said: "I don't think there can be any mistake about it. I am sure they are the enemy." "Enemy! Why, I have just left them myself. Cease firing, sir. What is your name?" rejoined the Confederate general. "I am Colonel —— of the —— Indiana. And pray, sir, who are you?" Thus made aware that he was with a Federal regiment, and that his only escape was to brazen it out, his dark blouse and the increasing obscurity happily befriending him, the Confederate general shook

ENGAGEMENT OF STARKWEATHER'S BRIGADE ON THE EXTREME UNION LEFT.

General J. C. Starkweather, in his official report, says that the brigade, consisting at the time of the 24th Illinois, 1st and 21st Wisconsin, and 79th Pennsylvania, "arrived on the field of battle at about 1:30 P. M., having marched twelve miles. . . Finding the troops already engaged well on the right, center, and left, and thinking the extreme left position most accessible, and, from appearances, one that should be held at all hazards, I placed my command at once in position facing the enemy's right." General McCook, in his report on the part taken by Starkweather's brigade, says that the 21st Wisconsin was stationed "in a corn-field, lying down, awaiting the approach of the enemy, and when he approached with his overwhelming force this new regiment poured into his ranks a most withering fire."

POSITION OF LOOMIS'S BATTERY ON ROUSSEAU'S LINE, LOOKING ACROSS DOCTOR'S CREEK.

Loomis's battery occupied the highest part of the ridge above H. P. Bottom's house, at about the center of Rousseau's line. Lytle's brigade extended from the battery across the old Mackville pike to the "burnt barn." Lytle's brigade was assailed from the direction of Bottom's house, and from the right flank. The attack upon the position held by Loomis's battery was made chiefly from the ridge in the middle distance of the picture on page 54. The Confederates gained the northeast side of that ridge by following down the dry bed of Doctor's Creek under the shelter of its west bank.

his fist in the Federal colonel's face, and promptly said: "I will show you who I am, sir. Cease firing at once!" Then, cantering down the line again, he shouted authoritatively to the men, "Cease firing!" Then, reaching the cover of a small copse, he spurred his horse and was soon back with his own corps, which he immediately ordered to open fire.

The battle of Perryville, a hard-fought fight against many odds, was merely a favorable incident which decided nothing. Our army, however, was elated and did not dream of a retreat, as we had held the field and bivouacked on it. But the commanding general, full of care, summoned his lieutenant-generals to a council in which both advised retreat.

The next day General Smith's army was called to Harrodsburg, where a junction of the two forces was effected, and where a position was selected to receive Buell's attack. This, however, not being made, Bragg was enabled to take measures for an immediate retrograde. Forrest was at once despatched by forced marches to take position at Murfreesboro', and prepare it for occupancy by the retreating Confederates.

The conduct of the retreat was intrusted to Polk. Our army fell back first to Camp Dick Robinson, whence the retreat began in earnest, a brigade of cavalry leading. . . .

About the 31st of October, 1862, General Bragg, having made a short visit to Richmond, there obtained the sanction of the Confederate Government for a movement into middle Tennessee. Returning to Knoxville, General Bragg made prep-

arations with the utmost rapidity for the advance to Murfreesboro', where General Breckinridge was already posted, and General Forrest was operating with a strong, active cavalry force. Our headquarters were advanced to Tullahoma on the 14th of November, and on the 26th to Murfreesboro'. Notwithstanding long marches and fighting, the condition of the troops was very good; and had they been well clad, the Confederate army would have presented a fine appearance.

On November 24th, 1862, the commands of Lieutenant-General Pemberton at Vicksburg, and that of General Bragg in Tennessee, were placed under General Joseph E. Johnston, and his official headquarters were established at Chattanooga. Immediately thereafter General Johnston visited Murfreesboro', where he passed some days devoted to a thorough inspection of the army. Our forces numbered somewhat over 40,000 men. General Johnston's visit was followed during the second week in December by that of President Davis and his aide, General Custis Lee. The President asked Bragg if he did not think he could spare a division of his army to reinforce Pemberton. Bragg assented and despatched a division of 8000 men under Stevenson. This step was contrary to the decided opinion previously expressed to Mr. Davis by General Johnston.

So well satisfied was General Bragg at having extricated his army from its perilous position in Kentucky, that he was not affected by the attacks upon him by the press for the failure of the campaign. He was cheerful, and would frequently join the staff about the camp-fire, and relate with

zest incidents of his services under General Taylor in Mexico. On the 26th General Wheeler, commanding the cavalry outposts, sent despatches in quick succession to headquarters reporting a general advance of Rosecrans's army. Soon all was bustle and activity. General Hardee's corps at Triune was ordered to Murfreesboro'. Camps at once broken up, and everything was made ready for active service. On the 27th of December our army was moving.

On Sunday, December 28th, Polk and Hardee met at General Bragg's headquarters to learn the situation and his plans. Rosecrans was advancing from Nashville with his whole army. Wheeler with his cavalry was so disposed at the moment as to protect the flanks, and, when pressed, to fall back toward the main army. Hardee's corps, consisting of the divisions of Breckinridge and Cleburne, with Jackson's brigade as a reserve, constituted our right wing, with its right resting on the Lebanon Pike and its left on the Nashville road. Polk's corps, composed of Withers's and Cheatham's divisions, was to take post with its right touching Hardee on the Nashville road, and its left resting on the Salem Pike; McCown's division was to form the reserve and to occupy our center. Such was the position of the Confederate army on the 29th of December.

On Tuesday, December 30th, Rosecrans was in our front, a mile and a half away. At 12 o'clock artillery on both sides was engaged. At 3 o'clock the Federal infantry advanced and attacked our lines, but were repulsed by the Louisiana and Alabama brigade, under Colonel Gibson, commanding in the absence of General Daniel Adams. But night

soon interposed, quiet prevailed, and the two armies bivouacked opposite to each other. General Bragg was on the field the entire day, but returned to his headquarters that evening at Murfreesboro'. He called his corps commanders together and informed them that his advices convinced him that Rosecrans, under cover of the day's attack, had been massing his troops for a move on our left flank. It was then agreed that Hardee should at once move to the extreme left Cleburne's division of his corps and the reserve (McCown), and that, next morning, Hardee should take command in that quarter and begin the fight.

At daylight on the 31st (Wednesday), Hardee, with Cleburne's and McCown's divisions, attacked McCook's corps of the Federal army. For a while the enemy were disorganized, many of the men being still engaged in cooking their breakfasts, but they very soon got under arms and in position, and resisted the attack with desperation. At this juncture Polk advanced with Withers's and Cheatham's divisions, and after hard fighting McCook's corps was driven back between three and four miles. Our attack had pivoted the Federals on their center, bending back their line, as one half-shuts a knife-blade. At 12 o'clock we had a large part of the field, with many prisoners, cannon, guns, ammunition, wagons, and the dead and wounded of both armies.

Between 2 and 3 o'clock, however, Rosecrans massed artillery on the favorable rising ground to which his line had been forced back. On this ground cedar-trees were so thick that his movements had not been perceived. Our line again advanced. Stewart's, Chalmers's, Donelson's, and

PERRYVILLE, KENTUCKY, LOOKING SOUTHEAST FROM THE MACKVILLE PIKE.

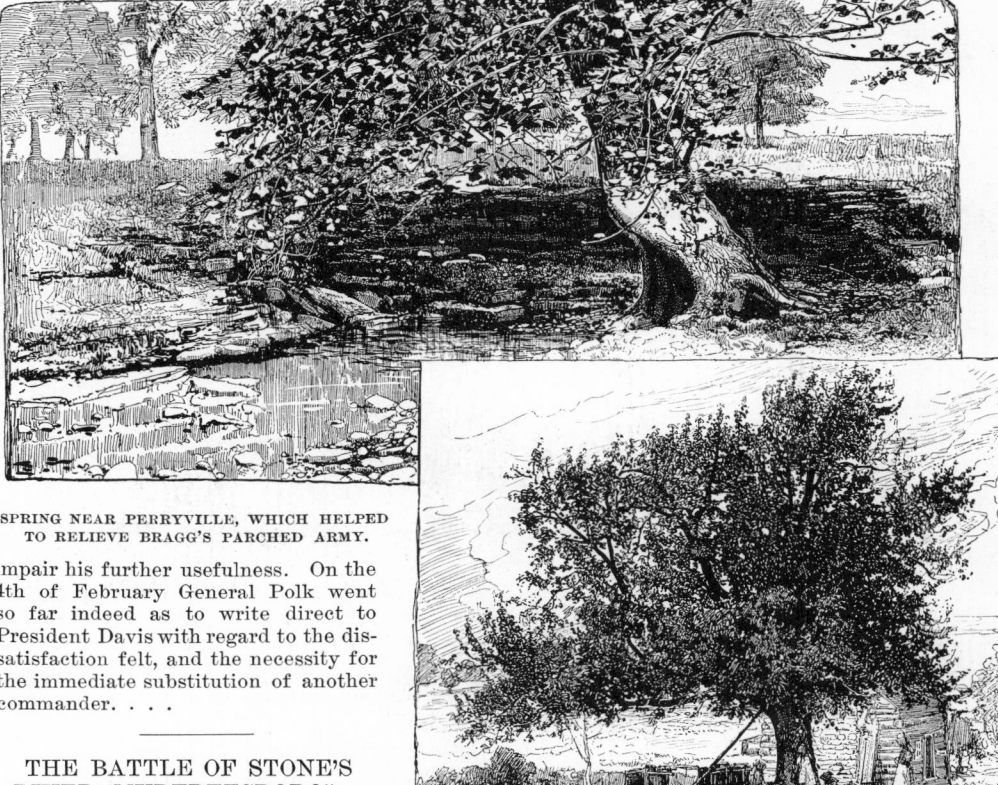

SPRING NEAR PERRYVILLE, WHICH HELPED TO RELIEVE BRAGG'S PARCHED ARMY.

PEAR-TREE, ONE HUNDRED YEARS OLD, AT THE LEFT OF ROUSSEAU'S POSITION, PERRYVILLE.

Maney's brigades, supported by Slocomb's, Cobb's, and Byrne's batteries, were hurled against the Federal line, but could not carry it. Reinforced by Gibson's and Jackson's brigades, another charge was ordered, but the position was not carried, and many were killed and wounded on our side.

A bitter cold night was now on us. We were masters of the field. The sheen of a bright moon revealed the sad carnage of the day, and the horrors of war became vividly distinct. That night General Bragg again made his headquarters at Murfreesboro', whence he gave orders for the care of the wounded. All the churches and public buildings were turned into hospitals. He announced to Richmond by telegraph: "God has granted us a happy New Year."

We had indeed routed the Federal right wing, but the bloody work was not over. During January 1st Rosecrans's army was intrenching itself, but General Bragg was of the opinion that their quiet meant a retreat.

During the morning of the 2d (Friday) quiet prevailed, except some shelling on our right. At about noon General Bragg determined to dislodge the force on his right. Orders were given to that end, and our best troops were carefully selected. Hanson's, Preston's, Gibson's, and Hunt's brigades, with Cobb's and Wright's batteries, were placed under Major-General Breckinridge. A gun fired by one of our batteries at 4 o'clock was the signal for the attack. After a fierce fight we carried the hill. The orders were to take its crest, and there remain intrenched. General Breckinridge endeavored to execute this order, but the commanders of the brigades engaged could not restrain the ardor of their men, who pushed on beyond support. The Federal batteries that had been massed on the other side of the stream now opened on them, and drove the Confederates back with terrible slaughter, fully 2000 of our men being killed and wounded in this attack. At 10 o'clock P. M. the news of this disastrous charge, led by the *élite* of the Confederate army, cast a gloom over all.

Saturday, January 3d, the two armies faced each other, with little fighting on either side.

The miscarriage of the 2d determined General Bragg to begin to fall back on Tullahoma; but all day of the 3d our forces maintained their line of battle taken up early that morning. That night the evacuation of Murfreesboro' was effected. General Rosecrans entered Murfreesboro' on Sunday, the 4th of January, 1863. Meantime his adversary was in full retreat on Tullahoma, thirty-six miles distant. By this time General Bragg's corps commanders, as well as their subordinates down to the regimental rank and file, scarcely concealed their want of confidence in him as the commander of the army. On the 11th of January he invited from his corps, division, and brigade commanders an expression of their opinion on that point, and their replies, while affirming their admiration for his personal courage, devotion to duty, and ability as an organizer, frankly confessed that his army had lost confidence to such an extent in his capacity for chief command as wholly to impair his further usefulness. On the 4th of February General Polk went so far indeed as to write direct to President Davis with regard to the dissatisfaction felt, and the necessity for the immediate substitution of another commander. . . .

THE BATTLE OF STONE'S RIVER (MURFREESBORO')— THE UNION SIDE.

BY G. C. KNIFFIN, LIEUT.-COLONEL, U. S. V.
A member of General Crittenden's staff.

ON the 26th of December, 1862, General W. S. Rosecrans, who on the 20th of October had succeeded General Buell in the command of the Army of the Cumberland, set out from Nashville with that army with the purpose of attacking the Confederate forces under General Braxton Bragg, then concentrated in the neighborhood of Murfreesboro', on Stone's River, Tenn.

The three corps into which the army was organized moved by the following routes: General Crittenden by the Murfreesboro' turnpike, arriving within two miles of Murfreesboro' on the night of the 29th; General Thomas's corps by the Franklin and Wilkinson turnpikes, thence by cross-roads to the Murfreesboro' pike, arriving a few hours later; and General McCook's corps, marching by the Nolensville pike to Triune, and bivouacking at Overall's Creek on the same night. . . .

Rosecrans reported his force actually engaged, December 31st, at 43,400, while Bragg placed his own force at 37,712. . . .

The plan of battle was as follows: General McCook was to occupy the most advantageous position, refusing his right as much as was practicable and necessary to secure it; to receive the attack of the enemy, or, if that did not come, to attack sufficiently to hold all the forces in his front. General Thomas and General Palmer were to open with skirmishing and engage the enemy's center and left as far as the river. Crittenden was to cross Van Cleve's division at the lower ford (covered and supported by Morton's Pioneers, 1700 strong), and to advance on Breckinridge. Wood's division was to cross by brigades at the upper ford, and, moving on Van Cleve's right, was to carry everything before it to Murfreesboro'. This move was

HOSPITAL KITCHEN.

GENERAL SAMUEL BEATTY'S BRIGADE (VAN CLEVE'S DIVISION) ADVANCING TO SUSTAIN
THE UNION RIGHT NEAR THE NASHVILLE PIKE.

POSITION OF MENDENHALL'S FIFTY-EIGHT GUNS (AS SEEN FROM THE EAST BANK ABOVE
THE FORD) WHICH REPELLED THE CHARGE OF BRECKINRIDGE, JANUARY 2, 1863.

intended to dislodge Breckinridge, and to gain the high ground east of Stone's River, so that Wood's batteries could enfilade the heavy body of troops massed in front of Negley and Palmer. The center and left, using Negley's right as a pivot, were to swing round through Murfreesboro' and take the force confronting McCook in rear, driving it into the country toward Salem. The successful execution of General Rosecrans's design depended not more upon the spirit and gallantry of the assaulting column than upon the courage and obstinacy with which the position held by the right wing should be maintained. Having explained this fact to General McCook, the commanding general asked him if, with a full knowledge of the ground, he could if attacked, hold his position three hours, — again alluding to his dissatisfaction with the direction which his line had assumed, but, as before, leaving that to the corps commander, — to which McCook replied, "I think I can."

Swift witnesses had borne to the ears of General Bragg the movements of General Rosecrans. He had in his army about the same proportion of raw troops to veterans as General Rosecrans, and the armies were equally well armed. By a singular coincidence Bragg had formed a plan identical with that of his antagonist. If both could have been carried out simultaneously the spectacle would have been presented of two large armies turning upon an axis from left to right. Lieutenant-General Hardee was put in command of the Confederate left wing, consisting of McCown's and Cleburne's divisions, and received orders to attack at daylight. Hardee's attack was to be taken up by Polk with the divisions of Cheatham and With-

ers, in succession to the right flank, the move to be made by a constant wheel to the right, on Polk's right flank as a pivot. The object of General Bragg was by an early and impetuous attack to force the Union army back upon Stone's River, and, if practicable, by the aid of the cavalry, cut it off from its base of operations and supplies by the Nashville pike.

As has been shown, the Union and Confederate lines were much nearer together on the Union right than on the left. In point of fact the distance to be marched by Van Cleve to strike Breckinridge on Bragg's right, crossing Stone's River by the lower ford, was a mile and a half. To carry out the order of General Bragg to charge upon Rosecrans's right, the Confederate left wing, doubled, with McCown in the first line and Cleburne in support, had only to follow at double-quick the advance of the skirmish line a few hundred paces, to find themselves in close conflict with McCook.

The Confederate movement began at daybreak. General Hardee moved his two divisions with the precision that characterized that able commander. McCown, deflecting to the west, as he advanced to the attack, left an opening between his right and Withers's left, into which Cleburne's division fell, and together the two divisions charged upon R. W. Johnson and Davis, while yet the men of those divisions were preparing breakfast. There was no surprise. The first movement in their front was observed by the Union skirmish line, but that first movement was a rush as of a tornado. The skirmishers fell back steadily, fighting, upon the main line, but the main line was overborne by the fury

of the assault. Far to the right, overlapping R. W. Johnson, the Confederate line came sweeping on like the resistless tide, driving artillerists from their guns and infantry from their encampments. Slowly the extreme right fell back, at first contesting every inch of ground. In Kirk's brigade 500 men were killed or wounded in a few minutes. Willich lost nearly as many. Goodspee's battery, on Willich's right, lost three guns. The swing of Bragg's left flank toward the right brought McCown's brigades upon the right of Davis's division. Leaving the detachments in R. W. Johnson's division to the attention of two of his brigades and Wheeler's cavalry, McCown turned McNair to the right, where Cleburne was already heavily engaged. Driving Davis's skirmishers before him, Cleburne advanced with difficulty in line of battle, bearing to the right over rough ground cut up with numerous fences and thickets, and came upon the main line at a distance of three-fourths of a mile from his place of bivouac. It was not yet daylight when he began his march, and he struck the Union line at six o'clock. General Davis now changed the front of Colonel Post's brigade nearly perpendicular to the rear.   .   .   .

In front of Post, the Confederates under McCown, in command of McNair's brigade of his own division, and Liddell of Cleburne's division, received a decided repulse; and Cleburne was for a time equally unsuccessful in pushing back the main Union line.

Three successive assaults were made upon this position. In the second, Vaughan's and Maney's brigades of Cheatham's division relieved Loomis's and Manigault's. In the third attack Post's bri-

gade was enveloped by Hardee's left, which, sweeping toward his rear, made withdrawal a necessity. Sill had been killed in the first assault. Schaefer's Union brigade was brought forward to the support of the front line. The dying order from General Sill to charge was gallantly obeyed, and Loomis was driven back to his first position. Manigault advanced at about 8 o'clock, and attacked directly in his front, but, meeting with the same reception, was compelled to retire. A second attack resulted like the first.

Rosecrans, having arranged his plan of battle, had risen early to superintend its execution. Crittenden, whose headquarters were a few paces distant, mounted at 6 A. M., and with his staff rode to an eminence, where Rosecrans, surrounded by his staff-officers, was listening to the opening guns on the right. The plan of Bragg was instantly divined, but no apprehension of danger was felt. Suddenly the woods on the right in the rear of Negley appeared to be alive with men wandering aimlessly in the direction of the rear. The roar of artillery grew more distinct, mingled with the continuous volleys of musketry. The rear of a line of battle always presents the pitiable spectacle of a horde of skulkers, men who, when tried in the fierce flame of battle, find, often to their own disgust, that they are lacking in the element of courage. But the spectacle of whole regiments of soldiers flying to the rear was a sight never seen by the Army of the Cumberland except on that occasion. Captain Otis, from his position on the extreme right, despatched a messenger, who arrived breathless, to inform General Rosecrans that the right wing was in rapid retreat. The as-

SCENE OF THE FIGHTING OF PALMER'S AND ROUSSEAU'S DIVISIONS.

In the distance between the railroad on the left and the pike in the center was the first position of Hazen's brigade of Palmer's division on Dec. 31. In the cedars on the right Neg-ley's division and the regulars of Rousseau's division were roughly handled. In the foreground are seen the batteries of Loomis and Guenther.

ADVANCE OF COLONEL M. B. WALKER'S UNION BRIGADE, AT STONE'S RIVER, ON THE EVENING OF JANUARY 2, 1863.

Walker's position is in the cedars near the right of Rousseau's line. In the right of the picture is seen the 4th Michigan Battery. The front line was composed of the 31st and 17th Ohio, and the second line of the 82d Indiana and 38th Ohio.

tounding intelligence was confirmed a moment later by a staff-officer from McCook, calling for reinforcements. "Tell General McCook," said Rosecrans, "to contest every inch of ground. If he holds them we will swing into Murfreesboro' and cut them off." Then Rousseau, with his reserves, was sent into the fight, and Van Cleve, who, in the execution of the initial movement on the left, had crossed Stone's River at 6 A. M. at the lower ford, and was marching in close column up the hill beyond the river (preparatory to forming a line of battle for a movement to the right, where Wood was to join him in an assault upon Breckinridge), was arrested by an order to return and take position on the turnpike facing toward the woods on the right. A few moments later this gallant division came dashing across the fields, with water dripping from their clothing, to take a hand in the fray. Harker's brigade was withdrawn from the left and sent in on Rousseau's right, and Morton's Pioneers, relieved at the ford by Price's brigade, were posted on Harker's right. The remaining brigades of Van Cleve's division (Beatty's and Fyffe's) formed on the extreme right, and thus an improvised line half a mile in extent presented a new and unexpected front to the approaching enemy. It was a trying position to these men to stand in line while the panic-stricken soldiers of McCook's beaten regiments, flying in terror through the woods, rushed past them. The Union lines could not fire, for their comrades were between them and the enemy. Rosecrans seemed ubiquitous. All these dispositions had been made under his personal supervision. While riding rapidly to the front, Colonel Garesché, his chief-of-staff, was killed at his side by a cannon-ball. Finding Sheridan coming out of the cedars into which Rousseau had just entered, Rosecrans directed Sheridan to the ammunition train, with orders to fill his cartridge-boxes and march to the support of Hazen's brigade, now hotly engaged on the edge of the Round Forest. The left was now exposed to attack by Breckinridge, and riding rapidly to the ford, Rosecrans inquired who commanded the brigade. "I do, sir," said Colonel Price. "Will you hold this ford?" "I will try, sir." "Will you hold this ford?" "I will die right here." "Will you hold this ford?" for the third time thundered the general. "Yes, sir," said the colonel. "That will do"; and away galloped Rosecrans to Palmer, who was contending against long odds for the possession of Round Forest. . . .

[The Confederate attack of December 31 was finally repulsed at the last position taken by the Union forces south and west of the cemetery. The decisive combat took place January 2 on the east bank of the river.]

General Bragg confidently expected to find the Union troops gone from his front on the morning of the 2d. His cavalry had reported the turnpike full of troops and wagons moving toward Nashville, but the force east of Stone's River soon attracted his attention. Reconnoissance by staff-officers revealed Beatty's line, enfilading Polk in his new position. It was evident that Polk must be withdrawn or Beatty dislodged. Bragg chose the latter alternative, and Breckinridge, against his earnest protest, was directed to concentrate his division and assault Beatty. Ten Napoleon guns were added to his command, and the cavalry was ordered to cover his right. The line was formed by placing Hanson's brigade of Kentuckians, who had thus far borne no part in the engagement, on the extreme left, supported by Adams's brigade, now commanded by Colonel Gibson. The Confederate Palmer's brigade, commanded by General Pillow, took the right of the line, with Preston in reserve. The artillery was ordered to follow the attack and go into position on the summit of the slope when Beatty should be driven from it. The total strength of the assaulting column was estimated by Bragg at six thousand men. His cavalry took no part in the action.

In the assault that followed a brief cannonade Hanson's left was thrown forward close to the river bank, with orders to fire once, then charge with the bayonet. On the right of Beatty was Colonel S. W. Price's brigade, and the charge made by Hanson's 6th Kentucky was met by Price's 8th Kentucky regiment, followed by Hanson and Pillow in successive strokes from right to left of Beatty's line. Overborne by numerical strength, the Union brigades of Price and Fyffe were forced back upon Grider, in reserve, the right of whose brigade was rapidly being turned by Hanson, threatening to cut the division off from the river. Beatty ordered retreat, and assailants and assailed moved in a mass toward the river. The space between the river bank and the ridge occupied by Grose now presented a scene of the wildest confusion. The pursuit led the Confederate column to the right of Grose, and Lieutenant Livingston opened upon it with his artillery, but he was quickly ordered across the river. Crittenden, turning to his chief-of-artillery, said, "Mendenhall, you must cover my men with your guns." Never was there a more effective response to such a request; the batteries of Swallow, Parsons, Estep, Stokes, Stevens, Standart, Bradley, and Livingston dashed forward, wheeled into position, and opened fire. In all, fifty-eight pieces of artillery played upon the enemy. Not less than one hundred shots per minute were fired. As the mass of men swarmed down the slope they were mowed down by the score. Confederates were pinioned to the earth by falling branches. For a few minutes the brave fellows held their ground, hoping to advance, but the west bank bristled with bayonets.

Hanson was mortally wounded, and his brigade lost over 400 men; the loss in the division was 1410. There was no thought now of attacking Grose, but one general impulse to get out of the jaws of death. The Union infantry was soon ordered to charge. Colonel John F. Miller with his brigade and two regiments of Stanley's was the first to cross the river, on the extreme left. He was quickly followed on the right by Davis and Morton, and by Hazen in the center. Beatty quickly re-formed his division and recrossed the river and joined in the pursuit. The artillery ceased firing, and the Union line with loud cheers dashed forward, firing volley after volley upon the fugitives, who rallied behind Robertson's battery and Anderson's brigade in the narrow skirt of timber from which they had emerged to the assault. The Union line advanced and took possession of the ground from which Beatty had been driven an hour before, and both armies bivouacked upon the battlefield. . . .

THE UNION LEFT AT STONE'S RIVER.

BY THOMAS L. CRITTENDEN, MAJOR-GEN., U. S. V.
Commanding the left wing at Stone's River.

THE battle of Stone's River, Tennessee, on the 31st of December, 1862, and the 2d of January, 1863, was one of the most fiercely contested and bloody conflicts of the war. The two armies that met in this conflict were made up of soldiers who, for the most part, had been disciplined by capable instructors and hardened by service in the field, both having made many long marches, and neither having been strangers to the perils of the battle-field. Moreover, these armies were ably commanded by graduates of the Military Academy at West Point — a military school, I think, not surpassed, if equaled, anywhere else. The duration of the battle, and the long list of the killed and wounded, show the stuff of which the two armies were composed. I do not think that two better armies, as numerous and so nearly matched in strength, ever met in battle.

I had the good fortune to command the left wing of our army and, thanks to the skill and bravery of the officers and men of my command, the enemy were not able to drive them from our first line of battle. On the 31st of December my extreme left was strongly posted, but my right was in an open field back from the stream. Still it was a fairly strong position by reason of the railroad and the

MAJOR-GENERAL B. F. CHEATHAM, C. S. A.

POSITION OF STARKWEATHER'S AND SCRIBNER'S BRIGADES ON JANUARY 1, 2, AND 3.

E. KIRBY SMITH,
LIEUTENANT-GENERAL, C. S. A.

railroad cut and the woods. Thomas's position in the center was not so strong as mine; of McCook's, on our right, I knew nothing; that it was less strong than ours, I presume from the fact that in spite of the most stubborn resistance McCook was driven back two miles or more, the whole right of the army hinging on its center, while the left held its ground. Thomas, with Rousseau's division, including a brigade of regulars (Lieutenant-Colonel O. L. Shepherd's), undertook to support McCook, but they were all driven along. Every time the right was driven in I thought (and I now think) that nothing but a most extraordinary blunder on the part of a soldier of the experience of Bragg hindered him from breaking Rosecrans's army in two and leaving me standing with my troops looking at Murfreesboro'. It is a pretty well-established maxim in military tactics that you should always press your advantage. Bragg had the advantage; all that he had to do (it seems to me) was to pursue it and leave me alone with my success. Instead of that, he attempted to drive the left; but he could not drive us; and meanwhile our right was reorganized. I did not know on the 31st when they would come right upon our rear. I was facing Murfreesboro'. My right division under Palmer changed its place somewhat, to conform to our movements on the right, but that line was maintained by stubborn fighting. Thomas was then not far back, and that helped me more. (McCook was too far away for any protection to my flank.) Rousseau's men were driven out of the woods, a regular dense thicket, and Shepherd's regulars suffered fearfully in there. They moved in by the head of column. There was no fighting of consequence on the 1st of January.

The last attack made by the enemy was upon my extreme left, on the 2d of January, and it was disastrous to them. Van Cleve's division, under Colonel Samuel Beatty, had crossed the river on the 1st, and Grose and Hazen had followed with their brigades on the 2d. The fight opened on Colonel Beatty's line and lasted about twenty minutes. Before this battle I had been inclined to underrate the importance of artillery in our war, but I never

knew that arm to render such important service as at this point. The sound judgment, bravery, and skill of Major John Mendenhall, who was my chief-of-artillery, enabled me to open 58 guns almost simultaneously on Breckinridge's men, and to turn a dashing charge into a sudden retreat and rout, in which the enemy lost 1700 or 1800 men in a few moments. I witnessed the effect of this cannonade upon the Confederate advance. Mendenhall's guns were about 100 yards back from the river. Van Cleve's division of my command was retiring down the opposite slope, before overwhelming numbers of the enemy, when the guns, the fire of which had been held till our men should no longer be exposed to it, opened upon the swarming enemy. The very forest seemed to fall before our fire, and not a Confederate reached the river. Mendenhall did not receive adequate recognition in the report of General Rosecrans.

As to our general's plan of battle, I don't remember that I was ever advised of it. The battle was fought according to the plan of General Bragg. Indeed, our uniform experience was — at Perryville, at Stone's River, at Chickamauga — that whenever we went to attack Bragg we were attacked by him, and so our plan had to be extemporized. I knew Bragg. His reputation was that of a martinet. He was a severe disciplinarian, a good soldier, and a hard fighter.

During the fight I had the experience of eating a horse-steak, the only one I ever tasted; it was simply because although we had supplies there we could n't get at them. I had to go to sleep without my wagon, and as I said something about being hungry, one of the men said: "General, I will get you a first-rate beefsteak." Next morning I found that the steak had been cut from a horse that

had been killed. I did n't know this at the time I ate it.

On the night of the 31st a wagon-train arrived from Nashville escorted by a thousand men, and these men, I learned, were sent back. I won't say whom they were under, but I know I felt and thought it was unwise that a thousand men who had n't been in the fight at all should be sent away. All the wagons in the world would n't have made me send back a thousand fresh men. They could have stayed there and eaten horse for a while until they had won the fight.

I regard Rosecrans as of the first order of military mind. He was both brave and generous, impulsively so; in fact, in his impulsiveness lay a military defect, which was to issue too many orders while his men were fighting. When I met him on the field on the 31st I saw the stains of blood on his breast, and exclaimed: "Are you wounded, General?" "Oh, no," said he, "that is the blood of poor Garesché, who has just been killed."

After the fight on the night of the 31st a number of general officers were assembled by Rosecrans's order, including McCook, Thomas, Stanley, and myself. There was some talk of falling back. I do not remember who started the subject, but I do remember that I expressed the opinion that my men would be very much discouraged to have to abandon the field after their good fight of the day, during which they had uniformly held their position. I spoke of the proposition as resembling the suggestion of General Wool to General Taylor at Buena Vista, when Taylor responded: "My wounded are behind me, and I will never pass them alive." Rosecrans called McCook to accompany him on a ride, directing us to remain until their return. McCook has since told me that the

purpose of this ride was to find a position beyond Overall's Creek to which the army might retire. Upon approaching the creek Rosecrans, perceiving mounted men moving up and down with torches, said to McCook: "They have got entirely in our rear and are forming a line of battle by torchlight." They returned then to where we were, and Rosecrans told us to go to our commands and prepare to fight or die. The explanation of the torches is that the men were making fires, and the torches were firing-brands being carried from one point to another by cavalrymen. I had received an order from General Rosecrans not to allow the men to make fires; but upon looking out of my quarters I discovered that the fires were already made from one end of my line to the other. I sent Rosecrans word that as the men were cold and were not being disturbed by the enemy, and as it would take all night to put out the fires, we had better leave them. The men would have suffered very much if they had stayed there all night without fire.

The battle was fought for the possession of middle Tennessee. We went down to drive the Confederates out of Murfreesboro', and we drove them out. They went off a few miles and camped again. And we, although we were the victors, virtually went into hospital for six months before we could march after them again. Whether we would take Murfreesboro' or go back to Nashville was doubtful until the last moment. As in most of our battles, our meager fruits resulted to either side from such partial victories as were for the most part won. Yet it was a triumph. It showed that in the long run the big purse and the big battalions — both on our side — must win; and it proved that there were no better soldiers than ours.

The results of the battle were not what we had hoped, and yet there was a general feeling of elation. One day, after we had gone into Murfreesboro', I accompanied General Rosecrans in a ride about our camp. We had come across some regiment or brigade that was being drilled, and they raised a shout, and as he rode along he took off his cap and said: "All right, boys, all right; Bragg 's a good dog, but Hold Fast 's a better." This well expressed my feeling as to the kind of victory we had won.

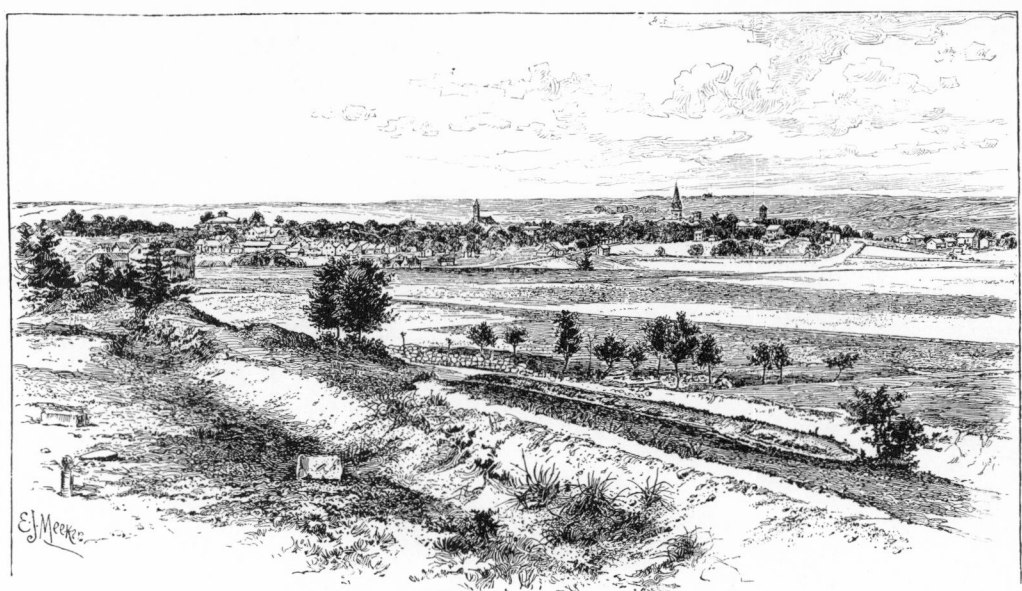

FREDERICKSBURG FROM THE FOOT OF WILLIS'S HILL.
From a war-time photograph.

In the middle-ground is seen the south end of the stone wall, and it may be seen that the front line of defense formed by the wall was continued still farther to the right by the sunken Telegraph road. At the base of the hill, this side of the stone wall, is seen an earth work which was a part of the second line. A third line was on the brow of this hill, now the National Cemetery. Between the steeples on the outskirts of Fredericksburg is seen the end of Hanover street, by which, and by the street in the right of the picture, the Union forces filed out to form for the assault.

In command of the Union forces at Fredericksburg.

THE BATTLE OF FREDERICKSBURG.

THE UNION SIDE—THE STORMING OF MARYE'S HEIGHTS.

BY DARIUS N. COUCH, MAJOR-GENERAL, U. S. V.
Commander of the Second Corps at the battle of Fredericksburg.

ON the evening of October 15th, 1862, a few days after McClellan had placed me in command of the Second Corps, then at Harper's Ferry, the commanding general sent an order for Hancock to take his division the next morning on a reconnoissance toward Charlestown, about ten miles distant. The division started in good season, as directed. About 10 in the morning General McClellan reined up at my headquarters, and asked me to go out with him to see what the troops were doing. Our people had met the enemy's outpost five miles from the Ferry, and, while artillery shots were being exchanged, both of us dismounted, walked away by ourselves, and took seats on a ledge of rocks. After a little while McClellan sent to an aide for a map of Virginia. Spreading it before us, he pointed to the strategic features of the valley of Shenandoah, and indicated the movements he intended to make, which would have the effect of compelling Lee to concentrate in the vicinity, I think, of Gordonsville or Charlottesville, where a great battle would be fought. Continuing the conversation, he said, "But I may not have command of the army much longer. Lincoln is down on me," and, taking a paper from his pocket, he gave me my first intimation of the President's famous letter. He read it aloud very carefully, and when it was finished I told him I thought there was no ill-feeling in the tone of it. He

thought there was, and quickly added, "Yes, Couch, I expect to be relieved from the Army of the Potomac, and to have a command in the West; and I am going to take three or four with me," calling off by their names four prominent officers. I queried if "so and so" would be taken along, naming one who was generally thought to be a great favorite with McClellan. His curt reply was, "No, I sha'n't have him."

This brief conversation opened a new world for me. I had never before been to any extent his confidant, and I pondered whether on a change of the commanders of the Army of the Potomac the War Department would allow him to choose the generals whose names had been mentioned. I wondered what would be the future of himself and those who followed his fortunes in that untried field. These and a crowd of other kindred thoughts quite oppressed me for several days. But as the time wore on, and preparations for the invasion of Virginia were allowed to go on without let or hindrance from Washington, I naturally and gladly inferred that McClellan's fears of hostile working against him were groundless. However, the blow came, and soon enough.

On the 8th of November, just at dark, I had dismounted, and, standing in the snow, was superintending the camp arrangements of my troops, when McClellan came up with his staff, accompanied by

General Burnside. McClellan drew in his horse, and the first thing he said was:

"Couch, I am relieved from the command of the army, and Burnside is my successor."

I stepped up to him and took hold of his hand, and said, "General McClellan, I am sorry for it." Then, going around the head of his horse to Burnside, I said, "General Burnside, I congratulate you."

Burnside heard what I said to General McClellan; he turned away his head, and made a broad gesture as he exclaimed:

"Couch, don't say a word about it."

His manner indicated that he did not wish to talk about the change; that he thought it was not good policy to do so, nor the place to do it. He told me afterward that he did not like to take the command, but that he did so to keep it from going to somebody manifestly unfit for it. I assumed that he meant Hooker. Those of us who were well acquainted with Burnside knew that he was a

brave, loyal man, but we did not think that he had the military ability to command the Army of the Potomac.

McClellan took leave on the 10th. Fitz-John Porter sent notes to the corps commanders, informing them that McClellan was going away, and suggesting that we ride about with him. Such a scene as that leave-taking had never been known in our army. Men shed tears, and there was great excitement among the troops.

I think the soldiers had an idea that McClellan would take care of them — would not put them in places where they would be unnecessarily cut up; and if a general has the confidence of his men he is pretty strong. But officers and men were determined to serve Burnside loyally.

A day or two afterward Burnside called the corps commanders together, mapped out a course that he intended to pursue, and among other things he said that he intended to double the army corps and he proposed to call the three new commands

—or doubles—"grand divisions." Under this arrangement my corps, the Second, and Willcox's, the Ninth, which had been Burnside's, formed the Right Grand Division under General Sumner. When Sumner and I arrived near Falmouth, opposite Fredericksburg, November 17th, we found the enemy in small force in readiness to oppose our crossing the Rappahannock. Everybody knew that Lee would rush right in; we could see it. If the pontoons had been there, we might have crossed at once. Yet we lay there nearly a month, while they were fortifying before our eyes; besides, the weather was against us. Under date of December 7th, my diary contains this entry, "Very cold; plenty of snow. Men suffering; cold outdoors, ice indoors in my room."

Sumner's headquarters were at the Lacy House, while the Second Corps lay back of the brow of the hill behind Falmouth.

On the night of the 9th, two nights before the crossing, Sumner called a council to discuss what we were to do, the corps, division, and brigade commanders being present. The result was a plain, free talk all around, in which words were not minced, for the conversation soon drifted into a marked disapprobation of the manner in which Burnside contemplated meeting the enemy.

Sumner seemed to feel badly that the officers did not agree to Burnside's mode of advance. That noble old hero was so faithful and loyal that he wanted, even against impossibilities, to carry out everything Burnside suggested. I should doubt if his judgment concurred. It was only chivalrous attachment to Burnside, or to any commander. But there were not two opinions among the subordinate officers as to the rashness of the undertaking.

Somebody told Burnside of our views, and he was irritated. He asked us to meet him the next night at the Lacy House. He said he understood, in a general way, that we were opposed to his plans. He seemed to be rather severe on Hancock—to my surprise, for I did not think that officer had said as much as myself in opposition to the plan of attack. Burnside stated that he had formed his plans, and all he wanted was the devotion of his men. Hancock made a reply in which he dis-

claimed any personal discourtesy, and said he knew there was a line of fortified heights on the opposite side, and that it would be pretty difficult for us to go over there and take them. I rose after him, knowing that I was the more guilty, and expressed a desire to serve Burnside, saying, among other things, that if I had ever done anything in any battle, in this one I intended to do twice as much. French came in while I was talking. He was rather late, and in his bluff way exclaimed: "Is this a Methodist campmeeting?"

The heights on the morning of the 11th, before the bridges were thrown across, did not offer a very ani-

mated scene, because the troops were mostly hidden. The bombardment for the purpose of dislodging the sharpshooters, who under cover of the houses were delaying the bridge-making, was terrific, while the smoke settled down and veiled the scene. After the bombardment had failed to dislodge the enemy, the 7th Michigan and the 19th and the 20th Massachusetts of Howard's division sprang into the pontoons, and rowing themselves over drove away Barksdale's sharpshooters. This gallant action enabled the engineers to complete the bridges. Howard's division was the first to cross by the upper bridge, his

advance having a lively fight in the streets of Fredericksburg. Hawkins's brigade of Willcox's corps occupied the lower part of the town on the same evening, and the town was not secured without desperate fighting. I went over the next morning, Friday, the 12th, with Hancock's and French's divisions. The remainder of Willcox's corps crossed and occupied the lower part of the town. There was considerable looting. I placed a provost-guard at the bridges, with orders that nobody should go back with plunder. An enormous pile of booty was collected there by evening. But there came a time when we were too busy to guard it, and I suppose it was finally carried off by another set of spoilers. The troops of the two corps bivouacked that night in the streets and were not permitted to make fires. Late on that day we had orders to be ready to cross Hazel Run, which meant that we were to join Franklin. That was the only proper move to make, since we had done just what the enemy wanted us to do

—had divided our army. The conditions were favorable for a change of position unknown to the enemy, since the night was dark and the next morning was foggy. But it would have been very difficult to make the movement. I was much worried in regard to building the necessary bridges over Hazel Run, and the dangers attending a flank movement at night in the presence of the enemy. But the order to march never came. The orders that were given by Burnside showed that he had no fixed plan of battle. After getting in the face of the enemy, his intentions seemed to be continually changing.

Early the next morning, Saturday, the 13th, I received orders to make an assault in front. My instructions came from General Sumner, who did not cross the river during the fight, owing to a special understanding with which I had nothing to do, and which related to his supposed rashness. At Fair Oaks, Antietam, and on other battle-fields, he had shown that he was a hard fighter. He was a grand soldier, full of honor and gallantry, and a man of great determination.

As I have said, on that Saturday morning we were enveloped in a heavy fog. . . . French was at once directed to prepare his division in three

THE BOMBARDMENT OF FREDERICKSBURG, DECEMBER 11, 1862.

THE PHILLIPS HOUSE, BURNSIDE'S HEADQUARTERS.
From a photograph taken while the house was burning.

HOT WORK FOR HAZARD'S BATTERY.

THE NINTH CORPS CROSSING BY THE PONTOON-BRIDGE TO THE STEAMBOAT LANDING AT THE LOWER END OF THE TOWN.

brigade lines for the advance, and Hancock was to follow with his division in the same order. The distance between the brigade lines was to be about 200 yards.

Toward 10 o'clock the fog began to lift; French reported that he was ready, I signaled to Sumner, and about 11 o'clock the movement was ordered to begin. French threw out a strong body of skirmishers, and his brigades filed out of town as rapidly as possible by two parallel streets, the one on the right, which was Hanover street, running into the Telegraph road, and both leading direct to Marye's Hill, the stronghold of the enemy. On the outskirts of the town the troops encountered a ditch, or canal, so deep as to be almost impassable except at the street bridges, and, one of the latter being partly torn up, the troops had to cross single file on the stringers. Once across the canal, the attacking forces deployed under the bank bordering the plain over which they were to charge. This plain was obstructed here and there by houses and fences, notably at a fork of the Telegraph road, in the narrow angles of which was a cluster of houses and gardens; and also on the parallel road just south of it, where stood a large square brick house. This cluster of houses and the brick house were the rallying-points for parts of our disordered lines of attack. The fork in the road and the brick house were less than 150 yards from the stone-wall, which covered also as much more of the plain to the left of the brick house. A little in advance of the brick house a slight rise in the ground afforded protection to men lying down against the musketry behind the stone-wall, but not against the converging fire of the artillery on the heights. My headquarters were in the field on the edge of the town, overlooking the plain.

A few minutes after noon French's division charged in the order of Kimball's, Andrews's, and Palmer's brigades, a part of Kimball's men getting into the cluster of houses in the fork of the road. Hancock followed them in the order of Zook's, Meagher's, and Caldwell's brigades, the two former getting nearer to the stone-wall than any who had

gone before, except a few of Kimball's men, and nearer than any brigade which followed them.

Without a clear idea of the state of affairs at the front, since the smoke and light fog veiled everything, I sent word to French and Hancock to carry the enemy's works by storm. Then I climbed the steeple of the court-house, and from above the haze and smoke got a clear view of the field. Howard, who was with me, says I exclaimed, "Oh, great God! see how our men, our poor fellows, are falling!" I remember that the whole plain was covered with men, prostrate and dropping, the live men running here and there, and in front closing upon each other, and the wounded coming back. The commands seemed to be mixed up. I had never before seen fighting like that, nothing approaching it in terrible uproar and destruction. There was no cheering on the part of the men, but a stubborn determination to obey orders and do their duty. I don't think there was much feeling of success. As they charged, the artillery fire would break their formation and they would get mixed; then they would close up, go forward, receive the withering

infantry fire, and those who were able would run to the houses and fight as best they could; and then the next brigade coming up in succession would do its duty and melt like snow coming down on warm ground.

I was in the steeple hardly ten seconds, for I saw at a glance how they were being cut down, and was convinced that we could not be successful in front, and that our only chance lay by the right. I immediately ordered Howard to work in on the right with the brigades of Owen and Hall, and attack the enemy behind the stone wall in flank, which was done. Before he could begin this movement both Hancock and French had notified me that they must have support or they would not be responsible for the maintenance of their position. Sturgis, of Willcox's corps, who had been supporting my left, sent the brigades of Ferrero and Nagle to the fruitless charge.

About two o'clock General Hooker, who was in command of the Center Grand Division (Stoneman's and Butterfield's corps) came upon the field. At an earlier hour Whipple's division of Stoneman's corps had crossed the river and relieved Howard on the right, so that the latter might join in the attack in the center, and Griffin's division of Butterfield's corps had come over to the support of Sturgis. Humphreys and Sykes, of the latter corps, came to my support. Toward 3 o'clock I received the following despatch:

"HEADQUARTERS, RIGHT GRAND DIVISION, ARMY OF THE POTOMAC, Dec. 13th, 1862.—2:40 P. M. GENERAL COUCH: Hooker has been ordered to put in everything. You must hold on until he comes in. By command of Brevet Major-General SUMNER, W. G. JONES, Lieut., Aide-de-camp, etc."

Hooker was the ranking general, and as I understood he was to take command of the whole fighting line, the putting in of his fresh men beside mine might make a success. His very coming was to me, therefore, like the breaking out of the sun in a storm. I rode back to meet him, told him what had been done, and said, "I can't carry that hill by a front assault; the only chance we have is to try to get in on the right." Hooker replied, "I will talk with Hancock." He talked with Hancock,

THE GROUND BETWEEN FREDERICKSBURG AND MARYE'S HEIGHTS.
From a war-time photograph.

CONFEDERATE WORKS ON WILLIS'S HILL, NOW THE SITE OF THE NATIONAL CEMETERY.
From a war-time photograph.

FRANKLIN'S BATTLE-FIELD AS SEEN FROM HAMILTON'S CROSSING.
Fredericksburg steeples in the distance. (From a sketch made in 1884.)

and after a few minutes said, "Well, Couch, things are in such a state I must go over and tell Burnside it is no use trying to carry this line here,"—or words to that effect,—and then he went off. His going away left me again in command. Burnside was nearly two miles distant. It was not much after 2 o'clock when he went away, and it was about 4 when he returned. This was after Humphreys had made his charge and the fighting for the day was substantially finished. We were holding our lines.

Hooker left word that Humphreys, whose division was ready to advance, should take his cue from me. Butterfield also gave Humphreys orders to that effect. After a lull in the battle General Caldwell, a brigade commander under Hancock, sent word to the latter that the enemy were retreating from Marye's house. It was probably only a shifting of the enemy's troops for the relief of the front line. But, assuming that the report was true, I said, "General Humphreys, Hancock reports the enemy is falling back; now is the time for you to go in!" He was ready, and his troops around him were ready. The order had evidently been expected, and after an interval of more than twenty-five years I well recollect the grim determination which settled on the face of that gallant hero when he received the words, "Now is the time for you to go in!" Spurring to his work he led his two brigades, who charged over precisely the same ground, but who did not get quite so near to the stone wall as some of French's and Hancock's men.

The musketry fire was very heavy, and the artillery fire was simply terrible. I sent word several times to our artillery on the right of Falmouth that they were firing into us and were tearing our own men to pieces. I thought they had made a mistake in the range. But I learned later that the fire came from the guns of the enemy on their extreme left.

Soon after 4 o'clock, or about sunset, while Humphreys was at work, Getty's division of Willcox's corps was ordered to the charge on our left by the unfinished railroad. I could see them being dreadfully cut up, although they had not advanced as far

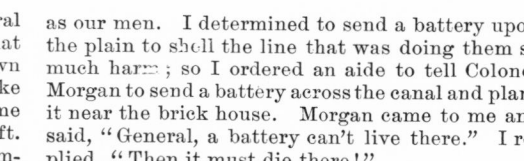

FRANKLIN'S MEN CHARGING ACROSS THE RAILROAD.

as our men. I determined to send a battery upon the plain to shell the line that was doing them so much harm; so I ordered an aide to tell Colonel Morgan to send a battery across the canal and plant it near the brick house. Morgan came to me and said, "General, a battery can't live there." I replied, "Then it must die there!"

Hazard took his battery out in gallant style and opened fire on the enemy's lines to the left of the Marye House. Men never fought more gallantly, and he lost a great many men and horses. When

Hooker came he ordered Frank's battery to join Hazard. But this last effort did not last long. In the midst of it I rode to the brick house, accompanied by Colonel Francis A. Walker, Lieutenant Cushing, and my orderly, Long. The smoke lay so thick that we could not see the enemy, and I think they could not see us, but we were aware of the fact that somebody in our front was doing a great deal of shooting. I found the brick house packed with men; and behind it the dead and the living were as thick as they could be crowded together. The dead were rolled out for shelter, and the dead horses were used for breastworks. I know I tried to shelter myself behind the brick house, but found I could not, on account of the men already there. The plain thereabouts was dotted with our fallen. I started to cross to the fork of the road where our men, under Colonel John R. Brooke, were holding the cluster of houses.

When it became dark the wounded were being brought off the plain, and Hooker was talking about relieving my men in front by putting in Sykes's division, and I said, "No! No men shall take the place of the Second Corps unless General Sumner gives the orders. It has fought and gained that ground and it shall hold it." Later the order came for Sykes to relieve the Second Corps, which was done about 11 o'clock.

That night was bitter cold, and a fearful one for the front line hugging the hollows in the ground, and for the wounded who could not be reached. It was a night of dreadful suffering. Many died of wounds and exposure, and as fast as men died

THE GRAND REVIEW AT FALMOUTH DURING PRESIDENT LINCOLN'S VISIT.
From a war-time sketch.

ABANDONING THE WINTER CAMP AT FALMOUTH.
From a war-time sketch.

they stiffened in the wintry air, and on the front line were rolled forward for protection to the living. Frozen men were placed for dumb sentries.

My corps again bivouacked in the town, and they were not allowed fires lest they should draw the fire of the enemy's artillery.

At 2 o'clock in the morning Burnside came to my headquarters near the center of the town. I was lying down at the time. He asked me to tell him about the battle, and we talked for about an hour. I told him everything that had occurred. "And now," I said, "General Burnside, you must know that everything that could be done by troops was done by the Second Corps." He said, "Couch, I know that; I am perfectly satisfied that you did your best." He gave no intimation of his plans for the next day. He was cheerful in his tone, and did not seem greatly oppressed, but it was plain that he felt he had led us to a great disaster, and one knowing him so long and well as myself could see that he wished his body was also lying in front of Marye's Heights. I never felt so badly for a man in my life.

The next day, Sunday, the 14th, our men began digging trenches along the edge of the town. We were on the alert, for there was some fear of an assault. Of course there is no need of denying that after the battle the men became strained. The pressure of a fight carries you through, but after it is all over and you have been whipped, you do not feel very pugnacious. The men, knowing that they had been unsuccessful, were in a nervous state, and officers suffered also from the reaction, the worst of it being that the mass of the army had lost confidence in its commander.

About midday of the 14th Burnside called a council of war, in which it was decided to fall back, but to hold Fredericksburg. No attack was made by us that day, though Burnside had said that he should renew the assault on Marye's Hill, with his old Ninth Corps, and that he would place himself at its head. General Getty of that corps, a very gallant officer, touched me as I passed him and

said: "I understand that Burnside has given out that he intends to lead seventeen regiments to the attack." He urged me strongly to dissuade him if possible, as it would be a perfect slaughter of men.

At the council Hooker expressed himself as against the movement of retreat, saying, "We must fight those people. We are over there and we must fight them." But, as I remember, he did not advocate the plan of holding Fredericksburg if we were not to renew the fight. I urged that the army was not in a condition, after our repulse, to renew the assault, but that we ought to hold Fredericksburg at all hazards. I had an argument with General Burnside upon that point, telling him that I was willing to have him throw all the responsibility upon me; that if we held the town we should have a little something to show for the sacrifice of the day before; that the people would feel we had not failed utterly. It was agreed that Fredericksburg should be held. Then Burnside dismissed us, and sent Hooker and myself to Fredericksburg to arrange for the defense. We held a council at the corner of Hanover street.

It was decided that Hooker's troops should hold the town. The question was how many men would he leave for that purpose, opinions varying from ten to eighteen thousand. My limit was ten thousand men. General Tyler turned to me and said: "Make it higher, General." We compromised on twelve thousand. We remained in the town on the 14th, and that evening my corps and the Ninth Corps recrossed the river. Next morning we found that Fredericksburg had been evacuated. When Willcox and I left, we thought, of course, it would be held. The talk was that during the night Hooker prevailed upon Burnside to evacuate the town. . . . After the battle Burnside tried to regain the confidence of the army, and there is no doubt that Sumner did a good deal to help him. . . .

When Hooker, on January 25th, was placed in command of the army, many of us were very much

surprised; I think the superior officers did not regard him competent for the task. He had fine qualities as an officer, but not the weight of character to take charge of that army. Nevertheless, under his administration the army assumed wonderful vigor. I have never known men to change from a condition of the lowest depression to that of a healthy fighting state in so short a time. President Lincoln, with his wife, came down to spend a few days with General Hooker, and to see the different officers and talk with them. To further that General Hooker gave a dinner party, at which all the corps commanders were present, and also Mr. Lincoln. Mr. Lincoln would talk to the officers on the subject that was uppermost in our minds —how we were to get the better of the enemy on the opposite hills. Before he went away he sent for Hooker and for me, I being second in command, and almost his last injunction was, "Gentlemen, in your next battle *put in all your men*." Yet that is exactly what we did not do at Chancellorsville.

We had a grand review of the army in honor of the President. The Second Corps paraded with Howard's Eleventh Corps, I think; for after I had saluted at the head of my corps I rode to the side of the President, who was on horseback, and while near him General Schurz approached at the head of his division. I said, "Mr. Lincoln, that is General Schurz," pronouncing it *Shurs*, after the American fashion. Mr. Lincoln turned to me and said, "Not *Shurs*, General Couch, but *Shoortz*," But he did it very pleasantly, and I was just a little surprised that our Western President should have the advantage of me. It was a beautiful day, and the review was a stirring sight. Mr. Lincoln, sitting there with his hat off, head bent, and seemingly meditating, suddenly turned to me and said, "General Couch, what do you suppose will become of all these men when the war is over?" And it struck me as very pleasant that somebody had an idea that the war would some time end.

THE CONFEDERATE SIDE.

THE DEFENSE OF MARYE'S HEIGHTS AND THE STONE WALL.

BY LAFAYETTE McLAWS, MAJOR-GENERAL, C. S. A.
Commander of McLaws's Division at Fredericksburg.

ON the 25th of November, 1862, my division marched into Fredericksburg, and shortly after, by direction of General Longstreet, I occupied the city with one of my brigades, and picketed the river with strong detachments from the dam at Falmouth to a quarter of a mile below Deep Run creek, the enemy's pickets being just across the river, within a stone's throw of mine. Detachments were immediately set at work digging rifle-pits close to the edge of the bank, so close that our men, when in them, could command the river and the shores on each side. The cellars of the houses near the river were made available for the use of riflemen, and zigzags were constructed to enable the men to get in and out of the rifle-pits under cover. All this was done at night, and so secretly and quietly that I do not believe the enemy had any conception of the minute and careful preparations that had been made to defeat any attempt to cross the river in my front. No provision was made for the use of artillery, as the enemy had an enormous array of their batteries on the heights above the town, and could have demolished ours in five minutes.

Two or three evenings previous to the Federal attempt to cross, I was with General Barksdale, and we were attracted by one or more of the enemy's bands playing at their end of the railroad bridge. A number of their officers and a crowd of their men were about the band cheering their national airs, the "Star Spangled Banner," "Hail Columbia," and others, once so dear to us all. It seemed as if they expected some response from us, but none was given until, finally, they struck up "Dixie," and then both sides cheered, with much

MAJOR-GENERAL LAFAYETTE McLAWS, C. S. A.

RUINS OF "MANSFIELD," ALSO KNOWN AS THE "BERNARD HOUSE."
From a war-time photograph.

10 A. M., when suddenly the tremendous array of the Federal artillery opened fire from the heights above the city.

It is impossible fitly to describe the effects of this iron hail hurled against the small band of defenders and into the devoted city. The roar of the cannon, the bursting shells, the falling of walls and chimneys, and the flying bricks and other material dislodged from the houses by the iron balls and shells, added to the fire of the infantry from both sides and the smoke from the guns and from the burning houses, made a scene of indescribable confusion, enough to appal the stoutest hearts! Under cover of this bombardment the Federals renewed their efforts to construct the bridge, but the little band of Mississippians in the rifle-pits under Lieutenant-Colonel John C. Fiser, 17th Mississippi, composed of his own regiment, 10 sharp-shooters from the 13th Mississippi, and 3 companies from the 18th Mississippi (Lieutenant-Colonel Luse), held their posts, and successfully repelled every attempt. The enemy had been committed to that point, by having used half their pontoons.

About 4:30 P. M. the enemy began crossing in boats, and the concentrated fire from all arms, directed against Barksdale's men in the rifle-pits, became so severe that it was impossible for them to use their rifles with effect.

As the main purpose of a determined defense, which was to gain time for the other troops to take position, had been accomplished, Colonel Fiser was directed to draw his command back from the river and join the brigade in the city; and just in time, for the enemy, no longer impeded by our fire, crossed the river rapidly in boats, and, forming on the flanks, rushed down to capture the men in the rifle-pits, taking them in the rear. Some of the men in the cellars, who did not get the order to retire, were thus captured, but the main body of them rejoined the brigade on Princess-Anne street, where it had been assembled, and all attempts made by the enemy, now crossing in large numbers, to gain possession of the city were defeated. The firing ceased by 7 o'clock, and as the grand division of Franklin had effected a crossing below the mouth of Deep Run, and thus controlled ground which was higher than the city, and other troops had crossed above the city, where, also, the ground was higher, so that our position would become untenable in the morning, I directed General Barksdale to retire to a strong position I had noticed along a sunken road cut through the foot of Marye's Hill and running perpendicular to the line of the enemy's advance. . . .

On the 12th close and heavy skirmishing was kept up between my advanced parties and the enemy, and whole divisions were employed in fortifying

laughter. Surmising that this serenade meant mischief, I closely inspected our bank of the river, and at night caused additional rifle-pits to be constructed to guard more securely the approaches to the bridge.

Early in the night of the 10th General Barksdale reported that his pickets had heard noises, as if the enemy were hauling pontoon-boats to the brink of the river. A dense fog had prevented a clear view. About 2 A. M. of the 11th, General Barksdale notified me that the movements on the other side indicated that the enemy were preparing to lay down the pontoon-bridges. I told him to let the bridge building go on until the enemy were committed to it and the construction parties were within easy range. At 4:30 he reported that the bridge was being rapidly constructed and was nearly half done, and he was about to open fire. I then ordered the signal to be given by firing two guns of J. P. W. Read's battery, posted on the highest point along my front, on the edge of the hills alongside the main road running to the city.

Previous notice had been sent to General Lee and to corps headquarters that the bridge was being constructed. With the sound of the cannon was mingled the rattle of the rifles of the Mississippi men, who opened a concentrated fire from the rifle-pits and swept the bridge, now crowded with the construction parties. Nine distinct and desperate attempts were made to complete the bridge, but every one was attended with such heavy loss from our fire that the efforts were abandoned until about

their positions and preparing for the coming assaults. The grounds in my front had been well studied by myself, in company with my brigade commanders and colonels of regiments, and all the details for the supply of ammunition, provisions, water, care for the wounded, and other necessary arrangements had been attended to, so that we waited for the enemy with perfect calmness and with confidence in our ability to repel them.

A heavy fog hung over the valley, concealing the town from our view, and until late in the day the banks below were not visible. As I was anxiously inquiring for some news from the pickets, since the point of attack had not yet been developed, my aide-de-camp, Captain H. L. P. King, volunteered to go to the river and collect information by personal observation, and I consented to his going, but did not send him. He rode off, and in about two hours returned, reporting that he had ridden down Deep Run as far as he could go in safety on horseback, and, dismounting and concealing his horse, had gone on foot down the run to its mouth, and from there he had watched the enemy crossing the river on two bridges. One or two hundred yards below the mouth of the run large bodies of infantry, artillery, and some cavalry had crossed, while heavy forces on the opposite side were waiting their turn to cross. On his return he had gone into a two-story wooden dwelling on the banks of the river, and had taken a leisurely view of the whole surroundings, confirming his observations taken from the mouth of Deep Run. This was a daring reconnoissance, as, at the time, none of our troops were within a mile of him. Up to this time the enemy had not shown us any very large body of troops, either in Fredericksburg, on the opposite side, or below.

On the 13th, during the early morning, a thick fog enveloped the town in my front and the valley of the river, but between 9 and 10 o'clock it lifted, and we could see on our right, below Deep Run, long lines of the enemy stretching down the river,

and near it, but not in motion. Reconnoitering parties on horseback were examining the grounds in front of our army, coming within range without being fired on. After they retired a strong body of infantry advanced from a point on the river, somewhat below my extreme right, as if to gain possession of the Bernard woods, but I had seven rifle-guns on the hill above those woods to meet this very contingency, and, these opening on this advancing body, it fell back to the river before coming within reach of Barksdale.

As the fog lifted higher, an immense column of infantry could be seen halted on the other side of the river, along the road leading from the hills beyond to the pontoon-bridges in front of the town, and extending back for miles, as it looked to us, and still we could not see the end. In Jackson's front the enemy had advanced, and their forming lines were plainly visible, while in Longstreet's front we could see no body of troops on the Fredericksburg side of the river. The indications were that Jackson was to receive the first blow, and General Longstreet came to me and said he was going over to that flank. I called his attention to the immense column of troops opposite us, on the other side of the river, with its head at the pontoon-bridges, crossing to Fredericksburg in our immediate front, and told him that in my judgment the most desperate assault was to be made to us on his front, and it would be developed close to us, without our knowing that it was forming, nor should we know when it commenced to move against us; that the assault would be sudden, and we should be ready to meet it, and that there were certainly as many of the enemy in that column threatening us as appeared in the lines opposite General Jackson. General Longstreet agreed with me, and remained.

Not long after, the grand division of General Franklin, in plain view from where we stood, was seen advancing in two lines against Jackson's front, marching in most magnificent order. No perceptible check could I observe in the advance, and the first line in good order entered the woods and was lost to our view. But the immediate crash of musketry and the thunder of artillery told of a desperate conflict, and we waited anxiously for some sign of the result. Soon masses of the enemy were seen emerging from the woods in retreat, and the whole body of the enemy marched back in the direction they came from, in excellent order, and very deliberately. Now began the trial against Longstreet's lines; but our confidence in our ability to resist all assaults against us had been wonderfully increased by seeing the repulse of Franklin. [See the narrative by General Reynolds on page 177.]

My line of defense was a broken one, running from the left along the sunken road, near the foot of Marye's Hill, where General Cobb's brigade (less the 16th Georgia) was stationed. During the 12th the defenses of this line had been extended

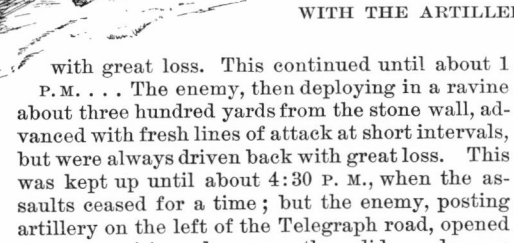

WITH THE ARTILLERY.

beyond the hill by an embankment thrown up to protect the right from sharpshooters, as also to resist assaults that might be made from that direction, and then the line was retired a hundred or more yards to the foot of the hills in the rear, along which was extended Kershaw's brigade of South Carolina troops, and General Barksdale's Mississippians, from left to right, the brigade of General Semmes being held in reserve. The Washington Artillery, under Colonel Walton, were in position on the crest of Marye's Hill over the heads of Cobb's men, and two brigades under General Ransom were held here in reserve. The heights above Kershaw and Barksdale were crowned with 18 rifle-guns and 8 smooth-bores belonging to batteries, and a number of smooth-bores from the reserve artillery. The troops could not be well seen by the enemy, and the artillery on my rear line was mostly concealed, some covered with brush. The enemy from their position could not see the sunken road near the foot of Marye's Hill, nor do I think they were aware, until it was made known to them by our fire, that there was an infantry

force anywhere except on top of the hill, as Ransom's troops could be seen there, in reserve, and the men in the sunken road were visible at a short distance only.

Soon after 11 A. M. the enemy approached the left of my line by the Telegraph road, and, deploying to my right, came forward and planted guidons or standards (whether to mark their advance or to aid in the alignment I do not know), and commenced firing; but the fire from our artillery, and especially the infantry fire from Cobb's brigade, so thinned their ranks that the line retreated without advancing, leaving their guidons planted. Soon another force, heavier than the first, advanced, and were driven back with great slaughter. They were met on retiring by reinforcements, and advanced again, but were again repulsed, with great loss. This continued until about 1 P. M. . . . The enemy, then deploying in a ravine about three hundred yards from the stone wall, advanced with fresh lines of attack at short intervals, but were always driven back with great loss. This was kept up until about 4:30 P. M., when the assaults ceased for a time; but the enemy, posting artillery on the left of the Telegraph road, opened on our position; however, they did no damage worth particularizing.

The batteries on Marye's Hill were at this time silent, having exhausted their ammunition, and were being relieved by guns from Colonel E. P. Alexander's battalion. Taking advantage of this lull in the conflict, the 15th South Carolina was brought forward from the cemetery, where it had been in reserve, and was posted behind the stone wall, supporting the 2d South Carolina regiment.

The enemy in the mean while formed a strong column of lines of attack, and advancing under cover of their own artillery, and no longer impeded by ours, came forward along our whole front in the most determined manner; but by this time, as just explained, I had lines four deep throughout the whole sunken road, and beyond the right flank. The front rank, firing, stepped back, and the next in rear took its place and, after firing, was replaced by the next, and so on in rotation. In this way the volley firing was made nearly continuous, and the file firing very destructive. The enemy were repulsed at all points.

THE SUNKEN ROAD UNDER MARYE'S HILL.
From a photograph taken in 1884.

NOTE.—In the background is seen the continuation of Hanover street, which on the left ascends the hill to the Marye Mansion. The little square field lies in the fork made by the former road and the Telegraph road. Nearly all that remained in 1884 of the famous stone wall is seen in the right of the picture. The horses are in the road, which is a continuation of the street south of Hanover street, and on which is the brick house mentioned in General Couch's article. The house in which General Cobb died would be the next object in the right of the picture if the foreground were extended.

In his official report General Kershaw, who succeeded General Cobb, thus describes the situation during the battle in that part of the road seen in the picture. "The road is about 25 feet wide, and is faced by a stone wall about 4 feet high on the city side. The road having been cut out of the side of the hill, in many places this last wall is not visible above the surface of the ground. The ground falls off rapidly to almost a level surface, which extends about 150 yards, then, with another abrupt fall of a few feet, to another plain which extends some 200 yards, and then falls off abruptly into a wide ravine, which extends along the whole front of the city and discharges into Hazel Run. I found, on my arrival, that Cobb's brigade, Colonel McMillan commanding, occupied our entire front, and my troops could only get into position by doubling on them. This was accordingly done, and the formation along most of the line during the engagement was consequently four deep. As an evidence of the coolness of the command, I may mention here that, notwithstanding that their fire was the most rapid and continuous I have ever witnessed, not a man was injured by the fire of his comrades. . . . In the mean time line after line of the enemy deployed in the ravine, and advanced to the attack at intervals of not more than fifteen minutes until about 4: 30 o'clock, when there was a lull of about a half-hour, during which a mass of artillery was placed in position in front of the town and opened upon our position. At this time I brought up Colonel De Saussure's regiment. Our batteries on the hill were silent, having exhausted their ammunition, and the Washington Artillery were relieved by a part of Colonel Alexander's battalion. Under cover of this artillery fire, the most formidable column of attack was formed, which, about 5 o'clock, emerged from the ravine, and, no longer impeded by our artillery, impetuously assailed our whole front. From this time until after 6 o'clock the attack was continuous, and the fire on both sides terrific. Some few, chiefly officers, got within 30 yards of our lines, but in every instance their columns were shattered by the time they got within 100 paces. The firing gradually subsided, and by 7 o'clock our pickets were established within 30 yards of those of the enemy.

"Our chief loss after getting into position in the road was from the fire of sharp-shooters, who occupied some buildings on my left flank in the early part of the engagement, and were only silenced by Captain [W.] Wallace, of the 2d Regiment, directing the continuous fire of one company upon the buildings. General Cobb, I learn, was killed by a shot from that quarter. The regiments on the hill suffered most, as they were less perfectly covered."

The last charge was made after sundown — in fact it was already dark in the valley. A Federal officer who was in that assault told me that the first discharge at them was a volley, and the bullets went over their heads "in sheets," and that his command was ordered to lie down, and did lie down for a full half-hour and then retired, leaving a large number of killed and wounded. The firing ceased as darkness increased, and about 7 P. M. the pickets of the opposing forces were posted within a short distance of each other, my pickets reporting noises as of movements of large bodies of troops in the city.

Thus ended the battle. The enemy remained in possession of the city until the night of the 15th, and then retired across the Rappahannock, resuming their former positions, and Kershaw's brigade of my division reoccupied the city. . . .

CROSSING THE RAPPAHANNOCK.

BY H. G. O. WEYMOUTH, U. S. V., CAPTAIN 19th MASSACHUSETTS REGIMENT.

ON the morning of the 11th of December, 1862, about two hours before daylight, the regimental commanders of Colonel Norman J. Hall's Third Brigade, of Howard's Second Division, Second Army Corps, were assembled at brigade headquarters to receive preliminary orders for the approaching battle. Our brigade commander informed us that our regiment was to be the first to cross the upper pontoon-bridge, which was to be laid by the engineer corps by daylight, and that we were to hold and occupy the right of the town until the whole army should have crossed, when the Right Grand Division, comprising the Second and Ninth Corps, would charge the heights, supported by artillery in front and on the right flank. On our arrival at the river at daylight we found but a very small section of the bridge laid, in consequence of the commanding position which the enemy held on the right bank of the river, secreted as they were behind fences made musket-proof by piling cord-wood and other materials against them. After a fruitless attempt of eight hours' duration to

lay the bridge where the enemy had absolute control of the river front, the idea was abandoned, and notice was sent down to us at the river that the enemy would be shelled from the heights, with orders to take to the pontoon-boats and cross and dislodge the enemy in order to enable the engineer corps to complete the bridge. The instant the artillery ceased firing, the 7th Michigan and 19th Massachusetts took to the boats and poled across the river under a heavy musketry fire from the enemy. The 7th Michigan was the first to make a landing, and marched up Farquhar street in a direct line from the bridge. They immediately became severely engaged, and the first two companies of the 19th Massachusetts that had crossed went forward and joined them. A few minutes later the remainder of the 19th crossed, formed in line on the bank of the river, left resting on Farquhar street, and advanced, deploying as skirmishers in order to drive back the enemy from the western part of the city. We were met with such resistance by Barksdale's brigade, very aptly styled by General Longstreet "Confederate hornets," that it was nearly dusk before we gained the north side of Caroline street. It was now apparent that our thin line could not make any farther advance against the

formidable barricades the enemy had erected on the south side of the street, consisting of barrels and boxes, filled with earth and stones, placed between the houses, so as to form a continuous line of defense, and the left of our line was forced to fall back down Farquhar street, fully one-half the distance from Caroline street. On reporting our position to a staff-officer our brigade commander ordered the 20th Massachusetts to clear the streets. They marched up Farquhar street in company or division front, and on reaching Caroline street wheeled to the right; but before the full regiment had entered the street the enemy, from their snug retreats, poured such a deadly fire on them as to force them to retire with great loss.

This action of the 20th enabled our left to regain our position on Caroline street, which was maintained until Barksdale withdrew his command to the heights, about an hour after dark. At about 11 o'clock General Howard crossed over to learn our position. Informing him that the enemy had retired in our front, I asked him if we should move forward. After making some inquiries concerning our right, he thought nothing would be gained by doing so. We remained in this position until about noon of the 13th.

BARKSDALE'S MISSISSIPPIANS OPPOSING THE LAYING OF THE PONTOON-BRIDGES.

CROSSING THE RIVER IN PONTOONS TO DISLODGE THE CONFEDERATE SHARP-SHOOTERS.

A HOT DAY ON MARYE'S HEIGHTS.

BY WILLIAM MILLER OWEN, FIRST LIEUTENANT, C. S. A.
Adjutant of the New Orleans "Washington Artillery," at the battle of Fredericksburg.

ON the night of the 10th of December we of the New Orleans Washington Artillery sat up late in our camp on Marye's Heights, entertaining some visitors in an improvised theater, smoking our pipes, and talking of home. A final punch having been brewed and disposed of, everybody crept under the blankets and was soon in the land of Nod. In an hour or two we were aroused by the report of a heavy gun. I was up in an instant, for if there should be another it would be the signal that the enemy was preparing to cross the river. Mr. Florence, a civilian in the bivouac, bounced as if he had a concealed spring under his blanket, and cried, "Wake up! wake up! what's that?" The deep roar of the second gun was heard, and we knew what we had to do. It was 4 o'clock. Our orders were that upon the firing of these signal guns we should at once take our places in the re-

doubts prepared for us on Marye's Hill and await developments. "Boots and saddles" was sounded, and the camp was instantly astir, and in the gray of the morning we were on the Plank road leading to the hill. The position reached, . . . the men made the redoubts as snug as possible, and finding the epaulements not to their liking, went to work with pick and shovel throwing the dirt a little higher, and fashioning embrasures to fire through. The engineers objected, and said they were "ruining the works," but the cannoneers said, "We have to fight here, not you; we will arrange them to suit ourselves." And General Longstreet approvingly said, "If you save the finger of a man's hand, that does some good." A dense fog covered the country, and we could not discern what was going on in the town.

The morning of the 12th was also foggy, and it was not until 2 P. M. that it cleared off, and then we could see the Stafford Heights across the river, densely packed with troops. At 3 P. M. a heavy column moved down toward one of the bridges near the gas works and we opened upon it, making some splendid practice and apparently stirring them up prodigiously, for they soon sought cooler localities. While our guns were firing the enemy's long-range batteries on the Stafford Heights opened upon us, as much as to say, "What are you about over there?" We paid no attention to their inquiry, as our guns could not reach them.

At dawn the next morning, December 13th, in the fresh and nipping air, I stepped upon the gallery overlooking the heights back of the little old-fashioned town of Fredericksburg. Heavy fog and mist hid the whole plain between the heights and the Rappahannock, but under cover of that fog and within easy cannon-shot lay Burnside's army. Along the heights, to the right and left of where I was standing, extending a length of nearly five miles, lay Lee's army. The bugles and the drum corps of the respective armies were now sounding reveille, and the troops were preparing for their early meal. All knew we should have a battle to-day, and a great one, for the enemy had crossed the river in immense force upon his pontoons during the night. On the Confederate side all was ready, and the shock was awaited with stubborn resolution. Last night we had spread our blankets upon the bare floor in the parlor of Marye's house, and now our breakfast was being prepared in its fire-place, and we were impatient to have it over. After hastily dispatching this light meal of bacon and corn-bread, the colonel, chief bugler, and I (the adjutant of the battalion) mounted our horses and rode out to inspect our lines. Visiting first the position of the 10-pounder Parrott rifle on the Plank road, we found Galbraith and his boys wide awake and ready for business. Across the Plank road, in an earthwork, was the battery of Donaldsonville Cannoneers, of Louisiana, all Creoles and gallant soldiers. Riding to the rear of Marye's house, we visited in turn the redoubts of Squires, Miller, and Eshleman, and found everything ready for instant action. The ammunition chests had been taken off the limbers and placed upon the ground behind the traverses close to the guns. The horses and limbers had been sent to the rear out of danger. We drew rein and spoke a few words to each in passing, and at the 3d Company's redoubt we were invited by Sergeant "Billy" Ellis to partake of some "café noir," which his mess had prepared in a horse bucket. Nothing loth, we drank a tin-cupful, and found, not exactly "Mocha," or "Java," but the best of parched corn. However, it was hot, the morning was raw, and it did very well.

At 12 o'clock the fog had cleared, and while we were sitting in Marye's yard smoking our pipes, after a lunch of hard crackers, a courier came to Colonel Walton, bearing a despatch from General

THE WASHINGTON ARTILLERY ON MARYE'S HILL FIRING UPON THE UNION COLUMNS FORMING FOR THE ASSAULT.

Longstreet for General Cobb, but, for our information as well, to be read and then given to him. It was as follows: "Should General Anderson, on your left, be compelled to fall back to the second line of heights, you must conform to his movements." Descending the hill into the sunken road, I made my way through the troops, to a little house where General Cobb had his headquarters, and handed him the despatch. He read it carefully, and said, "Well! if they wait for me to fall back, they will wait a long time." Hardly had he spoken, when a brisk skirmish fire was heard in front, toward the town, and, looking over the stone wall, we saw our skirmishers falling back, firing as they came; at the same time the head of a Federal column was seen emerging from one of the streets of the town. They came on at the double-quick, with loud cries of "Hi! Hi! Hi!" which we could distinctly hear. Their arms were carried at "right shoulder shift," and their colors were aslant the shoulders of the color-sergeants. They crossed the canal at the bridge, and, getting behind the bank to the low ground to deploy, were almost concealed from our sight. It was 12:30 P. M., and it was evident that we were now going to have it hot and heavy.

The enemy, having deployed, now showed him-

self above the crest of the ridge and advanced in columns of brigades, and at once our guns began their deadly work with shell and solid shot. How beautifully they came on! Their bright bayonets glistening in the sunlight made the line look like a huge serpent of blue and steel. The very force of their onset leveled the broad fences bounding the small fields and gardens that interspersed the plain. We could see our shells bursting in their ranks, making great gaps; but on they came, as though they would go straight through and over us. Now we gave them canister, and that staggered them. A few more paces onward and the Georgians in the road below us rose up, and, glancing an instant along their rifle barrels, let loose a storm of lead into the faces of the advance brigade. This was too much; the column hesitated, and then, turning, took refuge behind the bank. But another line appeared from behind the crest and advanced gallantly, and again we opened our guns upon them, and through the smoke we could discern the red breeches of the "Zouaves," and hammered away at them especially. But this advance, like the preceding one, although passing the point reached by the first column, and doing and daring all that brave men could do, recoiled under our canister and the bullets of the infantry in the

road, and fell back in great confusion. Spotting the fields in our front, we could detect little patches of blue—the dead and wounded of the Federal infantry who had fallen facing the very muzzles of our guns. Cooke's brigade of Ransom's division was now placed in the sunken road with Cobb's men. At 2 P.M. other columns of the enemy left the crest and advanced to the attack; it appeared to us that there was no end to them. On they came in beautiful array and seemingly more determined to hold the plain than before; but our fire was murderous, and no troops on earth could stand the *feu d'enfer* we were giving them. In the foremost line we distinguished the green flag with the golden harp of old Ireland, and we knew it to be Meagher's Irish brigade. The gunners of the two rifle-pieces, Corporals Payne and Hardie, were directed to turn their guns against this column; but the gallant enemy pushed on beyond all former charges, and fought and left their dead within five-and-twenty paces of the sunken road. Our position on the hill was now a hot one, and three regiments of Ransom's brigade were ordered up to reinforce the infantry in the road. We watched them as they came marching in line of battle from the rear, where they had been lying in reserve. They passed through our works and rushed down the hill with loud yells, and then stood shoulder to shoulder with the Georgians. The 25th North Carolina regiment, crossing Miller's guns, halted upon the crest of the hill, dressed its line, and fired a deadly volley at the enemy at close range, and then at the command "Forward!" dashed down the hill. It left dead men on Miller's redoubt, and he had to drag them away from the muzzles of his guns. At this time General Cobb fell mortally wounded, and General Cooke was borne from the field, also wounded. Among other missiles a 3-inch rifle-ball came crashing through the works and fell at our feet. Kursheedt picked it up and said, "Boys, let's send this back to them again"; and into the gun it went, and was sped back into the dense ranks of the enemy.

General Kershaw now advanced from the rear with two regiments of his infantry to reinforce the men in the sunken road, who were running short of ammunition, and to take command.

The sharp-shooters having got range of our embrasures we began to suffer. Corporal Ruggles fell mortally wounded, and Perry, who seized the rammer as it fell from Ruggles's hand, received a bullet in the arm. Rodd was holding "vent," and away went his "crazy bone." In quick succession Everett, Rossiter, and Kursheedt were wounded.

Falconer in passing in rear of the guns was struck behind the ear and fell dead. We were now so short-handed that every one was in the work, officers and men putting their shoulders to the wheels and running up the guns after each recoil. The frozen ground had given way and was all slush and mud. We were compelled to call upon the infantry to help us at the guns. Eshleman crossed over from the right to report his guns nearly out of ammunition; the other officers reported the same. They were reduced to a few solid shot only. It was now 5 o'clock P. M., and there was a lull in the storm. The enemy did not seem inclined to renew his efforts, so our guns were withdrawn, and the batteries of Woolfolk and Moody were substituted. The little whitewashed brick-house to the right of the redoubt we were in was so battered with bullets during the four hours and a half engagement that at the close it was transformed to a bright brick-dust red. An old cast-iron stove lay against the house, and as the bullets would strike it, it would give forth the sound of "bing! bing!" with different tones and variations. . . .

At 5:30 another attack was made by the enemy, but it was easily repulsed, and the battle of Fredericksburg was over, and Burnside was baffled and defeated.

IN FRONT OF THE STONE WALL.

BY JOHN W. AMES, BREVET BRIGADIER-GENERAL, U. S. V.

Captain 11th U. S. Infantry, Second Brigade of Regulars, at the battle of Fredericksburg.

ON Saturday, December 13th, our brigade had been held in reserve, but late in the day we were hurried to the battle only to see a field full of flying men and the sun low in the west shining red through columns of smoke — six deserted field-pieces on a slight rise of ground in front of us, and a cheering column of troops in regular march disappearing on our left. But the day was then over and the battle lost, and our line felt hardly bullets enough to draw blood before darkness put an end to the uproar of all hostile sounds, save desultory shell-firing. For an hour or two afterward shells from Marye's Heights traced bright lines across the black sky with their burning fuses. Then, by command, we sank down in our lines, to get what sleep the soggy ground and the danger might allow us.

COBB'S AND KERSHAW'S TROOPS BEHIND THE STONE WALL.

Experience had taught us that when the silent line of fire from the shells had flashed across the sky and disappeared behind us the scream and explosion that followed were harmless, but still it required some effort to overcome the discomfort of the damp ground, and the flash and report of bursting shells, and to drop quietly asleep at an order. We finally slept, but we were roused before midnight, and formed into line with whispered commands, and then filed to the right, and, reaching the highway, marched away from the town. There were many dead horses at exposed points of our turning and many more dead men. Here stood a low brick house, with an open door in its gable end, from which shone a light, and into which we peered when passing. Inside sat a woman, gaunt and hard-featured, with crazy hair and a Meg Merrilies face, still sitting by a smoking candle, though it was nearly two hours past midnight. But what woman could sleep, though never so masculine and tough of fiber, alone in a house between two hostile armies — two corpses lying across her door-steps, and within, almost at her feet, four more! So, with wild eyes and face lighted by her smoky candle, she stared across the dead barrier into the darkness outside with the look of one who heard and saw not, and to whom all sounds were a terror.

We formed in two lines, — the right of each resting near and in front of this small brick house, and the left extending into the field at right angles with the highway. Here we again bivouacked, finding room for our beds with no little difficulty, because of the shattered forms of those who were here taking their last long sleep. We rose early. The heavy fog was penetrating and chilly, and the damp turf was no warm mattress to tempt us to a morning nap. So we shook off sloth from our moistened bodies willingly, and rolling up the gray blankets set about breakfast. The bivouac breakfast is a nearer approach to its civilized congener than the bivouac bed. Coffee can be made hot and good in blackened tins; pork can be properly frizzled only on a stick over an open fire; hard tack is a better, sweeter morsel than the average American housewife has yet achieved with her saleratus, sour milk, "empt'ins," and what-not; and a pipe — who can estimate what that little implement has done for mankind? Certainly none better than those who have sought its solace after the bivouac breakfast that succeeds a bivouac bed, in December.

We now began to take note through the misty veil of the wreck of men and horses cumbering the ground about us, and a slight lifting of the gray fog showed us the story of yesterday's repeated assaults and repeated failures. When our pipes were exhausted we got up to inspect and criticise the situation. Just here was the wreck of a fence, which seemed to have been the high-tide mark of our advance-wave of battle. The fence was a barrier which, slight as it was, had turned back the already wavering and mutilated lines of assault. Almost an army lay about us and scattered back over the plain toward the town. Not only corpses, but many of the badly wounded, hardly distinguishable from the dead, were here too. To die, groveling on the ground or fallen in the mire, is dreadful indeed. The pallid faces, and the clammy hands clenching their muskets, looked ghastly by the fog-light. The new, bright blue overcoats only made the sight the ghastlier.

About eighty yards in front the plowed field was bounded by a stone wall, and behind the wall were men in gray uniforms moving carelessly about. This picture is one of my most distinct memories of the war — the men in gray behind this wall, talking, laughing, cooking, cleaning muskets, clicking locks — there they were! — Lee's soldiers! — the Army of Northern Virginia! We were so absurdly near this host of yesterday's victors that we seemed wholly in their hands and a part of their great mass; cut off and remote from the Federal army, and almost within the lines of the enemy — prisoners, of course. That was the immediate impression, as we stupidly gazed in the first moment of the awkward discovery.

But the sharp whistle of a bullet sounded in our ears, and a rebel's face peered through the puff of smoke, as he removed the rifle from his shoulder; then rapidly half a dozen more bullets whistled by us, and the warning sent us all to earth. . . .

The enemy riddled every moving thing in sight; horses tied to the wheels of a broken gun-carriage behind us; pigs that incautiously came grunting from across the road; even chickens were brought down with an accuracy of aim that told of a fatally short range, and of a better practice than it would have been wise for our numbers to face. They applauded their own success with a hilarity we could hardly share in, as their chicken-shooting was across our backs, leaving us no extra room for turning. But this was mere wantonness of slaughter, not indulged in when the higher game in blue uniform was in sight. The men who had left our ranks for water, or from any cause, before we were pinned to the earth, came back at great peril. Indeed, I believe not one of them reached our line again unhurt. Some were killed outright; others were mortally wounded, and died within a few steps of us; and several who tried to drag themselves away flat upon their faces were put out of their misery. This, too, showed us plainly what we might expect, and fixed our bounds to such segments of the fields as were hidden from the enemy. This was not alike throughout the line. At one point the exposure was absolute, and stillness as absolute was the only safety. A slight barrier was afterward formed at this point by a disposal of the dead bodies in front, so that the dead actually sheltered the living.

After two or three hours of this experience we became somewhat accustomed to the situation,—for man becomes accustomed to almost anything that savors of routine,—and learned with considerable exactness the limit inside which we might move with safety, and learned also of endurable constraint. It was somewhat curious to see how strong the tobacco hunger was with many—perhaps with most. Men would jump to their feet and run the length of a regiment to borrow tobacco, and in so doing run the gauntlet of a hundred shots. This was so rarely accomplished in entire safety that it won the applause of our line and hearty congratulations to any one fortunate enough to save his life and sweeten it with the savory morsel.

All this would have been ludicrous but for the actual suffering inflicted upon so many. Men were mortally hit, and there was no chance to bind up their wounds; they were almost as far beyond our help as if they had been miles away. A little was accomplished for their relief by passing canteens from hand to hand, keeping them close to the ground out of sight, and some of the wounded were where a little manipulation could be done in safety. It was sad to hear the cries fade away to low moans, and then to silence, without a chance to help. The laugh over a successful chase for tobacco would die away only to change into a murmur of indignation at the next cruel slaughter. A young officer, boyish and ruddy, fresh from a

THE STONE WALL UNDER MARYE'S HEIGHTS.
From a photograph taken immediately after Sedgwick carried the position by assault, at the second attack, May 3, 1863.

visit home, with brighter sword and shoulder-straps than most of us, raised his head to look at the enemy, and a bullet at once pierced his brain. Without a word or groan his head sank again, his rosy cheek grew livid, and his blood crimsoned his folded hands. Next a leg or arm was shattered as it became exposed in shifting from the wearisomeness of our position. Presently a system of reporting the casualties became established; the names of the injured were passed from mouth to mouth — "Captain M——, 17th, just killed"; "Private ——, Co. C, 11th ——, knocked over." Those who were fortunate enough to have paper and pencil, and elbow-room enough to get them from pocket-depths, kept a list of the names of the killed and wounded; the occupation this gave proved a blessing, for the hours were very long and weary. I suppose *ennui* is hardly the word where nerves are on the rack, and danger pinions one to a single spot of earth; yet something like *ennui* came over us. . . . I was called back to the dull wet earth and the crouching line at Fredericksburg by a request from Sergeant Read, who "guessed he could hit that cuss with a spy-glass" — pointing, as he spoke, to the batteries that threatened our right flank. Then I saw that there was commotion at that part of the Confederate works, and an officer on the parapet, with a glass was taking note of us. Had they discovered us at

last, after letting us lie here till high noon, and were we now to receive the plunging fire we had looked for all the morning? Desirable in itself as it might be to have "that cuss with a spy-glass" removed, it seemed wiser to repress Read's ambition. The shooting of an officer would dispel any doubts they might have of our presence, and we needed the benefit of all their doubts. Happily, they seemed to think us not worth their powder and iron.

Were we really destined to see the friendly shades of night come on and bring us release from our imprisonment? For the first time we began to feel it probable when the groups left the guns without a shot. I grew easy enough in mind to find that sleep was possible, and I was glad to welcome it as a surer refuge from the surroundings than the scrap of newspaper. It was a little discouraging to see a sleeping officer near me awakened by a bullet, but as his only misfortune, besides a disturbed nap, seemed to be a torn cap and scratched face, he soon wooed back the startled goddess. I had enjoyed sleep for its quiet and rest, but never before for *mere* oblivion.

When I returned to consciousness I found the situation unchanged, except that the list of casualties had been swelled by the constant rifle-practice, which was still as pitiless and as continuous as before. . . .

Slowly the sun declined. He had been our friend all day, shining through the December air with an autumn glow that almost warmed the chill earth; but at his last half-hour he seemed to hang motionless in the western sky. His going down would set us free; free from the fire that was galling and decimating us; free from the fear of guns on the right, and advance from the front; free from numbness, and constraint, and irksomeness, and free from the cold, wet earth. Also it would bring us messengers from the town to call us back from the exposed position and the field of dead bodies. But he lingered and stood upon the order of his going, until it seemed as if a Joshua of the Confederates had caused him to stand still.

When at last the great disk stood, large and red, upon the horizon, every face was turned toward it, forgetting constraint, thirst, tobacco, and rebel fire, in the eagerness to see the end of a day that had brought us a new experience of a soldier's life, and had combined the dangers of a battle-field and the discomfort of a winter's bivouac with many new horrors of its own.

At last the lingering sun went down. December twilights are short; the Federal line sprang to its feet with almost a shout of relief. The rebel fire grew brisker as they saw such a swarm of blue coats rising from the ground, but it was too late to see the foresights on the rifles, and shots unaimed were not so terrible as the hated ground. So we contemptuously emptied our rifles at them, and before the smoke rolled away the coming darkness had blotted out the wall and the hostile line.

With our line rose also a few men from the ghastly pile of yesterday's dead, who hobbled up on muskets used as crutches. These poor fellows had bound up their own wounds, and the coffee we had given them had cheered them into life and hope. Their cheerfulness grew into hilarity and merriment as they found themselves clear, at last, from the dead, and facing toward home, with a hope not by any means so impossible of realization as it had seemed not long before. Poor fellows! their joy was more touching than their sufferings — which, indeed, they seemed to have forgotten.

In our own brigade we found we had lost nearly

MAJOR-GENERAL J. B. KERSHAW, C. S. A.

150, out of a present-for-duty strength of about 1,000 men. This would have been a fair average loss in any ordinary battle, but we had suffered it as we lay on the ground inactive, without the excitement and dash of battle and without the chance to reply: a strain upon nerves and physical endurance which we afterward remembered as severer than many more fatal fields. In the midst of our buzz of relief and mutual congratulation, the expected summons came for us to fall back to the town. Once more we formed an upright line of battle, then faced by the rear rank and marched in retreat, with muffled canteens and many halts and facings about toward a possible pursuit. Reaching a slight bank, we descended to the meadow through which the Fredericksburg raceway was dug, and here we changed to a flank march and filed into the highway. The highway soon became a street, and we were once more in Fredericksburg. . . .

BRIGADIER-GENERAL ROBERT RANSOM,
C. S. A.

HAYS'S BRIGADE OF STONEWALL JACKSON'S CORPS, AT HAMILTON'S CROSSING.

JACKSON AT HAMILTON'S CROSSING.

BY J. H. MOORE, C. S. A.

THE morning of the 13th [of December] dawned with a dense fog enveloping the plain and city of Fredericksburg, through which the brilliant rays of the sun struggled about 10 in the morning. In front of the right of the Confederate army was displayed the vast force of Franklin, marching and countermarching, hastily seeking the places assigned for the coming conflict. Here was a vast plain, now peopled with an army worthy of its grand dimensions. A slight but dazzling snow beneath, and a brilliant sun above, intensified the leaping reflections from thousands of gleaming bayonets. Officers, on restless horses, rushed from point to point in gay uniforms. Field-artillery was whisked into position as so many fragile toys. Rank and file, foot and horse, small-arms and field-ordnance presented so magnificent a pageant as to call forth the unbounded admiration of their adversaries. In a word, this was the grandest martial scene of the war. The contrast between Stonewall Jackson's corps and Franklin's grand division was very marked, and so far as appearances went the former was hardly better than a caricature of the latter.

When all was in readiness, adjutants stepped to the front, and, plainly in our view, read the orders of the day. This done, the fatal advance across the plain commenced. With gay pennants, State, regimental, and brigade pennants flying, this magnificent army advanced in three closely compacted lines of battle. At intervals, in front, preceded by horse artillery, and flanked on either side by numerous field-pieces, hundreds of heavy field-pieces from the north bank of the Rappahannock belched forth their missiles of destruction and

swept the plain in advance of Franklin's columns, while at the same moment his smaller field-pieces in front and on the flanks joined in to sweep the open space on all sides. This mighty cannonading was answered by the Confederate ordnance. Onward, steady and unwavering, these three lines advanced, preceded by a heavy skirmish-line, till they neared the railroad, when Jackson's right and right center poured into these sturdy ranks a deadly volley from small-arms. Spaces, gaps, and wide chasms instantly told the tale of a most fatal encounter. Volley after volley of small-arms continued the work of destruction, while Jackson's artillery posted on the Federal left and at right angles to their line of advance kept up a withering fire on the lessening ranks. The enemy advanced far in front of the River road [and crossing the railroad charged the slopes upon which our troops were posted], but at length wavered, halted, and suddenly retreated to the protection of the railroad embankments. The struggle was kept up by sharp-shooters for some time, when another general advance was made against a furious cannonade of small-arms and artillery. Again the scene of destruction was repeated; still the Federals crossed the railroad, when a gap in Jackson's line between Archer's and Thomas's brigades was discovered by some of the assailants. This interval was rushed for by a part of Franklin's troops as a haven of safety, while the rest of his command were repulsed in the utmost confusion.

The extreme left of Archer's brigade, and the extreme right of Thomas's brigade, that is, the 14th Tennessee and 19th Georgia, commanded by Colonel Forbes, and a part of the 7th Tennessee, commanded by Colonel Goodner, of the former brigade, believing they were about to be surrounded, gave way. Their comrades on the right, unaware

BRIGADIER-GENERAL THOMAS R. R. COBB, C. S. A.
Killed at Fredericksburg.

of the condition of affairs on the left, and seeing the enemy routed in their front, were amazed at this confusion. Officers and men on the right were enraged at what seemed to be cowardice, and, rushing toward the broken lines, officers leveled their pistols and, with many privates, fired into these fleeing comrades.

Presently the true condition of affairs appeared when the victorious brigades of Franklin emerged from the woods. Line and field officers rushed to and fro, wildly shouting, "Into line, into line!" and, even in the face of a flanking foe, the gallant Colonel Turney, who temporarily commanded Archer's brigade, succeeded in re-forming his regiments at right angles to the former line of attack. This gave a brief check to the victors. Still the infantry and artillery fire scourged the line. The rout or capture of the Confederates seemed inevitable. Turney was struck by a Minié ball, which entered his mouth and came out at his neck, and his apparently lifeless body was hurriedly placed on a blanket, and four of his devoted followers attempted to carry him to the rear. They had not proceeded far when a shell burst among them, and they in turn lay helpless by the side of their bleeding commander. Colonel Goodner also did gallant service in preventing a rout, for, with the part of the 7th that still held its ground, he formed a line at right angles to their former position, and aided in checking this dangerous reverse.

Up to the time of the break in our line no one in the ranks apprehended any danger. Those in front and near this scene of defeat and confusion made desperate efforts to rally the men and prevent a stampede, for we looked for nothing but defeat or capture. We were unaware of the fact that we had any reserves. Presently Early's division, in the very mood and spirit that had characterized Archer's brigade before the breaking of the lines, came at double-quick to our relief, jesting and yelling at us: "Here comes old Jubal! Let old Jubal

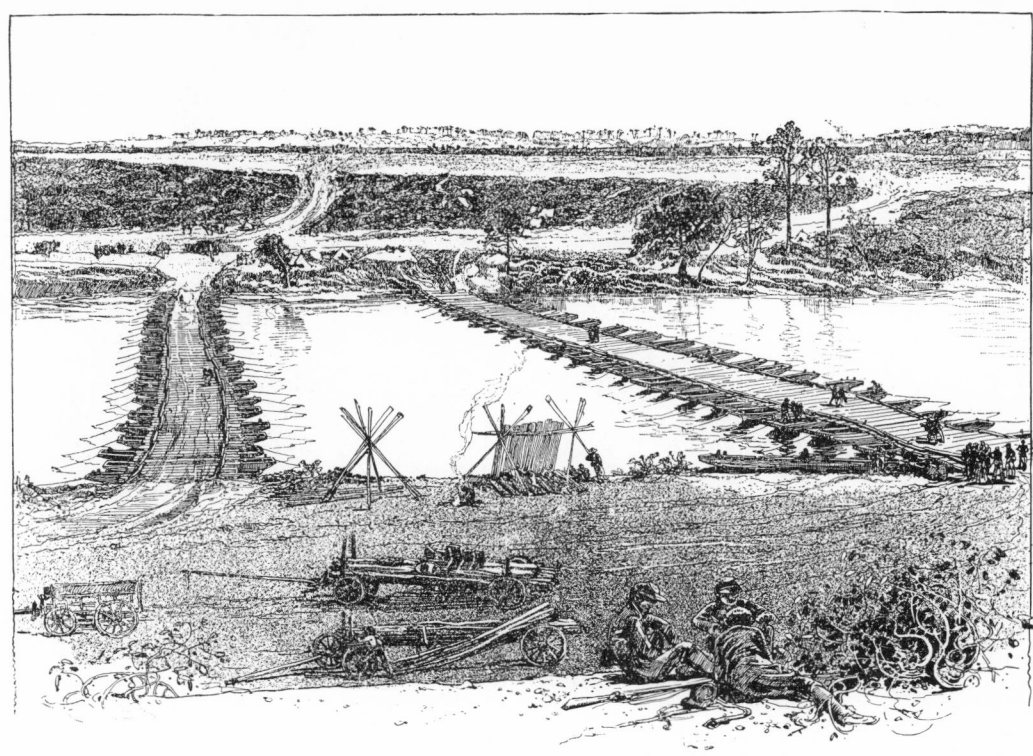

THE PONTOON-BRIDGES AT FRANKLIN'S CROSSING.
The hills occupied by Stonewall Jackson's command are seen in the distance.

straighten that fence! Jubal's boys are always getting Hill out o' trouble!"

A desperate encounter followed. The Federals fought manfully, but the artillery on our right, together with the small-arms, literally mowed them down. Officers and men lost courage at the sight of their lessening ranks, and in the utmost confusion they again sought the shelter of the railroad. Archer's brigade, of Jackson's corps, was on the extreme right of A. P. Hill's front line, composed of the following regiments, posted in the order named: 19th Georgia, 14th Tennessee, 7th Tennessee, 1st Tennessee, and extended from the interval or space left unoccupied by Gregg's brigade to the railroad curve near Hamilton's Crossing. We occupied ground slightly higher than the level of the plain over which the Federals had to pass. In our immediate rear and left was an irregular growth of timber of varied size, which obstructed the view in the direction of the Gregg interval.

As the battle opened in the morning, the enemy was plainly in our view, and we could distinctly see their approach to the railroad in our front and to the left, where in every attempt to advance they halted. Now and then they would make an effort to advance from the railroad to our lines. We who were on the right had no trouble to repulse those in our front, and, in fact, we successfully met every assault made on the right, and that, too, with little or no loss. We regarded the efforts of the Federals, so far as the right was concerned, as futile in the extreme. In fact, their assaults on this part of the line appeared like the marching of men to certain defeat and slaughter. Our infantry fire aided

by fifteen pieces of artillery placed at our right, did terrible execution as the poor fellows emerged from a slight railroad cut in front of a part of our line. [See the narrative by General Reynolds following.]

On the morning of the 13th General Jackson rode down his lines dressed in a new suit, presented to him, as we understood, by General Stuart. Some of our men facetiously remarked that they preferred seeing him with his rusty old cap on, as they feared he would n't get down to work. He inspected all of his positions, riding alone. After halting near the extreme right, the artillery fire was begun, and here I had an excellent opportunity to see him under fire. I watched him closely and was unable to detect the slightest change in his demeanor. In a few minutes he rode off in the direction of Lee's head-quarters.

A very general impression prevails, and it is in a great measure confirmed by writers on Fredericksburg, that Jackson's lines were strongly fortified. This is not correct: we had no time to construct anything like fortifications. D. H. Hill's division had been at Port Royal, eighteen miles below Fredericksburg, to prevent the Federals from crossing at that point; he left Port Royal after the enemy had abandoned the project of crossing there, and did not reach the position assigned him until about daylight of the morning of the battle.

The next morning the scenes of carnage were heart-sickening. To intensify the horrible picture, the dead and the mortally wounded were in many instances burned in the sedge-grass, which was set on fire by bursting shells.

GENERAL REYNOLDS'S ACCOUNT OF THE ENGAGEMENT AT HAMILTON'S CROSSING.

The report of General John F. Reynolds, commanding the First Corps, contains the following account of the engagement of his troops at Hamilton's Crossing: "About 8:30 A. M. Meade's division advanced across the Smithfield ravine, formed in column of two brigades, with the artillery between them, the Third Brigade marching by the flank on the left and rear. It moved down the river some 500 or 600 yards, when it turned sharp to the right and crossed the Bowling Green road. The enemy's artillery opened fire from the crest and the angle of the Bowling Green road. I directed General Meade to put his column directly for the nearest point of wood, and, having gained the crest, to extend his attack along it to the extreme point of the heights, where most of the enemy's artillery was posted. As the column crossed the Bowling Green road the artillery of his division was ordered into position on the rise of the ground between this road and the railroad; Cooper's and Ransom's batteries, to the front, soon joined by Amsden's to oppose those of the enemy on the crest, while Simpson's had to be thrown to the left, to oppose that on the Bowling Green road, which was taking the column in flank. Hall's battery was at the same time thrown to the front, on the left of Gibbon's division, which was advancing in line on Meade's right. The artillery combat here raged furiously for some time, until that of the enemy was silenced, when all of our batteries were directed to shell the wood, where his infantry was supposed to be posted. This was continued some half-hour, when the column of Meade, advancing in fine order and with gallant determination, was directed into the point of wood which extended this side of the railroad, with instructions, when they carried the crest and road which ran along it in their front, to move the First Brigade along the road, the Second Brigade to advance and hold the road, while the Third moved across the open field, to support the First in carrying the extreme point of the ridge. At this time I sent orders to General Gibbon to advance, in connection with General Meade, and carry the wood in his front. The advance was made under the fire of the enemy's batteries on his right and front, to which Gibbon's batteries replied, while those of Smith joined in on the right.

"Meade's division successfully carried the wood in front, crossed the railroad, charged up the slope of the hill, and gained the road and edge of the wood, driving the enemy from his strong positions in the ditches and railroad cut, capturing the flags of two regiments and sending about 200 prisoners to the rear. At the same time Gibbon's division had crossed the railroad and entered the wood, driving back the first line of the enemy and capturing a number of prisoners; but, from the dense character of the wood, the connection between his division and Meade's was broken. The infantry combat was here kept up with

great spirit for a short time, when Meade's column was vigorously assailed by the enemy's masked force, and, after a severe contest, forced back. Two regiments of Berry's brigade, Birney's division, arrived about this time, and were immediately thrown into the wood on Gibbon's left, to the support of the line; but they, too, were soon overpowered, and the whole line retired from the wood, Meade's in some confusion, and, after an ineffectual effort by General Meade and myself to rally them under the enemy's fire, that of the artillery having resumed almost its original intensity, I directed General Meade to re-form his division across the Bowling Green road, and ordered the remainder of Berry's brigade, which had come up, to the support of the batteries.

"The enemy, showing himself in strong force in the wood, seemed disposed to follow our retiring troops, but the arrival of the other brigades of Birney's division on the ground at this critical moment, to occupy our line of battle materially aided in saving Hall's battery, which was now seriously threatened by the enemy, and, together with our artillery fire, soon drove him to his sheltered positions and cover, from which his infantry did not again appear.

"General Gibbon's division was assailed in turn in the same manner, and compelled to retire from the wood soon after Meade's."

General Conrad Feger Jackson, commanding the Third Brigade of Meade's division, was killed within the enemy's lines. General Jackson was a native of Pennsylvania, and was appointed colonel of the 9th Pennsylvania Reserves in 1861. He commanded a brigade in Porter's Corps (fifth) in the Peninsula.

MAJOR-GENERAL W. B. FRANKLIN, U. S. V.
Commanding the left grand division at Fredericksburg. (From a photograph taken about 1884.)

THE RIGHT WING OF HOOKER'S ARMY CROSSING THE RAPPAHANNOCK AT KELLY'S FORD.

THE BATTLE OF CHANCELLORSVILLE.

THE UNION SIDE.

BY ALFRED PLEASONTON, BREVET MAJOR-GENERAL, U. S. A.
Commander of the Cavalry on the Field at Chancellorsville.

UNION CAVALRY-MAN'S HAT.

IN the latter part of April, 1863, General Hooker decided to undertake an offensive campaign with the Army of the Potomac against the Army of Northern Virginia, under General Lee. At this time the two armies faced each other: Lee's, numbering about 60,000 men, being at Fredericksburg, and the Army of the Potomac, numbering about 130,000 men, at Falmouth, on the north side of the Rappahannock River opposite Fredericksburg. Hooker directed three corps of the army, the First, the Third, and the Sixth, comprising 59,000 men, under the command of General Sedgwick, to cross the Rappahannock River below Fredericksburg and hold Lee's army in that position, while he himself moved secretly and with celerity three corps, the Fifth, the Eleventh, and the Twelfth, numbering 42,000 men, up the river, crossing it and concentrating them at Chancellorsville, ten miles west of Fredericksburg, with the purpose of moving down upon General Lee's army to take it in rear and flank — two divisions of the Second Corps being placed to cover Banks's Ford, the third division being left at Falmouth, while a brigade and battery were stationed at United States Ford to facilitate the crossing. The Cavalry Corps, with the exception of one small brigade of three regiments and a battery of horse artillery, which was left under my command with the army, was ordered

under the command of General Stoneman to make a raid in rear of Lee's army, and destroy his railroads and his communications with Richmond. . . .

The right wing of the army crossed Kelly's Ford on the morning of the 29th, and the Eleventh and Twelfth corps reached Germanna Ford that evening. I had the advance of this column with two regiments of cavalry and a battery of horse artillery; the third regiment of the cavalry brigade I sent with the Fifth Corps to Ely's Ford. In the afternoon, at Germanna Ford, I surprised and captured a picket of some fifty of Stuart's cavalry soldiers. With them was an engineer officer belonging to Stuart's staff. On searching the party, as is done with all prisoners, I found on this engineer officer a very bulky volume, which proved to be a diary that he had been keeping throughout the war. I spent the greater part of the night in reading it, in hopes of finding something that would be of advantage to us; nor was I disappointed. This diary stated that in the first week in March a council of war had been held at General Stuart's headquarters, which had been attended by Generals Jackson, A. P. Hill, Ewell, and Stuart. They were in conference over five hours, and came to the decision that the next battle would be at or near Chancellorsville, and that that position must be prepared. The next day, the 30th of April, I moved on toward Chancellorsville, and at 1 o'clock in the day I captured a courier or orderly from General Lee, who had a despatch from Lee, dated at Fredericksburg, noon of that day, and addressed to Major-General McLaws, stating that he had just been informed that the enemy

HOOKER'S HEADQUARTERS AT CHANCELLORSVILLE, SATURDAY MORNING, MAY 2.

had concentrated in force near Chancellorsville, inquiring why he had not been kept advised, and saying that he wished to see McLaws as soon as possible at headquarters. At 2 o'clock P. M., one hour later, I reported to General Hooker at Chancellorsville, and submitted to him the diary and General Lee's despatch, both of which he retained, and I suggested that we had evidently surprised General Lee by our rapid movements across the river, and, as Lee had prepared for a battle at Chancellorsville, we had better anticipate him by moving on toward Fredericksburg. A march of three or four miles would take us out of the woods into a more open country, where we could form our line of battle, and where our artillery could be used to advantage; we would then be prepared to move on Fredericksburg in the morning. Besides, such a movement would enable us to uncover Banks's Ford, which would shorten our communication with General Sedgwick over 5 miles, and bring us within 3½ miles of Falmouth by that Ford. . . .

[General Pleasonton's cavalry on the evening of the 30th developed the presence of Stuart's Confederates on the right rear of Hooker's army, masking Stonewall Jackson's movements. The narrative proceeds with the events in the Union lines after that information reached General Hooker.]

To move the army down on Fredericksburg with an unknown force on its rear and flank was a hazardous experiment. What could have been done with safety the day before now became doubtful, and it was this uncertainty that paralyzed the vigor and action of General Hooker throughout the 1st of May. Although he started the Second, Fifth, Twelfth, and Third corps in the direction of Tabernacle Church on the way to Fredericksburg, the movement was not of such a character as to bring success. Upon meeting a stubborn resistance from General Jackson's forces, and fearing that if he

should become deeply engaged a force from Spotsylvania would take him in the rear and flank, he withdrew the army and placed it in position at Chancellorsville.

From that time the whole situation was changed. Without striking a blow, the army was placed on the defensive. The golden moment had been lost, and it never appeared again to the same extent afterward — an illustration that soldiers' legs have as much to do with winning victories as their arms.

General Lee knew that General Hooker had taken his army back to its position at Chancellorsville. The Third Corps had already been taken from General Sedgwick at Fredericksburg, and at 2 o'clock on the morning of May 2d the First Corps was also ordered up to Chancellorsville, leaving Sedgwick with the Sixth Corps. These movements did not escape the attention of General Lee, so he decided to assume the offensive and put in operation the plan which had been suggested by Generals Jackson, A. P. Hill, Ewell, and Stuart, at their council of war in the first week in March. He left a sufficient force at Fredericksburg to watch Sedgwick, while with the bulk of his army he moved on Chancellorsville, sending a force under Generals Jackson, A. P. Hill, and Stuart, to make a turning movement and to attack the Union forces in the rear and right flank, and roll them up. Lee himself, in the mean time, with the remainder of his forces, occupied the attention of the left and center of Hooker's army, to prevent any interference with the flank movement. General Lee's strategy was the same that Hooker had carried out so successfully until he stopped at Chancellorsville. Lee was equally successful in his movements, and we will now investigate the causes of his failure to give the Army of the Potomac a crushing blow.

On the 2d day of May the right of the Army of the Potomac was the Eleventh Corps, in the woods

THE 29TH PENNSYLVANIA (OF KANE'S BRIGADE, GEARY'S DIVISION, TWELFTH CORPS) IN THE TRENCHES UNDER ARTILLERY FIRE, MAY 3.

near Dowdall's Tavern (Melzi Chancellor's); the Third Corps connected it with the Twelfth Corps at Fairview and Chancellorsville, facing south toward the woods; while the Second and the Fifth corps were posted to prevent any attack taking the position in the rear and flank from the east. Throughout the morning of the 2d of May, attacks were made on different portions of our line from the east to the west. These attacks occurred at intervals of an hour or more, but always farther to the west. I was satisfied this was done to withdraw our attention from the real point of attack, and I mentioned this to Hooker, who had become more and more impressed with the belief that the information contained in the diary of Stuart's engineer officer was correct, and that Lee had adopted a plan to carry it out.

In the afternoon of May 2d General Sickles, commanding the Third Corps, sent in word that the enemy were retreating toward Gordonsville, and that their wagons and artillery could be seen passing by the Furnace road some three miles to the south. General Hooker sent for me on receiving this report, and stated that he was not sure the enemy were retreating; that he wanted an officer of experience in that part of the field, and that he wished me to take my command there and keep him promptly informed of everything that was going on. I asked him if he considered me to be under the orders of any one. He replied quickly, "You are under my orders only; use your best judgment in doing whatever you think ought to be done."

On arriving at Hazel Grove, about one mile from Chancellorsville, I found that General Sickles was moving two of the divisions of the Third Corps in the direction of Catherine Furnace, and shortly after he became engaged there with a strong rear-guard. Hazel Grove was the highest ground in the neighborhood and was the key of our position, and I saw that if Lee's forces gained it the Army of the Potomac would be worsted.

General Sickles wanted some cavalry to protect his flanks, and I gave him the 6th New York. This left me with only the 8th and 17th Pennsylvania regiments and Martin's New York battery of horse artillery. I posted this command at the extreme west of the clearing, about two hundred yards from the woods in which the Eleventh Corps was encamped. This position at Hazel Grove was about a quarter of a mile in extent, running nearly northeast and southwest, but was in no place farther than two hundred yards from the woods, and on the south and east it sloped off into a marsh and a creek. It commanded the position of the army at Fairview and Chancellorsville and enfiladed our line. The moving out to the Furnace of the two divisions of the Third Corps left a gap of about a mile from Hazel Grove to the right of the Twelfth Corps. Shortly after General Sickles had been engaged at the Furnace, he sent me word that the enemy were giving way and cavalry could be used to advantage in pursuit. Before moving my command I rode out to the Furnace to comprehend the situation. It was no place for cavalry to operate, and as I could hear spattering shots going more and more toward the northwest, I was satisfied that the enemy were not retreating. I hastened back to my command at Hazel Grove; when I reached it, the Eleventh Corps to our rear and our right was in full flight, panic-stricken beyond description. We faced about, having then the marsh behind us. It was an ugly marsh, about fifty yards wide, and in the stampede of the Eleventh Corps, beef cattle, ambulances, mules, artillery, wagons, and horses

FROM A PHOTOGRAPH.

S. Hooker

became stuck in the mud, and others coming on crushed them down, so that when the fight was over the pile of debris in the marsh was many feet high. I saw that something had to be done, and that very quickly, or the Army of the Potomac would receive a crushing defeat. The two cavalry regiments were in the saddle, and as I rode forward Major Keenan of the 8th Pennsylvania came out to meet me, when I ordered him to take the regiment, charge into the woods, which, as we had previously stood, were to our rear, and hold the enemy in check until I could get some guns into position. He replied, with a smile at the size of the task, that he would do it, and started off immediately. Thirty men, including Major Keenan, Captain Arrowsmith, and Adjutant Haddock, never came back. I then directed Captain Martin to bring his guns into battery, load with double charges of canister, and aim them so that the shot would hit the ground half-way between the guns and the woods. I also stated that I would give the order to fire. Just then a handsome young lieutenant of the 4th U. S. Artillery, Frank B. Crosby (son of a distinguished lawyer of New York City), who was killed the next day, galloped up and said, "General, I have a battery of six guns; where shall I go? what shall I do?" I told him to place his battery in line on the right of Martin's battery, and gave him the same instructions I had given Martin as to how I wanted him to serve his guns. These 2 batteries gave me 12 guns, and to obtain more I then charged 3 squadrons of the 17th Pennsylvania Cavalry on the stragglers of the Eleventh Corps to clear the ground, and with the assistance of the rest of the regiment succeeded in placing 10 more pieces of artillery in line. The line was then ready for Stonewall Jackson's onset. It was dusk when his men swarmed out of the woods for a quarter of a mile in our front (our rear ten minutes before). They came on in line five and six deep, with but one flag—a Union flag dropped by the Eleventh Corps.

I suspected deception and was ready for it. They called out not to shoot, they were friends; at the same time they gave us a volley from at least five thousand muskets. As soon as I saw the flash I gave the command to fire, and the whole line of artillery was discharged at once. It fairly swept them from the earth; before they could recover themselves the line of artillery had been loaded and was ready for a second attack. After the second discharge, suspecting that they might play the trick of having their men lie down, draw the fire of the artillery, then jump up and charge before the pieces could be reloaded, I poured in the canister for about twenty minutes, and the affair was over.

When the Eleventh Corps was routed, the situation was this: The nearest infantry to me was the right of the Twelfth Corps, over a mile off, and engaged by the forces under General Lee, who was trying to prevent them from impeding the movements of General Jackson. The two divisions of the Third Corps were nearly a mile to the west, at the Furnace. Had Jackson captured the position at Hazel Grove, these two divisions would have been cut off from the army. He would have seen

REPULSE OF JACKSON'S MEN AT HAZEL GROVE, BY ARTILLERY UNDER GENERAL PLEASONTON.

General Hooker and his staff getting what troops he could to prevent the routed Eleventh Corps from demoralizing the rest of the army, and the fatal position which that portion of the army occupied rendered it an easy task to have crushed it. Neither the Second Corps nor the Twelfth Corps was in position to have defended itself against an attack by Jackson from Hazel Grove.

For half an hour General Jackson had the Army of the Potomac at his mercy. That he halted to re-form his troops in the woods, instead of forging ahead into the clearing, where he could re-form his troops more rapidly, and where he could have seen that he was master of the situation, turned out to be one of those fatalities by which the most brilliant prospects are sacrificed. When he advanced upon the artillery at Hazel Grove Jackson had another opportunity to win, if his infantry had been properly handled. The fire of his infantry was so high it did no harm; they should have been ordered to fire so low as to disable the cannoneers at the guns. Had his infantry fire been as effective as that of our artillery, Jackson would have carried the position. The artillery fire was effective because I applied to it that principle of dynamics in which the angle of incidence is equal to the angle of reflection,—that

is to say, if the muzzle of a gun is three feet from the ground and it is discharged so that the shot will strike the ground at a distance of one hundred yards, it will glance from the earth at the same angle at which it struck it, and in another one hundred yards will be three feet from the ground. I knew my first volley must be a crushing one, or Jackson, with his superior numbers, would charge across the short distance which separated us and capture the artillery before the guns could be reloaded.

After the fight at Hazel Grove I sent into the woods and captured a number of Jackson's men. I asked them to what command they belonged. One of them said to General A. P. Hill's corps, and added, "That was a pretty trick you played us this evening." I asked to what he referred. He replied, "By withdrawing your infantry, and catching us on your guns,"—thus showing that the flight of the Eleventh Corps was looked upon as a ruse. To my question, if they had suffered much, he said that they had been badly cut up; that General Jackson had been badly wounded; also General A. P. Hill, and their chief of artillery. I asked how he knew General Jackson had been wounded. He stated that he saw him when he was carried off the field

in a litter. This information I immediately reported to General Hooker, when he directed me to withdraw my command from that position and go into camp on the north side of the Rappahannock River. It was 4 A. M. of the 3d of May when I moved from Hazel Grove. Sickles, with the two divisions of the Third Corps, reached Hazel Grove from the Furnace between half-past nine and ten on the night of the 2d of May. Some of his troops had fighting in the woods before I left, but I am unable to say what was its character.

On the morning of the 3d of May (Sunday) General Stuart was in command of Jackson's forces, Jackson and A. P. Hill having been wounded, as reported by the prisoner taken the night before. Stuart prepared, with his usual impetuosity, to renew the attack early that morning, and by one of those unfortunate occurrences so prevalent during the war, he caught the Third Corps in motion to take up a new position, connecting with the Twelfth Corps at Fairview, and facing to the west. This withdrawal enabled Stuart to take the position at Hazel Grove from which Jackson had been repulsed the evening before. He saw its advantages at once, and, placing some thirty pieces of artillery there, he enfiladed the Twelfth Corps at Fairview and Chancellorsville, and punished the Third Corps severely. The Third Corps was fighting throughout the day under great disadvantages. To add to the embarrassments of the army, General Hooker that morning was disabled by a concussion, and the army was virtually without a head, the different corps commanders fighting their commands on the defensive. Such extraordinary conditions forced the Army of the Potomac to fall back from Chancellorsville and Fairview, and form a new line of battle to the north and some distance from Chancellorsville. This line presented a front to the enemy that could not be enfiladed or turned. Desultory fighting, especially with artillery, was kept up on the 4th of May; but Hooker's battle ended on the 3d, after the army had gained its new position.

It is useless to speculate what General Hooker would have done if he had not been disabled. Up to the evening of the 2d of May the enemy had suffered severely, while the Army of the Potomac had comparatively but few killed and wounded;

UNION TROOPS CROSSING THE RAPIDAN AT ELY'S FORD.

SECOND LINE OF UNION DEFENSE AT THE JUNCTION OF THE ROADS TO ELY'S AND
UNITED STATES FORDS.

but the unfortunate circumstances that contracted the lines of our army enabled the enemy to inflict the severest punishment upon all the troops that were engaged. In fact, the greatest injury was inflicted on the 3d of May, while the army had no commander. Had the First Corps, which had not been engaged, and the Fifth Corps, still fresh, been thrown into the action in the afternoon of Sunday, the 3d of May, when Lee's troops were exhausted from the struggle, they would certainly have made Chancellorsville what it should have been,—a complete success. These two corps mustered from 25,-000 to 30,000 men. There was no one to order them into the fight, and a second golden opportunity was lost. The army recrossed the Rappahannock River on the night of May 5th, and took up again the position at Falmouth which they had occupied before the campaign.

THE ELEVENTH CORPS AT CHAN-
CELLORSVILLE.

BY OLIVER O. HOWARD, MAJOR-GENERAL, U. S. A.
Commander of the Eleventh Corps.

THE country around Chancellorsville for the most part is a wilderness, with but here and there an opening. If we consult the recent maps (no good ones existed before the battle), we notice that the two famous rivers, the Rapidan and the Rappahannock, join at a point due north of Chancellorsville; thence the Rappahannock runs easterly for two miles, till suddenly at the United States Ford it turns and flows south for a mile and a half, and then, turning again, completes a horse-shoe bend. Here, on the south shore, was General Hooker's battle-line on the morning of the 2d of May, 1863. Here his five army corps, those

of Meade, Slocum, Couch, Sickles, and Howard, were deployed. The face was toward the south, and the ranks mainly occupied a ridge nearly parallel with the Rapidan. . . .

Our opponents, under General Robert E. Lee, the evening before, were about two miles distant toward Fredericksburg, and thus between us and Sedgwick. Lee had immediately with him the divisions of McLaws, Anderson, Rodes, Colston, and A. P. Hill, besides some cavalry under Stuart. He held, for his line of battle, a comparatively short front between the Rappahannock and the Catherine Furnace, not exceeding two miles and a half in extent. His right wing, not far from the river, was behind Mott's Run, which flows due east, and his left was deployed along the Catherine Furnace road.

Could Hooker, on the first day of May, have known Lee's exact location, he never could have had a better opportunity for taking the offensive. But he did not know, and after the few troops advancing toward Fredericksburg had met the approaching enemy he ordered all back to the "old position," the Chancellorsville line. . . .

On the preceding Thursday, the last of April, the three corps that constituted the right wing of the army, Meade's, Slocum's, and mine, had crossed from the north to the south side of the Rapidan, and by 4 o'clock in the afternoon had reached the vicinity of Chancellorsville, where Slocum, who was the senior commander present, established his headquarters. I, approaching from Germanna Ford, halted my divisions at Dowdall's Tavern and encamped them there. Then I rode along the Plank road through the almost continuous forest to the Chancellorsville House. There I reported to Slocum. He said that the orders were for me to cover the right of the general line, posting my command near Dowdall's Tavern. He pointed to a place on

the map marked "Mill" near there, on a branch of Hunting Run, and said, "Establish your right there." General Slocum promised, with the Twelfth Corps, to occupy the space between his headquarters and Dowdall's clearing; but, finding the distance too great, one of his division commanders sent me word that I must cover the last three-quarters of a mile of the Plank road. This was done by a brigade of General Steinwehr, the commander of my left division, though with regret on our part, because it required all the corps reserves to fill up that gap.

The so-called Dowdall's Tavern was at that time the home of Melzi Chancellor. He had a large family, including several grown people. I placed my headquarters at his house. In front of me, facing south along a curving ridge, the right of Steinwehr's division was located. He had but two brigades, Barlow on the Plank road and Buschbeck on his right. With them Steinwehr covered a mile, leaving but two regiments for reserve. These he put some two hundred yards to his rear, near the little "Wilderness Church."

Next to Steinwehr, toward our right, came General Carl Schurz's division. First was Captain Dilger's battery. Dilger was one of those handsome, hearty, active young men that everybody liked to have near. His guns pointed to the southwest and west, along the Orange Plank road. Next was Krzyzanowski's brigade, about half on the front and half in reserve. Schurz's right brigade was that of Schimmelfennig, disposed in the same manner, a part deployed and the remainder kept a few hundred yards back for a reserve. Schurz's front line of infantry extended along the old turnpike and faced to the southwest. The right division of the corps was commanded by General Charles Dev-

ens, afterward attorney-general in the cabinet of President Hayes. Devens and I together had carefully reconnoitered both the Orange Plank road and the old turnpike for at least three miles toward the west. After this reconnoissance he established his division,—the Second Brigade, under McLean, next to Schurz's first, and then pushing out on the pike for half a mile he deployed the other, Gilsa's, at right angles facing west, connecting his two parts by a thin skirmish-line. Colonel Gilsa's brigade was afterward drawn back, still facing west at right angles to the line, so as to make a more solid connection, and so that, constituting, as it did, the main right flank, the reserves of the corps could be brought more promptly to its support, by extending its right to the north, should an enemy by any possible contingency get so far around. A section of Dieckmann's battery which looked to the west along the old pike was located at the angle.

The reserve batteries, twelve guns, were put upon a ridge abreast of the little church and pointed toward the northwest, with a view to sweep all approaches to the north of Gilsa, firing up a gradually ascending slope. This ridge, where I stood during the battle, was central, and, besides, enabled the artillerymen to enfilade either roadway, or meet an attack from south, west, or north. Here epaulments for the batteries were constructed, and cross-intrenchments for the battery supports were dug, extending from the little church across all the open ground that stretched away from the tavern to the right of Devens's line.

To my great comfort, General Sickles's corps came up on Friday, May 1st, and took from our left Steinwehr's three-quarters of a mile of the Plank road. Thus he relieved from the front line Barlow's large brigade, giving me, besides the several

181

THE WILDERNESS CHURCH.

STAMPEDE OF THE ELEVENTH CORPS ON THE PLANK ROAD.

MAJOR-GENERAL CARL SCHURZ, U. S. V.

division reserves, General Barlow with 1500 men as a general reserve for the corps. These were massed near the cross-intrenchments, and held avowedly to support the batteries and protect General Devens's exposed right flank.

As to pickets, each division had a good line of them. My aide, Major Charles H. Howard, assisted in connecting them between divisions, and during the 2d of May that fearless and faithful staff-officer, Major E. Whittlesey, rode the entire circuit of their front to stimulate them to special activity. Those of Devens were "thrown out at a distance from a half-mile to a mile and stretching well around covering our right flank"; and the picket-posts in front on the pike were over two miles beyond the main line. . . .

Meanwhile the Confederate General Rodes had been reaching his place in the Wilderness. At 4 P. M. his men were in position; the line of battle of his own brigade touched the pike west of us with its right and stretched away to the north; beyond his brigade came Iverson's in the same line. On the right of the pike was Doles's brigade, and to his right Colquitt's. One hundred yards to rear was Trimble's division (Colston commanding), with Ramseur on the right following Colquitt. After another interval followed the division of A. P. Hill. The advance Confederate division had more men in it than there were in the Eleventh Corps, now in position. Counting the ranks of this formidable column, beginning with the enveloping skirmish line, we find 7, besides the 3 ranks of file-closers. Many of them were brought into a solid mass by the entanglements of the forest, and gave our men the idea that battalions were formed in close columns doubled on the center. With as little noise as possible, a little after 5 P.M., the steady advance of the enemy began. Its first lively effects, like a cloud of dust driven before a coming shower, appeared in the startled rabbits, squirrels, quail, and other game flying wildly hither and thither in evident terror, and escaping, where possible, into adjacent clearings.

The foremost men of Doles's brigade took about half an hour to strike our advance picket on the pike. This picket, of course, created no delay. Fifteen minutes later he reached our skirmishers, who seem to have resisted effectively for a few minutes, for it required a main line to dislodge them. Doles says, concerning the next check he received, "After a resistance of about ten minutes we drove him [Devens] from his position on the left and carried his battery of two guns, caissons, and horses." . . .

I sent out my chief-of-staff, Colonel Asmussen, who was the first officer to mount,—"The firing is in front of Devens; go and see if all is in order on the extreme right." He instantly turned and galloped away. I mounted and set off for a prominent place in rear of Schurz's line, so as to change front to the northwest of every brigade southeast of the point of attack, if the attack should extend beyond Devens's right flank; for it was divined at once that the enemy was now west of him. I could see numbers of our men—not the few stragglers that always fly like chaff at the first breeze, but scores of them—rushing into the opening, some with arms

and some without, running or falling before they got behind the cover of Devens's reserves, and before General Schurz's waiting masses could deploy or charge. The noise and the smoke filled the air with excitement, and to add to it Dieckmann's guns and caissons, with battery men scattered, rolled and tumbled like runaway wagons and carts in a thronged city. The guns and the masses of the right brigade struck the second line of Devens before McLean's front had given way; and, more quickly than it could be told, with all the fury of the wildest hailstorm, everything, every sort of organization that lay in the path of the mad current of panic-stricken men, had to give way and be broken into fragments.

My own horse seemed to catch the fury; he sprang—he rose high on his hind legs and fell over, throwing me to the ground. My aide-de-camp, Dessauer, was struck by a shot and killed, and for a few moments I was as helpless as any of the men who were speeding without arms to the rear. But faithful orderlies helped me to remount. Schurz was still doing all he could to face regiments about and send them to Devens's northern flank to

help the few who still held firm. Devens, already badly wounded, and several officers were doing similar work. I rode quickly to the reserve batteries. A staff-officer of General Hooker, Lieutenant-Colonel Joseph Dickinson, Assistant Adjutant-General, joined me there; my own staff gathered around me. I was eager to fill the trenches that Barlow would have held. Buschbeck's second line was ordered to change front there. His men kept their ranks, but at first they appeared slow. Would they never get there!

Dickinson said, "Oh, General, see those men coming from that hill way off to the right, and there's the enemy after them. Fire, oh, fire at them; you may stop the flight!"

"No, Colonel," I said, "I will never fire on my own men!"

As soon as our men were near enough the batteries opened, firing at first shells and then canister over their heads. As the attacking force emerged from the forest and rushed on, the men in front would halt and fire, and, while these were reloading, another set would run before them, halt and fire, in no regular line, but in such multitudes that our men went down before them like trees in a hurricane.

By extraordinary effort we had filled all our long line of cross-intrenchments, mainly with fragments of organizations and individual soldiers. Many officers running away stopped there and did what they could, but others shouted, "We've done all we can," and ran on. Schirmer managed the reserve artillery fairly. Dilger, the battery commander on Schurz's left, rolled the balls along the Plank road and shelled the wood. General Steinwehr was on hand, cool, collected, and judicious. Like Blair at Atlanta, he had made his men (who were south of Dowdall's) spring to the reverse side of their intrenchments and be ready to fire the instant it was possible.

Let us pause here a moment and follow Doles,

RACE ON THE PLANK ROAD FOR RIGHT OF WAY, BETWEEN THE NINTH MASSACHUSETTS BATTERY AND A BAGGAGE TRAIN.

who led the enemy's attack. He states that, after his first successful charge, "the command moved forward at the double-quick to assault the enemy, who had taken up a strong position on the crest of a hill in the open field." This position was the one on Hawkins's farm where Devens's and Schurz's reserves began their fight. But wave after wave of Confederate infantry came upon them, and even their left flank was unprotected the instant the runaways had passed it. To our sorrow, we, who had eagerly observed their bravery, saw these reserves also give way, and the hill and crest on Hawkins's farm were quickly in the hands of the men in gray.

Doles, who must have been a cool man to see so clearly amid the screeching shells and all the hot excitement of battle, says again: "He" (meaning our forces from Schimmelfennig's and Buschbeck's brigades, and perhaps part of McLean's, who had faced about and had not yet given way) "made a stubborn resistance from behind a wattling fence on a hill covered thickly with pines."

Among the stubborn fighters at this place was Major Jeremiah Williams. The enemy was drawing near him. His men fired with coolness and deliberation. His right rested among scrubby bushes and saplings, while his left was in comparatively open ground. The fire of the approaching enemy was murderous, and almost whole platoons of our men were falling; yet they held their ground. Williams waited, rapidly firing, till not more than thirty paces intervened, and then ordered the retreat. Out of 333 men and 16 commissioned officers in the regiment (the 25th Ohio), 130, including 5 officers, were killed or wounded. Major Williams brought a part of the living to the breastworks near me; the remainder, he says, were carried off to the rear by another regimental commander.

During the delays we had thus far caused to the first division of our enemy, all his rear lines had closed up, and the broad mass began to appear even below me on my left front to the south of Steinwehr's knoll. Then it was, after we had been fighting an hour, that Sickles's and Pleasonton's guns began to be heard, for they had faced about at Hazel Grove obliquely toward the northwest, and were hurrying artillery, cavalry, and infantry into position to do what they could against the attack now reaching them.

I had come to my last practicable stand. The Confederates were slowly advancing, firing as they came. The twelve guns of Schirmer, the corps chief of artillery, increased by a part of Dilger's battery, fired, at first with rapidity; but the battery men kept falling from death and wounds. Suddenly, as if by an order, when a sheet of the enemy's fire reached them, a large number of the men in the supporting trenches vacated their positions and went off.

No officers ever made more strenuous exertions than those that my staff and myself put forth to stem the tide of retreat and refill those trenches, but the panic was too great. Then our artillery fire became weaker and weaker.

I next ordered a retreat to the edge of the forest toward Chancellorsville, so as to uncover Steinwehr's knoll, the only spot yet firmly held. The

batteries, except four pieces, were drawn off and hurried to the rear. The stand at the edge of the forest was necessarily a short one.

General Steinwehr, being now exposed from flank and rear, having held his place for over an hour, drew off his small remnants and all moved rapidly through openings and woods, through low ground and swamps, the two miles to the first high land south of Hooker's headquarters.

Captain Hubert Dilger with his battery sturdily kept along the Plank road, firing constantly as he retired. The Confederate masses rushed after us in the forest and along all paths and roads with triumphant shouts and

GENERAL HOWARD STRIVING TO RALLY HIS TROOPS.

redoubled firing, and so secured much plunder and many prisoners.

It was after sundown and growing dark when I met General Hiram G. Berry, commanding a division of the Third Corps, as I was ascending the high ground above named. "Well, General, where now?" he asked. "You take the right of this road and I will take the left and try to defend it," I replied.

Our batteries, with many others, were on the

crest facing to the rear, and as soon as Steinwehr's troops had cleared the way these guns began a terrible cannonade and continued it into the night. They fired into the forest, now full of Confederates, all disorganized by their exciting chase, and every effort of the enemy to advance in that direction in the face of the fire was effectually barred by the

artillery and supporting troops. Stonewall Jackson fell that evening from bullet-wounds, in the forest in front of Berry's position. And here, on the forenoon of the next day, May 3d, the gallant General Berry met his death. It was here, too, that officers of the Eleventh Corps, though mortified by defeat, successfully rallied the scattered brigades and divisions, and, after shielding the batteries, went during the night to replace the men of the Fifth Corps and thereafter defend the left of the general line. . . . Jackson was victorious. Even his enemies praise him; but, providentially for us, it was the last battle that he waged against the American Union. . . .

HOOKER'S LEFT WING AT CHANCELLORSVILLE AND THE STORMING OF FREDERICKSBURG HEIGHTS

BY HUNTINGTON W. JACKSON, BREVET LIEUTENANT-COLONEL, U. S. V.

Aide-de-camp to General John Newton in the Assault on Marye's Heights.

. . . During the evening of the 2d of May Hooker sent word to Sedgwick "to take up his line on the Chancellorsville road and attack and destroy any forces he might meet." He also added that "he (Sedgwick) would probably fall upon the rear of Lee's forces, and between them they would use Lee up." If Hooker thought an insignificant force was in Sedgwick's front, the engagement soon to take place showed how mistaken he was. Sedgwick received the order about 11 o'clock at night. He at once advanced his command to the Bowling Green road and then marched by the right flank toward Fredericksburg. Newton's division was in the advance. The night was dark and the road made darker by the foliage of the trees on either side. The progress was necessarily slow. Frequent short halts were made while the skirmishers were feeling their way. Once, when the halt was prolonged and nothing broke the deep silence of the night except an occasional shot followed by the never-to-be-forgotten *ping* of the Minié ball, General Newton, who was riding with the third or fourth regiment from the advance, called out: "Is any one of my staff here?" Those present promptly responded, and I was directed to "ride ahead and tell Colonel Shaler to brush away the enemy's pickets." The road was filled with soldiers, some lying down, others resting on their guns, but a passage was quickly cleared. At Hazel Run Colonel Shaler and Colonel Hamblin were found standing together. Here the enemy made a determined resistance. Their pickets were but a few yards distant. On the other side of the creek the road made a sharp ascent and curved to the right. In a subdued tone Colonel Shaler said: "Colonel Hamblin, you have heard the order from General Newton?" At once Colonel Hamblin left. In a moment there was the noise of hurrying feet, the troops quickly disappeared in the dark; a shout, a bright, sudden flash, a roll of musketry followed, and the road was open.

It was the gray of morning when the advance reached the rear and left of Fredericksburg. A negro who came into the lines reported the heights occupied and that the enemy were cutting the canal to flood the roads. To ascertain whether this was true, another delay was caused. No one in the command was acquainted with the topography of the country, and the advance was compelled to move with great caution through the streets and in the outskirts of the town. As the morning dawned, Marye's Heights, the scene of the fierce attacks under Burnside in the previous December, were presented to our view. Several regiments were speedily moved along the open ground in the rear of the town toward the heights, and this movement discovered the enemy in force behind the famous stone wall at the base of the hill. Lee had left Early with his division and Barksdale's brigade, a force of about ten thousand men, to hold Freder-

THE CONFEDERATES CHARGING HOWARD'S BREASTWORKS ON THE PLANK ROAD, MAY 2.

RETREAT OF HOOKER'S RIGHT WING ACROSS THE RAPPAHANNOCK.

icksburg Heights. They were protected by strong works and supported by well-served artillery. It was at once felt that a desperate encounter was to follow, and the recollections of the previous disaster were by no means inspiriting.

It was Sunday morning, the 3d of May, and the weather was beautiful. The town was perfectly quiet, many of the inhabitants had fled, not a person was to be seen on the streets, and the windows and blinds of the houses were closed. The marks of the fierce cannonade to which the place had previously been exposed were everywhere visible.

As soon as practicable and as secretly as possible, Sedgwick prepared to attack the heights. Gibbon, of the Second Corps, who had been left on the north bank, crossed shortly after Sedgwick had captured the town and moved to the right, but his advance was stopped by the canal in front, over which it was impossible to lay bridges in face of the fire from the artillery and infantry on the hill. Sedgwick says, "Nothing remained but to carry the works by direct assault." The attack on Marye's Heights was made under direction of Newton. Two columns, each marching by fours, were formed on the Plank and Telegraph roads, and were supported by a line of infantry from the Light Brigade on the left, commanded by Colonel Burnham. The right column, under Colonel George C. Spear, was composed of the 61st Pennsylvania and the 43d New York. These two regiments belonged to the Light Brigade. This column was supported by the 67th New York and 82d Pennsylvania, under Colonel Alexander Shaler. The left column consisted of the 7th Massachusetts and the 36th New York, under Colonel Thomas D. Johns. The line of battle, commanded by Colonel Hiram Burnham, was composed of the 5th Wisconsin (acting as skirmishers), the 6th Maine, 31st New York (these three regiments also belonging to the Light Bri-

gade), and the 23d Pennsylvania. Howe's division was posted south of Hazel Run, and coöperated handsomely, capturing five guns.

The order to advance was given at 11 o'clock. Sedgwick and Newton with the deepest interest watched the attack from the garden of a brick residence situated on the outskirts of the town and to the left of the Telegraph road, which commanded a full view of the assault. The movements of the enemy showed that they were actively preparing to receive the attack, but the men behind the stone wall were concealed from view. As the left column emerged from the town and was passing near Sedgwick and Newton, the enemy's battery opened, and a portion of a bursting shell struck and killed Major Elihu J. Faxon, of the 36th New York, while mounted and riding with his command, and wounded several others. There was an exclamation of horror and a momentary scattering of the rear of the column, but the men quickly closed up and pressed on. Colonel Spear, commanding the right column, was killed at about the same time. Both columns and line, in light marching order, advanced at double-quick without firing a shot. The enemy kept up an incessant artillery fire, and the noise was deafening. Their musketry fire was reserved until our men were within easy range. Then a murderous storm of shot from the stone wall, and grape and canister from the hill, burst upon the columns and line. For a moment the head of the left column was checked and broken. The column on the right was also broken. Colonel Burnham's line of blue on the green field paused as if to recover breath, and slightly wavered. Sedgwick and Newton looked on with unconcealed anxiety, and turned to each other, but remained silent. The suspense was intense. Was it to be a victory or a defeat? Was the place a second time to be a "slaughter-pen"? Was the Sixth

Corps to be driven into the river? Staff-officers, waving their swords and hurrahing to the men, dashed down the Telegraph road. A blinding rain of shot pierced the air. It was more than human nature could face. The head of the column as it reached the lowest part of the decline near a fork in the road seemed to melt away. Many fell; others bending low to the earth hurriedly sought shelter from the undulations of ground and the fences and the two or three wooden structures along the road. Out of 400 comprising the 7th Massachusetts, 150 were killed and wounded. Colonel Johns, commanding, was severely wounded. Then, as if moved by a sudden impulse and nerved for a supreme effort, both columns and the line in the field simultaneously sprang forward. The stone wall was gained and the men were quickly over it. Just as my horse was jumping through a break in the wall one of the enemy, standing slightly to the left and about a horse's length from me, raised his gun and fired. The excitement of the hour must have unnerved his hand, for the ball *zipped* harmlessly by to my right. In a second a bayonet was thrust into his breast by one of our men on my left. Along the wall a hand-to-hand fight took place, and the bayonet and the butt of the musket were freely used. The brilliant and successful charge occupied perhaps ten or fifteen minutes, and immediately after the wall was carried the enemy became panic-stricken. In the flight they threw away guns, knapsacks, pistols, swords, and everything that might retard their speed. One thousand prisoners were taken, besides several battle-flags and pieces of artillery. The commander of a Louisiana battery handed his saber to Colonel Thomas S. Allen, of the 5th Wisconsin. This regiment out of 500 men lost 123, and the 6th Maine out of about the same number lost 167 in killed and wounded. Over 600 were killed and wounded

in the direct assault upon the heights, and the loss to the corps on the entire front was about 1000.

General G. K. Warren, who had arrived that morning with instructions from headquarters, said in his telegram to Hooker: "The heights were carried splendidly at 11 A. M. by Newton." Upon reaching the summit of the sharp hill, after passing through the extensive and well-wooded grounds of the Marye House, an exciting scene met the eye. A single glance exhibited to view the broad plateau alive with fleeing soldiers, riderless horses, and artillery and wagon trains on a gallop. The writer hurried back to Sedgwick, who was giving directions for Brooks and Howe to come up, and suggested that it was a rare opportunity for the use of cavalry. With evident regret Sedgwick replied that he did not have a cavalryman. The carrying of the heights had completely divided the enemy's forces, throwing either flank with much confusion on opposite roads, and it seemed as though a regiment of cavalry might not only have captured many prisoners, guns, ammunition, and wagons, but also have cleared the way for the corps almost as far as the immediate rear of Lee's army at Chancellorsville.

Newton's division, exhausted by the night march, the weight of several days' rations and sixty rounds of ammunition, and by the heat, fatigue, and excitement of battle, were allowed to halt for a short time. Many were soon asleep, while others made coffee and partook of their first meal that day.

Brooks's division soon came up from below Hazel Run, and took the advance. Newton and Howe followed. The enemy in the mean time had united their forces, and delayed the rapid advance by frequent stands, retiring successively from hill to hill, and opening with artillery. Ravines running at right angles to the main road and the rolling character of the country were favorable for imped-

THE WILDERNESS CHURCH (IN THE LEFT MIDDLE-GROUND) AND HAWKINS'S FARM (ON THE RIGHT) AS SEEN FROM THE PLANK ROAD IN FRONT OF DOWDALL'S TAVERN.

STAYING JACKSON'S ADVANCE, SATURDAY EVENING, MAY 2, WITH ARTILLERY PLACED ACROSS THE PLANK ROAD.

ing the pursuit, which was continued for three or four miles until we reached Salem Church, an unpretentious red-brick structure situated on a ridge covered with dense woods and undergrowth. To-day it bears many scars of the contest waged around it.

At this point the enemy were in position with four fresh brigades withdrawn from Hooker's front, and prepared to contest any farther advance. Lee had met with such complete success in his attack upon Hooker that he felt he could well spare these troops and not suffer. Brooks on the left of the road and Newton on the right quickly formed their commands and made several gallant assaults. The fight was very severe in the thick woods, and for a time was waged with varying success. The crest of the woods and a little school-house near the church were gained, and once it was thought they could be held, but the enemy, in superior numbers, pressed on, and the ground and the church were left in their possession. The contest did not last long, but nearly 1500 were killed and wounded. Bartlett's brigade, numbering less than 1500, lost 580 officers and men. That night the soldiers slept on their arms.

It was understood throughout the Sixth Corps that as soon as it should become engaged with the enemy Hooker would immediately attack in his front, and prevent any reinforcements from being sent against Sedgwick. All during that Sabbath day and the next the sound of Hooker's guns was

eagerly listened for. No sound would have been more welcome. But after 10 o'clock Sunday morning axes and spades were used at Chancellorsville more than the guns. The feeling became widely prevalent that the Sixth Corps would be compelled to take care of itself. At first it was cautiously whispered that Hooker had failed, and soon the worst was surmised, and it was concluded that no help could be expected from him. His dash, promptness, and confidence as a division and corps commander were gone.

Lee that night withdrew his troops, flushed with their brilliant success, from the front of Hooker, with the exception of Jackson's corps, and marched against Sedgwick. Still Hooker remained inactive; with a force greatly in excess of the enemy in his front, he made no effort to relieve Sedgwick from his perilous position. Works were thrown up by the enemy along the Salem Church ridge, and they extended their right until on Monday morning Marye's Heights and Fredericksburg, won at so great a sacrifice, were again theirs.

Sedgwick's position, as finally established, was in the shape of a horseshoe, both flanks resting on the river, the line covering Banks's Ford. His line of battle was between five and six miles in length. Frequent attempts had been made, during Sunday morning, to communicate with Banks's Ford and to direct the laying of pontoon-bridges, but for some time roving bodies of cavalry frustrated this. The late Colonel Henry W. Farrar,

then on the staff of Sedgwick, while carrying a message for this purpose, was captured and taken to Richmond. The 4th of May dragged wearily, skirmishing continued all day, the weather was hot, Sedgwick's position was most critical, and the keenest anxiety was felt. Lee was in our front with a force much larger than Sedgwick's then available command of about eighteen thousand men, and an attack was momentarily expected, but fortunately Lee consumed the whole day in establishing his lines. The greatest vigilance and activity were exercised by our men in throwing up rifle-pits. Hooker sent word to Sedgwick to look well to the safety of his corps, and either to fall back upon Fredericksburg or recross at Banks's Ford; he also added that he could do nothing to relieve him. Sedgwick accordingly intrusted Newton with the arrangements for the withdrawal. Newton quickly made himself acquainted with the roads leading to Banks's Ford and succeeded in establishing communication with General Henry W. Benham, who was in charge of the pontoons at that place.

At 6 o'clock in the evening the enemy attacked Brooks and Howe on the center and left, with the design of cutting off the corps from Banks's Ford. Howe not only maintained his position until nightfall, but also made several counter-charges, capturing several hundred prisoners. Brooks also held on until dark, but in retiring was closely pursued by the enemy. The whole corps then successfully fell back to Banks's Ford, and the long and painful suspense of the day was over. The picket line in front and on the left of Salem ridge was withdrawn by General David A. Russell in person. I had been directed to assist him. That sterling soldier, dismounted, moved along the line saying, "Quietly, men, quietly; don't make any noise"; but the jingle of the canteens and other unavoidable sounds on the evening air revealed the movement to the vigilant enemy, and they followed

closely, yelling and firing until the double-quick step brought us to our main column on the march, about a mile distant. Several of the enemy's scouts penetrated almost to the ford and threw up rockets to mark our position. The enemy's artillery responded to the signal, shelling both troops and bridges, but with little injury. During the night we recrossed the river, and took position to meet the enemy should they, as expected at the time, cross to the north side to renew their attack. . . .

THE CONFEDERATE SIDE.

STONEWALL JACKSON'S LAST BATTLE.

BY THE REV. JAMES POWER SMITH, CAPTAIN AND ASSISTANT ADJUTANT-GENERAL, C. S. A.

Aide-de-camp to General Jackson at the Battle of Chancellorsville.

AT daybreak on the morning of the 29th of April, 1863, sleeping in our tents at corps headquarters, near Hamilton's Crossing, we were aroused by Major Samuel Hale, of Early's staff, with the stirring news that Federal troops were crossing the Rappahannock on pontoons under cover of a heavy fog. General Jackson had spent the night at Mr. Yerby's hospitable mansion near by, where Mrs. Jackson [his second wife] had brought her infant child for the father to see. He was at once informed of the news, and promptly issued to his division commanders orders to prepare for action. At his direction I rode a mile across the fields to army headquarters, and, finding General Robert E. Lee still slumbering quietly, at the suggestion of Colonel Venable, whom I found stirring, I entered the general's tent and awoke him. Turning his feet out of his cot, he sat upon its side as I gave him the tidings from the front. Expressing no surprise, he playfully said: "Well, I thought I heard firing, and was beginning to think it was time some of you young fellows were

STONEWALL JACKSON GOING FORWARD ON THE PLANK ROAD IN ADVANCE OF HIS
LINE OF BATTLE.

fronting Hooker's advance from Chancellorsville, near the Tabernacle Church on the Plank road. To meet the whole Army of the Potomac, under Hooker, General Lee had of all arms about 60,000 men. General Longstreet, with part of his corps, was absent below Petersburg. General Lee had two divisions of Longstreet's corps, Anderson's, and McLaws's, and Jackson's corps, consisting of four divisions, A. P. Hill's, D. H. Hill's, commanded by Rodes, Trimble's, commanded by Colston, and Early's; and about 170 pieces of field-artillery. The divisions of Anderson and McLaws had been sent from Fredericksburg to meet Hooker's advance from Chancellorsville; Anderson on Wednesday, and McLaws (except Barksdale's brigade, left with Early) on Thursday. At the Tabernacle Church, about four miles east of Chancellorsville, the opposing forces met and brisk skirmishing began. On Friday, Jackson, reaching Anderson's position, took command of the Confederate advance, and urged on his skirmish line under Brigadier-General Ramseur with great vigor. How the muskets rattled along a front of a mile or two, across the unfenced fields, and through the woodlands! What spirit was imparted to the line, and what cheers rolled along its length, when Jackson, and then Lee himself, appeared riding abreast of the line along the Plank road! Slowly but steadily the line advanced, until at nightfall all Federal pickets and skirmishers were driven back upon the body of Hooker's force at Chancellorsville.

Here we reached a point, a mile and a half from Hooker's lines, where a road turns down to the left toward the old Catherine Furnace; and here at the fork of the roads General Lee and General Jackson spent the night, resting on the pine straw, curtained only by the close shadow of the pine forest. A little after nightfall I was sent by General Lee upon an errand to General A. P. Hill, on the old stone turnpike a mile or two north; and returning some time later with information of matters on our right, I found General Jackson retired to rest, and General Lee sleeping at the foot of a tree, covered with his army cloak. As I aroused the sleeper, he slowly sat up on the ground and said, "Ah, Captain, you have returned, have you? Come here and tell me what you have learned on the right." Laying his hand on me, he drew me down by his side, and, passing his arm around my shoulder, drew me near to him in a fatherly way that told of his warm and kindly heart. When I had related such information as I had secured for him, he thanked me for accomplishing his commission, and then said he regretted that the young men about General Jackson had not relieved him of annoyance, by finding a battery of the enemy which had harassed our advance, adding that the young men of that day were not equal to what they were when he was a young man. Seeing immediately that he was jesting and disposed to rally me, as he often did young officers, I broke away from the hold on me which he tried to retain, and, as he laughed heartily through the stillness of the night, I went off to make a bed of my saddle-blanket, and, with my head in my saddle, near my horse's feet, was soon wrapped in the heavy slumber of a wearied soldier.

Some time after midnight I was awakened by the chill of the early morning hours, and, turning over, caught a glimpse of a little flame on the slope above me, and, sitting up to see what it meant, I saw, bending over a scant fire of twigs, two men seated on old cracker boxes and warming their hands over the little fire. I had but to rub my eyes and collect my wits to recognize the figures of Robert E. Lee and Stonewall Jackson. Who can tell the story of that quiet council of war between two sleeping armies? Nothing remains on record to tell of plans discussed, and dangers weighed, and a great purpose formed, but the story of the great day so soon to follow.

It was broad daylight, and the thick beams of yellow sunlight came through the pine branches, when some one touched me rudely with his foot, saying: "Get up, Smith, the general wants you!" As I leaped to my feet the rhythmic click of the canteens of marching infantry caught my ear. Already in motion! What could it mean? In a moment I was mounted and at the side of the general, who sat on his horse by the roadside, as the long line of our troops cheerily, but in silence as directed, poured down the Furnace road. His cap was pulled low over his eyes, and, looking up from under the visor, with lips compressed, indicating the firm purpose within, he nodded to me, and in brief and rapid utterance, without a superfluous word, as though all were distinctly formed in his mind and beyond question, he gave me orders for our wagon and ambulance trains. From the open fields in our rear, at the head of the Catharpin road, all trains were to be moved upon that road to Todd's Tavern, and thence west by interior roads, so that our troops would be between them and the enemy at Chancellorsville. My orders having been delivered and the trains set in motion, I returned to the site of our night's bivouac, to find that General Jackson and his staff had followed the marching column.

Slow and tedious is the advance of a mounted officer who has to pass, in narrow wood roads through dense thickets, the packed column of marching infantry, to be recognized all along the line and good-naturedly chaffed by many a gay-spirited fellow: "Say, here's one of Old Jack's little boys; let him by, boys!" in the most patronizing tone. "Have a good breakfast this morning, sonny?" "Better hurry up, or you'll catch it for getting behind." "Tell Old Jack we're all a-comin'." "Don't let him begin the fuss till we get thar!" And so on, until about 3 P. M., after a ride of ten miles of tortuous road, I found the general, seated on a stump by the Brock road, writing this despatch, which, through the courtesy of the Virginia State Library, is given in facsimile [see page 188].

The place here mentioned as Chancellor's was also known as Dowdall's Tavern. It was the farm of the Rev. Melzi Chancellor, two miles west of Chancellorsville, and the Federal force found here and at Talley's, a mile farther west, was the Eleventh Corps, under General Howard. General Fitz Lee, with cavalry scouts, had advanced until he had view of the position of Howard's corps, and found them unsuspicious of attack.

coming to tell me what it was all about. Tell your good general that I am sure he knows what to do. I will meet him at the front very soon."

It was Sedgwick who had crossed, and, marching along the river front to impress us with his numbers, was now intrenching his line on the river road, under cover of Federal batteries on the north bank.

All day long we lay in the old lines of the action of December preceding, watching the operation of the enemy. Nor did we move through the next day, the 30th of April. During the forenoon of the 29th General Lee had been informed by Gen-

eral J. E. B. Stuart of the movement in force by General Hooker across the Rappahannock upon Chancellorsville; and during the night of Thursday, April 30th, General Jackson withdrew his corps, leaving Early and his division with Barksdale's brigade to hold the old lines from Hamilton's Crossing along the rear of Fredericksburg.

By the light of a brilliant moon, at midnight, that passed into an early dawn of dense mist, the troops were moved, by the Old Mine road, out of sight of the enemy, and about 11 A. M. of Friday, May 1st, they reached Anderson's position, con-

BRIGADIER-GENERAL F. T. NICHOLLS, C. S. A.

THE NEW CHANCELLOR HOUSE.

This picture is from a photograph taken at a reunion of Union and Confederate officers and soldiers in May, 1884. The original house was set on fire by Confederate shells on Sunday, May 3d, shortly after Hooker was injured while standing on the porch. The picture faces south. Jackson attacked the Eleventh Corps from the left (west) by the Plank road, which passes in front of the Chancellor House. The crossroad in the foreground leads northward to Ely's Ford, a crossing of the Rapidan, and United States Ford, a crossing of the Rappahannock.

MAJOR-GENERAL R. E. COLSTON, C. S. A.

Reaching the Orange Plank road, General Jackson himself rode with Fitz Lee to reconnoiter the position of Howard, and then sent the Stonewall brigade of Virginia troops, under Brigadier-General Paxton, to hold the point where the Germanna Plank road obliquely enters the Orange road. Leading the main column of his force farther on the Brock road to the old turnpike, the head of the column turned sharply eastward toward Chancellorsville. About a mile had been passed, when he halted and began the disposition of his forces to attack Howard. Rodes's division, at the head of the column, was thrown into line of battle, with Colston's forming the second line and A. P. Hill's the third, while the artillery under Colonel Stapleton Crutchfield moved in column on the road, or was parked in a field on the right. The well-trained skirmishers of Rodes's division, under Major Eugene Blackford, were thrown to the front. It must have been between 5 and 6 o'clock in the evening, Saturday, May 2d, when these dispositions were completed. Upon his stout-built, long-paced little sorrel, General Jackson sat, with visor low over his eyes and lips compressed, and with his watch in his hand. Upon his right sat General Robert E. Rodes, the very picture of a soldier, and every inch all that he appeared. Upon the right of Rodes sat Major Blackford.

"Are you ready, General Rodes?" said Jackson.

"Yes, sir!" said Rodes, impatient for the advance.

"You can go forward then," said Jackson.

A nod from Rodes was order enough for Blackford, and then suddenly the woods rang with the bugle call, and back came the responses from bugles on the right and left, and the long line of skirmishers, through the wild thicket of undergrowth, sprang eagerly to their work, followed promptly by the quick steps of the line of battle. For a moment all the troops seemed buried in the depths of the gloomy forest, and then suddenly the echoes waked and swept the country for miles, never failing until heard at the headquarters of Hooker at Chancellorsville — the wild "rebel yell" of the long Confederate lines.

Never was assault delivered with grander enthusiasm. Fresh from the long winter's waiting, and confident from the preparation of the spring, the troops were in fine condition and in high spirits. The boys were all back from home or sick leave. "Old Jack" was there upon the road in their midst; there could be no mistake and no failure. And there were Rodes and A. P. Hill. Had they not seen and cheered, as long and as loud as they were permitted, the gay-hearted Stuart and the long-bearded Fitz Lee on his fiery charger? Was not Crutchfield's array of brass and iron "dogs of war" at hand, with Poague and Palmer, and all the rest, ready to bark loud and deep with half a chance?

Alas! for Howard and his unformed lines, and his brigades with guns stacked, and officers at dinner or asleep under the trees, and butchers deep in the blood of beeves! Scattered through field and forest, his men were preparing their evening meal. A little show of earthwork facing the south was quickly taken by us in reverse from the west. Flying battalions are not flying buttresses for an army's stability. Across Talley's fields the rout begins. Over at Hawkins's hill, on the north of the road, Carl Schurz makes a stand, soon to be driven into the same hopeless panic. By the quiet Wilderness Church in the vale, leaving wounded and dead everywhere, by Melzi Chancellor's, on into the deep thicket again, the Confederate lines press forward, — now broken and all disaligned by the density of bush that tears the clothes away; now halting to load and deliver a volley upon some regiment or fragment of the enemy that will not move as fast as others. Thus the attack upon Hooker's flank was a grand success, beyond the most sanguine expectation.

The writer of this narrative, an aide-de-camp of Jackson's, was ordered to remain at the point where the advance began, to be a center of communication between the general and the cavalry on the flanks, and to deliver orders to detachments of artillery still moving up from the rear. A fine black charger, with elegant trappings, deserted by his owner and found tied to a tree, became mine only for that short and eventful nightfall; and about 8 P. M., in the twilight, thus comfortably mounted, I gathered my couriers about me and went forward to find General Jackson. The storm of battle had swept far on to the east and become more and more faint to the ear, until silence came with night over the fields and woods. As I rode along that old turnpike, passing scattered fragments of Confederates looking for their regiments, parties of prisoners concentrating under guards, wounded men by the roadside and under the trees at Talley's and Chancellor's, I had reached an open field on the right, a mile west of Chancellorsville, when, in the dusky twilight, I saw horsemen near an old cabin in the field. Turning toward them, I found Rodes and his staff engaged in gathering the broken and scattered troops that had swept the two miles of battle-field. "General Jackson is just ahead on the road, Captain," said Rodes; "tell him I will be here at this cabin if I am wanted." I had not gone a hundred yards before I heard firing, a shot or two, and then a company volley upon the right of the road, and another upon the left. A few moments farther on I met Captain Murray Taylor, an aide of A. P. Hill's, with tidings that Jackson and Hill were wounded, and some around them killed, by the fire of their own men. Spurring my horse into a sweeping gallop, I soon passed the Confederate line of battle, and, some three or four rods on its front, found the general's horse beside a pine sapling on the left, and a rod beyond a little party of men caring for a wounded officer. The story of the sad event is briefly told, and, in essentials, very much as it came to me from the lips of the wounded general himself, and in everything confirmed and completed by those who were eye-witnesses and near companions.

When Jackson had reached the point where his line now crossed the turnpike, scarcely a mile west of Chancellorsville, and not half a mile from a line of Federal troops, he had found his front line unfit for the farther and vigorous advance he desired, by reason of the irregular character of the fighting, now right, now left, and because of the dense thickets, through which it was impossible to preserve alignment. Division commanders found it more and more difficult as the twilight deepened to hold their broken brigades in hand. Regretting the necessity of relieving the troops in front, General Jackson had ordered A. P. Hill's division, his third

LEE AND JACKSON IN COUNCIL ON THE NIGHT OF MAY 1.

and reserve line, to be placed in front. While this change was being effected, impatient and anxious, the General rode forward on the turnpike, followed by two or three of his staff and a number of couriers and signal sergeants. He passed the swampy depression and began the ascent of the hill toward Chancellorsville, when he came upon a line of the Federal infantry lying on their arms. Fired at by one or two muskets (two musket-balls from the enemy whistled over my head as I came to the front), he turned and came back toward his line, upon the side of the road to his left. As he rode near to the Confederate troops, just placed in position and ignorant that he was in the front, the left company began firing to the front, and two of his party fell from their saddles dead—Captain Boswell, of the Engineers, and Sergeant Cunliffe, of the Signal Corps. Spurring his horse across the road to his right, he was met by a second volley from the right company of Pender's North Carolina brigade. Under this volley, when not two rods from the troops, the general received three balls at the same instant. One penetrated the palm of his right hand and was cut out that night from the back of his hand. A second passed around the wrist of the left arm and out through the left hand. A third ball passed through the left arm half-way from shoulder to elbow. The large bone of the upper arm was splintered to the elbow-joint, and the wound bled freely. His horse turned quickly from the fire, through the thick bushes which swept the cap from the general's head, and scratched his forehead, leaving drops of blood to stain his face. As he lost his hold upon the bridle-rein, he reeled from the saddle, and was caught by the arms of Captain Wilbourn, of the Signal Corps. Laid upon the ground, there came at once to his succor General A. P. Hill and members of his staff. The writer reached his side a minute after, to find General Hill holding the head and shoulders of the wounded chief. Cutting open the coat-sleeve from wrist to shoulder, I found the wound in the upper arm, and with my handkerchief I bound the arm above the wound to stem the flow of blood. Couriers were sent for Dr. Hunter McGuire, the surgeon of the corps and the general's trusted friend, and for an ambulance. Being outside of our lines, it was urgent that he should be moved at once. With difficulty litter-bearers were brought from the line near by, and the general was placed upon the litter and carefully raised to the shoulder, I myself bearing one corner. A moment after, artillery from the Federal side was opened upon us; great broadsides thundered over the woods; hissing shells searched the dark thickets through, and shrapnels swept the road along which we moved. Two or three steps farther, and the litter-bearer at my side was struck and fell; but, as the litter turned, Major Watkins Leigh, of Hill's staff, happily caught it. But the fright of the men was so great that we were obliged to lay the litter and its burden down upon the road. As the litter-bearers ran to the cover of the trees, I threw myself by the general's side and held him firmly to the ground as he attempted to rise. Over us swept the rapid fire of shot and shell—grape-shot striking fire upon the flinty rock of the road all around us, and sweeping from their feet horses and men of the artillery just moved to the front. Soon the firing veered to the other side of the road, and I sprang to my feet, assisted the general to rise, passed my arm around him, and with the wounded man's weight thrown heavily upon me, we forsook the road. Entering the woods, he sank to the ground from exhaustion; but the litter was soon brought, and again rallying a few men, we essayed to carry him farther, when a second bearer fell at my side. This time, with none to assist, the litter careened, and the general fell to the ground, with a groan of deep pain. Greatly alarmed, I sprang to his head, and, lifting his head as a stray beam of moonlight came through clouds and leaves, he opened his eyes and wearily said: "Never mind me, Captain, never mind me." Raising him again to his feet, he was accosted by Brigadier-General Pender: "Oh, General, I hope you are not seriously wounded. I will have to retire my troops to re-form them, they are so much broken by this fire." But Jackson, rallying his strength, with firm voice said: "You must hold your ground, General Pender; you must hold your ground, sir!" and so uttered his last command on the field. . . .

FACSIMILE OF STONEWALL JACKSON'S
LAST DESPATCH TO GENERAL LEE.

UNION CAVALRY SCOUTING IN FRONT OF THE CONFEDERATE ADVANCE.

THE BATTLE OF GETTYSBURG.

NARRATIVE OF EVENTS.*

PRELIMINARY.

AT the beginning of the Gettysburg campaign, June 3, 1863, the Confederate army, under command of General Robert E. Lee, was composed of three large corps under (1) Longstreet, (2) Ewell, and (3) A. P. Hill—about 70,000, including Stuart's cavalry force (11,000, and 16 guns), and batteries of artillery numbering 190 guns.

The Union army, then under command of General Joseph Hooker, was composed of seven small corps under (1) Reynolds, (2) Hancock, (3) Sickles, (5) Meade (succeeded by Sykes), (6) Sedgwick, (11) Howard, (12)

LEE'S INVASION OF PENNSYLVANIA.

BY JAMES LONGSTREET, LIEUT.-GENERAL, C. S. A.
Commander of the First Corps of Lee's Army at the Battle of Gettysburg.

. . . While General Lee was reorganizing his army he was also arranging the new campaign. Grant had laid siege to Vicksburg, and Johnston was concentrating at Jackson to drive him away. Rosecrans was in Tennessee and Bragg was in front of him. The force Johnston was concentrating at Jackson gave us no hope that he would have sufficient strength to make any impression upon Grant, and even if he could, Grant was in a position to reinforce rapidly and could supply his army with greater facility. Vicksburg was doomed unless we could offer relief by strategic move. I proposed to send a force through East Tennessee to join Bragg and also to have Johnston sent to join him, thus concentrating a large force against Rosecrans, crush out his army, and march against Cincinnati. That, I thought, was the only way we had to relieve Vicksburg. General Lee admitted the force of my proposition, but finally stated that he preferred to organize a campaign into Maryland and Pennsylvania, hoping thereby to draw the Federal troops from the southern points they occupied. After discussing the matter with him for several

Slocum—about 82,000 in all; a heavy cavalry force—about 11,000, and 27 guns—under Pleasonton, and batteries of artillery numbering 300 guns.

Lee was on the south side of the Rappahannock at and near Fredericksburg, guarding the road to Richmond. Hooker was opposite Lee on the north side of the river, guarding the road to Washington.

Lee determined to invade the Northern States. Hill's corps was ordered to remain at Fredericksburg, and the corps of Ewell and Longstreet to join Stuart's cavalry at Culpeper.

days, I found his mind made up not to allow any of his troops to go west. I then accepted his proposition to make a campaign into Pennsylvania, provided it should be offensive in strategy but defensive in tactics, forcing the Federal army to give us battle when we were in strong position and ready to receive them. One mistake of the Confederacy was in pitting force against force. The only hope we had was to outgeneral the Federals. We were all hopeful and the army was in good condition, but the war had advanced far enough for us to see that a mere victory without decided fruits was a luxury we could not afford. Our numbers were less than the Federal forces, and our resources were limited while theirs were not. The time had come when it was imperative that the skill of generals and the strategy and tactics of war should take the place of muscle against muscle. Our purpose should have been to impair the *morale* of the Federal army and shake Northern confidence in the Federal leaders. We talked on that line from day to day, and General Lee, accepting it as a good military view, adopted it as the key-note of the campaign. I suggested that we should have all the details and purposes so well arranged and so impressed upon our minds that when the critical moment should come, we could refer to our calmer moments and know we were carrying out our original plans. I stated to General Lee that if he would allow me to handle my corps so as to receive the attack of the Federal army, I would beat it off without calling on him for help except to guard my right and left, and called his attention to the battle of Fredericksburg as an instance of defensive warfare, where we had thrown not more than five thousand troops into the

GENERAL ROBERT E. LEE, C. S. A.
Confederate Commander at the Battle of Gettysburg.   (From a photograph taken after the war.)

fight and had beaten off two-thirds of the Federal army with great loss to them and slight loss to my own troops. I also called his attention to Napoleon's instructions to Marmont at the head of an invading army.

A few days before we were ready to move General Lee sent for General Ewell to receive his orders. I was present at the time and remarked that if we were ever going to make an offensive battle it should be done south of the Potomac — adding that we might have an opportunity to cross the Rappahannock near Culpeper Court House and

* The narrative notes standing at the heads of the articles on Gettysburg in the pages following are condensed from a work by Brevet Major-General Abner Doubleday, U. S. A., entitled "Gettysburg Made Plain," and published by The Century Co. General Doubleday commanded a division in the First Corps, Army of the Potomac, and during a portion of the battle he commanded the corps.

make a battle there. I made this suggestion in order to bring about a discussion which I thought would give Ewell a better idea of the plan of operations. My remark had the desired effect, and we talked over the possibilities of a battle south of the Potomac. The enemy would be on our right flank while we were moving north. Ewell's corps was to move in advance to Culpeper Court House, mine to follow, and the cavalry was to move along on our right flank to the east of us. Thus, by threatening his rear, we could draw Hooker from his position on Stafford Heights opposite Fredericksburg. Our movements at the beginning of the campaign were necessarily slow in order that we might be sure of having the proper effect on Hooker.

Ewell was started off to the valley of Virginia to cross the mountains and move in the direction of Winchester, which was occupied by considerable forces under Milroy. I was moving at the same time east of the Blue Ridge with Stuart's cavalry on my right so as to occupy the gaps from Ashby on to Harper's Ferry. Ewell, moving on through the valley, captured troops and supplies at Winchester, and passed through Martinsburg and Williamsport into Maryland. As I moved along the eastern slope of the Blue Ridge we heard from day to day of the movements of Hooker's army, and that he had finally abandoned his position on Stafford Heights, and was moving up the Potomac in the direction of Washington. Upon receipt of that information, A. P. Hill was ordered to draw off from Fredericksburg and follow the movements of General Ewell, but to cross the Potomac at Shepherdstown. When Hill with his troops and well-supplied trains had passed my rear, I was ordered to withdraw from the Blue Ridge, pass over to the west of the Shenandoah, and follow the movements of the other troops, only to cross the Potomac at Williamsport. I ordered General Stuart, whom I considered under my command, to occupy the gaps with a part of his cavalry and to follow with his main force on my right, to cross the Potomac at Shepherdstown, and move on my right flank. Upon giving him this order, he informed me that he had authority from General Lee to occupy the gaps with a part of his cavalry, and to follow the Federal army with the remainder. At the same time he expressed his purpose of crossing the river east of the Blue Ridge and trying to make way around the right of the Federal army; so I moved my troops independent of the cavalry, and, following my orders, crossed at Williamsport, came up with A. P. Hill in Maryland, and moved on thence to Chambersburg. . . . The two armies were then near each other, the Confederates being north and west of Gettysburg, and the Federals south and southeast. . . . On the 30th of June we turned our faces toward our enemy and marched upon Gettysburg. The Third Corps, under Hill, moved out first and my command followed.

AT CLOSE QUARTERS ON THE FIRST DAY AT GETTYSBURG.

NARRATIVE NOTES.

HOOKER SUSPECTS.

Hooker, seeing a great diminution of tents in his front, suspected that the Confederates were leaving Fredericksburg. He said to Sedgwick,—a life-long friend and classmate,—"John, go over there and see if the enemy have gone. They may have left merely their empty tents to deceive us."

So, on the 6th of June, Sedgwick threw bridges out, under cover of his artillery, and crossed the Rappahannock. He sent back word to Hooker, "There is a pretty stiff opposition; I think their main body must be still here." Hooker directed Pleasonton to take all the cavalry that could be spared and go to Culpeper, to ascertain if anything unusual was going on there. All of Stuart's cavalry and two-thirds of the Confederate army were in that vicinity.

BATTLE OF BRANDY STATION, JUNE 9TH.

Pleasonton, who was at Warrenton Junction, backed by two infantry brigades, slipped quietly down to the Rappahannock and bivouacked there without fire or light. At dawn the next morning he crossed the stream, completely surprised Stuart's cavalry, and very nearly captured his artillery. Unfortunately Colonel Benjamin F. Davis, who led the advance, was killed, and there was no officer at hand to take his place. This caused some delay and confusion, which gave the enemy time to rally and form line of battle.

After fighting all day against Stuart's cavalry, the enemy's infantry came up and Pleasonton retired. He reported to Hooker that two-thirds of the enemy were at Culpeper preparing to move on Washington.

Hooker sent troops up the Rappahannock to prevent Lee from crossing by the direct route.

Lee sent Ewell's corps to the Shenandoah valley with orders to clear out the Union troops under Milroy at Winchester and under Tyler at Martinsburg.

Hooker started toward Washington. Ewell gained possession of Winchester and Martinsburg, but not of Harper's Ferry.

There is a rocky and thickly wooded range of heights called the Bull Run Mountains, running from Leesburg south. As Hooker had not occupied them, but was farther to the east, Lee desired to do so, for it would give him a very strong position on Hooker's flank and bring him (Lee) very near to Washington. He therefore directed his cavalry to reconnoiter in that direction.

BATTLE OF ALDIE, JUNE 17TH.

Stuart's reconnoitering party met the Union cavalry at Aldie, and, after a hard battle, retreated.

A series of cavalry combats ensued, ending in the retreat of Stuart's cavalry behind the Blue Ridge.

LEE ENTERS PENNSYLVANIA.

Hooker was strongly posted east of the Bull Run range and could not be attacked with much chance of success. As Lee could not well remain inactive or retreat, he resolved to invade Pennsylvania. This was a hazardous enterprise, for Hooker might intervene between him and Richmond. Stuart's cavalry was left to prevent this catastrophe by guarding the passes in the Blue Ridge. Stuart was also directed to harass Hooker and attack his rear should he attempt to cross the Potomac in pursuit of Lee.

Lee reached Chambersburg with Longstreet's and Hill's corps. Ewell's corps was in advance at Carlisle and York, preceded by Jenkins's and by White's cavalry, threatening to cross the Susquehanna and take Harrisburg.

In the mean time Stuart's cavalry had crossed the Potomac near Seneca Creek above Washington, reached Rockville, near Washington, on its way north. Two of his brigades under Jones and Robertson were holding the gaps in the Blue Ridge without any enemy in front of them. Hooker's army was still at and near Frederick, Maryland.

A CHANGE OF UNION COMMANDERS.

On June 28th, Hooker determined to send Slocum's corps and the garrison of Harper's Ferry—the latter about 10,000 strong—to operate against Lee's rear. This was an excellent plan, but Hooker's superior, General Halleck, refused to allow him to remove the troops from Harper's Ferry; and Hooker said if he could not manage the campaign in his own way, he preferred to give up the command of the army. Halleck gladly relieved him, and Major-General George G. Meade, commander of the Fifth Corps, was assigned to the command in his place.

On June 28th, Lee learned from a scout that the Union army was in his rear and that his communication with Richmond was seriously endangered.

In this emergency he concluded to threaten Baltimore. As a preliminary measure he directed his entire army to move on Gettysburg. Stuart was intercepted at Hanover by Kilpatrick's division of cavalry, but managed to disengage himself from the contest and continue his journey to join Ewell at York. The latter was, however, on his way to Gettysburg, and Stuart . . . rode night and day to join Lee there. When he finally reached the field in the afternoon of the 2d, his horses were in bad condition from overwork, and his men were utterly exhausted.

General Reynolds commanded the left wing of the Union army, composed of the First, Eleventh, and Third corps. The advance of Hill's corps on the morning of July 1st struck Buford's division of Union cavalry a short distance to the west of Gettysburg.

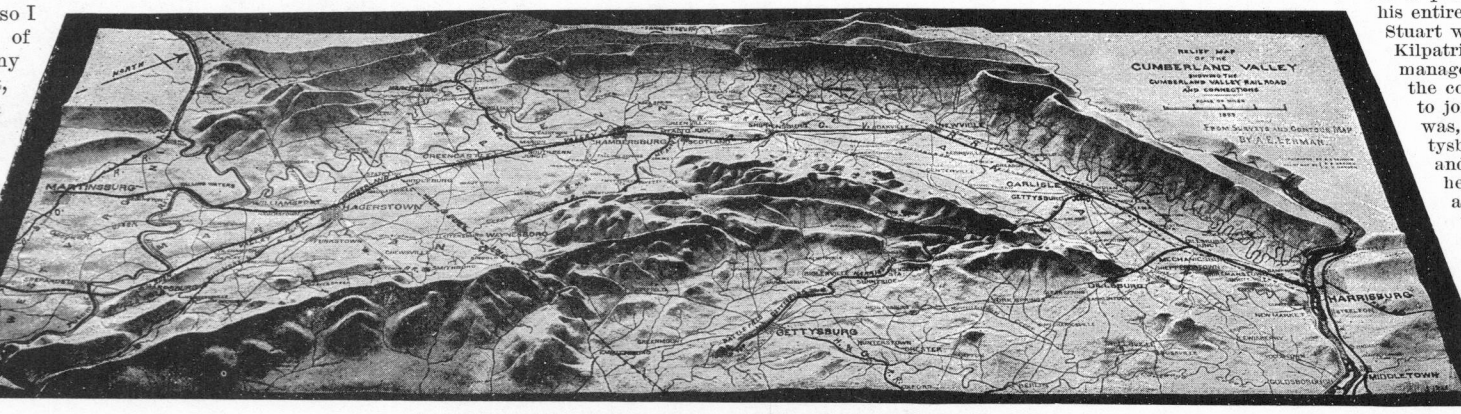

RELIEF MAP OF THE GETTYSBURG CAMPAIGN.
From a photograph of the original cast made by A. E. Lehman for the Cumberland Valley Railroad Company.

BUFORD'S CAVALRY OPPOSING THE CONFEDERATE ADVANCE UPON GETTYSBURG.

THE FIRST DAY AT GETTYSBURG.

BY HENRY J. HUNT, BREVET MAJOR-GENERAL, U. S. A.

Chief of artillery of the Army of the Potomac at the Battle of Gettysburg.

... On the night of June 30th Meade's headquarters and the Artillery Reserve were at Taneytown; the First Corps at Marsh Run, the Eleventh at Emmitsburg, Third at Bridgeport, Twelfth at Littlestown, Second at Uniontown, Fifth at Union Mills, Sixth and Gregg's cavalry at Manchester, Kilpatrick's at Hanover. ... Lee's whole army was nearing Gettysburg, while Meade's was scattered over a wide region to the east and south of that town.

Meade was now convinced that all designs on the Susquehanna had been abandoned; but as Lee's corps were reported as occupying the country from Chambersburg to Carlisle, he ordered, for the next day's moves, the First and Eleventh corps to Gettysburg under Reynolds, the Third to Emmitsburg, the Second to Taneytown, the Fifth to Hanover, and the Twelfth to Two Taverns, directing Slocum to take command of the Fifth in addition to his own. The Sixth Corps was left at Manchester, thirty-

four miles from Gettysburg, to await orders. But Meade, while conforming to the current of Lee's movement, was not merely drifting. The same afternoon he directed the chiefs of engineers and artillery to select a field of battle on which his army might be concentrated, whatever Lee's lines of approach, whether by Harrisburg or Gettysburg, — indicating the general line of Pike Creek as a suitable locality. Carefully drawn instructions were sent to the corps commanders as to the occupation of this line should it be ordered; but it was added that developments might cause the offensive to be assumed from present positions. These orders were afterward cited as indicating General Meade's intention not to fight at Gettysburg. They were, under any circumstances, wise and proper orders, and it would probably have been better had he concentrated his army behind Pike Creek rather than at Gettysburg; but events finally controlled the actions of both leaders.

At 8 A. M., July 1st, Buford's scouts reported Heth's advance on the Cashtown road, when Gamble's brigade formed on McPherson's Ridge, from the Fairfield road to the railroad cut; one section of Calef's Battery A, 2d United States, near the left of his line, the other two across the Chambersburg or Cashtown pike. Devin formed his disposable squadrons from Gamble's right toward Oak Hill, from which he had afterward to transfer them to the north of the town to meet Ewell. As Heth advanced, he threw Archer's brigade to the right, Davis's to the left of the Cashtown pike, with Pettigrew's and Brockenbrough's brigades in support. The Confederates advanced, skirmishing heavily with Buford's dismounted troopers. Calef's battery, engaging double the number of its own guns, was served with an efficiency worthy of its former reputation as "Duncan's battery" in the Mexican war, and so enabled the cavalry to hold their long line for two hours. When Buford's report of the enemy's advance reached Reynolds, the latter, ordering Doubleday and Howard to follow,

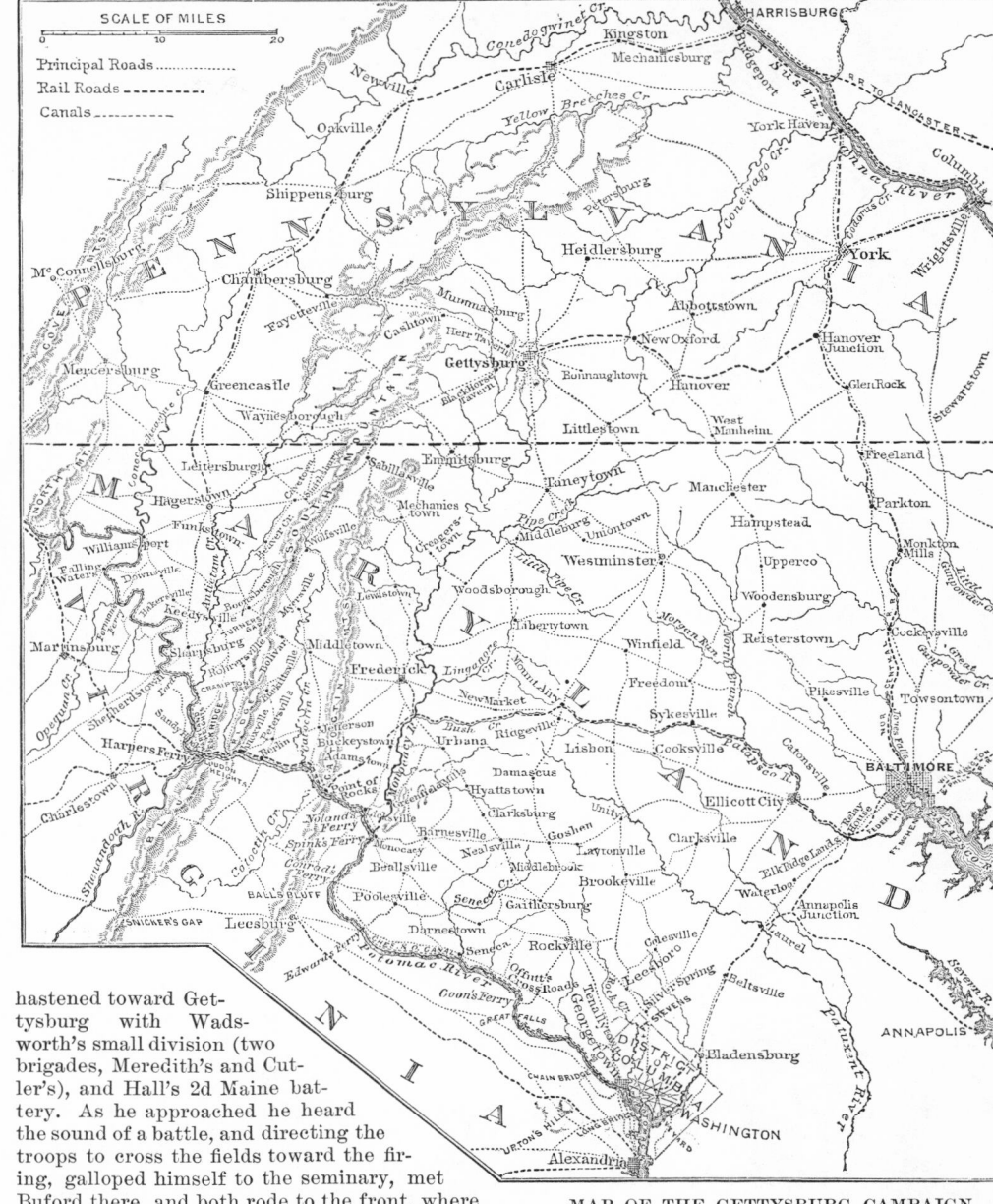

MAP OF THE GETTYSBURG CAMPAIGN.

hastened toward Gettysburg with Wadsworth's small division (two brigades, Meredith's and Cutler's), and Hall's 2d Maine battery. As he approached he heard the sound of a battle, and directing the troops to cross the fields toward the firing, galloped himself to the seminary, met Buford there, and both rode to the front, where the cavalry, dismounted, were gallantly holding their ground against heavy odds. After viewing the field, he sent back to hasten up Howard, and as the enemy's main line was now advancing to the attack, directed Doubleday, who had arrived in advance of his division, to look to the Fairfield road, sent Cutler with three of his five regiments north of the railroad cut, posted the other two under Colonel Fowler, of the 14th New York, south of the pike, and replaced Calef's battery by Hall's, thus relieving the cavalry. Cutler's line was hardly formed when it was struck by Davis's Confederate brigade on its front and right flank, whereupon Wadsworth, to save it, ordered it to fall back to Seminary Ridge. This order not reach-

ing the 147th New York, its gallant major, Harney, held that regiment to its position until, having lost half its numbers, the order to retire was repeated. Hall's battery was now imperiled, and it withdrew by sections, fighting at close canister range and suffering severely. Fowler thereupon changed his front to face Davis's brigade, which held the cut, and with Dawes's 6th Wisconsin — sent by Doubleday to aid the 147th New York — charged and drove Davis from the field. The Confederate brigade suffered severely, losing all its field-officers but two, and a large proportion of its men killed and captured, being disabled for further effective service that day. In the mean time Archer's Confederate

GENERAL LEE'S HEADQUARTERS ON THE CHAMBERSBURG PIKE.

LUTHERAN CHURCH ON CHAMBERSBURG STREET, GETTYSBURG, USED AS A HOSPITAL.

brigade had occupied McPherson's wood, and as the regiments of Meredith's "Iron Brigade" came up, they were sent forward by Doubleday, who fully recognized the importance of the position, to dislodge Archer. At the entrance of the wood they found Reynolds in person, and, animated by his presence, rushed to the charge, struck successive heavy blows, outflanked and turned the enemy's right, captured General Archer and a large portion of his brigade, and pursued the remainder across Willoughby Run. Wadsworth's small division had thus won decided successes against superior numbers, but it was at grievous cost to the army and the country, for Reynolds, while directing the opera-

THE LUTHERAN SEMINARY.
The upper picture from a war-time photograph.
Both pictures show the face of the seminary toward the town, and in the right-hand view is seen the Chambersburg Pike. On the first day, Buford and Reynolds used the cupola for observations; thereafter it was the chief signal-station and observatory for the Confederates.

tions, was killed in the wood by a sharp-shooter. It was not, however, until by his promptitude and gallantry he had determined the decisive field of the war, and had opened brilliantly a battle which required three days of hard fighting to close with a victory. To him may be applied, in a wider sense than in its original one, Napier's happy eulogium on Ridge: "No man died on that field with more glory than he; yet many died, and there was much glory."

After the repulse of Davis and Archer, Heth's division was formed in line mostly south of the Cashtown pike, with Pender's in second line, Pegram's and McIntosh's artillery (nine batteries) occupying all the commanding positions west of Willoughby Run. Doubleday reëstablished his former lines, Meredith holding McPherson's wood. Soon after, Rowley's and Robinson's divisions (two brigades each) and the four remaining batteries of the corps arrived. Rowley's division was thrown forward, Stone's brigade to the interval between Meredith and Cutler, and Biddle's with Cooper's battery to occupy the ridge between the wood and the Fairfield road. Reynolds's battery replaced

GETTYSBURG FROM OAK HILL.
Oak Hill is a mile north-west of Gettysburg, and the view here is south-east, showing Stevens Hall (named after Thaddeus Stevens), the preparatory department of the Pennsylvania College, on the left; then Culp's Hill; then Pennsylvania College, and, to the right of its cupola, the observatory on Cemetery Hill.

Hall's, and Calef's rejoined Gamble's cavalry, now in reserve. Robinson's division was halted near the base of Seminary Ridge. By this time, near noon, General Howard arrived, assumed command, and directed General Schurz, commanding the Eleventh Corps, to prolong Doubleday's line toward Oak Hill with Schimmelfennig's and Barlow's divisions and three batteries, and to post Steinwehr's division and two batteries on Cemetery Hill as a rallying-point. By 1 o'clock, when this corps was arriving, Buford had reported Ewell's approach by the Heidlersburg road,

and Howard called on Sickles at Emmitsburg and Slocum at Two Taverns for aid, to which both these officers promptly responded. It was now no longer a question of prolonging Doubleday's line, but of protecting it against Ewell whilst engaged in front with Hill. Schurz's two divisions, hardly 6000 effectives, accordingly formed line on the open plain half a mile north of the town. They were too weak to cover the ground, and a wide interval was left between the two corps, covered only by the fire of Dilger's and Wheeler's batteries (ten guns) posted behind it.

That morning, whilst on the march to Cashtown, Ewell received Hill's notice that his corps was advancing to Gettysburg, upon which he turned the heads of his own columns to that point. Reporting the change by a staff-officer to General Lee, Ewell was instructed that if the Federals were in force at Gettysburg, a general battle was not to be brought on until the rest of the army was up. Approaching Gettysburg, Rodes, guided by the sounds of battle, followed the prolongation of Seminary Ridge; Iverson's, Daniel's, and Ramseur's brigades on the western, O'Neal's and Doles's on the eastern

slope. Ewell, recognizing the importance of Oak Hill, ordered it to be occupied by Carter's artillery battalion, which immediately opened on both the Federal corps, enfilading Doubleday's line. This caused Wadsworth again to withdraw Cutler to Seminary Ridge, and Reynolds's battery was posted near McPherson's house, under partial cover. Stone therefore placed two of his three regiments on the Cashtown pike, so as to face Oak Hill. This left an interval between Stone and Cutler, through which Cooper and Reynolds could fire with effect, and gave to these lines a cross-fire on troops entering the angle between them. Robinson now sent his two brigades to strengthen Cutler's right. They took post behind the stone walls of a field, Paul's brigade facing west, Baxter's north. Rodes, regarding this advance as a menace, gave orders at 2:30 P. M. to attack. Iverson, sweeping round to his left, engaged Paul, who prolonged Cutler's line, and O'Neal attacked Baxter. The repulse of O'Neal soon enabled Baxter to turn upon Iverson. Cutler also attacked him in flank, and after losing 500 men killed and wounded, 3 of Iverson's regiments surrendered. General Robinson reports the capture of 1000 prisoners and 3 colors; General Paul

PENNSYLVANIA COLLEGE, GETTYSBURG.
The cupola was first used by Union officers, and then by Confederate, as a station for observation and signals. During the withdrawal of the First and Eleventh corps through the town, there was hard fighting in the college grounds.

was severely wounded, losing both eyes. Meanwhile Daniel's brigade advanced directly on Stone, who maintained his lines against this attack and also Brockenbrough's, of Hill's corps, but was soon severely wounded. Colonel Wister, who succeeded him, met the same fate, and Colonel Dana took command of the brigade. Ramseur, who followed Daniel, by a conversion to the left, now faced Robinson and Cutler with his own brigade, the remnant of Iverson's, and one regiment of O'Neal's, his right connecting with Daniel's left, and the fighting became hot. East of the ridge, Doles's brigade had been held in observation, but about 3:30 P. M., on the advance of Early, he sent his skirmishers forward and drove those of Devin — who had gallantly held the enemy's advance in check with his dismounted troopers — from their line and its hillock on Rock Creek. Barlow, considering this an eligible position for his own right, advanced his division, supported by Wilkeson's battery, and seized it. This made it necessary for Schurz to advance a brigade of Schimmelfennig's division to connect with Barlow, thus lengthening his already too extended line.

THE LINE OF DEFENSE AT THE CEMETERY GATE-HOUSE.

ASSAULT OF BROCKENBROUGH'S CONFEDERATE BRIGADE (HETH'S DIVISION) UPON THE
STONE BARN OF THE McPHERSON FARM.

The line of the stone barn was held by Stone's brigade, Pennsylvania Bucktails (Doubleday's division), its right resting on the Chambersburg pike (the left of the picture) and its left on the McPherson woods, where a part of Archer's Confederate brigade of Heth's division was captured by Meredith's brigade.

The arrival of Early's division had by this time brought an overwhelming force on the flank and rear of the Eleventh Corps. On the east of Rock Creek, Jones's artillery battalion, within easy range, enfiladed its whole line and took it in reserve, while the brigades of Gordon, Hays, and Avery in line, with Smith's in reserve, advanced about 4 P. M. upon Barlow's position, Doles, of Rodes's division, connecting with Gordon. An obstinate and bloody contest ensued, in which Barlow was desperately wounded, Wilkeson killed, and the whole corps forced back to its original line, on which, with the aid of Coster's brigade and Heckman's battery, drawn from Cemetery Hill, Schurz endeavored to rally it and cover the town. The fighting here was well sustained, but the Confederate force was overpowering in num-

bers, and the troops retreated to Cemetery Hill, Ewell entering the town about 4:30 P. M. These retrograde movements had uncovered the flank of the First Corps and made its right untenable.

Meanwhile, that corps had been heavily engaged along its whole line; for, on the approach of Rodes, Hill attacked with both his divisions. There were thus opposed to the single disconnected Federal line south of the Cashtown pike two solid Confederate ones which outflanked their left a quarter of a mile or more. Biddle's small command, less than a thousand men, after a severe contest was gradually forced back. In McPherson's wood and beyond, Meredith's and Dana's brigades repeatedly repulsed their assailants, but as Biddle's retirement uncovered their left, they too fell back to successive positions, from which they inflicted

HALL'S BATTERY ON THE FIRST DAY RESISTING THE CONFEDERATE ADVANCE ON THE CHAMBERSBURG ROAD

MAJOR-GENERAL GEORGE G. MEADE, U. S. A.
Union Commander at the Battle of Gettysburg.

heavy losses, until finally all three reached the foot of Seminary Ridge, where Colonel Wainwright, commanding the corps artillery, had planted twelve guns south of the Cashtown pike, with Stewart's battery, manned in part by men of the Iron Brigade, north of it. Buford had already thrown half of Gamble's dismounted men south of the Fairfield road. Heth's division had suffered so severely that Pender's had passed to its front, thus bringing fresh troops to bear on the exhausted Federal line.

It was about 4 P. M. when the whole Confederate line advanced to the final attack. On their right Gamble held Lane's brigade for some time in check, Perrin's and Scales's suffered severely, and Scales's was broken up, for Stewart, swinging half his guns, under Lieutenant Davison, upon the Cashtown pike, raked it. The whole corps being now heavily pressed and its right uncovered, Doubleday gave the order to fall back to Cemetery Hill, which was effected in comparatively good

order, the rear, covered by the 7th Wisconsin, turning when necessary to check pursuit. Colonel Wainwright, mistaking the order, had clung with his artillery to Seminary Hill, until, seeing the infantry retreating to the town, he moved his batteries down the Cashtown pike until lapped on both sides by the enemy's skirmishers, at close range, when he was compelled to abandon one gun on the road, all its horses being killed. The Eleventh Corps also left a disabled gun on the field. Of the troops who passed through the town, many, principally men of the Eleventh Corps, got entangled in the streets, lost their way, and were captured.

On ascending Cemetery Hill, the retreating troops found Steinwehr's division in position covered by stone fences on the slopes, and occupying by their skirmishers the houses in front of their line. As they arrived they were formed, the Eleventh Corps on the right, the First Corps on the left of Steinwehr. As the batteries came up,

MONUMENT IN THE GETTYSBURG CEMETERY.

they were well posted by Colonels Wainwright and Osborn, and soon a formidable array of artillery was ready to cover with its fire all the approaches. Buford assembled his command on the plain west of Cemetery Hill, covering the left flank and presenting a firm front to any attempt at pursuit. The First Corps found a small reinforcement awaiting it, in the 7th Indiana, part of the train escort, which brought up nearly five hundred fresh men. Wadsworth met them and led them to Culp's Hill, where, under direction of Captain Pattison of that regiment, a defensive line was marked out. Their brigade (Cutler's) soon joined them; wood and stone were plentiful, and soon the right of the line was solidly established.

NORTH-EAST CORNER OF THE McPHERSON WOODS, WHERE GENERAL REYNOLDS WAS KILLED.

MAJOR-GENERAL JOHN F. REYNOLDS, U. S. V.
Killed on the first day at Gettysburg. The uniform is that of a field-officer in the regular army.

Nor was there wanting other assurance to the men who had fought so long that their sacrifices had not been in vain. As they reached the hill they were received by General Hancock, who arrived just as they were coming up from the town, under orders from General Meade to assume the command. His person was well known; his presence inspired confidence, and it implied also the near approach of his army-corps. He ordered Wadsworth at once to Culp's Hill to secure that important position, and aided by Howard, by Warren who had also just arrived from headquarters, and by others, a strong line, well flanked, was soon formed.

General Lee, who from Seminary Hill had witnessed the final attack, sent Colonel Long, of his staff, a competent officer of sound judgment, to examine the position, and directed Ewell to carry it if practicable, renewing, however, his previous warning to avoid bringing on a general engagement until the army was all up. Both Ewell—who was making some preparations with a view to attack—and Long found the position a formidable one, strongly occupied and not accessible to artillery fire. Ewell's men were indeed in no condition for an immediate assault. Of Rodes's eight thousand, nearly three thousand were *hors de combat*. Early had lost over five hundred, and had but two brigades disposable, the other two having been sent on the report of the advance of Federal troops, probably the Twelfth Corps, then near by to watch the York road. Hill's two divisions had been very roughly handled, and had lost heavily, and he withdrew them to Seminary Hill as Ewell entered the town, leaving the latter with not more than eight thousand men to secure the town and the prisoners. Ewell's absent division (Edward Johnson's) was expected soon, but it did not arrive until near sunset, when the Twelfth Corps and Stannard's Vermont brigade were also up, and the Third Corps was arriving. In fact an assault by the Confederates was not practicable before 5:30 P. M., and after that the position was perfectly secure. For the first time that day the Federals had the advantage of position, and sufficient troops and artillery to occupy it, and Ewell would not have been justified in attacking without the positive orders of Lee, who was present and wisely abstained from giving them.

NARRATIVE NOTES.

BATTLE OF THE SECOND DAY.

The following diagram will explain the advantages and disadvantages of the battle-field.

The Union army was sheltered by the curved ridge. If it was desired to reinforce any part, it could be done by short lines,—chords of the arc,—and its movements being behind the ridge would be hidden from the view of its enemies.

As the Confederate army acted on the offensive it had

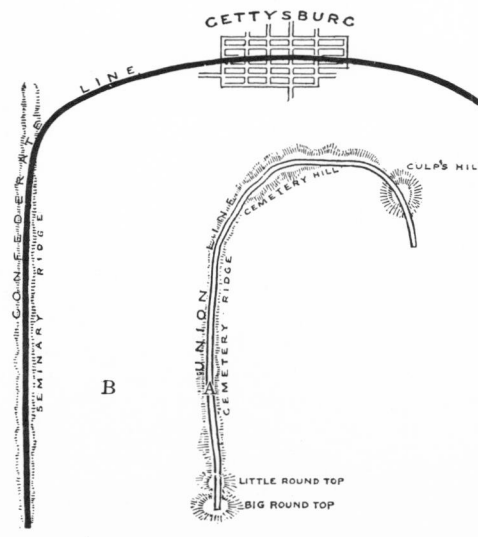

DIAGRAM OF THE GETTYSBURG BATTLE-FIELD.

to descend into the plain, where all its important operations were in full view of the Union signal-stations on the heights, where were officers with powerful glasses. To reinforce any part of the Confederate line required a long march around, on the circumference of the circle, which consumed much valuable time.

On the other hand the nature of the ground made the fire from the Union batteries diffusive, while the Confederate batteries were able to concentrate a heavy fire upon almost any point in front of them.

THE UNION ARMY REACHES GETTYSBURG.

Most of the troops, though worn out with hard marching, arrived by midday of July 2d. The Sixth Corps had thirty-four miles to march, and came later in the afternoon.

SICKLES MOVES IN ADVANCE.

In the preceding diagram, A marks the position to which Sickles had been assigned with the Third Corps. As the ridge disappears there for a considerable space, the ground is low, and, in the opinion of General Sickles, was unfavorable for defense. He therefore went out about three-quarters of a mile to some high ground in front (marked B on the diagram). General Meade, who visited the position, disapproved this movement.

Sickles was soon fiercely assailed by Longstreet's corps.

THE SECOND DAY—THE CONFEDERATE SIDE.

THE STRUGGLE FOR "ROUND TOP."

BY E. M. LAW, MAJOR-GENERAL, C. S. A.

Commanding a division in the assault on "Round Top."

. . . The Confederate line of battle occupied a ridge, partly wooded, with a valley intervening between it and the heights held by the Federal troops in front. The position occupied by the Federal left wing in front of us was fully disclosed to view, and it was certainly one of the most formidable it had ever been the fortune of any troops to confront. Round Top rose like a huge sentinel guarding the Federal left flank, while the spurs and ridges trending off to the north of it afforded unrivaled positions for the use of artillery. The puffs of smoke rising at intervals along the line of hills, as the Federal batteries fired upon such portions of our line as became exposed to view, clearly

showed that these advantages had not been neglected. The thick woods which in great part covered the sides of Round Top and the adjacent hills concealed from view the rugged nature of the ground, which increased fourfold the difficulties of the attack.

How far up the slope of Round Top the Federal left extended we could not tell, as the woods effectually concealed from view everything in that quarter.

Our order of attack — issued as soon as the two divisions of Longstreet's corps came into position on the line already described — was, that the movement should begin on the right, my brigade on that flank leading, the other commands taking it up successively toward the left. It was near 5 o'clock P. M. when we advanced to the attack. The artillery on both sides had been warmly engaged for about fifteen minutes, and continued to fire heavily until we became engaged with the Federal infantry, when the Confederate batteries ceased firing to avoid injury to our own troops, who were then, for the most part, concealed by the woods about the base of Round Top and the spurs to the north of it. General Wood was severely wounded in the arm by a shot from the Federal artillery as we moved into action.

Advancing rapidly across the valley which separated the opposing lines, — all the time under a heavy fire from the batteries, — our front line struck the enemy's skirmishers posted along the farther edge of the valley. Brushing these quickly away, we soon came upon their first line of battle, running along the slopes of the hills known as Devil's Den, to our left of Round Top, and separated from the latter by Plum Run valley. The fighting soon became close and severe. Exposed to the artillery fire from the heights in front and on our left, as well as to the musketry of the infantry, it required all the courage and steadiness of the veterans who composed the Army of Northern Virginia — whose spirit was never higher than then — to face the storm. Not one moment was lost. With rapidly thinning ranks the gray line swept on, until the blue line in front wavered, broke, and seemed to dissolve in the woods and rocks on the mountain-side. The advance continued steadily, the center of the division moving directly upon the guns on the hill adjoining Devil's Den on the north, from which we had been suffering so severely. In order to secure my right flank, I

I extended it well up on the side of Round Top, and my brigade, in closing to the right, left a considerable interval between its left and the right of the Texas brigade of Robertson. Into this interval I threw Benning's Georgia brigade, which had up to that time occupied the second line. At the same time seeing a heavy Federal force on Robertson's left, and no Confederate troops having come up to extend our line in that direction, Anderson's Georgia brigade, till then also in the second line, was thrown out on that flank.

Thus disposed, the division continued to move forward, encountering, as it ascended the heights around the battery on the spur and to the right and left of it, a most determined resistance from the Federal troops, who seemed to be continually reinforced. The ground was rough and difficult, broken by rocks and boulders, which rendered an orderly advance impossible. Sometimes the Federals would hold one side of the huge boulders on the slope until the Confederates occupied the other. In some cases my men, with reckless daring, mounted to the top of the large rocks in order to get a better view, and to deliver their fire with greater effect. One of these, Sergeant Barbee of the Texas brigade, having reached a rock a little in advance of the line, stood erect on the top of it, loading and firing as coolly as if unconscious of danger, while the air around him was fairly swarming with bullets. He soon fell helpless from several wounds; but he held his rock, lying upon the top of it until the litter-bearers carried him off.

In less than an hour from the time we advanced to the attack, the hill by Devil's Den opposite our center was taken, with three pieces of the artillery that had occupied it. The remaining piece was run down the opposite slope by the gunners, and escaped capture.

In the mean time my brigade, on the right, had swept over the northern slope of Round Top, cleared it of the enemy, and then, making a partial change of front to the left, advanced upon Little Round Top, which lay in rear of the spur on which the battery had been taken. This change of direction

THE "SLAUGHTER PEN" AT THE BASE AND ON THE LEFT SLOPE OF LITTLE ROUND TOP.

THE STRUGGLE FOR DEVIL'S DEN (LOOKING TOWARD THE CONFEDERATE LINES).

DEAD CONFEDERATE SHARP-SHOOTER IN THE DEVIL'S DEN.

soon exposed it to a flank attack on the right by fresh troops (Vincent's brigade), rendering it necessary to retire it to the general line.

While our center and right wing were engaged as I have described, Anderson's brigade, on the left, was subjected to great annoyance and loss by movements of the enemy upon its left flank, being frequently compelled to change the front of the regiments on that flank to repel attacks from that direction.

Up to this time I had seen nothing of McLaws's division, which was to have extended our left and to have moved to the attack at the same time. I therefore halted my line, which had become broken and disorganized by the roughness of the ground over which it had been fighting, and placing it in as advantageous a position as possible for receiving any attack that the Federals might be disposed to make, I hurried back to the ridge from which we had originally advanced. I found McLaws still in position there, his troops suffering considerably from a severe fire of artillery from the opposite hills. I was informed by General Kershaw, who held the right of this division, that although he understood the general instructions that the forward movement was to be taken up from the right, he had not yet received the order to move from his division commander. I pointed out the position of Hood's division, and urged the necessity of immediate support on its left. General Kershaw requested me to designate the point on which his right flank should be directed, and promptly moved to the attack, the movement being taken up by the whole division.

When Hood's division first attacked, General Meade, alarmed for the safety of his left wing, and doubtless fully alive to the importance of holding so vital a point as Round Top and its adjacent spurs, commenced sending reinforcements to the threatened points. We encountered some of these in our first advance, and others were arriving as McLaws came up on our left. In its advance this division extended from the "Peach Orchard" near the Emmitsburg road, on its left, to the "Wheatfield" north of the hill on which we had captured the Federal battery, where its right wing connected with my left. As McLaws advanced, we again moved forward on his right, and the fighting continued in "see-saw" style — first one side and then the other gaining ground or losing it, with small

LIEUTENANT BAYARD WILKESON HOLDING HIS BATTERY TO ITS WORK IN AN EXPOSED POSITION.

NOTE.—The death of Lieutenant Bayard Wilkeson, who commanded Battery G, Fourth U. S. Artillery, was one of the most heroic episodes of the fight. He was but nineteen years old and was the son of Samuel Wilkeson, who, as correspondent of the "New York Times," was at Meade's headquarters during the fight. Gen. John B. Gordon, finding it impossible to advance his Confederate division in the face of the fire of Wilkeson's battery, and realizing that if the officer on the horse could be disposed of the battery would not remain, directed two batteries of his command to train every gun upon him. Wilkeson was brought to the ground, desperately wounded, and his horse was killed. He was carried by the Confederates to the Alms House (or dragged himself there—the accounts differ), where he died that night. Just before he expired, it is said, he asked for water; a canteen was brought to him; as he took it a wounded soldier lying next to him begged, "For God's sake give me some?" He passed the canteen untouched to the man, who drank every drop it contained. Wilkeson smiled on the man, turned slightly, and expired.

UNION DEAD WEST OF THE SEMINARY.

196

advantage to either, until dark. At the close of the engagement Hood's division held the hill where the battery had been taken, and the ridge to its left —our right extending across Devil's Den and well up on the northwestern slope of Round Top.

During the night this line was strengthened by the construction of a breastwork of the loose stones that abounded all along the positions occupied by the troops, and the light of the next morning disclosed the fact that the Federal troops in front of us had improved their time in the same way. In fact, all through the night we could hear them at work as the rocks were dropped in place on the work, and no doubt they heard us just as distinctly, while we were engaged in the same life-preserving operation.

Though the losses had been severe on both sides, comparatively few prisoners had been taken. But early in the night, in the confusion resulting from the fight over such rugged ground, and the darkness of the wooded mountain-side, men of both armies, in search of their commands, occasionally wandered into the opposing picket-lines and were captured. Many of the Federal wounded were left in our lines on the ground from which their troops had been forced back, and some of ours remained in their hands in the most advanced positions which we had reached and had been compelled to abandon. Among these latter was Colonel Powell of the 5th Texas regiment, who was shot through the body and afterward died. Powell was a stout, portly man, with a full beard, resembling in many respects General Longstreet, and the first impression of his captors was that they had taken that officer. Indeed, it was asserted positively by some of the prisoners we picked up during the night that Longstreet was badly wounded and a prisoner in their hands, and they obstinately refused to credit our statements to the contrary. . . .

LONGSTREET'S ATTACK AT THE PEACH ORCHARD AND WHEAT-FIELD.

BY J. B. KERSHAW, MAJOR-GEN., C. S. A.
Commanding Kershaw's Brigade at Gettysburg.

MY brigade, composed of South Carolinians, the 2d, 3d, 7th, 8th, and 15th Carolina regiments, and the Third South Carolina battalion, constituted, with Semmes's, Wofford's,

VIEW OF CULP'S HILL FROM THE POSITION OF THE BATTERIES NEAR THE CEMETERY GATE.

1. Position of Stevens's 5th Maine Battery which enfiladed Early's division in the charge upon East Cemetery Hill. 2. Left of the line of field-works on Culp's Hill. 3. Position of the 33d Massachusetts behind the fence of a lane where the left of the Confederate charge was repulsed.

BREVET MAJOR-GENERAL DANIEL E. SICKLES, U. S. A.
Commanding the Third Army Corps at Gettysburg.

and Barksdale's brigades, the division of Major-General Lafayette McLaws, and that, with the divisions of Pickett and Hood, formed the First Corps, Army of Northern Virginia, known as Longstreet's. . . . At 3 P. M. the head of my column emerged from the woods, and came into the open field in front of the stone wall which extends along by Flaherty's farm, and to the east past Snyder's. Here we were in full view of the Federal position. Their main line appeared to extend from little Round Top, where their signal flags were flying, until it was lost to sight far away to the left. An advanced line occupied the Peach Orchard, heavily supported by artillery, and extended from that point toward our left along the Emmitsburg road. The intervening ground was occupied by open fields, interspersed and divided by stone walls. The position just here seemed almost impregnable. I immediately formed line of battle along the stone wall just mentioned, my left resting about Flaherty's house, and my right near Snyder's. This was done under cover of my skirmishers, who engaged those of the enemy near the Emmitsburg road. In the mean time I examined the position of the Federals with some care. I found them in superior force, strongly posted in the Peach Orchard, which bristled with artillery, with a main line of battle in their rear, and extending to, if not upon, Little Round Top, far beyond the point at which their left had been supposed to rest. To carry out my instructions would have been, if successful in driving the enemy from the Peach Orchard, to present my own right flank and rear to a large portion of the enemy's main line of battle. I therefore placed my command in position under the cover of the stone wall, and communicated the condition of matters to Major-General McLaws. The division was then formed on this line, Semmes's brigade two hundred yards in rear and supporting Kershaw's; Barksdale's on the left of Kershaw's, with Wofford's in Barksdale's rear supporting him. Cabell's battalion of artillery was placed along the wall to Kershaw's right, and the 15th South Carolina regiment, Colonel de Saussure, was thrown to their right to support them on that flank.

In the mean time General Hood's division was moving in our rear to the right, to gain the enemy's left flank, and I was directed to commence the attack as soon as General Hood became engaged, swinging around toward the Peach Orchard, and at the same time establishing connection with Hood on my right, and coöperating with him. It was understood that he was to sweep down the Federal lines in a direction perpendicular to our line of battle. I was informed that Barksdale would move with me and conform to my movement; that Semmes would follow me, and Wofford follow Barksdale. These instructions I received in sundry messages from General Longstreet and General McLaws, and in part by personal communication with him. In my center-front was a stone farm-house [supposed to be Rose's], with a barn also of stone. These buildings were about five hundred yards from our position, and on a line with the crest of the Peach Orchard hill.

The Federal infantry was posted along the front of the orchard, and also on the face looking toward Rose's. Six of their batteries were in position, three at the orchard near the crest of the hill, and the others about two hundred yards in rear, extending in the direction of Little Round Top. Behind Rose's was a morass, and, on the right of that, a stone wall running parallel with our line, some two hundred yards from Rose's. Beyond the morass was a stony hill, covered with heavy timber and thick undergrowth interspersed with boulders and large fragments of rock, extending some distance toward the Federal main line, and in the direction of Round Top, and to our left and in rear of the orchard and the batteries posted there. Beyond the stone wall last mentioned, and to the right of the stony hill, was a dense forest extending far to the right. From the morass a small stream ran into this wood and along the base of the mountain. Between the stony hill and the forest was an interval of about one hundred yards, only sparsely covered with a scrubby undergrowth, through which a narrow road led in the direction of the mountain. Looking down this road from Rose's a large wheat-field

was seen. In rear of the wheat-field, and between that and the mountain, there was a heavy force of Federals, posted in line behind a stone wall. Under my instructions I determined to move upon the stony hill, so as to strike it with my center, and thus attack the orchard on its left rear. About 4 o'clock I received the order to move, at a signal from Cabell's artillery. They were to fire for some minutes, then pause, and then fire three guns in rapid succession. At this I was to move without further orders. I communicated these instructions to the commanders of each of the regiments in my command, directing them to convey them to the company officers. They were told, at the signal, to order the men to leap the wall without further orders, and to align the troops in front of it. Accordingly, at the signal, the men leaped over the wall and were promptly aligned; the word was given, and the brigade moved off at the word, with great steadiness and precision, followed by Semmes with equal promptness. General Longstreet accompanied me in this advance on foot, as far as the Emmitsburg road. All the field and staff officers were dismounted on account of the many obstacles in the way. When we were about the Emmitsburg road, I heard Barksdale's drums beat the assembly, and knew *then* that I should have no immediate support on my left, about to be squarely presented to the heavy force of infantry and artillery at, and in rear of, the Peach Orchard. The 2d and 8th South Carolina regiments and James's (Third) battalion constituted the left wing of the brigade, and were then moving majestically across the fields to the left of the lane leading to Rose's, with the steadiness of troops on parade. They were ordered to change direction to the left, and attack the batteries in rear of the Peach Orchard, and accordingly moved rapidly on that point. In order to aid this attack,

the direction of the 3d and 7th regiments was changed to the left, so as to occupy the stony hill and wood. After passing the buildings at Rose's, the charge of the left wing was no longer visible from my position; but the movement was reported to have been magnificently conducted until the cannoneers had left their guns and the caissons were moving off, when the order was given to "move *by the right flank*," by some unauthorized person, and was immediately obeyed by the men. The Federals returned to their guns and opened on these doomed regiments a raking fire of grape and canister, at short distance, which proved most disastrous, and for a time destroyed their usefulness. Hundreds of the bravest and best men of Carolina fell, victims of this fatal blunder. While this tragedy was being enacted, the 3d and 7th regiments were conducted rapidly to the stony hill. In consequence of the obstructions in the way, the 7th Regiment had lapped the 3d a few paces, and when they reached the cover of the stony hill I halted the line at the edge of the wood for a moment, and ordered the 7th to move by the right flank to uncover the 3d Regiment, which was promptly done. It was, no doubt, this movement, observed by some one from the left, that led to the terrible mistake which cost so dearly.

The moment the line was rectified the 7th and

MAJOR-GENERAL E. M. LAW, C. S. A.

3d regiments advanced into the wood and occupied the stony hill, the left of the 3d Regiment swinging around and attacking the batteries to the left of that position, which, for the reasons already stated, had resumed their fire. Very soon a heavy column moved in two lines of battle across the wheat-field to attack my position in such a manner as to take the 7th Regiment in flank on the right. The right wing of this regiment was then thrown back to meet this attack, under the command of Lieutenant-Colonel Bland. I then hurried in person to General Semmes, then 150 yards in my right rear, to bring him up to meet the attack on my right, and also to bring forward my right regiment, the 15th, commanded by Colonel W. G. de Saussure, which, separated from the brigade by the artillery at the time of the advance, was cut off by Semmes's brigade. In the act of leading his regiment, this gallant and accomplished commander of the 15th had just fallen when I reached it. He fell some paces in front of the line, with sword drawn, leading the advance.

General Semmes promptly responded to my call, and put his brigade in motion toward the right, preparatory to moving to the front. While his troops were moving he fell, mortally wounded. Returning to the 7th Regiment, I reached it just as the advancing column of Federals had arrived at a point some two hundred yards off, whence they poured into us a volley from their whole line, and advanced to the charge. They were handsomely received and entertained by this veteran regiment, which long kept them at bay in its front. One regiment of Semmes's brigade came at a double-quick as far as the ravine in our rear, and checked the advance of the Federals in their front. There was still an interval of a hundred yards, or thereabout, between this regiment and the right of the 7th, and into this the enemy was forcing his way, causing my right to swing back more and more; still fighting, at a distance not exceeding thirty paces, until the two wings of the regiment were nearly doubled on each other.

About this time, the fire of the battery on my left having ceased, I sent for the 2d South Carolina regiment to come to the right. Before I could

GENERAL G. K. WARREN AT THE SIGNAL STATION ON LITTLE ROUND TOP.
From a sketch made at the time.

NOTE.—General Warren testified that he went to Little Round Top "by General Meade's direction." In a letter dated July 13th, 1872, General Warren says:

"Just before the action began in earnest, on July 2d, I was with General Meade, near General Sickles, whose troops seemed very badly disposed on that part of the field. At my suggestion, General Meade sent me to the left to examine the condition of affairs, and I continued on till I reached Little Round Top. There were no troops on it, and it was used as a signal station. I saw that this was the key to the whole position, and that our troops in the woods in front of it could not see the ground in front of them, so that the enemy would come upon them before they would be aware of it. The long line of woods on the west side of the Emmitsburg road (which road was along a ridge) furnished an excellent place for the enemy to form out of sight, so I requested the captain of a rifle-battery just in front of Little Round Top to fire a shot into these woods. He did so, and as the shot went whistling through the air the sound of it reached the enemy's troops and caused every one to look in the direction of it. This motion revealed to me the glistening of gun-barrels and bayonets of the enemy's line of battle, already formed and far outflanking the position of any of our troops; so that the line of his advance from his right to Little Round Top was unopposed. I have been particular in telling this, as the discovery was intensely thrilling to my feelings, and almost appalling. I immediately sent a hastily written despatch to General Meade to send a division at least to me, and General Meade directed the Fifth Army Corps to take position there. The battle was already beginning to rage at the Peach Orchard, and before a single man reached Round Top the whole line of the enemy moved on us in splendid array, shouting in the most confident tones. While I was still all alone with the signal officer, the musket-balls began to fly around us, and he was about to fold up his flags and withdraw, but remained, at my request, and kept waving them in defiance. Seeing troops going out on the Peach Orchard road, I rode down the hill, and fortunately met my old brigade. General Weed, commanding it, had already passed the point, and I took the responsibility to detach Colonel O'Rorke, the head of whose regiment I struck, who, on hearing my few words of explanation about the position, moved at once to the hill-top. About this time First Lieutenant Charles E. Hazlett of the Fifth Artillery, with his battery of rifled cannon, arrived. He comprehended the situation instantly, and planted a gun on the summit of the hill. He spoke to the effect that though he could do little execution on the enemy with his guns, he could aid in giving confidence to the infantry, and that his battery was of no consequence whatever compared with holding the position. He stayed there till he was killed. I was wounded with a musket-ball while talking with Lieutenant Hazlett on the hill, but not seriously; and, seeing the position saved while the whole line to the right and front of us was yielding and melting away under the enemy's fire and advance, I left the hill to rejoin General Meade near the center of the field, where a new crisis was at hand."

hear anything of them the enemy had swung around and lapped my whole line at close quarters, and the fighting was general and desperate all along the line, and so continued for some time. These men were brave veterans who had fought from Bull Run to Gettysburg, and knew the strength of their position, and so held it as long as it was tenable. The 7th Regiment finally gave way, and I directed Colonel Aiken to re-form it at the stone wall about Rose's. I passed to the 3d Regiment, then hotly engaged on the crest of the hill, and gradually swung back its right as the enemy made progress around that flank. Semmes's advanced regiment had given way. One of his regiments had mingled with the 3d, and amid rocks and trees, within a few feet of each other, these brave men, Confederates and Federals, maintained

a desperate conflict. The enemy could make no progress in front, but slowly extended around my right. Separated from view of my left, of which I could hear nothing, all my staff being with that wing, the position of the 15th Regiment being wholly unknown, the 7th having retreated, and nothing being heard of the other troops of the division, I feared the brave men around me would be surrounded by the large force of the enemy constantly increasing in numbers, and all the while gradually enveloping us. In order to avoid such a catastrophe, I ordered a retreat to the buildings at Rose's. On emerging from the wood as I followed the retreat, I saw Wofford riding at the head of his fine brigade, then coming in, his left being in the Peach Orchard, which was then clear of the enemy. His movement was such as to strike the stony hill

on the left, and thus turn the flank of the troops that had driven us from that position. On his approach the enemy retreated across the wheat-field, where, with the regiments of my left wing, Wofford attacked with great effect, driving the Federals upon and near to Little Round Top. I now ascertained that Barksdale had advanced upon the Peach Orchard after I had become engaged; that he had cleared that position with the assistance of my 8th South Carolina regiment, driving all before him, and, having advanced far beyond that point, until enveloped by superior forces, had fallen mortally wounded, and been left in the Federals' hands. He had passed too far to my left to afford me any relief except in silencing the batteries that had so cruelly punished my left. When Barksdale passed to the left, the regiments of my left wing moved up into the wood on the left of the stony hill, and maintained that position against heavy odds, until the advance of Wofford's brigade.

When the enemy fell back from the stony hill on General Wofford's advance, the 15th South Carolina and a portion of Semmes's brigade followed them and joined Wofford in his attack upon the retreating column. I rallied the remainder of my brigade and Semmes's at Rose's, with the assistance of Colonel Sorrel of Longstreet's staff, and advanced with them to the support of Wofford, taking position at the stone wall overlooking the forest to the right of Rose's house, some two hundred yards in front. Finding that Wofford's men were coming out, I retained them at that point to check any attempt of the enemy to follow. It was now

ABNER DOUBLEDAY,
BREVET MAJOR-GENERAL, U. S. A.

near nightfall, and the operations of the day were over. That night we occupied the ground over which we had fought, with my left at the Peach Orchard, on the hill, and gathered the dead and wounded—a long list of brave and efficient officers and men. Captain Cunningham's company of the 2d Regiment was reported to have gone into action with forty men, of whom but four remained unhurt to bury their fallen comrades. My losses exceeded 600 men killed and wounded—about one-half the force engaged. . . .

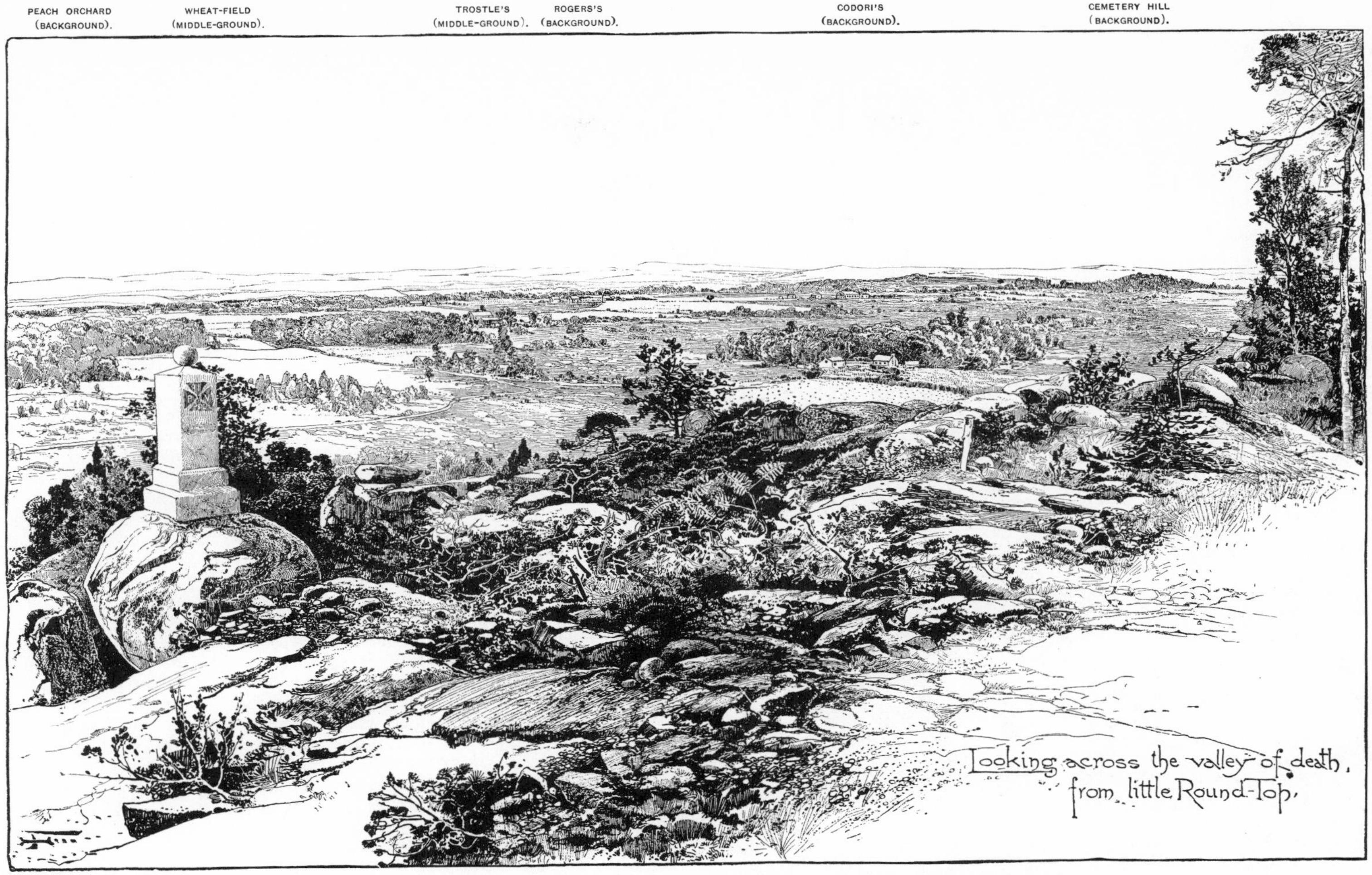

THE SECOND DAY— THE UNION SIDE.

BY HENRY J. HUNT, BREVET MAJOR-GEN., U. S. A.,
Chief of Artillery, A. P.

. . . As soon as Longstreet's attack commenced, General Warren was sent by General Meade to see to the condition of the extreme left. The duty could not have been intrusted to better hands. Passing along the lines he found Little Round Top, the key of the position, unoccupied except by a signal station. The enemy at the time lay concealed, awaiting the signal for assault, when a shot fired in their direction caused a sudden movement on their part which, by the gleam of reflected sunlight from their bayonets, revealed their long lines outflanking the position. Fully comprehending the imminent danger, Warren sent to General Meade for a division. The enemy was already advancing when, noticing the approach of the Fifth Corps, Warren rode to meet it, caused Weed's and Vincent's brigades and Hazlett's battery to be detached from the latter and hurried them to the summit. The passage of the six guns through the roadless woods and amongst the rocks was marvelous. Under ordinary circumstances it would have been considered an impossible feat, but the eagerness of the men to get into action with their comrades of the infantry, and the skilful driving, brought them without delay to the very summit, where they went immediately into battle. They were barely in time, for the enemy were also climbing the hill. A close and bloody hand-to-hand struggle ensued, which left both Round Tops in our possession. Weed and Hazlett were killed, and Vincent was mortally wounded—all young

men of great promise. Weed had served with much distinction as an artillerist in the Peninsular, Second Bull Run, and Antietam campaigns, had become chief of artillery of his army corps, and at Chancellorsville showed such special aptitude and fitness for large artillery commands that he was immediately promoted from captain to brigadier-general and transferred to the infantry. Hazlett was killed whilst bending over his former chief to receive his last message. Lieutenant Rittenhouse efficiently commanded the battery during the remainder of the battle.

The enemy, however, clung to the woods and rocks at the base of Round Top, carried Devil's

VIEW FROM THE POSITION OF HAZLETT'S BATTERY ON LITTLE ROUND TOP.

The Emmitsburg road passes the Peach Orchard, Roger's, and Codori's; the latter's buildings broke the center of Pickett's lines as they charged upon the ridge between Cemetery Hill and Little Round Top. (From photographs.)

Den and its woods, and captured three of Smith's guns, who, however, effectively deprived the enemy of their use by carrying off all the implements. The breaking in of the Peach Orchard angle exposed the flanks of the batteries on its crests, which retired firing, in order to cover the retreat of the infantry. Many guns of different batteries had to be abandoned because of the destruction of their horses and men; many were hauled off by hand; all the batteries lost heavily. Bigelow's 9th Massachusetts made a stand close by the Trostle house in the corner of the field through which he had retired fighting with prolonges fixed. Although already much cut up, he was directed by McGilvery to hold that point at all hazards until a line of artillery could be formed in front of the wood beyond Plum Run; that is, on what we have called the "Plum Run line." This line was formed by collecting the serviceable batteries and fragments of batteries that were brought off, with which, and Dow's Maine battery fresh from the reserve, the pursuit was checked. Finally some twenty-five guns formed a solid mass, which unsupported by infantry held this part of the line, aided General Humphrey's movements, and covered by its fire the abandoned guns until they could be brought off, as all were, except perhaps one. When, after accomplishing its purpose, all that was left of Bigelow's battery was withdrawn, it was closely pressed by Colonel Humphreys's 21st Mississippi, the only Confederate regiment which succeeded in crossing the run. His men had entered the battery and fought hand-to-hand with the cannoneers; one was killed while trying to spike a gun, and another knocked down with a hand-spike whilst endeavoring to drag off a prisoner. The battery went into action with 104 officers and men. Of the four battery officers one was killed, another mortally, and a third, Capt. Bigelow, severely wounded. Of 7 sergeants, 2 were killed and 4 wounded; or a total of 28 men, including 2 missing; and 65 out of 88 horses were killed or wounded. As the battery had sacrificed itself for the safety of the line, its work is specially noticed as typical of the service that artillery is not infrequently called upon to render, and did render in other instances at Gettysburg besides this one.

DEVIL'S DEN, FACING LITTLE ROUND TOP.

MAJOR-GENERAL WINFIELD SCOTT HANCOCK, U. S. A.
Commanding the Second Army Corps at Gettysburg. (From a photograph taken during the war, or soon after.)

When Sickles was wounded General Meade directed Hancock to take command of the Third as well as his own corps, which he again turned over to Gibbon. About 7:15 P. M. the field was in a critical condition. Birney's division was now broken up; Humphreys's was slowly falling back, under cover of McGilvery's guns; Anderson's line was advancing. On its right Barksdale's brigade, except the 21st Mississippi, was held in check only by McGilvery's artillery, to whose support Han-

cock now brought up Willard's brigade of the Second Corps. Placing the 39th New York in reserve, Willard with his other three regiments charged Barksdale's brigade and drove it back nearly to the Emmitsburg road, when he was himself repulsed by a heavy artillery and infantry fire, and fell back to his former position near the sources of Plum Run. In this affair Willard was killed and Barksdale mortally wounded. Meanwhile the 21st Mississippi crossed the run from the neighborhood of the Trostle house, and drove out the men of Watson's battery ("I," 5th United States), on the extreme left of McGilvery's line, but was in turn driven off by the 39th New York, led by Lieutenant Peeples of the battery, musket in hand, who thus recovered his guns, Watson being severely wounded.

Birney's division once broken, it was difficult to stem the tide of defeat. Hood's and McLaws's division — excepting Barksdale's brigade — compassed the Devil's Den and its woods, and as the Federal reinforcements from other corps came piecemeal, they were beaten in detail until by successive accretions they greatly outnumbered their opponents, who had all the advantages of position, when the latter in turn retired, but were not pursued. This fighting was confined almost wholly to the woods and wheat-field between the Peach Orchard and Little Round Top, and the great number of brigade and regimental commanders, as well as of inferior officers and soldiers, killed and wounded on both sides, bears testimony to its close and desperate character. General Meade was on the ground active in bringing up and putting in reinforcements, and in doing so had his horse shot under him. At the close of the day the Confederates held the base of the Round Tops, Devil's Den, its woods, and the Emmitsburg road, with skirmishers thrown out as far as the Trostle house; the Federals had the two Round Tops, the Plum Run line, and Cemetery Ridge. During the night the Plum Run line, except the wood on its left front (occupied by McCandless's brigade, Crawford's division, his other brigade being on Big Round Top), was abandoned; the Third Corps was massed to the left and rear of Caldwell's division, which had reoccupied its short ridge, with McGilvery's artillery on its crest. The Fifth Corps remained on and about Round Top, and a division [Ruger's] which had been detached from the Twelfth Corps returned to Culp's Hill.

When Longstreet's guns were heard, Ewell opened a cannonade, which after an hour's firing was overpowered by the Federal artillery on Cemetery Hill. Johnson's division then advanced, and found only one brigade — Greene's — of the Twelfth Corps in position, the others having been sent to the aid of Sickles at the Peach Orchard. Greene fought with skill and determination for two or three hours, and reinforced by seven or eight hundred men of the First and Eleventh corps, succeeded in holding his own intrenchments, the enemy taking possession of the abandoned works of Geary and Ruger. This brought Johnson's troops near the Baltimore pike, but the darkness prevented their seeing or profiting by the advantage then within their reach. When Ruger's division returned from Round Top, and Geary's from Rock

Creek, they found Johnson in possession of their intrenchments, and immediately prepared to drive him out at daylight.

It had been ordered that when Johnson engaged Culp's Hill, Early and Rodes should assault Cemetery Hill. Early's attack was made with great spirit, by Hoke's and Avery's brigades, Gordon's being in reserve; the hill was ascended through the wide ravine between Cemetery and Culp's hills, a line of infantry on the slopes was broken, and Wiedrich's Eleventh Corps and Rickett's reserve batteries near the brow of the hill were overrun; but the excellent position of Stevens's 12-pounders at the head of the ravine, which enabled him to sweep it, the arrival of Carroll's brigade sent unasked by Hancock, — a happy inspiration, as this line had been weakened to send supports both to Greene and Sickles, — and the failure of Rodes to coöperate with Early, caused the attack to miscarry. The cannoneers of the two batteries, so summarily ousted, rallied and recovered their guns by a vigorous attack — with pistols by those who had them, by others with hand-spikes, rammers, stones, and even fence-rails — the "Dutchmen" showing that they were in no way inferior to their "Yankee" comrades, who had been taunting them ever since Chancellorsville. After an hour's desperate fighting the enemy was driven out with heavy loss, Avery being among the killed. At the close of this second day a consultation of corps commanders was held at Meade's headquarters. I was not present, although summoned, but was informed that the vote was unanimous to hold our lines and await an attack for at least one day before taking the offensive, and Meade so decided.

THE THIRD DAY AT GETTYSBURG— THE UNION SIDE.

BY HENRY J. HUNT, BREVET MAJOR-GENERAL, U. S. A.
Chief of Artillery, Army of the Potomac.

IN view of the successes gained on the second day, General Lee resolved to renew his efforts. These successes were:

1st. *On the right*, the lodgment at the bases of the Round Tops, the possession of Devil's Den and its woods, and the ridges on the Emmitsburg road, which gave him the coveted positions for his artillery.

2d. *On the left*, the occupation of part of the intrenchments of the Twelfth Corps, with an outlet to the Baltimore pike, by which all our lines could be taken in reverse.

3d. *At the center*, the partial success of three of Anderson's brigades in penetrating our lines, from which they were expelled only because they lacked proper support. It was thought that better concert of action might have made good a lodgment here also.

Both armies had indeed lost heavily, but the account in that respect seemed in favor of the Confederates, or at worst balanced. Pickett's and Edward Johnson's divisions were fresh, as were Posey's and Mahone's brigades of R. H. Anderson's, and William Smith's brigade of Early's division. These could be depended upon for an assault; the others could be used as supports, and to follow up a success.

CONFEDERATE SKIRMISHERS AT THE FOOT OF CULP'S HILL.

The artillery was almost intact. Stuart had arrived with his cavalry, excepting the brigades of Jones and Robertson, guarding the communications; and Imboden had also come up. General Lee, therefore, directed the renewal of operations both on the right and left. Ewell had been ordered to attack at daylight on July 3d, and during the night reinforced Johnson with Smith's, Daniel's, and O'Neal's brigades. Johnson had made his preparations, and was about moving, when at dawn Williams's artillery opened upon him, preparatory to an assault by Geary and Ruger for the recovery of their works. The suspension of this fire was followed by an immediate advance by both sides. A conflict ensued which lasted with varying success until near 11 o'clock, during which the Confederates were driven out of the Union intrenchments by Geary and Ruger, aided by Shaler's brigade of the Sixth Corps. They made one or two attempts to regain possession, but were unsuccessful, and a demonstration to turn Johnson's left caused him to withdraw his command to Rock Creek. At the close of the war the scene of this conflict was covered by a forest of dead trees, leaden bullets proving as fatal to them as to the soldiers whose bodies were thickly strewn beneath them.

Longstreet's arrangements had been made to attack Round Top, and his orders issued with a view to turning it, when General Lee decided that the assault should be made on Cemetery Ridge by Pickett's and Pettigrew's divisions. with part of Trimble's. Longstreet formed these in two lines— Pickett on the right, supported by Wilcox; Pettigrew on the left, with Lane's and Scales's brigades under Trimble in the second line. Hill was ordered to hold his line with the remainder of his corps,— six brigades,—give Longstreet assistance if required, and avail himself of any success that might be gained. Finally a powerful artillery force, about one hundred and fifty guns, was ordered to prepare the way for the assault by cannonade. The necessary arrangements caused delay, and before notice of this could be received by Ewell, Johnson, as we

have seen, was attacked, so that the contest was over on the left before that at the center was begun. The hoped-for concert of action in the Confederate attacks was lost from the beginning.

On the Federal side Hancock's corps held Cemetery Ridge with Robinson's division, First Corps, on Hays's right in support, and Doubleday's at the angle between Gibbon and Caldwell. General Newton, having been assigned to the command of the first corps, *vice* Reynolds, was now in charge of the ridge held by Caldwell. Compactly arranged on its crest was McGilvery's artillery, forty-one guns, consisting of his own batteries, reinforced by others from the Artillery Reserve. Well to the right, in front of Hays and Gibbon, was the artillery of the Second Corps under its chief, Captain Hazard. Woodruff's battery was in front of Ziegler's Grove; on his left, in succession, Arnold's Rhode Island, Cushing's United States, Brown's Rhode Island, and Rorty's New York. In the fight of the preceding day the two last-named batteries had been to the front and suffered severely. Lieutenant T. Fred Brown was severely wounded, and his command devolved on Lieutenant Perrin. So great had been the loss in men and horses that they were now of four guns each, reducing the total number in the corps to twenty-six. Daniels's battery of horse artillery, four guns, was at the angle. Cowan's 1st New York battery, six rifles, was placed on the left of Rorty's soon after the cannonade commenced. In addition, some of the guns on Cemetery Hill, and Rittenhouse's on Little Round Top, could be brought to bear, but these were offset by batteries similarly placed on the flanks of the enemy, so that on the Second Corps line, within the space of a mile, were 77 guns to oppose nearly 150. They were on an open crest plainly visible from all parts of the opposite line. Between 10 and 11 A. M., everything looking favorable at Culp's Hill, I crossed over to Cemetery Ridge, to see what might be going on at other points. Here a magnificent display greeted my eyes. Our whole front for two miles was covered by batteries already

in line or going into position. They stretched— apparently in one unbroken mass—from opposite the town to the Peach Orchard, which bounded the view to the left, the ridges of which were planted thick with cannon. Never before had such a sight been witnessed on this continent, and rarely, if ever, abroad. What did it mean? It might possibly be to hold that line while its infantry was sent to aid Ewell, or to guard against a counter-stroke from us, but it most probably meant an assault on our center, to be preceded by a cannonade in order to crush our batteries and shake our infantry; at least to cause us to exhaust our ammunition in reply, so that the assaulting troops might pass in good condition over the half mile of open ground which was beyond our effective musketry fire. With such an object the cannonade would be long and followed immediately by the assault, their whole army being held in readiness to follow up a success. From the great extent of ground occupied by the enemy's batteries, it was evident that all the artillery on our west front, whether of the army corps or the reserve, must concur as a *unit*, . . . and beginning on the right, I instructed the chiefs of artillery and battery commanders to withhold their fire for fifteen or twenty minutes after the cannonade commenced, then to concentrate their fire with all possible accuracy on those batteries which were most destructive to us—but slowly, so that when the enemy's ammunition was exhausted, we should have sufficient left to meet the assault. I had just given these orders to the last battery on Little Round Top, when the signal-gun was fired, and the enemy opened with all his guns. From that point the scene was indescribably grand. All their batteries were soon covered with smoke, through which the flashes were incessant, whilst the air seemed filled with shells, whose sharp explosions, with the hurtling of their fragments, formed a running accompaniment to the deep roar of the guns. Thence I rode to the Artillery Reserve to order fresh batteries and ammunition to be sent up to the ridge as soon as the cannonade ceased; but both the reserve and the train had gone to a safer place. Messengers, however, had been left to receive and convey orders, which I sent by them; then I returned to the ridge. Turning into the Taneytown pike, I saw evidence of the necessity under which the reserve had "decamped," in the remains of a dozen exploded caissons, which had been placed under cover of a hill, but which the shells had managed to search out. In fact, the fire was more dangerous behind the ridge than on its crest. . . .

I now rode along the ridge to inspect the batteries. The infantry were lying down on its reverse slope, near the crest, in open ranks, waiting events. As I passed along, a bolt from a rifle-gun struck the ground just in front of a man of the front rank, penetrated the surface and passed under him, throwing him "over and over." He fell behind the rear rank, apparently dead, and a ridge of earth where he had been lying reminded me of the backwoods practice of "barking" squirrels. Our fire was deliberate, but on inspecting the chests I found that the ammunition was running low, and hastened to General Meade to advise its immediate cessation and preparation for the assault which would certainly follow. The headquarters building, immediately behind the ridge, had been aban-

JOHN L. BURNS, "THE OLD HERO OF GETTYSBURG."

Sergeant George Eustice, of Company F, 7th Wisconsin Volunteers, in a letter from Gilroy, Santa Clara County, California, gives this account of John Burns's action in the ranks of that regiment:

"It must have been about noon when I saw a little old man coming up in the rear of Company F. In regard to the peculiarities of his dress, I remember he wore a swallow-tailed coat with smooth brass buttons. He had a rifle on his shoulder. We boys began to poke fun at him as soon as he came amongst us, as we thought no civilian in his senses would show himself in such a place. Finding that he had really come to fight I wanted to put a cartridge-box on him to make him look like a soldier, telling him he could not fight without one. Slapping his pantaloons-pocket, he replied, 'I can get my hands in here quicker than in a box. I'm not used to them new-fangled things.' In answer to the question what possessed him to come out there at such a time, he replied that the rebels had either driven away or milked his cows, and that he was going to be even with them. About this time the enemy began to advance. Bullets were flying thicker and faster, and we hugged the ground about as close as we could. Burns got behind a tree, and surprised us all by not taking a double-quick to the rear. He was as calm and collected as any veteran on the ground. We soon had orders to get up and move about a hundred yards to the right, when we were engaged in one of the most stubborn contests I ever experienced. Foot by foot we were driven back to a point near the seminary, where we made a stand, but were finally driven through the town to Cemetery Ridge. I never saw John Burns after our movement to the right, when we left him behind his tree, and only know that he was true blue and grit to the backbone, and fought until he was three times wounded."

The 7th Wisconsin served in the "Iron Brigade," First Corps. Burns's bravery is mentioned in General Doubleday's official report.

THE 29TH PENNSYLVANIA FORMING LINE OF BATTLE ON CULP'S HILL, MORNING OF
THE THIRD DAY.

GENERAL GEORGE H. STEUART'S BRIGADE RENEWING THE CONFEDERATE ATTACK ON
CULP'S HILL, MORNING OF THE THIRD DAY.

doned, and many of the horses of the staff lay dead. Being told that the general had gone to the cemetery, I proceeded thither. He was not there, and on telling General Howard my object, he concurred in its propriety, and I rode back along the ridge, ordering the fire to cease. This was followed by a cessation of that of the enemy, under the mistaken impression that he had silenced our guns, and almost immediately his infantry came out of the woods and formed for the assault. On my way to the Taneytown road to meet the fresh batteries which I had ordered up, I met Major Bingham, of Hancock's staff, who informed me that General Meade's aides were seeking me with orders to "cease firing"; so I had only anticipated his wishes. The batteries were brought up, and Fitz-hugh's, Weir's, Wheeler's, and Parson's were put in near the clump of trees. Brown's and Arnold's batteries had been so crippled that they were now withdrawn, and Brown's was replaced by Cowan's. Meantime the enemy advanced, and McGilvery opened a destructive oblique fire, reinforced by that of Rittenhouse's six rifle-guns from Round Top, which were served with remarkable accuracy, enfilading Pickett's lines. The Confederate approach was magnificent, and excited our admiration; but the story of that charge is so well known that I need not dwell upon it further than as it concerns my own command. The steady fire from McGilvery and Rittenhouse, on their right, caused Pickett's men to "drift" in the opposite direction, so that the weight of the assault fell upon the positions occupied by Hazard's batteries. I had counted on an artillery cross-fire that would stop it before it reached our lines, but, except a few shots here and there, Hazard's batteries were

silent until the enemy came within canister range. They had unfortunately exhausted their long-range projectiles during the cannonade, under the orders of their corps commander, and it was too late to replace them. . . .

The losses in the batteries of the Second Corps were very heavy. Of the five battery commanders and their successors on the field, Rorty, Cushing, and Woodruff were killed, and Milne was mortally, and Sheldon severely, wounded at their guns. So great was the destruction of men and horses, that Cushing's and Woodruff's United States, and Brown's and Arnold's Rhode Island batteries were consolidated to form two serviceable ones. . . .

Whilst the main battle was raging, sharp cavalry combats took place on both flanks of the army. On the left the principal incident was an attack made by order of General Kilpatrick on infantry and artillery in woods and behind stone fences, which resulted in considerable losses, and especially in the death of General Farnsworth, a gallant and promising officer who had but a few days before been appointed brigadier-general and had not yet received his commission. On the right an affair of some magnitude took place between Stuart's command of four and Gregg's of three brigades; but Jenkins's Confederate brigade was soon thrown out of action from lack of ammunition, and two only of Gregg's were engaged. Stuart had been ordered to cover Ewell's left, and was proceeding toward the Baltimore pike, where he hoped to create a diversion in aid of the Confederate infantry, and in case of Pickett's success to fall upon the retreating Federal troops. From near Cress's Ridge, two and a half miles east of Gettysburg, Stuart commanded a view of the roads in rear of the Federal

lines. On its northern wooded end he posted Jackson's battery, and took possession of the Rummel farm buildings, a few hundred yards distant. Hampton and Fitzhugh Lee were on his left, covered by the wood, Jenkins and Chambliss on the right, along the ridge. Half a mile east on a low parallel ridge, the southern part of which bending west toward Cress's Ridge furnished excellent positions for artillery, was the Federal cavalry brigade of McIntosh, who now sent a force toward Rummel's, from which a strong body of skirmishers was thrown to meet them, and the battery opened. McIntosh now demanded reinforcements, and Gregg, then near the Baltimore pike, brought him Custer's brigade and Pennington's and Randol's batteries. The artillery soon drove the Confederates out of Rummel's, and compelled Jackson's Virginia battery to leave the ridge. Both sides brought up reinforcements and the battle swayed from side to side of the interval. Finally the Federals were pressed back, and Lee and Hampton, emerging from the wood, charged, sword in hand, facing a destructive artillery fire — for the falling back of the cavalry had uncovered our batteries. The assailants were met by Custer's and such other mounted squadrons as could be thrown in; a *mêlée* ensued, in which Hampton was severely wounded and the charge repulsed. Breathed's and McGregor's Confederate batteries had replaced Jackson's, a sharp artillery duel took place, and at nightfall each side held substantially its original ground. Both sides claim to have held the Rummel house. The advantage was decidedly with the Federals, who had foiled Stuart's plans. Thus the battle of Gettysburg closed as it had opened, with a very creditable cavalry battle. . . .

PICKETT'S CHARGE AND ARTILLERY FIGHTING AT GETTYSBURG.

BY E. PORTER ALEXANDER, BRIGADIER-GENERAL, C. S. A.

Chief of artillery of Longstreet's corps during the Battle of Gettysburg.

THE Reserve Artillery of Longstreet's corps, in the Gettysburg campaign, consisted of the Washington Artillery of New Orleans, then under Major Eshleman, nine guns, and my own battalion of twenty-six guns. Besides these, the artillery of the corps comprised Cabell's, Henry's, and Dearing's battalions of eighteen guns each. The latter battalions were usually attached, on the march, respectively to McLaws's, Hood's, and Pickett's divisions of infantry.

On the first of July, 1863, the Reserve Artillery was encamped near Greenwood, and we had no idea that the great battle of the campaign had already opened about eighteen miles away. Early in the night, however, rumors reached us that Hill's corps had been heavily engaged, and that Ewell's had come to his assistance; that the enemy had been driven some distance, but had finally made a stand in a very strong position. These rumors were soon followed by orders for the artillery to march at 1 o'clock for the front. There was little time to sleep before taking the road, and I think but few improved even that little.

We marched quite steadily, with a good road and a bright moon, until about 7 A. M. on the 2d, when we halted in a grassy open grove about a mile west of Seminary Ridge, and fed and watered. Here, soon afterward, I was sent for by General Long-

HENRY J. HUNT,
BREVET MAJOR-GENERAL, U. S. A., CHIEF OF
ARTILLERY, ARMY OF THE POTOMAC.

CHARGE OF
ALEXANDER'S ARTILLERY.

WILLIAM N. PENDLETON,
BRIGADIER-GENERAL, C. S. A., LEE'S CHIEF
OF ARTILLERY.

street, and, riding forward, found him with General Lee on Seminary Ridge. Opposite, about a mile away, on Cemetery Ridge, overlooking the town, lay the enemy, their batteries making considerable display, but their infantry, behind stone walls and ridges, scarcely visible. In between us were only gentle rolling slopes of pasture and wheat-fields, with a considerable body of woods to the right and front. The two Round Tops looked over everything, and a signal-flag was visible on the highest. Instinctively the idea arose, "If we could only take position here, and have them attack us through this open ground!" But I soon learned that we were in no such luck — the boot, in fact, being upon the other foot.

It was explained to me that our corps was to assault the enemy's left flank, and I was directed to reconnoiter it and then to take charge of all the artillery of the corps and direct it in the attack, leaving my own battalion to the command of Major Huger. I was particularly cautioned, in moving the artillery, to keep it out of sight of the signal station upon Round Top.

I immediately started on my reconnoissance, and in about three hours had a good idea of all the ground, and had Cabell's, Henry's, and my own battalions parked near where our infantry lines were to be formed and the attack begun. Dearing's battalion with Pickett's infantry was not yet up, and the Washington Artillery was left in reserve.

Through some blunder, part of our infantry had been marched on a road that brought them in sight of Round Top, and, instead of taking to the fields and hollows, they had been halted for an hour, and then had been countermarched and sent around by a circuitous road, via Black Horse Tavern, about five miles out of the way, thereby losing at least two hours.

We waited quite a time for the infantry, and I think it was about 4 o'clock when at last the word was given for Hood's division to move out and endeavor to turn the enemy's left, while McLaws

awaited the development of Hood's attack, ready to assault the Peach Orchard. Henry's battalion moved out with Hood and was speedily and heavily engaged; Cabell was ready to support him, and at once went into action near Snyder's house, about seven hundred yards from the Peach Orchard.

The Federal artillery was ready for us, and in their usual full force and good practice. The ground at Cabell's position gave little protection, and he suffered rapidly in both men and horses. To help him, I ran up Huger, with 18 guns of my own 26, to Warfield's house, within 500 yards of the Peach Orchard, and opened upon it. This made 54 guns in action, and I hoped they would crush that part of the enemy's line in a very short time, but the fight was longer and hotter than I expected. So accurate was the enemy's fire, that two of my guns were fairly dismounted, and the loss of men was so great that I had to ask General Barksdale, whose brigade was lying down close behind in the wood, for help to handle the heavy 24-pounder howitzers of Moody's battery. He gave me permission to call for volunteers, and in a minute I had eight good fellows, of whom, alas! we buried two that night, and sent to the hospital three others mortally or severely wounded. At last I sent for my other two batteries, but before they arrived McLaws's division charged past our guns, and the enemy deserted their line in confusion. Then I believed that Providence was indeed "taking the proper view," and that the war was very nearly over. Every battery was limbered to the front, and the two batteries from the rear coming up, all six charged in line across the plain and went into action again at the position the enemy had deserted. I can recall no more splendid sight, on a small scale,— and certainly no more inspiring moment during the war,— than that of the charge of these six batteries. An artillerist's heaven is to follow the routed enemy, after a tough resistance, and throw shells and canister into his disorganized and fleeing masses. Then the explosions of the guns sound louder and more powerful, and the very shouts of the gunners, ordering "Fire!" in rapid succession, thrill one's very soul. There is no excitement on earth like it. It is far prettier shooting than at a compact, narrow line of battle, or at another battery. Now we saw our heaven just in front, and were already breathing the very air of victory. Now we would have our revenge, and

make them sorry they had stayed so long. Everything was in a rush. The ground was generally good, and pieces and caissons went at a gallop, some cannoneers mounted, and some running by the sides — not in regular line, but a general race and scramble to get there first.

But we only had a moderately good time with Sickles's retreating corps after all. They fell back upon fresh troops in what seemed a strong position, extending along the ridge north of Round Top. Hood's troops under Law gained the slope of Little Round Top, but were driven back to its base. Our infantry lines had become disjointed in the advance, and the fighting became a number of isolated combats between brigades. The artillery took part wherever it could, firing at everything in sight, and a sort of pell-mell fighting lasted until darkness covered the field, and the fuses of the flying shells looked like little meteors in the air. But then both musketry and artillery slackened off, and by 9 o'clock the field was silent. It was evident that we had not finished the job, and would have to make a fresh effort in the morning. The firing had hardly ceased when my faithful little darky, Charley, came up hunting for me with a fresh horse, affectionate congratulations on my safety, and, what was equally acceptable, something to eat. Negro servants hunting for their masters was a feature of the landscape that night. I then found General Longstreet, learned what I could of the fortunes of the day on other parts of the field, and got orders for the morning. They were in brief that our present position was to be held, and the attack renewed as soon as Pickett arrived, and he was expected early. . . .

Early in the morning General Lee came around, and I was then told that we were to assault Cemetery Hill, which lay rather to our left. This necessitated a good many changes of our positions, which the enemy did not altogether approve of, and they took occasional shots at us, though we shifted about, as inoffensively as possible, and carefully avoided getting into bunches. But we stood it all meekly, and by 10 o'clock, Dearing having come up, we had seventy-five guns in what was virtually one battery, so disposed as to fire on Cemetery Hill and the batteries south of it, which would have a fire on our advancing infantry. Pickett's division had arrived, and his men were resting and eating. Along Seminary Ridge, a

short distance to our left, were sixty-three guns of A. P. Hill's corps, under Colonel R. L. Walker. As their distance was a little too great for effective howitzer fire, General Pendleton offered me the use of nine howitzers belonging to that corps. I accepted them, intending to take them into the charge with Pickett, so I put them in a hollow behind a bit of wood, with no orders but to wait there until I sent for them. About 11, some of Hill's skirmishers and the enemy's began fighting over a barn between the lines, and gradually his artillery and the enemy's took part, until over a hundred guns were engaged, and a tremendous roar was kept up for quite a time. But it gradually died out, and the whole field became as silent as a churchyard about 1 o'clock. The enemy aware of the strength of his position, simply sat still and waited for us. It had been arranged that when the infantry column was ready, General Longstreet should order two guns fired by the Washington Artillery. On that signal all our guns were to open on Cemetery Hill and the ridge extending toward Round Top, which was covered with batteries. I was to observe the fire and give Pickett the order to charge. I accordingly took position, about 12, at the most favorable point, just on the left of the line of guns, and with one of Pickett's couriers with me. Soon after I received the following note from Longstreet:—

"COLONEL: If the artillery fire does not have the effect to drive off the enemy or greatly demoralize him, so as to make our efforts pretty certain, I would prefer that you should not advise General Pickett to make the charge. I shall rely a great deal on your good judgment to determine the matter, and shall expect you to let General Pickett know when the moment offers."

This note rather startled me. If that assault was to be made on General Lee's judgment it was all right, but I did not want it made on mine. I wrote back to General Longstreet to the following effect:—

"GENERAL: I will only be able to judge of the effect of our fire on the enemy by his return fire, for his infantry is but little exposed to view, and the smoke will obscure the whole field. If, as I infer from your note, there is any alternative to this attack, it should be care-

PICKETT'S CHARGE.—THE MAIN COLLISION TO THE RIGHT OF THE "CLUMP OF TREES."

In this hand-to-hand conflict General Armistead, of Pickett's division, was killed, and General Webb, of Gibbon's division (Union), was wounded. (From the Cyclorama of Gettysburg, by permission of the National Panorama Company.)

fully considered before opening our fire, for it will take all the artillery ammunition we have left to test this one thoroughly, and if the result is unfavorable, we will have none left for another effort. And even if this is entirely successful, it can only be so at a very bloody cost."

To this presently came the following reply:

"COLONEL: The intention is to advance the infantry if the artillery has the desired effect of driving the enemy's off, or having other effect such as to warrant us in making the attack. When the moment arrives, advise General Pickett, and of course advance such artillery as you can use in aiding the attack."

I hardly knew whether this left me discretion or not, but at any rate it seemed decided that the artillery must open. I felt that if we went that far we could not draw back, but the infantry must go too. General A. R. Wright, of Hill's corps, was with me looking at the position when these notes were received, and we discussed them together. Wright said, "It is not so hard to *go* there as it looks; I was nearly there with my brigade yesterday. The trouble is to *stay* there. The whole Yankee army is there in a bunch."

I was influenced by this, and somewhat by a sort of camp rumor which I had heard that morning, that General Lee had said that he was going to send every man he had upon that hill. At any rate, I assumed that the question of supports had been well considered, and that whatever was possible would be done. But before replying I rode to see Pickett, who was with his division a short distance in the rear. I did not tell him my object, but only tried to guess how he felt about the charge. He seemed very sanguine, and thought himself in luck to have the chance. Then I felt that I could not make any delay or let the attack suffer by any indecision on my part. And, that General Longstreet might know my intention, I wrote him only this:

"GENERAL: When our artillery fire is at its best, I shall order Pickett to charge."

Then, getting a little more anxious, I decided to send for the nine howitzers and take them ahead of Pickett up nearly to musket range, instead of following close behind him as at first intended; so I sent a courier to bring them up in front of the infantry, but under cover of the wood. The courier could not find them. He was sent again, and only returned after our fire was opened, saying they were gone. I afterward learned that General Pendleton had sent for a part of them, and the others had moved to a neighboring hollow to get out of the line of the enemy's fire at one of Hill's batteries during the artillery duel they had had an hour before.

At exactly 1 o'clock by my watch the two signal-guns were heard in quick succession. In another minute every gun was at work. The enemy were not slow in coming back at us, and the grand roar of nearly the whole artillery of both armies burst in on the silence, almost as suddenly as the full notes of an organ would fill a church.

The artillery of Ewell's corps, however, took only a small part, I believe, in this, as they were too far away on the other side of the town. Some of them might have done good service from positions between Hill and Ewell, enfilading the batteries fighting us. The opportunity to do that was the single advantage in our having the exterior line, to compensate for all its disadvantages. But our line was so extended that all of it was not well studied, and the officers of the different corps had no opportunity to examine each other's ground for chances to coöperate.

The enemy's

MAJOR-GENERAL GEORGE E. PICKETT, C. S. A.

position seemed to have broken out with guns everywhere, and from Round Top to Cemetery Hill was blazing like a volcano. The air seemed full of missiles from every direction. The severity of the fire may be illustrated by the casualties in my own battalion under Major Huger.

Under my predecessor, General S. D. Lee, the battalion had made a reputation at the Second Manassas and also at Sharpsburg. At the latter battle it had a peculiarly hard time, fighting infantry and superior metal nearly all day, and losing about eighty-five men and sixty horses. Sharpsburg they called "artillery hell." At Gettysburg the losses in the same command, including the infantry that volunteered to help serve the guns, were 144 men and 116 horses, nearly all by artillery fire. Some parts of the Federal artillery suffered in the same proportion under our fire. I heard of one battery losing 27 out of 36 horses in ten minutes.

Before the cannonade opened I had made up my mind to give Pickett the order to advance within fifteen or twenty minutes after it began. But when I looked at the full development of the enemy's batteries, and knew that his infantry was generally protected from our fire by stone walls and swells of the ground, I could not bring myself to give the word. It seemed madness to launch infantry into that fire, with nearly three-quarters of a mile to go at midday under a July sun. I let the 15 minutes pass, and 20, and 25, hoping vainly for something to turn up. Then I wrote to Pickett: "If you are coming at all you must come at once, or I cannot give you proper support; but the enemy's fire has not slackened at all; at least eighteen guns are still firing from the cemetery itself." Five minutes after sending that message, the enemy's fire suddenly began to slacken, and the guns in the cemetery limbered up and vacated the position.

We Confederates often did such things as that to save our ammunition for use against infantry, but I had never before seen the Federals withdraw their guns simply to save them up for the infantry fight. So I said, "If he does not run fresh batteries in there in five minutes, this is our fight." I looked anxiously with my glass, and the five minutes passed without a sign of life on the deserted position, still swept by our fire, and littered with dead men and horses and fragments of disabled carriages. Then I wrote Pickett, urgently: "For God's sake, come quick. The eighteen guns are gone; come quick, or my ammunition won't let me support you properly."

I afterward heard from others what took place with my first note to Pickett.

Pickett took it to Longstreet, Longstreet read it, and said nothing. Pickett said, "General, shall I advance?" Longstreet, knowing it had to be, but unwilling to give the word, turned his face away. Pickett saluted and said, "I am going to move forward, sir," galloped off to his division, and immediately put it in motion.

Longstreet, leaving his staff, came out alone to where I was. It was then about 1:40 P. M. I explained the situation, feeling then more hopeful, but afraid our artillery ammunition might not hold out for all we would want. Longstreet said, "Stop Pickett immediately, and replenish your ammunition." I explained that it would take too long, and the enemy would recover from the effect our fire was then having, and we had, moreover, very little to replenish with. Longstreet said, "I don't want to make this attack. I would stop it now, but that General Lee ordered it and expects it to go on. I don't see how it can succeed." I listened, but did not dare offer a word. The battle was lost if we stopped. Ammunition was far too low to try anything else, for we had been fighting three days. There was a chance, and it was not my part to interfere. . While Longstreet was still speaking, Pickett's division swept out of the wood, and showed the full length of its gray ranks and shining bayonets, as grand a sight as ever a

man looked on. Joining it on the left Pettigrew stretched farther than I could see. General Dick Garnett, just out of the sick ambulance, and buttoned up in an old blue overcoat, riding at the head of his brigade, passed us and saluted Longstreet. Garnett was a warm personal friend, and we had not met before for months. We had served on the plains together before the war. I rode with him a short distance, and then we wished each other luck and a good-by, which was our last.

Then I rode down the line of guns, selecting such as had enough ammunition to follow Pickett's advance, and starting them after him as fast as possible. I got, I think, fifteen or eighteen in all, in a little while, and went with them. Meanwhile, the infantry had no sooner debouched on the plain than all the enemy's line, which had been nearly silent, broke out again with all its batteries. The eighteen guns were back in the cemetery, and a storm of shell began bursting over and among our infantry. All of our guns — silent as the infantry passed between them — reopened over their heads when the lines had got a couple of hundred yards away, but the enemy's artillery let us alone and fired only at the infantry. No one could have looked at that advance without feeling proud of it.

But, as our supporting guns advanced, we passed many poor, mangled victims left in its trampled wake. A terrific infantry fire was now opened upon Pickett, and a considerable force of the enemy moved out to attack the right flank of his line. We halted, unlimbered, and opened fire

upon it. Pickett's men never halted, but opened fire at close range, swarmed over the fences and among the enemy's guns — were swallowed up in smoke, and that was the last of them. The conflict hardly seemed to last five minutes before they were melted away, and only disorganized stragglers pursued by a moderate fire were coming back. Just then, Wilcox's brigade passed by us, moving to Pickett's support. There was no longer anything to support, and with the keenest pity at the useless waste of life, I saw them advance. The men, as they passed us, looked bewildered, as if they wondered what they were expected to do, or why they were there. However, they were soon halted and moved back. They suffered some losses, and we had a few casualties from canister sent at them at rather long range.

From the position of our guns the sight of this conflict was grand and thrilling, and we watched it as men with a life-and-death interest in the result. If it should be favorable to us, the war was nearly over; if against us, we each had the risks of many battles yet to go through. And the event culminated with fearful rapidity. Listening to the rolling crashes of musketry, it was hard to realize that they were made up of single reports, and that each musket-shot represented nearly a minute of a man's life in that storm of lead and iron. It seemed as if 100,000 men were engaged, and that human life was being poured out like water. As soon as it appeared that the assault had failed, we ceased firing in order to save ammunition in case the enemy should advance. But we held our ground as boldly as possible, though we were entirely without support, and very low in ammunition. The enemy gave us an occasional shot for a while, and then, to our great relief, let us rest. About that time General Lee, entirely alone, rode up and remained with me for a long time. He then probably first appreciated the full extent of the disaster as the disorganized stragglers made their way back past us. The Comte de Paris, in his excellent account of this battle, remarks that Lee,

THE CHARGE OF PICKETT, PETTIGREW, AND TRIMBLE.
From a war-time sketch from the Union position.

CEMETERY HILL.   CLUMP OF TREES.   ROUND TOPS.
PROFILE OF CEMETERY RIDGE AS SEEN FROM PICKETT'S POSITION BEFORE THE CHARGE.

as a soldier, must at this moment have foreseen Appomattox — that he must have realized that he could never again muster so powerful an army, and that for the future he could only delay, but not avert, the failure of his cause. However this may be, it was certainly a momentous thing to him to see that superb attack end in such a bloody repulse. But, whatever his emotions, there was no trace of them in his calm and self-possessed bearing. I thought at the time his coming there very imprudent, and the absence of all his staff-officers and couriers strange. It could only have happened by his express intention. I have since thought it possible that he came, thinking the enemy might follow in pursuit of Pickett, personally to rally stragglers about our guns and make a desperate defense. He had the instincts of a soldier within him as strongly as any man. Looking at Burnside's dense columns swarming through the fire of our guns toward Marye's Hill at Fredericksburg, he said: "It is well war is so terrible, or we would grow too fond of it." No soldier could have looked on at Pickett's charge and not burned to be in it. To have a personal part in a close and desperate fight at that moment would, I believe, have been at heart a great pleasure to General Lee, and possibly he was looking for one. We were here joined by Colonel Fremantle of Her Majesty's Coldstream Guards, who was visiting our army. He afterward published an excellent account of the battle in "Blackwood," and described many little incidents that took place here, such as General Lee's encouraging the retreating stragglers to rally as soon as they got back to cover, and saying that the failure was his fault, not theirs. Colonel Fremantle especially noticed that General Lee reproved an officer for spurring a foolish horse, and advised him to use only gentle measures. The officer was Lieutenant F. M. Colston of my staff, whom General Lee had requested to ride off to the right and try to discover the cause of a great cheering we heard in the enemy's lines. We thought it might mean an advance upon us, but it proved to be only a greeting to some general officer riding along the line.

That was the end of the battle. Little by little we got some guns to the rear to replenish and refit, and get in condition to fight again, and some we held boldly in advanced positions all along the line. Sharp-shooters came out and worried some of the men, and single guns would fire on these, sometimes very rapidly, and manage to keep them back; some parts of the line had not even a picket in front. But the enemy's artillery generally let us alone, and I certainly saw no reason to disturb the *entente cordiale*. Night came very slowly, but came at last; and about 10 the last gun was withdrawn to Willoughby Run, whence we had moved to the attack the afternoon before.

Of Pickett's three brigadiers, Garnett and Armistead were killed, and Kemper dangerously wounded. Fry, who commanded Pettigrew's brigade, which adjoined Garnett on the left, and in the charge was the brigade of direction for the whole force, was also left on the field desperately wounded. Of all Pickett's field-officers in the three brigades only one major came out unhurt. The men who made the attack were good enough: the only trouble was, there were not enough of them. . . .

PICKETT'S CHARGE.—LOOKING DOWN THE UNION LINES FROM THE "CLUMP OF TREES."
General Hancock and staff are seen in the left center of the picture.—This picture is from the Cyclorama of Gettysburg, by permission of the National Panorama Company.

LONGSTREET'S STORY OF THE GRAND CHARGE.

BY JAMES LONGSTREET, LIEUTENANT-GENERAL, C. S. A.

. . . About 1 o'clock everything was in readiness. The signal-guns broke the prevailing stillness, and immediately 150 Confederate cannon burst into a deafening roar, which was answered by a thunder almost as great from the Federal side. The great artillery combat proceeded. The destruction was, of course, not great; but the thunder on Seminary Ridge, and the echo from the Federal side, showed that both commanders were ready. The armies seemed like mighty wild beasts growling at each other and preparing for a death-struggle. For an hour or two the fire was continued, and met such steady response on the part of the Federals that it seemed less effective than we had anticipated. I sent word to Alexander that unless he could do something more, I would not feel warranted in ordering the troops forward. After a little, some of the Federal batteries ceased firing, possibly to save ammunition, and Alexander thought the most suitable time for the advance had come. He sent word to Pickett, and Pickett rode to my headquarters. As he came up he asked if the time for his advance had come. I was convinced that he would be leading his troops to needless slaughter, and did not speak. He repeated the question, and without opening my lips I bowed in answer. In a determined voice Pickett said: "Sir, I shall lead my division forward." He then remounted his horse and rode back to his command. I mounted my horse, and rode to a point where I could observe the troops. . . .

That day at Gettysburg was one of the saddest of my life. I foresaw what my men would meet, and would gladly have given up my position rather than share in the responsibilities of that day. It was thus I felt when Pickett at the head of 4900 brave men marched over the crest of Seminary Ridge and began his descent of the slope. As he passed he rode gracefully, with his jaunty cap raked well over on his right ear, and his long auburn locks, nicely dressed, hanging almost to his shoulders. He seemed rather a holiday soldier than a general at the head of a column which was about to make one of the grandest, most desperate assaults recorded in the annals of wars. Armistead and Garnett, two of his brigadiers, were veterans of nearly a quarter of a century's service. Their minds seemed absorbed in the men behind, and in the bloody work before them. Kemper, the other brigadier, was younger, but had experienced many severe battles. He was leading my old brigade that I had drilled on Manassas plains before the first battle on that noted field. The troops advanced in well-closed ranks and with elastic step, their faces lighted with hope. Before them lay the ground over which they were to pass to the point of attack. Intervening were several fences, a field of corn, a little swale running through it and then a rise from that point to the Federal stronghold. As soon as Pickett passed the crest of the hill, the Federals had a clear view and opened their batteries, and as he descended the eastern slope of the ridge his troops received a fearful fire from the batteries in front and from Round Top. The troops marched steadily, taking the fire with great coolness. As soon as they passed my batteries I ordered my artillery to turn their fire against the batteries on our right then raking my lines. They did so, but did not force the Federals to change the direction of their fire and relieve our infantry. As the troops were about to cross the swale I noticed a considerable force of Federal infantry moving down as though to flank the left of our line. I sent an officer to caution the division commanders to guard against that move. . . . After crossing the swale, the troops kept the same steady step, but met a dreadful fire at the hands of the Federal sharp-shooters; and as soon as the field was open the Federal infantry poured down a terrific fire which was kept up during the entire assault. The slaughter was terrible, the enfilade fire of the batteries on Round Top being very destructive. At times one shell would knock down five or six men. I dismounted to relieve my horse, and was sitting on a rail fence watching very closely the movements of the troops. As Pickett's division concentrated in making the final assault, Kemper fell severely wounded. As the division threw itself against the Federal line Garnett fell and expired. The Confederate flag was planted in the Federal line, and immediately Armistead fell mortally wounded at the feet of the Federal soldiers. The wavering divisions then seemed appalled, broke their ranks, and retired. Immediately the Federals swarmed around Pickett, attacking on all sides, enveloped and broke up his command, having killed and wounded more than two thousand men in about thirty minutes. They then drove the fragments back upon our lines. As they came back I fully expected to see Meade ride to the front and lead his forces to a tremendous counter-charge. Sending

CONFEDERATE ARTILLERYMEN AT DINNER.

CONFEDERATES WAITING FOR THE END OF THE ARTILLERY DUEL.

my staff-officers to assist in collecting the fragments of my command, I rode to my line of batteries, knowing they were all I had in front of the impending attack, resolved to drive it back or sacrifice my last gun and man. The Federals were advancing a line of skirmishers which I thought was the advance of their charge. As soon as the line of skirmishers came within reach of our guns, the batteries opened again and their fire seemed to check at once the threatened advance. After keeping it up a few minutes the line of skirmishers disappeared, and my mind was relieved of the apprehension that Meade was going to follow us.

General Lee came up as our troops were falling back, and encouraged them as well as he could; begged them to reform their ranks and reorganize their forces, and assisted the staff-officers in bringing them all together again. It was then he used the expression that has been mentioned so often: "It was all my fault; get together, and let us do the best we can toward saving that which is left us." . . .

FARNSWORTH'S CHARGE AND DEATH.

BY H. C. PARSONS, CAPTAIN, 1ST VERMONT CAVALRY.

Commanding the First Battalion in Farnsworth's Charge.

ON the eve of the battle of Gettysburg Captain Elon J. Farnsworth, of the 8th Illinois Cavalry, an aide on General Pleasonton's staff, was promoted for gallantry to be brigadier-general and given command of a brigade in Kilpatrick's division, consisting of the 5th New York, 18th Pennsylvania, 1st Vermont, and 1st West Virginia regiments.

On the evening of the 2d of July we were on Meade's right wing, and by noon of the third day of the battle we went into position on his left wing, near the enemy's artillery line, on the south end of Seminary Ridge. . . . Kilpatrick's orders were to press the enemy, to threaten him at every point, and to strike at the first opportunity, with an emphatic intimation that the best battle news could be brought by the wind. His opportunity had now come. If he could bring on a battle, drive back the Texas regiment, and break the lines on the mountain, Meade's infantry on Round Top would surely drive them into the valley, and then the five thousand cavalry in reserve could strike the decisive blow.

The 1st West Virginia was selected to attack the Texas regiment. The Third Battalion of the 1st Vermont was thrown out as skirmishers; the First and Second battalions were held for the charge on the mountain. The 1st West Virginia charged at our left and front down the open valley, nearly in the direction, but toward the right, of the Bushman house upon the 1st Texas regiment, which was in line behind a rail fence that had been staked and bound with withes. A thin line shot forward and attempted to throw the rails, tugging at the stakes, cutting with their sabers, and falling in the vain effort. The regiment came on in magnificent style, received a deadly volley before which it recoiled, rallied, charged the second time, and fell back with great loss.

I was near Kilpatrick when he impetuously gave the order to Farnsworth to make the last charge. Farnsworth spoke with emotion: "General, do you mean it? Shall I throw my handful of men over rough ground, through timber, against a brigade of infantry? The 1st Vermont has already been fought

half to pieces; these are too good men to kill." Kilpatrick said: "Do you refuse to obey my orders? If you are afraid to lead this charge, I will lead it." Farnsworth rose in his stirrups,—he looked magnificent in his passion,—and cried, "Take that back!" Kilpatrick returned his defiance, but, soon repenting, said, "I did not mean it; forget it." For a moment there was silence, when Farnsworth spoke calmly, "General, if you order the charge, I will lead it, but you must take the responsibility." I did not hear the low conversation that followed, but as Farnsworth turned away he said, "I will obey your order." Kilpatrick said earnestly, "I take the responsibility." . . . We rode out in columns of fours with drawn sabers. General Farnsworth, after giving the order to me, took his place at the head of the Second Battalion. In this action I commanded the First Battalion, and Major Wells commanded the Second. Captain Cushman and Lieutenant Watson rode with me; General Farnsworth and Adjutant-General Estes rode with Major Wells.

As the First Battalion rode through the line of our dismounted skirmishers, who were falling back, they cried to us to halt. As we passed out from the cover of the woods the 1st West Virginia was retiring in disorder on our left. A frantic horse with one leg torn off by a cannon-ball rushed toward us as if for protection. We rode through the enemy's skirmish line across the fields, over the low fences, past the Slyder house, and down the road. The sun was blinding; Captain Cushman shaded his eyes with his hand and cried, "An ambuscade!" We were immediately upon the enemy, within thirty paces, and the deadly volley which is referred to in the Confederate reports was fired, but it passed over our heads; although they report that half our saddles were emp-

tied, not a man was shot, yet the fire was the close and concentrated volley of a regiment. . . .

[After describing the charge of the two battalions over boulders and stone fences into the heart of the enemy's camps, and the return charge through two lines of Confederates, Captain Parsons concludes as follows:]

The whole number who rode with Farnsworth was about three hundred. Their casualties were sixty-five. They brought in over one hundred prisoners; they rode within the Confederate lines nearly two miles; they received at short range the direct or enfilading fire of three regiments of infantry and of a battery of artillery; they drew two regiments out of line and held them permanently in new positions, breaking the Confederate front and exposing it to an infantry charge if one had been immediately ordered. Their assault was so bold that the Confederates received it as the advance of a grand attack, and finding themselves exposed to infantry in front and cavalry in the rear, they were uncertain of their position. Why no advantage was taken of this it is not for us to explain. Why the infantry, when they heard fighting in Law's rear, or when, afterward, we delivered to their skirmish line our prisoners, did not advance and drive his brigade into the valley where it would have been exposed to a general flank attack, has never been explained; but it was not "a charge of madmen with a mad leader." We believed, and yet believe, that Farnsworth's charge was wisely ordered, well timed, well executed, and effective.

The behavior of the horses in this action was admirable. Running low and swift, as in a race; in their terror surrendering to their masters, and guiding at the slightest touch on the neck; never refusing a fence or breaking from the column; crowding together and to the front, yet taking or

BRIGADIER-GENERAL LEWIS A. ARMISTEAD, C. S. A.
Killed in Pickett's Charge.

CEMETERY RIDGE AFTER PICKETT'S CHARGE.
From a war-time sketch.

ELON J. FARNSWORTH,
BRIGADIER-GENERAL, U. S. V.
Killed in Farnsworth's Charge.

avoiding the obstacles with intelligence, they carried their riders over rocks and fallen timber and fences that the boldest hunter would hardly attempt to-day; and I doubt if there was a single fall of man or horse, except from the shot of the enemy. . . . There was no charging of cannon, no sabering of men. Farnsworth and his troopers understood that they were to draw the enemy's fire, to create a diversion, preparatory to the main movement. They were to ride as deep into the enemy's lines as possible, to disclose his plan and force his positions. The taking of the prisoners on the return was the accident, not the order, of the charge. There was no encouragement of on-looking armies, no cheer, no bravado; and each man felt, as he tightened his saber belt, that he was summoned to a ride to death.

Farnsworth fell in the enemy's lines with his saber raised, dead with five mortal wounds, and without fame. So fell this typical volunteer soldier of America—a man without military training or ambition, yet born with a genius for war which carried him to high command and to the threshold of a great career.

NARRATIVE NOTE.

Hancock rode along the line and made prompt dispositions to meet the coming storm. Gibbon's division, of the Second Corps, received and repelled the shock, while part of Doubleday's command, principally Stannard's Vermont brigade, struck the right flank of the main body and doubled it up in confusion so as greatly to impede its progress.

General Hancock was wounded by the side of Stannard.

Wilcox's and Perry's brigades, which should have guarded Pickett's right flank, became separated from it, and attacked the First Corps, commanded since the night of the first day by General Newton. Stannard turned about and took this second column in flank, drove it back, and again captured a large number of prisoners.

The whole plain was soon covered with fugitives, but, as no pursuit was ordered, General Lee in person succeeded in rallying them, and in re-forming the line of battle.

REPELLING LEE'S LAST BLOW AT GETTYSBURG.

BY EDMUND RICE, BREVET LIEUTENANT-COLONEL, U. S. A.

THE brigades of Harrow, Webb, and Hall, of Gibbon's division, Hancock's corps, occupied the crest on Cemetery Ridge on July 3d. The right of Hall's and the left of Webb's brigades were in a

FARNSWORTH'S CHARGE.

clump of trees, called by the enemy the salient of our position, and this grove was the focus of the most fearful cannonade that preceded Pickett's charge. One regiment, the 72d Pennsylvania, in Webb's command, was a little in rear of the left of its brigade; two regiments, the 19th Massachusetts and 42d New York, Colonel A. F. Devereux commanding, of Hall's brigade, were in rear of the right of their brigade.

From the opposite ridge, three-fourths of a mile away, a line of skirmishers sprang lightly forward out of the woods, and with intervals well kept moved rapidly down into the open fields, closely followed by a line of battle, then by another, and by yet a third. Both sides watched this never-to-be-forgotten scene,—the grandeur of attack of so many thousand men. Gibbon's division, which was to stand the brunt of the assault, looked with admiration on the different lines of Confederates, marching forward with easy, swinging step, and

the men were heard to exclaim: "Here they come!" "Here they come!" "Here comes the infantry!" Soon little puffs of smoke issued from the skirmish line, as it came dashing forward, firing in reply to our own skirmishers in the plain below, and with this faint rattle of musketry the stillness was broken; never hesitating for an instant, but driving our men before it, or knocking them over by a biting fire as they rose up to run in, their skirmish line reached the fences of the Emmitsburg road. This was Pickett's advance, which carried a front of five hundred yards or more. I was just in rear of the right of the brigade, standing upon a large boulder, in front of my regiment, the 19th Massachusetts, where, from the configuration of the ground, I had an excellent view of the advancing lines, and could see the entire formation of the attacking column. Pickett's separate brigade lines lost their formation as they swept across the Emmitsburg road, carrying with them their chain of skirmishers. They pushed on toward the crest, and merged into one crowding, rushing line, many ranks deep. As they crossed the road, Webb's infantry, on the right of the trees, commenced an irregular, hesitating fire, gradually increasing to a rapid file firing, while the shrapnel and canister from the batteries tore gaps through those splendid Virginia battalions.

The men of our brigade, with their muskets at the ready, lay in waiting. One could plainly hear the orders of the officers as they commanded, "Steady, men, steady! Don't fire!" and not a shot was fired at the advancing hostile line, now getting closer every moment. The heavy file firing on the right in Webb's brigade continued.

By an undulation of the surface of the ground to the left of the trees, the rapid advance of the dense line of Confederates was for a moment lost to view; an instant after they seemed to rise out of the earth, and so near that the expression on their faces was distinctly seen. Now our men knew that the time had come, and could wait no longer. Aiming low, they opened a deadly concentrated discharge upon the moving mass in their front. Staggered by the storm of lead, the charging line hesitated, answered with some wild firing which soon increased to a crashing roll of musketry, running down the whole length of their front, and then all that portion of Pickett's division which came within the zone of this terrible close musketry fire appeared to melt and drift away in the powder-smoke of both sides. At this juncture some one behind me gave the quick, impatient order, "Forward, men! Forward! Now is your chance!"

I turned and saw that it was General Hancock, who was passing the left of the regiment. He checked his horse and pointed toward the clump of trees to our right and front. I construed this into an order for both regiments — the 19th Massachusetts and the 42d New York — to run for the trees, to prevent the enemy from breaking through. The men on the left of our regiment heard my command, and were up and on the run forward before the 42d New York, which did not hear Hancock's order until Colonel Devereux repeated it to Colonel Mallon, had a chance to rise. The line formation of the two regiments was partially broken, and the left of the 19th was brought forward, as though it had executed a right half-wheel. All the men who were now on their feet could see, to the right and front, Webb's wounded men with a few stragglers and several limbers leaving the line, as the battle-flags of Pickett's division were carried over it. With a cheer the two regiments left their position in rear of Hall's right, and made an impetuous dash, racing diagonally forward for the clump of trees. Many of Webb's men were still lying down in their places in ranks, and firing at those who followed Pickett's advance, which, in the mean time, had passed over them. This could be determined by the puffs of smoke issuing from their muskets, as the first few men in gray sprang past them toward the cannon, only a few yards away. But for a few moments only could such a fire continue, for Pickett's disorganized mass rolled over, beat down, and smothered it.

One battle-flag after another, supported by Pickett's infantry, appeared along the edge of the trees, until the whole copse seemed literally crammed with men. As the 19th and 42d passed along the brigade line, on our left, we could see the men prone in their places, unshaken, and firing steadily to their front, beating back the enemy. I saw one leader try several times to jump his horse over our line. He was shot by some of the men near me.

The two regiments, in a disorganized state, were now almost at right angles with the remainder of the brigade — the left of the 19th Massachusetts being but a few yards distant — and the officers and men were falling fast from the enfilading fire of the hostile line in front, and from the direct fire of those who were crowded in among the trees. The advance of the two regiments became so thinned that for a moment there was a pause. Captain Farrell, of the 1st Minnesota, with his company, came in on my left. As we greeted each other he received his death-wound, and fell in front of his men, who now began firing. As I looked back I could see our men, intermixed with those who were driven out of the clump of trees a few moments before, coming rapidly forward, firing, some trying to shoot through the intervals and past those who were in front.

BATTLE BETWEEN THE UNION CAVALRY UNDER GREGG AND THE CONFEDERATE CAVALRY UNDER STUART.

The gap in the line seemed to widen, for the enemy in front, being once more driven by a terrible musketry in their very faces, left to join those who had effected an entrance through Webb's line.

The men now suffered from the enfilading fire of the enemy who were in the copse. Seeing no longer an enemy in front, and annoyed by this galling fire from the flank, the 7th Michigan and 59th New York, followed by the 20th Massachusetts and the regiments of Harrow's brigade, left their line, faced to the right, and in groups, without regimental or other organization, joined in the rush with those already at the edge of the clump of trees, all cheering and yelling, "Hurrah! for the white trefoil!" "Clubs are trumps!" "Forward the white trefoil!" [The badge of Gibbon's division — the Second, of the Second Corps — was a white trefoil.]

This was one of those periods in action which are measurable by seconds. The men near seemed to fire very slowly. Those in rear, though coming up at a run, seemed to drag their feet. Many were firing through the intervals of those in front, in their eagerness to injure the enemy. This manner

of firing, although efficacious, sometimes tells on friend instead of foe. A sergeant at my side received a ball in the back of his neck by this fire. All the time the crush toward the enemy in the copse was becoming greater. The men in gray were doing all that was possible to keep off the mixed bodies of men who were moving upon them swiftly and without hesitation, keeping up so close and continuous a fire that at last its effects became terrible. I could feel the touch of the men to my right and left, as we neared the edge of the copse. The grove was fairly jammed with Pickett's men, in all positions, lying and kneeling. Back from the edge were many standing and firing over those in front. By the side of several who were firing, lying down or kneeling, were others with their hands up, in token of surrender. In particular I noticed two men, not a musket-length away, one aiming so that I could look into his musket-barrel; the other, lying on his back, coolly ramming home a cartridge. A little farther on was one on his knees waving something white in both hands. Every foot of ground was occupied by men engaged in mortal combat, who were in every possible position which can be taken while under arms, or lying wounded or dead.

A Confederate battery, near the Peach Orchard, commenced firing, probably at the sight of Harrow's men leaving their line and closing to the right upon Pickett's column. A cannon-shot tore a horrible passage through the dense crowd of men in blue, who were gathering outside the trees; instantly another shot followed, and fairly cut a road through the mass. My thoughts were now to bring the men forward; it was but a few steps to the front, where they could at once extinguish that destructive musketry and be out of the line of the deadly artillery fire. Voices were lost in the uproar; so I turned partly toward them, raised my sword to attract their attention, and motioned to advance. They surged forward, and just then, as I was stepping backward with my face to the men, urging them on, I felt a sharp blow as a shot struck me, then another; I whirled round, my sword torn from my hand by a bullet or shell splinter. My visor saved my face, but the shock stunned me. As I went down our men rushed forward past me, capturing battle-flags and making prisoners.

Pickett's division lost nearly six-sevenths of its officers and men. Gibbon's division, with its leader wounded, and with a loss of half its strength, still held the crest.

CONFEDERATE PRISONERS ON THE BALTIMORE PIKE.

GENERAL LEE AFTER THE BATTLE.

BY JOHN D. IMBODEN, BRIGADIER-GENERAL, C. S. A.

Commanding a cavalry brigade at Gettysburg.

. . . When night closed the struggle, Lee's army was repulsed. We all knew that the day had gone against us, but the full extent of the disaster was only known in high quarters. The carnage of the day was generally understood to have been frightful, yet our army was not in retreat, and it was surmised in camp that with to-morrow's dawn would come a renewal of the struggle. All felt and appreciated the momentous consequences to the

THE RETREAT FROM GETTYSBURG.

cause of Southern independence of final defeat or victory on that great field.

It was a warm summer's night; there were few camp-fires, and the weary soldiers were lying in groups on the luxuriant grass of the beautiful meadows, discussing the events of the day, speculating on the morrow, or watching that our horses did not straggle off while browsing. About 11 o'clock a horseman came to summon me to General Lee. I promptly mounted and, accompanied by Lieutenant George W. McPhail, an aide on my staff, and guided by the courier who brought the message, rode about two miles toward Gettysburg to where half a dozen small tents were pointed out, a little way from the roadside to our left, as General Lee's headquarters for the night. On inquiry I found that he was not there, but had gone to the headquarters of General A. P. Hill, about half a mile nearer to Gettysburg. When we reached the place indicated, a single flickering candle, visible from the road through the open front of a common wall-tent, exposed to view Generals Lee and Hill seated on camp-stools with a map spread upon their knees. Dismounting, I approached on foot. After exchanging the ordinary salutations General Lee directed me to go back to his headquarters and wait for him. I did so, but he did not make his appearance until about 1 o'clock. when he came riding alone, at a slow walk, and evidently wrapped in profound thought.

When he arrived there was not even a sentinel on duty at his tent, and no one of his staff was awake. The moon was high in the clear sky, and the silent scene was unusually vivid. As he approached and saw us lying on the grass under a tree, he spoke, reined in his jaded horse, and essayed to dismount. The effort to do so betrayed so much physical exhaustion that I hurriedly rose, and stepped forward to assist him, but before I reached his side he had succeeded in alighting, and threw his arm across the saddle to rest, and, fixing his eyes upon the ground, leaned in silence and almost motionless upon his equally weary horse,— the two forming a striking and never-to-be-forgotten group. The moon shone full upon his massive features, and revealed an expression of sadness that I had never before seen upon his face. Awed by his appearance, I waited for him to speak until the silence became embarrassing, when, to break it and change the silent current of his thoughts, I ventured to remark, in a sympathetic tone, and in allusion to his great fatigue:

"General, this has been a hard day on you."

He looked up, and replied mournfully:

"Yes, it has been a sad, sad day to us," and immediately lapsed into his thoughtful mood and attitude. Being unwilling again to intrude upon

"CARRY ME BACK TO OLE VIRGINNY."

his reflections, I said no more. After perhaps a minute or two, he suddenly straightened up to his full height, and turning to me with more animation and excitement of manner than I had ever seen in him before, for he was a man of wonderful equanimity, he said in a voice tremulous with emotion:

"I never saw troops behave more magnificently than Pickett's division of Virginians did to-day in that grand charge upon the enemy. And if they had been supported as they were to have been,— but, for some reason not yet fully explained to me, were not,— we would have held the position and the day would have been ours." After a moment's pause he added in a loud voice, in a tone almost of agony, "Too bad! *Too bad!* OH! TOO BAD!"

I shall never forget his language, his manner, and his appearance of mental suffering. In a few moments all emotion was suppressed, and he spoke feelingly of several of his fallen and trusted officers; among others of Brigadier-Generals Armistead, Garnett, and Kemper, of Pickett's division. He invited me into his tent, and as soon as we were seated he remarked:

"We must now return to Virginia. As many of our poor wounded as possible must be taken home. I have sent for you because your men and horses are fresh and in good condition, to guard and conduct our train back to Virginia. The duty will be arduous, responsible, and dangerous, for I am afraid you will be harassed by the enemy's cavalry. How many men have you?"

"About 2100 effective present, and all well mounted, including McClanahan's six-gun battery of horse-artillery."

"I can spare you as much artillery as you require," he said, "but no other troops, as I shall need all I have to return safely by a different and shorter route than yours. The batteries are generally short of ammunition, but you will probably meet a supply I have ordered from Winchester to Williamsport. Nearly all the transportation and the care of all the wounded will be intrusted to you. You will recross the mountain by the Chambersburg road, and then proceed to Williamsport by any route you deem best, and without a halt till you reach the river. Rest there long enough to feed your animals; then ford the river, and do not halt again till you reach Winchester, where I will again communicate with you." . . .

NARRATIVE NOTES.

THE RETREAT.

The next day, July 4th, General Lee drew back his flanks and at evening began his retreat by two routes — the main body on the direct road to Williamsport through the mountains, the other via Chambersburg, the latter including the immense train of the wounded.

THE UNION CAVALRY IN PURSUIT.

Gregg's division (except Huey's brigade) was sent in pursuit by way of Chambersburg, but the enemy had too much the start to render the chase effective.

Kilpatrick, however, got in front of the main body on the direct route and, after a midnight battle at Monterey, fought during a terrific thunder-storm, succeeded in making sad havoc of Ewell's trains.

Buford's division of cavalry, aided by that of Kilpatrick, came near capturing Williamsport, defended by Imboden, with all of the Confederate trains, and the fresh ammunition so much needed by Lee, which had been galloping from Winchester almost without an escort, to meet him.

The opportune arrival of Stuart's cavalry, backed by infantry, forced Buford and Kilpatrick to fall back.

LEE REACHES WILLIAMSPORT.

Lee concentrated his army in the vicinity of Williamsport, but as French had destroyed his pontoon bridge, and as the Potomac had risen, he was unable to cross. He therefore fortified his position.

Meade did not follow Lee directly, but went around by way of Frederick. After considerable delay the Union army again confronted that of Lee, and were about — under orders from President Lincoln — to make an attack, when Lee slipped away on the night of July 14th to the Virginia side of the Potomac.

This ended the campaign of Gettysburg.

The Union loss was 3072 killed, 14,497 wounded, 5434 missing = Total, 23,003.

The Confederate loss was 2592 killed, 12,709 wounded, 5150 missing = Total, 20,451.

GOOD-BYE!

VICKSBURG FROM THE NORTH.
From a sketch made after the surrender.

CONFEDERATE RIVER-BATTERY ON THE RIDGE SOUTH OF VICKSBURG.
From a sketch made after the surrender.

THE SIEGE OF VICKSBURG.

NARRATIVE OF EVENTS.

Immediately after the fall of New Orleans in the spring of 1862 Farragut's fleet sailed up the Mississippi to Baton Rouge, a movement which threatened Natchez and Vicksburg, farther up the river. On May 18th the advance of the fleet, carrying a force of land troops 1400 strong, led by General Thomas Williams, anchored below Vicksburg and demanded the surrender of the town. After an extended reconnoissance the expedition retired to Baton Rouge May 25. In June and July further attempts were made by both the army and navy, but were unsuccessful. An expedition led by General John C. Breckinridge left Vicksburg in July, and attacked Baton Rouge August 5. Williams was killed, but the assault was repulsed. Breckinridge seized Port Hudson, near Baton Rouge, and fortified it. Baton Rouge was evacuated by the Union troops on the 20th.

The next attempt to reduce Vicksburg by land attack was made in November and December, 1862. Grant marched from Corinth southward late in November, and reached Oxford December 20. Meanwhile, Sherman started from Memphis with a river expedition, landed above Vicksburg, and assaulted the batteries and fortifications on Chickasaw Bluffs, on the 29th. He was repulsed, and the expedition withdrew to Milliken's Bend above the mouth of the Yazoo. About that time General John A. McClernand reached Sherman's camp as commander of the river expedition. He moved the army up the Arkansas River and captured Arkansas Post (Fort Hindman), with 5000 prisoners, January 11, 1863. (Other operations in Arkansas in 1862, subsequent to the decisive battle of Pea Ridge, March 8, were the organization of a Confederate army of 20,000 men at Little Rock; the occupation of Helena on the Mississippi by the Union army of General Curtis, and the campaign in northern Arkansas between Hindman's corps of Arkansans and the Union Army of the Frontier, under General James G. Blunt, ending in a severe battle at Prairie Grove, Ark., December 7.)

Grant's overland campaign against Vicksburg was interrupted by Confederate cavalry raids against his line of communications. Early in December General N. B. Forrest's mounted column was despatched from Bragg's army in central Tennessee into western Tennessee to cut the Mobile and Ohio Railway, and Earl Van Dorn, who had been appointed commander of a cavalry corps in Northern Mississippi, made a circuitous march from Grenada to Holly Springs, on the Mississippi Central, and destroyed Grant's main depot of supplies. The campaign was virtually abandoned after those raids, and Grant transferred his army to Young's Point, on the west bank of the Mississippi above Vicksburg, where it was united with McClernand's. Grant reached Young's Point in person early in February, and assumed chief command. Two months were passed in ineffectual efforts to reach high ground north of Vicksburg, and to cut ship-canals through which to pass the fleet and flank the stronghold.

THE UNION SIDE.

BY ULYSSES S. GRANT, GENERAL, U. S. A.
Commander of the besieging armies.

NOTE.—Pemberton's army of defense, over 50,000 strong, was intrenched on the high ground along the east bank of the Mississippi, extending from Haynes's Bluff, 11 miles north of Vicksburg, to Grand Gulf, 50 miles south. A small force was stationed at Jackson, 50 miles east of Vicksburg.

In April Grant marched with McClernand's column down the west bank of the river to a point opposite Grand Gulf. Sherman, meanwhile, threatened Haynes's Bluff. McClernand was ferried over to the east bank, at Bruinsburg, and on May 1 defeated the enemy at Port Gibson, turning Grand Gulf. Sherman then reached the front, and the united columns marched northeastward toward Jackson. McClernand again defeated the enemy at Raymond, near Jackson, May 12.

Meanwhile, General Joseph E. Johnston, who had been appointed to the command of the Confederate armies in the West, in November, 1862, was marching from Chattanooga to the relief of Pemberton. Sherman captured Jackson May 14, before Johnston reached there, and the latter moved around northward to form a junction with Pemberton, whom he ordered to abandon Vicksburg. Grant's advance intercepted Pemberton at Champion's Hill, midway between Jackson and Vicksburg. Defeated there, May 16, Pemberton retired westward across the Big Black. The next day he was again defeated at the crossings of the Big Black, and retreated to the defenses of Vicksburg. On the 19th, Grant's lines extended from Haynes's Bluff southward, inclosing the position on the east. An assault that day failed to carry the works, but advanced positions were secured where the troops were fully sheltered from the enemy's fire.

On the 22d another assault commenced at 10 o'clock, covered by a furious cannonade. The assailants reached the parapets of the enemy and planted their battle-flags upon them, but were unable to enter the works, and were withdrawn at dark.

. . . I now determined upon a regular siege,— to "out-camp the enemy," as it were, and to incur no more losses. The experience of the 22d convinced officers and men that this was best, and they went to work on the defenses and approaches with a will. With the navy holding the river the investment of Vicksburg was complete. As long as we could hold our position, the enemy was limited in supplies of food, men, and munitions of war, to what they had on hand. These could not last always.

The crossing of troops at Bruinsburg commenced April 30th. On the 18th of May the army was in rear of Vicksburg. On the 19th, just twenty days after the crossing, the city was completely invested and an assault had been made; five distinct battles — besides continuous skirmishing — had been fought and won by the Union forces; the capital of the State had fallen, and its arsenals, military manufactories, and everything useful for military purposes had been destroyed; an average of about 180 miles had been marched by the troops engaged; but 5 days' rations had been issued, and no forage; over 6000 prisoners had been captured, and as many more of the enemy had been killed or wounded; 27 heavy cannon and 61 field-pieces had fallen into our hands; 250 miles of the river, from Vicksburg to Port Hudson had become ours. The Union force that had crossed the Mississippi River up to this time was less than 43,000 men. One division of these — Blair's — only arrived in time to take part in the battle of Champion's Hill, but was not engaged there; and one brigade — Ransom's — of McPherson's corps reached the field after the battle. The enemy had at Vicksburg, Grand Gulf, Jackson, and on the roads between these places, over

GENERAL BLAIR'S DIVISION CROSSING BIG BLACK RIVER ON THE WAY TO VICKSBURG.

POSITION OF LOGAN'S DIVISION OF McPHERSON'S CORPS.

In the middle-ground is seen the main line of works, which on the right ascends the hill to the White House at the end of the curtain of trees. On the ridge to the left of the White House is the Union sap leading to the exploding mine under the Confederate fort near the Jackson road. Between the Union and Confederate lines, a little to the left of the center, are the trees that mark the conference between Grant and Pemberton, as seen in the picture on page 218.

LOGAN.   McPHERSON.   VICKSBURG.

EXPLOSION OF THE MINE UNDER THE CONFEDERATE FORT ON THE JACKSON ROAD.
From a sketch made at the time.

The foreground shows the Union sap near the White House, where stand Generals McPherson, Logan, and Leggett, with three other officers. In the distance is seen "Coonskin's" Tower, a lookout and perch for sharp-shooters, adjoining Battery Hickenlooper, near which were massed the troops that charged into the crater.

sixty thousand men. They were in their own country, where no rear-guards were necessary. The country is admirable for defense, but difficult to conduct an offensive campaign in. All their troops had to be met. We were fortunate, to say the least, in meeting them in detail: at Port Gibson, 7000 or 8000; at Raymond, 5000; at Jackson, from 8000 to 11,000; at Champion's Hill, 25,000; at the Big Black, 4000. A part of those met at Jackson were all that were left of those encountered at Raymond. They were beaten in detail by a force smaller than their own, upon their own ground. . . .

After the unsuccessful assault on the 22d, the work of the regular siege began. Sherman occupied the right, starting from the river above Vicksburg; McPherson the center (McArthur's division now with him); and McClernand the left, holding the road south to Warrenton. Lauman's division arrived at this time and was placed on the extreme left of the line.

In the interval between the assaults of the 19th and 22d, roads had been completed from the Yazoo River and Chickasaw Bayou, around the rear of the army, to enable us to bring up supplies of food and ammunition; ground had been selected and cleared, on which the troops were to be encamped, and tents and cooking utensils were brought up. The troops had been without these from the time of crossing the Mississippi up to this time. All was now ready for the pick and spade. With the two brigades brought up by McArthur, which reached us in rear of Vicksburg. and Lauman's division brought from Memphis, and which had just arrived, we had now about forty thousand men for the siege. Prentiss and Hurlbut were

ordered to send forward every man that could be spared. Cavalry especially was wanted to watch the fords along the Big Black, and to observe Johnston. I knew that Johnston was receiving reinforcements from Bragg, who was confronting Rosecrans in Tennessee. Vicksburg was so important to the enemy that I believed he would make the most strenuous efforts to raise the siege, even at the risk of losing ground elsewhere.

My line was more than fifteen miles long, extending from Haynes's Bluff to Vicksburg, thence south to Warrenton. The line of the enemy was about seven. In addition to this, having an enemy

CONFEDERATE LINES IN THE REAR OF VICKSBURG.
From a war-time photograph.

at Canton and Jackson, in our rear, who was being constantly reinforced, we required a second line of defense facing the other way. I had not troops enough under my command to man these. But General Halleck appreciated the situation, and, without being asked, forwarded reinforcements with all possible despatch.

The ground about Vicksburg is admirable for defense. On the north it is about two hundred feet above the Mississippi River at the highest point, and very much cut up by the washing rains; the ravines were grown up with cane and underbrush, while the sides and tops were covered with

a dense forest. Farther south the ground flattens out somewhat, and was in cultivation. But here, too, it was cut by ravines and small streams. The enemy's line of defense followed the crest of a ridge, from the river north of the city, eastward, then southerly around to the Jackson road, full three miles back of the city; thence in a southwesterly direction to the river. Deep ravines of the description given lay in front of these defenses.

As there is a succession of gullies, cut out by rains, along the side of the ridge, the line was necessarily very irregular. To follow each of these spurs with intrenchments, so as to command the slopes on either side, would have lengthened their line very much. Generally, therefore, or in many places, their line would run from near the head of one gully nearly straight to the head of another, and an outer work, triangular in shape, generally open in the rear, was thrown up on the point; with a few men in this outer work they commanded the approaches to the main line completely.

The work to be done to make our position as strong against the enemy as his was against us was very great. The problem was also complicated by our wanting our line as near that of the enemy as possible. We had but four engineer officers with us. Captain F. E. Prime, of the Engineer Corps, was the chief, and the work at the beginning was mainly directed by him. His health soon gave out, when he was succeeded by Captain Cyrus B. Comstock, also of the Engineer Corps. To provide assistants on such a long line, I directed that all officers who had been graduated at West Point, where they had necessarily to study mili-

THE FIGHT IN THE CRATER AFTER THE EXPLOSION OF THE UNION MINE UNDER THE CONFEDERATE FORT ON THE JACKSON ROAD, JUNE 25, 1863.

tary engineering, should, in addition to their other duties, assist in the work.

The chief quartermaster and the chief commissary were graduates. The chief commissary, now the commissary-general of the army [General Robert Macfeely], begged off, however, saying that there was nothing in engineering that he was good for, unless he would do for a sap-roller. As soldiers require rations while working in ditches as well as when marching and fighting, and we would be sure to lose him if he was used as a sap-roller, I let him off. The general is a large man—weighs two hundred and twenty pounds, and is not tall.

We had no siege-guns except six 32-pounders, and there were none in the West to draw from. Admiral Porter, however, supplied us with a battery of navy-guns of large caliber, and with these, and the field-artillery used in the campaign, the siege began. The first thing to do was to get the artillery in batteries, where they would occupy commanding positions; then establish the camps under cover from the fire of the enemy, but as near up as possible; and then construct rifle-pits and covered ways, to connect the entire command by the shortest route. The enemy did not harass us much while we were constructing our batteries. Probably their artillery ammunition was short; and their infantry was kept down by our sharp-shooters, who were always on the alert and ready to fire at a head whenever it showed itself above the rebel works.

In no place were our lines more than six hundred yards from the enemy. It was necessary, therefore, to cover our men by something more than the ordinary parapet. To give additional protection, sand-bags, bullet-proof, were placed along the tops of the parapets, far enough apart to make loop-holes for musketry. On top of these,

logs were put. By these means the men were enabled to walk about erect when off duty, without fear of annoyance from sharp-shooters. The enemy used in their defense explosive musket-balls, thinking, no doubt, that, bursting over the men in the trenches, they would do some execution; but I do not remember a single case where a man was injured by a piece of one of the shells. When they were hit, and the ball exploded, the wound was terrible. In these cases a solid ball would have hit as well. Their use is barbarous, because they produce increased suffering without any corresponding advantage to those using them. [See Colonel Lockett's statement on page 218.]

The enemy could not resort to the method we did to protect their men, because we had an inexhaustible supply of ammunition to draw upon, and used it freely. Splinters from the timber would have made havoc among the men behind.

There were no mortars with the besiegers, except what the navy had in front of the city; but wooden ones were made by taking logs of the toughest wood that could be found, boring them out for six- or twelve-pounder shells, and binding them with strong iron bands. These answered as coehorns, and shells were successfully thrown from them into the trenches of the enemy.

The labor of building the batteries and intrenching was largely done by the pioneers, assisted by negroes who came within our lines and who were paid for their work, but details from the troops had often to be made. The work was pushed forward as rapidly as possible, and when an advanced position was secured and covered from the fire of the enemy, the batteries were advanced. By the 30th of June there were 220 guns in position, mostly light field-pieces, besides a battery of heavy guns belonging to, manned, and commanded by the navy.

We were now as strong for defense against the garrison of Vicksburg as they were against us. But I knew that Johnston was in our rear, and was receiving constant reinforcements from the East. He had at this time a larger force than I had prior to the battle of Champion's Hill. . . .

On the 22d of June positive information was received that Johnston had crossed the Big Black River for the purpose of attacking our rear, to raise the siege and release Pemberton. The correspondence between Johnston and Pemberton shows that all expectation of holding Vicksburg had by this

DOUBLE CAVE IN THE RIGBY HILL.

We were now looking west, besieging Pemberton, while we were also looking east to defend ourselves against an expected siege by Johnston. But as against the garrison of Vicksburg we were as substantially protected as they were against us. When we were looking east and north we were strongly fortified, and on the defensive. Johnston evidently took in the situation, and wisely, I think, abstained from making an assault on us, because it would simply have inflicted loss on both sides without accomplishing any result.

We were strong enough to have taken the offensive against him; but I did not feel disposed to take any risk of loosing our hold upon Pemberton's army, while I would have rejoiced at the opportunity of defending ourselves against an attack by Johnston.

From the 23d of May the work of fortifying and pushing forward our position nearer to the enemy had been steadily progressing. At three points on the Jackson road in front of Ransom's brigade a sap was run up to the enemy's parapet, and by the 25th of June we had it undermined and the mine charged. The enemy had countermined, but did not succeed in reaching our mine. At this particular point the hill on which the rebel work stands rises abruptly. Our sap ran close up to the outside of the en-

"SKY PARLOR HILL," A CONFEDERATE SIGNAL-STATION DURING THE SIEGE, AND (PICTURES ABOVE AND BELOW) CAVES OF THE KIND IN WHICH RESIDENTS OF VICKSBURG SOUGHT REFUGE DURING THE BOMBARDMENT BY THE FLEET.
From photographs.

time passed from Johnston's mind. I immediately ordered Sherman to the command of all the forces from Haynes's Bluff to the Big Black River. This amounted now to quite half the troops about Vicksburg. Besides these, Herron's and A. J. Smith's divisions were ordered to hold themselves in readiness to reinforce Sherman. Haynes's Bluff had been strongly fortified on the land slide, and on all commanding points from there to the Big Black, at the railroad crossing, batteries had been constructed. The work of connecting by rifle-pits, where this was not already done, was an easy task for the troops that were to defend them.

CAVE NEAR THE MACHINE-SHOP.

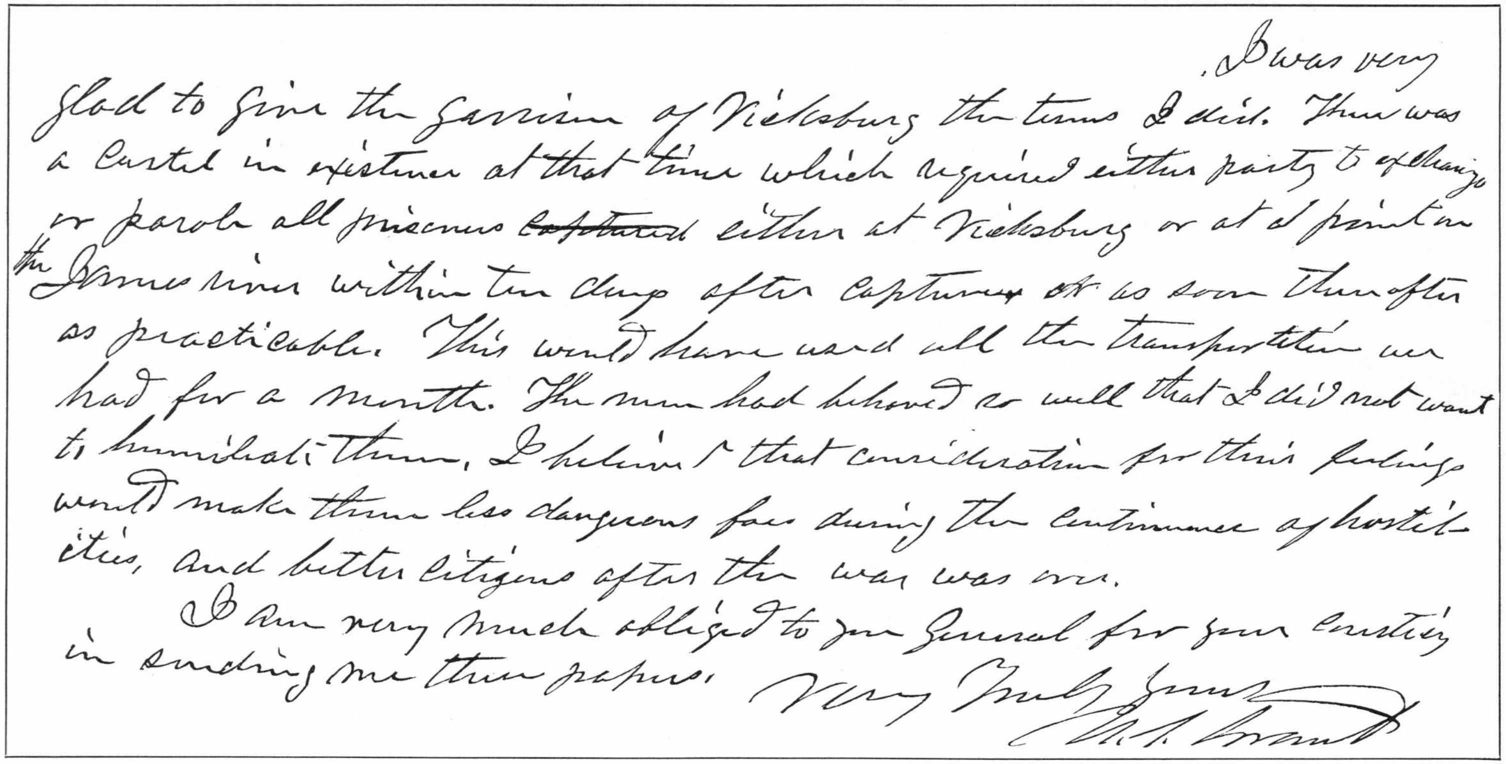

emy's parapet. In fact, this parapet was also our protection. The soldiers of the two sides occasionally conversed pleasantly across this barrier; sometimes they exchanged the hard bread of the Union soldiers for the tobacco of the Confederates; at other times the enemy threw over hand-grenades, and often our men, catching them in their hands, returned them.

Our mine had been started some distance back down the hill, consequently when it had extended as far as the parapet it was many feet below it. This caused the failure of the enemy in his search to find and destroy it. On the 25th of June, at 3 o'clock, all being ready, the mine was exploded. A heavy artillery fire all along the line had been ordered to open with the explosion. The effect was to blow the top of the hill off and make a crater where it stood. The breach was not sufficient to enable us to pass a column of attack through. In fact, the enemy, having failed to reach our mine, had thrown up a line farther back, where most of the men guarding that point were placed. There were a few men, however, left at the advance line, and others working in the counter-mine, which was still being pushed to find ours. All that were there were thrown into the air, some of them coming down on our side, still alive. I remember one colored man, who had been underground at work, when the explosion took place, who was thrown to our side. He was not much hurt, but was terribly frightened. Some one asked him how high he had gone up. "Dunno, Massa, but t'ink 'bout t'ree mile," was the reply. General Logan commanded at this point, and took this colored man to his quarters, where he did service to the end of the siege.

As soon as the explosion took place the crater was seized upon by two regiments of our troops who were near by, under cover, where they had been placed for the express purpose. The enemy made a desperate effort to expel them, but failed, and soon retired behind the new line. From here, however, they threw hand-grenades, which did some execution. The compliment was returned by our men, but not with so much effect. The enemy could lay their grenades on the parapet, which alone divided the contestants, and then roll them down upon us; while from our side they had to be thrown over the parapet, which was at considerable elevation. During the night we made efforts to secure our position in the crater against the missiles of the enemy, so as to run trenches along the outer base of their parapet, right and left; but the enemy

continued throwing their grenades, and brought boxes of field ammunition (shells), the fuses of which they would light with port-fires, and throw them by hand into our ranks. We found it impossible to continue this work. Another mine was consequently started, which was exploded on the 1st of July, destroying an entire rebel redan, killing and wounding a considerable number of its occupants, and leaving an immense chasm where it stood. No attempt to charge was made this time, the experience of the 25th admonishing us. Our loss in the first affair was about thirty killed and wounded. The enemy must have lost more in the two explosions than we did in the first. We lost none in the second.

From this time forward the work of mining and of pushing our position nearer to the enemy was prosecuted with vigor, and I determined to explode no more mines until we were ready to explode a number at different points and assault immediately after. We were up now at three different points, one in front of each corps, to where only the parapet of the enemy divided us.

At this time an intercepted despatch from Johnston to Pemberton informed me that Johnston intended to make a determined attack upon us, in order to relieve the garrison at Vicksburg. I knew the garrison would make no forcible effort to relieve itself. The picket lines were so close to each other — where there was space enough between the lines to post pickets — that the men could converse. On the 21st of June I was informed, through this means, that Pemberton was preparing to escape, by crossing to the Louisiana side under cover of night; that he had employed workmen in making boats for that purpose; that the men had been canvassed to ascertain if they would make an assault on the "Yankees" to cut their way out; that they had refused, and almost mutinied, because their commander would not surrender and relieve their sufferings, and had only been pacified by the assurance that boats enough would be finished in a week

to carry them all over. The rebel pickets also said that houses in the city had been pulled down to get material to build these boats with. Afterward this story was verified. On entering the city we found a large number of very rudely constructed boats.

All necessary steps were at once taken to render such an attempt abortive. Our pickets were doubled; Admiral Porter was notified so that the river might be more closely watched; material was collected on the west bank of the river to be set on fire and light up the river if the attempt was made; and batteries were established along the levee crossing the peninsula on the Louisiana side. Had the attempt been made, the garrison of Vicksburg would have been drowned or made prisoners on the Louisiana side. General Richard Taylor was expected on the west bank to coöperate in this movement, I believe, but he did not come, nor could he have done so with a force sufficient to be of service. The Mississippi was now in our possession from its source to its mouth, except in the immediate front of Vicksburg and Port Hudson. We had nearly exhausted the country, along a line drawn from Lake Providence to opposite Bruinsburg. The roads west were not of a character to draw supplies over for any considerable force.

By the 1st of July our approaches had reached the enemy's ditch at a number of places. At ten points we could move under cover to within from five to 100 yards of the enemy. Orders were given to make all preparations for assault on the 6th of July. The debouches were ordered widened, to afford easy egress, while the approaches were also to be widened to admit the troops to pass through four abreast. Plank and sand-bags, the latter filled with cotton packed in tightly, were ordered prepared, to enable the troops to cross the ditches.

On the night of the 1st of July Johnston was between Brownsville and the Big Black, and wrote Pemberton from there that about the 7th of the month an attempt would be made to create a diversion to enable him to cut his way out. Pemberton was a prisoner before this message reached him.

On July 1st Pemberton, seeing no hopes of outside relief, addressed the following letter to each of his four division commanders:

"Unless the siege of Vicksburg is raised, or supplies are thrown in, it will become necessary very shortly to evacuate the place. I see no prospect of the former, and there are many great, if not insuperable, obstacles in the way of the latter. You are therefore requested to inform me with as little delay as possible as to the condition of your troops, and their ability to make the

---

[Facsimile handwritten letter:]

I was very glad to give the garrison of Vicksburg the terms I did. There was a Cartel in existence at that time which required either party to exchange or parole all prisoners captured either at Vicksburg or at a point on the James river within ten days after capture or as soon thereafter as practicable. This would have used all the transportation we had for a month. The men had behaved so well that I did not want to humiliate them. I believed that consideration for their feelings would make them less dangerous foes during the continuance of hostilities, and better citizens after the war was over.

I am very much obliged to you General for your courtesy in sending me these papers.

Very Truly Yours

U. S. Grant

FACSIMILE OF PART OF A LETTER FROM GEN. GRANT TO GEN. MARCUS J. WRIGHT, C. S. A., DATED NEW YORK, NOV. 30, 1884.

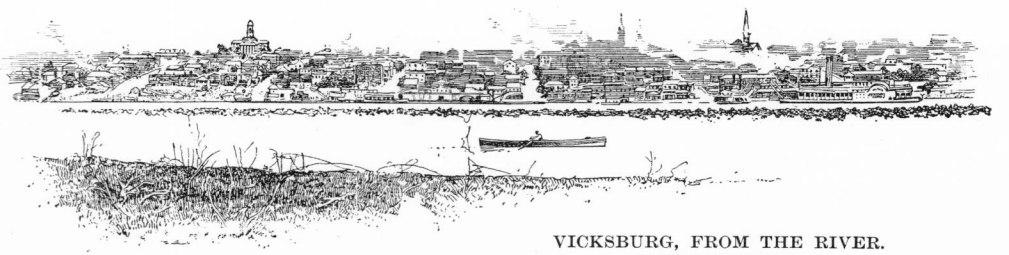

VICKSBURG, FROM THE RIVER.
From a photograph.

IN THE SAPS BETWEEN THE WHITE HOUSE
AND THE VICKSBURG CRATER, JULY 2, 1863.
From a sketch made at the time.

THE WHITE HOUSE, OR SHIRLEY, AT THE ENTRANCE TO McPHERSON'S SAPS AGAINST THE
"THIRD LOUISIANA REDAN," VICKSBURG.
From a war-time sketch.

marches and undergo the fatigues necessary to accomplish a successful evacuation."

Two of his generals suggested surrender, and the other two practically did the same; they expressed the opinion that an attempt to evacuate would fail. Pemberton had previously got a message to Johnston suggesting that he should try to negotiate with me for a release of the garrison with their arms. Johnston replied that it would be a confession of weakness for him to do so; but he authorized Pemberton to use his name in making such an arrangement.

On the 3d, about 10 o'clock A. M., white flags appeared on a portion of the rebel works. Hostilities along that part of the line ceased at once. Soon two persons were seen coming toward our lines bearing a white flag. They proved to be General Bowen, a division commander, and Colonel Montgomery, aide-de-camp to Pemberton, bearing the following letter to me:

"I have the honor to propose an armistice for —— hours, with a view to arranging terms for the capitulation of Vicksburg. To this end, if agreeable to you, I will appoint three commissioners, to meet a like number to be named by yourself, at such place and hour to-day as you may find convenient. I make this proposition to save the further effusion of blood, which must otherwise be shed to a frightful extent, feeling myself fully able to maintain my position for a yet indefinite period. This communication will be handed you, under a flag of truce, by Major-General John S. Bowen."

It was a glorious sight to officers and soldiers on the line where these white flags were visible, and the news soon spread to all parts of the command. The troops felt that their long and weary marches, hard fighting, ceaseless watching by night and day in a hot climate, exposure to all sorts of weather, to diseases, and, worst of all, to the jibes of many Northern papers that came to them, saying all their suffering was in vain, Vicksburg would never be taken, were at last at an end, and the Union sure to be saved.

Bowen was received by General A. J. Smith and asked to see me. I had been a neighbor of Bowen's in Missouri, and knew him well and favorably before the war; but his request was refused. He then suggested that I should meet Pemberton. To this I sent a verbal message saying that if Pemberton desired it I would meet him in front of McPherson's corps, at 3 o'clock that afternoon. I also sent the following written reply to Pemberton's letter:

"Your note of this date is just received, proposing an armistice for several hours, for the purpose of arranging terms of capitulation through commissioners to be appointed, etc. The useless effusion of blood you propose stopping by this course can be ended at any time you may choose, by the unconditional surrender of the city and garrison. Men who have shown so much endurance and courage as those now in Vicksburg will always challenge the respect of an adversary, and I can assure you will be treated with all the respect due to prisoners of war. I do not favor the proposition of appointing commissioners to arrange the terms of capitulation, because I have no terms other than those indicated above."

At 3 o'clock Pemberton appeared at the point suggested in my verbal message, accompanied by the same officers who had borne his letter of the morning. Generals Ord, McPherson, Logan, A. J. Smith, and several officers of my staff, accompanied me. Our place of meeting was on a hill-side within a few hundred feet of the rebel lines. Near by stood a stunted oak-tree, which was made historical by the event. It was but a short time before the last vestige of its body, root, and limb had disappeared, the fragments being taken as trophies. Since then the same tree has furnished as many cords of wood, in the shape of trophies, as "The True Cross."

Pemberton and I had served in the same division during a part of the Mexican war. I knew him very well, therefore, and greeted him as an old acquaintance. He soon asked what terms I proposed to give his army if it surrendered. My answer was the same as proposed in my reply to his letter. Pemberton then said, rather snappishly, "The conference might as well end," and turned abruptly as if to leave. I said, "Very well." General Bowen, I saw, was very anxious that the surrender should be consummated. His manners and remarks while Pemberton and I were talking showed this. He now proposed that he and one of our generals should have a conference. I had no objection to this, as nothing could be made binding upon me that they might propose. Smith and Bowen accordingly had a conference, during which Pemberton and I, moving some distance away toward the enemy's lines, were in conversation. After awhile Bowen suggested that the Confederate army should be allowed to march out with the honors of war, carrying their small-arms and field-artillery. This was promptly and unceremoniously rejected. The interview here ended, I agreeing, however, to send a letter giving final terms by 10 o'clock that night. I had sent word to Admiral Porter soon after the correspondence with Pemberton had commenced, so that hostilities might be stopped on the part of both army and navy. It was agreed on my parting with Pemberton that they should not be renewed until our correspondence should cease.

When I returned to my headquarters I sent for all the corps and division commanders with the army immediately confronting Vicksburg. (Half the army was from eight to twelve miles off, waiting for Johnston.) I informed them of the contents of Pemberton's letters, of my reply, and the

HEADQUARTERS OF THE UNION SIGNAL CORPS, VICKSBURG.
From a war-time photograph.

REAR-ADMIRAL PORTER'S FLOTILLA ARRIVING BELOW VICKSBURG ON THE NIGHT OF APRIL 16, 1863—IN THE FOREGROUND GENERAL W. T. SHERMAN GOING IN A YAWL TO THE FLAG-SHIP "BENTON."

substance of the interview, and was ready to hear any suggestion; but would hold the power of deciding entirely in my own hands. This was the nearest to a "council of war" I ever held. Against the general and almost unanimous judgment of the council, I sent the following letter:

"In conformity with agreement of this afternoon I will submit the following proposition for the surrender of the city of Vicksburg, public stores, etc. On your accepting the terms proposed I will march in one division as a guard, and take possession at 8 A. M. to-morrow. As soon as rolls can be made out and paroles be signed by officers and men, you will be allowed to march out of our lines, the officers taking with them their side-arms and clothing; and the field, staff, and cavalry officers one horse each. The rank and file will be allowed all their clothing, but no other property. If these conditions are accepted, any amount of rations you may deem necessary can be taken from the stores you now have, and also the necessary cooking-utensils for preparing them. Thirty wagons also, counting two-horse or mule teams as one, will be allowed to transport such articles as cannot be carried along. The same conditions will be allowed to all sick and wounded officers and soldiers as fast as they become able to travel. The paroles for these latter must be signed, however, whilst officers present are authorized to sign the roll of prisoners."

By the terms of the cartel then in force, prisoners captured by either army were required to be forwarded, as soon as possible, to either Aiken's Landing below Dutch Gap, on the James River, or to Vicksburg, there to be exchanged, or paroled until they could be exchanged. There was a Confederate Commissioner at Vicksburg, authorized to make the exchange. I did not propose to take him prisoner, but to leave him free to perform the functions of his office. Had I insisted upon an unconditional surrender, there would have been over thirty-odd thousand men to transport to Cairo, very much to the inconvenience of the army on the Mississippi; thence the prisoners would have had to be transported by rail to Washington or Baltimore; thence again by steamer to Aiken's—all at very great ex-

pense. At Aiken's they would have to be paroled, because the Confederates did not have Union prisoners to give in exchange. Then again Pemberton's army was largely composed of men whose homes were in the south-west; I knew many of them were tired of the war and would get home just as soon as they could. A large number of them had voluntarily come into our lines during the siege and requested to be sent north where they could get employment until the war was over and they could go to their homes.

Late at night I received the following reply to my last letter:

"I have the honor to acknowledge the receipt of your communication of this date, proposing terms of capitulation for this garrison and post. In the main, your terms are accepted; but, in justice both to the honor and spirit of my troops manifested in the defense of Vicksburg, I have to submit the following amendments, which, if acceded to by you, will perfect the agreement between us. At 10 o'clock A. M. to-morrow I propose to evacuate the works in and around Vicksburg, and to surrender the city and garrison under my command, by marching out with my colors and arms, stacking them in front of my present lines, after which you will take possession. Officers to retain their side-arms and personal property, and the rights and property of citizens to be respected."

This was received after midnight; my reply was as follows:

"I have the honor to acknowledge the receipt of your communication of 3d July. The amendment proposed by you cannot be acceded to in full. It will be necessary to furnish every officer and man with a parole signed by himself, which, with the completion of the roll of prisoners, will necessarily take some time. Again, I can make no stipulations with regard to the treatment of citizens and their private property. While I do not propose to cause them any undue annoyance or loss, I cannot consent to leave myself under any restraint by stipulations. The property which officers will be allowed to take with them will be as stated in my proposition of last evening; that is, officers will be allowed their private baggage and side-arms, and mounted officers one horse each. If you mean by your proposition

for each brigade to march to the front of the lines now occupied by it, and stack arms at 10 o'clock A. M., and then return to the inside and there remain as prisoners until properly paroled, I will make no objection to it. Should no notification be received of your acceptance of my terms by 9 o'clock A. M., I shall regard them as having been rejected, and shall act accordingly. Should these terms be accepted, white flags should be displayed along your lines to prevent such of my troops as may not have been notified from firing upon your men."

Pemberton promptly accepted these terms.

During the siege there had been a good deal of friendly sparring between the soldiers of the two armies, on picket and where the lines were close together. All rebels were known as "Johnnies"; all Union troops as "Yanks." Often "Johnny" would call, "Well, Yank, when are you coming into town?" The reply was sometimes: "We propose to celebrate the 4th of July there." Sometimes it would be: "We always treat our prisoners with kindness and do not want to hurt them"; or, "We are holding you as prisoners of war and while you are feeding yourselves." The garrison, from the commanding general down, undoubtedly expected an assault on the 4th. They knew from the temper of their men it would be successful when made, and that would be a greater humiliation than to surrender. Besides it would be attended with severe loss to them.

The Vicksburg paper, which we received regularly through the courtesy of the rebel pickets, said prior to the 4th, in speaking of the "Yankee" boast that they would take dinner in Vicksburg that day, that the best receipt for cooking rabbit was, "First ketch your rabbit." The paper at this time, and for some time previous, was printed

on the plain side of wall paper. The last was issued on the 4th, and announced that we had "caught our rabbit."

I have no doubt that Pemberton commenced his correspondence on the 3d for the twofold purpose; first, to avoid an assault, which he knew would be successful, and second, to prevent the capture taking place on the great national holiday,—the anniversary of the Declaration of American Independence. Holding out for better terms, as he did, he defeated his aim in the latter particular.

On the 4th, at the appointed hour, the garrison of Vicksburg marched out of their works, and formed line in front, stacked arms, and marched back in good order. Our whole army present witnessed this scene without cheering.

Logan's division, which had approached nearest the rebel works, was the first to march in, and the flag of one of the regiments of his division was soon floating over the court-house. Our soldiers were no sooner inside the lines than the two armies began to fraternize. Our men had had full rations from the time the siege commenced to the close. The enemy had been suffering, particularly toward the last. I myself saw our men taking bread from their haversacks and giving it to the enemy they had so recently been engaged in *starving out*. It was accepted with avidity and with thanks.

Pemberton says in his report: "If it should be asked why the 4th of July was selected as the day for surrender, the answer is obvious. I believed that upon that day I should obtain better terms. Well aware of the vanity of our foe, I knew they would attach vast importance to the entrance, on the 4th of July, into the stronghold of the great

REAR-ADMIRAL PORTER'S FLOTILLA PASSING THE VICKSBURG BATTERIES, NIGHT OF APRIL 16, 1863, THE FLAG-SHIP "BENTON" LEADING, FOLLOWED BY THE "LOUISVILLE," "LAFAYETTE," "GENERAL PRICE," "MOUND CITY," "PITTSBURG," "CARONDELET," AND "TUSCUMBIA"; AND THE TRANSPORTS "HENRY CLAY," "FOREST QUEEN," AND "SILVER WAVE." (FROM A WAR-TIME SKETCH.)

river, and that, to gratify their national vanity, they would yield then what could not be extorted from them at any other time." This does not support my view of his reasons for selecting the day he did for surrendering. But it must be recollected that his first letter asking terms was received about 10 o'clock A. M., July 3d. It then could hardly be expected that it would take 24 hours to effect a surrender. He knew that Johnston was in our rear for the purpose of raising the siege, and he naturally would want to hold out as long as he could. He knew his men would not resist an assault, and one was expected on the 4th. In our interview he told me he had rations enough to hold out some time. My recollection is two weeks. It was this statement that induced me to insert in the terms that he was to draw rations for his men from his own supplies.

On the 3d, as soon as negotiations were commenced, I notified Sherman, and directed him to be ready to take the offensive against Johnston, drive him out of the State, and destroy his army if he could. Steele and Ord were directed at the same time to be in readiness to join Sherman as soon as the surrender took place. Of this Sherman was notified.

I rode into Vicksburg with the troops, and went to the river to exchange congratulations with the navy upon our joint victory. At that time I found that many of the citizens had been living underground. The ridges upon which Vicksburg is built, and those back to the Big Black, are composed of a deep yellow clay, of great tenacity. Where roads and streets are cut through, perpendicular banks are left, and stand as well as if composed of stone. The magazines of the enemy were made by running passage-ways into this clay at places where there were deep cuts. Many citizens secured places of safety for their families by carving out rooms in these embankments. A door-way in these cases would be cut in a high bank, starting from the level of the road or street, and after running in a few feet a room of the size required was carved out of the clay, the dirt being removed by the door-way. In some instances I saw where two rooms were cut out, for a single family, with a door-way in the clay wall separating them. Some of these were carpeted and furnished with considerable elaboration. In these the occupants were fully secure from the shells of the navy, which were dropped into the city, night and day, without intermission. . . .

NARRATIVE NOTE.

FROM DONELSON AND NEW ORLEANS TO VICKSBURG — NAVAL OPERATIONS.

On the 9th of May, 1862, Commodore Foote (see page 36) was relieved from the command of the Western Flotilla by Flag-Officer Charles Henry Davis. On the 25th Charles Ellet's rams joined the fleet, and the combined forces bombarded Fort Pillow above Memphis, which the enemy abandoned June 4. Memphis fell June 6, after a battle between Davis's and Ellet's fleets on one side and Captain J. E. Montgomery's River Defense Fleet on the other. After the capture of Memphis, Davis sent an expedition up White River, and a combined land and naval attack on June 17 drove the enemy from the bluffs at St. Charles. During the fight a Confederate shell exploded the boilers of the ironclad *Mound City*.

Meanwhile, Farragut's fleet, operating on the lower Mississippi, passed the batteries at Vicksburg, June 26 to

28, and opened communication with Davis by means of Colonel Alfred W. Ellet's ram fleet, which met Farragut's vessels above Vicksburg July 1st. Farragut's fleet dropped down below Vicksburg on the night of the 15th, and Davis retired up the river to Helena. In October Davis was succeeded by David D. Porter, as acting rear-admiral. In November a fleet of gun-boats under Captain Henry Walke entered the Yazoo and cleared it of torpedoes and other obstructions to prepare for Sherman's operations at Chickasaw Bluffs. Porter led the fleet in person while the vessels engaged the batteries during Sherman's attack, and also in the attack on Arkansas Post, January 11, 1863. During the winter his gun-boats operated in the Yazoo, and the ram fleet under young Ellet performed brilliant

The "Osage"

The "Choctaw"

THE "BLACKHAWK," ADMIRAL PORTER'S
FLAG-SHIP, VICKSBURG, 1863.

services against the enemy's vessels at Vicksburg and in the Mississippi and the Red rivers below. In March two of Farragut's vessels ran the batteries at Port Hudson, and from that time on the fleets were in communication.

The naval operations directly connected with the attack upon Vicksburg were conducted by Rear-Admiral David D. Porter, of the Mississippi flotilla. On the night of April 16th he ran the Vicksburg batteries with the ironclads *Benton*, *Lafayette*, *Tuscumbia*, *Carondelet*, *Louisville*, *Mound City*, and *Pittsburg*, and the ram *General Price*. Thereafter that fleet occupied the river from Vicksburg to Grand Gulf. On the 29th of April it silenced the batteries at Grand Gulf.

After Grant invested Vicksburg on the east, Porter's upper fleet cleared the Yazoo River of obstructions and destroyed the Confederate navy-yard at Yazoo City, together with unfinished vessels, stores, etc., effectually guarding Grant's right flank.

During Grant's assault May 22, the lower fleet bombarded the hill and water batteries, and throughout the siege the mortar-boats shelled the city and the batteries on the heights. At times the gun-boats joined in the bombardment, notably on May 27, when the *Cincinnati* was sunk by fire from Fort Hill, and June 20. The navy threw 16,000 shells into the enemy's lines. Siege-guns, landed from the gun-boats and placed in position in rear of Vicksburg, were manned by naval crews under command of Lieutenants T. O. Selfridge and J. G. Walker.

INCIDENTS OF THE SIEGE OF VICKSBURG FROM THE CONFEDERATE SIDE.

BY COLONEL S. H. LOCKETT, C. S. A.
Chief engineer of the defenses.

. . . On the 25th the Federal dead and some of their wounded in the fight of the 22d were still in our

front and close to our lines. The dead had become offensive, and the living were suffering fearful agonies. General Pemberton, therefore, under a flag of truce, sent a note to General Grant proposing a cessation of hostilities for two and a half hours, so that the dead and dying men might receive proper attention. This was acceded to by General Grant, and from six o'clock until nearly dark both parties were engaged in performing funeral rites and deeds of mercy to the dead and wounded Federal soldiers. On this occasion I met General Sherman for the first time. Naturally, the officers of both armies took advantage of the truce to use their eyes to the best possible advantage. I was on the Jackson road redan, which had been terribly pounded and was the object of constant attention from a battery of heavy guns in its immediate front. The Federals were running toward it in a zigzag approach, and were already in uncomfortable proximity to it. While standing on the parapet of this work a Federal orderly came up to me and said that General Sherman wished to speak to me. Following the orderly, I reached a group of officers standing some two hundred yards in front of our line. One of these came forward, introduced himself as General Sherman, and said: "I saw that you were an officer by your insignia of rank, and have asked you to meet me, to put into your hands some letters intrusted to me by Northern friends of some of your officers and men. I thought this would be a good opportunity to deliver this mail before it got too old." To this I replied: "Yes, General, it would have been very old, indeed, if you had kept it until you brought it into Vicksburg yourself." "So you think, then," said the general, "I am a very slow mail route." "Well, rather," was the reply, "when you have to travel by regular approaches, parallels, and zigzags." "Yes," he said, "that is a slow way of getting into a place, but it is a very sure way, and I was determined to deliver those letters sooner or later."

The general then invited me to take a seat with him on an old log near by, and thus the rest of the time of the truce was spent in pleasant conversation. In the course of it the general remarked: "You have an admirable position for defense here, and you have taken excellent advantage of the ground." "Yes, General," I replied, "but it is equally as well adapted to offensive operations, and your engineers have not been slow to discover it." To this, General Sherman assented. Intentionally or not, his civility certainly prevented me from seeing many other points in our front that I as chief engineer was very anxious to examine.

The truce ended, the sharp-shooters immediately began their work and kept it up until darkness prevented accuracy of aim. Then the pickets of the two armies were posted in front of their respective lines, so near to each other that they whiled away the long hours of the night-watch with social chat. Within our lines the pick and shovel were the weapons of defense until the next morning.

On the night of the 26th, while we were trying to place an obstruction across the swamp between our right and the river, our working party and its support had a sharp engagement with a detachment of Federals who came to see what we were doing. We captured one hundred of our inquisitive friends, and retired without putting in the obstruction. At other parts of the line the work of making traverses, changing guns to more available points, making covered ways along the line and to the rear, and repairing damages, went on as vigorously as our means would allow.

The events of the 27th of May were varied by an attack on our river batteries by the fleet. The *Cincinnati* was badly crippled, and before reaching her former moorings she sank in water not deep enough to cover her deck. She was still within range of our guns, so that the efforts made by the Federals to dismantle her and remove her armament were effectually prevented.

By this time the Federal commander was evidently convinced that Vicksburg had to be taken by regular siege operations. By the 4th of June the Federals had advanced their parallels within 150 yards of our line. From them they commenced several double saps against our most salient works — the Jackson road redan, the Graveyard road redan, the Third Louisiana redan, on the left of the Jackson road, and the lunette on the right of the Baldwin's Ferry road. In each of these the engineer in charge was ordered to place thundering barrels and loaded shells with short-time fuses, as preparations for meeting assaults. The stockade redan and the stockade on its left, which had been constructed across a low place in our line, had by this time been nearly knocked to

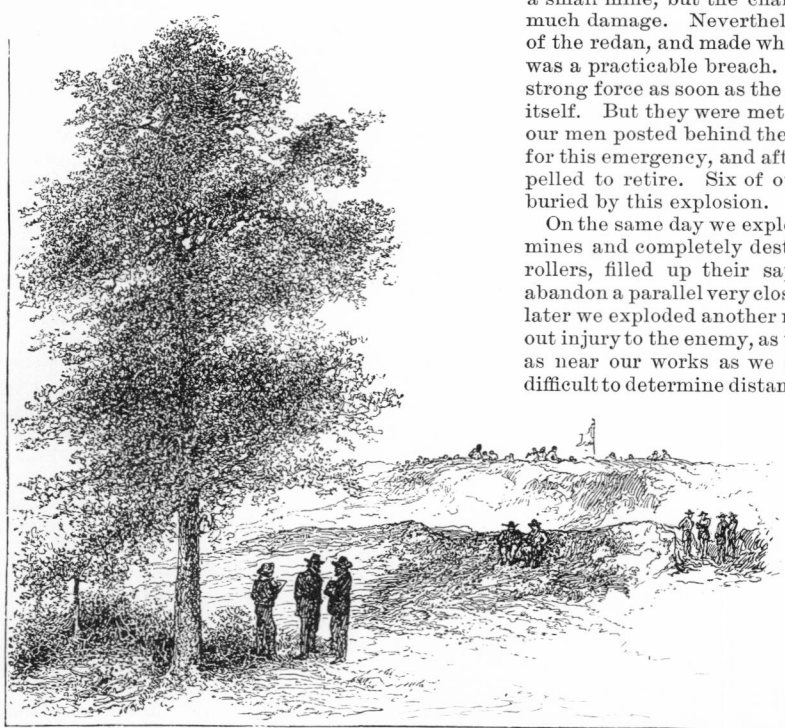

FIRST CONFERENCE BETWEEN GRANT AND PEMBERTON, JULY 3, 1863.
From a sketch made at the time.

NOTE.—Grant and Pemberton met near the tree and went aside to the earthwork, where they sat in conference. To their right is a group of four, including General John S. Bowen, C. S. A., General A. J. Smith, General James B. McPherson, and Colonel L. M. Montgomery. Under the tree are Chief-of-Staff John A. Rawlins, Assistant Secretary of War Charles A. Dana, and Theodore R. Davis, special artist, who made the above and many other sketches of the Vicksburg siege, in this work.

pieces by the enemy's artillery. A new line was therefore made to take its place when it should be no longer tenable. So, too, retrenchments, or inner lines, were ordered at all points where breaches seemed imminent or the enemy more than ordinarily near. These retrenchments served us excellently before the siege was terminated.

By the 8th of June, in spite of all efforts to prevent them, the enemy's sap-rollers had approached within sixty feet or two of our works. A private soldier suggested a novel expedient by which we succeeded in destroying the rollers. He took a piece of port-fire, stuffed it with cotton saturated with turpentine, and fired it from an old-fashioned large-bore musket into the roller, and thus set it on fire. Thus the enemy's sappers were exposed and forced to leave their sap and begin a new one some distance back. After this they kept their sap-rollers wet, forcing us to other expedients.* Our next effort was counter-mining. From the ditches of all the threatened works counter-mines were started on the night of the 13th of June. The Third Louisiana redan was located on a very narrow ridge and had no ditch. The counter-mines for it were therefore started from within by first sinking a vertical shaft, with the intention of working out by an inclined gallery under the enemy's sap. Before this work was completed the Federal sappers succeeded in getting under the salient of the redan, and on the 25th they exploded a small mine, but the charge was too small to do much damage. Nevertheless it tore off the vortex of the redan, and made what the Federals thought was a practicable breach. Into it they poured in strong force as soon as the explosion had expended itself. But they were met by a deadly volley from our men posted behind the retrenchment prepared for this emergency, and after heavy loss were compelled to retire. Six of our counter-miners were buried by this explosion.

On the same day we exploded two of our counter-mines and completely destroyed the enemy's sap-rollers, filled up their saps, and forced them to abandon a parallel very close to our line. Two days later we exploded another mine prematurely, without injury to the enemy, as they had not approached as near our works as we supposed. It was very difficult to determine distances underground, where we could hear the enemy's sappers picking, picking, picking, so very distinctly that it hardly seemed possible for them to be more than a few feet distant, when in reality they were many yards away.

* I think this may be the origin of General Grant's notion that we had explosive bullets. I certainly never heard of anything of the sort, and most surely would have made use of them if we had had them in circumventing the Federal engineers.—S. H. L. [See statement of General Grant, p. 213.]

GENERAL GRANT.   MASTER FRED. D. GRANT.   CHARLES A. DANA, ASSISTANT SECRETARY OF WAR.

UNION HEADQUARTERS, JULY 3.   GENERAL GRANT RECEIVING GENERAL PEMBERTON'S MESSAGE.
From a sketch made at the time.

NOTE—In his "Personal Memoirs" (C. L. Webster & Co.) General Grant says: "On leaving Bruinsburg for the front I left my son Frederick, who had joined me a few weeks before, on board of one of the gun-boats asleep, and hoped to get away without him until after Grand Gulf should fall into our hands; but on waking up he learned that I had gone, and being guided by the sound of the battle raging at Thompson's Hill — called the battle of Port Gibson — found his way to where I was. He had no horse to ride at the time, and I had no facilities for even preparing a meal. He therefore foraged around the best he could until he reached Grand Gulf. Mr. C. A. Dana, then an officer of the War Department, accompanied me on the Vicksburg campaign and through a portion of the siege. He was in the same situation as Fred so far as transportation and mess arrangements were concerned. The first time I call to mind seeing either of them, after the battle, they were mounted on two enormous horses, grown white from age, equipped with dilapidated saddles and bridles. Our trains arrived a few days later, after which we were all perfectly equipped. My son accompanied me throughout the campaign and siege, and caused no anxiety either to me or to his mother, who was at home. He looked out for himself and was in every battle of the campaign. His age, then not quite thirteen, enabled him to take in all he saw, and to retain a recollection of it that would not be possible in more mature years."

On the 29th of June the enemy had succeeded in getting close up to the parapet of the Third Louisiana redan. We rolled some of their unexploded 13-inch shells down upon them and annoyed them so much as to force them to stop operations. At night they protected themselves against this method of attack by erecting a screen in front of their sap.

This screen was made of heavy timbers, which even the shells could not move. I finally determined to try the effect of a barrel of powder. One containing 125 pounds was obtained, a time-fuse set to fifteen seconds was placed in the bung-hole, was touched off by myself with a live coal, and the barrel was rolled over the parapet by two of our sappers. The barrel went true to its destination and exploded with terrific force. Timbers, gabions, and facines were hurled into the air in all directions, and the sappers once more were compelled to retire. They renewed their operations, however, at night, and in a few days succeeded in establishing their mine under the redan, which they exploded at 1:30 o'clock P. M. on the 1st of July. The charge was enormous — one and a quarter tons, as I subsequently learned from the Federal engineer. The crater made was about twenty feet deep and fifty feet in diameter. The redan was virtually destroyed, and the explosive effect extended back

far enough to make a breach of nearly twenty feet width in the retrenchment across the gorge of the work. We expected an assault, but previous experience had made the enemy cautious. Instead, they opened upon the work a most terrific fire from everything that could be brought to bear upon it. Only a few minutes before the explosion I had been down in our counter-mine and had left seven men there, only one of whom was ever seen again; he, a negro, was blown over into the Federal lines, but not seriously hurt. The next thing for us to do was to stop the breach in our retrenchment. This we first tried to accomplish by heaving dirt into the breach with shovels from the two sides, but the earth was swept away by the storm of mis-

WOODEN COEHORN ON GRANT'S LINES.
From a sketch.

ARRIVAL OF GENERAL GRANT AT GENERAL PEMBERTON'S VICKSBURG HOUSE, JULY 4, 1863.
From a sketch made at the time.

LOGAN'S DIVISION ENTERING VICKSBURG BY THE JACKSON ROAD, JULY 4, 1863.
From a sketch made at the time.

siles faster than it could be placed in position. We then tried sand-bags, but they, too, were torn to shreds and scattered. Finally I sent for some tent flies and wagon covers, and with these great rolls of earth was prepared under cover and pushed into place, until at last we had something between us and the deadly hail of shot and shell and Minié balls. Playing into that narrow breach for nearly six hours were 2 9-inch Dahlgren guns, a battery of large Parrotts, one or more batteries of field-guns, a Coehorn mortar, and the deadliest fire of musketry ever witnessed by any of us there present. We stopped the breach, but lost in killed and wounded nearly one hundred men by the explosion and the subsequent fusillade. This was really the last stirring incident of the siege. On the 2d of July we exploded one of our mines somewhat prematurely, and we had ready for explosion 11 others, containing from 100 to 125 pounds of powder, and extending at a depth of 6 to 9 feet for a distance of from 18 to 20 feet in front of our works. The fuses were set and everything was primed and ready for the approach of the Federal sappers, but on the 3d of July the flag of truce stopped all operations on both sides, and the efficiency of our preparations was not put to the test.

The Federal engineers had similar preparations made for our destruction at several points. Their men had gradually closed up to our lines, so that at some portions, for a hundred yards or more, the thickness of our parapet was all that separated us. Fighting by hand-grenades was all that was possible at such close quarters. As the Federals had the hand-grenades and we had none, we obtained our supply by using such of theirs as failed to explode, or by catching them as they came over the parapet and hurling them back.

The causes that led to the capitulation are well known. We had been from the beginning short of ammunition, and continued so throughout in spite of the daring exploits of Lamar Fontaine, Captain E. J. Sanders, and Courier Walker, who floated down the river on logs and brought, respectively, 18,000, 20,000, and 200,000 caps. We were short of provisions, so that our men had been on quarter rations for days before the close of the siege; had eaten mule meat, and rats, and young shoots of cane, with a relish of epicures dining on the finest delicacies of the table. We were so short-handed that no man within the lines had ever been off duty more than a small part of each day; and in response to inquiries of the lieutenant-general commanding, every general officer and colonel had reported his men as physically exhausted and unfit for any duty but simply standing in the trenches and firing. Our lines were badly battered, many of our guns were dismounted, and the Federal forces were within less than a minute of our defenses, so that a single dash could have precipitated them upon us in overwhelming numbers. All of these facts were brought out in the council of war on the night of the 2d of July. After that General Pemberton said he had lost all hopes of being relieved by General Johnston; he had considered every possible plan of relieving ourselves, and to

LIEUTENANT-GENERAL J. C. PEMBERTON, C. S. A.
Commanding the besieged garrison of Vicksburg.

his mind there were but two alternatives — either to surrender while we still had ammunition enough left to give us the right to demand terms, or to sell our lives as dearly as possible in what he knew must be a hopeless effort to cut our way through the Federal lines. He then asked each officer present to give his vote on the question, *surrender or not?* Beginning with the junior officer present, all voted to surrender but two, — Brigadier-General S. D. Lee and Brigadier-General Baldwin, — and these had no reasons to offer. After all had voted, General Pemberton said: "Well, gentlemen, I have heard your votes, and I agree with your almost unanimous decision, though my own preference would be to put myself at the head of my troops and make a desperate effort to cut our way through the enemy. That is my only hope of saving myself from shame and disgrace. Far better would it be for me to die at the head of my army, even in a vain effort to force the enemy's lines, than to surrender it and live and meet the obloquy which I know will be heaped upon me. But my duty is to sacrifice myself to save the army which has so nobly done its duty to defend Vicksburg. I therefore concur with you, and shall offer to surrender this army on the 4th of July." Some objection was made to the day, but General Pemberton said: "I am a Northern man; I know my people; I know their peculiar weaknesses and their national vanity; I know we can get better terms from them on the 4th of July than any other day of the year. We must sacrifice our pride to these considerations." And thus the surrender was brought about.

During the negotiations we noticed that General Grant and Admiral Porter were communicating with each other by signals from a tall tower on land and a mast-head on Porter's ship. Our signal-service men had long before worked out the Federal code on the principle of Poe's "Gold Bug," and translated the messages as soon as sent. We knew that General Grant was anxious to take us all as prisoners to the Northern prison-pens. We also knew that Porter said he did not have sufficient transportation to carry us, and that in his judgment it would be far better to parole us and use the fleet in sending the Federal troops to Port Hudson and other points where they were needed. This helped to make General Pemberton more bold and persistent in his demands, and finally enabled him to obtain virtually the terms of his original proposition.

A few minutes after the Federal soldiers marched in, the soldiers of the two armies were fraternizing and swapping yarns over the incidents of the long siege. One Federal soldier seeing me on my little white pony, which I had ridden every day to and from and along the lines, sang out as he passed: "See here, Mister, — you man on the little white horse! Danged if you ain't the hardest feller to hit I ever saw; I've shot at you more 'n a hundred times!"

General Grant says there was no cheering by the Federal troops. My recollection is that on our right a hearty cheer was given by one Federal division "for the gallant defenders of Vicksburg!"

BREVET MAJOR-GENERAL J. M. BRANNAN,
U. S. A.
From a photograph taken in May, 1865.

CONFEDERATE LINE OF BATTLE IN THE CHICKAMAUGA WOODS.

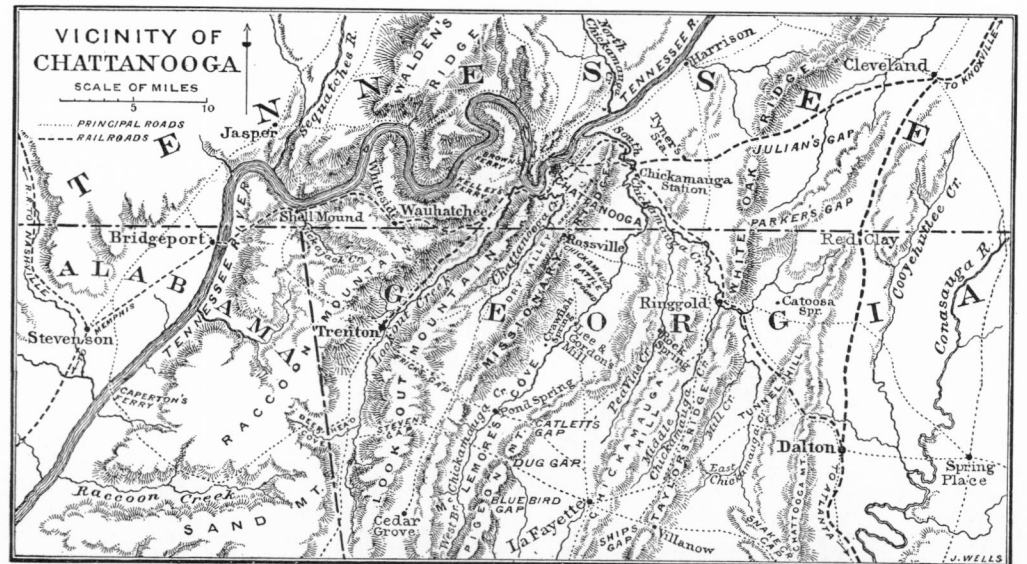

MAJOR-GENERAL JAMES A. GARFIELD,
U. S. V.
From a war-time photograph.

THE BATTLE OF CHICKAMAUGA.

NARRATIVE NOTE.

After the battle of Murfreesboro' (Stone's River), December 31, 1862-January 2, 1863, Rosecrans's army remained at Murfreesboro', facing Bragg's fortified camps at Shelbyville and Tullahoma. In June Rosecrans marched around Bragg's right flank, and compelled him to retreat to Chattanooga. After the surrender of Vicksburg and the battle of Gettysburg (July, 1863), Bragg was reinforced from Mississippi, and Longstreet was ordered to join him from Virginia.

Early in September Rosecrans crossed the Tennessee on the right (west) of Chattanooga, and advanced southward into Georgia. Bragg also marched southward, abandoning Chattanooga, which Rosecrans occupied,

THE CONFEDERATE SIDE.

THE GREAT ATTACK AT CHICKAMAUGA.

BY DANIEL H. HILL, LIEUTENANT-GENERAL, C.S.A.
Commander of a corps at the battle of Chickamauga.

ON the 13th of July, 1863, while in charge of the defenses of Richmond and Petersburg and the department of North Carolina, I received an unexpected order to go West. I was seated in a yard of a house in the suburbs of Richmond (the house belonging to Mr. Poe, a relative of the poet), when President Davis, dressed in a plain suit of gray and attended by a small escort in brilliant uniform, galloped up and said: "Rosecrans* is about to advance upon Bragg; I have

*At the beginning of the Civil War I was asked the question, "Who of the Federal officers are most to be feared?" I replied: "Sherman, Rosecrans, and McClellan. Sherman has genius and daring, and is full of resources. Rosecrans has fine practical sense, and is of a tough, tenacious fiber. McClellan is a man of talents, and his delight has always been in the study of military history and the art and science of war." Grant was not once thought of. The light of subsequent events thrown upon the careers of these three great soldiers has not changed my estimate of them; but I acquiesce in the verdict which has given greater renown to some of their comrades. . . .

I fought against McClellan from Yorktown to Sharpsburg (Antietam), I encountered Rosecrans at Chickamauga, and I surrendered to Sherman at Greensboro', N. C.—each of the three commanding an army.—D. H. H.

placing his army in position to cover its southern approaches. Bragg countermarched his army, and attacked Rosecrans on the 19th. The brunt of the fighting fell upon the Union left wing under Thomas, which Bragg attempted to crush in order to gain the Rossville road, the gateway to Chattanooga. The attack failed, but was resumed on the 20th. Polk commanded the Confederate right against Thomas, and Longstreet, who had reached the field during the night, commanded the left. Rosecrans strengthened Thomas by withdrawing troops from McCook's corps on the right.

General Hill's narrative is mainly a description of the decisive attack upon Rosecrans's right center and right.

found it necessary to detail Hardee to defend Mississippi and Alabama. His corps is without a commander. I wish you to command it." "I cannot

do that," I replied, "as General Stewart ranks me." "I can cure that," answered Mr. Davis, "by making you a lieutenant-general. Your papers will be ready to-morrow. When can you start?" "In twenty-four hours," was the reply. . . .

[An ineffectual attack by Polk upon Thomas opened the battle of the second day. General Hill proceeds:]

At 11 A. M. Stewart's division advanced under an immediate order from Bragg. His three brigades under Brown, Clayton, and Bate advanced with Wood of Cleburne's division, and, as General Stewart says, "pressed on past the corn-field in front of the burnt house, two or three hundred yards beyond the Chattanooga road, driving the enemy within his line of intrenchments. . . . Here they met a fresh artillery fire on front and flank, heavily supported by infantry, and had to retire."

This was the celebrated attack upon Reynolds and Brannan which led directly to the Federal disaster. In the mean time our right was preparing to renew the attack. I proposed to the wing commander, Polk, to make a second advance, provided fresh troops were sent forward, requesting that the gap in Breckinridge's left, made by the withdrawal of Helm, should be filled by another brigade. General J. K. Jackson's was sent for that purpose, but unfortunately took its position too far in rear to engage the attention of the enemy in front, and every advance on our right during the remainder of the day was met with flank and cross fire from that quarter. Gist's brigade and Liddell's division of Walker's corps reported to me. Gist immediately attacked with great vigor the log-works which had repulsed Helm so disastrously, and he in turn was driven back. Liddell might have made as great an impression by moving on the Chattanooga road as Breckinridge had done, but his strong brigade (Walthall's) was detached, and he advanced with Govan's alone, seized the road for the second time that day, and was moving behind the breastworks, when, a column of the enemy appearing on his flank and rear, he was compelled to retreat.

This was simultaneous with the advance of Stewart. The heavy pressure on Thomas caused Rosecrans to support him by sending the divisions of Negley and Van Cleve and Brannan's reserve brigade. In the course of these changes, an order to Wood, which Rosecrans claims was misinterpreted, led to a gap being left into which Longstreet stepped with the eight brigades (Bushrod Johnson's original brigade and McNair's, Gregg's, Kershaw's, Law's, Humphrey's, Benning's, and Robertson's) which he had arranged in three lines to constitute his grand column of attack. Davis's two brigades, one of Van Cleve's, and Sheridan's entire division were caught in front and flank and driven from the field. Disregarding the order of the day, Longstreet now gave the order to wheel to the right instead of the left, and thus take in reverse the strong position of the enemy. Five of McCook's brigades were speedily driven off the field. He es-

MAP OF THE CHICKAMAUGA CAMPAIGN.

LEE AND GORDON'S MILLS ON THE CHICKAMAUGA.

THE SNODGRASS FARM-HOUSE.

General Thomas's headquarters on the second day were in the field this side of the house. The hills called the "Horse-shoe," made famous by the defense of Brannan and Steedman, lie on the opposite side of the house.

timates their loss at forty per cent. Certainly that flank march was a bloody one. I have never seen the Federal dead lie so thickly on the ground, save in front of the sunken wall at Fredericksburg.

But that indomitable Virginia soldier, George H. Thomas, was there, and was destined to save the Union army from total rout and ruin, by confronting with invincible pluck the forces of his friend and captain in the Mexican war. Thomas had ridden to his right to hurry up reinforcements, when he discovered a line advancing, which he thought at first was the expected succor from Sheridan, but he soon heard that it was a rebel column marching upon him. He chose a strong position on a spur of Missionary Ridge, running east and west, placed upon it Brannan's division with portions of two brigades of Negley's; Wood's division (Crittenden's) was placed on Brannan's left. These troops, with such as could be rallied from the two broken corps, were all he had to confront the forces of Longstreet, until Steedman's division of Granger's corps came to his relief about 3 P. M. Well and nobly did Thomas and his gallant troops hold their own against foes flushed with past victory and confident of future success. His new line was nearly at right angles with the line of log-works on the west side of the Rossville road, his right being an almost impregnable wall-like hill, his left nearly an inclosed fortification. Our only hope of success was to get in his rear by moving far to our right, which overlapped the Federal left.

Bushrod Johnson's three brigades in Longstreet's center were the first to fill the gap left by Wood's withdrawal from the Federal right; but the other five brigades under Hindman and Kershaw moved promptly into line as soon as space could be found for them, wheeled to the right, and engaged in the murderous flank attack. On they rushed, shouting, yelling, running over batteries, capturing trains,

taking prisoners, seizing the headquarters of the Federal commander, at the Widow Glenn's, until they found themselves facing the new Federal line on Snodgrass Hill. Hindman had advanced a little later than the center, and had met great and immediate success. The brigades of Deas and Manigault charged the breastworks at double-quick, rushed over them, drove Laiboldt's Federal brigade of Sheridan's division off the field down the Rossville road; then General Patton Anderson's brigade of Hindman, having come into line, attacked and beat back the forces of Davis, Sheridan, and Wilder, in their front, killed the hero and poet General Lytle, took 1100 prisoners, 27 pieces of artillery, commissary and ordnance trains, etc. Finding no more resistance on his front and left, Hindman wheeled to the right to assist the forces of the center. The divisions of Stewart, Hood, Bushrod Johnson, and Hindman came together in front of the new stronghold of the Federals.

It was now 2:30 P. M. Longstreet, with his staff, was lunching on sweet-potatoes. A message came just then that the commanding general wished to see him. He found Bragg in rear of his lines, told him of the steady and satisfactory progress of the battle, that sixty pieces of artillery had been reported captured (though probably the number was overestimated), that many prisoners and stores had been taken, and that all was going well. He then asked for additional troops to hold the ground gained, while he pursued the two broken corps down the Dry Valley road and cut off the retreat of Thomas. Bragg replied that there was no more fight in the troops of Polk's wing, that he could give Longstreet no reinforcements, and that his headquarters would be at Reed's Bridge. He seems not to have known that Cheatham's division and part of Liddell's had not been in action that day.

Some of the severest fighting had yet to be done

after 3 P. M. It probably never happened before for a great battle to be fought to its bloody conclusion with the commanders of each side away from the field of conflict. But the Federals were in the hands of the indomitable Thomas, and the Confederates were under their two heroic wing commanders, Longstreet and Polk. In the lull of the strife I went with a staff-officer to examine the ground on our left. One of Helm's wounded men had been overlooked, and was lying alone in the woods, his head partly supported by a tree. He was shockingly injured.[*]

Hindman and Bushrod Johnson organized a column of attack upon the front and rear of the stronghold of Thomas. It consisted of the brigades of Deas, Manigault, Gregg, Patton, Anderson, and McNair. Three of the brigades, Johnson says, had each but five hundred men, and the other two were not strong. Deas was on the north side of the gorge through which the Crawfish road crosses, Manigault across the gorge and south, on the crest parallel to the Snodgrass Hill, where Thomas was. The other three brigades extended along the crest with their faces north, while the first two faced east. Kershaw, with his own and Humphreys's brigade, was on the right of Anderson, and was to coöperate in the movement. It began at 3:30 P. M. A terrific contest ensued. The bayonet was used,

* He belonged to Von Zinken's regiment, of New Orleans, composed of French, Germans, and Irish. I said to him: "My poor fellow, you are badly hurt. What regiment do you belong to?" He replied: "The Fifth Confederit, and a dommed good regiment it is." The answer, though almost ludicrous, touched me as illustrating the *esprit de corps* of the soldier — his pride in and his affection for his command. Colonel Von Zinken told me afterward that one of his desperately wounded Irishmen cried out to his comrades, "Charge them, boys; they have cha-ase (cheese) in their haversacks." Poor Pat, he has fought courageously in every land in quarrels not his own.—D. H. H.

and men were killed and wounded with clubbed muskets. A little after 4, the enemy was reinforced, and advanced, but was repulsed by Anderson and Kershaw.

General Bushrod Johnson claims that his men were surely, if slowly, gaining ground at all points, which must have made untenable the stronghold of Thomas. Relief was, however, to come to our men, so hotly engaged on the left, by the advance of the right. At 3 P. M. Forrest reported to me that a strong column was approaching from Rossville, which he was delaying all he could. From prisoners we soon learned that it was Granger's corps. We were apprehensive that a flank attack, by fresh troops, upon our exhausted and shattered ranks might prove fatal. Major-General Walker strongly advised falling back to the position of Cleburne, but to this I would not consent, believing that it would invite attack, as we were in full view. Cheatham's fine division was sent to my assistance by the wing commander. . . .

Longstreet was determined to send Preston with his division of three brigades under Gracie, Trigg, and Kelly, aided by Robertson's brigade of Hood's division, to carry the heights — the main point of defense. His troops were of the best material and had been in reserve all day; but brave, fresh, and strong as they were, it was with them alternate advance and retreat, until success was assured by a renewal of the fight on the right. At 3:30 P. M. General Polk sent an order to me to assume command of the attacking forces on the right and renew the assault. Owing to a delay in the adjustment of our lines, the advance did not begin until 4 o'clock. The men sprang to their arms with the utmost alacrity, though they had not heard of Longstreet's success, and they showed by their cheerfulness that there was plenty of "fight in them." Cleburne ran forward his batteries, some by hand,

MAJOR-GENERAL GEORGE H. THOMAS, U. S. A.
Commanding the Fourteenth Army Corps at Chickamauga.

val to retreat to Rossville, but, stout soldier as he was, he resolved to hold his ground until nightfall. An hour more of daylight would have insured his capture. Thomas had under him all the Federal army, except the six brigades which had been driven off by the left wing.

Whatever blunders each of us in authority committed before the battles of the 19th and 20th, and during their progress, the great blunder of all was that of not pursuing the enemy on the 21st. The day was spent in burying the dead and gathering up captured stores. Forrest, with his usual promptness, was early in the saddle, and saw that the retreat was a rout. Disorganized masses of men were hurrying to the rear; batteries of artillery were inextricably mixed with trains of wagons; disorder and confusion pervaded the broken ranks struggling to get on. Forrest sent back word to Bragg that "every hour was worth a thousand men." But the commander-in-chief did not know of the victory until the morning of the 21st, and then he did not order a pursuit. Rosecrans spent the day and the night of the 21st in hurrying his trains out of town. A breathing-space was allowed him; the panic among his troops subsided, and Chattanooga — the objective point of the campaign — was held. There was no more splendid fighting in '61, when the flower of the Southern youth was in the field, than was displayed in those bloody days of September, '63. But it seems to me that the *élan* of the Southern soldier was never seen after Chickamauga — that brilliant dash which had distinguished him was gone forever. He was too intelligent not to know that the cutting in two of Georgia meant death to all his hopes. He knew that Longstreet's absence was imperiling Lee's safety, and that what had to be done must be done quickly. The delay in striking was exasperating to him; the failure to strike after the success was crushing to all his longings for an independent South. He fought stoutly to the last, but, after Chickamauga, with the sullenness of despair and without the enthusiasm of hope. That "barren victory" sealed the fate of the Southern Confederacy.

THE UNION SIDE.

RECEIVING THE ATTACK.

BY EMERSON OPDYCKE, BREVET MAJOR-GENERAL, U. S. V.
Colonel of the 125th Ohio at the battle of Chickamauga.

. . . Rosecrans slowly concentrated his corps on the north bank of the Chickamauga River, at Lee and Gordon's Mills, twelve miles south of Chattanooga. Bragg decided to move down the valley up which he had retired because, first, of all the routes open to him that one was least obstructed; and, secondly, because it would continue his army near the railway of his supplies, which was also bringing him Longstreet.

Rosecrans did not get his corps united and well in position, before the enemy, on the 19th, began the battle of Chickamauga.

The country in which the next two days' operations took place lies between the river and Missionary Ridge, and was covered by woods of varying density, broken here and there by cleared fields. The Chickamauga River, winding slowly through the forest of the region, flows into the Tennessee eight miles above Chattanooga. Bragg's aim was to turn our left and gain the road into Chattanooga, now indispensable to the existence of our army. Thomas commanded our left; and as Bragg sent division after division against that wing, Rosecrans sent successive divisions to Thomas. The fighting was close and stubborn; batteries were taken and retaken till the day closed, without material advantage to either side. It was clear, however, that we were outnumbered; for, while we had put nearly every regiment into the action, the enemy, meeting us with equal numbers in line of battle, still had heavy reserves.

In the night both commanders prepared for the decisive conflict which all felt must come on the 20th. Still covering the Chattanooga road, Rosecrans placed his army in a somewhat better position, both flanks well refused. From left to right his divisions were: Baird's, R. W. Johnson's, Palmer's, Reynolds's, Brannan's, Negley's, Davis's, Sheridan's; Wood's and Van Cleve's were in reserve; and three brigades of Granger's corps were near Rossville, four miles away. Thomas commanded six divisions at the left, McCook two at the right, and Crittenden the two in reserve. Thomas covered his front with a slight barricade of rails and old logs found in the woods, and so greatly aided his men.

Early in the morning Thomas discovered, and reported to Rosecrans, that another division was needed to maintain our extreme left against the enemy's longer line. Rosecrans, therefore, brought Wood from reserve to relieve Negley, and ordered Negley at once to report his division to Thomas; and Thomas was informed that Negley would immediately join him at the left. But Negley, disappearing from the line, drifted away from the field to Rossville. Two of his brigades reached the left, but so far apart, and so ill-timed, as to be of little value. It is important to remember Negley's conduct, because from it came the misapprehensions that were soon to result in disaster to our right wing.

The Confederate plan was to turn and envelop our left, and then to advance upon our divisions in succession, and involve the whole in one common ruin. Their right wing was commanded by Polk, and their left by Longstreet.

Polk was ordered to begin the battle at day-

---

to within three hundred yards of the enemy's breastworks, pushed forward his infantry, and carried them. General J. K. Jackson, of Cheatham's division, had a bloody struggle with the fortifications in his front, but had entered them when Cheatham with two more of his brigades, Maney's and Wright's, came up. Breckinridge and Walker met with but little opposition until the Chattanooga road was passed, when their right was unable to overcome the forces covering the enemy's retreat. As we passed into the woods west of the road, it was reported to me that a line was advancing at right angles to ours. I rode to the left to

ascertain whether they were foes or friends, and soon recognized General Buckner. The cheers that went up when the two wings met were such as I had never heard before, and shall never hear again.

Preston gained the heights a half hour later, capturing 1000 prisoners and 4500 stand of arms. But neither right nor left is entitled to the laurels of a complete triumph. It was the combined attack which, by weakening the enthusiasm of the brave warriors who had stood on the defense so long and so obstinately, won the day.

Thomas had received orders after Granger's arri-

break, but the first shots were not heard before 8:30; and, in an hour, the action at the left became furious. Polk's right division began to envelop our left and to appear upon our rear; but Thomas hurried some reserves against it and drove it away in disorder. Having been able, in the absence of Negley's division, to find the way to our left and rear, the enemy would naturally reappear there with decisive numbers. Thomas, therefore, knowing nothing of Negley's conduct, and wishing to add only a division to his left, sent again and again for the promised reinforcements. The attack soon extended heavily to Johnson, Palmer, and Reynolds; and, by 10:30, lightly to Brannan. Naturally supposing that Negley had already reached Thomas, Rosecrans inferred, from the requests of Thomas and from other indications, that Bragg was moving his left wing to the extreme right of the Confederate line of battle. The conflict had been raging against Thomas for two hours, while Wood, Davis, and Sheridan were untouched; and, not suspecting that Longstreet (a reconnoissance of ten minutes would have developed it) was already formed for attack and about to advance in

full force against our right wing, Rosecrans, in the short space of fifteen minutes,—10:30 to 10:45,— ordered to his left Van Cleve, from the reserve, and Sheridan from the extreme right; and, by the blunder of an aide in wording an order, sent Wood out of line to "close up on Reynolds and support him as soon as possible," while McCook was to move Davis by the left flank into the position vacated by Wood. These disconnected and fatal movements of Van Cleve, Wood, Sheridan, and Davis were in progress when Longstreet attacked them with six divisions of the Confederate left wing. Disaster was the immediate and inevitable result.

Sheridan's routed division moved back to Rossville. Heroism could not save Davis; his division was overwhelmed, and scattered in fragments that were afterward collected behind Missionary Ridge. Wood's movement uncovered Brannan's right, and, in temporary confusion, that division hurried away to a new position. This exposed Reynolds's right, made it necessary for him to change front to the rear at right angles on his left; but *there* he held firmly to Palmer's right. The rush of disordered troops and artillery, disintegrating Van Cleve's division, destroyed its further usefulness in this battle. Rosecrans, seeing this appalling demolition of his right wing, and finding that the enemy had interposed between him and Thomas, hastened around to Rossville. Finding there men of Negley's division, which he had supposed to be with Thomas, Rosecrans thought the day lost, and deemed it his duty to hasten to Chattanooga, there to prepare for the reception and disposition of what *seemed to him* his disordered and defeated army. Rosecrans and Garfield, his chief-of-staff, separated at Rossville, Rosecrans riding to Chattanooga and Garfield to Thomas at the front. Rosecrans says that he sent Garfield to the front; while Garfield has many times said that he himself insisted upon going, that the sound of the battle proved that Thomas was still

HOUSE OF MR. J. M. LEE, CRAWFISH SPRINGS, ROSECRANS'S HEADQUARTERS BEFORE THE BATTLE, AND SITE OF THE UNION FIELD-HOSPITAL FOR THE RIGHT WING.
From a photograph taken in 1884.

holding the enemy in check. McCook and Crittenden soon joined Rosecrans at Chattanooga; but Thomas remained on the field. Brannan brought his division to a good position, but so far to the right of Reynolds that the space of a division lay open between them. While Wood was moving toward this gap, Longstreet, advancing to complete the work, came within musket-range.

The moment was critical, because if Wood should be unable to occupy and hold the gap, Longstreet would pass through, permanently cut off Brannan, again turn, and then overwhelm Reynolds, and attack the rear of Palmer, Johnson, and Baird, who were still confronted by Polk. Wood coolly changed front under fire, so as to face south instead of east, and caused one of his brigades to charge with fixed bayonets. The audacity of the charge probably made the enemy believe that there was force enough near to sustain it, for they soon bolted, and then fled out of range just before our bayonets reached their ranks. The needed moments were snatched from the enemy, and Wood brought his division into the gap between Reynolds and Brannan.

Except some fragments from the broken divisions, our line was now composed of Baird's, Johnson's, Palmer's, Reynolds's, Wood's, and Brannan's divisions, naming them from left to right. In front stood the whole army of the enemy, eager to fall upon us with the energy that comes from great success and greater hopes. But close behind our line rode a general whose judgment never erred, whose calm, invincible will never bent; and around him thirty thousand soldiers resolved to exhaust the last round of ammunition, and then to hold their ground with their bayonets. Soldiers thus inspired and commanded, are more easily killed than defeated.

For five long hours the shocks and carnage were

as close and deadly as men could make them. Thomas often came within speaking distance of his men, and wherever the energy of the attack most endangered our line, he strengthened it with cannon and regiments drawn from points in less peril; and when the soldiers asked for more ammunition Thomas said: "Use your bayonets." At about 3:30 in the afternoon I saw General Thomas looking in the direction of Chattanooga, watching with anxious interest a column of dust rising in the air. Our suspense was relieved when Granger and Steedman emerged from the dust, and Garfield dashed up to Thomas.

To prevent a turning movement on the road from Ringgold, through Rossville to Chattanooga, Granger, with three brigades, had been stationed on the Ringgold road; and, by a sound, soldierly judgment, leaving one brigade to do the work assigned to three, brought two brigades to the field. Thomas himself was then only a little way down the rear slope of the low ridge on which Wood's division was fighting, with every man in the line, and with no reserves. We were hard pressed, and many muskets became so hot that loading was difficult; but Thomas sent up two cannon with the words: "The position must be held." The reply was: "Tell General Thomas that we will hold the position or go to heaven from it."

At about 4 o'clock Longstreet drew back and asked for reinforcements, but was answered that the right wing was already so shattered that it could not aid him. He then brought forward his reserves and re-formed his lines; and extending beyond our right, advanced in a final attack.

Thomas ordered Granger's reinforcements to the right of Brannan, where the enemy had already begun to appear. The conflict there, and on the divisions of Brannan and Wood, was soon at its

GENERAL JOHN B. HOOD, C. S. A.
Commanding a corps at Chickamauga.

CRAWFISH SPRINGS.

fiercest. Our short-range ammunition from the cannon cut great gaps through the enemy's columns, and the steady volleys of musketry, aided by our bayonets, did their remorseless work for about thirty minutes; and then the Confederate left wing, shattered, bleeding, defeated, withdrew from sight. The battle was ended — Thomas had saved the army. . . .

REINFORCING GENERAL THOMAS.

BY J. S. FULLERTON, BREVET BRIGADIER-GEN-
ERAL, U. S. V.
At Chickamauga chief-of-staff to General Gordon Granger.

ON the 19th day of September, 1863, the Reserve Corps of the Army of the Cumberland, General Gordon Granger in command, was distributed over a long stretch of country, its rear at Murfreesboro' and its van on the battlefield of Chickamauga. These troops had been posted to cover the rear and left flank of the army. During September 19th, the first day of the battle, they were engaged in some skirmishing and stood at arms expecting an attack. On the evening of the 19th every indication pointed to a renewal of the battle early the next day. The night was cold for that time of the year. Tell-tale fires were prohibited. The men slept on their arms. All was quiet save in the field-hospitals in the rear. A bright moon lighted up the fields and woods.

Bragg is piling his whole army on Thomas? I am going to his assistance."

We quickly climbed down the rick, and, going to Steedman, Granger ordered him to move his command "over there," pointing toward the place from which came the sounds of battle. Colonel Daniel McCook was directed to hold fast at McAfee Church, where his brigade covered the Ringgold road. Before half-past 11 o'clock Steedman's command was in motion. Granger, with his staff and escort, rode in advance. Steedman, after accompanying them a short distance, rode back to the head of his column.

Thomas was nearly four miles away. The day had now grown very warm, yet the troops marched rapidly over the narrow road, which was covered ankle-deep with dust that rose in suffocating clouds. Completely enveloped in it, the moving column swept along like a desert sandstorm. Two miles from the point of starting, and three-quarters of a mile to the left of the road, the enemy's skirmishers and a section of artillery opened fire on us from an open wood. This force had worked round Thomas's left, and was then partly in his rear. Granger halted to feel them. Soon becoming convinced that it was only a large party of observation, he again started his column and pushed rapidly forward. I was then sent to bring up Colonel McCook's brigade, and put it in position to watch the movements of the enemy, to keep open the Lafayette road, and to cover the open fields between that point and the position held by Thomas. This brigade remained there the rest of the day. Our skirmishers had not gone far when they came upon Thomas's field-hospital, at Cloud's house, then swarming with the enemy. They came from the same body of Forrest's cavalry that had fired on us from the wood. They were quickly driven out, and our men were warmly welcomed with cheers from dying and wounded men.

A little farther on we were met by a staff-officer sent by General Thomas to discover whether we were friends or enemies; he did not know whence friends could be coming, and the enemy appeared to be approaching from all directions. All of this shattered Army of the Cumberland left on the field was with Thomas; but not more than one-fourth of the men of the army who went into battle at the opening were there. Thomas's loss in killed and wounded during the two days had been dreadful. As his men dropped out his line was contracted to half its length. Now its flanks were bent back, conforming to ridges shaped like a horse-shoe.

On the part of Thomas and his men there was no thought but that of fighting. He was a soldier who had never retreated, who had never been defeated. He stood immovable, the "Rock of Chickamauga." Never had soldiers greater love for a commander. He imbued them with his spirit, and their confidence in him was sublime.

To the right of Thomas's line was a gorge, then a high ridge, nearly at right angles thereto, running east and west. Confederates under Kershaw

Along the greater part of a front of eight miles the ground was strewn with the intermingled dead of friend and foe. The morning of Sunday, the 20th, opened with a cloudless sky, but a fog had come up from the warm water of the Chickamauga and hung over the battlefield until 9 o'clock. A silence of desertion was in the front. This quiet continued till nearly 10 o'clock; then, as the peaceful tones of the church-bells, rolling over the land from the east, reached the meridian of Chickamauga, they were made dissonant by the murderous roar of the artillery of Bishop Polk, who was opening the battle on Thomas's front. Granger, who had been ordered at all hazards to hold fast where he was, listened and grew impatient. Shortly before 10 o'clock, calling my attention to a great column of dust moving from our front toward the point from which came the sound of battle, he said, "They are concentrating over there. That is where we ought to be." The corps flag marked his headquarters in an open field near the Ringgold road. He walked up and down in front of his flag, nervously pulling his beard. Once stopping, he said, "Why the —— does Rosecrans keep me here? There is nothing in front of us now. There is the battle"— pointing in the direction of Thomas. Every moment the sounds of battle grew louder, while the many columns of dust rolling together here mingled with the smoke that hung over the scene.

At 11 o'clock, with Granger, I climbed a high hay-rick near by. We sat there for ten minutes listening and watching. Then Granger jumped up, thrust his glass into its case, and exclaimed with an oath:

"I am going to Thomas, orders or no orders!"

"And if you go," I replied, "it may bring disaster to the army and you to a court-martial."

"There's nothing in our front now but ragtag, bobtail cavalry," he replied. "Don't you see

(McLaws's division of Hood's corps) were passing through the gorge, together with Bushrod Johnson's division, which Longstreet was strengthening with Hindman's division; divisions were forming on this ridge for an assault; to their left the guns of a battery were being unlimbered for an enfilading fire. There was not a man to send against the force on the ridge, none to oppose this impending assault. The enemy saw the approaching colors of the Reserve Corps and hesitated.

At 1 o'clock Granger shook hands with Thomas. Something was said about forming to fight to the right and rear.

"Those men must be driven back," said Granger, pointing to the gorge and ridge. "Can you do it?" asked Thomas.

LIEUTENANT-GENERAL JOSEPH WHEELER, C. S. A.
Cavalry commander under Bragg at Chickamauga.

"Yes, my men are fresh, and they are just the fellows for that work. They are raw troops, and they don't know any better than to charge up there."

Granger quickly sent Aleshire's battery of 3-inch rifle guns which he brought up to Thomas's left to assist in repelling another assault about to be made on the Kelly farm front. Whitaker's and Mitchell's brigades under Steedman were wheeled into position and projected against the enemy in the gorge and on the ridge. With ringing cheers they advanced in two lines by double-quick — over open fields, through weeds waist-high, through a little valley, then up the ridge. The enemy opened on them first with artillery, then with a murderous musketry fire. When well up the ridge the men almost exhausted were halted for breath. They lay on the ground two or three minutes, then came the command, "Forward!" Brave, bluff old Steedman, with a regimental flag in his hand, led the way. On went the lines, firing as they ran and bravely receiving a deadly and continuous fire from the enemy on the summit. The Confederates began to break and in another minute were flying down the southern slope of the ridge. In twenty minutes from the beginning of the charge the ridge had been carried.

Granger's hat had been torn by a fragment of shell; Steedman had been wounded; Whitaker had been wounded, and four of his five staff-officers killed or mortally wounded. Of Steedman's two brigades, numbering 3500, twenty per cent. had been killed and wounded in that twenty minutes; and the end was not yet.

The enemy massed a force to retake the ridge. They came before our men had rested; twice they assaulted and were driven back. During one assault, as the first line came within range of our muskets, it halted, apparently hesitating, when we saw a colonel seize a flag, wave it over his head, and rush forward. The whole line instantly caught his enthusiasm, and with a wild cheer followed, only to be hurled back again. Our men ran down the ridge in pursuit. In the midst of a group of Confederate dead and wounded they found the brave colonel dead, the flag he carried spread over him where he fell.

Soon after 5 o'clock Thomas rode to the left of his line, leaving Granger the ranking officer at the center. The ammunition of both Thomas's and Granger's commands was now about exhausted. When Granger had come up he had given ammunition to Brannon and Wood, and that had exhausted his supply. The cartridge-boxes of both our own and the enemy's dead within reach had been emptied by our men. When it was not yet 6 o'clock, and Thomas was still on the left of his line, Brannan rushed up to Granger, saying, "The enemy are forming for another assault; we have not another round of ammunition — what shall we do?" "Fix bayonets and go for them," was the reply. Along the whole line ran the order, "Fix bayonets." On came the enemy — our men were lying down. "Forward," was sounded. In one instant they were on their feet. Forward they went to meet the charge. The enemy fled. So impetuous was this counter-charge that one regiment, with empty muskets and empty cartridge-boxes, broke through the enemy's line, which, closing in their rear, carried them off as in the undertow.

One more feeble assault was made by the enemy; then the day closed, and the battle of Chickamauga was over. Of the 3700 men of the Reserve Corps who went into the battle that afternoon, 1175 were killed and wounded; 613 were missing, many of whom were of the regiment that broke through the lines. Our total loss was 1788, nearly 50 per cent.

Gordon Granger was rough in manner, but he had a tender heart. He was inclined to insubordination, especially when he knew his superior to be wrong. Otherwise he was a splendid soldier. Rosecrans wrote of him, "Granger, great in battle."

GENERAL THOMAS'S BIVOUAC AFTER THE FIRST DAY'S BATTLE.

THE CRISIS AT CHICKAMAUGA.

BY GATES P. THRUSTON, BREVET BRIGADIER-GENERAL, U. S. V.
On the staff of General McCook at the battle of Chickamauga.

. . . When Longstreet struck the right, Rosecrans was near McCook and Crittenden. Seeing our line swept back, he hurried to Sheridan's force for aid. With staff and escort he recklessly strove to stem the tide. They attempted to pass to the left through a storm of canister and musketry, but were driven back.

All became confusion. No order could be heard above the tempest of battle. With a wild yell the Confederates swept on far to their left. They seemed everywhere victorious. Rosecrans was borne back in the retreat. Fugitives, wounded, caissons, escort, ambulances, thronged the narrow pathways. He concluded that our whole line had given way, that the day was lost, that the next stand must be made at Chattanooga. McCook and Crittenden, caught in the same tide of retreat, seeing only rout everywhere, shared the opinion of Rosecrans, and reported to him for instructions and coöperation.

Briefly, this is the story of the disaster on our right at Chickamauga: We were overwhelmed by numbers; we were beaten in detail. Thirty minutes earlier Longstreet would have met well-organized resistance. Thirty minutes later our marching divisions could have formed beyond his column of attack.

But Longstreet had now swept away all organized opposition in his front. Four divisions only of the Union army remained in their original position — Johnson, of McCook's corps; Palmer, of Crittenden's, and Baird and Reynolds, of Thomas's.

Three had been cut off and swept away. Longstreet's force separated them. He says he urged Bragg to send Wheeler's cavalry in pursuit. Strange to report, no pursuit was ordered.

An incident of the battle perhaps contributed to the delay. When Sheridan and others were sent to the left, the writer hastened down toward Crawfish Springs, instructed by McCook to order the cavalry to the left to fill the gaps made by the withdrawal of infantry. I was but fairly on the run when Longstreet struck our right. The storm of battle was sweeping over the ground I had just left. Hastily giving the orders and returning, I found the 39th Indiana regiment coming from a cross-road — a full, fresh regiment, armed with Spencer's repeating-rifles, the only mounted force in our army corps. Calling upon Colonel T. J. Harrison, its commander, to hurry to the left, we led the regiment at a gallop to the Widow Glenn's.

The sound of battle had lulled. No Union force was in sight. A Confederate line near by was advancing against the position. Harrison, dismounting his men, dashed at the enemy in a most effective charge. Wilder, coming up on our right, also attacked. Wilder had two regiments armed with the same repeating-rifles. They did splendid work. Longstreet told Wilder after the war that the steady and continued racket of these guns led him to think an army corps had attacked his left flank. Bragg, cautious by nature, hesitated. By the time he was ready to turn Longstreet's force against Thomas, valuable time had elapsed.

Brannan, partly knocked out of line, had gathered his division on a hill at right angles to his former position, and a half mile in rear of Reynolds's. General Wood came up with Harker's bri-

gade and part of George P. Buell's, and posted them near Brannan's left. Some of Van Cleve's troops joined them, and fragments of Negley's.

General Thomas, ignorant of these movements and of the disaster to the right of the Union army, had again been attacked by Breckinridge and Forrest. They were again in Baird's rear with increased force. Thomas's reserve brigades, Willich, Grose, and Van Derveer, hurried to meet the attack. After a fierce struggle the Confederates were beaten back. Thomas, expecting the promised assistance of Sheridan, had sent Captain Kellogg to guide him to the left. Kellogg, hurrying back, reported that he had been fired on by a line of Confederates advancing in the woods in rear of Reynolds, who held the center of our general line.

The men in gray were coming on the right instead of Sheridan! Wood and Harker hoped the force advancing in the woods on their new front was a friendly one. The National flag was waved; a storm of bullets was the response. It was Stewart and Bate coming with their Tennesseeans. They had finally forced their way across the ragged edge of the Federal right, and were following Hood. Fortunately Thomas had just repulsed Breckinridge's attack on his left, and Stanley, Beatty, and Van Derveer had double-quicked across the "horse-shoe" to our new right. They did not come a moment too soon. The improvised line of Federals thus hastily formed on "Battery Hill" now successfully withstood the assault of the enemy. The Union line held the crest. Longstreet was stayed at last. Gathering new forces, he soon sent a flanking column around our right. We could not extend our line to meet this attack. They had reached the summit, and were coming around still farther on through a protected ravine. For a time the fate of the Union army hung in the balance. All seemed lost, when unexpected help came from Gordon Granger, and the right was saved. . . .

LIEUTENANT-GENERAL N. B. FORREST, C. S. A.
Commanding a cavalry corps at Chickamauga.

THE ARMY OF THE CUMBERLAND IN FRONT OF CHATTANOOGA.
From a lithograph.

The picture shows the intrenchments occupied by three divisions of Thomas's corps. In the foreground is seen Fort Grose, manned on the left of the picture by the 24th Ohio and on the right by the 36th Indiana. Fort Negley is at the end of the line of works seen in the middle-ground, Lookout Mountain being in the distance.

CHATTANOOGA.

BY ULYSSES S. GRANT, GENERAL, U. S. A.
Commander of the Union Army at the Battle of Chattanooga.

NARRATIVE OF EVENTS LEADING TO CHATTANOOGA.

PORT HUDSON, DEC., 1862, TO JULY 8, 1863.

General Nathaniel P. Banks relieved General Butler commanding the Department of the Gulf in December, 1862, and acting under orders to coöperate with General McClernand's column on the upper Mississippi, he sent a detachment under General Cuvier Grover by water (under convoy of Farragut's gun-boats) to take possession of Baton Rouge. The Confederates evacuated the town December 16, and Banks's army occupied it as a base of operations against Port Hudson. Several attempts were made to flank the latter during the winter; and all failing, it was invested in May by a land column on the east. After an unsuccessful assault on May 27, which cost 1850 men, siege operations were commenced which resulted in its surrender July 8.

HELENA, JULY 4, 1863.

While Grant was marching on Vicksburg, General E. Kirby Smith, who had succeeded to the command of the Trans-Mississippi Department in February, 1863, organized an expedition at Little Rock to attack Helena as a means of relieving Vicksburg. The force was led by Generals T. H. Holmes and Sterling Price, who stormed the works, and were repulsed with heavy loss on July 4, the day of the fall of Vicksburg.

LITTLE ROCK, SEPT. 10, 1863.

The fall of Vicksburg and Port Hudson led to the reinforcement of the Union army in Missouri and Arkansas, where General John M. Schofield was in command. In August, Schofield sent General Frederick M. Steele from Helena against Little Rock. The Confederates under Price abandoned Little Rock without serious fighting on September 10.

JACKSON, MISS., JULY 8 TO 17, 1863.

Immediately upon the fall of Vicksburg all the Confederate troops in Mississippi not included in the surrender were concentrated at Jackson under General Joseph E. Johnston. Sherman marched against Jackson, and, after withstanding a vigorous siege of seven days, Johnston evacuated on the 16th. In September, Sherman's and McPherson's corps moved eastward to reinforce Rosecrans's army, which at the close of the month was practically shut up in Chattanooga Valley, with the Tennessee River in the rear and the Confederates strongly posted on commanding heights in front. Grant reached Chattanooga late in October, and assumed command. Rosecrans was relieved from the Army of the Cumberland by General George H. Thomas.

. . . Chattanooga is on the south bank of the Tennessee, where that river runs nearly due west. It is at the northern end of a valley five or six miles in width through which runs Chattanooga Creek. To the east of the valley is Missionary Ridge, rising from five to eight hundred feet above the creek, and terminating somewhat abruptly a half-mile or more before reaching the Tennessee. On the west of the valley is Lookout Mountain, 2200 feet above tide-water. Just below the town, the Tennessee makes a turn to the south and runs to the base of Lookout Mountain, leaving no level ground between the mountain and river. The Memphis and Charleston railroad passes this point, where the mountain stands nearly perpendicular. East of Missionary Ridge flows the South Chickamauga River; west of Lookout Mountain is Lookout Creek; and west of that, the Raccoon Mountain. Lookout Mountain at its northern end rises almost perpendicularly for some distance, then breaks off in a gentle slope of cultivated fields to near the summit, where it ends in a palisade thirty or more feet in height. On the gently sloping ground, between the upper and lower palisades, there is a single farm-house, which is reached by a wagon road from the valley to the east.

The intrenched line of the enemy commenced on the north end of Missionary Ridge and extended along the crest for some distance south, thence across Chattanooga Valley to Lookout Mountain. Lookout Mountain was also fortified and held by the enemy, who also kept troops in Lookout Valley and on Raccoon Mountain, with pickets extending down the river so as to command the road on the north bank and render it useless to us. In addition to this there was an intrenched line in Chattanooga Valley extending from the river east of the town to Lookout Mountain, to make the investment complete. Besides the fortifications on Missionary Ridge there was a line at the base of the hill, with occasional spurs of rifle-pits half-way up the front. The enemy's pickets extended out into the valley toward the town so far that the pickets of the two armies could converse. At one point they were separated only by the narrow creek which gives its name to the valley and town, and from which both sides drew water. The Union lines were shorter than those of the enemy.

Thus the enemy, with a vastly superior force, was strongly fortified to the east, south, and west, and commanded the river below. Practically the Army of the Cumberland was besieged. The enemy, with his cavalry north of the river, had stopped the passing of a train loaded with ammu-nition and medical supplies. The Union army was short of both, not having ammunition enough for a day's fighting. . . .

On the 26th Hooker crossed the river at Bridgeport and commenced his eastward march. At 3 o'clock on the morning of the 27th Hazen moved into the stream with his sixty pontoons and eighteen hundred brave and well-equipped men. Smith started enough in advance to be near the river when Hazen should arrive. There are a number of detached spurs of hills north of the river at Chattanooga, back of which is a good road parallel to the stream, sheltered from view from the top of Lookout. It was over this road Smith marched. At 5 o'clock Hazen landed at Brown's Ferry, surprised the picket-guard and captured most of it. By 7 o'clock the whole of Smith's force was ferried over and in possession of a height commanding the ferry. This was speedily fortified while a detail was laying the pontoon-bridge. By 10 o'clock the bridge was laid, and our extreme right, now in Lookout Valley, was fortified and connected with the rest of the army. The two bridges over the Tennessee River,—a flying one at Chattanooga and the new one at Brown's Ferry,—with the road north of the river, covered from both the fire and the view of the enemy, made the connection complete. Hooker found but slight obstacles in his way, and on the afternoon of the 28th emerged into Lookout Valley at Wauhatchie. Howard marched on to Brown's Ferry, while Geary, who commanded a division in the Twelfth Corps, stopped three miles south. The pickets of the enemy on the river below were cut off and soon came in and surrendered.

The river was now open to us from Lookout Valley to Bridgeport. . . . On the way to Chattanooga I had telegraphed back to Nashville for a good sup-

HAZEN'S MEN LANDING FROM PONTOON-BOATS AT BROWN'S FERRY.
From a war-time sketch.

ply of vegetables and small rations, which the troops had been so long deprived of. . . . Neither officers nor men looked upon themselves any longer as doomed. The weak and languid appearance of the troops, so visible before, disappeared at once. I do not know what the effect was on the other side, but assume it must have been correspondingly depressing. Mr. Davis had visited Bragg but a short time before, and must have perceived our condition to be about as Bragg described it in his subsequent report. "These dispositions," he said, "faithfully sustained, insured the enemy's speedy evacuation of Chattanooga, for want of food and forage. Possessed of the shortest route to his depot and the one by which reinforcements must reach him, we held him at our mercy, and his destruction was only a question of time." But the dispositions were not "faithfully sustained," and I doubt not that thousands of men engaged in trying to "sustain" them now rejoice that they were not.

There was no time during the rebellion when I did not think, and often say, that the South was more to be benefited by defeat than the North. The latter had the people, the institutions, and the territory to make a great and prosperous nation. The former was burdened with an institution abhorrent to all civilized peoples not brought up under it, and one which degraded labor, kept it in ignorance, and enervated the governing class. With the outside world at war with this institution, they could not have extended their territory. The labor of the country was not skilled, nor allowed to become so. The whites could not toil without becoming degraded, and those who did were denominated "poor white trash." The system of labor would have soon exhausted the soil and left the people poor. The non-slaveholders would have left the country, and the small slaveholder must have sold out to his more fortunate neighbors. Soon the slaves would have outnumbered the masters, and, not being in sympathy with them, would have risen in their might and exterminated them. The war was expensive to the South as well as to the North, both in blood and treasure; but it was worth all it cost.

The enemy was surprised by the movement which secured to us a line of supplies. He appreciated

VIEW OF CHATTANOOGA AND MOCCASIN POINT FROM THE SIDE OF LOOKOUT MOUNTAIN.
From a photograph.

its importance, and hastened to try to recover the line from us. His strength on Lookout Mountain was not equal to Hooker's command in the valley below. From Missionary Ridge he had to march twice the distance we had from Chattanooga, in order to reach Lookout Valley. But on the night of the 28th–29th [of October] an attack was made on Geary, at Wauhatchie, by Longstreet's corps. When the battle commenced, Hooker ordered Howard up from Brown's Ferry. He had three miles to march to reach Geary. On his way he was fired upon by rebel troops from a foot-hill to the left of the road, and from which the road was commanded. Howard turned to the left, and charged up the hill, and captured it before the enemy had time to in-

trench, taking many prisoners. Leaving sufficient men to hold this height, he pushed on to reinforce Geary. Before he got up, Geary had been engaged for about three hours against a vastly superior force. The night was so dark that the men could not distinguish one another except by the light of the flashes of their muskets. In the darkness and uproar Hooker's teamsters became frightened, and deserted their teams. The mules also became frightened, and, breaking loose from their fastenings, stampeded directly toward the enemy. The latter no doubt took this for a charge, and stampeded in turn. By 4 o'clock in the morning the battle had entirely ceased, and our "cracker line" was never afterward disturbed.

In securing possession of Lookout Valley, Smith lost one man killed and four or five wounded. The enemy lost most of his pickets at the ferry by capture. In the night engagement of the 28th–29th Hooker lost 416 killed and wounded. I never knew the loss of the enemy, but our troops buried over 150 of his dead, and captured more than 100.

Having got the Army of the Cumberland in a comfortable position, I now began to look after the remainder of my new command. Burnside was in about as desperate a condition as the Army of the Cumberland had been, only he was not yet besieged. He was a hundred miles from the nearest possible base, Big South Fork of the Cumberland River, and much farther from any railroad we had possession of. The roads back were over mountains, and all supplies along the line had long since been exhausted. His animals, too, had been starved, and their carcasses lined the road from Cumberland Gap, and far back toward Lexington, Kentucky. East Tennessee still furnished supplies of beef, bread, and forage, but it did not supply ammunition, clothing, medical supplies, or small rations, such as coffee, sugar, salt, and rice.

Stopping to organize his new command, Sherman had started from Memphis for Corinth on the 11th of October. His instructions required him to repair the road in his rear in order to bring up supplies. The distance was about 330 miles through a hostile country. His entire command could not have maintained the road if it had been completed. The bridges had all been destroyed by the enemy and much other damage done; a hostile community lived along the road; guerrilla bands infested the country, and more or less of the cavalry of the enemy was still in the west. Often Sherman's work was destroyed as soon as completed, though he was only a short distance away. . . . On November 1st, he crossed the Tennessee at Eastport, and that day was in Florence, Alabama, with the head of column, while his troops were still crossing at Eastport, with Blair bringing up the rear.

MILITARY BRIDGE OVER THE TENNESSEE RIVER AT CHATTANOOGA, BUILT IN OCTOBER, 1863.
From a photograph.

DEPARTURE OF THE FIRST HOSPITAL TRAIN FROM CHATTANOOGA, JANUARY, 1864, AND INTERIOR OF A HOSPITAL CAR.
From a war-time photograph.

Sherman's force made an additional army, with cavalry, artillery, and trains, all to be supplied by the single-track road from Nashville. All indications pointed also to the probable necessity of supplying Burnside's command, in East Tennessee, 25,000 more, by the same road. A single track could not do this. I therefore gave an order to Sherman to halt General G. M. Dodge's command of eight thousand men at Athens, and subsequently directed the latter to arrange his troops along the railroad from Decatur, north toward Nashville, and to rebuild that road. The road from Nashville to Decatur passes over a broken country, cut up with innumerable streams, many of them of considerable width, and with valleys far below the road-bed. All the bridges over these had been destroyed and the rails taken up and twisted by the enemy. All the locomotives and cars not carried off had been destroyed as effectually as they knew how to destroy them. All bridges and culverts had been destroyed between Nashville and Decatur, and thence to Stevenson, where the Memphis and Charleston and the Nashville and Chattanooga roads unite. The rebuilding of this road would give us two roads as far as Stevenson over which to supply the army. From Bridgeport, a short distance farther east, the river supplements the road. . . .

General Dodge had the work assigned him finished within forty days after receiving his orders. The number of bridges to rebuild was 182, many of them over deep and wide chasms. The length of road repaired was 182 miles. . . .

On the 4th of November Longstreet left our front with about 15,000 troops, besides Wheeler's cavalry, 5000 more, to go against Burnside. The situation seemed desperate, and was more exasperating because nothing could be done until Sherman should get up. The authorities at Washington were now more than ever anxious for the safety of Burnside's army, and plied me with despatches faster than ever, urging that something should be done for his relief. On the 7th, before Longstreet could possibly have reached Knoxville, I ordered General Thomas peremptorily to attack the enemy's right, so as to force the return of the troops that had gone up the valley. I directed him to take mules, officers' horses, or animals wherever he could get them, to move the necessary artillery. But he persisted in the declaration that he could not move a single piece of artillery, and could not see how he could possibly comply with the order. Nothing was left to be done but to answer Wash-

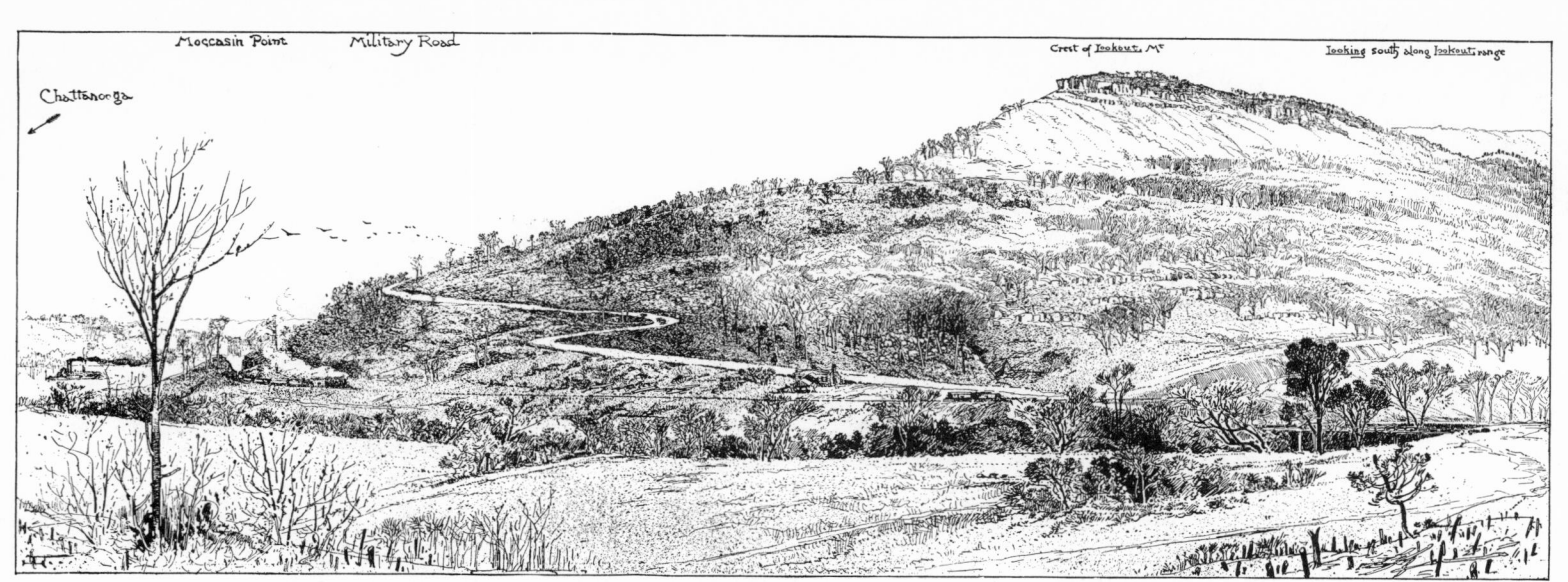

VIEW OF LOOKOUT MOUNTAIN FROM THE HILL TO THE NORTH, WHICH WAS GENERAL HOOKER'S POSITION DURING THE BATTLE ON THE MOUNTAIN, NOVEMBER 24, 1863.
The military road winding over the north slope of Lookout was built after Hooker captured the mountain. (From a war-time photograph.)

ington despatches as best I could, urge Sherman forward, although he was making every effort to get forward, and encourage Burnside to hold on, assuring him that in a short time he would be relieved. All of Burnside's despatches showed the greatest confidence in his ability to hold his position as long as his ammunition should hold out. He even suggested the propriety of abandoning the territory he held south and west of Knoxville, so as to draw the enemy farther from his base, and to make it more difficult for him to get back to Chattanooga when the battle should begin. Longstreet had a railroad as far as Loudon; but from

there to Knoxville he had to rely on wagon trains. Burnside's suggestion, therefore, was a good one, and it was adopted. . . .

Longstreet, for some reason or other, stopped at Loudon until the 13th. That being the terminus of his railroad communications, it is probable he was directed to remain there awaiting orders. He was in a position threatening Knoxville, and at the same time where he could be brought back speedily to Chattanooga. The day after Longstreet left Loudon, Sherman reached Bridgeport in person, and proceeded on to see me that evening, the 14th, and reached Chattanooga the next day. . . .

The next day after Sherman's arrival I took him, with Generals Thomas and Smith and other officers, to the north side of the river and showed them the round over which Sherman had to march, and pointed out generally what he was expected to do. I, as well as the authorities in Washington, was still in a great state of anxiety for Burnside's safety. Burnside himself, I believe, was the only one who did not share in this anxiety. Nothing could be done for him, however, until Sherman's troops were up. As soon, therefore, as the inspection was over, Sherman started for Bridgeport to hasten

matters, rowing a boat himself, I believe, from Kelley's Ferry. Sherman had left Bridgeport the night of the 14th, reached Chattanooga the evening of the 15th, made the above-described inspection the morning of the 16th, and started back the same evening to hurry up his command, fully appreciating the importance of time.

His march was conducted with as much expedition as the roads and season would admit of. By the 20th he was himself at Brown's Ferry with head of column, but many of his troops were far behind, and one division, Ewing's, was at Trenton, sent that way to create the impression that Lookout was to be taken from the south. Sherman received his orders at the ferry, and was asked if he could not be ready for the assault the following morning. News had been received that the battle had been commenced at Knoxville. Burnside had been cut off from telegraphic communication. The President, the Secretary of War, and General Halleck were in an agony of suspense. My suspense was also great, but more endurable, because I was where I could soon do something to relieve the situation. It was impossible to get Sherman's troops up for the next day. I then asked him if they could not be got up to make the assault on the morning of the 22d, and ordered Thomas to move on that date. But the elements were against us. It rained all the 20th and 21st. The river rose so rapidly that it was difficult to keep the pontoons in place. . . .

Meantime Sherman continued his crossing, without intermission, as fast as his troops could be got up. The crossing had to be effected in full view of the enemy on the top of Lookout Mountain. Once over, the troops soon disappeared behind the detached hills on the north side, and would not come to view again, either to watchmen on Lookout Mountain or Missionary Ridge, until they emerged between the hills to strike the bank of the river. But when Sherman's advance reached a point opposite the

GENERAL HOOKER AND STAFF ON THE HILL NORTH OF LOOKOUT CREEK, FROM WHICH HE DIRECTED THE BATTLE.
From a war-time photograph.

town of Chattanooga, Howard, who, it will be remembered, had been concealed behind the hills on the north side, took up his line of march to join the troops on the south side. His crossing was in full view both from Missionary Ridge and the top of Lookout, and the enemy, of course, supposed these troops to be Sherman's. This enabled Sherman to get to his assigned position without discovery.

On the 20th, when so much was occurring to discourage,—rains falling so heavily as to delay the passage of troops over the river at Brown's Ferry, and threatening the entire breaking of the bridge; news coming of a battle raging at Knoxville; of Willcox being threatened by a force from the east,—a letter was received from Bragg which contained these words:

"As there may still be some non-combatants in Chattanooga, I deem it proper to notify you that prudence would dictate their early withdrawal."

Of course I understood that this was a device intended to deceive; but I did not know what the intended deception was. On the 22d, however, a deserter came in who informed me that Bragg was leaving our front, and on that day Buckner's division was sent to reinforce Longstreet at Knoxville, and another division started to follow, but was recalled. The object of Bragg's letter, no doubt, was in some way to detain me until Knoxville could be captured, and his troops there be returned to Chattanooga.

During the night of the 21st the rest of the pontoon-boats, completed, one hundred and sixteen in all, were carried up to and placed in North Chickamauga. The material for the roadway over these was deposited out of view of the enemy within a few hundred yards of the bank of the Tennessee, where the north end of the bridge was to rest.

Hearing nothing from Burnside, and hearing much of the distress in Washington on his account, I could no longer defer operations for his relief. I determined therefore to do on the 23d, with the Army of the Cumberland, what had been intended to be done on the 24th.

The position occupied by the Army of the Cumberland had been made very strong for defense during the months it had been besieged. The line was about a mile from the town, and extended from Citico Creek, a small stream running near the base of Missionary Ridge and emptying into the Tennessee about two miles below the mouth of the South Chickamauga, on the left, to Chattanooga Creek on the right. All commanding points on the line were well fortified and well equipped with artillery. The important elevations within the line had all been carefully fortified and supplied with a proper armament. Among the elevations so fortified was one to the east of the town, named Fort Wood. It owed its importance chiefly to the fact that it lay between the town and Missionary Ridge, where most of the strength of the enemy was. Fort Wood had in it twenty-two pieces of artillery, most of which would reach the nearer points of the enemy's line. On the morning of the 23d, Thomas, according to instructions, moved Granger's corps of two divisions, Sheridan and T. J. Wood com-

THE BATTLE OF LOOKOUT MOUNTAIN.

From a painting lent by Captain W. L. Stork. The picture shows the Union troops fighting in the woods near the cliffs of Point Lookout.

Early in October, 1863, Jefferson Davis visited Lookout Mountain with General Bragg. As they approached the edge of the cliff, General Bragg, with a wave of the hand, alluded to "the fine view"; whereupon Major Robert W. Wooley, who had little faith in the military outlook, exclaimed to a brother officer, but so that all could hear: "Yes, it 's a fine view, but a —— bad prospect."

manding, to the foot of Fort Wood, and formed them into line as if going on parade—Sheridan on the right, Wood to the left, extending to or near Citico Creek. Palmer, commanding the Fourteenth Corps, held that part of our line facing south and southwest. He supported Sheridan with one division, Baird's, while his other division, under [R. W.] Johnson, remained in the trenches, under arms, ready to be moved to any point. Howard's corps was moved in rear of the center. The picket lines were within a few hundred yards of each other. At 2 o'clock in the afternoon all were ready to advance. By this time the clouds had lifted so that the enemy could see from his elevated position all that was going on. The signal for advance was given by a booming of cannon from Fort Wood and other points on the line. The rebel pickets were soon driven back upon the main guards, which occupied minor and detached heights between the main ridge and our lines. These too were carried before halting, and before the enemy had time to reinforce their advance guards. But it was not without loss on both sides. This movement secured to us a line fully a mile in advance of the one we occupied in the morning, and one which the enemy had occupied up to this time. The fortifications were rapidly turned to face the other way. During the following night they were made

strong. We lost in this preliminary action about eleven hundred killed and wounded, while the enemy probably lost quite as heavily, including the prisoners that were captured. With the exception of the firing of artillery, kept up from Missionary Ridge and Fort Wood until night closed in, this ended the fighting for the day.

The advantage was greatly on our side now, and if I could only have been assured that Burnside could hold out ten days longer I should have rested more easy. But we were doing the best we could for him and the cause. . . .

At 2 o'clock in the morning, November 24th, Giles A. Smith pushed out from the North Chickamauga with his 116 boats, each loaded with 30 brave and well-armed men. The boats, with their precious freight, dropped down quietly with the current to avoid attracting the attention of any one who could convey information to the enemy, until arriving near the mouth of South Chickamauga. Here a few boats were landed, the troops debarked, and a rush was made upon the picket-guard known to be at that point. The guard was surprised, and twenty of their number captured. The remainder of the troops effected a landing at the point where the bridge was to start, with equally good results. The work of ferrying over Sherman's command from the north side of the Tennessee was at once commenced, using the pontoons for the purpose. A steamer was also brought up from the town to assist. The rest of M. L. Smith's division came first, then the division of John E. Smith. The troops as they landed were put to work intrenching their position. By daylight the two entire divisions were over, and well covered by the works they had built.

The work of laying the bridge on which to cross the artillery and cavalry was now begun. The ferrying over of the infantry was continued with the steamer and the pontoons, taking the pontoons, however, as fast as they were wanted to put in their place in the bridge. By a little past noon the bridge was completed, as well as one over the South Chickamauga, connecting the troops left on that side with their comrades below, and all the infantry and artillery were on the south bank of the Tennessee.

Sherman at once formed his troops for assault on Missionary Ridge. By 1 o'clock he started, with M. L. Smith on his left, keeping nearly the course of Chickamauga River; J. E. Smith next, to the right and a little in the rear; then Ewing, still farther to the right, and also a little to the rear of J. E. Smith's command, in column ready to deploy to the right if an enemy should come from that direction. A good skirmish line preceded each of these columns. Soon the foot of the hill was reached; the skirmishers pushed directly up, followed closely by their supports. By half-past 3 Sherman was in possession of the height, without having sustained much loss. A brigade from each division was now brought up, and artillery was dragged to the top of the hill by hand. The enemy did not seem to have been aware of this movement until the top of the hill was gained. There had been a drizzling rain during the day, and the clouds were so low that Lookout Mountain and the top of

Missionary Ridge were obscured from the view of persons in the valley. But now the enemy opened fire upon their assailants, and made several attempts with their skirmishers to drive them away, but without avail. Later in the day a more determined attack was made, but this, too, failed, and Sherman was left to fortify what he had gained.

Sherman's cavalry took up its line of march soon after the bridge was completed, and by half-past 3 the whole of it was over both bridges, and on its way to strike the enemy's communications at Chickamauga Station. All of Sherman's command was now south of the Tennessee. During the afternoon General Giles A. Smith was severely wounded and carried from the field.

Thomas having done on the 23d what was expected of him on the 24th, there was nothing for him to do this day, except to strengthen his position. Howard, however, effected a crossing of Citico Creek and a junction with Sherman, and was directed to report to him. With two or three regiments of his command, he moved in the morning along the banks of the Tennessee and reached the point where the bridge was being laid. He went out on the bridge as far as it was completed from the south end, and saw Sherman superintending the work from the north side, moving himself south as fast as an additional boat was put in and the roadway put upon it. Howard reported to his new chief across the chasm between them, which was now narrow and in a few minutes was closed.

While these operations were going on to the east of Chattanooga, Hooker was engaged on the west. . . .

The side of Lookout Mountain confronting Hooker's command was rugged, heavily timbered, and full of chasms, making it difficult to advance with troops, even in the absence of an opposing force. Farther up the ground becomes more even and level, and was in cultivation. On the east side the slope is much more gradual, and a good wagon road, zigzagging up it, connects the town of Chattanooga with the summit.

Early in the morning of the 24th Hooker moved Geary's division, supported by a brigade of Cruft's, up Lookout Creek, to effect a crossing. The remainder of Cruft's division was to seize the bridge over the creek, near the crossing of the railroad. Osterhaus was to move up to the bridge and cross it. The bridge was seized by Grose's brigade after a slight skirmish with the picket guarding it. This attracted the enemy so that Geary's movement farther up was not observed. A heavy

SIGNAL CORPS, PRIVATE.

AMBULANCE CAMP.

mist obscured him from the view of the troops on the top of the mountain. He crossed the creek almost unobserved, and captured the picket of over forty men on guard near by. He then commenced ascending the mountain directly in his front. By this time the enemy was seen coming down from their camp on the mountain slope, and filing into their rifle-pits to contest the crossing of the bridge. By 11 o'clock the bridge was complete. Osterhaus was up, and after some sharp skirmishing the enemy was driven away, with considerable loss in killed and captured.

While the operations at the bridge were progressing, Geary was pushing up the hill over great obstacles, resisted by the enemy directly in his front, and in face of the guns on top of the mountain. The enemy, seeing their left flank and rear menaced, gave way and were followed by Cruft and Osterhaus. Soon these were up abreast of Geary, and the whole command pushed up the hill, driving the enemy in advance. By noon Geary had gained the open ground on the north slope of the mountain with his right close up to the base of the upper palisade, but there were strong fortifications in his front. The rest of the command coming up, a line was formed from the base of the upper palisade to the mouth of Chattanooga Creek.

Thomas and I were on the top of Orchard Knob. Hooker's advance now made our line a continuous one. It was in full view, extending from the Tennessee River, where Sherman had crossed, up Chickamauga River to the base of Missionary Ridge, over the top of the north end of the ridge, to Chattanooga Valley, then along parallel to the ridge a mile or more, across the valley to the mouth of Chattanooga

Creek, thence up the slope of Lookout Mountain to the foot of the upper palisade. The day was hazy, so that Hooker's operations were not visible to us except at moments when the clouds would rise. But the sound of his artillery and musketry was heard incessantly. The enemy on his front was partially fortified, but was soon driven out of his works. At 2 o'clock the clouds, which had so obscured the top of Lookout all day as to hide whatever was going on from the view of those below, settled down and made it so dark where Hooker was as to stop operations for the time. At 4 o'clock Hooker reported his position as impregnable. By a little after 5, direct communication was established, and a brigade of troops was sent from Chattanooga to reinforce him. These troops had to cross Chattanooga Creek, and met with some opposition, but soon overcame it, and by night the commander, General Carlin, reported to Hooker and was assigned to his left. . . .

The morning of the 25th opened clear and bright, and the whole field was in full view from the top of Orchard Knob. It remained so all day. Bragg's headquarters were in full view, and officers — presumably staff-officers — could be seen coming and going constantly.

The point of ground which Sherman had carried on the 24th was almost disconnected from the main ridge occupied by the enemy. A low pass, over which there is a wagon road crossing the hill, and near which there is a railroad tunnel, intervenes between the two hills. The problem now was to get to the latter. The enemy was fortified on the point, and back farther, where the ground was still higher, was a second fortification commanding the

first. Sherman was out as soon as it was light enough to see, and by sunrise his command was in motion. Three brigades held the hill already gained. Morgan L. Smith moved along the east base of Missionary Ridge; Loomis along the west base, supported by two brigades of John E. Smith's division; and Corse with his brigade was between the two, moving directly toward the hill to be captured. The ridge is steep and heavily wooded on the east side, where M. L. Smith's troops were advancing, but cleared and with a more gentle slope on the west side. The troops advanced rapidly and carried the extreme end of the rebel works. Morgan L. Smith advanced to a point which cut the enemy off from the railroad bridge and the means of bringing up supplies by rail from Chickamauga Station, where the main depot was located. The enemy made brave and strenuous efforts to drive our troops from the position we had gained, but without success. The contest lasted for two hours. Corse, a brave and efficient commander, was badly wounded in this assault. Sherman now threatened both Bragg's flank and his stores, and made it necessary for him to weaken other points of his line to strengthen his right. From the position I occupied I could see column after column of Bragg's forces moving against Sherman; every Confederate gun that could be brought to bear upon the Union forces was concentrated upon him. J. E. Smith, with two brigades, charged up the west side of the ridge to the support of Corse's command, over open ground, and in the face of a heavy fire of both artillery and musketry, and reached the very parapet of the enemy. He lay here for a time, but the enemy coming with a heavy force upon his right flank, he was compelled to fall back, followed by the foe. A few hundred yards brought Smith's troops into a wood, where they were speedily re-formed, when they charged and drove the attacking party back to his intrenchments.

Seeing the advance, repulse, and second advance of J. E. Smith from the position I occupied, I directed Thomas to send a division to reinforce him. Baird's division was accordingly sent from the right of Orchard Knob. It had to march a considerable distance, directly under the eyes of the enemy, to reach its position. Bragg at once commenced massing in the same direction. This was what I wanted. But it had now got to be late in the afternoon, and I had expected before this to see Hooker crossing the ridge in the neighborhood of Rossville, and compelling Bragg to mass in that direction also.

The enemy had evacuated Lookout Mountain during the night, as I expected he would. In crossing the valley he burned the bridges over Chattanooga Creek, and did all he could to obstruct the roads behind him. Hooker was off bright and early, with no obstructions in his front but distance and the destruction above named. He was detained four hours in crossing Chattanooga Creek, and thus was lost the immediate advantages I expected from his forces. His reaching Bragg's flank and extending across it was to be the signal for Thomas's assault of the ridge. But Sherman's condition was getting so critical that the assault for his relief could not be delayed any longer.

Sheridan's and Wood's divisions had been lying under arms from early in the morning, ready to move the instant the signal was given. I now directed Thomas to order the charge at once. I watched eagerly to see the effect, and became impatient at last that there was no indication of any charge being made. The center of the line which was to make the charge was near where Thomas and I stood together, but concealed from our view by the intervening forest. Turning to Thomas to inquire what caused the delay, I was surprised to see General Thomas J. Wood, one of the division commanders who were to make the charge, standing talking to him. I spoke to General Wood, asking him why he had not charged, as ordered an hour before. He replied very promptly that this was the first he had heard of it, but that he had been ready all day to move at a moment's notice. I told him to make the charge at once. He was off in a moment, and in an incredibly short time loud cheering was heard, and he and Sheridan were driving the enemy's advance before them toward Missionary Ridge. The Confederates were strongly intrenched on the crest of the ridge in front of us, and had a second line half-way down and another at the base. Our men drove the troops in front of the lower line of rifle-pits so rapidly, and followed them so closely, that rebel and Union troops went over the first line of works almost at the same time. Many rebels were captured and sent to the rear under the fire of their own friends higher up the hill. Those that were not captured retreated, and were pursued. The retreating hordes being between friends and pursuers, caused the enemy to fire high, to avoid killing their own men. In fact, on that occasion the Union soldier nearest the enemy was in the safest position. Without awaiting further orders or stopping to re-form, on our troops went to the second line of works; over that and on for the crest— thus effectually carrying out my orders of the 18th for the battle and of the 24th for this charge. I watched their progress with intense interest. The fire along the rebel line was terrific. Cannon and musket balls filled the air; but the damage done was in small proportion to the ammunition used. The pursuit continued until the crest was reached, and soon our men were seen climbing over the Confederate barrier at different points in front of both Sheridan's and Wood's divisions. The retreat of the enemy along most of his line was precipitate, and the panic so great that Bragg and his officers lost all control over their men. Many were captured and thousands threw away their arms in their flight.

Sheridan pushed forward until he reached the Chickamauga River at a point above where the enemy had crossed. He met some resistance from troops occupying a second hill in rear of Missionary Ridge, probably to cover the retreat of the main body and of the artillery and trains. It was now getting dark, but Sheridan, without halting on that account, pushed his men forward up this second hill slowly and without attracting the attention of the men placed to defend it, while he detached to the right and left to surround the position. The enemy discovered the movement before these dis-

THE CONFEDERATE LINE OPPOSED TO BAIRD'S DIVISION ON MISSIONARY RIDGE.
From the Cyclorama.

positions were complete, and beat a hasty retreat, leaving artillery, wagon trains, and many prisoners in our hands. To Sheridan's prompt movement the Army of the Cumberland and the nation are indebted for the bulk of the capture of prisoners, artillery, and small-arms that day. Except for his prompt pursuit, so much in this way would not have been accomplished.

While the advance up Missionary Ridge was going forward, General Thomas, with his staff, General Gordon Granger, commander of the corps making the assault, and myself and staff, occupied Orchard Knob, from which the entire field could be observed. The moment the troops were seen going over the last line of rebel defenses I ordered Granger to join his command, and mounting my horse I rode to the front. General Thomas left about the same time. Sheridan, on the extreme right, was already in pursuit of the enemy east of the ridge. Wood, who commanded the division to the left of Sheridan, accompanied his men on horseback, but did not join Sheridan in the pursuit. To the left, in Baird's front, where Bragg's troops had massed against Sheridan, the resistance was more stubborn, and the contest lasted longer. I ordered Granger to follow the enemy with Wood's division, but he was so much excited, and kept up such a roar of musketry in the direction the enemy had taken, that by the time I could stop the firing the

enemy had got well out of the way. The enemy confronting Sherman, now seeing everything to their left giving way, fled also. Sherman, however, was not aware of the extent of our success until after nightfall, when he received orders to pursue at daylight in the morning.

Hooker, as stated, was detained at Chattanooga Creek by the destruction of the bridges at that point. He got his troops over, with the exception of the artillery, by fording the stream, at a little after 3 o'clock. Leaving his artillery to follow when the bridges should be reconstructed, he pushed on with the remainder of his command. At Rossville he came upon the flank of a division of the enemy, which soon commenced a retreat along the ridge. This threw them on Palmer. They could make but little resistance in the position they were caught in, and as many of them as could do so escaped. Many, however, were captured. Hooker's position during the night of the 25th was near Rossville, extending east of the ridge. Palmer was on his left, on the road to Graysville.

During the night I telegraphed to Willcox that Bragg had been defeated, and that immediate relief would be sent to Burnside if he could hold out; to Halleck I sent an announcement of our victory, and informed him that forces would be sent up the valley to relieve Burnside.

Before the battle of Chattanooga opened I had taken measures for the relief of Burnside the moment the way should be clear. . . .

The victory at Chattanooga was won against great odds, considering the advantage the enemy had of position; and was accomplished more easily than was expected by reason of Bragg's making several grave mistakes: first, in sending away his ablest corps commander, with over 20,000 troops; second, in sending away a division of troops on the eve of battle; third, in placing so much of a force on the plain in front of his impregnable position.

It was known that Mr. Davis had visited Bragg on Missionary Ridge a short time before my reaching Chattanooga. It was reported and believed that he had come out to reconcile a serious difference between Bragg and Longstreet, and finding this difficult to do planned the campaign against Knoxville, to be conducted by the latter general. I had known both Bragg and Longstreet before the war, the latter very well. We had been three years at West Point together, and, after my graduation, for a time in the same regiment. Then we served together in the Mexican war. I had known Bragg in Mexico, and met him occasionally subsequently. I could well understand how there might be an irreconcilable difference between them.

Bragg was a remarkably intelligent and well-informed man, professionally and otherwise. He was also thoroughly upright. But he was possessed of an irascible temper, and was naturally disputatious. A man of the highest moral character and the most correct habits, yet in the old army he was in frequent trouble. As a subordinate he was always on the lookout to catch his commanding officer infringing upon his prerogatives; as a post

SIGNALING FROM THE MOUNTAIN.

commander he was equally vigilant to detect the slightest neglect, even of the most·trivial order.

I heard in the old army an anecdote characteristic of General Bragg. On one occasion, when stationed at a post of several companies, commanded by a field-officer, he was himself commanding one of the companies and at the same time acting post quartermaster and commissary. He was a first lieutenant at the time, but his captain was detached on other duty. As commander of the company he made a requisition upon the quartermaster — for something he wanted. As quartermaster he declined to fill the requisition, and indorsed on the back of it his reason for so doing. As company commander he responded to this, urging that his requisition called for nothing but what he was entitled to, and that it was the duty of the quartermaster to fill it. As quartermaster he still persisted that he was right. In this condition of affairs Bragg referred the whole matter to the commanding officer of the post. The latter, when he saw the nature of the matter referred, exclaimed: "My God, Mr. Bragg, you have quarreled with every officer in the army, and now you are quarreling with yourself."

Longstreet was an entirely different man. He was brave, honest, intelligent, a very capable soldier, subordinate to his superiors, just and kind to his subordinates, but jealous of his own rights, which he had the courage to maintain. He was never on the lookout to detect a slight, but saw one as soon as anybody when intentionally given.

It may be that Longstreet was not sent to Knoxville for the reason stated, but because Mr. Davis had an exalted opinion of his own military genius, and thought he saw a chance of "killing two birds with one stone." On several occasions during the war he came to the relief of the Union army by means of his *superior military genius*.

I speak advisedly when I say Mr. Davis prided himself on his military capacity. He says so himself virtually, in his answer to the notice of his nomination to the Confederate Presidency. Some of his generals have said so in their writings since the downfall of the Confederacy. Whatever the cause or whoever is to blame, grave mistakes were made at Chattanooga, which enabled us, with the undaunted courage of the troops engaged, to gain a great victory, under the most trying circumstances presented during the war, much more easily than could otherwise have been attained. If Chattanooga had been captured, East Tennessee would have followed without a struggle. It would have been a victory to have got the army away from Chattanooga safely. It was manifold greater to defeat, and nearly destroy, the besieging army.

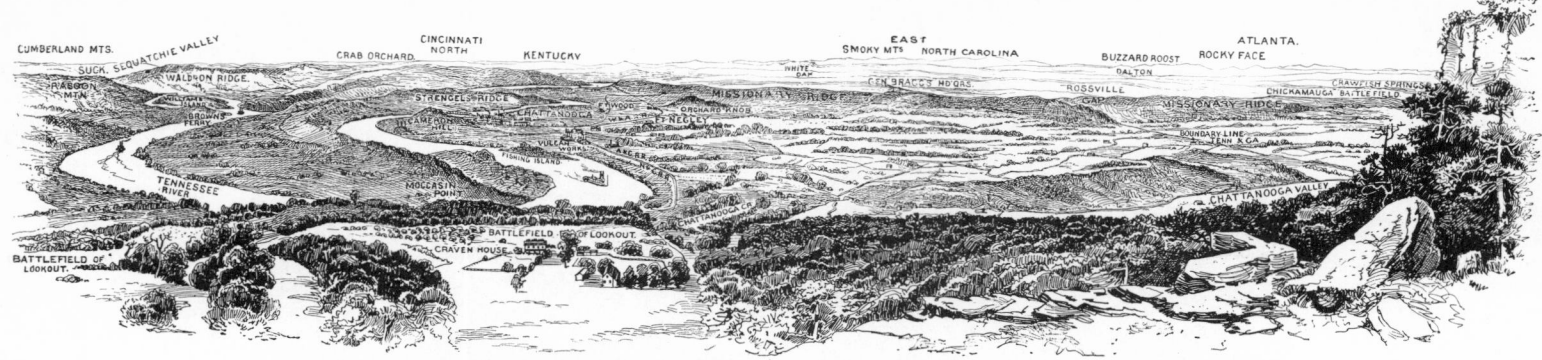

PANORAMIC VIEW OF THE CHATTANOOGA REGION FROM POINT LOOKOUT, ON LOOKOUT MOUNTAIN.
From a lithograph.

In this battle the Union army numbered in round figures about 60,000 men; we lost 752 killed, and 4713 wounded and 350 captured or missing. The rebel loss was much greater in the aggregate, as we captured, and sent North to be rationed there, over 6100 prisoners. Forty pieces of artillery, over seven thousand stand of small-arms, and many caissons, artillery wagons, and baggage wagons fell into our hands. The probabilities are that our loss in killed was the heavier, as we were the attacking party. The enemy reported his loss in killed at 361; but as he reported his missing at 4146, while we held over 6000 of them as prisoners, and there must have been hundreds, if not thousands, who deserted, but little reliance can be placed in this report. There was certainly great dissatisfaction with Bragg, on the part of the soldiers, for his harsh treatment of them, and a disposition to get away if they could. Then, too, Chattanooga following in the same half-year with Gettysburg in the East, and Vicksburg in the West, there was much the same feeling in the South at this time that there had been in the North the fall and winter before. If the same license had been allowed the people and the press in the South that was allowed in the North, Chattanooga would probably have been the last battle fought for the preservation of the Union.

Bragg's army now being in full retreat, the relief of Burnside's position at Knoxville was a matter for immediate consideration. Sherman marched with a portion of the Army of the Tennessee, and one corps of the Army of the Cumberland, toward Knoxville; but his approach caused Longstreet to abandon the siege long before these troops reached their destination. Knoxville was now relieved; the anxiety of the President was removed, and the loyal portion of the North rejoiced over the double victory: the raising of the siege of Knoxville and the victory at Chattanooga.

THE ASSAULT ON MISSIONARY RIDGE.

1. THE UNION SIDE, BY BREVET BRIGADIER-GENERAL JOSEPH S. FULLERTON, U. S. V.

. . . At twenty minutes before four the signal-guns were fired. Suddenly twenty thousand men rushed forward, moving in line of battle by brigades, with a double line of skirmishers in front, and closely followed by the reserves in mass. The big siege-guns in the Chattanooga forts roared above the light artillery and musketry in the valley. The enemy's rifle-pits were ablaze, and the whole ridge in our front had broken out like another Ætna. Not many minutes afterward our men were seen working through the felled trees and other obstructions. Though exposed to such a terrific fire, they neither fell back nor halted. By a bold and desperate push they broke through the works in several places and opened flank and reverse fires. The enemy was thrown into confusion, and took precipitate flight up the ridge. Many prisoners and a large number of small-arms were captured. The order of the commanding general had now been fully and most successfully carried out. But it did not go far enough to satisfy these brave men, who thought the time had come to finish the battle of Chickamauga. There was a halt of but a few minutes, to take breath and to re-form lines; then, with a sudden impulse, and without orders, all started up the ridge. Officers, catching their spirit, first followed, then led. There was no thought of supports or of protecting flanks, though the enemy's line could be seen, stretching on either side.

As soon as this movement was seen from Orchard Knob, Grant quickly turned to Thomas, who stood by his side, and I heard him say angrily:

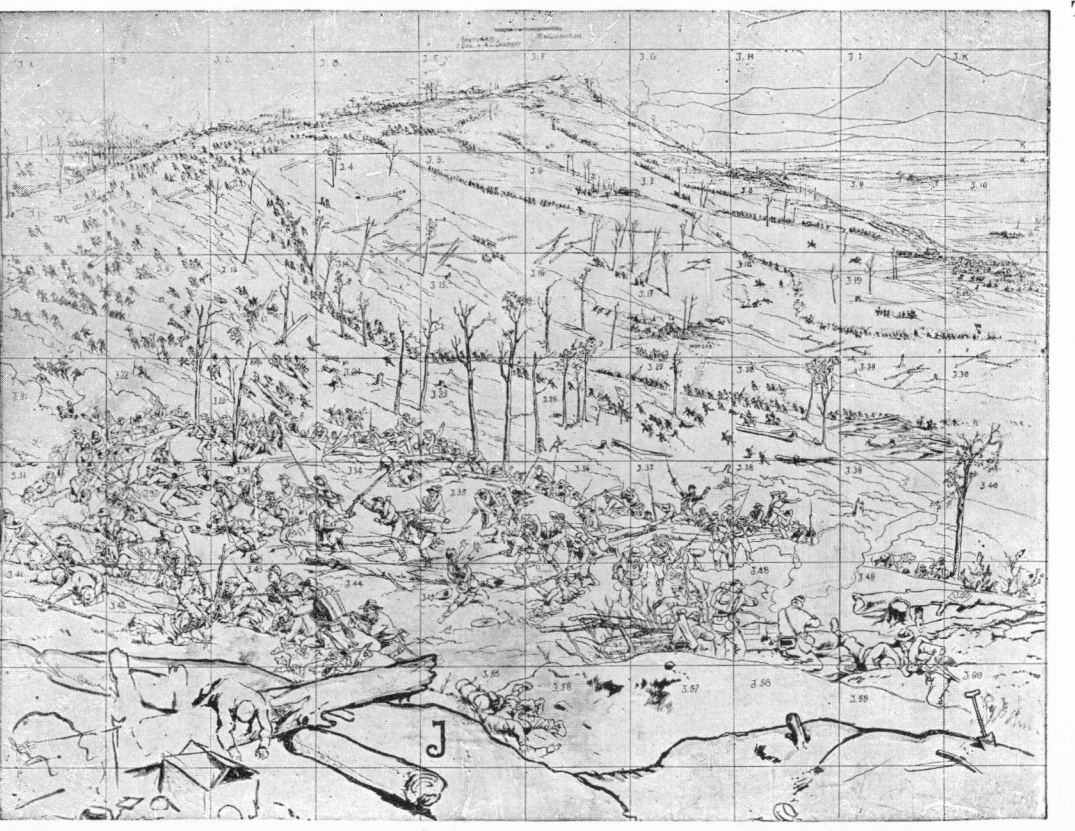

THE CHARGE UP MISSIONARY RIDGE BY BAIRD'S, WOOD'S, SHERIDAN'S, AND JOHNSON'S DIVISIONS.
From the rough sketch for one section of the Cyclorama of the Battle of Missionary Ridge.

"Thomas, who ordered those men up the ridge?" Thomas replied, in his usual slow, quiet manner: "I don't know; I did not." Then, addressing General Gordon Granger, he said, "Did you order them up, Granger?" "No," said Granger; "they started up without orders. When those fellows get started all hell can't stop them." General Grant said something to the effect that somebody would suffer if it did not turn out well, and then, turning, stoically watched the ridge. He gave no further orders.

As soon as Granger had replied to Thomas, he turned to me, his chief-of-staff, and said: "Ride at once to Wood, and then to Sheridan, and ask them if they ordered their men up the ridge, and tell them, if they can take it, to push ahead." As I was mounting, Granger added: "It is hot over there, and you may not get through. I shall send Captain Avery to Sheridan, and other officers after both of you." As fast as my horse could carry me, I rode first to General Wood, and delivered the message. "I did n't order them up," said Wood; "they started up on their own account, and they are going up, too! Tell Granger, if we are supported, we will take and hold the ridge!" As soon as I reached General Sheridan, Captain Avery got to General Sheridan, and delivered his message. "I did n't order them up," said Sheridan; "but we are going to take the ridge!" He then asked Avery for his flask and waved it at a group of Confederate officers, standing just in front of Bragg's headquarters, with the salutation, "Here's at you!" At once two guns — the "Lady Breckinridge" and the "Lady Buckner" — in front of Bragg's headquarters were fired at Sheridan and the group of officers about him. One shell struck so near as to throw dirt over Sheridan and Avery. "Ah!" said the general, "that is ungenerous; I shall take those guns for that!" Before Sheridan received the message taken by Captain Avery, he had sent a staff-officer to Granger, to inquire whether "the order given to take the rifle-pits meant the rifle-pits at the base, or those on the top of the ridge." Granger told this officer that "the order given was to take those at the base." Conceiving this to be an order to fall back, the officer, on his way to Sheridan, gave it to General Wagner, commanding the Second Brigade of the division, which was then nearly half-way up the ridge. Wagner ordered his brigade back to the rifle-pits at the base, but it only remained there till Sheridan, seeing the mistake, ordered it forward. It again advanced under a terrific fire.

The men, fighting and climbing up the steep hill, sought the roads, ravines, and less rugged parts. The ground was so broken that it was impossible to keep a regular line of battle. At times their movements were in shape like the flight of migratory birds — sometimes in line, sometimes in mass, mostly in V-shaped groups, with the points toward the enemy. At these points regimental flags were flying, sometimes drooping as the bearers were shot, but never reaching the ground, for other brave hands were there to seize them. Sixty flags were advancing up the hill. Bragg was hurrying large bodies of men from his right to the center. They could be seen hastening along the ridge. Cheatham's division was being withdrawn from

BAIRD'S DIVISION FIGHTING FOR THE CREST OF MISSIONARY RIDGE.
From the Cyclorama.

Sherman's front. Bragg and Hardee were at the center, urging their men to stand firm and drive back the advancing enemy, now so near the summit — indeed, so near that the guns, which could not be sufficiently depressed to reach them, became useless. Artillerymen were lighting the fuses of shells, and bowling them by hundreds down the hill. The critical moment arrived when the summit was just within reach. At six different points, and almost simultaneously, Sheridan's and Wood's divisions broke over the crest, — Sheridan's first, near Bragg's headquarters; and in a few minutes Sheridan was beside the guns that had been fired at him, and claiming them as captures of his division. Baird's division took the works on Wood's left almost immediately afterward; and then Johnson came up on Sheridan's right. The enemy's guns were turned upon those who still remained in the works, and soon all were in flight down the eastern slope. Baird got on the ridge just in time to change front and oppose a large body of the enemy moving down from Bragg's right to attack our left. After a sharp engagement, that lasted till dark, he drove the enemy back beyond a high point on the north, which he at once occupied.

The sun had not yet gone down, Missionary Ridge was ours, and Bragg's army was broken and in flight! . . .

Sheridan did not long stop to receive praise and congratulations. With two brigades he started down the Mission Mills road, and found, strongly

posted on a second hill, the enemy's rear. They made a stout resistance, but by a sudden flank movement he drove them from the heights and captured two guns and many prisoners. . . .

2. THE CONFEDERATE SIDE, BY GENERAL BRAXTON BRAGG, C. S. A.

About 11 A. M. the enemy's forces were being moved in heavy masses from Lookout and beyond to our front, while those in front extended to our right. They formed their lines with great deliberation just beyond the range of our guns and in plain view of our position. Though greatly outnumbered, such was the strength of our position that no doubt was entertained of our ability to hold it, and every disposition was made for that purpose. During this time they [the enemy] had made several attempts on our extreme right, and had been handsomely repulsed with very heavy loss by Major-General Cleburne's command, under the immediate directions of Lieutenant-General Hardee. . . . About 8:30 P. M. the immense force in the front of our left and center advanced in three lines, preceded by heavy skirmishers. Our batteries opened with fine effect, and much confusion was produced before they reached musket-range. In a short time the roar of musketry became very heavy, and it was soon apparent the enemy had been repulsed in my immediate front. While riding along the crest congratulating the troops, intelligence reached me that our line was

broken on my right, and the enemy had crowned the ridge. Assistance was promptly despatched to that point under Brigadier-General Bate, who had so successfully maintained the ground in my front, and I proceeded to the rear of the broken line to rally our retiring troops and return them to the crest to drive the enemy back. General Bate found the disaster so great that his small force could not repair it. About this time I learned that our extreme left had also given way, and that my position was almost surrounded. Bate was immediately directed to form a second line in the rear, where, by the efforts of my staff, a nucleus of stragglers had been formed upon which to rally. Lieutenant-General Hardee, leaving Major-General Cleburne in command on the extreme right, moved toward the left when he heard the heavy firing in that direction. He reached the right of Anderson's division just in time to find it had nearly all fallen back, commencing on its left, where the enemy had first crowned the ridge. By a prompt and judicious movement, he threw a portion of Cheatham's division directly across the ridge facing the enemy, who was now moving a strong force immediately on his left flank. By a decided stand here the enemy was entirely checked, and that portion of our force to the right remained intact. All to the left, however, except a portion of Bate's division, was entirely routed and in rapid flight. . . . A panic which I had never before witnessed seemed to have seized upon officers and men, and each seemed to be struggling for his personal safety, regardless of his duty or his character. In this distressing and alarming state of affairs General Bate was ordered to hold his position covering the road for the retreat of Breckinridge's command, and orders were immediately sent to Generals Hardee and Breckinridge to retire their forces upon the depot at Chickamauga. . . . No satisfactory excuse can possibly be given for the shameful conduct of our troops on the left in allowing their line to be penetrated. The position was one which ought to have been held by a line of skirmishers against any assaulting column, and wherever resistance was made the enemy fled in disorder after suffering heavy loss. Those who reached the ridge did so in a condition of exhaustion from the great physical exertion in climbing which rendered them powerless, and the slightest effort would have destroyed them. Having secured much of our artillery, they soon availed themselves of our panic, and turning our guns upon us enfiladed the lines, both right and left, rendering them entirely untenable. Had all parts of the line been maintained with equal gallantry and persistence, no enemy could ever have dislodged us, and but one possible reason presents itself to my mind in explanation of this bad conduct in veteran troops who never before failed in any duty assigned them, however difficult and hazardous: They had for two days confronted the enemy, marshaling his immense forces in plain view, and exhibiting to their sight such a superiority in numbers as may have intimidated weak-minded and untried soldiers. But our veterans had so often encountered similar hosts when the strength of position was against us, and with perfect success, that not a doubt crossed my mind.

GENERAL BURNSIDE AT THE CONFEDERATE COTTON BATTERY ON THE WHARF,
NEW BERNE.
From a war-time sketch.

FORTS ELLIS AND LANE IN THE DISTANCE.

BOMBARDMENT OF THE CONFEDERATE FORT THOMPSON DURING THE BATTLE OF NEW BERNE.
From a war-time sketch.

OPERATIONS ON THE ATLANTIC COAST.

NARRATIVE OF EVENTS.

The Confederate forts, Hatteras and Clark, at Hatteras Inlet, the main approach to Pamlico Sound, were reduced by a military and naval expedition led by General Benjamin F. Butler and Commodore Silas H. Stringham in August, 1861.

The fine harbor of Port Royal, South Carolina, was secured in November of the same year by a combined expedition under Commodore Samuel F. Du Pont and General Thomas W. Sherman. Forts Walker and Beauregard, at the entrance to the harbor, were reduced after five hours' bombardment.

The capture of Port Royal was followed by the abandonment by the Confederates of all the coast towns South of Charleston, except Savannah, which was defended by Fort Pulaski at the mouth of the river. In April, 1862, that stronghold was reduced by a remarkable bombardment from Union batteries erected on Tybee Island.

A strong blockade was maintained along the coast, but it was neutralized again and again by Confederate supply steamers, and also by cruisers, notably in front of Charleston and Wilmington. At Charleston, in the summer of 1862, the blockading fleet was effectually detroyed by Confederate rams.

The Confederates made three attempts to recapture New Berne, North Carolina, after it fell into Union possession, as narrated by General Burnside, below. All were failures. In the last, May 5, 1864, the ram *Albemarle* attempted to coöperate, but while passing through Albemarle Sound she was met and defeated by a fleet under Captain Melancton Smith.

Fort Fisher, a strong work at the mouth of Cape Fear River guarding Wilmington, held out until January, 1865 (see article by Captain Selfridge to follow), and, on the 22d of February, Wilmington fell into the hands of General John M. Schofield, with an army transferred from Tennessee, by way of Washington.

The following paper was read by General Burnside before the Soldiers' and Sailors' Historical Society of Rhode Island, July 7th, 1880, and is included here by permission of the Society, the text being somewhat abridged to conform to the plan of this work.

THE BURNSIDE EXPEDITION TO NORTH CAROLINA.

BY AMBROSE E. BURNSIDE, MAJOR-GENERAL, U. S. A.

Commander of the Forces in the North Carolina Campaign.

SOON after the 1st Rhode Island regiment was mustered out of service, I was appointed by President Lincoln to the office of brigadier-general. My commission was given to me August 6th, 1861, and I was ordered to report to General McClellan, who placed me in charge of the division and brigades which were formed of the new troops as they arrived in Washington. My duty was to look after the drill and discipline of these brigades, with a view to giving the men the efficiency necessary for assignment to the older divisions of the army, which were then organizing in Washington under the name of the Army of the Potomac. The duty was interesting in some respects, but was in the main somewhat tame, so that I very naturally desired more active duty.

One evening in the following October, General

GENERAL BURNSIDE'S HEADQUARTERS, ROANOKE ISLAND.
From a war-time sketch.

McClellan and I were chatting together over the affairs of the war, when I mentioned to him a plan for the formation of a coast division to which I had given some thought. After giving him a somewhat detailed account of the plan, he asked me to put it in writing as soon as possible, which was done. The next day it was presented to him, and it met his approval. He laid it before the Secretary of War, by whom it was also approved. The general details of the plan were briefly as follows: To organize a division of from 12,000 to 15,000 men, mainly from States bordering on the Northern sea-coast, many of whom would be familiar with the coasting trade, and among whom would be found a goodly number of mechanics; and to fit out a fleet of light-draught steamers, sailing vessels, and barges, large enough to transport the division, its armament and supplies, so that it could be rapidly thrown from point to point on the coast with a view to establishing lodgments on the Southern coast, landing troops, and penetrating into the interior, thereby threatening the lines of transportation in the rear of the main army then concentrating in Virginia, and holding possession of the inland waters on the Atlantic coast.

After the approval of the plan, I was ordered to New York to fit out the fleet; and on the 23d of October orders were issued establishing my headquarters for the concentration of the troops of the division at Annapolis. Troops arrived from time to time at Annapolis, and all went well in the camp, which was established on beautiful grounds just outside the town. . . .

I had organized the division into three brigades, which were placed in command of General J. G. Foster, General Jesse L. Reno, and General John G. Parke, three of my most trusted friends. We

of more than eighty. The harbor probably never presented a finer appearance than on that night. All the vessels were illuminated, and the air was filled with the strains of martial music and the voices of brave men. Not a man in the fleet knew his destination, except myself, the brigade commanders, and two or three staff-officers, yet there was no complaint or inquisitiveness, but all seemed ready for whatever duty was before them.

Sealed orders were given to the commanders of each vessel, to be opened at sea. Much discouragement was expressed by nautical men and by men high in military authority as to the success of the expedition. The President and General McClellan were both approached, and the President was frequently warned that the vessels were unfit for sea, and that the expedition would be a total failure. Great anxiety was manifested to know its destination, but the secret had been well kept at Washington and at our headquarters. As Mr. Lincoln afterward told me, one public man was very importunate, and, in fact, almost demanded that the President should tell him where we were going. Finally, the President said to him, "Now, I will tell you in great confidence where they are going, if you will promise not to speak of it to any one." The promise was given, and Mr. Lincoln said, "Well, now, my friend, the expedition is going to sea!" The inquirer left him without receiving

REAR-ADMIRAL L. M. GOLDSBOROUGH, U. S. N.
Flag-officer of the fleet in the Burnside Expedition.

had been cadets together at West Point, and I had always entertained for them the greatest confidence and esteem. In all future operations in the expedition, our close friendly relations were maintained, and I was never disappointed in any reliance which I had placed on their gallantry, skill, and integrity. I had been notified by General McClellan that our destination would be Hatteras Inlet, with a view to operations in the inland waters of North Carolina.

On the 5th of January the troops began to embark. During that day there were some delays, which resulted from inexperience in the manœuvering of the vessels and in the new work to which they were unaccustomed. On that night, snow to the depth of from two to three inches fell, which gave to the camp and surrounding country, on the morning of the 6th, a most picturesque appearance. Regiment after regiment struck their tents and marched to the point of embarkation, with bands playing, colors flying, and the men cheering and singing from lightness of heart. As they passed through the quaint old town of Annapolis, the lines of troops, with their dark uniforms and glittering bayonets, contrasted markedly with the snow-clad fields and trees. . . .'.

On the morning of the 9th, each vessel set sail, under orders to rendezvous at Fort Monroe, and there, by the night of the 10th, all had joined the *Supply* and other vessels, making altogether a fleet

any
further
information. In this
jocular manner
Mr. Lincoln was in
the habit of throwing off the cares of state; and it often occurs to me that but for that habit he would have been broken down under the great weight of public responsibility which rested upon him from the first day of the war to the termination of his noble life. In my opinion, no man has ever lived who could have gone through that struggle as he did. At no period of his life, I believe, was his heart ever stirred with a feeling of enmity or resentment against any one. He was actuated by the simple desire and determination to maintain the authority of the Government at all hazards.

On the night of the 11th the signal for sailing

was given, and very soon the fleet was under way. My headquarters were on board a large steamer, the *George Peabody*; but, with two or three of my staff-officers, I took for my headquarters during the voyage a small propeller called the *Picket*, in reality the smallest vessel in the fleet. I was moved to do this because of the great criticism which had been made as to the unseaworthiness of the vessels of the fleet, and because of a desire to show my faith in their adaptability to the service. Their weaknesses were known to me, but they were the best that could be procured, and it was necessary that the service should be performed even at the risk of losing life by shipwreck. The weather was threatening, but I did not foresee the storm by which we were afterward overtaken. At that time we had no weather signal reports; but, in any event, the sailing would not have been delayed, because the orders to proceed to our work were imperative. It was, of course, learned by all, after reaching the sea, that the destination of the fleet was Hatteras Inlet. . . .

From time to time we made efforts to cross the fleet from the inlet into Pamlico Sound, over what was called the swash, which separated it from the inlet. We had been led to believe that there were eight feet of water upon the swash, but when we arrived we discovered to our sorrow that there were but six feet, and as most of our vessels, as well as the vessels of the naval fleet which we found at Hatteras Inlet on our arrival, drew more water than that, it was necessary to deepen the channel by some process. The current upon the swash was very swift, a circumstance which proved to be much in our favor. Large vessels were sent ahead, under full steam, on the bar when the tide was running out, and then anchors were carried out by boats in advance, so as to hold the vessels in position. The swift current would wash the sand from under them and allow them to float, after which they were driven farther on by steam and anchored again, when the sand would again wash out from under them. This process was continued for days, until a broad channel of over eight feet was made, deep enough to allow the passage of the fleet into the sound. On the 26th, one of our largest steamers got safely over the swash and anchored in the sound, where some of the gun-boats had preceded them. By the 4th of February the entire fleet had anchored and had passed into the sound, and orders

were given for the advance on Roanoke Island. Detailed instructions were given for the landing of the troops and the mode of attack.

At an early hour on the morning of the 5th the start was made. The naval vessels, under Commodore Goldsborough, were in advance and on the flanks. The sailing vessels containing troops were taken in tow by the steamers. There were in all sixty-five vessels. The fleet presented an imposing appearance as it started up the sound. The day was most beautiful, and the sail was enjoyed beyond meas-

ure
by the
soldiers,
who had long
been so penned
up in the desolate
inlet. At sundown, signal was given to come to anchor within ten miles of Roanoke Island. At 8 o'clock the next morning the signal to weigh anchor was given, but our progress was very much retarded by a gale that sprung up; so we anchored, but very little in advance of our position of the night before. During that night all lights were carefully concealed. The naval vessels were well out in ad-

RUSH C. HAWKINS,
BREVET BRIGADIER-GENERAL, U. S. V.

vance to protect the transports from the inroads of the rebel gun-boats.

On the morning of the 7th the gun-boats passed inside the narrow passage known as Roanoke Sound, and were soon abreast of the lower part of Roanoke Island. Soon after the naval fleet had passed through, the transport fleet began its passage. The rebel gun-boats were seen close inshore under the batteries of the island. At half-past 10 o'clock a signal gun was fired from one of the forts, announcing our approach. At half-past 11, one of the naval vessels opened fire, which was replied to by the rebels. Signals were given by the commodore of the fleet to begin the action. By noon the firing became rapid, and soon after the engagement became general. The rebels had driven a line of piles across the main channel to obstruct the progress of our vessels, leaving a narrow space for themselves to retreat through; and as our naval vessels pressed them, they availed themselves of this means of safety. Our guns soon got the range of their batteries, and, by most extraordinary skill and rapidity of firing, almost silenced them. Just before noon, I ordered a reconnoissance by a small boat, with the view of ascertaining a point of landing. A young negro, who had escaped from the island on our arrival at Hatteras Inlet, had given me most valuable information as to the nature of the shore of the island, from which I had determined that our point of landing should be at Ashby's Harbor, which was nearly midway up the shore.

At 1 o'clock, the quarters of the garrison in one of the forts were fired by one of our shells. The rebel gun-boats retired up the sound, but still continued a brisk fire as they were followed by our vessels. Orders were given for the troops to land at 3 o'clock. The ground in the rear of Ashby's Harbor was cleared by shells from the naval vessels, and our large surf-boats were lowered, rapidly filled with troops, and towed up in long lines by light-draught vessels until they came near to the shore of the harbor, when each of the surf-boats was cut loose and steered for the shore. There was no obstruction to their landing. In less than an hour 4000 troops were ashore, and before midnight the entire force was landed, with the exception of one regiment, which was landed on the morning of the 8th. The advance of our troops was ordered on this morning, General Foster being in the advance and center, General Reno on the left, and General Parke on the right. Just above Ashby's Harbor the island from shore to shore was marshy, swampy ground. A causeway had been built up the center of the island, and on this, about one mile and a half from the harbor, was a fort, which was flanked by what seemed to

L. O'B. BRANCH,
BRIGADIER-GEN., C. S. A.
Commanding the Confederate forces at New Berne; killed at Antietam, Sept. 17, 1862. (From a photograph.)

UNION ASSAULT UPON THE FORT AT ROANOKE ISLAND.
Described in text below. (From a war-time sketch.)

be impassable ground; but it did not prove to be so to our troops. General Foster pressed the rebels in front, General Reno passed around the left with his brigade, often waist-deep in the marsh, through almost impenetrable thickets, until he gained the right flank of the enemy's line. General Parke performed equally good service on the right, and after advantageous positions had been obtained, the work was carried by a simultaneous assault, and from that time there was no hindrance to the march of our troops to the head of the island and to the forts on the shore, where the entire garrison was captured. The naval fleet pursued the rebel gun-boats, nearly all of which, however, were destroyed by their crews to prevent capture. The results of this important victory were great, particularly in inspiring the confidence of the country in the efficiency of its armies in the field.

The troops enjoyed their rest at Roanoke Island, but were not allowed to remain idle long. On the 26th of February, orders were given to make arrangements to embark for New Berne, and within four days they were all on board. On the 12th of March, the entire command was anchored off the mouth of Slocum's Creek, and about fourteen miles from New Berne. The approach to the city had been obstructed by piles and sunken vessels. About four miles from New Berne a large fort on the shore had been built, with a heavy armament, and a line

of earthworks extended from the fort inland a distance of some two miles, where it ended in almost impassable ground.

On the night of the 12th orders were given for landing, and on the morning of the 13th the troops were put ashore, in very much the same way that they had been at Roanoke. By 1 o'clock the debarkation was finished, and the troops were put in line of march. About this time the rain began to fall, and the road became almost impassable. No ammunition could be carried except what the men themselves could carry. No artillery could be taken except the small howitzers, which were hauled by the troops with drag-ropes. This was one of the most disagreeable and difficult marches that I witnessed during the war. We came in contact with the enemy's pickets just before dark, when it was decided to delay the attack until morning. That night a most dreary bivouac followed. Early the next morning, notwithstanding the fog, the disposition for the attack was made. General Foster was ordered to engage the enemy on the right, General Reno to pass around on the extreme left, and General Parke to occupy the center. We were much nearer to the enemy than we expected, and were soon in contact with them. General Foster rapidly closed with them, and met with severe resistance. He asked for reinforcements, but was told that every man had been ordered into action, and that there were no reserves. The contest was

sharp, but brief. The 4th Rhode Island broke the enemy's line near where it crossed the railroad, after which the enemy wavered, and a general advance of our whole line placed us in possession of the works. The enemy fled to New Berne, burning the bridge behind them. Our troops rapidly pursued, but the fact that they had to cross the river in boats prevented them from capturing the main body of the enemy. As it was, large numbers of prisoners and munitions fell into our hands. In the mean time the naval vessels had worked their way up to the city and aided in the transportation of the troops across, and New Berne was occupied on the afternoon of the 14th.

It still remained for us to reduce Fort Macon, Beaufort. To this work General Parke's brigade was ordered. The country between New Berne and Beaufort was immediately occupied, and a passage by hand-car was made between the two places, all the rolling stock having been run off the road. By the morning of the 11th of April regular siege operations had been begun by General Parke and were pressed rapidly forward, and by the 26th of April the garrison at Beaufort had been forced to surrender.

Thus another victory was to be inscribed upon our banner. The Rhode Island troops bore a most honorable part in this conflict. After that, several small expeditions were sent into the interior of the country, all of which were successful.

Much to my sorrow, on the 3d of the following July I was ordered to go to the peninsula to consult with General McClellan, and after that my duties as commanding officer in North Carolina ended; but a large proportion of the troops of the expedition served under me during the remainder of the war, as members of the gallant Ninth Corps.

The Burnside expedition has passed into history; its record we can be proud of. No body of troops ever had more difficulties to overcome in the same space of time. Its perils were both by land and water. Defeat never befell it. No gun was lost by it. Its experience was a succession of honorable victories.

VICE-ADMIRAL S. C. ROWAN, U. S. N.
Commander of the naval division at Roanoke Island.

"NEW IRONSIDES."　　　　　"KEOKUK."

BOMBARDMENT OF FORT SUMTER AND ADJACENT FORTS BY THE UNION FLEET, APRIL 7, 1863.

BEFORE CHARLESTON IN 1863.

BY MAJOR-GENERAL QUINCY A. GILLMORE, U. S. V.
Commanding the Department of the South.

NOTE.—As the city of Charleston was one of the two chief points through which munitions of war and other supplies from Europe were sent into the Confederacy, the United States Government was anxious to capture it. The Confederates under Beauregard strengthened and equipped Forts Sumter and Moultrie, and other defensive works in the harbor, constructed batteries, laid torpedoes in navigable streams near the city of Charleston, and kept a large force of men in the various garrisons, with reinforcements not far away.

On the 7th of April, 1863, Admiral Du Pont, with a fleet of monitors, unsuccessfully attacked Fort Sumter. Later the Union land forces, under General Quincy A. Gillmore, undertook the capture of Morris Island, held by the Confederates with infantry and artillery. From the position thus secured, and in coöperation with the fleet, Fort Sumter could then be successfully assailed, leaving a passage for the ships to enter the harbor and reach the city. Morris Island, with its powerful "Battery Wagner," was captured, but Sumter, though only a ruin, remained in the hands of the Confederates throughout the war. Charleston was not evacuated until February 17, 1865, and then only to furnish additional men to the army opposing Sherman's march.

The following is General Gillmore's account of the attack on Morris Island, and the storming of Battery Wagner.

. . . Between the middle of June and the 6th of July preparations for the descent upon Morris Island went quietly forward. It was deemed necessary that this attack should be a surprise in order to insure success. On the extreme northern end of Folly Island forty-seven field and siege guns and mortars were quietly placed in position, screened by thick undergrowth from the view of the enemy on the opposite side of Light-house inlet. . . .

On the evening of July 9th a small brigade was silently embarked in row-boats in Folly River, behind Folly Island. It was commanded by Brigadier-General George C. Strong, who had received orders to carry the south end of Morris Island by storm. By break of day the leading boats had reached Light-house inlet, where the column was halted under cover of marsh-grass to await orders. The point where the landing was to be made was still nearly a mile distant, and this stretch of river had to be passed in full view under fire. All our Folly Island batteries opened before sunrise, and soon after this four iron-clad monitors, led by Rear-Admiral Dahlgren, steamed up abreast of Morris Island and took part in the action. After the cannonade had lasted nearly two hours General Strong was signaled to push forward and make the attack. This was promptly and gallantly done under a hot fire. The men did not hesitate or waver for a moment. All the enemy's batteries on the south end of the island, containing eleven pieces of artillery, were captured in succession, and by 9 o'clock we occupied three-fourths of the island, with our skirmishers within musket range of Battery Wagner. Thus was the first step in the plan of joint operation successfully taken. The intense heat, which prostrated many of the men, forced a suspension of operations for the day.

Two unsuccessful attempts were made to carry Battery Wagner by assault. In the first, which took place at daybreak on the morning of July 11th, the parapet of the work was reached, but the supports recoiled under the heavy fire of grape and canister that met them, and the advantage gained could not be held. This repulse demonstrated the remarkable strength of the work and the necessity of establishing counter-batteries against it, which, with the coöperation of the fleet, might dismount the principal guns and either drive the enemy from it or open the way to a successful assault. After the first assault Battery Wagner was inclosed; it reached entirely across the island from water to water; it mounted some heavy guns for channel defense, and several siege-guns that swept the narrow beach over which we would have to approach from the south; and a large bomb-proof shelter afforded the garrison absolute protection when the fire became so hot that they could not stand to their guns or man the parapet. To us the place presented the appearance of a succession of low, irregular sand-hills like the rest of the island. Battery Gregg, on the north end of the island at Cumming's Point, was known to be armed with guns bearing on the channel. Of one important topographical change we were entirely ignorant. We did not know that the island at its narrowest point, between us and Battery Wagner, and quite near to the latter, had been worn away by the encroachments of the sea to about one-third the width shown on our lastest charts, and so much reduced in height that during spring-tides or heavy weather the waves swept entirely over it to the marsh in rear. Against us the fort presented an armed front about 800 feet in length, reaching entirely across the island, while our advance must be made over a strip of low shifting sand only about 80 feet wide, and two feet above the range of ordinary tides.

Between the 16th and 18th of July, as preliminary to a second attempt to get possession of Battery Wagner by assault, 41 pieces of artillery, comprising light rifles and siege-mortars, were put in position on an oblique line across the island at distances from the fort ranging from 1300 to 1900 yards. The rifles were intended principally to dismount the enemy's guns. Early in the afternoon of the 18th all these batteries opened fire, and the navy closed in on the fort and took an active and efficient part in the engagement. In a short time the work became absolutely silent on the faces looking toward us, and practically so on the sea front, from which at the beginning of the action a severe fire had been delivered against the fleet.

MAJOR-GENERAL QUINCY A. GILLMORE, U. S. A.
From a photograph.

The work was silenced for the time at least, but whether this was due to the injury inflicted on its armament, or to the inability of the men to stand to their pieces, or to these two causes combined, we had no means of knowing.

An assault was ordered. The time of evening twilight was selected for the storming party to advance, in order that it might not be distinctly seen from the James Island batteries on our extreme left, and from Fort Sumter and Sullivan's Island in our distant front. Brigadier-General Truman Seymour organized and commanded the assaulting column, composed of Brigadier-General G. C. Strong's brigade supported by the brigade of Colonel Haldimand S. Putnam. As the column left the line of our batteries and began its advance along the narrow strip of beach, a rapid fire was opened upon it from Fort Sumter and from the works on James Island and on Sullivan's Island. When it reached a point so near to Battery Wagner that the fire from our own guns and those of the navy had to be suspended from fear of destroying our own men, a compact and deadly sheet of musketry fire was instantly poured upon the advancing column by the garrison, which had suddenly issued forth from the security of the bomb-proof shelter. Although the troops went gallantly forward and gained the southeast bastion of the work and held it for more than two hours, the advantages which local knowledge and the deepening darkness gave the enemy forced a withdrawal. The repulse was complete, and our loss severe, especially in officers of rank. The gallant Strong, who had been the first man to land on Morris Island a few days before, actually leading his entire command in

THE "SWAMP ANGEL" IN POSITION.
From a sketch made at the time.

NOTE.—The 8-inch 200-pounder Parrott rifle gun, called the "Swamp Angel" by the soldiers, was used in bombarding the city of Charleston. The English journal, "Engineering," speaks of the construction of the battery upon which this gun was mounted as one of the most important engineering works done by either army. The gun exploded in the thirty-sixth discharge. It is now mounted as a monument in Trenton, New Jersey.

THE NIGHT ASSAULT ON BATTERY WAGNER, JULY 18, 1863.

the left and rear of the first parallel. Those in the second parallel were perilously near to Battery Wagner, the most advanced piece being only 820 yards distant from the guns of that work. One of the batteries was efficiently commanded by Commander Foxhall A. Parker, U. S. N. On the night of August 9th the position selected for the third parallel was reached by the flying sap, 330 yards in advance of the right of the second parallel. It was deemed inexpedient to push the approaches beyond this point until after the breeching batteries should open on Fort Sumter.

From this time forward the fire from the enemy's guns in our front and on our extreme left was severe and almost uninterrupted. . . . Finally some of the breeching batteries opened fire on the 17th of August, and by the 19th all were in successful operation. The result was soon clearly foreshadowed. Nothing, indeed, but the destruction of our guns, either by the enemy's shot or through their own inherent weakness, would long delay it. About 450 projectiles struck the fort daily, every one of which inflicted an incurable wound. Large masses of the brick walls and parapets were rapidly loosened and thrown down. The bulk of our fire was directed against the gorge and southeast face, which presented themselves diagonally to us. They were soon pierced through and through, and cut down on top to the casemate arches. The shot that went over them took the north and northwest faces in reverse.

The seven days' service of the breeching batteries, ending August 23d, left Fort Sumter in the condition of a mere infantry outpost, without the power to fire a gun heavier than a musket, alike incapable of annoying our approaches to Battery Wagner, or of inflicting injury upon the fleet. In this condition it remained for about six weeks. A desultory fire was kept up to prevent repairs, and on the 30th of August another severe cannonade was opened and continued for two days at the request of the admiral commanding, who contemplated entering the inner harbor on the 31st.

Some time before this the enemy began to remove the armament of Fort Sumter by night, and many of its guns were soon mounted in other parts of the harbor.

During the progress of the operations thus briefly outlined, the navy had most cordially coöperated whenever and wherever their aid could best be rendered. The service of the monitors was notably efficient in subduing the fire of Battery Wagner, which at times not only seriously retarded the labors of the sappers, but threatened the destruction of some of the most advanced of the breeching guns. While the breaching of Fort Sumter was still in progress, active work was resumed on the approaches to Battery Wagner by pushing the full sap from the left of the third parallel. Meanwhile, the spring-tides had come with easterly winds, flooding the trenches to the depth of two feet and washing down the parapets. The progress of the sap was hotly contested with both artillery and sharp-shooters. The latter had taken possession of a ridge about 240 yards in advance of the main work, where they had placed themselves under such cover that they could not be dislodged by our fire or the flank fire of the fleet, while that from their own guns in rear passed harmlessly over their heads. An attempt to capture this ridge having failed, a fourth parallel was established on the night of August 21st, about five hundred yards in advance of the third. From this point the ridge was carried [by the 24th Massachusetts] at the point of the bayonet on the 26th, under the direction of Brigadier-General Terry, and the fifth parallel was established thereon. The resistance to our advance now assumed a most obstinate and determined character, being evidently under skilful and intelligent direction, while the firing from the James Island batteries became more steady and accurate. . . .

In this emergency it was determined, as well to hasten the final result as to revive the flagging spirits of the men, to carry on simultaneously against Battery Wagner two distinct kinds of attack: First, to silence the work by an overpowering bombardment with siege and Coehorn mortars, so that our sappers would have only the James Island batteries to annoy them; and, second, to breach the bomb-proof shelter with our heavy rifles, and thus force a surrender. During the daytime the *New Ironsides*, Captain S. C. Rowan, was to coöperate with her eight-gun broadsides. These operations were actively begun at break of day on the 5th of September. . . .

The garrison soon sought safety in the bomb-proof shelter, and the fort showed but little sign of life. . . . Early on the night of September 6th our sap was pushed forward entirely beyond the south front of the work, and between the sea front and the water, crowning the crest of the counterscarp at the north or farthest end of that front, and completely masking all the guns of the work. An order was issued to carry the place the next morning by assault on the north front at the time of low tide, when the width of beach would be the greatest. . . . During the night the fort was evacuated with such celerity that only two boat-loads of men were captured.

These operations left the whole of Morris Island in our possession, and Fort Sumter in ruins and destitute of guns. A powerful armament was mounted on the north end of the island, to coöperate with the monitors when they should move in, and to prevent the remounting of guns on Fort Sumter. Early on the morning following the capture of Battery Wagner, the admiral, under a flag of truce, demanded the surrender of Fort Sumter. It was refused.

On the night of the 8th a naval assault was made on the work about midnight, and repulsed with considerable loss. . . .

THE BOAT ATTACK ON FORT SUMTER, NIGHT OF SEPT. 8, 1863.

that descent and in the daring assault that followed, was fatally wounded. . . . Colonel John S. Chatfield was mortally wounded; Colonel Haldimand S. Putnam and Colonel Robert G. Shaw were killed; and Brigadier-General Truman Seymour and several regimental commanders were wounded. . . .

To meet the contingency brought on by the failure it was determined to change slightly the prearranged order of operations by attempting the demolition of Fort Sumter with our heavy rifles, at a distance of two miles and upward, by firing over Battery Wagner and its garrison from ground already in our possession. . . .

The first parallel was established, July 19th, on the line occupied the day before by our batteries against Battery Wagner, and the second parallel on the night of the 23d by the flying sap, about six hundred yards in advance of the first. Eleven of the breeching guns against Fort Sumter were located in these two parallels, and the other seven to

CAPTAIN J. W. COOKE, C. S. N.
Commander of the "Albemarle."

THE FIRST BATTLE OF THE CONFEDERATE RAM "ALBEMARLE."

BY HER BUILDER, GILBERT ELLIOTT.
Volunteer aide to the commander of the ram during the engagement described.

IN the spring of 1864 it was decided at Confederate headquarters that an attempt should be made to recapture Plymouth. General Hoke was placed in command of the land forces, and Captain J. W. Cooke received orders to coöperate with the *Albemarle*, an ironclad then nearly finished. Accordingly Hoke's division proceeded to the vicinity of Plymouth and surrounded the town from the river above to the river below, and preparation was made to storm the forts and breastworks as soon as the *Albemarle* could clear the river front of the Federal war-vessels protecting the place with their guns.

On the morning of April 18th, 1864, the *Albemarle* left the town of Hamilton and proceeded down the river toward Plymouth, going stern foremost, with chains dragging from the bow, the rapidity of the current making it impracticable to steer with her head down-stream. She came to anchor about three miles above Plymouth, and a mile or so above the battery on the bluff at Warren's Neck, near Thoroughfare Gap, where torpedoes, sunken vessels, piles, and other obstructions had been placed. An exploring expedition was sent out, under command of one of the lieutenants, which returned in about two hours, with the report that it was considered impossible to pass the obstructions. Thereupon the fires were banked, and the officers and crew not on duty retired to rest.

Having accompanied Captain Cooke as a volunteer aide, and feeling intensely dissatisfied with the apparent intention of lying at anchor all that night, and believing that it was "then or never" with the ram if she was to accomplish anything, and that it would be foolhardy to attempt the passage of the obstructions and batteries in the daytime, I requested permission to make a personal investigation. Captain Cooke cordially assenting,

THE SINKING OF THE "SOUTHFIELD," APRIL 18, 1864.

and Pilot John Luck and two of the few experienced seamen on board volunteering their services, we set forth in a small lifeboat, taking with us a long pole, and arriving at the obstructions proceeded to take soundings. To our great joy it was ascertained that there was ten feet of water over and above the obstructions. This was due to the remarkable freshet then prevailing; the proverbial "oldest inhabitant" said, afterward, that such high water had never before been seen in Roanoke River. Pushing on down the stream to Plymouth, and taking advantage of the shadow of the trees on the north side of the river, opposite the town, we watched the Federal transports taking on board the women and children who were being sent away for safety, on account of the approaching bombardment. With muffled oars, and almost afraid to breathe, we made our way back up the river, hugging the northern bank, and reached the ram about 1 o'clock, reporting to Captain Cooke that it was practicable to pass the obstructions provided the boat was kept in the middle of the stream. Captain Cooke instantly aroused his men, gave the order to get up steam, slipped the cables in his impatience to be off, and started down the river. The obstructions were soon reached and safely passed, under a fire from the fort at Warren's Neck which was not returned. Protected by the ironclad shield, to those on board the noise made by the shot and shell as they struck the boat sounded no louder than pebbles thrown against an empty barrel. At Boyle's Mill, lower down, there was another fort upon which was mounted a very heavy gun. This was also safely passed, and we then discovered two steamers coming up the river. They proved to be the *Miami* and the *Southfield*.

The two ships were lashed together with long spars, and with chains festooned between them. The plan of Captain Flusser, who commanded, was to run his vessels so as to get the *Albemarle* be-

tween the two, which would have placed the ram at a great disadvantage, if not altogether at his mercy; but Captain Cooke ran the ram close to the southern shore, and then suddenly turning toward the middle of the stream, and going with the current, the throttles, in obedience to his bell, being wide open, he dashed the prow of the *Albemarle* into the side of the *Southfield*, making an opening large enough to carry her to the bottom in much less time than it takes to tell the story. Part of her crew went down with her.

The chain-plates on the forward deck of the *Albemarle* became entangled in the frame of the sinking vessel, and her bow was carried down to such a depth that water poured into her port-holes in great volume, and she would soon have shared the fate of the *Southfield*, had not the latter vessel reached the bottom, and then, turning over on her side, released the ram, thus allowing her to come up on an even keel. The *Miami*, right alongside, had opened fire with her heavy guns, and so close were the vessels that a shell with a ten-second fuse, fired by Captain Flusser, after striking the *Albemarle* rebounded and exploded, killing the gallant man who pulled the lanyard, tearing him almost to pieces. Notwithstanding the death of Flusser, an attempt was made to board the ram, which was heroically resisted by as many of the crew as could be crowded on the top deck, who were supplied with loaded muskets passed up by their comrades below. The *Miami*, a very fast side-wheeler, succeeded in eluding the *Albemarle* without receiving a blow from her ram, and retired below Plymouth, into Albemarle Sound.

Captain Cooke having successfully carried out his part of the programme, General Hoke attacked the fortifications the next morning and carried them. . . . During the attack the *Albemarle* held the river front, and all day long poured shot and shell into the resisting forts with her two guns.

COMMANDER C. W. FLUSSER, U. S. N.
In command of the "Miami." (Killed.)

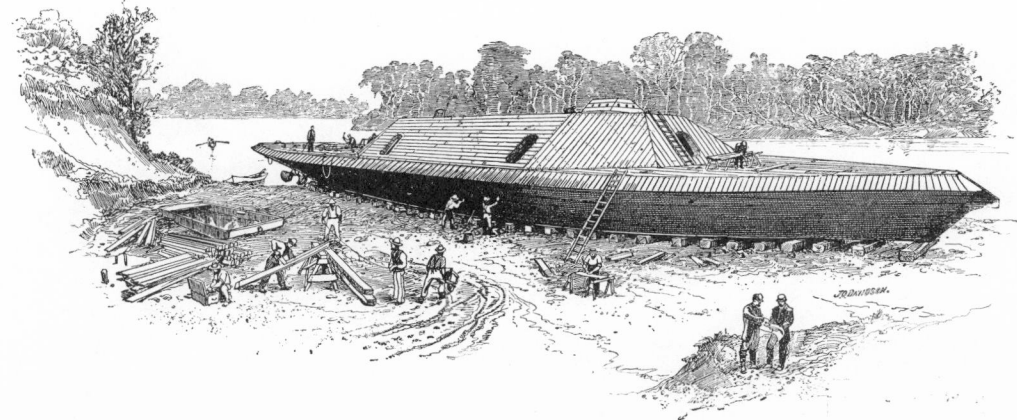

BUILDING THE "ALBEMARLE" AT EDWARDS'S FERRY.

THE DESTRUCTION OF THE "ALBEMARLE."

BY W. B. CUSHING, COMMANDER, U. S. N.
Leader of the expedition to sink the iron-clad ram.

IN September, 1864, the Government was laboring under much anxiety in regard to the condition of affairs in the sounds of North Carolina. Some months previous (April 19th) a rebel ironclad had made her appearance, attacking and recapturing Plymouth, beating our fleet, and sinking the *Southfield*. Some time after (May 5th), this ironclad, the *Albemarle*, had steamed out into the open sound and engaged seven of our steamers, doing much damage and suffering little. The *Sassacus* had attempted to run her down, but had failed, and had had her boiler exploded. The Government had no ironclad that could cross Hatteras bar and enter the sounds, and it was impossible for any number of our vessels to injure the ram at Plymouth.

At this stage of affairs Admiral S. P. Lee spoke to me of the case, when I proposed a plan for her capture or destruction. I submitted in writing two plans. The first was based upon the fact that through a thick swamp the ironclad might be approached to within a few hundred yards, whence India-rubber boats, to be inflated and carried upon men's backs, might transport a boarding-party of a hundred men ; in the second plan the offensive force was to be conveyed in two very small low-pressure steamers, each armed with a torpedo and a howitzer. In the latter (which had my preference), I intended that one boat should dash in, while the other stood by to throw canister and renew the attempt if the first should fail. It would also be useful to pick up our men if the attacking boat were disabled. Admiral Lee believed that the plan was a good one, and ordered me to Washington to submit it to the Secretary of the Navy. Mr. Fox, Assistant Secretary of the Navy, doubted the merit of the project, but concluded to order me to New York to "purchase suitable vessels."

Finding some boats building for picket duty, I selected two, and proceeded to fit them out. They were open launches, about thirty feet in length, with small engines, and propelled by a screw. A 12-pounder howitzer was fitted to the bow of each, and a boom was rigged out, some fourteen feet in length, swinging by a goose-neck hinge to the bluff of the bow. A topping lift, carried to a stanchion

THE "ALBEMARLE" READY FOR ACTION.

inboard, raised or lowered it, and the torpedo was fitted into an iron slide at the end. This was intended to be detached from the boom by means of a heel-jigger leading inboard, and to be exploded by another line, connecting with a pin, which held a grape shot over a nipple and cap. The torpedo was the invention of Engineer Lay of the navy, and was introduced by Chief-Engineer Wood. Everything being completed, we started to the southward, taking the boats through the canals to Chesapeake Bay. My best boat having been lost in going down to Norfolk, I proceeded with the other through the Chesapeake and Albemarle canal. Half-way through, the canal was filled up, but finding a small creek that emptied into it below the obstruction, I endeavored to feel my way through. Encountering a mill-dam, we waited for high water, and ran the launch over it ; below she grounded, but I got a flat-boat, and, taking out gun and coal, succeeded in two days in getting her through. Passing with but seven men through the canal, where for thirty miles there was no guard or Union inhabitant, I reached the sound, and ran before a gale of wind to Roanoke Island.

In the middle of the night I steamed off into the darkness, and in the morning was out of sight. Fifty miles up the sound I found the fleet anchored off the mouth of the river, and awaiting the ram's appearance. Here, for the first time, I disclosed

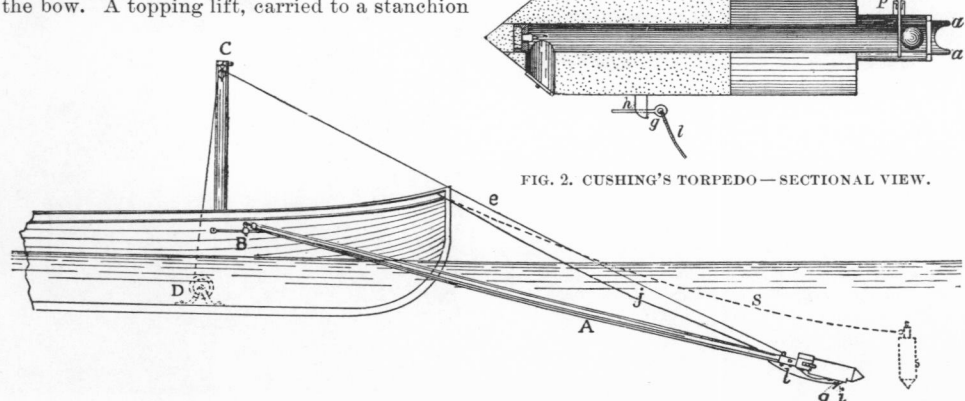

FIG 1. CUSHING'S LAUNCH AND TORPEDO—SHOWING METHODS OF WORKING.

FIG. 2. CUSHING'S TORPEDO—SECTIONAL VIEW.

to my officers and men our object, and told them that they were at liberty to go or not, as they pleased. These, seven in number, all volunteered. One of them, Mr. Howarth of the *Monticello*, had been with me repeatedly in expeditions of peril.

The Roanoke River is a stream averaging 150 yards in width, and quite deep. Eight miles from the mouth was the town of Plymouth, where the ram was moored. Several thousand soldiers occupied town and forts, and held both banks of the stream. A mile below the ram was the wreck of the *Southfield*, with hurricane deck above water, and on this a guard was stationed. Thus it seemed impossible to surprise them, or to attack with hope of success.

Impossibilities are for the timid: we determined to overcome all obstacles. On the night of the 27th of October we entered the river, taking in tow a small cutter with a few men, whose duty was to dash aboard the wreck of the *Southfield* at the first hail, and prevent a rocket from being ignited.

We passed within thirty feet of the pickets without discovery, and neared the vessel. I now thought that it might be better to board her, and "take her alive," having in the two boats twenty men well armed with revolvers, cutlasses, and hand-grenades. To be sure, there were ten times our number on the ship and thousands near by ; but a surprise is everything, and I thought if her fasts were cut at the instant of boarding, we might overcome those on board, take her into the stream, and use her iron sides to protect us afterward from the forts. Knowing the town, I concluded to land at the lower wharf, creep around, and suddenly dash aboard from the bank ; but just as I was sheering in close to the wharf, a hail came, sharp and quick, from the ironclad, and in an instant was repeated. I at once directed the cutter to cast off, and go down to capture the guard left in our rear, and, ordering all steam, went at the dark mountain of iron in front of us. A heavy fire was at once opened upon us, not only from the ship, but from men stationed on the shore. This did not disable us, and we neared them rapidly. A large fire now blazed upon the bank, and by its light I discovered the unfortunate fact that there was a circle of logs around the *Albemarle*, boomed well out from her side, with the very intention of preventing the action of torpedoes. To examine them more closely,

I ran alongside until amidships, received the enemy's fire, and sheered off for the purpose of turning, a hundred yards away, and going at the booms squarely, at right angles, trusting to their having been long enough in the water to have become slimy — in which case my boat, under full headway, would bump up against them and slip over into the pen with the ram. This was my only chance of success, and once over the obstruction my boat would never get out again. As I turned, the whole back of my coat was torn out by buckshot, and the sole of my shoe was carried away. The fire was very severe.

In a lull of the firing, the captain hailed us, again demanding what boat it was. All my men gave comical answers, and mine was a dose of canister from the howitzer. In another instant we had struck the logs and were over, with headway nearly gone, slowly forging up under the enemy's quarterport. Ten feet from us the muzzle of a rifle gun looked into our faces, and every word of command on board was distinctly heard.

My clothing was perforated with bullets as I stood in the bow, the heel-jigger in my right hand and the exploding-line in the left. We were near enough then, and I ordered the boom lowered until the forward motion of the launch carried the torpedo under the ram's overhang. A strong pull of the detaching-line, a moment's waiting for the torpedo to rise under the hull, and I hauled in the left hand, just cut by a bullet.

The explosion took place at the same instant that 100 pounds of grape, at 10 feet range, crashed among us, and the dense mass of water thrown out by the torpedo came down with choking weight upon us.

Twice refusing to surrender, I commanded the men to save themselves ; and, throwing off sword, revolver, shoes, and coat, struck out from my disabled and sinking boat into the river. It was cold, long after the frosts, and the water chilled the blood, while the whole surface of the stream was

COMMANDER W. B. CUSHING, U. S. N.

plowed up by grape and musketry, and my nearest friends, the fleet, were twelve miles away; but anything was better than to fall into rebel hands, so I swam for the opposite shore. As I neared it a man [Samuel Higgins, fireman], one of my crew, gave a great gurgling yell and went down.

The rebels were out in boats picking up my men; and one of the boats, attracted by the sound, pulled in my direction. I heard my own name mentioned, but was not seen. I now "struck out" down the stream, and was soon far enough away again to attempt landing. This time, as I struggled to reach the bank, I heard a groan in the river behind me, and, although very much exhausted, concluded to turn and give all the aid in my power to the officer or seaman who had bravely shared the danger with me.

Swimming in the night, with eye at the level of the water, one can have no idea of distance, and labors, as I did, under the discouraging thought that no headway is made. But if I were to drown that night, I had at least an opportunity of dying while struggling to aid another. Nearing the swimmer, it proved to be Acting Master's Mate Woodman, who said that he could swim no longer. Knocking his cap from his head, I used my right arm to sustain him, and ordered him to strike out. For ten minutes at least, I think, he managed to keep afloat, when, his physical force being completely gone, he sank like a stone.

Again alone upon the water, I directed my course toward the town side of the river, not making much headway, as my strokes were now very feeble, my clothes being soaked and heavy, and little chopseas splashing with choking persistence into my mouth every time I gasped for breath. Still, there was a determination not to sink, a will not to give up; and I kept up a sort of mechanical motion long after my bodily force was in fact expended. At last, and not a moment too soon, I touched the soft mud, and in the excitement of the first shock I half raised my body and made one step forward; then fell, and remained half in the mud and half in the water until daylight, unable even to crawl on hands and knees, nearly frozen, with my brain in a whirl, but with one thing strong in me — the fixed determination to escape.

As day dawned I found myself in a point of swamp that enters the suburbs of Plymouth, and not forty yards from one of the forts. The sun came out bright and warm, proving a most cheering visitant, and giving me back a good portion of the strength of which I had been deprived before. Its light showed me the town swarming with soldiers and sailors, who moved about excitely, as if angry at some sudden shock. It was a source of satisfaction to me to know that I had pulled the wire that set all these figures moving, but as I had no desire of being discovered my first object was to get into a dry fringe of rushes that edged the swamp; but to do this required me to pass over thirty or forty feet of open ground, right under the eye of a sentinel who walked the parapet.

Watching until he turned for a moment, I made a dash to cross the space, but was only half-way over when he again turned, and forced me to drop down, right between two paths, and almost entirely unshielded. Perhaps I was unobserved because of the mud that covered me and made me blend with

THE BLOWING-UP OF THE "ALBEMARLE."

the earth; at all events the soldier continued his tramp for some time, while I, flat on my back, lay awaiting another chance for action. Soon a party of four men came down the path at my right, two of them being officers, and passed so close to me as almost to tread upon my arm. They were conversing upon the events of the previous night, and were wondering "how it was done," entirely unaware of the presence of one who could give them the information. This proved to me the necessity of regaining the swamp, which I did by sinking my heels and elbows into the earth and forcing my body, inch by inch, toward it. For five hours then, with bare feet, head, and hands, I made my way where I venture to say none ever did before, until I came at last to a clear place, where I might rest upon solid ground. The cypress swamp was a network of thorns and briers that cut into the flesh at every step like knives; frequently, when the soft mire would not bear my weight, I was forced to throw my body upon it at length, and haul myself along by the arms. Hands and feet were raw when I reached the clearing, and yet my difficulties were but commenced. A working party of soldiers was in the opening, engaged in sinking some schooners in the river to obstruct the channel. I passed twenty yards in their rear through a corn furrow, and gained some woods below. Here I encountered a negro, and after serving out to him twenty dollars in greenbacks and some texts of Scripture (two powerful arguments with an old

darkey), I had confidence enough in his fidelity to send him into town for news of the ram.

When he returned, and there was no longer doubt that she had gone down, I went on again and plunged into a swamp so thick that I had only the sun for a guide and could not see ten feet in advance. About 2 o'clock in the afternoon I came out from a dense mass of reeds upon the bank of one of the deep, narrow streams that abound there, and right opposite to the only road in the vicinity. It seemed providential, for thirty yards above or below, I never should have seen the road, and might have struggled on until, worn out and starved, I should find a never-to-be-discovered grave. As it was, my fortune had led me to where a picket party of seven soldiers were posted, having a little flat-bottomed, square-ended skiff toggled to the root of a cypress tree that squirmed like a snake in the inky water. Watching them until they went back a few yards to eat, I crept into the stream and swam over, keeping the big tree between myself and them, and making for the skiff. Gaining the bank, I quietly cast loose the boat and floated behind it some thirty yards around the first bend, where I got in and paddled away as only a man could whose liberty was at stake.

Hour after hour I paddled, never ceasing for a moment, first on one side, then on the other, while sunshine passed into twilight and that was swallowed up in thick darkness, only relieved by the few faint star rays that penetrated the heavy swamp curtain on either side. At last I reached the mouth of the Roanoke, and found the open sound before me. My frail boat could not have lived in the ordinary sea there, but it chanced to be very calm, leaving only a slight swell, which was, however, sufficient to influence my boat, so that I was forced to paddle all upon one side to keep her on the intended course.

After steering by a star for perhaps two hours for where I thought the fleet might be, I at length discovered one of the vessels, and after a long time got within hail. My "Ship ahoy!" was given with the last of my strength, and I fell powerless, with a splash, into the water in the bottom of my boat, and awaited results. I had paddled

every minute for ten successive hours, and for four my body had been "asleep," with the exception of my arms and brain. The picket vessel, *Valley City*, upon hearing the hail, at once got under way, at the same time lowering boats and taking precaution against torpedoes. It was some time before they would pick me up, being convinced that I was the rebel conductor of an infernal machine, and that Lieutenant Cushing had died the night before. At last I was on board, had imbibed a little brandy and water, and was on my way to the flag-ship.

As soon as it became known that I had returned, rockets were thrown up and all hands were called to cheer ship, and when I announced success, all the commanding officers were summoned on board to deliberate upon a plan of attack. In the morning I was well again in every way, with the exception of hands and feet, and had the pleasure of exchanging shots with the batteries that I had inspected the day before. I was sent in the *Valley City* to report to Admiral Porter at Hampton Roads, and soon after Plymouth and the whole district of the Albemarle, deprived of the ironclad's protection, fell an easy prey to Macomb and our fleet.

NOTE BY THE CAPTAIN OF THE "ALBEMARLE."

The crew of the *Albemarle* numbered but sixty, too small a force to allow me to keep an armed watch on deck at night and to do outside picketing besides. Moreover, to break the monotony of the life and keep down ague, I had always out an expedition of ten men, who were uniformly successful in doing a fair amount of damage to the enemy.

It was about 3 A. M. The night was dark and slightly rainy, and the launch was close to us when we hailed and the alarm was given — so close that the gun could not be depressed enough to reach her; so the crew were sent in the shield with muskets, and kept up a heavy fire on the launch as she slowly forced her way over the chain of logs and ranged by us within a few feet. As she reached the bow of the *Albemarle* I heard a report as of an unshotted gun, and a piece of wood fell at my feet. Calling the carpenter, I told him a torpedo had been exploded, and ordered him to examine and report to me, saying nothing to any one else. He soon reported "a hole in her bottom big enough to drive a wagon in." By this time I heard voices from the launch: "We surrender," etc., etc., etc. I stopped our fire and sent out Mr. Long, who brought back all those who had been in the launch except the gallant captain and three of her crew, all of whom took to the water. Having seen to their safety, I turned my attention to the *Albemarle* and found her resting on the bottom in eight feet of water, her upper works above water.

That is the way the *Albemarle* was destroyed, and a more gallant thing was not done during the war. . . .

THE WRECK OF THE "ALBEMARLE."
From a photograph.

MAJOR-GENERAL ALFRED H. TERRY, U. S. A.
From a photograph.

THE BOMBARDMENT AND CAPTURE OF FORT FISHER.

BY THOMAS O. SELFRIDGE, JR., CAPTAIN, U. S. N.
Commander of a division in the naval column during the assault.

WHEN the Secretary of the Navy, Mr. Welles, recognizing the importance of closing the port of Wilmington, urged upon President Lincoln to direct a coöperation of the army, General Grant was requested to supply the necessary force from the troops about Richmond. As Fort Fisher lay within the territorial jurisdiction of General Butler, commanding the Department of Virginia and North Carolina, the troops were detailed from his command, and in the first attack Butler, with General Weitzel in immediate command of the troops, had control of the land operations. The naval command of the expedition having been declined by Admiral Farragut, on account of ill-health, Rear-Admiral Porter, who had so successfully coöperated with the army in opening the Mississippi, was selected, and was allowed to bring with him five of his officers, of whom the writer was one, being detailed for the command of the gun-boat *Huron*. The Atlantic and Gulf coasts being almost entirely in our possession, the Navy Department was able to concentrate before Fort Fisher a larger force than had ever before assembled under one command in the history of the American navy — a total of nearly 60 vessels, of which five were ironclads, including the *New Ironsides*, besides the three largest of our steam-frigates, viz., the *Minnesota*, *Colorado* and *Wabash*. The fleet arrived in sight of the fort on the morning of December 20th, 1864. . . .

[Bombardment was opened at intervals between the 20th and 25th, and on the last date was resumed with vigor to cover a land attack. The troops advanced to

THE BOMBARDMENT OF FORT FISHER, AS SEEN FROM THE MOUND BATTERY.

within a short distance of the fort, when Butler and Weitzel decided that the place could not be carried by storm. The second attack, January 15th, 1865, Captain Selfridge describes as follows:]

Upon receiving Admiral Porter's despatches, Mr. Welles again sought the coöperation of the army, to which General Grant at once acceded, sending back the same force of white troops, reinforced by two colored brigades under General Charles J. Paine, the whole under the command of Major-General Alfred H. Terry. While lying at Beaufort, Admiral Porter determined to assist in the land attack of the army by an assault upon the sea-face of Fort Fisher with a body of seamen. In a general order volunteers from the fleet were called for, and some two thousand officers and men offered themselves for this perilous duty.

General Terry arrived off Beaufort with his forces on the 8th of January, 1865, a plan of operations was agreed upon, and the 12th was fixed for the sailing of the combined force.

Upon the morning of the 13th the ironclads were sent in to engage the fort. Going in much closer than before, the monitors were within twelve hundred yards of the fort. Their fire was in consequence much more effective.

The remainder of the fleet were occupied till 2 P. M. in landing the troops and stores. This particular duty, the provisioning of the army, and the protection of its flank was afterward turned over to the lighter gun-boats, whose guns were too small to employ them in the bombardment of the fort, the whole under the charge of Commander J. H. Upshur, commanding the gun-boat *A. D. Vance*.

On the afternoon of the 13th the fleet, excepting the ironclads, which had remained in their first positions close to the fort, steamed into the several positions assigned them and opened a terrific fire. By placing a buoy close to the outer reef, as a guide, the leading ship, the *Minnesota*, was enabled to anchor nearer, and likewise the whole battle-line was much closer and their fire more effective, the best proof of which is the large number of guns

upon the land-face of the fort that was found to be destroyed or dismounted. The weight of fire was such that the enemy could make but a feeble reply. At nightfall the fleet hauled off, excepting the ironclads, which kept up a slow fire through the night.

During the 14th a number of the smaller gun-boats carrying 11-inch guns were sent in to assist in dismounting the guns on the land-face. Their fire was necessarily slow, and the presence of these small craft brought the enemy out of their bomb-proofs to open upon them, during which the *Huron* had her main-mast shot away. Upon seeing this renewal of fire, the *Brooklyn*, *Mohican*, and one or two other vessels were ordered in by Porter, and with this reinforcement the fire of the fort slackened. The bombardment from the smaller gun-boats and ironclads was kept up during the night. This constant duty day and night was very hard upon these small vessels, and the officers and crew of my own vessel, the *Huron*, were worn out.

Fort Fisher was at this time much stronger than at the first attack. . . . It was arranged that the grand bombardment should begin on the morning of the 15th, and the separate assaults of soldiers and sailors should take place at 3 P. M. A code of signals was agreed upon between the two commanders, and the assault was to be signaled to the fleet by a blowing of steam-whistles, whereupon their fire would be directed to the upper batteries. After the assault of the sailors had failed the *Ironsides* used her 11-inch guns with great effect in firing into the traverses filled with Confederates resisting the advance of the Union forces. At 9 A. M. the fleet was directed by signal to move in three divisions, and each ship took its prescribed place as previously indicated to her commander; consequently there was no disorder.

All felt the importance of this bombardment, and, while not too rapid to be ineffective, such a storm of shell was poured into Fort Fisher that forenoon, as I believe had never been seen before in any naval engagement. The enemy soon ceased to make any reply from their heavy guns, excepting

the "mound battery," which was more difficult to silence, while those mounted on the land-face were by this time disabled.

Before noon the signal was made for the assaulting column of sailors and marines to land. From thirty-five of the sixty ships of the fleet boats shoved off, making, with their flags flying as they pulled toward the beach in line abreast, a most spirited scene. The general order of Admiral Porter required that the assaulting column of sailors should be armed with cutlasses and pistols. It was also intended that trenches or covered ways should be dug for the marines close to the fort, and that our assault should be made under the cover of their fire; but it was impossible to dig such shelter trenches near enough to do much good under fire in broad daylight.

The sailors as they landed from their boats were a heterogeneous assembly, companies of two hundred or more from each of the larger ships, down to small parties of twenty each from the gun-boats. They had been for months confined on shipboard, had never drilled together, and their arms, the old-fashioned cutlass and pistol, were hardly the weapons to cope with the rifles and bayonets of the enemy. Sailor-like, however, they looked upon the landing in the light of a lark, and few thought the sun would set with a loss of one-fifth of their number.

After some discussion between Lieutenant-Commander K. R. Breese, and some of the senior officers, it was decided to form three divisions, each composed of men from the corresponding division squadrons of the fleet; the first division under the command of Lieutenant-Commander C. H. Cushman, the second under Lieutenant-Commander James Parker (who was Breese's senior but waived his rank, the latter being in command as the admiral's representative), the third under Lieutenant-Commander T. O. Selfridge, Jr.; a total of 1600 blue-jackets, to which was added a division of 400 marines under Captain L. L. Dawson.

The whole force marched up the beach and lay down under its cover just outside rifle range, await-

CAPTAIN T. O. SELFRIDGE, JR., U. S. N.
From a photograph.

ing the movements of the army. We were formed by the flank, and our long line flying numerous flags gave a formidable appearance from the fort, and caused the Confederates to divide their forces, sending more than one-half to oppose the naval assault.

At a preconcerted signal the sailors sprang forward to the assault, closely following the water's edge, where the inclined beach gave them a slight cover. We were opened upon in front by the great mound battery, and in flank by the artillery of the half-moon battery, and by the fire of a thousand rifles. Though many dropped rapidly under this fire, the column never faltered, and when the angle where the two faces of the fort unite was reached, the head halted to allow the rear to come up. This halt was fatal, for as the others came up they followed suit, and lay down till the space between the parapet and the edge of the water was filled. As the writer approached with the Third Division he shouted to his men to come on, intending to lead them to where there was more space; but, looking back, he discovered that his whole command, with few exceptions, had stopped and joined their comrades. Making his way to the front, close to the palisade, he found several officers, among whom were Lieutenant-Commanders Parker and Cushman. The situation was a very grave one. The rush of the sailors was over; they were packed like sheep in a pen, while the enemy were crowding the ramparts not forty yards away, and shooting into them as fast as they could fire. There was nothing to reply with but *pistols*. Something must be done, and speedily. There were some spaces in the palisade where it was torn away by the fire of the fleet, and an attempt was made to charge through, but we found a deep, impassable ditch, and those who got through were shot down. Flesh and blood could not long endure being killed in this slaughter pen, and the rear of the sailors broke, followed by the whole body, in spite of all efforts to rally them. It was certainly mortifying, after charging for a mile, under a most galling fire, to the very foot of the fort, to have the whole force retreat down the beach. It has been the custom, unjustly in my opinion, to lay the blame on the marines for not keeping down the fire till the sailors could get in. But there were but 400 of them against 1200 of the garrison: the former in the open plain, and with no

THE BOMBARDMENT OF FORT FISHER, JANUARY 15, 1865.

cover; the latter under the shelter of their ramparts. The mistake was in expecting a body of sailors, collected hastily from different ships, unknown to each other, armed with swords and pistols, to stand against veteran soldiers armed with rifles and bayonets. Another fatal mistake was the stopping at the sea angle. Two hundred yards farther would have brought us to a low parapet without palisade or ditch, where, with proper arms, we could have intrenched and fought. Some sixty remained at the front, at the foot of the parapet,

under cover of the palisade, until nightfall enabled them to withdraw. Among the number I remember Lieutenant-Commanders Breese, Parker, Cushman, Sicard; Lieutenants Farquhar, Lamson, S. W. Nichols, and Bartlett.

A loss of some three hundred in killed and wounded attests the gallant nature of the assault. Among these were several prominent officers, including Lieutenants Preston and Porter, killed, Lieut.-Commanders C. H. Cushman, W. N. Allen; Lieutenants G. M. Bache, R. D. Evans, wounded.

After their repulse the sailors did good service with the marines by manning the intrenchments thrown up across the peninsula, which enabled General Terry to send Abbott's brigade and Blackman's (27th U. S.) colored regiment to the assistance of the troops fighting in the fort. Here they remained till morning, when they returned to their respective ships. When the assault of the naval column failed, the *Ironsides* and the monitors were directed to fire into the gun traverses in advance of the positions occupied by the army, and by doing so greatly demoralized the enemy. About 8 P.M. that night the fort fell into our hands after the hardest fighting by our gallant troops, and with its capture fell the last stronghold of the Southern Confederacy on the Atlantic coast.

I will not go so far as to say the army could not have stormed Fort Fisher without the diversion afforded by the naval assault, for no soldiers during the war showed more indomitable pluck than the gallant regiments that stormed the fort on that afternoon; but I do say our attack enabled them to get into the fort with far less loss than they would otherwise have suffered.

As a diversion the charge of sailors was a success; as an exhibition of courage it was magnificent; but the material of which the column was composed, and the arms with which it was furnished, left no reasonable hope after the first onslaught had been checked that it could have succeeded.

While kept under the walls of the fort, I was an eye-witness to an act of heroism on the part of Assistant-Surgeon William Longshaw, a young officer of the medical staff, whose memory should ever be kept green by his corps, and which deserves more than this passing notice. A sailor too severely wounded to help himself had fallen close to the water's edge, and with the rising tide would have drowned. Dr. Longshaw, at the peril of his life, went to his assistance and dragged him beyond the incoming tide. At this moment he heard a cry from a wounded marine, one of a small group who, behind a little hillock of sand close to the parapet, kept up a fire upon the enemy. Longshaw ran to his assistance, and while attending to his wounds was shot dead. What made the action of this young officer even more heroic was the fact that on that very day he had received a leave of absence, but had postponed his departure to volunteer for the assault.

ASSAULT OF THE NAVAL COLUMN ON THE NORTHEAST SALIENT OF FORT FISHER.

GENERAL GRANT RECONNOITERING THE CONFEDERATE POSITION AT SPOTSYLVANIA COURT HOUSE.

From a sketch made at the time.

NOTE.—Mr. Reed, the artist, belonged to Bigelow's 9th Massachusetts battery (Warren's Corps), which, with a battery of the 5th Regular Artillery, was holding the Fredericksburg road, at the place where General Grant made his observation. The troops seen in the background are the 9th Massachusetts Volunteers, who at the time were crossing the road from the left toward the right of the line. The position was one looking directly toward the Court House proper, and was part of the line seized by Burnside's Corps on May 9th. Warren's Corps occupied it from the 14th to the 21st. Veterans will recognize this as a faithful portrait of the general as he appeared in the field during that campaign.

HEADQUARTERS OF THE ARMY OF THE POTOMAC AT BRANDY STATION.

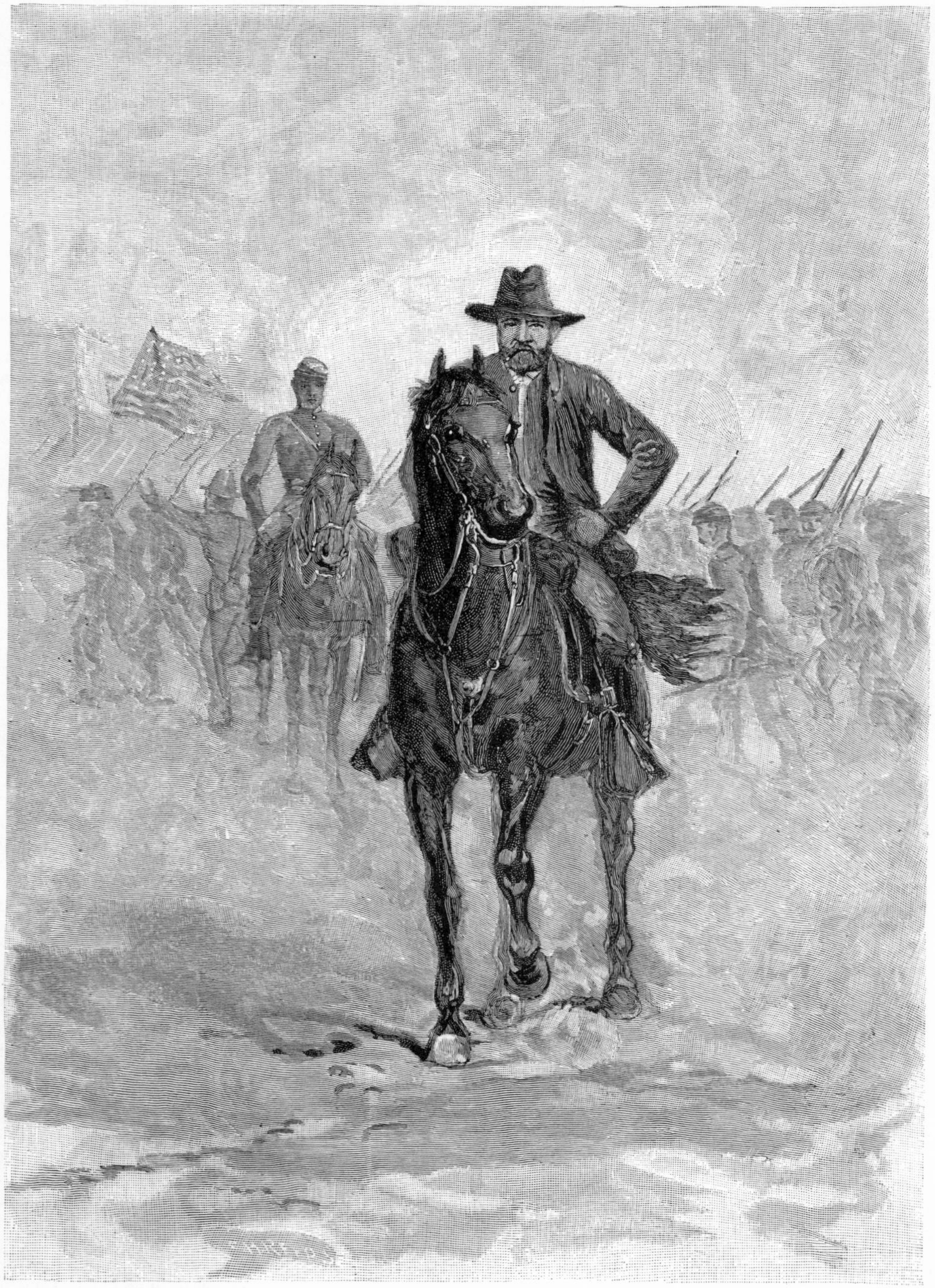

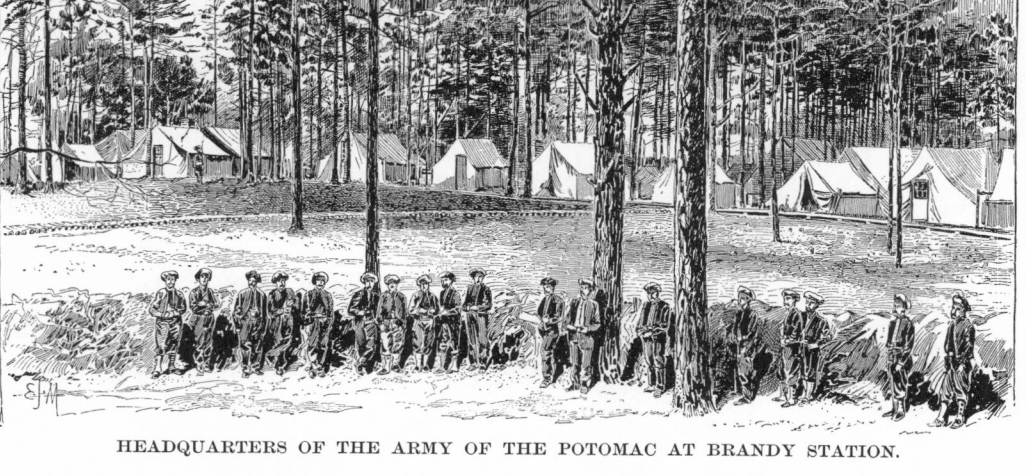

THE WILDERNESS CAMPAIGN.

NARRATIVE OF EVENTS.

Lee's retreat from Gettysburg to Virginia ended in placing his army in its former position at Culpeper. Longstreet's corps was transferred to the scene of Bragg's operations around Chattanooga, and fought at Chickamauga and Knoxville. After the battle of Chickamauga, the Eleventh and Twelfth Union Corps, under Howard and Slocum, were sent to Chattanooga. Late in September Meade pushed across the Rappahannock and Rapidan, forcing Lee to abandon Culpeper. As a counter move, Lee attempted to turn Meade's flank and get between the Army of the Potomac and Washington. Thereupon Meade retired slowly to Centreville. On October 14, General G. K. Warren (the new commander of the Fifth Corps) repulsed a desperate attack by A. P. Hill's corps at Bristoe. Lee followed Meade toward Centreville, but, without offering general battle, retired to the Rapidan. Meade pursued, and a brilliant action was fought at the crossing of the Rappahannock, November 7, between Russell's division of the Sixth Corps and Hays's division of Early's Corps. Russell stormed the Rappahannock redoubts and captured eight battle-flags with 2000 prisoners.

Meade crossed the Rappahannock, and on the 28th of November was south of the Rapidan confronting Lee, who had fortified the line of Mine Run, covering Orange Court House. On December 1 the army retreated to the north bank of the Rapidan without a battle, and established winter quarters. Lee remained at Orange Court House and Gordonsville, where Longstreet's Corps rejoined him in March, 1864.

The most noteworthy affair in Virginia during the winter was a Union cavalry raid in rear of Lee's army. The cavalcade, led by General Kilpatrick and Colonel Ulric Dahlgren, rode to the fortifications of Richmond without meeting serious opposition. Some sharp fighting took place in front of the Confederate works, and the raiders retreated down the Peninsula. Colonel Dahlgren was ambushed and killed during the retreat.

PREPARING FOR THE CAMPAIGN.*

BY ULYSSES S. GRANT, GENERAL, U. S. A.

MY commission as lieutenant-general was given to me on the 9th of March, 1864. On the following day I visited General Meade, commanding the Army of the Potomac, at his headquarters, Brandy Station, north of the Rapidan. I had known General Meade slightly in the Mexican war, but had not met him since until this visit. I was a stranger to most of the Army of the Potomac—I might say to all, except the officers of the regular army who had served in the Mexican war. There had been some changes ordered in the organization of that army before my promotion. One was the consolidation of five corps into three, thus throwing some officers of rank out of important commands. Meade evidently thought that I might want to make still one more change not yet ordered. He said to me that I might want an officer who had served with me in the West, mentioning Sherman especially, to take his place; if so, he begged me not to hesitate about making the change. He urged that the work before us was of such vast importance to the whole nation that the feeling or wishes of no one person should stand in the way of selecting the right men for all positions. For himself, he would serve to the best of his ability wherever placed. I assured him that I had no thought of substituting any one for him. As to Sherman, he could not be spared from the West.

This incident gave me even a more favorable opinion of Meade than did his great victory at Gettysburg the July before. It is men who wait to be selected, and not those who seek, from whom we may always expect the most efficient service. . . .

On the 23d of March I was back in Washington, and on the 26th took up my headquarters at Culpeper Court House, a few miles south of the headquarters of the Army of the Potomac.

Although hailing from Illinois myself, the State of the President,

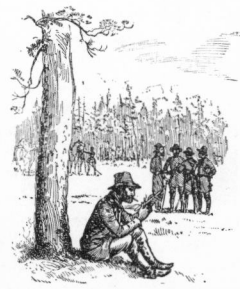

GENERAL GRANT WHITTLING DURING THE BATTLE OF THE WILDERNESS.

From a war-time sketch.

* "Personal Memoirs of U. S. Grant." Copyright, 1885, by U. S. Grant. All rights reserved.

MAJOR-GEN. JUDSON KILPATRICK, U. S. V.

SECOND DAY OF THE BATTLE OF THE WILDERNESS, MAY 6, 1864.
View toward Parker's store, from the Lacy house, the headquarters of Grant, Meade, and Warren.

COLONEL JOHN S. MOSBY, C. S. A.

I never met Mr. Lincoln until called to the capital to receive my commission as lieutenant-general. I knew him, however, very well and favorably from the accounts given by officers under me at the West who had known him all their lives. I had also read the remarkable series of debates between Lincoln and Douglas a few years before, when they were rival candidates for the United States Senate. I was then a resident of Missouri, and by no means a "Lincoln man" in that contest; but I recognized then his great ability.

In my first interview with Mr. Lincoln alone he stated to me that he had never professed to be a military man, or to know how campaigns should be conducted, and never wanted to interfere in them; but that procrastination on the part of commanders, and the pressure from the people at the North and from Congress, *which was always with him*, forced him into issuing his series of "Military Orders"—No. 1, No. 2, No. 3, etc. He did not know that they were not all wrong, and did know that some of them were. All he wanted, or had ever wanted, was some one who would take the responsibility and act, and call on him for all the assistance needed; he would pledge himself to use all the power of the Government in rendering such

assistance. Assuring him that I would do the best I could with the means at hand, and avoid as far as possible annoying him or the War Department, our first interview ended.

The Secretary of War I had met once before only, but felt that I knew him better. While I had been commanding in west Tennessee we had held conversations over the wires at night. He and Halleck both cautioned me against giving the President my plans of campaign, saying that he was so kind-hearted, so averse to refusing anything asked of him, that some friend would be sure to get from him all he knew. I should have said that in our interview the President told me that he did not want to know what I proposed to do. But he submitted a plan of campaign of his own which he wanted me to hear, and then dispose of as I pleased. He brought out a map of Virginia, on which he had evidently marked every position occupied by the Federal and Confederate armies up to that time. He pointed out on the map two streams which empty into the Potomac, and suggested that the army might be moved on boats and landed between the mouths of these streams. We would then have the Potomac to bring supplies, and the tributaries would protect our flanks while we moved out. I listened respectfully, but did not suggest that the same streams would protect Lee's flanks while he was shutting us up. I did not communicate my plans to the President or to the Secretary or to General Halleck.

On the 26th of March, with my headquarters at Culpeper, the work of preparing for an early campaign commenced. . . .

That portion of the Army of the Potomac not engaged in guarding lines of communication was on the northern bank of the Rapidan. The Army of Northern Virginia, confronting it on the opposite bank of the same river, was strongly intrenched and was commanded by the acknowledged ablest general in the Confederate army. The country back to the James River is cut up with many streams, generally narrow, deep, and difficult to cross, except where bridged. The region

is heavily timbered, and the roads are narrow and very bad after the least rain. Such an enemy was not, of course, unprepared with adequate fortifications at convenient intervals all the way back to Richmond, so that, when driven from one fortified position, they would always have another farther to the rear to fall back into. To provision an army, campaigning against so formidable a foe through such a country, from wagons alone, seemed almost impossible. System and discipline were both essential to its accomplishment. . . .

In one of my early interviews with the President I expressed my dissatisfaction with the little that had been accomplished by the cavalry so far in the war, and the belief that it was capable of accomplishing much more than it had done if under a thorough leader. I said I wanted the very best man in the army for that command. Halleck was present and spoke up, saying: "How would Sheridan do?" I replied: "The very man I want."

The President said I could have anybody I wanted. Sheridan was telegraphed for that day, and on his arrival was assigned to the command of the cavalry corps with the Army of the Potomac. . . .

By the 27th of April spring had so far advanced as to justify me in fixing a day for the great move. On that day Burnside left Annapolis to occupy Meade's position between Bull Run and the Rappahannock. Meade was notified and directed to bring his troops forward to his advance; on the following day Butler was notified of my intended advance on the 4th of May, and he was directed to move, the night of the same day, and get as far up the James River as possible by daylight, and push on from there to accomplish the task given him. He was also notified that reinforcements were being collected in Washington, which would be forwarded to him should the enemy fall back into the trenches at Richmond. . . .

While my headquarters were at Culpeper, from the 26th of March to the 4th of May, I generally visited Washington once a week to confer with the Secretary of War and the President. On the last occasion, a few days before moving, a circum-

stance occurred which came near postponing my part in the campaign altogether. Colonel John S. Mosby had for a long time been commanding a partizan corps, or regiment, which operated in the rear of the Army of the Potomac. On my return to the field on this occasion, as the train approached Warrenton Junction, a heavy cloud of dust was seen to the east of the road, as if made by a body of cavalry on a charge. Arriving at the junction, the train was stopped and inquiries were made as to the cause of the dust. There was but one man at the station, and he informed us that Mosby had crossed a few minutes before at full speed in pursuit of Federal cavalry. Had he seen our train coming, no doubt he would have let his prisoners escape to capture the train. I was on a special train, if I remember correctly, without any guard. Since the close of the war I have come to know Colonel Mosby personally, and somewhat inti-

MAJOR-GENERAL STEPHEN D. RAMSEUR, C. S. A.

mately. He is a different man entirely from what I had supposed. He is slender, not tall, wiry, and looks as if he could endure any amount of physical exercise. He is able, and thoroughly honest and truthful. There were probably but few men in the South who could have commanded successfully a separate detachment, in the rear of an opposing army and so near the border of hostilities, as long as he did without losing his entire command.

On this same visit to Washington I had my last interview with the President before reaching the James River. He had, of course, become acquainted with the fact that a general movement had been ordered all along the line, and seemed to think it a new feature in war. I explained to him that it was necessary to have a great number of troops to guard and to hold the territory we had captured, and to prevent incursions into the Northern States. These troops could perform this service just as well by advancing as by remaining still; and by advancing they would compel the enemy to keep detachments to hold them back or else lay his own territory open to invasion. "Oh! yes, I see that," he said. "As we say out West, if a man can't skin he must hold a leg while somebody else does." . . . Soon after midnight, May 3–4, the Army of the Potomac moved out from its position north of the Rapidan, to start upon that memorable campaign destined to result in the capture of the Confederate capital and the army defending it.

NOTE.—Grant's campaign from the Rapidan to the James is usually referred to as "The Wilderness Campaign." The first battle of the series took place in a region known as "The Wilderness."

THROUGH THE WILDERNESS. — THE CONFEDERATE SIDE.

BY E. M. LAW, MAJOR-GENERAL, C. S. A.
Commanding a brigade under Longstreet.

ON the 2d of May, 1864, a group of officers stood at the Confederate signal station on Clark's Mountain, Virginia, south of the Rapidan, and ex-

CONFEDERATE LINE WAITING ORDERS IN THE WILDERNESS.

amined closely through their field-glasses the position of the Federal army then lying north of the river in Culpeper county. The central figure of the group was the commander of the Army of Northern Virginia, who had requested his corps and division commanders to meet him there. Though some demonstrations had been made in the direction of the upper fords, General Lee expressed the opinion that the Federal army would cross the river at Germanna or Ely's. Thirty-six hours later General Meade's army, General Grant, now commander-in-chief, being with it, commenced its march to the crossings indicated by General Lee.

The Army of the Potomac, which had now commenced its march toward Richmond, was more powerful in numbers than at any previous period of the war. It consisted of three corps: the Second (Hancock's), the Fifth (Warren's), and the Sixth (Sedgwick's); but the Ninth (Burnside's) acted with Meade throughout the campaign. Meade's army was thoroughly equipped, and provided with every appliance of modern warfare. On the other hand, the Army of Northern Virginia had gained little in numbers during the winter just passed, and had never been so scantily supplied with food and clothing. The equipment as to arms was well enough for men who knew how to use them, but commissary and quartermasters' supplies were lamentably deficient. A new pair of shoes or an overcoat was a luxury, and full rations would have astonished the stomachs of Lee's ragged Confederates. But they took their privations cheerfully, and complaints were seldom heard. I recall an instance of one hardy fellow whose trousers were literally "worn to a frazzle" and would no longer adhere to his legs even by dint of the most persistent patching. Unable to buy, beg, or borrow another pair, he wore instead a pair of thin cotton

drawers. By nursing these carefully he managed to get through the winter. Before the campaign opened in the spring a small lot of clothing was received, and he was the first man of his regiment to be supplied.

I have often heard expressions of surprise that these ragged, bare-footed, half-starved men would fight at all. But the very fact that they remained with their colors through such privations and hardships was sufficient to prove that they would be dangerous foes to encounter upon the line of battle. The *morale* of the army at this time was excellent, and it moved forward confidently to the grim death-grapple in the wilderness of Spotsylvania with its old enemy, the Army of the Potomac.

General Lee's headquarters were two miles northeast of Orange Court House; of his three corps, Longstreet's was at Gordonsville, Ewell's was on and near the Rapidan, above Mine Run, and Hill's on his left, higher up the stream. When the Federal army was known to be in motion, General Lee prepared to move upon its flank with his whole force as soon as his opponent should clear the river and begin the march southward. The route selected by General Grant led entirely around the right of Lee's position on the river above. Grant's passage of the Rapidan was unopposed, and he struck boldly out on the direct road to Richmond. Two roads lead from Orange Court House down the Rapidan toward Fredericksburg. They follow the general direction of the river, and are almost parallel to each other, the "Old turnpike" nearest the river, and the "Plank road" a short distance south of it. The route of the Federal army lay directly across these two roads along the western borders of the famous Wilderness.

About noon on the 4th of May, Ewell's corps was put in motion on and toward the Orange turnpike, while A. P. Hill, with two divisions, moved parallel

with him on the Orange Plank road. The two divisions of Longstreet's corps, encamped near Gordonsville, were ordered to move rapidly across the country and follow Hill on the Plank road. Ewell's corps was the first to find itself in the presence of the enemy. As it advanced along the turnpike on the morning of the 5th, the Federal column was seen crossing it from the direction of Germanna Ford. Ewell promptly formed line of battle across the turnpike, and communicated his position to General Lee, who was on the Plank road with Hill. Ewell was instructed to regulate his movements by the head of Hill's column, whose progress he could tell by the firing in its front. . . .

General Warren, whose corps was passing when Ewell came up, halted, and turning to the right made a vigorous attack upon Edward Johnson's division, posted across the turnpike. J. M. Jones's brigade, which held the road, was driven back in confusion. Steuart's brigade was pushed forward to take its place. Rodes's division was thrown in on Johnson's right, south of the road, and the line thus reëstablished moved forward, reversed the tide of battle, and rolled back the Federal attack. The fighting was severe and bloody while it lasted. At some points the lines were in such close proximity in the thick woods which covered the battle-field that when the Federal troops gave way several hundred of them, unable to retreat without exposure to almost certain death, surrendered themselves as prisoners.

Ewell's entire corps was now up — Johnson's division holding the turnpike, Rodes's division on the right of it, and Early's in reserve. So far Ewell had been engaged only with Warren's corps, but Sedgwick's soon came up from the river and joined Warren on his right. Early's division was sent to meet it. The battle extended in that direction, with steady and determined attacks upon Early's front, until nightfall. The Confederates still clung to their hold on the Federal flank against every effort to dislodge them.

When Warren's corps encountered the head of Ewell's column on the 5th of May, General Meade is reported to have said: "They have left a division to fool us here, while they concentrate and prepare a position on the North Anna." If the stubborn resistance to Warren's attack did not at once convince him of his mistake, the firing that announced the approach of Hill's corps along the Plank road, very soon afterward, must have opened his eyes to the bold strategy of the Confederate commander. General Lee had deliberately chosen this as his battle-ground. He knew this tangled wilderness well, and appreciated fully the advantages such a field afforded for concealing his great inferiority of force, and for neutralizing the superior strength of his antagonist. General Grant's bold movement across the lower fords into the Wilderness, in the execution of his plan to swing past the Confederate army and place himself between it and Richmond, offered the expected opportunity of striking a blow upon his flank while his troops were stretched out on the line of march. The wish for such an opportunity was doubtless in a measure "father to the thought" expressed by General Lee three days before, at the signal station on Clark's Mountain.

Soon after Ewell became engaged on the Old turn-

**LIEUTENANT-GENERAL
RICHARD H. ANDERSON, C. S. A.**

pike, A. P. Hill's advance struck the Federal outposts on the Plank road at Parker's store, on the outskirts of the Wilderness. These were driven in, and followed up to their line of battle, which was so posted as to cover the junction of the Plank road with the Stevensburg and Brock roads, on which the Federal army was moving toward Spotsylvania. The fight began between Getty's division of the Sixth Corps, and Heth's division, which was leading A. P. Hill's column. Hancock's corps, which was already on the march for Spotsylvania by way of Chancellorsville, was at once recalled, and at 4 o'clock in the afternoon was ordered to drive Hill "out of the Wilder-

MAJOR-GENERAL FITZHUGH LEE, C. S. A.

ness." Cadmus Wilcox's division went to Heth's support, and Poague's battalion of artillery took position in a little clearing on the north side of the Plank road, in rear of the Confederate infantry. But there was little use for artillery on such a field, with the angry flashing and heavy roar of the musketry, mingled with the yells of the combatants as they swayed to and fro in the gloomy thickets. Among the killed were General Alexander Hays, of Hancock's corps, and General J. M. Jones, of Ewell's.

When the battle closed at 8 o'clock, General Lee sent an order to Longstreet to make a night march, so as to arrive upon the field at daylight the next morning. The latter moved at 1 A. M. of the 6th, but it was already daylight when he reached the Plank road at Parker's store, three miles in rear of Hill's battle-field. During the night the movements of troops and preparations for battle could be heard on the Federal line, in front of Heth's and Wilcox's divisions, which had so far sustained themselves against every attack by six divisions under General Hancock. But Heth's and Wilcox's men were thoroughly worn out. Their lines were ragged and irregular, with wide intervals, and in some places fronting in different directions. In the expectation that they would be relieved during the night, no effort was made to rearrange and strengthen them to meet the storm that was brewing.

As soon as it was light enough to see what little could be seen in that dark forest, Hancock's troops swept forward to the attack. The blow fell with greatest force upon Wilcox's troops south of the Orange Plank road. They made what front they could and renewed the fight, until, the attacking column overlapping the right wing, it gave way, and the whole line "rolled up" from the right and retired in disorder along the Plank road as far as the position of Poague's artillery, which now opened upon the attacking force. The Federals pressed their advantage and were soon abreast of the artillery on the opposite side, their bullets flying across the road among the guns where General Lee himself stood. For a while matters looked very serious for the Confederates. General Lee, after sending a messenger to hasten the

march of Longstreet's troops, and another to prepare the trains for a movement to the rear, was assisting in rallying the disordered troops, and directing the fire of the artillery, when the head of Longstreet's corps appeared in double column, swinging down the Orange Plank road at a trot. In perfect order, ranks well closed, and no stragglers, those splendid troops came on, regardless of the confusion on every side, pushing their steady way onward like "a river in the sea" of confused and troubled human waves around them. Kershaw's division took the right of the road, and, coming into line under a heavy fire, moved obliquely to the right (south) to meet the Federal left, which had "swung round" in that direction. The Federals were checked in their sweeping advance, and thrown back upon their front line of breastworks, where they made a stubborn stand. But Kershaw, urged on by Longstreet, charged with his whole command, swept his front, and captured the works.

Nearly at the same moment Field's division took the left of the road, with Gregg's brigade in front, Benning's behind it, Law's next, and Jenkins's following. As the Texans in the front lines swept past the batteries where General Lee was standing, they gave a rousing cheer for "Marse Robert," who spurred his horse forward and followed them in the charge. When the men became aware that he was "going in" with them, they called loudly to him to go back. "We won't go on unless you go back" was the general cry. One of the men dropped to the rear, taking the bridle turned the general's horse around, while General Gregg came up and urged him to do as the men wished. At that moment a member of his staff (Colonel Venable) directed his attention to General Longstreet, whom he had been looking for, and who was sitting on his horse near the Orange Plank road. With evident disappointment General Lee turned off and joined General Longstreet.

The ground over which Field's troops were advancing was open for a short distance, and fringed on its farther edge with scattered pines, beyond which began the Wilderness. The Federals [Webb's brigade of Hancock's corps] were advancing through the pines with apparent resistless force, when Gregg's eight hundred Texans, regard-

MAJOR-GENERAL G. W. C. LEE, C. S. A.

less of numbers, flanks, or supports, dashed directly upon them. There was a terrific crash, mingled with wild yells, which settled down into a steady roar of musketry. In less than ten minutes one-half of that devoted eight hundred were lying upon the field dead or wounded; but they had delivered a staggering blow and broken the force of the Federal advance. Benning's and Law's brigades came promptly to their support, and the whole swept forward together. The tide was flowing the other way. It ebbed and flowed many times that day, strewing the Wilderness with human wrecks. Law's brigade captured a line of log breastworks in its front, but had held them

MAJOR-GENERAL EDWARD JOHNSON, C. S. A.

LIEUTENANT-GENERAL WADE HAMPTON, C. S. A.

THROWING UP BREASTWORKS IN THE WILDERNESS.
From a sketch made at the time.

CAPTURE OF A PART OF THE BURNING UNION BREASTWORKS, MAY 6.
From a sketch made at the time.

only a few moments when their former owners [Webb's brigade] came back to claim them. The Federals were driven back to a second line several hundred yards beyond, which was also taken. This advanced position was attacked in front and on the right from across the Orange Plank road, and Law's Alabamians "advanced backward" without standing on the order of their going, until they reached the first line of logs, now in their rear. As their friends in blue still insisted on claiming their property, and were advancing to take it, they were met by a counter-charge and again driven beyond the second line. This was held against a determined attack, in which the Federal General Wadsworth was shot from his horse as he rode up close to the right of the line on the Plank road. The position again becoming untenable by reason of the movements of Federal troops on their right, Law's men retired a second time to the works they had first captured. And so, for more than two hours, the storm of battle swept to and fro, in some places passing several times over the same ground, and settling down at length almost where it had begun the day before.

About 10 o'clock it was ascertained that the Federal left flank rested only a short distance south of the Orange Plank road, which offered a favorable opportunity for a turning movement in that quarter. General Longstreet at once moved Mahone's, Wofford's, Anderson's, and Davis's brigades, the whole under General Mahone, around this end of the Federal line. Forming at right angles to it, they attacked in flank and rear, while a general advance was made in front. So far the fight had been one of anvil and hammer. But this first display of tactics at once changed the face of the field. The Federal left wing was rolled up in confusion toward the Plank road and then back upon the Brock road.

This partial victory had been a comparatively easy one. The signs of demoralization and even panic among the troops of Hancock's left wing, who had been hurled back by Mahone's flank attack, were too plain to be mistaken by the Confederates, who believed that Chancellorsville was about to be repeated. General Longstreet rode forward and prepared to press his advantage. Jenkins's fresh

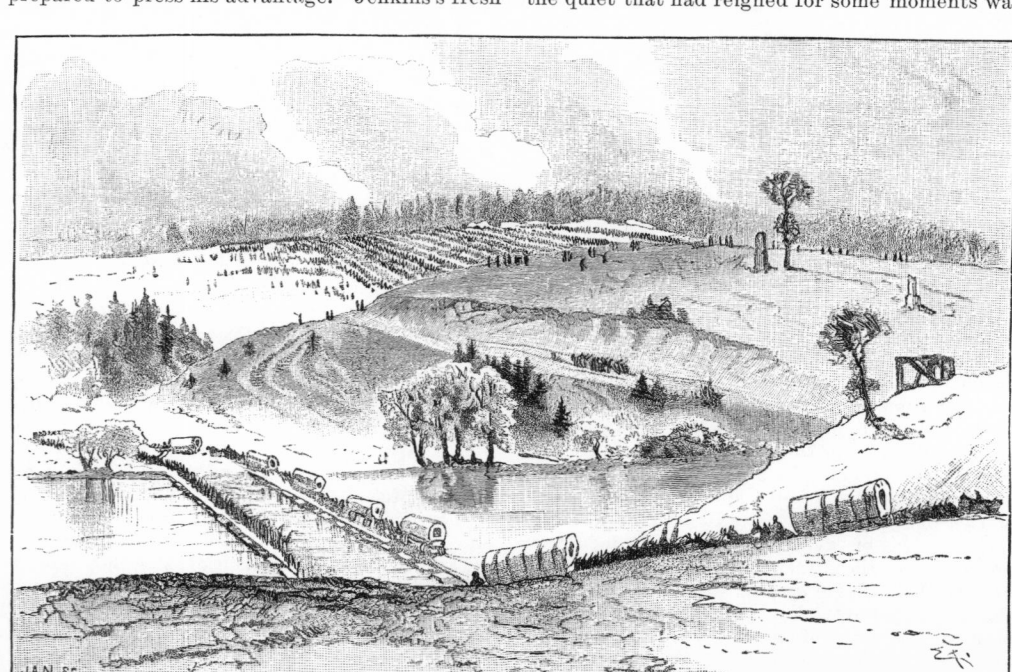

UNION TROOPS CROSSING THE RAPIDAN AT GERMANNA FORD, MAY 4, 1864.

brigade was moved forward on the Plank road to renew the attack, supported by Kershaw's division, while the flanking column was to come into position on its right. The latter were now in line south of the road and almost parallel to it. Longstreet and Kershaw rode with General Jenkins at the head of his brigade as it pressed forward, when suddenly the quiet that had reigned for some moments was broken by a few scattered shots on the north of the road, which were answered by a volley from Mahone's line on the south side. The firing in their front, and the appearance of troops on the road whom they failed to recognize as friends through the intervening timber, had drawn a single volley, which lost to them all the fruits of the splendid work they had just done. General Jenkins was killed and Longstreet seriously wounded by our own men. The troops who were following them faced quickly toward the firing and were about to return it; but when General Kershaw called out, "They are friends," every musket was lowered and the men dropped upon the ground to avoid the fire.

The head of the attack had fallen, and for a time the movements of the Confederates were paralyzed. Lee came forward and directed the dispositions for a new attack, but the change of commanders after the fall of Longstreet, and the resumption of the thread of operations, occasioned a delay of several hours, and then the tide had turned, and we received only hard knocks instead of victory. When at 4 o'clock an attack was made upon the Federal line along the Brock road, it was found strongly fortified, and stubbornly defended. The log breastworks had taken fire during the battle, and at one point separated the combatants by a wall of fire and smoke which neither could pass. Part of Field's division captured the works in their front, but were forced to relinquish them for want of support. Meanwhile Burnside's corps, which had reinforced Hancock during the day, made a vigorous attack on the north of the Orange Plank road. Law's (Alabama) and Perry's (Florida) brigades were being forced back, when, Heth's division coming to their assistance, they assumed the offensive, driving Burnside's troops beyond the extensive line of breastworks constructed previous to their advance. . . .

BREASTWORKS OF HANCOCK'S CORPS ON THE
BROCK ROAD—MORNING OF MAY 7.
From a sketch made at the time.

VIEW FROM NEAR THE WILDERNESS TAVERN,
LOOKING TOWARD THE BATTLE-FIELD—2 P. M., MAY 7.
From a sketch made at the time.

Both sides were now strongly intrenched, and neither could well afford to attack. And so the 7th of May was spent in skirmishing, each waiting to see what the other would do. That night the race for Spotsylvania began. General Lee had been informed by "Jeb" Stuart of the movement of the Federal trains southward during the afternoon. After dark the noise of moving columns along the Brock road could be heard, and it was at once responded to by a similar movement on the part of Lee. The armies moved in parallel columns separated only by a short interval. Longstreet's corps (now commanded by R. H. Anderson) marched all night and arrived at Spotsylvania at 8 o'clock on the morning of the 8th, where the ball was already in motion. Stuart had thrown his cavalry across the Brock road to check the Federal advance, and, as the Federal cavalry had failed to dislodge him, Warren's corps had been pushed forward to clear the way. Kershaw's, Humphreys's, and Law's brigades were at once sent to Stuart's assistance. The head of Warren's column was forced back and immediately commenced intrenching. Spotsylvania Court House was found occupied by Federal cavalry and artillery, which retired without a fight. The Confederates had won the race.

The troops on both sides were now rapidly arriving. Sedgwick's corps joined Warren's, and in the afternoon was thrown heavily against Anderson's right wing, which, assisted by the timely arrival of Ewell's corps, repulsed the attack with great slaughter. Hill's corps (now under command of General Early) did not arrive until the next morning, May 9th. General Lee's line now covered Spotsylvania Court House, with its left (Longstreet's corps) resting on the Po River, a small

stream which flows on the southwest; Ewell's corps in the center, north of the Court House, and Hill's on the right crossing the Fredericksburg road. These positions were generally maintained during the battles that followed, though brigades and divisions were often detached from their proper commands and sent to other parts of the field to meet pressing emergencies. . . .

THROUGH THE WILDERNESS.—THE UNION SIDE.

BY ALEXANDER S. WEBB, BREVET MAJOR-GENERAL, U. S. A.
Commanding a brigade under Hancock during the battle.

. . . As for the Wilderness, it was uneven, with woods, thickets, and ravines right and left. Tangled thickets of pine, scrub-oak, and cedar prevented our seeing the enemy, and prevented any one in command of a large force from determining accurately the position of the troops he was ordering to and fro. The appalling rattle of the musketry, the yells of the enemy, and the cheers of our own men were constantly in our ears. At times, our lines while firing could not see the array of the enemy, not fifty yards distant. After the battle was fairly begun, both sides were protected by log or earth breastworks.

For an understanding of the roads which shaped the movements in the Wilderness, cross the Rapidan from the north and imagine yourself standing on the Germanna Plank road, where the Brock road intersects it, a little south of Wilderness Tavern, and facing due west. In general, the Union right wing (Sedgwick) held the Germanna road, and the

left wing (Hancock) the Brock road, while the center (Warren) stretched across the obtuse angle formed by them. At the Lacy house, in this angle, Grant, Meade, and Warren established their headquarters during the day of the 5th. If, standing at the intersection of these roads, you stretch forward your arms, the right will correspond with the Orange turnpike, the left with the Orange Plank road. Down the Orange turnpike, on May 5th, Lee sent Ewell against Warren, while two divisions of A. P. Hill advanced by the Orange Plank road to check Hancock. Nearly a day later, Longstreet reached the field on the same road as Hill. The engagements fought on May 5th by Ewell on the Orange turnpike, and by A. P. Hill on the Orange Plank road, must be regarded as entirely distinct battles.

Warren received orders from Meade at 7:15 in the morning to attack Ewell with his whole force. General Sedgwick, with Wright's division and Neill's brigade of Getty's division, was ordered to move out, west of the Germanna Plank road, connecting with the Fifth Corps, which was disposed across the turnpike in advance of Wilderness Tavern. At this time also, General Hancock, at Chancellorsville, was warned by General Meade that the enemy had been met on the turnpike, and he was directed to halt at Todd's tavern until further orders. Meantime, Crawford's division of Warren's corps, between the turnpike and plank road, in advancing, found Wilson's cavalry skirmishing with what he supposed to be the enemy's cavalry. At 8 A. M., under orders, Crawford halted, and, hearing that our cavalry, at Parker's store, almost directly south of him, was in need of support, he sent out skirmishers to assist them. Those

skirmishers struck Hill's corps, moving down the Orange Plank road toward the Brock road. Thus at 8 A. M. General Grant and General Meade had developed the presence of Hill on their left and Ewell on their right. Getty's division of Sedgwick had reached Wilderness Tavern; and when it was learned that Hill was coming down the Orange Plank road, Getty was directed to move out toward him, by way of the Brock road, and drive Hill back, if possible, behind Parker's store.

On our right Johnson's division of Ewell was driven back along the Orange turnpike in confusion by General Griffin of Warren's corps. Ricketts and Wright of Sedgwick were delayed in reaching their position on the right of Warren, and for lack of such support Griffin's right brigade under Ayres was forced back and two guns were abandoned. Wadsworth, with his division of Warren's corps, supplemented by Dennison's brigade of Robinson's divi-

BRIGADIER-GENERAL
MICAH JENKINS, C. S. A.
Killed May 6, 1864. (From a tintype.)

MAJOR-GENERAL A. A. HUMPHREYS, U. S. V.
Chief-of-staff, Army of the Potomac.

sion, of the same corps, had started forward in a westerly direction, until he found himself with his left toward the enemy. McCandless's brigade of Crawford's division (also of Warren's corps) had endeavored to obtain a position on the left of Wadsworth, but lost its bearings in the entangled woods so that its left came in contact with Ewell's right, and it, as well as Wadsworth's left, was driven in by Daniel's and Gordon's brigades, forming the right of Ewell. Thus Crawford was left with his left flank in the air, and he of necessity was drawn in about 2 o'clock and posted about a mile southwest from the Lacy house, facing toward his first position at Chewning's house. Wadsworth finally took position on the left of Crawford, facing toward the south and west, with his back toward the Lacy house. Griffin, on Crawford's right, reached to the Orange turnpike. Wright's division of Sedgwick formed on the right of Griffin, with the left of Upton's brigade resting on the pike; then came the brigades of Penrose and Russell, then Neill's brigade of Getty's division. Soon after getting into position Neill and Russell were attacked by Johnson, who was repulsed. Still farther to the right, toward the Germanna Plank road, Seymour, of Ricketts's division, came up and took position. The entire Union front line was now intrenched.

At this time on the center and right Warren and Sedgwick were securely blocked by Ewell's single corps. On the left of the line the situation was this: At 11 A. M. Hancock, whose advance had passed Todd's tavern, received a despatch stating that the enemy was coming down the Orange Plank road in full force, and he was directed to move his corps up to the Brock road, due north. He was further informed that Getty had been sent to drive the enemy back, and must be supported immediately; that on the turnpike Griffin had been pushed back somewhat, and that he (Hancock) must push out on the Plank road and connect his right with Warren's left.

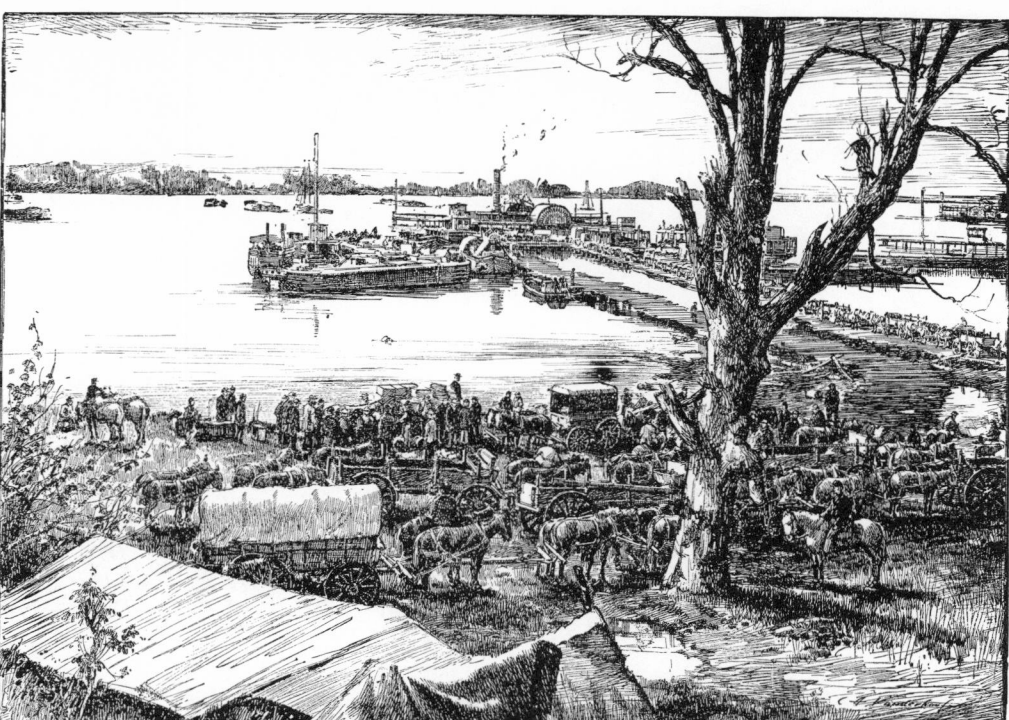

BELLE PLAIN, POTOMAC CREEK, A UNION BASE OF SUPPLIES.
From a photograph taken in 1864.

Hancock promptly started his column, and met General Getty at the junction of the Plank and Germanna roads. Getty's division was then in line of battle, along the Brock road, with Grant's brigade on the left of the Plank road, and Wheaton's and Eustis's brigades on the right of the road which the troops were intrenching. This was 2 P. M. of the 5th. Getty informed Hancock that there were two divisions of A. P. Hill out in his front, and Hancock directed the finishing of the works that had been begun, before any advance should be made. Hancock placed Birney's division on the left of Getty in two lines of battle along the Brock road, and Mott's and Gibbon's divisions on Birney's left; Barlow's divisions held the extreme left and formed an angle on the Brock road overlooking the bed of an unfinished railroad. Most of the artillery of Hancock's corps was posted with Barlow's division. Frank's brigade of Barlow's division was stationed partly across the Brock road, near the junction of the Brock road and a cross-road leading to the Catharpin road. All of Hancock's corps were directed to throw up breastworks of logs and earth, the intrenched line beginning at Getty's left and extending to Barlow's left, where it was refused to cover the flank. The second line, of the Second Corps, also threw up earthworks, and a third intrenched line was formed behind Birney and Mott nearest the Plank road.

At 4:30 P. M. Getty started to the attack, and marched but four hundred yards when he struck Heth's division of Hill's corps, and found the enemy in force, his right having been reinforced by Wilcox's division. Hancock threw forward Birney and Mott on the left of Getty, and put a section

of Ricketts's old battery on the Plank road. General Hancock says in his report: "The fight here became very fierce at once, the lines of battle were exceedingly close, the musketry continuous and deadly along the entire line." Carroll's and Owen's brigades of Gibbon's division were sent in to support Getty upon the Plank road. Colonel Carroll, an excellent fighting man, was wounded, but remained on the field. More to the left, Brooke and Smyth, of Barlow's division, attacked the right of Hill, and forced it back. About 4 o'clock, also, Wadsworth, who had been sent from his position near the Lacy house to strike across the country toward the Plank road, halted for the night in line of battle, facing nearly south between Tapp's house and the Brock road. This ended the operations of May 5th, leaving the Army of the Potomac in close contact with Ewell and Hill. During the night of the 5th orders were given for a general attack by Sedgwick, Warren, and Hancock at 5 o'clock the next morning.

Longstreet's arrival on the field was known and reported by General Hancock to General Meade at 7 A. M. on the 6th; indeed, it was found that Longstreet was present when, at 5 o'clock, my brigade (of Gibbon's division) was ordered to relieve General Getty. When I advanced I immediately became engaged with Field's division, consisting of Gregg's, Benning's, Daw's, and Jenkins's brigades, on the north side of the Orange Plank road.

Just before 5 o'clock the right of the line under Sedgwick was attacked by the Confederates, and gradually the firing extended along the whole front. Wadsworth's division fought its way across Hancock's front to the Plank road, and advanced along that road. Hancock pushed forward Birney with his own and Mott's divisions, Gibbon's division supporting, on the left of the Plank road, and soon drove his opponents from their rifle-pits, and for the time being appeared to have won a victory. His left, however, under Barlow, had not advanced. From information derived from prisoners and from the cavalry operating in the vicinity of Todd's tavern, it was believed at this time that Longstreet was working around the left to attack the line along the Brock road. Instead of attacking there, Longstreet moved to the support of Hill, and just as the Confederates gave away before Birney's assault, Longstreet's leading division, under General C. W. Field, reached Birney's battle-ground and engaged my line.

Thus at 8 o'clock Hancock was battling against both Hill and Longstreet. General Gibbon had command on the left. Hancock himself was looking out for the Plank road.

Warren's Fifth Corps, in front of Ewell, had obeyed the orders of General Grant, in making frequent and persistent attacks throughout the morning without success. The same may be said of Wright, of Sedgwick's Sixth Corps, who was attacking Ewell's left; but Ewell was too strongly intrenched to be driven back from his line by the combined Fifth and Sixth corps.

General Burnside, with the divisions of Wilcox and Potter, attempted to relieve Hancock by passing up between the turnpike and the Plank road to Chewning's farm, connecting his right with Warren

BREVET MAJOR-GENERAL M. C. MEIGS,
QUARTERMASTER-GENERAL, U. S. A.
From a photograph.

DISTRIBUTING AMMUNITION UNDER FIRE TO WARREN'S FIFTH CORPS, MAY 6.
From a sketch made at the time.

THE BURNING WOODS, MAY 6—RESCUING WOUNDED.
From a sketch made at the time.

and joining the right of Hancock, now held by my brigade. Burnside's other division, under Stevenson, moved up the Plank road in our support, and I placed four of his regiments, taken from the head of his column, on my right, then pressed to the rear and changed my whole line, which had been driven back to the Plank road, forward to its original line, holding Field's division in check with the twelve regiments now under my command. . . .

Burnside had finally become engaged far out on our right front; Potter's division came upon the enemy intrenched on the west side of a little ravine extending from Ewell's right. General Burnside says that after considerable fighting he connected his left with Hancock's right and intrenched.

Hancock was out of ammunition, and had to replenish the best way he could from the rear. At 3:45 P. M. the enemy advanced in force against him to within a hundred yards of his logworks on the left of the Plank road. The attack was of course the heaviest here. Anderson's division came forward and took possession of our line of intrenchments, but Carroll's brigade was at hand and drove them out at a double quick.

Now let us return to our right, and stand where General Meade and General Grant were, at the Lacy house. The battle was finished over on the left so far as Hancock and Burnside were concerned. Grant had been thoroughly defeated in his attempt to walk past General Lee on the way to Richmond. Shaler's brigade of Wright's division of Sedgwick's corps had been guarding the wagon-trains, but was now needed for the fight and had returned to the Sixth Corps lines. It was placed

on the extreme right on the Germanna Plank road, due north from where General Grant was standing. Shaler's brigade was close up to the enemy, as indeed was our whole line. Shaler was busy building

breastworks, when it was struck in the flank, rolled up in confusion, and General Seymour and General Shaler and some hundreds of his men were taken prisoners. But the brigade was not de-

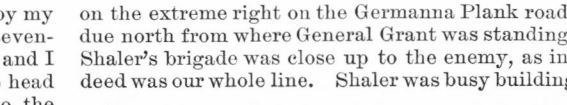

OUT OF THE WILDERNESS, SUNDAY MORNING, MAY 8—THE MARCH TO SPOTSYLVANIA.
From a sketch made at the time.

stroyed. A part of it stood, and, darkness helping them, the assailants were prevented from destroying Wright's division. Wright kept his men in order.

This is in fact the end of the battle of the Wilderness, so far as relates to the infantry. Our cavalry was drawn in from Todd's tavern and the Brock road. The enemy's cavalry followed them. They were all intrenched, and General Grant decided that night that he would continue the movement to the left, as it was impossible to attack a position held by the enemy in such force in a tangled forest. . . .

NOTE.—Warren's Fifth Corps led the advance of the Army of the Potomac from the Wilderness to Spotsylvania, and reached there on the 8th. Crawford's division attacked the Confederate center and developed a strongly intrenched line. On the 9th Burnside's corps arrived opposite the Confederate right and Hancock reached the field on the right of Warren. Sheridan's corps of 10,000 sabers cut loose from the main army and started on the memorable raid around Lee's army. That day, also, General Sedgwick was killed by a Confederate sharpshooter and General H. G. Wright assumed command of the Sixth Corps. On the 10th Hancock crossed the river Po, threatening the Confederate left, and, finding the position intrenched, retired under a heavy fire. Warren assailed the Confederate right center about 3 P. M., and was repulsed. Warren's attempt was followed by an attack all along the line. A picked storming column of Sixth Corps regiments, led by Colonel Emory Upton, penetrated beyond the second line of Confederate intrenchments, but was compelled to fall back. Burnside's troops pushed close up to the enemy's works on Lee's right and intrenched under fire. General T. G. Stevenson, commanding a division under Burnside, was killed while leading the advance. The assault generally failed. On the night of the 11th the Second and Sixth corps were massed opposite the Confederate center for a grand attack on the 12th.

MAJOR-GENERAL JOHN SEDGWICK, U. S. V.
Killed at Spotsylvania in the Wilderness Campaign, May 9, 1864. (From a photograph.)

IN THE RANKS AT THE BLOODY ANGLE,—SPOTSYLVANIA.

BY G. NORTON GALLOWAY,
A SOLDIER OF THE NINETY-FIFTH PENNSYL-
VANIA VOLUNTEERS.

. . . General Grant's orders to Hancock were to
assault at daylight on the 12th in coöperation with
Burnside on his left, while Wright and Warren were

held in readiness to assault on his right. The Confederate army was composed of three corps—Longstreet (now R. H. Anderson) on their left, Ewell in
the center, and A. P. Hill (now under Early) on
the right. The point to be assaulted was a salient
of fieldworks on the Confederate center, afterward called the "Bloody Angle." It was held by
General Edward Johnson's division. Here the
Confederate line broke off at an angle of ninety

STRUGGLING FOR THE WORKS AT THE "BLOODY ANGLE."

degrees, the right parallel, about the length of a
small brigade, being occupied by General George
H. Steuart's regiments. This point was a part or
continuation of the line of works charged and carried by General Upton on May 10th, and was considered to be the key to Lee's position.

Just as the day was breaking, Barlow's and Birney's divisions of Hancock's corps pressed forward
upon the unsuspecting foe, and leaping the breastworks, after a hand-to-hand conflict with the bewildered enemy, in which guns were used as clubs,
possessed themselves of the intrenchments. Over
three thousand prisoners were taken, including
General Johnson and General Steuart. Twenty
Confederate cannon became the permanent trophies of the day, twelve of them belonging to Page
and eight to Cutshaw.

Upon reaching the second line of Lee's works,
held by Wilcox's division, who by this time had
become apprised of the disaster to their comrades,
Hancock met with stern resistance, as Lee in the
mean time had been hurrying troops to Ewell from
Hill on the right and Anderson on the left, and
these were sprung upon our victorious lines with
such an impetus as to drive them hastily back
toward the left of the salient.

As soon as the news of Hancock's good and ill
success reached army headquarters, the Sixth Corps
— Upton's brigade being in advance — was ordered
to move with all possible haste to his support. At
a brisk pace we crossed a line of intrenchments a
short distance in our front, and, passing through a
strip of timber, at once began to realize our nearness to the foe. . . .

I cannot imagine how any of us survived the
sharp fire that swept over us at this point — a fire
so keen that it split the blades of grass all about us,
the Miniés moaning in a furious concert as they
picked out victims by the score.

The rain was still falling in torrents, and held the
country about in obscurity. The command was
soon given to my regiment, the 95th Pennsylvania
Volunteers, Captain Macfarlan commanding,—it
being the advance of Upton's brigade,—to "rise
up," whereupon with hurrahs we went forward,
cheered on by Colonel Upton, who had led us safe
through the Wilderness. It was not long before
we reached an angle of works constructed with
great skill. Immediately in our front an abatis had
been arranged consisting of limbs and branches in-
terwoven into one another, forming footlocks of the
most dangerous character. But there the works
were, and over some of us went, many never to return. At this moment Lee's strong line of battle,
hastily selected for the work of retrieving ill-for-
tune, appeared through the rain, mist, and smoke.
We received their bolts, losing nearly one hundred
of our gallant 95th. Colonel Upton saw at once
that this point must be held at all hazards; for if
Lee should recover the Angle, he would be enabled
to sweep back our lines right and left, and the
fruits of the morning's victory would be lost. The
order was at once given us to lie down and commence firing; the left of our regiment rested against
the works, while the right, slightly refused, rested
upon an elevation in front. And now began a desperate and pertinacious struggle.

Under cover of the smoke-laden rain the enemy
was pushing large bodies of troops forward, determined at all hazards to regain the lost ground.
Could we hold on until the remainder of our brigade
should come to our assistance? Regardless of the
heavy volleys of the enemy that were thinning our
ranks, we stuck to the position and returned the
fire until the 5th Maine and the 121st New York of
our brigade came to our support, while the 96th
Pennsylvania went in on our right; thus reinforced,
we redoubled our exertions. The smoke, which

BREVET MAJOR-GEN. EMORY UPTON, U. S. A.
From a photograph.

UPTON'S BRIGADE AT THE "BLOODY ANGLE."
After drawings by a participant.

MAJOR-GENERAL JOHN C. ROBINSON, U. S. V.
Wounded at Spotsylvania.

was dense at first, was intensified by each discharge of artillery to such an extent that the accuracy of our aim became very uncertain, but nevertheless we kept up the fire in the supposed direction of the enemy. Meanwhile they were crawling forward under cover of the smoke, until, reaching a certain point, and raising their usual yell, they charged gallantly up to the very muzzles of our pieces and reoccupied the Angle.

Upon reaching the breastwork, the Confederates for a few moments had the advantage of us, and made good use of their rifles. Our men went down by the score; all the artillery horses were down; the gallant Upton was the only mounted officer in sight. Hat in hand, he bravely cheered his men, and begged them to "hold this point." All of his staff had been either killed, wounded, or dismounted.

At this moment, and while the open ground in rear of the Confederate works was choked with troops, a section of Battery C, 5th United States Artillery, under Lieutenant Richard Metcalf, was brought into action and increased the carnage by opening at short range with double charges of canister. This staggered the apparently exultant enemy. In the maze of the moment these guns were run up by hand close to the famous Angle, and fired again and again, and they were only abandoned when all the drivers and cannoneers had fallen. The battle was now at white heat.

The rain continued to fall, and clouds of smoke hung over the scene. Like leeches we stuck to the work, determined by our fire to keep the enemy from rising up. Captain John D. Fish, of Upton's staff, who had until this time performed valuable service in conveying ammunition to the gunners, fell, pierced by a bullet. This brave officer seemed to court death as he rode back and forth between the caissons and cannoneers with stands of canister under his "gum" coat. "Give it to them, boys! I'll bring you the canister," said he; and as he turned to cheer the gunners, he fell from his horse mortally wounded. In a few moments the two brass pieces of the 5th Artillery, cut and hacked by the

bullets of both antagonists, lay unworked with their muzzles projecting over the enemy's works, and their wheels half sunk in the mud. Between the lines and near at hand lay the horses of these guns, completely riddled. The dead and wounded were torn to pieces by the canister as it swept the ground where they had fallen. The mud was halfway to our knees, and by our constant movement the fallen were almost buried at our feet. We now backed off from the breastwork a few yards, abandoning for a while the two 12-pounders, but still keeping up a fusillade. We soon closed up our shattered ranks and the brigade settled down again to its task. Our fire was now directed at the top of the breastworks, and woe be to the head or hand that appeared above it. In the mean time the New Jersey brigade, Colonel W. H. Penrose, went into action on our right, and the Third Brigade, General Eustis's, was hard at work. The Vermont brigade, under Colonel Lewis A. Grant, which had been sent to Barlow's assistance, was now at the Angle, and General Wheaton's brigade was deep in the struggle. The Second and Third divisions of the Sixth Corps were also ready to take part. . . .

Our losses were frightful. What remained of many different regiments that had come to our support had concentrated at this point, and had planted their tattered colors upon a slight rise of ground close to the Angle, where they stayed during the latter part of the day.

To keep up the supply of ammunition, pack-mules were brought into use, each animal carrying three thousand rounds. The boxes were dropped close behind the troops engaged, where they were quickly

opened by the officers or file-closers, who served the ammunition to the men. The writer fired four hundred rounds of ammunition, and many others as many or more. In this manner a continuous and rapid fire was maintained, to which for a while the enemy replied with vigor.

Finding that we were not to be driven back, the Confederates began to use more discretion, exposing themselves but little, using the loop-holes in their works to fire through, and at times placing the muzzles of their rifles on the top logs, seizing the trigger and small of the stock, and elevating the breech with one hand sufficiently to reach us. During the day a section of Cowan's battery took position behind us, sending shell after shell close over our heads, to explode inside the Confederate works. In like manner Coehorn mortars eight hundred yards in our rear sent their shells with admirable precision gracefully curving over us. Sometimes the enemy's fire would slacken, and the moments would become so monotonous that something had to be done to stir them up. Then some resolute fellow would seize a fence-rail or piece of abatis, and, creeping close to the breastworks, thrust it over among the enemy, and then drop on the ground to avoid the volley that was sure to follow. A daring lieutenant in one of our left companies leaped upon the breastworks, took a rifle that was handed to him, and discharged it among the foe. In like manner he discharged another, and was in the act of firing a third shot when his cap flew up in the air, and his body pitched headlong among the enemy.

On several occasions squads of disheartened Con-

federates raised pieces of shelter-tents above the works as a flag of truce; upon our slacking fire and calling to them to come in, they would immediately jump the breastworks and surrender. One party of twenty or thirty thus signified their willingness to submit; but owing to the fact that their comrades occasionally took advantage of the cessation to get a volley into us, it was some time before we concluded to give them a chance. With leveled pieces we called to them to come in. Springing upon the breastworks in a body, they stood for an instant panic-stricken at the terrible array before them; that momentary delay was the signal for their destruction. While we, with our fingers pressing the trigger, shouted to them to jump, their troops, massed in the rear, poured a volley into them, killing or wounding all but a few, who dropped with the rest and crawled in under our pieces, while we instantly began firing.

The battle, which during the morning raged with more or less violence on the right and left of this position, gradually slackened, and attention was concentrated upon the Angle. So continuous and heavy was our fire that the head logs of the breastworks were cut and torn until they resembled hickory brooms. Several large oak-trees, which grew just in the rear of the works, were completely gnawed off by our converging fire, and about 3 o'clock in the day fell among the enemy with a loud crash. . . .

NARRATIVE OF EVENTS.

Both Warren's and Burnside's troops coöperated in the attack headed by Hancock at the "Bloody Angle." Warren was quickly repulsed. Burnside made repeated attacks during the day. General R. B. Potter's division carried the enemy's works and was driven out again, but subsequently established connection with Hancock's line. The divisions of Generals O. B. Wilcox and Thomas L. Crittenden (formerly commanding a corps under Rosecrans in the West) advanced their lines by assault and intrenched close to the enemy's works. Six days, May 12 to 18, were passed by Grant in manœuvering and waiting for reinforcements. On the 19th, Ewell's corps attacked Grant's right flank, but was repulsed. On the

BREVET MAJOR-GENERAL ALEXANDER S.
WEBB, U. S. V.
Wounded at Spotsylvania.

McCOOL'S FARM-HOUSE, WITHIN THE "BLOODY ANGLE," SPOTSYLVANIA.
From a war-time photograph.

MAJOR-GENERAL WILLIAM FARRAR
SMITH, U. S. V.
Commanding the Eighteenth Army Corps
at Cold Harbor.

21st the army moved out by the left, past Lee's flank, toward Richmond. On the 23d the advance found Lee intrenched on the North Anna. After some fighting Grant moved onward past Lee's right without, however, crossing the North Anna. Meanwhile, Sheridan's cavalry had rejoined the army on the 25th, after a raid to Richmond, during which the Confederate cavalry was defeated in a brilliant action at Yellow Tavern, and its leader, the noted "Jeb" Stuart, killed. Sheridan led the advance of the army across the Pamunkey River, and on the 28th of May fought a heavy battle with Lee's cavalry at Hawe's shop. Numerous skirmishes and several serious actions followed, and on the 1st of June the armies again confronted each other at Cold Harbor, Lee, as usual, blocking Grant's road to Richmond.

COLD HARBOR.—THE UNION SIDE.

BY MARTIN T. McMAHON, BREVET-GEN., U. S. V.
Chief-of-staff to General H. G. Wright, Sixth Corps.

. . . On the afternoon of May 31st Sheridan, who was on the left flank of the army, carried, with his cavalry, a position near the old well and cross-roads known as Old Cold Harbor, and, with his men dismounted behind rough breastworks, held it against Fitzhugh Lee until night. To this point, during the night, marched the vanguard of the Army of the Potomac, the Sixth Corps, under Wright, over roads that were many inches deep in dust. The night was sultry and oppressive. Many of our horses and mules were dying of thirst, yet they had to be forced through streams without halting to drink. Frequent messengers from Sheridan came during the night, urging the importance of rapid movement. About 9 the next day (June 1st) the head of the column reached Sheridan's position, and the cavalry was withdrawn. The enemy, who had been seriously threatening Sheridan, withdrew from our immediate front to within their lines and awaited us, occupying a strong outer line of intrenchments in front of our center, somewhat in advance of their main position, which included that on which the battle of Gaines's Mill had been fought two years before. It covered the approaches to the Chickahominy, which was the last formidable obstacle we had to meet before standing in

front of the permanent works of Richmond. A large detachment, composed of the Eighteenth Corps and other troops from the Army of the James, under General W. F. Smith, had disembarked at White House on the Pamunkey, and was expected to connect that morning with the Sixth Corps at Cold Harbor. A mistake in orders caused an unnecessary march and long delay. In the afternoon, however, Smith was in position on the right of the Sixth Corps. Late in the afternoon both corps assaulted. The attack was made vigorously and with no reserves. The outer line in front of the right of the Sixth and the left of the Eighteenth was carried brilliantly, and the enemy was forced back, leaving several hundred prisoners in our hands. On the left, where Russell advanced, our losses were severe. The men went forward under a terrible fire from front and flank, until they were ordered to lie down under such shelter as was afforded by the ground and the enemy's

BRASS COEHORNS IN USE AT COLD HARBOR.
From a war-time sketch.

impenetrable slashing, to which they had advanced. Russell was wounded, but remained upon the field all day. This left the well and the old tavern at Cold Harbor in our rear, and brought us in front of the most formidable position yet held by the enemy. In front of him was a wooded country, interspersed with clearings here and there, sparsely populated, and full of swamps. Before daylight the Army of the Potomac stood together once more almost within sight of the spires of Richmond, and on the very ground where, under McClellan, they had defended the passage of the river they were now endeavoring to force.

On the 2d of June our confronting line, on which the burden of the day must necessarily fall, consisted of Hancock on the left, Wright in the center, and Smith on the right. Warren and Burnside were still farther to the right, their lines refused, or drawn back, in the neighborhood of Bethesda Church, but not confronting the enemy. The character of the country was such that at no point could the general direction of the various corps be seen for any considerable distance.

The enemy's general line, although refused at certain points and with salients elsewhere, because of the character of the country, was that of an arc of a circle, the concave side toward us, overlapping on both flanks the three corps intending to attack. The line of advance of Wright's command holding the center was therefore perpendicular to that of the enemy. Hancock's line, connecting with Wright's left, extended obliquely to the left and rear. A movement upon his part to the front must necessarily take him off obliquely from the line of advance of the center. The same was true of Smith's command upon the right. What resulted from this formation the 3d of June developed. No reconnoissance had been made other than the bloody one of the evening before. Every one felt that this was to be the final struggle. No further flanking marches were possible. Richmond was dead in front. No further wheeling of corps from right to left by the rear; no further dusty marches possible on that line, even "if it took all summer." The general attack was fixed for the afternoon of the 2d, and all preparations had been made when the order was countermanded and the attack postponed until half-past four the following morning. Promptly at the hour named on the 3d of June the men moved from the slight cover of the rifle-pits, thrown up during the night, with steady, determined advance, and there rang out suddenly on the summer air such a crash of artillery and musketry as is seldom heard in war. No great portion of the advance could be seen from any particular point, but those of the three corps that passed through the clearings were feeling the fire terribly. Not much return was made at first from our infantry, although the fire of our batteries was incessant. The time of actual advance was not over eight minutes. In that little period more men fell bleeding as they advanced than in any other like period of time throughout the war. A strange and terrible feature of this battle was that as the three gallant corps moved on, each was enfiladed while receiving the full force of the enemy's direct fire in front. The enemy's shell and shot were plunging through Hancock's battalions from his right. From the left a similarly destructive fire was poured in upon Smith, and from both flanks on the Sixth Corps in the center. At some points the slashings and obstructions in the enemy's front were reached. Barlow, of Hancock's corps, drove the enemy from an advanced position, but was himself driven out by the fire of their second line. R. O. Tyler's brigade (the Corcoran Legion) of the same corps swept over an advance work, capturing several hundred prisoners. One officer alone, the colonel of the 164th New York [James P. McMahon], seizing the colors of his regiment from the dying color-bearer as he fell, succeeded in reaching the parapet of the enemy's main works, where he planted his colors and fell dead near the ditch, bleeding from many wounds. Seven other colonels of Hancock's command died within those few minutes. No troops could stand against such a fire, and the order to lie down was given all along the line. At points where no shelter was afforded, the men were withdrawn to such cover as could be found, and the battle of Cold Harbor, as to its result at least, was over. Each corps commander reported and complained to General Meade that the other corps commanders, right or left, as the case might be, failed to protect him from enfilading fire by silencing batteries in their respective fronts: Smith, that he could go no farther until Wright advanced upon his left; Hancock, that it was useless for him to attempt a further advance until Wright advanced upon his right; Wright, that it was impossible for him to move until Smith and Hancock advanced to his support on the right and left to shield him from the enemy's enfilade. . . . Shortly after midday came the order to suspend for the present all further operations, and directing corps commanders to intrench, "including their advance positions," and directing also that reconnoissances be made, "with a view to moving against the enemy's works by regular approaches."

The field in front of us, after the repulse of the main attack, was indeed a sad sight. I remember at one point a mute and pathetic evidence of sterling valor. The 2d Connecticut Heavy Ar-

GENERAL GRANT AND STAFF AT BETHESDA CHURCH, NORTH OF COLD HARBOR.
General Grant is sitting with his back to the smaller tree. (From a war-time photograph.)

tillery, a new regiment eighteen hundred strong, had joined us but a few days before the battle. Its uniform was bright and fresh, therefore its dead were easily distinguished where they lay. They marked in a dotted line an obtuse angle, covering a wide front, with its apex toward the enemy, and there upon his face, still in death, with his head to the works, lay the colonel, the brave and genial Colonel Elisha S. Kellogg.

When night came on, the groans and moaning of the wounded, all our own, who were lying between the lines, were heartrending. Some were brought in by volunteers from our intrenchments, but many remained for three days uncared for beneath the hot summer suns and the unrefreshing dews of the sultry summer nights. The men in the works grew impatient, yet it was against orders and was almost certain death to go beyond our earthworks. An impression prevails in the popular mind, and with some reason perhaps, that a commander who

sends a flag of truce asking permission to bury his dead and bring in his wounded has lost the field of battle. Hence the reluctance upon our part to ask a flag of truce. In effect it was done at last on the evening of the third day after the battle, when, for the most part, the wounded needed no further care, and our dead had to be buried almost where they fell.

The work of intrenching could only be done at night. The fire of sharp-shooters was incessant, and no man upon all that line could stand erect and live an instant. This condition of things continued for twelve days and nights: Sharp-shooters' fire from both sides went on all day; all night the zigzags and parallels nearer to the enemy's works were being constructed. In none of its marches by day or night did that army suffer more than during those twelve days. Rations and ammunition were brought forward from parallel to parallel through the zigzag trenches,

and in some instances where regiments whose term of service had expired were ordered home, they had to leave the field crawling on hands and knees through the trenches to the rear At 9 o'clock every night the enemy opened fire with artillery and musketry along his whole line. This was undoubtedly done under suspicion that the Army of the Potomac had seen the hopelessness of the task before it and would withdraw in the night-time for another movement by the flank, and, if engaged in such a movement, would be thrown into confusion by this threat of a night attack. However, no advance was made by the enemy.

Another strange order came about this time. It opened with a preamble that inasmuch as the enemy had without provocation repeatedly opened fire during the night upon our lines, therefore, at midnight of that day, the corps commanders were directed to open fire from all their batteries generally upon the enemy's position and continue it until daylight. This was coupled with the proviso that if in the opinion of a corps commander the fire would provoke a return from the enemy which would inflict severe damage upon his troops, then he was exempted from the operation of the order. The commanders of the three corps holding the front communicated with one another by telegraph with this result: Smith was satisfied that the fire which he would provoke would inflict upon him disproportionate damage. Hancock for the same reason did not intend to open fire unless the fire provoked by the other corps reached his lines. Wright adopted the same rule of action. Twelve o'clock came, and the summer night continued undisturbed.

Thus things went on until the 15th of June. Preparations had been made in the mean time for the abandonment of the position and the withdrawal of the army to another line of operations. Yet the summer had scarcely begun. The army was withdrawn successfully and skilfully, and, crossing to the south bank of the James, entered upon the new campaign before Petersburg. . . .

"Cold Harbor," said General Grant, "is, I think, the only battle I ever fought that I would not fight over again under the circumstances" ("Around the World with General Grant," by John Russell Young, Vol. II., ch. XXXIV., p. 304); and again, in his "Memoirs," Vol. II., p. 276, "I have always regretted that the last assault at Cold Harbor was ever made."

COLD HARBOR.—THE CONFEDERATE SIDE.

BY GEORGE CARY EGGLESTON.
Sergeant-Major, Lamkin's Virginia Battery.

. . . When we reached Cold Harbor the command to which I belonged had been marching almost continuously day and night for more than fifty hours without food, and for the first time we knew what actual starvation was. It was during that march that I heard a man wish himself a woman,—the only case of the kind I ever heard of,—and he uttered the wish half in grim jest and made haste to qualify it by adding, "or a baby."

Yet we recovered our cheerfulness at once after taking the first nibble at the crackers issued to us

VIEW OF UNION BREASTWORKS ON THE COLD HARBOR LINE, JUNE 1.
From a sketch made at the time.

PENNSYLVANIA RESERVES RESISTING AN ATTACK NEAR THE BETHESDA CHURCH, JUNE 2.
From a sketch made at the time.

there, and made a jest of the scantiness of the supply. One tall, lean mountaineer, Jim Thomas by name, who received a slight wound every time he was under fire and was never sufficiently hurt to quit duty, was standing upon a bank of earth, slowly munching a bit of his last cracker, and watching the effect of some artillery fire which was in progress at the time, when a bullet carried away his cap and cut a strip of hair from his head, leaving the scalp for a space as bald as if it had been shaved with a razor. He sat down at once to nurse a sharp headache, and then discovered that the cracker he had held in his hand was gone, leaving a mere fragment in his grasp. At first he was in doubt whether he might not have eaten it unconsciously, but he quickly discovered that it had been knocked out of his hand and crushed to bits by a bullet, whereupon as he sat there in an exposed place, where the fire was unobstructed, he lamented his loss in soliloquy. "If I had eaten that cracker half an hour ago, it would have been safe," he said. "I should have had none left for next time, but I have none left as it is. That shows how foolish it is to save anything. Whew! how my head aches! I wish it was from over-eating, but even the doctor could n't lay it to that just now. The next time I stand up to watch the firing, I 'll put my cracker — if I have any — in a safe place down by the breastwork, where it won't get wounded, poor thing! By the way, here 's a little piece left, and that 'll get shot while I sit here talking." And with that he jumped down into the ditch, carefully placed the mouthful of hardtack at the foot of the works, and resumed his interested observation of the artillery duel.

Trifling of that kind was constant among the men throughout that terrible campaign from the Wilderness to Petersburg, and while it yielded nothing worth recording as wit or humor, it has always seemed to me the most remarkable and most significant fact in the history of the time. It revealed a capacity for cheerful endurance which alone made the campaign possible on the Confederate side. With mercenary troops or regulars the resistance that Lee was able to offer to Grant's tremendous pressure would have been im-

possible in such circumstances. The starvation and the excessive marching would have destroyed the *morale* of troops held together only by discipline. No historical criticism of our civil war can be otherwise than misleading if it omits to give a prominent place, as a factor, to the character of the volunteers on both sides, who, in acquiring the steadiness and order of regulars, never lost their personal interest in the contest, or their personal pride of manhood, as a sustaining force under trying conditions. If either force had lacked this element of personal heroism on the part of its men it would have been driven from the field long before the spring of 1865. It seems to me the most important duty of those who now furnish the materials out of which the ultimate history of our war will be constructed is to emphasize this aspect of the matter, and in every possible way to illustrate the part which the high personal character of the volunteers in the ranks played in determining the events of the contest. For that reason I like to record one incident which I had an opportunity to observe at Cold Harbor.

Immediately opposite the position occupied by the battery to which I belonged, and about six or eight hundred yards distant across an open field, lay a Federal battery, whose commander was manifestly a man deeply in earnest for other and higher reasons than those that govern the professional soldier: a man who fought well because he fought in what he felt to be his own cause and quarrel. His guns and ours were engaged almost continuously in an artillery duel, so that I became specially interested in him, particularly as the extreme precision of his fire indicated thoroughness and conscientiousness of work for months before the campaign began. One day — whether before or after the great assault I cannot now remember — that part of our line which lay immediately to the left of the position occupied by the battery to which I belonged was thrown forward to force the opposing Federal line back. It was the only large movement in the way of a charge over perfectly open ground that I ever had a chance to observe with an unobstructed view, and merely as a spectator. When we, with a few well-aimed shells, had

fired a barn that stood between the lines, and driven a multitude of sharp-shooters out of it, the troops to our left leaped over their works and with a cheer moved rapidly across the field. The resistance made to their advance was not very determined, — probably the Federal line at that point had been weakened by concentration elsewhere, — and after a brief struggle our men crossed the slight Federal earthworks and pressed their adversaries back into the woods and beyond my view. It was a beautiful operation to look at, and one the like of which a soldier rarely has an opportunity to see so well; but my attention was specially drawn to the situation of the artillery commander to whom I have referred as posted immediately in our front. His position was the pivot, the point where the Federal line was broken to a new angle, when that part of it which lay upon his right hand was pressed back while that on his left remained stationary. He fought like a Turk or a tiger. He directed the greater part of his rapid fire upon the advancing line of Confederates, but turned a gun every few moments upon our battery, apparently by way of letting us know that he was not unmindful of our attentions, even when he was so busily engaged elsewhere. The bending back of the line on his right presently subjected him to a murderous fire upon the flank and rear, a fire against which he had no protection whatever, while we continued a furious bombardment from the front. His position was plainly an untenable one, and, so far as I could discover with a strong glass, he was for a time without infantry support. But he held his ground and continued to fight in spite of all, firing at one time as from two faces of an acute triangle. His determination was superb, and the coolness of his gunners and cannoneers was worthy of the unbounded admiration which we, their enemies, felt for them. Their firing increased in rapidity as their difficulties multiplied, but it showed no sign of becoming wild or hurried. Every shot went straight to the object against which it was directed; every fuse was accurately timed, and every shell burst where it was intended to burst. I remember that in the very heat of the contest there came into my mind Bulwer's superb

description of Warwick's last struggle, in which he says that around the king-maker's person there "centered a little *war*," and I applied the phrase to the heroic fellow who was so superbly fighting against hopeless odds immediately in front of me. Several of his guns were dismounted, and his dead horses were strewn in rear. The loss among his men was appalling, but he fought on as coolly as before, and with our glasses we could see him calmly sitting on his large gray horse directing the work of his gunners and patiently awaiting the coming of the infantry support, without which he could not withdraw his guns. It came at last, and the batteries retired to the new line.

When the battalion was gone and the brief action over, the wreck that was left behind bore sufficient witness of the fearfulness of the fire so coolly endured. The large gray horse lay dead upon the ground; but we preferred to believe that his brave rider was still alive to receive the promotion which he had unquestionably won.

NOTE. — The effective strength of the Union army in the Wilderness is estimated at 118,000 of all arms.

On the 1st of June the Army of the Potomac, at and about Cold Harbor, numbered 103,875 "present for duty," and General W. F. Smith brought from the Army of the James about 10,000, exclusive of 2500 left to guard the landing at White House. The losses of this army (including those sustained by the reinforcements received at Spotsylvania and Smith's corps at Cold Harbor), from May 5th to June 15th, were as follows:

BATTLES, ETC.	Killed.	Wounded.	Captured or Missing.	Total.
The Wilderness	2246	12,037	3383	17,666
Spotsylvania	2725	13,416	2258	18,399
North Anna and Totopotomoy	591	2,734	661	3,986
Cold Harbor and Bethesda Church	1844	9,077	1816	12,737
Sheridan's first expedition	64	337	224	625
Sheridan's second expedition	150	741	625	1,516
Grand total from the Wilderness to the James	7620	38,342	8967	54,929

Lee's effective force at the commencement of the campaign was not less than 61,000. Reinforcements aggregating 14,400 men reached him after crossing the North Anna. The Confederate losses during the campaign are nowhere authoritatively stated.

A SHELL AT HEADQUARTERS.

THE GRAND STRATEGY OF THE LAST YEAR OF THE WAR, AND THE CAPTURE OF ATLANTA.

BY WILLIAM T. SHERMAN, GENERAL, U. S. A.
Commander of the Military Division of the Mississippi.

ON the 4th day of March, 1864, General U. S. Grant was summoned to Washington from Nashville to receive his commission of lieutenant-general, the highest rank then known in the United States, and the same that was conferred on Washington in 1798. He reached the capital on the 7th, had an interview for the first time with Mr. Lincoln, and on the 9th received his commission at the hands of the President, who made a short address, to which Grant made a suitable reply. He was informed that it was desirable that he should come east to command all the armies of the United States, and give his personal supervision to the Army of the Potomac. On the 10th he visited General Meade at Brandy Station, and saw many of his leading officers, but he returned to Washington the next day and went on to Nashville, to which place he had summoned me, then absent on my Meridian expedition. On the 18th of March he turned over to me the command of the Western armies, and started back for Washington, I accompanying him as far as Cincinnati. Amidst constant interruptions of a business and social nature, we reached the satisfactory conclusion that, as soon as the season would permit, all the armies of the Union would assume the "bold offensive" by "concentric lines" on the common enemy, and would finish up the job in a single campaign if possible. The main "objectives" were Lee's army behind the Rapidan in Virginia, and Joseph E. Johnston's army at Dalton, Georgia.

On reaching Washington, Grant studied with great care all the minutiæ of the organization, strength, qualities, and resources of each of the many armies into which the Union forces had resolved themselves by reason of preceding events, and in due time with wonderful precision laid out the work which each one should undertake. His written instructions to me at Nashville were embraced in the two letters of April 4th and April 19th, 1864, both in his own handwriting, which I still possess, and which, in my judgment, are as complete as any

of those of the Duke of Wellington contained in the twelve volumes of his published letters and correspondence.

With the month of May came the season for *action*, and by the 4th all his armies were in motion. The army of Butler at Fort Monroe was his left, Meade's army the center, and mine at Chattanooga his right. Butler was to move against Richmond on the south of James River, Meade straight against Lee, intrenched behind the Rapidan, and I to attack Joe Johnston and push him to and beyond Atlanta. This was as far as human foresight could penetrate. Though Meade commanded the Army of the Potomac, Grant virtually controlled it, and on the 4th of May, 1864, he crossed the Rapidan, and at noon of the 5th attacked Lee.

He knew that a certain amount of fighting, "killing," had to be done to accomplish his end, and also to pay the penalty of former failures. In the "wilderness" there was no room for grand strategy, or even minor tactics; but the fighting was desperate, the losses to the Union army being, according to Phisterer, 18,387, to the Confederate loss of 11,400 — the difference due to Lee's intrenchments and the blind nature of the country in which the battle was fought. On the night of May 7th both parties paused, appalled by the fearful slaughter; but Grant commanded, "Forward by the left flank." That was, in my judgment, the supreme moment of his life; undismayed, with a full comprehension of the importance of the work in which he was engaged, feeling as keen a sympathy for his dead and wounded as any one, and without stopping to count their numbers, he gave his orders calmly, specifically, and absolutely — "Forward to Spotsylvania." But his watchful and skilful antagonist detected his purpose, and, having the inner or shorter line, threw his army across Grant's path, and promptly fortified it. These field intrenchments are peculiar to America, though I am convinced they were employed by the Romans in Gaul in the days of Cæsar. Troops, halting for

From a photograph taken after the war.

the night or for battle, faced the enemy; moved forward to ground with a good outlook to the front; stacked arms, gathered logs, stumps, fence-rails, anything which would stop a bullet; piled these to their front, and, digging a ditch behind, threw the dirt forward, and made a parapet which covered their persons as perfectly as a granite wall.

When Grant reached Spotsylvania, May 8th, he found his antagonist in his front thus intrenched. He was delayed there till the 20th, during which time there was incessant fighting, because he was compelled to attack his enemy behind these improvised intrenchments. His losses, according to Phisterer, were 12,564, while the Confederates lost

9000. Nevertheless, his renewed order, "Forward by the left flank," compelled Lee to retreat to the defenses of Richmond.

Grant's "Memoirs" enable us to follow him day by day across the various rivers which lay between him and Richmond, and in the bloody assaults at Cold Harbor, where his losses are reported 14,931 to 1700 by his opponent. Yet ever onward by the left flank, he crossed James River and penned Lee and his Army of Northern Virginia within the intrenchments of Richmond and Petersburg for ten long months on the pure defensive, to remain almost passive observers of local events, while Grant's other armies were absolutely annihilating the Southern Confederacy.

While Grant was fighting desperately from the Rapidan to the James, there were two other armies within the same "zone of operations"—that "of the James" under General Butler, who was expected to march up on the south and invest Petersburg and even Richmond; and that of Sigel at Winchester, who was expected to march up the Valley of Virginia, pick up his detachments from the Kanawha (Crook and Averell), and threaten Lynchburg, a place of vital importance to Lee in Richmond. Butler failed to accomplish what was expected of him; and Sigel failed at the very start, and was replaced by Hunter, who marched up the valley, made junction with Crook and Averell at Staunton, and pushed on with commendable vigor to Lynchburg, which he invested on the 16th of June.

Lee, who had by this time been driven into Richmond with a force large enough to hold his lines of intrenchments and a surplus for expeditions, detached General Jubal A. Early with the equivalent of a corps to drive Hunter away from Lynchburg. Hunter, far from his base, with inadequate supplies of food and ammunition, retreated by the Kanawha to the Ohio River, his nearest base, thereby exposing the Valley of Virginia; whereupon Early, an educated soldier, promptly resolved to take advantage of the occasion, marched rapidly down this valley northward to Winchester, crossed the Potomac to Hagerstown, and thence boldly marched on Washington, defended at that time only by militia and armed clerks. Grant, fully alive to the danger,

GENERAL WILLIAM T. SHERMAN AT ATLANTA.
From a photograph.

GENERAL SHERMAN'S HEADQUARTERS AT THE HOWARD HOUSE, IN FRONT OF ATLANTA.
From a sketch made at the time.

despatched to Washington, from his army investing Petersburg, two divisions of the Sixth Corps, and also the Nineteenth Corps just arriving from New Orleans. These troops arrived at the very nick of time—met Early's army in the suburbs of Washington, and drove it back to the Valley of Virginia.

This most skilful movement of Early demonstrated to General Grant the importance of the Valley of Virginia, not only as a base of supplies for Lee's army in Richmond, but as the most direct, the shortest, and the easiest route for a "diversion" into the Union territory north of the Potomac. He therefore cast around for a suitable commander for this field of operations, and settled upon Major-General Philip H. Sheridan, whom he had brought from the West to command the cavalry corps of the Army of the Potomac.

Sheridan promptly went to his new sphere of operations [see p. 283], quickly ascertained its strength and resources, and resolved to attack Early in the position which he had chosen in and about Winchester, Va. He delivered his attack across broken ground on the 19th of September, beat his antagonist in fair, open battle, sending him "whirling up the valley," inflicting a loss of 5500 men to his own of 4873, and followed him up to Cedar Creek and Fisher's Hill. Early recomposed his army and fell upon the Union army on

the 19th of October at Cedar Creek, gaining a temporary advantage during General Sheridan's absence; but on his opportune return his army resumed the offensive, defeated Early, captured nearly all his artillery, and drove him completely out of his field of operations, eliminating that army from the subsequent problem of the war. Sheridan's losses were 5995 to Early's 4200; but these losses are no just measure of the results of that victory, which made it impossible to use the valley as a Confederate base of supplies and as an easy route for raids within the Union lines. General Sheridan then committed its protection to detachments, and with his main force rejoined Grant, who still held Lee's army inside his intrenchments at Richmond and Petersburg.

I now turn with a feeling of extreme delicacy to the conduct of that other campaign from Chattanooga to Atlanta, Savannah, and Raleigh, which with liberal discretion was committed to me by General Grant in his minute instructions of April 4th and April 19th, 1864. To all military students these letters must be familiar, because they have been published again and again, and there never was and never can be raised a question of rivalry or claim between us as to the relative merits of the manner in which we played our respective parts. We were as brothers—I the older man in years, he the higher in rank. We both believed in our heart of hearts that the success of the Union cause was not only necessary to the then generation of Americans, but to all future generations. We both professed to be gentlemen and professional soldiers, educated in the science of war by our generous Government for the very occasion which had arisen. Neither of us by nature was a combative man; but with honest hearts and a clear purpose to do what man could we embarked on that campaign, which I believe, in its strategy, in its logistics, in its grand and minor tactics, has added new luster to the old science of war. Both of us had at our front generals to whom in early life we had been taught to look up—educated and experienced soldiers like ourselves, not likely to make any mistakes, and each of whom had as strong an army as could be collected from the mass of the Southern people,—of the same blood as ourselves, brave, confident, and well-equipped; in addition to which they had the most decided advantage of operating in their own difficult country of mountain, forest, ravine, and river, affording admirable opportunities for defense, besides the other equally important advantage that we had to invade the country of our unqualified enemy, and expose our long lines of supply to the guerrillas of an "exasperated people." Again, as we advanced we had to leave guards to bridges, stations, and interme-

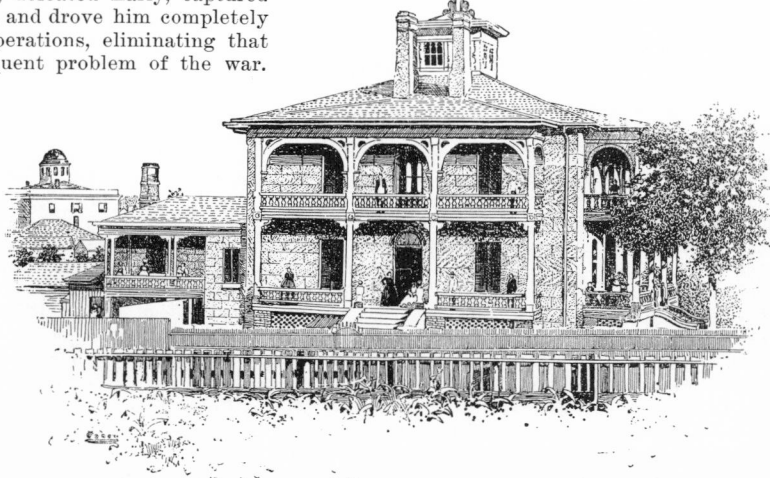

THE "CALICO HOUSE," GENERAL SHERMAN'S FIRST HEADQUARTERS IN ATLANTA.
Afterward the office of his engineers; also for several months a hospital. (From a photograph.)

MAJOR-GENERAL JACOB D. COX, U. S. V.
From a photograph.

ALLATOONA PASS, LOOKING NORTH—CORSE'S FORT ON THE LEFT.
From a war-time photograph.

MAJOR-GENERAL E. C. WALTHALL, C. S. A.
From a photograph.

diate depots, diminishing the fighting force, while our enemy gained strength by picking up his detachments as he fell back, and had railroads to bring supplies and reinforcements from his rear. I instance these facts to offset the common assertion that we of the North won the war by brute force and not by courage and skill.

On the historic 4th day of May, 1864, the Confederate army at my front lay at Dalton, Georgia [see p. 261], composed, according to the best authority, of about 45,000 men, commanded by Joseph E. Johnston, who was equal in all the elements of generalship to Lee, and who was under instructions from the war powers in Richmond to assume the offensive northward as far as Nashville. But he soon discovered that he would have to conduct a defensive campaign. Coincident with the movement of the Army of the Potomac, as announced by telegraph, I advanced from our base at Chattanooga with the Army of the Ohio, 13,559 men; the Army of the Cumberland, 60,773, and the Army of the Tennessee, 24,465,—grand total, 98,797 men and 254 guns.

I had no purpose to attack Johnston's position at Dalton in front, but marched from Chattanooga to feign at his front and to make a lodgment in Resaca, eighteen miles to his rear, on "his line of communication and supply." The movement was partly, not wholly, successful; but it compelled Johnston to let go Dalton and fight us at Resaca, where, May 13th-16th, our loss was 2747 and his 2800. I fought offensively and he defensively, aided by earth parapets. He then fell back to Calhoun, Adairsville, and Cassville, where he halted for the battle of the campaign; but for reasons given in his memoirs, he continued his retreat behind the next spur of mountains to Allatoona.

Pausing for a few days to repair the railroad without attempting Allatoona, of which I had personal knowledge acquired in 1844, I resolved to push on toward Atlanta by way of Dallas; Johnston quickly detected this, and forced me to fight him, May 25th-28th, at New Hope Church, four miles north of Dallas, with losses of 3000 to the Confederates and 2400 to us. The country was almost in a state of nature—with few or no roads, nothing that a European could understand; yet the bullet killed its victim there as surely as at Sevastopol.

Johnston had meantime picked up his detachments, and had received reinforcements from his rear which raised his aggregate strength to 62,000 men, and warranted him in claiming that he was purposely drawing us far from our base, and that when the right moment should come he would turn on us and destroy us. We were equally confident, and not the least alarmed. He then fell back to his position at Marietta, with Brush Mountain on his right, Kenesaw his center, and Lost Mountain his left. His line of ten miles was too long for his numbers, and he soon let go his flanks and concentrated on Kenesaw. We closed down in battle array, repaired the railroad up to our very camps, and then prepared for the contest. Not a day, not an hour, not a minute was there a cessation of fire. Our skirmishers were in absolute contact, the lines of battle and the batteries but little in rear of the skirmishers; and thus matters continued until June 27th, when I ordered a general assault, with the full coöperation of my great lieutenants, Thomas, McPherson, and Schofield, as good and true men as ever lived or died for their country's cause; but we failed, losing 3000 men, to the Confederate loss of 630. Still the result was that within three days Johnston abandoned the strongest possible position and was in full retreat for the Chat-

MAJOR-GENERAL JOHN M. PALMER, U. S. V.
From an ambrotype.

tahoochee River. We were on his heels; skirmished with his rear at Smyrna Church on the 4th day of July, and saw him fairly across the Chattahoochee on the 10th, covered and protected by the best line of field intrenchments I have ever seen, prepared long in advance. No officer or soldier who ever served under me will question the generalship of Joseph E. Johnston. His retreats were timely, in good order, and he left nothing behind. We had advanced into the enemy's country 120 miles, with a single-track railroad, which had to bring clothing, food, ammunition, everything requisite for 100,000 men and 23,000 animals. The city of Atlanta, the gate city opening the interior of the important State of Georgia, was in sight; its protecting army was shaken but not defeated, and onward we had to go—illustrating the principle that "an army once on the offensive must maintain the offensive."

We feigned to the right, but crossed the Chattahoochee by the left, and soon confronted our enemy behind his first line of intrenchments at Peach Tree Creek, prepared in advance for this very occasion. At this critical moment the Confederate Government rendered us most valuable service. Being dissatisfied with the Fabian policy of General Johnston, it relieved him, and General Hood was substituted to command the Confederate army [July 18th]. Hood was known to us to be a "fighter," a graduate of West Point of the class of 1853, No. 44, of which class two of my army commanders, McPherson and Schofield, were No. 1 and No. 7. The character of a leader is a large factor in the game of war, and I confess I was pleased at this change, of which I had early notice. I knew that I had an army superior in numbers and morale to that of my antagonist; but being so far from my base, and operating in a country devoid of food and forage, I was dependent for supplies on a poorly constructed railroad back to Louisville, five hundred miles. I was willing to meet the enemy in the open country, but not behind well-constructed parapets.

Promptly, as expected, General Hood sallied from his Peach Tree line on the 20th of July, about midday, striking the Twentieth Corps (Hooker), which had just crossed Peach Tree Creek by improvised bridges. The troops became commingled, and fought hand to hand desperately for about four hours, when the Confederates were driven back within their lines, leaving behind their dead and wounded. These amounted to 4796 men, to our loss of 1710. We followed up, and Hood fell back to the main lines of the city of Atlanta. We closed in, when again Hood, holding these lines with about one-half his force, with the other half made a wide circuit by night, under cover of the woods, and on the 22d of July enveloped our left flank "in air," a movement that led to the hardest battle of the campaign. [See page 266.] He encountered the Army of the Tennessee—skilled veterans who were always ready to fight, were not alarmed by flank or rear attacks, and met their assailants with heroic valor. The battle raged from noon to night, when the Confederates, baffled and defeated, fell back within the intrenchments of Atlanta. Their losses are reported 8499 to ours of 3641; but among our dead was McPherson, the commander of the Army of the Tennessee. While this battle was in progress, Schofield at the center and Thomas on the right made efforts to break through the intrenchments at their fronts, but found them too strong to assault.

The Army of the Tennessee was then shifted, under its new commander (Howard), from the extreme left to the extreme right, to reach, if possible, the railroad by which Hood drew his supplies, when, on the 28th of July, he repeated his tactics of the 22d, sustaining an overwhelming defeat, losing 4632 men to our 700. These three sallies convinced him that his predecessor, General Johnston, had not erred in standing on the defensive. Thereafter the Confederate army in Atlanta clung to its parapets. I never intended to assault these, but gradually worked to the right to reach and destroy his line of supplies, because soldiers, like other mortals, must have food. Our extension to the right brought on numerous conflicts, but nothing worthy of note, till about the end of August I resolved to leave one corps to protect our communications to the rear, and move with the other five to a point (Jonesboro') on the railroad twenty-six miles below Atlanta, *not* fortified. This movement was perfectly strategic, was successful, and resulted in our occupation of Atlanta, on the 2d of September, 1864. The result had a large effect on the whole country at the time, for solid and political reasons. I claim no special merit to myself, save that I believe I followed the teachings of the best masters of the "science of war" of which

I had knowledge; and, better still, I had pleased Mr. Lincoln, who wanted "success" very much. But I had not accomplished all, for Hood's army, the chief "objective," had escaped.

Then began the real trouble. We were in possession of Atlanta, and Hood remained at Lovejoy's Station, thirty miles south-east, on the Savannah railroad, with an army of about 40,000 veterans inured to war, and with a fair amount of wagons to carry his supplies, independent of the railroads. On the 21st of September he shifted his position to Palmetto Station, twenty-five miles south-west of Atlanta, on the Montgomery and Selma railroad, where he began systematic preparations for an aggressive campaign against our communications to compel us to abandon our conquests. Here he was visited by Mr. Davis, who promised all possible coöperation and assistance in the proposed campaign; and here also Mr. Davis made his famous speech, which was duly reported to me in Atlanta, assuring his army that they would make my retreat more disastrous than was that of Napoleon from Moscow. Forewarned, I took immediate measures to thwart his plans. One division was sent back to Rome, another to Chattanooga; the guards along our railroad were reinforced and warned of the coming blow. General Thomas was sent back to the headquarters of his department at Nashville, Schofield to his at Knoxville, while I remained in Atlanta to await Hood's "initiative." This followed soon. Hood, sending his cavalry ahead, crossed the Chattahoochee River at Cambelltown with his main army on the 1st of October, and moved to Dallas, detaching a strong force against the railroad above Marietta which destroyed it for fifteen miles, and then sent French's division to capture Allatoona. I followed Hood, reaching Kenesaw Mountain in time to see in the distance the attack on Allatoona, which was handsomely repulsed by Corse. Hood then moved westward, avoiding Rome, and by a circuit reached Resaca, which he summoned to surrender, but did not wait to attack. He continued thence the destruction of the railroad for about twenty miles to the tunnel, including Dalton, whose garrison he captured. I followed up to Resaca, then turned west to intercept his retreat down the Valley of Chattooga; but by rapid marching he escaped to Gadsden, on the Coosa, I halting at Gaylesville, whence to observe his further movements. Hood, after a pause,

UNION EARTHWORKS IN FRONT OF BIG AND LITTLE KENESAW.
From a war-time photograph.

crossed the mountains to Decatur, on the Tennessee River, which point, as it was defended by a good division of troops, he avoided, and finally halted opposite Florence, Alabama, on the Tennessee. Divining the object of his movement against our communications, which had been thus far rapid and skilful, I detached by rail General Schofield and two of my six corps to Nashville, all the reinforcements that Thomas deemed necessary to enable him to defend Tennessee, and began my systematic preparations for resuming the offensive against Georgia. Repairing the broken railroads, we collected in Atlanta the necessary food and transportation for 60,000 men, sent to the rear all impediments, called in all detachments, and ordered them to march for Atlanta, where by November 4th were assembled four infantry corps, one cavalry division, and 65 field guns, aggregating 60,598 men. Hood remained at Florence, preparing to invade Tennessee and Kentucky, or to follow me. We were prepared for either alternative.

According to the great Napoleon, the fundamental maxim for successful war is to "converge a superior force on the critical point at the critical time." In 1864 the main "objectives" were Lee's and Johnston's armies, and the critical point was thought to be Richmond or Atlanta, whichever should be longer held. Had General Grant overwhelmed and scattered Lee's army and occupied Richmond he would have come to Atlanta; but as I happened to occupy Atlanta first, and had driven Hood off to a divergent line of operations far to the west, it was good strategy to leave him to a subordinate force, and with my main army to join Grant at Richmond. The most practicable route to Richmond was nearly a thousand miles in dis-

tance, too long for a single march; hence the necessity to reach the sea-coast for a new base. Savannah, distant three hundred miles, was the nearest point, and this distance we accomplished from November 12th to December 21st, 1864. According to the Duke of Wellington, an army moves upon its belly, not upon its legs; and no army dependent on wagons can operate more than a hundred miles from its base, because the teams going and returning consume the contents of their wagons, leaving little or nothing for the maintenance of the men and animals at the front, who are fully employed in fighting; hence the necessity to "forage liberally on the country," a measure which fed our men and animals chiefly on the very supplies which had been gathered near the railroads by the enemy for the maintenance of his own armies. "The March to the Sea" was in strategy only a shift of base for ulterior and highly important purposes.

Many an orator in his safe office at the North had proclaimed his purpose to cleave his way to the sea. Every expedition which crossed the Ohio River in the early part of the war headed for the sea; but things were not ripe till the Western army had fought, and toiled, and labored down to Atlanta. Not till then did a "March to the Sea" become practicable and possible of grand results. Alone I never measured it as now my eulogists do, but coupled with Thomas's acts about Nashville, and those about Richmond directed in person by General Grant, the "March to the Sea," with its necessary corollary, the march northward to Raleigh, became vastly important, if not actually conclusive of the war. Mr. Lincoln was the wisest man of our day, and more truly and kindly gave voice to my secret thoughts and feeling when he

CONFEDERATES DRAGGING GUNS UP KENESAW MOUNTAIN.
From the "Valentine," published by the Western & Atlantic R. R. Co.

CONFEDERATE WORKS ON THE SOUTH BANK OF THE CHATTAHOOCHEE.

OPPOSING SHERMAN'S ADVANCE TO ATLANTA.

BY JOSEPH E. JOHNSTON, GENERAL, C. S. A.
Commander of Confederate army during the campaign from Dalton to Atlanta.

PRESIDENT DAVIS transferred me from the Department of Mississippi to the command of the Army of Tennessee by a telegram received December 18th, 1863, in the camp of Ross's brigade of cavalry near Bolton. I assumed that command at Dalton on the 27th. . . . In the inspections, which were made as soon as practicable, the appearance of the army was very far from being "matter of much congratulation." Instead of a reserve of muskets there was a deficiency of six thousand and as great a one of blankets, while the number of bare feet was painful to see. The artillery horses were too feeble to draw the guns in fields, or on a march, and the mules were in similar condition. . . . The last return of the army was of December 20th, and exhibited an effective total of less than 36,000, of whom 6000 were without arms and as many without shoes. . . .

The instruction, discipline, and spirit of the army were much improved between the 1st of January and the end of April, and its numbers were increased. The efforts for the latter object brought back to the ranks about five thousand of the men who had left them in the rout of Missionary Ridge. On the morning report of April 30th the totals were: 37,652 infantry, 2812 artillery with 112 guns, and 2392 cavalry. This is the report as corrected by Major Kinloch Falconer, assistant adjutant-general, from official records in his office. Sherman had assembled at that time an army of 98,797 men and 254 guns; but before the armies actually met, three divisions of cavalry under Generals Stoneman, Garrard, and McCook added 10,000 or 12,000 men to the number. The object prescribed to him by General Grant was "to move against John-

ston's army, to break it up, and to get into the interior of the enemy's country as far as he could, inflicting all the damage possible on their war resources."

The occupation of Dalton by General Bragg had been accidental. He had encamped there for a night in his retreat from Missionary Ridge, and had remained because it was ascertained next morning that the pursuit had ceased. Dalton is in a valley so broad as to give ample room for the deployment of the largest American army. Rocky-face, which bounds it on the west, terminates as an obstacle three miles north of the railroad gap, and the distance from Chattanooga to Dalton around the north end exceeds that through the railroad gap less than a mile; and a general with a large army, coming from Chattanooga to attack an inferior one near Dalton, would follow that route and find in the

MAJOR-GENERAL JOHN A. LOGAN.
From a photograph.

wrote me at Savannah from Washington under date of December 26th, 1864:

"When you were about leaving Atlanta for the Atlantic coast I was anxious, if not fearful; but feeling that you were the better judge, and remembering 'nothing risked, nothing gained,' I did not interfere. Now the undertaking being a success, the honor is all yours; for I believe none of us went further than to acquiesce; and taking the work of General Thomas into account, as it should be taken, it is indeed a great success. Not only does it afford the obvious and immediate military advantages, but in showing to the world that your army could be divided, putting the stronger part to an important new service, and yet leaving enough to vanquish the old opposing force of the whole, Hood's army, it brings those who sat in darkness to see a great light. But what next? I suppose it will be safer if I leave General Grant and yourself to decide."

So highly do I prize this testimonial that I preserve Mr. Lincoln's letter, every word in his own handwriting, unto this day; and if I know myself, I believe on receiving it I experienced more satisfaction in giving to his overburdened and weary soul one gleam of satisfaction and happiness, than of selfish pride in an achievement which has given me among men a larger measure of fame than any single act of my life. There is an old maxim of war that a general should not divide his forces in the presence of an enterprising enemy, and I confess that I felt more anxious for General Thomas's success than my own, because had I left him with an insufficient force it would have been adjudged ungenerous and unmilitary in me; but the result, and Mr. Lincoln's judgment *after* the event, demonstrated that my division of force was liberal, leaving to Thomas "enough to vanquish the old opposing force of the whole, Hood's army," and retaining for myself enough to march to the sea, and thence north to Raleigh, in communication with the old Army of

the Potomac which had so long and heroically fought for Richmond, every officer and soldier of which felt and saw the dawn of peace in the near approach of their comrades of the West, who, having finished their task, had come so far to lend them a helping hand if needed. I honestly believe that the grand march of the Western army from Atlanta to Savannah, and from Savannah to Raleigh, was an important factor in the final result, the overwhelming victory at Appomattox, and the glorious triumph of the Union cause.

Meantime Hood, whom I had left at and near Florence, 317 miles to my rear, having completely reorganized and resupplied his army, advanced against Thomas at Nashville [see p. 277], who had also made every preparation. Hood first encountered Schofield at Franklin, November 30th, 1864, attacked him boldly behind his intrenchments, and sustained a positive check, losing 6252 of his best men, including Generals Cleburne and Adams, who were killed on the very parapets, to Schofield's loss of 2326. Nevertheless he pushed on to Nashville, which he invested. Thomas, one of the grand characters of our civil war, nothing dismayed by danger in front or rear, made all his preparations with cool and calm deliberation; and on the 15th of December sallied from his intrenchments, attacked Hood in his chosen and intrenched position, and on the next day, December 16th, actually annihilated his army, eliminating it thenceforward from the problem of the war. Hood's losses were 15,000 men to Thomas's 3057. Therefore at the end of the year 1864, the conflict at the West was concluded, leaving nothing to be considered in the grand game of war but Lee's army, held by Grant in Richmond, and the Confederate detachments at Mobile and along the sea-board north of Savannah. . . .

broad valley a very favorable field.

Mr. Davis descants on the advantages I had in mountains, ravines, and streams, and General Sherman claims that those features of the country were equal to the numerical difference between our forces. I would gladly have given all the mountains, ravines, rivers, and woods of Georgia for such a supply of artillery ammunition, proportionally, as he had. Thinking as he did, it is strange that he did not give himself a decided superiority of actual strength, by drawing troops from his three departments of the Cumberland, the Tennessee, and the Ohio, where, according to Secretary Stanton's report of 1865, he had 139,000 men fit for duty. The country in which the two armies operated is not rugged; there is nothing in its character that gave advantage to the Confederates. Between Dalton and Atlanta the only mountain in sight of the railroad is Rocky-face, which aided the Federals. The small military value of mountains is indicated by the fact that in the Federal attack on June 27th our troops on Kenesaw suffered more than those on the plain.

During the previous winter Major-General Gilmer, chief engineer, had wisely made an admirable base for our army by intrenching Atlanta.

As a road leads from Chattanooga through Snake

MAJOR-GENERAL JOHN M. CORSE, U. S. V.
Who "Held the Fort" at Allatoona.

THE BATTLE OF ALLATOONA, OCTOBER 5, 1864.
From "The Mountain Campaigns in Georgia, or War Scenes on the W. & A.," published by the Western & Atlantic R. R. Co.

Creek Gap to the railroad bridge at Resaca, a light intrenchment to cover 3000 or 4000 men was made there; and to make quick communication between that point and Dalton, two rough country roads were so improved as to serve that purpose.

On the 1st of May I reported to the Administration that the enemy was about to advance, suggesting the transfer of at least a part of General Polk's troops to my command. Then the cavalry with convalescent horses was ordered to the front, — Martin's division to observe the Oostenaula from Resaca to Rome, and Kelly's little brigade to join the cavalry on the Cleveland road.

On the 4th the Federal army, including the troops from Knoxville, was at Ringgold. Next day it skirmished until dark with our advance guard of cavalry. This was repeated on the 6th. On the 7th it moved forward, driving our cavalry from Tunnel Hill, and taking a position in the afternoon in front of the railroad gap, and parallel to Rocky-face — the right a mile south of the gap, and the left near the Cleveland road.

Until that day I had regarded a battle in the broad valley in which Dalton stands as inevitable. The greatly superior strength of the Federal army

made the chances of battle altogether in its favor. It had also places of refuge in case of defeat, in the intrenched pass of Ringgold and in the fortress of Chattanooga; while we, if beaten, had none nearer than Atlanta, 100 miles off, with three rivers intervening. General Sherman's course indicating no intention of giving battle east of Rocky-face, we prepared to fight on either side of the ridge. . . . About 10 o'clock A. M. of the 13th the Confederate army moved from Dalton and reached Resaca just as the Federal troops approaching from Snake Creek Gap were encountering Loring's division a mile from the station. Their approach was delayed long enough by Loring's opposition to give me time to select the ground to be occupied by our troops. And while they were taking this ground the Federal army was forming in front of them. The left of Polk's corps occupied the west face of the intrenchment of Resaca. Hardee's corps, also facing to the west, formed the center. Hood's, its left division facing to the west and the two others to the northwest, was on the right, and, crossing the railroad, reached the Connasauga. The enemy skirmished briskly with the left half of our line all the afternoon.

On the 14th spirited fighting was maintained by the enemy on the whole front, a very vigorous attack being made on Hindman's division of Hood's corps, which was handsomely repulsed. In the mean time General Wheeler was directed to ascertain the position and formation of the Federal left. His report indicating that these were not unfavorable to an attack, Lieutenant-General Hood was directed to make one with Stewart's and Stevenson's divisions, strengthened by four brigades from the center and left. He was instructed to make a half change of front to the left to drive the enemy from the railroad, the object of the operation being to prevent them from using it. The attack was extremely well conducted and executed, and before dark (it was begun at 6 P. M.) the enemy was driven from his ground. This encouraged me to hope for a more important success; so General Hood was directed to renew the fight next morning. His troops were greatly elated by this announcement, made to them that evening.

On riding from the right to the left after nightfall, I was informed that the extreme left of our line of skirmishers, forty or fifty men, had been driven from their ground, — an elevation near the river, — and received a report from Major-General Martin that Federal troops were crossing the Oostenaula near Lay's Ferry on a pontoon bridge — two divisions having already crossed. In consequence of this, Walker's division was sent to Lay's Ferry immediately, and the order to General Hood was revoked; also, Lieutenant-Colonel S. W. Presstman, chief engineer, was directed to lay a pontoon bridge a mile above the railroad, and to have the necessary roadway made.

Sharp fighting commenced early on the 15th, and continued until night with so much vigor that many of the assailants pressed up to our intrenchments. All these attacks were repelled, however. In General Sherman's language, the sounds of musketry and cannon rose all day to the dignity of a battle.

Soon after noon intelligence was received from Major-General Walker, that the report that the enemy had crossed the Oostenaula was untrue. Lieutenant-General Hood was therefore again ordered to assail the enemy with the troops he had commanded the day before. When he was about

CONFEDERATE INTRENCHMENTS NEAR NEW HOPE CHURCH.

Hood marched back about two, and formed his corps facing to our right and rear. Being asked for an explanation, he replied that an aide-de-camp had told him that the Federal army was approaching on that road. Our whole army knew that to be impossible. It had been viewing the enemy in the opposite direction every day for two weeks. General Hood did not report his extraordinary disobedience—as he must have done had he believed the story upon which he professed to have acted. The time lost frustrated the design, for success depended on timing the attack properly. . . .

An attack, except under very unfavorable circumstances being impossible, the troops were formed in an excellent position along the ridge immediately south of Cassville, an elevated and open valley in front, and a deep one in rear of it. Its length was equal to the front of Hood's and Polk's and half of Hardee's corps. They were placed in that order from right to left.

As I rode along the line while the troops were forming, Gen. Shoup, chief of artillery, pointed out to me a space of 150 or 200 yards, which he thought might be enfiladed by artillery on a hill a half mile beyond Hood's right and in front of the prolongation of our line, if the enemy should clear away the thick wood that covered it and establish batteries. He was desired to point out to the officer who might command there some narrow ravines very near, in which his men could be shel-

to move forward, positive intelligence was received from General Walker that the Federal right was actually crossing the Oostenaula. This made it necessary to abandon the thought of fighting north of the river, and the orders to Lieutenant-General Hood were countermanded, but the order from corps headquarters was not sent to Stewart promptly, and consequently he made the attack unsustained, and suffered before being recalled.

The occupation of Resaca being exceedingly hazardous, I determined to abandon the place. So the army was ordered to cross the Oostenaula about midnight,—Hardee's and Polk's corps by the railroad and trestle bridges, and Hood's by that above, on the pontoons. . . .

In leaving Resaca I hoped to find a favorable position near Calhoun, but there was none; and the army, after resting 18 or 20 hours near that place, early in the morning of the 17th moved on seven or eight miles to Adairsville, where we were joined by the cavalry of General Polk's command, a division of 3700 men under General W. H. Jackson. Our map represented the valley in which the railroad lies as narrow enough for our army formed across it to occupy the heights on each side with its flanks, and therefore I intended to await the enemy's attack there; but the breadth of the valley far exceeded the front of our army in order of battle. So another plan was devised. Two roads lead southward from Adairsville,—one directly through Cassville; the other follows the railroad through Kingston, turns to the left there, and rejoins the other at Cassville. The interval between them is widest opposite Kingston, where it is about seven miles by the farm roads. In the expectation that a part of the Federal army would follow each road, it was arranged that Polk's corps should engage the column on the direct road when it should arrive opposite Kingston,—

Hood's, in position for the purpose, falling upon its left flank during the deployment. Next morning, when our cavalry on that road reported the right Federal column near Kingston, General Hood was instructed to move to and follow northwardly a country road a mile east of that from Adairsville, to be in position to fall upon the flank of the Federal column when it should be engaged with Polk. An order announcing that we were about to give battle was read to each regiment, and heard with exultation. After going some three miles, General

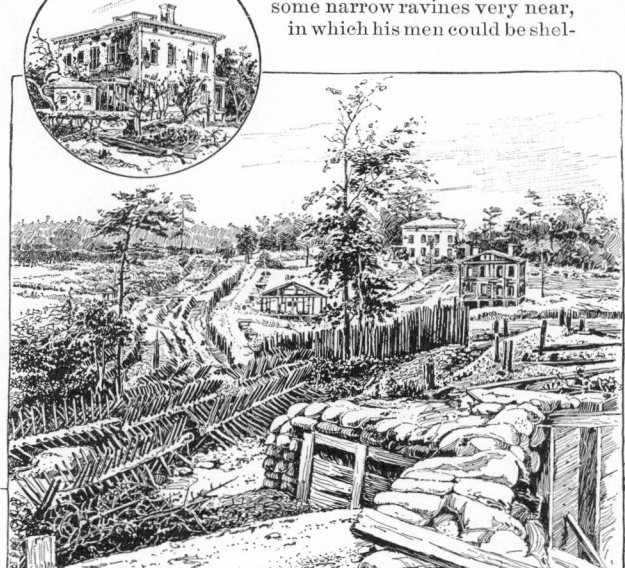

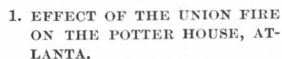

1. EFFECT OF THE UNION FIRE ON THE POTTER HOUSE, ATLANTA.
2. VIEW OF THE CONFEDERATE LINE AT THE POTTER HOUSE, LOOKING EASTWARD.
3. VIEW OF CONFEDERATE DEFENSES OF ATLANTA, LOOKING NORTHEAST.

tered from such artillery fire, and to remind him that while artillery was playing upon his position no attack would be made upon it by infantry. The enemy got into position soon after our troops were formed and skirmished until dark, using their field-

pieces freely. During the evening Lieutenant-Generals Polk and Hood, the latter being spokesman, asserted that a part of the line of each would be so enfiladed next morning by the Federal batteries established on the hill above mentioned, that they would be unable to hold their ground an hour; and therefore urged me to abandon the position at once. They expressed the conviction that early the next morning batteries would open upon them from a hill *then thickly covered with wood and out of range of brass field-pieces*. The matter was discussed perhaps an hour, in which time I became apprehensive that as the commanders of two-thirds of the army thought the position untenable, the opinion would be adopted by their troops, which would make it so. Therefore I yielded. Lieutenant-General Hardee, whose ground was the least strong, was full of confidence. Mr. Davis says ("Rise and Fall," Vol. II, p. 533) that General Hood asserts, in his report and in a book, that the two corps were on ground commanded and enfiladed by the enemy's batteries. On the contrary, they were on a hill, and the enemy were in a valley where their batteries were completely commanded by ours.

The army abandoned the ground before daybreak and crossed the Etowah after noon, and encamped near the railroad. Wheeler's cavalry was placed in observation above, and Jackson's below our main body.

No movement of the enemy was discovered until the 22d, when General Jackson reported their army moving toward Stilesboro', as if to cross the Etowah near that place; they crossed on the 23d. On the 24th Hardee's and Polk's corps encamped on the road from Stilesboro' to Atlanta, southeast of

Dallas, and Hood's four miles from New Hope Church, on the road from Allatoona. On the 25th the Federal army was a little east of Dallas, and Hood's corps was placed with its center at New Hope Church, Polk's on his left, and Hardee's prolonging the line to the Atlanta road, which was held by its left. A little before 6 o'clock in the afternoon Stewart's division in front of New Hope Church was fiercely attacked by Hooker's corps, and the action continued two hours without lull or pause, when the assailants fell back. The canister shot of the sixteen Confederate field-pieces and the musketry of five thousand infantry at short range must have inflicted heavy loss upon General Hooker's corps, as is proved by the name "Hell Hole," which, General Sherman says, was given the place by the Federal soldiers. Next day the Federal troops worked so vigorously, extending their intrenchments toward the railroad, that they skirmished very little. The Confederates labored strenuously to keep abreast of their work, but in vain, owing to greatly inferior numbers and an insignificant supply of intrenching tools. On the 27th, however, the fighting rose above the grade

THE BATTLE OF RESACA, GEORGIA, MAY 14, 1864.
From "The Mountain Campaigns in Georgia," etc. Published by The Western and Atlantic R. R. Co.

BREVET BRIG.-GEN. BENJAMIN HARRISON, U.S.V.
Commanding a brigade at Resaca. (From a photograph.)

of skirmishing, especially in the afternoon when at half-past 5 o'clock the Fourth Corps (Howard) and a division of the Fourteenth (Palmer) attempted to turn our right, but the movement, after being impeded by the cavalry, was met by two regiments of our right division (Cleburne's), and the two brigades of his second line brought up on the right of the first. The Federal formation was so deep that its front did not equal that of our two brigades; consequently those troops were greatly exposed to our musketry—all but the leading troops being on a hillside facing us. They advanced until their first line was within 25 or 30 paces of ours, and fell back only after at least 700 men had fallen dead in their places. When the leading Federal troops paused in their advance, a color-bearer came on and planted his colors eight or ten feet in front of his regiment, but was killed in the act. A soldier who sprang forward to hold up or bear off the colors was shot dead as he seized the staff. Two others who followed successively fell like him, but the fourth bore back the noble emblem. Some time after nightfall the Confeder-

ates captured above two hundred prisoners in the hollow before them. General Sherman does not refer to this combat in his "Memoirs," although he dwells with some exultation upon a very small affair of the next day at Dallas, in which the Confederates lost about three hundred killed and wounded, and in which he must have lost more than ten times as many.

In the afternoon of the 28th Lieutenant-General Hood was instructed to draw his corps to the rear of our line in the early part of the night, march around our right flank, and form it facing the left flank of the Federal line and obliquely to it, and attack at dawn—Hardee and Polk to join in the battle successively as the success on the right of each might enable him to do so. We waited next morning for the signal—the sound of Hood's musketry—from the appointed time until 10 o'clock, when a message from that officer was brought by an aide-de-camp to the effect that he had found R. W. Johnson's division intrenching on the left of the Federal line and almost at right angles to it, and asked for instructions. The message proved

that there could be no surprise, which was necessary to success, and that the enemy's intrenchments would be completed before we could attack. The corps was therefore recalled. It was ascertained afterward that after marching eight or ten hours Hood's corps was then at least six miles from the Federal left, which was little more than a musket-shot from his starting-point.

The extension of the Federal intrenchments toward the railroad was continued industriously to cut us off from it or to cover their own approach to it. We tried to keep pace with them, but the labor did not prevent the desultory fighting, which was kept up while daylight lasted. In this the great inequality of force compelled us to employ dismounted cavalry. On the 4th or 5th of June the Federal army reached the railroad between Ackworth and Allatoona. The Confederate forces then moved to a position carefully marked out by Colonel Presstman, its left on Lost Mountain, and its right, of cavalry, beyond the railroad and somewhat covered by Noonday Creek, a line much too long for our strength.

On the 8th the Federal army seemed to be near Ackworth, and our position was contracted to cover the roads leading thence to Atlanta. This brought the left of Hardee's corps to Gilgal Church, Polk's right near the Marietta and Ackworth road and Hood's corps massed beyond that road. Pine Mountain, a detached hill, was held by a division. On the 11th of June the left of the Federal army was on the high ground beyond Noonday Creek, its center a third of a mile in front of Pine Mountain and its right beyond the Burnt Hickory and Marietta road.

In the morning of the 14th General Hardee and I rode to the summit of Pine Mountain to decide if the outpost there should be maintained. General Polk accompanied us. After we had concluded our examination and the abandonment of the hill that night had been decided upon, a few shots were fired at us from a battery of Parrott guns a quarter of a mile in our front; the third of these passed through General Polk's chest, from left to right, killing him instantly. This event produced deep sorrow in the army, in every battle of which he had been distinguished. Major-General W. W. Loring succeeded to the command of the corps.

PART OF THE CONFEDERATE INTRENCHMENTS AT RESACA.

PART OF THE BATTLE-FIELD OF RESACA.

A division of Georgia militia under Major-General G. W. Smith, transferred to the Confederate service by Governor Brown, was charged with the defense of the bridges and ferries of the Chattahoochee, for the safety of Atlanta. On the 16th Hardee's corps was placed on the high ground east of Mud Creek, facing to the west. The right of the Federal army made a corresponding change of front by which it faced to the east. It was opposed in 'this manœuver by Jackson's cavalry as well as 2500 men can resist 30,000. The angle where Hardee's right joined Loring's left was soon found to be a very weak point, and on the 17th another position was chosen, including the crest of Kenesaw, which Colonel Presstman prepared for occupation by the 19th, when it was assumed by the army. In this position two divisions of Loring's corps occupied the crest of Kenesaw from end to end, the other division being on its right, and Hood's corps on the right of it, Hardee's extending from Loring's left across the Lost Mountain and Marietta road. The enemy approached as usual under cover of successive lines of intrenchments. In these positions of the two armies there were sharp and incessant partial engagements until the 3d of July. On the 21st of June the extension of the Federal line to the south, which had been protected by the swollen condition of Noses Creek, compelled the transfer of Hood's corps to our left. . . .

In the morning of the 27th, after a cannonade by all its artillery, the Federal army assailed the Confederate position, especially the center and right — the Army of the Cumberland advancing against the first, and that of the Tennessee against the other. Although suffering losses out of all proportion to those they inflicted, the Federal troops pressed up to the Confederate intrenchments in many places, maintaining the unequal conflict for two hours and a half, with the persevering courage of American soldiers. At 11:30 A. M. the attack had failed. . . .

As the extension of the Federal intrenched line

to their right had brought it nearer to Atlanta than was our left, and had made our position otherwise very dangerous, two new positions for the army were chosen, one nine or ten miles south of Marietta, and the other on the high ground near the Chattahoochee.

Colonel Presstman was desired to prepare the first for occupation, and Brigadier-General Shoup, commander of the artillery, was instructed to strengthen the other with a line of redoubts devised by himself.

The troops took the first position in the morning of the 3d, and as General Sherman was strength-

ening his right greatly, they were transferred to the second in the morning of the 5th. The cavalry of our left had been supported in the previous few days by a division of State troops commanded by Major-General G. W. Smith.

As General Sherman says, "It was really a continuous battle lasting from June 10th to July 3d." The army occupied positions about Marietta twenty-six days, in which the want of artillery ammunition was especially felt; in all those days we were exposed to an almost incessant fire of artillery as well as musketry — the former being the more harassing, because it could not be returned; for our supply of artillery ammunition was so small that we were compelled to reserve it for battles and serious assaults.

In the new position each corps had two pontoon-bridges laid. Above the railroad bridge the Chattahoochee had numerous good fords. General Sherman, therefore, directed his troops to that part of the river, ten or fifteen miles above our camp. On the 8th of July two of his corps had crossed the Chattahoochee and intrenched themselves. Therefore the Confederate army also crossed the river on the 9th.

About the middle of June Captain Grant of the engineers was instructed to strengthen the fortifications of Atlanta materially, on the side toward Peach Tree Creek, by the addition of redoubts and by converting barbette into embrasure batteries. I also obtained a promise of seven sea-coast rifles from General D. H. Maury [at Mobile], to be mounted on that front. Colonel Presstman was instructed to join Captain Grant with his subordinates, in this work of strengthening the defenses of Atlanta, especially between the Augusta and Marietta roads, as the enemy was approaching that side. For the same reason a position on the high ground looking down into the valley of Peach Tree Creek was selected for the army, from which it might engage the enemy if he should expose himself in the passage of the stream. The position of each division was marked and pointed out to its staff-officers.

On the 17th we learned that the whole Federal army had crossed the Chattahoochee; and late in the evening, while Colonel Presstman was receiving from me instructions for the next day, I received the following telegram of that date:

"Lieutenant-General J. B. Hood has been commissioned to the temporary rank of general under the late law of Congress. I am directed by the Secretary of War to inform you that, as you have failed to arrest the advance of the enemy to the vicinity of Atlanta, and ex-

EXTREME LEFT (VIEW LOOKING SOUTH) OF THE CONFEDERATE LINES AT RESACA.

The cluster of houses includes the railway station, the railway running generally parallel with the earthworks here seen, which in the distance descend to the Oostenaula River. The railway and wagon bridges over the Oostenaula, used alternately by the contending armies, are near the railway station.

press no confidence that you can defeat or repel him, you are hereby relieved from the command of the Army and Department of Tennessee, which you will immediately turn over to General Hood.

"S. COOPER, Adjutant and
Inspector-General."

Orders transferring the command of the army to General Hood were written and published immediately, and next morning I replied to the telegram of the Secretary of War:

"Your despatch of yesterday received and obeyed — command of the Army and Department of Tennessee has been transferred to General Hood. As to the alleged cause of my removal, I assert that Sherman's army is much stronger, compared with that of Tennessee, than Grant's compared with that of Northern Virginia. Yet the enemy has been compelled to advance much more slowly to the vicinity of Atlanta than to that of Richmond and Petersburg, and penetrated much deeper into Virginia than into Georgia. Confident language by a military commander is not usually regarded as evidence of competence."

General Hood came to my quarters early in the morning of the 18th, and remained there until nightfall. Intelligence was soon received that the Federal army was marching toward Atlanta, and at his urgent request I gave all necessary orders during the day. The most important one placed the troops in the position already chosen, which covered the roads by which the enemy was approaching. After transferring the command to General Hood, I described to him the course of action I had arranged in my mind. If the enemy should give us a good opportunity in the passage of Peach Tree Creek, I expected to attack him. If successful, we should obtain important results, for the enemy's retreat would be on two sides of a triangle and our march on one. If we should not succeed, our intrenchments would give us a safe refuge, where we could hold back the enemy until the promised State troops should join us; then, placing them on the nearest defenses of the place (where there were, or ought to be, seven sea-coast rifles, sent us from Mobile by General Maury), I would attack the Federals in flank with the three Confederate corps. If we were successful, they would be driven against the Chattahoochee below the railroad, where there are no fords, or away from their supplies, as we might fall on their left or right flank. If unsuccessful, we could take refuge in Atlanta, which we could hold indefinitely; for it was too strong to be taken by assault, and too extensive to be invested. This would win the campaign, the object of which the country supposed Atlanta to be. . . .

BATTLE OF ATLANTA, JULY 22, 1864—THE CONTEST ON BALD HILL: FOURTH DIVISION, FIFTEENTH CORPS IN THE FOREGROUND.
From the Panorama of "Atlanta."

HOOD'S SECOND SORTIE AT ATLANTA —BATTLE OF BALD HILL.

BY W. H. CHAMBERLIN, MAJOR, 81ST OHIO VOLUNTEERS.
Aide-de-camp to General Dodge at the battle of Bald Hill.

GENERAL Sherman's line lay east and northeast of Atlanta, with McPherson's Army of the Tennessee forming the extreme left, and extending some distance south of the Augusta railroad. General Logan's Fifteenth Corps, which joined the left of the Army of the Ohio, extended across the Augusta railroad, and General Blair's Seventeenth Corps extended the line southward, touching the McDonough road beyond what is now McPherson Avenue. The Sixteenth Corps, commanded by General Grenville M. Dodge, had been in reserve in rear of the Fifteenth Corps, north of the railroad, until July 21st, when General Fuller's division was placed in the rear of the center of the Seventeenth Corps. On the morning of July 22d a movement was begun, which afterward proved to have been the most fortunate for the Union army that could have been ordered, even if the intention of the enemy had been known to us.

It was to place the remainder of General Dodge's corps — General Sweeny's division — upon the left of the Seventeenth Corps. General Sweeny's division moved south of the railroad and halted, some time before noon, in open ground, sloping down toward a little stream, in the rear of General Fuller's division, which was in bivouac near the edge of a wood. Here, then, in the rear of the Seventeenth Corps, lay the two divisions of General Dodge's corps, as if in waiting for the approach of General Hardee's troops who had been marching nearly all night around Blair's left flank, and were even then making painfully slow progress, moving in line of battle through the thickets and obstructions that opposed their march. Our troops were really in waiting for the order to go to their new positions. General Dodge had been out on the left of General Blair's corps to select a place for his troops, and had succeeded in drawing a shell or two from the enemy's nearest earthwork. He had returned to General Fuller's headquarters, and had accepted that officer's invitation to a noonday lunch with him. In a few minutes his command would have been in motion for the front. If that had happened, and his corps had vacated the space it then held,

there would have been absolutely nothing but the hospital tents and the wagon trains to stop Hardee's command from falling unheralded directly upon the rear of the Fifteenth and Seventeenth corps in line. Upon what a slight chance, then, hung the fate of Sherman's army that day. . . .

Just here is a point upon which most of the accounts of the battle are wrong. They represent Dodge's corps to have been in motion. Fuller had bivouacked there the previous night. Sweeny's command, while technically in motion, had been halted, awaiting orders.

Just as General Dodge was about to dismount to accept General Fuller's hospitality, he heard firing in a southeasterly direction, to the rear of General Sweeny's division. He took no lunch. He was an intensely active, almost nervously restless, officer. He saw in an instant that something serious was at hand. He gave General Fuller orders to form his division immediately, facing southeastwardly, and galloped off toward Sweeny's division. He had hardly reached that command when Hardee's lines came tearing wildly through the woods with the yells of demons. As if by magic, Sweeny's division sprang into line. The two batteries of artillery (Loomis's and Laird's) had stopped on commanding ground, and were promptly in service. General Dodge's quick eye saw the proper disposition to be made of a portion of Colonel Mersy's brigade, and, cutting red tape, he delivered his orders direct to the colonels of the regiments. The orders were executed instantly, and the enemy's advance was checked. This act afterward caused trouble. General Dodge was not a West Point graduate, and did not revere so highly the army regulations as did General Sweeny, who had learned them as a cadet. Sweeny was much hurt by General Dodge's action in giving orders direct to regimental commanders, and pursued the matter so far as to bring on a personal encounter a few days after the battle, in which he came near losing his life at the hands of a hot-tempered officer. He was placed in arrest. The court-martial, however, did not consider his case until nearly the end of the war, when he was acquitted.

The battle of General Dodge's corps on this open ground, with no works to protect the troops of either side, was one of the fiercest of the war. General Dodge's troops were inspired by his courageous personal presence, for he rode directly along the lines, and must have been a conspicuous target for many a Confederate gun. His sturdy saddle-horse was worn out early in the afternoon, and was replaced by another. There was not a soldier who did not feel that he ought to equal his general in courage, and no fight of the war exhibited greater personal bravery on the part of an entire command than was shown here. Nor can I restrain a tribute to the bravery of the enemy. We had an advantage in artillery; they in numbers. Their assaults were repulsed, only to be fearlessly renewed, until the sight of dead and wounded lying in their way, as they charged again and again to break our lines, must have appalled the stoutest hearts. So persistent were their onslaughts that numbers were made prisoners by rushing directly into our lines.

When General Dodge rode from General Fuller's lunch toward the sound of the firing I rode with him. The first order he gave me was to return to General Fuller and direct him to close up his line on General Sweeny's right. Returning as soon as I could after delivering this order, I met General Dodge riding at full speed. As soon as he got within hearing distance he called out to me, "Go at once to General McPherson, on Blair's left, and tell him I need troops to cover my left. The enemy is flanking us." Wheeling my horse, I started back. As I went, the attack on Dodge's corps was in full force. Out in open ground, in full view as it was, I could not resist checking my horse for a moment to see the grand conflict. I remember yet how the sight of our banners advancing amid the smoke thrilled me as it gave them a new beauty, and the sound of our artillery, though it meant death to the

foe, fell upon our ears as the assurance of safety to us and to our flag.

General McPherson, from a point farther on, had witnessed the same scene. Lieut.-Col. W. E. Strong, his chief-of-staff, and the only staff-officer with him at that time, thus describes what they then saw:

"The enemy, massed in columns three or four lines deep, moved out of the dense timber several hundred yards from Dodge's position, and, after gaining fairly the open fields, halted and opened fire rapidly on the Sixteenth Corps. They, however, seemed surprised to find our infantry in line of battle prepared for attack, and, after facing for a few minutes the destructive fire from the divisions of Generals Fuller and Sweeny, fell back in disorder to the cover of the woods. Here, however, their lines were quickly re-formed, and they again advanced, evidently determined to carry the position. The scene at this time was grand and impressive. It seemed to us that every mounted officer of the attacking column was riding at the front or at the right or left of the first line of battle. The regimental colors waved and fluttered in advance of the lines, and not a shot was fired by

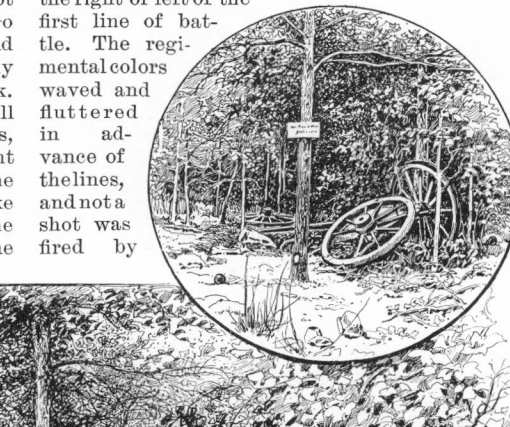

the rebel infantry, although their movement was covered by a heavy and well-directed fire of artillery, which was posted in the woods and on higher ground, and which enabled the guns to bear upon our troops with solid shot and shell by firing over the attacking column. It seemed impossible, however, for the enemy to face the sweeping, deadly fire from Fuller's and Sweeny's divisions, and the guns of Laird's 14th Ohio and Welker's batteries fairly mowed great swaths in the advancing columns. They showed great steadiness, and closed up the gaps and preserved their alignments; but the iron and leaden hail that was poured upon them was too much for flesh and blood to stand, and before reaching the center of the open fields the columns were broken and thrown into great confusion. Taking advantage of this, a portion of Fuller's and Sweeny's divisions, with bayonets fixed, charged the enemy and drove them back to the woods, taking many prisoners. The 81st Ohio (Colonel Adams) charged first, then the 39th Ohio (Colonel McDowell) and the 27th Ohio (Colonel Churchill). General McPherson's admiration for the steadiness and determined bravery of the Sixteenth Corps was unbounded."

While I was riding to find General McPherson,

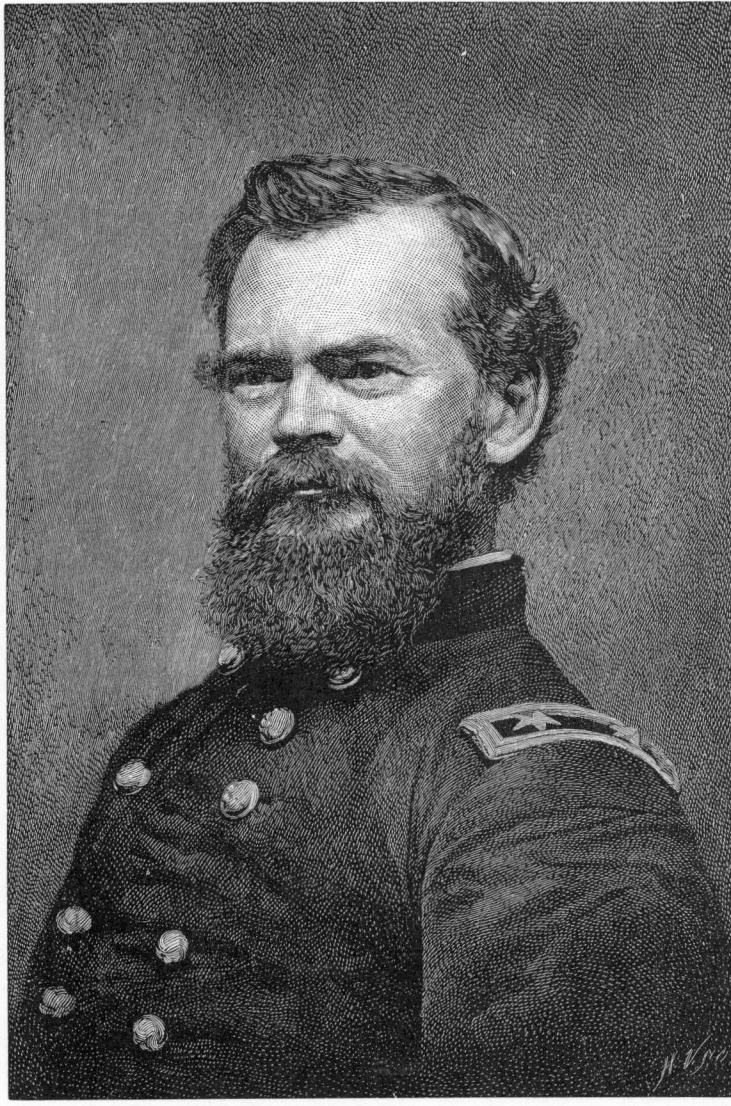

MAJOR-GENERAL JAMES B. McPHERSON, U. S. V. KILLED JULY 22, 1864.

he had just taken his eyes from the view of this splendid victory described by Colonel Strong, and had started ahead of me in the direction of Blair's left. Of course I did not find him. In a very few minutes after leaving Colonel Strong the brave general was dead, while I, following, was forced to deflect to the right, and reached our line at Giles A. Smith's division, at the point known then as Bald Hill. While in the act of asking there for a brigade for General Dodge's left, I heard a terrific yelling toward the left and rear, and, looking around, I saw a full Confederate line rushing out of the dense timber within easy hailing distance. I perceived at once that no brigade could be spared from that position for General Dodge. General Smith's troops quickly jumped to the other side of their works, prepared to meet this rear attack. The mounted officers, myself included, found some difficulty in getting their horses over the works

before the firing began. I then rode to General Harrow's division, next on the right, but he had no reserve troops to spare. Proceeding to General Morgan L. Smith's division, I met General John A. Logan, commander of the Fifteenth Corps, and he directed General Smith to weaken his front line by sending Martin's brigade to General Dodge's left.

Perhaps no better disposition of General Dodge's corps could have been made, if the intentions of General Hood had been known. But so much cannot be said of the position of General Blair's left. It has not escaped attention that Hood's ability to throw Hardee's corps into the position where it struck General Dodge that noonday was aided materially by the fact that General Sherman's usual cavalry flanking pickets were wanted. The cavalry had nearly all been sent to break railroads in Hood's rear. Nor does it appear that General Blair's infantry outposts were far enough

SCENE OF GENERAL McPHERSON'S DEATH, ON THE BATTLE-FIELD OF JULY 22.
From war-time photograph.

A 32-pounder cannon, set upon a granite block, now marks the spot of General McPherson's death. A large pine stands within a few feet of the monument, which faces a partly improved roadway that is called McPherson Avenue.

BATTLE OF ATLANTA, JULY 22.—RECAPTURE FROM THE CONFEDERATES OF DeGRESS'S BATTERY.

The view is west toward Atlanta; the Confederates in capturing the battery charged along the Georgia railroad from the rolling-mill, and took advantage of the cover of the railroad embankment and cut. (This picture is a reproduction from the Panorama of the Battle of Atlanta.)

advanced to give timely warning of the approach of an enemy.

I happened to be with General Logan when he received the order to take command of the Army of the Tennessee in place of General McPherson. I shall not easily forget the ride I had with him as he made his way to the point of danger, the left. Although whizzing balls sped about our ears as we entered the open ground near Dodge's position, and shells now and then exploded overhead, General Logan moved on the most direct line, and with no delay, to General Dodge's headquarters. He heard, in a few terse sentences, from General Dodge, how affairs stood there. Dodge's battle at that time was about won, and his command, after the enemy had spent its force in unsuccessful assaults, intrenched quickly, almost on the battle-line. Both General Fuller's and General Sweeny's divisions had captured battle-flags and prisoners. A part of General Fuller's command had changed front under fire with conspicuous bravery and steadiness, Fuller having himself planted the colors of the 27th Ohio, to indicate the new line. Among the regiments engaged were the 27th, 39th, 43d, and 81st Ohio; the 7th, 9th, 12th, 50th, 52d, 57th, 64th, and 66th Illinois, and the 2d Iowa. The brigade (Martin's) from the Fifteenth Corps did not take part in the action, and was subsequently sent farther to the rear to assist in the defense of Decatur.

What may be considered a separate action, although intended by Hood to be simultaneous, was the attack on the Fifteenth Corps, one division of

which (General Morgan L. Smith's) was driven from its line. This took place about 3 o'clock, after the Sixteenth Corps' fighting was mainly over. It was a part of the attack from the Atlanta defenses made by Hood on both the Seventeenth and Fifteenth corps.

When General Logan assumed command of the Army of the Tennessee he placed General Morgan L. Smith in command of the Fifteenth Corps, and General Lightburn succeeded to the command of Smith's division. This all happened just before Hood's attack on the Fifteenth Corps. The line had been weakened as before indicated, and the enemy succeeding in pushing a column through a cut in the Augusta railroad line, and driving back a portion of General Lightburn's troops and flanking the rest, the whole division, to use the language of General Lightburn's official report, "broke in confusion to the rear." This left in the enemy's hands sections of an Illinois battery (A, 1st Artillery) stationed near the railroad, and also DeGress's famous battery of four 20-pounder Parrotts, placed on the right of this division. General Lightburn's report is very brief. He simply says he checked the retreat of his division at the line occupied by his troops on the morning of that day, re-formed, and, with the assistance of General Wood's division and one brigade of the Sixteenth Corps, commanded by Captain Mersy, recaptured all the guns of Battery H, 1st Illinois (DeGress's), and two of Battery A. He had but six regiments in line when his division was driven back. . . .

THE BATTLE OF ATLANTA, JULY 22.
From the painting by James E. Taylor.

268

THE "LEXINGTON" PASSING OVER THE FALLS AT THE DAM.
From a war-time sketch.

THE DEFENSE OF THE RED RIVER.

NARRATIVE OF EVENTS.

The capture of Vicksburg and Port Hudson on the Mississippi, in 1863 (see p. 211), completely isolated the trans-Mississippi territory of the Confederacy, and the Union government determined, for political reasons, "to plant the flag in Texas." A detachment of the Nineteenth Corps, Army of the Gulf, under General W. B. Franklin, convoyed by the navy, went by sea, in September, to attempt the capture of Houston and Galveston. (An unsuccessful attack on Galveston had been made in January previous by a land and naval force led by General A. J. Hamilton.) Franklin's gun-boats were repulsed by Confederate batteries at Pass Franklin, on the 8th, and the expedition returned to New Orleans. In October General Banks, with the Thirteenth Corps, under General C. C. Washburne, sailed from New Orleans and seized Brazos Island, Brownsville, and Point Isabel, on the Rio Grande. Leaving the troops there in command of General N. J. T. Dana, Banks assembled an army and fleet and entered Red River in March, 1864. At the same time General Steele's column at Little Rock marched through Southern Arkansas toward the Red River to coöperate with Banks.

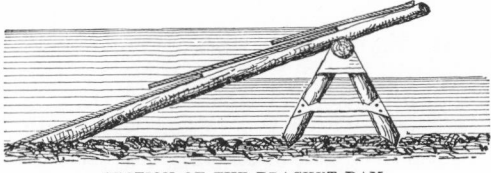

SECTION OF THE BRACKET DAM.

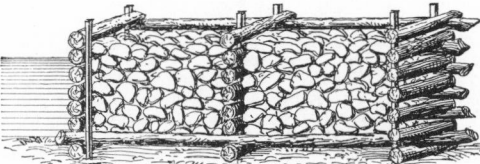

CRIB OF STONE AND BRICK.

SECTION OF THE TREE DAM.
FEATURES OF THE RED RIVER DAM.

BY E. KIRBY SMITH, GENERAL, C. S. A.
Commander of the Trans-Mississippi Department.

SOON after my arrival in the Trans-Mississippi Department, I became convinced that the valley of the Red River was the only practicable line of operations by which the enemy could penetrate the country. This fact was well understood and appreciated by their generals.

I addressed myself to the task of defending this line with the slender means at my disposal. Fortifications were erected on the lower Red River; Shreveport and Camden were fortified, and works were ordered on the Sabine and the crossings of the upper Red River. Depots were established on the shortest lines of communication between the Red River valley and the troops serving in Arkansas and Texas. These commands were directed to be held ready to move with little delay, and every preparation was made in advance for accelerating a concentration, at all times difficult over long distances, and through a country destitute of supplies and with limited means of transportation.

In February, 1864, the enemy were preparing in New Orleans, Vicksburg, and Little Rock for offensive operations. Though 25,000 of the enemy were reported on the Texas coast, my information convinced me that the valley of the Red River would be the principal theater of operations, and Shreveport the objective point of the columns moving from Arkansas and Louisiana.

On the 21st of February, General Magruder, commanding in Texas, was ordered to hold Green's division of cavalry in readiness to move at a moment's warning, and on the 5th of March the division was ordered to march at once to Alexandria and report to General Taylor, who had command in Louisiana. About that time the enemy commenced massing his forces at Berwick Bay.

On the 12th of March a column of ten thousand men, composed of portions of the Sixteenth and Seventeenth Army Corps under General A. J. Smith, moved down from Vicksburg to Simsport, and advanced with such celerity on Fort De Russy, taking it in reverse, that General Taylor was not allowed time to concentrate and cover this important work, our only means of arresting the progress of the gun-boats. The fall of this work and the im-

mediate movement of the enemy, by means of his transports, to Alexandria, placed General Taylor in a very embarrassing position. He extricated himself with his characteristic tact by a march of seventy miles through the pine woods. Banks now pressed forward from Berwick Bay, by the line of the Teche, and by the aid of steamers, on both the Mississippi and Red rivers, concentrated at Alexandria a force of over 30,000 men, supported by the most powerful naval armament ever employed on a river.

As soon as I received intelligence of the debarkation of the enemy at Simsport, I ordered General Price, who commanded in Arkansas, to despatch his entire infantry, consisting of Churchill's and Parsons's divisions, to Shreveport, and General Maxey to move toward General Price, and, as soon as Steele advanced, to join Price with his whole command, Indians included. The cavalry east of the Ouachita was directed to fall back toward Natchitoches, and subsequently to oppose, as far as possible, the advance of the enemy's fleet. It was under the command of General St. John R. Liddell. All disposable infantry in Texas was directed on Marshall, and although the enemy still had a force of several thousand on the coast, I reduced the number of men holding the defenses to an absolute minimum. General Magruder's field report shows that but 2300 men were left in Texas. Except these, every effective soldier in the department was put in front of Steele or in support of Taylor.

The enemy was operating with a force, according to my information, of full 50,000 effective men; with the utmost powers of concentration not 25,000 men of all arms could be brought to oppose his movements. Taylor had at Mansfield after the junction of Green, 11,000 effectives with 5000 infantry from Price's army in one day's march of him at Keachie. Price, with 6000 or 8000 cavalry, was engaged in holding in check the advance of Steele, whose column, according to our information, did not number less than 15,000 of all arms. Shreveport was made the point of concentration; with its fortifications covering the depots, arsenals, and shops at Jefferson, Marshall, and above, it was

MAJOR-GENERAL NATHANIEL P. BANKS, U. S. V.
In command of the Union forces in the Red River Campaign.

a strategic point of vital importance. All the infantry not with Taylor, opposed to Banks, was directed on Shreveport. Price with his cavalry command was instructed to delay the march of Steele's column whilst the concentration was being made. Occupying a central position at Shreveport, with the enemy's columns approaching from opposite directions, I proposed drawing them within striking distance, when, by concentrating upon and striking them in detail, both columns might be crippled or destroyed.

Banks pushed on to Natchitoches. It was expected he would be detained there several days in accumulating supplies. Steele on the Little Missouri and Banks at Natchitoches were but about one hundred miles from Shreveport or Marshall. The character of the country did not admit of their

ALEXANDRIA, ON THE RED RIVER.
From a war-time photograph.

THE CONFEDERATE FORT DE RUSSY, ABOUT TEN MILES BELOW ALEXANDRIA.
From a sketch made soon after it was captured.

forming a junction above Natchitoches, and if they advanced I hoped, by refusing one of them, to fight the other with my whole force.

It seemed probable at this time that Steele would advance first. When he reached Prairie d'Ane, two routes were open to him: the one to Marshall, crossing the river at Fulton, the other direct to Shreveport. I consequently held Price's infantry, under Churchill, a few days at Shreveport. Steele's hesitation and the reports of the advance of Banks's cavalry caused me, on the 4th of April, to move Churchill to Keachie, a point twenty miles in rear of Mansfield, where the road divides to go to Marshall and Shreveport. He was directed to report to General Taylor. I now visited and conferred with General Taylor. He believed that Banks could not yet advance his infantry across the barren country lying between Natchitoches and Mansfield. I returned to Shreveport and wrote General Taylor not to risk a general engagement, but to select a position in which to give battle should Banks advance, and by a reconnoissance in force to compel the enemy to display his infantry, and to notify me as soon as he had done so and I would join him in the front.

The reconnoissance was converted into a decisive engagement near Mansfield, on the 8th of April, with the advance of the enemy (a portion of the Thirteenth Corps and his cavalry), and by the rare intrepidity of Mouton's division resulted in a complete victory over the forces engaged. The battle of Mansfield was not an intentional violation of my instructions on General Taylor's part. The Federal cavalry had pushed forward so far in advance of their column as to completely cover its movement, and General Taylor reported to me by despatch at 12 meridian of the day on which the battle took place, that there was no advance made from Grand Ecore except of cavalry. In fact, however, General Franklin with his infantry was on the march, and at once pushed forward to the support of the cavalry. When General Mouton with his division drove in the cavalry, he struck the head of Franklin's troops, and by a vigorous and able attack without waiting for orders from Taylor, re-

pulsed and drove back Franklin's advance and opened the battle of Mansfield, which, when Taylor came to the front, with his accustomed boldness and vigor he pushed to a complete success.

Churchill, with his infantry under Tappan and Parsons, joined Taylor that night. The next morning Taylor, advancing in force, found the enemy in position at Pleasant Hill. Our troops attacked with vigor and at first with success, but, exposing their right flank, were finally repulsed and thrown into confusion. The Missouri and Arkansas troops, with a brigade of Walker's division, were broken and scattered. The enemy recovered cannon which we had captured the day before, and two of our pieces with the dead and wounded were left on the field. Our repulse at Pleasant Hill was so complete, and our command was so disorganized, that had Banks followed up his success vigorously he would have met but feeble opposition to his advance on Shreveport.

Having ridden forward at 2 A. M. on receipt of Taylor's report of the battle of Mansfield, I joined Taylor after dark on the 8th, a few yards in rear of the battle-field of that day. Polignac's (previously Mouton's) division of Louisiana infantry was all that was intact of Taylor's force. Assuming command, I countermanded the order that had been given for the retreat of Polignac's division, and was consulting with General Taylor when some stragglers from the battle-field, where our wounded were still lying, brought the intelligence that Banks had precipitately retreated after the battle, converting a victory which he might have claimed into a defeat. Our troops in rear rallied, and the field was next day occupied by us.

Banks continued his retreat to Grand Ecore, where he intrenched himself and remained until the return of his fleet and its safe passage over the bars, made especially difficult this season by the unusual fall of the river.

Our troops were completely paralyzed and disorganized by the repulse at Pleasant Hill, and the cavalry, worn by its long march from Texas, had been constantly engaged for three days, almost without food or forage. Before we could reorgan-

ize at Mansfield and get into condition to advance over the fifty-five miles of wilderness that separated our armies, the enemy had been reinforced and intrenched at Grand Ecore. The enemy held possession of the river until he evacuated Grand Ecore.

Steele was still slowly advancing from the Little Missouri to the Prairie d'Ane. I deemed it imprudent to follow Banks below Grand Ecore with my whole force, and leave Steele so near Shreveport. Even had I been able to throw Banks across the Atchafalaya, the high water of that stream would have arrested his farther progress. An intercepted despatch from General Sherman to General A. J. Smith, directing the immediate return of his force to Vicksburg, removed the last doubt in my mind that Banks would withdraw to Alexandria as rapidly as possible, and it was hoped the falls would detain his fleet there until we could dispose of Steele, when the entire force of the department would be free to operate against him. I confidently hoped, if I could reach Steele with my infantry, to beat him at a distance from his depot, in a poor country, and with my large cavalry force to destroy his army. The prize would have been the Arkansas Valley and the powerful fortifications of Little Rock. Steele's defeat or retreat would leave me in position promptly to support Taylor's operations against Banks.

Leaving Taylor with his cavalry, now under Wharton, and the Louisiana division of infantry under Polignac, to follow up Banks's retreat, and taking the Texas, Arkansas, and Missouri divisions of infantry, I moved against Steele's column in Arkansas. Steele entered Camden, where he was too strong for assault, but the capture of his train at the battle of Marks's Mill, on the 25th of April, forced him to evacuate Camden on the 28th, and the battle of Jenkins's Ferry on the Saline, April 30th, completed his discomfiture. He retreated to Little Rock. Churchill, Parsons, and Walker were at once marched across country to the support of Taylor, but before the junction could be effected Banks had gone.

To return to Taylor, after the enemy left Grand Ecore, General Taylor attacked his rear at Cloutier-

ville, whilst a detachment under Bee held the Federal advance in check at Monette's Ferry. General Taylor's force was, however, too weak to warrant the hope that he could seriously impede the march of Banks's column. After the latter reached Alexandria, General Taylor transferred a part of his command to the river below Alexandria, and with unparalleled audacity and great ability and success operated on the enemy's gun-boats and transports.

The construction of the dam, aided by a temporary rise in Red River, enabled Admiral Porter to get his fleet over the falls. Had he delayed but one week longer, our whole infantry force would have been united against him.

Banks evacuated Alexandria on the 12th and 13th of May, the fleet quitted the Red River, and the campaign ended with the occupation of all the country we had held at its beginning, as well as of the lower Teche. . . .

NOTE.—The Confederates remained in almost undisturbed possession of Texas until May 26, 1865, when General Smith surrendered the forces in the Trans-Mississippi Department to General Canby. Meanwhile, in Missouri and Arkansas the war continued throughout the year 1864. Steele retired from Red River toward Little Rock, followed by Generals Smith and Price, who attacked him at Jenkins's Ferry, the crossing of Saline River, April 30. After the battle Steele continued his march northward, and Price assembled a formidable column under Generals John S. Marmaduke, J. F. Fagan, and J. O. Shelby, to make an extensive raid into Missouri. He attempted to capture St. Louis, Jefferson City, and Lexington, successively, but was repulsed at every point. The Department of Missouri was then under Rosecrans, who had assumed command in January, 1864. General Pleasonton commanded the cavalry corps under Rosecrans, and General S. R. Curtis, with the Army of Kansas, took part in the campaign against Price, which extended over the months of September and October.

In General Price's report occurs the following summary of the campaign: "I marched 1434 miles, fought 43 battles and skirmishes, captured and paroled over 3000 Federal officers and men, captured 18 pieces of artillery, 3000 stand of small-arms, 16 stand of colors, . . . a great many wagons and teams, large numbers of horses, great quantities of subsistence and ordnance stores, . . . and destroyed property to the cost of $10,000,000. . . . I lost 10 pieces of artillery, 2 stand of colors, 1000 small-arms, while I do not think I lost 1000 prisoners. . . . I brought with me at least 5000 recruits."

THE "MONONGAHELA" RAMMING THE "TENNESSEE."

CAPTURE OF THE CONFEDERATE GUN-BOAT "SELMA" BY THE "METACOMET."

THE BATTLE OF MOBILE BAY.

WITH FARRAGUT ON THE "HARTFORD."

BY JOHN CODDINGTON KINNEY, FIRST LIEUTENANT, 13TH CONNECTICUT INFANTRY.
Acting signal-officer, U. S. A., on board of Admiral Farragut's flag-ship, the "Hartford."

NOTE.— Mobile was the only seaport of importance held by the Confederates on the coast of the east Gulf. Measures for its defense were commenced in January, 1861, by the authorities of Alabama, who placed garrisons in old Forts Morgan and Gaines, at the entrance to the bay. The defenses were subsequently increased until, in 1864, there were three lines of works encompassing the city and ten batteries commanding the lower channel. The blockade was generally effectual, but it was run by the notorious cruiser *Florida*, inward in September, 1862, and outward in January, 1863. After the Mississippi was opened by the capture of Vicksburg and Port Hudson, Farragut turned his attention to Mobile Bay. The Confederates were engaged in the construction of rams and ironclads at Mobile and above, and it was his desire to force the entrance into Mobile Bay and capture the forts that guarded it, before the new vessels could be finished. In the latter part of July, 1864, General Gordon Granger brought a land force from New Orleans to coöperate with Farragut.

. . . On the morning of August 4th a detachment of army signal-officers, under command of the late Major Frank W. Marston, arrived by tug from New Orleans. They were distributed among the principal vessels of the fleet, for the purpose of communicating with General Granger's force after the entrance into the bay had been effected, and it was the good fortune of the writer to be assigned to duty on the *Hartford*. In the afternoon of the same day, Admiral Farragut, with the commanding officers of the different vessels, made a reconnoissance on the steam-tender *Cowslip*, running inside of Sand Island, where the three monitors were anchored, and within easy range of both forts. . . .

The scene on the *Cowslip* that afternoon of the 4th of August was a notable one, as she steamed within the range of the forts. The central figure was the grand old admiral, his plans all completed, affable with all, evidently not thinking of failure as among the possibilities of the morrow, and filling every one with his enthusiasm. He was sixty-three years old, of medium height, stoutly built, with a finely proportioned head and smoothly shaven face, with an expression combining overflowing kindliness with iron will and invincible determination, and with eyes that in repose were full of sweetness and light, but, in emergency, could flash fire and fury. . . .

Before attempting to narrate the events of the next day, it may be well to give an idea of the situation. Mobile Bay gradually widens from the city to the gulf, a distance of thirty miles. The entrance is protected by a long, narrow arm of sand, with Fort Morgan on the extreme western point. Across the channel from Fort Morgan, and perhaps three miles distant, is Dauphine Island, a narrow strip of sand with Fort Gaines at its eastern end. Further to the west is little Fort Powell, commanding a narrow channel through which light-draught vessels could enter the bay. Between Dauphine Island and Fort Morgan, and in front of the main entrance to the bay, is Sand Island, a barren spot, under the lee of which three of our monitors were lying. The army signal-officers were sent on board the fleet, not with any intention of having their services used in passing the forts, but in order to establish communication afterward between the fleet and the army, for the purpose of coöperating in the capture of the forts. The primary objects of Admiral Farragut in entering the bay were to close Mobile to the outside world, to capture or destroy the *Tennessee*, and to cut off all possible means of escape from the garrisons of the forts. Incidentally, also, he desired to secure the moral effect of a victory, and to give his fleet, which had been tossed on the uneasy waters of the Gulf for many months, a safe and quiet anchorage. There was no immediate expectation of capturing the city of Mobile, which was safe by reason of a solid row of piles and torpedoes across the river, three miles below the city. Moreover, the larger vessels of the fleet could not approach within a dozen miles of the city, on account of shallow water. But the lower bay offered a charming resting-place for the fleet, with the additional attraction of plenty of fish and oysters, and an occasional chance to forage on shore.

At sunset the last orders had been issued, every commander knew his duty, and unusual quiet prevailed in the fleet. The sea was smooth, a gentle breeze relieved the midsummer heat, and the night came on serenely and peacefully, and far more quietly than to a yachting fleet at Newport. For the first hour after the candles were lighted below the stillness was almost oppressive. The officers of the *Hartford* gathered around the ward-room table, writing letters to loved ones far away, or giving instructions in case of death. As brave and thoughtful men, they recognized the dangers that they did not fear, and made provision for the possibilities of the morrow. But this occupied little time, and then, business over, there followed an hour of unrestrained jollity. Many an old story was retold and ancient conundrum repeated. Old officers forgot, for the moment, their customary dignity, and it was evident that all were exhilarated and stimulated by the knowledge of the coming struggle. There was no other "stimulation," for the strict naval rules prevented. Finally, after a half-hour's smoke under the forecastle, all hands turned in. The scene on the flag-ship was representative of the night before the battle throughout the fleet.

It was the admiral's desire and intention to get under way by daylight, to take advantage of the inflowing tide; but a dense fog came on after midnight and delayed the work of forming line.

It was a weird sight as the big ships "balanced to partners," the dim outlines slowly emerging like phantoms in the fog. The vessels were lashed together in pairs, fastened side by side by huge cables. All the vessels had been stripped for the fight, the top-hamper being left at Pensacola, and the starboard boats being either left behind or towed on the port side. The admiral's steam-launch, the *Loyall*, named after his son,[*] steamed alongside the flag-ship on the port side.

It was a quarter of six o'clock before the fleet was in motion. Meantime a light breeze had scattered the fog and left a clear, sunny August day. The line moved slowly, and it was an hour after starting before the opening gun was fired. This was a 15-inch shell from the *Tecumseh*, and it exploded over Fort Morgan. Half an hour afterward the fleet came within range, and the firing from the starboard vessels became general, the fort and the Confederate fleet replying. The fleet took position across the entrance to the bay and raked the advance vessels fore and aft, doing great damage, to which it was for a time impossible to make effective reply. Gradually the fleet came into close quarters with Fort Morgan, and the firing on both sides became terrific. The wooden vessels moved more rapidly than the monitors, and as the *Brooklyn* came opposite the fort, and approached the torpedo line, she came nearly alongside the rear monitor. To have kept on would have been to take

[*] Mrs. Farragut's maiden name was Loyall.

REAR-ADMIRAL JAMES E. JOUETT, U. S. N.
In command of the "Metacomet."

"TENNESSEE."   FORT MORGAN.   "HARTFORD."   "BROOKLYN."   SAND ISLAND LIGHT.

THE BATTLE OF MOBILE BAY, LOOKING SOUTH AND EASTWARD.
From a war-time sketch.

REAR-ADMIRAL THORNTON A. JENKINS, U. S. N.
In command of the "Richmond."

lead, with the ram *Tennessee* approaching and with the unknown danger of the torpedoes underneath. At this critical moment the *Brooklyn* halted and began backing and signaling with the army signals. The *Hartford* was immediately behind and the following vessels were in close proximity, and the sudden stopping of the *Brooklyn* threatened to bring the whole fleet into collision, while the strong inflowing tide was likely to carry some of the vessels to the shore under the guns of the fort.

On the previous night the admiral had issued orders that the army signal-officers were not to be allowed on deck during the fight, but were to go into the cockpit, on the lower deck, and assist surgeons. The reason assigned was that these officers would not be needed during the passage of the forts, but would be wanted afterward to open communication with the army, and that therefore it would be a misfortune to have any of them disabled. The two army signal-officers on the *Hartford* disrelished this order exceedingly, and, after consulting together, decided that in the confusion of the occasion their presence on deck would probably not be noticed, and that they would evade the command if possible. In this they were successful until shortly before passing Sand Island and coming within range of Fort Morgan. Then the executive officer, Lieutenant-Commander Lewis A. Kimberly, who never allowed anything to escape his attention, came to them very quietly and politely, and told them the admiral's order must be obeyed. We were satisfied from his manner that the surgeons had need of us, and, without endeavoring to argue the matter, made our way to the stifling hold, where Surgeon Lansdale and Assistant-Surgeon Commons, with their helpers, were sitting, with their paraphernalia spread out ready for use.

Nearly every man had his watch in his hand awaiting the first shot. To us, ignorant of everything going on above, every minute seemed an hour, and there was a feeling of great relief when the boom of the *Tecumseh's* first gun was heard. Presently one or two of our forward guns opened, and we could hear the distant sound of the guns of the

fort in reply. Soon the cannon-balls began to crash through the deck above us, and then the thunder of our whole broadside of nine Dahlgren guns kept the vessel in a quiver. But as yet no wounded were sent down, and we knew we were still at comparatively long range. In the intense excitement of the occasion it seemed that hours had passed, but it was just twenty minutes from the time we went below, when an officer shouted down the hatchway: "Send up an army signal-officer immediately; the *Brooklyn* is signaling." In a moment the writer was on deck, where he found the situation as already described. Running on to the forecastle, he hastily took the *Brooklyn's* message, which imparted the unnecessary information, "The monitors are right ahead; we cannot go on without passing them." The reply was sent at once from the admiral, "Order the monitors ahead and go on." But still the *Brooklyn* halted, while, to add to the horror of the situation, the monitor *Tecumseh*, a few hundred yards in the advance, suddenly careened to one side and almost instantly sank to the bottom, carrying with her Captain Tunis A. M. Craven and the greater part of his crew, numbering in all 114 officers and men. The pilot, John Collins, and a few men who were in the turret, jumped into the water and were rescued by a boat from the *Metacomet*, which, under charge of Acting Ensign Henry C. Nields, rowed up under the guns of the fort and through a deadly storm of shot and shell and picked them up. Meanwhile the *Brooklyn* failed to go ahead, and the whole fleet became a stationary point blank target for the guns of Fort Morgan and of the rebel vessels. It was during these few perilous moments that the most fatal work of the day was done to the fleet.

Owing to the *Hartford's* position, only her few bow guns could be used, while a deadly rain of shot and shell was falling upon her, and her men were being

cut down by scores, unable to make reply. The sight on deck was sickening beyond the power of words to portray. Shot after shot came through the side, mowing down the men, deluging the decks with blood, and scattering mangled fragments of humanity so thickly that it was difficult to stand on the deck, so slippery was it. The old expressions of the "scuppers running blood," "the slippery deck," etc., give but the faintest idea of the spectacle on the *Hartford*. The bodies of the dead were placed in a long row on the port side, while the wounded were sent below until the surgeons' quarters would hold no more. A solid shot coming through the bow struck a gunner on the neck, completely severing head from body. One poor fellow (afterward an object of interest at the great Sanitary Commission Fair in New York) lost both legs by a cannon-ball; as he fell he threw up both arms, just in time to have them also carried away by another shot. At one gun, all the crew on one side were swept down by a shot which came crashing through the bulwarks. A shell burst between the two forward guns in charge of Lieutenant Tyson, killing and wounding fifteen men. The mast upon which the writer was perched was twice struck, once slightly, and again just below the foretop by a heavy shell from a rifle on the Confederate gun-boat *Selma*. Fortunately the shell came tumbling end over end, and buried itself in the mast, butt-end first, leaving the percussion-cap protruding. Had it come point first, or had it struck at any other part of the mast than in the reinforced portion where the heel of the topmast laps the top of the lower mast, this contribution to the literature of the war would probably have been lost to the world, as the distance to the deck was about a hundred feet. As it was, the sudden jar would have dislodged any one from the cross-trees had not the shell been visible from the time

it left the *Selma*, thus giving time to prepare for it by an extra grip around the top of the mast. Looking out over the water, it was easy to trace the course of every shot, both from the guns of the *Hartford* and from the Confederate fleet. Another signal message from the *Brooklyn* told of the sinking of the *Tecumseh*, a fact known already, and another order to "go on" was given and was not obeyed.

Soon after the fight began, Admiral Farragut, finding that the low-hanging smoke from the guns interfered with his view from the deck, went up the rigging of the mainmast as far as the futtock-shrouds, immediately below the maintop. The pilot, Martin Freeman, was in the top directly overhead, and the fleet-captain was on the deck below. Seeing the admiral in this exposed position, where, if wounded, he would be killed by falling to the deck, Fleet-Captain Drayton ordered Knowles, the signal-quartermaster, to fasten a rope around him so that he would be prevented from falling.

Finding that the *Brooklyn* failed to obey his orders, the admiral hurriedly inquired of the pilot if there was sufficient depth of water for the *Hartford* to pass to the left of the *Brooklyn*. Receiving an affirmative reply, he said: "I will take the lead," and immediately ordered the *Hartford* ahead at full speed. As he passed the *Brooklyn* a voice warned him of the torpedoes, to which he returned the contemptuous answer, "Damn the torpedoes." This is the current story, and may have some basis of truth. But as a matter of fact, there was never a moment when the din of the battle would not have drowned any attempt at conversation between the two ships, and while it is quite probable that the admiral made the remark it is doubtful if he shouted it to the *Brooklyn*.

Then was witnessed the remarkable sight of the *Hartford* and her consort, the *Metacomet*, passing over the dreaded torpedo ground, and rushing ahead far in advance of the rest of the fleet, the extrication of which from the confusion caused by the

Brooklyn's halt required many minutes of valuable time. The *Hartford* was now moving over what is called the "middle ground," with shallow water on either side, so that it was impossible to move except as the channel permitted. Taking advantage of the situation, the Confederate gun-boat *Selma* kept directly in front of the flag-ship and raked her fore and aft, doing more damage in reality than all the rest of the enemy's fleet. The other gun-boats, the *Gaines* and the *Morgan*, were in shallow water on our starboard bow, but they received more damage from the *Hartford's* broadsides than they were able to inflict. Meanwhile the ram *Tennessee*, which up to this time had contented herself with simply firing at the approaching fleet, started for the *Hartford*, apparently with the intention of striking her amidships. She came on perhaps for half a mile, never approaching nearer than a hundred yards, and then suddenly turned and made for the fleet, which, still in front of the fort, was gradually getting straightened out and following the *Hartford*. This change of course on the part of the ram has always been a mystery. The captain of the ram, in papers published since the war, denies that any such move was made, but it was witnessed by the entire fleet, and is mentioned by both Admiral Farragut and Fleet-Captain Drayton in their official reports.

The *Hartford* had now run a mile inside the bay, and was suffering chiefly from the raking fire of the *Selma*, which was unquestionably managed more skilfully than any other Confederate vessel. Captain (now Admiral) Jouett, commanding the *Hartford's* escort, the *Metacomet*, repeatedly asked permission of the admiral to cut loose and take care of the *Selma*, and finally, at five minutes past eight, consent was given. In an instant the cables binding the two vessels were cut, and the *Metacomet*, the fastest vessel in the fleet, bounded ahead. The *Selma* was no match for her, and, recognizing her danger, endeavored to retreat up the bay. But she was speedily overhauled, and when a shot had wounded her captain and killed her first lieutenant she surrendered. Before this the *Gaines* had been crippled by the splendid marksmanship of the *Hartford's* gunners, and had run aground under the guns of the fort, where she was shortly afterward set on fire, the crew escaping to the shore. The gun-boat *Morgan*, after grounding for a few moments on the shoals to the east of Navy Cove, retreated to the shallow water near the fort, whence she escaped the following night to Mobile. The *Hartford*, having reached the deep water of the bay, about three miles north of Dauphine Island, came to anchor.

Let us now return to the other vessels of the fleet, which we left massed in front of Fort Morgan by the remarkable action of the *Brooklyn* in stopping and refusing to move ahead. When the ram *Tennessee* turned away from the *Hartford*, as narrated, she made for the fleet, and in their crowded and confused condition it seemed to be a matter of no difficulty to pick out whatever victims the Confederate commander (Admiral Franklin Buchanan) might desire, as he had done in 1861 when commanding the *Merrimac* in Hampton Roads. Before he could reach them the line had become straightened, and the leading vessels had passed the fort. . . .

Whatever damage was done by the *Tennessee* to

"GALENA."   "ITASCA."
THE "BROOKLYN" AFTER THE BATTLE OF MOBILE BAY.
From a sketch made at the time.

the fleet in passing the fort was by the occasional discharge of her guns. She failed to strike a single one of the Union vessels, but was herself run into by the *Monongahela*, Captain Strong, at full speed. The captain says in his report:

"After passing the forts I saw the rebel ram *Tennessee* head on for our line. I then sheered out of the line to run into her, at the same time ordering full speed as fast as possible. I struck her fair, and swinging around poured in a broadside of solid 11-inch shot, which apparently had little if any effect upon her."

This modest statement is characteristic of the writer, now dead, as are so many others of the conspicuous actors in that day's work. The *Monongahela* was no match for the *Tennessee*, but she had been strengthened by an artificial iron prow, and being one of the fastest — or rather, *least slow* — of the fleet, was expected to act as a ram if opportunity offered. Captain Strong waited for no orders, but seeing the huge ram coming for the fleet left his place in the line and attacked her as narrated. It was at this time that the *Monongahela's* first lieutenant, Roderick Prentiss, a brave and gifted young officer, received his death-wound, both legs being shattered.

At last all the fleet passed the fort, and while the ram ran under its guns the vessels made their way to the *Hartford* and dropped their anchors, except the *Metacomet*, *Port Royal*, *Kennebec*, and *Itasca*. After the forts were passed, the three last named had cut loose from their escorts and gone to aid the *Metacomet* in her struggle with the *Selma* and *Morgan*.

The thunder of heavy artillery now ceased. The crews of the various vessels had begun to efface the marks of the terrible contest by washing the decks and clearing up the splinters. The cooks were preparing breakfast, the surgeons were busily engaged in making amputations and binding arteries, and under canvas, on the port side of each vessel, lay the ghastly line of dead waiting the sailor's burial. As if by mutual understanding, officers who were relieved from immediate duty gathered in the ward-rooms to ascertain who of

their mates were missing, and the reaction from such a season of tense nerves and excitement was just setting in when the hurried call to quarters came and the word passed around, "The ram is coming."

The *Tennessee*, after remaining near Fort Morgan while the fleet had made its way four miles above to its anchorage — certainly as much as half an hour — had suddenly decided to settle at once the question of the control of the bay. Single-handed she came on to meet the whole fleet, consisting now of ten wooden vessels and the three monitors. At that time the *Tennessee* was believed to be the strongest vessel afloat, and the safety with which she carried her crew during the battle proved that she was virtually invulnerable. Fortunately for the Union fleet she was weakly handled, and at the end fell a victim to a stupendous blunder in her construction — the failure to protect her rudder-chains. The spectacle afforded the Confederate soldiers, who crowded the ramparts of the two forts, — the fleet now being out of range, — was such as has very rarely been furnished in the history of the world. To the looker-on it seemed as if the fleet was at the mercy of the ram, for the monitors, which were expected to be the chief defense, were so destitute of speed, and so difficult to manœuvre, that it seemed an easy task for the *Tennessee* to avoid them and sink the wooden vessels in detail. Because of the slowness of the monitors, Admiral Farragut selected the fastest of the wooden vessels to begin the attack. While the navy signals for a general attack of the enemy were being prepared, the *Monongahela* (Captain Strong) and the *Lackawanna* (Captain Marchand) were ordered by the more rapid signal-system of the army to "run down the ram," the order being immediately repeated to the monitors.

The *Monongahela*, with her prow already somewhat weakened by the previous attempt to ram, at once took the lead, as she had not yet come to

CAPTAIN TUNIS A. M. CRAVEN, U. S. N.
Captain Craven commanding the "Tecumseh," was one of 93 officers and men who went down with the ship and were drowned.

anchor. The ram from the first headed for the *Hartford*, and paid no attention to her assailants, except with her guns. The *Monongahela*, going at full speed, struck the *Tennessee* amidships — a blow that would have sunk almost any vessel of the Union navy, but which inflicted not the slightest damage on the solid iron hull of the ram. (After the surrender it was almost impossible to tell where the attacking vessel had struck.) Her own iron prow and cutwater were carried away, and she was otherwise badly damaged about the stern by the collision. The *Lackawanna* was close behind and delivered a similar blow with her wooden bow, simply causing the ram to lurch slightly to one side. As the vessels separated the *Lackawanna* swung alongside the ram, which sent two shots through her and kept on her course for the *Hartford*, which was now the next vessel in the attack. The two flag-ships approached each other, bow to bow, iron against oak. It was impossible for the *Hartford*, with her lack of speed, to circle around and strike the ram on her side; her only safety was in keeping pointed directly for the bow of her

THE BATTLE OF MOBILE BAY.
From a war-time sketch.

FORT GAINES. "GALENA." "ONEIDA." "ITASCA." "OSSIPEE." "CHICKASAW." "TENNESSEE." FORT MORGAN.

THE "HARTFORD" IN COLLISION WITH THE "TENNESSEE."
From a war-time sketch.

assailant. The other vessels of the fleet were unable to do anything for the defense of the admiral except to train their guns on the ram, on which as yet they had not the slightest effect.

It was a thrilling moment for the fleet, for it was evident that if the ram could strike the *Hartford* the latter must sink. But for the two vessels to strike fairly, bows on, would probably have involved the destruction of both, for the ram must have penetrated so far into the wooden ship that as the *Hartford* filled and sank she would have carried the ram under water. Whether for this reason or for some other, as the two vessels came together, the *Tennessee* slightly changed her course, the port bow of the *Hartford* met the port bow of the ram, and the ships grated against each other as they

BRIGADIER-GENERAL RICHARD L. PAGE,
C. S. A.
Commanding at Fort Morgan.

passed. The *Hartford* poured her whole port broadside against the ram, but the solid shot merely dented the side and bounded into the air. The ram tried to return the salute, but owing to defective primers only one gun was discharged. This sent a shell through the berth-deck, killing five men and wounding eight. The muzzle of the gun was so close to the *Hartford* that the powder blackened her sides.

The admiral stood on the quarter-deck when the vessels came together, and as he saw the result he jumped on the port-quarter-rail, holding to the mizzen-rigging, a position from which he might have jumped to the deck of the ram as she passed. Seeing him in this position, and fearing for his safety, Flag-Lieutenant Watson slipped a rope around him and secured it to the rigging, so that during the fight the admiral was twice "lashed to the rigging," each time by devoted officers who knew better than to consult him before acting. Fleet-Captain Drayton had hurried to the bow of the *Hartford* as the collision was seen to be inevitable, and expressed keen satisfaction when the ram avoided a direct blow.

The *Tennessee* now became the target for the whole fleet, all the vessels of which were making toward her, pounding her with shot, and trying to run her down. As the *Hartford* turned to make for her again, we ran in front of the *Lackawanna*, which had already turned and was moving under full headway with the same object. She struck us on our starboard side, amidships, crushing halfway through, knocking two port-holes into one, upsetting one of the Dahlgren guns, and creating general consternation. For a time it was thought that we must sink, and the cry rang out over the deck: "Save the admiral! Save the admiral!" The port boats were ordered lowered, and in their

haste some of the sailors cut the "falls," and two of the cutters dropped into the water wrong side up, and floated astern. But the admiral sprang into starboard mizzen-rigging, looked over the side of the ship, and, finding there were still a few inches to spare above the water's edge, instantly ordered the ship ahead again at full speed, after the ram. The unfortunate *Lackawanna*, which had struck the ram a second blow, was making for her once more, and, singularly enough, again came up on our starboard side, and another collision seemed imminent. And now the admiral became a trifle excited. He had no idea of whipping the rebels to be himself sunk by a friend, nor did he realize at the moment that the *Hartford* was as much to blame as the *Lackawanna*. Turning to the writer he inquired. "Can you say 'For God's sake' by signal?" "Yes, sir," was the reply. "Then say to the *Lackawanna*, 'For God's sake get out of our way and anchor!'" In my haste to send the message, I brought the end of my signal flag-staff down with considerable violence upon the head of the admiral, who was standing nearer than I thought, causing him to wince perceptibly. It was a hasty message, for the fault was equally divided, each ship being too eager to reach the enemy, and it turned out all right, by a fortunate accident, that Captain Marchand never received it. The army signal-officer on the *Lackawanna*, Lieutenant Myron Adams (now pastor of Plymouth Congregational Church in Rochester, N. Y.), had taken his station in the foretop, and just as he received the first five words, "For God's sake get out" —— the wind flirted the large United States flag at the mast-head around him, so that he was unable to read the conclusion of the message.

The remainder of the story is soon told. As the *Tennessee* left the *Hartford* she became the target

of the entire fleet, and at last the concentration of solid shot from so many guns began to tell. The flag-staff was shot away, the smoke-stack was riddled with holes and finally disappeared. The monitor *Chickasaw*, Lieutenant-Commander Perkins, succeeded in coming up astern, and began pounding away with 11-inch solid shot, and one shot from a 15-inch gun of the *Manhattan* crushed into the side sufficiently to prove that a few more such shots would have made the casement untenable. Finally, one of the *Chickasaw*'s shots cut the rudder-chain of the ram, and she would no longer mind her helm.

COMMANDER J. D. JOHNSTON, C. S. N.
Of the ram "Tennessee."

At the time, as Admiral Farragut says in his report, "she was sore beset. The *Chickasaw* was pounding away at her stern, the *Ossipee* was approaching her at full speed, and the *Monongahela*, *Lackawanna*, and this ship were bearing down upon her, determined upon her destruction." From the time the *Hartford* struck her she did not fire a gun. Finally the Confederate admiral, Buchanan, was severely wounded by an iron splinter or a piece of a shell, and just as she was about to strike her the *Tennessee* displayed a white flag, hoisted on an improvised staff through the grating over her deck. The *Ossipee* (Captain LeRoy) reversed her engine, but was so near that a harmless collision was inevitable. Suddenly the terrific cannonading ceased, and from every ship rang out cheer after cheer as the weary men realized that at last the ram was conquered and the day won. The *Chickasaw* took the *Tennessee* in tow and brought her to anchor near the *Hartford*. The impression prevailed at first that the *Tennessee* had been seriously injured by the ramming she had received and was sinking, and orders were signaled to send boats to assist her crew, but it was soon discovered that this was unnecessary. Admiral Buchanan surrendered his sword to Lieutenant Giraud, of the *Ossipee*, who was sent to take charge of the captured *Tennessee*. Captain Heywood, of the Marine Corps, was sent on board the ram with a guard of marines. On meeting Admiral Buchanan he could not resist the temptation to inform him that they had met before under different circumstances, the captain having been on the frigate *Cumberland* when she was sunk in Hampton Roads by Buchanan in the *Merrimac*. . . .

Fort Morgan was at once invested, and surrendered on the 23d of August.

ON BOARD THE RAM "TENNESSEE."

BY JAMES D. JOHNSTON, COMMANDER, C. S. N.

. . The heavier ships of the fleet, together with the monitors, steamed up the bay to a point about four miles above Fort Morgan, where they were in the act of anchoring when it was discovered that the ram was approaching with hostile intent. Upon this apparently unexpected challenge the fleet was immediately put in motion, and the heavier vessels seemed to contend with each other for the glory of

"LACKAWANNA." "WINNEBAGO."   "OSSIPEE."   "BROOKLYN." "TENNESSEE."   "ITASCA."   "RICHMOND."   "HARTFORD."   "CHICKASAW." FORT MORGAN.

SURRENDER OF THE "TENNESSEE," BATTLE OF MOBILE BAY.

sinking the daring rebel ram, by running themselves up on her decks, which extended some thirty feet at each end of the shield, and were only about eighteen inches above the surface of the water. So great was their eagerness to accomplish this feat that the *Lackawanna*, one of the heaviest steamers, ran bows on into the *Hartford*, by which both vessels sustained greater damage than their united efforts in this direction could have inflicted upon their antagonist.

Early in the action, the pilot of the *Tennessee* had been wounded by having the trap-door on the top of the pilot-house knocked down upon his head by a shot from one of the enemy's ships, which struck it on the edge while it was thrown back to admit of his seeing more clearly the position of the vessel. Thereafter I remained in the pilot-house for the purpose of directing the movements of the ram.

The monitors kept up a constant firing at short range. The two double-turreted monitors (*Chickasaw* and *Winnebago*) were stationed under the stern of the *Tennessee*, and struck the after end of her shield so repeatedly with 11-inch solid shot that it was found at the close of the action to be in a rather shaky condition. One of these missiles had struck the iron cover of the stern port and jammed it against the shield so that it became impossible to run the gun out for firing, and Admiral Buchanan, who superintended the battery during the entire engagement, sent to the engine-room for a machinist to back out the pin of the bolt upon which the port-cover revolved. While this was being done a shot from one of the monitors struck the edge of the port-cover, immediately over the spot where the machinist was sitting, and his remains had to be taken up with a shovel, placed in a bucket and thrown overboard. The same shot caused several iron splinters to fly inside of the shield, one of which killed a seaman, while another broke the admiral's leg below the knee. The admiral sent for me, and as I approached he quietly remarked, "Well, Johnston, they've got me. You'll have to look out for her now. This is your fight, you know." I replied, "All right, sir. I'll do the best I know how." While returning to the pilot-house I felt the vessel careen so suddenly as nearly to throw me off my feet. I discovered that the *Hartford* had run into the ram amidships, and that while thus in contact with her the Federal crew were using their small-arms by firing through the open ports. However, only one man was wounded in this way, the causes of all our other wounds

being iron splinters from the washers on the inner ends of the bolts that secured the plating. I continued on my way to the pilot-house, and upon looking through the narrow peep-holes in its sides to ascertain the position of the enemy's ships, I discovered that the wooden vessels had mostly withdrawn from the action, leaving it to the monitors to effect the destruction of the ram at their leisure. At this time both of my most efficient guns had been placed in broadside, because both the after and forward port-covers had been so effectually jammed against the shield as to block up the ports. The steering apparatus had been completely destroyed, as it had been plainly visible on the after-deck, and the smoke-stack had fallen, destroying the draught in such a degree as to render it impossible to keep steam enough to stem the tide, which was running out at the rate of over four miles an hour.

Realizing the impossibility of directing the firing of the guns without the use of the rudder, and that the ship had been rendered utterly helpless, I went to the lower deck and informed the admiral of her condition, and that I had not been able to bring a gun to bear upon any of our antagonists for nearly half an hour, to which he replied: "Well, Johnston, if you cannot do them any further damage you had better surrender." . . .

With this sanction the commander of the *Tennessee* soon hoisted the white flag, but not in time to escape ramming by one of the heaviest Union ships, which struck the ram on the starboard quarter.

As she did so her commander hailed, saying: "This is the United States steamer *Ossipee*. Hello, Johnston, how are you? Le Roy—don't you know me? I'll send a boat alongside for you." The boat came and conveyed me on board the *Ossipee*, at whose gangway I was met by her genial commander, between whom and myself a life-long friendship had existed. When I reached the deck of his ship, he remarked, "I'm glad to see you, Johnston. Here's some ice-water for you—I know you're dry; but I've something better than that for you down below." . . .

Within an hour after I was taken on board the *Ossipee*, Admiral Farragut sent for me to be brought on board his flag-ship, and when I reached her deck he expressed regret at meeting me under such circumstances, to which I replied that he was not half as sorry to see me as I was to see him. . . .

DEFENDING AN EMBRASURE.

HOOD'S INVASION OF TENNESSEE
AND THE BATTLES OF FRANKLIN AND NASHVILLE.

THE INVASION.*

BY J. B. HOOD, GENERAL, C. S. A.
Commanding the invading army.

. . . I remained two days at Cross Roads in serious thought and perplexity. I could not offer battle while the officers were *unanimous* in their opposition. Neither could I take an intrenched position with likelihood of advantageous results, since Sherman could do the same, repair the railroad, amass a large army, place Thomas in my front in command of the forces he afterward assembled at Nashville, and then, himself, move southward; or, as previously suggested, he could send Thomas into Alabama, whilst he marched through Georgia, and left me to follow in his rear. This last movement upon our part would be construed by the troops into a retreat, and could but result in disaster. In this dilemma I conceived the plan of marching into Tennessee with the hope to establish our line eventually in Kentucky, and determined to make the campaign which followed, unless withheld by General Beauregard or the authorities at Richmond. I decided to make provision for twenty days' supply of rations in the haversacks and wagons; to order a heavy reserve of artillery to accompany the army, in order to overcome any serious opposition by the Federal gun-boats; to cross the Tennessee at or near Guntersville, and again destroy Sherman's communications at Stevenson and Bridgeport; to move upon Thomas and Schofield, and to attempt to rout and capture their army before it could reach Nashville. I intended then to march upon that city, where I would supply the army and reinforce it, if possible, by accessions from Tennessee. I was imbued with the belief that I could accomplish this feat,

* Taken by permission (and condensed) from General Hood's work, "Advance and Retreat," published by General G. T. Beauregard for the Hood Orphan Memorial Fund: New Orleans, 1880.

afterward march northeast, pass the Cumberland River at some crossing where the gun-boats, if too formidable at other points, were unable to interfere, then move into Kentucky, and take position with our left at or near Richmond, and our right extending toward Hazel Green, with Pound and Stony gaps in the Cumberland Mountains at our rear.

In this position I could threaten Cincinnati, and recruit the army from Kentucky and Tennessee; the former State was reported, at this juncture, to be more aroused and embittered against the Federals than at any other period of the war. While Sherman was debating between the alternatives of following our army or marching through Georgia, I hoped, by rapid movements, to achieve these results.

If Sherman should cut loose and move south — as I then believed he would do after I left his front *without previously worsting him in battle* — I would occupy at Richmond, Kentucky, a position of superior advantage, as Sherman, upon his arrival at the sea-coast, would be forced to go on board ship, and, after a long détour by water and land, repair to the defense of Kentucky and Ohio or march direct to the support of Grant. If he should return to confront my forces, or follow me directly from Georgia into Tennessee and Kentucky, I hoped then to be in condition to offer battle; and, if blessed with victory, to send reinforcements to General Lee, in Virginia, or to march through the gaps in the Cumberland Mountains and attack Grant in rear. This latter course I would pursue in the event of defeat or of inability to offer battle to Sherman. If, on the other hand, he should march to join Grant, I could pass through the Cumberland gaps to Petersburg, and attack Grant in rear at least two weeks before he, Sherman, could render him assistance.

This move, I believed, would defeat Grant, and allow General Lee, in command of our combined armies, to march upon Washington or turn upon and annihilate Sherman. Such is the plan which, during the 15th and 16th, as we lay in bivouac near Lafayette, I maturely considered, and determined to carry out.

On the 17th the army resumed its line of march, and that night camped three miles from the forks of the Alpine, Gaylesville, and Summerville roads; thence it proceeded toward Gadsden. I proposed to move directly on to Guntersville and to take into Tennessee about one-half of Wheeler's cavalry (leaving the remainder to look after Sherman) and to have a depot of supplies at Tuscumbia in the event that I should meet with defeat in Tennessee.

Shortly after my arrival at Gadsden, General Beauregard reached the same point; I at once unfolded to him my plan, and requested that he confer apart with the corps commanders, Lieutenant-Generals Lee and Stewart and Major-General Cheatham. If after calm deliberation he deemed it expedient we should remain upon the Alabama line and attack Sherman, or take position, intrench, and finally follow on his rear when he should move south, I would of course acquiesce, albeit with reluctance. If, contrariwise, he should agree to my proposed plan to cross into Tennessee, I would move immediately to Guntersville, thence to Stevenson, Bridgeport, and Nashville.

This important question at issue was discussed during the greater part of one night, with maps before us. General Beauregard at length took the ground that, if I should engage in the projected campaign, it would be necessary to leave in Georgia all the cavalry at present with the army, in order to watch and harass Sherman in case he should move south, and to instruct Forrest to join me as soon as I should cross the Tennessee River. To this proposition I acceded. After he had held a separate conference with the corps commanders, we again debated several hours over the course of action to be pursued; and, during the interview, I discovered that he had gone to work in earnest to ascertain, in person, the true condition of the army; that he had sought information not only from the corps commanders, but from a number of officers, and had reached the same conclusion I had formed at Lafayette: that we were not competent to offer pitched battle to Sherman, nor could we follow him south without causing our retrograde movement to be construed by the troops into *a recurrence* of retreat, which would entail desertions and render the army of little or no use in its opposition to the enemy's march through Georgia. After two days' deliberation General Beauregard authorized me, on the evening of the 21st of October, to proceed to the execution of my plan of operations into Tennessee. General Beauregard's approval of a forward movement into Tennessee was soon made known to the army. The prospect of again entering that State created great enthusiasm, and from the different encampments arose at intervals that genuine Confederate shout so familiar to every Southern soldier, and which then betokened an improved state of feeling among the troops. With twenty days' rations in the haver-

sacks and wagons, we marched, on the 22d of October, upon all the roads leading from Gadsden in the direction of Guntersville, on the Tennessee River, and bivouacked that night in the vicinity of Bennettsville. . . .

. . . The Confederate army rested upon the banks of the Tennessee one month after its departure from Palmetto. It had been almost continuously in motion during the interim; by rapid moves and manœuvers, and with only a small loss, it had drawn Sherman as far north as he stood in the early spring. The killed and wounded at Allatoona had been replaced by absentees who returned to ranks, and, as usual in such operations, the number of desertions became of no consequence.

Notwithstanding my request as early as the 9th of October that the railroad to Decatur be repaired, nothing had been done on the 1st of November toward the accomplishment of this important object. I had expected upon my arrival at Tuscumbia to find additional supplies, and to cross the river at once. Unfortunately, I was constrained to await repairs upon the railroad before a sufficient amount of supplies could be received to sustain the army till it was able to reach middle Tennessee.

General Beauregard remained two weeks at Tuscumbia and in its vicinity, during which interval the inaugurated campaign was discussed anew at great length. General Sherman was still in the neighborhood of Rome, and the question arose as to whether we should take trains and return to Georgia to oppose his movements south, or endeavor to execute the projected operations into Tennessee and Kentucky. I adhered to the conviction I had held at Lafayette and Gadsden, and a second time desired General Beauregard to consult the corps commanders, together with other officers, in regard to the effect a return to Georgia would produce upon the army. I also urged the

BREVET MAJOR-GENERAL EMERSON OPDYCKE, U. S. V.

MAJOR-GENERAL PATRICK R. CLEBURNE, C. S. A.
Killed at Franklin, November 30, 1864.

consideration that Thomas would immediately overrun Alabama, if we marched to confront Sherman. I had fixedly determined, unless withheld by Beauregard or the authorities at Richmond, to proceed, as soon as supplies were received, to the execution of the plan submitted at Gadsden.

At this juncture I was advised of the President's opposition to the campaign into Tennessee previous to a defeat of Sherman in battle. The President was evidently under the impression that the army should have been equal to battle by the time it had reached the Alabama line, and was averse to my going into Tennessee. He was not, as were General Beauregard and myself, acquainted with its true condition. Therefore, a high regard for his views notwithstanding, I continued firm in the belief that the only means to checkmate Sherman, and coöperate with General Lee to save the Confederacy, lay in speedy success in Tennessee and Kentucky, and in my ability finally to attack Grant in rear with my entire force.

Although every possible effort was made to expedite the repairs upon the railroad, the work progressed slowly. Heavy rains in that section also interfered with the completion of the road. On the 13th I established my headquarters in Florence, upon the north branch of the Tennessee, and the following day General Forrest, with his command, reported for duty. On the 15th the remainder of Lee's corps crossed the river and bivouacked in advance also of Florence. Stewart's and Cheatham's corps were instructed to cross. About the time all necessary preparations verged to a completion, and I anticipated to move forward once more, heavy rains again delayed our supplies. Working parties were at once detailed and sent to different points on the railroad; wagons were also despatched to aid in the transportation of supplies. The officer in charge was instructed to require the men to labor unceasingly for the accomplishment of this important object. In the mean time information had reached me that Sherman was advancing south, from Atlanta. He

marched out of that fated city on the 16th. Thus were two opposing armies destined to move in opposite directions, each hoping to achieve glorious results.

I well knew the delay at Tuscumbia would accrue to the advantage of Sherman, as he would thereby be allowed time to repair his railroad, and at least start to the rear all surplus material. I believed, however, that I could still get between Thomas's forces and Nashville, and rout them; furthermore, effect such manœuvers as to insure to our troops an easy victory. These convictions counterbalanced my regret that Sherman was permitted to traverse Georgia unopposed.

General Beauregard had moved in the direction of Georgia to assemble all available forces to oppose Sherman's advance.

On the 19th the cavalry was ordered to move forward. The succeeding day Lee's corps marched to the front about ten miles on the Chisholm road, between the Lawrenceburg and Waynesboro' roads. On the 20th of November, Stewart's corps having crossed the Tennessee and bivouacked several miles beyond on the Lawrenceburg road, orders were issued that the entire army move at an early hour the next morning. Lee's and Stewart's corps marched upon the Chisholm and the Lawrenceburg roads, and Cheatham's upon the Waynesboro' road. Early dawn of the 21st found the army in motion. I hoped by a rapid march to get in rear of Schofield's forces, then at Pulaski, before they were able to reach Duck River. That night headquarters were established at Rawhide, twelve miles north of Florence on the Waynesboro' road. The march was resumed on the 22d and continued till the 27th, upon which date the troops, having taken advantage of every available road, reached Columbia, via Mount Pleasant. Forrest operated in our front against the enemy's cavalry, which he easily drove from one position to another.

The Federals at Pulaski became alarmed, and, by forced marches, reached Columbia, upon Duck River, in time to prevent our troops from cutting them off.

Colonel Presstman and his assistants laid the pontoons [over Duck River] during the night of the 28th, about three miles above Columbia; orders to move at dawn the following day having been issued to the two corps and the division above mentioned, I rode with my staff to Cheatham's right, passed over the bridge soon after daybreak, and moved forward at the head of Granbury's Texas brigade, of Cleburne's division, with instructions that the remaining corps and divisions follow, and at the same time keep well closed up during the march. . . .

THE UNION SIDE AT FRANKLIN AND NASHVILLE.

BY HENRY STONE, BREVET COLONEL, U. S. V.
A member of the staff of General Thomas.

NOTE.—Schofield retired from Columbia to Spring Hill, on the road to Franklin, where he was almost surrounded by Hood's army, and was compelled to cut his way out on the night of the 29th. By severe marching his troops reached Franklin, on the south bank of the Harpeth, during the 30th, and had barely completed a line of field-works when Hood's column rushed to the attack.

. . . The head of the column under General Cox reached the outskirts of Franklin about the same hour that the rear-guard was leaving Spring Hill. Here the tired, sleepy, hungry men, who had fought and marched, day and night, for nearly a week, threw up a line of earthworks on a slight eminence which guards the southern approach to the town, even before they made their coffee. Then they gladly dropped anywhere for the much-needed "forty winks." Slowly the rest of the weary column, regiment after regiment of worn-out men, filed into the works, and continued the line, till a complete bridge-head, from the river-bank above to the river-bank below, encircled the town. By noon of the 30th all the troops had come up, and the wagons were crossing the river, which was already fordable, notwithstanding the recent rains. The rear-guard was still out, having an occasional bout with the enemy.

MAJOR-GENERAL JAMES H. WILSON, U. S. V.
Commanding the Union Cavalry.

The Columbia Pike bisected the works, which at that point were built just in front of the Carter house, a one-story brick dwelling west of the pike, and a large gin-house on the east side. Between the gin-house and the river the works were partly protected in front by a hedge of Osage orange, and on the knoll, near the railroad cut close to the bank, were two batteries belonging to the Fourth Corps. Near the Carter house was a considerable thicket of locust-trees. Except these obstructions, the whole ground in front was entirely unobstructed and fenceless, and, from the works, every part of it was in plain sight. General Cox's division of three brigades, commanded that day, in order from left to right, by Colonels Stiles and Casement and General Reilly, occupied the ground between the Columbia Pike and the river above the town. The front line consisted of eight regiments, three in the works and one in reserve for each of the brigades of Stiles and Casement, while Reilly's brigade nearest the pike had but two regiments in the works, and two in a second line, with still another regiment behind that. . . .

General Wood's division of the Fourth Corps had gone over the river with the trains; and two brigades of Wagner's division, which had so valiantly stood their ground at Spring Hill and covered the rear since, were halted on a slope about half a mile to the front. Opdycke had brought his brigade within the works, and held them massed, near the pike, behind the Carter house. Besides the guns on the knoll, near the railroad-cut, there were six pieces in Reilly's works; four on Strickland's left; two on Moore's left, and four on Grose's left—in all, twenty-six guns in that part of the works, facing south, and twelve more in reserve, on or near the Columbia Pike.

As the bright autumn day, hazy with the golden light of an Indian summer atmosphere, wore away, the troops that had worked so hard looked hopefully forward to a prospect of ending it in peace and rest, preparatory either to a night march to Nashville, or to a reinforcement by Smith's corps

1. THE CARTER HOUSE, FROM THE SIDE TOWARD THE TOWN. 2. THE CARTER HOUSE, FROM THE CONFEDERATE SIDE. 3. FRONT VIEW OF THE CARTER HOUSE.
From photographs taken in 1884.

and General Thomas. But about 2 o'clock, some suspicious movements on the hills a mile or two away—the waving of signal flags and the deployment of the enemy in line of battle—caused General Wagner to send his adjutant-general, from the advanced position where his two brigades had halted, to his commanding general, with the information that Hood seemed to be preparing for attack. In a very short time the whole Confederate line could be seen, stretching in battle array, from the dark fringe of chestnuts along the river-bank, far across the Columbia Pike, the colors gaily fluttering and the muskets gleaming brightly, and advancing steadily, in perfect order, dressed on the center, straight for the works. Meantime General Schofield had retired to the fort, on a high bluff on the other side of the river, some two miles away, by the road, and had taken General Stanley with him. From the fort the whole field of operations was plainly visible. Notwithstanding all these demonstrations, the two brigades of Wagner were left on the knoll where they had been halted, and, with scarcely an apology for works to protect them, had waited until it was too late to retreat without danger of degenerating into a rout.

On came the enemy, as steady and resistless as a tidal wave. A couple of guns, in the advance line, gave them a shot and galloped back to the works. A volley from a thin skirmish-line was sent into

HILL NEAR NASHVILLE FROM WHICH BATE'S CONFEDERATE DIVISION WAS DRIVEN ON DECEMBER 16. (SEE PAGE 280.)
From a photograph taken in 1884.

THE BATTLE-FIELD OF FRANKLIN, TENNESSEE, LOOKING NORTH FROM GENERAL CHEATHAM'S HEADQUARTERS.

their ranks, but without causing any delay to the massive array. A moment more, and with that wild "rebel yell" which, once heard, is never forgotten, the great human wave swept along, and seemed to ingulf the little force that had so sturdily awaited it.

The first shock came, of course, upon the two misplaced brigades of Wagner's division, which, through some one's blunder, had remained in their false position until too late to retire without disaster. They had no tools to throw up works; and when struck by the resistless sweep of Cleburne's and Brown's divisions, they had only to make their way, as best they could, back to the works. In that wild rush, in which friend and foe were intermingled, and the piercing "rebel yell" rose high above the "Yankee cheer," nearly seven hundred were made prisoners. But worst of all for the Union side, the men of Reilly's and Strickland's brigades dared not fire, lest they should shoot down their own comrades, and the guns, loaded with grape and canister, stood silent in the embrasures. With loud shouts of "Let's go into the works with them," the triumphant Confederates, now more like a wild, howling mob than an organized army, swept on to the very works, with hardly a check from any quarter. So fierce was the rush that a number of the fleeing soldiers—officers and men—dropped ex-

hausted into the ditch, and lay there while the terrific contest raged over their heads, till, under cover of darkness, they could crawl safely inside the intrenchments. . . .

Colonel Emerson Opdycke, of Wagner's division, as already stated, had brought his brigade inside the works, and they were now massed near the Carter house, ready for any contingency. Two regiments of Reilly's brigade, the 12th and 16th Kentucky, which had reached Franklin about noon, had taken position a little in rear of the rest of the brigade, and thrown up works. As soon as the break was made in the lines, all these reserves rushed to the front, and after a terrific struggle succeeded in regaining the works. Opdycke's brigade, deploying as it advanced, was involved in as fierce a hand-to-hand encounter as ever soldiers engaged in. The two Kentucky regiments joined in the fight with equal ardor and bravery. A large part of Conrad's and Lane's men, as they came in, though wholly disorganized, turned about and gave the enemy a hot reception. Opdycke's horse was shot under him, and he fought on foot at the head of his brigade. General Cox was everywhere present, encouraging and cheering on his men. General Stanley, who, from the fort where he had gone with General Schofield, had seen the opening clash, galloped to

the front as soon as possible and did all that a brave man could until he was painfully wounded. Some of Opdycke's men manned the abandoned guns in Reilly's works; others filled the gap in Strickland's line. These timely movements first checked and then repulsed the assaulting foe, and soon the entire line of works was reoccupied, the enemy sullenly giving up the prize which was so nearly won. Stewart's corps, which was on Cheatham's right, filling the space to the river, kept abreast of its valiant companion, and, meeting no obstacle, reached the works near the Union left before Cheatham made the breach at the Columbia Pike. Owing to the peculiar formation of the field, the left of Stewart's line was thrown upon the same ground with the right of Cheatham's; the two commands there became much intermingled. This accounts for so many of General Stewart's officers and men being killed in front of Reilly's and Casement's regiments.

Where there was nothing to hinder the Union fire, the muskets of Stiles's and Casement's brigades made fearful havoc; while the batteries at the railroad-cut plowed furrows through the ranks of the advancing foe. Time after time they came up to the very works, but they never crossed them except as prisoners. More than one color-bearer was shot down on the parapet. It is impossible to exaggerate the fierce energy with which the Confederate soldiers, that short November afternoon, threw themselves against the works, fighting with what seemed the very madness of despair. There was not a breath of wind, and the dense smoke settled down upon the field, so that, after the first assault, it was impossible to see at any distance. Through this blinding medium, assault after assault was made, several of the Union officers declaring in their reports that their lines received as many as thirteen distinct attacks.

Between the gin-house and the Columbia Pike the fighting was fiercest, and the Confederate losses the greatest. Here fell most of the Confederate generals who, that fateful afternoon, madly gave up their lives; Adams of Stewart's corps—his horse astride the works, and himself within a few feet of them. Cockrell and Quarles, of the same corps, were severely wounded. In Cheatham's corps, Cleburne and Granbury were killed near the pike. On the west of the pike Strahl and Gist were killed, and Brown was severely wounded. General G. W. Gordon was captured by Opdycke's brigade, inside the works. . . .

Schofield retired his army during the night to Nashville, uniting with Thomas, who occupied an intrenched line inclosing the city on the east, south, and west, with the flanks resting upon the Cumberland River. On the 1st of December Hood's columns took up positions on a line of hills confronting the Union works, and threw up intrenchments. The interval between December 1 and 9 was passed by Thomas in organizing his forces for a decisive battle. His movement was further delayed by a severe storm of freezing rain, which set in on the 9th, and rendered the fields and roads ice-bound until the 14th. That night orders were given to attack next day.

It was not daylight, on the morning of the 15th of December, when the army began to move. In most of the camps reveille had been sounded at 4 o'clock, and by 6 everything was ready. It turned out a warm, sunny, winter morning. A dense fog at first hung over the valleys and completely hid all movements, but by 9 o'clock this had cleared away. General Steedman, on the extreme left, was the first to draw out of the defenses, and to assail the enemy at their works between the Nolensville and Murfreesboro' pikes. It was not intended as a real attack, though it had that effect. Two of Steedman's brigades, chiefly colored troops, kept two divisions of Cheatham's corps constantly busy, while his third was held in reserve; thus one Confederate corps was disposed of. S. D. Lee's corps, next on Cheatham's left, after sending two brigades to the assistance of Stewart, on the Confederate left, was held in place by the threatening position of the garrison troops, and did not fire a shot during the day. Indeed, both Cheatham's and Lee's corps were held, as in a vise, between Steedman and Wood. Lee's corps was unable to move or to fight. Steedman maintained the ground he occupied till the next morning, with no very heavy loss.

When, about 9 o'clock, the sun began to burn away the fog, the sight from General Thomas's position was inspiring. A little to the left, on Montgomery Hill, the salient of the Confederate lines, and not more than six hundred yards distant from Wood's salient, on Lawrens Hill, could be seen the advance line of works, behind which an unknown force of the enemy lay in wait. Beyond, and along the Hillsboro' Pike, were stretches of stone wall, with here and there a detached earthwork, through whose embrasures peeped the threatening artillery. To the right, along the valley of Richland Creek, the dark line of Wilson's advancing cavalry could be seen slowly making its difficult way across the wet, swampy, stumpy ground. Close in front, and at the foot of the hill, its right joining Wilson's left, was A. J. Smith's corps, full of cheer and enterprise, and glad to be once more in the open field. Then came the Fourth Corps, whose left, bending back toward the north, was hidden behind Lawrens Hill. Already the skirmishers were engaged, the Confederates falling back before the determined and steady pressure of Smith and Wood.

By the time that Wilson's and Smith's lines were fully extended and brought up to within striking distance of the Confederate lines, along the Hillsboro' Pike, it was noon. Post's brigade of Wood's old division (now commanded by General Sam Beatty),

which lay at the foot of Montgomery Hill, full of dash and spirit, had since morning been regarding the works at the summit with covetous eyes. At Post's suggestion, it was determined to see which party wanted them most. Accordingly, a charge was ordered—and in a moment the brigade was swarming up the hillside, straight for the enemy's advanced works. For almost the first time since the grand assault on Missionary Ridge, a year before, here was an open field where everything could be seen. From General Thomas's headquarters everybody looked on with breathless suspense, as the blue line, broken and irregular, but with steady persistence, made its way up the steep hillside against a fierce storm of musketry and artillery. Most of the shots, however, passed over the men's heads. It was a struggle to keep up with the colors, and, as they neared the top, only the strongest were at the front. Without a moment's pause, the color-bearers and those who had kept up with them, Post himself at the head, leaped the parapet. As the colors waved from the summit, the whole line swept forward and was over the works in a twinkling, gathering in prisoners and guns. Indeed, so large was the mass of the prisoners which a few minutes later was seen heading toward our own lines, that a number of officers at General Thomas's headquarters feared the assault had failed and the prisoners were Confederate reserves who had rallied and retaken the works. But the fear was only momentary; for the wild outburst of cheers that rang across the valley told the story of complete success.

Meanwhile, farther to the right, as the opposing lines neared each other, the sound of battle grew louder and louder, and the smoke thicker and thicker, until the whole valley was filled with the haze. It was now past noon, and at every point the two armies were so near together that an assault was inevitable. Hatch's division of Wilson's cavalry, at the extreme right of the continuous line, was confronted by one of the detached works which Hood had intended to be "impregnable"; and the right of McArthur's division of A. J. Smith's infantry was also within striking distance of it. Coon's cavalry brigade was dismounted and ordered to assault the works, while Hill's infantry brigade received similar orders. The two commanders moved forward at the same time, and entered the work together, Colonel Hill falling dead at the head of his command. In a moment the whole Confederate force in that quarter was routed

MAJOR-GENERAL J. B. STEEDMAN, U. S. V.
Commanding the provisional detachment.

and fled to the rear, while the captured guns were turned on them.

With the view of extending the operations of Wilson's cavalry still further to the right, and if possible gaining the rear of the enemy's left, the two divisions of the Twenty-third Corps that had been in reserve near Lawrens Hill were ordered to Smith's right, while orders were sent to Wilson to gain, if possible, a lodgment on the Granny White Pike. These orders were promptly obeyed, and Cooper's brigade on reaching its new position got into a handsome fight, in which its losses were more than the losses of the rest of the Twenty-third Corps during the two days' battle. [This brigade had not been engaged at Franklin.]

But though the enemy's left was thus rudely driven from its fancied security, the salient at the center, being an angle formed by the line along Hillsboro' Pike and that stretching toward the east, was still firmly held. Post's successful assault had merely driven out or captured the advance forces; the main line was intact. As soon as word came of the successful assault on the right, General Thomas sent orders to General Wood, commanding the Fourth Corps, to prepare to attack the salient. The staff-officer by whom this order was sent did not at first find General Wood; but see-

ing the two division commanders whose troops would be called upon for the work, gave them the instruction. As he was riding along the line he met one of the brigade commanders—an officer with a reputation for exceptional courage and gallantry—who, in reply to the direction to prepare for the expected assault, said, "You don't mean that we've got to go in here and attack the works on that hill?" "Those are the orders," was the answer. Looking earnestly across the open valley, and at the steep hill beyond, from which the enemy's guns were throwing shot and shell with uncomfortable frequency and nearness, he said, "Why, it would be suicide, sir; perfect suicide." "Nevertheless, those are the orders," said the officer; and he rode on to complete his work. Before he could rejoin General Thomas the assault was made, and the enemy were driven out with a loss of guns, colors, and prisoners, and their whole line was forced to abandon the works along the Hillsboro' Pike and fall back to the Granny White Pike. The retreating line was followed by the entire Fourth Corps (Wood's), as well as by the cavalry and Smith's troops; but night soon fell, and the whole army went into bivouac in the open fields wherever they chanced to be.

At dark, Hood, who at 12 o'clock had held an unbroken, fortified line from the Murfreesboro' to the Hillsboro' Pike, with an advanced post on Montgomery Hill and five strong redoubts along the Hillsboro' Pike, barely maintained his hold of a line from the Murfreesboro' Pike to the Granny White Pike, near which on two large hills the left of his army had taken refuge when driven out of their redoubts by Smith and Wilson. These hills were more than two miles to the rear of his morning position. . . .

The morning was consumed in moving to new positions. Wilson's cavalry, by a wide détour, had passed beyond the extreme Confederate left, and secured a lodgment on the Granny White Pike.

VIEW OF THE WINSTEAD HILLS, FRANKLIN, WHERE HOOD FORMED HIS LINE OF BATTLE.
From a photograph.

The right of Wagner's two brigades, in the advanced position, was posted behind the stone wall in the foreground. The Columbia Pike is shown passing over the hills on the left of the picture. (See pages 277, 278.)

But one avenue of escape was now open for Hood— the Franklin Pike. Gen Thomas hoped that a vigorous assault by Schofield's corps against Hood's left would break the line there, and thus enable the cavalry, relieved from the necessity of operating against the rebel flank, to gallop down the Granny White Pike to its junction with the Franklin, some six or eight miles below, and plant itself square across the only remaining line of retreat. If this scheme could be carried out, nothing but capture or surrender awaited Hood's whole army.

Meantime, on the National left, Colonel Post, who had so gallantly carried Montgomery Hill the morning before, had made a careful reconnoissance of Overton's Hill, the strong position on Hood's right. As the result of his observation, he reported to General Wood, his corps commander, that an assault would cost dear, but he believed it could be made successfully; at any rate he was ready to try it. The order was accordingly given, and everything prepared. The brigade was to be supported on either side by fresh troops to be held in readiness to rush for the works the moment Post should gain the parapet. The bugles had not finished sounding the charge, when Post's brigade, preceded by a strong line of skirmishers, moved forward, in perfect silence, with orders to halt for nothing, but to gain the works at a run. The men dashed on, Post leading, with all speed through a shower of shot and shell. A few of the skirmishers reached the parapet; the main line came within twenty steps of the works, when, by a concentrated fire of musketry and artillery from every available point of the enemy's line, the advance was momentarily checked, and, in another instant, Post was brought down by a wound, at first reported as mortal. This slight hesitation and the disabling of Post were fatal to the success of the assault. The leading and animating spirit gone, the line slowly drifted to its origi-

nal position, losing in those few minutes nearly 300 men; while the supporting brigade on its left lost 250.

Steedman had promised to coöperate in this assault, and accordingly Thompson's brigade of colored troops was ordered to make a demonstration at the moment Post's advance began. These troops had never before been in action and were now to test their mettle. There had been no time for a reconnoissance, when this order was given, else it is likely a way would have been found to turn the enemy's extreme right flank. The colored brigade moved forward against the works east of the Franklin Pike and nearly parallel to it. As they advanced, they became excited, and what was intended merely as a demonstration was unintentionally converted into an actual assault. Thompson, finding his men rushing forward at the double-quick, gallantly led them to the very slope of the intrenchments. But, in their advance across the open field, the continuity of his line was broken by a large fallen tree. As the men separated to pass it, the enemy opened an enfilading fire on the exposed flanks of the gap thus created, with telling effect. In consequence, at the very moment when a firm compact order was most needed, the line came up ragged and broken. Meantime Post's assault was repulsed, and the fire which had been concentrated on him was turned against Thompson. Nothing was left, therefore, but to withdraw as soon as possible to the original position. This was done without panic or confusion, after a loss of 467 men from the three regiments composing the brigade.

When it was seen that a heavy assault on his right, at Overton's Hill, was threatened, Hood ordered Cleburne's old division to be sent over to the exposed point, from the extreme left, in front of Schofield. About the same time General Couch, commanding one of the divisions of the Twenty-third Corps, told General Schofield that he believed he could carry the hill in his front, but doubted if he could hold it without assistance. The ground in front of General Cox, on Couch's right, also offered grand opportunities for a successful assault. Meantime the cavalry, on Cox's right, had made its way

beyond the extreme left flank of the enemy, and was moving northward over the wooded hills direct to the rear of the extreme rebel left.

General Thomas, who had been making a reconnoissance, had no sooner reached Schofield's front than General McArthur, who commanded one of Smith's divisions, impatient at the long waiting, and not wanting to spend the second night on the rocky hill he was occupying, told Smith that he could carry the high hill in front of Couch,—the same that Couch himself had told Schofield he could carry,—and would undertake it unless forbidden. Smith silently acquiesced, and McArthur set to work. Withdrawing McMillen's (his right) brigade from the trenches, he marched it by the flank in front of General Couch's position, and with orders to the men to fix bayonets, not to fire a shot, and neither to halt nor to cheer until they had gained the enemy's works, the charge was sounded. The gallant brigade, which had served and fought in every part of the Southwest, moved swiftly down the slope, across the narrow valley, and began scrambling up the steep hillside, on the top of which was the redoubt, held by Bate's division, and mounted also with Whitworth guns. The bravest onlookers held their breath as these gallant men steadily and silently approached the summit amid the crash of musketry and the boom of the artillery. In almost the time it has taken to tell the story they gained the works, their flags were wildly waving from the parapet, and the unmistakable cheer, "the voice of the American people," as General Thomas called it, rent the air. It was an exultant moment, but this was only a part of the heroic work of that afternoon. While McMillen's brigade was preparing for this wonderful charge, Hatch's division of cavalry, dismounted, had also pushed its way through the woods, and had gained the tops of two hills that commanded the rear of the enemy's works. Here, with incredible labor, they had dragged by hand two pieces of artillery, and, just as McMillen began his charge, these opened on the hill where Bate was, up the opposite slope of which the infantry were scrambling. At the same time Coon's brigade of Hatch's division, with resounding cheers, charged upon the enemy, and poured such volleys of musketry from their repeating-rifles as I have never heard equaled. Thus beset on both sides, Bate's people broke out of the works, and ran down the hill toward their right and rear as fast as their legs could carry them. It was more like a scene in a spectacular drama than a real incident in war. The hillside in front, still green, dotted with the boys in blue swarming up the slope; the dark background of high hills beyond; the lower-

OVERTON'S HOUSE, HOOD'S HEADQUARTERS AT NASHVILLE.
From a photograph taken in 1884.

ing clouds; the waving flags; the smoke slowly rising through the leafless tree-tops and drifting across the valleys; the whirlwind outburst of musketry; the ecstatic cheers; the multitude racing for life down into the valley below,—so exciting was it all, that the lookers-on instinctively clapped their hands, as at a brilliant and successful transformation scene, as indeed it was. For, in those few minutes, an army was changed into a mob, and the whole structure of the rebellion in the Southwest, with all its possibilities, was utterly overthrown. As soon as the other divisions farther to the left saw and heard the doings on their right, they did not wait for orders. Everywhere, by a common impulse, they charged the works in front, and carried them in a twinkling. General Edward Johnson and nearly all his division and his artillery were captured. Over the very ground where, but a little while before, Post's assault had been repulsed, the same troops now charged with resistless force, capturing fourteen guns and one thousand prisoners. Steedman's colored brigades also rallied and brought in their share of prisoners and other spoils of war. Everywhere the success was complete. . . .

NOTE.—The repulse of Hood virtually ended the war in the West north of Tennessee River. Thomas remained at Nashville, and Schofield, with the Army of the Ohio, was sent to North Carolina.

Hood retreated to Tupelo, and detachments of his army went to Mobile and to join Johnston in the Carolinas.

In January the Sixteenth Corps was organized from troops in Thomas's department, and sent to New Orleans under General A. J. Smith, to join in attacking Mobile. Mobile was defended by an army under General Dabney H. Maury, and the fleet of Commodore Farrand. General E. R. S. Canby, who had succeeded Banks, invested the place, and on the 8th and 9th of April, Spanish Fort and Fort Blakely fell by bombardment and assault, and the city was evacuated on the 11th.

Meanwhile, Wilson, starting from the banks of the Tennessee in March, had driven Forrest into central Alabama. He defeated him and captured Selma on April 2 and entered Montgomery on the 11th, the day Canby gained Mobile. From Montgomery Wilson moved eastward into Georgia, where his troopers intercepted the flight of Jefferson Davis. (See p. 320.) On May 4 Canby received the surrender of all the Confederate forces in Alabama and Mississippi.

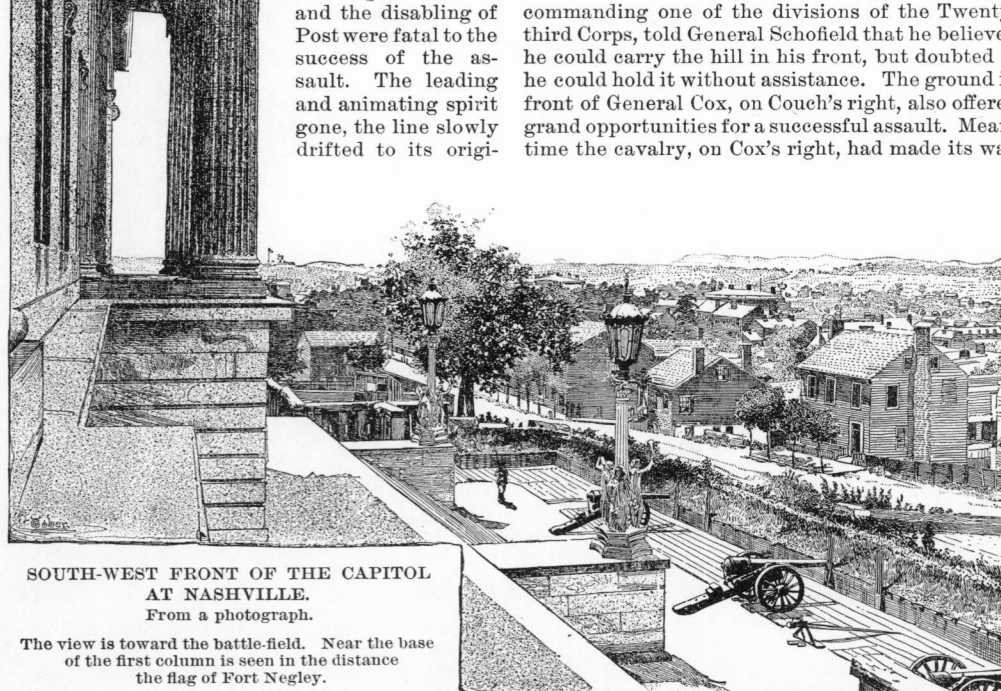

SOUTH-WEST FRONT OF THE CAPITOL
AT NASHVILLE.
From a photograph.

The view is toward the battle-field. Near the base of the first column is seen in the distance the flag of Fort Negley.

FORT STEVENS, WASHINGTON.
From a war-time photograph.

THE SHENANDOAH VALLEY CAMPAIGN.

NARRATIVE OF EVENTS.

The peculiar military advantages which the Confederates enjoyed while controlling the Shenandoah Valley (also called the Valley of Virginia) were first demonstrated in the first campaign of Bull Run (see p. 24 and following). Shortly after that event Stonewall Jackson assumed command of the Valley District. In March, 1862, Winchester was occupied by a Union force under General James Shields, which Jackson attacked near the hamlet of Kernstown, March 23. Defeated at Kernstown, Jackson retreated up the valley and a strong Union force under General Banks was assembled at Strasburg. In May Fremont entered the valley from West Virginia in support of Banks, and Jackson defeated his advance at McDowell, May 8. On the 23d, 24th, and 25th of May Jackson attacked Banks on the flank at Port Royal, Newton, and Winchester, and compelled him to retreat across the Potomac. Fremont, marching from Franklin, attempted to cut off Jackson's retreat up the valley, but was defeated at Cross Keys

June 8th, and Shields's division, marching to form a junction with Fremont, was defeated at Port Republic on the 9th. Soon after these successes Jackson's army joined Lee in front of Richmond to take part in the "Seven Days'" campaign (see p. 82 and following). The route of Lee's army lay through the valley during the invasions of Maryland and Pennsylvania in 1862 and 1863. At the beginning of Grant's campaign against Richmond in May, 1864, the Union troops in the valley were commanded by Sigel, the Confederates by General J. D. Imboden. Sigel attempted to advance up the valley. He was defeated at New Market on May 15th by Imboden and resigned the command to General David Hunter. Hunter moved on Lynchburg, where he was met by General Jubal Early, with a part of Lee's army, and compelled to retreat westward across the mountains. Early then marched down the valley, on his raid to Washington. Sigel, who had been retained in command along the Potomac, retired all his forces into Maryland.

EARLY'S MARCH TO WASHINGTON.*

BY JUBAL A. EARLY, LIEUTENANT-GENERAL, C. S. A.

ON the 12th of June, 1864, while the Second Corps (Ewell's) of the Army of Northern Virginia was lying near Gaines's Mill, in rear of Hill's line at Cold Harbor, I received orders from General Lee to move the corps, with two of the battalions of artillery attached to it, to the Shenandoah Valley; to strike Hunter's force in the rear and, if possible, destroy it; then to move down the valley, cross the Potomac near Leesburg, in Loudoun County, or at or above Harper's Ferry, as I might find most practicable, and threaten Washington city. I was further directed to communicate

with General Breckinridge, who would coöperate with me in the attack on Hunter and the expedition into Maryland. . . .

At Lynchburg I had received a telegram from General Lee, directing me, after disposing of Hunter, either to return to his army or to carry out the original plan, as I might deem most expedient. After the pursuit had ceased I received another despatch from him, submitting it to my judgment whether the condition of my troops would permit the expedition across the Potomac to be carried out, and I determined to take the responsibility of continuing it. On the 23d the march was resumed, and we reached Buchanan that night. On the 26th I reached Staunton in advance of the troops, and the latter came up next day, which was spent in reducing transportation and getting provisions from Waynesboro'.

During the night of the 4th [of July] the enemy evacuated Harper's Ferry, burning the railroad and pontoon bridges across the Potomac. It was

not possible to occupy the town of Harper's Ferry, except with skirmishers, as it was thoroughly commanded by the heavy guns on Maryland Heights; and the 5th was spent by Rodes's and Ramseur's divisions in demonstrating at that place. . . .

On the 10th the march was resumed at daylight, and we bivouacked four miles from Rockville, on the Georgetown pike, having marched twenty miles. McCausland, moving in front, drove a body of the enemy's cavalry before him, and had a brisk engagement at Rockville, where he encamped after defeating and driving off the enemy.

We moved at daylight on the 11th, McCausland on the Georgetown pike, while the infantry, preceded by Imboden's cavalry under Colonel Smith, turned to the left at Rockville, so as to reach the 7th street pike which runs by Silver Springs into Washington. Jackson's cavalry moved on the left flank. The previous day had been very warm, and the roads were exceedingly dusty, as there had been no rain for several weeks. The heat during the night had been very oppressive, and but little rest had been obtained. This day was an exceedingly hot one, and there was no air stirring. While marching, the men were enveloped in a suffocating cloud of dust, and many of them fell by the way from exhaustion. Our progress was therefore very much impeded, but I pushed on as rapidly as possible, hoping to get into the fortifications around Washington before they could be manned. Smith drove a small body of cavalry before him into the works on the 7th street pike, and dismounted his men and deployed them as skirmishers. I rode ahead of the infantry, and arrived in sight of Fort Stevens on this road a short time after noon, when I discovered that the works were but feebly manned.

Rodes, whose division was in front, was immediately ordered to bring it into line as rapidly as possible, throw out skirmishers, and move into the works if he could. My whole column was then moving by flank, which was the only practicable mode of marching on the road we were on, and before Rodes's division could be brought up we saw a cloud of dust in the rear of the works toward Washington, and soon a column of the enemy filed into them on the right and left, and skirmishers were thrown out in front, while an artillery fire was opened on us from a number of batteries. This defeated our hopes of getting possession of the works by surprise, and it became necessary to reconnoiter.

Rodes's skirmishers were thrown to the front, driving those of the enemy to the cover of the works, and we proceeded to examine the fortifications in order to ascertain if it was practicable to carry them by assault. They were found to be exceedingly strong, and consisted of what appeared to be inclosed forts for heavy artillery, with a tier of lower works in front of each, pierced for an immense number of guns, the whole being connected by curtains with ditches in front, and strengthened by palisades and abatis. The timber had been felled within cannon range all around and left on the ground, making a

formidable obstacle, and every possible approach was raked by artillery. On the right was Rock Creek, running through a deep ravine which had been rendered impassable by the felling of the timber on each side, and beyond were the works on the Georgetown pike, which had been reported to be the strongest of all. On the left, as far as the eye could reach, the works appeared to be of the same impregnable character.* This reconnoissance consumed the balance of the day.

* General Barnard, in his "Defences of Washington," thus describes the works:

"Every prominent point, at intervals of eight hundred to one thousand yards, was occupied by an inclosed field-fort; every important approach or depression of ground, unseen from the forts, swept by a battery for field-guns; and the whole connected by rifle-trenches which were in fact lines of infantry parapets, furnishing emplacement for two ranks of men, and affording covered communication along the line, while roads were opened wherever necessary, so that troops and artillery could be moved rapidly from one point of the immense periphery to another, or under cover, from point to point along the line. The counterscarps were surrounded by abatis; bomb-proofs were provided in nearly all the forts; all guns not solely intended for distant fire placed in embrasures and well traversed. All commanding points on which an enemy would be likely to concentrate artillery to overpower that of one or two of our forts or batteries were subjected not only to the fire, direct and cross, of many points along the line, but also from heavy rifled guns from distant points unattainable by the enemy's field-guns. With all these developments, the lines certainly approximated to the maximum degree of strength which can be attained from unrevetted earthworks. Inadequately manned as they were, the fortifications compelled at least a concentration and an arraying of force on the part of the assailants, and thus gave time for the arrival of succor."

LIEUTENANT-GENERAL JUBAL A. EARLY, C. S. A.
From a photograph.

* Condensed from General Early's "Memoir of the Last Year of the War for Independence in the Confederate States of America." Lynchburg: Published by Charles W. Button for the Virginia Memorial Association, 1867; here printed by permission of the author.

The rapid marching, and the losses at Harper's Ferry, Maryland Heights, and Monocacy, had reduced my infantry to about 8000 muskets. Of these a very large number were greatly exhausted by the last two days' marching, some having fallen by sunstroke, and not more than one-third of my force could have been carried into action. I had about forty pieces of artillery, of which the largest were 12-pounder Napoleons, besides a few pieces of horse-artillery with the cavalry. McCausland reported the works on the Georgetown pike too strongly manned for him to assault. After dark on the 11th I held a consultation with Major-Generals Breckinridge, Rodes, Gordon, and Ramseur, in which I stated to them the necessity of doing something immediately, as the passes of South Mountain and the fords of the Upper Potomac would soon be closed against us. After interchanging views with them, I determined to make an assault on the enemy's works at daylight next morning. But during the night a despatch was received from General Bradley T. Johnson from near Baltimore, that two corps had arrived from General Grant's army, and that his whole army was probably in motion. As soon as it was light enough to see, I rode to the front, and found the parapet lined with troops. I had, therefore, reluctantly to give up all hopes of capturing Washington, after I had arrived in sight of the dome of the Capitol, and given the Federal authorities a terrible fright.

Some of the Northern papers stated that, between Saturday and Monday, I could have entered the city; but on Saturday I was fighting at Monocacy, thirty-five miles from Washington, a force which I could not leave in my rear; and after disposing of that force and moving as rapidly as it was possible for me to move, I did not arrive in front of the fortifications until after noon on Monday, and then my troops were exhausted, and it required time to bring them up into line. I had then made a march, over the circuitous route by Charlottesville, Lynchburg, and Salem, down the valley and through the passes of the South Mountain, which, notwithstanding the delays in dealing with Hunter's, Sigel's, and Wallace's forces, is, for its length and rapidity, I believe, without a parallel in this or any other modern war. My small force had been thrown up to the very walls of the Federal capital, north of a river which could not be forded at any point within forty miles, and with a heavy force and the South Mountain in my rear—

the passes through which mountain could be held by a small number of troops. A glance at the map, when it is recollected that the Potomac is a wide river, and navigable to Washington for the largest vessels, will cause the intelligent reader to wonder, not why I failed to take Washington, but why I had the audacity to approach it as I did, with the small force under my command. It was supposed by some, who were not informed of the facts, that I delayed in the lower valley longer than was necessary; but an examination of the foregoing narrative will show that not one moment was spent in idleness. I could not move across the Potomac and through the passes of the South Mountain, with any safety, until Sigel was driven from, or safely housed in, the fortifications at Maryland Heights.

After abandoning the idea of capturing Washington I determined to remain in front of the fortifications during the 12th, and retire at night. Johnson had burned the bridges over the Gunpowder, on the Harrisburg and Philadelphia roads, threatened Baltimore, and started for Point Lookout; but the attempt to release the prisoners was not made, as the enemy had received notice of it in some way. On the afternoon of the 12th a heavy reconnoitering force was sent out by the enemy, which, after severe skirmishing, was driven back

by Rodes's division with but slight loss to us. About dark we commenced retiring, and did so without molestation. Passing through Rockville and Poolesville, we crossed the Potomac at White's Ford, above Leesburg, in Loudoun County, on the morning of the 14th, bringing off the prisoners captured at Monocacy, and our captured beef cattle and horses, and everything else, in safety.

SHERIDAN IN THE SHENANDOAH VALLEY.

BY WESLEY MERRITT, MAJOR-GENERAL, U. S. V.,
BRIGADIER-GENERAL, U. S. A.
Commanding the First Division of Cavalry.

UP to the summer of 1864 the Shenandoah Valley had not been to the Union armies a fortunate place either for battle or for strategy. A glance at the map will go far toward explaining this. The valley has a general direction from southwest to northeast. The Blue Ridge Mountains, forming its eastern barrier, are well defined from the James River above Lynchburg to Harper's Ferry on the Potomac. Many passes (in Virginia called "gaps") made it easy of access from the Confederate base of operations; and, bordered by a fruitful country filled with supplies, it offered a tempting highway for an army bent on a flanking march on Washington or the invasion of Maryland or Pennsylvania. For the Union armies, while it was an equally practicable highway, it led away from the objective, Richmond, and was exposed to flank attacks through the gaps from vantage-ground and perfect cover.

It was not long after General Grant completed his first campaign in Virginia, and while he was in front of Petersburg, that his attention was called to this famous seat of side issues between Union and Confederate armies. With quick military instinct he saw that the valley was not useful to the Government for aggressive operations. He decided that it must be made untenable for either army. In doing this he reasoned that the advantage would be with us, who did not want it as a source of supplies, nor as a place of arms, and against the Confederates, who wanted it for both. Accordingly, instructions were drawn up for carrying on a plan of devastating the valley in a way least injurious to the people. These instructions, which were intended for Hunter, were destined to be

THE BATTLE OF WINCHESTER—RICKETTS'S ADVANCE AGAINST RODES'S DIVISION ON THE MORNING OF SEPTEMBER 19, 1864.

MAJOR-GENERAL GEORGE A. CUSTER, U. S. V.
From a photograph.

IN THE VAN.

carried out by another, and how well this was accomplished it is my purpose to recount.

Hunter's failure to capture Lynchburg in the spring of 1864, and his retreat by a circuitous line opened the valley to General Early, who had gone to the relief of Lynchburg. Marching down the valley and taking possession of it without serious opposition, Early turned Harper's Ferry, which was held by a Union force under Sigel, and crossed into Maryland at Shepherdstown. The governors of New York, Pennsylvania, and Massachusetts were called on for hundred-days men to repel the invasion, and later the Army of the Potomac supplied its quota of veterans as a nucleus around which the new levies could rally. General Early marched on Washington, and on the 11th of July was in front of the gates of the capital. The following day, after a severe engagement in which the guns of Fort Stevens took part, he withdrew his forces through Rockville and Poolesville, and, crossing the Potomac above Leesburg, entered the Valley of Virginia through Snicker's Gap. Afterward, crossing the Shenandoah at the ferry of the same name, he moved to Berryville, and there awaited developments.

After the immediate danger to Washington had passed it became a question with General Grant and the authorities in Washington to select an officer who, commanding in the valley, would prevent further danger from invasion. After various suggestions, Major-General Philip H. Sheridan was selected temporarily for this command. His permanent occupation of the position was opposed by Secretary Stanton on the ground that he was too young for such important responsibility. On the 7th of August, 1864, Sheridan assumed command of the Middle Military Division, and of the army for the protection of the valley, afterward known as the "Army of the Shenandoah."

Naturally, on assuming command, Sheridan moved with caution. He was incited to this by his instructions, and inclined to it by his unfamiliarity with the country, with the command, and with the enemy he had to deal with. On the other hand, Early, who had nothing of these to learn, save the

mettle of his new adversary, was aggressive, and at once manœuvered with a bold front, seemingly anxious for a battle. The movements of the first few days showed, however, that Early was not disposed to give battle unless he could do so on his own conditions.

On the morning of the 10th of August, Sheridan, who had massed his army at Halltown, in front of Harper's Ferry, marched toward the enemy's communications, his object being to occupy Early's line of retreat and force him to fight before reinforcements could reach him. The march of my cavalry toward the Millwood-Winchester road brought us in contact with the enemy's cavalry on that road, and it was driven toward Kernstown. At the same time a brigade under Custer, making a reconnoissance on the Berryville-Winchester road, came on the enemy holding a defile of the highway, while "his trains and infantry were marching toward Strasburg." As soon as the retreat of the enemy was known to General Sheridan the cavalry was ordered to pursue and harass him. Near White Post, Devin came upon a strongly posted force, which, after a sharp fight, he drove from the field, and the division took position on the Winchester-Front Royal pike. The same day my division had a severe affair with infantry near Newtown, in which the loss to my second brigade was considerable.

On the 12th of August, the enemy having retired the night before, the cavalry pursued to Cedar Creek, when it came up with Early's rear-guard and continued skirmishing until the arrival of the head of the infantry column. The day following, the reconnoissance of a brigade of cavalry discovered the enemy strongly posted at Fisher's Hill. About this time Early received his expected reinforcements. General Sheridan, being duly informed of this, made preparations to retire to a position better suited for defense and adapted to the changed conditions of the strength of the two armies. . . .

About 2 P. M. on the 16th an attack was made . . . which resulted in the battle of Cedarville. . . . The Confederates were thrown into confusion and retreated, leaving 300 prisoners, together with two stand of colors. . . .

FROM A PHOTOGRAPH.

P. H. Sheridan

[Several other engagements took place between the troops of General Sheridan and General Early, leaving Sheridan master of the situation.]

On the 12th of September Sheridan had telegraphed Grant to the effect that it was exceedingly difficult to attack Early in his position behind the Opequon, which constituted a formidable barrier; that the crossings, though numerous, were deep, and the banks abrupt and difficult for an attacking force; and, in general, that he was waiting for the

chances to change in his favor, hoping that Early would either detach troops or take some less defensible position. His caution was fortunate at this time, and his fearlessness and hardihood were sufficiently displayed thereafter. In the light of criticisms, then, it is curious that the world is now inclined to call Sheridan reckless and foolhardy.

At 2 A. M. of September 19th Sheridan's army was astir under orders to attack Early in front of Winchester. . . . At daylight Wilson advanced

across the Opequon, and carried the earthwork which covered the defile and captured part of the force that held it. The infantry followed — Wright's corps first, with Getty leading, and Emory next. Between two and three miles from the Opequon, Wright came up with Wilson, who was waiting in the earthwork he had captured. There the country was suitable for the deployment of the column, which commenced forming line at once. Ramseur, with the bulk of the Confederate artillery, immediately opened on Wright's troops, and soon the Union guns were in position to reply. Wilson took position on the left of the Sixth Corps. Then followed a delay that thwarted the part of the plan which contemplated the destruction of Early's army in detail. Emory's command was crowded off the road in its march, and so delayed by the guns and trains of the Sixth Corps that it was slow getting on the field, and it was hours before the lines were formed. This delay gave the Confederates time to bring up the infantry of Gordon and Rodes. Gordon, who first arrived, was posted on Ramseur's left near the Red Bud, and when Rodes arrived with three of his four brigades, he was given the center. This change in the situation, which necessitated fighting Early's army in his chosen position, did not disconcert the Union commander. He had come out to fight, and though chafing at the unexpected delay, fight he would to the bitter end.

In the mean time the cavalry, which had been ordered to the right, had not been idle. Moving at the same time as did the rest of the army, my division reached the fords of the Opequon near the railroad crossing at early dawn. Here I found a force of cavalry supported by Breckinridge's infantry. After sharp skirmishing the stream was crossed at three different points, but the enemy contested every foot of the way beyond. The cavalry, however, hearing Sheridan's guns, and knowing the battle was in progress, was satisfied with the work it was doing in holding from Early a considerable force of infantry. The battle here continued for some hours, the cavalry making charges on foot or mounted according to the nature of the

HENRY E. DAVIES, JR.   D. MCM. GREGG.   PHILIP H. SHERIDAN.   WESLEY MERRITT.   A. T. A. TORBERT.   JAMES H. WILSON.

SHERIDAN AND SOME OF HIS GENERALS.
Facsimile of a photograph taken in 1864.

country, and steadily though slowly driving the enemy's force toward Winchester. Finally Breckinridge, leaving one brigade to assist the cavalry in retarding our advance, moved to the help of Early, arriving on the field about 2 P. M.

It was 11:30 A. M. before Sheridan's lines were ready to advance. When they moved forward, Early, who had gathered all his available strength, met them with a front of fire, and the battle raged with the greatest fury. The advance was pressed in the most resolute manner, and the resistance by the enemy being equally determined and both sides fighting without cover, the casualties were very great. Wright's infantry forced Ramseur and Rodes steadily to the rear, while Emory on the right broke the left of the enemy's line and threw it into confusion. At this time the Confederate artillery opened with canister at short range, doing fearful execution. This, coupled with the weakening of the center at the junction between Emory and Wright, and with a charge delivered on this junction of the lines by a part of Rodes's command, just arrived on the field, drove back the Union center. At this critical moment Russell's divi-

sion of Wright's corps moved into the breach on Emory's left, and, striking the flank of the Confederate troops who were pursuing Grover, restored the lines and stayed the Confederate advance. The loss to both sides had been heavy. General Russell of the Union army, and Generals Rodes and Godwin of the Confederate, were among the killed.

A lull in the battle now followed, which General Sheridan improved to restore his lines and to bring up Crook, who had not yet been engaged. It had been the original purpose to use Crook on the left to assist Wilson's cavalry in cutting off Early's retreat toward Newtown. But the stress of battle compelled Sheridan to bring his reserve in on the line, and accordingly Crook was ordered up on Emory's right, one brigade extending to the north of Red Bud Creek. At the same time Emory reformed his lines, placing Breckinridge's command in reserve. At this time Merritt, who with his cavalry had followed Breckinridge closely to the field, approached on the left rear of the Confederates, driving their flying and broken cavalry through the infantry lines. The cavalry then charged re-

peatedly into Early's infantry, first striking it in the rear, and afterward face to face as it changed front to repel the attack. These attacks were made by the cavalry without any knowledge of the state of the battle except what was apparent to the eye. First Devin charged with his brigade, returning to rally, with three battle-flags and over three hundred prisoners. Next Lowell charged with his brigade, capturing flags, prisoners, and two guns. After this the entire division was formed and charged to give the final coup.

At the time of this last charge the Union infantry advanced along the entire line and the enemy fled in disorder from the field, and night alone (for it was now dark) saved Early's army from capture. . . .

Early retreated to Fisher's Hill, where Sheridan again defeated him in battle on the 22d, pushing him hotly all the way up the valley as far as Staunton.

When the army commenced its return march, the cavalry was deployed across the valley, burning, destroying, or taking away everything of value, or likely to become of value, to the enemy. It was a severe measure, and appears severer now in the lapse of time; but it was necessary as a measure of war. The country was fruitful, and was the paradise of bushwhackers and guerrillas. They had committed numerous murders and wanton acts of cruelty on all parties weaker than themselves. Officers and men had been murdered in cold blood on the roads, while proceeding without a guard through an apparently peaceful country. The thoughtless had been lured to houses only to find, when too late, that a foe was concealed there, ready to take their lives if they did not surrender. It is not wonderful, then, that the cavalry sent to work the destruction contemplated did not at that time shrink from the duty. It is greatly to their credit that no personal violence on any inhabitant was ever reported, even by their enemies. The valley from Staunton to Winchester was completely devastated, and the armies thereafter occupying that country had to look elsewhere for their supplies. There is little doubt, however, that enough was left in the country for the subsistence of the people, for this, besides being contemplated by orders, resulted of necessity from the fact that, while the work was done hurriedly, the citizens had ample time to secrete supplies, and did so.

On the return of the army after the pursuit of the scattered remnants of Early's force, General Sheridan placed it in position on Cedar Creek north of the Shenandoah, Crook on the left, Emory in the center, and Wright in reserve. The cavalry was placed on the flanks. The occupation of Cedar Creek was not intended to be permanent; there were many serious objections to it as a position for defense. The approaches from all points of the enemy's stronghold at Fisher's Hill were through wooded ravines in which the growth and undulations concealed the movement of troops, and for this reason and its proximity to Fisher's Hill the pickets protecting its front could not be thrown, without danger of capture, sufficiently far to the front to give ample warning of the advance of the enemy. We have already seen how Sheridan took advantage of like conditions at Fisher's Hill. Early was now contemplating the surprise of his antagonist. . . .

On the 15th General Sheridan, taking with him Torbert with part of the cavalry, started for Washington, the design being to send the cavalry on a raid to Gordonsville and vicinity. The first camp was made near Front Royal, from which point the cavalry was returned to the army, it being considered safer to do so in consequence of a despatch intercepted by our signal officers from the enemy's station on Three Top Mountain, and forwarded to General Sheridan by General Wright. This despatch was as follows:

"To Lieutenant-General Early: Be ready to move as soon as my forces join you, and we will crush Sheridan.—Longstreet, Lieutenant-General."

In sending back the cavalry General Sheridan wrote to General Wright, directing caution on his part, so that he might be duly prepared to resist the attack in case the above despatch was genuine. Sheridan continued to Washington, and the cavalry resumed its station in the line of defense at Cedar Creek. At this time everything was quiet—suspiciously so.

On the 16th Custer made a reconnoissance in his front on the back road, but found no enemy outside the lines at Fisher's Hill. . . . On the 18th reconnoissances on both flanks discovered no sign of a movement by the enemy.

The result of the destruction of supplies in the Valley was now being felt by Early's troops. About this time he writes: "I was now compelled to move back for want of provisions and forage, or attack the enemy in his position with the hope of driving him from it; and I determined to attack." From reports made by General Gordon and a staff-officer who ascended Three Top Mountain to reconnoiter the Union position, and the result of a reconnoissance made at the same time by General Pegram toward the right flank of the Union army, General Early concluded to attack by secretly moving a force to turn Sheridan's left flank at Cedar Creek.

The plan of this attack was carefully made; the routes the troops were to pursue, even after the battle had commenced, were carefully designated. The attack was made at early dawn. The surprise was complete. Crook's camp, and afterward Emory's, was

THE SURPRISE AT CEDAR CREEK.
From a war-time sketch.
The right of the picture shows the Confederate flanking column attacking the left of the Nineteenth Corps from the rear. The Union troops, after a determined resistance, took position on the outer side of their rifle-pits.

attacked in flank and rear, and the men and officers driven from their beds, many of them not having the time to hurry into their clothes, except as they retreated half awake and terror-stricken from the overpowering numbers of the enemy. Their own artillery, in conjunction with that of the enemy, was turned on them, and long before it was light enough for their eyes, unaccustomed to the dim light, to distinguish friend from foe, they were hurrying to our right and rear intent only on their

VIEW ON THE VALLEY TURNPIKE WHERE SHERIDAN JOINED THE ARMY AT CEDAR CREEK.
From a photograph taken in 1885.

safety. Wright's infantry, which was farther removed from the point of attack, fared somewhat better, but did not offer more than a spasmodic resistance. The cavalry on the right was on the alert. The rule that in the immediate presence of the enemy the cavalry must be early prepared for attack resulted in the whole First Division being up with breakfast partly finished, at the time the attack commenced. A brigade sent on reconnoissance to the right had opened with its guns some minutes before the main attack on the left, for it had met the cavalry sent by Early to make a demonstration on our right.

The disintegration of Crook's command did not occupy many minutes. With a force of the enemy passing through its camp of sleeping men, and another powerful column well to their rear, it was not wonderful that the men as fast as they were awakened by the noise of battle thought first and only of saving themselves from destruction. The advance of Gordon deflected this fleeing throng from the main road to the rear, and they passed over to the right of the army and fled along the back road. Emory made an attempt to form line facing along the main road, but the wave of Gordon's advance on his left, and the thunders of the attack along the road from Strasburg, rendered the position untenable, and he was soon obliged to withdraw to save his lines from capture.

At this time there were hundreds of stragglers moving off by the right to the rear, and all efforts to stop them proved of no avail. A line of cavalry was stretched across the fields on the right, which halted and formed a respectable force of men, so far as numbers were concerned, but these fled and disappeared to the rear as soon as the force which held them was withdrawn. By degrees the strength of the battle died away. The infantry of the Sixth Corps made itself felt on the advance of the enemy, and a sort of confidence among the troops which had not fled from the field was being restored. A brigade of cavalry was ordered to the left to intercept the enemy's advance to Winchester. Taylor's battery of artillery, belonging to the cavalry, moved to the south, and, taking position with the infantry which was retiring, opened on the enemy. The artillery with the cavalry was the only artillery left to the army. The other guns had either been captured or sent to the rear. This battery remained on the infantry lines, and did much toward impeding the enemy's advance until the cavalry changed position to the Winchester-Strasburg road. This change took place by direction of General Torbert about 10 o'clock. In making it the cavalry marched through the broken masses of infantry direct to a point on the main road northeast of Middletown. The enemy's artillery fire was terrific. Not a man of the cavalry left the ranks unless he was wounded, and everything was done with the precision and quietness of troops on parade. General Merritt informed Colonel Warner of Getty's division, near which the cavalry passed, and which was at that time following the general retreat of the army, of the point where the cavalry would take position and fight, and Warner promised to notify General Getty, and no doubt did so, for that division of the Sixth Corps advanced to the position on the cavalry's right. Then Devin and Lowell charged

LIEUTENANT-GENERAL JOHN B. GORDON, C. S. A.
From a photograph.

and drove back the advancing Confederates. Lowell dismounted his brigade and held some stone walls whose position was suited to defense. Devin held on to his advance ground. Here the enemy's advance was checked for the first time, and beyond this it did not go.

The enemy's infantry sheltered themselves from our cavalry attacks in the woods to the left, and in the inclosures of the town of Middletown. But they opened a devastating fire of artillery. This was the state of affairs when General Sheridan arrived.

Stopping at Winchester over night on the 18th, on his way from Washington, General Sheridan heard the noise of the battle the following morning, and hurried to the field. His coming restored confidence. A cheer from the cavalry, which awakened the echoes of the valley, greeted him and spread the good news of his coming over the field. [See note at end of article.]

He rapidly made the changes necessary in the lines, and then ordered an advance. The cavalry on the left charged down on the enemy in their front, scattering them in all directions. The in-fantry, not to be out-done by the mounted men, moved forward in quick time and charged impetuously the lines of Gordon, which broke and fled. It took less time to drive the enemy from the field than it had for them to take it. They seemed to feel the changed conditions in the Union ranks, for their divisions broke one after another and disappeared toward their rear. The cavalry rode after them and over them, until night fell and ended the fray at the foot of Fisher's Hill. Three battle-flags and twenty-two guns were added to the trophies of the cavalry that day. Early lost almost all his artillery and trains, besides everything that was captured from the Union army in the morning.

The victory was dearly bought. The killed or mortally wounded included General Bidwell and Colonels Thoburn and Kitching, besides many other officers and men. Among the killed in the final charge by the cavalry at Cedar Creek was Colonel Charles Russell Lowell. He had been wounded earlier in the day, but had declined to leave the field.

The battle of Cedar Creek has been immortalized by poets and historians. The transition from defeat, rout, and confusion to order and victory, and all this depending on one man, made the country wild with enthusiasm. The victory was a fitting sequel to Winchester, a glorious prelude to Five Forks and Appomattox. . . .

NOTES ON "SHERIDAN'S RIDE."

In his "Personal Memoirs" (New York: C. L. Webster & Co., 1888), Vol. II., General Sheridan says that toward 6 A. M. of October 19th word was brought to him (at Winchester) of the artillery firing at Cedar Creek. Between half-past 8 and 9 o'clock, while he was riding along the main street of Winchester, toward Cedar Creek, the demeanor of the people who showed themselves at the windows convinced him that the citizens had received secret information from the battle-field, "and were in raptures over some good news." The narrative continues:

"For a short distance I traveled on the road, but soon found it so blocked with wagons and wounded men that my progress was impeded, and I was forced to take to the adjoining fields to make haste. . . .

"My first halt was made just north of Newtown, where

GENERAL CUSTER'S DIVISION RETIRING FROM MOUNT JACKSON, OCTOBER 7, 1864.

I met a chaplain digging his heels into the sides of his jaded horse, and making for the rear with all possible speed. I drew up for an instant, and inquired of him how matters were going at the front. He replied, 'Everything is lost; but all will be right when you get there'; yet, notwithstanding this expression of confidence in me, the parson at once resumed his breathless pace to the rear. At Newtown I was obliged to make a circuit to the left, to get around the village. I could not pass through it, the streets were crowded, but meeting on this détour Major McKinley, of Crook's staff, he spread the news of my return through the motley throng there.

"When nearing the Valley pike, just north of Newtown, I saw about three-fourths of a mile west of the pike a body of troops, which proved to be Ricketts's and Wheaton's divisions of the Sixth Corps, and then learned that the Nineteenth Corps had halted a little to the right and rear of these; but I did not stop, desiring to get to the extreme front. Continuing on parallel with the pike, about midway between Newtown and Middletown I crossed to the west of it, and a little later came up in rear of Getty's division of the Sixth Corps. When I arrived, this division and the cavalry were the only troops in the presence of and resisting the enemy; they were apparently acting as a rear-guard at a point about three miles north of the line we held at Cedar Creek when the battle began. General Torbert was the first officer to meet me, saying as he rode up, 'My God! I am glad you 've come.' . . .

"Jumping my horse over the line of rails, I rode to the crest of the elevation, and there, taking off my hat, the men rose up from behind their barricades with cheers of recognition. . . . I then turned back to the rear of Getty's division, and as I came behind it a line of regimental flags rose up out of the ground, as it seemed, to welcome me. They were mostly the colors of Crook's troops, who had been stampeded and scattered in the surprise of the morning. The color-bearers, having withstood the panic, had formed behind the troops of Getty. The line with the colors was largely composed of officers, among whom I recognized Colonel R. B. Hayes, since President of the United States, one of the brigade commanders. At the close of this incident I crossed the little narrow valley, or depression, in rear of Getty's line, and, dismounting on the opposite crest, established that point as my headquarters. . . . Returning to the place where my headquarters had been established, I met near them Ricketts's division, under General Keifer, and General Frank Wheaton's division, both marching to the front. When the men of these divisions saw me they began cheering and took up the double-quick to the front, while I turned back toward Getty's line to point out where these returning troops should be placed.

"All this had consumed a great deal of time, and I concluded to visit again the point to the east of the Valley pike, from where I had first observed the enemy, to see what he was doing. Arrived there, I could plainly see him getting ready for attack, and Major Forsyth now suggested that it would be well to ride along the line of battle before the enemy assailed us, for although the troops had learned of my return, but few of them had seen me. Following his suggestion I started in behind the men, but when a few paces had been taken I crossed to the front, hat in hand, passed along the entire length of the infantry line; and it is from this circumstance that many of the officers and men who then received me with such heartiness have since supposed that that was my first appearance on the field. But at least two hours had elapsed since I reached the ground, for it was after midday when this incident of riding down the front took place, and I arrived not later, certainly, than half-past ten o'clock."

General Emory says in his "Narrative":

"This electric message from General Sheridan put every man on his feet. . . . Very soon the pickets came in, quickly followed by the enemy's infantry. Our first line [Grover] then rose up *en masse* and delivered their fire, and the enemy disappeared. There was not a sound of musket or gun for twenty minutes following. The First Division was deployed to the right of the Second, and the charge commenced. . . . The enemy resisted at every strong fence and ditch and other obstacle with great bravery, but still the line swept on. The First Brigade (Colonel Edwin P. Davis) of the First Division (Dwight's), which was on the extreme right, with unparalleled intrepidity and fleetness completely enveloped the enemy, so that one hour before the sun set . . . the troops were in complete command . . . of the camp they had occupied in the morning." . . .

UNION BATTERY NEAR DUNN'S HOUSE, PETERSBURG.
From a war-time photograph.

THE SIEGE OF PETERSBURG,

AND THE BATTLE OF THE CRATER.

NARRATIVE OF EVENTS.

The Union government obtained a foothold in southeastern Virginia by the Confederate abandonment of Norfolk and Suffolk, during McClellan's advance up the Peninsula in 1862. Petersburg, however, was an important link in the line of communications between Richmond and the Carolinas, and was early placed in a state of defense.

In April, 1864, General Beauregard assumed command of the Confederate department which included Petersburg, and began to collect forces from the coast for operations along the James River, in anticipation of an attack by Grant south of Richmond. Simultaneous with the movement of the Army of the Potomac from the Rapidan, May 4, the Army of the James, under General B. F. Butler, sailed from Fortress Monroe up James River, and seized City Point and Bermuda Hundred.

The cavalry division under General A. V. Kautz, marching from Suffolk, joined on the 10th, after destroying the bridges on the Weldon road, south of Petersburg, and delaying reinforcements for Beauregard. After intrenching Bermuda Hundred, Butler destroyed the railroad between Richmond and Petersburg, and on the 13th and 14th his troops carried a portion of the first line of defenses at Drewry's Bluffs, near Richmond. On the 16th, Beauregard attacked Butler and forced him back to his intrenchments in the narrow neck of land between the Appomattox and the James. Beauregard intrenched in front of Butler in a manner which enabled him to hold the line with a slight force and spare the bulk of his army for the defense of Richmond. The Eighteenth Corps of Butler's army reinforced Grant at Cold Harbor [see p. 254].

On June 9 Butler sent the Tenth Corps, under General Q. A. Gillmore, and Kautz's cavalry to attack Petersburg [see following]. Gillmore and Kautz returned to Bermuda Hundred after their fruitless errand. While the Army of the Potomac was crossing the James on the 14th and 15th of June [see p. 255], Smith's corps, which had rejoined Butler, marched on Petersburg and assaulted the outer line of defenses late on the 15th, carrying them for a distance of two miles and a half in the northeast of the city. Hancock and Burnside reached the field that night, and on the night of the 16th the assaults were renewed, and portions of the Confederate second line were captured.

THE SIEGE OF PETERSBURG.—1. SHARP-SHOOTERS ON THE LINE OF THE EIGHTEENTH CORPS. 2. BIVOUAC OF THE FIFTH CORPS IN THE RIFLE-PITS.

RESERVOIR HILL, WHERE KAUTZ'S ADVANCE WAS STOPPED, JUNE 9, 1864.

The spires of Petersburg are seen to the left of the reservoir. In front of the reservoir is the ravine of Lieutenant's Creek that encircles the eastern outskirts of the city and afforded the Confederates a concealed and convenient way by which either wing of their lines could be reinforced by troops from the other. (From a photograph made in 1886.)

Meanwhile, Beauregard had strengthened the garrison by drawing troops from the defenses of Richmond. On the 17th the Fifth Corps reached Petersburg and the assaults were pressed all along the line. Burnside carried an advanced position and intrenched it, though losing heavily in the operation. On the 18th Lee's troops arrived, and the Union assaults made that day with great vigor, especially by Hancock, were decisively repulsed. Siege lines were then established and gradually extended east and south of the city. Butler's intrenched position at Bermuda Hundred became a base for extended movements north of the James, which gradually enveloped Richmond on the east.

FIRST ATTACKS ON PETERSBURG.

BY AUGUST V. KAUTZ, BREVET MAJOR-GENERAL, U. S. A.

Commanding the Cavalry Division, Army of the James.

THE Cavalry Division of the Army of the James was organized in the last days of April, 1864. Through the personal application of Lieutenant-General Grant I was selected and promoted to be Brigadier-General of Volunteers to organize and command it. I found the troops of which it was to be made up encamped in rear of Portsmouth, Va., picketing the line of the Blackwater River, on the 20th of April. As first organized it was arranged as follows: First Brigade, 3d New York, and 1st District of Columbia Cavalry, Colonel S. H. Mix commanding. Second Brigade, 11th and 5th Pennsylvania Cavalry, Colonel S. P. Spear commanding. A section of 3-inch rifles of the 4th Wisconsin Battery was temporarily assigned. The division numbered less than 2800 men, all told. . . .

On the night of the 8th of June, General Butler having perfected a plan for the capture of Petersburg, the cavalry moved in conjunction with a brigade of white troops under Colonel J. R. Hawley and a part of Hinks's colored division; the whole commanded by General Gillmore. The infantry was expected to threaten Petersburg from the City Point road, while the cavalry made a détour to the Jerusalem plank-road, where the enemy's line was believed to be weak. It was agreed that if the cavalry carried this line, General Gillmore was to assault the line in his front. The distance the

cavalry had to march took up more time than was anticipated, and the line was not carried until just before noon of the 9th, and General Gillmore, having exhausted his patience, was far on his way back to City Point at that time. The line, where the Jerusalem road entered it, was held by about two hundred Second Class militia, and was easily carried, and had the infantry been at hand to support the cavalry Petersburg could have been taken and held at this time. The Cavalry Division, however, had only about thirteen hundred serviceable men on this occasion, and could not hold the advantage gained without sufficient infantry support. The advance penetrated to the water-works, where it was confronted by a battery in position, and the rear of the cavalry was threatened by the enemy holding the line on the City Point front, and was therefore compelled to retire with the captured prisoners, and returned to Bermuda Hundred, where we arrived after dark. Shortly after this affair General Gillmore was relieved from the command of the Tenth Corps.

On the 15th of June, the Eighteenth Corps under General W. F. Smith having rejoined Butler, after its detachment to Cold Harbor, another effort was made to take Petersburg, with this difference in the plan, that while the cavalry should distract the enemy as much as possible in the direction of the Jerusalem plank-road, the Eighteenth Corps was to carry the line on the City Point side. The cavalry, having driven in the enemy's pickets on the City Point road, moved to the left and was engaged the entire day exposed mainly to artillery fire, without any apparent action on the part of the Eighteenth Corps. We believed ourselves again deserted, and at seven in the evening the cavalry was withdrawn, and the column was just fairly on the return when the noise of the assault so long expected broke upon us about four miles to our right. It was all over in a few moments, and, as we subsequently learned, General Smith had carried the entire line in his front. The Army of the Potomac began to arrive on the night of the 15th, and was on hand to support the Eighteenth Corps in the position it had captured. . . .

REPELLING THE FIRST ASSAULT ON PETERSBURG.

BY R. E. COLSTON, BRIGA-
DIER-GENERAL, C. S. A.
Provisional Commander of the
Post of Petersburg.

AT the end of April, 1864, I was transferred from the Department of Georgia to that of Virginia and was assigned by General H. A. Wise to the provisional command of the post of Petersburg, which I had already held from January to March, 1863. General Wise returned to Petersburg about June 1st, and I remained there while waiting for another assignment.

At that time the lines covering Petersburg on the south side of the Appomattox formed a semicircle of about eight miles,

HEADQUARTERS OF GENERAL GRANT AND BASE OF SUPPLIES, CITY POINT, ON THE JAMES RIVER.
From an oil-painting.

development, resting upon the river at each extremity. With the exception of a few lunettes and redoubts at the most commanding positions, they were barely marked out, and a horseman could ride over them without the least difficulty almost everywhere, as I myself had done day after day for weeks just before the fight. They differed *in toto* from the shortened and formidable works constructed later by General Lee's army.

On the 9th of June the lines were entirely stripped of regular troops, with the exception of Wise's brigade on our extreme left, and of Sturdivant's battery of four guns. Every other regiment had been ordered across the James to aid General Lee on the north side. A few skeleton companies of home guards (less than 150 men) occupied the redoubts half a mile from the river on the left, which were armed with heavy artillery. Then came a gap of a mile and a half to lunette 16, occupied by 30 home guards with 4 pieces of stationary artillery. One mile farther to the right were two howitzers of Sturdivant's battery; one mile farther still were lunettes 26, 27, and 28, at the intersection of the lines with the Jerusalem road; but neither there nor for four miles more to the river on our right was there a man or gun.

During the night of June 8th–9th General Kautz and Colonel Spear, with four regiments of cavalry and 4 pieces of artillery, crossed the Appomattox on a pontoon-bridge, about 7 miles below Petersburg, and on the morning of the 9th they made their appearance in front of the left of our lines, while the Federal gun-boats opened a heavy fire upon Fort Clifton and other positions on the river. The alarm-bell was rung in the city about 9 o'clock, and every man able to shoulder a musket hurried out to the lines. Colonel F. H. Archer, a veteran of the Mexican war, who had commanded a Confederate battalion in my brigade in 1862, but now

commanding the Home Guards, hastened to take position at lunettes Nos. 27 and 28 on the Jerusalem road with 125 men. This force was composed of Second Class Reserves, men exempted from active service on account of age or infirmities, and boys under conscription age, who had had no military training. Very few of them wore a uniform, and they were armed with inferior muskets and rifles, for all the best arms had to be reserved for troops in the field.

At the first sound of alarm I mounted my horse, hastened to report to General Wise and to offer my services. He thanked me warmly, saying that he was just going across the river to bring up the reserve infantry as promptly as possible, together with other reinforcements, and directed me to take command of all the forces in the lines and use them according to my judgment, with only one specific order, viz., that lunette No. 16 must be held at any hazard. He added as he turned his horse's head: "For God's sake, General, hold out till I come back, or all is lost!"

At lunette No. 16 I found the men at their guns, but the enemy were not yet in sight. They had reconnoitered from a distance the positions on our left; seeing heavy guns on the works, and not aware of the very small number of the defenders, they had continued their reconnoissance toward the right, nearly hidden from our view by the wooded and undulating character of the ground. We had no scouts or mounted men to send out for information. I had been at lunette 16 about an hour, and it was nearly 11 o'clock, when a courier arrived fom Petersburg with a note from General Wise, saying that the enemy were advancing by the Jerusalem road upon Colonel Archer's position, and that reinforcements were on the way. I left my aide, Lieutenant J. T. Tosh, in command at lunette 16, with orders not to leave that position

until relieved. I galloped on alone toward the Jerusalem road, and when half-way there I heard the rattle of musketry from that point. Being just then at the position of Sturdivant's section, I ordered the sergeant to bring on one of his howitzers to lunette 28, and hastened toward it, catching glimpses of Federal cavalry still moving to our right, parallel to our intrenchments. Arrived at lunettes 27 and 28 I found that Colonel Archer had disposed his small force very judiciously in the low trenches. A wagon had been overturned across the road and, together with a hastily built rail-fence, formed a pretty good barricade. A detachment of Federal cavalry had just made a spirited charge and been checked by this obstruction and by the scattering fire of the militia. Several dead horses, some sabers and carbines, and a couple of prisoners were the tokens of the repulse, and the men were in high spirits at their success in this their first fight. It was evident, however, that the enemy had only been feeling the position and were preparing for a more serious attack. Their line was visible on the edge of the woods back of the Gregory house, and our slender ranks were extended to the right and left to present an equal front. In a few minutes the howitzer that I had ordered up came in sight and was welcomed with cheers by our men. I placed it in lunette 28, and took my position in the trenches, which did not cover us more than waist-high.

Very soon an advance was made by the enemy's dismounted skirmishers, while a mounted line in close order appeared behind the Gregory house. I impressed upon the men the necessity of holding their fire until the enemy were at close range, and this direction was well observed. But the howitzer opened fire and the Federal skirmishers fell back under cover and commenced a continuous fire of small-arms. A number of their men had taken

position in the Gregory house and were shooting, from the windows and from the garret, some firing through openings made by knocking off the shingles. I directed the artillery sergeant to send a few shells at the house to dislodge them, but the distance was so short that the shells passed through the building before exploding, and failed to set it on fire as I had hoped. Meanwhile the mounted line, some three hundred yards back, presented a tempting mark and I told the sergeant to give them canister. To my intense vexation he replied that he had not a single charge of canister with his piece. I then directed him to shell the mounted line, but several shells passed over the line and burst harmlessly beyond it. I now ordered him to cut the fuse at the closest notch, and, pointing the piece myself very low, I had the satisfaction of seeing the shell explode just in front of the line of cavalry and make a great gap in its ranks, causing its immediate retreat.

All this time the bullets were flying uncomfortably thick and close, but I saw no signal of another advance. Meanwhile our men, closely hugging the low breastworks and holding back their fire, were suffering no harm. In about half an hour a cannon shot was fired at us, then another, followed

MAJOR-GENERAL M. C. BUTLER, C. S. A.
Commanding a cavalry brigade during the siege of Petersburg.

VIEW OF THE CONFEDERATE LINE TAKEN UP BY GENERAL BEAUREGARD, JUNE 18. FROM A POINT ON THE UNION PICKET LINE TO THE FRONT AND LEFT OF FORT HASKELL.
From a sketch made in 1886.

by others in quick succession. The enemy had paused while waiting for the arrival of their battery. So far from being dismayed, the brave civilians around me, with Colonel Archer at their head, offered to charge the battery, but I knew that the moment they left the cover of the trenches to cross the open ground they would be destroyed by the breech-loading carbines of the dismounted men supporting the battery and far overlapping our front. Our only hope was in delay. . . .

But the end was very near. The enemy, sheltered by the Gregory house and the defective construction of our works, which allowed approach under cover to within fifty yards, redoubled the fire of their skirmishers and artillery; while a line in open order, overlapping both our flanks, advanced, firing rapidly. The brave militia discharged their pieces at close range. Numbers of them fell killed or wounded, and before the survivors could reload the enemy turned our left flank and more of our men fell by bullets that struck us in the rear from lunette No. 26, which we had not had men enough to occupy. Yet those heroic citizens held their ground. In the heat of the fight I picked up and discharged at the enemy two or three of the muskets dropped by our fallen men. We were now hemmed in on three sides, and only a narrow path leading through an abrupt ravine offered a way of escape. The howitzer, which continued its fire to the last, was captured while limbering up, the horses being shot in their traces, and two artillerymen killed. Some of the militia were killed or wounded with the bayonet or carbine butts, and many were captured. Our shattered remnants made their way down and across the ravine and re-formed at my command on Reservoir Hill, in order, if needed, to support Graham's battery, which had just arrived and unlimbered on the top of the hill.

After driving us from the trenches the enemy paused awhile to call in their dismounted men and to send to their rear our wounded and prisoners. They then formed in mounted column, with a few files thrown forward in open order. They advanced upon the main road, evidently expecting to enter the city without further opposition.

The moments gained at such fearful cost barely gave time for Graham's battery to cross the bridge. They came up Sycamore street at full gallop and

unlimbered on the summit of Reservoir Hill just as the head of the Federal column was coming down the opposite slope into the hollow. The battery opened fire, and with rapidity and precision hurled a storm of shell and canister upon the approaching cavalry. The enemy, who thought themselves already in possession of the city, halted in surprise. But just at this moment, while they were yet hesitating, Dearing's cavalry, which had followed after Graham's battery, charged upon Kautz's and Spear's column with irresistible impetuosity. The latter wheeled about, but re-formed on the top of the next hill and gallantly endeavored to make a stand there, being joined by another column advancing upon the Blandford road. But this also was checked by a section of Sturdivant's battery, which came on their flank from another road. Under the fire of artillery and the charge of Dearing's cavalry the enemy retreated.

CARRYING POWDER TO THE MINE.

THE BATTLE OF THE PETERSBURG CRATER.

BY WILLIAM H. POWELL, MAJOR, U. S. A.
Aide-de-camp to General Ledlie during the charge at the Crater.

BY the assaults of June 17th and 18th, 1864, on the Confederate works at Petersburg, the Ninth Corps, under General Burnside, gained an advanced position beyond a deep cut in the railroad, within 130 yards of the enemy's main line and confronting a strong work called by the Confederates Elliott's Salient, and sometimes Pegram's Salient. In rear of that advanced position was a deep hollow. A few days after gaining this position Lieutenant-Colonel Henry Pleasants, who had been a mining engineer and who belonged to the 48th Pennsylvania Volunteers, composed for the most part of miners from the upper Schuylkill coal region, suggested to his division commander, General Robert B. Potter, the possibility of running a mine under one of the enemy's forts in front of the deep hollow. This proposition was submitted to General Burnside, who approved of the measure, and work was commenced on the 25th of June. If ever a man labored under disadvantages, that man was Colonel Pleasants. In his testimony before the Committee on the Conduct of the War, he said:

"My regiment was only about four hundred strong. At first I employed but a few men at a time, but the number was increased as the work progressed,

until at last I had to use the whole regiment — non-commissioned officers and all. The great difficulty I had was to dispose of the material got out of the mine. I found it impossible to get any assistance from anybody; I had to do all the work myself. I had to remove all the earth in old cracker boxes; I got pieces of hickory and nailed on the boxes in which we received our crackers, and then iron-clad them with hoops of iron taken from old pork and beef barrels. . . . Whenever I made application I could not get anything, although General Burnside was very favorable to it. The most important thing was to ascertain how far I had to mine, because if I fell short of or went beyond the proper place, the explosion would have no practical effect. Therefore I wanted an accurate instrument with which to make the necessary triangulations. I had to make them on the farthest front line, where the enemy's sharp-shooters could reach me. I could not get the instrument I wanted, although there was one at army headquarters, and General Burnside had to send to Washington and get an old-fashioned theodolite, which was given to me. . . . General Burnside told me that General Meade and Major Duane, chief engineer of the Army of the Potomac, said the thing could not be done — that it was all clap-trap and nonsense; that such a length of mine had never been excavated in military operations, and could not be; that I would either get the men smothered, for want of air, or 'crushed by the falling of the earth; or the enemy would find it out and it would amount to nothing. I could get no boards or lumber supplied to me for my operations. I had to get a pass and send two companies of my own regiment, with wagons, outside of our lines to rebel saw-mills, and get lumber in that way, after having previously got what lumber I could by tearing down an old bridge. I had no mining picks furnished me, but had to take common army picks and have them straightened for my mining picks. . . . The only officers of high rank, so far as I learned, that favored the enterprise were General Burnside, the corps commander, and General Potter, the division commander."

On the 23d of July Colonel Pleasants had the whole mine ready for the placing of the powder. With proper tools and instruments it could have been done in one-third or one-fourth of the time. The greatest delay was occasioned by taking out the material, which had to be carried the whole length of the gallery. Every night the pioneers of Colonel Pleasant's regiment had to cut bushes to cover the fresh dirt at the mouth of the gallery; otherwise the enemy could have observed it from trees inside his own lines.

BREVET BRIGADIER-GENERAL
HENRY PLEASANTS, U. S. V.

PROFILE OF THE GROUND BETWEEN THE CRATER AND THE MOUTH OF THE MINE.
From a sketch made in 1886.

The main gallery was 510 $\frac{8}{10}$ feet in length. The left lateral gallery was thirty-seven feet in length and the right lateral thirty-eight feet. The magazines, eight in number, were placed in the lateral galleries—two at each end a few feet apart in branches at nearly right angles to the side galleries, and two more in each of the side galleries similarly placed by pairs, situated equidistant from each other and the end of the galleries.

It had been the intention of General Grant to make an assault on the enemy's works in the early part of July; but the movement was deferred in consequence of the work on the mine, the completion of which was impatiently awaited. As a diversion Hancock's corps and two divisions of cavalry had crossed to the north side of the James at Deep Bottom and had threatened Richmond. A part of Lee's army was sent from Petersburg to checkmate this move, and when the mine was ready to be sprung Hancock was recalled in haste to Petersburg. When the mine was ready for the explosives General Meade requested General Burnside to submit a plan of attack. . . .

With a view of making the attack, the division of colored troops, under General Edward Ferrero, had been drilling for several weeks, General Burnside thinking that they were in better condition to head a charge than either of the white divisions. They had not been in any very active service. On the other hand, the white divisions had performed very arduous duties since the beginning of the campaign, and before Petersburg had been in such proximity to the enemy that no man could raise his head above the parapets without being fired at. They had been in the habit of using every possible means of covering themselves from the enemy's fire.

General Meade objected to the use of the colored troops, on the ground, as he stated, that they were a new division and had never been under fire, while this was an operation requiring the very best troops. General Burnside, however, insisted upon his programme, and the question was referred to General Grant, who confirmed General

Meade's views, although he subsequently said in his evidence before the Committee on the Conduct of the War:

"General Burnside wanted to put his colored division in front, and I believe if he had done so it would have been a success. Still I agreed with General Meade as to his objections to that plan. General Meade said that if we put the colored troops in front (we had only one division) and it should prove a failure, it would then be said, and very properly, that we were shoving these people ahead to get killed because we did not care anything about them. But that could not be said if we put white troops in front."

The mine was charged with only 8000 pounds of powder, instead of 14,000, as asked for, the amount having been reduced by order of General Meade; and while awaiting the decision of General Grant on the question of the colored troops, precise orders for making and supporting the attack were issued by General Meade.

In the afternoon of the 29th of July, Generals Potter and O. B. Willcox met together at General Burnside's headquarters, to talk over the plans of the attack, based upon the idea that the colored troops would lead the charge, and while there the message was received from General Meade that General Grant disapproved of that plan, and that General Burnside must detail one of his white divisions to take the place of the colored division. This was the first break in the original plan. There were then scarcely twelve hours, and half of these at night, in which to make this change—and no possible time in which the white troops could be familiarized with the duties expected of them in connection with the assault.

General Burnside was greatly disappointed by this change; but he immediately sent for General

Ledlie, who had been in command of the First Division only about six weeks. Upon his arrival General Burnside determined that the three commanders of his white divisions should "pull straws," and Ledlie was (as he thought) the unlucky victim. He, however, took it good-naturedly, and, after receiving special instructions from General Burnside, proceeded with his brigade commanders to ascertain the way to the point of attack. This was not accomplished until after dark on the evening before the explosion.

The order of attack, as proposed by General Burnside, was also changed by direction of General Meade with the approval of General Grant. Instead of moving down to the right and left of the crater of the mine, for the purpose of driving the enemy from their intrenchments, and removing to that extent the danger of flank attacks, General Meade directed that the troops should push at once for the crest of Cemetery Hill. . . .

(The writer of this article was serving as judge-advocate of Ledlie's division, and also performed the duties of aide-de-camp to General Ledlie at the time of the explosion. When the orders were published for the movement he and Lieutenant George M. Randall, also of the regular army, and aide-de-camp to General Ledlie, were informed that they must accompany the advance troops in the attack.)

At 3:30 A.M. Ledlie's division was in position, the Second Brigade, Colonel E. G. Marshall, in front, and that of General W. F. Bartlett behind it, the men and officers in a feverish state of expectancy, the majority of them having been awake all night. Daylight came slowly, and still they stood with every nerve strained prepared to move forward the instant an order should be given. Four

o'clock arrived, officers and men began to get nervous, having been on their feet four hours; still the mine had not been exploded. General Ledlie then directed me to go to General Burnside and report to him that the command had been in readiness to move since 3:30 A.M., and to inquire the cause of the delay of the explosion. I found General Burnside in rear of the fourteen-gun battery, delivered my message, and received the reply from the general information that there was some trouble with the fuse dying out, but that an officer had gone into the gallery to ignite it again, and that the explosion would soon take place.

[Sergeant Henry Rees entered the mine and found that the fuse had died out at the first splicing. He cut the fuse above the charred portion; on his way out for materials he met Lieutenant Jacob Douty, who assisted in making a fresh splice, which was a success.]

I returned immediately, and just as I arrived in rear of the First Division the mine was sprung. It was a magnificent spectacle, and as the mass of earth went up into the air, carrying with it men, guns, carriages, and timbers, and spread out like an immense cloud as it reached its altitude, so close were the Union lines that the mass appeared as if it would descend immediately upon the troops waiting to make the charge. This caused them to break and scatter to the rear, and about ten minutes were consumed in re-forming for the attack.

(Immediately following the explosion the heavy guns along the line opened a severe fire.)

Not much was lost by this delay, however, as it took nearly that time for the cloud of dust to pass off. The order was then given for the advance. As no part of the Union line of breastworks had been removed (which would have been an arduous as well as hazardous undertaking), the troops clambered over them as best they could. This in itself broke the ranks, and they did not stop to reform, but pushed ahead toward the crater, about 130 yards distant, the débris from the explosion having covered up the abatis and *chevaux-de-frise* in front of the enemy's works.

THE CONFEDERATE SIDE OF THE CRATER, LOOKING TOWARD THE UNION LINES.
From a sketch made in 1886, taken from the road back of the crater, and nearly half-way to the cemetery crest. On the left is the swale where Mahone's troops formed for the counter-charge.

EXPLOSION OF THE MINE.
From a sketch made at the time.

THE CHARGE TO THE CRATER.
From a sketch made at the time.

Little did these men anticipate what they would see upon arriving there: an enormous hole in the ground about 30 feet deep, 60 feet wide, and 170 feet long, filled with dust, great blocks of clay, guns, broken carriages, projecting timbers, and men buried in various ways—some up to their necks, others to their waists, and some with only their feet and legs protruding from the earth. One of these near me was pulled out, and proved to be a second lieutenant of the battery which had been blown up. The fresh air revived him, and he was soon able to walk and talk. He was very grateful and said that he was asleep when the explosion took place, and only awoke to find himself wriggling up in the air; then a few seconds afterward he felt himself descending, and soon lost consciousness.

The whole scene of the explosion struck every one dumb with astonishment as we arrived at the crest of the débris. It was impossible for the troops of the Second Brigade to move forward in line, as they had advanced; and, owing to the broken state they were in, every man crowding up to look into the hole, and being pressed by the First Brigade, which was immediately in rear, it was equally impossible to move by the flank, by any command, around the crater. Before the brigade commanders could realize the situation, the two brigades became inextricably mixed, in the desire to look into the hole.

However, Colonel Marshall yelled to the Second Brigade to move forward, and the men did so, jumping, sliding, and tumbling into the hole, over the débris of material, and dead and dying men, and huge blocks of solid clay. They were followed by General Bartlett's brigade. Up on the other

side of the crater they climbed, and while a detachment stopped to place two of the dismounted guns of the battery in position on the enemy's side of the crest of the crater, a portion of the leading brigade passed over the crest and attempted to re-form. In doing so members of these regiments were killed by musket-shots from the rear, fired by the Confederates who were still occupying the traverses and intrenchments to the right and left of the crater. These men had been awakened by the noise and shock of the explosion, and during the interval before the attack had recovered their equanimity, and when the Union troops attempted to re-form on the enemy's side of the crater, they had faced about and delivered a fire into the backs of our men. This coming so unexpectedly caused the forming line to fall back into the crater.

Had General Burnside's original plan, providing that two regiments should sweep down inside the enemy's line to the right and left of the crater, been sanctioned, the brigades of Colonel Marshall

THE APPROACH TO THE CRATER AS SEEN FROM A POINT SOUTH-EAST OF THE MOUTH OF THE MINE.
From a sketch made in 1886.

and General Bartlett could and would have re-formed and moved on to Cemetery Hill before the enemy realized fully what was intended; but the occupation of the trenches to the right and left by the enemy prevented re-formation, and there being no division, corps, or army commander present to give orders to other troops to clear the trenches, a formation under fire from the rear was something no troops could accomplish.

After falling back into the crater a partial formation was made by General Bartlett and Colonel Marshall with some of their troops, but owing to the precipitous walls the men could find no footing except by facing inward, digging their heels into the earth, and throwing their backs against the side of the crater, or squatting in a half-sitting, half-standing posture, and some of the men were shot even there by the fire from the enemy in the traverses. It was at this juncture that Colonel Marshall requested me to go to General Ledlie and

explain the condition of affairs, which he knew that I had seen and understood perfectly well. This I did immediately.

While the above was taking place the enemy had not been idle. He had brought a battery from his left to bear upon the position, and as I started on my errand the crest of the crater was being swept with canister. Special attention was given to this battery by our artillery, but for some reason or other the enemy's guns could not be silenced. Passing to the Union lines under this storm of canister, I found General Ledlie and a part of his staff ensconced in a protected angle of the works. I gave him Colonel Marshall's message, explained to him the situation, and Colonel Marshall's reasons for not being able to move forward. General Ledlie then directed me to return at once and say to Colonel Marshall and General Bartlett that it was General Burnside's order that they should move forward immediately. This message was delivered. But the firing on the crater now was incessant, and it was as heavy a fire of canister as was ever poured continuously upon a single objective point. It was as utterly impracticable to re-form a brigade in that crater as it would be to marshal bees into line after upsetting the hive; and equally as impracticable to re-form outside of the crater, under the severe fire in front and rear, as it would be to hold a dress parade in front of a charging enemy. Here, then, was the second point of advantage lost by the fact that there was no person present with authority to change the programme to meet the circumstances. Had a prompt attack of the troops to the right and left of the crater been made as soon as the leading brigade had passed into the crater, or even fifteen minutes afterward, clearing the trenches and diverting the fire of the enemy, success would have been inevitable, and particularly would this have been the case on the left of the crater, as the small fort immediately in front of the Fifth Corps was almost, if not entirely, abandoned for a while after the explosion of the mine, the men running away from it as if they feared that it was to be blown up also.

Whether General Ledlie informed General Burnside of the condition of affairs as reported by me I do not know; but I think it likely, as it was not long after I had returned to the crater that a brigade of the Second Division (Potter's) under the command of Brigadier-General S. G. Griffin advanced its skirmishers and followed them immediately, directing its course to the right of the crater. General Griffin's line, however, overlapped the crater on the left, where two or three of his regiments sought shelter in the crater. Those on the right passed over the trenches, but owing to the

peculiar character of the enemy's works, which were not single, but complex and involuted and filled with pits, traverses, and bomb-proofs, forming a labyrinth as difficult of passage as the crater itself, the brigade was broken up, and, meeting the severe fire of canister, also fell back into the crater, which was then full to suffocation. Every organization melted away, as soon as it entered this hole in the ground, into a mass of human beings clinging by toes and heels to the almost perpendicular sides. If a man was shot on the crest he fell and rolled to the bottom of the pit.

From the actions of the enemy, even at this time, as could be seen by his moving columns in front, he was not exactly certain as to the intentions of the Union commander; he appeared to think that possibly the mine explosion was but a feint and that the main attack would come from some other quarter. However, he massed some of his troops in a hollow in front of the crater, and held them in that position.

Meantime General Potter, who was in rear of the Union line of intrenchments, being convinced that something ought to be done to create a diversion and distract the enemy's attention from this point, ordered Colonel Zenas R. Bliss, commanding his

UNION TROOPS.

THE BATTLE OF THE CRATER.
From an oil-painting.

CONFEDERATES CHARGING.

First Brigade, to send two of his regiments to support General Griffin, and with the remainder to make an attack on the right. Subsequently it was arranged that the two regiments going to the support of General Griffin should pass into the crater, turn to the right, and sweep down the enemy's lines. Colonel Bliss was partly successful, and obtained possession of some 200 or 300 yards of the line, and one of the regiments advanced to within 20 or 30 yards of the battery whose fire was so severe on the troops; but it could make no further headway for lack of support—its progress being impeded by slashed timber, while an unceasing fire of canister was poured into the men. They therefore fell back to the enemy's traverses and intrenchments.

At the time of ordering forward Colonel Bliss's command General Potter wrote a despatch to General Burnside, stating that it was his opinion, from what he had seen, and from the reports he had received from subordinate officers, that too many men were being forced in at this one point; that the troops there were in confusion, and it was absolutely necessary that an attack should be made from some other point of the line, in order to divert the enemy's attention and give time to straighten

out our line. To that despatch he never received an answer. Orders were, however, being constantly sent to the three division commanders of the white troops to push the men forward as fast as could be done, and this was, in substance, about all the orders that were received by them during the day up to the time of the order for the withdrawal.

When General Willcox came with the Third Division to support the First, he found the latter and three regiments of his own, together with the regiments of Potter's Second Division which had gone in on the right, so completely filling up the crater that no more troops could be got in there, and he therefore ordered an attack with the remainder of his division on the works of the enemy to the left of the crater. This attack was successful, so far as to carry the intrenchments for about 150 yards; but they were held only for a short time.

Previous to this last movement I had again left the crater and gone to General Ledlie, and had urged him to try to have something done on the right and left of the crater—saying that every man who got into the trenches to the right or left of it used them as a means of escape to the crater, and the enemy was reoccupying them as fast as

our men left. All the satisfaction I received was an order to go back and tell the brigade commanders to get their men out and press forward to Cemetery Hill. This talk and these orders, coming from a commander sitting in a bomb-proof inside the Union lines, were disgusting. I returned again to the crater and delivered the orders, which I knew beforehand could not possibly be obeyed; and I told General Ledlie so before I left him. Upon my return to the crater I devoted my attention to the movements of the enemy, who was evidently making dispositions for an assault.

About two hours after the explosion of the mine (7 o'clock) and after I had returned to the crater for the third time, General Edward Ferrero, commanding the colored division of the Ninth Corps, received an order to advance his division, pass the white troops which had halted, and move on to carry the crest of Cemetery Hill at all hazards. . . .

Had any one in authority been present when the colored troops made their charge [see p. 293], and had they been supported, even at that late hour in the day, there would have been a possibility of success; but when they fell back and broke up in disorder, it was the closing scene of the tragedy. The rout of the colored troops was followed up by a feeble attack from the enemy, more in the way of a reconnoissance than a charge; but the attack was repulsed by the troops in the crater and in the intrenchments, and the Confederates retired.

It was now evident that the enemy did not fear a demonstration from any other quarter, as they began to collect their troops for a decisive assault. On observing this I left the crater and reported to General Ledlie, whom I found seated in a bomb-proof with General Ferrero, that some means ought to be devised for withdrawing the mass of men from the crater without exposing them to the terrific fire which was kept up by the enemy; that if some shovels and picks could be found, the men in an hour could open a covered way by which they could be withdrawn; that the enemy was making every preparation for a determined assault on the crater, and, disorganized as the troops were, they could make no permanent resistance. Not an implement of any kind could be found; indeed, the

BREVET MAJOR-GENERAL HENRY G. THOMAS, U. S. V.

proposition was received with disfavor. Matters remained *in statu quo* until about 2 P. M., when the enemy's anticipated assault was made.

About 9:30 A. M. General Meade had given positive orders to have the troops withdrawn from the crater. To have done so under the severe fire of the enemy would have produced a stampede, which would have endangered the Union lines, and might possibly have communicated itself to the troops that were massed in rear of the Ninth Corps. General Burnside thought, for these and other reasons, that it would be possible to leave his command there until nightfall, and then withdraw it. There was no means of getting food or water to them, for which they were suffering. The midsummer sun caused waves of moisture produced by the exhalation from this mass to rise above the crater. Wounded men died there begging piteously for water, and soldiers extended their tongues to dampen their parched lips until their tongues seemed to hang from their mouths. Finally, the enemy, having taken advantage of our inactivity to mass his troops, was seen to emerge from the swale between the hill on which the crater was situated and that of the cemetery. On account of this depression they could not be seen by our artillery, and hence no guns were brought to bear upon them. The only place where they could be observed was from the crater. But there was no serviceable artillery there, and no infantry force sufficiently organized to offer resistance when the enemy's column pressed forward. All in the crater who could possibly hang on by their elbows and toes lay flat against its conical wall and delivered their fire; but not more than a hundred men at a time could get into position, and these were only armed with muzzle-loading guns, and in order to re-load they were compelled to face about and place their backs against the wall.

The enemy's guns suddenly ceased their long-continued and uninterrupted fire on the crater, and the advancing column charged in the face of feeble resistance offered by the Union troops. At this stage they were perceived by our artillery, which opened a murderous fire, but too late. Over the crest and into the crater they poured, and a hand-to-hand conflict ensued. It was of short duration, however; crowded as our troops were, and without organization, resistance was vain. Many men were bayoneted at that time—some probably that would not have been, except for the excitement of battle. About 87 officers and 1652 men of the Ninth Corps were captured, the remainder retiring to our own lines, to which the enemy did not attempt to advance. Among the captured was General William F. Bartlett. Earlier in the war he had lost a leg, which he replaced with one of cork. While he was standing in the crater, a shot was heard to strike with the peculiar thud known to those who have been in action, and the general was seen to totter and fall. A number of officers and men immediately lifted him, when he cried out, "Put me any place where I can sit down." "But you are wounded, General, are n't you?" was the inquiry. "My leg is shattered all to pieces," said he. "Then you can't sit up," they urged; "you'll have to lie down." "Oh, no!" exclaimed the general, *"it's only my cork leg that's shattered!"* . . .

THE CHARGE OF THE COLORED DIVISION.

BY HENRY GODDARD THOMAS, BREVET MAJOR-GENERAL, U. S. V.

Commanding Second Brigade of Colored Troops at the Battle of the Crater.

GUIDON OF THOMAS'S BRIGADE OF THE COLORED DIVISION — SHADED PARTS, GREEN; THE FIELD, WHITE.

. . . For some time previous to the explosion of the mine it was determined by General Burnside that the colored division should lead the assault. The general tactical plan had been given to the brigade commanders (Colonel Sigfried and myself), with a rough outline map of the ground, and directions to study the front for ourselves. But this latter was impracticable except in momentary glimpses. The enemy made a target of every head that appeared above the work, and their marksmanship was good. The manner of studying the ground was this: Putting my battered old hat on a ramrod and lifting it above the rampart just enough for them not to discover that no man was under it, I drew their fire; then stepping quickly a few paces to one side, I took a hasty observation.

About 11 P. M., July 29th, a few hours before the action, we were officially informed that the plan had been changed, and our division would not lead.

We were then bivouacking on our arms in rear of our line, just behind the covered way leading to the mine. I returned to that bivouac dejected and with an instinct of disaster for the morrow. As I summoned and told my regimental commanders, their faces expressed the same feeling.

Any striking event or piece of news was usually eagerly discussed by the white troops, and in the ranks military critics were as plenty and perhaps more voluble than among the officers. Not so with the blacks; important news such as that before us, was usually followed by long silence. They sat about in groups, "studying," as they called it. They waited, like the Quakers, for the spirit to move; when the spirit moved, one of their singers would uplift a mighty voice, like a bard of old, in a wild sort of chant. If he did not strike a sympathetic chord in his hearers, if they did not find in his utterance the exponent of their idea, he would sing it again and again, altering sometimes the words, more often the music. If his changes met general acceptance, one voice after another would chime in; a rough harmony of three parts would add itself; other groups would join his, and the song would become the song of the command.

The night we learned that we were to lead the charge the news filled them too full for ordinary utterance. The joyous negro guffaw always breaking out about the camp-fire ceased. They formed circles in their company streets and were sitting on the ground intently and solemnly "studying." At last a heavy voice began to sing,

> "We-e looks li-ike me-en a-a-marchin' on,
> We looks li-ike men-er-war."

Over and over again he sang it, making slight

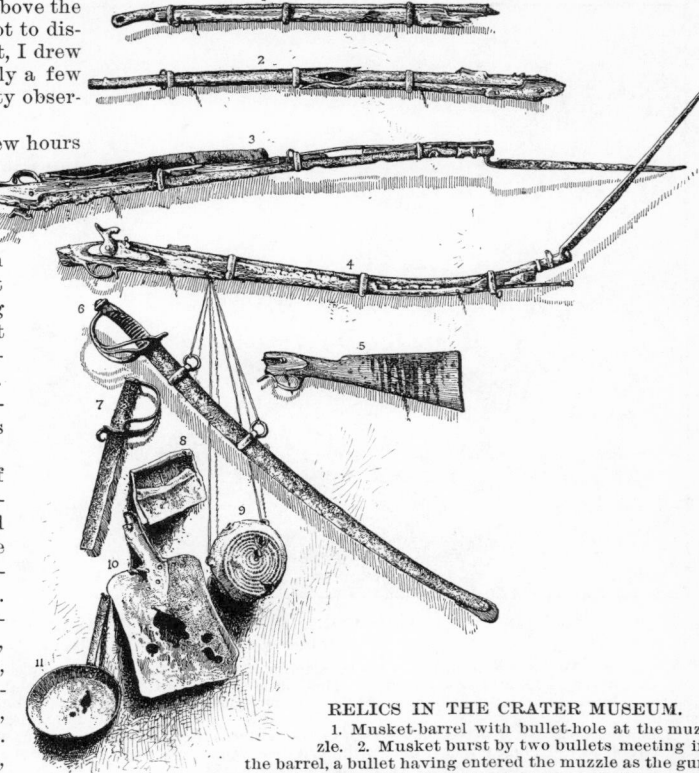

RELICS IN THE CRATER MUSEUM.

1. Musket-barrel with bullet-hole at the muzzle. 2. Musket burst by two bullets meeting in the barrel, a bullet having entered the muzzle as the gun was discharged. 3. Musket struck by six bullets, one embedding itself in the barrel near the bayonet. 4. Musket bent after having been cocked and capped. 5. Musket-stock covered with blood, found in a bomb-proof. 6. Sword found in a bomb-proof. 7. Broken sword. 8. Lining of a cartridge-box. 9. Canteen perforated by bullets. 10. Shovel having bullet-holes, found on the Union picket line in front of the crater. 11. Frying-pan having bullet-holes; taken out of the crater.

changes in the melody. The rest listened to him intently; no sign of approval or disapproval escaped their lips or appeared on their faces. All at once, when his refrain had struck the right response in their hearts, his group took it up, and shortly half a thousand voices were upraised extemporizing a half dissonant middle part and bass. It was a picturesque scene—these dark men, with their white eyes and teeth and full red lips, crouching over a smoldering camp-fire, in dusky shadow, with only the feeble rays of the lanterns of the first sergeants and the lights of the candles dimly showing through the tents. The sound was as weird as the scene, when all the voices struck the low E (last note but one), held it, and then rose to A with a *portamento* as sonorous as it was clumsy. Until we fought the battle of the crater they sang this every night to the exclusion of all other songs. After that defeat they sang it no more. . . .

Finally, about 7:30 A. M., we got the order for the colored division to charge. My brigade followed Sigfried's at the double-quick. Arrived at the crater, a part of the First Brigade entered. The crater was already too full; that I could easily see. I swung my column to the right and charged over the enemy's rifle-pits connecting with the crater on our right. These pits were different from any in our lines—a labyrinth of bomb-proofs and

SONG OF THE COLORED DIVISION BEFORE CHARGING INTO THE CRATER.

THE CRATER, AS SEEN FROM THE UNION SIDE.
From a sketch made at the time.

THE CONFEDERATE LINE AS RECONSTRUCTED AT THE CRATER.
From a drawing made by Lieutenant Henderson after the battle.

In October, 1887, Major James C. Coit, of Cheraw, South Carolina, wrote as follows with regard to this picture, and the Confederate battery, under his command, bearing on the crater:

"I am satisfied that I made that sketch of the crater. I had sent the sketch home after the battle, and had given some of the officers on the lines copies. It was made when I was in front of the Federal lines under the flag of truce for burying the dead. One gun that was blown up by the explosion fell between the lines, as represented in the sketch.

"My guns [Coit's battalion] were all upon the front line up to the time of the explosion of the mine. After that time one of my batteries was placed upon a second line, upon the Jerusalem plank-road immediately in rear of the crater. I also had a mortar-battery between the crater and the cemetery, about 150 yards in rear of the battery that was so effective on the day of the explosion. This battery [Wright's], where I was during the engagement, was just across the ravine to our left of the crater and just in rear of our infantry line, about 300 yards distant from the crater. It was erected there to defend Elliott's Salient. It bore directly upon the crater, and was the only battery which could reach the Federal troops in advancing to our lines and after they occupied the crater. It commanded the ground from the Federal main line to the Jerusalem plank-road in rear of the crater. General Potter was unable to silence it, or even to do us any serious injury, because he could not fire directly upon its front. From this position, which was very elevated, I had a view of the whole field from the Federal main line to the ridge or plank-road. I saw all the movements of the Federal troops from the beginning to the end of the fight. I remember particularly being struck with the gallantry of one of the Federal officers, with a flag in one hand and waving his sword in the other, mounting our works."

magazines, with passages between. My brigade moved gallantly on right over the bomb-proofs and over the men of the First Division. As we mounted the pits, a deadly enfilade from eight guns on our right and a murderous cross-fire of musketry met us. Among the officers, the first to fall was the gallant Fessenden of the 23d Regiment. Ayres and Woodruff of the 31st dropped within a few yards of Fessenden, Ayres being killed, and Woodruff mortally wounded. Liscomb of the 23d then fell to rise no more; and then Hackhiser of the 28th and Flint and Aiken of the 29th. Major Rockwood of the 19th then mounted the crest and fell back dead, with a cheer on his lips. Nor were these all; for at that time hundreds of heroes "carved in ebony" fell. These black men commanded the admiration and respect of every beholder.

The most advantageous point for the purpose, about eight hundred feet from the crater, having been reached, we leaped from the works and endeavored to make a rush for the crest. Captain Marshall L. Dempcy, and Lieutenant Christopher Pennell, of my staff, and four white orderlies with the brigade guidon accompanied me, closely followed by Lieutenant-Colonel Ross, leading the 31st Regiment. At the instant of leaving the works

Ross was shot down; the next officer in rank, Captain Wright, was shot as he stooped over him. The men were largely without leaders, and their organization was destroyed. Two of my four orderlies were wounded: one, flag in hand; the remaining two sought shelter when Lieutenant Pennell, rescuing the guidon, hastened down the line outside the pits. With his sword uplifted in his right hand and the banner in his left, he sought to call out the men along the whole line of the parapet. In a moment, a musketry fire was focused upon him, whirling him round and round several times before he fell. Of commanding figure, his bravery was so conspicuous that, according to Colonel Weld's testimony, a number of his (Weld's) men were shot because, spell-bound, they forgot their own shelter in watching this superb boy, who was an only child of an old Massachusetts clergyman, and to me as Jonathan was to David.

The men of the 31st making the charge were being mowed down like grass, with no hope of any one reaching the crest, so I ordered them to scatter and run back. The fire was such that Captain Dempcy and myself were the only officers who returned, unharmed, of those who left the works for that charge.

We were not long back within the honeycomb of passages and bomb-proofs near the crater before I received this order from the division commander: "Colonels Sigfried and Thomas, if you have not already done so, you will immediately proceed to take the crest in your front." My command was crowded into the pits, already too full, and were sandwiched, man for man, against the men of the First Division. They were thus partly sheltered from the fire that had reduced them coming up; but their organization was almost lost. I had already sent word to General Burnside by Major James L. Van Buren, of his staff, that unless a movement simultaneous with mine was made to the right, to stop the enfilading fire, I thought not a man would live to reach the crest; but that I would try another charge in about ten minutes, and I hoped to be supported. I then directed the commanders of the 23d, 28th, and 29th regiments to get their commands as much together and separated from the others as possible in that time, so that each could have a regimental following, for we were mixed up with white troops, and with one another to the extent of almost paralyzing any effort. We managed to make the charge, however, Colonel Bross of the 29th leading. The 31st had been so shattered, was so diminished, so largely without officers, that I got what was left of them out of the way of the charging column as much as possible. This column met the same fate in one respect as the former. As I gave the order, Lieutenant-Colonel John A. Bross, taking the flag into his own hands, was the first man to leap from the works into the valley of death below. He had attired himself in full uniform, evidently with the intent of inspiring his men. He had hardly reached the ground outside the works before he fell to rise no more. He was conspicuous and magnificent in his gallantry. The black men followed into the

jaws of death, and advanced until met by a charge in force from the Confederate lines.

I lost in all 36 officers and 877 men,—total, 913. The 23d Regiment entered the charge with eighteen officers; it came out with seven. The 28th entered with eleven officers, and came out with four. The 31st had but two officers for duty that night. . . .

NOTE.—The battle of the "Crater" ended for the time being the attempts of Grant to take Petersburg by direct assault. Hancock's corps, Gregg's cavalry division, and a force from Butler's army advanced up the north bank of the James in August to threaten Richmond, and at the same time Warren's corps marched out of the works at Petersburg and seized the Weldon railroad, at Globe Tavern, south of the city. The Confederates made repeated and desperate attacks to dislodge Warren, but were repulsed. Later Hancock and Gregg recrossed the James and proceeded to destroy the Weldon road beyond Warren's position. A desperate battle ensued at Reams's Station on August 20th.

In September operations were continued north of the James. On the 29th the Tenth Corps, under General D. B. Birney, and the Eighteenth, under General E. O. C. Ord, carried Fort Harrison, opposite Drewry's Bluffs, by storm, but were repulsed in a desperate assault on Fort Gilmer, a strong work nearer to Richmond.

In October an expedition under Hancock attempted to seize the South Side railroad, a line west of the Weldon road, but it proved to be within the enemy's intrenchments and the expedition retired after a sharp battle at Hatcher's Run. Further movements on the left were the expedition, December 7th to 10th, under Warren, by which the Weldon railroad was destroyed as far as Hicksford, and the combined movement, February 5th to 7th, under Warren and Humphreys (who on the 28th of November succeeded to the command of Hancock's Corps), which resulted in extending the Union intrenchments to Hatcher's Run, after some severe fighting with the troops of A. P. Hill and Gordon. The renewal of these operations in the spring of 1865 led to the campaign of Five Forks. Sheridan's cavalry joined the besieging army March 24th, and on the 29th started on the march around Lee's right flank.

Meanwhile, on the 25th, Gordon's corps breached Grant's lines at Fort Stedman, and fighting over the intrenchments continued until the grand assaults which terminated the siege on April 2d. (See p. 308.)

THE CONFEDERATE CRUISER "ALABAMA."

This sketch was made from a photograph (of a drawing) which Captain Semmes gave to a friend, with the remark that it was a correct picture of his ship. On the stocks, and until she went into commission, the *Alabama* was known as "No. 290," that being her number on the list of ships built by the Lairds. According to the volume, "Our Cruise in the Confederate States' War Steamer *Alabama*," she was a bark-rigged wooden propeller, of 1040 tons' register; length of keel, 210 feet; length over all, 220; beam, 32; depth, 17. She carried two horizontal engines, each of 300 horse-power; she had stowage for 350 tons of coal. All her standing rigging was of wire. She had a double wheel placed just before the mizzen-mast, and on it was inscribed the motto, "*Aide toi et Dieu t'aidera.*"

The bridge was in the center, just before the funnel. She carried five boats; cutter and launch amidships, gig and whale-boat between the main and mizzen-mast, and dingey astern. The main deck was pierced for twelve guns. She had an elliptic stern, billet head, and high bulwarks. Her cabin accommodations were first-class; and her ward-room was furnished with a handsome suite of state-rooms. The starboard steerage was for midshipmen, the port for engineers. Next came the engine-room, coal-bunkers, etc.; then the berth-deck, accommodating 120 men. Under the ward-room were store-rooms, and under the steerage were shell-rooms. Just forward of the fire-room came the hold, next the magazines, and, forward of all, the boatswain's and sail-maker's store-rooms. The hold was all under the berth-deck.

THE DUEL BETWEEN THE "ALABAMA" AND THE "KEARSARGE."

NOTE.—The Confederate Government sent out during the progress of the war a number of cruisers to attack the commerce of the United States. Most of them were built abroad; several of them in England. The most famous of these was the *Alabama*, which sailed from Liverpool on the 29th of July, 1862, on the day that the law officers of the Crown rendered an opinion that the vessel was clearly intended for warlike use against the United States, and recommended that she be seized at once. She was fitted up in one of the islands of the Azores, and for two years was a terror to the commerce of the United States, until finally sunk by the *Kearsarge*.

FROM THE DECK OF THE "ALABAMA."

BY JOHN McINTOSH KELL, EXECUTIVE OFFICER OF THE "ALABAMA."

. . . Our little ship was now showing signs of the active work she had been doing. Her boilers were burned out, and her machinery was sadly in want of repairs. She was loose at every joint, her seams were open, and the copper on her bottom was in rolls. We therefore set our course for Europe, and on the 11th of June, 1864, entered the port of Cherbourg, and applied for permission to go into dock. There being none but national docks, the Emperor had first to be communicated with before permission could be granted, and he was absent from Paris. It was during this interval of waiting, on the third day after our arrival, that the *Kearsarge* steamed into the harbor, for the purpose, as we learned, of taking on board the prisoners we had landed from our last two prizes. Captain Semmes, however, objected to this on the ground that the *Kearsarge* was adding to her crew in a neutral

port. The authorities conceding this objection valid, the *Kearsarge* steamed out of the harbor, without anchoring. During her stay we examined her closely with our glasses, but she was keeping on the opposite side of the harbor, out of the reach of a very close scrutiny, which accounts for our not detecting the boxing to her chain armor. After she left the harbor Captain Semmes sent for me to his cabin, and said: "I am going out to fight the *Kearsarge*; what do you think of it?" We discussed the battery, and especially the advantage the *Kearsarge* had over us in her 11-inch guns. She was built for a vessel of war, and we for speed, and though she carried one gun less, her battery was more effective at point-blank range. While the *Alabama* carried one more gun, the *Kearsarge* threw more metal at a broadside; and while our guns were more effective at long range, her 11-inch guns gave her greatly the advantage at close range. She also had a slight advantage in her crew, she carrying 163, all told, while we carried 149. Considering well these advantages, Captain Semmes communicated through our agent to the United States consul that if Captain Winslow would wait outside the harbor he would fight him as soon as we could coal ship.

Accordingly on Sunday morning, June 19th, between 9 and 10 o'clock, we weighed anchor and stood out of the western entrance of the harbor, the French iron-clad frigate *Couronne* following us. The day was bright and beautiful, with a light breeze blowing. Our men were neatly dressed, and our officers in full uniform. The report of our going out to

REAR-ADMIRAL SEMMES, C. S. N., CAPTAIN OF THE "ALABAMA."
From a photograph taken in England after the loss of his ship.

fight the *Kearsarge* had been circulated, and many persons from Paris and the surrounding country had come down to witness the engagement. With a large number of the inhabitants of Cherbourg they collected on every prominent point on the shore that would afford a view seaward. As we rounded the breakwater we discovered the *Kearsarge* about seven miles to the northward and eastward. We immediately shaped our course for her, called all hands to quarters, and cast loose the starboard battery. Upon reporting to the captain that the ship was ready for action, he directed me to send all hands aft, and mounting a gun-carriage, he made the following address:

"OFFICERS AND SEAMEN OF THE 'ALABAMA': You have at length another opportunity of meeting the enemy—the first that has been presented to you since

you sank the *Hatteras*! In the mean time you have been all over the world, and it is not too much to say that you have destroyed, and driven for protection under neutral flags, one-half of the enemy's commerce, which at the beginning of the war covered every sea. This is an achievement of which you may well be proud, and a grateful country will not be unmindful of it. The name of your ship has become a household word wherever civilization extends! Shall that name be tarnished by defeat? The thing is impossible! Remember that you are in the English Channel, the theater of so much of the naval glory of our race, and that the eyes of all Europe are at this moment upon you. The flag that floats over you is that of a young Republic, which bids defiance to her enemy's whenever and wherever found! Show the world that you know how to uphold it! Go to your quarters."

In about forty-five minutes we were somewhat over a mile from the *Kearsarge*, when she headed

"KEARSARGE."   FIGHTING IN A CIRCLE.   "ALABAMA."

for us, presenting her starboard bow. At a distance of a mile we commenced the action with our 100-pounder pivot-gun from our starboard bow. Both ships were now approaching each other at high speed, and soon the action became general with broadside batteries at a distance of about five hundred yards. To prevent passing, each ship used a strong port helm. Thus the action was fought around a common center, gradually drawing in the circle. At this range we used shell upon the enemy. Captain Semmes, standing on the horse-block abreast the mizzen-mast with his glass in hand, observed the effect of our shell. He called to me and said: "Mr. Kell, use solid shot; our shell strike the enemy's side and fall into the water." We were not at this time aware of the chain armor of the enemy, and attributed the failure of our shell to our defective ammunition.* After using solid shot for some time, we alternated shell and shot. The enemy's 11-inch shells were now doing severe execution upon our quarter-deck section. Three of them successively entered our 8-inch pivot-gun port: the first swept off the forward part of the gun's crew; the second killed one man and wounded several others; and the third struck the breast of the gun-carriage, and spun

* On the coast of Brazil we had had some target practice at one of our prizes. Many of our fuses proved defective. Upon visiting the target I found that one of the 100-pounder shells had exploded on the quarter-deck, and I counted fifteen marks from its missiles, which justifies me in asserting that had the 100-pound shell which we placed in the stern-post of the *Kearsarge* exploded, it would have changed the result of the fight. I at once examined every fuse and cap, discarding the apparently defective, and at the same time made a thorough overhauling of the magazine, as I thought; but the action with the *Kearsarge* proved that our entire supply of powder was damaged. The report from the *Kearsarge's* battery was clear and sharp, the powder burning like thin vapor, while our guns gave out a dull report, with thick and heavy vapor.—J. McI. K.

around on the deck until one of the men picked it up and threw it overboard. Our decks were now covered with the dead and the wounded, and the ship was careening heavily to starboard from the effects of the shot-holes on her water-line.

Captain Semmes ordered me to be ready to make all sail possible when the circuit of fight should put our head to the coast of France; then he would notify me at the same time to pivot to port and continue the action with the port battery, hoping thus to right the ship and enable us to reach the coast of France. The evolution was performed beautifully, righting the helm, hoisting the head-sails, hauling at the fore try-sail sheet, and pivoting to port, the action continuing almost without cessation.

This evolution exposed us to a raking fire, but, strange to say, the *Kearsarge* did not take advantage of it. The port side of the quarter-deck was so encumbered with the mangled trunks of the dead that I had to have them thrown overboard, in order to fight the after pivot-gun. I abandoned the after 32-pounder, and transferred the men to fill up the vacancies at the pivot-gun under the charge of young Midshipman Anderson, who in the midst of the carnage filled his place like a veteran. At this moment the chief engineer came on deck and reported the fires put out, and that he could no longer work the engines. Captain Semmes said to me, "Go below, sir, and see how long the ship can float." As I entered the ward-room the sight was indeed appalling. There stood Assistant-Surgeon Llewellyn at his post, but the table and the patient upon it had been swept away from him by an 11-inch shell, which opened in the side of the ship an aperture that was fast filling the ship with water.

It took me but a moment to return to the deck and report to the captain that we could not float ten minutes. He replied to me, "Then, sir, cease firing, shorten sail, and haul down the colors; it

will never do in this nineteenth century for us to go down, and the decks covered with our gallant wounded." The order was promptly executed, after which the *Kearsarge* deliberately fired into us five shot.* I ordered the men to stand to their quarters and not flinch from the shot of the enemy; they stood every man to his post most heroically. With the first shot fired upon us after our colors were down, the quartermaster was ordered to show a white flag over the stern, which order was executed in my presence. When the firing ceased Captain Semmes ordered me to despatch an officer to the *Kearsarge* to say that our ship was sinking, and to ask that they send boats to save our wounded, as our boats were disabled. The dingey, our smallest boat, had escaped damage. I despatched Master's-

* In Captain Winslow's letter (dated Cherbourg, June 21st, 1864) to the Secretary of the Navy, he says: "Toward the close of the action between the *Alabama* and this vessel, all available sail was made on the former for the purpose of again reaching Cherbourg. When the object was apparent the *Kearsarge* was steered across the bow of the *Alabama* for a raking fire; but before reaching this point the *Alabama* struck. Uncertain whether Captain Semmes was using some *ruse*, the *Kearsarge* was stopped"—and, I may add, continued his fire, for by his own words he thought Captain Semmes was making some ruse. The report that the *Alabama* fired her guns after the colors were down and she had shortened sail is not correct. There was a cessation in the firing of our guns when we shifted our battery to port, after which we renewed the action.

Almost immediately afterward the engineer reported the fires put out, when we ceased firing, hauled down the colors, and shortened sail. There was *no* gun fired from the *Alabama* after that. Captain Winslow may have thought we had surrendered when we ceased firing and were in the act of shifting the battery; but the idle report that junior officers had taken upon themselves to continue the action after the order had been given to cease firing is not worthy of notice. I did not hear the firing of a gun, and the discipline of the *Alabama* would not have permitted it.—J. McI. K.

In the letter from which Captain Kell quotes, Captain Winslow does not speak of "continuing his fire." But in his detailed report (dated July 30th, 1864) Captain Winslow says of the *Alabama*, after she had winded and set sail: "Her port broadside was presented to us, with only two guns bearing, not having been able, as I learned afterward, to shift over but one. I saw now that she was at our mercy, and a few more guns well directed brought down her flag. I was unable to ascertain whether it had been hauled down or shot away; but a white flag having been displayed over the stern our fire was reserved. Two minutes had not more than elapsed before she again opened on us with the two guns on the port side. This drew our fire again, and the *Kearsarge* was immediately steamed ahead and laid across her bows for raking. The white flag was still flying, and our fire was again reserved. Shortly after this her boats were seen to be lowering, and an officer in one of them came alongside and informed us the ship had surrendered and was fast sinking."

mate Fullman with the request. No boats appearing, I had one of our quarter-boats lowered, which was slightly injured, and I ordered the wounded placed in her. Dr. Galt, the surgeon who was in charge of the magazine and shell-room division, came on deck at this moment and was at once put in charge of the boat, with orders to "take the wounded to the *Kearsarge*." They shoved off just in time to save the poor fellows from going down in the ship.

I now gave the order for every man to jump overboard with a spar and save himself from the sinking ship. To enforce the order, I walked forward and urged the men overboard. As soon as the decks were cleared, save of the bodies of the dead, I returned to the stern-port, where stood Captain Semmes with one or two of the men and his faithful steward, who, poor fellow! was doomed to a watery grave, as he could not swim. The *Alabama's* stern-port was now almost at the water's edge. Partly undressing, we plunged into the sea, and made an offing from the sinking ship, Captain Semmes with a life-preserver and I on a grating.

The *Alabama* settled stern foremost, launching her bows high in the air. Graceful even in her death-struggle, she in a moment disappeared from the face of the waters. The sea now presented a mass of living heads, striving for their lives. Many poor fellows sank for the want of timely aid. Near me I saw a float of empty shell-boxes, and called to one

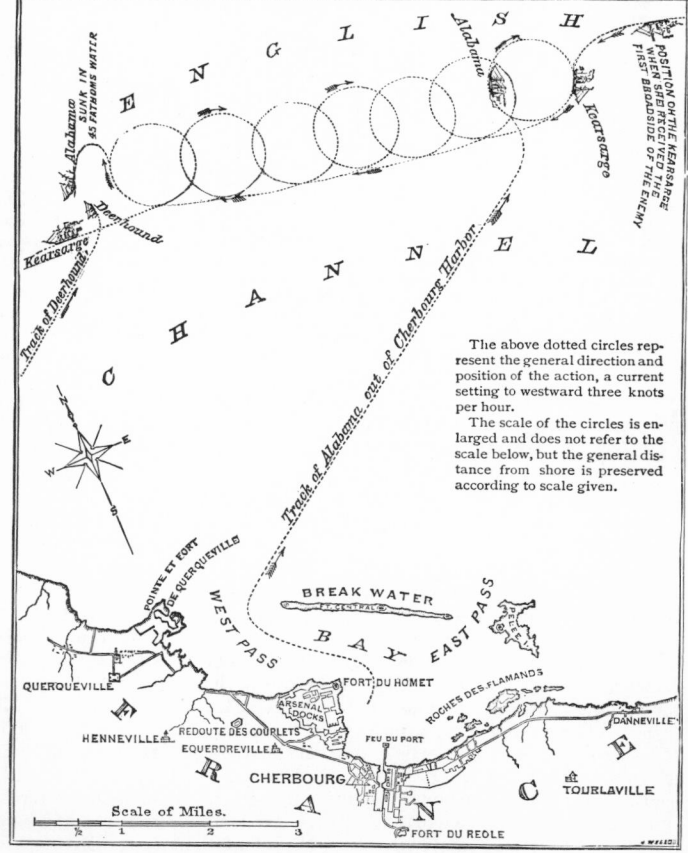

CHART OF THE ACTION OFF CHERBOURG.

The above dotted circles represent the general direction and position of the action, a current setting to westward three knots per hour.

The scale of the circles is enlarged and does not refer to the scale below, but the general distance from shore is preserved according to scale given.

of the men, a good swimmer, to examine it; he did so and replied, "It is the doctor, sir, dead." Poor Llewellyn! he perished almost in sight of his home. The young midshipman, Maffitt, swam to me and offered his life-preserver. My grating was not proving a very buoyant float, and the white-caps breaking over my head were distressingly uncomfortable, to say the least. Maffit said: "Mr. Kell, take my life-preserver, sir; you are almost exhausted." The gallant boy did not consider his own condition, but his pallid face told me that his heroism was superior to his bodily suffering, and I refused it. After twenty minutes or more I heard near me some one call out, "There is our first lieutenant," and the next moment I was pulled into a boat, in which was Captain Semmes, stretched out in the stern-sheets, as pallid as death. He had received during the action a slight contusion on the hand, and the struggle in the water had almost exhausted him. There was also several of our crew in the boat, and in a few moments we were alongside a little steam-yacht, which had come among our floating men, and by throwing them ropes had saved many lives. Upon reaching her deck, I ascertained for the first time that she was the yacht *Deerhound*, owned by Mr. John Lancaster, of England. In looking about I saw two French pilot-boats engaged in saving our crew, and finally two boats from the *Kearsarge*. To my surprise I found on the yacht Mr. Fullam, whom I had despatched in the dingey to ask that boats be sent to save our wounded. He reported to me that our shot had literally torn her casing from the chain armor of the *Kearsarge*, indenting the chain in many places, which explained Captain Semmes's observation of the effect of our shell upon the enemy, "that they struck the sides and fell into the water."

Captain Winslow, in his report, states that his ship was struck twenty-five or thirty times, and I doubt if the *Alabama* was struck a greater number of times. I may not, therefore, be bold in asserting that had not the *Kearsarge* been protected by her iron cables, the result of the fight would have been different. Captain Semmes felt the more keenly the delusion to which he fell a victim (not knowing that the *Kearsarge* was chain-clad) from the fact that he was exceeding his instructions in seeking an action with the enemy; but to seek a fight with an ironclad he conceived to be an unpardonable error. However, he had the satisfaction of knowing she was classed as a wooden gun-boat by the Federal Government; also that he had inspected her with most excellent glasses, and so far as outward appearances showed, she displayed no chain armor. At the same time it must be admitted that Captain Winslow had the right unquestionably to protect his ship and crew. In justice to Captain Semmes I will state that the battle would never have been fought had he known that the *Kearsarge* wore an armor of chain beneath her outer covering.* Thus was the *Alabama* lost by an error, if you please, but, it must be admitted, a *most pardonable* one, and not until "Father Neptune" claimed her as his own did she lower her colors.

The 11-inch shells of the *Kearsarge* did fearful work, and her guns were served beautifully, being aimed with precision, and deliberate in fire. She came into action magnificently. Having the speed of us, she took her own position and fought gallantly. But she tarnished her glory when she fired upon a fallen foe. It was high noon of a bright, beautiful day, with a moderate breeze blowing to waft the smoke of battle clear, and nothing to obstruct the view at five hundred yards. The very fact of the *Alabama* ceasing to fire, shortening sail, and hauling down her colors simultaneously, must have attracted the attention of the officer in command of the *Kearsarge*. Again, there is no reason given why the *Kearsarge* did not steam immediately into the midst of the crew of the *Alabama*, after their ship had been sunk, and, like a brave and generous foe, save the lives of her enemies, who had fought nobly as long as they had a plank to stand upon. Were it not for the timely presence of the kind-hearted Englishman and the two French pilot-boats, who can tell the number of us that would have rested with our gallant little ship beneath the waters of the English Channel? I quote the following from Mr. John Lancaster's letter to the London "Daily News": "I presume it was because he [Captain Winslow] *would* not or could not save them himself. The fact is that if the captain and crew of the *Alabama* had depended for safety altogether upon Captain Winslow, not one-half of them would have been saved." *

The following is an extract from Mr. John Lancaster's log, dated "Steam-yacht *Deerhound*, off Cowes":

"SUNDAY, June 19th, 9 A. M.

"Got up steam and proceeded out of Cherbourg harbor. Half-past ten observed the *Alabama* steaming out of the harbor toward the Federal steamer *Kearsarge*. Ten minutes past eleven, the *Alabama* commenced firing with her starboard battery, the distance between the contending vessels being about one mile. The *Kearsarge* immediately replied with her starboard guns. A very sharp, spirited fire was kept up, shot sometimes being varied by shells. In manœuvering, both vessels made seven complete circles at a distance of from a quarter to half a mile. At 12 a slight intermission was observed in the *Alabama's* firing, the *Alabama* making head-sail, and shaping her course for the land, distant about nine miles. At 12:30, observed the *Alabama* to be disabled and in a sinking state. We immediately made toward her and in passing the *Kearsarge* were requested to assist in saving the *Alabama's* crew. At 12:50, when within a distance of two hundred yards, the *Alabama* sunk. We then lowered our two boats, and with the assistance of the *Alabama's* whale-boat and dingey, succeeded in saving about forty men, including Captain Semmes and thirteen officers. At 1 P. M. we started for Southampton."

When Mr. Lancaster approached Captain Semmes, and said, "I think every man has been picked up; where shall I land you?" Captain Semmes replied, "I am now under the English colors, and the sooner you put me with my officers and men on English soil, the better." The little yacht moved rapidly away at once, under a press of steam, for Southampton. Armstrong, our second lieutenant, and some of our men who were saved by the French pilot-boats, were taken into Cherbourg. Our loss was 9 killed, 21 wounded, and 10 drowned.

It has been charged that an arrangement had been entered into between Mr. Lancaster and Captain Semmes, previous to our leaving Cherbourg, that in the event of the *Alabama* being sunk the *Deerhound* would come to our rescue. Captain Semmes and myself met Mr. Lancaster for the first time when rescued by him, and he related to us the

THE ELEVEN-INCH FORWARD PIVOT-GUN ON THE "KEARSARGE" IN ACTION.

*Surgeon Browne points out that the advantage derived from the chain armor was immaterial. It was a device that Captain Semmes also might have employed.

*In his report of June 21st, 1864, Captain Winslow said:

"It was seen shortly afterward that the *Alabama* was lowering her boats, and an officer came alongside in one of them to say that they had surrendered and were fast sinking, and begging that boats would be despatched immediately for the saving of life. The two boats not dis-

abled were at once lowered, and as it was apparent the *Alabama* was settling, this officer was permitted to leave in his boat to afford assistance. An English yacht, the *Deerhound*, had approached near the *Kearsarge* at this time, when I hailed and begged the commander to run down to the *Alabama*, as she was fast sinking and we had but two boats, and assist in picking up the men. He answered affirmatively and steamed toward the *Alabama*, but the latter sank almost immediately."

circumstance that was the occasion of his coming out to see the fight. Having his family on board, his intention was to attend church with his wife and children, when the gathering of the spectators on the shore attracted their attention, the report having been widely circulated that the *Alabama* was to go out that morning and give battle to the *Kearsarge*. The boys were clamorous to see the fight, and after a family discussion as to the propriety of going out on the Sabbath to witness a naval combat, Mr. Lancaster agreed to put the question to vote at the breakfast-table, where the youngsters carried their part by a majority. Thus many of us were indebted for our lives to that inherent trait in the English character, the desire to witness a "passage at arms."

That evening we landed in Southampton, and were received by the people with every demonstration of sympathy and kindly feeling. Thrown upon their shores by the chances of war, we were taken to their hearts and homes with that generous hospitality which brought to mind with tenderest feeling our own dear Southern homes in *ante-bellum* times. To the Rev. F. W. Tremlett, of Belsize Park, London, and his household, I am indebted for a picture of English home life that time cannot efface, and the memory of which will be a lasting pleasure till life's end.

FROM THE DECK OF THE "KEARSARGE."

BY JOHN M. BROWNE, SURGEON OF THE "KEARSARGE."

ON Sunday, the 12th of June, 1864, the *Kearsarge*, Captain John A. Winslow, was lying at anchor in the Scheldt, off Flushing, Holland. The cornet suddenly appeared at the fore, and a gun was fired. These were unexpected signals that compelled absent officers and men to return to the ship. Steam was raised, and as soon as we were off, and all hands called, Captain Winslow gave the welcome news of a telegram from Mr. Dayton, our Minister to France, announcing that the *Alabama* had arrived the day previous at Cherbourg; hence the urgency of departure, the probability of an encounter, and the expectation of her capture or destruction. The crew responded with cheers. The succeeding day witnessed the arrival of the *Kearsarge* at Dover for despatches, and the day after (Tuesday) her appearance off Cherbourg, where we saw the Confederate flag flying within the breakwater. As we approached, officers and men gathered in groups on deck, and looked intently at the "daring rover" that had been able for two years to escape numerous foes and to inflict immense damage on our commerce. She was a beautiful specimen of naval architecture. The surgeon went on shore and obtained *pratique* (permission to visit the port) for boats. Owing to the neutrality limitation, which would not allow us to remain in the harbor longer than twenty-four hours, it was inexpedient to enter the port. We placed a vigilant watch by turns at each of the harbor entrances, and continued it to the moment of the engagement.

On Wednesday Captain Winslow paid an official visit to the French admiral commanding the maritime district, and to the United States commercial agent, bringing on his return the unanticipated news that Captain Semmes had declared his intention to fight. At first the assertion was barely credited, the policy of the *Alabama* being regarded as opposed to a conflict, and to escape rather than to be exposed to injury, perhaps destruction; but the doubters were half convinced when the so-called challenge was known to read as follows:

"C. S. S. 'ALABAMA,' CHERBOURG, June 14th, 1864.

"To A. BONFILS, Esq., CHERBOURG. SIR: I hear that you were informed by the U. S. Consul that the *Kearsarge* was to come to this port solely for the prisoners landed by me, and that she was to depart in twenty-four hours. I desire you to say to the U. S. Consul that my intention is to fight the *Kearsarge* as soon as I can make the necessary arrangements. I hope these will not detain me more than until to-morrow evening; or after the morrow morning at furthest. I beg she will not depart before I am ready to go out.

"I have the honor to be, very respectfully,

"Your obedient servant,

"R. SEMMES, Captain."

This communication was sent by Mr. Bonfils, the Confederate States Commercial Agent, to Mr. Liais, the United States Commercial Agent, with a request that the latter would furnish a copy to Captain Winslow for his guidance. There was no other challenge to combat. The letter that passed between the commercial agents *was* the challenge about which so much has been said. Captain Semmes informed Captain Wins-

CLOSE OF THE COMBAT—THE "KEARSARGE" GETTING INTO POSITION TO RAKE THE "ALABAMA."

low through Mr. Bonfils of his intention to fight; Captain Winslow informed Captain Semmes through Mr. Liais that he came to Cherbourg to fight, and had no intention of leaving. He made no other reply.

Captain Winslow assembled the officers and discussed the expected battle. It was probable the two ships would engage on parallel lines, and the *Alabama* would seek neutral waters in event of defeat; hence the necessity of beginning the action several miles from the breakwater. It was determined not to surrender, but to fight until the last, and, if need be, to go down with colors flying. Why Captain Semmes should imperil his ship was not understood, since he would risk all and expose the cause of which he was a selected champion to a needless disaster, while the *Kearsarge*, if taken or destroyed, could be replaced. It was therefore concluded that he would fight because he thought he would be the victor.

Preparations were made for battle, with no relaxation of the watch. Thursday passed; Friday came; the *Kearsarge* waited with ports down, guns pivoted to starboard, the whole battery loaded, and shell, grape, and canister ready to use in any mode of attack or defense; yet no *Alabama* appeared. French pilots came on board and told of unusual arrangements made by the enemy, such as the hurried taking of coals, the transmission of valuable articles to the

RETURNING FOR THE WOUNDED.

shore, such as captured chronometers, specie, and the bills of ransomed vessels; and the sharpening of swords, cutlasses, and boarding-pikes. It was reported that Captain Semmes had been advised not to give battle; that he replied he would prove to the world that his ship was not a privateer, intended only for attack upon merchant vessels, but a true man-of-war; further, that he had consulted French officers, who all asserted that in his situation they would fight. Certain newspapers declared that he ought to improve the opportunity afforded by the presence of the enemy to show that his ship was not a "corsair," to prey upon defenseless merchantmen, but a real ship-of-war, able and willing to fight the "Federal" waiting outside the harbor. It was said the *Alabama* was swift, with a superior crew, and it was known that the ship, guns, and ammunition were of English make.

A surprise by night was suggested, and precautionary means were taken; everything was well planned and ready for action, but still no *Alabama* came. Meanwhile the *Kearsarge* was cruising to and fro off the breakwater. A message was brought from Mr. Dayton, our Minister to Paris, by his son, who with difficulty had obtained permission from the French admiral to visit the *Kearsarge*. Communication with either ship was prohibited, but the permission was given upon the promise of Mr. Dayton to return on shore directly after the delivery of the message. Mr. Dayton expressed the opinion that Captain Semmes would not fight, though acknowledging the prevalence of a contrary belief in Cherbourg. He was told that, in the event of battle, if we were successful the colors would be displayed at the mizzen as the flag of victory. He went on shore with the intention of leaving for Paris without delay. In taking leave of the French admiral the latter advised Mr. Dayton to remain over night, and mentioned the fixed purpose of Captain Semmes to fight on the following day, Sunday; and he gave the intelligence that there could be no further communication with the *Kearsarge*. Mr. Dayton passed a part of Saturday night trying to procure a boat to send off the acquired information, but the vigilance along the coast made his efforts useless. He remained, witnessed the battle, telegraphed the result to Paris, and was one of the first to go on board and offer congratulations.

At a supper in Cherbourg on Saturday night, several officers of the *Alabama* met sympathizing friends, the coming battle being the chief topic of conversation. Confident of victory, they proclaimed the intent to sink the "Federal" or gain a "corsair." They rose with promises to meet the following night to repeat the festivity as victors, were escorted to the boat, and departed with cheers and best wishes for a successful return.

Sunday, the 19th, came; a fine day, atmosphere somewhat hazy, little sea, light westerly wind. At 10 o'clock the *Kearsarge* was near the buoy marking the line of shoals to the eastward of Cherbourg, at a distance of about three miles from the entrance. The decks had been holystoned, the bright work cleaned, the guns polished, and the crew were dressed in Sunday suits. They were inspected at quarters and dismissed to attend divine service. Seemingly no one thought of the enemy; so long awaited and not appearing, speculation as to her coming had nearly ceased. At 10:20 the officer of the deck reported a steamer approaching from Cherbourg,—a frequent occurrence, and consequently it created no surprise. The bell was tolling for service when some one shouted, "She's coming, and heading straight for us!" Soon, by the aid of a glass, the officer of the deck made out the enemy, and shouted, "The *Alabama!*" and calling down the ward-room hatch repeated the cry, "The *Alabama!*" The drum beat to general quarters; Captain Winslow put aside the prayer-book, seized the trumpet, ordered the ship about, and headed seaward. The ship was cleared for action, with the battery pivoted to starboard.

The *Alabama* approached from the western entrance, escorted by the French iron-clad frigate *Couronne*, flying the pennant of the commandant of the port, followed in her wake by a small fore-and-aft-rigged steamer, the *Deerhound*, flying the flag of the Royal Mersey Yacht Club. The commander of the frigate had informed Captain Semmes that his ship would escort him to the limit of the French waters. The frigate, having convoyed the *Alabama* three marine miles from the coast, put down her helm, and steamed back into port without delay.

The steam-yacht continued on, and remained near the scene of action.

Captain Winslow had assured the French admiral that in the event of an engagement the position of the ship should be far enough from shore to prevent a violation of the law of nations. To avoid a question of jurisdiction, and to avert an escape to neutral waters in case of retreat, the *Kearsarge* steamed to sea, followed by the enemy, giving the appearance of running away and being pursued. Between six and seven miles from the shore the *Kearsarge*, thoroughly ready, at 10:50 wheeled, at a distance of one and a quarter miles from her opponent, presented the starboard battery, and steered direct for her, with the design of closing or of running her down. The *Alabama* sheered and presented her starboard battery. More speed was ordered, the *Kearsarge* advanced rapidly, and at 10:57 received a broadside of solid shot at a range of about eighteen hundred yards. This broadside cut away a little of the rigging, but the shot mostly passed

THE CREW OF THE "KEARSARGE" AT QUARTERS.
From a photograph.

over or fell short. It was apparent that Captain Semmes intended to fight at long range.

The *Kearsarge* advanced with increased speed, receiving a second and part of a third broadside, with similar effect. Captain Winslow wished to get at short range, as the guns were loaded with five-second shell. Arrived within nine hundred yards, the *Kearsarge*, fearing a fourth broadside, and apprehensive of a raking, sheered and broke her silence with a starboard battery. Each ship was now pressed under a full head of steam, the position being broadside, both employing the starboard guns.

Captain Winslow, fearful that the enemy would make for the shore, determined with a port helm to run under the *Alabama's* stern for raking, but was prevented by her sheering and keeping her broadside to the *Kearsarge*, which forced the fighting on a circular track, each ship, with a strong port helm, steaming around a common center, and pouring its fire into its opponent a quarter to half a mile away. There was a current setting to westward three knots an hour.

The action was now fairly begun. The *Alabama* changed from solid shot to shell. [Commander Kell (see p. 266) says the *Alabama* began with shell.] A shot from an early broadside of the *Kearsarge* carried away the spanker-gaff of the enemy, and caused his ensign to come down by the run. This incident was regarded as a favorable omen by the men, who cheered and went with increased confidence to their work. The fallen ensign reappeared at the mizzen. The *Alabama* returned to solid shot, and soon after fired both shot and shell to the end. The firing of the *Alabama* was rapid and wild, getting better near the close; that of the *Kearsarge* was deliberate, accurate, and almost from the beginning productive of dismay, destruction, and death. [Captain Semmes in his official report says : "The firing now became very hot, and the enemy's shot and shell soon began to tell upon our hull. knocking down, killing, and disabling a number of men in different parts of the ship."] The *Kearsarge* gunners had been cautioned against firing without direct aim, and had been advised to point the heavy guns below rather than above the water-line, and to clear the deck of the enemy with the lighter ones. Though subjected to an incessant storm of shot and shell, they kept their stations and obeyed instructions.

The effect upon the enemy was readily perceived, and nothing could restrain the enthusiasm of our men. Cheer succeeded cheer; caps were thrown in the air or overboard ; jackets were discarded ; sanguine of victory, the men were shouting, as each projectile took effect: "That is a good one!" "Down, boys!" "Give her another like the last!" "Now we have her!" and so on, cheering and shouting to the end.

After the *Kearsarge* had been exposed to an uninterrupted cannonade for eighteen minutes, a 68-pounder Blakely shell passed through the starboard bulwarks below the main rigging, exploded upon the quarter-deck, and wounded three of the crew of the after pivot-gun. With these exceptions not an officer or man received serious injury. The three unfortunate men were speedily taken below, and so quietly was the act done that at the termination of the fight a large number of the men were unaware that any of their comrades were wounded. Two shots entered the ports occupied by the thirty-twos, where several men were stationed, one taking effect in the hammock-netting, the other going through the opposite port, yet none were hit. A shell exploded in the hammock-netting and set the ship on fire ; the alarm calling for fire-quarters was sounded, and men who had been detailed for such an emergency put out the fire, while the rest stayed at the guns.

It is wonderful that so few casualties occurred on board the *Kearsarge*, considering the number on the *Alabama* — the former having fired 173 shot and shell, and the latter nearly double that number. The *Kearsarge* concentrated her fire and poured in the 11-inch shells with deadly effect. One penetrated the coal-bunker of the *Alabama*, and a dense cloud of coal-dust arose. Others struck near the water-line between the main and mizzen masts, exploded within board, or, passing through, burst beyond. Crippled and torn, the *Alabama*, moved

REAR-ADMIRAL JOHN A. WINSLOW, CAPTAIN OF THE "KEARSARGE."
From a photograph taken soon after the fight.

THE BOAT FROM THE "ALABAMA" ANNOUNCING THE SURRENDER AND ASKING FOR ASSISTANCE.
The picture shows shot-marks in the thin deal covering of the chain armor amidships.

less quickly and began to settle by the stern, yet did not slacken her fire, but returned successive broadsides without disastrous result to us.

Captain Semmes witnessed the havoc made by the shells, especially by those of our after pivot-gun, and offered a reward to any one who would silence it. Soon his battery was turned upon this particular offending gun. It was in vain, for the work of destruction went on. We had completed the seventh rotation on the circular track and had begun the eighth, when the Alabama, now settling, sought to escape by setting all available sail (fore-trysail and two jibs), left the circle amid a shower of shot and shell, and headed for the French waters; but to no purpose. In winding, the Alabama presented the port battery, with only two guns bearing, and showed gaping sides, through which the water washed. The Kearsarge pursued, keeping on a line nearer the shore, and with a few well-directed shots hastened the sinking. Then the Alabama was at our mercy. Her colors were struck, and the Kearsarge ceased firing. I was told by our prisoners that two of the junior officers swore they would never surrender, and in a mutinous spirit rushed to the two port guns and opened fire upon the Kearsarge. [See page 266.] Captain Winslow, amazed at this extraordinary conduct of an enemy who had hauled down his flag in token of surrender, exclaimed, "He is playing us a trick; give him another broadside." Again the shot and shell went crashing through her sides,

and the Alabama continued to settle by the stern. The Kearsarge was laid across her bows for raking, and in position to use grape and canister.

A white flag was then shown over the stern of the Alabama and her ensign was half-masted, union down. Captain Winslow for the second time gave orders to cease firing. Thus ended the fight, after a duration of one hour and two minutes. Captain Semmes, in his report, says: "Although we were now but four hundred yards from each other, the enemy fired upon me five times after my colors had been struck. It is charitable to suppose that a ship-of-war of a Christian nation could not have done this intentionally." He is silent as to the renewal by the Alabama of the fight after his surrender—an act which, in Christian warfare, would have justified the Kearsarge in continuing the fire until the Alabama had sunk beneath the waters.

Boats were now lowered from the Alabama. Her master's-mate, Fullam, an Englishman, came alongside the Kearsarge with a few of the wounded, reported the disabled and sinking condition of his ship, and asked for assistance. Captain Winslow inquired, "Does Captain Semmes surrender his ship?" "Yes," was the reply. Fullam then solicited permission to return with his boat and crew to assist in rescuing the drowning, pledging his word of honor that when this was done he would come on board and surrender. Captain Winslow granted the request. With less generosity he could have detained the officer and men, supplied their places in the boat from his ship's company, secured more prisoners and afforded equal aid to the distressed. The generosity was abused, as the sequel shows. Fullam pulled to the midst of the drowning, rescued several officers, went to the yacht, Deerhound, and cast his boat adrift, leaving a number of men struggling in the water.

It was now seen that the Alabama was settling fast. The wounded, and the boys who could not swim, were sent away in the quarter-boats, the waist-boats having been destroyed. Captain Semmes dropped his sword into the sea and jumped overboard with the remaining officers and men.

Coming under the stern of the Kearsarge from the windward, the Deerhound was hailed, and her commander requested by Captain Winslow to run down and assist in picking up the men of the sinking ship. Or, as her owner, Mr. John Lancaster, re-

ported: "The fact is, that when we passed the Kearsarge the captain cried out, 'For God's sake, do what you can to save them'; and that was my warrant for interfering in any way for the aid and succor of his enemies." The Deerhound was built by the Lairds at the same time and in the same yard with the Alabama. Throughout the action she kept about a mile to the windward of the contestants. After being hailed she steamed toward the Alabama, which sank almost immediately after. This was at 12:24. The Alabama sank in forty-five fathoms of water, at a distance of about four and a half miles from the breakwater, off the west entrance. She was severely hulled between the main and mizzen masts, and settled by the stern; the main-mast, pierced by a shot at the very last, broke off near the head and went over the side, the bow lifted high from the water, and then came the end. Suddenly assuming a perpendicular position, caused by the falling aft of the battery and stores, straight as a plumb-line, stern first, she went down, the jib-boom being the last to appear above water. Thus sank the terror of merchantmen, riddled through and through, and as she disappeared to her last resting-place there was no cheer; all was silent.

The yacht lowered her two boats, rescued Captain Semmes (wounded in the hand by broken iron rigging), First Lieutenant Kell, twelve officers, and twenty-six men, leaving the rest of the survivors to the two boats of the Kearsarge. Apparently aware that the forty persons he had rescued would be claimed, Mr. Lancaster steamed away as fast as he could, direct for Southampton, without waiting for such surgical assistance as the Kearsarge might render. Captain Winslow permitted the yacht to secure his prisoners, anticipating their subsequent surrender. Again his confidence was misplaced, and he afterward wrote: "It was my mistake at the moment that I could not recognize an enemy who, under the garb of a friend, was affording assistance." The aid of the yacht, it is

presumed, was asked in a spirit of chivalry, for the Kearsarge, comparatively uninjured, with but three wounded, and a full head of steam, was in condition to engage a second enemy. Instead of remaining at a distance of about four hundred yards from the Alabama, and from this position sending two boats, the other boats being injured, the Kearsarge by steaming close to the settling ship, and in the midst of the defeated, could have captured all — Semmes, officers, and men. Captain Semmes says: "There was no appearance of any boat coming to me from the enemy after the ship went down. Fortunately, however, the steam-yacht Deerhound, owned by a gentleman of Lancashire, England, Mr. John Lancaster, who was himself on board, steamed up in the midst of my drowning men, and rescued a number of both officers and men from the water. I was fortunate enough myself thus to escape to the shelter of the neutral flag, together with about forty others, all told. About this time the Kearsarge sent one, and then, tardily, another boat."

This imputation of inhumanity is contradicted by Mr. Lancaster's assertion that he was requested to do what he could to save "the poor fellows who were struggling in the water for their lives."

The Deerhound edged to the leeward and steamed rapidly away. An officer approached Captain Winslow and reported the presence of Captain Semmes and many officers on board the English yacht. Believing the information authentic, as it was obtained from the prisoners, he suggested the expediency of firing a shot to bring her to, and asked permission. Captain Winslow declined, saying "it was impossible; the yacht was simply coming round." Meanwhile the Deerhound increased the distance from the Kearsarge; another officer spoke to him in similar language, but with more positiveness. Captain Winslow replied that no Englishman who carried the flag of the Royal Yacht Squadron could so act. The Deerhound continued her

THE SINKING OF THE "ALABAMA."

300

flight, and yet another officer urged the necessity of firing a shot. With undiminished confidence Captain Winslow refused, saying the yacht was "simply coming round," and would not go away without communicating. The escape of the yacht and her coveted prize was manifestly regretted. The famed *Alabama*, "a formidable ship, the terror of American commerce, well armed, well manned, well handled," was destroyed, "sent to the bottom in an hour," but her commander had escaped; the victory seemed already lessened. It was held by the Navy Department that Captain Semmes violated the usages of war in surrendering to Captain Winslow through the agency of one of his officers and then effecting an escape during the execution of the commission; that he was a prisoner of the United States Government from the moment he sent the officer to make the surrender.* . . .

The *Kearsarge* received twenty-eight shot and shell, of which thirteen were in the hull, the most efficient being abaft the mainmast. A 100-pounder rifle shell entered at the starboard quarter and lodged in the stern-post. The blow shook the ship from stem to stern. Luckily the shell did not explode, otherwise the result would have been serious, if not fatal. A 32-pounder shell entered forward of the forward pivot port, crushing the waterways, raising the gun and carriage, and lodged, but did not explode, else many of the gun's crew would likely have been injured by the fragments and splinters. The smoke-pipe was perforated by a rifle shell, which exploded inside and tore a ragged hole nearly three feet in diameter, and carried away three of the chain guys. Three boats were shattered. The cutting away of the rigging was mostly about the mainmast. The spars were left in good order. A large number of pieces of burst shell were gathered from the deck and thoughtlessly thrown overboard. . . .

At 3:10 P. M. the *Kearsarge* anchored in Cherbourg harbor close by the ship-of-war *Napoleon*, and was soon surrounded by boats of every description filled with excited and inquisitive people. Ambulances, by order of the French admiral, were

* The controversy in reference to the *Deerhound* is summarized thus in a letter from Professor James Russell Soley, U. S. N. :

"A neutral ship, in general, could have no right to take part in hostilities even to the extent of rescuing the drowning sailors of a belligerent, their situation being a part and a consequence of the battle. In the case of the *Deerhound*, however, the interference was directly authorized by Captain Winslow's request, addressed to Mr. Lancaster, and therefore the latter committed no breach of neutrality in taking the prisoners on board. Once on board the English yacht, however, they were as free as air. So far from its being the obligation of the *Deerhound* to surrender them, the obligation was exactly the other way. Their surrender would have been as gross a violation of neutrality toward the Confederates as their unauthorized rescue would have been toward the Union Government. Captain Winslow was therefore perfectly right in refusing to detain the *Deerhound*, since the conduct of the yacht was the necessary and logical consequence of his own act. The point where he was clearly in the wrong was in making the request in the first place. What he should have done, as Surgeon-General Browne clearly intimates, was to have steamed up close to the sinking *Alabama*, and saved her people himself, instead of remaining four hundred yards off."

It will be noticed that this statement leaves untouched the question of the right of a prisoner to escape after surrender and before delivering himself up.

THE UNITED STATES SCREW-SLOOP "KEARSARGE" AT THE TIME OF THE ENCOUNTER WITH THE "ALABAMA."

When the "Kearsarge" was at the Azores, a few months before the fight with the "Alabama," Midshipman Edward E. Preble made a mathematically correct drawing of the ship, and from a photograph of that drawing the above picture was made. After the fight alterations were made in the "Kearsarge" which considerably changed her appearance.

sent to the landing to receive the wounded, and thence they were taken to the Hôpital de la Marine, where arrangements had been made for their reception. Dr. Galt and all the prisoners except four officers were paroled and sent on shore before sunset. Secretary Welles soon after expressed his disapprobation of this action. . . .

Captain Semmes in his official report says:

"At the end of the engagement it was discovered, by those of our officers who went alongside the enemy's ship with the wounded, that her midship section on both sides was thoroughly iron-coated. The planking had been ripped off in every direction by our shot and shell, the chain broken and indented in many places, and forced partly into the ship's side. The enemy was heavier than myself, both in ship, battery, and crew; but I did not know until the action was over that she was also iron-clad."

The ships were well matched in size, speed, armament, and crew, showing a likeness rarely seen in naval battles. The number of the ship's company of the *Kearsarge* was 163. That of the *Alabama*, from the best information, was estimated at 150.

The chain plating was made of one hundred and twenty fathoms of sheet-chains of one and seventeenths inch iron, covering a space amidships of forty-nine and one-half feet in length by six feet two inches in depth, stopped up and down to eye-bolts with marlines, secured by iron dogs, and employed for the purpose of protecting the engines when the upper part of the coal-bunkers was empty, as happened during the action. The chains were concealed by one-inch deal-boards as a finish. The chain plating was struck by a 32-pounder shot in the starboard gangway, which cut the chain and bruised the planking; and by a 32-pounder shell, which broke a link of the chain, exploded, and tore away a portion of the deal covering. Had the shot been from the 100-pounder rifle the result would have been different, though without serious damage, because the shot struck five feet above the water-line, and if sent through the side would have cleared the machinery and boilers. It is proper,

therefore, to assert that in the absence of the chain armor the result would have been nearly the same, notwithstanding the common opinion at the time that the *Kearsarge* was an "ironclad" contending with a wooden ship. The chains were fastened to the ship's sides more than a year previous to the fight, while at the Azores. It was the suggestion of the executive officer, Lieutenant-Commander James S. Thornton, to hang the sheet-chain (or spare anchor-cable) over the sides, so as to protect the midship section, he having served with Admiral Farragut in passing the forts to reach New Orleans, and having observed its benefit on that occasion. The work was done in three days, at a cost for material not exceeding seventy-five dollars. In our visit to European ports, the use of sheet-chains for protective purposes had attracted notice and caused comment. It is strange that Captain Semmes did not know of the chain armor; supposed spies had been on board and had been shown through the ship, as there was no attempt at concealment; the same pilot had been employed by both ships, and had visited each during the preparation for battle. The *Alabama* had bunkers full of coal, which brought her down in the water. The *Kearsarge* was deficient in seventy tons of coal of her proper supply, but the sheet-chains stowed outside gave protection to her partly-filled bunkers.

This Sunday naval duel was fought in the presence of more than 15,000 spectators, who, upon the heights of Cherbourg, the breakwater, and rigging of men-of-war, witnessed "the last of the *Alabama*." Among them were the captains, their families, and crews of two merchant ships burnt by the daring cruiser a few days before her arrival at Cherbourg, where they were landed in a nearly destitute condition. Many spectators were provided with spy-glasses and camp-stools. The *Kearsarge* was burning Newcastle coals, and the *Alabama* Welsh coals, the difference in the amount of smoke enabling the movements of each ship to be distinctly traced. An excursion train from Paris arrived in the morning, bringing hundreds of plea-

sure-seekers, who were unexpectedly favored with the spectacle of a sea-fight. A French gentleman at Boulogne-sur-Mer assured me that the fight was the conversation of Paris for more than a week.

NOTE.—Twelve Confederate cruisers figured in the so-called "*Alabama* Claims" settlement with England. Named in the order of the damage inflicted by each, these cruisers were: the *Alabama*, *Shenandoah*, *Florida*, *Tallahasse*, *Georgia*, *Chickamauga*, *Sumter*, *Nashville*, *Retribution*, *Jeff. Davis*, *Sallie*, and *Boston*. The actual losses inflicted by the *Alabama* ($7,050,293.76, according to claims for ships and cargoes filed up to March 15th, 1872) were only about $400,000 greater than those inflicted by the *Shenandoah*. The sum total of the claims filed against the twelve cruisers, for ships and cargoes, up to March 15th, 1872, was $19,782,917.60, all but about six millions of it being charged to the account of the *Alabama* and *Shenandoah*.

On May 8th, 1871, the Treaty of Washington was concluded, in accordance with which a Tribunal of Arbitration was appointed, which assembled at Geneva. It consisted of Count Frederick Sclopis, named by the King of Italy; Mr. Jacob Staempfli, named by the President of the Swiss Confederation; Viscount d'Itajuba, named by the Emperor of Brazil; Mr. Charles Francis Adams, named by the President of the United States; and Sir Alexander Cockburn, named by the Queen of Great Britain. The Counsel of Great Britain was Sir Roundell Palmer (afterward Lord Selborne). The United States was represented by William M. Evarts, Caleb Cushing, and Morrison R. Waite. Claims were made by the United States for indirect and national losses, as well as for the actual private losses represented by nearly twenty millions on ships and cargoes.

The Tribunal decided that England was in no way responsible for the $1,781,915.43 of losses inflicted by the *Tallahassee*, *Georgia*, *Chickamauga*, *Nashville*, *Retribution*, *Jeff. Davis*, *Sallie*, *Boston*, and *Sumter*; and on September 14th, 1872, it awarded $15,500,000 damages for actual losses of ships and cargoes and interest, on account of the *Alabama*, the *Florida* and her tenders, and the *Shenandoah* after she left Melbourne.

THE SHELL IN THE STERN-POST OF THE "KEARSARGE."

The charge was withdrawn from the shell, which was boxed in, and in that condition it remained for months, until the ship reached Boston, where, when the vessel was repaired, a section of the stern-post containing the embedded shell was cut away and sent to the Navy Department, and was finally deposited in the Ordnance Museum, at the Navy Yard, Washington.—J. M. B.

MARCHING THROUGH GEORGIA.

RAILWAY DESTRUCTION AS A MILITARY ART.

SHERMAN'S MARCH FROM ATLANTA THROUGH GEORGIA AND THE CAROLINAS.

FROM ATLANTA TO SAVANNAH.

BY OLIVER O. HOWARD, MAJOR-GENERAL, U. S. A.
Commanding the right wing of Sherman's army.

WHEN Sherman decided to march South from Atlanta, he ordered to Thomas at Nashville, Schofield with the Twenty-third Corps, Stanley with the Fourth Corps, all the cavalry, except Kilpatrick's division, all the detachments drawn back from the railway line, and such other troops, including A. J. Smith's, as Sherman's military division could furnish. Sherman reserved for his right wing my two corps, the Fifteenth and Seventeenth; and for his left wing the Fourteenth and Twentieth under Slocum. Mine, the Army of the Tennessee, numbered 33,000; Slocum's, the "Army of Georgia," 30,000; Kilpatrick's division of cavalry, 5000; so that the aggregate of all arms was 68,000 men. All surplus stores and trains were sent back to Tennessee. The railway south of the Etowah was next completely demolished. Under the ef-

RAISING THE UNION FLAG OVER THE OLD STATE-HOUSE, COLUMBIA.

ficient management of Colonel O. M. Poe, Sherman's chief engineer, all that was of a public nature in Atlanta which could aid the enemy was destroyed. Wrecked engines, bent and twisted iron rails, blackened ruins and lonesome chimneys saddened the hearts of the few peaceful citizens who remained there.

Behold now this veteran army thus reorganized and equipped, with moderate baggage and a few days' supply of small rations, but with plenty of ammunition, ready to march anywhere Sherman might lead. Just before starting, Sherman had a muscular lameness in one arm that gave him great trouble. On a visit to him I found his servant bathing and continuously rubbing the arm. As I understood the general's ruling, I would command next to him, because I had from the President an assignment to an army and a department. I was therefore especially anxious to know fully his plans, and plainly told him so. While the rubbing went on he explained in detail what he proposed and pointed significantly to Goldsboro', North Carolina, on his map, saying, "I hope to get there." On November 15th we set forth in good earnest. Slocum, Sherman accompanying him, went by the Augusta Railroad, and passed on through Milledgeville. I followed the Macon Railroad, and for the first seven days had Kilpatrick with me.

Notwithstanding our reduction of the impedimenta, our wagon trains were still long, and always a source of anxiety. Pushing toward Macon, I found some resistance from General G. W. Smith's new levies. The crossing of the Ocmulgee, with its steep and muddy banks, was hard enough for the trains. I protected them by a second demonstration from the left bank against Macon.

Smith crossed the river and gave us battle at Griswoldville. It was an affair of one division,—that of Charles R. Woods,—using mainly Walcutt's brigade. Smith was badly defeated, and during the mêlée our trains were hurried off to Gordon and parked there in safety. Here, at Gordon, Sherman, from Milledgeville, came across to me. Slocum had enjoyed a fine march, having had but little resistance. The stories of the mock Legislature at the State capital, of the luxurious supplies enjoyed all along, and of the constant fun and pranks of "Sherman's Bummers," rather belonged to that route than ours. Possibly we had more of the throngs of escaping slaves, from the baby in arms to the old negro hobbling painfully along the line of march — negroes of all sizes, in all sorts of patched costumes, with carts and broken-down horses and mules to match.

We brought along our wounded (over 200, I believe) in ambulances, and though they were jolted over corduroy roads and were much exposed to hardship, and participated in the excitements of the march, they all reached Savannah without the loss of a life. Our system of foraging was sufficiently good for the army, but the few citizens, women and children, who remained at home, suffered greatly. We marched our divisions on parallel roads when we could find them; but sometimes, using rails or newly cut poles, made our roads through swamps and soft ground, employing thousands of men. Arriving at the Oconee, Osterhaus found a wooded valley, with lagune bridges and a narrow causeway, on his road. A division of Hardee's, who himself had left Hood and gone to Savannah to command what Confederates he could hastily gather, had marched out to meet us and was intrenched on the east bank. Artillery and infantry fire swept our road. Osterhaus, excited by the shots, came to me shaking his head and asking how we could get any further. "Deploy your skirmishers more and more till there is no reply," I said. He did so. A half mile above he was able to send over among the cypresses a brigade in boats. The Confederate division gave

way and fled. Then shortly our bridge was laid on the main road and we marched on. Blair, who had returned from his furlough before we left Atlanta, crossed and kept the left bank of the Ogeechee, and Sherman usually accompanied him. Blair's knowledge and hospitality attracted him. So the armies went on meeting an increased resistance, but were not much delayed till we got to the Savannah Canal. Captain Duncan from my cavalry escort had carried Sherman's messages down the Ogeechee in a boat past Confederate guards and torpedoes, and gone out to sea. He was picked up by a United States vessel and his message taken to the admiral. Hence navy and provision ships were waiting off the headlands, uncertain just where Sherman would secure a harbor.

Owing to swamps and obstructed roads and Hardee's force behind them, we could not enter Savannah. Our food was getting low. True, Sherman had sent Kilpatrick to try and take Fort McAllister, a strong fort which held the mouth of the Ogeechee. But as its capture was too much for the cavalry, I asked Sherman to allow me to take that fort with infantry. Hazen's division was selected. My chief engineer, Reese, with engineers and pioneers and plenty of men to help him, in three days repaired the burnt bridge, over 1000 feet long, near King's house. Hazen, ready at the bridge, then marched over and took Fort McAllister by assault, which Sherman and I witnessed from the rice mill, some miles away on the other bank of the Ogeechee. Now we connected with the navy, and our supplies flowed in abundantly. Slocum soon put a force beyond the Savannah. Hardee, fearing to be penned up, abandoned his works and fled during the night before Slocum had seized his last road to the east. On December 21st the campaign culminated as Sherman entered Savannah. He sent the following despatch to President Lincoln, which he received Christmas Eve: "I beg to present to you, as a Christmas gift, the city of Savannah, with one hundred and fifty heavy guns and plenty of ammunition, and also about twenty-five thousand bales of cotton."

SHERMAN'S ARMY LEAVING ATLANTA.
From a sketch made at the time.

FROM SAVANNAH TO FAYETTEVILLE.

BY HENRY W. SLOCUM, MAJOR-GENERAL, U. S. V.
Commanding the left wing of Sherman's army.

. . . About one month was spent in Savannah in clothing the men and filling the trains with ammunition and rations. Then commenced the movement which was to make South Carolina feel the severities of war. . . . On leaving Savannah our right wing threatened Charleston and the left again threatened Augusta, the two wings being again united in the interior of South Carolina, leaving the Confederate troops at Augusta with almost a certainty that Charleston must fall without a blow from Sherman. On the arrival of the left wing at Sister's Ferry on the Savannah, instead of finding, as was anticipated, a river a few yards in width which could be easily crossed, they found a broad expanse of water which was utterly impassable. The continuous rain-fall had caused the river to overflow, so that the lowland on the South Carolina side was covered with water, extending nearly half a mile from the river. We were delayed several days in vain efforts to effect a crossing, and were finally compelled to await the falling of the waters. Our pontoon-bridge was finally constructed and the crossing commenced. Each regiment as it entered South Carolina gave three cheers. The men seemed to realize that at last they had set foot on the State which had done more than all others to bring upon the country the horrors of civil war. In the narrow road leading from the ferry on the South Carolina side torpedoes had been planted, so that several of our men were killed or wounded by treading upon them. This was unfortunate for that section of the State. Planting torpedoes for the defense of a position is legitimate warfare, but our soldiers regarded the act of placing them in a highway where no contest was anticipated as something akin to poisoning a stream of water; it is not recognized as fair or legitimate warfare. If that section of South Carolina suffered more severely than any other it was due in part to the blundering of people who were more zealous than wise.

About February 19th the two wings of the army were reunited in the vicinity of Branchville, a small village on the South Carolina Railroad at the point where the railroad from Charleston to Columbia branches off to Augusta. Here we resumed the work which had occupied so much of our time in Georgia, viz., the destruction of railroads.*

Having effectually destroyed over sixty miles of railroads in this section, the army started for Columbia, the capital of South Carolina, each corps taking a separate road. . . . During the night of February 17th the greater portion of the city of Columbia was burned. The lurid flames could easily be seen from my camp, many miles distant. Nearly all the public buildings, several churches,

---

*A knowledge of the art of building railroads is certainly of more value to a country than that of the best means of destroying them; but at this particular time the destruction seemed necessary, and the time may again come when such work will have to be done. Lest the most effectual and expeditious method of destroying railroad tracks should become one of the lost arts, I will here give a few rules for the guidance of officers who may in future be charged with this important duty. It should be remembered that these rules are the result of long experience and close observation. A detail of men to do the work should be made on the evening before operations are to commence. The number to be detailed being, of course, dependent upon the amount of work to be done, I estimate that one thousand men can easily destroy about five miles of track per day, and do it thoroughly. Before going out in the morning the men should be supplied with a good breakfast, for it has been discovered that soldiers are more efficient at this work, as well as on the battle-field, when their stomachs are

GENERAL SHERMAN SENDING HIS LAST TELEGRAM BEFORE CUTTING THE WIRES AND ABANDONING ALL COMMUNICATION WITH THE NORTH.
From a sketch made at the time.

full than when they are empty. The question as to the food to be given the men for breakfast is not important, but I suggest roast turkeys, chickens, fresh eggs, and coffee, for the reason that in an enemy's country such a breakfast will cause no unpleasantness between the commissary and the soldiers, inasmuch as the commissary will only be required to provide the coffee. In fact it has been discovered that an army moving through a hostile but fertile country, having an efficient corps of foragers (vulgarly known in our army as "bummers"), requires but few articles of food, such as hard-tack, coffee, salt, pepper, and sugar. Your detail should be divided into three sections of about equal numbers. I will suppose the detail to consist of three thousand men. The first thing to be done is to reverse the relative positions of the ties and iron rails, placing the ties up and the rails under them. To do this, Section No. 1, consisting of one thousand men, is distributed along one side of the track, one man at the end of each tie. At a given signal each man seizes a tie, lifts it gently till it assumes a vertical position, and then at another signal pushes it forward so that when it falls the ties will be over the rails. Then each man loosens his tie from the rail. This done, Section No. 1 moves forward to another portion of the road, and Section No. 2 advances and is distributed along the portion of the road recently occupied by Section No. 1. The duty of the second section is to collect the ties, place them in piles of about thirty ties each — place the rails on the top of these piles, the center of each rail being over the center of the pile, and then set fire to the ties. Section No. 2 then follows No. 1. As soon as the rails are sufficiently heated Section No. 3 takes the place of No. 2; and upon this devolves the most important duty, viz., the effectual destruction of the rail. This section should be in command of an efficient officer who will see that the work is not slighted. Unless closely watched, soldiers will content themselves with simply bending the rails around trees. This should never be permitted. A rail which is simply bent can easily be restored to its original shape. No rail should be regarded as properly treated till it has assumed the shape of a doughnut; it must not only be bent, but twisted. To do the twisting, Poe's railroad hooks are necessary, for it has been found that the soldiers will not seize the hot iron bare-handed. This, however, is the only thing looking toward the destruction of property which I ever knew a man in Sherman's army to decline doing. With Poe's hooks a double twist can be given to a rail, which precludes all hope of restoring it to its former shape except by re-rolling.—H. W. S.

HOOK USED BY GENERAL SHERMAN'S ARMY FOR TWISTING AND DESTROYING RAILROAD IRON.

an orphan asylum, and many of the residences were destroyed. The city was filled with helpless women and children and invalids, many of whom were rendered houseless and homeless in a single night. No sadder scene was presented during the war. The suffering of so many helpless and innocent persons could not but move the hardest heart. The question as to who was immediately responsible for this disaster has given rise to some controversy. I do not believe that General Sherman countenanced or was in any degree responsible for it. I believe the immediate cause of the disaster was a free use of whisky (which was supplied to the soldiers by citizens with great liberality). A drunken soldier with a musket in one hand and a match in the other is not a pleasant visitor to have about the house on a dark, windy night, particularly when for a series of years you have urged him to come, so that you might have an opportunity of performing a surgical operation on him.

From Columbia the army moved toward Fayetteville—the left wing crossing the Catawba River at Rocky Mount. While the rear of the Twentieth Corps was crossing, our pontoon-bridge was swept away by flood-wood brought down the river, leaving the Fourteenth Corps on the south side. This caused a delay of three days, and gave rise to some emphatic instructions from Sherman to the commander of the left wing—which instructions resulted in our damming the flood-wood to some extent, but not in materially expediting the march.

On the 3d of March we arrived at Cheraw, where we found a large supply of stores sent from Charleston for safe-keeping. . . . The march through South Carolina had been greatly delayed by the almost incessant rains and the swampy nature of the country. More than half the way we were compelled to corduroy the roads before our trains could be moved. To accomplish this work we had been supplied with axes, and the country was covered with saplings well suited to the purpose.

Three or four days prior to our arrival at Fayetteville General Sherman had received information that Wilmington was in possession of General Terry, and had sent two messengers with letters

GENERAL WM. B. HAZEN.　　GENERAL W. T. SHERMAN.　　GENERAL HENRY W. SLOCUM.
GENERAL O. O. HOWARD.　　GENERAL JOHN A. LOGAN.　　GENERAL JEFF. C. DAVIS.　　GENERAL J. A. MOWER.
From a photograph.

informing Terry when he would probably be at Fayetteville. Both messengers arrived safely at Wilmington, and on Sunday, the day after our arrival at Fayetteville, the shrill whistle of a steam-boat floating the Stars and Stripes announced that we were once more in communication with our own friends. As she came up, the banks of the river were lined by our soldiers, who made the welkin ring with their cheers. The opening of communication with Wilmington not only brought us our mails and a supply of clothing, but enabled us to send to a place of safety thousands of refugees and contrabands who were following the army and seriously embarrassing it. We were dependent upon the country for our supplies of food and forage, and every one not connected with the army was a source of weakness to us. On several occasions on the march from Atlanta we had been compelled to drive thousands of colored people back, not from lack of sympathy with them, but simply as a matter of safety to the army. The refugee-train following in the rear of the army was one of the most singular features of the march. Long before the war, the slaves of the South had a system of communication by which important

information was transmitted from one section of the country to another. The advance of Sherman's army through a section never before visited by a Union soldier was known far and wide many miles in advance of us. It was natural that these poor creatures, seeking a place of safety, should flee to the army, and endeavor to keep in sight of it. Every day as we marched on we could see, on each side of our line of march, crowds of these people coming to us through roads and across the fields, bringing with them all their earthly goods, and many goods which were not theirs. Horses, mules, cows, dogs, old family carriages, carts, and whatever they thought might be of use to them was seized upon and brought to us. They were allowed to follow in rear of our column, and at times they were almost equal in numbers to the army they were following. As singular, comical, and pitiable a spectacle was never before presented. One day a large family of slaves came through the fields to join us. The head of the family, a venerable negro, was mounted on a mule, and safely stowed away behind him in pockets or bags attached to the blanket which covered the mule were two little pickaninnies, one on each

side. This gave rise to a most important invention, i. e., "the best way of transporting pickaninnies." On the next day a mule appeared in column, covered by a blanket with two pockets on each side, each containing a little negro. Very soon old tent-flies or strong canvas was used instead of the blanket, and often ten or fifteen pockets were attached to each side, so that nothing of the mule was visible except the head, tail, and feet, all else being covered by the black woolly heads and bright shining eyes of the little darkies. Occasionally a cow was made to take the place of the mule; this was a decided improvement, as the cow furnished rations as well as transportation for the babies. Old stages, family carriages, carts and lumber wagons filled with bedding, cooking utensils and "traps" of all kinds, with men, women, and children loaded with bundles, made up the balance of the refugee-train which followed in our rear. As all the bridges were burned in front of us, our pontoon-trains were in constant use, and the bridges could be left but a short time for the use of the refugees. A scramble for precedence in crossing the bridge always occurred. The firing of a musket or pistol in rear would bring to the refugees visions of guerrillas, and then came a panic. As our bridges were not supplied with guard-rails, occasionally a mule would be crowded off, and with its precious load would float down the river.

Having thoroughly destroyed the arsenal buildings, machine-shops, and foundries at Fayetteville, we crossed the Cape Fear River on the 13th and 14th and resumed our march. We were now entering upon the last stage of the great march which was to unite the Army of the West with that of the East in front of Richmond. If this march could be successfully accomplished the Confederacy was doomed. General Sherman did not hope or expect to accomplish it without a struggle. He anticipated an attack and made provision for it. He ordered me to send my baggage-trains under a strong escort by an interior road on my right, and to keep at least four divisions with their artillery on my left, ready for an attack. . . . Our march to this point had been toward Raleigh. We now took the road leading to Goldsboro'.

MARCHING WITH SHERMAN THROUGH THE CAROLINAS.

BY DANIEL OAKEY, CAPTAIN 2D MASSACHUSETTS VOLUNTEERS.

. . . We were proud of our foragers. They constituted a picked force from each regiment, under an officer selected for the command, and were remarkable for intelligence, spirit, and daring. Before daylight, mounted on horses captured on the plantations, they were in the saddle and away, covering the country sometimes seven miles in advance. Although I have said "in the saddle," many a forager had nothing better than a bit of carpet and a rope halter; yet this simplicity of equipment did not abate his power of carrying off hams and sweet-potatoes in the face of the enemy. The foragers were also important as a sort of advance guard, for they formed virtually a curtain of mounted infantry screening us from the inquisitive eyes of parties of Wheeler's cavalry, with whom they did not hesitate to engage when it was a question of a rich plantation.

When compelled to retire, they resorted to all the tricks of infantry skirmishers, and summoned reinforcements of foragers from other regiments to help drive the "Johnnies" out. When success crowned their efforts, the plantation was promptly stripped of live stock and eatables. The natives were accustomed to bury provisions, for they feared their own soldiers quite as much as they feared ours. These subterranean stores were readily discovered by the practised "Yankee" eye. The appearance of the ground and a little probing with a ramrod or a bayonet soon decided whether to dig. Teams were improvised; carts and vehicles of all sorts were pressed into the service and loaded with provisions. If any antiquated militia uniforms were discovered, they were promptly donned, and a comical procession escorted the valuable train of booty to the point where the brigade was expected to bivouac for the night. The regimentals of the past, even to those of revolutionary times, were often conspicuous.

On an occasion when our brigade had the advance, several parties of foragers, consolidating themselves, captured a town from the enemy's cavalry, and occupied the neighboring plantations. Before the arrival of the main column hostilities had ceased; order had been restored, and mock arrangements were made to receive the army. Our regiment in the advance was confronted by a picket dressed in continental uniform, who waved his plumed hat in response to the gibes of the men, and galloped away on his bareback mule to apprise his comrades of our approach. We marched into the town and rested on each side of the main street. Presently a forager, in ancient militia uniform indicating high rank, debouched from a side street to do the honors of the occasion. He was mounted on a raw-boned horse with a bit of carpet for a saddle. His old plumed chapeau in hand, he rode with gracious dignity through the street, as if reviewing the brigade. After him came a family carriage laden with hams, sweet-potatoes, and other provisions, and drawn by two horses, a mule, and a cow, the two latter ridden by postilions.

The march through Georgia has been called a grand military promenade, all novelty and excitement. But its moral effect on friend and foe was

CONTRABANDS IN THE WAKE OF SHERMAN'S ARMY.

immense. It proved our ability to lay open the heart of the Confederacy, and left the question of what we might do next a matter of doubt and terror. It served also as a preliminary training for the arduous campaign to come. Our work was incomplete while the Carolinas, except at a few points on the sea-coast, had not felt the rough contact of war. But their swamps and rivers, swollen and spread into lakes by winter floods, presented obstructions almost impracticable to an invading army, if opposed by even a very inferior force. The beginning of our march in South Carolina was pleasant, the weather favorable, and the country productive. Sometimes at the midday halt a stray pig that had cunningly evaded the foragers would venture forth in the belief of having escaped "the cruel war," and would find his error, alas! too late, by encountering our column. Instantly an armed mob would set upon him, and his piercing shrieks would melt away in the scramble for fresh pork. But the midday sport of the main column and the happy life of the forager were sadly interrupted. The sun grew dim, and the rain came and continued. A few of our excellent foragers were reported captured by Wheeler's cavalry, while we sank deeper and deeper in the mud as we approached the Salkehatchie Swamp, which lay between us and the Charleston and Augusta railroad. As the heads of column came up, each command knew what it had to do. General Mower and G. A. Smith got their divisions across by swimming, wading, and floating, and effected lodgments in spite of the enemy's fire. An overwhelming mass of drenched and muddy veterans swept away the enemy, while the rest of our force got the trains and artillery over by corduroying, pontooning, and bridging. It seemed a grand day's work to have accomplished, as we sank down that night in our miry bivouac. The gallant General Wager Swayne lost his leg in this Salkehatchie en-

counter. Luckily for him and others we were not yet too far from our friends to send the wounded back, with a strong escort, to Pocotaligo.

We destroyed about forty miles of the Charleston and Augusta railroad, and, by threatening points beyond the route we intended to take, we deluded the enemy into concentrating at Augusta and other places, while we marched rapidly away, leaving him well behind, and nothing but Wade Hampton's cavalry, and the more formidable obstacle of the Saluda River and its swamps, between us and Columbia, our next objective. As the route of our column lay west of Columbia, I saw nothing of the oft-described and much-discussed burning of that city.

During the hasty removal of the Union prisoners from Columbia two Massachusetts officers managed to make their escape. Exhausted and almost naked, they found their way to my command. My mess begged for the privilege of caring for one of them. We gave him a mule to ride with a comfortable saddle, and scraped together an outfit for him, although our clothes were in the last stages. Our guest found the mess luxurious, as he sat down with us at the edge of a rubber blanket spread upon the ground for a table-cloth, and set with tin cups and platters. Stewed fighting-cock and bits of fried turkey were followed by fried corn-meal and sorghum. Then came our coffee and pipes, and we lay down by a roaring fire of pine-knots, to hear our guest's story of life in a rebel prison. Before daybreak the tramp of horses reminded us that our foragers were sallying forth. The red light from the countless camp-fires melted away as the dawn stole over the horizon, casting its wonderful gradations of light and color over the masses of sleeping soldiers, while the smoke from burning pine-knots befogged the chilly morning air. Then the bugles broke the impressive stillness, and the roll of drums was heard on all sides. Soon the scene was alive with blue coats and the hubbub of roll-

calling, cooking, and running for water to the nearest spring or stream. The surgeons looked to the sick and footsore, and weeded from the ambulances those who no longer needed to ride.

It was not uncommon to hear shots at the head of the column. The foragers would come tumbling back, and ride alongside the regiment, adding to the noisy talk their account of what they had seen, and dividing among their comrades such things as they had managed to bring away in their narrow escape from capture. A staff-officer would gallop down the roadside like a man who had forgotten something which must be recovered in a hurry. At the sound of the colonel's ringing voice, silence was instant and absolute. Sabers flashed from their scabbards, the men brought their guns to the "carry," and the battalion swung into line at the roadside; cats, fighting-cocks, and frying-pans passed to the rear rank; officers and sergeants buzzed around their companies to see that the guns were loaded and the men ready for action. The color-sergeant loosened the water-proof cover of the battle-flag, a battery of artillery flew past on its way to the front, following the returning staff-officer, and we soon heard the familiar bang of shells. Perhaps it did not amount to much after all, and we were soon swinging into "route step" again.

At times when suffering from thirst it was hard to resist the temptation of crystal swamp water, as it rippled along the side of a causeway, a tempting sight for the weary and unwary. In spite of oft-repeated cautions, some contrived to drink it, but these were on their backs with malarial disease at the end of the campaign, if not sooner.

After passing Columbia there was a brief season of famine. The foragers worked hard, but found nothing. They made amends, however, in a day or two, bringing in the familiar corn-meal, sweet-potatoes, and bacon.

We marched into Cheraw with music and with colors flying. Stacking arms in the main street, we proceeded to supper, while the engineers laid the pontoons across the Pedee River. The railing of the town pump, and the remains of a buggy, said to belong to Mr. Lincoln's brother-in-law, Dr. Todd, were quickly reduced to kindling-wood to boil the coffee. The necessary destruction of property was quickly accomplished, and on we went. A mile from the Lumber River the country, already flooded ankle-deep, was rendered still more inhospitable by a steady down-pour of rain. The bridges had been partly destroyed by the enemy, and partly swept away by the flood. An attempt to carry heavy army wagons and artillery across this dreary lake might have seemed rather foolhardy, but we went to work without loss of time. The engineers were promptly floated out to the river, to direct the rebuilding of bridges, and the woods all along the line of each column soon rang with the noise of axes. Trees quickly became logs, and were brought to the submerged roadway. No matter if logs disappeared in the floating mud; thousands more were coming from all sides. So, layer upon layer, the work went bravely on. Soon the artillery and wagons were jolting over our wooden causeway. As my regiment was the rear-guard for the day, we had various offices to perform for the train, and it was midnight before we saw the last wagon over

A BIVOUAC AMONG THE GEORGIA PINES.

INCIDENT OF SHERMAN'S MARCH—THE FATE OF THE RAIL FENCE.

and could have no safeguards. The country was necessarily left to take care of itself, and became a "howling waste." The "coffee-coolers" of the Army of the Potomac were archangels compared to our "bummers," who often fell to the tender mercies of Wheeler's cavalry, and were never heard of again, earning a fate richly deserved.

On arriving within easy distance of the Cape Fear River, where we expected to communicate with the navy, detachments were sent in rapid advance to secure Fayetteville. Our division, after a hard day of corduroying in various spots over a distance of twelve miles, went into camp for supper, and then, taking the plank-road for Fayetteville, made a moonlight march of nine miles in three hours, but our friends from the right wing arrived there before us.

Hardee retired to a good position at Averysboro', where Kilpatrick found him intrenched and too strong for the cavalry to handle unassisted. It was the turn of our brigade to do special duty, so at about 8 o'clock in the evening we were ordered to join the cavalry. We were not quite sure it rained, but everything was dripping. The men furnished themselves with pine-knots, and our weapons glistened in the torch-light, a cloud of black smoke from the torches floating back over our heads. The regimental wits were as ready as ever, and amid a flow of lively badinage we toiled on through the mud.

When the column was halted for a few minutes to give us an opportunity of drawing breath, I found Sergeant Johnson with one arm in the mud up to the elbow. He explained that he was trying to find his shoe. We floundered on for five miles, and relieved a brigade of Kilpatrick's men whom we found in some damp woods. There was a comfort in clustering round their camp-fires, while they retired into outer darkness to prepare for the morning attack. But the cavalry fire-side was only a temporary refuge from the storm, for we also had to depart into the impenetrable darkness beyond, to await in wet line of battle the unforeseen. Those who were exhausted sank down in the mud to sleep, while others speculated on the future.

ADVANCING UNDER DIFFICULTIES.

DESTROYING A RAILROAD.

the bridge by the light of our pine torches. It seemed as if that last wagon was never to be got over. It came bouncing and bumping along, its six mules smoking and blowing in the black, misty air. The teamster, mounted on one of the wheelers, guided his team with a single rein and addressed each mule by name, reminding the animal of his faults, and accusing him of having among other peculiarities, "a black military heart." Every sentence of his oath-adorned rhetoric was punctuated with a dexterous whip-lash.

At last, drenched to the skin and covered with mud, I took my position on the bridge, seated in a chair which one of my men had presented to me, and waited for the command to "close up."

As we passed the wagon camp, there was the deafening, indescribable chorus of mules and teamsters, besides the hoarse shouting of quartermasters and wagon-masters plunging about on horse-

back through the mud, to direct the arriving teams into their places. But it all died away in the distance as we marched on to find the oozy resting-place of the brigade. The army had been in bivouac some hours, and countless camp-fires formed a vast belt of fire that spread out into the black night.

As we advanced into the wild pine regions of North Carolina, the natives seemed wonderfully impressed at seeing every road filled with marching troops, artillery and wagon-trains. They looked destitute enough as they stood in blank amazement gazing upon the "Yanks" marching by. The scene before us was very striking; the resin pits were on fire, and great columns of black smoke rose high into the air, spreading and mingling together in gray clouds, and suggesting the roofs and pillars of a vast temple. All traces of habitation were left behind, as we marched into that grand forest with its beautiful carpet of pine-needles. The straight trunks of the pine-tree shot up to a great height and then spread out into a green roof, which kept us in perpetual shade. As night came on, we found that the resinous sap in the cavities cut in the trees to receive it, had been lighted by "bummers" in our advance. The effect of these peculiar watch-fires on every side, several feet above the ground, with flames licking their way up the tall trunks, was peculiarly striking and beautiful. But it was sad to see this wanton destruction of property, which, like the firing of the resin pits, was the work of "bummers," who were marauding through the country committing every sort of outrage. There was no restraint except with the column or the regular foraging-parties. We had no communications,

THE STORMING OF THE LITTLE SALKEHATCHIE RIVER BY WEVER'S BRIGADE OF
THE FIFTEENTH CORPS.
From a war-time sketch.

THE ROAD FROM McPHERSONVILLE. SHERMAN AND HIS STAFF PASSING THROUGH
WATER AND MIRE.
From a sketch made at the time.

The clear wintry dawn disclosed a long line of blue-coats spread over the ground in motionless groups. This was the roaring torch-light brigade of the night before. The orders "Fall in!" "Forward!" in gruff tones broke upon the chilly air, and brought us shivering to our feet. We moved to the edge of the woods with the cavalry. The skirmish-line, under Captain J. I. Grafton, had already disappeared into the opposite belt of woods, and evidently were losing no time in developing the enemy and ascertaining his force. They were drawing his fire from all points, indicating a force more than double that of our brigade. Dismounted cavalry were now sent forward to prolong the skirmish-line. Captain Grafton was reported badly wounded in the leg, but still commanding with his usual coolness. Suddenly he appeared staggering out of the wood into the open space in our front, bareheaded, his face buried in his hands, his saber hanging by the sword-knot from his wrist, one leg bound up with a handkerchief, his uniform covered with blood; in a moment he fell toward the colors. Officers clustered about him in silence, and a gloom spread through the brigade as word passed that Grafton was dead.

The main column was now arriving, and as the troops filed off to the right and left of the road, and the field-guns galloped into battery, we moved forward to the attack. The enemy gave us a hot reception, which we returned with a storm of lead. It was a wretched place for a fight. At some points we had to support our wounded until they could be carried off, to prevent their falling into the swamp water, in which we stood ankle-deep. Here and there a clump of thick growth in the black mud

broke the line as we advanced. No ordinary troops were in our front. They would not give way until a division of Davis's corps was thrown upon their right, while we pressed them closely. As we passed over their dead and wounded, I came upon the body of a very young officer, whose handsome, refined face attracted my attention. While the line of battle swept past me I knelt at his side for a moment. His buttons bore the arms of South Carolina. Evidently we were fighting the Charleston chivalry. Sunset found us in bivouac on the Goldsboro' road, and Hardee in retreat.

As we trudged on toward Bentonville, distant sounds told plainly that the head of the column was engaged. We hurried to the front and went into action, connecting with Davis's corps. Little opposition having been expected, the distance be-

tween our wing and the right wing had been allowed to increase beyond supporting distance in the endeavor to find easier roads for marching as well as for transporting the wounded. The scope of this paper precludes a description of the battle of Bentonville, which was a combination of mistakes, miscarriages, and hard fighting on both sides. It ended in Johnston's retreat, leaving open the road to Goldsboro', where we arrived ragged and almost barefoot. While we were receiving letters from home, getting new clothes, and taking our regular doses of quinine, Lee and Johnston surrendered, and the great conflict came to an end.

CONCLUDING NOTE.

On leaving Fayetteville, Sherman directed his march toward Goldsboro', his army proceeding in two columns on roads several miles apart. Howard commanded the right wing, Slocum the left. Hardee's Confederates

from Savannah, reinforced by the garrison from Charleston, slowly retreated in face of the Union advance.

On the 19th of March, Slocum's column was checked near Bentonville by the stubborn resistance of a long line of the enemy, strongly intrenched. A Confederate deserter informed General Slocum that General Joseph E. Johnston was on his front at the head of a large army, and preparing to crush Sherman's columns in detail. Johnston, who was assigned to the command of the Department of the Carolinas on the 23d of February previous, had united with Hardee's force, three strong detachments from Hood's Army of the Tennessee, under Beauregard, Cheatham and Wheeler, Hampton's cavalry and Hoke's division of infantry from Virginia and Bragg's Army of North Carolina,* and was able to muster 25,000 to 30,000 men for battle. Slocum threw up slight intrenchments, covering the Fayetteville and Goldsboro' road near the intersection of that road with the one leading from Bentonville southward to Clinton, and received the Confederate assaults. These were repeated several times with great gallantry. During the night of the 19th and on the 20th Howard's advance brigades reached the field, having marched at the sound of the firing to Slocum's aid. On the 21st Sherman's united army enveloped Johnston's line on three sides, and during the night the latter retreated toward Raleigh.

From Bentonville Sherman continued his march to Goldsboro', which was already occupied by the Army of the Ohio, under Schofield, and the Tenth Corps, Army of the James, under General A. H. Terry. Schofield and Terry had occupied Wilmington after its evacuation by Bragg, February 22d, and opened the road to Goldsboro', encountering Bragg on the south bank of the Neuse and at Kingston, March 8th and 10th.

Sherman's army reached Goldsboro' about the 25th, and went into camp. On the 5th of April the general announced in a confidential order to his chief subordinates that the next objective would be the union of his armies at some point north of the Roanoke with those then operating under Grant against Lee. The 11th was the

* After the battle of Chattanooga General Bragg acted as confidential military adviser to President Davis, and in November, 1864, assumed command of the Department of North Carolina.

BENTONVILLE THE MORNING AFTER THE BATTLE.—THE SMOKE IS FROM RESIN THAT
WAS FIRED BY THE CONFEDERATES.
From a sketch made at the time.

date fixed for the movement to the new position, but on the morning of the 6th news of the fall of Richmond and the retreat of Lee toward North Carolina was received at Sherman's headquarters. Instead of marching to the Roanoke, Sherman moved toward Johnston's bivouac at Smithfield, a point midway between Goldsboro' and Raleigh. Reaching Smithfield on the 12th, Sherman found Johnston in retreat toward Raleigh. The next day a courier rode through Sherman's camps shouting "Grant has captured Lee's army!"

Sherman at once ordered his troops in motion to cut off Johnston's retreat southward, but before the movement commenced Johnston asked for a cessation of hostilities with a view of surrender. While on the way to meet Johnston, Sherman received a despatch announcing the assassination of the President. A conditional treaty was signed by Sherman and Johnston on the 18th, but was disapproved by the new executive, Vice-President Johnson, and on the 21st Grant ordered hostilities resumed against Johnston's command. Further negotiations under a flag of truce resulted in the surrender of Johnston's army on the 26th, upon the same terms Lee received from Grant (see p. 315). After the surrender Sherman's army marched to Washington by way of Richmond, Spotsylvania, Fredericksburg, and Manassas.

SHERIDAN AND HIS GENERALS RECONNOITERING AT FIVE FORKS.

upon a very animated discussion of the coming movements.

After his twenty-minutes' talk with Grant, Sheridan mounted his horse, and, waving us a good-by with his hand, rode off to Dinwiddie. The next morning, the 31st, he reported that the enemy had been hard at work intrenching at Five Forks and to a point about a mile west of there. Lee had been as prompt as Grant to recognize that Five Forks was a strategic point of great importance, and, to protect his right, had sent Pickett there with a large force of infantry and nearly all the cavalry. The rain continued during the night of the 30th, and on the morning of the 31st the weather was cloudy and dismal.

General Grant had expected that Warren would be attacked that morning, and had warned him to be on the alert. Warren advanced his corps to ascertain with what force the enemy held the White Oak road and to try to drive him from it; but before he had gone far he met with a vigorous assault. When news came of the attack General Grant directed

FIVE FORKS AND THE FALL OF PETERSBURG.

BY HORACE PORTER, BREVET BRIGADIER-GENERAL, U. S. A.

A member of General Grant's staff.

IT was 9 o'clock in the morning of the 29th of March, 1865. General Grant and the officers of his staff had bidden good-by to President Lincoln and mounted the passenger car of the special train that was to carry them from City Point to the front, and the signal was given to start; the train moved off—Grant's last campaign had begun. Since 3 o'clock that morning the columns had been in motion and the Union army and the Army of Northern Virginia were soon locked in a death-grapple. The President remained at City Point, where he could be promptly informed of the progress of the movement. . . . The general sat down near the end of the car, drew from his pocket the flint and slow-match that he always carried, which, unlike a match, never missed fire in a gale of wind, and was soon wreathed in the smoke of the inevitable cigar. I took a seat near him with several other officers of the staff, and he at once began to talk over his plans in detail. They had been discussed in general terms before starting out from City Point. It was his custom, when commencing a movement in the field, to have his staff-officers understand fully the

objects he wished to accomplish, and what each corps of the army was expected to do in different emergencies, so that these officers, when sent to distant points of the line, might have a full comprehension of the general's intentions, and so that, when communication with him was impossible or difficult, they might be able to instruct the subordinate commanders intelligently as to the intentions of the general-in-chief.

For a month or more General Grant's chief apprehension had been that the enemy might suddenly pull out from his intrenchments and fall back into the interior, where he might unite with General Joe Johnston against Sherman and force our army to follow Lee to a great distance from its base. General Grant had been sleeping with one eye open and one foot out of bed for many weeks, in the fear that Lee would thus give him the slip. . . . Referring to Mr. Lincoln, he said: "The President is one of the few visitors I have had who has not attempted to extract from me a knowledge of my plans. He not only never asked them, but says it is better he should not know them, and then

he can be certain to keep the secret. He will be the most anxious man in the country to hear the news from us, his heart is so wrapped up in our success, but I think we can send him some good news in a day or two." I never knew the general to be more sanguine of victory than in starting out on this campaign.

When we reached the end of the railroad we mounted our horses, which had been carried on the same train, started down the Vaughan road, and went into camp for the night in a field just south of that road, close to Gravelly Run. . . .

While standing in front of the general's tent on the morning of the 30th, discussing the situation with several others on the staff, I saw General Sheridan turning in from the Vaughan road with a staff-officer and an escort of about a dozen cavalrymen, and coming toward our headquarters camp. He was riding his white pacer, a horse which had been captured from General Breckinridge's adjutant-general at Missionary Ridge. But, instead of striking a pacing gait now, it was at every step driving its legs knee-deep into the quicksand with the regularity of a pile-driver. As soon as Sheridan dismounted, he was asked with much eagerness about the situation on the extreme left. He took a decidedly cheerful view of matters, and entered

me to go to the spot and look to the situation of affairs there. I found Ayres's division had been driven in, and both he and Crawford were falling back upon Griffin. Miles, of Humphreys's corps, was sent to reinforce Warren, and by noon the enemy was checked. As soon as General Grant was advised of the situation, he directed General Meade to take the offensive vigorously. . . .

I found Sheridan a little north of Dinwiddie Court House, and gave him an account of matters on the left of the Army of the Potomac. He said he had had one of the liveliest days in his experience, fighting infantry and cavalry with cavalry only, but that he was concentrating his command on the high ground just north of Dinwiddie, and would hold that position at all hazards. . . .

This proved to be one of the busiest nights of the whole campaign. Generals were writing despatches and telegraphing from dark till daylight. Staff-officers were rushing from one headquarters to another, wading through swamps, penetrating forests, and galloping over corduroy roads engaged in carrying instructions, getting information, and making extraordinary efforts to hurry up the movement of the troops.

The next morning, April 1st, General Grant said to me: "I wish you would spend the day

RAILROAD MORTAR, PETERSBURG.

Pickett's intrenched line began. . . .

Ayres threw out a skirmish-line and advanced across an open field, which sloped down gradually toward the dense woods, just north of the White Oak road. He soon met with a fire from the edge of this woods, a number of men fell, and the skirmish-line halted and seemed to waver. Sheridan now began to exhibit those traits that always made him such a tower of strength in the presence of an enemy. He put spurs to his horse and dashed along in front of the line of battle from left to right, shouting words of encouragement and having something cheery to say to every regiment. "Come on, men," he cried. "Go at 'em with a will. Move on at a clean jump or you'll not catch one of them. They're all getting ready to run now, and if you don't get on to them in five minutes, they'll every one get away from you! Now go for them." Just then a man on the skirmish-line was struck in the neck; the blood spurted as if the jugular vein had been cut. "I'm killed!" he cried, and dropped on the ground. "You're not hurt a bit," cried Sheridan; "pick up your gun, man, and move right on to the front." Such was the electric effect of his words that the poor fellow snatched up his musket and rushed forward a dozen paces before he fell never to rise again. The line of battle of weather-beaten veterans was now moving right along down the slope toward the woods with a steady swing that boded no good for Pickett's command, earth-works or no earth-works. Sheridan was mounted on his favorite black horse "Rienzi," that had carried him from Winchester to Cedar Creek, and which Buchanan Read made famous for all time by his poem of "Sheridan's Ride." The roads were muddy, the fields swampy, the undergrowth dense, and "Rienzi," as he plunged and curveted, dashed the foam from his mouth and the mud from his heels. Had the Winchester pike been in a similar condition, he would not have made his famous twenty miles without breaking his own neck and Sheridan's too. . . .

Soon Ayres's men met with a heavy fire on their left flank, and had to change direction by facing more toward the west. As the troops entered the woods and moved forward over the boggy ground and struggled through the dense undergrowth, they were staggered by a heavy fire from the angle and fell back in some confusion. Sheridan now rushed into the midst of the broken lines, and cried out: "Where is my battle-flag?" As the sergeant who carried it rode up, Sheridan seized the crimson and white standard, waved it above his head, cheered on the men, and made heroic efforts to close up the ranks. Bullets were hum-

with Sheridan's command, and send me a bulletin every half-hour or so, advising me fully as to the progress of his movements. You know my views, and I want you to give them to Sheridan fully. Tell him the contemplated movement is left entirely in his hands, and he must be responsible for its execution. I have every confidence in his judgment and ability. I hope there may now be an opportunity of fighting the enemy's infantry outside of its fortifications."

I set out with half a dozen mounted orderlies to act as couriers in transmitting field bulletins. . . . About 1 o'clock it was reported by the cavalry that the enemy was retiring to his intrenched position at Five Forks, which was just north of the White Oak road, and parallel to it, his earth-works running from a point about three-quarters of a mile east of Five Forks to a point a mile west, with an angle or crotchet about one hundred yards long thrown back at right angles to his left to protect that flank. Orders were at once given to the Fifth Corps to move up the Gravelly Run Church road to the open ground near the church, and form in order of battle, with Ayres on the left, Crawford on his right, and Griffin in rear as a reserve. . . .

But the movement was slow, the required formation seemed to drag, and Sheridan, chafing with impatience and consumed with anxiety, became as restive as a racer when he nears the score and is struggling to make the start. He made every possible appeal for promptness, he dismounted from his horse, paced up and down, struck the clinched fist of one hand into the palm of the other, and fretted like a caged tiger. He said at one time: "This battle must be fought and won before the sun goes down. All the conditions may be changed in the morning; we have but a few hours of daylight left us. My cavalry are rapidly exhausting their ammunition, and if the attack is delayed much longer they may have none left." And then another batch of staff-officers were sent out to gallop through the mud and hurry up the columns.

At 4 o'clock the formation was completed, the order for the assault was given, and the struggle for

ming like a swarm of bees. One pierced the battle-flag, another killed the sergeant who had carried it, another wounded Captain A. J. McGonnigle in the side, others struck two or three of the staff-officers' horses. All this time Sheridan was dashing from one point of the line to another, waving his flag, shaking his fist, encouraging, threatening, praying, swearing, the very incarnation of battle. It would be a sorry soldier who could help following such a leader. Ayres and his officers were equally exposing themselves at all points in rallying the men, and soon the line was steadied, for such material could suffer but a momentary check. Ayres, with drawn saber, rushed forward once more with his veterans, who now behaved as if they had fallen back to get a "good-ready," and with fixed bayonets and a rousing cheer dashed over the earth-works, sweeping everything before them, and killing or capturing every man in their immediate front whose legs had not saved him.

Sheridan spurred "Rienzi" up to the angle, and with a bound the horse carried his rider over the earth-works, and landed in the midst of a line of prisoners who had thrown down their arms and were crouching close under their breast-works. Some of them called out, "Whar do you want us all to go to?" Then Sheridan's rage turned to humor, and he had a running talk with the "Johnnies" as they filed past. "Go right over there," he said to them, pointing to the rear. "Get right along, now. Drop your guns; you'll never need them any more. You'll all be safe over there. Are there any more of you? We want every one of you fellows." Nearly 1500 were captured at the angle.

An orderly here came up to Sheridan and said: "Colonel Forsyth of your staff is killed, sir." "It's no such thing," cried Sheridan. "I don't believe a word of it. You'll find Forsyth's all right." Ten

minutes after Forsyth rode up. It was the gallant General Frederick Winthrop who had fallen in the assault and had been mistaken for him. Sheridan did not even seem surprised when he saw Forsyth, and only said: "There, I told you so." I mention this as an instance of a peculiar trait of Sheridan's character, which never allowed him to be discouraged by camp rumors, however disastrous.

The dismounted cavalry had assaulted as soon as they heard the infantry fire open. The natty cavalrymen, with tight-fitting uniforms, short jackets, and small carbines, swarmed through the pine thickets and dense undergrowth, looking as if they had been especially equipped for crawling through knot-holes. Those who had magazine guns created a racket in those pine woods that sounded as if a couple of army corps had opened fire.

The cavalry commanded by the gallant Merritt made a final dash, went over the earth-works with a hurrah, captured a battery of artillery, and scattered everything in front of them. Here Custer, Devin, Fitzhugh, and the other cavalry leaders were in their element, and vied with each other in deeds of valor. Crawford's division had advanced in a northerly direction, marching away from Ayres and leaving a gap between the two divisions. General Sheridan sent nearly all of his staff-officers to correct this movement, and to find General Warren, whom he was anxious to see.

Sheridan had that day fought one of the most interesting technical battles of the war, almost perfect in conception, brilliant in execution, strik-

FIRST WAGON-TRAIN ENTERING PETERSBURG.

309

ingly dramatic in its incidents, and productive of immensely important results.

About half-past seven o'clock I started for general headquarters. . . . General Grant was sitting with most of the staff about him before a blazing camp-fire. He wore his blue cavalry overcoat, and the ever-present cigar was in his mouth. I began shouting the good news as soon as I got in sight, and in a moment all but the imperturbable general-in-chief were on their feet giving vent to wild demonstrations of joy. For some minutes there was a bewildering state of excitement, grasping of hands, tossing up of hats, and slapping of each other on the back. It meant the beginning of the end — the reaching of the "last ditch." It pointed to peace and home. Dignity was thrown to the winds. The general, as was expected, asked his usual question: "How many prisoners have been taken?" This was always his first inquiry when an engagement was reported. No man ever had such a fondness for taking prisoners. I think the gratification arose from the kindness of his heart, a feeling that it was much better to win in this way than by the destruction of human life. I was happy to report that the prisoners this time were estimated at over five thousand, and this was the only part of my recital that seemed to call forth a responsive expression from his usually impassive features. After having listened to the description of Sheridan's day's work, the general, with scarcely a word, walked into his tent, and by the light of a flickering candle took up his "manifold writer," a small book which retained a copy of the matter written, and after finishing several despatches handed them to an orderly to be sent over the field wires, came out and joined our group at the camp-fire, and said as coolly as if remarking upon the state of the weather: "I have ordered an immediate assault along the lines." This was about 9 o'clock.

General Grant was anxious to have the different commands [in front of Petersburg] move against the enemy's lines at once, to prevent Lee from withdrawing troops and sending them against Sheridan.

The hour for the general assault was now fixed at 4 the next morning. . . . At 4:45 there was a streak of gray in the heavens which soon revealed another streak of gray in the works opposite, and the charge was ordered. The thunder of hundreds of guns shook the ground like an earthquake, and soon the troops were engaged all along the lines. The general awaited the result of the assault at headquarters, where he could be easily communicated with, and from which he could give general directions.

At a quarter past five a message came from Wright that he had carried the enemy's line and was pushing in. Next came news from Parke, that he had captured the outer works in his front, with 12 pieces of artillery and 800 prisoners. . . .

Soon Ord was heard from, having broken through the intrenchments. Humphreys, too, had been doing gallant work; at half-past seven the line in his front was captured, and half an hour later Hays's division of his corps had carried an important earth-work, with three guns and most of the garrison. . . .

The general and staff now rode out to the front, as it was necessary to give immediate direction to

UNION ARTILLERY AT PETERSBURG PROTECTED BY MANTELETS.
From a war-time sketch.

the actual movements of the troops, and prevent confusion from the overlapping and intermingling of the several corps as they pushed forward. He urged his horse over the works that Wright's corps had captured, and suddenly came upon a body of three thousand prisoners marching to the rear. His whole attention was for some time riveted upon them, and we knew he was enjoying his usual satisfaction in seeing them. Some of the guards told the prisoners who the general was, and they became wild with curiosity to get a good look at him. Next he came up with a division of the Sixth Corps flushed with success, and rushing for-

ward with a dash that was inspiriting beyond description. When they caught sight of the leader, whom they had patiently followed from the Rapidan to the Appomattox, their cheers broke forth with a will and their enthusiasm knew no bounds. The general galloped along toward the right, and soon met Meade, with whom he had been in constant communication, and who had been pushing forward the Army of the Potomac with all vigor. Congratulations were quickly exchanged, and both went to pushing forward the work. General Grant, after taking in the situation, directed both Meade and Ord to face their commands toward the east,

and close up toward the inner lines which covered Petersburg. Lee had been pushed so vigorously that he seemed for a time to be making but little effort to recover any of his lost ground, but now he made a determined fight against Parke's corps, which was threatening his inner line on his extreme left and the bridge across the Appomattox. Repeated assaults were made, but Parke resisted them all sucessfully, and could not be moved from his position. Lee had ordered Longstreet from the north side of the James, and with these troops reinforced his extreme right. General Grant dismounted near a farm-house which stood on a knoll within a mile of the enemy's extreme line, and from which he could get a good view of the field of operations. He seated himself at the foot of a tree, and was soon busy receiving despatches and writing orders to officers conducting the advance. The position was under fire, and as soon as the group of staff-officers was seen the enemy's guns began paying their respects. This lasted for nearly a quarter of an hour, and as the fire became hotter and hotter several of the officers, apprehensive of the general's safety, urged him to move to some less conspicuous position, but he kept on writing and talking without the least interruption from the shots falling around him, and apparently not noticing what a target the place was becoming. After he had finished his despatches, he got up, took a view of the situation, and as he started toward the other side of the farm-house said, with a quizzical look at the group around him: "Well, they do seem to have the range on us." The staff was now sent to various points of the advancing lines, and all was activity in pressing forward the good work. By noon, nearly all the outer line of works was in our possession, except two strong redoubts which occupied a commanding position, named respectively Fort Gregg and Fort Whitworth. The general decided that these should be stormed, and about 1 o'clock three of Ord's brigades swept down upon Fort Gregg. . . .

About this time Miles had struck a force of the enemy at Sutherland's Station on Lee's extreme right, and had captured two pieces of artillery and nearly a thousand prisoners. At 4:40 the general, who had been keeping Mr. Lincoln fully advised of the history that was so rapidly being made that day, sent him a telegram inviting him to come out the next day and pay him a visit. A prompt reply came back from the President, saying: "Allow me to tender you and all with you the nation's grateful thanks for the additional and magnificent success. At your kind suggestion, I think I will meet you to-morrow."

Prominent officers now urged the general to make an assault on the inner lines and capture Petersburg that afternoon, but he was firm in his resolve not to sacrifice the lives necessary to accomplish such a result. He said the city would undoubtedly be evacuated during the night, and he would dispose the troops for a parallel march westward, and try to head off the escaping army. And thus ended the eventful Sunday.

The general was up at daylight the next morning, and the first report brought in was that Parke had gone through the lines at 4 A. M., capturing a few skirmishers, and that the city had surren-

THE CAPTURE OF EWELL'S CORPS, APRIL 6, 1865.
From a sketch made at the time.

dered at 4:28 to Colonel Ralph Ely. A second communication surrendering the place was sent in to Wright. The evacuation had begun about 10 the night before, and was completed before 3 on the morning of the 3d. Between 5 and 6 A. M. the general had a conference with Meade, and orders were given to push westward with all haste. About 9 A. M. the general rode into Petersburg. . . .

Soon an officer came with a despatch from Sheridan, who had been reinforced and ordered to strike out along the Danville railroad, saying he was already nine miles beyond Namozine Creek and pressing the enemy's trains. The general was anxious to move westward at once with the leading infantry columns, but Mr. Lincoln had telegraphed that he was on his way, and the general, though he had replied that he could not wait for his arrival, decided to prolong his stay until the President came up. Mr. Lincoln, accompanied by his little son "Tad," dismounted in the street and came in through the front gate with long and rapid strides, his face beaming with delight. He seized General Grant's hand as the general stepped forward to greet him, and stood shaking it for some time and pouring out his thanks and congratulations with all the fervor of a heart that seemed overflowing with its fullness of joy. I doubt whether Mr. Lincoln ever experienced a happier moment in his life. The scene was singularly affecting and one never to be forgotten. He then said: "Do you know, General, I have had a sort of sneaking idea for some days that you intended to do something like this, though I thought some time ago that you would so manœuvre as to have Sherman come up and be near enough to coöperate with you."

"Yes," replied the general, "I thought at one time that Sherman's army might advance so far as to be in supporting distance of the Eastern armies when the spring campaign against Lee opened, but I have had a feeling that it is better to let Lee's old antagonists give his army the final blow and finish up the job. If the Western armies were even to put in an appearance against Lee's army, it might give some of our politicians a chance to stir up sectional feeling in claiming everything for the troops from their own section of country. The Western armies have been very successful in their campaigns, and it is due to the Eastern armies to let them vanquish their old enemy single-handed."

"I see, I see," said Mr. Lincoln, "but I never thought of it in that light. In fact, my anxiety has been so great that I did n't care where the help came from so the work was perfectly done." . . .

At 12:30 the general wrote a telegram to Weitzel at Richmond, asking news from him, and showed it to the President before sending it. The general hoped that he would hear before he parted with the President that Richmond was in our possession, but after the interview had lasted about an hour and a half, the general said he must ride on to the front and join Ord's column, and took leave of the President, who shook his hand cordially, and with great warmth of feeling wished him God-speed and every success.

The general and staff had ridden as far as Sutherland's Station, about nine miles, when a despatch from Weitzel overtook him, which had come by a roundabout way. It read: "We took Richmond at 8:15 this morning. I captured many guns. Enemy left in great haste. The city is on fire in two places. Am making every effort to put it out." . . .

Grant and Meade both went into camp at Sutherland's Station that evening, the 3d. . . .

"WITH FATE AGAINST THEM."
From the painting by Gilbert Gaul.

diers were at hand, and, after the arrest of a few ringleaders and the more riotous of their followers, a fair degree of order was restored. But Richmond saw few sleeping eyes during the pandemonium of that night. . . . Either incendiaries, or (more probably) fragments of bombs from the arsenals, had fired various buildings, and the two cities, Richmond and Manchester, were like a blaze of day amid the surrounding darkness. Three high arched bridges were in flames; beneath them the waters sparkled and dashed and rushed on by the burning city. Every now and then, as a magazine exploded, a column of white smoke rose up as high as the eye could reach, instantaneously followed by a deafening sound. The earth seemed to rock and tremble as with the shock of an earthquake, and immediately afterward hundreds of shells would explode in air and send their iron spray down far below the bridge. As the immense magazines of cartridges ignited, the rattle as of thousands of musketry would follow, and then all was still for the moment, except the dull roar and crackle of the fast-spreading fires. At dawn we heard terrific explosions about "The Rocketts," from the unfinished ironclads down the river.

By daylight on the 3d, a mob of men, women, and children, to the number of several thousands, had gathered at the corner of 14th and Cary streets and other outlets, in front of the bridge, attracted by the vast commissary depot at that point; for it must be remembered that in 1865 Richmond was a half-starved city, and the Confederate Government had that morning removed its guards and abandoned the removal of the provisions, which was impossible for the want of transportation. The depot doors were forced open and a demoniacal struggle for the countless barrels of hams, bacon, whisky, flour, sugar, coffee, etc., etc., raged about the buildings among the hungry mob. The gutters ran whisky, and it was lapped as it flowed down the streets, while all fought for a share of the plunder. The flames came nearer and nearer, and at last caught in the commissariat itself.

At daylight the approach of the Union forces could be plainly discerned. After a little came the clatter of horses' hoofs galloping up Main street. . . . We saw another string of horsemen in blue pass up Main street, then we saw a dense column

THE FALL OF RICHMOND.

I. THE EVACUATION.—BY CLEMENT SULIVANE, CAPTAIN, C. S. A.

ABOUT 11:30 A. M. on Sunday, April 2d,[*] a strange agitation was perceptible on the streets of Richmond, and within half an hour it was known on all sides that Lee's lines had been broken below Petersburg; that he was in full retreat on Danville; that the troops covering the city at Chaffin's and Drewry's Bluffs were on the point of being withdrawn, and that the city was forthwith to be abandoned. A singular security had been felt by the citizens of Richmond, so the news fell like a bomb-shell in a peaceful camp, and dismay reigned supreme.

All that Sabbath day the trains came and went, wagons, vehicles, and horsemen rumbled and dashed to and fro, and in the evening, ominous groups of ruffians—more or less in liquor—began to make their appearance on the principal thoroughfares of the city. As night came on pillage and rioting and robbing took place. The police and a few sol-

[*] Mr. Davis attended morning service at St. Paul's Church, where he received a despatch, on reading which he left the church to prepare for the departure of the Government.

or black, and make them assist in extinguishing the flames. General Devens's division marched into the city, stacked arms, and went to work. Parsons's engineer company assisted by blowing up houses to check its advance, as about every engine was destroyed or rendered useless by the mob. In this manner the fire was extinguished and perfect order restored in an incredibly short time after we occupied the city. There was absolutely no plundering upon the part of our soldiers; orders were issued forbidding anything to be taken without remuneration, and no complaints were made of infringement of these orders. General G. F. Shepley was placed on duty as military governor. He had occupied a similar position in New Orleans after its capture in 1862, and was eminently fitted for it by education and experience. As we entered the suburbs the general ordered me to take half a dozen cavalrymen and go to Libby Prison, for our thoughts were upon the wretched men whom we supposed were still confined within its walls. It was very early in the morning, and

CITIZENS OF RICHMOND IN CAPITOL SQUARE DURING THE CONFLAGRATION.

of infantry march by, seemingly without end; we heard the very welkin ring with cheers as the United States forces reached Capitol Square, and then we turned and slowly rode on our way.

II. THE OCCUPATION.—BY THOMAS THATCHER GRAVES, AIDE-DE-CAMP ON THE STAFF OF GENERAL WEITZEL.

. . . As we approached the inner line of defenses we saw in the distance divisions of our troops, many of them upon the double-quick, aiming to be the first in the city; a white and a colored division were having a regular race, the white troops on the turnpike and the colored in the fields. As we neared the city the fires seemed to increase in number and size, and at intervals loud explosions were heard.

On entering we found Capitol Square covered with people who had fled there to escape the fire and were utterly worn out with fatigue and fright. Details were at once made to scour the city and press into service every able-bodied man, white

we were the first Union troops to arrive before Libby. Not a guard, not an inmate remained; the doors were wide open, and only a few negroes greeted us with, "Dey 's all gone, massa!"

The next day after our entry into the city, on passing out from Clay street, from Jefferson Davis's house, I saw a crowd coming, headed by President Lincoln, who was walking with his usual long, careless stride, and looking about with an interested air and taking in everything. Upon my saluting he said: "Is it far to President Davis's house?" I accompanied him to the house, which was occupied by General Weitzel as headquarters. The President had arrived about 9 o'clock, at the landing called Rocketts, upon Admiral Porter's flag-ship, the *Malvern*, and as soon as the boat was made fast, without ceremony, he walked on shore, and started off uptown. As soon as Admiral Porter was informed of it he ordered a guard of marines to follow as escort; but in the walk of about two miles they never saw him, and he was directed by negroes. At the Davis house, he was shown into

the reception-room, with the remark that the housekeeper had said that that room was President Davis's office. As he seated himself he remarked, "This must have been President Davis's chair," and, crossing his legs, he looked far off with a serious, dreamy expression.

At length he asked me if the housekeeper was in the house. Upon learning that she had left he jumped up and said, with a boyish manner, "Come, let 's look at the house!" We went pretty much over it; I retailed all that the housekeeper had told me, and he seemed interested in everything. As we came down the staircase General Weitzel came, in breathless haste, and at once President

Lincoln's face lost its boyish expression as he realized that *duty* must be resumed. Soon afterward Judge Campbell, General Anderson (Confederates), and others called and asked for an interview with the President. It was granted, and took place in the parlor with closèd doors.

I accompanied President Lincoln and General Weitzel to Libby Prison and Castle Thunder, and heard General Weitzel ask President Lincoln what he (General Weitzel) should do in regard to the conquered people. President Lincoln replied that he did not wish to give any orders on that subject, but, as he expressed it, "If I were in your place I'd let 'em up easy, let 'em up easy." . . .

THE SURRENDER AT APPOMATTOX.

BY HORACE PORTER, BREVET BRIGADIER-GENERAL, U. S. A.
Aide to General Grant at the time of the surrender.

A LITTLE before noon on the 7th of April, 1865, General Grant, with his staff, rode into the little village of Farmville, on the south side of the Appomattox River, a town that will be memorable in history as the place where he opened the correspondence with Lee which led to the surrender of the Army of Northern Virginia. He drew up in front of the village hotel, dismounted, and established headquarters on its broad piazza. News came in that Crook was fighting large odds with his cavalry on the north side of the river, and I was directed to go to his front and see what was necessary to be done to assist him. I found that he was being driven back, the enemy (Munford's and Rosser's cavalry divisions under Fitzhugh Lee) having made a bold stand north of the river. Humphreys was also on the north side, isolated from the rest of our infantry, confronted by a large portion of Lee's army, and having some very heavy fighting. On my return to general headquarters that evening Wright's corps was ordered to cross the river and move rapidly to the support of our troops there. Notwithstanding their long march that day, the men sprang to their feet with a spirit that made every one marvel at their pluck, and came swinging through the main street of the village with a step that seemed as elastic as on the first day of their toilsome tramp. It was now dark, but they spied

the general-in-chief watching them with evident pride from the piazza of the hotel.

Then was witnessed one of the most inspiring scenes of the campaign. Bonfires were lighted on the sides of the street, the men seized straw and pine knots, and improvised torches; cheers arose from throats already hoarse with shouts of victory, bands played, banners waved, arms were tossed high in air and caught again. The night march had become a grand review, with Grant as the reviewing officer.

Ord and Gibbon had visited the general at the hotel, and he had spoken with them as well as with Wright about sending some communication to Lee that might pave the way to the stopping of further bloodshed. Dr. Smith, formerly of the regular army, a native of Virginia and a relative of General Ewell, now one of our prisoners, had told General Grant the night before that Ewell had said in conversation that their cause was lost when they crossed the James River, and he considered that it was the duty of the authorities to negotiate for peace then, while they still had a right to claim concessions, adding that now they were not in condition to claim anything. He said that for every man killed after this somebody would be responsible, and it would be little better than murder. He could not tell what General Lee would do, but he hoped he would at

THE RUINS OF RICHMOND BETWEEN THE CANAL BASIN AND CAPITOL SQUARE.
From a war-time photograph.

PRESIDENT LINCOLN LEAVING THE DAVIS MANSION.
From a sketch made at the time.

APPOMATTOX COURT HOUSE.
From a war-time photograph.

once surrender his army. This statement, together with the news that had been received from Sheridan saying that he had heard that General Lee's trains of provisions which had come by rail were at Appomattox, and that he expected to capture them before Lee could reach them, induced the general to write the following communication:

"HEADQUARTERS, ARMIES OF THE U. S.
5 P. M., April 7th, 1865.
"GENERAL R. E. LEE, Commanding C. S. A.

"The results of the last week must convince you of the hopelessness of further resistance on the part of the Army of Northern Virginia in this struggle. I feel that it is so, and regard it as my duty to shift from myself the responsibility of any further effusion of blood by asking of you the surrender of that portion of the Confederate States army known as the Army of Northern Virginia. U. S. GRANT, Lieutenant-General."

This he intrusted to General Seth Williams, adjutant-general, with directions to take it to Humphreys's front, as his corps was close up to the enemy's rear-guard, and have it sent into Lee's lines. The general decided to remain all night at Farmville and await the reply from Lee, and he was shown to a room in the hotel in which, he was told, Lee had slept the night before. Lee wrote the following reply within an hour after he received General Grant's letter, but it was brought in by rather a circuitous route and did not reach its destination till after midnight:

"APRIL 7TH, 1865.

"GENERAL: I have received your note of this date. Though not entertaining the opinion you express of the hopelessness of further resistance on the part of the Army of Northern Virginia, I reciprocate your desire to avoid useless effusion of blood, and therefore before con-

sidering your proposition, ask the terms you will offer on condition of its surrender. R. E. LEE, General.
"LIEUTENANT-GENERAL U. S. GRANT,
Commanding Armies of the U. S."

The next morning before leaving Farmville the following reply was given to General Williams, who again went to Humphreys's front to have it transmitted to Lee:

"APRIL 8TH, 1865.
"GENERAL R. E. LEE, Commanding C. S. A.

"Your note of last evening in reply to mine of the same date, asking the conditions on which I will accept the surrender of the Army of Northern Virginia, is just received. In reply I would say that, peace being my great desire, there is but one condition I would insist upon,—namely, that the men and officers surrendered shall be disqualified for taking up arms against the Government of the United States until properly exchanged. I will meet you, or will designate officers to meet any officers you may name for the same purpose, at any point agreeable to you, for the purpose of arranging definitely the terms upon which the surrender of the Army of Northern Virginia will be received.
"U. S. GRANT,
Lieutenant-General."

There turned up at this time a rather hungry-looking gentleman in gray, in the uniform of a

THE VILLAGE OF APPOMATTOX COURT HOUSE. THE McLEAN HOUSE ON THE RIGHT.
From a war-time sketch.

colonel, who proclaimed himself the proprietor of the hotel. He said his regiment had crumbled to pieces, he was the only man left in it, and he thought he might as well "stop off" at home. His story was significant as indicating the disintegrating process that was going on in the ranks of the enemy.

General Grant had been marching most of the way with the columns that were pushing along south of Lee's line of retreat; but expecting that a reply would be sent to his last letter and wanting to keep within easy communication with Lee, he decided to march this day with the portion of the Army of the Potomac that was pressing Lee's rear-guard. After issuing some further instructions to Ord and Sheridan, he started from Farmville, crossed to the north side of the Appomattox, conferred in person with Meade, and rode with his columns. Encouraging reports came in all day, and that night headquarters were established at Curdsville in a large white farm-house, a few hundred yards from Meade's camp. The general and several of the staff had cut loose from the headquarters trains the night he started to meet Sheridan at Jetersville, and had neither baggage nor camp-equipage. The general did not even have his sword with him. This was the most advanced effort yet made at moving in "light march-

ing order," and we billeted ourselves at night in farm-houses, or bivouacked on porches, and picked up meals at any camp that seemed to have something to spare in the way of rations. This night we sampled the fare of Meade's hospitable mess, and once more lay down with full stomachs.

General Grant had been suffering all the afternoon from a severe headache, the result of fatigue, anxiety, scant fare, and loss of sleep, and by night it was much worse. He had been induced to bathe his feet in hot water and mustard, and apply mustard plasters to his wrists and the back of his neck, but these remedies afforded little relief. The dwelling we occupied was a double house. The general threw himself upon a sofa in the sitting-room on the left side of the hall, while the staff-officers bunked on the floor of the room opposite to catch what sleep they could. About midnight we were aroused by Colonel Charles A. Whittier of Humphreys's staff, who brought another letter from Lee. Rawlins at once took it into General Grant's room. It was as follows:

"APRIL 8TH, 1865.

"GENERAL: I received at a late hour your note of to-day. In mine of yesterday I did not intend to propose the surrender of the Army of Northern Virginia, but to ask the terms of your proposition. To be frank, I do not think the emergency has arisen to call for the surrender of this army, but, as the restoration of peace should be the sole object of all, I desired to know whether your proposals would lead to that end. I cannot, therefore, meet you with the view to surrender the Army of Northern Virginia; but as far as your proposal may effect the Confederate State forces under my command, * and tend to the restoration of peace, I should be pleased to meet you at 10 A. M. to-morrow on the old stage road to Richmond, between the picket-lines of the two armies.
"R. E. LEE, General.
"LIEUTENANT-GENERAL U. S. GRANT."

* Since February 9th, 1865, Lee had been general-in-chief of all the Confederate armies, and, evidently, was aiming here at a treaty of peace and general surrender.

General Grant had been able to get but very little sleep. He now sat up and read the letter, and after making a few comments upon it to General Rawlins lay down again on the sofa.

About 4 o'clock on the morning of the 9th I rose and crossed the hall to ascertain how the general was feeling. I found his room empty, and upon going out of the front door saw him pacing up and down in the yard holding both hands to his head. Upon inquiring how he felt, he replied that he had had very little sleep, and was still suffering the most excruciating pain. I said: "Well, there is one consolation in all this, General: I never knew you to be ill that you did not receive some good news. I have become a little superstitious regarding these coincidences, and I should not be surprised if some good fortune overtook you before night." He smiled and said: "The best thing that can happen to me to-day is to get rid of the pain I am suffering." We were soon joined by some others of the staff, and the general was induced to go over to Meade's headquarters with us and get some coffee, in the hope that it would do him good. He seemed to feel a little better now, and after writing the following letter to Lee and despatching it he prepared to move forward. The letter was as follows:

"APRIL 9TH, 1865.

"GENERAL: Your note of yesterday is received. I have no authority to treat on the subject of peace. The meeting proposed for 10 A. M. to-day could lead to no good. I will state, however, that I am equally desirous for peace with yourself, and the whole North entertains the same feeling. The terms upon which peace can be had are well understood. By the South laying down their arms, they would hasten that most desirable event, save thousands of human lives, and hundreds of millions of property not yet destroyed. Seriously hoping that all our difficulties may be settled without the loss of another life, I subscribe myself, etc.,

"U. S. GRANT, Lieutenant-General.
"GENERAL R. E. LEE."

It was proposed to him to ride during the day in a covered ambulance which was at hand, instead of on horseback, so as to avoid the intense heat of

APPOMATTOX STATION, VA.

the sun, but this he declined to do, and soon after mounted "Cincinnati" and struck off toward New Store. From that point he went by way of a cross-road to the south side of the Appomattox with the intention of moving around to Sheridan's front. While riding along the wagon road that runs from Farmville to Appomattox Court House, at a point eight or nine miles east of the latter place, Lieutenant Charles E. Pease of Meade's staff overtook him with a despatch. It was found to be a reply from Lee, which had been sent in to our lines on Humphreys's front. It read as follows:

"APRIL 9TH, 1865.

"GENERAL: I received your note of this morning on the picket-line, whither I had come to meet you and ascertain definitely what terms were embraced in your proposal of yesterday with reference to the surrender of this army. I now ask an interview, in accordance with the offer contained in your letter of yesterday, for that purpose. R. E. LEE, General.

"LIEUTENANT-GENERAL U. S. GRANT."

Pease also brought a note from Meade, saying that at Lee's request he had read the communication addressed to General Grant and in consequence of it had granted a short truce.

The general, as soon as he had read these letters, dismounted, sat down on the grassy bank by the roadside, and wrote the following reply to Lee:

"APRIL 9TH, 1865.

"GENERAL R. E. LEE, Commanding C. S. Army:

"Your note of this date is but this moment (11:50 A. M.) received, in consequence of my having passed from the Richmond and Lynchburg road to the Farmville and Lynchburg road. I am at this writing about four miles west of Walker's Church, and will push forward to the front for the purpose of meeting you. Notice sent to me on this road where you wish the interview to take place will meet me.

"U. S. GRANT, Lieut.-General."

MCLEAN'S HOUSE, APPOMATTOX COURT HOUSE.
From a photograph.

He handed this to Colonel Babcock of the staff, with directions to take it to General Lee by the most direct route. Mounting his horse again the general rode on at a trot toward Appomattox Court House. When five or six miles from the town, Colonel Newhall, Sheridan's adjutant-general, came riding up from the direction of Appomattox and handed the general a communication. This proved to be a duplicate of the letter from Lee that Lieutenant Pease had brought in from Meade's lines. Lee was so closely pressed that he was anxious to communicate with Grant by the most direct means, and as he could not tell with which column Grant was moving he sent in one copy of his letter on Meade's front and one on Sheridan's. Colonel Newhall joined our party, and after a few minutes' halt to read the letter we continued our ride toward Appomattox. On the march I had asked the general several times how he felt. To the same question now he said, "The pain in my head seemed to leave me the moment I got Lee's letter." The road was filled with men, animals, and wagons, and to avoid these and shorten the distance we turned slightly to the right and began to "cut across lots"; but before going far we spied men conspicuous in gray, and it was seen that we were moving toward the enemy's left flank, and that a short ride farther would take us into his lines. It looked for a moment as if a very awkward condition of things might possibly arise, and Grant become a prisoner in Lee's lines instead of Lee in his. Such a circumstance would have given rise to an important cross-entry in the system of campaign bookkeeping. There was only one remedy—to retrace our steps and strike the right road, which was done without serious discussion. About 1 o'clock the little village of Appomattox Court House, with its half-dozen houses, came in sight, and soon we were entering its single street. It is situated on some rising ground, and beyond the country slopes down into a broad valley. The enemy was seen with his columns and wagon trains covering the low ground. Our cavalry, the Fifth Corps, and part of Ord's command were occupying the high ground to the

south and west of the enemy, heading him off completely. Generals Sheridan and Ord, with a group of officers around them, were seen in the road, and as our party came up General Grant said: "How are you, Sheridan?" "First-rate, thank you; how are you?" cried Sheridan, with a voice and look that seemed to indicate that on his part he was having things all his own way. "Is Lee over there?" asked General Grant, pointing up the street, having heard a rumor that Lee was in that vicinity. "Yes, he is in that brick house," answered Sheridan. "Well, then, we'll go over," said Grant.

The general-in-chief now rode on, accompanied by Sheridan, Ord, and some others, and soon Colonel Babcock's orderly was seen sitting on his horse in the street in front of a two-story brick house, better in appearance than the rest of the houses. He said General Lee and Colonel Babcock had gone into this house a short time before, and he was ordered to post himself in the street and keep a lookout for General Grant, so as to let him know where General Lee was. Babcock told me afterward that in carrying General Grant's last letter he passed through the enemy's lines and found General Lee a little more than half a mile beyond Appomattox Court House. He was lying down by the roadside on a blanket which had been spread over a few fence rails on the ground under an apple-tree, which was part of an orchard. This circumstance furnished the only ground for the widespread report that the surrender occurred under an apple-tree. Babcock dismounted upon coming near, and as he approached on foot, Lee sat up, with his feet hanging over the roadside embankment. The wheels of the wagons in passing along the road had cut away the earth of this embankment and left the roots of the tree projecting. Lee's feet were partly resting on these roots. One of his staff-officers came forward, took the despatch which Babcock handed him and gave it to General Lee. After reading it, the general rose and said he would ride forward on the road on which Babcock had come, but was apprehensive that hostilities might begin in the mean time, upon the termination of the temporary truce, and asked Babcock to write a line to Meade informing him of the situation. Babcock wrote accordingly, requesting Meade to maintain the truce until positive orders from General Grant could be received. To save time it was arranged that a Union officer, accompanied by one of Lee's officers, should carry this letter through the enemy's lines. This route made the distance to Meade nearly ten miles shorter than by the roundabout way of the Union lines. Lee now mounted his horse and directed Colonel Charles Marshall, his military secretary, to accompany him. They started for Appomattox Court House in company with Babcock and followed by a mounted orderly. When the party reached the village they met one of its residents, named Wilmer McLean, who was told that General Lee wanted to occupy a convenient room in some house in the town. McLean ushered them into the sitting-room of one of the first houses he came to, but upon looking about and finding it quite small and meagerly furnished, Lee proposed finding something more commodious and better fitted for the occasion. McLean then conducted the party to his own house, about the best one in the town, where they awaited General Grant's arrival.

The house had a comfortable wooden porch with seven steps leading up to it. A hall ran through the middle from front to back, and on each side was a room having two windows, one in front and one in rear. Each room had two doors opening into the hall. The building stood a little distance back from the street, with a yard in front, and to the left was a gate for carriages and a roadway running to a stable in rear. We entered the grounds by this gate and dismounted. In the yard were seen a fine large gray horse, which proved to be General Lee's, and a good-looking mare belonging to Colonel Marshall. An orderly in gray was in charge of them, and had taken off their bridles to let them nibble the grass.

General Grant mounted the steps and entered the house. As he stepped into the hall Colonel Babcock, who had seen his approach from the window, opened the door of the room on the left, in which he had been sitting with General Lee and Colonel Marshall awaiting General Grant's arrival. The general passed in, while the members of the staff, Generals Sheridan and Ord, and some general officers who had gathered in the front yard, remained outside, feeling that he would probably want his first interview with General Lee to be, in a measure, private. In a few minutes Colonel Babcock came to the front door and, making a motion with his hat toward the sitting-room, said: "The general says, come in." It was then about half-past one of Sunday, the 9th of April. We entered, and found General Grant sitting at a marble-topped table in the center of the room, and Lee sitting beside a small oval table near the front window, in the corner opposite to the door by which we entered, and facing General Grant. Colonel Marshall, his military secretary, was standing at his left. We walked in softly and ranged ourselves quietly about the sides of the room, very much as people enter a sick-chamber when they expect to find the patient dangerously ill. Some found seats on the sofa and the few chairs which constituted the furniture, but most of the party stood.

The contrast between the two commanders was striking, and could not fail to attract marked attention as they sat ten feet apart facing each other. General Grant, then nearly forty-three years of age,

1   2   3   4   5   6   7 8   9   10   11   12 13   14   15

THE SURRENDER AT APPOMATTOX.
Based upon the lithograph called "The Dawn of Peace." By permission of W. H. Stelle.
2. General Robert E. Lee.   1. Colonel Charles Marshall, of General Lee's Staff.   8. Lieutenant-General Ulysses S. Grant.   15. Major-General Philip H. Sheridan.   7. Major-General Edward O. C. Ord.   14. Brevet Major-General Rufus Ingalls.   10. Brigadier-General John A. Rawlins, Chief-of-Staff; other members of General Grant's Staff: 4. Major-General Seth Williams.   12. Brevet Major-General John G. Barnard.   9. Colonel Horace Porter.   3. Colonel Orville E. Babcock.   5. Colonel Ely S. Parker.   6. Colonel Theodore S. Bowers.   11. Colonel Frederick T. Dent.   13. Colonel Adam Badeau.

was five feet eight inches in height, with shoulders slightly stooped. His hair and full beard were a nut-brown, without a trace of gray in them. He had on a single-breasted blouse, made of dark-blue flannel, unbuttoned in front, and showing a waistcoat underneath. He wore an ordinary pair of top-boots, with his trousers inside, and was without spurs. The boots and portions of his clothes were spattered with mud. He had had on a pair of thread gloves, of a dark-yellow color, which he had taken off on entering the room. His felt "sugar-loaf" stiff-brimmed hat was thrown on the table beside him. He had no sword, and a pair of shoulder-straps was all there was about him to designate his rank. In fact, aside from these, his uniform was that of a private soldier.

Lee, on the other hand, was fully six feet in height, and quite erect for one of his age, for he was Grant's senior by sixteen years. His hair and full beard were a silver-gray, and quite thick, except that the hair had become a little thin in front. He wore a new uniform of Confederate gray, buttoned up to the throat, and at his side he carried a long sword of exceedingly fine workmanship, the hilt studded with jewels. It was said to be the sword that had been presented to him by the State of Virginia. His top-boots were comparatively new, and seemed to have on them some ornamental

stitching of red silk. Like his uniform, they were singularly clean, and but little travel-stained. On the boots were handsome spurs, with large rowels. A felt hat, which in color matched pretty closely that of his uniform, and a pair of long buckskin gauntlets lay beside him on the table. We asked Colonel Marshall afterward how it was that both he and his chief wore such fine toggery, and looked so much as if they had turned out to go to church, while with us our outward garb scarcely rose to the dignity even of the "shabby-genteel." He enlightened us regarding the contrast, by explaining that when their headquarters wagons had been pressed so closely by our cavalry a few days before, and it was found they would have to destroy all their baggage, except the clothes they carried on their backs, each one, naturally, selected the newest suit he had, and sought to propitiate the god of destruction by a sacrifice of his second-best.

General Grant began the conversation by saying: "I met you once before, General Lee, while we were serving in Mexico, when you came over from General Scott's headquarters to visit Garland's brigade, to which I then belonged. I have always remembered your appearance, and I think I should have recognized you anywhere." "Yes," replied General Lee, "I know I met you on that occasion, and I have often thought of it and tried to recollect

how you looked, but I have never been able to recall a single feature." After some further mention of Mexico, General Lee said: "I suppose, General Grant, that the object of our present meeting is fully understood. I asked to see you to ascertain upon what terms you would receive the surrender of my army." General Grant replied: "The terms I propose are those stated substantially in my letter of yesterday—that is, the officers and men surrendered to be paroled and disqualified from taking up arms again until properly exchanged, and all arms, ammunition, and supplies to be delivered up as captured property." Lee nodded an assent, and said: "Those are about the conditions which I expected would be proposed." General Grant then continued: "Yes, I think our correspondence indicated pretty clearly the action that would be taken at our meeting; and I hope it may lead to a general suspension of hostilities, and be the means of preventing any further loss of life."

Lee inclined his head as indicating his accord with this wish, and General Grant then went on to talk at some length in a very pleasant vein about the prospects of peace. Lee was evidently anxious to proceed to the formal work of the surrender, and he brought the subject up again by saying:

"I presume, General Grant, we have both carefully considered the proper steps to be taken, and I would suggest that you commit to writing the terms you have proposed, so that they may be formally acted upon."

"Very well," replied General Grant, "I will write them out." And calling for his manifold order-book, he opened it on the table before him and proceeded to write the terms. The leaves had been so prepared that three impressions of the writing were made. He wrote very rapidly, and did not pause until he had finished the sentence ending with "officers appointed by me to receive them." Then he looked toward Lee, and his eyes seemed to be resting on the handsome sword that hung at that officer's side. He said afterward that this set him to thinking that it would be an unnecessary humiliation to require the officers to surrender their swords, and a great hardship to deprive them of their personal baggage and horses, and after a short pause he wrote the sentence: "This will not embrace the side-arms of the officers, nor their private horses or baggage." When he had finished the letter he called Colonel (afterward General) Ely S. Parker, one of the military secretaries on the staff, to his side and looked it over with him, and directed him as they went along to interline six or seven words and to strike out the word "their," which had been repeated. When this had been done, he handed the book to General Lee and asked him to read over the letter. It was as follows:

APPOMATTOX CT. H., VA., APRIL 9TH, 1865.
"GENERAL R. E. LEE, Commanding C. S. A.

"GENERAL: In accordance with the substance of my letter to you of the 8th inst., I propose to receive the surrender of the Army of Northern Virginia on the following terms, to wit: Rolls of all the officers and men to be made in duplicate, one copy to be given to an officer to be designated by me, the other to be retained by such officer or officers as you may designate. The officers to give their individual paroles not to take up arms against the Government of the United States until properly [exchanged], and each company or regimental commander to sign a like parole for the men of their commands. The arms, artillery, and public property to be parked, and stacked, and turned over to the officers appointed by me to receive them. This will not embrace the side-arms of the officers, nor their private horses or baggage. This done, each officer and man will be allowed to return to his home, not to be disturbed by the United States authorities so long as they observe their paroles and the laws in force where they may reside.

"Very respectfully,
"U. S. GRANT, Lieutenant-General."

Lee took it and laid it on the table beside him, while he drew from his pocket a pair of steel-rimmed spectacles and wiped the glasses carefully with his handkerchief. Then he crossed his legs, adjusted the spectacles very slowly and deliberately, took up the draft of the letter, and proceeded to read it attentively. It consisted of two pages. When he reached the top line of the second page, he looked up, and said to General Grant: "After the words 'until properly,' the word 'exchanged' seems to be omitted. You doubtless intended to use that word."

"Why, yes," said Grant; "I thought I had put in the word 'exchanged.'"

"I presumed it had been omitted inadvertently," continued Lee, "and with your permission I will mark where it should be inserted."

"Certainly," Grant replied.

Lee felt in his pocket as if searching for a pencil, but did not seem to be able to find one. Seeing this and happening to be standing close to him, I handed him my pencil. He took it, and laying the paper on the table noted the interlineation. During the rest of the interview he kept twirling this pencil in his fingers and occasionally tapping the top of the table with it. When he handed it back it was carefully treasured by me as a memento of the occasion. When Lee came to the sentence about the officers' side-arms, private horses, and baggage, he showed for the first time during the reading of the letter a slight change of countenance, and was evidently touched by this act of generosity. It was doubtless the condition mentioned to which he particularly alluded when he looked toward General Grant as he finished reading, and said with some degree of warmth in his manner: "This will have a very happy effect upon my army."

General Grant then said: "Unless you have

UNION SOLDIERS SHARING THEIR RATIONS WITH THE CONFEDERATES.
From a sketch made at the time.

some suggestions to make in regard to the form in which I have stated the terms, I will have a copy of the letter made in ink and sign it."

"There is one thing I would like to mention," Lee replied after a short pause. "The cavalrymen and artillerists own their own horses in our army. Its organization in this respect differs from that of the United States." This expression attracted the notice of our officers present, as showing how firmly the conviction was grounded in his mind that we were two distinct countries. He continued: "I would like to understand whether these men will be permitted to retain their horses?"

"You will find that the terms as written do not allow this," General Grant replied; "only the officers are permitted to take their private property."

Lee read over the second page of the letter again, and then said:

"No, I see the terms do not allow it; that is clear." His face showed plainly that he was quite anxious to have this concession made, and Grant said very promptly, and without giving Lee time to make a direct request:

"Well, the subject is quite new to me. Of course I did not know that any private soldiers owned their animals, but I think this will be the last battle of the war,—I sincerely hope so,—and that the surrender of this army will be followed soon by that of all the others, and I take it that most of the men in the ranks are small farmers, and as the country has been so raided by the two armies, it is doubtful whether they will be able to put in a crop to carry themselves and their families through the next winter without the aid of the horses they are now riding, and I will arrange it in this way: I will not change the terms as now written, but I will instruct the officers I shall appoint to receive the paroles

to let all the men who claim to own a horse or mule take the animals home with them to work their little farms." (This expression has been quoted in various forms and has been the subject of some dispute. I give the exact words used.)

Lee now looked greatly relieved, and though anything but a demonstrative man, he gave every evidence of his appreciation of this concession, and said, "This will have the best possible effect upon the men. It will be very gratifying and will do much toward conciliating our people." He handed the draft of the terms back to General Grant, who called Colonel T. S. Bowers of the staff to him and directed him to make a copy in ink. Bowers was a little nervous, and he turned the matter over to Colonel (afterward General) Parker, whose handwriting presented a better appearance than that of any one else on the staff. Parker sat down to write at the table which stood against the rear side of the room. Wilmer McLean's domestic resources in the way of ink now became the subject of a searching investigation, but it was found that the contents of the conical-shaped stoneware inkstand which he produced appeared to be participating in the general breaking up and had disappeared. Colonel Marshall now came to the rescue, and pulled out of his pocket a small boxwood inkstand, which was put at Parker's service, so that, after all, we had to fall back upon the resources of the enemy in furnishing the stage "properties" for the final scene in the memorable military drama.

Lee in the mean time had directed Colonel Marshall to draw up for his signature a letter of acceptance of the terms of surrender. Colonel Marshall wrote out a draft of such a letter, making it quite formal, beginning with "I have the honor to reply to your communication," etc. General Lee took it,

and, after reading it over very carefully, directed that these formal expressions be stricken out and that the letter be otherwise shortened. He afterward went over it again and seemed to change some words, and then told the colonel to make a final copy in ink. When it came to providing the paper, it was found we had the only supply of that important ingredient in the recipe for surrendering an army, so we gave a few pages to the colonel. The letter when completed read as follows:

"HEADQUARTERS, ARMY OF NORTHERN VIRGINIA.
APRIL 9TH, 1865.
"GENERAL: I received your letter of this date containing the terms of the surrender of the Army of Northern Virginia as proposed by you. As they are substantially the same as those expressed in your letter of the 8th inst., they are accepted. I will proceed to designate the proper officers to carry the stipulations into effect.
"R. E. LEE, General.
"LIEUTENANT-GENERAL U. S. GRANT."

While the letters were being copied, General Grant introduced the general officers who had entered, and each member of the staff, to General Lee. The general shook hands with General Seth Williams, who had been his adjutant when Lee was superintendent at West Point, some years before the war, and gave his hand to some of the other officers who had extended theirs, but to most of those who were introduced he merely bowed in a dignified and formal manner. He did not exhibit the slightest change of features during this ceremony until Colonel Parker of our staff was presented to him. Parker was a full-blooded Indian, and the reigning Chief of the Six Nations. When Lee saw his swarthy features he looked at him with evident surprise, and his eyes rested on him for several seconds. What was passing in his mind probably no one ever knew, but the natural surmise was that he at first mistook Parker for a negro, and was struck with astonishment to find that the commander of the Union armies had one of that race on his personal staff.

Lee did not utter a word while the introductions were going on, except to Seth Williams, with whom he talked quite cordially. Williams at one time referred in rather jocose a manner to a circumstance which occurred during their former service together, as if he wanted to say something in a good-natured way to break up the frigidity of the conversation, but Lee was in no mood for pleasantries, and he did not unbend, or even relax the fixed sternness of his features. His only response to the allusion was a slight inclination of the head. General Lee now took the initiative again in leading the conversation back into business channels. He said:

"I have a thousand or more of your men as prisoners, General Grant, a number of them officers whom we have required to march along with us for several days. I shall be glad to send them into your lines as soon as it can be arranged, for I have no provisions for them. I have, indeed, nothing for my own men. They have been living for the last few days principally upon parched corn, and we are badly in need of both rations and forage. I telegraphed to Lynchburg, directing several train-loads of rations to be sent on by rail from there, and when they arrive I should be glad to have the present wants of my men supplied from them."

At this remark all eyes turned toward Sheridan, for he had captured these trains with his cavalry the night before, near Appomattox Station. General Grant replied: "I should like to have our men sent within our lines as soon as possible. I will take steps at once to have your army supplied with rations, but I am sorry we have had no forage for the animals. We have had to depend upon the country for our supply of forage. Of about how many men does your present force consist?"

"Indeed, I am not able to say," Lee answered after a slight pause. "My losses in killed and wounded have been exceedingly heavy, and, besides, there have been many stragglers and some deserters. All my reports and public papers, and, indeed, my own private letters, had to be destroyed on the march, to prevent them from falling into the hands of your people. Many companies are entirely without officers, and I have not seen any returns for several days; so that I have no means of ascertaining our present strength."

General Grant had taken great pains to have a daily estimate made of the enemy's forces from all the data that could be obtained, and, judging it to be about 25,000 at this time, he said: "Suppose I send over 25,000 rations, do you think that will be a sufficient supply?" "I think it will be ample," remarked Lee, and added with considerable earnestness of manner, "and it will be a great relief, I assure you."

General Grant now turned to his chief commissary, Colonel (now General) M. R. Morgan, who was present, and directed him to arrange for issuing the rations. The number of officers and men surrendered was over 28,000. As to General Grant's supplies, he had ordered the army on starting out to carry twelve days' rations. This was the twelfth and last day of the campaign.

Grant's eye now fell upon Lee's sword again, and it seemed to remind him of the absence of his own, and by way of explanation he said to Lee:

"I started out from my camp several days ago without my sword, and as I have not seen my headquarters baggage since, I have been riding about without any side-arms. I have generally worn a sword, however, as little as possible, only during the actual operations of a campaign." "I am in the habit of wearing mine most of the time," remarked Lee; "I wear it invariably when I am among my troops, moving about through the army."

General Sheridan now stepped up to General Lee and said that when he discovered some of the Confederate troops in motion during the morning, which seemed to be a violation of the truce, he had sent him (Lee) a couple of notes protesting against this act, and as he had not had time to copy them he would like to have them long enough to make copies. Lee took the notes out of the breast-pocket of his coat and handed them to Sheridan with a few words expressive of regret that the circumstance had occurred, and ,intimating that it must have been the result of some misunderstanding.

After a little general conversation had been indulged in by those present, the two letters were signed and delivered, and the parties prepared to separate. Lee before parting asked Grant to notify Meade of the surrender, fearing that fighting might break out on that front and lives be uselessly lost. This request was complied with, and two Union officers were sent through the enemy's lines as the shortest route to Meade — some of Lee's officers accompanying them to prevent their being interfered with. At a little before 4 o'clock General Lee shook hands with General Grant, bowed to the other officers, and with Colonel Marshall left the room. One after another we followed, and passed out to the porch. Lee signaled to his orderly to bring up his horse, and while the animal was being bridled the general stood on the lowest step and gazed sadly in the direction of the valley beyond where his army lay — now an army of prisoners. He smote his hands together a number of times in an absent sort of a way; seemed not to see the group.of Union officers in the yard who rose respectfully at his approach, and appeared unconscious of everything about him. All appreciated the sadness that overwhelmed him, and he had the personal sympathy of every one who beheld him at this supreme moment of trial. The approach of his

"LEE HAS SURRENDERED TO GRANT!"

horse seemed to recall him from his reverie, and he at once mounted. General Grant now stepped down from the porch, and, moving toward him, saluted him by raising his hat. He was followed in this act of courtesy by all our officers present; Lee raised his hat respectfully, and rode off to break the sad news to the brave fellows whom he had so long commanded.

General Grant and his staff then mounted and started for the headquarters camp, which, in the mean time, had been pitched near by. The news of the surrender had reached the Union lines, and the firing of salutes began at several points, but the general sent orders at once to have them stopped, and used these words in referring to the occurrence: "The war is over, the rebels are our countrymen again, and the best sign of rejoicing after the victory will be to abstain from all demonstrations in the field."

Mr. McLean had been charging about in a manner which indicated that the excitement was shaking his system to its nervous center, but his real trials did not begin until the departure of the chief actors in the surrender. Then the relic-hunters charged down upon the manor-house and made various attempts to jump Mr. McLean's claims to his own furniture. Sheridan set a good example, however, by paying the proprietor twenty dollars in gold for the table at which Lee sat, for the purpose of presenting it to Mrs. Custer, and handed it over to her dashing husband, who started off for camp bearing it upon his shoulder. Ord paid forty dollars for the table at which Grant sat, and afterward presented it to Mrs. Grant, who modestly declined it, and insisted that Mrs. Ord should become its possessor. Bargains were at once struck for all the articles in the room, and it is even said that some mementos were carried off for which no coin of the realm was ever exchanged.

Before General Grant had proceeded far toward camp he was reminded that he had not yet announced the important event to the Government. He dismounted by the roadside, sat down on a large stone, and called for pencil and paper. Colonel (afterward General) Badeau handed his order-book to the general, who wrote on one of the leaves the following message, a copy of which was sent to the nearest telegraph station. It was dated 4 : 30 P. M. :

"HON. E. M. STANTON, Secretary of War, Washington: General Lee surrendered the Army of Northern Virginia this afternoon on terms proposed by myself. The accompanying additional correspondence will show the conditions fully. U. S. GRANT, Lieutenant-General."

Upon reaching camp he seated himself in front of his tent, and we all gathered around him, curious to hear what his first comments would be upon the crowning event of his life. But our expectations were doomed to disappointment, for he appeared to have already dismissed the whole subject from his mind, and turning to General Rufus Ingalls, his first words were: "Ingalls, do you remember that old white mule that so-and-so used to ride when we were in the city of Mexico?" "Why, perfectly," said Ingalls, who was just then in a mood to remember the exact number of hairs in the mule's tail if it would have helped to make matters agreeable. And then the general-in-chief went on to recall the antics played by that animal during an excursion to Popocatapetl. It was not until after supper that he said much about the surrender, when he talked freely of his entire belief that the rest of the rebel commanders would follow Lee's example, and that we would have but little more fighting, even of a partizan nature. He then surprised us by announcing his intention of starting to Washington early the next morning. We were disappointed at this, for we wanted to see something of the opposing army, now that it had become civil enough for the first time in its existence to let us get near it, and meet some of the officers who had been acquaintances in former years. The general, however, had no desire to look at the conquered, and but little curiosity in his nature, and he was anxious above all things to begin the reduction of the military establishment and diminish the enormous expense attending it, which at this time amounted to about four millions of dollars a day. When he considered, however, that the railroad was being rapidly put in condition and that he would lose no time by waiting till noon of the next day, he made up his mind to delay his departure.

ROBERT E. LEE.
From a photograph taken before the war.

his hat. The officers present gave a similar salute, and then grouped themselves around the two chieftains in a semicircle, but withdrew out of ear-shot. General Grant repeated to us that evening the substance of the conversation, which was as follows:

Grant began by expressing a hope that the war would soon be over, and Lee replied by stating that he had for some time been anxious to stop the further effusion of blood, and he trusted that everything would now be done to restore harmony and conciliate the people of the South. He said the emancipation of the negroes would be no hindrance to the restoring of relations between the two sections of the country, as it would probably not be the desire of the majority of the Southern people to restore slavery then, even if the question were left open to them. He could not tell what the other armies would do or what course Mr. Davis would now take, but he believed it would be best for their other armies to follow his example, as nothing could be gained by further resistance in the field. Finding that he entertained these sentiments, General Grant told him that no one's influence in the South was so great as his, and suggested to him that he should advise the surrender of the remaining armies and thus exert his influence in favor of immediate peace. Lee said he could not take such a course without consulting President Davis first. Grant then proposed to Lee that he should do so, and urged the hastening of a result which was admitted to be inevitable. Lee, however, was averse to stepping beyond his duties as a soldier, and said the authorities would doubtless soon arrive at the same conclusion without his interference. There was a statement put forth that Grant asked Lee to see Mr. Lincoln and talk with him as to the terms of reconstruction, but this was erroneous. I asked General Grant about it when he was on his death-bed, and his recollection was distinct that he had made no such suggestion. I am of opinion that the mistake arose from hearing that Lee had been requested to go and see the "President" regarding peace, and thinking that this expression referred to Mr. Lincoln, whereas it referred to Mr. Davis. After the conversation had lasted a little more than half an hour, and Lee had requested that such instructions be given to the officers left in charge to carry out the details of the surrender, that there might be no misunderstanding as to the form of paroles, the manner of turning over the property, etc., the conference ended. The two

commanders lifted their hats and said good-by. Lee rode back to his camp to take a final farewell of his army, and Grant returned to McLean's house, where he seated himself on the porch until it was time to take his final departure. During the conference Ingalls, Sheridan, and Williams had asked permission to visit the enemy's lines and renew their acquaintance with some old friends, classmates, and former comrades in arms who were serving in Lee's army. They now returned, bringing with them Cadmus M. Wilcox, who had been General Grant's groomsman when he was married; Longstreet, who had also been at his wedding; Heth, who had been a subaltern with him in Mexico, besides Gordon, Pickett, and a number of others. They all stepped up to pay their respects to General Grant, who received them very cordially and talked with them until it was time to leave. The hour of noon had now arrived, and General Grant, after shaking hands with all present who were not to accompany him, mounted his horse, and started with his staff for Washington without having entered the enemy's lines. Lee set out for Richmond, and it was felt by all that peace had at last dawned upon the land. The charges were now withdrawn from the guns, the camp-fires were left to smolder in their ashes, the flags were tenderly furled,—those historic banners, battle-stained, bullet-riddled, many of them but remnants of their former selves, with scarcely enough left of them on which to imprint the names of the battles they had seen,—and the Army of the Union and the Army of Northern Virginia turned their backs upon each other for the first time in four long, bloody years.

GENERAL LEE AND COLONEL MARSHALL LEAVING McLEAN'S HOUSE
AFTER THE SURRENDER.
From a sketch made at the time.

were coming and going, so that I was unable to write without interruption until about 10 o'clock, when General Lee, finding that the order had not been prepared, directed me to get into his ambulance, which stood near his tent, and placed an orderly to prevent any one from approaching me.

"I sat in the ambulance until I had written the order, the first draft of which (in pencil) contained an entire paragraph that was omitted by General Lee's direction. He made one or two verbal changes, and I then made a copy of the order as corrected, and gave it to one of the clerks in the adjutant-general's office to write in ink. I took the copy, when made by the clerk, to the general, who signed it, and other copies were then made for transmission to the corps commanders and the staff of the army. All these copies were signed by the general, and a good many persons sent other copies which they had made or procured, and obtained his signature. In this way many copies of the order had the general's name signed as if they were originals, some of which I have seen."

NOTE—The text of the order as issued was as follows: "HEADQUARTERS, ARMY OF NORTHERN VIRGINIA, April 10th, 1865. After four years of arduous service, marked by unsurpassed courage and fortitude, the Army of Northern Virginia has been compelled to yield to overwhelming numbers and resources. I need not tell the survivors of so many hard-fought battles, who have remained steadfast to the last, that I have consented to this result from no distrust of them, but, feeling that valor and devotion could accomplish nothing that could compensate for the loss that would have attended the continuation of the contest, I have determined to avoid the useless sacrifice of those whose past services have endeared them to their countrymen.

"By the terms of the agreement, officers and men can return to their homes, and remain there until exchanged. You will take with you the satisfaction that proceeds from the consciousness of duty faithfully performed; and I earnestly pray that a merciful God will extend to you his blessing and protection.

"With an increasing admiration of your constancy and devotion to your country, and a grateful remembrance of your kind and generous consideration of myself, I bid you an affectionate farewell. R. E. LEE, General."

That evening I made full notes of the occurrences which took place during the surrender, and from these the above account has been written.

There were present at McLean's house, besides Sheridan, Ord, Merritt, Custer, and the officers of Grant's staff, a number of other officers and one or two citizens who entered the room at different times during the interview.

About 9 o'clock on the morning of the 10th General Grant with his staff rode out toward the enemy's lines, but it was found upon attempting to pass through that the force of habit is hard to overcome, and that the practice which had so long been inculcated in Lee's army of keeping Grant out of his lines was not to be overturned in a day, and he was politely requested at the picket-lines to wait till a message could be sent to headquarters asking for instructions. As soon as Lee heard that his distinguished opponent was approaching, he was prompt to correct the misunderstanding at the picket-line, and rode out at a gallop to receive him. They met on a knoll that overlooked the lines of the two armies, and saluted respectfully, by each raising

GENERAL LEE'S FAREWELL ADDRESS TO HIS ARMY.

THE following account of the preparation of the Farewell Address of General Lee to his army is taken from a letter written by Lieutenant-Colonel Charles Marshall, of General Lee's staff, to General Bradley T. Johnson, dated Sep. 27th, 1887:

"General Lee's order to the Army of Northern Virginia at Appomattox Court House was written the day after the meeting at McLean's house, at which the terms of the surrender were agreed upon. That night the general sat with several of us at a fire in front of his tent, and after some conversation about the army, and the events of the day, in which his feelings toward his men were strongly expressed, he told me to prepare an order to the troops.

"The next day it was raining, and many persons

Handwritten telegram text:

At Lees 7½ P.M. 30 May '64

Genl G T Beauregard
Hancocks House —

If you cannot determine what troops to you
Can spare the Dept Cannot — The result will
be disaster if your delay will be disaster —
Butters troops will be with Grant tomorrow

R E Lee

2 7/340 Cp

AUTOGRAPH TELEGRAM OF GENERAL LEE.

LAST DAYS OF THE CONFEDERACY.*

BY BASIL W. DUKE, BRIGADIER-GENERAL, C. S. A.

NARRATIVE OF EVENTS.

On Sunday, April 9th, President Lincoln reached Washington on his return from his visit to the field of operations on the James, having left Richmond on the 6th. (See p. 312.) On the night of Friday, the 14th, the President visited Ford's Theatre, where he was shot by John Wilkes Booth. The next morning about 7 o'clock Mr. Lincoln died. Booth escaped from the city, and, guided by some Confederates, crossed the Potomac near Port Tobacco, Maryland, to Virginia. On Monday, the 24th, he crossed the Rappahannock from Port Conway to Port Royal and took refuge in a barn, where he was found on Wednesday, the 26th, by a detachment of Company L, 16th New York Cavalry, and killed. The assassination of the President was the result of a conspiracy. Mr. Seward, the Secretary of State, was also attacked on the evening of April 14th by Lewis Payne, a fellow-conspirator, and was severely injured. The following persons were tried before a military commission convened at Washington, May 9th, 1865, on the charge of conspiracy to assassinate the President and other high officers of the Government: David E. Herold, G. A. Atzerodt, Lewis Payne, Michael O'Laughlin, Edward Spangler, Samuel Arnold, Mary E. Surratt, and Doctor Samuel A. Mudd. Herold, Atzerodt, Payne, and Mrs. Surratt were hanged; O'Laughlin, Arnold, and Mudd were sentenced to be imprisoned for life, and Spangler for six years.

On Sunday, the 2d of April, on receipt of despatches from General Lee that the army was about to evacuate the Petersburg and Richmond lines, Mr. Davis assembled his cabinet and directed the removal of the public archives, treasure, and other property to Danville, Virginia. The members of the government left Richmond during the night of the 2d, and on the 5th Mr. Davis issued a proclamation stating that Virginia would not be abandoned. Danville was placed in a state of defense, and Admiral Raphael Semmes was appointed a brigadier-general in command of the defenses, with a force consisting of a naval brigade and two battalions of infantry. Upon the surrender of Lee and his army (April 9th), the Confederate Government was removed to Greensboro', North Carolina. On the 18th Mr. Davis and part of his cabinet and his personal staff, accompanied by a wagon-train, containing the personal property of the members of the Government and the most valuable archives, started for Charlotte, North Carolina.

. . . At Charlotte we found General Ferguson's brigade of cavalry; the town was also crowded with paroled soldiers of Lee's army and refugee officials from Richmond. On the next day Mr. Davis arrived, escorted by the cavalry brigades of General Dibrell, of Tennessee, and Colonel W. C. P. Breckinridge, of Kentucky.

In response to the greeting received from the citizens and soldiery, Mr. Davis made a speech which has been the subject of much comment, then and since. I heard it, and remember nothing said by him that could warrant much either of commendation or criticism. In the course of his remarks a despatch was handed him by some gentleman in the crowd, who, I have been told since, was the mayor of Charlotte. It announced the assassination of Mr. Lincoln. Mr. Davis read it aloud, making scarcely any comment upon it at all. He certainly used no unkind language, nor did he display any feeling of exultation. The impression produced on my mind by his manner and few words was that he did not credit the statement.

General John C. Breckinridge, who was then Secretary of War, had not accompanied Mr. Davis to Charlotte, but had gone to General Johnston's headquarters at Greensboro', and was assisting in the negotiations between Johnston and Sherman.

When General Breckinridge reached Charlotte, about two days after Mr. Davis's arrival, he was under the impression that the cartel he had helped to frame would be ratified by the Federal Government and carried into effect. I saw him and had a long conversation with him immediately upon his arrival. He was in cheerful spirits, and seemed to

*Condensed from "The Southern Bivouac" for August, 1886. When the campaign opened in 1865, General Duke commanded a brigade of cavalry in Southwestern Virginia. On the surrender of Lee he was ordered to report with his command to General Johnston in North Carolina.

NOTE.—In his "Memoirs of Robert E. Lee" (J. M. Stoddart & Co.) General A. L. Long says of this scene: "When, after his interview with Grant, General Lee again appeared, a shout of welcome instinctively ran through the army. But instantly recollecting the sad occasion that brought him before them, their shouts sank into silence, every hat was raised, and the bronzed faces of the thousands of grim warriors were bathed with tears.

"As he rode slowly along the lines hundreds of his devoted veterans pressed around the noble chief, trying to take his hand, touch his person, or even lay a hand upon his horse, thus exhibiting for him their great affection. The general then, with head bare and tears flowing freely down his manly cheeks, bade adieu to the army. In a few words he told the brave men who had been so true in arms to return to their homes and become worthy citizens."

GENERAL LEE'S RETURN TO HIS LINES AFTER THE SURRENDER.
From a war-time sketch.

think the terms obtained some mitigation of the sting of defeat and submission.

In the afternoon of that day General Johnston telegraphed that the authorities at Washington refused to recognize the terms upon which he and Sherman had agreed, that the armistice had been broken off, and that he would surrender, virtually, upon any terms offered him. Upon the receipt of this intelligence Mr. Davis resolved at once to leave Charlotte and attempt to march, with all the troops willing to follow him, to Generals Taylor and Forrest, who were somewhere in Alabama. He was accompanied by the members of his cabinet and his staff, in which General Bragg was included. The brigades of Ferguson, Dibrell, Breckinridge, and mine composed his escort, the whole force under the command of General Breckinridge.

At Abbeville, South Carolina, Mr. Davis held a conference with the officers in command of the troops composing his escort, which he himself characterized as a council of war, and which I may be justified, therefore, in so designating. It was, perhaps, the last Confederate council of war held east of the Mississippi River, certainly the last in which Mr. Davis participated. We had gone into camp in the vicinity of the little town, and, although becoming quite anxious to understand what was going to be done, we were expecting no immediate solution of the problem. We were all convinced that the best we could hope to do was to get Mr. Davis safely out of the country, and then obtain such terms as had been given General Johnston's army, or, failing in that, make the best of our way to the

trans-Mississippi. The five brigade commanders [S. W. Ferguson, George G. Dibrell, J. C. Vaughn, Basil W. Duke, and W. C. P. Breckinridge] each received an order notifying him to attend at the private residence in Abbeville, where Mr. Davis had made his headquarters, about 4 o'clock of that afternoon. We were shown into a room, where we found Mr. Davis and Generals Breckinridge and Bragg. No one else was present. I had never seen Mr. Davis look better or show to better advantage. He seemed in excellent spirits and humor; and the union of dignity, graceful affability, and decision, which made his manner usually so striking, was very marked in his reception of us. After some conversation of a general nature, he said: "It is time that we adopt some definite plan upon which the further prosecution of our struggle shall be conducted. I have summoned you for consultation. I feel that I ought to do nothing now without the advice of my military chiefs." He smiled rather archly as he used this expression, and we could not help thinking that such a term addressed to a handful of brigadiers, commanding altogether barely three thousand men, by one who so recently had been the master of legions was a pleasantry, yet he said it in a way that made it a compliment.

After we had each given, at his request, a statement of the equipment and condition of our respective commands, Mr. Davis proceeded to declare his conviction that the cause was not lost any more than hope of American liberty was gone amid the sorest trials and most disheartening reverses of the Revolutionary struggle; but that energy, courage, and constancy might yet save all. "Even," he said, "if the troops now with me be all that I can for the present rely on, three thousand brave men are enough for a nucleus around which the whole people will rally when the panic which now afflicts them has passed away." He then asked that we should make suggestions in regard to the future conduct of the war.

We looked at each other in amazement and with a feeling a little akin to trepidation, for we hardly knew how we should give expression to views diametrically opposed to those he had uttered. Our respect for Mr. Davis approached veneration, and notwithstanding the total dissent we felt, and were obliged to announce, to the programme he had indicated, that respect was rather increased than diminished by what he had said.

I do not remember who spoke first, but we all expressed the same opinion. We told him frankly that the events of the last few days had removed from our minds all idea or hope that a prolongation of the contest was possible. The people were not panic-stricken, but broken down and worn out. We said that an attempt to continue the war, after all means of supporting warfare were gone, would be a cruel injustice to the people of the South. We would be compelled to live on a country already impoverished, and would invite its further devastation. We urged that we would be doing a wrong to our men if we persuaded them to such a course; for if they persisted in a conflict so hopeless they would be treated as brigands, and would forfeit all chance of returning to their homes.

He asked why then we were still in the field. We answered that we were desirous of affording him an opportunity of escaping the degradation of capture, and perhaps a fate which would be direr to the people than even to himself, in still more embittering the feeling between the North and South. We said that we would ask our men to follow us until his safety was assured, and would risk them in battle for that purpose, but would not fire another shot in an effort to continue hostilities.

He declared, abruptly, that he would listen to no suggestion which regarded only his own safety. He appealed eloquently to every sentiment and reminiscence that might be supposed to move a Southern soldier, and urged us to accept his views. We remained silent, for our convictions were un-

shaken; we felt responsible for the future welfare of the men who had so heroically followed us; and the painful point had been reached, when to speak again in opposition to all that he urged would have approached altercation. For some minutes not a word was spoken. Then Mr. Davis rose and ejaculated bitterly that all was indeed lost. He had become very pallid, and he walked so feebly as he proceeded to leave the room that General Breckinridge stepped hastily up and offered his arm.

I have undertaken to narrate very briefly what occurred in a conference which lasted for two or three hours. I believe that I have accurately given the substance of what was said; and that where I have put what was said by Mr. Davis in quotation marks, I have correctly reproduced it, or very nearly so. . . .

Mr. Davis, having apparently yielded to the advice pressed upon him, that he should endeavor to escape, started off with a select party of twenty, commanded by Captain Given Campbell, of Kentucky, one of the most gallant and intelligent officers in the service. I knew nearly all of these twenty personally. Among them were Lieutenants Lee Hathaway and Winder Monroe of my brigade.

THE GRAND REVIEW OF UNION TROOPS IN WASHINGTON AT THE CLOSE OF THE WAR.

Escort and commander had been picked as men who could be relied on in any emergency, and there is no doubt in my mind that, if Mr. Davis had really attempted to get away or reach the trans-Mississippi, this escort would have exhausted every expedient their experience could have suggested, and, if necessary, fought to the death to accomplish his purpose. I have never believed, however, that Mr. Davis really meant or desired to escape after he became convinced that all was lost. I think that, wearied by the importunity with which the request was urged, he seemingly consented, intending to put himself in the way of being captured. I am convinced that he quitted the main body of the troops that they might have an opportunity to surrender before it was too late for surrender upon terms, and that he was resolved that the small escort sent with him should encounter no risk in his behalf. I can account for his conduct upon no other hypothesis. He well knew—and he was urgently advised—that his only chance of escape was in rapid and continuous movement. He and his party were admirably mounted, and could easily have outridden the pursuit of any party they were not strong enough to fight. Therefore, when he

deliberately procrastinated as he did, when the fact of his presence in that vicinity was so public, and in the face of the effort that would certainly be made by the Federal forces to secure his person, I can only believe that he had resolved not to escape. . . .

NOTE—Jefferson Davis was captured on the 10th of May near Irwinsville, Georgia, by a detachment of the 4th Michigan Cavalry (belonging to General R. H. G. Minty's division of General James H. Wilson's cavalry corps), under Lieutenant-Colonel Benjamin D. Pritchard. Wilson possessed knowledge of Davis's movements and had ordered Minty's troops to picket the line of the Ockmulgee. Pritchard left Macon, Georgia, on the 7th, and was moving south along the west bank of the Ocmulgee when he crossed the route on which Mr. Davis and his party were moving with about twenty-four hours' start of their pursuers. A detachment of the 1st Wisconsin Cavalry (belonging to General John T. Croxton's division), under Lieutenant-Colonel Henry Harnden, was following Mr. Davis in the direct road to Irwinsville, and Pritchard, making a swift march on another road, came upon the fugitives in their camp, and arrested Mr. Davis just as the advance of Harnden's command reached the scene.

Among those who surrendered at the time, besides Mr. Davis's family and the guard, were Mr. Reagan and Colonels Lubbock, Johnston, and Harrison. General Breckinridge and Colonel Wood escaped, and made their way to Florida, whence they sailed to Cuba in an open boat. Mr. Judah P. Benjamin had already left the party, and made his escape through Florida to the sea-coast, thence to the Bahamas in an open boat.

On the 29th of May, 1865, President Johnson issued a proclamation of amnesty to all persons (with some notable exceptions) who had participated in the rebellion, and who should make oath to support the Constitution and the Union, and the proclamations and laws relating to emancipation. Among the exceptions, besides certain civil and diplomatic officers and agents, and others, were the officers of the Confederate service above the rank of colonel in the army and that of lieutenant in the navy, and those who had been educated at the United States Military and Naval Academies.

Amnesty was further extended by proclamations, on September 7th, 1867, and December 25th, 1868. In the first the military exceptions made in the amnesty of May 29th, 1865, were reduced to ex-Confederate officers above the rank of brigadier-general in the army, and of captain in the navy, and in the second all exceptions were removed, and the pardon was unconditional and without the formality of any oath.

Mr. Davis was imprisoned at Fort Monroe immediately after his arrest, and was indicted on the charge of treason, by a Grand Jury in the United States Court for the District of Virginia at Norfolk, May 13th, 1866. On May 13th, 1867, he was released on a bail-bond of $100,000 signed by Cornelius Vanderbilt, Gerrit Smith, and Horace Greeley, and in December, 1868, a *nolle prosequi* was entered in the case.

THE GRAND REVIEW.

BY H. W. SLOCUM, MAJOR-GENERAL, U. S. V.

. . . We went into camp in the vicinity of Alexandria, my own headquarters being very near the place I had occupied during the first winter of the war, when McClellan was organizing the Army of the Potomac. We were soon informed that the final scene of the war was to be a grand review of all the troops by the President and his Cabinet. All the foreign ministers resident in Washington, the governors of the States, and many other distinguished people had been invited to be present. The Eastern troops were to be reviewed on the 23d of May, and the Western on the day following. The leading officers of Sherman's command were invited to the stand to witness the review of the Army of the Potomac, and they gladly accepted the invitation. After the close of the review of that army, several of our officers assembled at Sherman's headquarters to discuss matters and prepare for the work to be done next day. In speaking of the review of the Army of the Potomac Sherman said: "It was magnificent. In dress, in soldierly appearance, in precision of alignment and marching we cannot beat those fellows." All present assented to this statement. Some one then suggested that we should not make the attempt, but should pass in review "as we went marching through Georgia"; that the foragers, familiarly known among us as "bummers," should form part of the column. This suggestion seemed to strike General Sherman favorably, and instructions were issued to carry it into effect. Early on the following morning the head of our column started up Pennsylvania Avenue and soon passed the reviewing stand, which was filled with distinguished people from all parts of the country. Sherman's men certainly presented a very soldierly appearance. They were proud of their achievements, and had the swing of men who had marched through half a dozen States. But the feature of the column which seemed to interest the spectators most was the attachments of foragers in rear of each brigade. At the review the men appeared "in their native ugliness" as they appeared on the march through Georgia and the Carolinas. Their pack-mules and horses, with rope bridles or halters, laden with supplies such as they had carried on the march, formed part of the column. It was a new feature in a grand review, but one which those who witnessed it will never forget.

Soon after the review the troops were ordered into various camps, where the paymaster paid them his last visit, and then they separated, never again to meet in large bodies, except on Memorial Day, the 30th of May, of each year, when they meet to honor the memory of comrades who gave their lives for their country, and at annual reunions of regimental associations, when they assemble to renew the ties of comradeship formed during the struggle of more than four years' duration, which cost us hundreds of thousands of lives and thousands of millions of treasure, but which has conferred, even upon the defeated South, blessings that more than compensate the country for all her losses.

NOTES ON THE UNION AND CONFEDERATE ARMIES.

IN a statistical exhibit of deaths in the Union army, compiled (1885), under the direction of Adjutant-General Drum, by Joseph W. Kirkley, the causes of death are given as follows: Killed in action, 4142 officers, 62,916 men; died of wounds received in action, 2223 officers, 40,789 men, of which number 99 officers and 1973 men were prisoners of war; died of disease, 2795 officers and 221,791 men, of which 83 officers and 24,783 men were prisoners; accidental deaths (except drowned), 142 officers and 3972 men, of which 2 officers and 5 men were prisoners; drowned, 106 officers and 4838 men, of which 1 officer and 6 men were prisoners; murdered, 37 officers and 483 men; killed after capture, 14 officers and 90 men; committed suicide, 26 officers and 365 men; executed by United States military authorities, 267 men; executed by the enemy, 4 officers and 60 men; died from sunstroke, 5 officers and 308 men, of which 20 men were prisoners; other known causes, 62 officers and 1972 men, of which 7 officers and 312 men were prisoners; causes not stated, 28 officers and 12,093 men, of which 9 officers and 2030 men were prisoners. Total, 9584 officers and 349,944 men, of which 219 officers and 29,279 men were prisoners. Grand aggregate, 359,528; aggregate deaths among prisoners, 29,498. Since 1885 the Adjutant-General has received evidence of the death in Southern prisons of 694 men not previously accounted for, which increases the number of deaths among prisoners to 30,192, and makes a grand aggregate of 360,222.

On the 13th of April, 1865, the Secretary of War ordered the enrolment discontinued. The work of mustering out volunteers began April 29th, and up to August 7th 640,806 troops had been discharged; on September 14th the number had reached 741,107, and on November 15th 800,963.

On November 22d, 1865, the Secretary of War reported that Confederate troops surrendered and were released on parole, as follows:

Army of Northern Virginia, commanded by General R. E. Lee	27,805
Army of Tennessee and others, commanded by General Joseph E. Johnston	31,243
General Jeff. Thompson's Army of Missouri	7,978
Miscellaneous paroles, Department of Virginia	9,072
Paroled at Cumberland, Maryland, and other stations	9,377
Paroled by General Edward M. McCook in Alabama and Florida	6,428
Army of the Department of Alabama, General Richard Taylor	42,293
Army of the Trans-Mississippi Department, General E. Kirby Smith	17,686
Paroled in the Department of Washington	3,390
Paroled in Virginia, Tennessee, Alabama, Louisiana, and Texas	13,922
Surrendered at Nashville and Chattanooga, Tennessee	5,029
	174,223

COMPARATIVE STATEMENT OF THE NUMBER OF MEN FURNISHED THE UNITED STATES ARMY AND NAVY, AND OF THE DEATHS IN THE ARMY, 1861–5.

States, Territories, etc.	*Men furnished.* *White troops.*	*Sailors & marines.*	*Colored troops.*	*Total.*	*Aggregate of deaths.*
Alabama	2,576	......	......	2,576	345
Arkansas	8,289	......	......	8,289	1,713
California	15,725	......	......	15,725	573
Colorado	4,903	......	......	4,903	323
Connecticut	51,937	2,163	1,764	55,864	5,354
Dakota	206	......	.....	206	6
Delaware	11,236	94	954	12,284	882
Dist. of Columbia	11,912	1,353	3,269	16,534	290
Florida	1,290	......	......	1,290	215
Georgia	......	......	......	....	15
Illinois	255,057	2,224	1,811	259,092	34,834
Indiana	193,748	1,078	1,537	196,363	26,672
Iowa	75,797	5	440	76,242	13,001
Kansas	18,069	......	2,080	20,149	2,630
Kentucky	51,743	314	23,703	75,760	10,774
Louisiana	5,224	.....	.....	5,224	945
Maine	64,973	5,030	104	70,107	9,398
Maryland	33,995	3,925	8,718	46,638	2,982
Massachusetts	122,781	19,983	3,966	146,730	13,942
Michigan	85,479	498	1,387	87,364	14,753
Minnesota	22,913	3	104	24,020	2,584
Mississippi	545	....	......	545	78
Missouri	100,616	151	8,344	109,111	13,885
Nebraska	3,157	......	......	3,157	239
Nevada	1,080	......	......	1,080	33
New Hampshire	32,930	882	125	33,937	4,882
New Jersey	67,500	8,129	1,185	76,814	5,754
New Mexico	6,561	......	......	6,561	277
New York	409,561	35,164	4,125	448,850	46,534
North Carolina	3,156	......	......	3,156	360
Ohio	304,814	3,274	5,092	313,180	35,475
Oregon	1,810	......	......	1,810	45
Pennsylvania	315,017	14,307	8,612	337,936	33,183
Rhode Island	19,521	1,878	1,837	23,236	1,321
Tennessee	31,092	......	......	31,092	6,777
Texas	1,965	......	......	1,965	141
Vermont	32,549	619	120	33,288	5,224
Virginia	....	......	......	....	42
Washington	964	......	......	964	22
West Virginia	31,872	......	196	32,068	4,017
Wisconsin	91,029	133	165	91,327	12,301
Indian Nations	....	......	......	*3,530	1,018
Colored Troops	....	......	99,337	†90,337	‡36,847
	2,494,592	101,207	178,975	2,778,304	
Veteran Reserve Corps					1,672
U. S. Veteran Volunteers (Hancock's Corps)					106
U. S. Volunteer Engineers and Sharp-shooters					552
U. S. Volunteer Infantry					243
General and general staff-officers, U. S. Volunt'rs					239
Miscellaneous U. S. Volunt'rs (brigade bands, etc.)					232
Regular Army					5,798
Grand aggregate					§359,528

* Indians. † Number not credited to any State.

‡ Includes losses in all colored organizations excepting three regiments from Massachusetts whose deaths aggregate 574.

§ Increased by additional evidence since 1885 to 360,222.

NOTES TO THE ADJOINING TABLE.

Figures in the column of deaths, opposite names of States, represent only such as occurred among *white troops* (losses among colored troops and Indians being given at the foot of the table). The table does not indicate losses among sailors and marines.

The colored soldiers organized under the authority of the General Government and not credited to any State were recruited as follows: In Alabama, 4969; Arkansas, 5526; Colorado, 95; Florida, 1044; Georgia, 3486; Louisiana, 24,052; Mississippi, 17,869; North Carolina, 5035; South Carolina, 5462; Tennessee, 20,133; Texas, 47; Virginia, 5723.

There were also 5896 negro soldiers enlisted at large, or whose credits are not specially expressed by the records.

The number of officers and men of the Regular Army among whom the casualties herein noted occurred is estimated at 67,000; the number in the Veteran Reserve Corps was 60,508; and in Hancock's Veteran Corps, 10,883.

The other organizations of white volunteers, organized directly by the U. S. authorities, numbered about 11,000.

In 82 national cemeteries (according to the report of June 30th, 1888) 325,230 men are buried; 176,397 being known, and 148,833 unknown dead. These numbers include 1136 at Mexico City, most of whom lost their lives in the Mexican war; about 9500 Confederates; and about 8500 civilians.

The following table, made from official returns, shows the whole number of men enrolled (present and absent) in the active armies of the Confederacy:

	Jan. 1, 1862.	*Jan.* 1, 1863.	*Jan.* 1, 1864.	*Jan.* 1, 1865.
Army of Northern Va	84,225	144,605	92,050	155,772
Dep't of Richmond	......	7,820	8,494	16,601
Dep't of Norfolk	16,825	......	......	......
Dep't of the Peninsula	20,138	......	......	......
Dep't of Fredericksb'g	10,645	......	......	......
Dep't of N. C	13,656	40,821	9,876	5,187
Dep't of Miss. and E. La.	4,390	73,114	46,906	32,148
Dep't of S. C. and Ga.	40,955	27,052	65,005	53,014
Dep't of Pensacola	18,214	......	......	......
Dep't of N. Orleans	10,318	......	......	......
Dep't of the Gulf	......	10,489	17,241	12,820
Western Dep't	24,784	......	......	......
Army of Tenn.	......	82,799	88,457	86,995
Dep't of Ky	39,565	......	......	......
Dep't of East Tenn	......	18,768	52,821	......
Dep't of Northwest	4,296	......	......	......
Dep't of Western Va	......	10,116	18,642	7,138
Trans-Miss. Dep't	*30,000	*50,000	73,289	*70,000
Aggregate	318,011	465,584	472,781	439,675

* Estimated.

Very few, if any, of the local land forces, and none of the naval, are included in the tabular exhibit. If we take the 472,000 men in service at the beginning of 1864, and add thereto at least 250,000 deaths occurring prior to that date, it gives over 700,000. The discharges and desertions would probably increase the number to over 1,000,000. No data exists for a reasonably accurate estimate of Confederate losses.

GRAND REVIEWING STAND IN FRONT OF THE WHITE HOUSE, WASHINGTON, MAY 23–24, 1865.

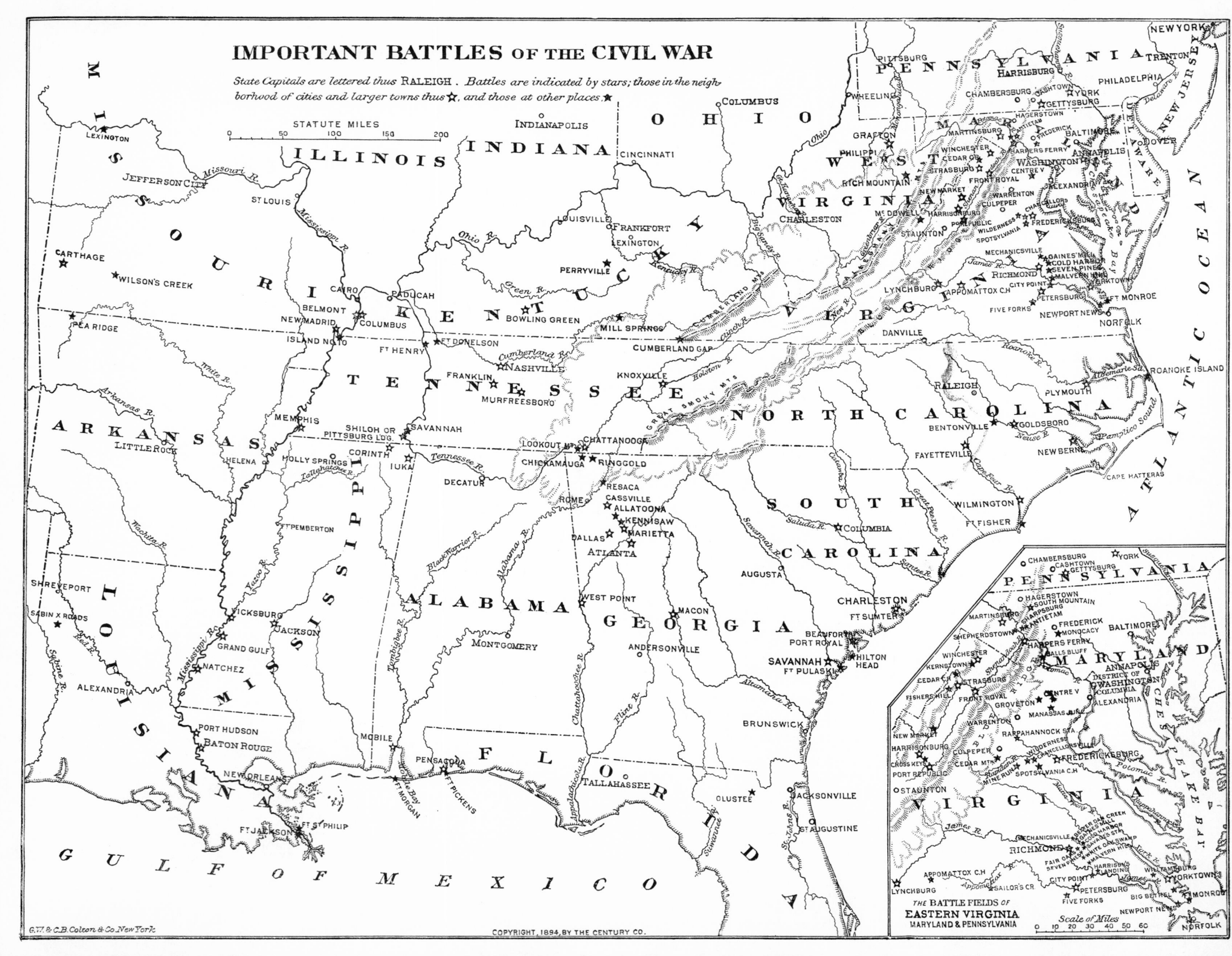

IMPORTANT BATTLES OF THE CIVIL WAR

State Capitals are lettered thus RALEIGH. *Battles are indicated by stars; those in the neighborhood of cities and larger towns thus* ☆, *and those at other places.* ★

STATUTE MILES

THE BATTLE FIELDS *OF*
EASTERN VIRGINIA
MARYLAND & PENNSYLVANIA

Scale of Miles

G.W. & C.B. Colton & Co. New York

COPYRIGHT, 1894, BY THE CENTURY CO.

ALPHABETICAL INDEX OF SUBJECTS

TABLE OF CONTENTS

TABLE OF CONTENTS —CONTINUED